Psychology of Classroom Learning
An Encyclopedia

Psychology of Classroom Learning
An Encyclopedia

VOLUME 2
k–z

Eric M. Anderman
EDITOR IN CHIEF

Lynley H. Anderman
CO-EDITOR

MACMILLAN REFERENCE USA
A part of Gale, Cengage Learning

GALE
CENGAGE Learning

Detroit • New York • San Francisco • New Haven, Conn • Waterville, Maine • London

GALE
CENGAGE Learning™

Psychology of Classroom Learning: An Encyclopedia
Eric M. Anderman, Editor in Chief
Lynley H. Anderman, co-editor

Project Editor: Miranda H. Ferrara

Production Technology Support: Luann Brennan, Mark Springer, Mike Weaver

Manuscript Editors: Bryan Aubrey, Melodie Monahan

Proofreader: John K. Krol

Indexer: Do Mi Stauber Indexing Service

Product Design: Pamela A. E. Galbreath

Imaging: Lezlie Light

Graphic Art: GGS Information Services, Inc.

Rights Acquisition and Management: Margaret Abendroth, Beth Beaufore, Dean Dauphinais

Composition: Evi Abou-El-Seoud, Mary Beth Trimper

Manufacturing: Wendy Blurton

Product Manager: Leigh Ann Cusack

Publisher: Jay Flynn

For product information and technology assistance, contact us at **Gale Customer Support, 1-800-877-4253.** For permission to use material from this text or product, submit all requests online at **www.cengage.com/permissions.** Further permissions questions can be emailed to **permissionrequest@cengage.com**

Since this page cannot legibly accommodate all copyright notices, the credits constitute an extension of the copyright notice.

Cover photographs reproduced by permission of Swerve/Alamy (Interior of American High School, Boston, Massachusetts); LWA-Dann Tardif/Zefa/Corbis (Students and Teacher Using Laptop in Classroom); JLP/Jose Luis Pelaez/Zefa/Corbis (Student Writing Languages on Blackboard); Pierre Tremblay/Masterfile www.masterfile.com (Students and Teacher in Classroom).

While every effort has been made to ensure the reliability of the information presented in this publication, Gale, a part of Cengage Learning, does not guarantee the accuracy of the data contained herein. Gale accepts no payment for listing; and inclusion in the publication of any organization, agency, institution, publication, service, or individual does not imply endorsement of the editors or publisher. Errors brought to the attention of the publisher and verified to the satisfaction of the publisher will be corrected in future editions.

EDITORIAL DATA PRIVACY POLICY: Does this product contain information about you as an individual? If so, for more information about our editorial data privacy policies, please see our Privacy Statement at www.gale.cengage.com.

Library of Congress Cataloging-in-Publication Data

Psychology of classroom learning : an encyclopedia / Eric M. Anderman, editor-in-chief; Lynley H. Anderman, co-editor.
   v. cm.
   Includes bibliographical references and index.
   ISBN 978-0-02-866167-4 (set : hardcover) -- ISBN 978-0-02-866168-1 (vol. 1) -- ISBN 978-0-02-866169-8 (v. 2)
   1. Learning, Psychology of--Encyclopedias. I. Anderman, Eric M. II. Anderman, Lynley Hicks.

LB1060.P89 2009
370.15'2303--dc22   2008008737

Gale
27500 Drake Rd.
Farmington Hills, MI, 48331-3535

ISBN-13: 978-0-02-866167-4 (set)   ISBN-10: 0-02-866167-2 (set)
ISBN-13: 978-0-02-866168-1 (vol. 1)   ISBN-10: 0-02-866168-0 (vol. 1)
ISBN-13: 978-0-02-866169-8 (v. 2)   ISBN-10: 0-02-866169-9 (vol. 2)

This title is also available as an e-book.
ISBN-13: 978-0-02-866170-4 ISBN-10: 0-02-866170-2
Contact your Gale, a part of Cengage Learning sales representative for ordering information.

Printed in the United States of America
1 2 3 4 5 6 7 11 10 09 08

Editorial Board

Contents

K

KNOWLEDGE

One of the main goals of cognitive psychology is to understand the relationship between knowledge and learning. To do so, researchers developed the *information processing model* (IPM) in the early 1950s, which has been used as the modal model of cognition since that time. The IPM consists of three main components, including sensory memory, working memory, and long-term memory (Neath & Surprenant, 2003). Sensory memory processes incoming sensory information for very brief periods of time, usually one-half to three seconds. The amount of information held at any given moment in sensory memory is limited to five to seven discrete elements such as letters of the alphabet or pictures of human faces. Working memory refers to real-time information processing in which meaning is assigned to incoming information from a text, pictures, or math problem. Long-term memory refers to a permanent repository of knowledge in memory. To use a computer analogy, sensory memory corresponds to inputting information via the keyboard, working memory corresponds to information current on the computer screen, and long-term memory corresponds to the computer's hard drive.

CATEGORIES OF KNOWLEDGE

Information processing theory assumes that ongoing mental activity in working memory is aided by different types of information in long-term memory that supports thinking and problem solving. At least three categories of knowledge are stored in long-term memory, including declarative, procedural, and self-regulatory knowledge (Anderson, 1976; Tulving, 1972). Declarative knowledge refers to the facts and concepts. Procedural knowledge refers to how to do things. Self-regulatory knowledge refers to knowledge individuals have about themselves as learners, what they know, and how to control their learning. All three types of knowledge are important. However, even large amount of declarative and procedural knowledge, without self-regulatory knowledge to support it, does little to help people survive and adapt successfully.

Declarative knowledge is a broad category that includes facts, concepts, and the relationships between concepts that lead to an integrated conceptual understanding of a domain of knowledge. Declarative knowledge includes thousands of facts such as the names of colors, numbers, coins, and trees. Concepts consist of two or more units of factual information that are used to understand a broader phenomenon such as human rights or social justice. Often concepts are phenomena that can be described abstractly, such as freedom or happiness, even though these phenomena do not exist in the physical world. Declarative knowledge also includes integrated conceptual knowledge that is sometimes referred to as *structural knowledge* or *mental models* (Halpern, 2003).

One of the most important organizational units in memory is the *schema*, which refers to an organized body of information about some distinct domain of knowledge. For example, every adult has a "car schema" in which information about different types of cars is organized. A car schema could be organized in several ways using either the cost or size of the car to generate subcategories. Anyone asked to name a luxury car could quickly name cars such as Rolls Royce or Bentley as examples. Most other people who share the same cultural group would have this information organized in a similar way as well.

Procedural knowledge is knowledge about how to do things, ranging from simple action sequences such as brushing one's teeth, to complex actions such as driving a car. Most adults possess an enormous amount of procedural knowledge, which enables them to perform complex activities such as grocery shopping easily because those procedures are automated though practice. Although there are many different types of action sequences, there are three sequences of special importance, including complex scripted actions, algorithms, and heuristics that are stored as single entities in memory.

Scripts refer to extended action sequences and plans that are stored in memory as single units of knowledge. Each person possesses thousands of scripts, for activities such as getting dressed, driving a car, dining at restaurants, and social interactions that save enormous amounts of time because scripts can be activated intact from memory. Scripts are analogous to schemata. Whereas schemata help individuals organize declarative knowledge about a topic or domain, scripts help people organize and remember steps in a complicated action sequence. Algorithms and heuristics can be thought of as "mini-scripts." An algorithm is a rule for solving a specific problem that always works, whereas a heuristic is a rule of thumb for solving a problem that often works, but not always. For example, an algorithm could be used to compute the average of 1,000 scores by adding all the scoring and dividing the total by the number of scores. A simple heuristic could also be used to estimate the average by sampling seven scores at random, rank ordering the scores, and using the middle score as an estimate.

Self-regulatory knowledge is knowledge about how to regulate one's memory, thought, and learning (Schunk & Zimmerman, 2006). Declarative and procedural knowledge alone are not sufficient to be an adaptive learner. In addition, individuals must possess knowledge about themselves as learners and about the skills they need to learn effectively. Self-regulatory knowledge can be divided into two types, including domain specific knowledge and domain general knowledge (Alexander, 2003). The former is knowledge individuals possess about themselves with regard to a domain such as mathematics or a sub-domain such as geometry. In contrast, the latter includes general knowledge such as learning strategies that enable people to adapt and self-regulate across all domains.

Domain specific knowledge refers to knowledge that is encapsulated within a particular domain of learning such as mathematics, history, and literature. Sometimes domain specific knowledge is referred to as *topic knowledge*, although this term suggests knowledge about a specific topic such as geometry within a broader domain such as mathematics. Domain specific knowledge is extremely important in the development of expertise and skilled

problem solving (Ericsson, 2003). Cognitive psychologists once believed that it was possible to capture the knowledge of experts through interviews and observation, and in turn, help novices become experts quickly. However, researchers discovered that experts become experts slowly through years of hard work, deliberate practice, and guidance from other experts. Most experts have deep knowledge in one domain, yet shallow knowledge in other domains, due in large part to the amount of time they invest in developing expertise in their chosen domain. Expertise in one domain usually does not transfer spontaneously to other domains, although it can be facilitated through direct instruction and analogical cues, which help the learner understand the relationship between two different problems.

Domain general knowledge refers to knowledge that is equally useful to learners across domains and topics. Domain general knowledge often is referred to as *metacognitive knowledge,* which includes knowledge of cognition and regulation of cognition (Schraw, 2006). The former includes strategy knowledge and conditional knowledge, while the latter includes knowledge of regulatory skills such as planning, monitoring, and evaluation of learning. Metacognitive knowledge enables learners to identify problems and self-correct by changing strategies.

TEACHER KNOWLEDGE

Like other experts, skilled teachers possess different types of knowledge that facilitates classroom practice. Shulman (1987) suggested that skilled teachers possess knowledge about domain content, pedagogy, learners and student development, as well as educational contexts, and educational ends, purposes and values. Many educators view content and pedagogical knowledge as essential to effective teaching. Content knowledge refers to knowledge in a particular domain, such as mathematics, science, social studies, reading, and language arts. Pedagogical content knowledge has been defined as "a collection of teacher professional constructions, as a form of knowledge that preserves that planning and wisdom of practice that the teacher acquires when repeatedly teaching a certain topic" (Hashweh, 2005, p. 273).

Content knowledge is domain-specific in nature, whereas many teachers have endorsed domain-general pedagogy that emphasizes constructivist teaching. The fundamental idea of constructivism is allowing students to connect to the learning environment through problem-based learning, inquiry activities, and dialogues with others. By allowing students to construct knowledge as learners, the educational goal is to help them think critically about concepts. There are many strategies that a teacher might employ when teaching a particular content areas: (a) scaffolding, which allows the learner to make sense of complex tasks; (b) modeling, which requires the teacher to think aloud about problem solving; while (c) coaching, guiding, and advising requires the teacher to probe the students' thinking. Experiences should be genuine and relevant to the learners and inquiry is used as an approach for students to engage in discovery learning.

IMPLICATIONS FOR LEARNING AND TEACHING

Knowledge facilitates information processing and long-term learning by providing an integrated conceptual network of information in long-term memory. Knowledge in isolation (i.e., inert knowledge) is of little value, whereas organized knowledge is powerful because it enables people to sort and store information in memory, predict and judge, and evaluate their learning accurately. Knowledge also enables individuals to process information more efficiently (Neath & Surprenant, 2003).

Recent research emphasizes the importance of constructed knowledge, distributed cognition, and distributed knowledge. *Constructivism* refers to the assumption that knowledge is constructed actively by learners, rather than transmitted passively through lecture, discussion, or observation. Constructivism assumes that active learning is better because knowledge is understood in a deeper, more relevant way. An extension of constructivism is the assumption that knowledge and learning are more sophisticated when mutually shared across multiple learners in an active dialogue. This is referred to often as *distributed cognition*. In contrast, *distributed knowledge* refers to knowledge that is distributed across two or more individuals, but may be distributed across hundreds of individuals, such as knowledge about complex technological products. Knowledge can also be distributed between humans and human artifacts such as books and tools such as calculators.

Distributed cognition and knowledge are topics of considerable debate for both practical and theoretical reasons. Many educators assume that mutually constructed meaning is more dynamic than individually constructed meaning, and some believe that knowledge exists only as a distributed set of beliefs and assumptions across multiple individuals (Zhang & Patel, 2006). In addition, many have argued that complex ideas and knowledge require multiple contributors to exist at all. From a theoretical standpoint, researchers are interested in how to best foster distributed cognition across multiple people and/or machines, and how to represent knowledge in human and machine databases in a distributed manner.

Like students, teachers possess different types of knowledge that are essential to effective teaching (Shulman,

1987). Teachers develop this knowledge slowly over time, often taking 5 to 10 years of teaching practice to develop deep expertise. Both students and teachers construct most higher-order conceptual knowledge through personal experiences, reflection on experiences, and dialogue with other students and teachers (Ericsson, 2003). Individuals also construct metacognitive knowledge that enables them to self-regulate within their domain of expertise. Constructed *executive knowledge* is assumed to be stored in long-term memory in sophisticated schemata and scripts that enable the individual to perform a variety of complex skills with a high degree of efficiency.

SEE ALSO *Information Processing Theory; Knowledge Representation.*

BIBLIOGRAPHY

Alexander, P. A. (2003). The development of expertise: The journey from acclimation to proficiency. *Educational Researcher, 32,* 10–14.

Anderson, J. R. (1976). *Language, memory, and thought.* Mahwah, NJ: Erlbaum.

Ericsson, K. A. (2003). The acquisition of expert performance as problem solving. In J. E. Davidson & R. J. Sternberg (Eds.), *The psychology of problem solving* (pp. 31–83). Cambridge, England: Cambridge University Press.

Halpern, D. F. (2003). *Thought and knowledge: An introduction to critical thinking* (4th ed.). Mahwah, NJ: Erlbaum.

Hashweh, M. Z. (2005). Teacher pedagogical constructions: a reconfiguration of pedagogical content knowledge. *Teacher and Teaching: Theory and Practice 11*(3), 273–292.

Neath, I., & Surprenant, A. M. (2003). *Human memory: An introduction to research, data, and theory* (2nd ed.). Pacific Grove, CA: Brooks/Cole Publishing.

Schraw, G. (2006). Knowledge: Structures and processes. In P. Alexander & P. Winne (Eds.), *Handbook of educational psychology* (2nd ed., pp. 245–264). San Diego, CA: Academic Press.

Schunk, D. H., & Zimmerman, B. J. (2006). Competence and control beliefs: Distinguishing the means and the ends. In P. Alexander & P. Winne (Eds.), *Handbook of educational psychology* (2nd ed., pp. 349–367). San Diego, CA: Academic Press.

Shulman, L. (1987). Knowledge and teaching: foundations of the new reform. *Harvard Educational Review 57,* 1–22.

Tulving, E. T. (1972). Episodic and semantic memory. In E. Tulving & W. Donaldson (Eds.), *Organization of memory* (pp. 381–403). San Diego, CA: Academic Press.

Zhang, J., & Patel, V. (2006). Distributed cognition, representation, and affordance. *Pragmatics & Cognition 14,* 333–341.

Gregory Schraw
Michelle Vander Veldt
Lori Olafson

KNOWLEDGE REPRESENTATION

Knowledge representation refers to how knowledge is stored in long-term memory. Researchers have been keenly interested in this topic for over 50 years and a number of models of knowledge representation have been developed (Miyaki & Shah, 1999). There are four main families of models that are of interest to researchers. These include network, production, dual coding, and connectionist models. Each model is summarized below, compared to other models, and briefly discussed regarding its contributions to understanding learning in the classroom.

NETWORK MODELS

Network models of knowledge representation became popular in the 1960s. Early models focused on the hierarchical representation of declarative knowledge in memory and the relationship between different knowledge units (Quillian, 1968; Collins & Quillian, 1969). Network models possess three major components, including nodes in which a specific unit of information is stored, properties of information within nodes, and relational links among nodes. This can be explained by reference to the domain of animals. Subsumed within this domain are different types of animals such as birds, fish, and mammals. Network models envisioned each of these categories as nodes, while each node possessed a number of essential properties. The "animal" node included properties such as "breathes, eats, has skin." The "bird" node included properties such as "has wings, has feathers, and flies" whereas the "fish" node included different properties such as "has fins, has gills, and swims." Network models emphasized parsimony in mental representation; thus, properties included in a superordinate node were not replicated at a subordinate node. Because birds and fish are both animals, it was not necessary to include the property "has skin" because this property was included already in the "animal" node.

Quillian (1968) proposed five different kinds of relational links between nodes, including superordinate and subordinate, modifier, disjunctive, conjunctive, and residual links. These links specified whether properties of one node were shared with another node. For example, the fact that all animals have skin is a superordinate link that is true of all other links subsumed beneath it unless otherwise noted as a disjunctive link. Network models based on the notion of nodes, properties, and links helped explain how people remember information in an efficient manner and why it is relatively easy to search memory and make simple judgments, such as whether a canary eats and has skin.

The search process of memory was explained by the concept of spreading activation of attention among nodes.

Some concepts activated particular nodes and activation would spread to adjacent nodes. For example, the word "camel" would activate the "mammal" node and all properties of mammals would be activated, whereas properties of distance nodes such as fish would not be activated. Thus, activation spread through memory both vertically and horizontally. Activation spread vertically in an upward (i.e., camel to mammal) or downward (i.e., camel to dromedary). Activation also spread horizontally (i.e., camel to horse, camel to mule). Activation typically spreads further in a horizontal versus vertical direction, although activation is constrained in part by the situational demands of learning.

The idea that memory is organized into nodes of specific information that are interrelated to other nodes has been a lasting idea. Almost all other models of knowledge representation incorporate the idea of node, although what a node includes varies from model to model. The assumption that nodes have properties and are linked in a manner that indicates the type of relationship between nodes has not fared as well. Early network models provided a useful description of how declarative knowledge was represented in long-term memory, but they failed to explain the construction and representation of procedural and self-regulatory knowledge. Network models also paved the way for the development of schema theory in the 1970s, which spawned hundreds of practical experiments about the effect of schemata on learning and memory.

In recent years, a new class of network models has appeared that focuses on higher order processes such as complex problem solving, creativity, and metacognition (Griffiths, Steyvers & Tenenbaum, 2007). These models frequently describe excitatory and inhibitory processes similar to those described in connectionist models. This new breed of semantic network models often provides a better account of complex mental processes, such as understanding the overall gist of text or conversation.

PRODUCTION SYSTEM MODELS

Production models of knowledge representation and learning were first developed in the 1970s. One goal of these models was to explain a broader array of memory phenomena such as procedural learning, in addition to the representation of declarative knowledge. The most comprehensive production model is the ACT-R model (Adaptive Character of Thought, Revised) by John Anderson (1996, 2000). Anderson's model developed from the human associative learning (HAM) model proposed by Anderson and Bower (1973).

ACT-R proposes three interactive memory systems that support adaptive thinking, including declarative knowledge, procedural knowledge, and working memory. The declarative knowledge component consists of schemata and chunks within schemata that encode specific declarative knowledge units. The procedural knowledge component consists of production rules that break down complex action sequences into a number of "if-then" steps, which enable the learner to perform complex actions using a series of simple steps. Declarative and procedural components are connected to each other, as well as a working memory system in which activated declarative and procedural units are used to solve problems, make decisions, and adapt to environmental conditions.

ACT-R differs from earlier network models in that it proposes production rules, which are combined into production systems, which enable the brain to represent complex actions. A production rule specifies the action to be taken to achieve a specific goal and the conditions under which each action is taken. For example, imagine that a person has a ring of five keys and needs to open an office door. This scenario can be represented as a simple production as follows: IF a person must open a door, THEN he or she must insert key one and open the door; IF key one fails to open the door THEN the person must insert key two, and so on.

This production rule could be subdivided further into finer grained production rules that specify how to use each key until the correct key is identified, or none of the keys open the door. In addition, conditions could be added to each substep in the production sequence to assist the learner. For instance, one might add a condition statement, instructing the person not to attempt to use long, narrow keys with square heads because these keys often open car doors rather than office doors.

Anderson states that complex cognitive activity can be understood and explained in terms of small productions, based on simple units of declarative and procedural knowledge. This suggests that learning is a systematic process of acquiring declarative and procedural knowledge through experience and using this knowledge under specific conditions to execute complex actions, which themselves are comprised of many small productions. The theory of ACT-R also discusses how individuals construct and infer new knowledge based on past experiences. Thus, the theory is not entirely experience driven. Nevertheless, ACT-R views learning as a systematic process of acquiring the right knowledge and using that knowledge under the right conditions. Using knowledge repeatedly (i.e., practicing) increases the speed and accuracy of productions. Tuning productions to varying conditions also increases the efficiency of learning and performance.

Like network models, ACT-R postulates a process of spreading activation among declarative and procedural knowledge units during the execution of production sequences. Anderson (1996) provides sophisticated weighting systems, which serve as algorithms for which production rules to apply under particular conditions. Activation spreads among production rules as a function of conditions and weights, which highlight some rules and downplay others. Activation is not necessarily hierarchical from superordinate to subordinate nodes, as is often the case in network models. Thus, production systems tend to be less hierarchical than networks.

Production system models have two clear advantages over earlier network models. First, they incorporate procedural knowledge into the model and explain how procedural and declarative knowledge are interrelated through working memory. Second, they do an excellent job of explaining incremental skill acquisition and the development of expertise. Production systems have been used to create and model intelligent tutoring systems that might take the place of human tutors. One potential criticism is that production systems are highly mechanistic; that is, they postulate that learning and performance is the sum and nothing more than the sum of a sequence of discrete productions. Related to this criticism is the fact that production systems highlight the role of experience and direct leaning and downplay rational reflection and the role of discovery and creativity.

DUAL CODING MODELS

Dual coding theory (DCT) was first postulated by Alan Pavio in the early 1970s and continues to be an important model of processing and knowledge representation in long-term memory (Pavio, 2007). DCT postulates two separate modular stores in long-term memory that include visual-spatial and verbal representation systems. Both systems are assumed to be functionally separate, yet interconnected. This means that visual-spatial and verbal long-term memories can perform tasks independent of one another, yet are able to pool resources when necessary. A number of researchers have speculated that dual-coding systems may be reflected in neurological differences between the brain's right and left hemispheres (Pavio, 2007). DCT also postulates that some learners may have a visual-spatial or verbal preference for information processing.

DCT hypothesizes different representational systems for each of the two codes. The visual-spatial system uses mental images as the primary representational code, while the verbal system uses speech as the primary code. DCT assumes that every object and concept has a verbal label in verbal memory, whereas not every object or concept has an imaginal label in visual-spatial memory. Specifically, some concepts such as "automobiles" have concrete referents, while some concepts such as "affection" do not. DCT refers to this distinction as concrete versus abstract concepts.

The most important assertion of DCT is that concrete concepts may be easier to process and learn because mental activity can be distributed across the two stores

Four models of knowledge representation in long term memory

	Network	Production system	Dual coding	Connectionist
Type of architecture	Hierarchical	Non-hierarchical production rules	Modular; two separate modules	Non-hierarchical distributed neural networks
Important components	Nodes, properties, relational links	Production rules and systems of rules	Verbal and visual-spatial stores networks	Units (explicit and hidden); weighted connections; neural networks
Important processes	Spreading activation	Spreading activation	Separate storage systems with separate resources	Activation; forward and back propagation
Strengths	Simple; does good job of modeling hierarchical relationship of declarative knowledge	Models procedural knowledge. Explains development of expertise	Explains differences in visual vs. verbal processing and recall	Modeled after brain physiology. Can be tested using computer simulations. Generalizes to other life forms.
Weaknesses	Does not explain procedural, conceptual or self-regulatory knowledge	Mechanistic. Places strong role on experience and practice rather than reflection.	Does not explain integrated visual-verbal representations.	Very data-driven Removes "mind" from learning.

Table 1 ILLUSTRATION BY GGS INFORMATION SERVICES. CENGAGE LEARNING, GALE.

(Reed, 2006; Sadoski, 2005). Thus, a word such as "cat" can be represented separately in each storage system, whereas a word such as "truth" presumably is represented only in the verbal system. Two implications follow from this assumption. One is that information that is concrete in nature or that can be visualized will be better learned (Sadoski, Goetz, & Rodriguez, 2000). This has led to a great deal of research on the use of mnemonic techniques. A second implication is that visual information such as pictures in a book, summary tables, graphs, charts, and other visual aids should facilitate learning (Schnotz, 2002).

Research findings generally support the two-store model proposed by dual coding theory. DCT seems to be especially useful as an explanation of beginning reading processes such as vocabulary learning. It also explains why words are easier to learn in context as well as in the presence of visual aids such as pictures. In contrast, the theory does not explain well how congenitally blind individuals learn or how students create integrated visual-verbal representations in memory.

CONNECTIONIST MODELS

Connectionist models of knowledge representation and learning became popular in the 1980s and sometimes are referred to as neural networks or parallel distributed processing (PDP) models (Neath & Suprenant, 2003). Connectionist models represent an important paradigm shift from network and production system models because they de-emphasize the intentional role of the learner, while emphasizing the role of experience in building neural pathways and connections, as well as assumptions about cognitive architecture (Bechtel & Abrahamsen, 2002).

Although a great deal of attention has been devoted to connectionist models the past 20 years, especially the seminal work of Rumelhart and McClelland (1986), their origin can be traced to earlier researchers such as Selfridge (1959).

Connectionist models differ from network and production models in two ways. The first difference is that previous cognitive models used a computer metaphor to describe human information processing. In this view, information passes through an initial sensory system, is acted upon in working memory, and represented in permanent store in long-term memory. Connectionist models replaced the computer metaphor with a neural pathway metaphor modeled on the human brain. In this view, information is represented as patterns of activation across a variety of units, which correspond to neurons in the human brain.

A second difference is that network and production models focus on the representation of discrete units of information within a node in memory (e.g., a fact or a simple production rule), whereas connectionist models view knowledge representation as continuous across a number of interconnected units in memory. Thus, information such as facts, concepts, and production rules are not represented within single nodes, but distributed across nodes.

Connectionist models propose a rather simple architecture based on units, which maintain elementary information, typically simpler than corresponding nodes in network and production models. Multiple units are connected to create information that one might label as facts or concepts. The connectivity pattern among these units is of utmost importance. Any given unit may be connected to many other units, using a number of different connectivity patterns. Thus, one unit may be part of different knowledge representations much like a single light in a theatre marquee may be used to spell different words. Connectionist theories have proposed different types of units. The most important of these are input units, output units, and hidden units, which are mediating connections between inputs and outputs.

Each unit has an activation value assigned to it under different processing conditions. Activation spreads throughout the system, but depends in part on the connectivity pattern among units, as well as connection weights, which determine whether one unit contributes more activation than another unit. There are a variety of activation algorithms; however, the two most important are forward (i.e., input to output units) and backward propagation (i.e., output to input units). Training (i.e., learning) in a connectionist network occurs as units are activated and deactivated, and connection weights change due to environmental conditions and feedback to the connectionist network through back propagation.

Connectionist models have several strengths and weaknesses. Strengths include their close physiological analogy to the human brain, the fact that their major claims can be tested using computer simulations, and that they provide a general theory of learning that is not unique to humans, but explains how learning may occur in other mammalian and non-mammalian life forms. Possible weaknesses, depending upon one's theoretical point of view, is that connectionist models are too bottom-up (i.e., learning occurs exclusively through experience and data-based feedback), and the mind is removed from models of learning (i.e., the role of rational reflection and inference construction is downplayed).

COMPARING THE FOUR MODELS

Each of the models described above has unique strengths. Table 1 provides a summary of these, as well as the main assumptions of each model. Several points should be considered regarding Table 1. First, each of the models is speculative and incomplete in nature. A large number of studies have supported some, but not all, of the assumptions of each of the models. Currently, there are few cross-model comparisons that definitely support one of the four hypothesized representational architectures. Second, all of the models emphasize the bottom-up nature of learning from experience. Network models are most likely to emphasize the role of higher-order knowledge, whereas connectionist models are least likely to make assumptions about higher-order knowledge or conscious self-regulatory skills. Third, all have useful implications for understanding learning.

IMPLICATIONS FOR LEARNING

Theories and models of knowledge representation all agree on two important implications for learning. One is that knowledge is represented in complex, multi-dimensional ways in memory. The models in Table 1 assume that learners possess higher-order knowledge that develops from simpler knowledge representations. In addition, all the models assume that knowledge is modular in nature (i.e., partitioned in memory into functional units), albeit each model postulates different modules such as concepts embedded in schemata (i.e., networks), separate declarative and procedural representations (i.e., production systems), or imaginal and verbal processing systems (i.e., dual coding).

A second implication is that knowledge is acquired very slowly. Concepts, schemata, and procedural skills are built up slowly over time, automated over hundreds of hours of practice, and often honed under the watchful eye of mentors and master teachers. From an educational perspective, it seems naïve to expect students to become highly knowledgeable within a domain without years of exposure and practice within that domain. Observing and modeling the performance of an expert helps novices develop the knowledge and skills necessary to perform at a high level of expertise.

One important difference among the four perspectives described above is how they address very complex representations such as mental models (Radvansky, 2006). A mental model is a cognitive representation of a complex process (e.g., flying a jet), spatial map (e.g., mental navigational map of New York City), or explanatory model of some phenomenon (e.g., Big Bang Theory). Many experts would agree that constructing mental models and using them to reason and solve problems is the height of cognition. Nevertheless, it is unclear presently how individuals construct mental models, represent them in memory, or use them to make complex decisions (Dougherty, Franco-Watkins, & Thomas, 2008). Network and production system models seem better suited to explain them, whereas connectionist models often deny the necessity of complex representations like mental models. Understanding the representation of complex mental phenomenon such as a mental model remains an important goal of cognitive psychology.

SEE ALSO *Information Processing Theory; Knowledge.*

BIBLIOGRAPHY

Anderson, J. R. (1996). ACT: A simple theory of complex cognition. *American Psychologist, 51,* 255–365.

Anderson, J. R. (2000). *Cognitive psychology and its implication* (5th ed.). New York: Worth.

Anderson, J. R., & Bower, G. H. (1973). *Human associative memory.* Washington, DC: Winston.

Bechtel, W., & Abrahamsen, A. (2002). *Connectionism and the mind: Parallel processing, dynamics, and evolution in networks* (2nd ed.). London: Blackwell Publishers.

Collins, A. M., & Quillian, M. R. (1969). Retrieval time from semantic memory. *Journal of Verbal Learning and Verbal Behavior, 8,* 240–248.

Dougherty, Franco-Watkins, A. M., & Thomas, R. (2008). Psychological plausibility of the theory of probabilistic mental models and the fast and furious heuristic. *Psychological Review, 115,* 199–213.

Griffiths, T. L., Steyvers, M., & Tenenbaum, J. B. (2007). Topics in semantic representation. *Psychological Review, 114,* 211–244.

Miyake, A., & Shah, P. (1999). Toward unified theories of working memory: Emerging general consensus, unresolved theoretical issues, and future research directions. In A. Miyake & P. Shah (Eds.), *Models of working memory: Mechanisms of active maintenance and executive control.* Cambridge, England: Cambridge University Press.

Neath, I., & Surprenant, A. M. (2003). *Human memory: An introduction to research, data, and theory* (2nd ed.). Pacific Grove, CA: Brooks/Cole.

Pavio, A. (2007). *Mind and its evolution: A dual coding theoretical approach.* Mahwah, NJ: Erlbaum.

Quillian, M. R. (1968). Semantic memory. In M. Minsky (Ed.), *Semantic information processing,* (pp. 21–56). Cambridge, MA: MIT Press.

Radvansky, G. A. (2006). *Human memory.* Boston: Pearson.

Reed, S. K. (2006). Cognitive architectures for multimedia learning. *Educational Psychologist, 41,* 87–98.

Rumelhart, D. E., McClelland, J. L., and the PDP Research Group. (1986). *Parallel distributed processing: Explorations in the microstructure of cognition: Vol. 1. Foundations.* Cambridge, MA: MIT Press.

Sadoski, M. (2005). A dual coding view of vocabulary learning. *Reading & writing Quarterly, 21,* 221–238.

Sadoski, M., Goetz, E. T., & Rodriguez, M. (2000). Engaging texts: Effects of concreteness on comprehensibility, interest, and recall in four text types. *Journal of Educational Psychology, 92,* 85–95.

Schnotz, W. (2002). Towards an integrated view of learning from text and visual displays. *Educational Psychology Review, 14,* 101–120.

Selfridge, O. G. (1959). Pandemonium: A paradigm for learning. In *The mechanization of thought processes.* London: H. M. Stationery Office.

Gregory Schraw

KOHLBERG, LAWRENCE
1927–1987

Lawrence Kohlberg (1927–1987) was a psychologist who drew on education, anthropology, and philosophy, to inform his work on the development of moral judgment and on moral behavior. Kohlberg was raised in Bronxville, New York, and attended Phillips Academy, an elite board-

Lawrence Kohlberg. BARRY DONAHUE. COURTESY OF HARVARD OFFICE OF NEWS AND PUBLIC AFFAIRS.

ing school. After World War II he assisted in smuggling European Jewish refugees to Palestine. This work, a turning point in Kohlberg's interest in morality, was documented in his first article, "Beds for Bananas" (1948). At the age of 21, Kohlberg enrolled as an undergraduate at the University of Chicago and earned his bachelor's degree within a year. Kohlberg continued studying at the University of Chicago in pursuit of a degree in clinical psychology; he was inspired by Jean Piaget's work to interview children and adolescents about morality, which was the focus of his dissertation. Kohlberg completed his doctoral degree in 1958. He held a faculty position at the University of Chicago department of psychology for six years before joining the Graduate School of Education at Harvard in 1968. Kohlberg was devoted to developing his research and mentoring students at Harvard until his death in 1987.

Kohlberg's work was particularly influenced by the philosophies of Socrates, John Locke, Thomas Jefferson, and John Stuart Mill, as well as the works of Jean Piaget and John Dewey. Just as Socrates thrived on dialogue and conflict, Kohlberg viewed such interactions as essential for his development. Thus, many of his critics could also be considered his collaborators. Most notably, this group includes feminist psychologist Carol Gilligan, who began teaching at Harvard with Erik Erickson in 1967. After meeting her in 1968, Kohlberg invited Gilligan to collaborate on a study and, in 1970, to become his teaching and research assistant. Colleagues and friends, the pair coauthored a book and several papers. In 1982, Gilligan authored *In a Different Voice*, in which she challenged Kohlberg's work by calling for the inclusion of female populations and women's perspectives in morality research. Though at odds with each other in their publications Kohlberg and Gilligan continued to teach together, actually teaching about their disagreements.

Kohlberg's initial contribution to educational psychology set the stage for the remainder of his work. Previous theories on morality assumed that society or adults imposed morality on children or that moral judgments were based on avoiding negative feelings. In contrast, Kohlberg asserted that children are moral philosophers whose ability to formulate their own moral decisions develops with experience. For his doctoral dissertation, Kohlberg interviewed 72 White Chicago boys about the Heinz dilemma: Heinz, a man without the means to buy the drug necessary to save his wife's life, steals the drug from the pharmacist. Based on the boys' responses and influenced by Piaget's theory of developmental stages, Kohlberg identified six stages of moral judgment development contained within three levels. The preconventional level includes stage 1, punishment and obedience orientation, and stage 2, instrumental relativist orientation. The conventional level includes stage 3, interpersonal concordance orientation, and stage 4, society maintaining orientation. The postconventional or principled level includes stage 5, social contract orientation, and stage 6, universal ethics principles. Seeking to validate his theory, Kohlberg developed an interview protocol and scoring guidelines (moral judgment interview) and gathered longitudinal and cross-cultural data. These studies included a 22-year study with data collected every three years and over forty studies conducted in Western and non-Western countries. Generally, these studies found support for Kohlberg's theory.

Although widely known for his theoretical and empirical work, Kohlberg focused increasingly on practical applications of his work. He consulted on and created moral education programs for schools, universities, prisons, and community organizations. The most radical of these programs was his "just community approach" in which organizations are fully democratic. Kohlberg helped several schools adopt this approach in which every student and staff member has an equal voice, and an equal vote, in every school decision. One decision at the Cluster School in Cambridge, Massachusetts, allowed students to leave school early if there was no elective course they wanted to attend. Elsa Wasserman, a Cluster School counselor, reported that the students felt a rare sense of commitment to the school and to fellow students due to the just community approach.

The impact of Kohlberg's work is not that he provided a definitive answer to a particular psychological question, but that he breathed new life into the formulation of questions and the pursuit of answers. Kohlberg brought a new perspective and new methodology to moral development inquiry and encouraged students and colleagues to challenge his and others' work by bringing their own perspectives to bear on issues. Thus, whereas Kohlberg's theory of moral development is so highly regarded that it is included in nearly every psychology textbook, Kohlberg's work as a whole energized the field, actually diversifying the perspectives and approaches represented in the moral development research conducted by other researchers.

SEE ALSO *Moral Development.*

BIBLIOGRAPHY

WORKS BY

Kohlberg, L. (1948). Beds for bananas. *Menorah Journal, 36,* 385–399.

Kohlberg, L. (1969). Stage and sequence: The cognitive developmental approach to socialization. In D. A. Goslin (Ed.), *Handbook of socialization theory and research* (pp. 347–380). Chicago: Rand McNally.

Kohlberg, L. (1984). *The psychology of moral development.* San Francisco: Harper & Row.

Kohlberg, L., & Mayer, R. (1972). Development as the aim of education. *Harvard Educational Review, 42,* 449–496.

Power, F. C., Higgins, A., & Kohlberg, L. (1989). *Lawrence Kohlberg's approach to moral education.* New York: Columbia University Press.

WORKS ABOUT

Kuchinke, K. P. (2001). Lawrence Kohlberg. In J. A. Palmer (Ed.), *Fifty modern thinkers on education: From Piaget to the present* (pp. 188–193). New York: Routledge.

Walsh, C. (2000, October 1). Reconstructing Larry: Assessing the legacy of Lawrence Kohlberg. *Ed. Magazine.* Retrieved April 9, 2008, from www.gse.harvard.edu/news/features/larry10012000_page1.html.

Anne S. Beauchamp

L

LANGUAGE IMPAIRMENTS

SEE *Speech and Language Impairments.*

LAVE, JEAN
1939–

Jean Lave is a social anthropologist, whose work on learning as an integral aspect of social practice has been a major influence on thinking in several fields, including cultural studies, sociolinguistics, organizational studies, human geography, and of course education. That so many disciplines have been influenced by her work speaks to the power of her insights.

Born in 1939, Jean Lave received her BA in anthropology from Stanford University and her PhD in social anthropology from Harvard University. She has taught at the University of California at Irvine and at Berkeley. She has done fieldwork research on the nexus of social practice, learning, and identity in a variety of settings, including Indian communities in Brazil, tailor apprentices in Africa, and shoppers in the United States. Subsequently, in the context of an ethno-historical study of the port trade undertaken with Paul Duguid, Lave investigated the complex identities of British families in Portugal (see the book *History in Person*). She has received several awards, including in 1994 the Sylvia Scribner Research Award from the American Educational Research Association in recognition of the influence of her work on thinking and research in education.

Those who have had the privilege to work with her know Lave as an exceptional teacher and collaborator, who practices her theorizing and invests in it her deep concern about the social production of marginalization. For her, in both her theory and her life, the production of knowledge is a fundamentally social enterprise. The book *Understanding Practice*, which she edited with Seth Chaiklin, reflects this ability to open spaces for learning together: It was the result of a highly collaborative two-part conference, during which a group of scholars met initially without position papers, but collaborated until a major contribution had been published.

Lave is best known for her seminal writing on situated learning, which she describes as "changing participation in changing practices." In their book *Situated Learning*, she and Etienne Wenger introduced the now widely adopted concepts of "legitimate peripheral participation" and "communities of practice."

But it is important to place these contributions in the context of Lave's intellectual trajectory. On the one hand, these developments were the result of two decades of careful studies of learning as situated in activity. Early in her career, Lave did an ethnographic study of apprenticeship among Vai and Gola tailors in Liberia, a study summarized in *Situated Learning* and analyzed in more details in a subsequent book *Apprenticeship in Critical Ethnography*. This ethnography convinced Lave that knowing and learning had to be understood as situated in the activities and trajectories of the apprentices whose new skills were part of their becoming tailors. Back in the United States, she applied the insights of the tailor study to understand the use of mathematics by shoppers in grocery stores. This study examined the complex relations among persons in action, social contexts, and knowledge-ability, and yielded an insightful critique of purely cognitive perspectives on learning laid out in her ground-breaking book *Cognition in Practice*.

On the other hand, communities of practice and legitimate peripheral participation are not isolated concepts. They are part and parcel of a broader framework, a learning theory anchored in a "historical, dialectical, social practice theory." (Lave, 1996, p. 150) This theory places learning in the context of the lived experience of persons in the socially constituted world—with its histories, cultures, institutions, identities, generations, claims to knowledge, and their contested production and reproduction in communities of practice. A person always participates in multiple communities of practice, and learning entails the development of an identity across practices.

Turning this theoretically and ethnographically informed gaze on the classroom, Lave questions some fundamental assumptions about schooling. She uses insights from apprenticeship to challenge the privileged status of teaching and to argue that learning, not teaching, is the primary phenomenon—for both students and teachers—learning as the fashioning of a trajectory of identity. Listening to students, she hears them talk about the work of entering their social reality rather than school subjects. She suggests that to advance teaching, "teachers need to know about the powerful identity-changing communities of practice of their students, which define the conditions of their work" (Lave, 1996, p. 159).

Her focus on social practice provides both a theoretical framework and a body of field research to analyze the classroom as a unique place of practice, with its own logic, politics, and history. This yields three fundamental questions about classroom teaching:

What is the practice of the classroom as a historically specific setting for learning?

How is the practice of the classroom related to "mature practices" in the world?

How is the practice of the classroom related to the everyday lives of students more broadly?

That these three questions seem natural to educators in the early 2000s is a tribute to the influence of Jean Lave.

BIBLIOGRAPHY

Lave, J. (1988). *Cognition in practice: Mind, mathematics, and culture in everyday life.* New York: Cambridge University Press.

Lave, J. (1993). The practice of learning. In Chaiklin, S., & Lave, J. (Eds.), *Understanding practice: perspectives on activity and context.* New York: Cambridge University Press.

Lave, J. (1996). Teaching, as learning, in practice. *Mind, Culture and Activity 3,* 149-164.

Lave, J. (2001). Getting to be British. In Holland, D., & Lave, J. (Eds.), *History in person: Enduring struggle, contentious practice, intimate identities.* Santa Fe, NM: School of American Research Press.

Lave, J., & Wenger, E. (1991). *Situated Learning: Legitimate Peripheral Participation.* New York: Cambridge University Press.

Etienne Wenger
John D. Smith
Marc Coenders

LEARNED HELPLESSNESS

Learned helplessness results from experiencing uncontrollable events that cause individuals to expect future lack of control. It is characterized by decreased motivation, failure to learn, and negative emotions such as sadness, anxiety, and frustration. The learned helpless response pattern was discovered accidentally during the mid-1960s in the study of animal learning: Psychologist Martin Seligman observed that after exposure to inescapable electric shock some dogs passively accepted the shock even when they could take action to turn it off. The so-called helpless dog puzzle initiated decades of research and theory on learned helplessness that covered various topics, including passivity in laboratory rats, clinical depression, children's classroom behavior, success in selling insurance policies, and mortality in nursing homes.

Learned helplessness is formally defined as a disruption in motivation, affect, and learning following exposure to noncontingent (uncontrollable) outcomes. There are three crucial elements to its definition: contingency, cognition, and behavior. Contingency refers to the objective relationship between actions and outcomes; for helplessness to occur there must be no relationship between a person's actions and the outcome he or she experiences. Cognition refers to how individuals perceive the contingency, explain it, and extrapolate from this understanding. The perception of uncontrollability (noncontingency) may be accurate or inaccurate, but once it occurs individuals attempt to explain it. From this explanation they make extrapolations about the future and, when learned helplessness occurs, they expect that their behavior will not influence future outcomes. Behavior refers to the observable effects of being exposed to uncontrollable outcomes. Most often it involves a sense of giving up—weaker attempts to control the situation or even failure to try to do so at all—a behavior incompatible with new learning. The response is also accompanied by negative emotions such as anxiety and sadness.

LEARNED HELPLESSNESS IN CHILDREN

It was not long before the idea of learned helplessness was extended to child behavior. In the early 1970s, Carol Dweck demonstrated that some children adopted the view that once failure occurred the situation was out of their control and that there was nothing they could do. Specifically, she used children's explanations for failure on a questionnaire to study two groups, those who viewed failure as due to insufficient effort and those who did not. She was able to document two response patterns to failure by having fifth and sixth grade students talk out loud while attempting problems too difficult for their age level immediately after successfully solving age-appropriate problems. She labeled the patterns learned helpless and mastery oriented.

The learned helpless pattern, shown by children whose questionnaire responses did not invoke insufficient effort for failure, involved denigrating their abilities upon encountering failure, overestimating the number of problems they did not solve, and expressing considerable self-doubt. Their performance deteriorated as they were less likely to solve problems after experiencing failure even when the problems were identical to those solved before the failure. Integral to this response pattern is the experience of negative feelings, including anxiety, sadness, and expressed boredom. Thus, the helpless pattern comprises a reaction to failure that undermines the self and impairs performance.

The mastery oriented pattern, in contrast, leads to increased motivation in the face of failure. Children who demonstrate this response pattern typically show some form of self-instruction or self-monitoring when they encounter failure. Their mood remains positive and they maintain the belief in their ability to perform well. Their optimistic view is matched by their behavior as most (over 80%) maintain or improve their problem-solving strategies and they solve just as many, or more, problems as they did prior to experiencing failure. In sum, these children view failure as a challenge and as a learning opportunity, not as an indictment of their ability.

These response patterns show that the differences are not due to ability. Children who display learned helpless versus mastery oriented patterns perform equally well prior to encountering failure, but those who are mastery oriented show superior performance following a failure experience. About 80% to 85% of all students clearly demonstrate one of the response patterns with students of all abilities falling into each group. It is therefore not uncommon to find very intelligent, bright students who are learned helpless, a group that is all too easily overlooked in the classroom.

LEARNED HELPLESSNESS IN THE CLASSROOM

Because the patterns described were identified in rigorous experimental studies, it is important to note that they have also been shown to occur on typical classroom tasks. Specifically, children who encountered confusing instructions in a questionnaire booklet in the classroom performed differently on subsequent questions depending on whether they fell into learned helpless or mastery oriented groups. Under these circumstances, the number of children answering all questions correctly was lower for those showing the learned helpless response pattern (34.6%) as compared to the mastery oriented pattern (71.9%). When, however, the instructions were clear, there was no appreciable difference in the performance of helpless (76.6%) and mastery (68.4%) groups.

Learned helplessness in the classroom can result from teacher behavior. This discovery emerged from the observation that girls in grade school receive higher grades and less negative feedback in the classroom than boys. Although the feedback girls receive confirms their

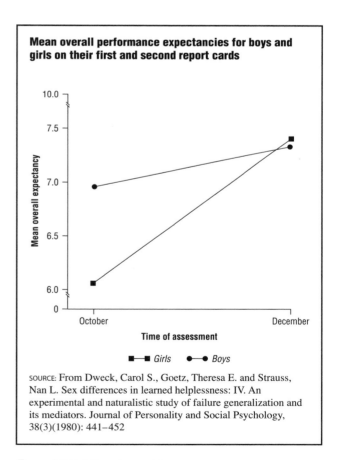

SOURCE: From Dweck, Carol S., Goetz, Theresa E. and Strauss, Nan L. Sex differences in learned helplessness: IV. An experimental and naturalistic study of failure generalization and its mediators. Journal of Personality and Social Psychology, 38(3)(1980): 441–452

Figure 1 ILLUSTRATION BY GGS INFORMATION SERVICES. CENGAGE LEARNING, GALE.

competence they tend to question their ability in the face of failure, putting them at greater risk of displaying learned helplessness. In an attempt to address this conundrum, Dweck and colleagues observed the pattern of evaluative feedback given to boys and girls in grade school classrooms (Dweck et al., 1978). They found that the contingencies of feedback differed in that 45% of boys' work-related feedback referred to its nonintellectual aspects (e.g., neatness) whereas for girls the feedback referred almost exclusively to its intellectual quality. Teachers also more frequently ascribed boys' failures to lack of motivation. They then conducted an experiment to show that both boys and girls who received the teacher-girl contingency were more likely to view subsequent failure feedback from that evaluator as indicative of their ability.

The teacher-boy feedback pattern allows boys to avoid ascribing failure to their ability and to even blame the teacher for negative feedback, allowing them to enter a new grade with high expectations of success. This option is less likely for those experiencing the teacher-girl contingency as the areas of academic performance remain similar; hence, failure attributed to lack of ability will remain relevant. If correct, boys should be able to enter a new grade level with higher expectancies for success as compared to girls, but these differences should decrease as children experience evaluation from the new teacher. This is precisely what Dweck, Goetz, and Strauss (1980) found when expected success was assessed at the beginning of a school year (October) and later in the year (December).

There is some evidence that the learned helpless and mastery oriented patterns are socialized by parents. For example, parents who attribute their children's failures to their children's ability tend to have children who display helpless behaviors (Fincham & Cain, 1986). Observation of third grade children and their mothers performing a series of solvable and insolvable problem-solving tasks showed that mastery oriented children had mothers who increased task-focused teaching behaviors and maintained high-positive affect during the insolvable puzzles, whereas mothers of children showing learned helplessness reciprocated their child's negative affect. Similarly, when children mentioned performance goals, mothers of the learned helpless group responded by focusing on performance, whereas mothers in the mastery oriented group redirected attention by focusing on a learning goal (e.g., "Let's see if we can figure out a pattern here").

IMPLICATIONS OF LEARNED HELPLESS FOR EDUCATORS

Attempts to remediate learned helplessness have largely focused on changing the ability attributions associated with learned helplessness to effort attributions (e.g., "Work harder and you'll do better"). These attempts efforts have met with limited success possibly because little attention has been given to the perceived credibility of the feedback. When credible, such feedback likely increases motivation, but it may be demoralizing if not credible. Effort attribution feedback is likely most successful in the early stages of learning and for difficult tasks, when greater effort can produce better results and its credibility is high. However, Dale Schunk has found that ability feedback (e.g., "You're good at this") given when children succeeded early in the course of learning enhanced achievement better than effort feedback.

Although feedback that focuses on controllable attributions (e.g., effort, strategy use) is widely recommended, research suggests that focusing students' attention on the goal of learning rather than on showing how well they can perform has beneficial effects in combating helplessness. Success obtained in attempts to remediate learned helpless responding has occurred largely in short term interventions, and it remains to be determine how best to produce lasting changes. In view of evidence that a relationship develops over time between learned helplessness patterns and children's achievement level (Fincham, Hokoda, & Sanders, 1989), there is an urgent need to address this gap in researchers' knowledge.

SEE ALSO *Attribution Theory; Attributional Retraining.*

BIBLIOGRAPHY

Dweck, C. S., Davidson, W., Nelson, S., & Bradley, E. (1978). Sex differences in learned helplessness: II. The contingencies of evaluative feedback in the classroom and III. An Experimental Analysis. *Developmental Psychology* 14(3), 268–276.

Fincham, F. D., & Cain, K. M. (1986). Learned helplessness in humans: A developmental analysis. *Developmental Review* 6(4), 301–333.

Fincham, F. D., Hokoda, A., & Sanders, R., Jr. (1989). Learned helplessness, test anxiety, and academic achievement: A longitudinal analysis. *Child Development* 60(1), 138–145.

Hokoda, A., & Fincham, F. D. (1995). Origins of children's helpless and mastery achievement patterns in the family. *Journal of Educational Psychology* 87(3), 375–385.

Peterson, C., Maier, S. F., & Seligman, M. S. (1993). *Learned helplessness: A theory for the age of personal control.* Oxford: Oxford University Press.

Schunk, D. H. (1984). Sequential attributional feedback and children's achievement behaviors. *Journal of Educational Psychology* 76(6), 1159–1169.

Frank D. Fincham

LEARNING AND TEACHING FOREIGN LANGUAGES

Although a large proportion of the world's population speaks two (or more) languages, the psychological study of second/foreign language learning is not commonplace. Typically, courses in second language learning are not offered in departments of psychology; thus, few students ever have the opportunity to avail themselves of such knowledge. This is unfortunate because psychology has much to offer to the field of foreign language instruction. Almost everyone has studied a second language at some time in their schooling, but only a few psychologists have developed a specialized interest in learning and teaching a second language (e.g., Bialystok, 2001; Hakuta, 1986; Hamers & Blanc, 2000; Rivers, 1964; Krashen, 1981).

The relevance of second language learning and teaching for psychology is as critical as any topic having to do with the intricacies involved in any aspect of human learning. The goal here is to discuss a few of the psychological questions involved in second language learning and to provide a theoretical and empirical understanding for why the learning and teaching of foreign languages is a legitimate area of work for psychologists (see McLaughlin, 1987; Padilla, 2006). This discussion will be framed around key questions in the field of language education.

METHODS FOR TEACHING A NEW LANGUAGE TO STUDENTS

Over the years many methods for teaching a new language have evolved. The most longstanding method and the one that has been most heavily influenced by the work of psychologists is the Audio-Lingual Method (Rivers, 1964). The goal in this method is to overlearn the target language through communicative drills directed by the teacher. The idea is to use the target language to the point that it becomes automatic and in the process new habits in the language are formed that overcome the tendency to rely on first language habits. In this method new vocabulary and grammatical structures are presented through teacher-directed dialogue drills, as well as heavy reliance on language lab drills organized around imitation and repetition drills. Students' correct responses are positively reinforced. Listening and speaking in the second language are the objectives in this method. Students' native language habits are considered as interfering, thus the use of the native language is restricted in the classroom. This method emphasizes proper pronunciation, simple everyday dialogues, and correct grammar.

In recent years there has been a gradual shift in language education to an approach that favors communicative competence in the second language. This is called the Communicative Approach. The goal of this approach is to teach students the new language through classroom activities that engage students in the process of negotiating meaning in everyday conversations, rather than in teacher-directed repetitions of contrived dialogues. Students are taught to be communicators, not learners merely of vocabulary and grammar as in the audio-lingual method. In this approach to teaching a new language, the emphasis is on developing motivation to learn through establishing meaningful, purposeful things to do with the new language (see Padilla, 2006). Individuality in using the new language is encouraged, as well as cooperation with peers, which promotes a sense of personal competence in the use of the target language.

DEFINING FOREIGN LANGUAGE AND SECOND LANGUAGE EDUCATION

The social context in which a new language is learned is the deciding factor in determining whether the new language is identified as a foreign or second language. For example, a program that teaches students English in school in the United States is referred to as English as a second language (ESL) instruction. However, in the same school and down the hall from the ESL classroom, a teacher may be instructing students in Spanish, French, or Japanese. Because these languages are not the primary medium of communication in the United States, students in these classes are learning a foreign language (FL). The distinction is subtle but important. English language learners (ELLs) are immersed in English and get much more authentic English input from native speakers than students learning a foreign language (e.g., French) since this is not the medium of everyday communication in the United States. Thus, English learners have many sources (e.g., peers and mass media) and opportunities for receiving English language input. In contrast, students learning a foreign language in an American school typically have only their teacher to rely on for authentic language input. The distinctions in language learning contexts are important because they reveal how language instruction is planned and implemented.

An important contrast between foreign language education and English language instruction is that in an FL class students are not expected to develop proficiency in one or two years of instruction. Even students who reach the advanced placement level in an FL are seldom capable of showing a high level of oral proficiency in the FL. However, in ESL instruction students are expected to be mainstreamed into English-only classrooms within one or two years. For many learners this is an unreasonable expectation that often creates other related school achievement difficulties. Thus, expectations differ depending on whether the discussion is about learning a second or a foreign language.

ELEMENTS INVOLVED IN LEARNING A SECOND LANGUAGE

Language learning is complex, whether the language is acquired in infancy as a first language or later in life as a second or third language. The learning process consists of acquiring a language system, rather than learning a series of disconnected components. A language system consists of not only grammatical rules and vocabulary, but also the proper way to use language, such as requesting information, inviting a friend to a social event, thanking a person for a kind act, or greeting a stranger. In addition, a language system includes discourse, whereby speakers learn what to say to whom and when.

In their research on bilingualism, Hamers and Blanc (2000) studied how bilinguals carry out a large variety of cognitive tasks in the two languages. Bilingualism involves having a command of the linguistic system—the phonology, morphology, syntax, semantics, and pragmatics—that constitute the essence of each language, but it also means being able to keep the languages separate cognitively when necessary, and strategies to search the memory store in one language in order to use the information in the other language.

The specific elements of the language system learned in a second language classroom vary by language. For example, the student learning Chinese or Farsi must learn an entirely new orthography, whereas students learning Spanish will only have minor differences in alphabets to contend with (Akamatsu, 2002). Some languages will have very different sentence structures compared to English; others will appear to be more familiar. However, familiarity with the language system alone is not enough to enable students to engage in successful communicative activities. Learners also acquire the strategies that assist them in bridging communication gaps that result from differences of language and culture. Examples of these strategies include circumlocution (saying things in different ways), using context clues, understanding, interpreting, producing gestures effectively, asking for and providing clarification, and negotiating meaning with others.

In language learning and teaching an important concept is comprehensible input. Students can only learn what they understand and in language teaching this means that the teacher must make content comprehensible. There is a theoretical debate about what exactly comprehensible input is and how it advances a learner's knowledge of a new language (Sanz, 2005). However, at a practical level teachers understand that with early to intermediate language learners, teaching for comprehension includes providing many nonverbal clues such as pictures, objects, demonstrations, gestures, and intonation cues. As competency in the language develops, other strategies include using hands-on activities and coopera-

tive or peer tutoring techniques. As learners' vocabulary and knowledge of the language expands, they are able to comprehend more information. Ultimately, mastery demands that learners understand what the teacher is saying in class or what a native speaker is saying in a real-life context as well as the appropriate conversational interactive exchanges in and out of the classroom. Sound strategies for teaching languages to students who differ by their level of proficiency have been incorporated into a compendium, "Standards for Foreign Language Learning in the 21st Century" (National Standards in Foreign Language Education Project, 1999). All of the professional language associations have endorsed the Standards and they are a critical element in teacher education programs today. In fact, education students must demonstrate mastery of these Standards in order to receive their teaching credential to teach a foreign language.

THE ROLE OF MOTIVATION

Gardner (1985) studied a variety of psychological and social variables in examining the role of motivation in second language learning. According to Gardner, anyone who seeks to learn a second language recognizes the potential value of speaking a new language and must be motivated to learn the language for one of two reasons: instrumental purposes (e.g., to get a job or to meet a school graduation requirement) or for integrative purposes (e.g., to understand better how native speakers of the language think and behave). Motivation underlies the learning of language because it addresses the goals and expectations of the learner as well as the teacher. If a person is only interested in enough survival skills in a new language to be able to secure employment then the level of attainment will be different from learners who want to read and discuss the important literature of another culture. In an extension of Gardner's research, Sung and Padilla (1998) found an "ethnic heritage-related motivation" for learning Chinese, Korean, or Japanese. Students who wanted to learn the language of their ancestors were more motivated to learn these more difficult languages, especially if their parents also wanted them to learn the language. Thus, knowing students' reasons for learning a second language enables teachers to plan an appropriate curriculum.

TIME INVOLVED IN LEARNING A SECOND LANGUAGE

How long it takes to learn a second language is an important pedagogical as well as psychological question because the answer depends in part on the learner's age, aptitude, personality, and motivation. If a person wants just enough language to be able to interact on a social level with native speakers, he or she will spend considerably less time learning the new language than a person who wants to be able to succeed academically in a classroom in the new language and compete with native speakers.

The learning of basic survival communication skills in a new language takes a few months to a year or two depending on the amount of language input the learner receives from native speakers of the target language, the accuracy of second language output demanded by the context, the motivation of the learner, and the amount of practice in listening and speaking the new language. This depends too on the age of the learner. The knowledge of the new language that a child would need to interact with native speakers on the playground is different from what would be required of a university student who intends to study in Spain or China and take academic coursework in Spanish or Mandarin with native students. The time needed to master a second language for interpersonal communication is considerably less than the time required to master second language oral and literacy (reading and writing) skills in order to do academic level courses with native speakers of the second language.

In sum, there is no one answer to the question of how much time is necessary to learn a second language. The answer depends on expectations of what language skills (oral, listening, reading, or writing) and level of proficiency are desirable in the student. If the goal is basic survival skills, the amount of time needed will be far less than if the aim is to develop a high level of communicative competency.

ATTAINING PROFICIENCY IN A SECOND LANGUAGE

A learner who is proficient in a second language is able to exhibit a high level of accuracy in the second language. This includes being able to use the new language with grammatical accuracy in ways that are contextually and culturally authentic. Accuracy pertains to the precision of the message in terms of fluency, grammar, vocabulary, pronunciation, and cultural appropriateness. When language practice reflects real-world use, it forms the foundation for developing proficiency. This is true regardless of age, grade level, and type of language instruction offered the student.

The demands of accuracy in a second language, as can be seen, are high. There are four modes of expression—listening, speaking, reading, and writing—that constitute the paths by which information and concepts are transmitted from one person to another. Listening and reading are receptive skills; speaking and writing are productive skills. Students cannot create the language they are learning without first receiving input from teachers, peers, and the media. Thus, developing proficiency in each of these modes reinforces proficiency in the other modes. For

example, learning to read in a new language facilitates vocabulary acquisition, which augments speaking and writing in the second language. Thus, all four modes of expression are important elements in language learning, and their use is required in all formal classroom contexts.

Bialystok (2001) has shown that language input provided to language learners and the language output expected of them must be developmentally appropriate in two senses: (1) appropriate to the developing level of second language learning that the person has attained, and (2) appropriate to the cognitive and linguistic level of the student in his or her first language. In first language acquisition research shows that parents simplify their language input to their young children by speaking slower, frequent repetition, and simplified vocabulary and grammar. Hakuta (1985) argues that good language teachers use these same strategies in the early stages of ESL or FL instruction.

As the learner advances in the acquisition of the second language, three categories of discourse describe language use on the basis of receptive and productive skills. The categories are: interactive comprehension and production, receptive comprehension, and comprehensible production. Examples of interactive comprehension and production include telephone conversations and correspondence with friends through e-mail or instant messaging. These activities provide for an exchange of ideas. If one person does not understand the interchange, it is relatively simple to achieve understanding by seeking clarification. The interactive comprehension and production category of discourse is common in the social use of language.

Receptive comprehension refers to activities such as reading a book in a science class or viewing a video in a history class, activities that preclude seeking clarification from the author or narrator. In these situations, readers or listeners rely solely on their reservoir of concepts and language decoding skills for comprehension. Receptive comprehension becomes increasingly important with each grade level because students are required to do more reading and to integrate the information acquired with new knowledge presented by the teacher. Teachers are very important in this stage since they can provide valuable strategies to help students advance to more complex language structures.

Comprehensible production is critical because it shows what a learner is capable of doing in their new language (e.g., completing a job application, making an oral class presentation). During such activities the second language user makes a presentation or writes a letter that precludes any seeking of clarification of meaning by the reader or listener. This places a responsibility on the second language user to communicate with clarity and accuracy. The comprehensible production category of discourse is common in the academic use of language. Further, many high-stakes tests (e.g., AP tests in a foreign language) include a writing component that requires students to produce an essay that is scored not only for grammaticality, but for the persuasiveness of an argument.

METHODS FOR TEACHING A SECOND LANGUAGE

Many strategies have evolved over the years to teach a second or foreign language to students. It is beyond the scope of this entry to cover all the methods that can be found in schools. However, two such methods used at the elementary school level will be described.

Foreign Language in the Elementary School. In this model a second language is presented as a distinct subject—much like science or social studies—that is typically taught at least three to five times per week, with classes lasting anywhere from 20 to 50 minutes. Most FLES programs focus on teaching the four communication skills, as well as the culture of the speakers of the language being learned. Some programs called content-based or content-enriched programs incorporate themes and objectives from the regular academic curriculum as a vehicle for developing foreign language skills. Depending on the frequency and time devoted to language instruction and the opportunities provided for practicing the language, children can attain substantial second language proficiency.

Immersion Programs. Immersion programs have grown in popularity in Canada and the United States since the late 1970s (Padilla, 2006). In an immersion program English-speaking children spend part or all of the school day learning a second language (e.g., French, Spanish, Japanese). In a full (total) immersion program, students learn all subjects (e.g., math, social studies, science) in the second language. Partial immersion programs operate on the same principle, but only a portion of the curriculum is presented in the second language. Partial immersion programs are generally more common than full immersion programs. In this type of program students may learn social studies and math in the second language for part of the day, and science and language arts in English for the remainder of the day. In both full and partial immersion, the second language is the medium for the content instruction rather than the subject of instruction. Students enrolled in immersion programs work toward full proficiency in the second language and usually reach a higher level of language competence than students participating in FLES or other types of language programs. The research findings supporting this conclusion are well established.

In conclusion, there are many ways in which psychologists can contribute to the study of foreign language teaching and learning. Psychologists have much to give to educators and parents who want to know more about the latest research in cognition and language and how this applies to learning a second language.

BIBLIOGRAPHY

Akamatsu, N. (2002). A similarity in word-recognition procedures among second language readers with different first language backgrounds. *Applied Psycholinguistics, 23*(1), 117–133.

Bialystok, E. (2001). *Bilingualism in Development: Language, Literacy, and Cognition.* New York: Cambridge University Press.

Gardner, R. C. (1985). *Social psychology and second language learning: The role of attitudes and motivation.* London: Edward Arnold.

Hakuta, K. (1986). *Mirror of language: The debate on bilingualism.* New York: Basic Books.

Hamers, J. F., & M. H. Blanc. (2000). *Bilinguality & bilingualism* (2nd ed.). Cambridge, England: Cambridge University Press.

Krashen, S. D. (1981). *Principles and practice in second language acquisition.* English Language Teaching series. London: Prentice-Hall International (UK) Ltd.

McLaughlin, B. (1987). *Theories of second language acquisition.* London: Edward Arnold.

National Standards in Foreign Language Education Project. (1999). *Standards for foreign language learning in the 21st century.* Lawrence, KS: Allen Press.

Padilla, A. M. (2006). Second language learning: Issues in research and teaching. In P. A. Alexander and P. H. Wine (Eds.), *Handbook of educational psychology* (2nd ed.). Mahwah, NJ: Erlbaum.

Rivers, W. M. (1964). *The psychologist and the foreign-language teacher.* Chicago: University of Chicago Press.

Sanz, C. (Ed.) (2005). *Mind & context in adult second language acquisition.* Washington, DC: Georgetown University Press.

Sung, H., & Padilla, A. M. (1998). Student motivation, parental attitudes, and involvement in the learning of Asian languages in elementary and secondary schools. *Modern Language Journal 82*(2), 205–216.

Amado M. Padilla
Ali Borjian

LEARNING AND TEACHING MATHEMATICS

Major theoretical approaches to learning and teaching mathematics have been developed from three psychological perspectives of human learning. The *social constructivist approach* to mathematical learning emphasizes classroom learning as a process of both individual and

Doing a problem on the board helps students share solutions and strategies with the whole class. © **TERRY VINE/CORBIS.**

social construction. Critical to this framework is the need for mathematics teachers to construct a form of practice that fits with their students' ways of learning mathematics (Wood, Cobb, & Yackel, 1995). "The most basic responsibility of constructivist teachers is to learn the mathematical knowledge of their students and how to harmonize their teaching methods with the nature of that mathematical knowledge" (Steffe & Wiegel, 1992, p. 17). This is the planning whereby teachers plant powerful mathematical ideas in a personally meaningful context for students to investigate. Cobb, Wood, and Yackel (1993) further elaborate on teachers' responsibility in the mathematics classroom as playing the dual role of fostering the development of conceptual knowledge among students and facilitating the constitution of what is often referred to as taken-as-shared knowledge in the classroom community. This is the teaching in which, without direct access to one another's understanding, members of the classroom community achieve through social interaction a sense of some aspects of knowledge being shared, promoted by classroom social norms understood by members as constitut-

ing effective participation in the mathematics classroom community.

The underlying metaphor of social constructivism is *persons in conversation,* which highlights the critical role of language (see Ernest, 1996). For example, when teaching the theorem that the sum of the three inner angles of a triangle is 180 degrees, a teacher practicing social constructivism would present the idea of moving the three angles together to calculate the sum and would then have students talk about or share their ideas about moving angles. Manipulatives would be provided to students so that they could take a triangle apart and experiment with different ways of making three angles come together. Students would find that many of their ideas about moving angles would produce three angles forming a straight line indicating 180 degrees. This physical construction would then be followed by another "talk point" for students promoted by the teacher about how to move angles mathematically for geometric proof. Students, now with papers and pencils, would engage in continuing conversation about moving angles mathematically with the main idea being creating equal angles in different places in order to pull three angles together (the mathematical construction would refer frequently to the physical construction). The language elements are always critical during the whole process from moving angles physically to moving angles mathematically.

The cognitive science approach to mathematical learning emphasizes the nature of knowledge representation (this separates cognitive psychologists from constructivist theorists). Representation in mathematical learning can take on different forms: cognitive (the internal representation of a learner's knowledge), mathematical (the mathematical representation of a mathematical structure), symbolic (the external representation of a mathematical notation), explanatory (the model and theory developed to account for cognitive structures and processes), and computational (the hypothetical mental representation in computer programs based on observed human behaviors) (see English & Halford, 1995). These representations provide a way to construct cognitive models of mental structures of mathematical knowledge and cognitive processes of mathematical learning. Cognitive processes operate on cognitive representations (mental structures) that are viewed as a network of interrelated mathematical ideas.

The quality of mathematical learning is measured through the number of connections that learners can make among mental representations and the strength of each connection (Hiebert & Carpenter, 1992). The notion of connected representation "provides an effective link between theoretical cognitive issues and practical classroom issues" (English & Halford, 1995, p. 13). Cognitive science has proven to be the most effective way to investigate problem-solving behaviors in mathematics. In addition to solid mathematical knowledge, successful problem solving in mathematics is found to require "a repertoire of general problem-solving heuristics" that remind mathematics educators of the classic work of Polya (1957) (English & Halford, 1995, p. 14).

For example, English and Halford (1995) argued that "a mental model of the relations between numbers themselves" is needed to truly understand numbers (p. 60). The mental model starts with a correspondence between a number and a set of objects (e.g., 5 corresponds to five apples). Relations between numbers can then correspond to relations between sets. Because the set of five apples has more objects (members) than the set of three apples, 5 is larger than 3. Students establish the mental model of number by experimenting with sets of objects to reinforce the correspondence between number relations and set relations. Without this mental model, most students would have to rely on the succession relation to understand numbers, with rote learning emphasizing the counting order of the numbers. Obviously, the notion that 5 is larger than 3 because 5 comes after 3 is at best vague and fuzzy to most students.

The sociocultural approach to mathematical learning emphasizes the effort to situate mathematical ideas within culturally organized activities. Because education is a process of enculturation (or socialization), it is important for learners to engage in social interaction with more knowledgeable experts in what Lev Vygotsky called the *zone of proximal development* and for teachers to use culturally developed sign systems and culturally appropriate artifacts as psychological tools for instruction (Vygotsky, 1978). "The qualities of thinking [and learning] are actually generated by the organizational features of the social interaction" (van Oers, 1996, p. 93). Internalization is another central notion in Vygotsky's cultural-historical theory of human development which "appears first between people as an intermental category and then within the child as an intramental category" (Vygotsky, 1960, p. 197–198). Particularly relevant to mathematics education is the notion that "learning is the initiation into a social tradition [of mathematical inquiry, mathematical discovery, mathematical argument, and so on]" (Solomon, 1989, p. 150).

With enculturation as the emphasis, a teacher who employs the sociocultural approach to teach mathematics would design a learning task through which students can interact with experts. Simply put, it is a process of guided participation and interaction of learning by solving problems just beyond a student's current capability with the help of a more expert other via scaffolding. Experts do not necessarily imply mathematicians. Teachers are most often the experts in real classrooms, and continuing professional development strengthens their expertise in mathematics. In addition, teaching assistants, advanced peers, and even parents can all be trained to become mathematics experts in real classrooms.

For the theorem that the sum of the three inner angles of a triangle is 180 degrees, experts would ask well-thought questions around the main idea of creating equal angles in different places so that the three angles can be pulled together to examine the sum. These questions prepare students for the demonstration of experts who would show students how to move one angle (both physically and mathematically), would have students comment on the move, and would ask students to move the other angles following a similar strategy. Observing students closely, experts would alert students of wrong moves, would point out reasons for wrong moves, and would demonstrate correct moves repeatedly. This modeling and coaching process between experts and students, often considered apprenticeship in nature, is the very foundation of the sociocultural approach that requires social participation and interaction of the whole classroom community. Finally, experts would evaluate with students on different strategies of moving angles and would reason with them on the best way to move angles.

The whole interaction between experts and students would end up with the establishment (or enculturation) of an important mathematical tradition (or practice) on the use of auxiliary lines for geometric proof. As a result, experts would have trained students on geometric proof in a way very similar to how masters would have trained apprentices in, say, furniture building.

LEARNING GOALS FOR MATHEMATICS EDUCATION

"Students must learn mathematics with understanding, actively building new knowledge from experience and prior knowledge" (National Council of Teachers of Mathematics [NCTM], 2000, p. 11). The mathematics education research community has been fairly united in identifying understanding as the major learning goal for mathematics education—teaching mathematics for understanding. Simon (2006) stated:

> Recent discourse in mathematics education has coalesced around the importance of focusing on and fostering students' mathematical understanding. This agreement among mathematics educators has led to a commitment to generate new learning goals for students that are less skewed in favor of skill and facts learning and more focused on student thinking. (p. 359)

Although mathematics education has a long history, teaching mathematics for understanding is a fairly new notion.

Believing that two effectively different subjects are taught under the same name called mathematics, Richard Skemp published his classic paper on mathematical understanding in 1976. He distinguished between *instrumental understanding* (knowing how) and *relational understanding* (knowing both how and why). According to Skemp (1976), there are three advantages in instrumental understanding of mathematics: (a) easier to understand, (b) more immediate and more apparent rewards, and (c) quicker in getting correct answers. But the metaphor for instrumental understanding is *getting an instruction to go to a certain place* (i.e., still not knowing how to go to any new place). There are four advantages in relational understanding of mathematics: (a) more adaptable to new tasks, (b) easier to remember, (c) effective as a goal in itself, and (d) organic in quality. The metaphor for relational understanding is *getting a map to go to a certain place* (i.e., knowing how to go to any new place).

It is common among teachers to use rhymes to help students understand mathematical properties. Such an effort in many cases results in instrumental understand-ing. For example, many teachers use the following rhyme to help students understand (or memorize) the order of number operation: *Please* (parenthesis) *Excuse* (exponential) *My* (multiplication) *Dear* (division) *Aunt* (addition) *Sally* (subtraction). Many students who have gained instrumental understanding through this teaching practice would mistakenly believe that, for example, they should do addition before subtraction because of the order shown in the rhyme. This rhyme does not illustrate the fact that there are equivalent levels of operation. The order of operation does not matter between multiplication and division. Neither does it between addition and subtraction.

In contrast to instrumental understanding, relational understanding aims to make students know the very reason behind every mathematical action (or manipulation). For example, when solving the equation $2X-4 = 8$, for X, a teacher adopting instrumental understanding would procedurally have students move the 4 from the left side of the equation to the right side. Their instrumental understanding also reminds them to change the sign of the number (in this case from negative to positive): $2X = 8 + 4$ or $2X = 12$. However, many students have no understanding of why this rule governs this mathematical action. Instead of having students learn this procedural rule, a teacher adopting relational understanding would emphasize properties of equation operation, such as the one that adding the same number to both sides of an equation keeps equality. Therefore, students with relational understanding would perform: $2X-4 + 4 = 8 + 4$ resulting in $2X = 12$.

Instrumental understanding produces procedural knowledge, whereas relational understanding produces conceptual knowledge. Hiebert and Lefevre (1986) defined conceptual knowledge as "knowledge that is rich in relationships ... a network in which the linking relationships are as prominent as the discrete pieces of information" (pp. 3–4, cited in Simon, 2006). This is the reason why effective classroom teaching for mathematical understanding often emphasizes one key aspect of understanding: connection.

Researchers have increasingly recognized the importance of affect-related factors in mathematical learning and teaching. Stuart (2000) stated that "mathematics is like a sport: [performance is] 90 percent mental—one's mathematics confidence—and 10 percent physical— one's mathematics competence in performing mathematical skills" (p. 330–331). After a review of studies, Eynde, de Corte, and Verschaffel (2002) noted that both affective and cognitive factors play a key role as the constituting elements of the learning process:

> Motivation and volition (i.e., the conative factors) are no longer seen as just the fuel or the engine of the

REFORM AND CONTROVERSY IN MATHEMATICS INSTRUCTION

Between 1955 and 1975 mathematics education in the United States underwent major—and expensive—curricular reforms called "modern mathematics" or "new math." The movement took various and sometimes contradictory forms with uneven implementation and outcomes. In 1989 the National Research Council (NRC) published *Everybody Counts: A Report to the Nation on the Future of Mathematics Education*. It identified some of the successes and failures of the reform movement:

- Some important aspects, such as a renewed emphasis on geometry, probability, and statistics, were widely adopted.
- Applications of mathematics to other fields, such as biology and business, became accepted components of mathematics curricula.
- Some attempts at deepening mathematical understanding, such as sets and commutative law, were poorly applied and became the butt of public ridicule.
- By moving the curricula into unfamiliar territory, teachers and schools lost the confidence of parents and the community.

Everybody Counts outlined some of the lessons learned from these attempts at curricular reform:

- The wholesale adoption by school districts of an intact outside curriculum is destined for failure.
- Superficial district-wide curricular overhauls can be disastrous.
- Improvement in mathematics curricula and instruction requires a major public information campaign, strong leadership from teachers, parents, professionals, and politicians, and strong public support.

The NRC report identified ongoing transitions in mathematics education:

- from minimal mathematics for the majority of students and advanced mathematics for the gifted few to a common core of mathematics instruction for all students
- from an authoritarian "transmission of knowledge" to student-centered "stimulation of learning"
- from public indifference or hostility toward mathematics to a recognition of its importance in contemporary society
- from a focus on routine skills to developing broad-based mathematical abilities, including discerning relationships, logical reasoning, and using a wide variety of methods for solving new problems
- from preparation for subsequent math courses to topics with relevance for the present and future needs of students
- from an emphasis on paper-and-pencil calculations to the use of calculators and computers
- from a public perception of mathematics as a static set of rules to an appreciation of mathematics as an active science of patterns.

The National Council of Teachers of Mathematics (NCTM) published their landmark *Curriculum and Evaluation Standards for School Mathematics* in the same year as the NRC report. Among the NCTM's recommendations:

- Voluntary acceptance of national standards based on the work of the NCTM to establish a common philosophy and framework for mathematics education
- Local implementation of reform involving the entire community
- The study of mathematics during every school year, including a broad range of mathematical subjects, the use mathematics in other classes, and the active engagement of students in learning
- The involvement of parents in demanding that schools meet the NCTM standards, encouraging their children to continue studying math, expecting homework to involve more than routine computations, and supporting teachers in curricular improvements
- An upgrading of the teaching profession, with teachers working together, familiarizing themselves with issues of mathematical education, examining current practice, and debating new proposals, and team teaching at the elementary level

- Designing appropriate assessments for future needs
- Strengthening college mathematics.

In 2000 the NCTM published *Principles and Standards for School Mathematics (PSSM)*, a refinement of the 1989 standards, outlining a common foundation for mathematics education for all students from preschool through grade 12. Its numerous recommendations for reform were generated from a set of principles:

- The Equity Principle: high expectations and strong support for all students, including an end to tracking that permanently excludes groups of students from a challenging comprehensive mathematics program to be replaced by structures that accommodate differences
- The Curriculum Principle: a consistent curriculum through the grade levels that draws on research for implementing standards and is chosen with input from families and the community
- The Teaching Principle: teacher understanding of what students know and need to learn and challenging and supporting them; teachers adapting to changing curricula and technologies and incorporating new knowledge about how students learn mathematics; improved pre-service education, professional development, and collaboration
- The Learning Principle: students have time and opportunity to learn mathematics with understanding and to build on prior knowledge

and experience; elementary students study mathematics for at least one hour per day with well-prepared teachers who enjoy math, including team teaching and the use of specialists; middle and high school students take the equivalent of one year of mathematics at each grade level, spending a substantial amount of time each day on work that keeps them engaged in mathematical learning

- The Assessment Principle: multiple forms of assessment that are aligned with instructional goals and provide teachers and students with useful information
- The Technology Principle: equitable allocation and utilization of technology that is embedded in the curriculum and enhances teaching and learning.

The *PSSM* stressed the urgent need for mathematics specialists to work with teachers, administrators, families, and community members.

In 2006 the NCTM published *Curriculum Focal Points for Prekindergarten through Grade 8 Mathematics*, which was—at least in part—a response to criticism that the *PSSM* had led to curricula lacking basic instruction in arithmetic. However controversy over new standards and teaching methods remained at least as heated as that over the new math in the 1960s and 1970s.

Margaret Alic

learning process, but are perceived as fundamentally determining the quality of the learning. In a similar way, self-confidence and positive emotions (affective factors) are no longer considered as just positive side effects of learning, but become important constituent elements of learning and problem solving. (p. 14)

NCTM has been highlighting five new goals for mathematical learning and teaching since 1989 when it published the first-ever curriculum standards. Two of the five new goals are affective in nature: (a) students learn to value mathematics, and (b) students become confident in their ability to do mathematics.

CHALLENGES FOR EFFECTIVE MATHEMATICS INSTRUCTION

As early as 1985, Slavin and Karweit stated that "one of the most troublesome and enduring problems of mathematics instruction is accommodating heterogeneity in student

preparation and learning rate" (p. 351). The problem of classroom heterogeneity is much more pronounced in mathematics than in any other school subject because mathematics is structured in the most highly sequential fashion among all school subjects—access to and performance in mathematics courses are determined by prior success in particular courses often referred to as prerequisites that systematically regulate student performance and progress in mathematics (see Oakes, 1990). This means that mathematical problems and difficulties accumulate, and the degree of classroom heterogeneity enlarges over time.

Traditionally, there are two ways to deal with the problem of classroom heterogeneity. One is ability grouping at various levels: (a) grouping students within a class (e.g., regular mathematics groups and advanced mathematics groups), (b) grouping classes within a school (e.g., curriculum tracking and curriculum placement), and (c) grouping schools within a district (e.g., special education programs and magnet programs for gifted students). The other prevalent way to accommodate classroom heterogeneity is individualized instruction in which students work on learning materials at their own level and rate with frequent assistance from teachers.

NCTM (1989) introduced another means to accommodate diverse learning needs: *content differentiation.* This concept emphasizes that the depth to which a topic is explored should depend on the level of abstraction at which students are capable or operating. To apply this concept, classroom teachers make concrete examples and applications of a topic open to all students to learn but make higher levels of abstraction and generalization available to, but not required of, all students. Classroom heterogeneity remains a major challenge in mathematics instruction today because the effectiveness of ability group and individualized instruction has been challenged, and the concept of content differentiation is difficult to implement even for experienced teachers.

A related, but largely isolated, challenge in mathematics instruction is the presence, in some cases substantial, of English as a second language (ESL) students. ESL students face enormous difficulties in mathematical learning because both mathematics and the language that carries it are foreign to them. NCTM (1994) clarifies that all students, regardless of their language or cultural background, must study a core curriculum in mathematics based on its curriculum standards. In 1991 NCTM recommended five major changes in mathematics classroom to help ESL students succeed in mathematics: (a) selecting mathematics tasks that engage students' interests and intellect, (b) orchestrating classroom discourse in ways that promote the investigation and growth of mathematical ideas, (c) using, and helping students use, technology and other tools to pursue mathematical investigations; (d) seeking, and helping students seek, connections to previous and developing knowledge; and (e) guiding individual, small-group, and whole-class work (students benefit from a variety of instructional settings in the classroom).

EFFECTIVE INSTRUCTIONAL TECHNOLOGY FOR MATHEMATICS EDUCATION

Various types of instructional technology (IT) have been developed to enhance mathematical learning and teaching. Lou, Abrami, and d'Apollonia (2001) classified IT into five major categories according to its educational functions: (a) tutorial, (b) communication media, (c) exploratory environment, (d) tools, and (e) programming language (with limited application so far). Tutorial refers to programs that can directly teach mathematics by creating a stimulating environment in which information, demonstration, and practice are shared with students.

Computer-assisted instruction (CAI) and various mathematics games (e.g. Math Blaster) are typical examples. Research points to CAI as a potentially effective mechanism for teaching students (including those with special needs), with increased mathematics performance as positive outcomes (e.g., Xin, 1999).

Communication media refers to communication tools such as email, computer-supported-collaborative learning (CSCL) systems, videoconferencing, and the Internet. These tools promote effective communication and information sharing. Multimedia program and videoconferencing have begun to emerge as potentially effective tools for mathematical learning and teaching (e.g., Irish, 2002; SBC Knowledge Ventures, 2005). For example, videoconferencing is found to help meet state and national curriculum standards, reach new heights in staff professional development, and help students take classes not offered at their school. In particular, students involved in the operation of the videoconferencing equipment benefit the most by having learned both subject contents and technical skills.

Exploratory environment seek to encourage active learning through discovery and exploration. Logo, simulations, and hypermedia-based learning are typical examples. One of the hypermedia-based learning programs in mathematics is the Adventures of Jasper Woodbury, a mathematics program developed at the Vanderbilt University and widely used around the world. Based on the theory of anchored instruction, the program uses video and multimedia computing technology to provide problem-scenarios to help students develop skills and knowledge for problem solving and critical thinking. Implementation of this program has yielded positive findings (e.g., Mushi, 2000; Shyu, 1999).

Tools serve the technological purpose of making learning and teaching attractive, effective, and efficient. Word processors, PowerPoint, spreadsheet, Geometer's Sketchpad, data-analysis software, and various virtual manipulatives are typical examples. In mathematics classrooms, particularly at the elementary level, manipulatives are used extensively to help students build a foundation for understanding abstract mathematical concepts. Accessed via the Internet, virtual manipulatives are replicas of real manipulatives and capable of connecting dynamic visual images with abstract symbols (a limitation of regular manipulatives). A variety of studies have examined the use of virtual manipulative tools in mathematics classrooms and have found positive effects on student mathematics achievement and attitude toward mathematics (e.g., Moyer & Bolyard, 2002; Reimer & Moyer, 2005; Suh, Moyer, & Heo, 2005).

ASSESSING MATHEMATICAL LEARNING AND TEACHING

As an emerging concept, classroom assessment is different from student assessment in that the goal of classroom assessment is to understand learners' learning in order to improve teachers' teaching. Based on results of a comprehensive review of empirical research on whether classroom assessment can benefit learning (in mathematics, science, and English) by Black and Wiliam (1998), Harlen and Winter (2004) offered this summary:

> [There is] convincing evidence that classroom assessment raises students' attainment when it has these key characteristics: that information is gathered about the processes and products of learning and is used to adapt teaching and learning; that learners receive feedback that enables them to know how to improve their work and take forward their learning; that teachers and learners share an understanding of the goals of particular pieces of work; that learners are involved in assessing their work (both self- and peer-assessment); that pupils are actively involved in learning rather than being passive recipients of information. (p. 390)

Some developments have also occurred in student assessment. There have been calls for traditional large-scale assessments not only to measure (or assess) but also improve (or support) student mathematical learning. Chudowsky and Pellegrino (2003) argued that large-scale assessments can and should do a much better job of "gauging student learning, holding education systems accountable, signaling worthy goals for students and teachers to work toward, and providing useful feedback for instructional decision making" (p. 75). As one of the efforts, large-scale tests are moving toward a closer alignment with mathematics curriculum and instruction.

Portfolios are emerging as a popular alternative student assessment. A portfolio is a purposeful collection of a students' work as indicators of their effort, progress, and achievement over time to gauge their cognitive and affective development. For mathematical learning, the purpose of a portfolio is to understand "student thinking, student's growth over time, mathematical connections, student views of themselves as mathematicians, and the problem solving process" (Stenmark, 1991, p.37). However, there ought to be a note of caution on alternative student assessments. Herman and Winters (1994) discussed the lack of empirical evidence on claims of advantages of portfolios over traditional student assessments. Carney (2001) noted that the research literature on portfolios did not change much from 1994 to 2001. An inspection of the leading *Journal for Research in Mathematics Education* shows again the lack of empirical research on all forms of alternative assessments since 2001.

RESEARCH-GROUNDED CURRICULUM AND INSTRUCTION PROJECTS IN MATHEMATICS

After an evaluation of current mathematics curriculum projects based on his Curriculum Research Framework, Clements (2004) ranked the Realistic Mathematics Education (RME), the Investigations in Number, Data, and Space (Investigations), Everyday Mathematics, and the Connected Mathematics Project (CMP) as (large-scale) research-based curriculum projects in mathematics education. The RME actually is a learning and teaching theory about mathematics education, developed by the Freudenthal Institute in the Netherlands. Freudenthal (1991) views mathematics as connected to reality and as a human activity. "Realistic" refers not only to the connection of mathematics with the real world and everyday life but also to problems real in mind of students. The RME organizes mathematics education into a process of guided reinvention to allow students to experience the similarity between the process by which mathematics is learned and the process by which mathematics is invented. "Invention" emphasizes the need to develop steps in the learning process, and "guided" emphasizes the need to create an instructional environment for the learning process. The RME can be characterized as making good use of (a) contexts (phenomenological exploration), (b) models (instrument bridging), (c) productions and constructions from students (student contribution), (d) educational interactions (interactivity), and (e) intertwining (of various learning strands).

The Investigations is a complete K-5 reform-based mathematics curriculum developed under the leadership of Dr. Susan Russell at TERC in Cambridge, Massachusetts. It designs activity-based investigations to encourage students to think creatively, develop their own problem-solving strategies, and work cooperatively. In addition to talking, writing, and drawing about mathematics, students use manipulatives, calculators, and computers to explore mathematical concepts and procedures. Classroom assessment is embedded within each investigation for improvement in teaching. Studies are in favor of Investigations students in (a) straight calculation problems (basic facts and whole number operations), (b) understanding of number concepts and number relationships, (c) word problems and complex calculation problems, and (d) performance in a high-stakes standardized test (administered in Massachusetts). Studies also indicate that Investigations works well with students across all mathematics achievement levels.

Research and development of Dr. Max Bill and his colleagues during the 1980s and 1990s resulted in the University of Chicago School Mathematics Project. The major component, Everyday Mathematics, is a research-based K-6 curriculum, with the goal to significantly improve both curriculum and instruction for all students to learn mathematics. The project began with a research phase in which a thorough review was conducted of existing research on mathematics curriculum and instruction with an emphasis on mathematical thinking. This review study was accompanied by interviews of hundreds of K-3 children and surveys of curricular and instructional practices in other countries. The research phase eventually established several basic principles to guide the curriculum development, including that (a) students learn mathematics from their own experiences obtained in an environment in which mathematics is rooted in real life, learners are actively involved in learning, and teachers provide learners with rich and meaningful mathematical contexts; (b) K-6 mathematics curriculum should build on an intuitive and concrete foundation, gradually shifting children to an abstract and symbolic foundation; and (c) teachers are the key factor in the success of any curriculum project, requiring adequate attention to their working lives.

Based on these principles, curriculum at each grade level went through a 3-year development cycle (1 year of writing, 1 year of extensive field testing, and 1 year of revising) with collaboration between mathematicians, education specialists, and classroom teachers. This unique development process has resulted in a comprehensive K-6 curriculum with a sequence of instruction carefully building upon and extending knowledge and skills obtained in the previous learning experience.

Led by Dr. Glenda Lappan at Michigan State University, the Connected Mathematics Project (CMP) is a research-based and field-tested middle school mathematics curriculum, different from many existing mathematics curricula because it takes a problem-centered curricular approach to develop powerful mathematical concepts, skills, and procedures with a focus on the ways of mathematical thinking and reasoning. CMP emphasizes the following principles reflecting both research and policy stances in mathematics education regarding what truly supports mathematical learning and teaching: (a) curriculum should be built around a number of "big" mathematical ideas, (b) underlying concepts, skills, or procedures should be in an appropriate developmental sequence; (c) an effective curriculum should be coherent connecting investigation to investigation, unit to unit, and grade to grade; (d) focus of classroom instruction should be inquiry and investigation of mathematical ideas embedded in rich problem situations, (e) mathematical tasks should be the primary vehicle for student engagement, (f) mathematical ideas should be explored deeply enough to enable students to make sense of them, (g) curriculum should develop student ability to reason effectively with information represented in multiple formats (graphic, numeric, symbolic, and verbal) and to

interchange flexibly among these representations, and (h) curriculum should reflect the information-processing capability of technology and appreciate how technology is fundamentally changing the way that people learn and apply mathematics.

Most reforms in mathematics instruction can be reasonably characterized as standards-based (referring to the 1989 NCTM Standards) and inquiry-oriented (referring to the hands-on and minds-on discovery approach). Different instructional reforms employ different strategies to promote standards and discoveries in mathematics. Some of them are research-grounded reforms, such as QUASAR (Quantitative Understanding: Amplifying Student Achievement and Reasoning), a national project particularly aimed at improving mathematics instruction for socially disadvantaged middle school students (see Silver & Stein, 1996). The most influential of the research-grounded instructional reforms in mathematics may well be the Cognitively Guided Instruction (CGI). Based on their research, Dr. Thomas Carpenter and Dr. Elizabeth Fennema at the University of Wisconsin at Madison led the development of the CGI approach to teaching mathematics (e.g., Carpenter, Fennema, Franke, & Empson, 1999).

Essentially, CGI encourages mathematics teachers to utilize what they know about the mathematical understanding of their students to select or create mathematical problems, promote students to think about the problems, stimulate students with a well-designed sequence of questions to guide them gradually to approach or discover the solutions, and facilitate discussion and idea-sharing throughout the entire instruction. The CGI instruction basics for teachers can be roughly summarized as: (a) giving sufficient waiting or thinking time for students to respond, (b) allowing free use of all materials to assist problem solving, (c) creating context of problem solving relevant to students, (d) reading a problem multiple times as necessary, (e) focusing on thinking process rather than product, (f) asking for and probing into students' explanations to learn about their mathematical thinking, (g) analyzing wrong answers from students with the whole class, (h) sharing solutions and strategies with the whole class, (i) promoting students to compare solutions to identify best problem-solving strategies, and (j) delaying symbol manipulations.

BIBLIOGRAPHY

Black, P., & Wiliam, D. (1998). Assessment and classroom learning. *Assessment in Education, 5,* 1–74.

Carpenter, T. P., Fennema, E., Franke, M. L., & Empson, S. B. (1999). *Children's mathematics: Cognitively guided instruction.* Portsmouth, NH; Heinemann and Reston, VA: National Council of Teachers of Mathematics.

Carney, J. (2001). *Electronic and traditional portfolios as tools for teacher knowledge representation.* Unpublished doctoral dissertation, University of Washington, Seattle.

Chudowsky, N., & Pellegrino, J. W. (2003). Large-scale assessments that support learning: What will it take? *Theory into Practice, 42,* 75–83.

Clements, D. H. (2004, April). *Curriculum research: Toward a framework for research-based curricula.* Paper presented at the annual meeting of the American Educational Research Association, San Diego, CA.

Cobb, P., Wood, T., & Yackel, E. (1993). Discourse, mathematical thinking, and classroom practice. In E. Forman, N. Minick, & A. Stone (Eds.), *Contexts for learning: Sociocultural dynamics in children's development* (pp. 91–119). New York: Oxford University Press.

English, L., & Halford, G. S. (1995). *Mathematics education: Models and processes.* Mahwah, NJ: Erlbaum.

Ernest, P. (1996). Varieties of constructivism: A framework for comparison. In L. P. Steffe, P. Nesher, P. Cobb, G. A. Goldin, & B. Greer (Eds.), *Theories of mathematical learning* (pp. 335–350). Mahwah, NJ: Erlbaum.

Eynde, P. O., de Corte, E., & Verschaffel, L. (2002). Framing students' mathematics-related beliefs: A quest for conceptual clarity and a comprehensive categorization. In G. C. Leder, E. Pehkonen, & G. Törner (Eds.), *Beliefs: A hidden variable in mathematics education?* (pp. 13–38). Dordrecht, The Netherlands: Kluwer.

Freudenthal, H. (1991). *Revisiting mathematics education.* Dordrecht: The Netherlands: Kluwer.

Harlen, W., & Winter, J. (2004). The development of assessment for learning: Learning from the case of science and mathematics. *Language Testing, 21,* 390–408.

Herman, J. L., & Winters, L. (1994) Portfolio research: A slim collection. *Educational Leadership, 52,* 48–55.

Hiebert, J., & Carpenter, T. P. (1992). Learning and teaching with understanding. In D. A. Grouws (Ed.), *Handbook of research in mathematics teaching and learning* (pp. 65–97). New York: Macmillan.

Hiebert, J., & Lefevre, P. (1986). Conceptual and procedural knowledge in mathematics: An introductory analysis. In J. Hiebert (Ed.), *Conceptual and procedural knowledge: The case of mathematics* (pp. 1–27). Hillsdale, NJ: Erlbaum.

Irish, C. (2002). Using peg and keyword mnemonics and computer-assisted instruction to enhance basic multiplication performance in elementary students with learning and cognitive disabilities. *Journal of Special Education Technology, 17*(4), 29–40.

Lou, Y., Abrami, P. C., & d'Apollonia, S. (2001). Small group and individual learning with technology: A meta-analysis. *Review of Educational Research, 71,* 449–521.

Moyer, P. S., & Bolyard, J. (2002). Exploring representation in the middle grades: Investigations in geometry with virtual manipulatives. *Australian Mathematics Teacher, 58,* 19–25.

Mushi, S. (2000). *Use of interactive video technology to teach middle school mathematics in Chicago, September–November, 2000. Final Evaluation Report.* Chicago: Northeastern Illinois University.

National Council of Teachers of Mathematics. (1989). *Curriculum and evaluation standards for school mathematics.* Reston, VA: Author.

National Council of Teachers of Mathematics. (1991). *Professional standards for teaching mathematics.* Reston, VA: Author.

National Council of Teachers of Mathematics. (1994). *News Bulletin.* Reston, VA: Author.

National Council of Teachers of Mathematics. (2000). *Principles and standards for school mathematics.* Reston, VA: Author.

Oakes, J. (1990). *Multiplying inequalities: The effects of race, social class, and tracking on opportunities to learn mathematics and science.* Santa Monica, CA: Rand.

Polya, G. (1957). *How to solve it* (2nd ed.). New York: Doubleday.

Reimer, K., & Moyer, P. S. (2005). Third-graders learn about fractions using virtual manipulatives: A classroom study. *Journal of Computers in Mathematics and Science Teaching, 24,* 5–25.

SBC Knowledge Ventures. (2005). *SBC videoconference adventures.* San Antonio, TX: Author.

Shyu, H. Y. (1999). Effects of media attributes in anchored instruction. *Journal of Educational Computing Research, 21,* 119–139.

Silver, E. A., & Stein, M.K. (1996). The QUASAR project. *Urban Education, 30,* 476–521.

Simon, M. A. (2006). Key developmental understandings in mathematics: A direction for investigating and establishing learning goals. *Mathematical Thinking and Learning, 8,* 359–371.

Skemp, R. (1976). Instrumental understanding and relational understanding. *Mathematics Teaching, 77,* 20–26.

Slavin, R. E., & Karweit, N. L. (1985). Effects of whole class, ability grouped, and individualized instruction on mathematics achievement. *American Educational Research Journal, 22,* 351–367.

Solomon, Y. (1989). *The practice of mathematics.* London, Routledge.

Steffe, L., & Wiegel, H. (1992). On reforming practice in mathematics education. *Educational Studies in Mathematics, 23,* 445–465.

Stenmark, J. K. (1991). *Mathematics assessment: Myths, models, good questions.* Reston, VA: National Council of Teachers of Mathematics.

Stuart, V.B. (2000). Math curse or math anxiety? *Teaching Children Mathematics, 6,* 330–336.

Suh, J., Moyer, P. S., & Heo, H. (2005). Examining technology uses in the classroom: Developing fraction sense using virtual manipulative concept tutorials. *Journal of Interactive Online Learning, 3*(4), 1–21.

van Oers, B. (1996). Learning mathematics as a meaningful activity. In L. P. Steffe, P. Nesher, P. Cobb, G. A. Goldin, & B. Greer (Eds.), *Theories of mathematical learning* (pp. 91–113). Mahwah, NJ: Erlbaum.

Vygotsky, L. S. (1960). *Razvitie vysshikh psikhicheskikh funktsii* [The development of the higher mental functions]. Moscow: Akad. Ped. Nauk. RSFSR.

Vygotsky, L. S. (1978). *Mind and society: The development of higher psychological processes.* Cambridge, MA: Harvard University Press.

Wood, T., Cobb, P., & Yackel, E. (1995). Reflections on learning and teaching mathematics in elementary school. In L. Steffe & J. Gale (Eds.), *Constructivism in education* (pp. 401–422). Hillsdale, NJ: Erlbaum.

Xin, J. F. (1999). Computer-assisted cooperative learning in integrated classrooms for students with and without disabilities. *Information Technology in Childhood Education, 1,* 61–78.

Xin Ma

LEARNING AND TEACHING READING

Helping students become good readers is an important part of the education process. Students need to be able to gain information from a variety of texts, know how to access texts to solve problems, and be able to critically examine information presented through texts. However, providing reading instruction that develops such abilities can be a complex and challenging task. Therefore, this entry was designed to provide readers with some of the more prominent theoretical positions and instructional techniques that can be used to provide students with excellent reading instruction. This entry is meant to serve as a brief introduction and broad overview for teaching reading.

PREVALENT THEORIES IN READING INSTRUCTION

Exemplary reading teachers often have strong background knowledge in theories of reading and can apply them to their instruction (Pressley, Allington, Wharton-MacDonald, Block, & Morrow, 2001). Theoretical knowledge allows teachers to make more informed decisions about their instruction and helps them know why one technique may be better than another. Three theories are presented in this section: (a) schema theory, (b) socio-cultural theory, and (c) identity theory. Each theory offers a different way to understand the reading process and reading instruction.

Schema Theory. Schema theory states that individuals will draw on their knowledge of the world in order to help them understand what they read (Anderson, 2004). How well people can understand what they read is connected to the topic being presented and the amount of knowledge they hold about it. Different interpretations of text can result from different amounts and types of background knowledge on a given topic. Schemas exist for such areas as the content being presented in a text (people, ideas, and places), the processes for reading and comprehending (knowing how to identify words, summarize, locate the main idea), and for different genres of text (mysteries, autobiographies, web sites). Reading comprehension is likely to be limited if a person does not possess sufficient background information for the information being presented.

Socio-Cultural Theory. Socio-cultural theory suggests that people's experiences at home, at school, and in their communities can influence their reading development. Students' views of reading, and the purposes of it, are often shaped at home before they enter kindergarten. When students read books or are asked to engage in reading activities, they draw on previous social and cultural experiences to help them understand what they should do and why. Students use their knowledge about what is valued to inform how they read and comprehend texts. Students from diverse cultural backgrounds may engage with reading activities in ways that are not valued by schools and that teachers consider unacceptable. Understanding that students' different approaches to reading are connected to their social and cultural backgrounds can allow teachers to provide more personalized assistance.

Identity Theory. Identity theory suggests that how students read texts and apply reading instruction will be connected to how they identify themselves as readers and how they want to be identified by their peers, teachers, or family members (Gee, 2002). In school, teachers often communicate what it means to be identified as a good or poor reader. Students who identify themselves as poor readers may disengage from reading because they are afraid that doing so will publicly reveal their weaknesses and allow a negative identity to be assigned to them. Teachers may interpret students' decisions as a desire not to learn and may respond by limiting the personal help they provide. Students who are identified as good readers or who show they are trying to become good readers are more likely to receive additional, personalized help.

IMPORTANT GOALS IN READING INSTRUCTION

An overall goal of reading instruction is to help students learn how to create new knowledge from what they read and apply it to specific problems in every day life. Helping students reach such a goal requires instruction in many small goals throughout their school careers. The critical goals in reading instruction discussed here are to develop students' (a) concepts about print, (b) phonics knowledge, (c) vocabulary knowledge, (d) fluency, and (e) comprehension abilities.

Concepts about Print. For beginning readers, developing concepts about print is often the first step in learning how to read. Concepts about print include understanding (a) about how to hold, open, and turn pages in books,

Because students' reading levels likely vary, the type of reading instruction they need also varies. **RICHARD HUTCHINGS / PHOTO RESEARCHERS, INC.**

(b) that text is read from left to right and top to bottom, (c) that printed words have meaning, and (d) there is a one-to-one match between spoken and written words (Tompkins, 2006). As students develop their concepts about print they learn how to interact with texts in ways that will help them gain meaning from them as they read. Students should have developed strong concepts about print by the end of kindergarten.

Phonics Knowledge. Phonics is the correspondence between letters and sounds (Stahl, 2002). Knowing the sound that the letter *s* makes and that this sound is different from the letter *n* is an example of phonics knowledge. Reading cannot take place without understanding the sounds letters make. Readers rely on their knowledge of phonics whenever they come across an unknown word and must sound it out.

Vocabulary Knowledge. Vocabulary knowledge is critical to students' success at reading. A central goal of vocabulary knowledge is to help students develop full word knowledge (Allen, 1999). Full word knowledge means that students know multiple meanings for a given word and/or different ways a given word can be used. It is not necessary, or possible, to have full word knowledge for every word. For most words, students will have partial knowledge. They will know one definition for the word and be able to use it in a sentence. The more words students have at the partial and full knowledge level, the better their comprehension of text. Students who have limited partial and full word knowledge in the early grades often have reading difficulties later in school if their vocabulary is not fully developed.

Fluency. Fluency is the ability to read words accurately, quickly, and with expression (Rasinski, 2006). Students with poor fluency abilities read words slowly, in isolation, and often without any inflection. They tend to focus more on how to say the words and less on what the words in a sentence or paragraph mean. Students may read at faster or slower rates depending on the difficulty of the text being read, and their fluency abilities may change depending on the genre of the text being read. Most students should be able to read fluently by third grade.

Comprehension. Comprehending texts involves extracting meaning as well as creating it (Snow & Sweet, 2003). Students must be able to locate main ideas and facts within a text and use that information to further their understanding of a concept or idea. Comprehension strategies can be taught that assist students in making meaning from texts. Examples of comprehension strategies include visualizing, asking questions, and summarizing what was read.

CHALLENGES IN CREATING EFFECTIVE READING INSTRUCTION

Helping students meet the above goals requires providing them with effective reading instruction. Effective reading instruction, however, is not solely about teaching students a specific set of skills and providing opportunities for them to apply what they have learned. Teachers must often be responsive to numerous challenges, including (a) instructing students with a variety of reading abilities, (b) being able to differentiate instruction, and (c) finding appropriate texts.

In any classroom, teachers may have students reading on grade level as well as several years above or below. By fourth grade, many students are likely to be classified as struggling readers (Curtis, 2004). Struggling readers read one or more years below grade level but do not have an identified learning disability. They need additional comprehension instruction and texts on their current reading level (Allington, 2007; Duke & Pearson, 2002).

Because students' reading levels likely vary, the type of reading instruction they need also varies. Teachers need to assess students' strengths and weaknesses as readers and then create a plan of instruction that is appropriate for their needs. Not all students need the same type of instruction, read the same texts, or participate in the same activities. Such instruction requires a great deal of organization as well as detailed knowledge about assessment, cognitive reading processes, and reading instruction.

As teachers attempt to differentiate their instruction, they typically find that the textbooks they want students to read are too difficult for most of their students to comprehend, even those reading on grade level. Difficult texts can hinder students' abilities to learn content and improve as readers (Fordham, 2006). Teachers need to seek out additional texts that students can read and learn from with limited support.

EFFECTIVE TECHNIQUES IN READING INSTRUCTION

In teaching reading teachers can use a number of effective techniques. The techniques discussed here serve as an introduction to some of the more popular methods used in the early 2000s.

Word Walls. Word walls (Cunningham, 2000) are alphabetical lists of high-frequency words that are posted in the classroom. They help students develop their word recognition and fluency abilities. Walls are added to on a regular basis as new words are introduced. Examples of words that might be found on word walls are *a, no, of, she, has,* and *when.*

Repeated Readings. Repeated readings help to develop students' fluency, word recognition, concepts of print, and comprehension abilities (Topping, 2006). Students read texts or have texts read to them multiple times. When teachers read aloud, students can follow along, read aloud, or echo the teachers' words. Teachers may wish to point to the words as they read aloud. Students can also engage in repeated readings by reading with a partner or listening to a book on tape.

Centers. Centers allow students to practice previously taught reading skills on their own or with peers. Effective centers require students to read, write, and discuss what they are doing. For example, students might be asked to read a story on their own, create a written response, and then share and explain their response with a peer.

Guided Reading. Guided reading allows students to apply reading strategies they have been taught while reading texts that are an appropriate difficulty for them (Fountas & Pinnell, 1996). Teachers work with four to six students who need similar types of reading instruction. Teachers first introduce a text that students can read on their own with little support. Teachers may provide a brief lesson that focuses on one or two strategies they want students to apply when reading. Teachers observe the students reading and provide additional assistance as needed. As students progress, they read more difficult books and use more strategies.

Authentic Instruction. Authentic instruction (Duke, Purcell-Gates, Hall, & Tower, 2006) can improve students' comprehension of non-fiction texts and increase their understanding of text features such as headings, indexes, and table of contents as early as second grade. Students read and use non-fiction texts in ways that mirror how texts are used outside school. For example, students might choose to read non-fiction texts in order to answer their own questions about the world. Authentic instruction helps students learn how (a) to generate their own questions about a topic being studied and then (b) use a variety of texts to locate their answers.

Literature Circles. In literature circles, students come together in small groups to read and discuss a common text (Daniels, 2001). Students read a selected portion of the text, complete a written response, and engage in a discussion with group members. Students' responses can include: (a) summarizing, (b) creating a picture, (c) making connections to other texts or experiences, or (d) developing meanings for new vocabulary.

Literature circles help students learn basic reading skills such as how to summarize and locate main ideas in texts. They also help students learn more complex skills, including how (a) to discuss how they made sense of a text, (b) support their interpretations of text, and (c) make connections across multiple texts.

ASSESSING READING ABILITIES

Assessing students' reading abilities allows teachers to understand their strengths and weaknesses as readers and can be used to inform reading instruction. The assessments presented here are ones that teachers can do on their own and with few materials. Each provides information about students' abilities as it pertains to one or more of the five goals discussed earlier.

Running Records. Running records assess students' fluency and word recognition abilities (Davenport, 2002). Teachers listen to students read a portion of text aloud. They place a check mark next to the words students read correctly and note any miscues made. Miscues are "unexpected responses that do not match the text" (Goodman, 1994, p. 1096) and are not considered to be mistakes. Miscues are based on students' current knowledge about the topic they are reading as well as how language is constructed. Teachers review their notes to examine what, if any, miscues students made when reading and look for patterns that may exist.

Retelling. Retellings provide information about how well students (a) comprehend passages, (b) can identify story elements in narratives, (c) can identify main ideas, and (d) can communicate the passage in an order that makes sense (Gredler & Johnson, 2004). Students read a text silently and then explain the text as though they were talking to someone who had never read it before. If students leave out information, teachers may ask them a question to see if they can identify a particular aspect and then note that the help was provided.

Informal Reading Inventories. Informal reading inventories (IRI) allow teachers to determine the level of text students can read on their own. They also provide teachers with information about students' fluency, word recognition, and comprehension abilities. IRIs allow teachers to develop a broader picture of students' abilities to read and comprehend text (Cooper & Kiger, 2008).

In an IRI, students read aloud a passage for which they can accurately read a minimum of 90 percent of the words. Students read individual word lists, written from a pre-primer through twelfth-grade level, to determine the level of the passage they should read. Teachers conduct a running record as the passage is read. Students then retell the passage. Finally, teachers engage students in a series of comprehension questions which range in difficulty. Students' responses to the questions can provide insight about how well they can locate basic facts in text and make inferences.

Narrative Comprehension. Narrative comprehension assessments help determine young children's abilities to comprehend narrative texts (Paris & Hoffman, 2004). The assessment can be used with children who may or may not be able to read. Students examine wordless picture books, explain what they think is taking place, and answer comprehension questions. The assessment shows how well children can recall important details from text, make inferences, and make connections across the story.

RESEARCH-BASED CURRICULUM PROGRAMS

There are numerous research-based curriculum programs teachers can use for reading instruction. The ones described here help students develop the goals described earlier and also draw on many of the effective teaching techniques. Teachers may find that these programs provide ways to address some of the instructional challenges they may encounter.

Concept-oriented Reading Instruction (CORI). CORI increases elementary students' abilities to read science texts while increasing their science knowledge and motivation (Guthrie, Wigfield, & Perencevich, 2004). Students receive instruction on how to apply comprehension strategies to science texts and learn how such skills as summarizing, asking and answering questions, and locating information. As students read and learn about science, their intrinsic motivation, or personal desire to learn, is expected to increase. In the CORI program, students participate in activities, including (a) engaging with the world outside school, (b) reading a variety of texts, and (c) working with others. The CORI program follows a consistent pattern of instruction that is intended to help students develop in each of these areas.

Four Blocks. The Four Blocks program helps beginning readers learn how to read and can also assist students in third and fourth grade who may have reading difficulties (Cunningham, Hall, & Sigmon, 2000). It is made up of four different approaches that students experience each day: (a) guided reading, (b) self-selected reading, (c) writing, and (d) working with words. The Four Blocks program was designed to help teachers work with students who vary in their reading abilities but without relying on ability grouping. The Four Blocks approach helps students develop their phonics, comprehension, and fluency abilities.

Open Court Reading. The Open Court Reading program is a commercially produced series of basals for students in grades K–6 (McGraw Hill, 2002). The reading program was based on research findings that support students' development as readers. Teachers can use a script when teaching lessons.

In kindergarten and first grade, the emphasis is on teaching decoding skills. The emphasis on decoding often results in students having strong decoding abilities and a greater understanding of sound-letter relationships. Beginning in second grade, a greater emphasis is placed on developing comprehension and fluency. The program is often criticized for failing to help students develop abilities to discuss texts and do more than comprehend at a literal level (Wilson, Martens, & Arya, 2005). However, Open Court has also been recognized for aligning its instruction with reading research.

BIBLIOGRAPHY

Allen, J. (1999). *Words, words, words.* Portsmouth, NH: Heinemann.

Allington, R. L. (2007). Intervention all day long: New hope for struggling readers. *Voices from the Middle, 14,* 3–17.

Anderson, R. C. (2004). Role of the readers' schema in comprehension, learning, and memory. In R. B. Ruddell and N. J. Unrau (Eds.), *Theoretical models and processes of reading* (5th ed., pp. 594–606). Newark, DE: International Reading.

Cooper, J. D., & Kiger, N. D. (2008). *Literacy assessment: Helping teachers plan instruction.* Boston, MA: Houghton Mifflin.

Cunningham, P. M. (2000). *Phonics they use: Words for reading and writing* (3rd ed.). New York: HarperCollins.

Cunningham, P. M., Hall, D. P., & Sigmon, C. M. (2000). *The teachers' guide to the four blocks: A multimethod, multilevel framework for grades 1–3.* Greensboro, NC: Carson-Dellosa.

Daniels, H. (2001). *Literature circles: Voice and choice in book clubs and reading groups.* Portland, ME: Stenhouse.

Davenport, M. R. (2002). *Miscues not mistakes: Reading assessment in the classroom.* Portsmouth, NH: Heinemann.

Duke, N. K., & Pearson, P. D. (2002). Effective practices for developing reading comprehension. In A. E. Farstrup & S. J. Samuels (Eds.), *What research has to say about reading instruction* (3rd. ed.). Newark, DE: International Reading.

Duke, N. K., Purcell-Gates, V., Hall, L. A., & Tower, C. (2006). Authentic literacy activities for developing comprehension and writing. *The Reading Teacher, 60*(4), 344–355.

Fordham, N. (2006). Crafting questions that address comprehension strategies in content area reading. *Journal of Adolescent and Adult Literacy, 49,* 390–396.

Fountas, I. C., & Pinnell, G. S. (1996). *Guided reading: Good first teaching for all children.* Portsmouth, NH: Heinemann.

Gee, J. (2002). Identity as an analytic lens for research in education. *Review of Research in Education, 25,* 99–125.

Goodman, K. S. (1994). Reading, writing, and written texts: A transactional sociopsycholinguistic view. In R. B. Ruddell & N.J. Unrau (Eds.), *Theoretical models and processes of reading.* 4th ed. (pp. 1093–1130). Newark, DE: International Reading.

Gredler, M. E., & Johnson, R. L. (2004). *Assessment in the literacy classroom.* Boston: Pearson.

Guthrie, J. T., Wigfield, A., & Perencevich, K. C. (Eds.). (2004). *Motivating reading comprehension: Concept-oriented reading instruction.* Mahwah, NJ: Erlbaum.

McGraw Hill. (2007). *Results with open-court reading.* New York: McGraw Hill.

Paris, S., & Hoffman, J. V. (2004). Reading assessments in kindergarten through third grade: Findings from the Center for the Improvement of Early Reading Achievement. *Elementary School Journal, 105,* 199–219.

Pressley, M., Allington, R. L., Wharton-McDonald, R. Block, C. C., & Morrow, L. M. (2001). *Learning to read: Lessons from exemplary first-grade classrooms.* New York: Guilford Press.

Rasinski, T. V. (2006). A brief history of reading fluency. In S. J. Samuels & A. E. Farstrup (Eds.), *What research has to say about fluency instruction* (pp. 4–23). Newark, DE: International Reading.

Stahl, S. (2002). Saying the "p" word: Nine guidelines for exemplary phonics instruction. In *The international reading association's evidence-based reading instruction. Putting the National Reading Panel Report into practice* (pp. 61–68). Newark, DE: International Reading.

Snow, C. E., & Sweet, A. P. (2003). Reading for comprehension. In A. P. Sweet and C. E. Snow (Eds.), *Rethinking reading comprehension* (pp. 1–11). New York: Guilford Press.

Tompkins, G. E. (2006). *Literacy for the 21st century: A balanced approach.* 4th ed. Upper Saddle River, NJ: Pearson, Merrill, Prentice Hall.

Topping, K. J. (2006). Building reading fluency: Cognitive, behavioral, and socioemotional factors and the role of peer-mediated learning. In S. J. Samuels & A. E. Farstrup (Eds.), *What research has to say about fluency instruction* (pp. 106–129). Newark, DE: International Reading.

Wilson, P. G., Martens, P., & Arya, P. (2005). Accountability for reading and readers: What the numbers don't tell. *The Reading Teacher, 58,* 622–631.

Leigh A. Hall

LEARNING AND TEACHING SCIENCE

In 1983 the National Commission for Excellence in Education released its report, *A Nation at Risk*, announcing that U.S. schools had undergone a precipitous 20-year decline in the quality of mathematics and science education. The result was an intense new focus on research into how children learn science and how best to teach it, culminating with the release of *Benchmarks for Science Literacy* (BSL) in 1993 by Project 2061 of the American Association for the Advancement of Science (AAAS) and *The National Science Education Standards* (NSES) in 1996 by the National Research Council (NRC) of the National Academy of Sciences. States and local school districts began instituting reforms and setting new standards.

However, after 15 years of standards-based reform American students exhibited little improvement in science achievement, and the achievement gap between majority students and economically disadvantaged and non-Asian minority students remained large. As the first decade of the 21st century neared its end it was apparent that 25 years of intensive research into learning and teaching science had not been effectively translated into classroom practice.

GOALS FOR SCIENCE LEARNING

Although there are ongoing efforts to encourage young people—particularly females and minorities—to pursue careers in science and technology, most researchers agree that the primary goal of K-12 science learning should be the creation of a scientifically literate population. Scientific literacy can be defined as a basic understanding of science, an appreciation of how science shapes society and culture, and the ability to reason scientifically. Many American adults lack the basic understanding of science that is required for making informed decisions about the many scientific issues affecting their lives. Therefore some educators go further, defining the primary goal of science education as providing students with the information and tools to become lifelong science learners who can adapt to the technological innovations that will be at the center of life in the 21st century.

For many educators learning goals have become synonymous with standards—national, state, and local school district determinations of what students should know, understand, and be able to do in scientific subjects at specific grade levels. National standards are delineated in the BSL and NSES.

The 2007 NRC report, *Taking Science to School*, cites the development of scientifically proficient students as a key goal: "Students who are proficient in science:

1. know, use, and interpret scientific explanations of the natural world;

2. generate and evaluate scientific evidence and explanations;

3. understand the nature and development of scientific knowledge; and;

4. participate productively in scientific practices and discourse" (p. 36).

K-12 science education standards usually cite scientific thinking as a primary educational objective, and competence in scientific investigation as a goal from the earliest grades. According to these standards students should be able to:

- Formulate a question;
- Design an investigation;
- Analyze data;
- Draw conclusions.

HOW STUDENTS LEARN SCIENCE

It has been apparent since at least the late 1970s that traditional methods of teaching science—lectures, textbooks, memorization of facts, theorems, and formulas—have little to do with learning science. Furthermore with the explosion in scientific knowledge in the latter half of the 20th century, information was often obsolete before it could even be taught. Rather, a large body of research has clearly demonstrated that children learn science by doing science—a process called inquiry-based learning, a form of constructivist instruction. With inquiry-based learning students investigate and discover on their own, in addition to reading and receiving instruction and guidance.

Inquiry-based science learning generally begins with observing, describing, and reflecting on objects and phenomena, leading to the formulation of questions and identifying assumptions about those objects and phenomena. Students then acquire more knowledge, using books and other sources to determine what is already known from experimental evidence. The next step in inquiry-based learning is to test explanations in a variety of ways. Students plan investigations and use tools to collect, analyze, and interpret data. They propose explanations, make predictions, and communicate their ideas, results, and conclusions.

Hands-on or exploratory learning stresses the importance of scientific experiences for developing skills. For young children these skills include observation and comparison, measurement, and classification, in addition to communication. More advanced skills involve inferring relationships, formulating hypotheses, and predicting outcomes. Students learn to identify and control variables, methods of gathering, organizing, and recording data, and how to draw conclusions.

CONCEPTUAL CHANGE

In contrast to the old-fashioned view that young children think in simple concrete terms, research has shown that the thinking of even very young children is quite sophisticated and that they are capable of thinking in both concrete and abstract terms. They utilize a range of reasoning processes—including causal reasoning and distinguishing between reliable and unreliable sources of information—that form the basis of scientific thinking.

Perhaps most importantly a large body of research has shown that children do not start school as blank slates upon which scientific knowledge can be written. Rather, children come to school with their own conceptual resources, already knowing a great deal about the natural world and having formulated their own scientific ideas. However, children also vary greatly in their early learning experiences and opportunities, which may be influenced by race, ethnicity, language, gender, culture, and socioeconomic background. Thus they differ in their conceptual resources and in what they are capable of learning at a given age.

Because many scientific concepts are not intuitive, children often have deeply entrenched misconceptions about nature, and these misconceptions often prove to be barriers to learning science. In the late 1970s cognitive researchers began interviewing students to assess their understanding of scientific concepts. They found that many students had trouble, not because the concepts were inherently difficult, but rather because they conflicted with the students' entrenched misconceptions. Furthermore, the memorization of scientific facts and formulas could disguise these underlying misconceptions. Among the topics about which students often hold misconceptions are force and motion, the particulate theory of matter, heat and temperature, electricity, optics, and evolution.

Learning science requires not just knowledge of key facts and concepts but an understanding of how facts and concepts relate to each other and their implications and applications. This may require a large-scale reorganization of knowledge and in-depth conceptual change to overcome prior misconceptions. These processes take time and require that children work with the same ideas and concepts in different ways over weeks, months, and years. According to Posner and colleagues (1982), four conditions must be met for conceptual change to occur: Students must be dissatisfied with their current conceptions because they conflict with observations or contain discrepancies; students must understand the new idea; they must be able to reconcile the new idea with their own ideas; and they must find the new idea useful and amenable to further testing.

Strike, Posner, and colleagues' general model of conceptual change applied the philosophy of science to the learning of science. Since then the conceptual change approach has become a basic tenet of teaching science. By first assessing prior knowledge, students' knowledge can be built upon, and misconceptions and potential misunderstandings can be addressed. The goal is for students to discover or recreate concepts on their own. Posner and colleagues proposed that having students work through problems with different explanations and compare the results led the students to recognize the shortcomings of their explanations and strengthened the scientific concept.

FURTHER THEORIES OF SCIENCE TEACHING

In addition to the importance of conceptual understanding, most contemporary theories of science teaching involve support for constructivist practices—active, inquiry-based, and collaborative strategies that utilize experimentation and other scientific methods to teach scientific reasoning within the context of specific science content. Because science is, in essence, a social process, research suggests that it should be taught as such, with emphasis on working in groups and whole-class and small-group discussions, questioning, and communication that enhance the development of scientific literacy.

Scientific discussions, explanations, and evaluation of evidence differ from those activities in other subjects and in everyday life. Students need instructional support to learn the language and practices of scientific experimentation, interpretation, and discussion. Many attempts at hands-on discovery learning have proved unproductive due to lack of guidance. In constructivist inquiry-based learning the teacher acts as a coach, introducing basic information and new concepts as required and guiding group discussions.

Finally, there is a consensus among researchers that science curricula, textbooks, national, state, and local standards and assessments contain far too many disconnected topics. Most research indicates that it is far more productive to focus on core ideas, which are explored in depth progressively through grades K-8.

EFFECTIVE INSTRUCTIONAL STRATEGIES

There exists a large body of research on effective means for promoting conceptual change. Building from misconceptions can be effective: For example, young children may find that their preconceived ideas about why weather changes conflict with their observations, so the teacher introduces the concepts of air movement and weather fronts. In a conceptual change approach the teacher provides an introduction, including a review and motivating experiences. This is followed by focus, in which the students observe an event, pose a problem, and formulate ideas and explanations. The challenge presents a conflicting question or discrepancy and the students then develop new ideas. Application involves solving problems using the new ideas and engages the students in discussion and debate. Finally, the teacher or students, or both, summarize the results and connect them with other lessons.

Discovery argumentation, using cycles of model-based reasoning, has been found to be effective with students from elementary school through high school. The *bridging analogies* strategy introduces a target situation in which the students' initial intuition conflicts with a scientific principle. This is followed by an *anchoring intuition,* a situation in which intuition agrees with scientific principle. At first the students see the two situations as completely different. A series of bridging analogies or intermediate models are then presented in which the situations are intermediate between the target and the anchor. Following cycles of reasoning the students develop a new model that they can test. Nuthall found that upper-elementary students required three or four experiences with new scientific ideas before the concepts enter their long-term memory.

Know-Want-Learn (KWL) charts help students visualize what they already know and what they want to learn and then conclude with what they have learned. Hershberger and colleagues (2006) have modified KWL to Know-Learning-Evidence-Wonder (KLEW), emphasizing observation, evidence, and further investigation. Yet another variation includes "know and think," to encourage students to share their initial ideas and realize that what they think they know can change as a result of inquiry.

Research indicates that from the earliest grades designing and conducting experiments and investigations helps students understand scientific concepts. With guidance students can follow the scientific method by formulating hypotheses and designing and carrying out experiments and collecting evidence that is used to evaluate the hypotheses. This process conforms to several of the teaching guidelines presented in the AAAS's Project 2061 research-based *Science for All Americans* (1989):

- "Teaching should be consistent with the nature of scientific inquiry."

- "Science teaching should reflect scientific values."

- Scientific knowledge should be presented in the context of the processes by which it was arrived at.

Learning-cycle approaches can actively engage students in the processes of science through collaborative inquiry into interesting and familiar phenomena. First fully described in 1967 by Karplus and Thier, the learning-cycle approach alternates hands-on exploration and applications and "minds-on" activities through interactions with the teacher, other students, and texts. Over the years numerous studies have supported the effectiveness of the learning cycle, particularly when all three phases of the cycle are utilized, and exploration precedes the introduction of concepts and terminology.

Rodger W. Bybee's 1997 5-E model is a learning-cycle modification: Engage, Explore, Explain, Elaborate, and Evaluate. The Launch, Explore, Summarize (LES) model is a condensed version of the 5-E model. Aaron D. Isabelle (2007) has described applying the "storyline approach" to LES to incorporate conceptual change.

Using questions, objects, or visuals the teacher elicits the students' prior knowledge and discusses the concept addressed in a story. The teacher then reads a story from the history of science, discusses the factual and fictional aspects of the story, and connects the ideas in the story with the original discussion.

Studies have repeatedly found that discussion is an important science learning tool for even the youngest students. Effective "talking science" can include practice using scientific terms in sentences, discussing intuitive theories, reading different types of science writing, and translating between scientific and colloquial questions and statements.

Finally, the guidelines set forth in *Science for All Americans* include:

- Teaching should include the history of science and societal and multicultural perspectives.

- Inquiry should lead to a satisfying conclusion.

- Curiosity and creativity should be fostered.

- Questioning should be encouraged and dogma avoided.

- The aesthetics of scientific phenomena should be emphasized.

- Local resources should be utilized.

- "Teaching should take its time."

Consistent with this last point is a recommendation from researchers and reformers that students should study in great depth the core explanatory ideas in science rather than quickly traversing many different ideas, which permits only shallow understanding.

APPROPRIATE ASSESSMENT

Research has shown that large-scale standardized tests alone are not a valid method for assessing scientific understanding. Generally these tests measure knowledge of discrete pieces of information rather than structured knowledge of science. However ongoing, appropriately designed assessment is an important component of science teaching and learning. Performance-based or alternative assessments may include:

- Performing a task or experiment

- Describing an exploration or the solution to a problem

- An essay

- A portfolio

- Student-teacher discussions

- Worksheets

- Journals

Formative assessment is used by teachers to adapt instruction and by students to improve learning. Formative assessment involves a three-step feedback process:

- Setting a learning goal

- Assessing the gap between the goal and the student's understanding

- Using feedback to eliminate the gap.

For example, a teacher may learn from a series of questions that students have not understood a concept and decide to modify a subsequent lesson to reinforce that concept. Likewise, students may modify their own work after comparing it to the teacher's example.

Achievements to be assessed include:

- Inquiry skills

- Knowledge and understanding of facts, concepts, principles, laws, and theories

- Understanding of the nature and functions of science

- Scientific reasoning abilities

- Using science to make decisions and develop opinions on issues

- The ability to communicate clearly about science.

The Lawrence Hall of Science's Science Education for Public Understanding Program (SEPUP), an issue-based 6-12 curriculum, works with the University of California's Berkeley Evaluation and Assessment (BEAR) Center. The SEPUP/BEAR system scores students on five concepts and abilities:

- Designing and conducting investigations

- Identifying objective scientific evidence and evaluating various solutions to a problem on the basis of evidence

- Understanding concepts and their problem-solving applications

- Communicating scientific information, including explaining methodologies, presenting results, and justifying conclusions

- Group interactions including collaborating on tasks and contributing ideas.

CHALLENGES TO EFFECTIVE INSTRUCTION

Research has consistently identified teacher proficiency as a major challenge in science education. Most K-8 teachers have little background in science and little training in teaching science. Schools often struggle just to teach basic literacy and math skills, and the science curriculum may

be nonexistent. Many teachers tell researchers that the major impediments to their science teaching are their own lack of knowledge combined with inadequate facilities, supplies, and preparation time. Furthermore, children arrive at school with very different experiences and attitudes toward science. Recognizing and addressing these differences poses a special challenge to teachers.

The inquiry-based approach, which requires teachers to guide student experimentation and discussion while incorporating specific learning goals, is a major paradigm shift for many teachers. In addition preparation for government-mandated high-stakes standardized testing and the demand that teachers strictly adhere to applicable science standards are often incompatible with student-centered, hands-on science instruction.

Finally, most science curricula and textbooks provide neither continuity for students nor guidance for teachers. Project 2061's analysis of science textbooks found them to be of almost uniformly poor quality, superficially covering a large number of topics with little attention to concepts. Although researchers agree that the science curriculum is far too broad, there is little agreement about which topics to emphasize and which to eliminate.

RESEARCH-GROUNDED CURRICULUM PROJECTS

Concept-Oriented Reading Instruction (CORI) is a research program that integrates science inquiry and reading using the following support strategies to motivate students:

- Student autonomy

- Competence

- Learning goals

- Real-world interactions.

Elementary students are introduced to a complex domain such as ecology or the solar system. After several weeks they select a specific topic within the domain and choose related books to read. They receive help in finding and using resources and communicating what they have learned. Students also participate in related activities such as field trips, collecting, and experimentation. In a study of third and fifth graders in three schools, CORI students, as compared with students in the traditional science program,

- Reported greater interest in reading science

- Exhibited better reading comprehension of science texts

- Scored higher on standardized tests.

Several innovative curricula connect students with other students and with professional scientists. In the Global Learning and Observations to Benefit the Environment (GLOBE) project K-12 students worldwide study earth sciences in partnership with scientists. GLOBE has been shown to improve math, science, and geography skills, and students and teachers report increased interest in and awareness of environmental issues and satisfaction at having contributed to scientific research.

The Web-based Integrated Science Environment (WISE), developed by Marcia Linn and her colleagues, uses browser-based inquiry activities that enable middle and high school students to critique evidence, compare scientific arguments, and design solutions to scientific problems. WISE projects are interdisciplinary scientific issues and include hands-on data collection, online modeling, and design activities, as well as peer interaction and collaboration. The Center for Learning Technologies in Urban Schools (LeTUS) has developed very influential curriculum projects. The center is a collaboration of researchers at the University of Michigan and Northwestern University with Detroit and Chicago public schools. The center has developed inquiry-based instruction that has been shown to promote growth in conceptual understanding and reasoning. Students engage in projects around "driving questions," core explanatory questions about interesting topics that motivate inquiry. The North Dakota State University World Wide Web Instructional Committee (WWWIC), an interdisciplinary research team, has developed multi-user, interactive virtual environments (IVEs) for teaching high-school science. In "Geology Explorer" students examine an alien planet and conduct geologic tests. In "Virtual Cell" students enter a simulated cell and perform biological experiments. A decade of research has shown that IVEs improve student achievement and problem-solving skills.

BIBLIOGRAPHY

American Association for the Advancement of Science Project 2061 (1989). *Science for all Americans: Education for a changing future*. Retrieved April 21, 2008, from http://www.project2061.org/publications/sfaa/default.htm.

American Association for the Advancement of Science Project 2061 (1993). *Benchmarks for science literacy*. New York: Oxford University Press.

American Association for the Advancement of Science (2006). *Project 2061 textbook evaluations*. Retrieved April 21, 2008, from http://www.project2061.org/publications/textbook/default.htm.

Bennett, J. (2004). *Teaching and learning science: A guide to recent research and its applications*. New York: Continuum.

Bybee, R. W. (1997). Achieving scientific literacy: From purposes to practices. Portsmouth, NH: Heinemann.

Bybee, R. W. (Ed.). (2002). *Learning science and the science of learning: Science educators' essay collection*. Arlington, VA: NSTA Press.

Committee on Science Learning, Kindergarten through Eighth Grade. (2007). In R. A. Duschl, H. A. Schweingruber, & A. W. Shouse (Eds.), *Taking science to school: Learning and teaching science in K-8*. Washington, DC: National Academies Press.

diSessa, A. A., & Minstrell, J. (1998). Cultivating conceptual change with benchmark lessons. In J. G. Greeno & S. V. Goldman (Eds.), *Thinking practices in mathematics and science learning*. Mahwah, NJ: Erlbaum.

diSessa, A. A., & Sherin, B. (1998). What changes in conceptual change? *International Journal of Science Education, 20*, 1155–1191.

The GLOBE program. (2007). Retrieved April 21, 2008, from http://www.globe.gov/r/homepage.

Guthrie, J. T. (2006). *Concept-oriented reading instruction*. Retrieved April 21, 2008, from http://www.cori.umd.edu/.

Hershberger, K., Zembal-Saul, C., & Starr, M. L. (2006, February). Methods and strategies: Evidence helps the KWL get a KLEW. *Science and Children*, 50–53.

Isabelle, A. D. (2007). Teaching science using stories: The storyline approach. *Science Scope, 31,* 16–25.

Karplus, R., & Thier, H. D. (1967). *A new look at elementary school science*. Chicago: Rand McNally.

Lawrence Hall of Science. (2007). *SEPUP: The science education for public understanding program*. Retrieved April 21, 2008, from http://www.lawrencehallofscience.org/sepup/.

Martin, R., Sexton, C., & Franklin, T. (2005). *Teaching science for all children: Inquiry lessons for constructing understanding*. Boston: Pearson/A and B.

Michaels, S., Shouse, A. W., & Shweingruber, H. A. (2007). *Ready, set, science!: Putting research to work in K-8 science classrooms*. Washington, DC: National Academies Press.

National Commission on Excellence in Education. (1983). *A nation at risk: The imperative for educational reform*. Washington, DC: U.S. Department of Education.

National Committee on Science Education Standards and Assessment, National Research Council. (1996). *National science education standards*. Washington, DC: National Academies Press.

North Dakota State University. (2000). *World wide web instructional committee*. Retrieved April 21, 2008, from http://www.ndsu.nodak.edu/instruct/mcclean/wwwic/.

Nuthall, G. (1999). The way students learn: Acquiring knowledge from an integrated science and social studies unit. *The Elementary School Journal, 99*: 303–341.

Posner, G., Strike, K., Hewson, P., & Gertzog, W. (1982). Accommodation of a scientific conception: Toward a theory of conceptual change. *Science Education, 66*, 211–227.

Rhoton, J., & Shane, P. (Eds.). (2006). *Teaching science in the 21st century*. Arlington, VA: NSTA Press.

Strike, K., & Posner, G. (1985). A conceptual change view of learning and understanding. In L. West & A. L. Pines (Eds.), *Cognitive structure and conceptual change* (pp. 211–231). Orlando, FL: Academic Press.

Strike, K. A., & Posner, G. J. (1992). A revisionist theory of conceptual change. In R. A. Duschl & R. J. Hamilton (Eds.), *Philosophy of science, cognitive psychology, and educational theory and practice.* Albany, NY: State University of New York Press.

WISE (2007). Retrieved April 21, 2008, from http://wise.berkeley.edu/.

Margaret Alic

LEARNING AND TEACHING WRITING

Writing is a very demanding and complex task. Even a seemingly simple text, such as *Cat in the Hat*, can require considerable effort and expertise. It took Dr. Seuss well over a year to write the book, and he noted that "every word is a struggle—every sentence like a pang of birth."

Writing is a goal directed and self-sustained activity requiring the skillful management of the writing environment; the constraints imposed by the writing topic; the intentions of the writer(s), and the processes, knowledge, and skills involved in composing (Zimmerman & Reisemberg, 1997). It entails much more than this, however, as writing is a social activity involving either an implicit or explicit dialogue between writer(s) and reader(s). Writing is further shaped by the community of the writer. For example, written discourse differs considerably amongst a community of friends sharing ideas via email and texts written by biologists (Nystrand, 2006). Moreover, writing competence in one social community does not ensure competence in another. For instance, a good technical writer may not be a good novelist. What and how people write is also influenced by the cultural, societal, institutional, political, and historical background in which they are situated (Schultz & Fecho, 2000). To illustrate, students' concepts about writing are shaped, at least in part, by institutional decisions about pedagogy and curriculum. If a school's writing program places a heavy emphasis on correct form, students' revising efforts will most likely involve editing. A different approach to revising is likely, though, if form is deemphasized and meaning and process are stressed.

WRITING THEORIES AND MODELS

Given its complexity, it is not surprising that there is currently no model or theory of writing that fully or adequately captures it. One conceptual approach to studying writing focuses mostly on the individual writer and concentrates on understanding the cognitive and the motivational processes involved in composing (Graham, 2006). This cognitive or cognitive/motivational approach is exemplified in an influential model of writing developed by Hayes (1996). In his model, he takes into account, at least in part, the interaction between the task environment for writing and the internal capabilities of the writer. The task environment includes both a social component (e.g., the audience, other texts read while writing, and collaborators) as well as a physical component (e.g., text read so far and the writing medium, such as a word processor).

Internal factors include four main elements. First, cognitive processes: text interpretation, reflection, and text production. These processes allow the writer to form an internal representation of the writing task that can be acted upon; devise a plan to reach one or more writing goals; draw conclusions about the audience and possible writing content; use cues from the writing plan or text produced so far to retrieve semantic information that is then turned into written sentences; and evaluate plans and text and modify them as needed. Second, motivation, which includes the goals, predispositions, beliefs, and attitudes that influence the writing process. Third, long-term memory—knowledge of the writing topic and audience as well as linguistic and genre knowledge, including task schemas that specify how to carry out particular writing tasks. Fourth, working memory, which serves as an interface between cognitive processes, motivation, and memory, providing a space for holding information and ideas for writing as well as carrying out cognitive activities that require the writer's conscious attention.

In the model proposed by Hayes (1996) only limited attention is devoted to the social nature of writing. The influence of writing community, culture, society, institution, politics, and history are mostly ignored. One or more of these factors are captured in sociocultural theories of writing. For example, Russell (1997) developed a theory for explaining how macro-level social and political forces influence micro-level writing actions and vice versa. A basic unit in this model is an activity system, which examines how actors (an individual, dyad, or collective—perceived in social terms and taking into account the history of their involvement in the activity system) use concrete tools (e.g., writing) to accomplish some action with some outcome (this is accomplished in a problem space where subjects use tools in an ongoing interaction with others to shape an object over time in a shared direction).

Russell's theory also employs the concept of genre, "as typified ways of purposefully interacting in and among some activity system(s)" (p. 513). Genres are stabilized through regularized use of tools within and among individuals, creating a relatively predictable way of interacting with others, but they are only stabilized-for-now structures, as they are subject to change depending upon the context. Newcomers to an established activity system appropriate some of the routinized tools used by others (e.g., a particular structure for writing), but interactions between and among individuals and activity systems can change typified ways of acting

Primary grade students mastering basic writing skills. © **PHOTOCRETE, 2008. USED UNDER LICENSE FROM SHUTTERSTOCK.COM.**

(i.e., genres), as they may be modified or abandoned in response to changing conditions. Activity theory provides a method for describing and analyzing activity systems for writing and how they interact with macro-level activity systems involving academic discipline, culture, institution, society, and so forth.

To illustrate activity theory in action an example is given below of how political, institutional, societal, community, cultural, and historical factors might influence what happens in a second-grade class focusing on story writing. In this particular instance, the teacher's decision to concentrate on story writing was shaped by the district curriculum guide and the state's high-stakes testing program (story writing was emphasized in both) as well as the teacher's and her students' interest in story telling. The way in which story writing was introduced and taught was influenced by the teachers' beliefs about how to teach (which was previously influenced by her teacher preparation program, her own teachers as a child, and the culture of the school). In providing story writing instruction, the teacher used the same general routinized approach that she had applied when teaching personal narratives and other types of writing. Students also continued to generate papers using the same general script they had been using since the

start of the school year: selecting a topic, briefly planning what to say, making a draft, sharing it with a peer, revising and editing it, and sharing part or all of it with the class and at home.

While this script for writing was followed by most students, some of them modified it by eliminating a step (e.g., planning) or adding ones (e.g., sharing plans with a peer). The last of these modifications had a ripple effect in the classroom, as almost all of the students started sharing their plans with a peer. To provide students with concrete examples of stories, the teacher read traditional stories to the children (stories taken from her own dominant culture). However, one child brought to class a book of stories from Africa. He asked the teacher if they could try writing stories like those in his book. This request changed the focus of story writing in the class, as the teacher encouraged students to write stories from cultures other than their own, and several of the students' parents were asked to share their favorite stories from their culture with the class.

WRITING DEVELOPMENT

Not surprisingly, these two basic approaches to conceptualizing writing have led to different views of writing development. For example, Graham (2006) argued that four catalysts spur writing development. These involve changes in writer's strategic or self-regulatory behaviors (e.g., becoming more sophisticated in planning), motivation (e.g., heightened sense of efficacy about one's writing capabilities), knowledge (e.g., increased knowledge about the attributes and structures of different types of writing), and skills (e.g., automatization of handwriting and spelling and proficiency in sentence construction). These catalysts all reside within the individual, and this approach to development is consistent with cognitive/motivational theories of writing.

In contrast, Schultz and Fecho (2000) offer a different view of writing development—one that is consistent with sociocultural theories of writing. They argue that writing development reflects and contributes to the social, historical, political, and institutional contexts in which it occurs; varies across the school, home, and work contexts in which it is situated; is shaped by the curriculum and pedagogical decisions made by teachers and schools; tied to the social identity of the writer(s), and is greatly influenced by the social interactions surrounding writing.

These two approaches (and the theories underlying them) clearly privilege different aspects of writing and writing development. However, neither is complete, as cognitive/motivational views pay relatively little attention to context, and sociocultural views do not adequately address how individual factors shape writing development.

LEARNING GOALS AND TEACHING WRITING

The primary learning goals in schools during the primary grades are for students to master basic writing skills (such as handwriting, spelling, grammar, and sentence construction); begin to develop the strategic process needed to write effectively (e.g., planning, gathering and organizing information, monitoring, evaluating, revising, and so forth), acquire fundamental knowledge about writing (e.g., knowledge about the characteristics of good writing, needs of audiences, and so forth), learn to use electronic tools for composing (e.g., word processing and publishing tools), start to develop a life-long love for writing, and use writing for various purposes (e.g., communicate, inform, entertain, persuade, reflect, and so forth).

As students move into middle and high school, these same goals remain in play (although it is typically assumed that students have mastered some basic skills such as handwriting and spelling), with an emphasis on increasing students' competence as writers. Although students continue to write for a variety of purposes, using writing as a method for displaying subject-matter knowledge and as a tool for learning about such content becomes more prevalent. In some content areas (e.g., history), discourse genres typically used by that academic profession may be emphasized. At the college level, instructors may continue to emphasize more general writing development (especially for weaker writers), but as students enter classes in their majors, it is expected that they will learn the discourse styles and genres of that academic domain.

While states, school districts, and most schools have relatively clear goals for what students are to learn, there is no consensus on how to teach writing. The most prominent approach to writing instruction in the United States is the process approach (this is the only research-grounded general approach to writing instruction that has been extensively studied). This method is based on both cognitive/motivational and sociocultural views of writing. It involves extended opportunities for writing; writing for real audiences; engaging in cycles of planning, translating, and reviewing; personal responsibility and ownership of writing projects; high levels of student interactions, creation of a supportive writing environment; self-reflection and evaluation; and personalized individual assistance and instruction. This approach may only be effective, however, with teachers who are committed to its use and are trained in how to implement it. In a review of 21 studies, Graham and Perin (2007) found that this approach had little to no impact when these conditions were not met.

One concern with the process approach is that there may not be enough emphasis on explicitly teaching skills and strategic processes. The available empirical evidence indicates that directly and systematically teaching sentence construction skills and strategies for planning, revising, and editing as well as summarizing information can have a positive impact on improving the quality of students' writing (Graham & Perin, 2007). There is also some evidence that embedding more systematic instruction within the context of the process approach has a value-added impact on students' writing.

Students' writing skills can also be enhanced by providing them with assistance that helps them carry out one or more writing processes. Effective forms of support include clear and reachable writing assignment goals; help from peer(s) to carry out some aspect of the writing process; activities that help students generate, organize, and evaluate possible ideas for writing; examples of good writing that serve as a model for students; and technological supports such as word processing (Graham & Perin, 2007).

At present, it is not clear how these forms of effective writing practice should be combined or what amount of each should be provided. It is important to note that the identification of evidence-based practices in writing is far from complete. There are many practices in which there is at least some empirical evidence to support their effectiveness (this includes practices such as teaching vocabulary as a way to improve writing and having students assess their writing using a rubric). It is also certain that there are many scientifically untested practices used by teachers that will prove to be effective when evaluated by researchers. The study of exceptional teachers of writing provides one possible approach for identifying practices that merit such assessment.

There is one research-grounded treatment that has a strong impact on improving how well students write, especially struggling writers. This involves explicitly teaching students how to plan, revise, and edit their papers (teachers model how to use strategies and provide students with guided practice aimed at promoting effective and independent use). In 20 experimental studies reviewed by Graham and Perin (2007), such instruction improved the quality of students' writing in every single investigation. Particularly effective was a specific model for teaching writing strategies. The Self-Regulated Strategy Development model (see Harris, Graham, & Mason, 2006) not only involves modeling and guided practice, students are also taught the knowledge and skills needed to apply the strategies as well as procedures for regulating their use. Furthermore, this instruction is criterion- instead of time-based. This means that instruction continues for youngsters until they reach mastery, instead of providing a set number of instructional sessions.

ASSESSMENT AND EVALUATION OF WRITING

Many procedures used to assess and evaluate writing quality are drawn from cognitive theories of writing. A cognitive approach to writing supposes that text production is a finalized and complete activity, in which several complex cognitive processes are activated. Therefore, assessment and evaluation of writing quality relies on the final product. Past research has focused on two measures of writing quality: subjective and objective. Subjective (or qualitative) measures use raters to evaluate writing quality based on one or more scales, whereas objective (or quantitative) measures consist of countable indices of writing sub-components.

Holistic, analytic, and primary-trait scoring are the three main subjective methods of evaluating writing quality. Frequently used, holistic scoring reflects a rater's overall impression of the writing, compared to other writing samples in the group. Holistic scoring is norm-referenced; that is, it provides a single score that ranks students within a particular group. Some holistic scoring methods also are criterion-referenced, using pre-determined characteristics

of writing quality in the scoring process. Holistic scoring is the most economical method of scoring direct writing assignments (Scherer, 1985). One drawback to holistic scoring is that it does not provide instructional guidance for areas of concern within a writing sample.

Analytic scales and primary-trait scales address the need for assessment to inform instruction. Analytic scales are criterion-referenced and provide separate scores in predetermined areas of good writing, such as organization or development of the composition. They are the most reliable of all direct scoring assessment procedures (Scherer, 1985), although they take longer to score. One specific analytic scale, 6 Traits (and its later version: 6 + 1 Traits) has been used extensively in elementary and secondary schools. The 6 + 1 traits involve ideation, organization, voice, vocabulary sentence structure, conventions, and publication. Although developed for assessment, 6 Traits has been used as a method for writing instruction (see Graham & Perin, 2007, for a meta-analysis on the use of rubrics as an instructional method) and curriculum alignment, despite a lack of empirical research supporting its use for these situations.

Similar to analytic scales, primary trait scales also are criterion referenced. However, they differ from analytic scales in that the scoring guide is developed based on the specific purpose of each writing assignment. They can be used to assess the primary goal of the writing assignment (e.g., coherence of an argument) or to reflect genre-specific requirements (e.g., plot development).

Although in widespread use in both teaching and research, subjective measures of writing quality require scorer judgment and may be unreliable if extensive training and scoring directions are not provided. Other factors increase the variability of human scorers, such as fatigue, mood, and motivation (Freedman & Calfee, 1983). Computer-based scoring can parallel human graders; however, some scholars object to the validity of automated essay scoring (e.g., Ericsson & Haswell, 2006).

Reflecting a more sociocultural theory of writing, portfolio assessment collects several writing samples across different writing purposes and genres to gain a broader view of a student's writing ability. A good model of portfolio assessment includes the final product along with the drafts and revisions, allowing teachers to evaluate progress from start to finish. Some researchers advocate that portfolio assessment encourages students to develop writing over multiple occasions, rather than just a single sitting. Others believe that portfolios encourage more collaboration with peers rather than being teacher-centered, and that they are more consistent with teaching pedagogy (Murphy, 1994). Some districts and states collect student writing portfolios and then assess the written compositions using holistic, analytic, or primary-trait scoring methods. One concern with portfolio assessment is the time and cost to gather and evaluate each student's writing, whether in the classroom or in large-scale testing.

Objective measures of writing include the number of words written, percentage of correctly spelled words, or percentage of correct word sequences, among others. Objective measures are moderately correlated with subjective measures of writing quality (Espin, Shin, Deno, Skare, Robinson, & Benner, 2000); however, they often focus on one aspect of writing and serve as indirect measures of writing quality. Generally, these measures have been used in formative evaluation, allowing teachers to make changes to a student's instructional program based on frequent assessment.

Concerns over how to adequately assess and evaluate the quality of student writing have plagued the field for decades. The multiple purposes of writing, a lack of agreement on how to teach writing, and the increase of large-scale writing assessment have contributed to the debate. Any writing assessment method must meet standards of reliability and validity, while addressing legitimate needs for efficiency and a linkage between assessment and instruction.

BIBLIOGRAPHY

Espin, C. A., Shin, J., Deno, S. L., Skare, S., Robinson, S., & Benner, B. (2000). Identifying indicators of written expression proficiency for middle school students. *The Journal of Special Education, 34*(3), 140–153.

Freedman, S. W., & Calfee, R. C. (1983). Holistic assessment of writing: experimental design and cognitive theory. In P. Mosenthal, L. Tamor, & S. A. Walmsley (Eds.), *Research on writing: Principles and methods* (pp. 75–98). New York: Longman.

Graham, S. (2006). Writing. In P. Alexander & P. Winne (Eds.), *Handbook of educational psychology* (pp. 457–478). Mahwah, NJ: Erlbaum.

Graham, S., & Perrin, D. (2007). A meta-analysis of writing instruction for adolescent students. *Journal of Educational Psychology, 99,* 445–476.

Harris, K. R., Graham, S., & Mason, L. (2006). Improving the writing, knowledge, and motivation of struggling young writers: Effects of Self-Regulated Strategy development with and without peer support. *American Educational Research Journal, 43,* 295–340.

Hayes, J. (1996). A new framework for understanding cognition and affect in writing. In M. Levy & S. Ransdell (Eds.), *The science of writing: Theories, methods, individual differences, and applications* (pp. 1–27). Mahwah, NJ: Erlbaum.

Murphy, S. (1994). Writing portfolios in K-12 schools: Implications for linguistically diverse students. In L. Black, D. A. Daiker, & G. Stygall (Eds.), *New directions in portfolio assessment: Reflective practice, critical theory, and large-scale scoring* (pp. 140–156). Portsmouth, NH: Heinemann.

Nystrand, M. (2006). The social and historical context for writing research. In C. MacArthur, S. Graham, & J.

Fitzgerald (Eds.), *Handbook of writing research* (pp. 11–27). New York: Guilford.

Russell, D. (1997). Rethinking genre in school and society: An activity theory analysis. *Written Communication, 14,* 504–554.

Scherer, D. L. (1985). *Measuring the measurements: A study of evaluation of writing. An annotated bibliography.* (ERIC Document Reproduction Service No. 260455)

Schultz, K., & Fecho, B. (2000). Society's child: Social context and writing development. *Educational Psychology, 35,* 51–62.

Shermis, M. D., & Burstein, J. (2003). *Automated essay scoring: A cross-disciplinary perspective.* Hillsdale, NJ: Erlbaum.

White, E. M. (1985). *Teaching and assessing writing.* San Francisco: Jossey-Bass.

Zimmerman, B., & Reisemberg, R. (1997). Becoming a self-regulated writer: A social cognitive perspective. *Contemporary Educational Psychology, 22,* 73–101.

Steve Graham
Natalie G. Olinghouse

LEARNING DISABILITIES

Children and adults classified as learning disabled (LD) are individuals of normal intelligence who suffer mental information processing difficulties that influence their academic performance. Several types are referred to as LD, reflecting a heterogeneous group of individuals with intrinsic disorders that are manifested by specific difficulties in the acquisition and use of listening, speaking, reading, writing, reasoning, or mathematical abilities (Hammill, 1990). These definitions assume that the learning difficulties of such individuals are as follows:

1. Not due to poor instruction, but to specific psychological processing problems (e.g., remembering the association between sounds and letters) deriving from a neurological, constitutional, and/or biological base;

2. Not due to inadequate opportunity to learn, general intelligence, or to significant physical or emotional disorders;

3. Not manifested in all aspects of learning but specific to an academic behavior, for example, deficits in reading, but not arithmetic.

In several LD studies, children and adults with LD are operationally defined as having general IQ scores above 85 and standardized reading and/or math scores below the 25th percentile. The incidence of children with LD is conservatively estimated to reflect 2% of the public school population. LD is the largest category of children served in special education.

ASSESSMENT ISSUES

Problems of definition have severely affected the field of LD as a discipline because considerable latitude exists among psychologists in defining LD. This latitude is influenced by social/political trends as well as non-operational definitions of LD. The field is further exacerbated by the fact that the number of individuals classified with LD increased dramatically between 1985 and the early 2000s.

One impediment to advances in the field is unresolved issues related to discrepancy and another related to the importance of IQ. Traditionally, studies of children with LD have relied primarily on uncovering a significant discrepancy between achievement in a particular academic domain and general intellectual ability. The implicit assumption for using discrepancy scores is that individuals who experience reading, writing, and/or math difficulties, unaccompanied by a low IQ, are distinct in cognitive processing from slow or low achievers (e.g., Fletcher et al., 1992). This assumption is equivocal (e.g., Hoskyn & Swanson, 2000; Stuebing et al., 2002). Many studies have compared LD children with reading disabilities (RD, i.e., children with discrepancies between IQ and reading) with non-discrepancy defined poor readers (i.e., children whose IQ scores are in the same low range as their reading scores) and found that these groups are more similar in mental processing difficulties than different (Hoskyn & Swanson, 2000; Stuebing et al., 2002). As a result, some researchers have suggested dropping the requirement of average intelligence, in favor of a view by which children with reading problems are best conceptualized as existing at the extreme end of a continuum from poor to good readers (Stanovich & Siegel, 1994).

With the Individuals with Disabilities Education Improvement Act (IDEA, 2004), the United States federal government recognized potential problems with the IQ-discrepancy method by formally stating that the IQ-achievement discrepancy method was not necessary for LD diagnosis. To facilitate identifying children with LD, three criteria were added to the law:

States are not required to use a severe discrepancy between intellectual ability and achievement.

The procedure must include a process in which the children's response to scientifically based research interventions is considered in the assessment process.

States are permitted to use alternative research-based procedure to determine a specific learning disability.

Changes in the law were based on the assumption that IQ levels in children with low reading scores were irrelevant to a valid classification of LD. One alternative approach is referred to as response to instruction (RTI).

The goal of RTI is to monitor the intensity of instruction and make systematic changes in the instructional context as a function of a student's overt performance. This is done by considering various tiers of instructional intensity. As of 2008, RTI as an assessment approach for defining LD has a weak experimental base. There have been no controlled studies randomly assigning children seriously at risk for LD to assessment and/or delivery models (e.g., tiered instruction vs. special education (resource room placement) that have measured outcomes on key variables (e.g., overidentification, stability of classification, academic and cognitive growth in response to treatment). In addition, different states and school districts variously interpret how RTI should be implemented further undermining any uniformity between the science of instruction and assessment of children at risk for LD.

The validity of using discrepancy as a basis for defining LD, however, is not easily confirmed. Hoskyn and Swanson (2000) found in a synthesis of the literature that although children with RD and poor readers share some deficits in phonological processing and automaticity (naming speed), the RD group's performance was superior to poor readers on measures of syntactical knowledge, lexical knowledge, and spatial ability (also see Fuchs et al., 2000). Another finding was that cognitive differences between the two ability groups are more obvious in the earlier grades. Perhaps more important, a meta-analysis of the intervention literature (Swanson & Hoskyn, 1998) found that students with LD and low achievers differ in the magnitude of their responsiveness to treatment. Review of several intervention studies suggests that students who have low reading scores (25th percentile) but average IQ scores were less responsive to interventions than children whose reading and IQ scores were in the same low range (25th percentile) (also see Swanson & Hoskyn, 1998, pp. 300-301).

Typically, researchers who study the processing difficulties of children with LD do not use discrepancy criteria (Swanson, 1989). The majority of researchers rely on cut off scores on standardized measures above a certain criterion of general intelligence measures (e.g., standard score > 85) and cut-off scores below a certain criterion (e.g., standard score < 85) on primary academic domains (e.g., reading and mathematics).

SUBTYPES

Because of the heterogeneity of individuals classified as LD, several subtypes have been discussed in the literature. However, some subtypes have been considered invalid because (a) the particular subtypes do not respond differently to instructional programs when compared to other subtypes, and/or (b) the skills deficient in a particular subtype is not relevant to the academic areas important in the school context.

There are two subtypes, however, with extensive research that are relevant to the school context: reading disabilities and mathematical disabilities. These subtypes are defined by standardized (normed referenced) and reliable measures of intelligence and achievement. The most commonly used intelligence tests are from the Wechsler measures and common achievement tests that include measures of word recognition or identification (i.e., Wide Range Achievement Test, Woodcock Reading Mastery Test, Kaufman Test of Educational Achievement, Peabody Individual Test) and arithmetic calculation (all the aforementioned tests and the Key Math Diagnostic Test). In general, individuals with IQ scores equal to or above a Full Scale IQ score of 85 and reading subtest scores equal to below the 25th percentile and/or arithmetic subtest score equal to or below the 25th percentile constitute two high incidence disorders within LD: reading disabilities and math disabilities.

In terms of reading disabilities, Siegel (1989; 2003) argues that fundamental to evaluating reading disabilities is focus on word recognition measures because they capture more basic cognitive processes and responses than reading comprehension. Her research shows that difficulties in phonological processing are fundamental problems for children with reading disabilities, a problem that continues to adulthood. She also indicates that there is no evidence to suggest that development of decoding skills is a result of a specific instruction in grapheme-phoneme conversion rules. Her work and the work of others find that there are three processes critical in analysis of reading disabilities: those related to phonological processing (ability to segment sounds), syntactical processing, and working memory (combination of transient memory and long term memory).

In terms of math disabilities, Geary (1993, 2003) finds that children with arithmetic problems do not necessarily differ from academically normal peers in terms of the types of strategies used to solve simple arithmetic problems. Differences, however, are found in the percentage of retrieval and counting errors. Children with math disabilities have long-term memory representations of arithmetic facts that are not correct. He provides taxonomy of three general subtypes of mathematical disability: those related to procedural errors, those related to semantic memory, and those with visual/spatial difficulties. He indicates that the ability to retrieve basic arithmetic facts from long-term memory is a defining feature of math disabilities.

HISTORY AND INSTRUCTIONAL TRENDS

The term *learning disabilities* was first introduced in a speech by Samuel Kirk delivered in 1963 at Chicago Conference on Children with Perceptual Handicaps. Clinical studies prior to 1963 showed that a group of children who suffered perceptual, memory, and attention difficulties related to their poor academic performance but who were not intellectually retarded, were not being adequately served in the educational context.

Regarding the history of LD as a field, Wiederholt (1974) indicated that its unique focus was on identifying and remediating specific psychological processing difficulties. Popular intervention approaches during the 1960s and 1970s focused on visual-motor, auditory sequencing, or visual perception training exercises. Several criticisms were directed at these particular interventions on methodological and theoretical grounds.

By the late 1970s, dissatisfaction was expressed with a processing orientation to remediation of learning disabilities and with the influence of federal regulations in the U.S. (Public Law 94-142) remediation programs focused on basic skills such as reading and mathematics. The focus on basic skills rather than psychological processes was called direct instruction. The mid 1980s witnessed a shift from the more remedial-academic approach of teaching to instruction that included both basic skills and cognitive strategies (ways to better learn new information and efficiently access information from long-term memory). Children with LD were viewed as experiencing difficulty in regulating their learning performance. An instructional emphasis was placed on teaching students to check, plan, monitor, test, revise, and evaluate their learning during their attempts to learn or solve problems.

The early 1990s witnessed a resurgence of direct instruction intervention studies, primarily influenced by reading research, which suggested that a primary focus of intervention should be directed to phonological skills. The rationale was that because a large majority of children with learning disabilities suffer problems in reading, some of these children's reading problems are exacerbated because of lack of systematic instruction in processes related to phonological awareness (the ability to hear and manipulate sounds in words and understand the sound structure of language). This view gave rise to several interventions which emphasized phonics instruction and intense individual one-to-one tutoring to improve children's phonological awareness of word structures and sequences.

SCIENTIFICALLY BASED TREATMENTS

Some experimental research shows that children with LD can be assessed and significant gains can be made in academic performance as a function of treatment (see Vellutino et al., 2004). However, considerable evidence suggests that some children with normal intelligence when exposed to the best instructional condition fail to efficiently master skills in reading, mathematic, and/or writing (e.g., Fuchs & Fuchs, 1998; Torgesen, 2000). Some literature suggests that LD individuals are less responsive than generally poor readers to intervention (e.g., Swanson & Hoskyn, 1998) and these academic problems persist into adulthood (e.g., Ransby & Swanson, 2003). Further, these difficulties in academic mastery reflect fundamental deficits in processing, such as phonological processing and working memory (Swanson & Siegel, 2001).

Swanson, Hoskyn and Lee (1999) provided a comprehensive analysis of the experimental intervention literature on LD. Their synthesis of methodologically sound studies (those with well-defined control groups and clearly identified LD samples) found that positive outcomes in remediating academic behaviors (e.g., reading, writing, mathematics) were directly related to a combination of direct and strategy instructional models. These models included a graduated sequence of steps with multiple opportunities for overlearning the content and skills, cumulative review routines, mass practice, and teaching of all component skills to a level that shows mastery. The interventions involved (a) teaching a few concepts and strategies well rather than superficially, (b) teaching students to monitor their performance, (c) teaching students when and where to use the strategy in order to enhance generalization, (d) teaching strategies as an integrated part of an existing curriculum, and (e) providing teaching that includes a great deal of supervised student feedback and practice.

Swanson (2000) found that two critical instructional components underlie successful instructional interventions for children with LD. One component was explicit practice that includes activities related to distributed review and practice, repeated practice, sequenced reviews, daily feedback, and/or weekly reviews. The other component was advanced organizers, and these studies included activities (a) directing children to focus on specific material or information prior to instruction, (b) directing children about task concepts or events before beginning, and/or (c) the teacher stating objectives of instruction.

SEE ALSO *Attention Deficit Hyperactivity Disorder (ADHD); Direct Instruction; Individualized*

Education Program (IEP); Learning and Teaching Mathematics; Learning and Teaching Reading; Meta-Analysis; Special Education; Strategies Instruction.

BIBLIOGRAPHY

Fletcher, J. M., Francis, D. J., Rourke, B. P., Shaywitz, S. E., & Shaywitz, B. A. (1992). The validity of discrepancy-based definitions of reading disabilities. *Journal of Learning Disabilities, 25,* 555–561.

Fuchs, L. S., & Fuchs, D. (1998). Treatment validity: A unifying concept for reconceptualizing identification of learning disabilities. *Learning Disabilities Research and Practice, 13,* 204–219.

Fuchs, D., Fuchs, L., Mathes, P. G., & Lipsey, M. E. (2000). Reading differences between low-achieving students with and without reading disabilities: A meta-analysis. In G. Gersten, E. P. Schiller, & S. Vaughn (Eds.), *Contemporary Special Education Research* (pp. 105–136). Mahwah, NJ: Erlbaum.

Hammill, D. (1990). On defining learning disabilities: An emerging consensus. *Journal of Learning Disabilities, 23,* 74–84.

Hoskyn, M., & Swanson, H. L. (2000). Cognitive processing of low achievers and children with reading disabilities: A selective review of the published literature. *School Psychology Review, 29,* 102–119.

Geary, D. (1993). Mathematical disabilities: Cognitive, neuropsychological, and genetic components. *Psychological Bulletin, 114,* 345–362.

Geary, D. (2003). Learning disabilities in arithmetic: Problem solving differences and cognitive deficits. In H. L. Swanson, K. M. Harris, & S. Graham (Eds.), *Handbook of Learning Disabilities* (pp. 199–212). New York: Guilford.

Ransby, M., & Swanson, H. L. (2003). Reading comprehension skills of young adults with childhood dyslexia. *Journal of Learning Disabilities, 36,* 538–555.

Shaywitz, S. E., Fletcher, J. M., Holahan, J. M., Shneider, A. E., Marchione, K. E., Stuebing, K. K., et al. (1999). Persistence of dyslexia: The Connecticut longitudinal study at adolescence. *Pediatrics, 104,* 1351–1359.

Siegel, L. S. (1989). IQ is irrelevant to the definition of learning disabilities. *Journal of Learning Disabilities, 22,* 469–478.

Siegel, L.S. (2003). Basic cognitive processes and reading disabilities. In H. L. Swanson, K. M. Harris, & S. Graham (Eds.), *Handbook of Learning Disabilities* (pp. 158–181). New York: Guilford.

Stanovich, K., & Siegel, L. S. (1994). Phenotypic performance profile of children with reading disabilities: A regression-based test of the phonological-core variable-difference model. *Journal of Educational Psychology, 86,* 24–53.

Stuebing, K. K., Fletcher, J. M., LeDoux, J. M., Lyon, G. R., Shaywitz, S. E., & Shaywitz, B. A. (2002). Validity of IQ-discrepancy classifications of reading disabilities: A meta-analysis. *American Educational Research Journal, 39,* 469–518.

Swanson, H. L. (1989). Operational Definitions of LD: An overview. *Learning Disability Quarterly, 14,* 242–254.

Swanson, H. L. (2000). Searching for the best model for instructing students with LD: A component and composite analysis. *Educational and Child Psychology, 17,* 101–121.

Swanson, H. L., & Hoskyn, M. (1998). Experimental intervention research on students with learning disabilities: A meta-analysis of treatment outcomes. *Review of Educational Research, 68,* 277–321.

Swanson, H. L., Hoskyn, M., Lee, C. (1999). Interventions for Students with Learning Disabilities: A meta-analysis of Treatment Outcomes. New York: Guilford.

Swanson, H. L., & Siegel, L. S. (2001). Learning disabilities as a working memory deficit. *Issues in Education: Contributions from Educational Psychology, 7,* 1–48.

Torgesen, J. K. (2000). Individual differences in response to early interventions in reading: The lingering problem of treatment resisters. *Learning Disabilities Research and Practice, 15,* 55–64.

Vellutino, F. R., Fletcher, J. M., Snowling, M. J., & Scanlon, D. (2004). Specific reading disability (dyslexia): What have we learned in the past four decades? *Journal of Child Psychology and Psychiatry, 45,* 2–40.

Weiderholt, L. (1974). Historical perspective on the education of the learning disabled. In L. Mann & D. Sabatino (Eds.), *The second review of special education* (pp. 103–152). Austin: Pro-Ed.

H. Lee Swanson
Danielle Edelston

LEARNING IN INFORMAL SETTINGS

Educational research typically explores how and what students learn and tends not to examine where students learn. The assumption is people learn in school. With some notable and impressive exceptions (e.g., Resnick, 1987), the subject of setting for learning simply has not been of critical importance to educational researchers. However, it is the central question for researchers who study learning in informal settings.

School is a physical setting operating roughly from nine in the morning until three in the afternoon for thirteen years of childhood. It is the formal setting for learning. But what are informal learning settings? Any visitor to the Metropolitan Museum of Art or to the Vatican would be amused to hear them referred to as informal. Should three friends exploring a neighborhood creek on a Saturday afternoon be as participating in an informal learning setting, or should some notion of structure and intentionality be included in defining such settings?

By structure, researchers assume that the informal learning does not simply happen in some place and time other than school, but that such places have reasonable physical and temporal boundaries. There has to be some sense of a setting to informal learning settings. Thus, they can be a museum, a concert auditorium, a farm, even a baseball field, but probably they are not parks, the dinner table during an interesting discussion, or a toy store.

This distinction leads to the notion of intentionality. Not all museum visits have learning as a goal, and a visit to a toy store could possibly be primarily educational in nature. It depends in part on the purpose for the visit. Jackson (1968) writes about intentionality as being a key distinguishing feature of teaching, and the concept generalizes well here. Many settings can provide the opportunity for learning, but not all do, nor do all settings at all times. Thus, informal settings for learning may be defined here as those circumstances outside school in which learning is clearly at least one of the goals of the event.

An informal learning setting should be a setting bound by space and time, and its intended use should be educational during the activities under consideration, for example, a class trip to a natural history museum to learn about the First Nations people who lived in the area and that the class is studying in school. It could be a small group of students going to an art museum to look at Islamic art in relation to a special report that they are writing on geometry. Or it could be a high school cooperative vocational program in which students enhance applied mathematics skills.

Informal learning settings have structure and intentionality. But should the term also include individuals of school age who are learning school-related subject matter (perhaps broadly defined) on their own in informal settings, what Falk and Dierking call "free-choice learning" (Dierking & Falk, 2003; Falk, 2005)? This would then

Students learning about art at a museum. **GETTY IMAGES.**

include family outings to informal learning settings, and programs developed by institutions to teach children in various areas, but that are not directly related to schools themselves. Finally, there is the increasingly looming question of the Internet. At the Timeline of Art History section of the Web site maintained by the Metropolitan Museum of Art, one can spend weeks learning about cultures from all over the world and all through the history of humankind. Should the definition of informal learning settings include virtual locations as well as physical ones?

These possibilities have been presented for two purposes: first, to limit what will be discussed in the remainder of this entry; and second, and the more important part, to suggest the incredible variety, potential, and power of learning in informal settings. There is a spectrum of possible definitions of learning in informal settings. At what might be called the narrow end of the spectrum, the definition from the perspective of the individual might be: "I am at this place at this time to learn something that is related somehow to what I am learning in school." At the broad end, the perspective might be: "I am not in school and yet I am learning." Although the broader end is clearly the more intriguing one, the narrower end is of great concern to those who are interested in building strong and useful relationships between schools and cultural institutions (and other institutions), and this relationship is the focus here. It is strongly related (perhaps identical) to Eshach's 2007 notion of non-formal learning. Eshach differentiates formal learning (school-based), informal learning (everything individuals learn outside of school), and non-formal learning (learning in a planned situation or organization, but not in school).

LIMITED RESEARCH

Traditionally, school learning in informal settings has been characterized by the one-time school trip visit to the museum, zoo, local company, or performing arts venue. Often, preparatory activities and auxiliary materials accompany such visits. But research literature says little regarding the efficacy of such programs to produce what might be called school-based learning. Griffin (2004) reviewed the literature on such trips and finds that in terms of statistically significant gains on cognitive measures related to school subjects, the evidence is equivocal at best. Bowker (2002) looked at factors that influence learning in museums and again found that the literature does not speak with a single voice. There are some indications of generalizable findings, such as the need for students to have some time on their own in a school visit and the strong possibility that the increase in interest associated with museum visits pays off in subsequent classroom learning (Borun, Flexer, Casey, & Baum,

1983). But, in general, the conclusion one has to reach is that there simply is not a whole lot of literature demonstrating the efficacy of the single-trip museum visit in terms of the kinds of learning that are valued in schools.

Although perhaps a bit depressing, this finding is not particularly surprising. There are a number of natural constraints on finding such effects, including the difficulty of studying the phenomenon in a rigorous fashion, the limited time frame of the museum encounter, and the frequent lack of congruence between what the museum has to offer and what the students are learning in school. The question that is raised by the paucity of research documenting the efficacy of school/museum interactions is: Do museums actually contribute to the learning of school-related material? That is, is the research scarce because it is hard to produce, or is it scarce because there is no real learning?

REFRAMING THE QUESTION

Basically, the answer to that question is that it is the wrong question. It is the wrong question for researchers and evaluators to have asked, and to a degree, the wrong questions for museum educators to have tried to live up to. For too many years, those concerned with education in informal settings have tried to show that museums can lead to higher test scores of one form or another. But the logical linkage between what a museum has to offer and what is measured on school tests is tenuous, and the path from one to another is often tortuous. This is not meant as a critique of either cultural institutions or the institution of school testing; both have their place. It is simply a statement that it is hard to find one's way from one place to another. As an example of the nature of the problem, a federally funded, three-year project at the Isabella Stewart Gardner Museum found that students in the project used critical thinking skills more in looking at art than children not in the program but that there was no discernible effect on standardized test scores (National School Boards Association, 2007). And this was for an extensive program. When one considers the additional constraints of a one-time visit to a museum, complete with bus trips, packed lunches, lining up, getting coats off and back on again, the difficulty in finding statistically significant findings on test scores comes more into focus.

Fortunately, better questions are being posed in the early 2000s. Researchers have stopped looking at informal learning settings as adjuncts to schools and have begun looking at them for what they can offer and excel at. Schauble and her colleagues argue that researchers need to include issues such as the sparking and maintenance of motivation and personal development when considering the impact of museum visits (Schauble et al.,

1996). Hooper-Greenhill (2004) addresses this issue as well, arguing that researchers need to consider broader educational goals, which she calls generic learning outcomes, instead of more subject or unit-within-subject specific goals. Citing efforts by Great Britain's Economic and Social Research Council

Teaching and Learning Research Programme, she lists (among others) as possible goals:

positive identities of students as learners

knowledge and skill acquisition

acquisition of values and dispositions of a learning society

development of personal, community and societal concerns

One might reasonably ask if these are properly school-related learnings. Perhaps in a No Child Left Behind world, one might have difficulty in finding such statements in the masses of standards that define each state's desiderata for student growth. But the list cited in Hooper-Greenhill aligns quite nicely with New Zealand's "Key Competencies," the centerpiece of its national curriculum document (Ministry of Education, 2007):

Thinking

Using language, symbols, and texts

Managing self

Relating to others

Participating and contributing

It is perfectly reasonable to wonder, at this point, if museum education researchers have such difficulty in documenting small and specific effects, why would one expect to find broader effects. The answer is that is what museums do, when they are working well. They engender broader considerations and ideas, cause people to reflect beyond the visit, and encourage people to think in ways that perhaps they had not before. Although it is entirely possible to visit a museum and not be intrigued by anything in the collection, Carr (2006) argues that the very existence of objects of value and veneration should engender questions in the visitor. The visitor may ask about who made the artifacts, why they are important, and why they are displayed in a museum. Visitors may wonder about what the display means to them personally and how the displayed objects related. When individuals start to ask such questions and seek answers to them, learning occurs in various ways. First, knowledge is gained from the content and context of the objects themselves. Second, there is skill development in learning how to find answers to questions. Third, individuals often place themselves in the context of the objects,

leading to an exploration of a sense of community and identity.

DOCUMENTING A REVISED PERSPECTIVE

If, indeed, one can argue successfully that the learning that occurs in museums is of this broader and more substantial kind, how might one go about documenting such learning? This is a serious challenge, but one worth taking up. And there have been several promising starts. Leinhardt and Crowley (2002) begin from the perspective that one should be open to capture the learning as it occurs in the informal learning setting as opposed to determining what that learning should be a priori and then seeing if one can find the preconceived learning. This is a remarkable insight and one that might be well extended to learning in schools as well. Their approach to finding that learning is to have museum visitors fitted with recording devices so that they can listen to their conversations with others as they go to a museum, visit it, and return home from their visit. Leinhardt and Crowley call their approach, "learning conversations." Although their approach is costly, time-consuming, and can only sample very few participants, their results are nonetheless impressive. It is clear from their research that individuals in informal learning settings engage in conversations during and following visits that reflect authentic engagement with museum artifacts. They argue convincingly that the scope and level of these conversations, in comparison to conversations prior to the experience, are the types of experiences that lead to meaningful learning.

Bamberger and Tal (2007) utilized multiple observations in looking at the effects of choice on student learning. They video taped museum visits, conducted semi-structured interviews, and used questionnaires (the authors refer to them as worksheets). The data were coded so as to allow for assessment of those activities known to be related to student learning: student questioning, linkage to prior knowledge, scaffolding. As with the Leinhardt and Crowley approach, the authors did not look for specific learnings, but for the evidence of learning in general.

Finally, Smith and Waszkielewicz (2007) found that individuals (adults in this case) in an art museum were more likely to rate themselves highly in terms of thinking about interpersonal, intrapersonal, and societal concerns and issues while in the middle of a museum visit than at the beginning or the end of the visit. Like the two studies mentioned above, these authors gathered information on visitors during the museum visit. Their approach, however, used a fairly standard questionnaire format that allowed for the gathering of a quite large sample and replication over two museums using the same approach.

The research on learning in informal settings may not yield exactly what one might anticipate or, at the outset, even hope for. But as is so often the case in research, the new horizons are more intriguing than the old ones. As researchers learn that informal learning settings may or may not provide much support for acquiring everyday school objectives (as important as they are), they learn that they may well support broader and deeper goals. Educators look for growth in personal development, the ability to analyze and critique, a sense of belonging to structures and communities larger than one's own immediate group; they hope to make ties to the past and make conscious hope for better futures. What they find will almost certainly be different from what they envision, but the trip should be an enjoyable and rewarding one.

SEE ALSO *Guided Participation; Sociocultural Theory.*

BIBLIOGRAPHY

Bamberger, Y., & Tal, T. (2007). Learning in a personal context: Levels of choice in a free choice learning environment in science and natural history museums. *Science Education, 91*(1), 75–95.

Borun, M., Flexer, B., Casey, A., & Baum, L. (1983). *Planets and pulleys: Studies of class visits to a science museum.* Washington, DC: ASTC.

Bowker, R. (2002). Evaluating teaching and learning strategies at the Eden Project. *Evaluation and Research in Education, 16*(3), 123–135.

Carr, D. (2006). *A place not a place: Reflection and possibility in museums and libraries.* Lanham, MD: Alta Mira Press.

Dierking, L. D., & Falk, J. H. (2003). Optimizing out-of-school time: The role of free-choice learning. *New Directions for Youth Development, 97,* 75–88.

Eshach, H. (2007). Bridging in-school and out-of-school learning: Formal, non-formal, and informal. *Journal of Science Education and Technology, 16*(2), 171–190.

Falk, J. H. (2005). Free-choice environmental learning: Framing the discussion. *Environmental Education Research, 11*(3), 265–280.

Griffin, J. (2004). Research on students and museums: Looking more closely at the students in school groups. *Science Education, 88* (Suppl.1), S59–S70.

Hooper-Greenhill, E. (2004). Measuring learning outcomes in museums, archives, and libraries: The learning impact research project. *International Journal of Heritage Studies, 10*(2), 151–174.

Jackson, P. W. (1968). *Life in classrooms.* New York: Holt, Rinehart, and Winston.

Leinhardt, G., & Crowley, K. (2002). Objects of learning, objects of talk: Changing minds in museums. In S. Paris (Ed.), *Multiple perspectives on children's object-centered learning* (pp. 301–324). Mahwah, NJ: Erlbaum.

Ministry of Education. (2007). *The New Zealand curriculum.* Wellington, NZ: Learning Media.

National School Boards Association. (2007, May). Art improves critical thinking. *American School Board Journal, 8.*

Resnick, L. B. (1987). The 1987 presidential address: Learning in and out of school. *Educational Researcher, 16*(9), 13–20.

Schauble, L., Beane, D. B., Coates, G. D., Martin, L. M. W., & Sterling, P. V. (1996). Outside the classroom walls: Learning in informal environments. In L. Schauble & R. Glaser (Eds.), *Innovations in learning: New environments for education* (pp. 5–24). Mahwah, NJ: Erlbaum.

Smith, J. K., & Waszkielewicz, I. (2007). *The civilizing influence of art museum visitation.* Paper presented at annual meeting of the American Psychological Association, San Francisco, CA, 2007.

Smith, J. K. & Wolf, L. F. (1995, July). *Measurement and evaluation techniques for museum evaluation.* Paper presented at the annual meeting of the Visitor Studies Association, St. Paul, MN.

Jeffrey K. Smith

LEARNING STYLES

Learning styles theory is based on the understanding that differences between individuals' processing capabilities lead to significantly different learning requirements. Learning style theorists argue that these capabilities are fairly fixed, and most of the proponents believe that, in order for individuals to be successful learners, instruction needs to be matched to the individuals' learning preferences. While there is intuitive appeal in the notion that designing instruction to meet individual learning styles leads to improved academic achievement, there is a dearth of evidence to indicate that this concept has any validity. In fact, rather than increasing success in the classroom, research indicates that attempts to match instruction to specific learning styles fails to lead to improvements in student learning. Further, by limiting—rather than expanding—the range of educational approaches provided to learners, the use of learning styles has the potential to increase, rather than alleviate, the difficulties students experience in their learning.

LEARNING STYLES DESCRIBED

According to Vicki Snider (1990; 1992), learning styles are an outgrowth of the process approaches of the 1960s and 1970s—although the construct is meant to describe differences between learners rather than to identify disorders (e.g., visual or auditory preferences rather than a visual-processing disability). Learning styles based education is also considered to be a form of aptitude-treatment interaction. Aptitude-treatment interactions are meant to identify individuals' distinct characteristics (aptitudes) and match these with specific treatments (for example, instructional approaches) in order to produce statistically improved outcomes (in this case, significantly improved learning).

The learning styles construct also encompasses a range of models, including learning preferences (for example, global versus analytical or visual versus auditory learners), cognitive styles (e.g., field dependence versus field independence or reflective versus impulsive), and personality types (e.g., the Myers-Briggs types). This range of models makes it difficult to develop a consistent definition of learning styles. However, there are two traits that appear to be constant across most descriptions of learning styles. First, learning styles are generally seen as fixed; that is, individuals have certain aptitudes that result from their natural tendencies or predispositions. Second, by matching learners with particular attributes to complementary instructional approaches, it becomes possible to increase their ability to process information.

So, for example, in terms of natural predispositions, field dependent individuals are identified by the difficulty they experience differentiating a particular item, or figure, as distinct from a complex background, or the surrounding field. Field independent individuals, by contrast, can be identified by their ability to readily distinguish between the two. Continuing with this example, field dependent individuals are considered to be social learners who benefit from collaboration and extrinsic motivation, whereas field independent individuals are considered to be independent learners who are intrinsically motivated and work best on their own. The argument continues that, by designing learning opportunities that take into account these innate preferences, it should be possible to improve the learning of both types of students.

ACADEMIC USEFULNESS

According to Ronald Hyman and Barbara Rosoff, in order to be a useful addition to the field of education, there are certain criteria that the learning styles construct would need to meet. First, the concept of learning styles needs to be clearly defined, both to allow ready identification of particular types of learners and to ensure effective communication regarding how best to meet these various learners needs. Next, it is important that accurate and efficient assessment measures be created to enable the easy identification of these distinct learning styles. Finally, there would need to be specific instructional approaches that lead to improved academic achievement when matched to students with a particular learning style (and, following from this, that are ineffective when matched with students who demonstrate alternative learning styles). Unfortunately, despite decades of research, the field of learning styles based education has failed to make significant progress in any of these areas.

Inconsistency of Definitions. There are numerous learning style models (71 according to a major review by

Coffield and his colleagues), many of which differ in terms of the attributes their proponents identify as critical to individual differences. In fact, although there is some degree of overlap, the advocates of these various models focus on an extensive array of qualities that they believe to be central to improving academic achievement. For example, some models look at environmental (e.g., temperature and sound), emotional (e.g., motivation and persistence), sociological (e.g., working alone or with others), and physical traits (e.g., time of day and need for mobility). Others consider the dimensions of perception (concrete or abstract) and ordering (sequential or random). Yet others define learners on two independent dimensions, cognitive organization (holistic or analytic) and mental representation (verbal or imagery). Ultimately, the fact that there are so many different models with such disparate views of what constitutes learning styles makes it nearly impossible to develop a cohesive definition upon which the field can build.

Assessing Learning Styles. In terms of the effectiveness of learning styles assessments, there are two ways in which these measures are problematic. The first and more serious issue is that, without a unifying definition of learning styles, it is impossible to develop a cohesive means of evaluating the construct. In other words, given the fragmented nature of the field, it is unclear how valid any assessment measure could be. Despite this problem, assessment measures have been developed for a number of individual models. However, Steven Stahl notes that these are generally considered to have low reliabilities for standardized procedures; for example, when individuals complete a particular evaluation at two different points in time (test-retest), the results are very often inconsistent. There are two possible explanations for this difference; either individuals' learning styles change quite significantly over relatively short periods of time or the assessments themselves fail to measure what they are meant to measure. Either way, the disparity undermines confidence in these assessments.

The Usefulness of Learning Styles. Given the above critique, it is apparent that the concept of learning styles is problematic. In fact, from the late 1970s onward, a number of major literature reviews set out to evaluate the research conducted on learning styles (or its predecessor aptitude-treatment interactions). Each of these reviews independently reached the same conclusion: There is a striking lack of evidence indicating that the matching of learners with particular modes of instruction, whether based on self-reported or observed learning preferences, is an effective means of improving academic achievement.

For example, both Vicki Snider (1992) and Steven Stahl discuss numerous attempts to improve learners' reading ability by matching students who demonstrate particular types of modality preferences with the corresponding form of reading instruction. In these studies, visual or global learners have been taught using either whole word or whole language methods and auditory or analytic learners have been taught using a decoding or phonics-based approach. Results indicated that, despite the attempts to match children to the instructional approach that best complements their learning styles, there was no effect on reading achievement. One reason may be that, rather than possessing a particular learning style, students have different instructional needs at different points in their development.

According to many literacy researchers, early or emergent readers have been shown to benefit from more holistic approaches that emphasize concepts of print, language experience, and phonemic awareness. Once students have established these concepts, a focus on word recognition through phonics or decoding instruction is appropriate. As students develop comfort with the alphabetic principle, another shift occurs, and students consolidate their understanding of letter-sound correspondences and begin to develop their reading fluency. Using the most popular model for reading styles to describe what is occurring during these stages, the same student could be classified as a global or visual learner at the emergent stage, an analytic or auditory learner as the focus shifts to word recognition, and finally a global or visual learner again as the individual starts to develop reading fluency. Rather than arguing that students respond to a single type of instruction, it becomes apparent that what constitutes appropriate instruction changes as learners' needs change.

MULTICULTURAL LEARNING STYLES

Another problem that arises with the learning styles construct involves its application to broad cultural classifications. Advocates of this argument propose that students from various ethnic and cultural groups learn in fundamentally different ways from one another and that the education gap that exists between more successful white students and their lower achieving peers from different cultures (e.g., African American, Hispanic, Native American) is the result of culturally incompatible teaching. However, Craig Frisby argues that this contention is based upon several flawed assumptions; these range from the notion discussed above that learning styles and learning styles assessments are valid and reliable to the view that the members of various cultures must be taught in unique ways in order to demonstrate academic success. For example, according to some theorists, students from certain cultures prefer one modality over another and learn best when instruction is matched to those prefer-

ences. That is, some students are said to favor a lecture format and prefer having their work laid out in a step-by-step manner (analytic or auditory learners), whereas others are said to learn better when they have the opportunity to derive information though graphics and their material is presented holistically (global or visual learners), and still others are said to need to reinforce what they are learning through physical approaches in order to be successful (kinesthetic or tactile learners).

However, it is likely that students learn best, not as the result of a dominant processing preference being matched to its corresponding instructional approach, but as a result of educators' designing instructional approaches that are appropriate for the learning requirements of a particular situation. So that even auditory learners will develop a deeper understanding of, say, certain scientific concepts when given the opportunity to see a demonstration of that concept, than when they simply hear about that concept through a lecture. Similarly, most visual learners will develop a richer appreciation of a musical score after hearing a recording of it than they would after reading a critique of it. Likewise, although only some learners are classified as kinesthetic learners, it seems unlikely that individuals with other learning styles preferences will become competent at tennis simply by watching other players play the game or by learning about the steps involved in a serve without actually practicing it. Using these examples, it seems reasonable to argue that the modality people prefer has more to do with the nature of a given task than it has to do with individuals from certain cultural backgrounds having a cluster of learning requirements that develop out of a set of predetermined learning preferences.

ALTERNATIVES TO LEARNING STYLES

If learning styles are not the key to improved academic achievement, then what is? There are several educational approaches that can assist all learners, but are especially effective for those learners who are experiencing difficulties in the classroom. First, Vicki Snider (1990) suggests that teachers incorporate instruction that makes use of multiple modalities. Multimodality instruction differs from modality matching in that it incorporates visual, auditory, and tactile processing rather than just relying on one of these elements; such instruction has been shown to be effective with a range of learners, including those who are struggling with a particular curriculum. Second, when students encounter difficulty with their learning, rather than simply re-presenting the information in the same manner, teachers should consider where breakdowns may be occurring and how alternative ways of presenting the information can help students better develop their understanding of the material at hand (e.g., scaffolding, the presentation of additional examples, collaborative discussions).

Finally, instruction in cognitive strategies should be considered in concert with these other instructional methods. Barak Rosenshine defines cognitive strategies as approaches, such as question-generation and summarizing, which help students succeed with complex learning tasks, such as comprehension, problem solving, and writing. What is important about cognitive strategies is that, unlike learning styles, there is a substantial body of research to demonstrate that these approaches lead to greater academic achievement and that this achievement occurs with a range of learners across ages, gender, culture, and socioeconomic background. Perhaps more importantly, each of these three principles can be integrated into any learning environment without relying on the limitations of learning styles or learning styles based education.

SEE ALSO *Cognitive Strategies; Metacognition.*

BIBLIOGRAPHY
Coffield, F., Moseley, D., Hall, E., & Ecclestone, K. (2004). Learning styles and pedagogy in post-16 learning: A systematic and critical review. Retrieved April 16, 2008, from http://www.lsda.org.uk/files/PDF/1543.pdf.

Curry, L. (1990). A critique of the research on learning styles. *Educational Leadership 48*(2), 50–52, 54–56.

Frisby, C. L. (1993). One giant step backward: Myths of black cultural learning styles. *School Psychology Review, 22*(3), 535–557.

Hyman, R., & Rosoff, B. (1984). Matching learning and teaching styles: The jug and what's in it. *Theory into Practice 23*(1), 35–43.

Kavale, K. A., & Forness, S. R. (1987). Substance over style: Assessing the efficacy of modality testing and teaching. *Exceptional Children 54*(3), 228–239.

Rosenshine, B. Advances in research on instruction. (1997). In J.W. Lloyd, E. J. Kameanui, & D. Chard (Eds.), *Issues in educating students with disabilities* (pp. 197–221). Mahwah, NJ: Erlbaum.

Stahl, S. A. (1999). Different strokes for different folks? A critique of learning styles. Retrieved April 16, 2008, from http://www.aft.org/pubs-reports/american_educator/fall99/DiffStrokes.pdf.

Snider, V. E. (1990). What we know about learning styles from research in special education. *Educational Leadership 48*(2), 53.

Snider, V. E. (1992). Learning styles and learning to read: A critique. *Remedial and Special Education 13*(1), 6–18.

Melanie R. Kuhn

LONGITUDINAL RESEARCH

Educational researchers and practitioners are often interested in questions about how individuals grow and develop over time. For example, how rapidly does a student's understanding of various mathematical concepts changes during secondary school? (Ai, 2002). To effectively answer such questions, *longitudinal data* (Singer & Willett, 2003) must be collected in which the same information may be obtained from individuals at different times. For example, to study the development of mathematics achievement during secondary school, yearly mathematics achievement tests could be administered. Longitudinal data is contrasted with *cross-sectional data*, in which information is collected from individuals at one point in time (e.g., mathematics achievement tests of children of different ages at the same point in time). While cross-sectional data is easier to collect than longitudinal data, it cannot be used to accurately answer questions about change.

This entry provides an example of the use of longitudinal data to study change in mathematics achievement during secondary school. The research addresses the following questions:

1. How much does mathematics achievement change during secondary school?

2. In what ways do trajectories of mathematics achievement differ across students?

3. Does mathematics achievement development differ as a function of student race?

These questions are addressed by fitting a statistical model called the *multilevel model for change* to five years of mathematics achievement data collected as part of the *Longitudinal Study of American Youth* (LSAY), a national longitudinal study of U.S. secondary school students (Miller, Kimmel, Hoffer, & Nelson, 2000). LSAY data were collected from 5,945 students over 7 years, beginning in the fall of 1987 when the students were in either 7th or 10th grade. A primary focus of the LSAY was on measuring students' mathematics achievement over time, using items from the National Assessment of Educational Progress. Here, in the example, are analyses of mathematics achievement data from a sub-sample of 1,322 White and African American students between 7th grade and 11th grade, asking about the effects of race on changes in the mathematics achievement over time.

THE MULTILEVEL MODEL FOR CHANGE

When studying change over time, the first questions are about each person's individual change trajectory. For example, does a particular student's mathematics achievement

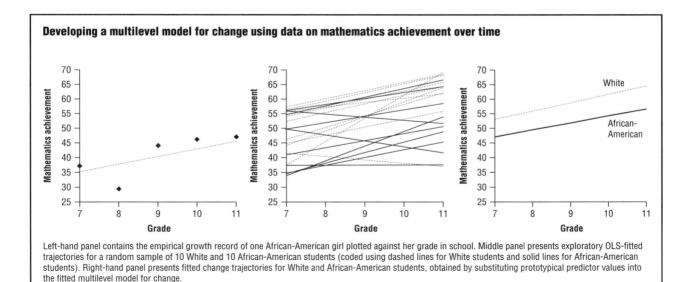

Developing a multilevel model for change using data on mathematics achievement over time

Left-hand panel contains the empirical growth record of one African-American girl plotted against her grade in school. Middle panel presents exploratory OLS-fitted trajectories for a random sample of 10 White and 10 African-American students (coded using dashed lines for White students and solid lines for African-American students). Right-hand panel presents fitted change trajectories for White and African-American students, obtained by substituting prototypical predictor values into the fitted multilevel model for change.

Figure 1 ILLUSTRATION BY GGS INFORMATION SERVICES. CENGAGE LEARNING, GALE.

improve rapidly during secondary school? Does another student's achievement increase less rapidly? Might yet another student's achievement actually decrease over time? These questions are addressed with the *level-1 statistical model*, or individual growth model, which represents the change that, according to the hypothesis, each member of the population will experience during the time period under study.

To develop an understanding of the level-1 model, the left-hand panel of Figure 1 should be considered, in which the researchers have plotted the mathematics achievement (MATHACH) of one African American girl from the dataset against her grade, between 7th and 11th grade. For this girl, mathematics achievement improves steadily over time. This upward trend is summarized in the empirical growth record by superimposing a fitted ordinary least squares (OLS) "achievement on grade" linear regression line. Observations based on this plot suggest two important components of this level-1 statistical model. First, the model should capture systematic underlying change in mathematics achievement over time (represented by the fitted growth trajectory plotted in Figure 1). Second, the model must account for differences between observed values of mathematics achievement (represented by the datapoints plotted in Figure 1), and the predicted values from the fitted growth trajectory. These observations lead the researchers to hypothesize the following level-1 model:

$$Y_{ij} = \left[\pi_{0i} + \pi_{1i}(GRADE_{ij} - 7) \right] + \epsilon_{ij} \quad (1)$$

This model asserts that, in the population of students from which this sample was drawn, Y_{ij}, the observed value of *MATHACH* for student i at time j is constituted from two important parts. The first part—in brackets in equation (1)—describes the underlying true change for this student as a linear function of his (or her) grade in school (*GRADE$_{ij}$*). This trajectory is characterized by two individual growth parameters, π_{0i} and π_{1i}, which determine its shape for the *ith* student. The intercept, π_{0i}, represents student i's true mathematics achievement in 7th grade. (This interpretation applies because the researchers centered *GRADE* in the level-1 model by subtracting the constant "7" from it.) The slope, π_{1i}, represents the yearly rate of change of student i's true mathematics achievement. The second part of the level-1 model is a random error term (ϵ_{ij}), which accounts for the difference between individual i's true and observed value of *MATHACH*, on occasion j. This level-1 residual represents that part of student i's value of *MATHACH* at time j not predicted by grade level.

In specifying a level-1 model, it is implicitly assumed that all students' true individual change trajectories have a common algebraic form, here represented by a straight line. But because all the students have their own value of the intercept and slope parameters, everyone does not necessarily follow exactly the same trajectory. Students' true mathematics achievement levels in seventh grade may vary, as may their rates of true change in achievement. Therefore, we may study inter-individual differences in individual growth trajectories by studying inter-individual variation in individual growth parameters. These observations form the foundation of the *level-2 statistical model*.

At level-2—the "between-person" or inter-individual level—questions are asked about predictors of change. Here, in the mathematics achievement example, at level-2 it was asked whether the average African American seventh grader has lower mathematics achievement than the average White seventh grader, and also whether rates of change in mathematics achievement differ as a function of race. These questions are addressed by modeling the relationship between inter-individual differences in the change trajectories (i.e., intercept and slope parameters) and student characteristics (here, race). To develop an intuition about the level-2 model, the middle panel of Figure 1 should be examined. It represents an exploratory analysis in which the researchers have plotted fitted OLS individual growth trajectories for a random subset of 10 White and 10 African American students (solid lines represent African American students and dashed lines represent White students). As noted for the single student in the left panel, mathematics achievement increases over time for most students. In addition, African American students seem to have generally lower mathematics achievement scores in seventh grade than do White students, and their rates of increase in achievement over time are not as large. But the substantial inter-individual heterogeneity in growth trajectories within groups should also be noted. Not all African American students have lower intercepts than do White students; many of them have higher mathematics achievement in seventh grade. Similarly, not all African American students have less steep slopes; some of them have very rapid increases in mathematics achievement over time. Furthermore, within both groups there are students whose mathematics achievement actually decreases over time.

The level-2 model must simultaneously account for both these general patterns (the between-group differences in intercepts and slopes) and inter-individual heterogeneity that remains within groups. This suggests that an appropriate level-2 model would have outcomes that are the level-1 individual growth parameters themselves (the π_{0i} and π_{1i} parameters from equation (1)). In addition, the level-2 model must specify the relationship between each individual growth parameter and predictor *AFAM* (0 = White, 1 = African American). Finally, the level-2 model must allow even individuals who share common predictor values to differ in their individual change trajectories, by permitting random variation in the individual growth parameters across students. These considerations lead to the following level-2 model:

$$\pi_{0i} = \gamma_{00} + \gamma_{01} AFAM_i + \zeta_{0i}$$
$$\pi_{1i} = \gamma_{10} + \gamma_{11} AFAM_i + \zeta_{1i}$$
(2)

Equation (2) has two main components which simultaneously treat the intercept (π_{0i}) and the slope (π_{1i})

of a student's growth trajectory as level-2 outcomes that are associated with predictor *AFAM*. The level-2 model contains four parameters known collectively as the fixed effects—γ_{00}, γ_{01}, γ_{10}, and γ_{11}—that capture systematic inter-individual differences in change trajectories. In equation (2), γ_{00} and γ_{10} are level-2 intercepts; γ_{01} and γ_{11} are level-2 slopes. γ_{00} represents the average true seventh grade mathematics achievement for White students in the population, while γ_{01} represents the hypothesized population difference in average true initial status between African American and White students. Similarly, γ_{10} represents the population average true annual rate of change in mathematics achievement for White students, while γ_{11} represents the hypothesized population difference in average true annual rate of change between African American and White students. The level-2 slopes, γ_{01} and γ_{11}, jointly capture the effects of *AFAM*. If γ_{01} and γ_{11} are non-zero, the average population trajectories in true mathematics achievement differ between the two racial groups; on the other hand, if γ_{01} and γ_{11} are both 0, then the trajectories do not differ by race. These two level-2 slope parameters therefore address the question: What is the difference in the average trajectory of true change in mathematics achievement between White students and African American students?

Results of fitting a multilevel model for change to data (*n*=1,322)

		Parameter	Estimate (*s.e.*)
Fixed Effects			
Initial status, π_{0i}	Intercept	γ_{00}	53.02*** (0.26)
	AFAM	γ_{01}	−5.93*** (0.80)
Rate of change, π_{1i}	Intercept	γ_{10}	2.87*** (0.08)
	AFAM	γ_{11}	−0.48* (0.23)
Variance Components			
Level-1:	Within-person, ε_{ij}	σ_ε^2	37.17*** (0.86)
Level-2:	In initial status, ζ_{0i}	σ_0^2	59.05*** (3.23)
	In rate of change, ζ_{1i}	σ_1^2	3.19*** (0.29)
	Covariance between ζ_{0i} and ζ_{1i}	σ_{01}	6.18*** (0.69)

~ $p < .10$; * $p < .05$; ** $p < .01$; *** $p < .001$

This model predicts mathematics achievement between grades 7 and 11 as a function of (GRADE-7) at level-1 and race (AFAM) at level-2.

Table 1 ILLUSTRATION BY GGS INFORMATION SERVICES. CENGAGE LEARNING, GALE.

An important feature of both the level-1 and level-2 models is the presence of the residuals (ε_{ij} at level-1 and ζ_{0i} and ζ_{1i} at level-2). As is the case with most residuals, researchers are usually less interested in their specific values than in their variability. Level-1 residual variance, σ_ε^2, summarizes the scatter of the level-1 residuals around each person's true change trajectory, in the population. The level-2 residual variances, σ_0^2 and σ_1^2, summarize the population inter-individual variation in true individual intercept and slope around their averages that is left over after controlling for the effect of *AFAM*.

As a final question at level-2, the researchers consider a potential association between seventh grade mathematics achievement and change in achievement. For example, do students with higher seventh grade mathematics achievement also experience larger gains in achievement? The researchers permit this possibility by allowing the level-2 residuals to be correlated. Their population covariance, σ_{01}, summarizes the association between true seventh grade math achievement and true rate of change in achievement, controlling for race.

INTERPRETING THE FITTED MULTILEVEL MODEL FOR CHANGE

Estimates from the fitted multilevel model for change are presented in Table 1. Substituting the $\hat{\gamma}'s$ from Table 1 into the hypothesized level-2 model in equation (2), the following fitted level-2 model is obtained:

$$\hat{\pi}_{0i} = 53.02 - 5.93 AFAM_i$$
$$\hat{\pi}_{1i} = 2.87 - .48 AFAM_i \tag{3}$$

The first part of this fitted model describes the estimated effects of *AFAM* on true seventh grade mathematics achievement; the second part describes its estimated effects on the annual rate of true change in mathematics achievement. Beginning with the first part of the fitted model, it is estimated that true seventh grade mathematics achievement for the average White student is 53.02. For the average African American seventh grader, it is estimated that true seventh grade mathematics achievement is 5.93 points lower (47.09). In addition, the researchers reject (at the .001 level) the null hypotheses that γ_{00} and γ_{01} are 0 and conclude that the average White student had non-zero true mathematics achievement in seventh grade (hardly surprising) and that there is a statistically significant difference in the average true seventh grade mathematics achievement of White students compared with their African American peers.

In the second part of the fitted model, it is estimated that the annual rate of true change in mathematics achievement for the average White student is 2.87 points per year. For the average African American student, it is estimated to be nearly half a point lower (at 2.39). In rejecting (at the .001 level) the null hypothesis on γ_{10}, it is concluded that the average White student experienced a statistically significant increase in true mathematics achievement over time. Because the researchers also reject (at the .05 level) the null hypothesis on γ_{11}, they conclude that differences between African American and White students in their annual rates of true change are also statistically significant. The estimated mathematics achievement for the average White student increased 11.48 points from 7th grade to 11th grade, while the increase for African American students was two points lower (9.56). African American students begin seventh grade with lower average mathematics achievement than their White counterparts, and the achievement gap increases over time.

Another way of interpreting the estimated fixed effects is to plot fitted trajectories for prototypical individuals. For this particular model, only two prototypes are possible: an African American student (*AFAM*=1) and a White student (*AFAM*=0). Substituting these predictor values into equation (3) yields the estimated seventh grade mathematics achievement and annual growth rates for each:

When *AFAM* = 0:

$$\hat{\pi}_{0i} = 53.02 - 5.93(0) = 53.02$$
$$\hat{\pi}_{1i} = 2.87 - .48(0) = 2.87$$

When *AFAM* = 1:

$$\hat{\pi}_{0i} = 53.02 - 5.93 = 47.09$$
$$\hat{\pi}_{1i} = 2.87 - .48(1) = 2.39 \tag{4}$$

These estimates are then substituted into the level-1 model in equation (1) to obtain the fitted individual change trajectories:

When *AFAM* = 0:

$$\hat{Y}_{ij} = 53.02 + 2.87(GRADE_{ij} - 7)$$

When *AFAM* = 1:

$$\hat{Y}_{ij} = 47.09 + 2.39(GRADE_{ij} - 7) \tag{5}$$

These fitted trajectories are plotted in the right-hand panel of Figure 1, and reinforce the numeric conclusions articulated above. In comparison to White students, the average African American student has lower mathematics achievement in seventh grade and a slower rate of increase in mathematics achievement.

The estimated variance components assess the amount of outcome variability left after including the predictor *AFAM*. The level-1 residual variance, ε_{ij}, summarizes the population variability in average student's outcome values around their own true change trajectory. Its estimate here is 37.17. Rejection of the associated null hypothesis test (at the .001 level) suggests the existence of additional within-person outcome variability that may be predictable in subsequent analyses by time-varying predictors other than time.

The level-2 variance components, σ_0^2 and σ_1^2, summarize the variability in true seventh grade achievement and rate of true change remaining after controlling for *AFAM*. Tests associated with these variance components evaluate whether there is any remaining outcome variation that could potentially be explained by further predictors at level-2. For these data, the researchers reject both of these null hypotheses (at the .001 level), and conclude that additional level-2 predictors may help explain some of this residual variation. Finally, the level-2 covariance component, σ_{01} is considered. The researchers reject the null hypothesis on the covariance and conclude that the intercepts and slopes of the individual true change trajectories are indeed correlated in the population. Controlling for student race, on average, African American and White students who have higher true mathematics achievement in seventh grade also have greater rates of increase in true mathematics achievement between 7th and 11th grade.

The mathematics achievement example presented in this entry has many features that simplify analysis and interpretation. However, the multilevel model for change is a very flexible, powerful method for analyzing longitudinal data and may be used to address quite complex longitudinal research questions. Five of these possibilities may be considered here. First, although only one predictor has been included in the analysis, it is straightforward to examine the impact of additional substantive level-2 predictors. For example, in addition to the race variable studied here, it could also be asked whether girls and boys have different mathematics achievement trajectories or whether there is an impact of various instructional methods on the development of mathematics achievement. Second, while all students in the example were assessed on exactly five occasions (a balanced design), the model may also be fitted to longitudinal datasets containing individuals with varying numbers of measurement occasions (an unbalanced design). Third, here measures of mathematics achievement that were taken in the fall of every year were analyzed, but occasions of measurement need not be equally spaced and different participants can have different data collection schedules. Fourth, individual change can be represented not only as a linear function presented here, but also curvilinear and discon-

tinuous functions representing substantively interesting hypotheses of change in educational outcomes over time. Finally, in addition to time-invariant predictors of change, such as race and gender, the effects of predictors whose values change over time can also be estimated, such as type and level of mathematics course in which a student is enrolled each year. Readers wishing to learn more about using longitudinal data to analyze change over time should consult books devoted to the topic, including Diggle, Heagerty, Liang, and Zeger (2002); Fitzmaurice, Laird, and Ware (2004); Hedeker and Gibbons (2006); Raudenbush and Bryk (2002); Singer and Willett (2003); Snijders and Bosker (1999); Verbeke and Molenberghs (2000); Walls and Schafer (2006); and Weiss (2005).

SEE ALSO *Cross-Sectional Research Designs; Research Methods: An Overview.*

BIBLIOGRAPHY

Ai, X. (2002). Gender differences in growth in mathematics achievement: Three-level longitudinal and multilevel analyses of individual, home, and school influences. *Mathematical Thinking and Learning, 4,* 1–22.

Diggle, P., Heagerty, P., Liang, K-Y., & Zeger, S. (2002). *Analysis of longitudinal data* (2nd ed.). New York: Oxford University Press.

Fitzmaurice, G. M., Laird, N. M., & Ware, J. H. (2004). *Applied longitudinal analysis.* New York: Wiley.

Hedeker, D., & Gibbons, R. D. (2006). *Longitudinal data Analysis.* New York: Wiley.

Kreft, I. G. G., & de Leeuw, J. (1998). *Introducing multilevel modeling.* Thousand Oaks, CA: Sage.

Miller, J. D., Kimmel, L., Hoffer, T. B., & Nelson, Cynthia. (2000). *Longitudinal study of American youth: User's manual.* Chicago: International Center for the Advancement of Scientific Literacy, Northwestern University.

Raudenbush, S. W., & Bryk, A. S. (2002). *Hierarchical linear models: Applications and data analysis methods* (2nd ed.). Thousand Oaks, CA: Sage.

Singer, J. D., & Willett, J. B. (2003). *Applied longitudinal data analysis: Modeling change and event occurrence.* New York: Oxford University Press.

Snijders, T. A. B., & Bosker, R. (1999). *Multilevel analysis: An introduction to basic and advanced multilevel modeling.* London: Sage.

Verbeke, G., & Molenberghs, G. (2000). *Linear mixed models for longitudinal data.* New York: Springer.

Walls, T. A., & Schafer, J. L. (2006). *Models for intensive longitudinal data.* New York: Oxford University Press.

Suzanne E. Graham
Judith D. Singer
John B. Willett

M

MACCOBY, ELEANOR E(MMONS)
1917–

Eleanor Maccoby's work on gender development, on the impact of divorce on children and families and parent-child interactions, and on child rearing practices has greatly informed the field of human development. In 1970, with Miriam Zellner, Maccoby described the underlying psychological concepts fueling various Project Follow Through programs (a government funded educational reform similar to Head Start). Their work, which focused on facilitating at-risk students' academic and social development, continues to be at the forefront of research in educational psychology and school reform. Similarly, Maccoby's research on the biological underpinnings of gender identity (1974, with Carol Jacklin) continues to help inform educators about the within-group differences of male and female groups, as well as the rather limited between-group differences of children's behavior and socialization practices. In addition, Maccoby's gender segregation research highlights the adult controlled contextual aspects of educational environments that reinforce and further promote children's (particularly girls') preferences for same sex playmates and peer groups through adolescence.

Born in 1917, Eleanor Maccoby began her college career at Reed College in 1934 and later transferred and received her BS in psychology from the University of Washington in 1939. After working for the Department of Agriculture's Division of Program Surveys as a study director, Maccoby completed her MS in 1949 from the University of Michigan, as well as her PhD in experimental psychology in 1950. While at Michigan she taught survey research methods and served as study director in the Survey Research Center (APA). Maccoby completed her dissertation in B.F. Skinner's lab; however, over time her theoretical interests shifted from behaviorism to learning theory, cognitive development, and interaction. Her early work with Robert Sears and Harry Levin at Harvard on parent-child interactions continues to be influential. At Harvard (1950–1958), Maccoby was an instructor and lecturer in the Department of Social Relations (APA). She joined the faculty of the Department of Psychology at Stanford University in 1958 and was awarded emerita status in 1987. Since that time Maccoby has continued her research and commentary on topics ranging from the lifespan development of gender differences and socialization processes to adaptive outcomes of divorce and the impact of media exposure on children and families, as well as out of the home childcare.

Maccoby's publications number well over 100, including her most cited co-authored book with Carol Jacklin, *Psychology of the Sex Differences* (1974). The work of *Sex Differences* was instrumental in summarizing extant literature on gender differences, encompassing more than 1,300 previous works. Also important is her work on the Stanford Longitudinal Study (1984, with Jacklin), which used a cross-sequential design to provide a comprehensive description of the development of same-sex play groups and group processes. Throughout Maccoby's career her research has focused on in-depth longitudinal analyses of human development, and it has offered great insight into the role that teachers can play in students' lives, as well as the impact parenting style on children's development.

Maccoby is the recipient of numerous distinguished and lifetime career awards and positions, including the American Psychological Association (APA), Division 7 Gordon Stanley Hall Award in 1982, the American Educational Research Association's Distinguished Contributions in Educational Research Award in 1984; the Society for Research in Child Development (SRCD's) Award for Distinguished Scientific Contributions to Child Development in 1987; the APA's Distinguished Scientific Contribution Award in 1988; and the American Psychological Foundation's Gold Medal Award for Lifetime Achievement in the Science of Psychology in 1996 (APA, 2007). In addition, she was the first female chair of the Department of Psychology at Stanford. As of 2007 she was a member of the National Academy of Sciences and had served as president of SRCD and the Consortium of Social Science Association (APA).

BIBLIOGRAPHY

WORKS BY

Maccoby, E. E., & Zellner, M. (1970). *Experiments in primary education: Aspects of project follow through.* New York: Harcourt Brace Jovanovich.

Maccoby, E. E., & Jacklin, C. N. (1974). *The psychology of sex differences.* Stanford, CA: Stanford University Press.

Maccoby, E. E. & Jacklin, C. N (1984). *Gender segregation in childhood. Advances in Child Development and Behavior, 20,* 239-287.

Maccoby, E. E., Mnookin, R. H., Depner, C. E., & Peters, H. E. (1992). *Dividing the child: Social and legal dilemmas of custody.* Cambridge, MA: Harvard University Press.

Buchanan, C. M., Maccoby, E. E., & Dornbusch, S. M. (1996). *Adolescents after divorce.* Cambridge, MA: Harvard University Press.

Maccoby, E. E. (1998). *The two sexes: Growing up apart, coming together.* Cambridge, MA: Belknap Press of the Harvard University Press.

WORKS ABOUT

Eleanor Maccoby. (2007). Retrieved April 10, 2008, from http://www.apa.org/Science/wist/maccoby.html.

Tierra M. Freeman

MAEHR, MARTIN L.
1932–

Martin L. Maehr was born in 1932 in Guthrie, Oklahoma. Maehr grew up in Perry, Oklahoma, where his father was a principal, and later a professor of educational psychology and administrator at Concordia College in Nebraska. Maehr married his wife Jane in 1959. He received his bachelor of arts and master of divinity degrees from Concordia Seminary in St. Louis. He then went on to doctoral study in psychology and education at the University of Nebraska. Maehr's dissertation was titled, "The Effect of Food Deprivation on Binocular Conflict," and his advisor was Warren R. Baller.

Maehr first studied for the ministry, with the expectation of teaching at a liberal arts college. He planned to enter a graduate program in classics, studying Greek and Latin, but a college administrator who was a friend of his family advised him to study educational psychology, because the university was investing resources into that area and not into classics. Maehr later met Dr. Robert E. Stake, a psychometrician. Stake encouraged Maehr's interests in psychology, which led to his dissertation research and later to experimental research on social motivation and achievement in school settings. Maehr has stated that his dissertation work, combined with several courses in counseling and social psychology, ultimately led to his career studying motivation.

Maehr's first academic position as an assistant professor was at Concordia Senior College in Ft. Wayne, Indiana. After several years of teaching, Maehr received a postdoctoral research fellowship from the National Institute of Mental Health that allowed him to conduct research in social psychology at Syracuse University. This was a turning point in Maehr's career, and in 1967 he moved to the University of Illinois Urbana-Champaign, where he served as director and professor at the Institute for Child Behavior and Development, as professor of educational psychology, and as associate dean for graduate and international programs. In 1992 Maehr moved to the University of Michigan, where he became director of the combined program in education and psychology, and a professor of education and psychology.

Maehr has published widely in the field of achievement motivation. His early work in motivation examined a variety of topics, including self-concept, Atkinson's theory of achievement motivation, and the "Pygmalion" effect. In 1976 Maehr published an influential article in *Review of Educational Research* titled "Continuing motivation: An analysis of a seldom considered educational outcome." In that article Maehr argued that motivation to continue engaging in academic tasks is an important, yet undervalued outcome, that should be fostered in classrooms.

During his time at the University of Illinois, Maehr worked alongside a number of other motivation researchers, including John Nichols, Carol Ames, and Carol Dweck. The conversations and collaborations between and among these scholars ultimately led to the development of goal orientation theory, and Maehr was one of the major contributors to this extremely influential framework for the study of motivation. His work involved measurement development, the application of goal theory to classroom and school reform, and the relation of goal orientation theory to both school leadership and school culture. Along with the late Carol Midgley and other collaborators at the University of Michigan, Maehr helped to develop the *Patterns of Adaptive Learning Survey* (PALS), which is one of the most widely used measures of achievement goals in the world. He also published several climate and leadership inventories with Larry Braskamp. Maehr also collaborated with other motivation researchers, including Avi Kaplan, Tim Urdan, Dennis McInerney, Leslie Fyans, and Eric M. Anderman.

At the University of Michigan, Maehr collaborated extensively with Midgley and the late Paul R. Pintrich. Maehr and Midgley worked together on several large-scale projects. One of the most notable involved work on motivation-based school reform in elementary and middle schools; Maehr and Midgley and their students worked with teachers, administrators, and parents in order to change the policies and practices of schools to become more aligned with the pursuit of mastery goals. That work resulted in the publication of a book, *Transforming School Cultures*, in 1996. Maehr worked with Pintrich on many projects, including the editing of several editions of the well-regarded Advances in Motivation and Achievement series as well as other volumes on academic motivation.

Maehr published extensively. In addition to the Advances in Motivation series, he wrote and edited numerous other books, and published over 100 peer-reviewed articles and book chapters. His research was funded by the National Institutes of Health, the U.S. Department of Education, National Science Foundation, and the Spencer Foundation. He is a fellow of the American Psychological Association and the American Psychological Society.

Maehr retired from his position at the University of Michigan in 2005. However, he remained extremely active as Emeritus Professor of Education and Psychology at Michigan, and as the co-principal investigator on a large-scale NSF-funded project examining the assessment of motivation, and a study funded by the Spencer Foundation examining Middle Eastern students in public schools in the United States.

BIBLIOGRAPHY

WORKS BY

Maehr, M. L. (1976). Continuing motivation: An analysis of a seldom considered educational outcome. *Review of Educational Research, 46*, 443–462.

Maehr, M. L. (1994). Culture and achievement motivation. *American Psychologist, 29*, 887–896.

Maehr, M. L., & Kleiber, D. A. (1981). The graying of achievement motivation. *American Psychologist, 36*, 787–799.

Maehr, M. L., & McInerney, D. M. (2004). Motivation as personal investment. In D. M. McInerney & S. Van Etten (Eds.), *Sociocultural influences on motivation and learning*, Vol. 4. Big theories revisited. Greenwich, CT: Information Age Publishing.

Maehr, M. L., & Midgley, C. (1991). Enhancing student motivation: A school-wide approach. *Educational Psychologist, 26*, 399–427.

Eric M. Anderman

MASTERY LEARNING

Few programs have been implemented as broadly or evaluated as thoroughly over the last four decades in education as those associated with mastery learning. Programs based on mastery learning principles operate today in nations throughout the world and at every level of education. When compared to traditionally taught classes, students in mastery learning classes consistently have been shown to learn better, reach higher levels of achievement, and develop greater confidence in their ability to learn and in themselves as learners (Guskey, 1997, 2001).

THE DEVELOPMENT OF MASTERY LEARNING

Although the basic tenets of mastery learning can be traced to such early educators as Comenius, Pestalozzi, and Herbart (Bloom, 1974), most modern applications stem from the writings of Benjamin S. Bloom of the University of Chicago. In the mid-1960s Bloom began a series of investigations on the variation that existed in student learning outcomes. He recognized that while

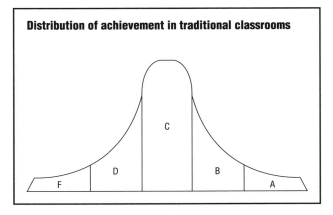

Figure 1 ILLUSTRATION BY GGS INFORMATION SERVICES. CENGAGE LEARNING, GALE.

students vary widely in their learning rates, virtually all learn well when provided with the necessary time and appropriate learning conditions. If teachers could provide the time and more appropriate conditions, Bloom reasoned that nearly all students could reach a high level of learning.

To determine how this might be practically achieved, Bloom first considered how teaching and learning take place in typical group-based classrooms. He observed that most teachers begin by dividing the concepts and skills that they want students to learn into smaller learning units. Following instruction on the unit, teachers administer an assessment to determine how well students have learned those concepts and skills. Based on the assessment results, students are sorted, ranked, and assigned grades. The assessment signifies to students the end of the unit and the end of the time they need to spend working on the unit material. It also represents their one and only chance to demonstrate what they have learned.

When teaching and learning proceed in this manner, Bloom found that only a small number of students learns well and the pattern of student achievement was similar to the normal curve distribution shown in Figure 1.

Seeking a strategy that would produce better results, Bloom drew upon two sources of information. He first considered the ideal teaching and learning situation in which an excellent tutor is paired with each student. In other words, Bloom tried to determine what crucial elements in one-to-one tutoring could be transferred to group-based instructional settings. Second, he reviewed descriptions of the learning strategies of academically successful students in group-based learning environments that distinguish them from their less successful classmates.

Bloom saw value in organizing the concepts and skills to be learned into units and assessing students' learning at the end of each unit as useful instructional techniques. But the classroom assessments most teachers used seemed to do little more than show for whom their initial instruction was and was not appropriate. Bloom believed that a far better approach would be for teachers to use their classroom assessments as learning tools, and then to follow those assessments with a feedback and corrective procedure. In other words, instead of using assessments only as evaluation devices that mark the end of each unit, Bloom recommended using them as part of the instructional process to identify individual learning difficulties (feedback) and to prescribe remediation procedures (correctives).

This is precisely what takes place when an excellent tutor works with an individual student. If the student makes a mistake, the tutor first points out the error (feedback) and then follows up with further explanation and clarification (correctives) to ensure the student's understanding. Similarly, academically successful students typically follow up the mistakes they make on quizzes and assessments. They ask the teacher about the items they missed, look up the answer in the textbook or other resources, or rework the problem or task so that they do not repeat those errors.

With this in mind, Bloom outlined an instructional strategy to make use of this feedback and corrective procedure, labeling it "Learning for Mastery" (Bloom, 1968), and later shortening it to simply "Mastery Learning" (Bloom, 1971a). With this strategy, teachers first organize the concepts and skills they want students to learn into learning units that typically involve about a week or two of instructional time. Following initial instruction on the unit, teachers administer a brief quiz or assessment based on the unit's learning goals. Instead of signifying the end of the unit, however, this assessment's purpose is to give students information, or "feedback," on their learning. To emphasize this new purpose Bloom suggested calling it a *formative assessment*, meaning "to inform or provide information" (see Scriven, 1967). A formative assessment identifies for students precisely what they have learned well to that point, and what they need to learn better (Bloom, Hastings, & Madaus, 1971).

Paired with each formative assessment are specific "corrective" activities for students to use in correcting their learning difficulties. Most teachers match these "correctives" to each item or set of prompts within the assessment so that students need work on only those concepts or skills not yet mastered. In other words, the correctives are "individualized." They may point out additional sources of information on a particular concept, such as page numbers in the textbook or workbook where the concept is discussed. They may identify alternative learning resources such as different textbooks, learning kits, alternative materials, CDs, videos, or Web-based instructional lessons. Or they may simply suggest sources of additional practice, such as study guides, computer exercises, independent or guided practice activities, or collaborative group activities.

With the feedback and corrective information gained from the formative assessment, each student has a detailed prescription of what more needs to be done to master the concepts or skills from the unit. This "just-in-time" correction prevents minor learning difficulties from accumulating and becoming major learning problems. It also gives teachers a practical means to vary and differentiate their instruction in order to better meet students' individual learning needs. As a result, many more students learn well, master the important learning goals in each unit, and gain the necessary prerequisites for success in subsequent units.

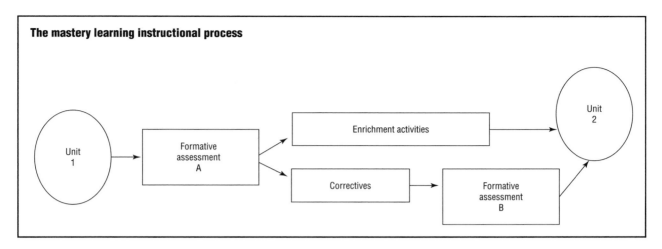

Figure 2 ILLUSTRATION BY GGS INFORMATION SERVICES. CENGAGE LEARNING, GALE.

When students complete their corrective activities after a class period or two, Bloom recommended they take a second formative assessment. This second, "parallel" assessment covers the same concepts and skills as the first, but is composed of slightly different problems or questions, and serves two important purposes. First, it verifies whether or not the correctives were successful in helping students overcome their individual learning difficulties. Second, it offers students a second chance at success and, hence, has powerful motivational value.

Some students, of course, will perform well on the first assessment, demonstrating that they have mastered the unit concepts and skills. The teacher's initial instruction was highly appropriate for these students and they have no need of corrective work. To ensure their continued learning progress, Bloom recommended that teachers provide these students with special "enrichment" or "extension" activities to broaden their learning experiences. Enrichment activities typically are self-selected by students and might involve special projects or reports, academic games, or a variety of complex, problem-solving tasks. Figure 2 illustrates this instructional sequence.

Bloom believed that through this process of formative classroom assessment, combined with the systematic correction of individual learning difficulties, all students could be provided with a more appropriate quality of instruction than is possible under more traditional approaches to teaching. As a result, nearly all might be expected to learn well and truly master the unit concepts or learning goals (Bloom, 1976; 1977). This, in turn, would drastically reduce the variation in students' achievement levels, eliminate achievement gaps, and yield a distribution of achievement more like that shown in Figure 3.

Bloom emphasized, however, that reducing variation in students' achievement does not imply making all students the same. Even under these more favorable learning conditions, some students undoubtedly will learn more than others, especially those involved in enrichment activities. But by recognizing relevant, individual differences among students and then altering instruction to better meet their diverse learning needs, Bloom believed the variation among students in how well they learn specific concepts or master a set of articulated learning goals could eventually reach a "vanishing point" (Bloom, 1971b). In other words, *all* students would be helped to learn well the knowledge and skills prescribed in the curriculum.

MISINTERPRETATIONS OF MASTERY LEARNING

In some instances "mastery learning" has been confused with the concept of "mastery goals" used in motivation research (Ames, 1992; Dweck, 1986). Although theoretically related, these concepts are quite distinct. "Mastery learning" relates to a theory about learning and an accompanying set of instructional strategies, as described above. "Mastery goals," on the other hand, concern a central distinction drawn by achievement goal theorists between striving to acquire skill and develop understanding (mastery goals), and striving to demonstrate superiority relative to others (performance or ability goals) (Butler, 2000). Mastery goals are typically associated with defining competence relative to task demands, attributing outcomes to effort, preferring challenging tasks, perceiving difficulty as an indication of the need for further learning, and responding to difficulty by seeking help and additional information. In contrast, performance or ability goals lead to defining competence relative to others, attributing outcomes to ability, interpreting difficulty as indicative of low ability, and refraining from exposing inadequate ability by seeking help (Butler, 2007). Hence, while the criterion-referenced orientation of mastery learning clearly focuses on mastery goals, the concepts are quite different.

Another misinterpretation stems from some early attempts to apply mastery learning that were based on narrow and inaccurate understandings of Bloom's theory. These efforts focused only on low-level cognitive skills, attempted to break learning down into small segments, and insisted that students "master" each segment before being permitted to move on. Teachers were regarded in these programs as little more than managers of materials and record-keepers of student progress. Unfortunately, similar misinterpretations of mastery learning continue (e.g., Prawat, 1992; Satterly, 1981).

Nowhere in Bloom's writing, however, can this kind of narrowness and rigidity be found. In fact, Bloom emphasized quite the opposite. He considered thoughtful and reflective teachers vital to the successful implementation of mastery learning and continually stressed flexibility in its application. In his earliest description of the process Bloom wrote:

> There are many alternative strategies for mastery learning. Each strategy must find some way of dealing with individual differences in learners through some means of relating the instruction to the needs and characteristics of the learners. . . . The nongraded school (Goodlad & Anderson, 1959) is one attempt to provide an organizational structure that permits and encourages mastery learning. (Bloom, 1968, pp. 7–8)

Bloom further emphasized his belief that instruction in mastery learning classrooms should focus on higher level learning goals, not simply basic skills. He noted:

> I find great emphasis on problem solving, applications of principles, analytical skills, and creativity. Such higher mental processes are emphasized because this type of learning enables the individual to relate his or her learning to the many problems he or she encounters in day-to-day living. These abilities are stressed because they are retained and utilized long after the individual has forgotten the detailed specifics of the subject matter taught in the schools. These abilities are regarded as one set of essential characteristics needed to continue learning and to cope with a rapidly changing world. (Bloom, 1978, p. 578)

Modern research studies have shown mastery learning to be particularly effective when applied to instruction focusing on higher level learning goals such as problem solving, drawing inferences, deductive reasoning, and creative expression (Arredondo & Block, 1990; Blakemore, 1992; Clark, Guskey, & Benninga, 1983;

Kozlovsky, 1990; Mevarech, 1980, 1981, 1985; Mevarech, & Werner, 1985; Soled, 1987). When well implemented, the process helps teachers improve student learning in a broad range of learning goals from basic skills to highly complex cognitive processes.

RESEARCH RESULTS AND IMPLICATIONS

Despite the modest nature of the changes required to implement mastery learning, extensive research evidence gathered in Asia (Kim et al., 1969, 1970; Wu, 1994), Australia (Chan, 1981), Europe (Dyke, 1988; Langeheine, 1992; Mevarech, 1985, 1986; Postlethwaite & Haggarty, 1998; Reezigt & Weide, 1990, 1992; Yildiran, 2006), South America (Cabezon, 1984), and the United States (Anderson, 1994; Block, Efthim, & Burns, 1989; Guskey & Pigott, 1988; Walberg, 1984, 1988), shows the careful and systematic application of mastery learning principles can lead to significant improvements in student learning. Some researchers even suggest that the superiority of Japanese students in international comparisons of achievement in mathematics operations and problem solving may be due largely to the widespread use in Japan of instructional practices similar to mastery learning (Nakajima, 2006; Waddington, 1995).

Long-term investigations have yielded similarly impressive results. A study by Whiting, Van Burgh, and Render (1995), for example, representing 18 years of data gathered from more than 7,000 high school students showed mastery learning to have remarkably positive influence on students' test scores and grade point averages as well as their attitudes toward school and learning. Another field experiment conducted in elementary and middle school classrooms showed that the implementation of mastery learning led to significantly positive increases in students' academic achievement and their self-confidence (Anderson, Barrett, Huston, Lay, Myr, Sexton, & Watson, 1992). Even more impressive, a comprehensive, meta-analysis review of the research on mastery learning by Kulik, Kulik, & Bangert-Drowns (1990a) concluded:

> We recently reviewed meta-analyses in nearly 40 different areas of educational research (J. Kulik & Kulik, 1989). Few educational treatments of any sort were consistently associated with achievement effects as large as those produced by mastery learning. In evaluation after evaluation, mastery programs have produced impressive gains. (p. 292)

Research evidence also shows that the positive effects of mastery learning are not limited to cognitive or achievement outcomes. The process also yields improvements in students' confidence in learning situations, school attendance rates, engagement in class activities, attitudes toward learning, and a variety of other affective

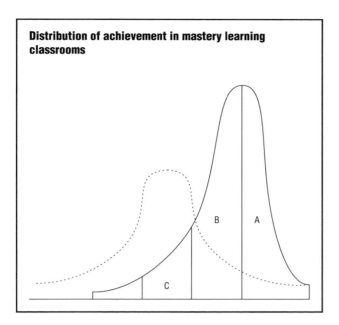

Distribution of achievement in mastery learning classrooms

Figure 3 ILLUSTRATION BY GGS INFORMATION SERVICES. CENGAGE LEARNING, GALE.

measures (Block & Burns, 1976; Block, Efthim, & Burns, 1989; Guskey & Pigott, 1988, Whiting & Render, 1987).

It should be noted that one review of the research on mastery learning, contrary to all others, indicated that the process had essentially no effect on student achievement (Slavin, 1987). This finding surprised not only scholars familiar with the vast research literature on mastery learning showing it to yield very positive results, but also large numbers of practitioners who had experienced its positive impact firsthand. A close inspection of this review shows, however, that it was conducted using techniques of questionable validity (Joyce, 1987; Hiebert, 1987), employed capricious selection criteria (Anderson & Burns, 1987; Kulik, Kulik, & Bangert-Drowns, 1990b), reported results in a biased manner (Bloom, 1987; Walberg, 1988), and drew conclusions not substantiated by the evidence presented (Guskey, 1987, 1988a). Most importantly, two much more extensive and methodologically sound reviews published since (Guskey & Pigott, 1988; Kulik, Kulik, & Bangert-Drowns, 1990a) have verified mastery learning's consistently positive impact on a broad range of student learning outcomes and, in one case (i.e., Kulik, Kulik, & Bangert-Drowns, 1990b), showed clearly the distorted nature of this earlier report.

Researchers in the 21st century generally recognize the value of the central elements of mastery learning and their importance in effective teaching at any level of education. Similar elements provide the foundation for more recently developed instructional approaches including differentiated instruction (Tomilson, 2003) and understanding by design (Wiggins & McTighe, 2005). As a result, fewer studies focus on the mastery learning process, *per se*. Instead, researchers are looking for ways to enhance results further, adding additional elements to the mastery learning process that positively contribute to student learning in hopes of attaining even more impressive gains (Bloom, 1984a, 1984b, 1988; Walberg, 1990). Recent work on the integration of mastery learning with other innovative strategies appears especially promising (Arredondo & Block, 1990; Guskey, 1988b, 1990a, 1990b; 1997b; Motamedi & Sumrall, 2000).

Mastery learning will not solve all the complex problems facing educators. Nevertheless, careful attention to the elements of mastery learning allows educators at all levels to make great strides in their efforts to reduce the variation in student achievement, close achievement gaps, and help all children to learn excellently.

BIBLIOGRAPHY

Ames, C. (1992). Goals, structures, and student motivation. *Journal of Educational Psychology, 84*(2), 261–272.

Anderson, L. W., & Burns, R. B. (1987). Values, evidence, and mastery learning. *Review of Educational Research, 57,* 215–223.

Anderson, S. A. (1994). *Synthesis of research on mastery learning.* (ERIC Document Reproduction Service No. ED 382 567).

Anderson, S., Barrett, C., Huston, M., Lay, L., Myr, G., Sexton, D., et al. (1992). *A mastery learning experiment* (Tech. Rep.). Yale, MI: Yale Public Schools.

Arredondo, D. E., & Block, J. H. (1990). Recognizing the connections between thinking skills and mastery learning. *Educational Leadership, 47*(5), 4–10.

Blakemore, C. L. (1992). Comparison of students taught basketball skills using mastery and nonmastery learning methods. *Journal of Teaching in Physical Education, 11*(3), 235–247.

Block, J. H., & Burns, R. B. (1976). Mastery learning. In L. Shulman (Ed.), *Review of research in education* (Vol. 4, pp. 3–49). Itasca, IL: Peacock.

Block, J. H., Efthim, H. E., & Burns, R. B. (1989). *Building effective mastery learning schools.* New York: Longman.

Bloom, B. S. (1968). Learning for mastery. *Evaluation Comment, 1*(2), 1–12.

Bloom, B. S. (1971a). Mastery learning. In J. H. Block (Ed.), *Mastery learning: Theory and practice* (pp. 47–63). New York: Holt, Rinehart & Winston.

Bloom, B. S. (1971b). *Individual differences in school achievement: A vanishing point?* Bloomington, IN: Phi Delta Kappan International.

Bloom, B. S. (1974). An introduction to mastery learning theory. In J. H. Block (Ed.), *Schools, society and mastery learning* (pp. 3–14). New York: Holt, Rinehart & Winston.

Bloom, B. S. (1976). *Human characteristics and school learning.* New York: McGraw-Hill.

Bloom, B. S. (1977). Favorable learning conditions for all. *Teacher, 95*(3), 22–28.

Bloom, B. S. (1978). New views of the learner: Implications for instruction and curriculum. *Educational Leadership, 35*(7), 563–576.

Bloom, B. S. (1984a). The 2 sigma problem: The search for methods of group instruction as effective as one-to-one tutoring. *Educational Researcher, 13*(6), 4–16.

Bloom, B. S. (1984b). The search for methods of group instruction as effective as one-to-one tutoring. *Educational Leadership, 41*(8), 4–18.

Bloom, B. S. (1987). A response to Slavin's mastery learning reconsidered. *Review of Educational Research, 57*(4), 507–508.

Bloom, B. S. (1988). Helping all children learn in elementary school and beyond. *Principal, 67*(4), 12–17.

Bloom, B. S., Hastings, J. T., & Madaus, G. (1971). *Handbook on formative and summative evaluation of student learning.* New York: McGraw-Hill.

Butler, R. (2000). What learners want to know: The role of achievement goals in shaping information seeking, learning, and interest. In C. Sansone & J. M. Harackiewicz (Eds.), *Intrinsic and extrinsic motivation: The search for optimal motivation and performance* (pp. 161–194). San Diego, CA: Academic Press.

Butler, R. (2007). Teachers' achievement goal orientations and associations with teachers' help seeking: Examination of a novel approach to teacher motivation. *Journal of Educational Psychology, 99*(2), 241–252.

Cabezon, E. (1984). *The effects of marked changes in student achievement patterns on the students, their teachers, and their parents: The Chilean case.* Unpublished doctoral dissertation, University of Chicago.

Chan, K. S. (1981). *The interaction of aptitude with mastery versus non-mastery instruction: Effects on reading comprehension of grade three students.* Unpublished doctoral dissertation, University of Western Australia, Perth, Australia.

Clark, C. R., Guskey, T. R., & Benninga, J. S. (1983). The effectiveness of mastery learning strategies in undergraduate education courses. *Journal of Educational Research, 76*(4) 210–214.

Dweck, C. S. (1986). Motivational processes affecting learning. *American Psychologist, 41*(10), 1040–1048.

Dyke, W. E. (1988, April). *The immediate effect of a mastery learning program on the belief systems of high school teachers.* Paper presented at the annual meeting of the American Educational Research Association, New Orleans, LA.

Goodlad, J. I., & Anderson, R. H. (1959). *The nongraded elementary school.* New York: Harcourt Brace.

Guskey, T. R. (1987). Rethinking mastery learning reconsidered. *Review of Educational Research, 57*(2), 225–229.

Guskey, T. R. (1988a). Response to Slavin: Who defines best? *Educational Leadership, 46*(2), 26–27.

Guskey, T. R. (1988b). Mastery learning and mastery teaching: How they complement each other. *Principal, 68*(1), 6–8.

Guskey, T. R. (1990a). Cooperative mastery learning strategies. *Elementary School Journal, 91*(1), 33–42.

Guskey, T. R. (1990b). Integrating innovations. *Educational Leadership, 47*(5), 11–15.

Guskey, T. R. (1997a). *Implementing Mastery Learning* (2nd ed.). Belmont, CA: Wadsworth.

Guskey, T. R. (1997b). Putting it all together: Integrating educational innovations. In S. J. Caldwell (Ed.), *Professional Development in Learning-Centered Schools* (pp. 130–149). Oxford, OH: National Staff Development Council.

Guskey, T. R. (2001). Mastery learning. In N. J. Smelser & P. B. Baltes (Eds.), *International Encyclopedia of Social and Behavioral Sciences* (pp. 9372–9377). Oxford, England: Elsevier Science.

Guskey, T. R., & Pigott, T. D. (1988). Research on group-based mastery learning programs: A meta-analysis. *Journal of Educational Research, 81*(4), 197–216.

Hiebert, E. H. (1987). The context of instruction and student learning: An examination of Slavin's assumptions. *Review of Educational Research, 57,* 337–340.

Joyce, B. (1987). A rigorous yet delicate touch: A response to Slavin's proposal for 'best-evidence' reviews. *Educational Researcher, 16*(4), 12–14.

Kim, H., et al. (1969). *A study of the Bloom strategies for mastery learning.* Seoul: Korean Institute for Research in the Behavioral Sciences. (in Korean).

Kim, H., et al. (1970). *The Mastery Learning Project in the middle schools.* Seoul: Korean Institute for Research in the Behavioral Sciences. (in Korean).

Kozlovsky, J. D. (1990). Integrating thinking skills and mastery learning in Baltimore County. *Educational Leadership, 47*(5), 6.

Kulik, C. C., Kulik, J. A., & Bangert-Drowns, R. L. (1990a). Effectiveness of mastery learning programs: A meta-analysis. *Review of Educational Research, 60,* 265–299.

Kulik, J. A., & Kulik, C. C. (1989). Meta-analysis in education. *International Journal of Educational Research, 13*(2), 221–340.

Kulik, J. A., Kulik, C. C., & Bangert-Drowns, R. L. (1990b). Is there better evidence on mastery learning? A response to Slavin. *Review of Educational Research, 60,* 303–307.

Langeheine, R. (1992). *State mastery learning: Dynamic models for longitudinal data.* Paper presented at the annual meeting of the American Educational Research Association, San Francisco.

Mevarech, Z. R. (1980). *The role of teaching learning strategies and feedback-corrective procedures in developing higher cognitive achievement.* Unpublished doctoral dissertation, University of Chicago.

Mevarech, Z. R. (1981, April). *Attaining mastery on higher cognitive achievement.* Paper presented at the annual meeting of the American Educational Research Association, Los Angeles.

Mevarech, Z. R. (1985). The effects of cooperative mastery learning strategies on mathematical achievement. *Journal of Educational Research, 78*(6), 372–377.

Mevarech, Z. R. (1986). The role of a feedback-corrective procedure in developing mathematics achievement and self-concept in desegregated classrooms. *Studies in Educational Evaluation, 12*(1), 197–203.

Mevarech, Z. R., & Werner, S. (1985). Are mastery learning strategies beneficial for developing problem solving skills? *Higher Education, 14*(4), 425–432.

Motamedi, B., & Sumrall, W. J. (2000). Mastery learning and contemporary issues in education. *Action in Teacher Education, 22*(1), 22–32.

Nakajima, A. (2006). A powerful influence on Japanese education. In T. R. Guskey (Ed.), *Benjamin S. Bloom:*

Portraits of an educator (pp. 109–111). Lanham, MD: Rowman & Littlefield Education.

Postlethwaite, K., & Haggarty, L. (1998). Towards effective and transferable learning in secondary school: The development of an approach based on mastery learning. *British Educational Research Journal, 24*(3), 333–353.

Prawat, R. S. (1992). Teachers' beliefs about teaching and learning: A constructivist perspective. *American Journal of Education, 100,* 354–395.

Reezigt, B. J., & Weide, M. G. (1990, April). *The effects of group-based mastery learning on language and arithmetic achievement and attitudes in primary education in the Netherlands.* Paper presented at the annual meeting of the American Educational Research Association, Boston.

Reezigt, G. J., & Weide, M. G. (1992, April). *Mastery learning and instructional effectiveness.* Paper presented at the annual meeting of the American Educational Research Association, San Francisco.

Satterly, D. (1981). *Assessments in schools.* Oxford, UK: Blackwell.

Scriven, M. S. (1967). The methodology of evaluation. In R. W. Tyler, R. M. Gagne, & M. Scriven (Eds.), *Perspectives of curriculum evaluation* (pp. 39–83). AERA Monograph Series on Curriculum Evaluation. No. 1. Chicago: Rand McNally.

Slavin, R. E. (1987). Mastery learning reconsidered. *Review of Educational Research, 57*(2), 175–213.

Soled, S W. (1987, April). *Teaching processes to improve both higher and lower mental process achievement.* Paper presented at the annual meeting of the American Educational Research Association, Washington, DC.

Tomilson, C. (2003). *Fulfilling the promise of the differentiated classroom: Strategies and tools for responsive teaching.* Alexandria, VA: Association for Supervision and Curriculum Development.

Waddington, T. (1995, April). *Why mastery matters.* Paper presented at the annual meeting of the American Educational Research Association, San Francisco.

Walberg, H. J. (1984). Improving the productivity of America's schools. *Educational Leadership, 41*(8), 19–27.

Walberg, H. J. (1988). Response to Slavin: What's the best evidence? *Educational Leadership, 46*(2), 28.

Walberg, H. J. (1990). Productive teaching and instruction: Assessing the knowledge base. *Phi Delta Kappan, 71,* 470–478.

Whiting, B., & Render, G. F. (1987). Cognitive and affective outcomes of mastery learning. A review of sixteen semesters. *The Clearing House, 60*(6), 276–280.

Whiting, B., Van Burgh, J. W., & Render, G. F. (1995). Mastery learning in the classroom. Paper presented at the annual meeting of the American Educational Research Association, San Francisco.

Wiggins, G., & McTighe, J. (2005). *Understanding by design* (2nd ed.). Alexandria, VA: Association for Supervision and Curriculum Development.

Wu, W. Y. (1994, April). *Mastery learning in Hong Kong: Challenges and prospects.* Paper presented at the annual meeting of the American Educational Research Association, New Orleans, LA.

Yildiran, G. (2006). *Multicultural applications of mastery learning.* Istanbul, Turkey: Faculty of Education, Bogazici University.

Thomas R. Guskey

MATHEMATICS, LEARNING AND TEACHING

SEE *Learning and Teaching Mathematics.*

MCKEACHIE, WILBERT J(AMES)
1921–

The life of arguably one of the most influential educational psychologists began humbly in a one-room school house in White Lake, Michigan. With his father as the lone teacher, Wilbert (Bill) J. McKeachie (born August 24, 1921) began a journey of life-long learning that spanned nine decades. His life experiences include serving as a church minister, a mathematics teacher, a naval radar officer, president of multiple academic organizations, and a marriage to the same woman (Ginny) for 65 years.

After graduating from Michigan State Normal College (later Eastern Michigan University), he spent four months teaching mathematics and serving as a United Methodist minister in Trout Lake, a small town in Michigan's Upper Peninsula. His application for clergy deferment was denied, and in January 1943 he reported for naval training in San Francisco. From June 1943 until the end of World War II, he served as a radar officer on the USS *Guest.* Every destroyer in the *Guest*'s fleet was hit, and eight of nine were sunk. Only the *Guest* survived.

Upon his return from war, McKeachie entered the doctoral program in psychology at the University of Michigan. He studied the then-emerging field of personality and social psychology, exploring issues of group formation and conformity, under Michigan's department chair Donald G. Marquis. When McKeachie received his degree, Marquis convinced him to forgo opportunities to join the faculty at other universities and instead stay at Michigan and coordinate the introductory psychology program. McKeachie joined the faculty at Michigan in 1948 and officially retired in 1992, although he continued his work as an emeritus professor into the early 2000s.

His honors and awards (over 30 citations) reflect the many spheres on which his career had an influence. Most notable among them are the Thorndike Award for Outstanding Research from APA Division 15, APA's Centennial Award for Outstanding Contribution, American Psychological Foundation Gold Medal Award, and APA's Presidential Citation.

In addition to these awards, McKeachie led several academic organizations. He served as president of the American Psychological Association, the American Psychological Foundation, the American Association for Higher Education, and was founding president of the Educational, Instructional, and School Psychology Division of the International Association of Applied Psychology. McKeachie served on the editorial boards of 20 journals and on governing boards of 17 organizations in higher education, many times serving in multiple capacities. (For example, he served in 22 different leadership positions for the American Psychological Association alone.)

Picking the most significant research contributions of someone with more than 390 publications is difficult. Still, three can be highlighted here. His signature written work is arguably his internationally recognized book *Teaching Tips*, as of 2008 in its twelfth edition. This book started as mimeographed copies of pedagogical strategies that he distributed to his teaching assistants in 1951. The book appeared in several languages and was widely respected by university professors. With its wide-ranging content—from test-writing to leading discussions to establishing good relations with university support staff—it is the quintessential survival guide for new faculty.

Second, the modern-day freshman-experience course has roots in McKeachie's work. These courses, along with the spate of related books, can arguably be traced to McKeachie's course entitled "Learning to Learn," which he first offered at Michigan in 1971. Like most of his work, the course was ahead of its time. It was his attempt to bring what were, at the time, pioneering concepts of motivation and cognition to help college students become better learners. The result was a national trend of most universities offering such courses.

Third, McKeachie was instrumental in securing funding for the National Center for Research to Improve Post-Secondary Teaching and Learning, which was housed at Michigan for five years. The most fruitful product from the center's existence was the Motivated Strategies for Learning Questionnaire (MSLQ), a self-report instrument designed to assist college students in assessing their learning strategies and motivation. Its subscales include what became fundamental concepts in the field of educational psychology such as self-efficacy, critical thinking, and goal orientation. The MSLQ has been used in hundreds of universities, dozens of countries, and translated into several languages.

Lest McKeachie be known as a one-sided academic with no interests or skills outside his career, it is worth noting that he was an amateur music composer, producing a range of works that include his high school fight song in 1939, a civil rights song in the 1960s, and several pieces that were sung by his own First Baptist Church of Ann Arbor. He also had a talent for pitching fastpitch softball. He pitched games in seven decades (from the 1930s to the 1990s), accumulating more than 900 victories. These and other accomplishments, too numerous to mention, demonstrate how his original love of learning that began in White Lake, Michigan, spread across his whole life.

BIBLIOGRAPHY

WORKS BY

Eble, K. E., & McKeachie, W. J. (1985). *Improving undergraduate education through faculty development.* San Francisco: Jossey-Bass.

Hartley, J., & McKeachie, W. J. (Eds.). (1990). *Teaching psychology: A handbook: readings from teaching of psychology.* Hillsdale, NJ: Erlbaum.

McKeachie, W. J. (1960). *Teaching tips: A guide-book for the beginning college teacher* (4th ed.). Ann Arbor, MI: G. Wahr.

McKeachie, W. J. (1969, 1978, 1986, 1994). *Teaching tips: A guidebook for the beginning college teacher.* (6th ed., 7th ed., 8th ed., 9th ed.). Lexington, MA: Heath.

McKeachie, W. J. (Ed.). (1980). *Learning, cognition, and college teaching.* San Francisco: Jossey-Bass.

McKeachie, W. J. (1999, 2002, 2006). *McKeachie's teaching tips: Strategies, research, and theory for college and university teachers* (10th ed., 11th ed., 12th ed.). Boston: Houghton Mifflin.

McKeachie, W. J., & Doyle, C. L. (1966, 1970, 1976). *Psychology.* Reading, MA: Addison-Wesley.

McKeachie, W. J., Isaacson, R. L., & Milholland, J. E. (1964). *Research on the characteristics of effective college teaching.* Ann Arbor: University of Michigan Press.

Walker, E. L., & McKeachie, W. J. (1967). *Some thoughts about teaching the beginning course in psychology.* Belmont, CA: Brooks Cole.

WORKS ABOUT

Davis, S. F., & Buskist, W. (2002). *The teaching of psychology: Essays in honor of Wilbert J. McKeachie and Charles L. Brewer.* Mahwah, NJ: Erlbaum.

Pintrich, P. R., Brown, D. R., & Weinstein, C. E. (Eds.). (1994). *Student motivation, cognition, and learning: essays in honor of Wilbert J. McKeachie.* Hillsdale, NJ: Erlbaum.

Scott VanderStoep

MEMORY

Alan Baddeley's 1999 book describes the case of Clive Wearing, a talented musician who in 1985 fell ill with a viral infection that resulted in encephalitis which caused extensive brain damage. Wearing could no longer remember what happened more than a few minutes before. He continued to believe that he had just regained consciousness and kept a diary in which he constantly recorded that belief. Wearing could, however, still play music. Thus, some kind of memory remained intact. His case demonstrates the importance of memory.

In 1968 Atkinson and Shiffrin developed a model consisting of three different kinds of memory: sensory, short term, and long term (Atkinson & Shiffrin, 1968). Sensory memory is very brief, lasting about 1/3 of a second (Sperling, 1960). Short-term memory is temporary memory storage. It has limited capacity and duration. Long-term memory is a more enduring memory.

SHORT-TERM MEMORY AND WORKING MEMORY

Miller described the capacity of short-term memory (STM) storage as 7 ± 2 bits of information (Miller, 1956). Contents in short-term memory last about 20 to 30 seconds unless an individual rehearses or elaborates on the material. There are two kinds of rehearsal: maintenance rehearsal and elaborative rehearsal. Maintenance rehearsal involves the repetition of the contents of STM; elaborative rehearsal involves a deeper form of rehearsal by which people connect the to-be-remembered information to what they already know. One way to reduce the demands on working memory involves chunking information, or grouping bits of information. For example, when trying to remember the phone number 555-1212, it easier to remember two chunks ("555" and "1212") rather than the seven individual numbers. Information is lost from short-term memory through decay and interference. Decay occurs when information is not used, and it simply fades from memory. Interference occurs when something else gets in the way of recall.

The probability of recalling information presented in a list is influenced by the position of the information in the list, a phenomenon known as the *serial position effect*. Recency effects indicate that items from the end of a list will be recalled, and primacy effects indicate that words at the beginning of a list will be recalled. Recognizing the limits of short-term memory, teachers can keep their instructions brief and provide opportunities for rehearsal.

A MODEL OF WORKING MEMORY

Working memory is a term used to describe a limited, though active, memory system. It differs from short-term memory in that it includes manipulation functions as well as storage. Baddeley proposed that working memory has a number of subsystems that are coordinated by a *central executive* (Baddeley, 1990). The first of these subsystems is the *phonological loop system*, which processes speech or auditory information. It consists of a passive phonological store and an articulatory rehearsal process.

The Phonological Loop System. The phonological loop processes verbal information. Evidence for it includes the phonological similarity effect, the unattended speech effect and the word length effect. People make more errors if the words they are asked to recall are similar in sound to one another (Baddeley, 1993). When individuals are asked to perform a verbal task (e.g., reading) with speech in the background, performance is impaired, a phenomenon known as the *unattended speech effect*. Verbal information that is presented auditorially is processed automatically. A third source of evidence in support of the phonological loop is found in the *word length effect*. There is a link between memory span and the length of words to be recalled.

The Visuospatial Sketchpad. A second subsystem in Baddeley's model is the *visuospatial sketchpad*, which is used for processing visual or spatial material or both. The results of a 1968 study by Brooks showed that when an individual engages in a visuospatial task such as pointing while performing a visual imagery task, the same processing capacity is being used. If the form of the task (verbal or visual) and that of the response (verbal or visual) are the same, performance is impaired.

The Executive System. The central executive system of working memory controls the phonological loop and the visuospatial sketchpad. It is an attentional control system with limited capacity (Baddeley, 1993). Daneman and Carpenter's 1980 study explored the relationship between working memory and reading comprehension by asking individuals to read passages that contained inconsistencies due to the presence of words with more than one meaning. Individuals with low working memory spans were able to come to the correct conclusion only 25% of the time. Individuals with high working memory spans were able to keep the initial information in working memory until they encountered the information that clarifies the passage. Additional research suggests that the functioning of the central executive system is the key difference between good and poor comprehenders (Oakhill, 1982, 1984; Oakhill, Yuill, & Parkin, 1986).

MEMORY DIFFICULTIES OF CHILDREN WITH SPECIAL NEEDS

When instructions are complicated or lengthy, there is a risk that students will not remember them. If students fail to follow instructions, it may be that the instructions exceeded their working memory's capacity for processing information. Interruptions are frequent in elementary school classes and it seems reasonable to assume that the constant interruption can produce interference effects. Working memory is involved in such tasks as reading comprehension, writing, problem solving, and mathematics (Swanson & Siegel, 2001).

Individuals with a large working memory span utilize cognitive resources more efficiently while reading, and as a result have more resources for storage while comprehending the text (Swanson & Siegel, 2001). Students must also retrieve information from long-term memory to include in their writing. Maintaining ideas and choosing among them while actually producing text can make heavy demands on memory capacity. Some learners have difficulty writing because of limited working memory capacity.

Students with learning disabilities frequently have deficits in working memory (Swanson & Siegel, 2001). In particular, they have difficulty with reading comprehension because of deficits in the phonological loop. Such difficulties are problematic on tasks that require a learner to retain information in mind for a short period while also carrying out further activities. This skill is very important in reading tasks in which information that is coming in must be stored temporarily while other information is being processed (Swanson & Alexander, 1997). Difficulties with working memory can also interfere with writing, because efforts to record ideas may interfere with maintenance rehearsal in working memory.

Students and teachers can use a variety of strategies to reduce the demands on working memory. Children often count on their fingers, thus giving themselves a visible record of their cognitive activity rather than relying on memory. Other strategies for supporting working memory include presenting information in multiple modalities, allowing students to record their ideas before writing, or using speech-to-text software to reduce the burden on working memory. Using an external representation can reduce the demands on working memory.

LONG-TERM MEMORY

Researchers have described several types of long-term memory. The Atkinson and Shiffrin model was based on the duration of memory. Processing was divided among sensory, short-term, and long-term memory. This model was very useful, but it does not provide a complete description of how memory works.

There are several ways to distinguish between various kinds of long-term memories. One important distinction is between episodic and semantic memory (Tulving, 1972). Episodic memory is memory of events and typically includes sensory information (things seen, heard, or smelled, and so on). Such memories often have heightened emotional content (happy, sad, fearful). These memories are embedded in a specific context—a specific time and place. In contrast, semantic memory is memory of verbal information or declarative knowledge—that is, knowledge about facts. For example, knowing one's address is an example of declarative knowledge. It is separate from sensory information and not tied to particular experiences. Combining episodic and semantic memories makes information more memorable and retrievable.

Semantic memory is memory for meaning and is thought to be organized like a network. In 1969 Collins and Quillian proposed the earliest network model of semantic memory. In this model, semantic networks are made up of a network of related propositions, the smallest units of meaning that can be verified as true or false. A proposition involves linking two concepts by a relationship. Connections between ideas also vary in strength and frequency of use. These factors are more important than the actual categorical structures.

A second distinction in types of memory is between declarative and procedural memory. Declarative memory is like semantic memory. For example, a person might have declarative memories about the structure of a bicycle. In contrast, procedural memory is memory about how to do something. In the example given above, Clive Wearing had retained procedural memory of how to play music.

IMAGES

Responding to a question about an image takes about the same amount of time as responding to a picture (Kosslyn, 1976). In one study, participants were asked to form a mental image of a cat. They were then asked questions such as, "Does the cat have a head?" and "Does the cat have claws?" Responses to the latter question took longer, as participants appeared to scan the image.

Image information is thought to be stored in piecemeal fashion in long-term memory. Images are created by activating the overall or global shape of the image; elaborations are then added to create a complete image (Kosslyn, 1980, 1983). More detailed images take longer to retrieve. Images are thought to be stored in a non-image format that specifies a *recipe* for constructing the image. As with the processing of language, processing images takes time.

SCHEMAS AND SCRIPTS

Semantic memory is organized in complex networks. Complex understanding of a domain will result in a dense network of interconnected propositions about that domain. *Schemas* refer to organized sets of propositions about a topic (Bartlett, 1932). Learners' available schemas influence how they interact with the environment.

The learner's schemas may be altered as a result of interacting with the environment.

A schema that describes the typical sequence of events in a situation is called a *script*, or *event schema*. For example, when people go to a restaurant, they usually expect actions to unfold in a particular way. Another type of script is a story grammar that can help students to understand and remember stories (Gagné, Yekovich, & Yekovich, 1993).

LEVELS OF PROCESSING

In 1972 Craik and Lockhart proposed an alternative theory of memory. It suggested that memory differences are not so much a function of duration as of depth of processing (Craik & Lockhart, 1972). They showed that students who attended to meaning performed significantly better than those who attended to surface features of the words. Craik and Lockhart argued that the differences in performance reflected differences in depth of processing.

Craik and Lockhart's concept of levels of processing helped shift the emphasis in the study of memory from storage to processing. The Atkinson and Shiffrin model defined memory systems in terms of the storage/duration of memories and described very short stores (sensory and short-term memory) and very long-term stores (long-term memory). The levels of processing theory focuses on the likelihood of retrieval as a function of how effortful and meaningful the initial encoding was.

ENCODING: ORGANIZATION, PRACTICE, AND ELABORATION

Encoding is the taking in of information. The probability that information will be retrieved or remembered depends on the quality of encoding. Key processes in good encoding are organization, practice, and elaboration. It is easier to learn organized material than it is to learn disorganized material.

Practice helps develop good memory. Material that is used more often is remembered more easily. However, there are different ways of practicing. Distributed practice is much more effective than massed practice. Distributed practice is done over a period of time, with varying intervals between rehearsals of the information. Remembering involves using the cues available to assist remembering but also involves generating cues that help remembering. Distributed practice allows students to practice both of these skills. Massed practice, in contrast, involves engaging in extensive practice at one time, such as studying all night before an exam. This can be somewhat effective for an immediate task but is unlikely to lead to long-term recall of information.

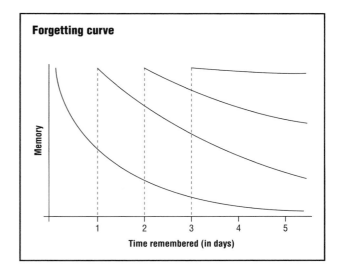

ILLUSTRATION BY GGS INFORMATION SERVICES. CENGAGE LEARNING, GALE.

Elaboration also helps in encoding and retrieval. It involves connecting new information with prior knowledge or to images or other enhancements of the information to be learned. Images in particular are powerful aids to memory and are frequently used to elaborate on information.

IMAGERY AND VISUAL LEARNING STRATEGIES

Dual-coding theory (Paivio, 1986) explains why images are helpful in remembering. According to this theory, images and words are represented differently, as *imagens* and *logogens*. When the two forms of representations are linked, the memory for the information is stronger. Baddeley's findings on the separate working memory systems for visual and verbal information also support the importance of presenting and learning information in both visual and verbal forms (Baddeley, 1999). Visual strategies such as concept maps and graphic organizers integrate verbal, visual, and spatial information to enhance encoding and retrieval.

RETRIEVAL AND FORGETTING

Remembering can occur through either recognition memory or recall. Recognition memory responds to cues. Responding to multiple-choice tests can require recognition memory because the cues provided by the options from which one may choose will provide some assistance to memory. When information is recalled, one must generate information without cues. Responding to an essay question, for example, requires that one generate and organize the content.

Retrieval occurs within a semantic network because activation is spread from one node to another. Related ideas are triggered. The specific linkages will vary from one person to another. Because of the structure of a network, retrieval can involve reconstructing the links between propositions and ideas.

Forgetting occurs when there is interference or decay. When material is encoded in an organized manner, more cues are encoded, thus making retrieval easier. Also, information that is used more frequently is easier to recall. Material that is not encoded in an organized way and not used often is more likely to be forgotten. This is so because in a propositional network model of memory, retrieval occurs through a process of spreading activation. When one node in a network is triggered, related nodes are also triggered as activation spreads along the links to them. When these links are used often, less activation is needed to generate the connecting node. If the nodes are highly interconnected with many links, forgetting is less likely, but retrieval may take longer. In a curious irony, the more people know, the longer it may take them to verify that they know it.

Forgetting occurs when information is not used. If students have not practiced solving geometry problems for a year, they are likely to have forgotten the steps in doing so. Forgetting also occurs because of interference.

BRAIN PROCESSES AND MEMORY

A number of structures in the medial temporal lobes of the brain are important for memory. They include the amygdala, the hippocampus, and the rhinal cortex that underlies the amygdala and hippocampus. The hippocampus plays a key role in the storage of new memories (Gazzaniga & Heatherton, 2003). The hippocampus and surrounding rhinal cortex are the most important areas for the consolidation of memory (Eichenbaum, 2002; Gazzaniga & Heatherton, 2003). The frontal lobes are also considered important for memory; although people who experience damage to the frontal lobes do not suffer dramatic memory loss, they may have difficulty remembering the order of events. Brain-imaging studies show that when people try to remember a list of words, the frontal lobes light up (Buckner, Kelly, & Petersen, 1999). The frontal lobes are more active when a task requires deeper encoding.

SEE ALSO *Cognitive Strategies; Information Processing Theory.*

BIBLIOGRAPHY

Atkinson, R. C., & Shiffrin, R. M. (1968). Human memory: A proposed system and its control processes. In K. W. Spence & J. T. Spence (Eds.), *The psychology of learning and motivation* (Vol. 2, pp. 89–195). Orlando, FL: Academic Press.

Baddeley, A. (1990). *Human memory.* Needham Heights, MA: Allyn & Bacon.

Baddeley, A. (1993). *Using your memory: A user's guide.* London: Penguin Books.

Baddeley, A. (1999). *Essentials of human memory.* Hove, United Kingdom: Psychology Press.

Buckner, R. L., Kelly, W. M., & Petersen, S. E. (1999). Frontal cortex contributes to human memory formation. *Nature Neuroscience, 2,* 311–314.

Craik, F. I. M., & Lockhart, R. S. (1972). Levels of processing: A framework for memory research. *Journal of Verbal Learning and Verbal Behavior, 11,* 671–684.

Daneman, M., & Carpenter, P. A. (1980). Individual differences in working memory and reading. *Journal of Verbal Learning and Verbal Behavior, 19,* 450–466.

Eichenbaum, H. (2002). *The cognitive neuroscience of memory.* Boston: Oxford University Press.

Gagné, E. D., Yekovich, C. W., & Yekovich, F. R. (1993). *The cognitive psychology of school learning* (2nd ed.). Boston: Little, Brown.

Gazzaniga, M. S., & Heatherton, T. F. (2003). *Psychological science.* New York: Norton.

Kosslyn, S. M. (1976). Can imagery be distinguished from other forms of internal representation? Evidence from studies of information retrieval times. *Memory and Cognition, 4,* 291–297.

Kosslyn, S. M. (1980). *Image and mind.* Cambridge, MA: Harvard University Press.

Kosslyn, S. M. (1983). *Ghosts in the mind's machine.* New York: Norton.

Miller, G. A. (1956). The magical number seven, plus or minus two: Some limits on our capacity for processing information. *Psychological Review, 6,* 81–97.

Oakhill, J. V. (1982). Constructive processes in skilled and less skilled comprehender's memory for sentences. *British Journal of Psychology, 73,* 13–20.

Oakhill, J. V. (1984). Inferential and memory skills in children's comprehension of stories. *British Journal of Educational Psychology, 54,* 31–39.

Oakhill, J. V., Yuill, N., & Parkin, A. (1986). On the nature of the differences between skilled and less skilled comprehenders. *Journal of Research in Reading, 9,* 80–91.

Paivio, A. (1986). *Mental representation: A dual coding approach.* New York: Oxford University Press.

Swanson, H. L., & Alexander, J. E. (1997). Cognitive processes as predictors of word recognition and reading comprehension in learning-disabled and skilled readers: Revisiting the specificity hypothesis. *Journal of Educational Psychology, 89,* 128–158.

Swanson, H. L., & Siegel, L. (2001). Learning disabilities as working memory deficit. *Issues in Education, 7,* 1–48.

Tulving, E. (1972). Episodic and semantic memory. In E. Tulving & W. Donaldson (Eds.), *Organization of memory* (pp. 381–403). New York: Academic Press.

Angela M. O'Donnell

MENTAL RETARDATION

With the advent of the Binet test in the early 20th century, professionals were provided with a way of quantifying intelligence and defining the condition subsequently known as mental retardation. Later, the American Association on Mental Retardation (AAMR) assumed a leading role in defining mental retardation for professional audiences. The AAMR definition was updated frequently in response to changes in the way that mental retardation was conceptualized by those in the field. As of the early 2000s AAMR definition states: "Mental retardation is a disability characterized by significant limitations both in intellectual functioning and in adaptive behavior as expressed in conceptual, social, and practical adaptive skills. This disability originates before age 18" (American Association on Mental Retardation, 2002). Examiners use standardized tests to assess intellectual and adaptive behavior functioning. As a part of the standardization process for these measures, normative groups are used to determine age based deviation scores that have a mean of 100 and, usually, a standard deviation of 15 points. Significant limitations are present when these scores are more than two standard deviations below the mean (i.e., a score of 70–75 allowing for the standard error of measurement for the specific assessment instrument used).

The AAMR definitions have typically been incorporated into current versions of other diagnostic systems. For example, the language of the 1992 AAMR definition is clearly evident in the *Diagnostic and Statistical Manual of Mental Disorders–IV TR* (APA, 2000). In contrast, state educational agencies vary considerably in which definition of mental retardation is used to establish eligibility guidelines. A survey of state agencies conducted by Denning, Chamberlain, and Polloway (2000) revealed that the 1983 AAMR definition of mental retardation was being used in 86 percent of the states in either verbatim or an adapted version and that only 7.9 percent of the states had incorporated the 1992 AAMR definition in an adapted or verbatim format. Moreover, 5.9 percent of the states used alternative definitions. The reasons for these differences in definition were not readily apparent from the published report.

In the early 2000s, the term *mental retardation* is rapidly falling into disfavor among professionals, families, and self-advocates. There is considerable pressure to change the term to something that is perceived as less stigmatizing, such as intellectual disability. Intellectual disability is the term that is currently used in many other English speaking countries, and, perhaps for that reason, this term was chosen by the American Association on Mental Retardation as a replacement in its organization name. The American Association on Intellectual and Developmental Disabilities is in concert with other prominent organizations such as the International Association for the Scientific Study of Intellectual Disabilities and the President's Committee for People with Intellectual Disabilities. Although there is increasing momentum for widespread change in terminology, the term mental retardation remains imbedded in public policy. For example, a diagnosis of mental retardation is typically required to establish eligibility for state and federal disability programs such as the Individuals with Disabilities Education Improvement Act of 2004, Social Security Disability Insurance, and the Medicaid Home and Community Based Waiver. Schalock, Luckasson, and Shogren have argued that "intellectual disability covers the same population of individuals who were diagnosed previously with mental retardation in number, kind, level, type and duration of the disability, and the need of people with this disability for individualized services and supports" (2007, p. 120). Although it is relatively easy for a professional association to adopt a change in terminology, as of 2007 it is expected to be some time before other associations and governmental entities would follow suit no matter how much the change is needed.

ASSESSMENT

Contemporary definitions of mental retardation require assessment of general intellectual functioning and adaptive behavior to determine a diagnosis. General intellectual functioning is measured by an individually administered, standardized intelligence test. Measures appropriate for school age children include the Wechsler Preschool and Primary Scale of Intelligence (3rd ed.), the Differential Ability Scales-II, the Wechsler Intelligence Scale for Children (4th ed.), Kaufman Assessment Battery for Children-II, and Stanford-Binet (5th ed.). Test selection is based on the chronological age of the child and the child's general level of functioning as well as the test's ability to clearly differentiate among children who perform at the lower end of a particular test. Given the likelihood that a child with mental retardation may also have sensory impairment or physical disability or be nonverbal, assessments have to be highly individualized and require the use of specialized measures designed for these populations. For example, intelligence tests appropriate for nonverbal or hearing impaired students are the Test of Nonverbal Intelligence-3 and the Leiter International Performance Scale (Rev.). In general, intellectual assessments for children with mental retardation require an examiner with considerable skill and experience in the assessment of children with special needs (Sattler & Hoge, 2006).

Adaptive behavior is typically assessed by informant report given the need for information about typical behavior that would go beyond that observed in a formal testing situation. Informants can include parents, teachers, or some other adult with considerable knowledge of the child's daily functioning. Measures of adaptive behavior assess personal and social competence in meeting common life demands as determined by the child's chronological age as well as the child's cultural background. Examples of areas assessed by these measures include: communication and language skills, social and interpersonal skills, gross and fine motor skills, and degree of independence in daily living skills. There are several well standardized measures available as of 2007, including the Adaptive Behavior Assessment System-II, Scales of Independent Behavior (Rev.) and the Vineland Adaptive Behavior Scales-II. These instruments vary in their coverage, but all assess skills and abilities consistent with the conceptual, social, and practical dimensions of adaptive behavior in the 2002 AAMR definition as well as the specific adaptive skill areas delineated in the DSM–IV TR (2000) (i.e. communication, self-care, home living, social skills, community use, self-direction, health and safety, functional academics, leisure skills, and work skills—for adults only).

CHARACTERISTICS OF MENTAL RETARDATION

Children with mental retardation are typically identified because they do not keep pace with developmental expectations in cognitive, language, social, and motor functioning. Typically, significant developmental delays in early childhood are predictive of poor academic functioning in childhood, as compared with same-age peers. Considerable study has been directed toward identifying the cognitive difficulties associated with mental retardation. Most of this work was conducted using experimental designs based on the deficit model of mental retardation. That is, comparisons were made between children with mental retardation and their same chronological age peers. Using this framework, nearly every cognitive process studied revealed dramatic differences between the two groups. The areas of study included attention, working memory, perceptual organizational skills, verbal problem solving, visual-spatial problem solving, vocabulary, language and abstract reasoning, among others. Subsequent studies have adopted a developmental perspective, in which the functioning of children with mental retardation is compared with typically developing children of comparable developmental level. Although some differences remain, it is clear that children with mental retardation generally follow the same developmental pathways as their typically developing peers but at a slower rate and do not ultimately attain as high a level.

Similarly, slower progress in attaining independence in meeting common life demands, or adaptive behavior, characterize children with mental retardation. It is a matter of some debate as to whether the observed deficits in adaptive behavior are a function of deficits in intellectual functioning. In fact, empirical studies indicate a high degree of correlation between measures of intelligence and adaptive behavior suggesting that they are not entirely independent entities. Moreover, some authors suggest that there are unique aspects of adaptive functioning that are not tapped by existing measures. These attributes include social intelligence, social competence, vulnerability, gullibility, and credulity. Greenspan (1999) argues that deficits in these areas contribute to the victimization of children with mental retardation as well as social and economic exploitation.

INDIVIDUAL DIFFERENCES AMONG CHILDREN WITH MENTAL RETARDATION

Throughout the 20th century, people realized that there are demonstrable and clinically relevant differences among people with mental retardation. Traditionally this differentiation was based on level of functioning. The terms mild, moderate, severe, and profound are in the early 2000s used in DSM–IV TR to designate levels of mental retardation that correspond to standard deviation units below the mean. Mild mental retardation is defined as between two and three standard deviations below the mean, moderate mental retardation is between three and four and so on. These categories have endured because there are clear differences among the levels in both cognitive performance and adaptive functioning. A similar subgroup classification system, using different terminology (i.e., educable, trainable, severe/profound), is still employed by some state education departments (Denning et al., 2000).

In 1992 the American Association on Mental Retardation published a revision of its classification manual that represented a paradigm shift for the field. In this system, reliance on a deficit oriented approach (i.e., mild, moderate, severe, and profound) was supplanted by a supports-based approach to describing the individual needs of persons with mental retardation. By so doing the severity level descriptions were abandoned and a diagnosis of mental retardation was based solely on IQ and adaptive functioning scores below 70 to 75. The new classification system required description of the degree of support needed to maximize a person's performance across a variety of functioning areas. Support was defined in terms of intensity and duration and categorized as intermittent, limited, extensive, and pervasive. Support needs were designated for each area of functioning— recognizing that an individual may require more intensive supports in some areas as contrasted with others. Accordingly, a person might require extensive supports in academic activities and intermittent support in self-care activities. Ultimately this information could inform intervention planning and enhance the person's overall functioning level. The AAMR (later AAIDD) published a Supports Intensity Scale for use with adults, with a children's version of the Supports Intensity Scale expected to follow.

A emphasis within the field as of 2007 is to focus on etiology in describing subgroups of children with mental retardation. For example, research aimed at defining the behavioral characteristics, or phenotypes, of various genetic disorders is moving ahead at an accelerated rate. Although a great deal of research has been focused on Fragile x, Angelman, Prader-Willi, Smith Magenis, and Williams syndromes, much was also published on Down syndrome. Studies of specific genetic disorders have yielded information regarding cognition, language and communication, visual-spatial skills, social development, and maladaptive behavior that has implications for educational professionals (Fidler, Hodapp, & Dykens, 2002).

INTERVENTIONS AND INSTRUCTIONAL PROCEDURES IN THE EARLY 2000S

Beginning with the Education for All Handicapped Children Act in 1975, the Individualized Education Plan has been the blueprint for educational services provided to children with mental retardation. This act established that all children, regardless of ability, were guaranteed a free and appropriate public education in the United States. The early 21st century version of this landmark legislation is known as the Individuals with Disabilities Education Improvement Act of 2004. A guiding principle of this legislation is that services should be provided in the least restrictive environment. That is, children with disabilities should receive educational services with their typically developing peers to the greatest degree possible. The goal for students with disabilities is inclusion within the general education setting. Inclusion means more than physical presence in the classroom or other education setting. Various practices are used to facilitate inclusion such as cooperative learning and peer tutoring experiences as well as instructional tools or strategies that enhance the salience of the academic content. Generally speaking, children with needs for extensive or pervasive supports spend the majority of their day in self-contained educational settings while children with less intense support needs may spend the majority of their day in a general education class with special education teacher services.

Early 2000s legislation such as the No Child Left Behind Act has reinforced the view that children with disabilities, including mental retardation, should graduate from public schools with basic or fundamental knowledge in mathematics, literacy, science and technology, practical skills sufficient to be self-supporting upon graduation, and problem-solving skills that foster lifelong learning. The success with which students with mental retardation achieve these skills varies considerably. For those who experience the greatest challenge with the general curriculum, efforts have yielded a functional curriculum that provides critical skills needed to participate in daily routines. These skills include independent living skills, communication, social skills, academic skills, and transition and community living skills. Support within the general education curriculum for children with mild mental retardation can be achieved in several different ways such as the use of accommodations that provide equal access to learning, curriculum modifications based on the child's current level of academic mastery, and adaptations of instructional methods to facilitate completion of assigned tasks.

Instructional procedures vary according to the needs of individual children. In general, children with mental retardation require explicit instruction if they are to succeed in school. Research has focused on a variety of methods to maximize instructional outcome and to promote generalization to real world settings. Examples of these methods include encouraging choice-making and self determination to enhance motivation to learn, teaching self-monitoring skills to encourage independence in completing academic tasks, and embedding instruction within activities to promote stimulus generalization and student motivation while distributing instructional trials over longer periods of time.

ISSUES RELATED TO ASSESSMENT AND INSTRUCTION

Children with mental retardation are likely also to have other deficits, such as cerebral palsy, seizure disorders, and sensory impairment (such as hearing and/or visual problems). In general, children with severe or profound mental retardation are at greater risk for these associated conditions as compared with children with mild or moderate mental retardation. Children with mental retardation are also at increased risk for health conditions that may affect their attendance at school as well as their participation in school activities. Finally, children with mental retardation are also at greater risk for speech problems. These difficulties can include difficulty with articulation as well as voice problems such as abnormal pitch or voice intensity.

Psychiatric diagnoses are more common among children with mental retardation as compared with their typically functioning peers. Epidemiological studies suggest that the risk may be as much as four times greater. For example, a study of 10,000 children aged 5 to 15 years in Great Britain revealed that 39 percent of children with mental retardation met DSM-IV and ICD-10 criteria for at least one psychiatric disorder as compared with 8.1 percent of children without mental retardation (Emerson, 2003). The reasons for this increased risk are not well known. Generally it is believed that the increased prevalence of sensory disorders, epilepsy, and brain damage associated with many specific etiologies play a role as does atypical developmental experience. It could well be that many children do not meet the criteria for a diagnosis of mental disorder but do manifest sub-threshold levels of particular symptoms that warrant intervention. The terms *behavior problems* or *behavior disorders* are often used to describe such cases.

The emphasis on studying behavioral phenotypes associated with particular etiologies has revealed co-occurring behavior problems and psychiatric disorders. These associations include attention-deficit hyperactivity disorder in fetal alcohol syndrome, anxiety in Williams syndrome, oppositional and defiant behavior in Smith-Magenis and Down syndromes, and self-injury in Lesch-Nyhan, Prader-Willi, Smith-Magenis, and Fragile x syndromes. Moreover, epidemiological studies indicate that as many as 75 percent of children with autism also have mental retardation. These children can be particularly challenging in the school setting when they exhibit property destruction, physical aggression, self-injury, and tantrums.

SEE ALSO *Special Education.*

BIBLIOGRAPHY

American Association on Mental Retardation. (2002). *Mental retardation: Definition, classification, and systems of supports* (10th ed.). Washington, DC: Author.

American Psychiatric Association. (2000). *Diagnostic and statistical manual of mental disorders.* 4th ed. Washington, DC: Author.

Denning, C. B., Chamberlain, J. A., & Polloway, E. A. (2000). An evaluation of state guidelines for mental retardation: Focus on definition and classification practices. *Education and Training in Mental Retardation and Developmental Disabilities 35,* 226–232.

Emerson, E. (2003). Prevalence of psychiatric disorders in children and adolescents with and without intellectual disability. *Journal of Intellectual Disability Research 47,* 51–58.

Fidler, D. J., Hodapp, R. M., & Dykens, E. M. (2002). Behavioral phenotypes and special education: Parent report of educational issues for children with Down syndrome, Prader-Willi syndrome, and Williams syndrome. *Journal of Special Education 36,* 80–88.

Greenspan, S. (1999). A contextualist perspective on adaptive behavior. In R. L. Schalock & D. L. Braddock (Eds.), *Adaptive behavior and its measurements: Implications for the field of mental retardation.* Washington, DC: American Association on Mental Retardation.

Sattler, J. M., & Hoge, R. D. (2006). *Assessment of children: Behavioral, social, and clinical foundations* (5th ed.). San Diego: Jerome M. Sattler.

Schalock, R. L., Luckasson, R. A., & Shogren, K. A. (2007). The renaming of mental retardation: Understanding the change to the term intellectual disability. *Intellectual and Developmental Disabilities 45,* 116–124.

Wehmeyer, M. L., & Agran, M. (2005). *Mental retardation and intellectual disabilities: Teaching students using innovative and research-based strategies.* Columbus, OH: Merrill Prentice Hall.

William E. MacLean, Jr.

META-ANALYSIS

The term meta-analysis, first coined by Gene Glass in 1976, refers to a statistical technique used to synthesize data from separate comparable studies in order to obtain a quantitative summary of research addressing a common question. In 1904 Karl Pearson published what is believed to be the first meta-analysis, examining the effectiveness of a vaccine against typhoid. In 1932 Ronald Fisher, in his classic text *Statistical Methods for Research Workers,* presented a technique for combining the p values that came from statistically independent tests of the same hypothesis. However, meta-analysis began to gain widespread use beginning in the 1960s with the tremendous growth in social scientific research and increasing interest in its social policy implications (Chalmers, Hedges, & Cooper, 2002). During the 1970s and 1980s, many of the techniques first invented by Pearson and Fisher were rediscovered and more sophisticated techniques were developed with the work of Gene Glass, Barry McGaw, and Mary Lee Smith (1981), John Hunter, Frank Schmidt, and Greg Jackson (1982), Robert Rosenthal (1984), and Larry Hedges and Ingram Olkin (1985).

Prior to the widespread use of meta-analysis, researchers relied on a narrative approach to summarize and integrate research on a specific topic. However, traditional narrative reviews have been criticized because, although they can provide a meticulous list of multiple tests of a hypothesis, they often fail to fully and accurately integrate findings and are prone to allowing the biases of the reviewer to enter into conclusions. Just as in the traditional narrative review of research, the aim of a meta-analysis is to summarize the results of past studies, suggest potential reasons for inconsistencies in past research findings, and direct future investigations. However, although meta-analysis has the same goals as the traditional narrative review, many limitations of the narrative review can be addressed by using statistical procedures to combine the results of previous studies (Cooper & Rosenthal, 1980). In the early 2000s, meta-analysis is an accepted and respected technique across many disciplines from psychology and education to medicine and public policy.

META-ANALYTIC PROCEDURES

Prior to conducting a meta-analysis, the researcher must first define the problem to be addressed by the meta-analysis, collect research relevant to the problem, and evaluate the quality of the data (Cooper, 1998). After these steps have been completed, then a meta-analysis can be conducted and the results interpreted.

Often the purpose of a meta-analysis is to answer three questions. First, does variable X have an effect on variable Y? Second, how much of an effect does variable X have on Y? Finally, are there moderating variables that can explain why the effect of X on Y varies from one study to the next? To answer the first two questions, meta-analysts will (a) calculate an effect size for the outcomes of hypothesis tests in every study and (b) average these effect sizes across hypothesis tests to estimate general magnitudes of effect and calculate confidence intervals as a test of the null hypothesis. In order to examine the question of moderating variables, meta-analysts will also (c) conduct homogeneity analyses in order to assess whether variations in outcomes exist and what features of comparisons might account for that variation, if it exists. The procedures for conducting a meta-analysis are described in detail in Cooper (1998), Cooper and Hedges (1994), Hedges and Olkin (1985), and Lipsey and Wilson (2001).

Estimating Effect Sizes. Cohen (1988) defined an effect size as "the degree to which the phenomenon is present in the population, or the degree to which the null hypothesis is false" (pp. 9–10). There are many different metrics to describe an effect size. Generally, each metric is associated with particular research designs. Although numerous estimates of effect size are available, three dominate the literature. The first, called the d-index by Cohen (1988), is a scale-free measure of the separation between two group means that is used when one variable in the relation is dichotomous and the other is continuous. Calculating the d-index for any study involves dividing the difference between the two group means by either their average standard deviation or the standard deviation of the control group. Another effect size metric is the r-index, or the Pearson product-moment correlation coefficient. Typically it is used to measure the degree of linear relation between two continuous variables. The third effect size metric is the odds ratio. The odds ratio is applicable when both variables are dichotomous and findings are presented as frequencies or proportions. The index is often used in studies of educational interventions when the outcome of interest is drop-out or retention rates.

Averaging Effect Sizes. The primary findings of meta-analyses are the average effect sizes and measures of dispersion that accompany them. State-of-the art meta-analytic procedures call for the weighting of effect sizes when they are averaged across studies. In the weighted procedure, each independent effect size is first multiplied by the inverse of its variance and the sum of these products is then divided by the sum of the inverses. The weighting procedure is generally preferred because it gives greater weight to effect sizes based on larger samples and larger samples give more precise population estimates. Confidence intervals are then calculated to test the null hypothesis that the difference between two means, or the size of a correlation or odds ratio, is zero.

Homogeneity Analyses. In addition to the confidence interval as a measure of dispersion, meta-analysts usually carry out homogeneity analyses. Homogeneity analyses allow the meta-analyst to explore whether effect sizes vary from one study to the next. A homogeneity analysis compares the amount of variance in an observed set of effect sizes with the amount of variance that would be expected by sampling error alone and provides calculation of how probable it is that the variance exhibited by the effect sizes would be observed if only sampling error were making them different. If there is greater variation in effects than would be expected by chance, then the meta-analyst can begin the process of examining moderators of comparison outcomes.

Moderator Analyses. Homogeneity analyses also allow the meta-analyst to test hypotheses about why the outcomes of studies differ. First, the meta-analyst calculates average effect sizes for different subgroups of studies, comparing the average effect sizes for different methods, types of programs, outcome measures, or participants. Then, homogeneity analyses are used to statistically test whether these factors are reliably associated with different magnitudes of effect. As previously suggested, homogeneity analyses assess whether sampling error alone accounts for variation or whether the features of studies, samples, treatment designs, or outcome measures also explain variations in the strength and/or direction of effect sizes across various groupings. This test is analogous to conducting an analysis of variance, in that a significant homogeneity statistic indicates that at least one group mean differs from the others.

Alternatively, meta-regression can be used to examine whether particular characteristics of studies are related to the sizes of the treatment effect. However, unlike the strategy previously discussed, meta-regression allows the meta-analyst to explore the relationship between continuous, as well as categorical, characteristics and effect size, and allows the effects of multiple factors to be investigated simultaneously (Thompson & Higgins, 2002).

COMPLEX DECISIONS IN META-ANALYSIS

When conducting primary research, investigators encounter decision points at which they have multiple choices about how to proceed. Meta-analysts must make decisions concerning how to handle multiple effect sizes coming from the same sample since this violates the assumption of most meta-analytic procedures that effect sizes are independent data points. Meta-analysts employ multiple approaches to handling non-independent tests. Some treat each effect size as independent so that no within-study information is lost, regardless of the number that come from the same study. However, this strategy violates the assumption that the estimates are independent and results of studies will not be weighted equally in any overall conclusion about results. Rather, studies will contribute to the overall effect in relation to the number of statistical tests contained in it.

Others use the study as the unit of analysis. In this strategy, a mean or median result is calculated to represent the study. This strategy ensures that the assumption of independence is not violated and that each study contributes equally to the overall effect. However, some within study information may be lost in this approach. As of 2007 the preferred approach is to use a shifting unit of analysis (Cooper, 1998). Here, each study is allowed to contribute as many effects as there are categories in the given analysis, but effects within any category are averaged. This shifting unit of analysis approach retains as much data as possible from each study while holding to a minimum any violations of the assumption that data points are independent.

Meta-analysts also have to decide whether a fixed-effects or random-effects model of error underlies the generation of study outcomes (Hedges & Vevea, 1998). In a fixed-effects model of error, all studies are assumed to be drawn from a common population. As such, variance in effect sizes is assumed to reflect only sampling error, that is, error solely due to participant differences. In a random-effects model of error, studies are expected to vary also as a function of features that can be viewed as random influences. Thus, in a random-effect analysis, study-level variance is assumed to be present as an additional source of random influence. If it is the case that the meta-analyst suspects a large number of these additional sources of random error, then a random-effects model is most appropriate in order to take these sources of variance into account. If the meta-analyst suspects that the data are most likely little affected by other sources of random variance, then a fixed-effects model can be applied. However, it is often difficult to decide whether there may be sources of random error affecting results. Consequently, the most conservative approach is to conduct all analyses twice, once employing fixed-effect assumptions and once using random-effect assumptions. Differences in results based on which set of assumptions is used can be incorporated into the interpretation and discussion of findings.

ALTERNATIVE APPROACHES TO META-ANALYSIS

While the inverse-variance method deriving from Hedges and Olkin (1985) described above has the most widespread use, alternative approaches to meta-analysis exist. In particular, approaches deriving from both Rosenthal (1984) and Hunter, Schmidt, and Jackson (1982) are commonly used.

Like the inverse-variance method, the Rosenthal technique converts study findings into standard index of effect and combines them to produce weighted means. However, unlike the Hedges and Olkin approach to estimate the overall significance of the effect, Rosenthal suggests combining the probabilities of each effect size. Further, heterogeneity is examined informally using diffuse and focused comparisons.

In the Hunter, Schmidt, and Jackson (1982; Hunter & Schmidt, 2004) approach, study findings are also converted into standard index of effect and combined to produce weighted means. However, untransformed effect size estimates weighted by the sample size of the study are used to compute the weighted mean effect size. Further, heterogeneity in effect sizes across studies is examined by comparing the observed variation in obtained effect sizes with the variation expected due to sampling error, that is, the expected variance in effect sizes given that all observed effects are estimating the same underlying population value. However, a formal statistical test of the difference between these two values is typically not carried out. Rather, the meta-analyst adopts a critical value for the ratio of observed-to-expected variance to use as a means for rejecting the null hypothesis. In this approach, the meta-analyst might also adjust effect sizes to account for methodological artifacts such as sampling error, range restrictions, or unreliability of measurements. This method has been applied most often in the areas of industrial and organizational psychology.

ADVANTAGES OF META-ANALYSIS

There are a number of advantages of meta-analysis over traditional narrative techniques for synthesizing research (see Rosenthal & DiMatteo, 2001, for a full review). First, the structured methodology of meta-analysis requires careful review and analysis of all contributing research. As such, meta-analysis overcomes much of the bias associated with the reliance on single studies or subsets of studies that inevitably occurs in narrative reviews of a literature. Second, meta-analysis allows even small and non-significant effects to contribute to the overall conclusions and avoids wasting data because a sample size was too small and significance was not achieved.

Third, meta-analysis allows the synthesist to ask questions about variables that moderate effects. Specifically, even if no individual study has compared results of different methods, types of programs, outcome measures, or participants, by comparing results across studies the synthesist can get a first hint about whether these variables would be important to look at in future research and/or as guides to policy. Without the aid of statistics, the synthesist simply examines the differences in outcomes across studies, groups them informally by study features, and decides whether the feature is a significant predictor of variation in outcomes. At best, this method is imprecise. At worst, it leads to incorrect inferences. In contrast, meta-analysis provides a formal means for testing whether different features of studies explain variation in their outcomes.

LIMITATIONS OF META-ANALYSIS

Despite many advantages, meta-analysis has been criticized for a number of legitimate limitations and concerns. First, while many meta-analysts go to great lengths to locate as much relevant research as possible, missing data as a result of the literature search procedures on the part of the synthesist or data censoring on the part of primary researchers, editors, or publishers is often inevitable. When data are systematically missing, not only is the size of the sample gathered for the research synthesis reduced, but the representativeness of the sample and the validity of the results are compromised, regardless of the quality of the meta-analysis in all other respects (Rothstein, Sutton, Borenstein, 2005). A number of techniques have been developed in order to assess the possible presence of data censoring and the implications of this threat to the validity of the conclusions drawn from the meta-analysis (see Rothstein, Sutton, Borenstein, 2005, for full review).

Second, meta-analysis is sometimes criticized for combining research of varying quality using various methods and samples. Because a meta-analysis is only as good as the primary research it is cumulating, it is important that the meta-analyst believes that each finding is testing the same relationship and that the primary researchers made valid assumptions when they computed the results of their statistical tests. Of course, research quality can also be used as a moderator variable in the meta-analysis.

Third, while educational psychology research often examines the combination and interaction of many variables in multifactorial models, including regression analyses,

meta-analysis is focused on individual effects. Consequently, there is some loss of information in meta-analysis because it remains difficult to include studies in which complex models were used to analyze data.

Finally, synthesis-based evidence should not be interpreted as supporting statements about causality. When different study characteristics are found associated with the effects of a treatment, the synthesist should recommend that future researchers examine these factors within a single experiment.

DIRECTING RESEARCH AND INFORMING EDUCATIONAL POLICY

With the ever growing volume of primary research on various education related topics, meta-analysis has become an essential tool among school policy makers and practitioners for coping with the overwhelming number of results. In the early 2000s, meta-analysis is often used to guide policy and practice in the classroom. Topics have ranged from the effectiveness of homework, access to special education, or the relationship between class size and achievement to the effect of providing rewards on intrinsic motivation or the relationship between race and achievement motivation. Further, often a synthesis of the current research leaves as many questions unanswered as it answers. However, it provides a comprehensive guide to direct future research. Clearly, the synthesist faces a number of complex issues in conducting a meta-analysis. However, if social science research is to contribute to rational decision making, then rigorous, systematic syntheses of research are a most critical component in researchers' methodological toolbox. Meta-analysis facilitates the attainment of these necessary standards.

SEE ALSO *Research Methods: An Overview.*

BIBLIOGRAPHY

Chalmers, I., Hedges, L. V., & Cooper, H. (2002). A brief history of research synthesis. *Evaluation & the Health Professions, 25,* 12–37.

Cohen, J. (1988). *Statistical Power Analysis in the Behavioral Sciences.* Hillsdale, NJ: Erlbaum.

Cooper, H. M. (1998). *Synthesizing Research: A Guide for Literature Reviews* (3rd ed.). Thousand Oaks, CA: Sage.

Cooper, H., & Hedges, L.V. (1994). *Handbook of Research Synthesis.* New York: Russell Sage.

Cooper, H. M., & Rosenthal, R. (1980). Statistical versus traditional procedures for summarizing research findings. *Psychological Bulletin, 87,* 442–449.

Fisher, R. A. (1932). *Statistical methods for research workers.* London: Oliver & Boyd.

Glass, G. V, McGaw, B., & Smith, M. L. (1981). *Meta-analysis in social research.* Beverly Hills, CA: Sage.

Hedges, L. V., & Olkin, I. (1985). *Statistical methods for meta-analysis.* Orlando, FL: Academic Press.

Hedges, L. V., & Vevea, J. L. (1998). Fixed and random effects models in meta-analysis. *Psychological Methods, 3,* 486–504.

Hunter, J. E., Schmidt, F. L., & Jackson, G. B. (1982). *Meta-analysis: Cumulating research findings across studies.* Beverly Hills, CA: Sage.

Hunter, J. E., & Schmidt, F. L. (2004). *Methods of meta-analysis: Correcting error and bias in research findings* (2nd ed.) Thousand Oaks, CA: Sage.

Lipsey, M. W., & Wilson, D. B. (2001). *Practical meta-analysis.* Thousand Oaks, CA: Sage.

Pearson, K. (1904). Report on certain enteric fever inoculation statistics. *British Medical Journal, 3,* 1243–1246.

Rosenthal, R. (1984). *Meta-analytic procedures for social research.* Beverly Hills, CA: Sage.

Rosenthal, R. & DiMatteo, M. R. (2001). Meta-analysis: Recent developments in quantitative methods for literature reviews. *Annual Review of Psychology, 52,* 59–82.

Rothstein, H. R., Sutton, A. J. & Borenstein, M. (2005). *Publication bias in meta-analysis: Prevention, assessment and adjustments.* London: Wiley.

Thompson, S. G., & Higgins, J. P. T. (2002). How should meta-regression analyses be undertaken and interpreted? *Statistics in Medicine, 21,* 1559–1573.

Erika A. Patall
Harris Cooper

METACOGNITION

Learning depends, in part, on the effective use of basic cognitive processes such as memory and attention, the activation of relevant background knowledge, and the deployment of cognitive strategies to achieve particular goals. To ensure that the basic processes are used effectively, that the activated knowledge is indeed relevant, and that appropriate strategies are being deployed, learners also need to have awareness and control of their cognitive processes. This higher-level cognition was given the label metacognition by American developmental psychologist John Flavell (1976).

The term metacognition literally means cognition about cognition, or more informally, thinking about thinking. Flavell defined metacognition as knowledge about cognition and control of cognition. The knowledge component encompasses what one knows about cognition, including knowledge about oneself as a learner, about aspects of the task at hand, and about strategies needed to carry out the task effectively. The control component encompasses the strategies one uses to make cognitive progress, such as planning how to approach a task, evaluating progress as the task is being completed, and changing tactics if difficulties arise.

HISTORICAL ROOTS OF INQUIRY IN METACOGNITION

Research on metacognition had its origins in the 1970s work of Flavell (1976, 1979) and another prominent developmental psychologist, Ann Brown (1943–1999). This work focused on children's metamemory, that is, their knowledge and control of their memory processes. In a landmark study, Kreutzer, Leonard, and Flavell, interviewed children in kindergarten and grades 1, 3, and 5 to determine their knowledge of how their memories work. Open-ended questions were asked about a variety of hypothetical situations tapping knowledge of person, task, and strategy variables influencing memory. For example, children were asked how they could be sure to remember to take their skates to school with them the next day and how they would remember a phone number, and whether it would be easier or harder to remember a list of words they had already studied. Responses revealed that even the youngest children had some knowledge of the workings of their memory, but that older children had greater insights.

Brown's early interest in metacognition was reflected in the title of a 1978 chapter, ''Knowing when, where, and how to remember: A problem of metacognition.'' Her 1970s research on how well children were able to assess their readiness to be tested on recall of simple materials, such as pictures of common objects, evolved naturally into research on the role of metacognition in studying academic materials and comprehending prose. Her 1980 chapter in a book on theoretical models of reading introduced metacognition to the community of reading researchers and helped to fuel the most active line of domain-specific inquiry in metacognition.

Although Flavell and Brown are credited with introducing the term metacognition, they were not the first to study phenomena that was to be called metacognitive. From the beginning of the twentieth century reading researchers were documenting the importance of monitoring and regulating one's comprehension processes. Memory researchers were studying feelings of knowing and memory monitoring from at least the 1960s. Information processing models from the 1970s included executive control systems that regulate basic cognitive processes.

In addition, Soviet psychologist Lev Vygotsky (1896–1934) and Swiss psychologist Jean Piaget (1896–1980) included processes regarded as metacognitive in their theories of children's thinking. Vygotsky theorized that children develop the capacity for self-regulation through interaction with more knowledgeable others. These individuals initially assume responsibility for monitoring progress, setting goals, planning activities, allocating attention, and so on. Gradually, responsibility for these executive processes is given over to the child, who becomes increasingly capable of regulating his or her own cognitive activities. This transition from other-regulation to self-regulation is in the early 2000s regarded as a hallmark of metacognitive development. Piaget theorized that peers challenge one another's thoughts and thus advance their cognitive development. Inducing children to reflect on their own thinking is in fact inducing metacognition.

Vygotsky's theory provides the foundation for contemporary classroom interventions that begin with explicit instruction on the part of the teacher, followed by modeling and guided practice of cognitive and metacognitive strategies, with a gradual release of responsibility to the student.

Piaget's theory has been built upon by contemporary researchers, including Palincsar and Brown, to reveal that peer discussion and collaboration help students to monitor their own understanding and build new strategic capabilities.

IMPORTANCE OF METACOGNITION IN THEORIES OF LEARNING AND INSTRUCTION

The implicit focus on metacognitive processes in early theories of information processing and cognitive development gave way to an explicit focus in contemporary theories of learning and instruction. Within a decade of the seminal work of Flavell and Brown, hundreds of laboratory studies had accumulated showing that metacognitive knowledge and control were associated with more successful cognitive performance, and applied research confirmed the practical importance of metacognition in the classroom. When students have knowledge and control of their own cognitive processes, learning is enhanced; this assertion holds regardless of the domain of learning, whether reading, writing, science, mathematics, or any other activity that involves thinking.

Evidence that metacognition is firmly entrenched in theorizing about how students learn comes from two influential national committees charged with reviewing and synthesizing the research on learning in the 1990s. Early in the decade a taskforce of the American Psychological Association, under the leadership of Nadine Lambert and Barbara McCombs, developed a set of learner-centered psychological principles intended as guidelines for school redesign and reform. Informing the principles was a model of learning that integrated the following factors: cognitive, metacognitive, motivational, affective, developmental, social, and individual differences. Metacognition was featured in one of the 14 learner-centered principles: "Thinking about thinking: Higher order strategies for selecting and monitoring mental operations facilitate creative and critical thinking." In justifying this principle the authors noted that instructional approaches that foster metacognition can enhance not only student learning but also student responsibility for learning.

Later in the 1990s a committee of the National Research Council, led by John Bransford, Ann Brown, and Rodney Cocking, similarly concluded that metacognition is a key factor in learning that should be deliberately cultivated. They emphasized the particularly important role that metacognition plays in promoting transfer of learning. That is, students can more readily apply knowledge acquired in one context to another context if they have more awareness of themselves as learners, if they monitor their strategies and resources, and if they assess their readiness for tests and other performances.

Although metacognition is a term that may still need to be defined to the general public, it is well represented in most college-level textbooks in cognitive, developmental, and educational psychology. Further information about the role of metacognition to learning and instruction can be found in numerous articles, chapters, and edited books, including those by DeSoete and Veenman; Hacker, Dunlosky and Graesser; Hartman; Israel and colleagues; Miller; Paris; Schneider and Lockl; Schraw and Impara; and Sternberg.

DEVELOPMENTAL AND INDIVIDUAL DIFFERENCES IN METACOGNITION

The early research on metacognition was conducted by developmental psychologists whose particular interest was in age-related changes. Flavell, Brown, and their colleagues documented substantial growth in knowledge and control of memory. Researchers demonstrated similar developmental trends in other cognitive enterprises, including communication, comprehension, problem solving, and attention. A consistent pattern in the domain of reading documented in the early years by Baker and Brown but still found in the early 2000s is that younger readers have little awareness that they must attempt to make sense of text; they focus on reading as a decoding process, rather than as a meaning-getting process.

Metacognitive growth is gradual throughout childhood, adolescence, and even into adulthood.

One cannot simply assert that an individual has or does not have metacognition. Metacognition is not a unitary construct, either across domains or within domains, nor is the deployment of a metacognitive strategy all or none. There are degrees in the effectiveness with which strategies can be applied. Children show primitive abilities to plan and check their activities on simple tasks during the preschool years, but even advanced students in higher education show metacognitive limitations on more difficult tasks.

A parallel line of inquiry that grew up alongside the developmental work focused on individual differences in metacognition, typically involving comparisons of better and poorer students, or students with and without a learning disability. Again, the pattern has been quite consistent, with better students demonstrating more knowledge and control of the processes involved in a given domain, whether it is studying, reading, writing, mathematics, or scientific problem solving. Ability-related differences in knowledge about cognition, like developmental differences, have been documented in countless studies, across age groups ranging from early childhood through later adulthood.

The compelling body of descriptive evidence that younger and less-skilled students have limited metacognitive knowledge and control led psychologists to ask whether metacognition could be deliberately fostered and if so, whether it would enhance children's success in school. Experimental research conducted as early as the 1980s provided an affirmative answer. Although the evidence became clear that increasing students' metacognitive awareness and control can improve learning, Baker points out that the relation between metacognition and learning is not unidirectional. Rather, reciprocal causation is most likely; that is, improvements in metacognition contribute to improvements in learning, which in turn contribute to further improvements in metacognition.

ASSESSMENT OF METACOGNITION

A variety of approaches have been used to measure metacognition, and considerable controversy exists as to the best ways to assess it. The tools that one selects must be suited to the developmental levels of the students and the purposes of the assessments. Multiple measures are recommended because they can provide converging evidence; if the same findings are obtained with different tools, the researcher or educator can be more confident in his or her conclusions.

The most frequently used approach to assess both metacognitive knowledge and metacognitive control is to ask students directly what they know or what they do while engaging in particular cognitive activities. Verbal reports are typically elicited through structured interviews, such as that originally used by Flavell, or by questionnaires that include multiple response options to a series of items. Most questionnaires are domain specific (e.g., they focus only on reading or only on math), but some are intended to be more domain general. A domain-specific inventory might tap a student's understanding of variables that affect reading outcomes and of strategies that are effective for comprehending text. An example of a well-validated inventory is Mokhtari and Reichard's Metacognitive Awareness of Reading Strategies Inventory. A domain-general inventory might assess an individual's knowledge about cognition (including declarative, procedural, and conditional knowledge) and regulation of cognition (including planning, monitoring, debugging, and evaluating learning). An example of a well-validated inventory is Schraw and Dennison's Metacognitive Awareness Inventory. Another valuable self-report option for assessing metacognitive control is to ask students to think aloud about what they are doing and thinking as they solve a problem or read a text.

Technological advances have led to more sophisticated and sensitive ways of assessing metacognitive control. Students can be asked to engage in a task while process measures are being collected online. For example, to assess metacognitive control during reading, a passage may be presented to the reader on a computer screen. Patterns of movement through the text are collected automatically, revealing whether the reader paused at a particular point, whether he or she looked back at previous text, or whether he or she jumped ahead. In many cases, the texts participants read contain errors that were deliberately introduced to make the text difficult to understand. Patterns of movement through the texts reveal processes of comprehension monitoring, or the lack thereof. These process measures are often supplemented by asking readers to reflect on what they were thinking or to answer follow-up comprehension questions. Online processing tasks can also be used to track cognitive monitoring while performing other activities such as mathematical problem solving, writing, computer programming, and vocabulary learning. An advantage of these approaches is that they reveal what students actually do instead of what they say they do. Research using online measures reveals the same developmental and ability-related differences documented through verbal reports.

Still another general approach to assessing metacognition is used primarily by researchers studying basic cognitive processes. In judgments of learning tasks, students are presented with to-be-learned material, such as a list of words or a passage, and they are given a test over the material. They are then asked to judge how well they learned the material or how well they answered the comprehension questions. Judgments of learning are then examined in relation to actual performance. A related approach assesses feelings of knowing or knowledge monitoring; it involves presenting students with material and asking them how well they think they would perform on a test. For example, they might be presented with a list of vocabulary words and asked how many they would be able to define or a set of math problems and asked how many they can solve. They are then asked to complete the task, and their performance is compared to their predictions. Even students at the college level generally are not very good at monitoring their learning, but research has shown that a host of factors influences their success, such as item difficulty and familiarity of the to-be-learned materials, and that they can be taught to monitor more effectively.

Researchers are the most frequent users of metacognitive assessments, but classroom teachers and school psychologists have also become interested in evaluating their students' metacognitive knowledge and control. According to Baker and Cerro, it is important to be mindful of the limitations of the tools that are used and the conclusions that can be drawn. For example, a limitation of questionnaires is that there is not necessarily a correspondence between what people say they do and what they actually do. Comparisons of questionnaire responses with performance measures on a given task often yield rather low correlations. In addition, people often respond according to what they think they should say, rather than what they actually believe or do. Despite their limitations, verbal reports can be valid and reliable sources of information about cognitive processes when carefully elicited and interpreted, as can more direct processing measures.

INSTRUCTIONAL IMPLICATIONS

Classroom-based intervention studies began to be implemented in the 1980s shortly after laboratory studies provided solid evidence that metacognitive knowledge and control could be fostered through direct instruction. These interventions typically are domain specific, undertaken not with the goal of increasing metacognition for its own sake, but rather with the goal of increasing learning. Teacher-led interventions using metacognitively oriented reading instruction have resulted in gains in students' metacognition as well as comprehension. One program developed by Michael Pressley and colleagues, known as Transactional Strategies Instruction, is effective with children as early as second grade. Similarly, teacher-led interventions have been devised and successfully implemented to help students plan, monitor, and evaluate their own thinking during mathematical problem solving. Peer collaboration and discussion play a vital role in the classroom as students make explicit their cognitive processes, assumptions, and strategies. Evidence that metacognitive intervention is effective is in the early 2000s so strong that disciplinary organizations and national panels recommend that metacognition be included in teacher preparation and in classroom curricula.

SEE ALSO *Brown, Ann Leslie; Cognitive Strategies; Piaget, Jean; Pressley, G. Michael; Reciprocal Teaching; Self-Regulated Learning; Theories of Learning; Theory of Mind; Vygotsky, Lev Semenovich.*

BIBLIOGRAPHY

Baker, L. (2008). Metacognitive development in reading: Contributors and consequences. In K. Mokhtari & R. Sheorey (Eds.), *Reading strategies of first and second language learners: See how they read.* Norwood, MA: Christopher Gordon.

Baker, L., & Brown, A. L. (1984). Metacognitive skills and reading. In P. D. Pearson, M. Kamil, R. Barr, & P. Mosenthal (Eds.), *Handbook of research in reading* (Vol. 1, pp. 353–395). New York: Longman.

Baker, L., & Cerro, L. (2000). Assessing metacognition in children and adults. In G. Schraw & J. Impara (Eds.), *Issues in the measurement of metacognition* (pp. 99–145). Lincoln: Buros Institute of Mental Measurements, University of Nebraska.

Bransford, J. D., Brown, A. L., & Cocking, R. R. (Eds.). (2000). *How people learn: Brain, mind, experience, and school.* Washington, DC: National Academy Press.

Brown, A. L. (1978). Knowing when, where, and how to remember: A problem of meta-cognition. In R. Glaser (Ed.), *Advances in instructional psychology* (Vol. 2, pp. 77–165). Hillsdale, NJ: Erlbaum.

Brown, A. L. (1980). Metacognitive development and reading. In R. J. Spiro, B. C. Bruce, & W. F. Brewer (Eds.), *Theoretical issues in reading comprehension* (pp. 453–482). Hillsdale, NJ: Erlbaum.

Brown, R., Pressley, M., Van Meter, P., & Schuder, T. (1996). A quasi-experimental validation of transactional strategies instruction with low-achieving second-grade readers. *Journal of Educational Psychology, 88,* 18–37.

Desoete, A., & Veenman, M. (Eds.) (2006). *Metacognition in mathematics education.* Hauppauge, NY: Nova Science.

Flavell, J. H. (1976). Metacognitive aspects of problem solving. In L. B. Resnick (Ed.), *The nature of intelligence* (pp. 231–235). Hillsdale, NJ: Erlbaum.

Flavell, J. H. (1979). Metacognition and cognitive monitoring: A new area of cognitive-developmental inquiry. *American Psychologist, 34,* 906–911.

Hacker, D. J., Dunlosky, J., & Graesser, A. C. (Eds.). (1998). *Metacognition in educational theory and practice.* Mahwah, NJ: Erlbaum.

Hartman, H. J. (Ed.). (2001). *Metacognition in learning and instruction: Theory, research and practice.* New York: Springer.

Israel, S. E., Block, C. C., Bauserman, K. L., & Kinnucan-Welsch (Eds.). (2005). *Metacognition in literacy learning: Theory, assessment, instruction, and professional development.* Mahwah, NJ: Erlbaum.

Kreutzer, M. A., Leonard, C., & Flavell, J. H. (1975). An interview study of children's knowledge about memory. *Monographs of the Society for Research in Child Development, 40,* 313–319.

Lambert, N. M., & McCombs, B. L. (Eds.). (1998). *How students learn: Reforming schools through learner-centered education.* Washington, DC: American Psychological Association.

McCormick, C. (2003). Metacognition and learning. In Reynolds, W. M., Miller, G. J., & Weiner, I. B. (Eds.). *Handbook of psychology,* Vol. 7, *Educational psychology.* New York: Wiley.

Mokhtari, K., & Reichard, C. A. (2002). Assessing students' metacognitive awareness of reading strategies. *Journal of Educational Psychology, 94,* 249–259.

Myers, M., & Paris, S. G. (1978). Children's metacognitive knowledge about reading. *Journal of Educational Psychology, 70,* 680–690.

Palincsar, A. S., & Brown, A. L. (1984). Reciprocal teaching of comprehension-fostering and comprehension-monitoring activities. *Cognition and Instruction, 1,* 117–175.

Paris, S. G. (2002). When is metacognition helpful, debilitating, or benign? In P. Chambres, M. Izaute, & P. Marescaux (Eds.), *Metacognition: Process, function and use* (pp. 105–120). Boston: Kluwer.

Schneider, W., & Lockl, K. (2002). The development of metacognitive knowledge in children and adolescents. In T. Perfect & B. Schwartz (Eds), *Applied metacognition* (pp. 224–257). Cambridge, UK: Cambridge University Press.

Schraw, G., & Dennison, R. S. (1994). Assessing metacognitive awareness. Contemporary *Educational Psychology, 19,* 460–475.

Schraw, G., & Impara, J. (Eds.). (2000). *Issues in the measurement of metacognition.* Lincoln, NE: Buros Institute of Mental Measurements.

Sternberg, R. J. (1998). Metacognition, abilities, and developing expertise: What makes an expert student? *Instructional Science, 26,* 127–140.

Vygotsky, L. S. (1978). *Mind in society.* Cambridge, MA: Harvard University Press.

Linda Baker

MI THEORY

SEE *Multiple Intelligences.*

MICROGENETIC RESEARCH

How do children learn? Developmental or educational psychologists would seem to be the experts to turn to in seeking answers to this question. Yet, for a long time, developmental psychologists devoted themselves to understanding how children's knowledge and understanding changes, but they did not directly examine the process by means of which these changes occur. Instead, the typical method was to study what children of one age understand and compare that to what children a few years older understand. Researchers then made inferences about what developed between the two ages. But clearly these inferences were indirect. No one had observed the change occurring within the individual child.

THE 1982 RESEARCH BY KUHN AND PHELPS

The microgenetic method has changed this. Its goal is direct observation of the change process as it occurs in individual children.

Its defining characteristic is that an individual encounters the same or similar problem over frequent occasions, allowing the researcher to observe how the individual's approaches to the problem change over time. Although the method has precursors in the work of Werner (1948), the first modern study featuring the microgenetic method was published by Kuhn and Phelps in 1982. They observed fourth grade students engaged in a scientific inquiry task. Students observed that one combination of liquid chemicals (e.g., A, B, and C) turned the mixture cloudy and another combination (e.g., B, C, and D) did not. The student's task was to experiment with the set of liquids to determine which of the individual liquids played a role in producing the chemical change and which did not.

Students of this age found the task difficult and typically did not succeed in drawing valid conclusions during their first attempt. But the critical feature of the method is that the student encounters the task not just once but a number of times, typically over a period of weeks or months. What Kuhn and Phelps observed is that over this course of time most students' performance improved in two ways. First, the conclusions got better. A student was more likely to correctly identify the components of the mixture that played a causal role in producing the outcome, as well as identify those components that played no causal role. But second, and equally important, the strategies by means of which a student generated those conclusions also underwent change. Specifically, the student displayed a number of different strategies to apply to the problem, and what changed over time was the frequency with which they were applied. More advanced and effective strategies—the ones that yielded valid conclusions—began to be used more frequently, while the less advanced, ineffective strategies that led to invalid conclusions became less frequent.

Exactly how did this change take place? Kuhn and Phelps found that some, but only a minority, of children showed an abrupt shift from predominant use of weak strategies to predominant use of strong strategies. These individuals discovered the best way to approach the problem quite suddenly, their approach took a sharp turn, and they rarely used the poorer strategies again. These children, however, were in the minority. For the majority of children, change took place much more gradually as better strategies increased in frequency and poorer ones decreased. Moreover, this change was not a smooth, continuous one. A better strategy might appear once but then not be used again until several sessions later. Or once this better strategy became predominant, a weak strategy that had not been used for some time might reappear. Change, in other words, was overall in a positive direction, but the progress was not even or constant.

An implication is that change entails two components—consolidation and mastery of the stronger strategies, leading to more frequent usage. and inhibition of the weaker strategies. Both are necessary for success. Much of the evidence from microgenetic studies suggests that the inhibition component may be the more challenging of the two. This conclusion is significant because it reverses previous conceptions of development.

A SIMILAR PROCESS ACROSS DIVERSE DOMAINS AND AGE GROUPS

Other studies since the one by Kuhn and Phelps have confirmed these basic findings over a wide range of cognitive tasks, including many that figure prominently in classroom instruction, and age groups. (For reviews of research see Siegler & Crowley, 1991; Kuhn, 1995; Miller & Coyle, 1999; Siegler, 2006). Chen and Siegler (2000), for example, observed changes in frequency of usage among 2-year-olds in the multiple strategies they exhibited to reach a desirable out-of-reach toy—reaching with their hands, asking for an adult's help or using an available tool. Siegler and Chen (1998) observed the strategies of 5-year-olds over time in making judgments about the operation of a balance scale. Alibali (1999) identified and followed over time ten different strategies that third and fourth graders used in solving mathematical equality problems (3 + x = 9). Thornton (1999) studied 5-year-olds playing the game of Twenty Questions.

Not only did she see strategy change over time; she also found that the type of strategy that was initially predominant was predictive of the degree of progress children showed. Children who initially asked only entirely specific questions ("Is it the red car?") were less likely to progress than were those who initially included at least some less specific questions (e.g., "Is it the car?") in their repertories. These were the children most likely to progress to consistent usage of the most effective strategies (e.g., "Is it one of the cars?") Other studies have similarly found initial variability to be a predictor of change.

The microgenetic method has produced many of the kinds of changes with practice in school-related tasks that educators hope to see, making it possible to better understand them (Kuhn, 2005). Dean and Kuhn (2007) used a microgenetic method to follow changes over time in fourth graders' scientific reasoning. Students had to discover which of multiple potential variables did and did not make a difference to an outcome, as they worked on multiple problems over a number of months.

Dean and Kuhn found not only that students' knowledge and the strategies used to generate that knowledge improved over time, but also that this improvement was better maintained, compared to a condition involving brief direct instruction of the effective strategy.

Finally, Kuhn, Goh, Iordanou, and Shaenfield (in press) observed change over time in sixth graders' argumentation strategies as they worked in pairs debating a social issue with a pair of peers who held an opposing view. Although they received no formal instruction, their argumentation skills showed improvement when assessed individually (without peer support) on a new topic.

LEARNING AND DEVELOPMENT

How and why does the microgenetic method work? Ideally, frequent exercise serves simply to speed up the change process, allowing the researcher to examine it, without altering its essential characteristics. A concern is that this acceleration might change characteristics of the process, if so limiting what can be learned about such changes as they occur in an entirely natural environment. Studies that have compared change patterns under microgenetic conditions with those observed over a much longer time period using longitudinal methods, however, find that the patterns observed under the two conditions are comparable (Siegler & Svetina, 2002). What differs is the length of time over which they take place.

But this does not mean that there is no difference between the comparatively rapid cognitive changes that have typically been called learning and the slower changes that have been referred to as development. The distinction between development and learning is a long-standing one that has been important to developmental psychologists, and there is no indication that it should be discarded.

While the microgenetic method has contributed to making the dividing line between learning and development less firm than it was once thought to be, it does not follow that there remain no useful distinctions at all. Learning what songs are on this week's Top 10 List and learning that conflicting ideas can both be right are different kinds of learning in numerous important respects (among them generalizabilty, reversibility, and universality of occurrence). What is important is recognizing the process of change as one that has multiple parameters. When the process is examined microgenetically, it becomes possible to begin to characterize it in terms of many such parameters. The distinction between development and learning is also indicated by the fact that microgenetic studies have typically shown change to occur more rapidly in older children or adults than in their younger counterparts (Kuhn & Pease, 2006; Kuhn, Garcia-Mila, Zohar, & Andersen, 1995). The older individuals apparently bring something to the learning process that the younger ones have not yet developed.

METASTRATEGIC MANAGEMENT

Another important question that has been asked about the strategy change that microgenetic studies reveal is the degree to which it occurs under the individual's conscious monitoring and control. Because inhibition of less effective strategies is involved, the development of conscious awareness, monitoring, and management of one's own learning processes—executive or metastrategic functions—have been suggested as playing an important role. Some microgenetic researchers, such as Siegler (2000, 2006; Siegler & Jenkins, 1989), emphasize the need for associations with the more frequent, less effective strategies to be weakened, as well as associations with more effective strategies strengthened. Others, such as Kuhn and colleagues (Kuhn, 2001; Kuhn & Dean, 2004) emphasize relinquishment of less effective strategies as a more formidable obstacle than strengthening new ones. These researchers propose that knowledge at a meta-level is as important as that at the performance level and plays a major role in what happens there. If so, the changes that occur at the strategic level in microgenetic studies should be accompanied by changes at the metastrategic level and studies by Kuhn and colleagues provide evidence that this is the case (Dean & Kuhn, 2007; Kuhn & Pearsall, 1998; Kuhn, Garcia-Mila, Zohar, & Andersen, 1995).

In the study by Kuhn and Pearsall, for example, during repeated engagement over several months with a scientific investigation task students were asked at several points to explain to a new student how to do the task. This measure of metastrategic understanding showed advances over time, as did measures of strategic performance. Kuhn and Pease (2006) showed that metastrategic monitoring and management of performance also increase over longer periods of time, as a part of normal cognitive development. They studied the performance of 12-year-olds and young adults in learning a simple set of causal relations, and they attributed the adults' superior performance to enhanced meta-level monitoring and management.

MICROGENETIC RESEARCH IN THE CLASSROOM

Although classroom teachers are unlikely to use it to conduct formal research studies, the microgenetic method clearly has a place in the classroom. Teachers are using the microgenetic method in an informal, naturalistic way when they assign their students the same or a similar task repeatedly over a period of time, for example, to carry out two-digit multiplication or to select a book to read and to write a book report on it. Teachers expect to see changes over time in the strategies a student brings to bear on the task and in the product that results. The findings from more formal microgenetic research offer teachers a framework for conceptualizing and monitoring such changes. They suggest that teachers have many strategies they might usefully consider in observing a student's progress over time. These include not only the product of the student's efforts—the work the student submits for a grade—but also what strategies the student has applied to generate this product, how the individual has changed over time, whether the student needs more help in inhibiting ineffective strategies or in consolidating the use of effective ones, and, perhaps most significant of all, what progress the student is making in coming to monitor and manage his or her own learning.

SEE ALSO *Piaget, Jean; Strategy Development.*

BIBLIOGRAPHY

Alibali, M. W. (1999). How children change their minds: Strategy change can be gradual or abrupt. *Developmental Psychology, 35,* 127–145.

Chen, Z., & Siegler, R. S. (2000). Across the great divide: Bridging the gap between understanding of toddlers' and older children's thinking. *Monographs of the Society for Research in Child Development, 65,* No. 2 (Whole No. 261).

Chinn, C. A. (2006). The microgenetic method: Current work and extensions to classroom research. In J. L. Green, G. Camilli, & P. Elmore (Eds.), *Handbook of complementary methods in education research* (pp. 439–456). Washington, DC: American Educational Research Association.

Dean, D., & Kuhn, D. (2007). Direct instruction vs. discovery: The long view. *Science Education, 91,* 384–397.

Kuhn, D. (2001). Why development does (and doesn't) occur: Evidence from the domain of inductive reasoning. In R. Siegler & J. McClelland (Eds.), *Mechanisms of cognitive development: Neural and behavioral perspectives.* Mahwah, NJ: Erlbaum.

Kuhn, D. (2005). *Education for thinking.* Cambridge, MA: Harvard University Press.

Kuhn, D., Garcia-Mila, M., Zohar, A., & Andersen, C. (1995). Strategies of knowledge acquisition. *Society for Research in Child Development Monographs, 60* (4), Serial No. 245.

Kuhn, D., Goh, W., Iordanou, K., & Shaenfield, D. (in press). Arguing on the computer: A microgenetic study of developing argument skills in a computer-supported environment. *Child Development.*

Kuhn, D., & Pearsall, S. (1998). Relations between metastrategic knowledge and strategic performance. *Cognitive Development, 13,* 227–247.

Kuhn, D., & Pease, M. (2006). Do children and adults learn differently? *Journal of Cognition and Development, 7,* 279–293.

Kuhn, D., & Phelps, E. (1982). The development of problem solving strategies. In H. Reese (Ed.), *Advances in child development and behavior, 17,* 1–44.

Miller, P. H., & Coyle, T. R. (1999). Developmental change: Lessons from microgenesis. In E. K. Scholnick, K. Nelson, S. A. Gelman, & P. H. Miller (Eds.), *Conceptual development: Piaget's legacy* (pp. 209–239). Mahwah, NJ: Erlbaum.

Siegler, R. (2006). Microgenetic studies of learning. In D. Kuhn & R. Siegler (Eds.), (W. Damon & R. Lerner, Series eds.), *Handbook of Child Psychology: Vol. 2. Cognition, Perception, and Language.* (6th edition). Hoboken, NJ: Wiley.

Siegler, R. S., & Chen, Z. (1998). Developmental differences in rule learning: A microgenetic analysis. *Cognitive Psychology, 36,* 273–310.

Siegler, R. S., & Crowley, K. (1991). The microgenetic method: A direct means for studying cognitive development. *American Psychologist, 46,* 606–620.

Siegler, R. S., & Jenkins, E. A. (1989). *How children discover new strategies.* Hillsdale, NJ: Erlbaum.

Siegler, R. S., & Svetina, M. (2002). A microgenetic/cross-sectional study of matrix completion: Comparing short-term and long-term change. *Child Development 73,* 793–809.

Thornton, S. (1999). Creating the conditions for cognitive change: The interaction between task structures and specific strategies. *Child Development, 70,* 588–603.

Deanna Kuhn

MIDDLE SCHOOL, TRANSITION TO

SEE *School Transitions: Middle School.*

MIDGLEY, CAROL
1933–2001

Carol Midgley was born in 1933 and grew up on Long Island, New York. For her undergraduate education, she attended the University of Vermont, where she met her future husband, Rees. The couple moved to Ann Arbor, Michigan, in 1961, where they raised their three children. Carol Midgley devoted much time to volunteer work, particularly in education. She was an activist whose mission was to improve public schools. Her efforts led to the implementation of open classrooms and "small houses" in local elementary and middle schools; she later worked with other members of her community to create Community High School, a school designed to focus on the academic and socio-emotional need of early adolescents.

Midgley returned to graduate school in the 1980s and received her Ph.D. in educational psychology from the University of Michigan in 1987. Her research focused on academic motivation during adolescence, with a particular emphasis on early adolescence. At Michigan, Midgley engaged in collaborative work with her mentor, Jacquelynne Eccles. They worked on a study designed to examine why women often opted out of studying mathematics, even when their performance was good. Midgley then worked on a large-scale study with Eccles, Allan Wigfield, and other colleagues, examining the transition from elementary school into middle school (MSALT—The Michigan Study of Adolescent Transitions). That study was originally designed to examine changes in expectancies and values in early adolescents as they transitioned from elementary school into middle school. It was the first study of school transitions that examined both within-year and between-year changes in motivation. Results of the study indicated that students' expectancies and values do change as students move into

middle school, and these changes are often in a negative direction. The focus on changes in expectancies and values of early adolescents across the transition countered the commonly held assumption that the observed drop in motivation was due to puberty.

Midgley and Eccles used stage-environment fit theory to explain these negative shifts in motivation. They argued that the environment in middle school was antithetical to the developmental needs of early adolescents, and that this mismatch between school environments and adolescents' needs contributed to the downward shift in motivation. As an example, they noted that early adolescents need cognitively challenging and interesting work, whereas the curricula that are presented in many middle schools are often repetitive and boring.

When later asked about Midgley's work on collaborative projects, Eccles noted that Midgley's involvement in all of these projects was critical: "We couldn't have done it without her."

In 1989 Midgley accepted a position as a research scientist in the Combined Program in Education and Psychology at the University of Michigan. There, Midgley began a long collaboration with Martin Maehr and also began mentoring her own graduate students. At this time, Midgley became particularly interested in goal orientation theory. Her career shifted at this point as she dedicated much of her future work to her original interest in school reform.

Midgley and her colleagues first worked in elementary schools, helping teachers to focus instruction on mastery goals (i.e., effort, improvement, and self-comparisons). Midgley then received funding from the U. S. Department of Education to work with educators on school reform, using a goal theory approach. Along with Maehr and their graduate students, Midgley immersed herself in collaborative work with several elementary and middle schools in Michigan. The goal of these studies was for educators to examine the types of achievement goals that they foster in their students (i.e., mastery or performance goals), and then to work with those educators to change instructional practices, so that the focus of instruction would be on mastery rather than performance. This work was both arduous and inspiring; it resulted in many publications and a book co-authored with Maehr. The work demonstrated that goal theory could be used to effectively guide school reform, and that educators could change their practices to focus on mastery.

Midgley later received funding from the William T. Grant Foundation to study the development of achievement goals during adolescence. This longitudinal work examined changes in goals and goal structures, as well as the relations of these changes to adolescent well being. Midgley also received funding, with her colleague Julianne Turner, from the Spencer Foundation; that study examined students' avoidance beliefs and behaviors in mathematics classrooms before and after the transition into middle school. The study used both quantitative and qualitative methods to examine the effects of instructional practices on avoidance behaviors. Result of the study indicated that students displayed fewer avoidance behaviors (i.e., self-handicapping, avoidance of help-seeking) when students perceived a mastery goal structure in math classrooms.

Under Midgley's direction, she and her students developed the Patterns of Adaptive Learning Survey (PALS). The PALS is an instrument that measures personal goal orientations and classroom goal structures. The instrument is widely recognized in the field. It has been translated into several languages and used with many thousands of students across the world.

Midgley died in 2001. Her legacy lives on, as her work on adolescent motivation continues to influence both research and policy in the United States and abroad. She is arguably one of the most cited researchers in the field of academic motivation. She mentored a large group of graduate students who continue to pursue her goals of improving education for adolescents.

BIBLIOGRAPHY

WORKS BY

Eccles, J. S., & Midgley, C. (1989). Stage/environment fit: Developmentally appropriate classrooms for early adolescents. In C. Ames & R. Ames (Eds.), *Research on motivation in education* (Vol. 3, pp. 139–186). New York: Academic Press.

Maehr, M. L., & Midgley, C. (1996). *Transforming school cultures.* Boulder, CO: Westview Press.

Midgley, C. (Ed.). (2002). *Goals, goal structures, and patterns of adaptive learning.* Mahwah, NJ: Erlbaum.

Midgley, C., & Edelin, K. (1998). Middle school reform and early adolescent well-being: The good news and the bad. *Educational Psychologist, 33,* 195–206.

Midgley, C., Feldlaufer, H., & Eccles, J. S. (1989). Change in teacher efficacy and student self- and task-related beliefs in mathematics during the transition to junior high school. *Journal of Educational Psychology, 81,* 247–258.

Midgley, C., Feldlaufer, H., & Eccles, J. S. (1989b). Student-teacher relations and attitudes toward mathematics before and after the transition to junior high school. *Child Development, 60,* 375–395.

Midgley, C., Kaplan, A., & Middleton, M. (2001). Performance-approach goals: Good for what, for whom, under what circumstances, and at what cost? *Journal of Educational Psychology, 93,* 77–86.

Midgley, C., Kaplan, A., Middleton, M., Urdan, T., Maehr. M. L., Hicks, L., et al. (1998). Development and validation of scales assessing students' achievement goal orientation. *Contemporary Educational Psychology, 23,* 113–131.

The Students of Dr. Carol Midgley

MISDIAGNOSES OF DISABILITIES

Focus on misdiagnoses of special education disabilities has centered predominantly on the overrepresentation of Black males in mental retardation classrooms. While it is unknown how many misdiagnoses occur each year, they have been systematically and historically documented across all ethnic minority populations (e.g., Hispanic, Native American, and Asian American) and special education categories (Reschley, 1981). Indeed, ethnic disproportionalities have been reported in specific learning disability (Barona, Santos de Barona, & Faykus, 1993; Payette & Clarizio, 1994) and in emotionally disturbed (Harris-Murri, King, & Rostenberg, 2006; Yeh, Forness, Ho, McCabe, & Hough, 2004), whereas in gifted and talented classrooms, ethnic minorities and females are under-represented and have a lower retention rate than their white, male counterparts (Moore, Ford, & Milner, 2005).

Based on these findings, researchers in psychology and education have emphasized the importance of cultural sensitivity and awareness in professionals who refer, test, and diagnose disabled children, especially minorities. In particular, the ways in which standardized tests are used and interpreted have been criticized given the weight an IQ score has on every special education diagnoses (e.g., Reschley, 1981). Because of an IQ phenomenon known as the Flynn effect, however, each one of the over 2 million children who are evaluated every year on IQ tests as part of their special education evaluation is at risk for misdiagnosis, regardless of ethnicity and gender.

USE OF IQ IN DETERMINING DIAGNOSES AND SERVICES

IQ tests are used in all special education diagnosis decisions, but they play a fundamental role in mental retardation (MR) and specific learning disability (SLD) diagnoses. Under federal guidelines, a child who displays "significantly subaverage general intellectual functioning, with deficits in adaptive behavior, and manifested during the developmental period (prior to age 18), that adversely affects a child's educational performance" will receive MR services (*Assistance to States for the Education of Children with Disabilities*, 2006, p. 46756). While each state has the flexibility to develop its own criteria (as long as it does not conflict with the criteria set forth by IDEA), "significantly subaverage general intellectual functioning" is usually determined by an IQ score of 70 points or below, as recommended by the American Psychiatric Association (APA, 1994) and the American Association of Intellectual and Developmental Disabilities (formerly known as the American Association of Mental Retardation; AAMR 1992). Often, obtaining an

IQ score below the cut-off of 70 points is enough to meet the criteria for mental retardation or MR.

Under the same guidelines, SLD is defined as "a disorder in one or more of the basic psychological processes involved in understanding or in using language, spoken or written, that may manifest itself in an imperfect ability to listen, think, speak, read, write, spell, or to do mathematical calculations" (*Assistance to States for the Education of Children with Disabilities,* 2006, p. 46757). There is much variability, however, between states on the ways in which SLD is diagnosed. A commonly used method is to determine if a student's IQ is significantly higher than his or her achievement test score, although this methodology is highly criticized among researchers and practitioners (e.g., Reschley & Hosp, 2004) and is no longer required in the Code of Federal Regulations. Regardless, a child must display at least average intellectual functioning (usually defined as an IQ of 85 points or higher) in order to qualify for SLD services. Thus, many educational diagnoses require scoring above or below a specific IQ score cut-off to qualify.

SLD is an umbrella term for a diverse array of cognitive disabilities that can range from brain injury to dyslexia. Therefore, services can range from providing students with extra time on tests to hiring resource room specialists. While the latter services can be costly, they are implemented less frequently than the former services, which are substantially less expensive. Therefore, while SLD is the most common special education diagnosis, accounting for almost half (48.5%) of the five million children in special education in 2002 (U.S. Department of Education, 2004), the costs of providing SLD services can vary widely.

MR, by contrast, is far less frequently diagnosed, accounting for less than 10% of the special education population (U.S. Department of Education, 2004). It is, however, a more consistent and costly set of services, compared to SLD. Common services offered to MR students include modified regular assignments and more extensive educational interventions, such as receiving one-to-one instructions in a self-contained classroom, instruction from specialists, and trained aides (Singer, Butler, Palfrey, & Walker, 1986).

THE FLYNN EFFECT

The Flynn effect refers to the steady rise in IQ scores seen between 1945 and the early 2000s. It is named after James Flynn (1984, 1987), the political scientist credited with its most extensive documentation. Flynn and others (e.g., Te Nijenhuis & Van der Flier, 2007; Rodgers & Wanstrom, 2007) have observed this systematic IQ rise in 29 nations, spanning 5 continents, including both developed and developing nations. The estimated magnitude of these gains range between 5 to 25 points within a single generation, depending on the country and type of IQ test used. In the United States, this rise is estimated to be approximately 3 points a decade on the Wechsler Intelligence Scale for Children (WISC) and the Stanford-Binet measures.

The reason for the wide range in gains between (as well as within) countries can be attributed to the IQ test that is used. Gains are higher on measures that rely heavily on tests of fluid abilities, or on-the-spot reasoning and abstract abilities, than they are on tests of crystallized abilities, or accumulated knowledge. Tests of crystallized intelligence, such as the vocabulary and arithmetic subtests on the WISC, show very small gains (only 2 to 3 points) between 1947 and 2002. Whereas subtests tests that measure abstract reasoning, visual cognition, on-the-spot reasoning, and working memory show gains up of 25 points during the same time period (Flynn, 2007).

The Flynn effect is measured in terms of IQ gains that result from people doing significantly better on an old IQ test that was created as far back as 25 years before their time (and has not been changed in that interval) when compared to their performance on a more current test whose content has been updated. In other words, as IQ test norms get older, people perform better on them, raising the mean IQ by several points within a matter of years. Specifically, within 20 years, the average IQ in the U.S. population rose from 100 to 106. To compensate for this upward creep, IQ tests are re-normed, at which point the test is made harder. Re-normed tests reset the mean back to 100, which in turn, hides the previous gains from the old norm. Therefore, the same person will score higher on an outdated, old IQ test compared to a brand new IQ test, even if both tests are administered on the same day.

THE FLYNN EFFECT AND MR/SLD DIAGNOSES

Given the fluctuations in IQ created by the Flynn effect when old IQ tests are re-normed, coupled with the heavy use of IQ cut-off scores, the diagnoses of MR and SLD are problematic. While scores rise and thus as more students surpass the 70 IQ cut-off, fewer students are classified MR. Similarly, more students are classified SLD as more students surpass the 85 IQ cut-off. Thus, the discrepancy between IQ and achievement widens. Both of these trends occur regardless of the students' actual cognitive ability. When scores fall with the onset of new IQ norms, these diagnostic trends will reverse; suddenly, MR diagnoses will increase, while SLD diagnoses will decrease. Again, these changes will occur not because the child's cognitive ability has changed but because the child was tested on a new IQ norm.

While Flynn's seminal analyses excluded individuals with cognitive disabilities, several studies have directly explored the Flynn effect among children in special education. Many researchers have reported that children receiving special education services lose, on average, some 5 to 9 IQ points when tested on a newly normed IQ test (e.g., Wechsler, 1991). More alarmingly, Kanaya, Scullin, and Ceci (2003), using a nationally diverse sample, found that over 30% of the students in their sample who tested above the MR cut-off score of 70 points on the WISC-R (Wechsler 1974) tested below the cut-off when retested on the newer normed WISC-III (Wechsler, 1991). This, in turn, resulted in a threefold increase in MR diagnoses, simply due to the test norms used and the year tested even though the students' actual cognitive ability did not decline.

In addition, among children initially diagnosed with SLD on the WISC-R, Gaskill and Brantley (1996) found that more than 40% of the students in their sample no longer met the criteria for SLD when retested on the newer, harder WISC-III. This finding was replicated by Truscott and Frank (2001) who found that the number of SLD diagnoses in a school district decreased with the introduction of the new norm as students no longer had a significant discrepancy between their IQ scores and achievement test scores.

Therefore, MR and SLD students were measured as having a significant drop in IQ when retested on a newer norm, and this drop often leads to a change in their diagnosis. More in-depth analyses also suggest there are individual differences in the Flynn effect. For example, Kanaya, Ceci, and Scullin (2005) discovered a larger Flynn effect among younger children tested on the original WISC norms (Wechsler, 1949), compared to older children on subsequent WISC-R norms. In addition, findings by Sanborn, Truscott, Phelps, and McDougal (2003) suggest that the Flynn effect is diminished in SLD children at lower IQ levels when compared to SLD children at higher IQ levels.

RESEARCH IMPLICATIONS FOR PROFESSIONALS

Due to the Flynn effect and the use of IQ cut-off scores in special education policies, children are diagnosed based on the year tested and test norms used rather than their actual cognitive ability. Therefore, children who are tested on old IQ norms and misdiagnosed due to their inflated scores will not qualify for or receive the resources of the appropriate education that is guaranteed to them by law. After the initial diagnosis, in order to accommodate changes that may occur in children's needs over time, federal guidelines require periodic re-evaluations for all children in special education. An IQ test is often administered as part of this re-evaluation to determine if the current educational program is meeting the children's needs and if services should be modified or discontinued. At this time, children run the risk of receiving a diagnosis based on a norm that has continued to age since their initial diagnosis, thus obtaining a further inflated score. Therefore, the services provided and the financial costs of providing them to disabled children can vary widely throughout the course of those children's education.

Consequently, the services and resources provided to misdiagnosed children will change independent of their actual cognitive ability and educational needs. In other words, schools will misallocate their financial resources and the students may not receive the services they need. Such findings and implications call into question the use of IQ cut-off scores in special education diagnoses and suggest that researchers, teachers, administrators, and policy makers must recognize the role of the Flynn effect when determining the educational needs of children with disabilities.

BIBLIOGRAPHY

American Association of Mental Retardation. (2002). *Mental retardation: Definition, classification, and systems of supports* (10th ed.). Annapolis, MD: Author.

American Psychiatric Association. (1994). *Diagnostic and Statistic Manual* (4th ed.). Washington, DC: Author.

Assistance to States for the Education of Children with Disabilities. (2006). 71 Fed. Reg. 46753.

Barona, A., Santos de Barona, M., & Faykus, S. P. (1993). The simultaneous effects of sociocultural variables and WISC-R factors on MR, LD and non placement of ethnic minorities in special education. *Education and Training in Mental Retardation, 28,* 66–74.

Flynn, J. R. (1984). The mean IQ of Americans: Massive gains 1932 to 1978. *Psychological Bulletin, 95,* 29–51.

Flynn, J. R. (1987). Massive IQ gains in 14 nations: What IQ tests really measure. *Psychological Bulletin, 101,* 171–191.

Flynn, J. R. (2007). *What is intelligence?* New York: Cambridge University Press.

Gaskill III, F. W., & Brantley, J. C. (1996). Changes in ability and achievement scores over time: Implications for children classified as learning disabled. *Journal of Psychoeducational Assessment, 14,* 220–228.

Harris-Murri, N., King, K., & Rostenberg, D. (2006). Reducing disproportionate minority representation in special education programs for students with emotional disturbances: Toward a culturally responsive response to intervention model. *Education and Treatment of Children, 29,* 779–799.

Kanaya, T., Ceci, S. J., & Scullin, M. H. (2005). Age differences in secular IQ trends: An individual growth modeling approach. *Intelligence, 33,* 613–621.

Kanaya, T, Scullin, M. H., & Ceci, S. J. (2003). The Flynn effect and U.S. policies: The impact of rising IQ scores on American society via mental retardation diagnoses. *American Psychologist, 58,* 1–13.

Moore, III, J. L., Ford, D. Y., & Milner, H. R. (2005). Recruitment is not enough: Retaining African American students in gifted education. *Gifted Children Quarterly, 49,* 51–67.

Payette, K. A., & Clarizio, H. F. (1994). Discrepant team decisions: The effects of race, gender, achievement, and IQ on LD eligibility. *Psychology in the Schools, 31,* 40–48.

Reschley, D. J. (1981). Psychological testing in educational classification and placement. *American Psychologist, 36,* 1094–1102.

Reschly, D. J., & Hosp, J. L. (2004). State SLD identification policies and practices. *Learning Disability Quarterly, 27,* 197–213.

Rogers, J. L., & Wanstrom, L. (2007). Identification of a Flynn effect in the NLSY: Moving from the center to the boundaries. *Intelligence, 35,* 187–196.

Sanborn, K. J., Truscott, S. D., Phelps, L., & McDougal, J. L. (2003). Does the Flynn effect differ by IQ level in samples of students classified as learning disabled? *Journal of Psychoeducational Assessment, 21,* 145–159.

Singer, J. D., Butler, J. A., Palfrey, J. S., & Walker, D. K. (1986). Characteristics of special education placements: Findings from probability samples in five metropolitan school districts. *Journal of Special Education, 20,* 319–337.

Te Nijenhuis, J., & Van der Flier, H. (2007). The secular rise in IQs in the Netherlands: Is the Flynn effect on *g*? *Personality and Individual Differences, 43,* 1259–1265.

Truscott, S. D., & Frank, A. J. (2001). Does the Flynn effect affect IQ scores of students classified as SLD? *Journal of School Psychology, 39,* 319–334.

U.S. Department of Education (2004). *Twenty-sixth annual report to Congress on the implementation of the Individuals with Disabilities Education Act.* Washington, DC: Author.

Wechsler, D. (1949). *The Wechsler Intelligence Scale for Children Manual.* New York: Psychological Corporation.

Wechsler, D. (1974). *The Wechsler Intelligence Scale for Children* (Rev. manual). New York: Psychological Corporation.

Wechsler, D. (1991). *The Wechsler Intelligence Scale for Children Manual* (3rd ed.). New York: Psychological Corporation.

Yeh, M., Forness, S. R., Ho, J., McCabe, K., & Hough, R. L. (2004). Parental etiological explanations and disproportionate racial/ethnic representation in special education services for youths with emotional disturbance. *Behavioral Disorders, 29,* 348–358.

Tomoe Kanaya
Stephen J. Ceci

MODELING

Modeling describes the process of learning or acquiring new information, skills, or behavior through observation, rather than through direct experience or trial-and-error efforts. Learning is viewed as a function of observation, rather than direct experience (Holland & Kobasigawa, 1980). When viewed as a process of learning, there are three elements involved in modeling: the model, or the person observed, the observer, the individual who acquires new knowledge or skills as a result of observing the model, and reinforcement, which, in part, determines which behaviors will be repeated. These three factors interact to affect behavior. Reinforcement entails the use of reinforcers (primary or secondary) to increase or decrease the likelihood of future behavior. Through observation of models, a student may learn to hit a baseball (motor skills), how best to interact with members of the opposite sex (social skills), or how to perform double-column addition (intellectual skills). Models can be real—people the student observes directly (e.g. teachers, parents, coaches), or they can be symbolic—characters in books, movies, and television. In either form, real or symbolic, it is difficult to imagine any society in which modeling has not played a crucial role in the transmission of knowledge, skills, and behaviors from one generation to the next.

MODELING EFFECTS ON LEARNING AND BEHAVIOR

Bandura and Walters (1963) concluded that the observation of models can result in one of three outcomes: (a) the modeling or observational learning effect, (b) the inhibitory or disinhibitory effect, and (c) the eliciting effect (which has also been referred to, by Holland and Kobasigawa, 1980, as the social facilitation or response facilitation effect). The modeling effect refers to the acquiring of new behavior as a result of observing a model, real or abstract. Learning how to hit a baseball can come from watching the coach directly or from watching a famous baseball player demonstrate the skill on a best-selling instructional video. The inhibitory or disinhibitory effect refers to the strengthening or weakening of behaviors as a result of observing a model. Many students will be inhibited about acting out in class simply by observing a classmate being punished for a particular behavior. Conversely, some students will be disinhibited, or will be more likely to act out, when they observe that same behavior not being punished. The eliciting effect occurs when a previously learned behavior happens more frequently as a result of observing a model being reinforced for the same behavior. Although it is similar in nature to the modeling effect and disinhibitory effect, Bandura (1971) suggests that the eliciting effect is unique for a couple of reasons. He notes:

> Response facilitation effects can be distinguished from observational learning and disinhibition by the fact that no new responses are acquired, and disinhibitory processes are not involved because the behavior in question is socially sanctioned and, therefore, is unencumbered by restraints. (p. 656)

Advertisers rely on the eliciting effect to sell their products by trying to convince people that purchasing their special brand of product (e.g. jeans, perfume, car), will make them more attractive, sophisticated, or likeable in the eyes of others.

ROLE OF MODEL, OBSERVER, AND REINFORCEMENT

As has been discussed, modeling, or learning as a function of observation, involves the model, the observer, patterns of reinforcement, and how these factors interact to influence behavior or learning. Attributes typically associated with effective models include power, prestige, competence, and warmth or caring. Models that demonstrate one or more of these characteristics are likely to have a stronger influence on the observer (Bandura, 1986). On the part of the observer, in order for modeling to be effective, there are four processes that must take place: attention, retention, reproduction, and motivation. First, the observer must pay attention. People are more likely to pay attention to models in a position of power (e.g., President of the United States) or prestige (e.g., music or movie star), who demonstrate competence (e.g., recognized expert), or show warmth (e.g., a caring teacher) toward the observer. Second, the observer must be able to retain what has been observed by encoding it in long-term memory. Effective teachers incorporate modeling in lesson plans and activities that facilitate long-term learning of information and skills. Third, the observers must be able to reproduce what has been observed. Not only do they need to possess the physical capacity, but they must also believe that that are capable of reproducing the behavior or task. Lastly, the student must be motivated for modeling to be effective. When a student observes other students in the class being reinforced by the teacher for speaking up during a class discussion on World War II, this may motivate the student to overcome his or her shyness and contribute to future class discussions. At the same time, when a teacher ridicules wrong answers from students, other students are less likely to be motivated to speak up for fear of also being ridiculed if they give the wrong answer.

Much in the same way as it functions in operant conditioning, reinforcement (type and frequency) influences the response patterns of observed behavior in the process of modeling. Rather than having a direct influence, however, such as in operant conditioning, reinforcement in modeling has a more indirect role in the learning of new behavior. When individuals observe behavior being punished or rewarded in others, this may lead to the vicarious reinforcement of that behavior in the individual. According to Bandura and Walters (1963), reinforcement in modeling operates in one of four ways, three at the level of the observer, and one at the level of the model. At the level of observer, there is increased likelihood that an observed behavior will be imitated if: (a) the observer is directly reinforced by the model, such as when a teacher praises a student for correctly doing a math problem just demonstrated on the board; (b) the imitated behavior is reinforced by its own consequences, such as a mother's excitement to the child who says "mommy" for the first time; or (c) the observer experiences vicarious reinforcement, such as the shy student who speaks up more in class after observing the teacher respond positively to other students who have done so. Reinforcement occurs at the level of the model when being imitated becomes reinforcing in itself, such as the father who feels proud because his son's batting performance improves as a result of instruction from the father. The father will be more likely, in this case, to continue with the instruction because the outcome is reinforcing the modeled behavior.

Modeling as a process of learning draws heavily from a variety of theoretical sources, including behaviorism (classical and operant conditioning), social learning and social cognitive theory, information processing theory, and sociocultural theory. In order to understand how characteristics of the model, the observer, and reinforcement interact to affect learning and behavior, it is necessary to understand how the various theories have uniquely contributed to our current understanding of modeling.

MODELING AND EARLY LEARNING THEORY

In early theories of human learning, namely behaviorism (i.e., classical and operant conditioning), theorists such as Ivan Pavlov (1849–1936), John B. Watson (1878–1958), and B.F. Skinner (1904–1990) used animal experiments to search out and verify explanations for human behavior. In classical conditioning, Pavlov discovered that dogs could be conditioned to respond in a certain way through the pairing of different stimuli in the environment. From this perspective, learning was viewed as a stimulus-response (S-R) relationship. A stimulus (in the environment) could be manipulated to elicit a particular response (in the individual). In classical conditioning, the focus is on how involuntary responses, such as salivating, are elicited as a result of changes in environmental conditions. As such, classical conditioning only describes one way that learning can occur in animals and humans, rather than having practical applications for classroom management. It was not until the later work of Skinner, in which he introduced the notion of reinforcement, that learning theory began to have practical implications for the classroom and student learning.

Lefrançois (2000) writes, "Simply put, Skinner's model of operant conditioning describes learning as an increase in the probability of occurrence of an operant (emitted response) as a function of reinforcement" (p. 123). With operant conditioning, Skinner expanded the behaviorist model of learning from (S-R) to include reinforcement, in which learning was viewed as (S)timulus-(R)esponse-(R)einforcement-(R)esponse, in which the increased or decreased likelihood of a behavior was contingent upon the type and frequency of reinforcement used. Types of reinforcement include positive reinforcement, negative reinforcement, and

MODELING IN THE CLASSROOM

To model a Venn diagram for early elementary students, the teacher, Ms. Lopez, first accesses the students' background knowledge. She then models completing a Venn diagram using think-alouds.

Ms. Lopez: "Girls and boys, yesterday we talked about how apples and oranges are similar and how they are different. Today I'm going to show you how we can organize that information in a Venn diagram. Raise your hand if you've seen a Venn diagram. [Show a blank Venn diagram.] We can use a Venn diagram to organize information about two items that we are comparing and contrasting. Information that applies to both is written in the area in the middle where the two circles overlap."

On the Elmo, Ms. Lopez draws a Venn diagram: "First, I make sure that my paper has the long sides at the top and bottom. I'll draw a big circle on the right side of the paper. That's where I'll write everything about only apples, so I'll write 'Apples' above that circle. My second circle will be on the left side of the paper, but watch carefully. The second circle is going to overlap the first one and the overlap is big enough for me to write things there. I'll label the left circle 'Oranges' because that's where I'm going to write everything about only oranges. Over the center part, where the two circles overlap, I'll write 'Both.'"

"The first thing I have to do is remember what I know about apples and oranges. I know that apples are red, so I'll write 'red' in the circle labeled 'apples.' Since I wrote about the color of apples, I need to write about the color of oranges across from that in the Venn diagram. I'll write 'orange' in the circle labeled 'Oranges' directly across from 'red' in the 'Apples' side. We want to keep our comparisons across from each other so we can see them easily when we look at the Venn diagram."

Ms. Lopez finishes writing and looks at the class. "Let me think about what else I know about apples and oranges. I can compare their skin. Apples have skin you can eat, so I'll write 'have skin you can eat' in the 'Apple' side of the Venn diagram. We have to peel oranges and don't eat their skin, so I'll write 'can't eat the skin/peel' in the 'Orange' side."

"I know they're both fruit, so I'll write 'fruit' in the overlapping part under 'Both' because that fact is about both apples and oranges."

Ms. Lopez continues her think-aloud, saying, "Let me see. We get juice from both fruits, so I can include that in the section about both," as she continues to fill in the Venn diagram.

"What else do I know about apples and oranges? I know. Oranges have segments and apples are solid fruit, so I'll write 'segments' in the 'Orange' section and 'no segments' in the 'Apple' section."

Ms. Lopez continues entering facts about apples and oranges until the diagram is complete frequently reminding the students that they need to be careful to write in the information that compares things directly across from each other in their sides of the Venn diagram so the information is organized.

Heidi H. Denler

punishment I and II. Frequency of reinforcement refers to schedules of reinforcement, such as continuous or intermittent. Some researchers (e.g., Masia & Chase, 1997) have linked operant conditioning with observational learning by pointing out that reinforcement plays a crucial role in determining the likelihood that an observed behavior will be imitated. Further, Bandura (1977) noted that imitation itself is a class of operants that is strongly influenced by patterns of reinforcement.

MODELING AND SOCIAL LEARNING THEORY

Bandura played a crucial role in bridging the gap between behavioral theory, with its focus on direct experience, and social learning theory, in which many believed that much of human learning occurred through the process of socialization. Rather than having to be "conditioned" (classical conditioning) or "shaped" (operant conditioning), Bandura and other early social learning theorists posited that the adults in any society transferred the skills and knowledge of that society from one generation to the next through a socialization process. Miller (1983) notes that it was at this point that learning theory moved strictly from the realm of the laboratory and into the real world as a way to explain human learning.

Miller (1983) also notes that two major shifts occurred in the history of social learning theory. First was the early work by Bandura and others demonstrating that imitation was linked with operant conditioning through reinforcement, or, that observed behavior was more likely to be imitated when it was reinforced in some way. This presented a major shift in learning theory because, for the first time, behavior was not viewed as only being a function of direct experience. The second major shift occurred with the work of Bandura and Walters in the 1960s and 1970s in which they argued that observational learning could occur without demonstrating a particular behavior. With behaviorism's focus on observed and measurable behavior, the assumption was that learning only occurred to the extent that it could be measured. Bandura (1965) referred to the latter as "no-trial learning." With these shifts came an increasing focus on how models and observers influenced the learning process, especially in Bandura's 1986 model of reciprocal determinism.

MODELING AND COGNITIVE PROCESSES

As discussed earlier, models can affect behavior in one of three ways, including the modeling effect, the inhibitory or disinhibitory effect, and the eliciting effect. With Bandura's reciprocal determinism model of learning, greater attention was paid to how the individual (observer) played a role in the learning process, especially in how cognitive and motivational processes influenced individual perceptions of observed events. Bandura (1986) notes that the greater the cognitive ability and prior knowledge on the part of the individual, the greater the perceptive ability of what is being observed. According to social cognitive theory, self-efficacy and self-regulation are important processes related to modeling in achievement contexts (i.e. school outcomes). Similarly, information processing theorists have clarified how such processes as encoding, retrieval, long- and short-term memory, and metacognition can also influence observational learning (Schunk & Zimmerman, 1996). In both cases the focus is placed on how observers perceive and process the information they are observing, and to a larger degree how capable they will be in reproducing the observed skill or behavior. Bandura (1986) refers to modeling as an "information-processing activity in which information about the structure of behavior and about environmental events is transformed into symbolic representations that serve as guides for action" (p. 51). Bandura suggests that modeling, on the part of the observer, is governed by four processes: attention, retention, production, motivation (see previous discussion on these processes for further detail).

MODELING SOCIOCULTURAL THEORY

In many ways, Lev Vygotsky's sociocultural theory of intellectual development combines many of the impor-

tant aspects of modeling in a way that illustrates the importance of observation in the process of learning. Vygotsky hypothesized that larger cultural and social systems played an essential role in the acquisition of language skills, intellectual development, and ultimately in becoming literate in the traditions and knowledge of a greater society (John-Steiner & Mahn, 1996). Without actually using the term modeling, Vygotsky described a process of intellectual development that started at the level of observation and eventually moved to the level of internalization. Many students are familiar with terms such as apprentice and the zone of proximal development, where through observation and reinforcement (i.e., scaffolding), students develop ever more sophisticated views of the world. While not using the exact terms, Vygotsky suggested that the tools of any society, which could be viewed as symbolic models, and teachers, who are examples of real-life models, are essential in helping children internalize and integrate skills and knowledge that are first perceived at the level of observation.

MODELING AS A MODE FOR LEARNING

Modeling is one of the most efficient modes of learning of any new skill or knowledge (Bandura, 1986). It is difficult to imagine any society that has not relied on models in one form or another to transmit the most important and basic cultural values, customs and beliefs from one generation to the next. If all of human learning had occurred at the level of direct experience or trial-and-error efforts, human progress would have occurred at a much slower rate. From childhood through adulthood, modeling plays a key role in the acquisition and development of cognitive and metacognitive skills, fine motor skills, interpersonal skills, and later professional skills. Each of these is gained primarily through the process of observation.

Motor skill acquisition and development occur as children observe parents, siblings, and peers interact with their worlds. From the simplest act of learning how to pick up and use a fork to the complex and multifaceted process of driving a car, all of these skills are acquired through the observation of models. Which skills are learned and repeated by the observer will ultimately depend upon the types of reinforcement received, as well as how capable or motivated the observer is to repeat those behaviors.

Learning simple cognitive skills, such as basic arithmetic or reading skills, as well as more complex cognitive skills, such as critical thinking or problem solving, are facilitated when models verbalize their own thought processes as they engage in these activities. Thoughts are thus made observable, and potentially modeled, through overt verbal representation of the model's actions. Modeling both thoughts and actions has several helpful features that contribute to its effectiveness in producing lasting improvements in cognitive skills. Nonverbal modeling gains and holds attention, which is often difficult to sustain by talk alone. It also provides an informative semantic context within which to imbed verbalized rules. Behavioral referents confer meaning on cognitive abstractions. Moreover, verbalized rules and strategies can be reiterated in variant forms as often as needed to impart a cognitive skill without taxing observers' interest by using different exemplars. In addition, the more and varied application can deepen understanding of generative rules.

According to the social cognitive model of learning, the acquisition of metacognitive and self-regulatory skills and competence first develops through social interaction, otherwise known as observational learning (Schunk & Zimmerman, 1996). Schunk and Zimmerman suggest that in developing what they call self-regulatory competence, students need to be given opportunities to practice the various strategies associated with self-regulated learning in order to fully develop and master this set of skills. Mastering these skills is made easier when models provide "guidance, feedback, and social reinforcement during practice."

MODELING AND COGNITIVE APPRENTICESHIP

Cognitive apprenticeship (Collins, Brown, & Newman, 1989; Collins, Brown, & Holum, 1991) incorporates key aspects of modeling, self-regulation and mastery learning. In cognitive apprenticeship, in which "thinking is made visible," teachers can utilize or combine various methods (i.e., modeling, coaching, scaffolding, articulation, reflection, and exploration) to help students build on their prior knowledge in a way that allows them to become self-regulated learners. Collins and his colleagues (1991) contend that through modeling, coaching, and scaffolding, which they refer to as the "core" of cognitive apprenticeship, students develop and acquire an integrated set of skills through the processes of "observation and guided practice."

Cognitive apprenticeship differs from traditional apprenticeship in three important ways. First, in traditional apprenticeships, the process of learning usually involves easily observable tasks. The carpenter learns his trade by following the example of the more experienced craftsman. There is little difficulty learning the "thinking" behind the successful completion of a particular task or process. In cognitive apprenticeships, the model, perhaps a teacher, has the difficult challenge of "making thinking visible," while usually engaging in an abstract task or process. Further, in cognitive apprenticeships, both the model's and the observer's thinking need to be made explicit. For the model, this is to ensure that the observer understands the how, why, and when of solving a particular problem. For the observer, this is to ensure that he or she receives proper feedback and support (i.e., scaffolding) during the learning process. Second, in traditional apprenticeships, the process of learning usually occurs in authentic settings while engaging in actual tasks. The learning is situated in a context and presents both the model and the observer the opportunity to engage in and understand not only the final product, but also how the final product is achieved. In a cognitive apprenticeship model, such as learning in the classroom, the process of learning occurs at the abstract level. Learning at the abstract level may lead to difficulty with transfer, or the ability to generalize newly acquired skills and knowledge in future activities.

To enhance learning in a cognitive apprenticeship model, Collins, Brown, and Holum (1991) offer a few suggestions for teachers. First, they suggest that teachers offer students a variety of tasks that range from "systematic to diverse." By presenting a diversity of tasks, teachers challenge students to generalize what they have observed. Second, they encourage teachers to help students reflect on their experiences in ways that help students "articulate the elements that are common across tasks" (p. 41). Lastly, they suggest helping students to understand the relevance of what they learn in order to motivate them to utilize newly acquired skills and knowledge in future endeavors. Clearly, the cognitive apprenticeship model requires that both the model and observer be active members of the learning process.

Models and modeling play an essential role in observational learning. At its core, modeling refers to imitation as a function of observation; however, it is much more than simple mimicry (Bandura, 1986). As a process of learning, modeling draws from various theoretical perspectives, including behaviorism (classical and operant conditioning), social learning and social cognitive theory, sociocultural theory, and information processing theory to explain how the model, the observer, and patterns of reinforcement interact to affect learning and behavior. Contrary to earlier views of learning, modeling assumes that individuals can learn vicariously through the experiences of others. In addition, learning is assumed to occur even in the absence of a direct demonstration of a particular learned skill or behavior. It may simply be a matter of choice on the part of the individual not to perform the newly acquired skill. Models can be either real or abstract, and have been shown to influence behavior in one of three ways: (a) the observational learning or modeling effect, (b) the inhibitory or disinhibitory effect, and (c) the eliciting effect. In order for modeling to be effective, the observer must be able to attend to, retain, reproduce, and be motivated to perform the observed behavior.

Contemporary views of modeling have linked this process of learning with the acquisition of fine and basic motor skills, interpersonal skills, cognitive development, and metacognition and self-regulation. Most contemporary views link aspects of the model, the observer, and reinforcement in a way as to explain new and effective ways of learning. One example of this would be cognitive apprenticeship (Collins et al., 1991), in which teachers, as effective models, make their thinking explicit to help student growth and development. As Schunk and Zimmerman (1996) have noted, when models also provide assistance and guided practice, student learning is enhanced.

SEE ALSO *Bandura, Albert; Cognitive Apprenticeship; Social Cognitive Theory.*

BIBLIOGRAPHY

Bandura. A. (1965a). Vicarious processes: A case of no-trial learning. In L. Berkowitz (Ed.), *Advances in Experimental Social Psychology, II* (pp. 1–55). New York: Academic Press.

Bandura, A. (1971). Psychotherapy based upon modeling principles. In A. E. Bergin & S. L. Garfield (Eds.), *Handbook of psychotherapy and behavior change: An empirical analysis* (pp. 653–708). New York: Wiley.

Bandura, A. (1977). *Social learning theory.* Englewood Cliffs, NJ: Prentice-Hall.

Bandura, A. (1986). *Social foundations of thought and action: A social cognitive theory.* Englewood Cliffs, NJ: Prentice-Hall.

Bandura, A., & Walters, R. (1963). *Social learning and personality development.* New York: Holt, Rinehart, & Winston.

Collins, A., Brown, J. S., & Holum, A. (1991). Cognitive apprenticeship: Making thinking visible. *American Educator, 6*(11), 38–46.

Collins, A., Brown, J. S., & Newman, S. E. (1989). Cognitive apprenticeship: Teaching the crafts of reading, writing, and mathematics. In L. B. Resnick (Ed.), *Knowing, learning, and instruction* (pp. 453–494). Hillsdale, NJ: Erlbaum.

Duncan, S. L. S. (1996). Cognitive apprenticeship in classroom instruction: Implications for industrial and technical teacher education. *Journal of Industrial Teacher Education, 33,* 66–86.

Holland, C. J., & Kobasigawa, A. (1980). Observational learning: Bandura. In G. M. Gazda & R. J. Corsini (Eds.), *Theories of learning: A comparative approach* (pp. 370–403). Itasca, IL: F. E. Peacock.

John-Steiner, V., & Mahn, H. (1996). Sociocultural contexts for teaching and learning. In D. C. Berliner & R. C. Calfee (Eds.), *Handbook of educational psychology* (pp. 125–151). New York: Macmillan.

Lefrançois, G. R. (2000). *Theories of human learning* (4th ed.). Belmont, CA: Wadsworth/Thomson Learning.

Masia, C. L., & Chase, P. N. (1997). Vicarious learning revisited: A contemporary behavior analytic interpretation. *Journal of Behavior Therapy & Experimental Psychiatry, 28*(1), 41–51.

Miller, P. H. (1983). *Theories of developmental psychology.* San Francisco: W. H. Freeman.

Schunk, D. H., & Zimmerman, B. J. (1996). Self-regulation and learning. In D. C. Berliner & R. C. Calfee (Eds.), *Handbook of educational psychology* (pp. 59–78). New York: Macmillan.

Christian E. Mueller

MORAL DEVELOPMENT

Morality refers to a doctrine or system of beliefs, values, or principles that govern human conduct in two ways: by prescribing positive behaviors that benefit others and by proscribing negative actions that harm others. The former set of behaviors, often called prosocial behaviors, include sharing, helping, and comforting. In terms of moral judgment, these actions are viewed as good and ought to be carried out. The latter type of actions, often referred to as inhibitory or negative morality, include violations of others' rights and welfare, such as hitting, harming, and otherwise injuring others physically or psychologically, actions viewed as bad which one ought not to do.

While defining morality might be a fairly straightforward matter, speculations about its origins and development have proved far more contentious. So, too, has the role of schools and classroom teachers in promoting its growth. This entry offers a summary of the major differing views on the origins of morality and its development. It focuses on two forms of moral development—judgment and identity—that have generated decades of empirical research and have affected moral/character education in the United States. In the context of describing the normative developmental changes that occur from early childhood through late adolescence, the entry explores the roles of gender, ethnicity, and culture on moral development. The role schools and teachers in fostering moral development is considered next, with a set of recommendations for educators.

MORAL DEVELOPMENT: SUMMARY OF PSYCHOLOGICAL PERSPECTIVES

In the field of psychology, morality and its development has been variously defined by different types of psychologists. Psychoanalysts, such as Sigmund Freud (1856–1939), believe that morality is rooted in the avoidance of guilt and shame and that its development is a product of the super-ego. In a similar vein, some developmental and social psychologists, such as Martin Hoffman and Jonathan Haidt, respectively, point to emotions as the basis of morality. According to Hoffman, as well as evolutionary psychologists, the origins of these moral emotions or senses date back many millennia to what has been called the ancestral environment or environment of evolutionary adaptation. While modern speculation about the biological and evolutionary basis of morality dates back to Charles Darwin's *The Descent of Man*, it has experienced a resurgence in the 21st century as findings from neuroscience have emerged.

Behavioral psychologists, most famously B. F. Skinner (1904–1990), offer a starkly contrasting view of the origins and development of morality regarding the mind of the newborn as a so-called blank slate, devoid of any inherent moral emotions or inclinations whatsoever. Direct experiences and the consequences they beget are the sole sources of all learning, moral and otherwise. In short, moral values are essentially synonymous with cultural mores. Morality has no biological or evolutionary basis, nor is it motivated by emotions, conscience, or judgment; it is simply those behaviors reinforced as good or bad, driven by the rewards they beget or the punishments they offset.

Despite the historic importance and one-time ascendancy of the foregoing views, the work of cognitively oriented developmental psychologists has dominated the field of moral psychology since the 1960s. Rooted in seminal work on moral judgment by Jean Piaget (1896–1980), Lawrence Kohlberg (1969) created a three-level, six-stage cognitive-structural model of the growth in moral reasoning and judgment. Like emotion-based theories, cognitive-structuralism posits that biology is important to moral development (though in terms of maturation of cognitive capacities, not the possession of inherent emotions). Like behavioral views, cognitive-structuralism posits that the environment plays a critical role in moral learning (though through thoughtful discussions of moral dilemmas, not mindless associations between behaviors and reinforcers). Given the enormous influence of Kohlberg's work on the field of moral psychology and education, his theory is described in more detail below. Before doing so, a brief discussion follows below of the important view of moral development that developed since about the 1980s.

While Kohlberg's theory and research continued to influence the field, the last quarter of the 20th century witnessed the gradual rise of empirical and theoretical work on the development of moral self-understanding and identity. The interest in moral identity and its role in moral behavior was brought into focus with Augusto Blasi's 1980 review of empirical research on moral cognition and moral action. After describing the relatively modest relations between moral judgment and moral behavior, Blasi posited that the observed gap might be explained by moral identity or the extent to which moral values and goals are regarded as core or essential aspects of the self. Individuals with strong or well developed

sense of the self-as-moral would be more likely to act in accordance in with their moral judgments. The critical mechanism is a sense of personal responsibility to act and the concomitant need to maintain "self-consistency" (Blasi, 1983). Blasi's groundbreaking work on moral identity spawned much theoretical and empirical research, which is explored below.

MORAL JUDGMENT DEVELOPMENT: KOHLBERG'S COGNITIVE-STRUCTURAL MODEL

Based on his longitudinal study of 75 males as well as numerous cross-cultural studies in disparate countries (e.g., Canada, Mexico, Taiwan, Turkey), Kohlberg posited that moral judgment develops along a three-level, six-stage continuum. Each of the three levels is composed of two stages, which describe the structure of thinking individuals use as they reason through a moral dilemma. The Moral Judgment of Interview (MJI) consists of five moral dilemmas (i.e., paragraph-length hypothetical vignettes in which the protagonist faces a decision that pits two moral values against each other). In the classic Heinz and the Drug dilemma, for example, issues of life and property rights are put at odds, and one must decide whether the Heinz should steal a drug that might save the life of his wife. However, it is not the determined course of action itself (steal/do not steal) that is used to score one's level and stage moral judgment. Rather, it is reasoning that one employs to render the decision that is of greatest interests to cognitive-structural theorists such as Kohlberg.

The first or preconventional level of development is characterized by largely egocentric reasoning, where good or right actions are defined in terms of their consequences to the self. At stage one, the first and most primitive form of reasoning, there is an unquestioning deference to superior power (e.g., "might makes right") and the physical consequences of action (regardless of meaning or value) dictate whether it is good or bad. At stage two, right action consists of that which instrumentally satisfies one's own needs and the needs of others. While elements of fairness and reciprocity are present, they are construed in a physical, pragmatic manner (e.g., "you scratch my back and I'll scratch yours") and not in terms of justice. Empirical research suggests that these two stages of reasoning are typical of children aged 4 through 10.

The second or conventional level of development morality is seen as conforming to and even maintaining the expectations, rules, and norms of the one's family, group, or society.

Kohlberg referred to stage three as "good-boy-good-girl orientation" because of its emphasis on pleasing others by conforming to stereotypical images of various social roles (e.g., being a "good son" by helping your mother with chores or a "good husband" by sacrificing your own safety for that of your wife). At stage four a higher level of abstraction is achieved and employed in moral reasoning. Rather than conforming to familial roles and expectations, the emphasis is now on maintaining law and order. Right behavior consists of doing one's duty, showing respect for authority and maintaining the given social systems (e.g., legal, religious). Empirical research suggests that these two stages of reasoning are typical during late childhood (Stage Three) and adolescence (Stage Four).

Finally, the fifth or postconventional level of development is characterized by a significant shift from given norms and conventions toward autonomous moral principles and values. At stage five, a "social-contract orientation" is achieved, and right action is defined in terms of general rights and standards. While still possessing legalistic overtones, reasoning at this stage involves a clear awareness of the relativism of personal values and opinions. Accordingly, an emphasis is placed upon procedural rules for reaching consensus and the possibility of changing the law (not simply conforming to it) to maximize social utility. At stage six, moral development reaches its pinnacle, and reasoning is characterized by consideration of universal moral principles. Prominent among these principles is respect for life and the notion of that all humans—regardless of class, color, and creed—possess an inherent dignity and worth that cannot be bought or bartered. Empirical research suggests that relatively few people achieve stage five reasoning and fewer still stage six. Indeed, stage six was all but removed from the model in the later 1980s because so few people demonstrated such thinking, and it is not included in the definitive scoring manual for the MJI (Anne Colby & Kohlberg, 1987).

CRITICISMS AND CORRECTIVES TO KOHLBERG AND COGNITIVE-STRUCTURALISM

As with any theory, Kohlberg's model of moral development is not without shortcomings and vocal critiques. Three of these are discussed below.

Gender Bias. Perhaps the most famous criticism of Kohlberg's theory was launched from within his own research group at Harvard University. In the late 1970s Carol Gilligan began to raise concerns about gender bias in the theory, suggesting that justice-based philosophical orientation of the model emphasized traditional masculine values and traits (e.g., individual rights, rationality, and impartiality) and thus marginalized traditional feminine values and traits (e.g., interpersonal care, intuition,

and social relations). Her book, *In a Different Voice*, which offered an alternative stage model of care-based moral development, was widely read, if not fully embraced. This and other prominent books on caring inspired numerous empirical investigations into the question of gender differences in moral orientation and judgment. These investigations lend some credence to Gilligan's critique but taken together show that gender differences are not as great as she claims (e.g., Walker, 2006). Where, for example, Gilligan posits a dichotomy—males are justice oriented and females are care oriented—the research indicated that males and females possess both justice- and care-based orientations (with females being only slightly more care oriented). With regard to moral reasoning itself, the vast majority (86%) of the 80 MJI studies reviewed by Walker revealed no such differences. Nonetheless, Gilligan's critique was in important one that pushed the field of moral psychology beyond its philosophical moorings in formal ethics and liberal social science.

Cultural Differences. A second and equally heated debate that Kohlberg's theory generated concerns his claims of universality; that is, that people the world over—from tribal nomads to inner-city urbanites—undergo the same six-stage developmental progression in their capacity to reason morally. In the most comprehensive review of this claim, involving 45 cross-cultural studies using the MJI, John Snarey reported general support for it but with a few major caveats. Chief among these is a bias favoring complex urban societies and middle-class populations (i.e., both score slightly higher). Similarly, cross-cultural studies employing the Defining Issues Test (i.e., a widely used pen and paper adaptation of the MJI) have shown educational attainment to be the single best predictor of moral reasoning scores. Age, gender, and ethnicity explain relatively little variance (if any at all) once education is accounted for.

It is important to keep in mind Kohlberg's model and these empirical studies focus on only one component of moral functioning: the development of moral judgment. Even if people across the globe exhibit the same invariant cognitive-developmental progression in their capacity to reason through a set of standardized hypothetical dilemmas, there remains plenty of room for cultural variation in the content, prioritizing, commitment to and expression of moral values and judgments. The work of cultural psychologists such as Richard Schweder and Hazel Markus provides great insights into some of these differences. So, too, does the work social-cognitive domain theorists such as Elliot Turiel, Larry Nucci, and Judith Smetana. They point to distinctions between three domains of judgment: the personal, social conventional, and moral. In doing so, domain theorists distinguish cultural mores from moral principles and identify where they may overlap and conflict. Furthermore, domain theorists believe that each domain has its own developmental trajectory. This conjecture is meant to serve as a corrective to Kohlberg's model, which is seen as conflating the personal and conventional with the moral.

The Thought/Action Problem. Perhaps that most enduring and damning shortcoming of Kohlberg's theory relates to his claim that moral judgment "can be a quite powerful and meaningful predictor of action" (Kohlberg & Candee, 1984, p. 397). As noted above, Blasi's 1980 review of the literature investigating the relations between moral reasoning and moral action suggested otherwise. This finding was not news to philosophers who had long since been writing about the thought/action problem. And, of course, most people need only look at their histories to find examples of behavioral engagement at odds with moral judgment. In educational settings, the epidemic of academic cheating offers a disconcerting illustration of the phenomenon: Most students cheat, even if they believe it is wrong or unjustifiable to do so. In short, while judgment may be a necessary component of moral action, it alone is not sufficient to compel it. Blasi's review made this clear and in doing so ushered in a new era of theorizing and research on moral motivation, one focusing on moral self, identity, personality, and character.

MORAL IDENTITY: BLASI'S SELF MODEL AND ITS LEGACY

It is important to note at the outset that despite the theory's limitations in predicting behavior, Blasi does not seek to rid moral psychology of its interest in moral judgment. He recognizes its importance, regarding it as necessary but insufficient in explaining the complexity of human moral motivation and functioning. In particularly, the movement (or lack thereof) from thought to action needs further explanation, and Blasi's self model offers one. Rooted in the work of Eric Erikson (1902–1994) and Jane Loevinger (1918–2008), Blasi posits that the observed gap might be explained by moral identity, that is, the extent to which one regards moral values and goals as core or essential aspects of the self, "those aspects without which the individual would see himself or herself to be radically different" (Blasi, 1984, p. 131). Individuals with strong or well-developed sense of the self-as-moral are more likely to act to in accord with their moral judgments. The critical mechanism is a sense of personal responsibility to act and the concomitant need to maintain self-consistency.

Blasi's self model also suggests that moral identity is not a unitary construct. Whereas some individuals may see honesty and fairness as essential aspects of themselves, other individuals may highlight compassion and caring for others as most salient to their sense of self-as-moral. In *Varieties of Moral Personality*, philosopher Owen Flanagan (1991) echoes Blasi's conjecture, arguing that "ethical goodness is realized in a multiplicity of ways" (p. 332). Lawrence Walker and his colleagues conducted several studies of moral maturity and exemplarity, focusing on three types: just, brave, and caring (see Walker, 2004). Research on moral identity has extended into domains beyond, but related to, the moral domain. Jim Younnis and Miraday Yates's work on civic identity provides a good example.

Finally, Blasi contends that moral identity is developmental in nature, that how the "essential self" is perceived and defined changes over time. Moreover, the centrality of morality to the self varies between individuals; the self comprises many qualities and their hierarchical ordering varies from person to person. In their seminal work on the development of self-understanding through childhood and adolescence, Damon and Hart found that moral qualities such as honesty and loyalty did not become a part of study participants' self-definitions until they reached adolescence. In the twenty years since Damon and Hart's 1988 book *Self-understanding in Childhood and Adolescence* was published, very little progress was made in creating a model of moral identity development comparable to Kohlberg's model of moral judgment development. It is clear that just as very few people ever achieve stage six reasoning ability, very few experience a full integration of morality and self. In their landmark 1992 study *Some Do Care: Contemporary Lives of Moral Commitment*, Anne Colby and William Damon give insights into the lives of people with extraordinary commitment to moral causes and actions. For these exceptional individuals, morality has been so completely integrated into their sense of self that they report feeling as though they had no choice. Though in a different way, this sense of not choosing but rather acting automatically is at the heart of the connections between moral expertise and schema accessibility that Daniel Lapsley and Darcia Narvaez (2004) make in their social-cognitive approach to moral development.

MORAL EDUCATION: INTEGRATIVE ETHICAL EDUCATION AND OTHER APPROACHES

Most Americans embrace the idea that public school curricula include some form of moral or character education. Indeed, the moral and civic purposes of education have a long history in both Western and Eastern political thought. The content and form as well as demand for moral education has varied greatly over time, even within the brief history of U.S. democracy (see Colby et al., 2003). This does not mean moral education is without its detractors or that there is no lively debate about the "what" and "how" of moral teaching and learning. Nonetheless, in the early 2000s there was increasing concessions and convergence among once divergent camps in the field. Traditional character educators, whose chief objective was the inculcation for moral virtues such as honesty and chastity, have now conceded that moral reasoning has a place in the curriculum. Meanwhile, cognitive-developmentalists such as Kohlberg have realized the motivational value of character traits.

This transformation and its history are beyond the scope of this entry, but interested readers should consult William Damon's 2002 *Bringing in a New Era of Character Education* and Daniel Lapsley and Clark Power's 2005 *Character Psychology and Character Education*. In addition, Larry Nucci's 2002) *Education in the Moral Domain* and Nel Noddings's 2002 *Educating Moral People: A Caring Alternative to Character Education* are excellent resources for classroom teachers as they strike a balance between theory and practice. Rheta DeVries and Betty Zan's 1994 *Moral Children: Constructing a Constructivist Atmosphere in Early Education* remains a long-standing and oft-cited guide for educators.

From these books and numerous other resources, the following sampling of recommendations for classroom practices rooted in Darcia Narvaez's 2006 "Integrative Ethical Education" (IEE). As the name suggests, IEE explicitly brings together traditional character education and cognitive-developmental approaches. It is also rooted the four component model of moral functioning (Rest, 1986), which highlights the need to foster growth in students' moral 1) sensitivity, 2) judgment, 3) motivation, and 4) action.

Moral Sensitivity. According to Rest, moral sensitivity is the first component of moral functioning. While psycho-analysts, emotion-based theorists, evolutionary psychologists, and domain theorists all contend that some degree of moral emotional awareness and sensitively is bred in the bone, all would also agree that the social environment and education are important in turning on and tuning in moral emotions and sensitivity. Teachers seeking to foster students' moral sensitivity should create learning environments and curricula that offer frequent exposure to moral emotions, virtues, concepts, and issues; they should help students take the perspective of others (e.g., classmates, historical figures, contemporary politicians,), and they should call attention to examples of caring and justice as well as insensitively and injustice, including bias, sexism, and racism. In doing so, teachers can help students identify moral emotions and issues and express and manage them.

Moral Judgment. Firmly rooted in Kohlberg's cognitive-structuralist model, this component of functioning concerns the capacity to interpret complex moral dilemmas. Whether real or hypothetical, moral dilemmas require people to discern the competing interests and values at stake and to render a judgment that—depending on the nature of the dilemma—gives due weight to one's own well-being, concern for others, respect for law and tradition, and principles of justice. To foster these capacities educators should engage students in dilemma discussions. Doing so effectively, however, is not easy.

Moral Motivation. This component has been relabeled numerous times in the literature (motivation, commitment, and focus) as it is probably the broadest of the four. After all, the motivation to act or not to do so is a multifaceted phenomenon contingent on both personal and environmental factors. As described above, one of the most important personal factors is moral identity. Students who see themselves as moral beings are more likely to act like moral beings. Teachers can foster students' moral identity development by exposing them to moral exemplars (e.g., honest, brave, caring) and by creating opportunities for students' to clarify and cultivate the meaning and importance of moral values and goals in their lives. Moral motivation and identity are also strengthened when educators create school and classroom cultures in which making the right choice and being a good citizen in the community are recognized and rewarded.

Moral Action. The final component of moral functioning is moral action. Even if students possess the necessary sensitivity, judgment, and motivation to act rightly, they may not possess the needed skills or know-how to do so. Resolving conflicts with others, challenging bias and racism when they occur, and taking the initiative to start or even lead good works are not easy tasks. Educators must teach these skills by creating authentic opportunities for students to practice and hone them. Community service projects and school-based organizations offer venues for such skill development. Teachers should both encourage and mentor students' efforts to address social, moral, civic, and political issues that affect them and their communities.

Moral learning in classrooms does not only occur through formal curriculum or extra-curricular programming. The "hidden curriculum" of schooling, as Philip Jackson famously called it, consists of (often unexamined) norms and policies that collectively give form and meaning to a wide range of behaviors. School governance structures, disciplinary procedures, the allocation of rewards, norms of teacher-student interaction, all communicate morally laden values. Issues of fairness, due process, equal opportunity, respect for differences, and equity in the distribution of scarce resources and rewards (such as teacher attention and grades) permeate the institution of public education. These factors should not be ignored. Teachers must be mindful of the rules, procedures, and norms they establish in their classroom, and they must be mindful of how they go about following them. When possible, students should be included in the process of establishing the governance structures and disciplinary procedures of their school and classroom communities; they should be given a voice in the process and on-going responsibility for ensuring that the place in which they live and learn is fair, just, and caring.

SEE ALSO *Adolescence; Cheating; Early Childhood Development; Gilligan, Carol; Kohlberg, Lawrence; Moral Education; Prosocial Behavior.*

BIBLIOGRAPHY

Blasi, A. (1980). Bridging moral cognition and moral action: A critical review of the literature. *Psychological Bulletin, 88*(1), 1–45.

Blasi, A. (1983). Moral cognition and moral action: A theoretical perspective. *Developmental Review, 3*(2), 178–210.

Blasi, A. (1984). Moral identity: Its role in moral functioning. In W. M. Kurtines & J. L. Gewirtz (Eds.), *Morality, moral behavior, and moral development* (pp. 128–139). New York: Wiley.

Colby, A., & Damon, W. (1992). *Some do care: Contemporary lives of moral commitment.* New York: Free Press.

Colby, A., Ehrlich, T., Beaumont, E., & Stephens, J. (2003). *Educating citizens: Preparing America's undergraduates for lives of moral and civic responsibility.* San Francisco: Jossey-Bass.

Colby, A., & Kohlberg, L. (1987). *The measurement of moral judgment* (Vol. 2). New York: Cambridge University Press.

Damon, W., & Hart, D. (1988). *Self-understanding in childhood and adolescence.* New York: Cambridge University Press.

Darwin, C. (1981). *The descent of man.* Princeton, NJ: Princeton University Press. (Original work published 1871)

Erikson, E. H. (1968). *Identity: Youth and crisis.* New York: Norton.

Flanagan, O. J. (1991). *Varieties in moral personality: Ethics and psychological realism.* Cambridge, MA: Harvard University Press.

Freud, S. (1949). *The ego and the id.* London: Hogarth Press.

Gilligan, C. (1982). *In a difference voice: Psychological theory and women's development.* Cambridge, MA: Harvard University Press.

Haidt, J. (2001). The emotional dog and its rational tail: A social intuitionist approach to moral judgment. *Psychological Review, 108*(4), 814–834.

Hoffman, M. L. (2001). *Empathy and moral development: Implications for caring and justice.* Cambridge, UK: Cambridge University Press.

Jackson, P. (1968). *Life in classrooms.* New York: Holt, Rinehart and Winston.

Kohlberg, L. (1969). Stage and sequence: The cognitive developmental approach to socialization. In D. A. Goslin (Ed.), *Handbook of socialization theory and research* (pp. 347–480). Chicago: Rand McNally.

Kohlberg, L., & Candee, D. (1984). The relationship of moral judgment to moral action. In W. M. Kurtines & J. L. Gewirtz (Eds.), *Morality, moral behavior, and moral development* (pp. 52–73). New York: Wiley.

Lapsley, D. K., & Narvaez, D. (2004). A social-cognitive approach to the moral personality. In D. K. Lapsley & D. Narvaez (Eds.), *Moral development, self, and identity* (pp. 189–212). Mahwah, NJ: Erlbaum.

Loevinger, J., & Wessler, R. (1970). *Measuring ego development: Vol. 1. Construction and use of a sentence completion test.* San Francisco: Jossey-Bass.

Markus, H., & Kitayama, S. (1991). Culture and the self: Implications for cognition, emotion, and motivation. *Psychological Bulletin, 98,* 224–253.

Narvaez, D. (2006). Integrative ethical education. In M. Killen & J. G. Smetana (Eds.), *Handbook of moral development* (pp. 703–732). Mahwah, NJ: Erlbaum.

Noddings, N. (1984). *Caring: A feminine approach to ethics and moral education.* Berkeley: University of California Press.

Nucci, L. (2001). *Education in the moral domain.* Cambridge, UK: Cambridge University Press.

Piaget, J. (1932). *The moral judgment of the child* (M. Gabain, Trans.). Glencoe, IL: Free Press.

Shweder, R. A. (1991). *Thinking through cultures: Expeditions in cultural psychology.* Cambridge, MA: Harvard University Press.

Skinner, B. F. (1971). *Beyond freedom and dignity.* New York: Knopf.

Smetana, J. G. (2006). Social-cognitive domain theory: Consistencies and variations in children's moral and social judgments. In M. Killen & J. G. Smetana (Eds.), *Handbook of moral development* (pp. 53–119). Mahwah, NJ: Erlbaum.

Snarey, J. R. (1985). Cross-cultural universality of social-moral development: A critical review of Kohlbergian research. *Psychological Bulletin, 97*(2), 202–23.

Turiel, E. (1983). *The development of social knowledge: Morality and convention.* New York: Cambridge University Press.

Walker, L. J. (2004). Gus in the gap: Bridging the judgment-action gap in moral functioning. In D. K. Lapsely & D. Narvaez (Eds.), *Moral development, self, and identity* (pp. 1–20). Mahwah, NJ: Erlbaum.

Walker, L. J. (2006). Gender and morality. In M. Killen & J. G. Smetana (Eds.), *Handbook of moral development* (pp. 93–115). Mahwah, NJ: Erlbaum.

Youniss, J., & Yates, M. (1997). *Community service and social responsibility in youth.* Chicago: University of Chicago Press.

Jason M. Stephens
GNA Garcia

MORAL EDUCATION

Every society is concerned about fostering moral character in children and forming responsible citizens. Controversy often accompanies these interests because adults do not always agree about what moral character is or how to cultivate it. Does a person with moral character support societal traditions, much like a tribal leader does, or challenge them, as did Jesus and Martin Luther King Jr.? What exactly do children need to learn in order to be engaged citizens? Further, do children develop moral character through exhortation or through lived experience? Questions like these are debated..

The debate over defining moral education is often pitched between two seemingly opposed perspectives: traditional character education, focused on the development of specific kinds of virtuous traits and habits (Narvaez, 2006) and rational moral education, which focuses on moral judgment and reasoning regarding justice and fairness. The integrative ethical education model (IEE) described below embraces both traditions. IEE defines moral education as the development of moral expertise, which requires both virtue, as intuitions and skills, and moral cognition, as reasoning, imagination, and understanding.

HISTORY OF MORAL EDUCATION

The practices of contemporary moral character education can be traced to ancient Greek philosophers such as Socrates, Plato, and Aristotle (Lapsley & Narvaez, 2006; Nucci & Narvaez, in press). The Socratic emphasis on virtue emphasized the mind, particularly philosophical thinking and reasoning. Socrates's own pedagogy—known as the Socratic method—used successive questions to guide students from ignorance to understanding. Knowing what is good was considered the sufficient condition for individuals to be considered good and virtuous. The Socratic emphasis on right thinking and reasoning echoes throughout the philosophy of his student, Plato, in his *The Republic* in which Plato seeks to define justice.

Aristotle's teachings and philosophy emphasized the practice of good actions, not only reason, as a means to living a life of virtue. With the tutelage of mentors and moral exemplars, Aristotle came to believe that the virtuous life is attainable through the practice of specific habits and virtues. Aristotle's philosophy of virtue laid the foundation for contemporary paradigms of character education.

The moral philosophy of early Greek thinkers, coupled with Christian theology, morality, and practice, provided a social and educational foundation in European and American societies from the Middle Ages to modern times. The intersection of moral philosophy and religion was especially evident in colonial U.S. schools; indeed, in the eighteenth and nineteenth centuries, U.S. schools aimed to develop students with good character through reading Bible stories and exhortations, what is considered traditional character education.

In the twentieth century, the explicit Protestant Christian theology of education became less congruous with the religious identity of many new immigrant citizens. Teachers could no longer rely on the assumption of a single universal religious identity as the foundation of

moral formation. At the same time, theoretical and empirical challenges were levied against moral character education in general. Among many provocative findings, the early work of Hartshorne and May, in *Studies in the Nature of Character* (1928–1930), concluded pessimistically that little if any universality or transfer of character existed across situations and general incongruence was demonstrated between moral knowledge and moral action.

Empirical challenges to moral character education and a changing social landscape precipitated a general decline in the interest and application of traditional character education in schools in the mid-twentieth century. The study of moral character education in many ways shifted to the psychological arena as issues of personality or values. Values clarification became a way for educators to discuss values without advocating any one in particular.

In the widespread move against behaviorism in psychology, Lawrence Kohlberg brought the developmental work of Swiss psychologist, Jean Piaget (1896–1980), to the United States. Inspired by Piaget, Kohlberg (1984) spawned the cognitive development approach to moral education as a counterweight to traditional character education and its collection of virtues. Kohlberg was concerned about the conventional condemnation of people such as Martin Luther King Jr., who were viewed as common criminals breaking the law. Kohlberg saw that civil rights demonstrators had a higher moral purpose in breaking the law, but he wondered how to prove that was true.

Integrative ethical education—ethical skills

Ethical sensitivity
Understand emotional expression
Take the perspectives of others
Connecting to others
Responding to diversity
Controlling social bias
Interpret situations
Communicate well

Ethical judgments
Understand ethical problems
Using codes & identifying judgment criteria
Reasoning critically
Reasoning ethically
Understand consequences
Reflect on process and outcome
Coping and resiliency

Ethical focus
Respecting others
Cultivate conscience
Help others
Being a community member
Finding meaning in life
Valuing traditions & institutions
Developing ethical identity & integrity

Ethical action
Resolving conflicts and problems
Assert respectfully
Taking initiative as a leader
Planning to implement decisions
Cultivate courage
Persevering
Working hard

SOURCE: Narvaez (2006).

ILLUSTRATION BY GGS INFORMATION SERVICES. CENGAGE LEARNING, GALE.

Kohlberg examined the moral development of a cohort of boys through childhood and adolescence. Looking for underlying patterns, he presented his subjects with moral dilemmas and perceived a three-level, six-stage progression in their thinking over time, moving from preconventional thinking to conventional to postconventional (Preconventional level: 1. avoid punishment, 2. Prudence and Simple Exchange; Conventional level: 3. Interpersonal Harmony and Concordance, 4. law and order; Postconventional level: 5. social contract, and 6. universal moral principles). Kohlberg proposed that with age and experience, each person moves from simple to more complex notions of moral reasoning, some moving farther up the stages than others. Each stage is more adequate than the previous one to solve complex moral problems. Kohlberg's basic theory was validated around the world, although there is some controversy about the nature and universality of the higher stages.

In order to stimulate moral reasoning development beyond that promoted by everyday experience, Kohlberg and his students developed the dilemma discussion method. The classic example is the "Heinz Dilemma" in which Heinz, a man of modest means, cannot afford the costly cure for his dying wife. Unable to appeal to the druggist or secure the necessary funds, Heinz breaks into the pharmacy and takes the medicine to save his wife. After the dilemma is presented, students take a position on whether he should steal the drug, and then they participate in small and large group discussions about the reasons for one action or another.

In his later years, Kohlberg and colleagues (Power, Higgins & Kohlberg, 1989) focused on a true-to-life cognitive developmental method, the just community, modeled on some features of the Jewish kibbutz. Implemented in schools and prisons, emphasis was placed upon developing adolescents' ties to community expectations (concerns of Stages 3 and 4) through democratic decision making of community rules (concern of Stage 5). Although an extremely demanding method, the "just community school" approach leads to increased trust, obedience, and loyalty among students, as well as moral stage growth.

NEWER APPROACHES

Newer generations of empirically derived approaches to moral character development developed in the late 20th century. Three are briefly described.

Child Development Project. The Child Development Project (CDP) was founded in the late 1970s as a comprehensive, systems-based approach for fostering positive and pro-social development of elementary-aged children. The CDP focuses on the home and classroom community as the formative contexts for moral character develop-

ment. Similar to Kohlberg's just community model, the intentional democratic structure of the CDP classroom promotes a sense of belonging, cooperation among peers, and sharing of values. A core theoretical component of the CDP is that participatory membership in a caring community, engagement in trusting interpersonal relationships, and collaborative learning experiences provide the necessary curricular and pedagogical foundation for pro-social development.

Teachers and parents become models and guides for the students, provide scaffolding for complex activities and concepts, and support students in their collaboration with peers and development of pro-social skills. CDP curricular materials engage the cognitive, behavioral, and affective components of pro-social development through supportive relationships with an adult, positive interactions with peers, experiences of perspective taking, understanding of values, and discussion of moral issues (see the Web site maintained by the Developmental Studies Center).

Students who participated in CDP demonstrated increased pro-social behavior, increased sense of school community, improved self-concept, and other positive outcomes (e.g., Battistich, Solomon, Watson, & Schaps, 1997). Most notable among the many positive findings was that sense of community was positively related to several key variables of interest such as conflict resolution skills, academic engagement, and concern for others.

Building Assets. It is widely accepted that parents are the primary moral educators of their children. Moral education and formation is more robust, however, when the moral instruction of the parents and family structure are resonant throughout the community (e.g., school, business, media). The Search Institute is a non-profit organization that promotes community-based positive youth development by deepening relationships and asset building. A list of forty positive assets (e.g., family support, adult role models, caring, peaceful conflict resolution) represent the internal and external values and competencies needed for healthy development and fundamental moral education (see the Web site maintained by the Search Institute). Greater numbers of assets are related to fewer risk behaviors. Through Search Institute programs, young people work with peers and adults in the community to deepen relationships, affirm the positive development of youth, and create and uphold institutions that promote an environment and experience that support positive and moral growth. This model has been linked with positive cognitive, affective, and behavioral change—such as increased moral action—in diverse contexts and communities (Benson, Leffert, Scales, & Blyth, 1998).

Social and Emotional Learning. Moral education occurs across diverse contexts (e.g., home, school, work) and through a variety of methods (e.g., direct instruction, experiential learning, counter-examples). But what are the underlying requisite skills for successful engagement in these moral contexts and activities? Social and emotional learning (SEL) is a theoretical and empirical domain that accentuates emotional intelligence as a suite of necessary skills for successful development. The SEL framework affirms the primacy of parents as moral educators and the importance of asset building within the community for successful development but focuses on specific social and emotional skills for life success. The Collaborative for Academic, Social, and Emotional Learning (CASEL) was founded in the 1990s to further explore how academic achievement skills are related to skills necessary for succeeding in life, both the private sphere of family and the public one of work. When children are emotionally and socially competent (e.g., self aware, respectful of others, able to manage conflict) they are better prepared to make moral and ethical decisions, to engage the moral messages of the community and to build assets from them (Lemerise & Arsenio, 2000). Emotional competencies provide the necessary intrapersonal and interpersonal foundation for successful moral judgment and action. Additionally, when SEL skills are taught in schools, students demonstrate increased engagement with learning and academic achievement.

Integrative Approaches. In the 1990s and early 2000s, there was a renewed interest in reconciling the divergence between traditional character education and rational moral education. Tom Lickona has collected the best concrete ideas and put them together in user-friendly books for elementary teachers. For example, Lickona and Davidson (2006) developed a model for helping high school students to develop both performance character and moral character.

The Integrative Ethical Education model (IEE; Narvaez, 2006) provides a broad, research-based framework for moral character development. It outlines an intentional, holistic, comprehensive, empirically derived approach to moral character education. Rooted in what was intuited by ancient philosophers and confirmed by modern science regarding how to cultivate human flourishing, this approach suggests five steps for educators to follow.

Step 1: Establish a caring relationship with each student. One of the most important protective factors against poor outcomes for a child are caring relationships, first, with an adult in the family, second, with an adult outside the family (Masten & Coatsworth, 1998). Teachers can provide the one relationship that supports a child.

Step 2: Establish a climate supportive of achievement and ethical character. A positive climate meets the needs of the child and fosters a sense of belonging to the larger group (Baumeister & Leary, 1995). Prosocial behavior is nurtured in climates that foster flourishing and the "developmental assets" that support resiliency (Benson et al., 1998). A caring classroom (and school) climate with high expectations is related both to high achievement and to moral behavior (Zins et al., 2004). In a caring classroom, discipline is not punishment but is coached character development.

Step 3: Teach ethical skills across the curriculum and extra-curriculum using a novice-to-expert pedagogy. The four component model (Narvaez & Rest, 1995) provides a functional view of moral behavior. Skills for each of the four components (ethical sensitivity, judgment, focus, action) have been identified. Best practice instruction provides opportunities for students to develop more accurate and better organized representations and the procedural skills required to use them. Children must experience an expert-in-training pedagogy for each skill that they learn. Teachers can set up instruction to help students develop appropriate knowledge by designing lessons according to the following four levels of activities: (1) immersion in examples and opportunities; (2) attention to facts and skills; (3) practice procedures; (4) integration of knowledge and procedures.

Step 4: Foster student self-authorship and self-regulation. Individuals can be coached not only in skills and expertise but in domain-specific self-efficacy and self-regulation (Zimmerman, Bonner, & Kovach, 2002). The most successful students learn to monitor the effectiveness of the strategies they use to solve problems and, when necessary, alter their strategies for success. Students can learn the metacognitive skills that moral experts have, for example, self-monitoring of attention away from temptations, self-cheerleading when energy flags, and selecting or designing the environment to maximize goal completion.

Step 5: Restore the village through asset-building communities and coordinated developmental systems. Truly democratic ethical education empowers all involved—educators, community members, and students—as they form a learning community together, developing ethical skills and self-regulation for both individual and community actualization. The purpose of ethical behavior is to live a good life in the community. Together, community members work out basic questions

628

such as the following: How should we get along in our community? How do we build up our community? How do we help one another flourish? Each individual lives within an active ecological context in which, ideally, the entire community builds ethical skills together.

The debate over what constitutes moral character education and the proper formation of good citizens continues in the 2000s. Three main categories or genres have emerged as approaches: traditionalist, humanist, and integrationist. The traditionalist genre is characterized by its focus on the development of specific kinds of virtuous traits or habits. Contemporary traditionalist perspectives often focus on a subset of virtues (e.g., Character Counts!). The humanist genre is characterized by the work of the philosophers John Dewey (1859–1952) and Nel Noddings (b. 1929), which focused on the role of experiences and, in particular, the quality of relationships in education and moral character development. Their work is typified by classrooms as democratic, participatory, and caring environments wherein students engage in collaborative endeavors. Finally, integrationists, as the name implies, incorporate traditional character education and rational moral judgment within the context of caring relationships and a caring community. Rational moral education is differentiated from traditional character education by its focus on moral judgment and reasoning oriented toward justice and fairness. Whereas traditional character education is concerned with the explicit formation of specific kinds of character (specific habits), rational moral judgment is concerned with developing the intellectual tools for moral reasoning and judgment. Although these two schools of moral education have been cast as divergent and mutually exclusive, integrative models of moral character education incorporate traditional virtue ethics and moral reasoning exercises within a caring environment for a truly comprehensive model of moral character education (Narvaez, 2006).

SEE ALSO *Cheating; Moral Development; Service-Learning.*

BIBLIOGRAPHY

Battistich, V., Solomon, D., Watson, M., & Schaps, E. (1997). Caring school communities. *Educational Psychologist, 32,* 137–151.

Benson, P. L., Leffert, N., Scales, P. C., & Blyth, D. A. (1998). Beyond the 'village' rhetoric: Creating healthy communities for children and adolescents. *Applied Developmental Science, 2*(3), 138–159.

Kohlberg, L. (1984). *The psychology of moral development: Essays on moral development* (Vol. 2). New York: Harper & Row.

Lapsley, D. K., & Narvaez, D. (2006). Character education. In W. Damon & R. Lerner, (Eds.), *Handbook of child psychology* (Vol. 4). New York: Wiley.

Lemerise, E. A., & Arsenio, W. F. (2000). An integrated model of emotion processes and cognition in social information processing. *Child Development, 71,* 107–118.

Lickona, T., & Davidson, M. (2006). *Smart & good high schools: Integrating excellence and ethics for success in school, work, and beyond.* New York: Center for the 4th and 5th Rs.

Masten, A. S., & Coatsworth, D. J. (1998). The development of competence in favorable and unfavorable environments: Lessons from research on successful children. *American Psychologist, 53,* 205–220.

Narvaez, D. (2006). Integrative ethical education. In M. Killen & J. G. Smetana, (Eds.), *Handbook of moral education* (pp. 703–733). Mahwah, NJ: Erlbaum.

Narvaez, D., & Rest J. P. (1995). The four components of acting morally. In W. Kurtines & J. Gewirtz (Eds.), *Moral behavior and moral development: An introduction* (pp. 385–400). New York: McGraw-Hill.

Nucci, L. P., & Narvaez, D. (Eds.) (in press). *Handbook of moral and character education.* New York: Routledge.

Power, F. C., Higgins, A., & Kohlberg, L. (1989). *Lawrence Kohlberg's approach to moral education.* New York: Columbia University Press.

Wynne, E. A., & Ryan, K. (1993). *Reclaiming our schools.* New York: Merrill.

Zimmerman, B. J., Bonner, S., & Kovach, R. (2002). *Developing self-regulated learners.* Washington, D.C.: American Psychological Association.

Zins, J. E., Weissberg, R. P., & Wang, M. C. (2004). *Building academic success on social and emotional learning: What does the research say?* New York: Teachers College Press.

Anthony C. Holter
Darcia Narvaez

MULTICULTURAL EDUCATION

Multicultural education encompasses theories and practices that strive to promote equitable access and rigorous academic achievement for students from all diverse groups, so that they can work toward social change. As a process of educational reform in PK-12 schools, higher education, and increasingly in out-of-school contexts, multicultural education challenges oppression and bias of all forms, and acknowledges and affirms the multiple identities that students bring to their learning.

Scholars have provided a range of definitions of multicultural education since the late years of the civil rights movement. A common theme that researchers of multicultural education underscore is that to maintain its critical analysis of power, multicultural education must be constructed within its history and roots in the civil rights movement (Banks 2004; Grant, Elsbree & Fondrie, 2004; Gay, 2004; Nieto & Bode, 2008; Sleeter & Bernal, 2004). To construct an analysis of power within school reform, several multicultural educators have defined multicultural education as a matrix of practices and concepts rather than a singular static notion. Three major definitions of multicultural educations are reviewed below.

BANKS'S FIVE DIMENSIONS OF MULTICULTURAL EDUCATION

James A. Banks (1979), a leading scholar in the field, argued in the early development of the field of multicultural education that "educators should carefully define concepts such as multiethnic and multicultural education and delineate the boundaries implied by these concepts" (p. 237). His later work continued to emphasize this point (2006). Banks has historically advanced a definition of multicultural education as a broad concept and extrapolated on five dimensions (1991, 2004, 2006). He formulated the five specific dimensions as *content integration, knowledge construction process, prejudice reduction, equity pedagogy,* and *empowering school culture and social structure* (2004).

Content integration deals with the infusion of various cultures, ethnicities, and other identities to be represented in the curriculum. The *knowledge construction process* involves students in critiquing the social positioning of groups through the ways that knowledge is presented, for example in scientific racism or the Eurocentric view of the "discovery" of America. *Prejudice reduction* describes lessons and activities that teachers implement to assert positive images of ethnic groups and to improve intergroup relations. *Equity pedagogy* concerns modifying teaching styles and approaches with the intent of facilitating academic achievement for all students. *Empowering school culture* describes the examination of the school culture and organization by all members of school staff with the intent to restructure institutional practices to create access for all groups (Banks, 2004). While highlighting the interrelatedness of the five dimensions Banks promotes deliberate attention to each.

NIETO'S SEVEN CHARACTERISTICS OF MULTICULTURAL EDUCATION

Another leading scholar, Sonia Nieto, offered a definition of multicultural education in 1992 that continues to influence discourse in the field (Nieto, 1992, Nieto & Bode, 2008). Nieto's definition of the characteristics of "multicultural education in a sociopolitical context" addresses the context of communities, and the process of education, in terms of elasticity rather than as a fixed and static form (2008, p. 7). She focuses on seven characteristics of multicultural education: "*antiracist, basic, important for all students, pervasive, education for social justice, a process* and *critical pedagogy*" (Nieto & Bode, 2008, p. 44).

Antiracist education makes antidiscrimination explicit in the curriculum and teaches students the skills to combat racism and other forms of oppression. *Basic education* advances the basic right of all students to engage in core academics and arts; it addresses the urgent need for students to develop social and intellectual skills to expand understanding in a diverse society. That multicultural education is *important for all students* challenges the commonly held misunderstanding that it is only for students of color, multilingual students, or special interest groups. Rather, all students deserve and need an education that is inclusive and rigorous. The *pervasive* nature of multicultural education emphasizes an approach that permeates the entire educational experience, including school climate, physical environment, curriculum, and relationships. In education for *social justice* teachers and students put their learning into action. Students learn that they have the power to make change as apprentices in a democratic society. Multicultural education as a *process* highlights the ongoing, organic development of individuals and educational institutions involving relationships among people. It also points to the intangibles of multicultural education that are less recognizable than specific curriculum content, such as expectations of student achievement, learning environments, students' learning preferences, and cultural variables that influence the educational experience. *Critical pedagogy* draws upon experiences of students through their cultural, linguistic, familial, academic, artistic and other forms of knowledge. It also takes students beyond their own experiences and enables them to understand perspectives with which they disagree, as well as to think critically about multiple viewpoints, leading to praxis, or reflection combined with action (Freire, 2000).

Nieto's emphasis on critical pedagogy draws on the work of Freire (2000), linking multicultural education with wider issues of power, including socioeconomic and political equality, in what May (1999) calls "critical multiculturalism."

FIVE APPROACHES TO MULTICULTURAL EDUCATION

Christine Sleeter and Carl Grant connect the role of sociopolitical power to define multicultural education. Sleeter and Grant's article in *Harvard Educational Review* (Sleeter & Grant, 1987) provided an extensive review of the literature on multicultural education and explained five approaches. This work became a cornerstone of the field, upon which Sleeter and Grant (2006) continue to build. A brief overview and analysis of the five approaches articulated by Sleeter and Grant is provided here.

The goal of the first approach, which Sleeter and Grant call *Teaching the Exceptional and the Culturally Different,* is to equip students with the academic skills,

Multicultural education acknowledges and affirms the multiple identities that students bring to their learning. WILL & DENI MCINTYRE/ PHOTO RESEARCHERS, INC.

concepts, and values to function in American society's institutions and culture. The positive attribute of this approach is that it spurred the movement toward modifying instruction and curriculum, commonly called differentiated instruction. Critics, however, claim that it has a tendency to emphasize an assimilationist perspective that positions students as holding deficits.

The second approach, *Human Relations*, consists of developing positive relationships among diverse groups and individuals to fight stereotyping and promote unity. Reducing prejudice and hostility are admirable goals, but according to its critics this approach tends to simplify culture and identity and avoids analyzing the causes of discrimination and inequality. Without a critical perspective, the Human Relations approach runs the risk of falling into the trap of feel-good tactics that are too soft on academic achievement.

Single-Group Studies is the third approach in the Sleeter and Grant analysis. The goal is to engage in an in-depth, comprehensive study that moves specific groups from the margins by providing information about the group's history, including experiences with oppression and resistance to that oppression. The hope is to reduce stratification and create greater access to power. While there are many positive components to this approach, viewing it as a beginning or entry level approach to multicultural education may be the most appropriate appraisal of it. Criticism of this approach cites the unintentional effect of keeping groups such as people of color, women, people with disabilities, and working class people segregated and out of the mainstream curriculum. Other potential pitfalls are the possibility of promoting cultural separatism and the tendency for this approach to be implemented as a mere add-on.

The fourth approach to multicultural education is self-reflexively dubbed *multicultural education.* Sleeter and Grant use this seemingly redundant title to clarify this approach since so many other practices, such as those described in the first three approaches, are sometimes referred to as multicultural education. They cite Gollnick (1980) to explain that the multicultural education approach promotes a range of goals: the value of cultural diversity, human rights, respect for differences, alternative life choices, social justice, equal opportunity, and equitable distribution of power. There are several criticisms of this approach that are discussed later in this entry. The most severe criticism argues that multicultural education promotes "particularism" and weakens social unification and academic rigor (Ravitch, 1990). Some scholars within the field of multicultural education point to the need for more attention to social structural inequalities and for teaching students the skills to challenge the disparities resulting from inequitable power structures.

The fifth approach, which is the approach Sleeter and Grant advocate, is *Education that is Multicultural and Social Reconstructionist,* which describes a complete redesign of an educational program. The notion of reconstructionism draws from Brameld's framework to offer a critique of modern culture (Sleeter & Grant, 2006). Such a redesign recommends addressing issues and concerns that affect students of diverse groups, encouraging students to take an active stance by challenging the status quo, and calling on students to collectively speak out and effect change by joining with other groups in examining common or related concerns (Sleeter & Grant, 1987, 2006).

CURRICULUM DESEGREGATION AND EQUITY PEDAGOGY

The three major definitions of multicultural education by Banks, Nieto, and Sleeter and Grant helped to launch the field and continue to sustain a discourse that is constantly evolving. Geneva Gay (2004) has referenced the "shifting contours of multicultural education" and some of the reasons for the developmental changes in its intention, implementation, and effectiveness (p. 193). She demonstrates how multicultural education has changed over time by discussing it as a relatively young field, stemming from the time of *Brown v. Board of Education* (1954), that has grown through developmental phases. Gay emphasizes how multicultural education's translation into practice is an ongoing dimension of its development. She cites two avenues for implementing educational equality within multicultural education: *curriculum desegregation* and *equity pedagogy.*

Curriculum desegregation requires analysis from every discipline and should not be relegated to the task of social studies and language arts. Gay points to several scholars who assert typologies that explain progression from simplistic curriculum reform to more comprehensive and complex forms. Other examples include lesson plans for specific subject areas. Gay (2003) also describes developmental paradigms that bridge multicultural theory and practice, pointing out that individual and institutional competencies vary widely, and that becoming a multi-

cultural educator is a process. In this she echoes one of Nieto's seven characteristics (Bode & Nieto, 2008).

Instructional approaches and the shift to *equity pedagogy* are closely linked to the implementation of multicultural education through refining curriculum content (Gay, 2004). Gay explains that multicultural education places value on "*how* to effectively teach diverse students as a well as *what* to teach them." Achieving educational equity is a multi-dimensional goal that is addressed in the proposal for culturally responsive teaching, which consists of many domains:

> The major domains include multicultural content; pluralistic classroom climates and learning environments; teacher attitudes and expectations toward diversity; building community among diverse learners; caring across cultures; use of multiple teaching techniques that are congruent with the cultural backgrounds, values, experiences, and orientations of different ethnic groups; developing personal efficacy and an ethos of success among diverse students; and using culturally informed assessment procedures to determine learning needs, knowledge acquisition, and skill proficiencies. (Gay, 2004, p. 214)

Citing a number of educational researchers who have demonstrated the effectiveness of multicultural education and its role in advancing academic achievement and participation in a democratic society, Gay confirms that educational desegregation and equality are advanced by multicultural education as the field continues to evolve:

> Evidence increasingly indicates that multicultural education makes schooling more relevant and effective for Latino American, Native American, Asian American, and Native Hawaiian students as well. . . . Students perform more successfully on all levels when there is greater congruence between their cultural backgrounds and such school experiences as task interest, effort, academic achievement, and feelings of personal efficacy or social accountability. (Gay, 2003, p. 35)

INTERSECTIONS AND COMMONALITIES

These researchers' explications of multicultural education deal with anti-racism, anti-oppression, and head-on indictments of policies and practices of schools and governments that maintain status quo privilege, power, and unequal schooling conditions. The aim of creating a more just society, by educating students for high academic achievement in which they become critically reflective and socially engaged is articulated by Banks (2004), Nieto & Bode (2008), Sleeter and Grant (2006) and Gay (2003, 2004). These aims remain consistent for multicultural educators as they reflect on challenges of the field.

SELF-REFLEXIVE CRITIQUES FROM WITHIN THE FIELD

Despite the historical assertions of scholarship and efforts to inform the field of education, especially teacher education, the socially transformative qualities of multicultural education have not been universally understood or embraced. The uneven understandings of multicultural education theory have led to some critiques within the field. Sleeter and Bernal (2004) note that as more and more people have taken up and used multicultural education, it has come to be understood in a wide variety of meanings: "Ironically, (given its historical roots), a good deal of what occurs within the arena of multicultural education today does not address the power relations critically, particularly racism" (p. 240). This point is a prevalent concern among multicultural educators. McLaren and Torres (1999) argue, "in general, discourses in the US that deal with multiculturalism deal very little with the concept of racism and focus instead on the politics and affirmation of difference" (p. 44). Nieto, Bode, Raible, and Kang (2008) concur: "the political and transformative theories of multicultural education have often been neglected when translated into practice. As a result, even though multicultural education has made an important contribution to schools and communities, few long-term institutional changes have taken root" (p. 178). Gloria Ladson-Billings (2004) demands an examination of the intertwining of racialized identities with the political and economic history, and current social order of the United States. She notes a "new citizenship" being taken up by some people of color "who want to remake their world into a more just and equitable one" (p. 117). She sees the challenge for educators "to reveal and incite the power of democratic ideals for marginalized students in U.S. schools" (p. 122).

The challenge of translating multicultural theory into practice and maintaining a critical, transformative focus is increased by the contemporary globalized social order that is exponentially changing the way in which many scholars and educators understand culture and identity. For example, a great deal of research and practice in multicultural education has been influenced by questions of how culture might be defined or understood. Historically, in U.S. society and in many school contexts, the very notions of culture and difference have been delineated into static objects, as a metaphorical flag to wave. In that historical conception, culture is viewed as thing to have, rather than a practice of living, learning, performing, negotiating, and translating multiple experiences for oneself and one's community. This static framework for viewing culture implies that human identity, and by extension, human knowledge and student achievement, is contained by set boundaries and will remain unchanged.

Such a viewpoint is often referred to as a "modernist" conception of culture and cultural identity, which is challenged by postmodern concepts in multicultural education (Dolby, 2000, Nieto, Bode, Kang & Raible, 2008). The understanding of culture as fluid and performative as opposed to a static fixture relates to other contemporary inquiries into human identity, such as questions about whether race is an inherent biological fact or a social construct. In 1998 the American Anthropological Association published a "Statement on Race" that indicted the attempts throughout U.S. history to establish division among biological populations as arbitrary and subjective by asserting "present-day inequalities between so-called racial groups are not consequences of their biological in heritance but products of historical and contemporary social, economic, educational and political circumstances" (p. 713).

Postmodern scholars criticize the argument that race is a biological rather than a social mechanism as an "essentialist" notion of race. Yet it is critical to note that abolishing notions of race does not end racism. Each scholarly definition of multicultural education reviewed here regards multicultural education as an anti-racist enterprise that assertively seeks to reduce prejudice. Yet these scholars point out that racism remains a stark reality and needs to be addressed by multicultural education even while contemporary discourse of identities call the notion of race into question (Nieto, Bode, Kang, & Raible, 2008).

Nieto, Bode, Kang, & Raible (2008) ask how multicultural education might transcend typically essentialist notions of race and other identities to reach a more nuanced, critical understanding of multicultural perspectives. As scholars of multicultural education reconceptualize the social constructs of race and racism, they acknowledge that multiple identities work in confluence in the anti-oppression goals of multicultural education. These identities, in addition to race, include social class, ethnicity, religion, language, age, ability/disability, sexual orientation, religion, gender, and other differences. However, because listing these identities as separate labels conflicts with postmodern frameworks on identity that insist identities and cultures are not static but shift and evolve in context, multicultural curriculum and instruction must evolve in a similar manner.

HETEROGENEITY AND HOMOGENEITY

Critical understandings of multicultural education address arguments about whether multicultural education should focus on differences or commonalities across and between ethnic groups. However, when multicultural education is understood within the multiple dimensions advanced by Banks (2006), Gay (2004), Nieto (2008) and Sleeter and Grant (2006) it cannot be viewed as an either/or enterprise.

Critics regard multicultural education, with its excessive emphasis on race and ethnicity, as divisive. They accuse its proponents of teaching to special interest groups to "disunite America" (Schlesinger, 1998). Many critics argue that teaching to a specific group emphasizes self-esteem at the expense of academic rigor. However, multicultural education insists on employing a range of strategies that aim for rigorous academic achievement for all students. Some of these educational strategies may involve inclusion of the knowledge, experiences, perspectives, and accomplishments of previously marginalized groups. This would be one of many approaches to multicultural education. Moreover, multicultural education asserts American ideals by upholding the unalienable constitutional right for every student to be prepared for full participation in a democratic society. However, a critical perspective demands that educators view the broad sociopolitical context of individuals and institutions, rather than labeling students or compartmentalizing them into rigid boxes. Such rigidity runs the risk of participating in and reinforcing stereotypes. At the same time, as Gay (2004) pointed out, the project of culturally responsive teaching requires addressing students' cultural backgrounds through curriculum and pedagogy. Sleeter (2001) provided in-depth analysis of the critiques of multicultural education, addressing both the conservative and radical left critiques of multicultural education. Noteworthy among her multiple findings was that most of the conservative critics ignore the research by scholars in the field of multicultural education (Sleeter, 2001, p. 85).

In summary, the scholars in the field have asserted that multicultural education is a matrix of several dimensions, qualities, and approaches that encompass theories and practices as a process of educational reform. Multicultural education promotes equitable access and rigorous academic achievement for all students so that they can work toward social change.

SEE ALSO *Culturally Relevant Pedagogy.*

BIBLIOGRAPHY

American Anthropological Association. (1998, September). AAA statement on race. *American Anthropologist, new series, 100(3),* 712–713.

Banks, J. A., (1979). Shaping the future of multicultural education. *The Journal of Negro Education 48*(Summer), 237–252.

Banks, J. A. (1991). The dimensions of multicultural education. *Multicultural Leader,* 4, 5–6.

Banks, J. A. (2004). Multicultural education: Historical development, dimensions, and practices. In J. A. Banks & C. A. McGee Banks (Eds.), *Handbook of research on multicultural education* (2nd ed., pp. 3–29). San Francisco: Jossey-Bass.

Banks, J. A. (2006). *Cultural diversity and education* (5th ed.). Boston: Allyn & Bacon.

Bode, P. (2005). *Multicultural art education: Voices of art teachers and students in the postmodern era.* Unpublished doctoral dissertation, University of Massachusetts, Amherst.

Brameld, T. (1956). *Toward a reconstructed philosophy of education.* New York: Holt, Reinhart & Winston.

Brown v. Board of Education. 347 U.S. 483 (1954).

Dolby, N. (2000). Changing selves: Multicultural education and the challenge of new identities. *Teachers College Record 102*(5), 898–912.

Freire, P. (2000). *Pedagogy of the oppressed* (M. B. Ramos, Trans.). New York: Continuum. (Original work published 1970).

Gay, G. (2003). The importance of multicultural education. *Educational Leadership 61*(4), 30–35.

Gay, G. (2004). Beyond Brown: Promoting equality through multicultural education. *Educational Leadership 19*(3), 192–216.

Gollnick, D. M. (1980). Multicultural education. *Viewpoints in Teaching and Learning, 56,* 1–17.

Grant, C. A., Elsbree, A. R., & Fondrie, S. (2004). A decade of research on the changing terrain of multicultural education research. In J. A. Banks & C. A. McGee Banks (Eds.), *Handbook of research on multicultural education* (2nd ed., pp. 184–207). San Francisco: Jossey-Bass.

Ladson-Billings, G. (2004). Culture versus citizenship: The challenge of racialized citizenship in the United States. In J. Banks (Ed.), *Diversity and citizenship education: Global perspectives* (pp.99–126). San Francisco: Jossey-Bass.

May, S. (1999). Towards critical multiculturalism. In S. May (Ed.), *Critical multiculturalism: Rethinking multicultural and antiracist education* (pp. 1–9). London: Falmer Press.

McCarty, T. L. (2002). *A place to be Navajo: Rough Rock and the struggle for self-determination in indigenous schooling.* Mahwah, NJ: Erlbaum.

McLaren, P., & Torres, R. (1999). Racism and multicultural education: Rethinking "race" and "whiteness" in late capitalism. In S. May (Ed.), *Critical multiculturalism: Rethinking multicultural and antiracist education* (pp. 42–76). London: Falmer Press.

Moll, L. C., Amanti, C., Neff, D., & Gonzalez, N. (1992). Funds of knowledge for teaching: Using a qualitative approach to connect homes and classrooms. *Theory into Practice, 31*(1), 132–141.

Nieto, S. (1992). *Affirming diversity: The sociopolitical context of multicultural education.* Mahwah, NJ: Erlbaum.

Nieto, S., & Bode, P. (2008). *Affirming diversity, The Sociopolitical context of multicultural education* (5th ed.). Boston: Allyn & Bacon.

Nieto, S., Bode, P., Kang, E. & Raible, J. (2008). Identity, Community and Diversity: Retheorizing multicultural curriculum for the postmodern era. In F. M. Connelly, M. F. He, & J. Phillion (Eds.), *The Sage handbook of curriculum and instruction.* Thousand Oaks, CA: Sage.

Park, C. C., Goodwin, A. L., & Lee, S. J. (Eds.). (2001). *Research on the education of Asian and Pacific Americans.* Greenwich, CT: Information Age.

Ravitch, D. (1990). Diversity and democracy: Multicultural Education in America. *American Educator, 141*(1), 16–20, 46–68.

Schlesinger, Jr., A. M. (1998). *The disuniting of America: Reflections on a multicultural society.* New York: Norton.

Sleeter, C. (2001). An analysis of the critiques of multicultural education. In J. A. Banks & C. A. McGee Banks (Eds.), *Handbook of research on multicultural education* (pp. 81–94). San Francisco: Jossey-Bass.

Sleeter, C. E., & Bernal, D. D. (2004). Critical pedagogy, critical race theory, and antiracist education: Implications for multicultural education. In J. A. Banks & C. A. McGee Banks (Eds.), *Handbook of research on multicultural education* (2nd ed., pp. 240–258). San Francisco: Jossey-Bass.

Sleeter, C. E., & Grant, C. (1987). An analysis of multicultural research in the United States. *Harvard Educational Review, 57*(4), 421–445.

Sleeter, C. E., & Grant, C. (2006). *Making choices for multicultural education: Five approaches to race, class, and gender* (5th ed.). Hoboken, NJ: Wiley.

Tharp, R. G., & Gallimore, R. (1988). *Rousing minds to life: Teaching, learning, and schooling in social context.* Cambridge, England: Cambridge University Press.

Patty Bode

MULTIPLE INTELLIGENCES

The theory of multiple intelligences, or MI theory, developed by Howard Gardner in the early 1980s, posits that individuals possess eight or more relatively autonomous intelligences that they use to solve problems and create products relevant to the societies in which they live. The eight intelligences identified by MI theory are linguistic, logical-mathematical, spatial, musical, bodily-kinesthetic, naturalistic, interpersonal, and intrapersonal. In conceiving of intelligence as multiple rather than unitary, the theory of multiple intelligences offers a very different perspective on human capabilities and potential than traditional conceptions of intelligence as measured by IQ tests.

GENERAL INTELLIGENCE VERSUS MI THEORY

The traditional conception of intelligence often referred to as IQ first came about in France in the early 1900s when psychologist Alfred Binet developed a 30-item intelligence test for identifying French school children in need of special education. Binet's work was popularized in the United States by Stanford psychologist Lewis Terman who published a revision of Binet's test in 1916 that came to be known as the Stanford-Binet scale.

Around the same time that Binet was developing his scale, English psychologist Charles Spearman (1904)

published a paper on general intelligence in which he asserted that all forms of intellectual activity stem from a unitary or general ability for problem-solving. While Binet had developed his scale with the goal of predicting children's school performance and not as a measure of intelligence across all endeavors, the results of his and Terman's work were taken as support of Spearman's theory. Spearman's conception of general intelligence became the prevailing view of intelligence over the course of the 20th century, though it did have its critics. Both Thorndike (1927) and Thurstone (1938) were prominent researchers who argued that an individual's intellectual abilities could not be measured by a single construct. Nonetheless, the conception of intelligence as a unitary ability gained hegemony among both psychologists and lay-people.

A challenge to this view of intelligence came in 1983 when Gardner laid out his theory of multiple intelligences in a work titled *Frames of Mind*. Gardner's theory emerged from his consideration of several simple but powerful questions:

> Are the brilliant chess player, violinist and athlete "intelligent" in their respective disciplines? If they are, then why do our tests of "intelligence" fail to identify them? In general, why does the traditional construct of intelligence fail to take into account such large areas of human endeavor? (Gardner, 2006, p. 6)

In these words, Gardner voices his concerns with the intelligence test designed by Binet and its underlying acceptance of intelligence as a single, unitary construct. In *Frames of Mind*, Gardner (1983) lays out his own conception of intelligence which differs from Binet's in several fundamental ways. First, proponents of Binet's conception of intelligence typically define intelligence as the trait or quality measured by an intelligence test. As psychologist E.G. Boring (1923) famously declared, "Intelligence is what the tests test" (p. 35). Gardner (2006), in contrast, defines intelligence as "an information-processing potential to solve problems or create products that are valued in at least one culture" (p. 235). Second, the traditional conception of intelligence conceives of a high IQ score as indicative of an individual's ability to be high achieving across a wide range of endeavors. In contrast, MI theory argues that individuals who demonstrate a particular aptitude in one intelligence will not necessarily demonstrate a similar aptitude in another intelligence. For example, an individual who demonstrates an impressive level of musical intelligence may be far less skilled when it comes to bodily-kinesthetic or spatial intelligence, or vice-versa. Finally, while most proponents of general intelligence regard intelligence as an innate trait which one can do little to change, multiple intelligences theory conceives of intelligence as a combination of heritable potentials and of skills that can be acquired and enhanced by appropriate experiences. In other words, while one individual may be born with a strong potential for musical intelligence, another individual can strengthen his or her musical intelligence through study and practice.

A common misunderstanding regarding MI theory is that people possess some intelligences and not others. According to MI theory, with the exception of individuals suffering from severe brain damage, all individuals possess the full range of intelligences. Thus, an individual's profile of intelligence may include a relatively low aptitude for musical intelligence, but that individual is misunderstanding MI theory if he or she claims to have no musical intelligence. Another misunderstanding is that every individual is superior in at least one of the intelligences. Individuals do differ in their levels of strength and weakness for each of the intelligences; however, there is no guarantee that every individual will demonstrate superior aptitude in at least one intelligence (Gardner, 1983).

IDENTIFYING AN INTELLIGENCE

Multiple intelligences theory has proved controversial in the psychology world. Perhaps the main source of this controversy is the evidence upon which the theory is based. Many other theories of intelligence are based entirely upon empirical data collected from psychometric instruments or experimental studies. These studies typically involve presenting subjects with a number of test items that are believed to measure intellectual capabilities. MI theory came about differently. Rather than conducting a series of experiments, Gardner (1983) developed his theory of multiple intelligences by synthesizing research from fields as diverse as evolutionary biology, neuroscience, anthropology, psychometrics as well as psychological studies of prodigies and savants. By drawing upon findings from these many diverse sources, Gardner developed the following set of criteria for identifying an intelligence:

It should be seen in relative isolation in prodigies, autistic savants, stroke victims or other exceptional populations.

It should have a distinct developmental trajectory.

It should have some basis in evolutionary biology.

It should be susceptible to capture in symbol systems.

It should be supported by evidence from psychometric tests of intelligence.

It should be distinguishable from other intelligences through experimental psychological tasks.

It should demonstrate a core, information-processing system. (Gardner, 1998).

Through application of these criteria, Gardner identified eight distinct intelligences. Linguistic intelligence allows individuals to create and understand products involving language such as poems, political speeches, and newspaper articles. Logical-mathematical intelligence allows individuals to develop equations and proofs, make calculations, and solve abstract problems. Scientists, analytic philosophers, and computer programmers typically possess profiles of intelligence high in logical-mathematical intelligence. Spatial intelligence enables individuals to use maps and other forms of graphic information in order to navigate around or through complex terrains. Musical intelligence allows individuals to create and interpret different types of sound patterns and combinations. Bodily-kinesthetic intelligence involves using one's own body to create products or solve problems. Dancers, artists, and surgeons all require a profile of intelligence high in bodily-kinesthetic intelligence. Interpersonal intelligence captures an individual's ability to observe and understand other people's moods, desires, skills, motivations, and intentions while intrapersonal intelligence reflects an individual's ability to recognize and assess these characteristics within himself.

Gardner's original theory of multiple intelligences identified the seven intelligences described here. However, in the mid-1990s, Gardner found that naturalistic intelligence met the above criteria for identification as an intelligence as well. According to Gardner, naturalistic intelligence enables individuals to recognize and distinguish among products of the natural world such as animals, plants, rock configurations, and weather formations. Individuals with high levels of naturalistic intelligence might be drawn to careers in botany, meteorology, and veterinary science.

Yet another misconception about MI theory is that intelligences are constantly being identified and added. This misconception comes about in part because of the literally hundreds of psychologists, educators, and writers who have begun writing about various intelligences since Gardner's original publication of *Frames of Mind* in 1983. In truth, however, naturalistic intelligence is the only intelligence that Gardner has identified and added to the original set of intelligences originally described in *Frames of Mind*. Between the early 1980s and the early 2000s, researchers have suggested a number of additional intelligences, including moral intelligence, humor intelligence, cooking intelligence, and even sexual intelligence. However, as of 2007, none of these suggested intelligences has met the criteria cited above for identification as a unique intelligence.

One partial exception is the proposal of existential intelligence (Gardner, 1999). Existential intelligence has been described as the intelligence of big questions—a capacity to consider issues of life, death, love, war, and being. One might expect philosophers, poets, and theologians to demonstrate a particular aptitude for existential intelligence. Gardner (2006) has referred to existential intelligence as a half-intelligence because research to date has found existential intelligence to meet several of the criteria for identification as a unique intelligence but not all of them. Thus, it is not yet clear whether existential intelligence warrants identification as its own unique intelligence or whether the capacity to reflect upon big questions is better conceived of as a component of one or more of the existing eight intelligences. As of 2007, Gardner has held off on classifying existential intelligence as a full-fledged ninth intelligence.

Of course, it is entirely possible that early decades of the 21st century, research in fields such as genetics or neuroscience will demonstrate that existential intelligence or other intelligences do meet the criteria for inclusion as an intelligence. It is also possible—perhaps even likely—that research in these fields will reveal that hitherto identified intelligences such as logical-mathematical intelligence consist of several sub- or component intelligences. As brain imaging techniques improve and researchers' understanding of the human genome increases, there is little doubt that MI theory will adapt and change. That said, the precise number and boundary of the intelligences is less important than the overarching principle of MI theory: namely, that intelligence is better understood as multiple and specific rather than unitary and general (Chen & Gardner, 2005; Gardner, 2006b).

APPLICATIONS OF MI THEORY

Multiple intelligences theory has had a substantial impact upon the world of education; however, Gardner did not develop MI theory with an intended educational agenda or audience. Rather, Gardner developed his theory of multiple intelligences with the goal of drawing upon dramatic advances in the fields of neuroscience, biology, and psychology to offer an alternative way of thinking about human cognition. Nonetheless, numerous educators embraced the idea of multiple intelligences almost from its inception. Hundreds of schools, teachers, and researchers at all different levels and in many different countries and settings have applied MI theory to the practice of education various ways. Examples include schools that use MI theory to provide teachers with a common vocabulary for discussing the learning of individual students. Other schools teach students about the concept of intrapersonal intelligence in order to encourage them to reflect upon their own strengths and weaknesses. Still other schools seek to deepen student engagement by designing curricula that draw upon different intelligences in students' investigation of a particular topic.

One of the first schools to draw extensively upon the principles of MI theory was the Key Learning Community in Indianapolis, Indiana. The Key Learning Community was founded by a team of teachers in 1987 with the mission of giving "equal emphasis for every student to each of the eight areas of intelligence: linguistic, musical, logical-mathematical, naturalistic, spatial, bodily-kinesthetic, interpersonal and intrapersonal" (Key Learning Community, 2007). The Key Learning Community regards MI theory as the cornerstone of its educational program, and, according to the Key Learning Community principal, the school's schedule "allows students to study all eight intelligences during the regular school day" (Key Learning Community, 2007). Interest in the work of the Key Learning Community has been widespread. The school hosts a formal visitors' program and annual summer institute which draw educators from across the United States and world interested in seeing the "world's first multiple intelligence school" in action.

If the Key Learning Community represents one of the earliest applications of MI theory, then Danfoss Universe represents one of the most ambitious. Danfoss Universe is a 10-acre science experience park that opened in Sonderberg, Denmark, in 2005. The park is divided into three parts: the outdoor park, a museum, and the Explorama. The Explorama is a museum-sized building with more than 50 different activities designed to teach visitors about their various intelligences (Danfoss Universe, 2007). For example, an intrapersonal exhibit called Mindball challenges contestants to lower their own stress levels deliberately; if they can do so, an electrode headband converts this reduction in stress into a force that can propel a ping pong ball into the orbit of the opponent. An exhibit on musical intelligence enables participants to create their own melodies on a theremin, one of the earliest electronic musical instruments. Finally, an exhibit on linguistic intelligence gives participants the opportunity to practice a few Japanese words and then examine a visual representation of their vocalization superimposed over that of a native Japanese speaker. Through trial and error, participants can improve their tone and pronunciation. With these and many other exhibits, Danfoss Universe encourages visitors to the Explorama to reflect upon their own profiles of intelligence. Moreover, in a subsequent addition, visitors have a chance to predict their performances on the various activities. At the end of their visit, they can compare their predictions with the actual outcome—another, quite veridical measure of intrapersonal intelligence.

RESEARCH ON MI THEORY

Since the late 1970s, numerous researchers have investigated the influence of MI theory. Here, two such studies are particularly notable, though in very different ways. Project Spectrum was a 10-year study conducted from 1984 to 1993 that sought to identify intellectual strengths in young children and then investigate the impact of an MI-based intervention program on first grade students at risk for school failure. As part of this study, both teachers and researchers observed at-risk first graders over the course of the school year as they participated in learning center activities designed to assess the absolute and relative strengths of the eight intelligences. From this study, Chen and Gardner (2005) report that "At-risk students, although they often perform poorly in traditional academic areas, are not necessarily low performers in all areas of learning" (p. 90). Chen and Gardner (2005) further report that identifying and nurturing these at-risk children's strengths led to statistically significant increases in these children's self-direction, self-confidence, positive classroom behavior, positive affect, self-monitoring, and active engagement. In short, then, it seems that using MI theory to identify children's profiles of intelligence and relative strengths can play a role in deepening these children's engagement and academic achievement.

A second study, the Project on Schools Using Multiple Intelligences Theory (SUMIT), was a three-year national study conducted from 1997 to 2000 that involved site visits, data analysis, and interviews with teachers at 41 schools that employed MI theory in some capacity. From this study, Kornhaber, Fierros and Veneema (2004) report that, after drawing upon MI theory, 78% of the schools in their study reported improved standardized test scores; 78% reported improved academic performance by students with learning difficulties; and 81% reported improvements in student discipline. More than half of these schools attributed these improvements to the implementation of curriculum and practices inspired by MI theory. Both Project Spectrum and Project SUMIT, then, seem to offer clear evidence of the promise that multiple intelligences theory holds for educators, schools, student performance, and school culture.

Part of the landscape in psychology and education since the early 1980s, MI theory has demonstrated considerable staying power. Its fate within psychology is likely to depend less on further tinkering with psychometric instruments and more on the convergence of evidence from neuroscience and genetics. These ongoing lines of research will indicate whether intellect is in fact pluralistic and, if so, whether the delineation suggested by Gardner comports with emerging data. Within education, MI theory promises to continue to appeal to teachers whose daily experience supports a view of young persons as having quite individual profiles of intellectual strengths and weaknesses. Whether the policies supported by governments will honor these individual differences or seek to ignore or reduce them through the administration of standard curricula and assessments remains to be seen.

SEE ALSO *Gardner, Howard.*

BIBLIOGRAPHY

Binet. A., & Simon, T. (1916). *The development of intelligence in children.* Baltimore, Williams & Wilkins. (Reprinted 1973, New York: Arno Press; 1983, Salem, NH: Ayer Company).

Boring, E. G. (1923, June 6). Intelligence as the tests test. *New Republic.* 35: 35-37.

Chen, J.-Q., & Gardner, H. (2005). Multiple Intelligences: Assessment based on multiple-intelligence theory. pp. 105-121. In D. Flanagan & P. Harrison (Eds.), *Contemporary intellectual assessment: theories, tests and issues.* New York: Guilford Press.

Danfoss universe. (2007). Retrieved April 16, 2008, from http://www.danfossuniverse.com.

Gardner, H. (1983). *Frames of mind: The theory of multiple intelligences.* New York: Basic Books.

Gardner, H. (1998). A multiplicity of intelligences. *Scientific American Presents: Exploring Intelligence, 9*(4), 19-23.

Gardner, H. (1999). *Intelligence reframed: Multiple intelligences for the 21st century.* New York: Basic Books.

Gardner, H. (2006). *Multiple intelligences: New horizons.* New York: Basic Books.

Key learning community. (2007). Retrieved April 16, 2008, from http://www.616.ips.k12.in.us.

Kornhaber, M., Fierros, E., & Veneema, S. (2004). *Multiple intelligences: Best ideas from research and practice.* Boston: Pearson Education.

Spearman, C. (1904). General intelligence, objectively determined and measured. *American Journal of Psychology, 15,* 201–293.

Terman, L. (1916). *The measurement of intelligence: An explanation of and complete guide for the use of the Stanford revision and extension of the Binet-Simon scale.* Boston: Houghton Mifflin.

Thorndike, E.L (1927). *The measurement of intelligence.* New York: Bureau of Publications, Teachers College.

Thurstone, L. L. (1938). *Primary mental abilities.* Chicago: University of Chicago Press.

Scott Seider
Howard Gardner

N

NEO-PIAGETIAN THEORIES OF DEVELOPMENT

In his 1992 review of Jean Piaget's theory, Harry Beilin compared its influence on the study of cognitive development to that of Shakespeare on English literature. Any theorist who has studied cognitive development in children from the middle of the twentieth century onward has been a neo-Piagetian in that broad sense. However, the subject of this entry is a smaller group of researchers who have called themselves neo-Piagetians. Because the *neo-* label directs attention back to a theory's origins, most neo-Piagetian researchers eventually chose other names that focused on their theories' new elements. Thus Kurt Fischer's neo-Piagetian theory became known as skill theory (Fischer & Pipp, 1984; Schwartz & Fischer, 2004) and Robbie Case's evolved into central conceptual structure theory (Griffin, 2004).

HOW NEO-PIAGETIAN THEORIES DIFFER FROM PIAGET'S THEORY

Neo-Piagetian theorists kept Piaget's idea that the progress of cognitive development is more like climbing a series of stairs (the stages) than walking smoothly up a ramp. They also agreed with Piaget that biological maturation sets broad upper limits on the kinds of thinking children are capable of doing at particular ages. All of the neo-Piagetians also shared Piaget's conviction that children's thinking reflects their developing internal mental structures (Case & Okamoto, 1996). However, each of the neo-Piagetians combined this general premise with ideas about the influence of experience on development

that were more analytically specific and more attuned to cultural and individual differences than anything found in Piaget's theory. For example, they considered how biological maturation of the central nervous system during the first years of life increases the speed with which children process information—an idea introduced in 1970 by Pascual-Leone. The neo-Piagetians linked that maturing processing speed to increases in working memory capacity that, in turn, set upper limits on the complexity of problems a child is likely to be able to solve.

The neo-Piagetians also have drawn on information-processing and linguistic theorists' ideas about the content-domain specificity of cognition. Piaget's theory evolved to include provisions for unevenness in the sophistication of a child's reasoning across different kinds of problems, but this domain specificity is more fundamental to neo-Piagetian theories. The influence of the information-processing paradigm also is evident in the neo-Piagetians' tendency to analyze Piaget's and other cognitive tasks in ways that highlight why one problem may be more or less difficult than another, even within the same content domain. Australian neo-Piagetian Graeme Halford (Andrews & Halford, 2002) became especially well known for his focus on this kind of task analysis.

The neo-Piagetians also adopted principles from social-cognitive theories such as that of Lev Vygotsky. These principles allowed them to give more extensive consideration than can be found in Piaget's work regarding how culturally determined experiences and minute-by-minute interactions with teachers and peers influence a child's intellectual performance. Although biology sets upper limits on performance, a child's culture and everyday

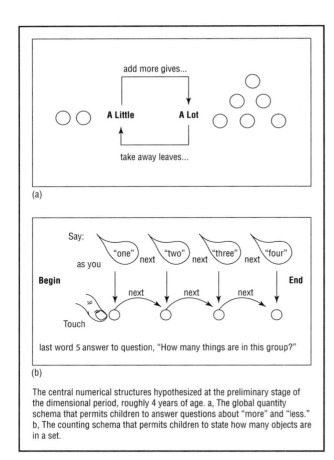

The central numerical structures hypothesized at the preliminary stage of the dimensional period, roughly 4 years of age. a, The global quantity schema that permits children to answer questions about "more" and "less." b, The counting schema that permits children to state how many objects are in a set.

Figure 1 ILLUSTRATION BY GGS INFORMATION SERVICES. CENGAGE LEARNING, GALE.

experience might not provide the information and practice needed for development up to that limit. Neo-Piagetian theories include mechanisms to account for cultural and socio-economic differences in patterns or rates of cognitive development. These theories also are compatible with the idea that individual children differ in their ability to absorb the experiences available in their culture.

With their joint consideration of biology, the precise requirements for doing a task, and the contributions of experience, the neo-Piagetian theorists have elaborated on possible mechanisms of developmental change, the *how* of development that was only sketched in very general terms by Piaget (Case, 1984; Case, 1996; Griffin, 2004; Schwartz & Fischer, 1994).

The neo-Piagetians' interests in mechanisms of development and in optimizing learning offer educators more explicit guidance than is available in Piaget's theory. A number of neo-Piagetians have proposed theories with relevance for classroom practices. However, Canadian psychologist Robbie Case (1945–2000) prob-

ably is the neo-Piagetian whose work has had the most influence on education.

OVERVIEW OF CASE'S THEORY

Case might be considered the quintessential neo-Piagetian researcher because he dedicated his own theorizing and research efforts to working explicitly within the historical framework of Piaget's ideas. However, Case tried to remedy some of the deficiencies in Piaget's theory by incorporating ideas and methods from other traditions, especially Vygotsky's social-constructivist theory, information-processing theories, linguistics, and new findings in developmental neuroscience (Case, 1996).

Like Piaget's own grand theory, Case's neo-Piagetian theory is hard to summarize because it developed—changing substantially across the span of Case's own research career and with work that his colleagues continued after his death. In his early work, Case focused on the broad implications of central processing speed and working memory span (e.g., Case, Kurland, & Goldberg, 1982). These ideas were retained in later versions of the theory, but there was more attention to the nature and development of children's mental representations in each of several cognitive domains—the central conceptual structures. In a 1996 monograph, Case and his colleagues investigated central conceptual structures underlying reasoning about number, space, and narrative (Case, 1996). All of these structures were described as going through stages that were labeled pre-dimensional, unidimensional, bidimensional, and integrated bidimensional and that characterized children's thought at about ages 4, 6, 8, and 10 years. Figures 1 and 2 show the central conceptual structures for number hypothesized to be characteristic of middle-class children in a technological society at about age 4 years (Figure 1) and at about age 6 years (Figure 2). Figure 1 shows that typical 4-year-olds, who are in the pre-dimensional stage, have not yet coordinated two ideas about number—the idea of comparisons between smaller and larger quantities and the idea of counting off a set of objects, saying number names in sequence. In contrast, typical 6-year-olds (Figure 2) have a unidimensional central numerical structure that coordinates several ideas along a number line that they can use to do a variety of arithmetic reasoning tasks.

Case and his colleagues (Case, 1996) also described how a sequence of increasingly complete and coherent central conceptual structures might organize children's developing reasoning in other content domains besides number. Although these domain-limited structures were expected to develop more or less in synchrony because they were all affected by common biological limits, the content of each structure also was expected to be influenced by

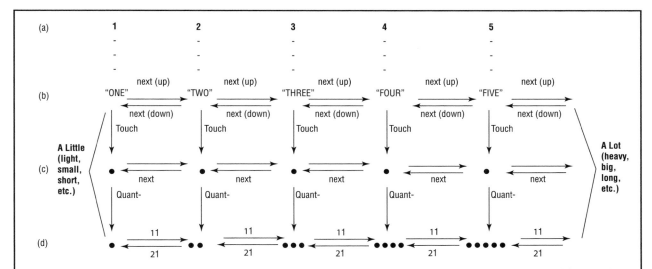

The central numerical structure (the "mental number line") hypothesized to emerge at around 6 years as a result of the elaboration and merging of the two earlier schemas shown in Fig. 1 above. The four rows indicate, respectively, (a) knowledge of written numerals, (b) knowledge of number words, (c) a pointing routine for "tagging" objects while counting, and (d) knowledge of cardinal set values. The vertical arrows indicate the knowledge that each row maps conceptually on to the next; the horizontal arrows indicate an understanding of the relation between adjacent items. The external brackets indicate the knowledge that the entire structure can be used as a vehicle for determining the relative amount of quantities composed of identical units (weight, height, length, etc.).

Figure 2 ILLUSTRATION BY GGS INFORMATION SERVICES. CENGAGE LEARNING, GALE.

cultural and individual experience, which gave them some independence from one another.

The idea that biological maturation limits the speed with which a child of a given age is likely to be able to process information, or think, is central to Case's interpretation of development. With increasing age, the child's neurons become more extensively coated with a fatty myelin sheath, which speeds transmission of information along the nerve fiber. Another key change with age is that the pattern of connections among the nerve cells in the brain becomes better specialized—unneeded connections drop out and important ones are strengthened with a combination of time and experience. Because older children can think faster than younger children, they can keep more concepts in mind at the same time. Case and his colleagues first demonstrated the link between thinking speed and memory span in a study of counting speed and memory for digits (Case et al., 1982). The principle extends far beyond arithmetic. In any content domain, familiarity and practice can help children process information more quickly and solve more complex problems. However, chronological age and biological maturation set limits on how much can be achieved with practice.

In Case's theory, one of children's developing mental structures is devoted to the representation of space. These spatial structures are reflected in children's drawings, which become increasingly organized along multiple spatial axes as children grown older. A 4-year-old's figure is likely to be floating in space, but a 6-year-old's drawing of a person usually stands on a ground line and may be accompanied by other objects, such as an animal or tree, arrayed along the same horizontal axis. Dealing with the vertical and depth dimensions comes later, and it is not until age 10 years or more that children coordinate all of these dimensions well. Even precociously talented young artists are not likely to represent spatial axes in a way much beyond that typical of their chronological age, although their drawings of each figure may be beautifully detailed and realistic (Case & Okamoto, 1996). Thinking in a coordinated way about multiple dimensions of space also is important in playing games such as checkers, in reading or drawing maps, and in making scientific judgments about relations within a series of objects (Case, 1996).

The ways in which culture might influence the separate development of various central conceptual structures was illustrated dramatically in a study comparing children who had experienced Western technological culture and schooling with those who had not. Case's colleague Fiati found that children who were living in isolated rural villages in the Volta region of central Africa and who had not experienced any Western-style schooling, performed at the same levels as urban children their age on tasks involving the coordination of ideas in a story, a task hypothesized to

ROBBIE CASE

Canadian psychologist Thomas Robert "Robbie" Case was born in Barrie, Ontario, in 1944. After earning a B.Sc. in psychology from McGill University in 1965, he taught high school English and physics in a kibbutz in Israel for a year. Case received his M.A. (1968) and Ph.D. (1971) in education from the University of Toronto's Ontario Institute for Studies in Education (OISE). He was a professor at the University of California-Berkeley and at Stanford before becoming director of the University of Toronto Institute of Child Study, where he remained until his death in 2000.

Case's research centered on child cognitive development, exploring the development of young children's thinking patterns, aiming to improve how special needs and impoverished students learned. He included Piagetian theories with his findings to create most advantageous instruction for these students, especially in math. Just before his death, Case began to apply his findings about children to civilizations, working with social scientist Tom Rohlen.

Case contributed chapters to numerous books and wrote many theses, grants, and journal articles, as well as *Intellectual Development: Birth to Adulthood* (1985) and *The Mind's Staircase* (1992). He also served as a consulting reviewer for several editorial boards.

Heidi H. Denler

depend on Case's central conceptual structure for narrative. This showed that there was nothing generally wrong with the children's ability to do complex thinking. However, life in the village had offered very little experience with numerical tasks, and the children's performance on tasks involving Case's central conceptual structure for numbers (see Figure 1) was immature. In less extreme cross-cultural comparisons, Case and his colleagues found that central conceptual structures developed at about the same rate for children in the United States, Canada, China, and Japan. However, socio-economic differences within a culture could be associated with large differences in developmental rate (Case, 1996; Case, Griffin, & Kelly, 2001).

EDUCATIONAL APPLICATIONS OF CASE'S THEORY

Although some of Case's early theorizing concerned development in infancy and the toddler years (Case,

1985), much of his work was concerned with how children's thinking changes between about age 4 and age 10 or so (Case, 1996). This makes his work especially relevant for educators working with children in preschool and elementary school.

A major implication of Case's work, consistent with the implications of information-processing theories, is that young children should not be expected to think about too many new ideas at once. For example, typical 6-year-olds are much more likely to give the correct answer to the problem "6 + 2 = ?" than they are to the related problem "6 + ? = 8", which is expressed with a missing addend. To solve a missing addend problem, a child needs to understand several unfamiliar symbols. Case (1978) found that children were more successful with missing addend problems if they were gradually introduced to the non-numerical elements of an equation before doing the arithmetic. Throughout his career, Case was concerned with analyzing exactly what a child needed to know and manipulate in order to solve common school problems and with how age and cultural experience may have left some children unable to meet classroom expectations (Case, Griffin, & Kelly, 2001).

When everyday experience has not helped children develop a particular kind of central conceptual structure, carefully planned instruction has been shown to help children catch up. One of Case's colleagues, Sharon Griffin, developed a compensatory education program for first graders from low-income families that she called Rightstart (Griffin, 2004; Griffin, Case, & Siegler, 1994). The goal of this program was to give these children lessons that would fill in gaps in their central conceptual structure for numbers (Figure 2). Children in the program and those in a control group were pre- and posttested using exams containing items influenced by Case's theory, and those who had been in the Rightstart program did better on the posttest.

Case's theory also has contributed to the design of more effective instruction on problems that are likely to be difficult for all children, regardless of their family background, such as understanding rational numbers. Rational numbers are percentages, decimals, and fractions. These topics usually are introduced in the late elementary years and often are not mastered fully even by adults. Moss and Case (1999) found that fourth graders achieved a deeper understanding of rational numbers in a curriculum that focused on step-by-step teaching of a conceptual structure for these numbers. The curriculum started with percentages, using exercises that involved observing and manipulating liquids in beakers and other objects that were partly full. Discussion at this point was all in terms of percentages. Then children were introduced to decimal notation using large number lines on the floor, and links between decimal fractions and percentages were emphasized. Finally, traditional fractional notation was taught and linked with the other two forms of rational number notation. Children who experienced this curriculum had a deeper understanding of rational numbers than children in a control group.

SEE ALSO *Information Processing Theory; Piaget, Jean; Vygotsky, Lev Semenovich.*

BIBLIOGRAPHY

Andrews, G., & Halford, G. S. (2002). A complexity metric applied to cognitive development. *Cognitive Psychology, 45,* 153–219.

Beilin, H. (1992). Piaget's enduring contribution to developmental psychology. *Developmental Psychology, 28,* 191–204.

Case, R. (1978). Intellectual development from birth to adulthood: A neo-Piagetian approach. In R. S. Siegler (Ed.), *Children's thinking: What develops?* Hillsdale, NJ: Erlbaum.

Case, R. (1984). The process of stage transition: A neo-Piagetian view. In R. J. Sternberg (Ed.), *Mechanisms of cognitive development* (pp. 19–44). New York: W. H. Freeman.

Case, R. (1985). *Intellectual development: Birth to adulthood.* New York: Academic Press.

Case, R. (1996). Introduction: Reconceptualizing the nature of children's conceptual structures and their development in middle childhood. In R. Case & Y. Okamoto, *The role of central conceptual structures in the development of children's thought.* Monographs of the Society for Research in Child Development (pp. 1–26), Serial No. 246, Vol. 6.

Case, R., Griffin, S., & Kelly, W. M. (2001). Socioeconomic differences in children's early cognitive development and their readiness for schooling. In S. L. Golbeck (Ed.), *Psychological perspectives on early childhood education: Reframing dilemmas in research and practice* (pp. 37–63). Mahwah, NJ: Erlbaum.

Case, R., Kurland, D. M., & Goldberg, J. (1982). Operational efficiency and the growth of short-term memory span. *Journal of Experimental Child Psychology, 33,* 386–404.

Fiati, T. A. (1992). Cross-cultural variation in the structure of children's thought. In R. Case, *The mind's staircase: Exploring the conceptual underpinnings of children's thought and knowledge* (pp. 319–342). Hillsdale, NJ: Erlbaum.

Fischer, K. L., & Pipp, S. L. (1984). Processes of cognitive development: Optimal level and skill acquisition. In R. J. Sternberg (Ed.), *Mechanisms of cognitive development* (pp. 45–80). New York: W. H. Freeman.

Griffin, S. (2004). Contributions of central conceptual structure theory to education. In A. Demetriou and A. Raftopoulos (Eds.), *Cognitive developmental change: Theories, models, and measurement* (pp. 264–295). Cambridge, UK: Cambridge University Press.

Griffin, S., Case, R., & Siegler, R. S. (1994). Rightstart: Providing the central conceptual prerequisites for first formal learning of arithmetic to students at risk for school failure. In K. McGilly (Ed.), *Classroom lessons: Integrating cognitive theory and classroom practice* (pp. 25–49). Cambridge, MA: MIT Press.

Moss, J., & Case, R. (1999). Developing children's understanding of the rational numbers: A new model and an experimental curriculum. *Journal for Research in Mathematics Education, 30,* 122–147.

Pascual-Leone, J. (1970). A mathematical model for the transition rule in Piaget's developmental stages. *Acta Psychologica, 32,* 301–345.

Schwartz, M., & Fischer, K. W. (2004). Building general knowledge and skill: Cognition and microdevelopment in science learning. In A. Demetriou & A. Raftopoulos (Eds.), *Cognitive developmental change: Theories, models, and measurement* (pp. 157–185). Cambridge, UK: Cambridge University Press.

Vygotsky, L. S. (1978). *Mind in society: The development of higher psychological processes.* Cambridge, MA: Harvard University Press.

Nancy Ewald Jackson

NORM-REFERENCED SCORING

Norm-referenced scoring is the process of comparing one person's score relative to a group in order to determine the relative standing of that person to the group in the area being testing (Thorndike, 2005). It is comparing one's score relative to the performance of others. Norm-referenced scoring is then a system of rank ordering and a way to give meaning to raw scores. Raw norm-referenced scoring does not indicate mastery and/or competency of skills. The group being compared against in norm-referenced scoring is termed the normative group or normative sample. The normative group should be representative of the person that is being compared against it (i.e., gender, race, geographical region, age, acculturation, language) in order for the scores to be meaningful.

Several key factors should be considered before using a norm-referenced assessment. One important factor is that the norming is recent, meaning that the sample that was used to collect the data is relatively recent. A good rule is to make sure that the norming data is no more than 10 years old. Also the normative groups should have been fairly large. Other important factors to consider are the reliability and validity of the scores that are given. Reliability refers to precision of scores. A highly reliable score is one which the tested person would achieve again if the same test were given a second time. Validity refers to the idea that the score is truly measuring what it purports to measure. Reliability and validity are reported in a range from zero to one. The closer to one the reported number is, the more reliable and valid the measure.

Norm-referenced scores are derived scores that can be reported in multiple forms. Raw scores (the actual number of items answered correctly) are not reported in norm-referenced scoring but are instead used to derive all other types of scores that can be reported. Norm-referenced scores can be reported in either a developmental format or a relative standing format. Both formats have strengths and weaknesses associated with them.

DEVELOPMENTAL SCORES

Developmental scores are ordinal scores, ordered from best to worst or worst to least in which adjacent values indicate a higher or lower value (Thorndike, 2005). There are two forms of developmental scores: age-equivalent or grade equivalent. The norms in these forms are then the average raw score of a particular age or grade indicated in the norm sample. For example, when using age-equivalents, an age equivalent of 12 would have been calculated in the norm sample by averaging all raw scores obtained by 12-year-olds. This calculation works in the same manner for grade equivalents. To say that a child is scoring at the third grade level indicates that a child obtained a raw score that was equivalent to the average raw score of third graders in the normative group. This statement does not, however, indicate in which way the score was obtained. The questions answered correctly by the person may be different from which questions were answered correctly in the norm sample. There is not an equal interval between scores. Age and grade equivalent scores have the advantage of seeming to be easily interpretable. A person's level of performance is compared to familiar milestones of age or education, which makes them easily explainable to a person with limited knowledge of score interpretation. For example, it is easy for a teacher to tell parents that their child is reading at a third grade level.

There are several drawbacks, though. Typically in the norm sample, representation of every month in school or every age is not possible. For example, the norm sample may have included students in grade 2.0, 3.0, and 4.0. The average raw score is easily obtained for those grades. But raw scores that fall in between these levels have to be translated into grade equivalents. Therefore, if a raw score of 30 indicated a grade equivalent of 2.0, and a raw score of 38 indicated a grade equivalent of 3.0, the raw scores of 31 to 37 have to be interpolated (assigned arithmetically to grades between or inside those tested (Thorndike, 2005). Not all grade or age equivalents may be assigned a raw score and there may not be equal intervals between scores or equal growth between years. For example, a raw score of 35 may translate into an age-equivalent of 7 years, a raw score of 36 may translate into an age-equivalent of 7 years, 1 month, and a raw score of 38 may translate in to an age-equivalent of 7 years, 8 months. Also, there may be possible raw scores that fall outside average raw scores obtained in the norm sample, which would then require extrapolation (arithmetically calculating outside the range tested) for those raw scores. For example, Test A has raw scores possible from 0 to 40. Grades 3.0 to 6.0 were included in the norm sample, and a raw score of 34 was the average for a sixth grader. The raw score of 40 falls outside the norm sample and would be calculated to be a grade equivalent greater than 6.0. Another important consideration with grade and age equivalents is whether there is meaning in assigning this type of score. For example, in most cases these types of score lose meaning in high school subject matter assessments. If a student is able to take biology in any grade of high school, it would not make sense then to administer a biology test and then to tell a student that he or she performed at, for example, a ninth grade equivalent.

SCORES OF RELATIVE STANDING

Scores of relative standing can also be broken into several formats: standard scores, scaled scores, and percentiles. These types of scores are useful for interpreting scores when grade or age is not a concern. Standard scores represent deviations (or the scatter of individual scores in the norm group) from the mean (Thorndike, 2005). Standard scores are considered to be at equal intervals; the difference between two points is the same throughout the scale. Standard scales are useful when the norm group is distributed among all scores possible. The standard score may be reported as a z-score, where the mean (or average) raw score is transformed to equal zero. Fifty percent of all scores will then fall above zero and 50% will fall below zero. This type of score is often complicated because raw scores may indicate a negative standard score. To help with this problem, standard scores are typically converted into other scaling systems which are easily comparable and retain the same properties. For example, the average IQ standard score of 100 is equivalent to a z-score of zero. A scaled score is a standard score that has been converted to a mean of 10 with a standard deviation of three.

Percentile equivalents are also directly comparable to standard scores. A percentile is the percentage of people in the norm group that the test taker performed as well as or better than (Thorndike, 2005). For example, a percentile score of 67 would indicate that a person performed as well or better than 67 percent of the norm sample. Percentile scores have one crucial difference from the scaled scores. Percentiles are not in an equal interval format. There is smaller variation in the percentiles nearer the mean and larger variation in the percentiles further from the mean. For example, there is little difference in raw scores that equate to percentile ranking of 50 or 55, whereas there is typically a great difference between the raw scores that compute to percentile rankings of 90 and 95.

Overall normative scoring is useful for making comparisons of performance against a similar group but not useful for determining mastery of content.

SEE ALSO *Criterion-Referenced Tests; Standardized Testing.*

BIBLIOGRAPHY
Thorndike, R. M. (2005). *Measurement and evaluation in psychology and education.* Upper Saddle River, NJ: Prentice Hall.

Krista Healy

NORM-REFERENCED TESTING

Norm-referenced testing is integral to the practice of psychological and educational testing. Originated in the work of modern statistics, this assessment method assumes that human traits and characteristics, such as intelligence, academic achievement, and behavior, are distributed along a normal probability or bell-shaped curve (hereafter, referred to as the normal curve). The normal curve represents the norm or average performance of a population and the scores that are above and below the average within that population. The norms for a test include percentile ranks, standard scores, and other statistics for the norm group on which the test was standardized. A certain percentage of the norm group falls within various ranges along the normal curve. Depending on the range within which test scores fall, scores correspond to various descriptors ranging from deficient to superior.

A Norm-Referenced Test (NRT) compares an examinee's test performance to those of the examinee's same-age peers from the test's norm group. This comparison permits a more meaningful interpretation of the individual's score. An examinee's test score is compared to that of a norm group by converting the examinee's raw scores into derived or scale scores. As shown in Figure 1, derived scores correspond to the normal curve, thus providing an interpretive framework for examinees administered the NRT. The norm group can consist of a larger population, such as a representative population of children from the United States (i.e., a national norm group), or it can consist of a smaller, more limited population, such as all children in an individual school or school district (i.e., a local norm group).

DERIVED SCORES

The conversion of examinees' raw scores into derived scores provides a system of common metrics that facilitate test interpretation. There are multiple derived scores reported for NRTs; however, the more common ones used for interpretive purposes are standard scores, standard deviations, scale scores, T-scores, percentile ranks, age-equivalent scores, and grade-equivalent scores. A standard score has a statistical mean or average of 100

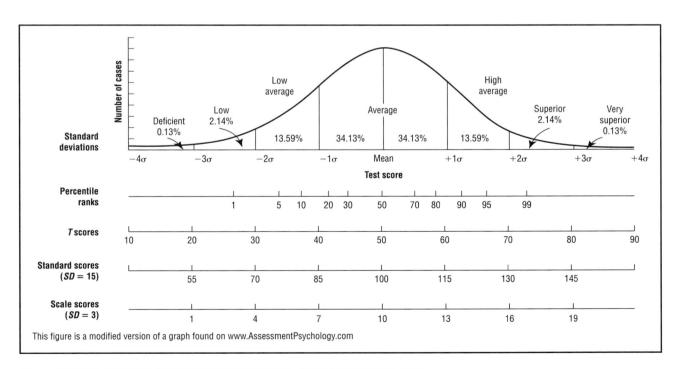

Figure 1 ILLUSTRATION BY GGS INFORMATION SERVICES. CENGAGE LEARNING, GALE.

and conveys how far an examinee's test score varies or deviates from the average of the distribution. The extent to which a score varies or deviates from the average is expressed as a standard deviation. For example, a standard score of 115 on a NRT, such as an intelligence quotient (IQ) test, is one standard deviation above the mean of 100 and falls within the High Average range.

Scale scores yield information about an examinee's performance on a sub-domain or subtest of a NRT. These scores have a mean or average of 10 and a standard deviation of 3 points. Therefore, a scale score of 7 on a NRT subtest indicates that the examinee's skill, as measured by the subtest, is one standard deviation below the mean of 10 and corresponds to the Low Average range. T-scores are a different distribution of standard scores in that the mean of the distribution is 50 with a standard deviation of 10 points. NRTs assessing behavior typically report T-scores. Consequently, a T-score of 60 on a behavior rating scale is one standard deviation above the mean of 50 and corresponds to the High Average/ At-Risk range. Percentile ranks indicate an examinee's position relative to the norm group. A percentile rank is a point in the distribution at or below which a certain percentage of scores falls. A child obtaining a percentile rank of 85 on an intelligence test indicates that the child's performance is equal to or greater than 85 percent of the child's same-age peers in the test's norm group. It does not mean the child obtained 85 percent of items correct on the NRT.

Grade- and age-equivalent scores are two of the most commonly used scores to report test results, yet they are also commonly misunderstood. These scores indicate that a student has attained the same raw scores (or number of items correct) as the average student of a certain grade or age level in the test's norm group. For example, if a student obtains a grade-equivalent score of 4.5 on a test of basic reading skills, this means the student obtained the same raw score as the average student in the fifth month of the fourth grade in the test's norm group. It does not mean the student acquired or demonstrated the same level of proficiency consistent with curricular expectations as the average student in the fifth month of the fourth grade at the student's school. Likewise, if a student obtains an age-equivalent score of 8.0 years on a test of basic reading skills, this means the student obtained the same raw score as the average 8-year-old student in the test's norm group. It does not mean the student acquired or demonstrated the same level of proficiency consistent with curricular expectations as the average 8-year-old student in the student's school. Consequently, grade and age-equivalent scores should not be interpreted literally. It is critical that test administrators and consumers understand the meaning and interpretation of these and other derived scores, as

misinterpretation can lead to serious consequences for the examinee, including possible misdiagnosis, misclassification, and/or inappropriate educational placement and services. Sattler and Lyman provide further, extensive information about these and other derived scores used for testing interpretive purposes.

Of note is the fact that NRTs are imperfect by nature. The scores yielded by NRTs are referred to as observed scores versus absolute or true scores. An observed score is one attained by an examinee, whereas a true score is one that is error-free and hypothetical in nature. For this reason, norm-referenced standard test scores have bands of error, which are expressed as either 90 percent or 95 percent confidence intervals. The 90 percent confidence interval indicates the range of standard scores within which an examinee's true score would fall 90 out of 100 times on repeated assessments. Likewise, the 95 percent confidence interval, a more conservative estimate, indicates the standard score range within which an examinee's true score would fall 95 out of 100 times on repeated assessments.

REVIEWING THE ADEQUACY OF A NORM GROUP

It is necessary to examine key characteristics of a test's norm group to ensure the adequacy of the norms, hence, the appropriateness of the test. Manuals that come with commercially developed tests should provide this information. According to Salvia and Ysseldyke, some of the important characteristics of a test's norm group are: a) the representativeness of the group, b) the number of individuals in the group, and c) the relationship of the norms to the purpose of testing. Adequate representation is dependent, in part, upon the demographic characteristics of the individuals in the norm sample, including their age, sex, race/ethnicity, parent education level, and geographic location. It is important that the sample of individuals in the norm group be proportioned across the aforementioned variables according to their prevalence in the reference population.

For example, the norm group of an intelligence test developed in the United States for children ages 6 years, 0 months to 16 years, 11 months, should include representative proportions of children within this age range according to selected demographic variables based on U.S. Bureau of the Census data. The age of the norms (i.e., the difference in time between the year in which the norm group was administered the test and the year an examinee is administered the test) is also a critical dimension when evaluating the representational aspect. In order for a norm group to be representative, it must be current. Reschly suggests that test norms older than 10 to 12 years may lead to inflated test scores, based on research indicating that intelligence in the general population increases at a rate of approximately three points per decade. The test consumer should be aware that the older the norm group is, hence, the older the test norms are, the less accurately the group and norms represent the current reference population.

The number of individuals comprising the norm group is also important because a large norm group assures reliability of the test as well as representation of outliers in the reference population. Salvia and Ysseldyke recommend that the norm group should contain at least 100 subjects per age or grade level. Also of crucial significance is the relationship of the norms to the purpose of testing. For example, if the purpose of testing is to determine how a child performed on a school district reading assessment, the norms developed for the district for that particular test administration would be the most appropriate reference of comparison. If the purpose is to ascertain how a child is performing intellectually, then the norms of a nationally standardized test of intelligence would be the most appropriate reference of comparison.

Finally, norms that include the performance of individuals with special needs are an important consideration for accurate representation, particularly when evaluating individuals for eligibility for special education services and program placement. To the extent that test norms are adequate, they allow for meaningful comparisons and accurate information about the population. The Standards for Educational and Psychological Testing (AERA et al., 1999) states: "Norms, if used, should refer to clearly described populations. These populations should include individuals or groups to whom test users will ordinarily wish to compare their own examinees" (p. 55). To this end, test users must determine the applicability of a test to any given individual or group.

STRENGTHS AND WEAKNESSES OF NORM-REFERENCED TESTS

Ornstein describes a number of strengths of NRTs, including but not limited to the following: a) they assume statistical rigor in that they are reliable (i.e., dependable and stable) and valid (i.e., measure what they are reported to measure); b) the quality of test items is generally high in that they are developed by test experts, pilot tested, and undergo revision prior to publication and use; and c) administration procedures are standardized and the test items are designed to rank examinees for the purpose of placing them in specific programs or instructional groups. Stewart and Kaminski report that local norms, based on the test performance of students from a specific locale, have the added advantage of providing meaningful information regarding average performance, for example, in a particular school or school district. These authors report many other advantages of using local norms, including

that they decrease the likelihood of bias in educational decision-making because a student's test performance is compared to other students whose demographic and background factors are similar. In addition, they afford school systems the opportunity to compare data on students' educational outcomes to instructional curricula to which students have already been exposed. Furthermore, local norms are useful in facilitating decisions such as identifying the educational needs of students, determining standards for student progress, and identifying and making decisions about students' eligibility for Chapter I, English as a Second Language, and academically gifted programs. Finally, these norms are useful for identifying students at risk for school failure.

The predominant criticism of NRTs is that their content is seldom aligned with curricular content taught in educational settings (with the exception of locally normed tests). Good and Salvia refer to the match between the items on a norm-referenced achievement test and the content taught in a curriculum as content validity. The underlying assumption of content validity is that the items on a NRT should correspond to the content of the curriculum taught in a classroom. Results of a NRT devoid of content validity make it difficult to determine effective interventions that are needed for a student experiencing academic and/or behavioral challenges. Also, NRTs do not allow for monitoring academic progress over an extended period of time; instead, they provide an index of achievement or performance in comparison to a norm group at one specific point in time. Furthermore, an underlying assumption of NRTs is that examinees have had opportunities to acquire skills and experiences comparable to those of examinees in the norm group.

If disparities exist between examinees and the norm group in terms of skills and experiences, the conclusions based on the examinee's test performance may be misleading. "When a child's general background experiences differ from those of the children on whom a test was standardized, then the use of the norms of that test as an index for evaluating that child's current performance or for predicting future performances may be inappropriate" (Salvia & Ysseldyke, 1991, p. 18). This potential problem is tied to the issue of cultural fairness, which has been the subject of significant consideration in test development and research. Essentially, no test is completely culturally fair. The responsibility for school practitioners is to ensure that a child's level of acculturation (i.e., the extent to which an individual has adjusted to the culture in which he or she lives) is considered when choosing a NRT. Flanagan & Ortiz have done extensive research on acculturation and language differences in the assessment of diverse children, and they provide in-depth information and guidelines on this topic.

With respect to limitations of local norms, Stewart and Kaminski cite misinterpretation as a primary disadvantage. Like the point made by Salvia and Ysseldyke, the group to whom a child's performance is compared should be well-defined (e.g., the age and grade of the students comprising the reference group as well as the size and stability of the group). Also, information about the measures administered to students as well as how the scores were derived should be provided. Stewart and Kaminski emphasize that the knowledge of how a student's performance in a particular subject area using local norms compares with that of their performance using national norms is quite significant. For example, a child may perform in the High Average tier of the local norm group in a particular subject area yet perform in the Below Average tier when tested on a nationally normed test in the same subject area. To report how the child performed only in relation to the local norms would be misleading.

THE STATUS OF NORM-REFERENCED TESTING

In part, due to the shortcomings of NRTs, other types of assessments are used to assess individuals' aptitudes and abilities. Such methods include Curriculum Based Measurement (CBM) as articulated by Shinn; the Dynamic Indicators of Basic Early Literacy Skills (DIBELS) as described by Good, Gruba, and Kaminski; and Curriculum Based Assessment (CBA) as described by Gravois and Gickling. Collectively, these methods use curriculum materials as the basis for assessing and monitoring students' academic progress. CBM and DIBELS assessment results are linked directly to instructional interventions, whereas CBA is used primarily to assess and modify a student's instructional environment for the purpose of placing the student in the most appropriate curriculum.

The Individuals with Disabilities Education Improvement Act passed in 2004 allowed states, for the first time, to use a student's response to scientific, research-based interventions as a basis for determining eligibility in the Specific Learning Disability (SLD) category of special education programs. This procedure, commonly referred to as Response to Intervention (RTI), is a significant shift from the traditional ability-achievement discrepancy model used in determining SLD eligibility. Although states have the option to continue using the ability-achievement discrepancy model, RTI, undoubtedly, will decrease the role of NRTs in qualifying students as learning disabled. Be that as it may, it is indisputable that NRTs facilitate meaningful comparisons between a student's test performance and that of the student's same-age peers in a test's norm group, and they will continue to be used and valued in the general education and special education arenas. It is also evident that CBA, DIBELS, CBM, and RTI procedures play a

significant role in instructional decision making and in the early 2000s were gaining an increasing role in special education eligibility decisions. Using a combination of these two assessment paradigms may well be the optimal solution for serving the educational needs of all children.

SEE ALSO *Standardized Testing.*

BIBLIOGRAPHY

American Educational Research Association, American Psychological Association, & the National Council on Measurement in Education (1999). *Standards for educational and psychological testing.* Washington, DC: American Educational Research Association.

Flanagan, D. P., & Ortiz, S.O. (2007). *Essentials of cross-battery assessment* (2nd ed.). New York: Wiley.

Good, R. H., Gruba, J., & Kaminski, R. A. (2002). Best practices in using Dynamic Indicators of Basic Early Literacy Skills (DIBELS) in an outcomes-driven model. In A. Thomas & J. Grimes (Eds.), *Best practices in school psychology IV* (pp. 699–720). Bethesda, MD: National Association of School Psychologists.

Good, R. H., & Salvia, J. (1988). Curriculum bias in published, norm-referenced reading tests: Demonstrable effects. *School Psychology Review, 17*(1), 51–60.

Gravois, T. A., & Gickling, E. E. (2002). Best practices in curriculum-based assessment. In A. Thomas & J. Grimes (Eds.), *Best practices in school psychology IV* (pp. 885–898). Bethesda, MD: National Association of School Psychologists.

Lyman, H. B. (1998). *Test scores and what they mean* (6th ed.). Boston: Allyn and Bacon.

Ornstein, A. C. (1993). Norm-referenced and criterion-referenced tests: An overview. *NASSP Bulletin, 77*(555), 28–39.

Reschly, D. J., Myers, T. G., & Hartel, C. R. (Eds.) (2002). *Mental retardation: Determining eligibility for social security benefits.* Washington, DC: National Academy Press.

Salvia, J., & Ysseldyke, J. E. (1991). *Assessment* (5th ed.). Boston: Houghton Mifflin.

Satter, J. M. (2001). *Assessment of children: Cognitive applications* (4th ed.). San Diego: Jerome M. Sattler.

Shinn, M. R. (2002). Best practices in using curriculum-based measurement in a problem-solving model. In A. Thomas & J. Grimes (Eds.), *Best practices in school psychology IV* (pp. 671–697). Bethesda, MD: National Association of School Psychologists.

Stewart, L. H., & Kaminski, R. (2002). Best practices in developing local norms for academic problem solving. In A. Thomas & J. Grimes (Eds.), *Best practices in school psychology IV* (pp. 737–752). Bethesda, MD: National Association of School Psychologists.

Harriett H. Ford

NORMAL DISTRIBUTION

The normal distribution is a widely used statistical tool. The normal distribution is often referred to as a *bell curve*, given its bell-type shape and perfect symmetry. The normal curve represents a distribution of individuals and generally indicates that most individuals are typical or normal on a particular measurement, but some individuals differ from that norm; as one moves further and further away from the center of the normal curve, individuals tend to exhibit characteristics that are more atypical of the norm. Normal distributions describe many phenomena. A normal distribution also is a fundamental mathematical assumption of many commonly used statistical techniques. The normal distribution can be used for many purposes, including calculating probabilities, examining students' performance on tests relative to the performance of other students, determining when certain students' scores are unusual or highly atypical, and deriving common metrics to compare students' scores across a variety of different assessments. The normal curve is the basis of many commonly used educational measures, including the SAT, the GRE, and many commonly used intelligence tests.

Many of the variables that are studied by educational researchers are assumed to come from a population of scores that are distributed normally. The normal distribution first was discussed by de Moivre in the 1700s; however, the normal distribution did not begin to be used as a statistical tool until mathematicians such as Pierre-Simon Laplace (1749–1827) and Carl Friedrich Gauss (1777–1855) began to study the distribution (Walker, 1934). The basic idea underlying the normal distribution is that as one examines large samples of individuals, the distribution of those individuals on many characteristics will often (but certainly not always) approximate a normal distribution. This is because most individuals will be typical or in the middle on the curve, whereas there will be fewer individuals who will be either extremely low or high on any given measure.

To start with a concrete example, image a distribution of SAT scores for first year students at a particular university. Most students will receive scores that are near the mean (and the median, and the mode), which would be displayed in the middle of a normal distribution. However, there are a few students who score extremely high (e.g., a perfect score of 800), and a few students who score extremely low on the SAT; those students' scores would be expressed at the extreme ends or *tails* of the normal distribution. This same type of curve would be evident for many other samples (e.g., the weight of bumblebees, the height of elephants, the number of barks emitted per day by pet dogs, IQ scores of third graders, etc.). In all of these cases, most measures will hover near a mean score, some will differ slightly from the mean, and there will always be a few cases that will be extremely low or high.

MEASURES USED TO ASSESS NORMALCY

Although the normal distribution is often what people expect to see, many distributions turn out not to look exactly like a perfect bell curve. There are a number of criteria that can be used to assess the normality of a curve. The criteria often provide information regarding how much a particular distribution differs from a normal distribution.

First, distributions can be skewed. A distribution is skewed when the mean of a sample differs from the median. When the mean exceeds the median, a distribution will be positively skewed, or skewed to the right; when the mean is less than the median, the distribution will be negatively skewed, or skewed to the left. A skewed distribution is one that contains extreme scores at either end of the distribution; this causes one tail of the curve to look as if it is stretched outward. For example, if a researcher examined a distribution of family income in a particular neighborhood where a billionaire lived, then the distribution would be positively skewed, because this one extremely high income would affect the shape of the distribution by literally *pulling* the distribution to the right by affecting the mean. Statisticians often indicate the level of skewness with a numerical value; a curve with a skewness of zero is a perfect normal distribution; in contrast, a curve with a skewness greater than or equal to $\pm$ 2.0 is quite highly skewed. A positive skewness value indicates that the distribution is skewed to the right (i.e., the mean is larger than the median), whereas a negative skewness value indicates that the distribution is skewed to the left (i.e., the mean is smaller than the median).

Second, distributions also can be described in terms of their kurtosis. The term *kurtosis* refers to how flat or peaked a curve is. In terms of kurtosis, the normal curve is mesokurtic (i.e., neither too peaked or flat). In contrast, distributions that are rather flat and have high standard deviations are referred to as platykurtic distribution, whereas distributions with a thin, tall center and a low standard deviation are referred to as leptokurtic distributions. A platykurtic distribution might occur when there is a large amount of variability in a measure (e.g., scores on an achievement test in a particular school vary greatly, from some very low scores to some average scores to some very high scores); in contrast, a leptokurtic distribution might occur when there is little variability in a measure (e.g., scores on an achievement test for most students in the school were all very close to each other, with little variability).

INTERPRETATIONS OF THE NORMAL CURVE

The normal curve is generally measured in standard deviation units, most commonly referred to as z-scores. The normal distribution has a mean z-score of zero and a standard deviation of 1.0. A z-score for any individual can be determined by subtracting the mean score of the distribution from the individual's specific score and then dividing by the standard deviation of the distribution.

One of the most interesting mathematical features of the normal curve is that the percentage of scores that fall within certain areas under the curve are consistent across all normal distributions. Mathematically, exactly 34.13% of the area under the normal curve falls between the middle of the curve (which is also the mean, median, and mode), and one standard deviation above the mean (or one z-score above the mean); similarly, exactly 34.13% of the area under the curve also falls between the middle of the curve and one standard deviation below the mean. The percentage of area under the curve decreases as the number of standard deviation units one moves away from the mean increases. Thus an additional 13.59% of the area under the curve falls between both +1 and +2 standard deviations above the mean, and -1 and -2 standard deviations below the mean; an additional 2.15% of the area under the normal curve falls between ± 2 and ±3 standard deviations above and below the mean (Sprinthall, 1997). The percentages of the area under the curve continue to remain identical on both the left and right-hand sides of the normal distribution as one proceeds up through higher standard deviations (z-scores). The exact percentage of area under the normal curve between any z-score and the mean can be determined by using a z-score table, which can be found in most introductory statistics text books.

Normal curves are also related to percentile scores, which are commonly used by many educational practitioners. This is particularly important, because educators often need to report and interpret individual students'

test scores for parents. A percentile is the point in a distribution below which a certain percentage of scores fall; thus a student who scored in the 60th percentile on an examination scored higher than 60% of the students who took that examination (this does not mean that the student correctly answered 60% of the questions on the examination). On a normal distribution, the 50th percentile corresponds with the middle of the curve, or a z-score of zero. When z-scores are positive, percentile measures will be above 50, whereas when z-scores are negative, percentile measures will be below 50.

Some other scores that are typically used in the field of education also can be expressed in terms of normal distributions. One of these is T scores, which have a mean of 50 and a standard deviation of 10; another is a stanine score, which divides the normal distribution into nine distinct units. Thus a mean T score (50) corresponds to the 50th percentile, to a z-score of zero, and to a stanine score of 5.

SEE ALSO *Standardized Testing.*

BIBLIOGRAPHY

De Moivre, A. D. (2000). *The Doctrine of Chances: A Method of Calculating the Probabilities of Events in Play.* New York: Chelsea. (Originally published in 1716)

Sprinthall, R. C. (1997). *Basic statistical analysis* (5th ed.). Needham Heights, MA: Allyn & Bacon.

Walker, H. M. (1934). Bi-Centenary of the Normal Curve. *Journal of the American Statistical Association, 29,* 72–75.

Eric M. Anderman

O

OBJECTIVE TEST ITEMS

An objective test item is defined as one for which the scoring rules are so exhaustive and specific that they do not allow scorers to make subjective inferences or judgments; thereby, any scorer that marks an item following the rules will assign the same test score. Objective tests began to be used early in the twentieth century as a means of evaluating learning outcomes and predicting future achievement, and their high reliability and predictive validity led to the gradual replacement of the essay test.

One common misconception about the objective test item is that it is limited to testing specific, often trivial, factual details, which would sometimes lead to the use of an essay or performance test to assess students' comprehension of broader principles or their ability to apply them. However, as Robert Ebel pointed out, well written objective tests (especially multiple choice tests) can actually assess such higher-order abilities to some extent. While it is true that some types of knowledge or abilities cannot be assessed by objective tests, educators also should keep in mind that what test items can assess depends largely on the skills and effort of the test constructor, rather the test format per se.

OBJECTIVE TEST FORMATS

A variety of different types of objective test formats can be classified into two categories: a selected response format, in which examinees select the response from a given number of alternatives, including true/false, multiple choice, and matching test items; and a constructed response format, in which examinees are required to produce an entire response, including short answer test items. This distinction is sometimes captured in terms of recognition and recall. These two general categories are further divided into basic types of objective tests, illustrated in the following examples (Figure 1).

The true/false test is the simplest form of selected response formats. True/false tests are those that ask examinees to select one of the two choices given as possible responses to a test question. The choice is between true and false, yes and no, right and wrong, and so on. A major advantage of the true/false test is its efficiency as it yields many independent responses per unit of testing time. Therefore, teachers can cover course material comprehensively in a single test. However, one apparent limitation of the true/false test is its susceptibility to guessing. It should be noted, however, that test givers can attenuate the effects of guessing by increasing the number of items in a test. In addition, some guessing might reflect partial knowledge, which would provide a valid indication of achievement.

Another selected response format type is the multiple-choice test, which has long been the most widely used among the objective test formats. Multiple-choice test items require the examinee to select one or more responses from a set of options (in most cases, 3–7). The correct alternative in each item is called the answer (or the key), and the remaining alternatives are called distracters. Examinees have less chance of guessing the correct answer to a multiple-choice test question compared to a true/false test question. In addition, the distracter an examinee selects may provide useful diagnostic information.

Related to the multiple-choice test is the matching test, which consists of a list of premises, a list of responses, and

---

Examples of objective test items

Letter symbols in parentheses indicate correct answers

True/false test item

(1) True/false items are those that ask examinees to supply a word, phrase, or number that answers a question or completes a sentence. (F)

Multiple-choice test item

(2) Which of the following situations will change the standardized regression coefficient in simple linear regression analysis? (C)

A The criterion variable is doubled.
B A constant value of 10 is added to the predictive variable.
C The predictive variable is squared.

Matching test item

(3) **Directions**: The first column below lists historical events. For each event, find the date it occurred on in the second column, and write the letter of the date on the line to the left of each event. Each date in the second column may be used once, more than once, or not at all.

(B) 1. Flight to Varennes   A. 1785–1789
(D) 2. Beginning of the First French Empire   B. 1790–1794
(C) 3. Coup of 18 Brumaire   C. 1794–1799
(A) 4. Attack on the Bastille prison   D. 1800–1804
(B) 5. Thermidorian Reaction

Short answer item

(4) What is the name of the capital city of Japan?   (Tokyo)

Figure 1 ILLUSTRATION BY GGS INFORMATION SERVICES. CENGAGE LEARNING, GALE.

---

directions for matching the two. Examinees must match each premise with one of the responses on the basis of the criteria described in the directions. A major strength of the matching test is that it is space-saving and, therefore, can be used to assess several important learning targets at once.

A typical example of a constructed-response format is the short-answer test, which asks examinees to supply a word, phrase, or number that answers a question or completes a sentence. Sometimes it is called a completion or fill-in-the-blank test. Although what a short-answer test item can assess is generally more limited to factual information, it does not require the development of plausible distracters. Moreover, short-answer items are much less susceptible to guessing than selected-response format items.

HOW TO CONSTRUCT OBJECTIVE TEST ITEMS

Basically, scoring objective test items is easy: It only requires one to follow the scoring rules. However, constructing good objective test items requires much more skill and effort. The first step is to develop a set of test specifications that can serve to guide the selection of test items. A table of specifications (or test blueprint) is a useful tool for this purpose. This tool is usually a two-way grid that describes content areas to be covered by the test as the row headings and skills and abilities to be developed (i.e., instructional objectives) as the column headings (Figure 2). After specifying the content and ability covered by the test using the

table of specifications, the appropriate test item format is selected for each item. At this point, not only objective test items but also other types of test items—essay test or performance assessment—should be considered, depending on the learning outcomes to be measured.

The next step is to create specific test items. Typically, it is particularly important for objective test items to be written in clear and unambiguous language to allow examinees to demonstrate their attainment of the learning objectives. If complex wording is used, the item simply reflects reading comprehension ability. It is also important for each objective test item to focus on an important aspect of the content area rather than trivial details. Asking trivial details not only makes the test items unnecessarily difficult, it also obscures what the test constructor really wants to measure. Similarly, relatively novel material should be used when creating items that measure understanding or the ability to apply principles. Items created by copying sentences verbatim from a textbook only reflect rote memory, rather than higher-order cognitive skills.

Many other specific rules exist for constructing objective test items. Test constructors must be very careful that examinees with little or no content knowledge cannot arrive at the correct answer by utilizing the characteristics of the test format that are independent of specific content knowledge. Jason Millman and his colleagues called this skill of the examinees "test-wiseness." For example, in multiple-choice test items, all options

An example table of specifications (test blue print)				
	Skills and abilities			
Content areas	Knowledge	Comprehension	Application, analysis, or synthesis	Total (%)
1. Univariate analysis: Central tendency and variability	3	2	1	6 (24)
2. Bivariate analysis: Correlation and regression analysis	2	3	3	8 (32)
3. Statistical hypothesis testing: Concepts, methods, and interpretation	1	3	2	6 (24)
4. Comparison of means: Paired t-test and analysis of variance (ANOVA)	1	2	2	5 (20)
Total (%)	7 (28)	10 (40)	8 (32)	25

Figure 2 ILLUSTRATION BY GGS INFORMATION SERVICES. CENGAGE LEARNING, GALE.

should be grammatically correct with respect to the stem (questions or incomplete statements preceding options), and key words from a stem, or their synonyms, should not be repeated in the correct option. Any violation of these rules would obviously provide an advantage for testwise examinees. Test composers should also equalize the length of the options of an item and avoid using specific determiners such as *all, always,* and *never* because some testwise examinees know that the correct option is frequently long and without such specific determiners. Robert Thorndike and Anthony Nitko have provided more comprehensive guidelines, with detailed explanations for constructing objective test items.

EFFECT OF OBJECTIVE TEST ITEMS ON TEACHING AND LEARNING

One common criticism of objective test items is that students are encouraged toward rote learning and other surface-processing strategies. Another related criticism is that objective tests, if used to evaluate the educational attainment of schools, encourage teachers to place undue emphasis on factual knowledge and disregard the understanding of students in the classrooms. Some evidence suggests that both are the case.

Kou Murayama, in a series of studies, investigated the effects of objective test items on the use of learning strategies. In one study, junior high school students participated in a history class for five days and took either an essay or short-answer test at the end of each day. Results showed that in the last day, those who took the short-answer tests used more rote learning strategies and fewer deep-processing strategies than those who took the essay tests. George Madaus reviewed much literature about the effects of standardized testing on what is taught at schools and found that teachers pay particular attention to the form of the questions and adjust their instruction accordingly, suggesting that objective tests could narrow instruction to the detriment of higher-order skills. Madaus argued that high-stakes tests—

tests that are used to make important decisions such as the ranking of schools—have much more influence on teaching.

However, educators should be reminded that objective test items are not limited to testing for specific factual knowledge. Well written items may not have such negative effects on students' use of learning strategies or teachers' teaching styles. Thus, it is not the objective test items per se that should be changed. What is important is to change the stereotypical beliefs that objective test items require only rote learning of factual knowledge and avoid poorly constructed objective test items.

SEE ALSO *Standardized Testing.*

BIBLIOGRAPHY

Ebel, R. L., & Frisbie, D. A. (1991). *Essentials of educational measurement* (5th ed.). Englewood Cliffs, NJ: Prentice Hall.

Madaus, G.. F. (1998). "The influence of testing on the curriculum." In L. N. Tanner (Ed.), *Critical issues in curriculum* (pp. 83–121). Chicago: University of Chicago Press.

Millman, J., Bishop, C. H., & Ebel, R. L. (1965): "An analysis of test-wiseness." *Educational and psychological measurement, 25*(3), 707–726.

Murayama, K. (2003). "Test format and learning strategy use." *Japanese Journal of Educational Psychology, 51*(1), 1–12.

Nitko, A. J. (2004). *Educational assessment of students* (4th ed.). Upper Saddle River, NJ: Merrill.

Thorndike, R. M. (1997). *Measurement and evaluation in psychology and education* (6th ed.). Upper Saddle River, NJ: Merrill.

Kou Murayama

OGBU, JOHN U(ZO)
1939–2003

John Uzo Ogbu was born in Nigeria on May 9, 1939. He earned a BA in anthropology at the University of California Berkeley in 1965, followed by an MA in 1969, and PhD in 1971. He taught at Berkeley from 1970 until his death on August 20, 2003. His most influential contribution to education is his cultural-ecological theory, a grand theory explaining why some groups tend to experience low academic achievement and others do not. This work responds to other explanations for low minority group achievement such as cultural mismatch.

Cultural mismatch (also referred to as cultural discontinuity or cultural differences) suggests that minority students experience low academic achievement because some aspects of their cultures—language, dialect, perception of time and space, attitude toward collectivism and individualism—do not match the school culture. This mismatch puts them at a disadvantage compared to students who share cultural background with school teachers, text books authors, and standardized test writers. If cultural mismatch is powerful, asked Ogbu, why do immigrant minority groups such as Punjabis and Chinese that experience cultural mismatch and discrimination show relatively high academic achievement?

To answer this question Ogbu distinguished voluntary and involuntary minorities. Voluntary minorities are those who come to a society of their own choice, often through immigration. Involuntary minorities are those who come to a society through enslavement, conquest, or colonization. Voluntary minorities do not experience persistent or pervasive low achievement, whereas involuntary (castelike) nonimmigrant minorities do. In the United States, Africans (like Ogbu) and Vietnamese are voluntary minorities, and African Americans and Native Americans are involuntary minorities. While Ogbu's theory focuses on Black academic disengagement and low achievement, it is intended as a theory of how voluntary and involuntary minorities fare in societies around the world.

According to his theory, involuntary immigrants experience a history of discrimination and prejudice that causes them to turn to each other in collective identity. If they know that they cannot turn to the dominant culture for help or support, they become more dependent upon and supportive of other members of their group. As they experience this fictive kinship, they also experience oppositional collective identity in which they reject behaviors and activities that represent the dominant, oppressor group. This pattern has been labeled "fear of acting White." Ogbu helped popularize, but did not invent, this label in an article that he co-authored with Signithia Fordham. According to Fordham and Ogbu, attitudes and behaviors that mark acting White include speaking standard English, listening to White music such as rock and roll or classical music, working hard in school, and getting good grades, which means students may actively undermine their own achievement in order to show solidarity with their group and to avoid feeling not truly Black.

Ogbu's theory has generated considerable research, commentary, and criticism. Criticisms include lack of attention to social class and gender, misuse of the term *caste*, and misconceptions regarding the social construction of race. Perhaps of most interest to educators, it has been criticized for blaming the victim. For example, in his last book (2003), about students in Shaker Heights, Ohio, he wrote that "Black students did not generally work hard" (p. 17) and "Black parents' educational strategies are not adequate and not effective in helping their children succeed in Shaker Heights schools" (p. 279). The theory has also been criticized because, while it purports to pay attention to history, it ignores historical facts about the avid pursuit of education by African Americans. Research generated by his theory, such as Bergin and Cooks (2002), showed that for some students, merely achieving high grades was not enough to elicit accusations of acting white. In addition, the theory has been criticized for not proposing solutions.

However, in his 2003 book, *Black American students in an affluent suburb: A study of academic disengagement,* Ogbu began to outline policy implications of his work. He suggested those policies will fail that do not address the community forces that foster underachievement. He was dubious about interventions such as school choice, cooperative learning approaches that capitalize on the assumption that Black and other minority groups value cooperation and collaboration, and culturally responsive education that supports cultural practices and learning styles allegedly common to African Americans. He wrote that they did not address community forces that foster avoidance of hard work. He recommended that schools implement minority achievement programs that reform community forces to support academic achievement. Such programs should demonstrate the link between schooling and adult futures, teach good study habits, and expose students to successful Black role models who thrived in school. The intent would be to create a collective identity that facilitates rather than undermines academic achievement.

BIBLIOGRAPHY

WORKS BY

Fordham, S., & Ogbu, J. U. (1986). Black students' school success: Coping with the "burden of 'acting White.'" *Urban Review 18*(3), 176–206.

Ogbu, J. U. (1978). *Minority education and caste: The American system in cross-cultural perspective.* New York: Academic Press.

Ogbu, J. U. (1987). Variability in minority school performance: A problem in search of an explanation. *Anthropology and Education Quarterly 18*(4), 312–334.

Ogbu, J. U. (2004). Collective identity and the burden of "acting White" in black history, community, and education. *Urban Review 36*(1), 1–35.

Ogbu, J. U., with Davis, A. (2003). *Black American students in an affluent suburb: A study of academic disengagement.* Mahwah, NJ: Erlbaum.

Ogbu, J. U., & Simons, H. D. (1998). Voluntary and involuntary minorities: A cultural-ecological theory of school performance with some implications for education. *Anthropology and Education Quarterly 29*(2), 155–188.

WORKS ABOUT

Bergin, D. A., & Cooks, H. C. (2002). High school students of color talk about accusations of "acting White." *Urban Review, 34*(2), 113–134.

Berube, M. R. (2000). *Eminent educators: studies in intellectual influence.* Westport, CT: Greenwood Press.

David A. Bergin

OPERANT CONDITIONING

Operant conditioning is defined as the use of consequences to modify the occurrence and form of behavior. "To put it very simply, behavior that is followed by pleasant consequences tends to be repeated and thus learned. Behavior that is followed by unpleasant consequences tends not to be repeated and thus not learned" (Alberto & Troutman, 2006, p. 12). Operant conditioning is specifically limited to voluntary behavior, that is, emitted responses, which distinguishes it from respondent or Pavlovian conditioning, which is limited to reflexive behavior (or elicited responses).

Operant conditioning was developed by B. F. Skinner (1904–1990), a psychologist at Harvard University, in 1938, and has continued into the early 2000s to be a popular approach for influencing behavior. Although the model was originally applied to animal learning (rats, pigeons; Skinner, 1938; 1963), it was subsequently commonly applied in educational settings. The model involves the operations of positive reinforcement, negative reinforcement, extinction, response cost punishment, and punishment with aversives, each of which is described below in this entry.

ASSUMPTIONS RELATED TO LEARNING

Gredler (2005) offers the following assumptions as the foundation of operant conditioning:

Learning is behavioral change (meaning that observers conclude that learning has occurred when behavior changes).

Behavioral change (i.e., learning) is related to changes in environmental events (these events being precursors of and consequences of an action).

One can determine relationships between behavior and the environment only if the characteristics of the behavior and the experimental conditions under which it occurs are defined in physically observable terms and observed under controlled conditions (the process must be systematic, observable, and controlled).

The only acceptable sources of information about the causes of specific behaviors are data from the experimental study of behavior (people must observe both the behavior and its causes).

The appropriate data source is the behavior of the individual (rather than the observers' expectations or inferences).

Of prime importance in the operant conditioning model is the focus on relationships between environmental events and behavior defined in physical terms, with an avoidance of the use of *inner states* as explanations.

VARIATIONS OF THE MODEL

There are four contexts or types of operant conditioning: positive reinforcement, negative reinforcement, positive (or response-cost) punishment, and negative punishment (or punishment with aversives) (Landrumm & Kauffman, 2006). The last three of these are all associated with aversiveness or aversive control while only one, positive reinforcement, is associated with positive control. Thus, researchers can distinguish between two variations of the model, a positive one and a negative one. (There is also extinction, which occurs when reinforcement following behavior is discontinued, causing the behavior itself to eventually be discontinued.)

In the positive version of the model, a person who emits a desired behavior (e.g., raising her hand and waiting to be called on) receives something good—a positive consequence (referred to as positive reinforcement). This may be a smile or praise or a piece of candy. The result of the reinforcement is that the behavior is strengthened, that is, its likelihood of subsequent occurrence increases. This represents a positive form of control.

In the negative version of the model there are three possible consequences. One is to avoid something bad—negative reinforcement. If a student raises her hand and waits to be called on, rather than speaking out, there is no positive consequence, only the avoidance of a negative one. A second is to receive something bad—punishment with aversives—which may take the form of being yelled at or ridiculed, hence reducing the tendency to speak out (or, perhaps, just suppressing it temporarily). The last negative approach, response-cost punishment, represents being deprived of something good, that is, a previously earned reinforcer being removed because of an undesirable behavior such as talking out in class, rather than raising one's hand and waiting to be called on (Walker, Shea, & Bauer, 2004). The punishment might be being placed in time-out or sent to the principal's office. These three approaches all represent aversive control, which may be associated with anxiety and fear (Skinner, 1953), and they may not result in a diminution of the strength of the undesirable response.

Another variation of the model is based on who or what precedes or occasions a response. After repeatedly pairing a response with a stimulus that precedes it, called a discriminative stimulus (S^D), the response will only occur in the presence of S^D, not in its absence. Such a response is said to be under stimulus control. "A behavior under stimulus control will continue to occur in the presence of the S^D, even when reinforcement is infrequent" (Alberto & Troutman, 2006, p. 306). Examples of stimulus control are answering telephones only when they ring (the sound of the ring serving as a discriminative stimulus), driving through intersections when the light is green (the S^D), not when it is red (although this is an imperfect S^D, because drivers often run red lights), and paying attention in class (a response) when being watched by the teacher (an S^D).

COMPONENTS AND ACTIVITIES OF THE MODEL THAT AFFECT EDUCATIONAL OUTCOMES

Various different positive reinforcers can be used to increase the likelihood of desired behavior in the classroom. They appear in the form of (a) consumable (e.g., candy), social (e.g., praise), (b) activity (e.g., time on the computer), (c) exchangeable (e.g., points or stickers), and (d) tangible (e.g., getting to sit in one's favorite chair). Activity reinforcers are among the most educationally relevant, since the activity can be done with educational value such as doing a jigsaw puzzle or watching an instructional video. However, it is of critical importance that the desired behavior immediately precede the activity reinforcer rather than follow it in order for the reinforcer to strengthen the response (this is called the Premack Principle, after David Premack, its discoverer), and in some cases this may be difficult to arrange, as, for example, when the activity reinforcer is a field trip (Kazdin, 2001).

Various reinforcement schedules (Skinner, 1969) have an effect on educational outcomes by affecting the likelihood of a particular response. A continuous reinforcement schedule, wherein every occurrence of a desired operant response is followed by a reinforcement, is desirable when operant conditioning is first taking place. However, once the desired response occurs on a regular basis, it

can be maintained by only occasional or intermittent reinforcement, thereby lessening the load on the teacher.

There are four possible intermittent reinforcement schedules: fixed ratio, fixed interval, variable ratio, and variable interval. In an educational setting (as in most settings), the two variable schedules best maintain the desired behavior, primarily because of their unpredictability. For example, if students were given the opportunity to listen to music, a reinforcement, after handing in some number of completed assignments, they would be more motivated to hand in completed assignments if the number required was not always the same (variable ratio) or the time during which they had to be handed in was not always the same (variable interval). By comparison, in the fixed interval schedule, where the reinforcement is provided after the desired behavior has been performed for a fixed amount of time (say 10 minutes), it does not take students long to realize that they can do nothing for nine and a half minutes and then perform the behavior to get the reinforcement. Similarly, if the fixed ratio is 4:1, students will perform the behavior four times in a row, and then relax after receiving the reinforcement.

Operant conditioning is a vehicle for teachers to achieve behavior modification in order to improve classroom management and facilitate learning. There are three techniques employed in particular to facilitate learning: prompting, chaining, and shaping. Prompting involves giving students cues (called *discriminative stimuli* in the lexicon of operant conditioning) to help them perform a particular behavior. When students are learning to read, a teacher may help them by sounding out a word (just as when actors forget their lines, someone prompts them by saying their next line). Prompting helps to make the unfamiliar become more familiar, but, if used too often, students can become dependent on it, so teachers should withdraw prompts as soon as adequate student performance is obtained (a process called *fading*). Also, teachers should be careful not to begin prompting students until students try a performing task without extra help.

Learning complex behaviors can also be facilitated through an operant conditioning technique called *chaining*, a technique for connecting simple responses in sequence to form a more complex response that would be difficult to learn all at one time. Each cue or discriminative stimulus leads to a response that then cues the subsequent behavior, enabling behaviors to be chained together. Skinner taught pigeons to steer torpedoes toward enemy vessels in World War II by chaining together responses that adjusted the direction of a torpedo relative to the target as it appeared on a screen. Although the technique was not actually used in the war, it appeared in trial runs that it would work successfully.

The third, and perhaps most generalizable technique is called *shaping,* a process of reinforcing each form of the behavior that more closely resembles the final version. It is used when students cannot perform the final version and are not helped by prompting. Shaping involves gradually changing the response criterion for reinforcement in the direction of the target behavior. If the student is given 10 math problems, for example, and gets three of them right, the student gets a reinforcement. On the next set of problems, the student needs to get six right for a reinforcement, then 10. By shifting the criterion for reinforcement, or successive approximations, a student's behavior is shaped in the direction of ultimate success.

According to Landrum and Kauffman, "Despite a rich history and extensive empirical underpinnings, the behavioral perspective on teaching and management is not highly regarded in the education community" (2006, p. 47). Its critics contend it is an unfeeling approach more suited to animals than to humans (Landrum & Kauffman, 2006). Nevertheless, operant conditioning is commonly used in classrooms and is viewed by many teachers as an effective approach to improving classroom practice. It provides teachers with a set of tools for improving classroom management and student learning.

SEE ALSO *Applied Behavior Analysis; Classical Conditioning; Skinner, B(urrhus) F(rederic).*

BIBLIOGRAPHY

Alberto, P. A., & Troutman, A. C. (2006). *Applied behavior analysis for teachers* (7th ed.). Upper Saddle River, NJ: Pearson/Prentice Hall.

Gredler, M. E. (2005). *Learning and instruction: Theory into practice* (5th ed.). Upper Saddle River, NJ: Pearson/Prentice Hall.

Kazdin, A. E. (2001). *Behavior modification in applied settings* (6th ed.). Belmont, CA: Wadsworth.

Landrum, T. J., & Kauffman, J. M. (2006). Behavioral approaches to classroom management. In C. M. Evertson & C. S. Weinstein (Eds.), *Handbook of classroom management: Research, practice and contemporary issues.* Mahwah, NJ: Erlbaum.

Skinner, B. F. (1938). *The behavior of organisms.* New York: Appleton-Century-Crofts.

Skinner, B. F. (1953). *Science and human behavior.* New York: Macmillan.

Skinner, B. F. (1963). Operant behavior. *American Psychologist, 18,* 503–515.

Skinner, B. F. (1969). *Contingencies of reinforcement.* New York: Appleton-Century-Crofts.

Walker, J. E., Shea, T. M., & Bauer, A. M. (2004). *Behavior management: A practical approach for educators.* Upper Saddle River, NJ: Pearson/Prentice Hall.

Bruce W. Tuckman

OPPORTUNITY/ ACHIEVEMENT GAP

Among the wide-ranging challenges facing American educators, perhaps no issue is more pressing than the inequity in student achievement among racial/ethnic and socioeconomic groups—a problem that in the early 2000s is somewhat contentiously referred to as the achievement gap.[1] Since the early 1970s, analyses of nationally representative survey data have documented a persistent history of achievement differences, according to which Whites and especially east Asians enjoy relatively high average student performance while African Americans and some Hispanic subgroups experience relatively low average student performance. Moreover, children whose families are on the lower rungs of the social class ladder average far lower achievement and educational attainment levels than their wealthier counterparts. Thus, it is important to recognize that what is often characterized as a single gap between White students and all minority students is more accurately portrayed as multiple gaps between and within racial and social class groups.

However gaps are measured—whether by pre-school vocabulary, elementary school grades, middle school standardized test scores, or high school or college completion rates—the fact that there is a continuing history of race and social class differences in U.S. education is not debatable. Perhaps the best evidence comes from the National Assessment of Educational Progress (NAEP), widely known as the nation's report card. NAEP trend data demonstrate persistent, if somewhat fluctuating, racial test score gaps going back to 1971. Although Black-White and Hispanic-White gaps in mathematics and reading steadily narrowed between 1971 and 1988, trends toward test score convergence reversed in the late 1980s. Some gaps stabilized and others actually widened throughout the 1990s. Since 1999, however, Black-White and Hispanic-White math and reading test score gaps have held fairly constant across age groups—with the exception of slight convergence in the Hispanic-White math gap and the Black-White reading gap among 9-year-olds. This convergence is trumpeted by the U.S. Department of Education as evidence of the impact of the No Child Left Behind Act (NCLB) of 2001.

Figure 1 presents cross-sectional analyses of fourth and eighth grade students' mathematics and reading results from the 2007 main NAEP.[2] Whites and Asian Pacific Americans score above national averages at both grade levels. Asian fourth grade students exceed the national math mean by .48 standard deviations (.50 SD approximates one year of academic growth) outperforming by .19 SD their White counterparts who also score above the national average. African Americans and Hispanics score below the national average in fourth and eighth grade. The math gap is especially pronounced for

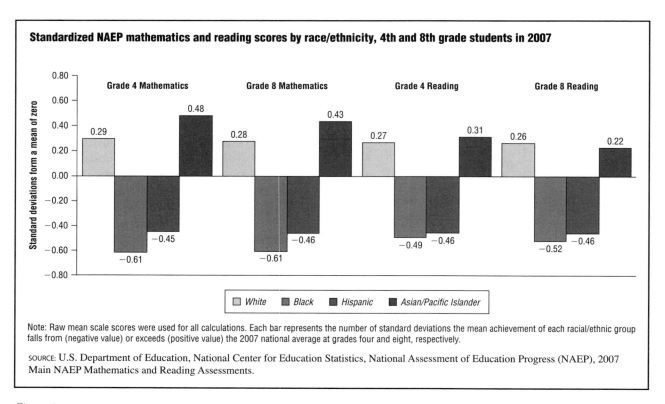

Standardized NAEP mathematics and reading scores by race/ethnicity, 4th and 8th grade students in 2007

Note: Raw mean scale scores were used for all calculations. Each bar represents the number of standard deviations the mean achievement of each racial/ethnic group falls from (negative value) or exceeds (positive value) the 2007 national average at grades four and eight, respectively.

SOURCE: U.S. Department of Education, National Center for Education Statistics, National Assessment of Education Progress (NAEP), 2007 Main NAEP Mathematics and Reading Assessments.

Figure 1 ILLUSTRATION BY GGS INFORMATION SERVICES. CENGAGE LEARNING, GALE.

African Americans (.61 SD below the mean), whereas Hispanic students score approximately .46 SD below the national average in mathematics and reading at both grade levels.

While standardized achievement data reveal students' relative mastery of specific knowledge and skills, still other data document differences in group-level educational attainment by alternate measures. For instance, according to the National Center for Education Statistics, high school dropout rates for Blacks and especially Hispanics substantially exceed those for Whites and Asians. Although the gap between Blacks and Whites narrowed significantly between 1965 and 2005, the disparity in the graduation rates of Hispanics versus other racial/ethnic groups persists at double-digit rates. The alarmingly high Hispanic high school dropout rate—1.4 million Hispanics between the ages of 16 and 24 were dropouts in 2005 (NCES, 2005)—is in fact twice that of Blacks and more than three times that of Whites and Asians (see Figure 2).[3] These numbers prefigure similar trends in educational attainment at the college level, as Hispanics are about half as likely as their non-Hispanic peers to complete four years of college (Vernez & Mizell, 2002).

Dramatic demographic changes in the United States only heighten the importance of these described gaps in academic performance. Population trend data indicate that by 2025 fully one quarter of all U.S. K-12 students will be of Spanish-speaking origin. At the same time the standards-based accountability movement in education, on the rise since the late 1980s and focusing especially on state assessments and K-12 test scores, has shone a bright light on unrelenting racial/ethnic and socioeconomic differences in academic performance. Many policymakers have redoubled their efforts (perhaps sometimes only symbolically) to achieve group-level equality of educational outcomes, if not inputs. Tellingly, the preamble to NCLB explicitly states the goal of eliminating test-score outcome gaps by the year 2014. In other words, during the first two decades of the 21st century, official interest in these described achievement gaps in American education may be at an all-time high.

MEASURING CONSEQUENCES

Policymakers are increasingly aware that the importance of closing gaps goes well beyond presumed links between improved minority student performance and improved job prospects for minorities. The moral and civic imperative to eliminate gaps is strong, but on a simply utilitarian rationale it can also be said that better educated students earn higher incomes, live healthier lives, pay

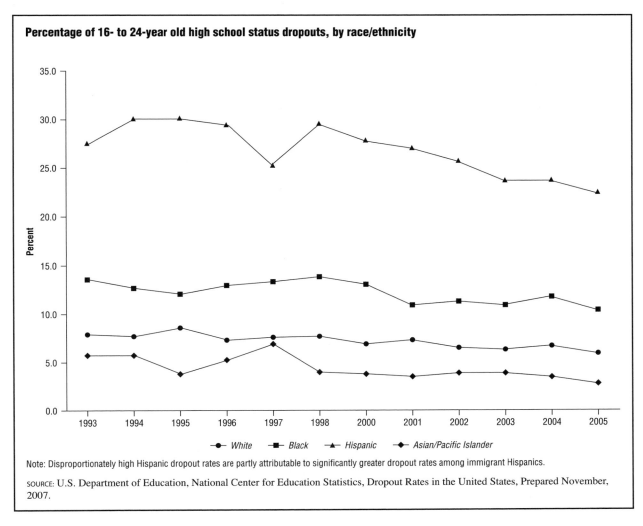

Figure 2 ILLUSTRATION BY GGS INFORMATION SERVICES. CENGAGE LEARNING, GALE.

higher taxes, and are less likely to be involved in crime. Columbia University's Henry Levin is a renowned researcher in the study of educational inequality and its costs. Working on the premise that high school graduation should serve as a minimal threshold for the standard of adequate education, he has investigated costs to society should educators fail to succeed in aiding greater numbers of students to procure a high school diploma. The report focuses on those individuals who at age 20 were not high school graduates in 2005, a group of approximately 700,000. The findings are sobering: For each of these individuals, over $200,000 is lost to society in federal, state, and local tax revenues and costs to the public health and criminal justice systems over the lifetime of each dropout. When aggregated the fiscal consequences to society for this single group of 700,000 students who leave school without high school diplomas

is the staggering sum of $148 billion in lost tax revenues and additional public expenditures over the lifetime. Clearly it is in the nation's best interest to reduce dropout rates, particularly among non-Asian minorities, and to ensure that all children secure an adequate education (Levin et al., 2007).

GAPS EMERGE ON THE POLICY AGENDA

James Coleman was a sociologist at Johns Hopkins University when his controversial 1966 report to the U.S. Congress, *Equality of Educational Opportunity*, became the first national study to offer a systemic description of racial/ethnic differences in academic achievement among children of various ages. Prior to the Coleman Report, investigations of this nature had been focused on educational inputs: School effectiveness was measured by the resources that

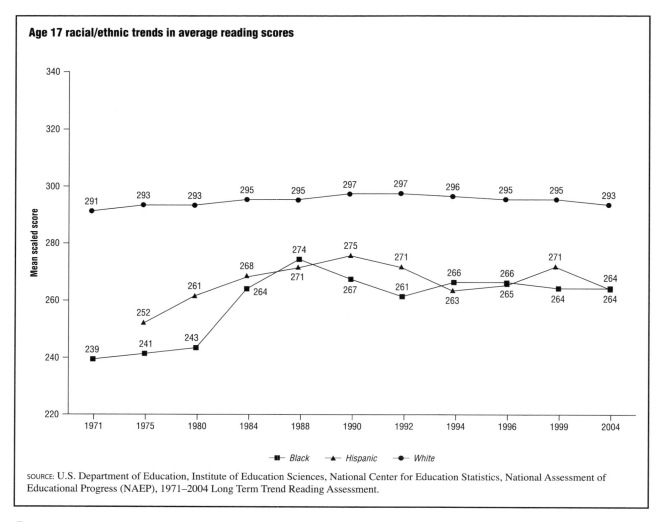

Age 17 racial/ethnic trends in average reading scores

SOURCE: U.S. Department of Education, Institute of Education Sciences, National Center for Education Statistics, National Assessment of Educational Progress (NAEP), 1971–2004 Long Term Trend Reading Assessment.

Figure 3 ILLUSTRATION BY GGS INFORMATION SERVICES. CENGAGE LEARNING, GALE.

went into schools, not the quality of the students who came out of them. To his surprise Coleman found that (1) while schools certainly influence student achievement—much of what tests measure must be learned in schools—and (2) although school quality varies widely in the United States, the large documented differences in the quality of schools attended by Black and White children fail to explain most of the difference in average levels of achievement between Blacks and Whites (Rothstein, 2004). These rather controversial findings have been cross-examined by many researchers. Few, if any, dispute Coleman's fundamental claims. Those who point to schools alone when searching for answers to stubborn outcome gaps may be ignoring the fact that children spend the vast majority of their waking hours each year somewhere other than the formal school setting. As developmental psychologist Urie Bronfenbrenner's ecological systems theory emphasizes, children are

enveloped within families and they navigate social life with peers. They reside in neighborhoods and communities where schools are charged with their formal education, which takes place largely within individual classrooms. Each of these overlapping networks and domains conditions students' educational performance in ways that are not mutually exclusive. Children lead nested lives.

Soon after publication of the Coleman Report, the federal government allotted substantial resources across multiple levels in an attempt to close the family/school/community input gap. In fact, desegregation in the wake of the 1964 Civil Rights Act combined with the Great Society's War on Poverty programs (including Head Start and compensatory Title I funding) helped reduce glaring resource inequities and coincided with nearly 20 years of steady progress in reducing both the Black-White and Hispanic-White test score gaps since 1971, per Figure 3.

However, by the time U.S. Secretary of Education Terrel Bell released the landmark 1983 report to Congress, *A Nation at Risk*, concerns about inequality on the domestic front were pushed into the background, giving way to a growing preoccupation with educational efficiency and global competitiveness. Thus, targeted programs for the poor and compensatory education reforms were rolled back throughout the 1980s. By 1988 the progress in narrowing educational opportunity and achievement gaps had stalled.

The widening of test score gaps in the late 1980s went largely unnoticed until 1994 when experimental psychologist Richard Herrnstein and political scientist Charles Murray published *The Bell Curve* to much fanfare and subsequent controversy. Their conclusions about the genetic inevitability of the gap were deduced from the research of others and resurrected in particular the much disputed claims of education psychologist Arthur Jensen, which were first published in 1969 in the *Harvard Educational Review*[4]. When a special task force of the American Psychological Association reviewed the data used by Herrnstein and Murray the association arrived at a much different conclusion: The paucity of direct evidence of the Black-White differential in psychometric intelligence simply could not support the genetic hypothesis. Richard E. Nisbett, a professor of psychology at the University of Michigan, has charged the authors of *The Bell Curve* with having provided a "shockingly incomplete and biased" reading of the research (Nisbett, 1998, p. 96). As of 2008, what all psychologists agree upon is that a person's developed capacity for intelligent behavior often differs in predictable ways from the person's hereditary potential. So-called intelligence or aptitude tests measure the development of innate abilities. The collective research of American psychology leads one to conclude that environmental factors explain far more of the variance in achievement than the number of Blacks or Whites in a person's family tree (Neisser et al., 1996).

SOURCES OF THE GAPS

When people turn to an examination, then, of contextual factors contributing to socioeconomic and racial education gaps, the breadth and depth of their sources quickly becomes apparent. Because causes are layered and overlapping, they are best considered simultaneously across domains. From a top-down structural perspective one might perceive broad economic conditions as being linked to, say, state and local tax rate policies that bear directly, if also differentially, upon community labor markets and housing values—which, in turn, dictate school finance schemes. There are indeed sizeable gaps in educational resources that differentiate communities serving White and minority children. From a less structural, bottom-up perspective, concentrated on student effort and family influence, one sees substantial variation in parents' approach to child rearing. Whether children are talked at or listened to, how frequently they read and are read to, and whether or not they attend quality preschool and summer school are important factors that are conditioned by parents' effort and resources. Children's friends and peers pick up where families leave off, exerting increasing influence as students progress through schooling. In short, there is a dynamic and sometimes transformative relationship between the practices of real people—including students, parents, and peers—and the structures of school, society, and even history (Ortner, 2006).

Figure 4 shows a nested, albeit by no means exhaustive, depiction of the many structural and individual-level factors that have been examined to understand the causes of the gap. The embedded domains are not mutually exclusive categories. Rather, they are composed of related factors that act upon one another in complex ways that are often difficult to observe and quantify. One challenge, therefore, is to determine the extent to which the attributes of formal institutional settings and those of less formal student, family, peer group, and neighborhood and societal-level influences contribute to the gaps. A few of the better documented causes of these gaps are noted below.

Re-segregation and the Distribution of Teacher Quality. In June 2007, a divided U.S. Supreme Court restricted the ability of public school districts to use race in determining which schools students can attend. Most voluntary desegregation efforts by school districts are now unconstitutional. According to Professor Gary Orfield of the UCLA Civil Rights Project, the re-segregation of U.S. schools has accelerated since the early 1990s and continues to grow in all parts of the country, most conspicuously among African Americans and Hispanics. Not since President Lyndon Johnson signed the Civil Rights Act have schools been as segregated as they are as of 2008. When people ask what it is about segregated schools that contributes to the racial achievement gap many point to course offerings, the composition of the student body, and perhaps especially the instruction gap. In a 1991 study of 900 Texas school districts, Harvard University's Achievement Gap Initiative director, Professor Ronald Ferguson, found that nearly all of the school-level variation in the gap in achievement between Blacks and Whites was attributable to systematic differences in the skills of their teachers. The simple fact is that far fewer of the best prepared teachers are teaching in schools where the vast majority of students are Black and/or Hispanic. These disparities in access to high-quality teachers and teaching are large and growing worse (Darling-Hammond, 2007).

Although quality teachers are important, it is nevertheless the case that most of the group-level variation in student achievement outcomes can be attributed to factors

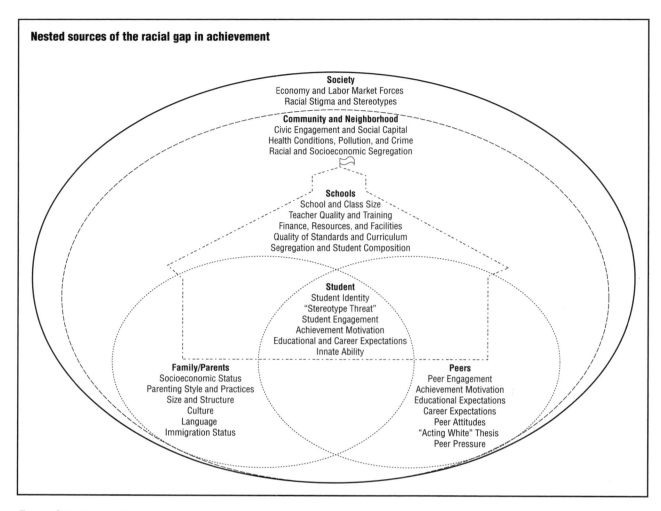

Figure 4 ILLUSTRATION BY GGS INFORMATION SERVICES. CENGAGE LEARNING, GALE.

outside of schools. As findings based on and replicating the Coleman Report have time and again demonstrated, other structural conditions and individual-level factors apart from schools also affect gaps in achievement.

Socioeconomic Status and Parenting. Socioeconomic status (SES), a measure of parental education, employment, and income is among the most powerful predictors of student achievement. Many prominent social scientists have shown that the correlation between SES and race is inevitably linked to diminished access to quality education for underrepresented minorities, and thus, not surprisingly, to patterned racial inequality in educational outcomes. While only 7 percent of White mothers in the Early Childhood Longitudinal Study of the Kindergarten Class of 1998–1999 (ECLS-K) had failed to complete high school, a full 18 percent of Black mothers and 35 percent of Latina mothers had failed to do so. Likewise,

only 15 percent of White children (and 11 percent of Asians) under the age of 18 were living in poverty in 2005 compared to almost one-third of all Black and Hispanic children (NCES, 2006). Not only are Black and Hispanic children more likely to have parents who have not completed high school and are poor, but they are also more likely to attend schools with other poor children. To the degree that both family poverty and school poverty affect academic achievement, Hispanic and Black students are twice disadvantaged (Rumberger, 2007).

Some understanding of how SES influences achievement is provided by psychologists who study the interactions between parents and children. The research of psychologist Laurence Steinberg at Temple University indicates that a lack of school-specific knowledge and a lack of opportunity (good parenting takes a lot of time) are what differentiate high and low SES parents in their parenting styles and approaches to raising children (Steinberg, 1996).

Other research conducted by Betty Hart and Todd Risley, child psychologists at the University of Kansas, links children's language development to parents' communication style. In a well-known 1995 study, they found that by age 3 the children of professionals had vocabularies of about 1,100 words—the children of welfare parents had vocabularies of about half as many words as their peers not living in poverty. Comparing children's vocabulary scores with their home life, Hart and Risley concluded that children's vocabulary correlated most closely to the number of words the parents spoke to their child. In addition, the number and kinds of words that children heard varied markedly by social class. In short, early childhood parenting practices and communication styles matter greatly and are patterned along class lines.

To reiterate, only about one-third of the racial gap in achievement can be attributed to what goes on in schools. Moreover, emerging research consensus indicates that family socioeconomic status accounts for at least another one-third of the gap in educational outcomes (Hedges and Nowell, 1999). While the effect of schools on a child's academic achievement is near impossible to isolate from other influences (including family SES), many researchers agree that even eliminating vast resource differences between schools and among families would not entirely close the racial gap in achievement. In fact, one of the most perplexing aspects of the racial test score gap is its persistence among even middle-class students and among students at the top of the achievement spectrum—the very pool from which the nation's leaders are drawn (Jencks & Phillips, 1998).

Individual Identity and Stereotype Threat. The work of Stanford social psychologist Claude Steele helps to interpret the persistent achievement gaps even among students who are enrolled in the most competitive U.S. universities. In spite of the many obstacles that inhibit educational achievement among non-Asian minority students, many forge ahead to attain high levels of academic success. Some minorities within the academic vanguard, however, may encounter further achievement barriers corresponding to their relative identification with schooling. In his groundbreaking work on how stereotypes interact with students' identities to shape educational performance, Steele (1997) explains what he calls "stereotype threat." According to Steele, stereotype threat arises when school-identified African Americans are in a situation or doing something for which a negative stereotype about one's group applies and must therefore be disconfirmed. Thus, stereotypes become particularly threatening for those who associate their identity and self-worth with success in a domain where their own group has been obviously stereotyped. So above and beyond the K-12 instruction gap and the socioeconomic inequality noted above, stereotypes

about groups can influence the identity formation and cognitive functioning of individual group members. The burden of heightened awareness about stereotypes and social stigma affects especially test score outcome gaps among students of color who are otherwise apparently advantaged.

SOCIETY'S INTEREST IN ELIMINATING ACHIEVEMENT GAPS

The coincidence of dramatic changes in U.S. demographics and new information about gaps accompanying the standards movement has led policymakers to increase pressure particularly on schools to demonstrate annual progress in student achievement for all students. That achievement gaps and disproportionately high dropout rates among non-Asian minorities have re-emerged on the policy agenda may seem relatively unsurprising in light of research demonstrating that the average high school graduate pays nearly $140,000 more in taxes over the course of a lifetime than a high school dropout. Baby Boomers whose overall well-being depends on the productivity of subsequent generations are concerned that the population base of American voters and taxpayers will increasingly come to be made up of persons less educated than they themselves were. Yet regardless of all researchers know about the incidence, consequences, and the causes of these gaps, government policy has only partially responded to this crisis. Even as most educational reform proceeds through almost entirely school-centered efforts to eliminate group-level achievement differences, the finding of the Coleman Report bears repeating: No more than 40% of the racial gap in educational outcomes can be attributed to the schools themselves (in isolation of other non-school factors). The ability to respond to the achievement gap problem will ultimately depend on whether people recognize and act on the broad range of factors that collectively shape student achievement.

NOTES

1. The very term "achievement gap" is considered by many to be a problematic misnomer. By reframing group-level differences in academic outcomes as the shameful product of a long history of discriminatory gaps in educational *inputs*, Gloria Ladson-Billings, in her 2005 presidential address to the American Educational Research Association, asserted that the so-called achievement gap is more accurately portrayed as an historically accumulated "educational debt" still owed underrepresented minority and poor students (Ladson-Billings, 2006).

2. Main NAEP data are not available for 12th graders in 2007.

3. It should be noted, however, that Hispanics are also making real educational gains over generations—improvements that are obscured by the continuing influx of new immigrants (Smith, 2003).

4. Jensen argued that programs like Head Start, which tried to boost the academic performance of minority children, were doomed to failure because I.Q. was so heavily genetic and impervious to environmental influences (Gladwell, 2007).

SEE ALSO *Ability Grouping; Culturally Relevant Pedagogy.*

BIBLIOGRAPHY

Bronfenbrenner, U. (1979). *The ecology of human development: Experiments by nature and design.* Cambridge, MA: Harvard University Press.

Coleman, J. S., Campbell, E., Hobson, C., McPartland, J., Mood, A., Weinfield, F., & York, R. (1966). *Equality of educational opportunity.* Washington, DC: U.S. Government Printing Office.

Darling-Hammond, L. (2007). The flat earth and education: How America's commitment to equity will determine our future. *Educational Researcher, 36,* 318–34.

Ferguson, R. F. (1991). Paying for public education: New evidence on how and why money matters. *Harvard Journal on Legislation, 28,* 465–98.

Gladwell, M. (2007). None of the above: What I.Q. doesn't tell you about race. *The New Yorker,* (17 Dec. 2007), 92–96.

Hart, B., & Risley, T. R. (1995). *Meaningful differences in the everyday experience of young American children.* Baltimore, MD: Paul H. Brookes.

Hedges, L. V., & Nowell, A. (1999). Changes in the Black-White gap in achievement test scores. *Sociology of Education, 7,* 111–35.

Herrnstein, R., & Murray, C. (1994). *The bell curve: Intelligence and class structure in American life.* New York: Free Press.

Jencks, C., & Phillips, M. (Eds.). (1998). *The Black-White test score gap.* Washington, DC: Brookings Institution Press.

Jensen, A. R. (1969). How much can we boost IQ and scholastic achievement? *Harvard Educational Review, 39,* 1–123.

Ladson-Billings, G. J. (2006). From the achievement gap to the education debt: Understanding achievement in U.S. schools. *Educational Researcher, 35,* 3–12.

Levin, H. M., Belfield, C., Muennig, P., & Rouse, C. (2007). The costs and benefits of an excellent education for all of America's children. *Center for Cost Based Studies.* Columbia University.

National Commission on Excellence in Education. (1983). *A Nation at risk: The imperative for educational reform.* Washington, DC: U.S. Department of Education.

Neisser, U. et al. (1996). Intelligence: Knowns and unknowns. *American Psychologist, 51,* 77–101.

Nisbett, R. E. (1998). Race, genetics, and IQ. In C. Jencks & M. Phillips (Eds.), *The Black-White test score gap* (pp. 86–102). Washington DC: Brookings Institution.

Orfield, G., & Lee, C. (2007). *Historic reversals, accelerating resegregation, and the need for new integration strategies.* Los Angeles: Civil Rights Project/Proyecto Derechos Civiles at UCLA.

Ortner, S. B. (2006). *Anthropology and social theory: Culture, power, and the acting subject.* Duke University Press.

Rothstein, R. (2004). *Class and schools: Using social, economic, and educational reform to close the Black-White achievement gap.* Economic Policy Institute. Teachers College, Columbia University.

Rumberger, R. W. (2007). Parsing the data on student achievement in high-poverty schools. *North Carolina Law Review, 86,* 1293–1314.

Smith, J. P. (2003). Assimilation across the Latino generations. *American Economic Review, 93,* 315–19.

Steele, C. M. (1997). A threat in the air: How stereotypes shape intellectual identity and performance. *American Psychologist, 52,* 613–29.

Steinberg, L. (1996). *Beyond the classroom: Why school reform has failed and what parents need to do.* New York: Simon & Schuster.

U.S. Department of Education, National Center for Education Statistics (NCES). (2005). *Dropout rates in the United States: 2005.* Washington, DC: U.S. Government Printing Office.

U.S. Department of Education, National Center for Education Statistics (NCES). (2006). *Digest of educational statistics: 2006.* Washington, DC: U.S. Government Printing Office.

Vernez, G., & Mizell, L. (2002). *Goal: To double the rate of Hispanics earning a bachelor's degree.* Santa Monica: RAND Corporation, Center for Research on Immigration Policy.

Robert K. Ream
Jose A. Espinoza
Sarah M. Ryan

ORTHOPEDIC IMPAIRMENTS

Orthopedic impairments are the most common of physical disabilities. A physical disability is any condition that interferes with a student's ability to use his or her body. The term *physical disabilities* may be used interchangeably when referring to orthopedic impairments. In 2004 the U.S. Department of Education reported that 74,000 students between age 6 and 21 received special education services under the orthopedic impairments disability category.

ORTHOPEDIC IMPAIRMENT DEFINITION

According to the Individuals with Disabilities Education Improvement Act of 2004 (IDEA), orthopedic impairment is as follows: "a severe orthopedic impairment that adversely affects a child's educational performance. The term includes impairments due to the effects of congenital anomaly (e.g., clubfoot, absence of some member, etc.), impairments due to the effects of disease (e.g., poliomyelitis, bone tuberculosis, etc.), and impairments from other causes (e.g., cerebral palsy, amputations, and fractures or burns that cause contractures)" (Pierangelo & Giuliani, 2007, p. 268).

Skeletal system impairments that involve the joints, bones, limbs, and associated muscles represent the musculoskeletal disorders. Orthopedic impairments often are divided into three main categories to help characterize the potential problems and learning needs of the students involved. These categories are neuromotor impairments, musculoskeletal disorders, and degenerative diseases. Although neuromotor impairments involve the central nervous system (brain, spinal cord, or nerves that send impulses to muscles), they also affect a child's ability to move, use, feel, or control certain parts of the body. Clinically, they are separate and distinct types of disabilities with entirely different causes from musculoskeletal disorders, but they result in similar limitations in movement. Some examples of neuromotor impairments are spina bifida, cerebral palsy, and spinal cord injuries. Musculoskeletal disorders include defects or diseases of the bones and muscles, such as limb deficiency or clubfoot. Degenerative diseases are those that affect motor movement such as muscular dystrophy.

Orthopedic impairments involve a wide range of causes and a diverse group of students. Some children have impairments caused by congenital anomalies, whereas others have experienced injuries or conditions that have resulted in orthopedic impairments. Congenital causes include cerebral palsy, osteogenesis imperfecta, joint deformity, and muscular dystrophy. Motor vehicle accidents, sports injuries, premature birth, and other injuries and conditions may cause orthopedic impairments. Burns and broken bones can result in damage both to bones and muscles. Some children have their impairments from birth, while others acquire a physical disability, so age of onset varies widely. There does not appear to be any trend toward greater incidence of orthopedic impairment in boys or girls or based on cultural or racial factors.

Some children with skeletal deformities have surgery. Others have to use various types of braces, prosthetic, and orthotic devices before, after, or in place of surgery. Others may use adapted wheelchairs. Many children identified with severe and multiple disabilities have an orthopedic impairment that must be considered when assessing and establishing services.

ASSESSING ORTHOPEDIC IMPAIRMENTS

Evaluating children with orthopedic impairments can be complicated because there are so many different types of disabilities and causes of impairment. Most orthopedic impairments are identified before a child enters school, but sometimes they are missed or do not appear until a

later age. A teacher may notice signs of poor coordination, frequent accidents, or complaints of acute or chronic pain.

The assessment must include a thorough medical evaluation of the child's orthopedic impairment by a licensed physician. Other data generally include documentation of observations and assessments of how the orthopedic impairment affects the child's ability to learn in the educational environment, as well as observations concerning mobility and activities of daily living. It is important to assess a student's social and physical adaptive behaviors through various checklists, inventories, rating scales, and interviews with those who know the child best. The severity of functional limitations must be such that they adversely impact the child's education performance.

A social history supplements the medical history, as does basic screening information on hearing, vision, speech and language skills, and development in areas such as cognition and social/emotional, or self-help behaviors. A team approach is taken for assessment and recommendations. The team that assesses a child with an orthopedic impairment must involve a parent and at least one of the child's general education classroom teacher(s). It should also include a licensed special education teacher, school counselor and/or psychologist, a licensed physician, and other profession personnel as appropriate. For example, a licensed physical therapist or occupational therapist should assess specific motor dysfunction in gross and fine motor development, neuromuscular development, daily living activities, sensory integration, and the need for adaptive equipment. The assessment also considers the permanent nature of the child's impairment. Usually the condition will not be considered an orthopedic impairment if it is not going to last at least 60 days.

More than one test always should be used to evaluate a child's needs for services. In all, the assessment must take into consideration the entire education from all angles, not just physical access to buildings, computers, libraries, or equipment that facilitates learning. For instance, a child may need to receive occupational therapy or other treatments, requiring time away from the general education classroom. Educators will need to develop adaptive strategies and adopt a hands-off approach at times to help students develop some independence. Then, too, social and peer issues also must be considered. The final evaluation should describe how the orthopedic impairment adversely affects a student's areas of development.

CHARACTERISTICS OF CHILDREN WITH ORTHOPEDIC IMPAIRMENTS

Children with orthopedic impairments have a wide range of characteristics that are specific to the underlying diagnosis. Therefore, it is difficult, perhaps even impossible, to generalize about the students in this category. For example, a child with a spinal cord injury could have immobility limited to one side of his or her body, just the arms or legs, or total paralysis. A child with cerebral palsy may have movement but need a wheelchair because he or she has slow, uncontrolled movements that make it difficult to walk.

It also is difficult to know prior to a thorough assessment, including input from medical professionals, what types of associated symptoms to expect. However, many students with orthopedic impairments have problems with motor skills, such as those involved in using standard writing tools, turning pages or books, or exploring and participating in typical classroom activities. Some students have associated speech impairments or multiple disabilities that may affect particular academic areas.

Some students with physical disabilities may lack common experiences and knowledge or common places, items, and activities as compared with general education students. This is due to a lack of mobility and, if their condition has existed since birth, the lack of typical childhood play and exploration. These students' social interactions often are limited because of limited motor, self-help, and self-care skills. Sometimes, standard instructional materials includes mention of objects and experiences or assumes comprehension that is beyond the experience and background of the child with an orthopedic impairment. Children with orthopedic impairments may have pain and discomfort, may sleep poorly and therefore be fatigued in class, and may be on medications. They also may miss school more frequently than other students because of their medical conditions.

Poor self-concept and poor self-advocacy skills may affect an individual student's performance or behavior. Some students with orthopedic impairments feel helpless or depressed as a result of their physical disability.

Some diseases, such as muscular dystrophy, are progressive, which means a child's need for services is likely to increase and certainly to change throughout the continuum of education. Other orthopedic impairments, particularly those caused by injury or temporary impairments from surgery, may lessen over time. Advances in medical care have allowed for better diagnosis and treatment of some disorders and diseases that cause orthopedic impairments. It is important to realize that some children with orthopedic impairments also face issues related to having both chronic and terminal illness.

EXAMPLES OF ORTHOPEDIC DISORDERS

More than 50 diseases and disorders are associated with orthopedic impairments. Along with subgroup types for these disorders. Spina bifida, scoliosis, cerebral palsy, and muscular dystrophy are some of the more well-known

conditions that cause orthopedic impairments in children. Spina bifida is a cleft spine, or incomplete closure of the spinal column. It is the most common permanently disabling birth defect. Spina bifida occulta is the mildest and most common form; next in severity is meningocele. With this type, the spinal cord develops normally, but the meninges, or protective covering, push through the opening in the vertebrae. Meningocele can be repaired surgically. Myelomeningocele is the most severe form of spina bifida. The bones of the spinal cord do not completely form and the spinal canal is incomplete, resulting in the spinal cord and meninges protruding out of the child's back. Spina bifida may be associated with hydrocephalus.

Scoliosis is a side-to-side curvature of the spine, measured by x-ray examination as greater than 10 degrees. It makes the shoulders, hips, or both appear uneven and can cause pain in the back. Most cases of scoliosis have no known cause, and although scoliosis can occur in children with other orthopedic impairments, it normally occurs in otherwise healthy children.

Cerebral palsy (CP) includes a number of chronic disorders that impair movement control. They appear early in life and generally do not worsen as children age. Cerebral palsy affects about 500,000 people in the United States; about 8,000 infants and 1,500 preschool-age children are diagnosed with it each year. Cerebral palsy is caused by injury to parts of the brain that control the ability to use muscles. The injury can occur before birth, during delivery, or soon after birth. Early signs normally appear by the time a child is 18 months of age. The three main types of CP are spastic, where muscle tone is too high or too tight; athetoid or dyskinetic CP, which can affect the whole body with slow, uncontrolled movements and low muscle tone; and mixed CP, a combination of the symptoms from both athetoid and spastic CP. A child with mixed CP has some muscles that are too tight and others that are too loose so that some movements are involuntary and mobility is limited in other areas by stiffness.

Muscular dystrophy (MD) is a group of genetic diseases characterized by progressive muscle weakness. The muscles most affected by MD vary, as do the types of the disease. Some are ultimately fatal, such as Duchenne muscular dystrophy, which also is the most severe form and the most common form affecting children. Although Duchenne MD results from a defective gene, it often occurs in families with no known history of the disease. Muscle weakness, rapid progression, and difficulty with motor skills are some of the characteristics of Duchenne MD. It primarily affects boys and symptoms usually begin in early childhood. There are several forms of muscular dystrophy, each with unique characteristics.

For example, Emery-Dreiffus MD typically causes symptoms in late childhood and early adolescence.

EDUCATIONAL PRACTICES

Several laws ensure an inclusive education for students with physical disabilities. The Individuals with Disabilities Education Improvement Act (IDEA) was introduced in 1975 and passed in 1990. It was reauthorized in 1997 and 2004 and includes provisions for children with orthopedic impairments as defined above. Students with orthopedic impairments also may be eligible for accommodations for general classroom inclusion under Section 504 of the Vocational Rehabilitation Act, passed in 1973. In addition, the Americans with Disabilities Act (ADA), which was passed in 1990, includes provisions concerning discrimination against individuals with disabilities and requirements that school facilities are accessible to all.

Placement is a key consideration for students with orthopedic impairments. The goal is inclusion in general education classes, but some students may need services from resource rooms, special classes, schools, or residential facilities, as well as hospital or homebound programs. In 2004, the U.S. Department of Education reported that about 46% of school-age children receiving special education services under the orthopedic impairments category were educated in general education classrooms. Setting up the appropriate placement, services, and environment begins with asking the student what he or she needs and evolves through the assessment and individualized education plan (IEP) process.

Students with orthopedic impairments may present unique challenges in adapting instructional environments that call for creative solutions. Some students may be paralyzed and require assistance moving from place to place. A student may require assistance with basic self-care such as toileting. These and other needs call on teachers to perform duties that historically have not been part of their role in school. Becoming familiar with orthotics, prostheses, adaptive devices, and the specific characteristics of a student's impairment can improve the experience for student and teacher.

To assist with academic tasks, a teacher might secure papers to a student's work area with tape, clipboards, or magnets; place rubber strips or pads on work tools such as rulers and calculators to help keep them from slipping during use; and provide writing instruments that require less pressure to produce a mark, such as felt-tip pens or soft lead pencils. Communication technology can assist the student and teacher in the classroom as well.

Specialists such as physical therapists and orthopedic therapists will be involved in the educational assessment and often will have ongoing involvement in the care of students with orthopedic impairment. States may have specific qualification requirements for teachers who participate in special education programs for children with orthopedic impairments, including basic study of disabilities, anatomy, physiology, and therapeutic movement.

ASSESSMENT AND INSTRUCTIONAL ISSUES

The varying degrees and types of physical disabilities can present special challenges to those local schools and educators who instruct students with orthopedic impairments. Providing the least restrictive environment and promoting eventual independence for students with physical disabilities requires addressing each case specifically, working in a team approach with the student, parents, and education and health professionals to provide a plan that best meets the student's needs. It is important that the teacher can carry over techniques from these professionals into the classroom.

Alliance of state laws with IDEA is an important consideration. The team must consider all applicable laws and regulations in planning for the education of a child with a physical disability. This work includes testing of students under state and federal guidelines such as the No Child Left Behind (NCLB) Act, which was signed into law in 2002 by President George W. Bush. The act revised the Elementary and Secondary Education Act, which is the primary federal law in pre-collegiate education. NCLB requires annual testing of all students in reading and math proficiency.

The NCLB Act initially allowed up to 1% of special education students to take alternate tests; in 2005 the number was raised to 3%. Students may take alternative tests if they meet certain legal criteria. Several options are available, including having different achievement criteria or taking the regular assessment with approved accommodations or modifications.

SEE ALSO *Individualized Education Program (IEP); Special Education.*

BIBLIOGRAPHY

Algozzine, B., & Ysseldyke, J. (2006). *Assisting students with medical, physical, and multiple disabilities: A practical guide for every teacher.* Thousand Oaks, CA: Corwin Press.

American Academy of Special Education Professionals. (2006). Orthopedic impairments. Retrieved April 16, 2008, from http://aasep.org/professional-resources/exceptionalstudents/orthopedicimpairment/index.html#c2738.

Baumberger, J. P., & Harper R. E. (2007). *Assisting students with disabilities: A handbook for school counselors* (2nd ed.). Thousand Oaks, CA: Corwin Press.

Dutton, M. (2005). *Orthopaedic examination, evaluation, and intervention: A pocket handbook.* New York: McGraw-Hill.

Educating the child with a disability or other special needs. (2007). *Exceptional Parent, 37,* 104–108.

Hannell, G. (2006) *Identifying children with special needs: Checklists and action plans for teachers.* Thousand Oaks, CA: Corwin Press.

Duchenne muscular dystrophy. (2007). Muscular Dystrophy Association. Retrieved April 16, 2008, from http://www.mda.org/publications/tchrdmd/.

National Association of Parents with Children in Special Education. (2007). Exceptional children and disability information. Orthopedic impairments. Retrieved April 16, 2008, from http://www.napcse.org/exceptionalchildren/orthopedicimpairments.php.

National Dissemination Center for Children with Disabilities. (2004). Disability fact sheet no. 2: Cerebral Palsy. Retrieved April 16, 2008, from http://www.nichcy.org/pubs/factshe/fs2.pdf.

National Dissemination Center for Children with Disabilities. (2004). Disability fact sheet no. 12: Spina Bifida. Retrieved April 16, 2008, from http://www.nichcy.org/pubs/factshe/fs12.pdf.

Pierangelo, R., & Giuliani, G. (2007). *The educator's manual of disabilities and disorders.* San Francisco, CA: Wiley & Sons.

Teresa Odle

P

PARENT INVOLVEMENT

Parental involvement in education and, its related term, family school relationships, have been conceptualized through multiple disciplinary lenses and through educational agency, as well as from local, state, and federal policy perspectives. Parental involvement in education and family school relations are terms that have been used interchangeably. However, there are subtle distinctions. Family-school relations are often conceptualized as the interactions, especially the communication, between families and schools pertaining to academic progress of students, academic or behavioral problems, and expectations for home engagement. This is the type of involvement that is often included in school policies pertaining to involvement. It is also evident in federal policies such as the No Child Left Behind Act, which defines parental involvement in education as "the participation of parents in regular, two-way and meaningful communication involving student academic learning and other school activities" (107th Congress, 2002).

More broadly, parental involvement in education has been defined as "parents' interactions with schools and with their children to promote academic success" (Hill et al., 2004). Such interactions extend beyond the engagement with schools, to the home life and the expectations and values for education that are communicated directly and indirectly to children. These conceptualizations focus on individual students and their families. Other disciplines, such as economics, have defined it in a way that gives parental involvement a different focus or level of analysis.

Within the field of economics, parental involvement in education is often defined collectively across parents within schools and across schools within districts, rather than at the individual or family level. Parental involvement has been conceptualized as "collective parental pressure" on schools or the impact of collective utilization of school policies such as school choice, exiting public schools and district assignments in favor of private, charter, and magnet schools (Epple & Romano, 1998; McMillan, 2000). Collective parental pressure can also occur through organized parent-teacher associations or simply through concerned parents monitoring the schools. It can impact school quality and climate and, in turn, school performance. In addition, economic conceptualizations include parental influence by voting for (or against) school board members, school district budgets (e.g., levies, bonds), and involvement in school governance and administration. These, in turn, impact school processes and learning outcomes (Jimenez & Sawada, 1999; Nechyba, McEwan, & Older-Aguilar, 1999). In addition to focusing on collective influence of parents, the outcomes of interest often are focused at the collective performance of schools or school districts, rather than individual students' academic progress. The involvement of just a few parents may influence the quality of instruction in a classroom or a school and, thereby, influence the academic development of many students (McMillan, 2000).

There are at least three theories that have guided research and practice (Comer, 1995; Epstein, 1987; Grolnick & Slowiaczek, 1994). Each of these theories conceptualize parental involvement in education as a multi-dimensional construct that includes communication between families and schools, parental involvement in education at school (e.g., volunteering at school) and parental involvement at home (e.g., helping with homework; providing educational experiences outside of school). Whereas these theories were based on elementary school contexts, additional research identifies appropriate types of involvement for middle and high school. For example, some theories distinguish involvement that reflects "academic socialization" such as communicating the importance or value of education and linking schoolwork to students' interests or goals (Hill & Tyson, 2007) and "structural involvement," which includes providing students with the space, materials and expectations for achievement that is especially important for adolescents (Chao, 2000).

Assessments of parental involvement vary widely across studies and typically reflect assessments from parent, teachers, and students' perspectives. As research shows that these reports are often only moderately correlated with one another, their often unique relation with academic outcomes supports the premise that each reporter has a unique and important perspective (Reynolds, 1991). There are few "gold standard" measures of parental involvement and family school relations. However, most measures attempt to account for frequency of involvement, especially frequency of communication and parental visits to the school. Longer and more detailed measures attempt to account for who initiated contact. Initiation is important because parents and teachers tend to initiate contact for different reasons (Epstein, 1996). Teachers tend to initiate contact, beyond the regulated parent-teacher conferences, in the context of academic or behavioral problems. Parents, in contrast, tend to initiate contact for more proactive reasons and their initiated contact is positively associated with achievement.

DEVELOPMENTAL TRENDS

Beyond the variations in assessments of parental involvement, there are some consistent developmental trends in the normative levels of parental involvement in education. In general, parents tend to be more involved in their children's education when the children are younger, especially in elementary school, than they are in middle and high school (Eccles & Harold, 1996; Stevenson & Baker, 1987). School transitions (i.e., school entry; middle school and high school transitions) mark times when parental involvement changes in amount or type. Schools may be more or less welcoming; parents may feel more or less efficacious about being involved. Despite lower mean levels of involvement in middle and high school, parental involvement in education remains positively associated with academic outcomes (Hill et al., 2004). However, the types of involvement that are most influential for adolescents are not accounted for in extant theories and measures of involvement and, thus, one can conclude

that parental involvement does not decline during middle and high school but changes form and shape (Hill & Taylor, 2004).

DEMOGRAPHIC FACTORS

In addition to changes across developmental stages, demographic factors shape the type, amount, and influence of parental involvement. The most notable are socioeconomic and ethnic/cultural factors. Motivations for parental involvement are based in parents' perceived role in their children's academic lives, a role which is culturally derived. Further, families' experiences with and perceptions of their ethnic minority status vis-à-vis the school culture and population influence their engagement with their children's schooling. Extant literature suggests that there are socioeconomic and ethnic differences in levels of involvement and its influence on achievement. For example, being college educated and from higher income levels is associated with higher levels of involvement in children's schooling (Kohl, Lengua, McMahon, & Conduct Problems Prevention Research Group, 2000; Moles, 1993; Reynolds, Mavrogenes, Bezruczko, & Hagemann, 1996).

However, the research on ethnic differences is less conclusive. Some find that African Americans and Latinos are involved less than Euro Americans (Moles, 1993; Reynolds, Mavrogenes, Bezruczko, & Hagemann, 1996), others find no differences (Harris, Kagey, & Ross, 1987; Hill & Craft, 2003) and still others find that African Americans and Latinos have high expectations and involvement in their children's education (Chavkin & Williams, 1989; Lopez, Sanchez, & Hamilton, 2000). In contrast, Asian American families have been found to have the lowest levels of involvement in their children's education, especially when involvement is defined by interactions with the school (Kao, 1995; Sui-Chi & Willms, 1996). Variations across studies may be due to types of measurement and potential confounds between ethnicity and other demographic factors such as socioeconomic status and community resources. For example, the extent to which Latino families were the numerical minority within their communities and their children were numerical minorities among the school population influenced the amount and effectiveness of parental involvement in education (Rodriguez, 2002).

Beyond mean level differences, ethnic and socioeconomic differences have been documented in the goals for involvement and in the associations with academic outcomes. African American and Latino families often report that one of the reasons for being involved at school is to demonstrate to their children's teachers that they are committed to their children's education (Gutman & McLoyd, 2002). This is a goal that is often necessary because of biases teachers often hold about the academic potential of

African American and Latino children and the value their parents place on education (Ferguson, 1998; Hill, 2001; Lareau, 1987). This goal is unnecessary for Euro American and Asian American families, who often benefit from positive stereotypes held by teachers and other school personnel. Further, there is evidence that processes by which involvement influences vary by ethnicity and socio-economic status. Hill and Craft (2003) found that parental involvement was associated with academic outcomes because it increased academic skills for African Americans. In contrast, for Euro Americans, it improved social and emotional competence in children (Hill & Craft, 2003). Similarly, parental involvement was differentially associated with achievement based on whether parents had college degrees (Hill et al., 2004).

Despite differences in the amount and types of involvement across demographic background, parental involvement and family school relations are positively associated with academic achievement and children's aspirations (Hill & Taylor, 2004). Two meta-analyses have been conducted on the extant literature that attest to its positive influence. Meta-analyses aggregate across empirical studies to ascertain a level of effect in a way that accounts for differences in sample size and quality of measurement. Looking at studies across developmental levels, the relation is positive and practically meaningful (Fan & Chen, 2001). The relation is strongest for parents' expectations and aspirations for their children. For studies focusing specifically on middle school age children, a developmental stage that is notable for its issues of adjustment, the relation is also positive (Hill & Tyson, 2007). The strongest positive influence was for involvement characterized as "academic socialization," defined as communicating the importance or value of education and linking schoolwork to students' interests or goals. Interestingly, for middle school students, parental assistance with homework was negatively associated with achievement (Hill & Tyson, 2007).

Given the positive influence parents have on their children's academic development, many programs and policies look toward involving parents as a way to mitigate gaps in achievement and help children reach their potential. Among the barriers to parental involvement, the most significant ones include conflicting schedules (time), feeling unwelcomed and unappreciated, and feeling unheard. Creating ways for parents to interact with teachers and school personnel as their schedule permits will improve communication. This may include the use of technology, including e-mail, e-bulletin boards, and voice mail (Bouffard, 2006). Further, schools and families may differ in their implicit and explicit expectations for parental involvement. Communications between families and schools that affirm and celebrate differences, acknowledge and build upon strengths, and make explicit the goals and assumptions of involvement are essential in helping families feel welcomed and involved.

SEE ALSO *Parenting Styles.*

BIBLIOGRAPHY

107th Congress. (2002). *Public Law 107-110, The No Child Left Behind Act of 2001.* Retrieved April 16, 2008, from http://www.ed.gov/policy/elsec/leg/esea02/107-110.pdf.

Bouffard, S. M. (2006). *'Virtual' parental involvement: The role of the Internet in parent-school communication.* Unpublished doctoral dissertation, Duke University, Durham, NC.

Chao, R. K. (2000). Cultural explanations for the role of parenting in the school success of Asian American children. In R. W. Taylor & M. C. Wang (Eds.), *Resilience across contexts: Family, work, culture, and community* (pp. 333–363). Mahwah, NJ: Erlbaum.

Chavkin, N. F., & Williams, D. L. (1989). Low income parents' attitudes toward parental involvement in education. *Journal of Sociology and Social Welfare, 16*(3), 17–28.

Comer, J. P. (1995). *School Power: Implications of an intervention project.* New York: Free Press.

Eccles, J. S., & Harold, R. D. (1996). Family involvement in children's and adolescents' schooling. In A. Booth & J. F. Dunn (Eds.), *Family-school links: How do they affect educational outcomes* (pp. 3–34). Mahwah, NJ: Erlbaum.

Epple, D., & Romano, R. (1998). Competition between public and private schools, vouchers, and peer group effects. *American Economic Review, 88,* 33–63.

Epstein, J. L. (1987). Toward a theory of family-school connections: Teacher practices and parent involvement. In K. Hurrelman, F. X. Kaufman & F. Losel (Eds.), *Social intervention: Potential and constraints* (pp. 121–136). Berlin: Water de Gruyter.

Epstein, J. L. (1996). Perspectives and previews on research and policy for school, family, and community partnerships. In A. Booth & J. F. Dunn (Eds.), *Family school links: How do they affect educational outcomes* (pp. 209–246). Mahwah, NJ: Erlbaum.

Fan, X., & Chen, M. (2001). Parental involvement and students' academic achievement: A meta-analysis. *Educational Psychology Review, 13*(1), 1–22.

Ferguson, R. F. (1998). Teachers' perceptions and expectations and the Black-White test score gap. In C. Jencks & M. Phillips (Eds.), *The Black-White test score gap.* Washington, DC: Brookings Institution Press.

Grolnick, W. S., & Slowiaczek, M. L. (1994). Parents' involvement in children's schooling: A multidimensional conceptualization and motivation model. *Child Development, 65,* 237–252.

Gutman, L. M., & McLoyd, V. C. (2002). Parents' management of their children's education within the home, at school, and in the community: An examination of African-American families living in poverty. *Urban Review, 32*(1), 1–24.

Harris, L., Kagey, M., & Ross, J. (1987). A child resource policy: Moving beyond dependence on school and family. *Phi Delta Kappan, 68,* 575–580.

Henderson, A. T., Mapp, K. L., Johnson, V. R. & Davies, D. (2007). *Beyond the bake sale: The essential guide to family-school partnerships.* New York: The New Press.

Hill, N. E. (2001). Parenting and academic socialization as they relate to school readiness: The roles of ethnicity and family income. *Journal of Educational Psychology, 93,* 686–697.

Hill, N. E., Castellino, D. R., Lansford, J. E., Nowlin, P., Dodge, K. A., Bates, J. E., et al. (2004). Parent academic involvement as related to school behavior, achievement, and aspirations: Demographic variations across adolescence. *Child Development, 75*(5), 1491–1509.

Hill, N. E., & Craft, S. A. (2003). Parent-school involvement and school performance: Mediated pathways among socioeconomically comparable African American and Euro-American families. *Journal of Educational Psychology, 95,* 74–83.

Hill, N. E., & Taylor, L. C. (2004). Parental School Involvement and Children's Academic Achievement: Pragmatics and Issues. *Current Directions in Psychological Science, 13*(4), 161–164.

Hill, N. E., & Tyson, D. F. (2007). Parental involvement in middle school: A meta-analytic assessment of strategies that promote achievement. *Manuscript Submitted for Publication, Duke University, Durham, NC.*

Jimenez, E., & Sawada, Y. (1999). Do community-managed schools work? An evaluation of El Salvador's EDUCO program. *The World Bank Economic Review, 13,* 415–441.

Kao, G. (1995). Asian Americans as model minorities? A look at their academic performance. *American Journal of Education, 103*(2), 121–159.

Kohl, G. O., Lengua, L. J., McMahon, R. J., & Conduct Problems Prevention Research Group. (2000). Parent involvement in school: Conceptualizing multiple dimensions and their relations with family and demographic risk factors. *Journal of School Psychology, 38,* 501–523.

Lareau, A. (1987). Social class differences in family-school relationships: The importance of cultural capital. *Sociology of Education, 60,* 73–85.

Lopez, L. C., Sanchez, V. V., & Hamilton, M. (2000). Immigrant and native-born Mexican-American parents' involvement in a public school: A preliminary study. *Psychological Reports, 86*(2), 521–525.

McMillan, R. (2000). Competition, parental involvement, and public school performance. In J. R. Hines (Ed.), *National tax association proceedings* (pp. 150–155). Washington, DC: National Tax Association.

Moles, O. C. (1993). Collaborations between schools and disadvantaged parents: Obstacles and openings. In N. F. Chavkin (Ed.), *Families and schools in a pluralistic society* (pp. 21–49). Albany, NY: State University of New York Press.

Nechyba, T., McEwan, P., & Older-Aguilar, D. (1999). The impact of family and community resources on student outcomes: An assessment of the international literature with implications for New Zealand. Retrieved April 16, 2008, from http://www.educationcounts.govt.nz/publications/schooling/6846.

Patrikakou, E. N., Weissberg, R. P., Redding, S. & Walberg, H. J. (Eds.). (2005). *School-family partnerships for children's success.* New York: Teachers College Press.

Reynolds, A. J. (1991). Comparing measures of parental involvement and their effects on academic achievement. *Early Childhood Research Quarterly, 7,* 441–462.

Reynolds, A. J., Mavrogenes, N. A., Bezruczko, N., & Hagemann, M. (1996). Cognitive and family-support mediators of preschool effectiveness: A confirmatory analysis. *Child Development, 67,* 1119–1140.

Rodriguez, J. L. (2002). Family environment and achievement among three generations of Mexican American high school students. *Applied Developmental Science, 6,* 88–94.

Stevenson, D. L., & Baker, D. P. (1987). The family school relation and the child's school performance. *Child Development, 58,* 1348–1357.

Sui-Chi, H. E., & Willms, D. J. (1996). Effects of parental involvement on eighth grade achievement. *Sociology of Education, 69,* (126–141).

Nancy E. Hill

PARENTING STYLES

Parenting style refers to the normative patterns of behavior and tactics that parents use to socialize and control their children. Early work on parenting styles in the 1950s (e.g., Sears, Maccoby, & Levin, 1957) documented that adults who were nurturing and able to exert control were especially influential on children's development of self-regulated and disciplined behavior. Others (Lewin, Lippitt, & White, 1939) documented that adult leadership styles in classroom-like settings resulted in different levels of engagement on the part of children, with relatively warm and egalitarian styles resulting in greater task involvement, more self-regulated and autonomous behavior, and more competent performance than either highly controlling or permissive styles. From this work evolved a general approach to the study of parenting styles focused on socialization strategies reflecting demandingness and responsiveness. Demandingness, or control, refers to the degree to which parents attempt to integrate a child into the family social system by enforcing family rules and standards for behavior, setting expectations that are developmentally appropriate, and providing structure; responsiveness, or warmth, refers to parental attempts to support the development of their child's individuality and self-assertive tendencies by being attentive to the child's emotional well-being, special needs, and interests.

BAUMRIND'S TYPOLOGY OF PARENTING STYLES

Following this early work, Diana Baumrind (1971) conducted extensive observations of parents interacting with their children in their homes and concluded that four dimensions of parent-child interactions reflecting types of responsiveness and control could predict reliably children's social, emotional, and cognitive functioning. Parental control reflected consistent enforcement of rules, provision of structure to children's activities, and persistence in gaining child compliance; maturity demands reflected expectations to perform up to one's potential, and demands for self-reliance and self-control; clarity of communication reflected the extent to which parents solicit children's opinions and feelings, and use reasoning to obtain compliance; and nurturance reflected parental expressions of warmth and approval as well as conscientious protection of children's physical and emotional well-being.

These dimensions were then used to develop a typology of qualitatively different parenting styles based on levels of responsiveness and control: authoritative, authoritarian, permissive indulgent, and permissive uninvolved (Baumrind, 1971; Maccoby & Martin, 1983). Authoritative parenting is responsive and demanding in that parents communicate high expectations, provide clear standards for behavior, monitor child behavior, and discipline based on reasoning and explanation rather than power assertion or withdrawal of love. Authoritarian parenting is similar to authoritative parenting in terms of being demanding; however, parents are described as less responsive in that they are more likely to use power assertive disciplinary techniques and rely on love withdrawal to gain child obedience. Permissive indulgent parents display relatively high levels of responsiveness but low levels of control. Specifically, this style is typified by low levels of control and maturity demands, but high levels of solicitation and demonstrations of warmth. In contrast, permissive uninvolved parenting is described as being relatively low on both warmth and control. At its extreme, this style is considered to be rejecting or neglectful of children.

CORRELATES OF PARENTING STYLES

There is widespread recognition that Baumrind's dimensions describe socialization processes central to the development of childhood and adolescent social and cognitive competence (Grusec & Goodnow, 1994; Maccoby & Martin, 1983). Baumrind's studies established that elementary-aged children of authoritative parents display adaptive levels of self-reliance and self-esteem, and socially responsible, independent, and achievement-oriented behavior; children with authoritarian parents display relatively less independent behavior and lower levels of self-reliance and self-esteem; and children with permissive parents display less positive behavior and self-reliance but high levels of self-esteem. Work by Steinberg and his colleagues (Steinberg, Lamborn, Darling, Mounts, & Dornbusch, 1994) supported the validity of the four-dimension typology in that adolescents with authoritative parents fared best with respect to a range of social, emotional, and academic competencies; students with authoritarian parents reported relatively lower levels of psychological well-being; those with indulgent parents were characterized as enjoying high levels of psychological and emotional well-being but lower levels of achievement

The four parenting styles and their effects

The authoritative parent
Affectionate and engaged
Sets limits and enforces consequences
Uses reason, logic, and appropriate negotiation
Empowers a child's decision making

His or her child is likely to be
Happy, responsible, and kind
Good at problem-solving
Self-motivated and confident
Cooperative
An excellent student
A leader

The authoritarian parent
Emotionally aloof
Bossy; likely to say, "Because I said so"
Uses physical punishment or verbal insults
Dismisses a child's feelings.

His or her child is likely to be
Moody and anxious
Well-behaved
An average to good student
A follower

The permissive parent
Affectionate
Anxious to please, ends every sentence by asking, "OK?"
Indulgent
Can't say no and stick to it
Easily manipulated

His or her child is likely to be
Demanding and whiny
Easily frustrated
Lacking kindness and empathy
A poor to average student
A follower

The passive parent
Emotionally removed or indifferent
Uninvolved
Abdicates discipline
Inconsistent and unpredictable

His or her child is likely to be
Clingy and needy
Inappropriate and rude
Likely to get into trouble
A poor student
A follower

ILLUSTRATION BY GGS INFORMATION SERVICES. CENGAGE LEARNING, GALE.

coupled with higher levels of misconduct; and students with uninvolved/neglectful parents were characterized as demonstrating the lowest levels of competence in all areas. Moreover, over the course of the high school years, the academic functioning of adolescents with neglectful parents declined and levels of delinquency and internalizing symptoms such as depression increased significantly, especially in comparison to that of students with authoritative parents.

Other researchers have documented similar advantages for children with authoritative parents such that they demonstrate competent social interaction skills, self-reliant and independent problem solving, emotional well-being and overall psychological adjustment, and few maladaptive internalizing and externalizing behaviors (Grusec & Goodnow, 1994; Pomerantz, Grolnick, & Price, 2005). These children enjoy academic success, demonstrate socially responsible and prosocial forms of classroom behavior, and competent relationships with their peers. They also report strong intrinsic interest in learning, positive beliefs about ability and control, and mastery goal orientations toward learning (see Wigfield, Eccles, Schiefele, Roeser, & Davis-Kean, 2006). It is important to note, however, that few of these findings reflect comparisons of parenting styles based on

Baumrind's typology, but rather on parenting described more generally along dimensions of control or warmth or in terms of authoritative versus non-authoritative parenting.

CLASS, ETHNICITY, AGE, AND GENDER

The benefits of authoritative parenting have been documented mostly in samples of middle-class families in industrialized Western societies. However, some evidence indicates that parenting in working class and low socioeconomic status families tends to be more authoritarian, with fathers using power assertive discipline more often than mothers. Children raised in more communal and extended family networks such as those found in Native American cultures, tend to be treated more permissively than European American children. Chinese mothers tend to demonstrate more controlling, authoritarian parenting practices than their European American counterparts (Fisher & Lerner, 2005). Research on age-related differences suggests that as children get older, outward displays of warmth and affection and direct disciplinary encounters by parents lessen, as verbal communication and discussion increase. Parents also tend to provide greater opportunities for autonomy and self-regulation as children enter adolescence and early adulthood (Maccoby, 2007).

Despite these group-level differences, the positive effects of responsiveness and developmentally appropriate levels of control are quite similar for all children. However, work on gender differences suggests that girls tend to be generally more susceptible to socialization practices than boys, whereas parental control tends to be more critical for boys' well-being than for girls' (Pomerantz et al., 2005; Weiss & Schwartz, 1996). Authoritative parenting also tends to predict social competence and adaptive psychological functioning for African American, Asian American, European American, and Hispanic American children; positive relations between authoritative parenting and academic outcomes have been found mostly for European American children.

CONCEPTUAL AND METHODOLOGICAL ISSUES

Although findings have been fairly robust and consistent with respect to the benefits of responsive and demanding parenting, several conceptual and methodological issues preclude strong conclusions about the effects of parenting styles on children. A central issue is that most researchers document parenting on the part of just one parent, most often the mother. Little is known about the frequency with which both parents display similar parenting styles or about the effects of discordant styles on children's development. Similarly, few studies document parenting styles

within the context of broader family systems. It also is not clear how consistent parenting styles are across contexts and age of the child. In this regard, the degree to which consistency moderates the effects of parenting styles on child outcomes is not known. However, inconsistent parenting has been related to aggressive and noncompliant behavior throughout childhood and adolescence (Wentzel, 1994).

Additional concerns surround the methods employed to document parenting styles (Maccoby, 2007). In studies of young children, observations of mother-child interactions during prescribed laboratory-based activities typically are used to identify specific parenting styles. Or mothers are asked to self-report on their parenting behaviors. In the case of observational studies, issues focus on how to capture behavior in real time and take into account the sequential and reciprocal nature of parent-child interactions. Decisions concerning whether to interpret interactions as a function of time, event, or context also are cause for debate. The use of mothers' reports has been met with concern given the psychological investment that mothers have in presenting themselves and their children in the best light. In studies of older children, self-report methodologies typically are used to ask children about their parents' behavior. In this case, researchers place importance on children's cognitive understanding of their parents' actions rather than on objective forms of behavior. However, the degree to which these reports are reliable and valid assessments of parents' behavior as opposed to characteristics of the child is not well understood.

Of final interest are the processes and mechanisms by which parenting styles might have their influence on child outcomes. To illustrate, reasons for why responsive parenting should be related to a child's academic performance have not been well articulated. Darling and Steinberg (1993) argued that parenting styles are part of a more complex system of parental inputs that include goals and expectations for their children (e.g., expectations for academic performance) and provisions of opportunities, resources, and instruction (e.g., academic enrichment programs, help with homework) targeted at achieving specific outcomes (e.g., mastery of academic subject matter). Additional research and theorizing that clarifies these possibilities is needed.

SEE ALSO *Parent Involvement.*

BIBLIOGRAPHY

Baumrind, D. (1971). Current patterns of parental authority. *Developmental Psychology Monograph, 4,* (1, Pt.2).

Darling, N., & Steinberg, L. (1993). Parenting style as context: An integrative model. *Psychological Bulletin, 113*(3), 487–49.

Fisher, B. C., & Lerner, M. R. (2005). *Encyclopedia of applied developmental science.* Vol. 2. Thousand Oaks, CA: Sage Publications.

Grusec, J. E., & Goodnow, J. J. (1994). Impact of parental discipline methods on the child's internalization of values: A reconceptualization of current points of view. *Developmental Psychology, 30*(1), 4–19.

Lewin, K., Lippitt, R., & White, R. K. (1939). Patterns of aggressive behavior in experimentally created "social climates." *Journal of Social Psychology, 10,* 271–299.

Maccoby, E. E. (2007). Historical overview of socialization research and theory. In J. E. Grusec & P. D. Hastings (Eds.), *Handbook of socialization: Theory and research* (pp. 13–41). New York, NY: Guilford Press.

Maccoby, E. E., & Martin, J. A. (1983). Socialization in the context of the family: Parent-child interaction. In P. H. Mussen (Ed.), *Handbook of child psychology.* Vol. 4: *Socialization, personality, and social development* (pp. 1–101). New York: Wiley.

Pomerantz, E. M., Grolnick, W. S., & Price, C. E. (2005). The role of parents in how children approach achievement. In A. J. Elliot & C. S. Dweck (Eds.), *Handbook of Competence and Motivation.* New York: Guilford Press.

Sears, R. R., Maccoby, E. E., & Levin, H. (1957). *Patterns of child rearing.* Evanston, IL: Row, Peterson.

Steinberg, L., Lamborn, S. D., Darling, N., Mounts, N. S., & Dornbusch, S. M. (1994). Over-Time Changes in Adjustment and Competence among Adolescents from Authoritative, Authoritarian, Indulgent, and Neglectful Families. *Child Development, 65*(3), 754–770.

Weiss, L. H., & Schwartz, J. C. (1996). The relationships between parenting types and older adolescents' personality, academic achievement, adjustment, and substance use. *Child Development, 67,* 2101–2114.

Wentzel, K. R. (1994). Family functioning and academic achievement in middle school: A social-emotional perspective. *Journal of Early Adolescence, 14,* 268–291.

Wigfield, A., Eccles, J. S., Schiefele, U., Roeser, R., & Davis-Kean, P. (2006). Development of achievement motivation. In W. Damon and N. Eisenberg (Eds.), *Handbook of child psychology* (Vol. 3, 6th ed. pp. 933–1002). New York: Wiley.

Kathryn R. Wentzel
Shannon L. Russell

PEER RELATIONSHIPS

This entry contains the following:

OVERVIEW

Experiences with peers constitute an important developmental context for children and adolescents (Rubin, Bukowski, & Parker, 2006). Children's experiences with peers occur on several different levels: general interactions with peers, friendships, and in groups. Social competence reflects a child's capacity to engage successfully with peers at different levels. This section will provide an introduction and overview of friendships, peer groups, and sociometric status, with attention to developmental changes that occur during childhood and adolescence.

FRIENDSHIPS

Friendship refers to a close, mutual and voluntary relationship. For many decades Harry Stack Sullivan's 1953 theorizing has provided a conceptual framework for the development and functions of friendships. Sullivan described friendships as providing the following functions: (a) offering consensual validation, (b) bolstering feelings of self-worth, (c) providing affection and a context for intimate disclosure, (d) promoting interpersonal sensitivity, and (e) setting the foundation for romantic and parental relationships. Sullivan believed these functions developed during childhood and that true friendships were formed around the age of 9 or 10.

More recently, Thomas Berndt's 2004 study described four types of support that friends provide for each other: informational support, instrumental support, companionship support, and esteem support.

Informational support refers to guidance and advice in personal problems with parents, romantic relationships, teachers or other friends. Instrumental support refers to help on any type of task, such as homework or chores. Companionship support refers to reliance on friends to do things with, such as someone to eat lunch with or go to a dance or sporting event. Esteem support refers to the encouragement friends provide both when life is going well (e.g., congratulating each other) and when life does not go as one hoped (e.g., consoling in the face of failure).

In general as individuals move from childhood to adolescence, they spend more time with their peers and less time with their family. There is less adult supervision when they are with their friends and increasingly they have more friends of the opposite sex (Brown, 2005). In addition, individuals' conceptions of friendships change as they progress through childhood and adolescence.

Friendship conceptions are measured by asking children questions such as "What is a best friend?" For very young children, friendship conceptions are driven by the social activities in which they are engaged. As they age, children become more sophisticated in their notions of friendship. Generally, friendship conceptions progress from concrete to more abstract with age. During childhood and into adolescence, friendships become more stable as well as increasingly characterized as reciprocal and intimate. The development of children's friendship conceptions has been studied by Robert Selman and James Youniss. Selman (1980) emphasized the evolving perspective-taking abilities that underlie the changes in friendship conceptions. Youniss (1980) emphasized the importance of reciprocity in the development of children's friendship conceptions.

PEER GROUPS

The term *peer group* refers to an individual's small, relatively intimate group of peers who interact on a regular basis (often referred to as a clique). Peer groups consist of individuals who share friendship, hang around and talk to each other as well as do activities together. As children develop into adolescents, they spend an increasing amount of time with their peers compared to their parents or other adults (Csikszentmihalyi & Larson, 1974). The nature of peer groups also changes during adolescence. Typically, in early adolescence peer groups are single-sex but by middle adolescence mixed-sex peer groups are more prevalent. During late adolescence peer groups start to disintegrate as individuals spend more time as part of a romantic couple (see Brown, 2005 for a review).

Research has documented that peer groups exhibit similarity in many characteristics and attributes. The tendency of individuals to affiliate with others who share similar attributes is a social dynamic called homophily. Homophily of peer group beliefs and behaviors has been found across a wide range of outcomes. For example, adolescent peer groups have been found to be more homogeneous than the student body as a whole on reported frequency of smoking, drinking, drug use, and dating (see Rubin and colleagues, 2006, for a review). Homophily of peer groups has also been found among peers along academic characteristics such as GPA, college aspirations, time on homework, and general engagement in schoolwork. Two processes contribute to homophily: socialization and selection. Socialization refers to the tendency for friends to influence similar attributes in each other over time. Selection refers to the tendency for individuals to choose friends with similar attributes.

Socialization (also referred to as peer influence or peer pressure) most likely manifests itself in both direct and indirect ways. For example, social reinforcement may play a role. Beliefs and behaviors that are discouraged or received negatively by the peer group are less likely to be displayed again by an individual. Conversely, beliefs and behaviors that are encouraged or positively received by the peer group are more likely to surface again in the presence of one's peers. However, peer influence is also likely to occur in less direct ways. For example, modeling processes are likely to be involved in peer influence. Observing a friend's commitment to schoolwork or voicing a belief about the meaning of school could introduce an individual to new behaviors and viewpoints. Depending on the consequences, observation of a model can strengthen or weaken the likelihood that the observer will engage in such behavior or adopt such beliefs in the future (Bandura, 1986). Finally, peer influence is also likely to occur through subtle means such as gossip, teasing, and humor. Gossiping about others, for example, is a means of clearly communicating unacceptable behavior without direct confrontation (Eder & Sanford, 1986). Thus, students share experiences and exchange information (in subtle and not so subtle ways) and out of these interactions among peer group members a context emerges regarding norms and values. This peer group context is likely to influence many outcomes, including adolescents' motivation and engagement in school (Kindermann, 1993; Ryan, 2001).

SOCIOMETRIC STATUS

Sociometric status is distinct from friendship or peer group membership and concerns overall peer acceptance (i.e. the experience of being liked or disliked by peers). Research in the field of developmental psychology has a long tradition of using sociometric assessment techniques to assess peer acceptance. Sociometric assessment techniques are used to identify who is liked or disliked. For example, children might be asked to nominate three to five peers who they "really like," or "like to play with," or "do not like" or "do not like to play with." The peer nominations are then used to classify students into different social status categories. Coie, Dodge and Coppotelli (1982) devised five different categories that are widely used by researchers: (a) popular children who receive many positive and few negative nominations, (b) average children who receive an average number of positive and negative nominations, (c) neglected children who receive few positive and negative nominations, (d) rejected children who receive few positive and many negative nominations, and (e) controversial children who receive many positive and many negative nominations.

Much research has examined the characteristics of children classified as popular, average, neglected, rejected, and controversial (see Rubin and colleagues, 2006, for a review). While there are some general trends there is variability within each group. Popular children tend to be sensitive, cooperative, easily join others in social activities, and often take on a leadership role. Neglected children are low in peer interaction of any kind and generally do not call attention to themselves. Rejected children are the most at risk. Researchers have distinguished between rejected children who are aggressive, those who are withdrawn, and those who are aggressive-withdrawn. In the short-term, aggressive, rejected children have conduct problems and antisocial behavior in school. Withdrawn children report feeling lonely, are more depressed, and have low self-image. Aggressive-withdrawn children are the most at risk for all of these problems. In the long-term, rejected children are more at risk for mental health problems, delinquency, low achievement, and dropping out of school. Controversial children have characteristics that are represented in many of the groups.

It is important to note that there are other measures of peer acceptance or social status besides sociometric techniques. For example, researchers have measured popularity in different ways. The sociometric tradition asks children to list who they like and who they dislike in a classroom. Another way is to ask children directly to identify who is popular or ask them to rate their own popularity (referred to as perceived popularity). Different measures highlight different aspects of peer acceptance and social status. Sociometric techniques highlight the likeability of students whereas the measures of perceived popularity highlight social centrality and visibility. Researchers interested in aggression have noted that these different measures can lead to different conclusions about how the peer system operates. For example, sociometric popular children tend not to be aggressive but there is a positive correlation between perceived popularity ratings and aggression (Cillesen & Rose, 2005).

BIBLIOGRAPHY

Bandura, A. (1986). *Social foundations of thought and action: A social cognitive theory.* Englewood Cliffs, NJ: Prentice Hall.

Berndt, T. J. (2004). Children's friendships: Shifts over a half century in perspectives on their development and their effects. *Merrill Palmer Quarterly, 50,* 206–223.

Brown, B. (2005). Adolescent relationships with their peers. In R. M. Lerner and L. Steinberg (Eds.), *Handbook of Adolescent Psychology.* Hoboken, NJ: Wiley.

Cillesen, A. H. N., & Rose, A. J. (2005). Understanding popularity in the peer system. *Current Directions in Psychological Science, 14,* 102–105.

Coie, J. D., Dodge, K. A., & Coppotelli, H. (1982). Dimensions of types of social status: A cross-age perspective. *Developmental Psychology, 18,* 557–560.

Eder, D., & Sanford, S. (1986). The development and maintenance of interactional norms among early adolescents. In *Sociological studies of child development* (Vol. 1, pp. 283–300). Greenwich, CT: JAI Press.

Kindermann, T. A. (1993). Natural peer groups as contexts for individual development: The case of children's motivation in school. *Developmental Psychology, 29,* 970–977.

Rubin, K. H., Bukowski, W. M., & Parker, J. G. (2006). Peer interactions, relationships and groups. In W. Damon, R. M. Lerner, & N. Eisenberg (Eds.), *Handbook of child psychology: Vol. 3. Social, emotional, and personality development* (6th ed., pp. 571–645). New York: Wiley.

Ryan, A. M. (2001). The peer group as a context for the development of young adolescents' motivation and achievement. *Child Development, 72,* 1135–1150.

Selman, R. (1980). *The growth of interpersonal understanding: Developmental and clinical analyses.* New York: Academic Press.

Sullivan, H. S. (1953). *The Interpersonal Theory of Psychiatry.* New York: Norton.

Youniss, J. (1980). *Parents and peers in social development: A Piaget-Sullivan perspective.* Chicago: University of Chicago Press.

Allison M. Ryan

FRIENDSHIPS

Relationships with peers are of central importance to children throughout childhood and adolescence. Children who enjoy positive relationships with peers experience levels of emotional well-being, beliefs about the self, and values for prosocial forms of behavior and social interaction that are stronger and more adaptive than do children without positive peer relationships. They also tend to be engaged in and even excel at academic tasks more than those who have peer relationship problems (Rubin, Bukowski, & Parker, 2006; Wentzel, 2005).

Researchers who study peer relationships typically focus on one of two peer contexts: children's dyadic friendships and their larger peer groups and crowds (Rubin et al., 2006). The major distinction between friendships and involvement with the broader peer group is that friendships reflect relatively private, egalitarian relationships often formed on the basis of idiosyncratic criteria. In contrast, peer groups are defined by publicly acknowledged and therefore easily identified and predictable characteristics that are valued by the group. Larger peer groups often are comprised of students who have formed close dyadic friendships with each other. However, friendships are enduring aspects of children's peer relationships at all ages, whereas peer groups and crowds emerge primarily in the middle school years, peak at the beginning of high school, and then diminish in prevalence as well as influence by the end of high school (Brown, 1989).

FUNCTIONS, QUALITIES, AND CORRELATES OF FRIENDSHIPS

Friendships have been described most often with respect to their qualities and functions (Newcomb & Bagwell, 1996; Parker & Asher, 1993). They provide a source of companionship and entertainment; help in solving problems, personal validation, and emotional support; and especially during adolescence, offer a foundation for identity development. Research on friendship formation based on interviews and observations of children at school suggests that positive friendships are most likely to be developed and maintained over time when children display personal attributes such as the ability to communicate responsively, exchange information, and establish common ground, and when they can self-disclose, extend and elaborate the activities of others, resolve conflict, and provide emotional support (Gottman, 1983). These characteristics tend to differ as a function of age. Young children describe their friendships in terms of specific overt characteristics such as spending time together or having common interests; older children are more likely to include psychological characteristics such as intimacy, self-disclosure, loyalty, and commitment in describing their friends. Friendships also become more stable as children develop (Rubin et al., 2006).

Researchers also have documented differences in the quality and type of interactions that children have with friends and with non-friends (Newcomb & Bagwell, 1995). In this research, friendships are determined most often on the basis of students' nominations of their best friends at school, which are then matched to determine reciprocity, or best friendships. Characteristics of reciprocated friends are then compared to those of children who do not mutually nominate each other. These studies indicate that when children interact with friends they display significantly greater amounts of social contact such as talking, cooperation, and positive affect, they demonstrate more concern with resolving interpersonal conflicts and are less likely to instigate conflict, and they are more productive and use resources more efficiently when engaged in cognitive-related tasks together than they do with non-friends. Relationships of friends also are characterized as more balanced with respect to mutuality and reciprocity, as having stronger affective bonds, and stronger levels of mutual trust and commitment than those of non-friends. Compared to non-friends, friends also have in common more interests, values, activities, levels of prosocial as well as aggressive behavior, and personality characteristics (Wentzel, 2005). Research on school-based motivation indicates that friends are similar in the degree to which they value academic achievement, set goals for educational accomplishments, and pursue goals to behave in prosocial ways (e.g., Wentzel, Barry, & Caldwell, 2004).

Moreover, researchers have studied the relations of having friends to children's development (Wentzel, 2005). For the most part, simply having one friend as opposed to no friends appears to be related to a range of positive outcomes for students of all ages (e.g., Parker & Asher, 1983). When compared to their peers without friends, children with reciprocated friendships tend to be more sociable, cooperative, self-confident, independent, emotionally supportive, altruistic and prosocial, and less aggressive. Elementary school and middle school students with friends also tend to earn better grades and score higher on standardize tests, and to be more involved and engaged in school-related activities than those who do not have reciprocated friendships. Children without friends are

often more lonely, emotionally distressed, and depressed than children with friends.

The supportive function of friendships is demonstrated in research showing that students who make school transitions with friends show overall better adjustment during and after transition periods (e.g., when they enter formal schooling, middle school, and high school) than those who do so without friends (e.g., Ladd & Price, 1987; Wentzel et al., 2004). Students who have established friendships with classmates also are more likely to enjoy a relatively safe school environment and are less likely to be the targets of peer-directed violence and harassment than their counterparts without friends (e.g., Schwartz et al., 2000). This safety net that friends appear to provide each other is critical in that peer-directed violence and harassment is a fairly pervasive problem in U.S. schools and can have an enormous negative impact on students' social and emotional functioning.

Although the importance of friendships in early development should not be understated, it is well documented that friendships play their most pivotal role in development during the adolescent years (Youniss & Smollar, 1989). During this time friendships are believed to provide a unique avenue for identity development; furthermore, during this time the strongest relationship between the experience of positive friendships and the numerous associated positive outcomes are found. In this stage of development, children exhibit increased psychological investment in their peers and dependence on friends for support.

HOW FRIENDSHIPS INFLUENCE DEVELOPMENT

It is likely that significant associations between having friends and other positive competencies partly reflect the fact that students who demonstrate competence in one domain of functioning (i.e., making friends) often do so in other domains. Of interest, however, is the extent to which these significant relations also reflect a process whereby change in competencies occurs as a result of friend influence (Hartup, 1966). For instance, simply having a close friend might have developmental significance for healthy adjustment over time. Individuals also might adopt or develop specific behavioral styles or interests because they are considered to be desirable characteristics of their close friends.

In general, however, there are many unanswered questions concerning how friendships exert their influence on development. Some of these questions concern the timing, stability, and quality of friendships. For example, one unknown concerns whether there are critical periods during which friendships have more powerful effects on certain developmental outcomes.. Can a child be friendless in middle school, establish a friendship in high school, and still experience the protective effects friendships are proposed to offer? Some researchers have suggested that the cumulative experience of friendships is important to development rather than any one particular friendship in one place or time (Hartup & Stevens, 1997). Another question concerns the directionality of influence: Do children have high quality friendships because they already possess the necessary skills to make friends, or do they develop positive social skills within the context of their friendships? As of 2007, empirical evidence that addresses these questions is limited. Longitudinal studies that assess the characteristics of both friends at multiple points in time are necessary to determine the nature and magnitude of change in each individual over time. There is also an evident gap in the literature addressing friendships outside the classroom or school. The role of neighborhood friends or friendships within a family network in development and learning are in the early 2000s studied infrequently.

In spite of these limitations, presumably some form of influence from friends is likely to take place. If such influence does occur, however, an important question is why. Explanations of influence often focus on the likelihood that positive emotional attachments to friends promote healthy psychological functioning; feelings of relatedness and belonging that results from having friends are believed to contribute directly to positive feelings of self-worth and self-esteem. In turn, these levels of emotional well-being are believed to contribute to adaptive functioning in social as well as academic domains. Substantial evidence based on children at all ages supports this perspective (Wentzel, 2005).

Some scholars posit an observational learning explanation of influence in which a friend models behavior that is subsequently adopted by a child who observes the behavior (Wentzel et al., 2004). Empirical findings provide support for this position in that children have the opportunity to observe their friends' behavior with greater frequency than non-friends' behavior. In addition, behavior that is learned by observing others is likely to be enacted to the extent that an individual is motivated to do so (Bandura, 1986). Therefore, a child's behavior might become more similar to a friend's behavior because of a change in underlying motivational processes such as goals and self-concept. Research on motivation documents that peers serve as powerful models that influence the development of academic self-efficacy, especially when children observe similar peers who demonstrate successful ways to cope with failure (Schunk, 1987). These modeling effects are especially likely to occur when students are friends, although students who have higher achieving friends tend to have lower levels of self-efficacy than those with lower-achieving friends (Altermatt & Pomerantz, 2005).

Finally, theorists have proposed that positive interactions with peers contribute directly to intellectual development and functioning. For example, Piaget (1965) argued that mutual discussion, perspective taking, and conflict resolution with peers can motivate the accommodation of new and more sophisticated approaches to intellectual problem solving. Research has supported his position in that active discussion, problem solving, and elaborative feedback among peers are associated with advances in a range of cognitive competencies, including problem-solving skills, conceptual understanding, and meta-cognitive reasoning in samples ranging from preschool to high school (Gauvain & Perez, 2007). Of relevance for understanding the influence of friends on cognitive development is research indicating that interactions with friends rather than acquaintances tend to yield more predictable cognitive advances, presumably because friends have well-established interaction patterns and are sensitive to each other's interests and needs. In this regard, working with friends rather than acquaintances tends to result in positive outcomes for girls more than for boys (Newcomb & Bagwell, 1995).

SCHOOL-BASED INFLUENCES ON STUDENTS' FRIENDSHIPS

Of final interest for educators and practitioners is evidence that teachers can have a significant influence on the nature and establishment of students' friendships (e.g., Donohue, Perry, & Weinstein, 2003; Stormshack, Bierman, Bruschi, Dodge, & Coie, 1999). For example, teachers' perceptions of students' academic aptitude, intelligence, and tendency to misbehave are related to students' choice of friends. Elementary-aged students appear to be aware of the categorizations their teachers make about their classmates and will reject or accept them based on characteristics such as their troublesomeness or smartness accordingly. Students perceived to be smart are consistently viewed in a more positive light, whereas those ranked as troublemakers tend to be socially rejected. This phenomenon is especially true for girls.

The instructional approach a teacher adopts, and the resulting classroom organization, also has an impact on students' opportunities to make friends (Epstein, 1983). Adolescents with teachers who employ learner-centered practices (e.g. involve students in decision making, emphasize the importance of building positive social relationships) as opposed to teacher-centered practices (e.g. focus on rote learning, evaluation) report having more close friends and obtain a greater number of friendship nominations in general. Middle and high school students in classrooms where frequent interactions with classmates are condoned, that is, where students are encouraged to talk to each other about class assignments, to work in small groups, and to move about while working on activities, also are less likely to be socially isolated or rejected by their classmates, enjoy greater numbers of friends, and experience more diversity and stability in their friendships. The degree to which middle schools and high schools are ethnically diverse, as opposed to having clear majority and minority groupings, also can influence the nature and stability of students' friendships (Urberg, Degirmencioglu, Tolson, & Hallidayscher, 1995).

BIBLIOGRAPHY

Altermatt, E. R., & Pomerantz, E. M. (2005). The implications of having high-achieving versus low-achieving friends: A longitudinal analysis. *Social Development, 14*, 61–81.

Bandura, A. (1986). *Social foundations of thought and action: A social cognitive theory.* Englewood Cliffs, NJ: Prentice-Hall.

Brown, B. B. (1989). The role of peer groups in adolescents' adjustment to secondary school. In T. J. Berndt & G. W. Ladd (Eds.), *Peer relationships in child development* (pp. 188–215). New York: Wiley.

Donohue, K., Perry, K., & Weinstein, R. (2003). Teachers' classroom practices and children's rejection by their peers. *Applied Developmental Psychology, 24*, 91–118.

Epstein, J. L. (1983). The influence of friends on achievement and affective outcomes. In J. L. Epstein & N. Karweit (Eds.), *Friends in school* (pp. 177–200). New York: Academic Press.

Gauvain, M., & Perez, S. M. (2007). The socialization of cognition. In J. E. Grusec & P. Hastings (Eds.), *Handbook of socialization: Theory and research* (pp. 588–613). New York: Guilford.

Gottman, J. M. (1983). How children become friends. *Monographs of the Society for Research in Child Development, 48* (3, Serial No. 201).

Hartup, W. W. (Ed.). (1966). *The young child: Reviews of research.* Washington, DC: National Association for the Education of Young Children.

Hartup, W. W., & Stevens, N. (1997). Friendships and adaptation in the life course. *Psychological Bulletin, 121*, 355–370.

Ladd, G. W., & Price, J. M. (1987). Predicting children's social and school adjustment following the transition from preschool to kindergarten. *Child Development, 58*, 1168–1189.

Newcomb, A. F., & Bagwell, C. L. (1995). Children's friendship relations: A meta-analytic review. *Psychological Bulletin, 117*, 306–347.

Newcomb, A. F., & Bagwell, C. L. (1996). The developmental significance of children's friendship relations. In W. M. Bukowski, A. F. Newcomb, & W. W. Hartup (Eds.), *The company they keep: Friendship during childhood and adolescence* (pp. 289–321). New York: Cambridge University Press.

Parker, J. G., & Asher, S. R. (1993). Friendship and friendship quality in middle childhood: Links with peer group acceptance and feelings of loneliness and social dissatisfaction. *Developmental Psychology, 29*, 611–621.

Piaget, J. (1965). *The moral judgment of the child.* New York: Free Press. (Originally published in 1932).

Rubin, K. H., Bukowski, W., & Parker, J. (2006). Peer interactions, relationships, and groups. In N. Eisenberg (Ed),

Handbook of Child Psychology: Social, emotional, and personality development (pp. 571–645). New York: Wiley.

Schunk, D. H. (1987). Peer models and children's behavioral change. *Review of Educational Research, 57*, 149–174.

Schwartz, D., Dodge, K. A., Pettit, G. S., Bates, J. E., & Conduct Problems Prevention Research Group. (2000). Friendship as a moderating factor in the pathway between early harsh home environment and later victimization in the peer group. *Developmental Psychology, 36*, 646–662.

Stormshack, E., Bierman, K., Bruschi, C., Dodge, K., & Coie, J. (1999). The relation between behavior problems and peer preference in different classroom contexts. *Child Development, 70*, 169–182.

Urberg, K. A., Degirmencioglu, S. M., Tolson, J. M., & Hallidayscher, K. (1995). The structure of adolescent peer networks. *Developmental Psychology, 31*, 540–547.

Wentzel, K. R. (2005). Peer relationships, motivation, and academic performance at school. In A. Elliot & C. Dweck (Eds.), *Handbook of Competence and Motivation* (pp. 279–296). New York: Guilford.

Wentzel, K. R., Barry, C., & Caldwell, K. (2004). Friendships in Middle School: Influences on motivation and school adjustment. *Journal of Educational Psychology, 96*, 195–203.

Youniss, J., & Smollar, J. (1989). Adolescents' interpersonal relationships in social context. In T. J. Berndt & G. Ladd (Eds.), *Peer relationships in child development* (pp. 300–316). New York: Wiley.

Kathryn R. Wentzel
Sandra A. Baker

PEER GROUPS

Peers constitute one of the most important contexts for child development and socialization. Beyond their function as companions in leisure activities they serve as sources of instrumental and emotional support, help a child formulate values and beliefs, and oversee a child's adherence to behavioral norms of the peer culture and broader society. Much of a child's interactions with peers takes place in peer groups, making it important for others to understand how peer groups are organized, how they operate, and how these factors change from early childhood through adolescence. North American youth are more likely to encounter peers in schools than any other single social context, making schools a major locus of peer group interactions (Brown, 2004). This entry gives an overview of child and adolescent peer groups, paying particular attention to the role that schools play in these groups.

EARLY EXPERIENCES WITH PEER GROUPS

During the toddler and preschool era, young people's interactions with peers tend to be organized and closely supervised by adults, giving young people little opportunity to choose their peer groups (Ladd & Golter, 1988). Moreover, peer groups are often ephemeral, emerging from a specific, structured activity (such as a play group organized by parents) and dissolving when the activity ends. In this context children are expected to master the tasks of group entry and group interaction. According to Putallaz and Gottman (1981), those who can adjust to the group's ongoing interests, rather than disrupting group functioning by trying to impose their own agenda, are more successful entering groups and better prepared to participate in the peer groups that will emerge in school settings.

Once young people enter more stable peer settings, such as a school classroom, they can exercise more choice in their peer associates and their groups become more stable. Nevertheless, Kindermann (1993) notes that in these early school years peer groups feature high turnover in membership from one month to the next. Most groups are formed among youth who have ample opportunity to interact (e.g., live in the same neighborhood or are in the same classroom at school) and share a strong interest in the activity that inspires the group's formation. Once past the preschool years, both girls and boys show a preference for forming groups of same-sex peers, an inclination that Ennett and Bauman (1996) found will continue until middle adolescence.

PEER GROUPS IN MIDDLE CHILDHOOD

As young people move past early childhood and the primary grades of elementary school, peer group interactions typically expand. Young people try to join structured after-school activities or organize informal after-school interactions that include the friends they have in school classrooms. Despite this behavior, peer group membership remains highly volatile. Cairns and his colleagues (1995) found that, over the course of a school year, the core of a group may remain intact while more peripheral members float among groups, but it is unlikely that a group will experience no changes in membership over this time period. One reason for this flux is the rather loose structure of peer groups that characterizes middle childhood. Shrum and Cheek (1987) reported that in any given classroom several sets of students will band together into cliques, but collectively they may constitute little more than half of the students in a class. Other students will seem to have attachments to two or more cliques and often serve as a conduit of information between groups (someone who can facilitate a child's transfer between cliques). Still others may bond together in a close friendship and confine interactions to the dyad, while a small cadre of students can be regarded as isolates without close relationships with any classmates (although they may have strong ties to a friend or clique outside the

classroom). Researchers disagree about the percentage of youth who belong to cliques, largely because of differences in the ways that these groups are defined or identified. It seems, however, as if membership in a tight-knit peer group actually diminishes across time, contradicting the stereotype of early adolescents as highly clique oriented (Shrum & Cheek, 1987).

More consensus exists on the average size of peer groups. Cliques usually contain between five and eight members. Ladd (1985) found that boys' groups tend to be larger than those of girls, possibly in order to facilitate boys' more active pursuits (e.g., sports) on the playground. Also, according to Ladd (1985), children who are well liked by classmates belong to larger cliques than peers who are generally disliked.

Cliques bring together children who share common interests and social backgrounds (socioeconomic status or ethnicity). One might also expect clique members to share similar personality dispositions or temperaments, but this is not always so. Whereas many people believe that relatively aggressive youth coalesce into peer groups that are distinct from those of nonaggressive youth, Farmer and colleagues (2002) discovered that aggressive children actually are widely dispersed among cliques. However, cliques do vary in the average level of aggressiveness of group members, and this group average correlates significantly with the level of academic and social adjustment of group members (Farmer et al., 2002). If a student who is relatively aggressive and disliked by peers belongs to a relatively aggressive peer group, the child will have difficulty mastering the social skills necessary to move into a more prosocial peer group and gain a more favorable reputation among classmates.

As is true among older youth or adults, children are inclined to favor members of their peer group over outsiders. They recognize and accentuate group differences in attitudes and behaviors. Toward the end of childhood, however, young people are likely to differentiate highly regarded, core group members from more peripheral and less popular members, especially if these peripheral members do not adhere closely to group norms. A child may even favor peers who are members of so-called outgroups over fellow clique-mates who tend to deviate from the clique's norms, especially if the peers in the out-group are not highly committed to their group's norms (Abrams, Rutland, & Cameron, 2003). Bigler, Brown, and Markell (2001) demonstrated that school adults can exacerbate rivalries and hostilities among peer groups by calling attention to the groups (e.g., allowing children to form their own work groups or teams at recess), even if the adults show no favoritism of one group over another.

EXPANSION OF PEER GROUPS
IN ADOLESCENCE

The peer group system grows more complex in early adolescence, especially if young people move from neighborhood-based elementary schools to larger secondary schools that are no longer based on self-contained classrooms. The most significant change is the emergence of a second layer of peer groups, often referred to as crowds. In contrast to cliques, which identify students who routinely interact with each other, crowds differentiate individuals who share a similar reputation or image among peers, whether or not the crowd members routinely interact with one another (Brown, 2004).

Crowds are organized around the most salient features of the peer social system. They also tend to address developmental mandates of adolescence as a life stage (Brown, Mory, & Kinney, 1994). In the dominant mainstream of American culture, young people of this age are expected to become more autonomous from adults, cultivate a sense of identity, and master the skills necessary to participate in heterosocial interactions and relationships that form the normative social patterns of adulthood. Accordingly, peer crowds reflect different prototypic identities or lifestyles, based on individual abilities and interests: jocks, brains, delinquents, partyers, goths, skaters, and so on. Crowds also tend to be arranged in a social hierarchy, according to their status among peers (Brown et al., 1994). Sometimes group status forms the basis for a crowd's name: populars, nerds, rejects. Important cultural elements endemic to a particular school or community may also be reflected in the crowd system, such as when groups emerge that are based on ethnic background, religious orientation, or family economic background. Thus, the crowd with which an adolescent is associated by peers is an indicator of the child's status, public identity, and values or behavior patterns that are most noticeable to peers.

The importance of belonging to a crowd grows through early adolescence, peaks in middle adolescence (about the beginning of high school), then fades (Brown, Eicher, & Petrie, 1986). Nevertheless, Schwendinger and Schwendinger (1989) reported that even in middle adolescence, not all young people are associated definitively with one particular crowd. Some display a "split image," in which peers associate them with two different crowds, whereas others are not well enough known by peers to place in any crowd. It appears to be more difficult for adolescents to change crowd affiliations than it is to change clique membership.

In addition to their role in identity development, crowds help to regulate social interactions by indicating which peers are acceptable candidates for friendship or dating relationships (Brown et al., 1994). Crowds at either end of the status hierarchy in Eckert's 1989 study

of high school youth displayed rivalries or animosities that precluded close relationships between members. These may be manifest in physical confrontations, such as between rival gangs, but they are more likely to be expressed in verbal exchanges or criticisms of the rival group. Research by Cillessen and Mayeux (2004) revealed that members of high status groups are rated by peers as more verbally aggressive than low status crowd members. Their aggressive behaviors often serve to affirm and reinforce their superior status in the peer system. But there is a price to pay for such aggression, in that members of high status crowds are not necessarily well liked by peers.

Although there are strong antipathies or rivalries among certain crowds in a school, there can be close affinities among other combinations of crowds. This fact may explain why, at least in high school, Urberg, Degirmencioglu, Tolson, and Halliday-Scher (1995) found that friendship groups often contain members of multiple crowds. The inclination to form cliques from within a given crowd appears to be stronger among certain crowds than others, and during early adolescence rather than later years (Kinney, 1993). However, patterns of exclusiveness in clique formation can be exacerbated in schools or communities that emphasize distinctions among students by virtue of residence, ethnicity, religion, or other demographic markers.

Ethnographers who have studied clique dynamics have focused on early adolescent groups of high-status girls. They have observed a complex structure that involves multiple roles and a hierarchy of authority, often enforced through a pattern of relational aggression that makes the groups appear to undermine members' psychological well-being (Adler & Adler, 1998). It is unlikely that the same structure and group dynamics typify adolescent cliques, especially after the middle school years. Finders (1997), for example, found that within-group relations were much less intense and more supportive in a lower status girls' clique than the high-status counterpart in the middle school that she studied.

A major function of adolescent cliques is to socialize youth into heterosexual roles and relationships (Connolly, Furman, & Konarski, 2000; Dunphy, 1963). Accordingly, although same-sex groups still dominate the adolescent social landscape, mixed-sex cliques become increasingly common. Youth who are involved in mixed sex groups begin dating and romantic relationships earlier and with more confidence than young people who remain in single-sex cliques (Connolly et al., 2000).

Peer groups are instrumental in promoting prosocial behavior, such as academic achievement, as well as antisocial activities, depending upon the norms of the group. In Ellis and Zarbatany's 2007 study of Canadian youth, group influences toward deviant behavior were significant only among low-status cliques, whereas group influences toward prosocial behavior were strongest in cliques of high-status students. Cliques do not have equal influence on all members. Tarrant, MacKenzie, and Hewitt (2006) found that those who identify strongly with their clique are more subject to its influence than members with more casual ties to the group. Cliques have indirect as well as direct effects on members' behavior and well-being. Lansford and colleagues (2003) reported that a strong and supportive friendship group can moderate the negative impact of poor parenting on young people.

As is the case for childhood cliques, schools can affect the dynamics of adolescent peer groups. Sponsoring ethnically based clubs or organizations helps to legitimize ethnically oriented crowds. Favoring one group of students over another (e.g., spotlighting athletes or giving them special consideration) can boost the cliques or crowds to which that group belongs. Separating students by academic ability or English language fluency creates divisions in the student body that affect the formation of friendship groups.

COALESCENCE OF CROWDS IN LATE ADOLESCENCE

By the final years of high school, most students have begun to solidify their sense of identity, located enduring friendships, and grown more comfortable with heterosocial activities. Having thus facilitated adolescent development, peer crowds diminish in importance and influence. In fact, the boundaries between crowds often dissipate, making it difficult to discern a crowd's members and making friendship groups that cut across several crowds more common (Brown et al., 1994). Young people's attention turns away from crowds, back toward their circle of friends. Peer groups function more as support systems than as powerful entities that direct student behavior, which helps to prepare students for the type of peer group experiences they are likely to encounter in adulthood.

BIBLIOGRAPHY

Abrams, D., Rutland, A., & Cameron, L. (2003). The development of subjective group dynamics: Children's judgments of normative and deviant in-group and out-group individuals. *Child Development, 74,* 1840–1856.

Adler, P. A., & Adler, P. (1998). *Peer power: Preadolescent culture and identity.* New Brunswick, NJ: Rutgers University Press.

Bigler, R. S., Brown, C. S., Markell, M. (2001). When groups are not created equal: Effects of group status on the formation of intergroup attitudes in children. *Child Development, 72,* 1151–1162.

Brown, B. B. (2004). Adolescents' relationships with peers. In R. M. Lerner & L. Steinberg (Eds.), *Handbook of Adolescent Psychology* (2nd ed., pp. 363–394). New York: Wiley.

Brown, B. B., Eicher, S. A., & Petrie, S. D. (1986). The importance of peer group ("crowd") affiliation in adolescence. *Journal of Adolescence, 9,* 73–96.

Brown, B. B., Mory, M., & Kinney, D. A. (1994). Casting adolescent crowds in relational perspective: Caricature, channel, and context. In R. Montemayor, G. R. Adams, & T. P. Gullotta (Eds.), *Advances in adolescent development: Vol. 6. Personal relationships during adolescence* (pp. 123–167). Newbury Park, CA: Sage.

Cairns, R. B., Leung, M.-C., Buchanan, L., & Cairns, B. D. (1995). Friendships and social networks in childhood and adolescence: Fluidity, reliability, and interrelations. *Child Development, 66,* 1330–1345.

Cillessen, A. H. N., & Mayeux, L. (2004). From censure to reinforcement: Developmental changes in the association between aggression and social status. *Child Development, 75,* 147–163.

Connolly, J., Furman, W., & Konarski, R. (2000). The role of peers in the emergence of heterosexual romantic relationships in adolescence. *Child Development, 71,* 1395–1408.

Dunphy, D. C. (1963). The social structure of urban adolescent peer groups. *Sociometry, 26,* 230–246.

Eckert, P. (1989). *Jocks and burnouts: Social categories and identity in the high school.* New York: Teachers College Press.

Ellis, W. E., & Zarbatany, L. (2007). Peer group status as a moderator of group influence on children's deviant, aggressive, and prosocial behavior. *Child Development, 78,* 1240–1254.

Ennett, S., & Bauman, K. (1996). Adolescent social networks: School, demographic, and longitudinal considerations. *Journal of Adolescent Research, 11,* 194–215.

Farmer, T. W., Leung, M., Rodkin, P. C., Cadwallader, T. W., Pearl, R., et al. (2002). Deviant or diverse peer groups? The peer affiliations of aggressive elementary students. *Journal of Educational Psychology, 94,* 611–620.

Finders, M. J. (1997). *Just girls: Hidden literacies and life in junior high.* New York: Teachers College Press.

Kindermann, T.A. (1993). Natural peer groups as contexts for individual development: The case of children's motivation in school. *Developmental Psychology, 29,* 970–977.

Kinney, D. (1993). From "nerds" to "normals": Adolescent identity recovery within a changing social system. *Sociology of Education, 66,* 21–40.

Ladd, G. W. (1983). Social networks of popular, average, and rejected children in school settings. *Merrill-Palmer Quarterly, 29,* 283–307.

Ladd, G. W., & Golter, B. S. (1988). Parents' management of preschoolers' peer relations: Is it related to children's social competence? *Developmental Psychology, 24,* 109–117.

Lansford, J. E., Criss, M. M., Petit, G. S., Dodge, K. A., & Bates, J. E. (2003). Friendship quality, peer group affiliation, and peer antisocial behavior as moderators of the link between negative parenting and adolescent externalizing behavior. *Journal of Research on Adolescence, 13,* 161–184.

Putallaz, M., & Gottman, J. M. (1981). An interactional model of children's entry into peer groups. *Child Development, 52,* 986–994.

Schwendinger, H., & Schwendinger, J.(1985). *Adolescent Subcultures and Delinquency.* New York: Praeger.

Shrum, W., & Cheek, N. H. (1987). Social structure during the school years: Onset of the degrouping process. *American Sociological Review, 52*, 218–223.

Tarrant, M., MacKenzie, L., & Hewitt, L.A. (2006). Friendship group identification, multidimensional self-concept, and experience of developmental tasks in adolescence. *Journal of Adolescence, 29*, 627–640.

Urberg, K. A., Degirmencioglu, S. M., Tolson, J. M., & Halliday-Scher, K. (1995). The structure of adolescent peer networks. *Developmental Psychology, 31*, 540–547.

B. Bradford Brown

PEER PRESSURE

Peer pressure is the influence that a group has on an individual. Although in common parlance peer pressure is frequently used to describe a negative influence, peer pressure can be both positive and negative. Young people are more susceptible to peer pressure at certain stages of development, but everyone is influenced by peers to some degree, even adults.

TYPES OF PEER PRESSURE

Peer pressure has been of interest to researchers for decades. In a series of experiments performed in 1955 and 1956, researcher Solomon Asch demonstrated the power of peer pressure to make otherwise intelligent individuals go against the evidence of their own eyes. He showed participants a straight line on a card and asked them to pick out which straight line on another card matched it. The straight lines on the second card were of quite different lengths, and when subjects performed the task alone they chose the correct line more than 99% of the time. However, when confederates of Asch became involved, the situation changed drastically. When every confederate chose the same, incorrect, line, the participant would choose the same, incorrect, line more than 36% of the time (Asch 1955). In general, the more confederates participating and choosing the incorrect line, the stronger this effect was found to be. This clearly demonstrated that, among the college student participants at least, the opinion of the group could exert such a strong influence that it could cause participants to choose against their better judgment. Interestingly, when even one confederate chose the correct line participants were more much more likely to choose the correct line (Asch 1956). This suggests that peer pressure is reduced when the group is not unanimous.

Asch's study was alarming because it showed that the influence of peers on judgment is so strong that it could make even intelligent college students choose the opinion of a group over the evidence of their own eyes. Since his groundbreaking experiments thousands of studies have been done demonstrating the presence of peer pressure on children and adolescents in dozens of different situations and at nearly every age. Much of this research has focused on negative peer pressure, the peer pressure most likely to be of concern to parents and educators.

Peer pressure has the capacity to be an extremely negative influence on a child or adolescent. Many studies have documented that children whose friends engage in negative or antisocial activities, such as smoking or using drugs, are much more likely to engage in such behaviors themselves. Salvy and colleagues' 2007 study even found that overweight girls who ate with a friend who was also overweight consumed more calories on average than overweight girls who ate with friends who were of normal weight. This kind of influence on day-to-day habits, outside even the realm of traditional antisocial activity, demonstrates how prevalent peer influence can be. Ad campaigns such as the "just say no" campaign of the 1980s and early 1990s and the "above the influence" campaign, begun in the mid 2000s, are aimed at encouraging children and adolescents to recognize the influence of peer pressure and to overcome its pressure to engage in antisocial activities.

Although peer pressure is most frequently used in conversation with a negative connotation, not all peer pressure is negative. Peer pressure is a necessary and important part of development. It helps to socialize children, provide a sense of identity, and can encourage positive behaviors. Peer pressure can encourage children and adolescents to strive for excellence in areas such as sports, theater, and science. Peer pressure might make children feel pressured to take an honors class with all of their friends, which would not necessarily be right for every child but would by no means be antisocial. Peer pressure is an important fact of life at all ages; it is even a significant motivator for adults. A 2006 report to the House Science and Technology subcommittee reported peer pressure more effective at making American adults conserve energy than concern for the environment, the desire to save money, or even social responsibility. Given that peer pressure exists at all ages, it may be more effective to help children and adolescents identify negative peer pressure than to try to eliminate peer pressure.

SUSCEPTIBILITY TO PEER PRESSURE

Susceptibility to peer pressure varies with age and specific personal traits. In general, the role of peer pressure increases with age into adolescence. When children are very young, parents and other caregivers tend to choose play groups and babysitting situations. Parents limit the amount of time they allow children they believe to be bad influences to have contact with their children. Very young children also tend to spend less time in the company of other children and more time with parents or other adult figures. Therefore, the presence of peer pressure is somewhat limited. As children enter school full time and begin to spend more of the day playing with peers outside the direct supervision of adults the potential for peer pressure increases.

Research is somewhat divergent about what age group is most susceptible to peer pressure. Some research indicates that the influence of peers steadily increases through middle school and peaks during the later years of high school. Recent research has suggested that this may not be the case. A 2007 study by Steinberg and Monahan found that resistance to the influence of peer pressure actually increases fairly linearly between ages 14 and 18, and does not increase significantly after that. They found that among the participants studied, ranging in age from 10 to 30, resistance to peer influence did not increase significantly from ages 10 to 14 or after age 18 (Steinberg, 2007).

In addition to changing with age, susceptibility to peer pressure also varies by individual. Children who have low self-confidence and a low sense of agency are more likely to be influenced by their peers. Children who are somewhat ostracized form the general group of peers may gravitate towards children who have also been ostracized, who may be more likely to engage in antisocial behavior. Children who are pushed out of the group may feel more pressure to conform in an attempt to be accepted by a group, even if the group is not engaging in prosocial activities.

FRIENDS VERSUS PEERS

Peer influence can come from many areas. It is not often found in the guise of one adolescent telling another adolescent directly, "Hey, everybody's doing it." It is usually more subtle but in many ways more insidious than that. Peer pressure most often comes from a peer group larger than the set of friends that the child or adolescent regularly interacts with. In this way peer pressure can be exerted indirectly, such as when everyone in school wears a certain type of sneakers or carries a certain brand of backpack. Although the influence is extremely dispersed, and it is not likely anyone will directly tell the children they need to buy those shoes or that backpack. the influence is none the less extremely strong.

Friendship group refers to the group of friends with which children or adolescents spend most of their time; the group to which they most closely relates. Friendship choice is often influenced by habits and interests the child already has. For example, an adolescent who smokes is more likely to be friends with a group of adolescents who also smoke than an adolescent who does not. Although already occurring traits can heavily influ-

ence friendship group choice, once the group has formed the members exert increased pressure on one another to conform.

Friendship groups are more likely than peer groups to exert direct, spoken pressure on a child or adolescent. The pressure to conform to the friendship group is also greater because fear of losing the primary friendship group can be severe. The friendship group can also help the child or adolescent resist pressure by the larger peer group to engage in antisocial activities. As was shown in the Asch experiment, even one other person standing against the group can provide enough incentive for individuals to go with their beliefs instead of with the group.

SEE ALSO *Self-Esteem.*

BIBLIOGRAPHY

Asch, S. E. (1955). Opinions and social pressure. *Scientific American, 193,* 31–35.

Asch, S. E. (1956). Studies of independence and conformity: A minority of one against unanimous majority. *Psychological Monographs: General and Applied, 70,* 1–69.

Cotterell, J. (2007). *Social networks in youth and adolescence.* New York: Routledge.

Hoffman, B., Monge, P., Chou, C., & Valente, T. (2007). Perceived peer influence and peer selection on adolescent smoking. *Addictive Behaviors, 38*(2), 1546–1555.

Perkins, H.W. (Ed.). (2003). *The social norms approach to prevent school and college age substance abuse: A handbook for educators, counselors, and clinicians.* San Francisco: Jossey-Bass.

Salvy, S., Romero, N., Pauch, R., & Epstein, L. H. (2007). Peer influence on pre-adolescent girls' snack intake: effect of weight status. *Appetite, 49*(1), 177–183.

Steinberg, L., & Monahan, K. (2007). Age difference in resistance to peer influence. *Developmental Psychology, 43*(6), 1531–1544.

Helen Davidson

SOCIOMETRIC STATUS

Sociometry is defined as the quantitative measurement of social relationships. Jacob Moreno (1889–1974) is considered the founder of sociometric analysis, with his 1934 book *Who Shall Survive?* Sociometry, as Moreno and others since have envisioned it, has two major objectives. The first is to describe the structure of the peer group as a whole, for example, by creating sociograms or visual diagrams of peer group structure. The second objective is to assess the status of individuals within the group. Sociologists have generally been more interested in group structure, while social and developmental psychologists have tended to focus more on the sociometric status of individuals, although there is considerable overlap between the sociological and psychological research on this topic. Bukowski and Cillessen provide an excellent review of the history of sociometry that explains its development during the twentieth century.

A vast number of empirical studies have investigated sociometric status among schoolchildren in the classroom setting. In the U.S. educational system, children spend an enormous amount of time with same-age peers in the classroom, so it is critically important to understand how each child fits within that group and to understand what are the consequences, both short-term and long-term, of having a particular status within the group. Furthermore, particularly in younger grades, the classroom setting provides researchers with a readily available, relatively self-contained peer group, which enables them to conduct sophisticated quantitative analyses of peer status and obtain very rich information about how the peer group functions and its effects on individual children.

MEASURING SOCIOMETRIC STATUS

The most common method of measuring sociometric status is to collect confidential nominations from the members of a peer group regarding who each person likes and who each person dislikes within the group. Occasionally, teachers, parents, or trained behavioral observers provide the data, but peer nominations are usually considered the best form of measurement. Peers understand the group from the inside, rather than viewing it from the outside, as others do. Also, the measurements are more direct with peers ("Who do you like?") than with teachers or observers ("Who is well-liked by peers?"). Furthermore, while there will be some degree of bias no matter what the source of information is (parents, teachers, observers, or peers), one can obtain more reliable information by surveying a large group of peers than one would get from a single individual such as a teacher or an observer. Often researchers use multiple sources for collecting the data, and they can learn a great deal about peer status by examining the similarities and differences among these various sources of information.

Sociometric status is usually measured by counting the number of liked votes and the number of disliked votes that each person receives from peers, a method that was introduced into developmental psychology by Coie, Dodge, and Coppotelli in the early 1980s. There is some controversy from an ethical perspective about whether to include the negative (disliked) nominations when collecting data or simply collect the positive (liked) nominations only. Some teachers, parents, and/or school administrators believe that asking about disliking will lead some children to be ostracized when they would not have been so otherwise. However, others argue that these measures are simply assessing relationships and attitudes that already exist. More importantly, the prob-

lem with not using negative nominations is that there is a substantial difference between failing to name someone as liked and actually naming the person as disliked. Only by using both types of nominations can researchers categorize children into the five different categories of sociometric status (described below) upon which most of the research in this field is based.

The five-category model proposed by Coie and colleagues involves counting the number of votes received by each student for liking and disliking and standardizing those votes within the classroom. In some cases, children are allowed to make an unlimited number of nominations, while in other cases, they are restricted to a specific number of nominations, (three, for example). Also, sometimes the nominations are only for same-sex peers (especially in younger grades) and sometimes they are across both genders. The first two categories that can be derived from these nominations differ along a dimension of social preference. The first category is sociometrically popular, which includes children who receive a large number of liked nominations and very few if any disliked nominations. The second category, sociometrically rejected, includes children who receive a large number of disliked nominations and very few if any liked nominations. The popular children are (obviously) more preferred than the rejected children. The next two categories differ along a second dimension, called social impact. These categories are sociometrically controversial, which includes children who receive many liked nominations and many disliked nominations, and sociometrically neglected, which includes children who receive very few of either type of nomination. The controversial children, who receive high numbers of both types of nominations, have more impact or prominence in the peer group than do neglected children, who receive low numbers of liked and disliked nominations. Finally, the last category is sociometrically average, which includes everyone who is not particularly high or low on either type of nomination.

BEHAVIORAL AND COGNITIVE CHARACTERISTICS OF STATUS GROUPS

Much research on sociometric status has focused on the rejected category (see Asher and Coie for a comprehensive review of peer rejection). The reason for this focus is that rejected children are most at risk for current and future behavioral problems. However, researchers have examined the behavioral characteristics and cognitive thought patterns of children in all these categories, as well as the antecedents and consequences of membership in a particular status group. What follows is a brief review of this research.

Five major sociometric statuses and their characteristics

Status	Sociometric ratings	Characteristics
Popular	• Many well-liked ratings, few disliked ratings • Many positive ratings	• Popular and have many friends • Viewed as leaders • Friendly and sociable • Cooperative and helpful • Understand social cues well and have high levels of social competence • Respect authority • Follow social rules • Described as having a good sense of humor and being positive
Controversial	• Both well-liked and disliked ratings • Ratings highly variable with many at each extreme	• Disruptive and aggressive • Socially competent • Active • Disregard social rules • Viewed as leaders and as having an impact on peer group • Perceived as having both positive and negative attributes • Share characteristics of both the popular and rejected aggressive groups
Neglected	• Ratings are near the mean on scores of social preference and social impact • No extreme positive or negative ratings • This is the most unstable of statuses	• Ignored or over looked by peers • Not treated poorly but not treated well by peers • Solitary and withdrawn • Not aggressive • Do not differ behaviorally from either the popular or average group
Average	• Ratings are near the mean on scores of social preference and social impact • No extreme positive or negative ratings	• Perceived as neither popular nor unpopular • High levels of positive social behaviors • High levels of social competence
Rejected	• Many disliked and very few well-liked ratings • Many negative ratings	• Associated with future maladaptive behaviors • Difficulties reading social cues
Rejected aggressive		• Perceived as bossy, non-cooperative, and impulsive • Aggressive and disruptive • Viewed as bullies • Externalize problems
Rejected withdrawn		• Perceived as sad and depressed • Do not actively engage in classroom activities • Have high negative self-perceptions • Actively ignored by classmates and often victims of bullying

SOURCE: Paige Shalter Bruening

ILLUSTRATION BY GGS INFORMATION SERVICES. CENGAGE LEARNING, GALE.

Researchers have determined behavioral profiles for the various status categories, and this research is nicely summarized in a review article by Newcomb, Bukowski, and Pattee. Sociometrically popular children tend to be helpful, cooperative, sociable, and demonstrate leadership within the peer group. Sociometrically rejected children tend to fall into two subgroups: rejected-aggressive and rejected-withdrawn. Rejected-aggressive children are physically aggressive and bullying toward peers, while rejected-withdrawn children are often the victims of aggression by other children. Both groups display maladaptive behavior that makes it difficult for these individuals to get along with other children. Controversial children share characteristics with both popular and rejected children. They are very active in the peer group and demonstrate leadership and cooperativeness, but they also tend to display aggres-

sion toward peers and do not abide by the rules. The neglected category is not stable over time; in other words, if a child is categorized as neglected during one measurement session, he or she is likely not to have that same status if measurements are taken several months or a year later. Although the neglected category may seem to be similar to the rejected-withdrawn group, there are important differences between the two. Rejected-withdrawn children are actively ostracized by the peer group, while neglected children are essentially ignored and not treated particularly well or particularly poorly by peers.

In addition to behavioral differences, children in the various status groups also differ in their patterns of thinking. Rejected-aggressive children tend to make hostile attributions regarding other children's behavior, whereas rejected-withdrawn children tend to make self-defeating attributions that interfere with their ability to make friends. Also, rejected children are less accurate overall than are other status groups at interpreting peers' behavior. Popular and average children have higher levels of social competence and are able to achieve their goals more readily in social situations than are rejected children.

ANTECEDENTS AND CONSEQUENCES OF SOCIOMETRIC STATUS

As one might imagine, children in these different status categories have different prognoses for future success. Longitudinal studies that follow children as they grow older (such as the study by Hymel, Rubin, Rowden, and LeMare) and retrospective studies that look at the childhood experiences of adults have both shown that early peer rejection is associated with later mental health problems, criminal behavior, and early school withdrawal. Rejected-aggressive children are more likely to engage in impulsive and delinquent behavior, while rejected-withdrawn children are more likely to suffer from depression and anxiety. Rejected children as a whole display maladaptive behavior as early as infancy, demonstrating more difficult temperaments and more insecure attachment to parents than do those from other status groups.

It is very important to note that most of the research on antecedents and consequences of sociometric status has been correlational rather than causal in nature. In other words, researchers have not established that temperament and attachment problems or faulty thinking patterns cause sociometric rejection, nor have they established that being sociometrically rejected in school causes later problems in life. There might be other variables as yet uninvestigated which could be responsible for the child's status as well as his or her past and future problems. If there is not a causal relationship between status and these other variables, it means that helping children to be more accepted by their peers will not necessarily improve their outcomes later in life.

Furthermore, it is important to realize that the link between sociometric status and present and future problems may be moderated or weakened by other variables. For example, research on friendships (such as the study by Parker and Asher) shows that friendship and peer status are two independent constructs, and children may have close dyadic friendships regardless of their status in the overall peer group. Having such friendships can make adjustment much easier for rejected children, and not having such friendships can attenuate the positive effects of being sociometrically popular.

GENDER AND DEVELOPMENTAL DIFFERENCES

Sociometric status differs somewhat depending on gender and stage of development. Rejected boys are distinguished from popular boys primarily based on aggression levels, whereas popular and rejected girls differ primarily in the degree to which they cooperate with others. Boys tend to display more physical aggression, while girls display indirect or relational aggression (spreading rumors or excluding or ostracizing peers). From a developmental perspective, a number of researchers have examined the stability of sociometric status over time and have found that status remains fairly stable over a child's time in school and often carries over to a new school environment. More interesting from a developmental point of view is the way in which children's and adolescents' stereotypes about popularity change as they grow older. If status is measured by asking about peers' reputation ("Who is popular in the peer group?" or "Who is unpopular?"), the results are very different from the findings on sociometric status, especially for older children and adolescents. Peers whom children name as popular may have more in common with sociometrically controversial children than with sociometrically popular children. A cross-sectional study by LaFontana and Cillessen shows that peers with a popular reputation are more dominant, demonstrate both prosocial and antisocial behaviors, and possess more resources such as money, athletic ability, and physical attractiveness, than do sociometrically popular peers. The differences between sociometrically popular and perceived popular children increase with age, peaking in middle school and early adolescence. Girls reach this peak somewhat earlier than do boys.

CAVEATS AND FUTURE DIRECTIONS

Despite the massive amount of research on sociometric status, there are several limitations to this literature. Most of the research has focused on the United States, so researchers do not know whether the same principles hold true in other cultures. There is a heavy emphasis on the role of cognition because the cognitive perspective dominated developmental psychology during the 1980s and 1990s when much of this research took place. There is also a strong emphasis on the individual and how he or she is affected by sociometric status. Future research must focus more on dyads and groups as the units of analysis. Much of the research has taken place with racially undiverse populations. Only in the early part of the twenty-first century did researchers begin in earnest to explore gender and ethnic differences in sociometric status. Finally, interventions depend on whether researchers view certain behaviors as adaptive or maladaptive. For example, is the aggression that reputationally popular children display considered good (assertiveness) or bad (bullying)? Should it be encouraged or discouraged? Parents, teachers, and researchers must work together to determine the future direction of research on sociometric status.

BIBLIOGRAPHY

Asher, S., & Coie, J. (Eds.). (1990). *Peer rejection in childhood.* New York: Cambridge University Press.

Berndt, T., & Ladd, G. (Eds.). (1989). *Peer relationships in child development.* New York: Wiley.

Bukowski, W. M., & Cillessen, A. H. N. (1998). *Sociometry then and now: Building on six decades of measuring children's experiences with the peer group.* San Francisco: Jossey-Bass.

Coie, J. D., Dodge, K. A., & Coppotelli, H. (1982). Dimensions and types of social status: A cross-age perspective. *Developmental Psychology, 18,* 557–570.

Hymel, S., Rubin, K. H., Rowden, L., & LeMare, L. (1990). Children's peer relationships: Longitudinal prediction of internalizing and externalizing problems from middle to late childhood. *Child Development, 61,* 2004–2021.

LaFontana, K. M., & Cillessen, A. H. N. (2002). Children's perceptions of popular and unpopular peers: A multimethod assessment. *Developmental Psychology, 38,* 635–647.

Moreno, J. L. (1934). *Who shall survive? A new approach to the problem of human interrelations.* Washington, DC: Nervous and Mental Disease.

Newcomb, A. F., Bukowski, W. M., & Pattee, L. (1993). Children's peer relations: A meta-analytic review of popular, rejected, neglected, controversial, and average sociometric status. *Psychological Bulletin, 113,* 99–128.

Parker, J. G., & Asher, S. R. (1993). Friendship and friendship quality in middle childhood: Links with peer group acceptance and feelings of loneliness and social dissatisfaction. *Developmental Psychology, 29,* 611–621.

Rubin, K. H., Bukowski, W. M., & Parker, J. G. (2006). Peer Interactions, relationships, and groups. In N. Eisenberg, W. Damon, & R. M. Lerner (Eds.), *Handbook of child psychology: Vol. 3. Social, emotional, and personality development* (6th ed., pp. 571–645). Hoboken, NJ: John Wiley & Sons.

Kathryn M. LaFontana

PEER TUTORING

Peer tutoring is an intervention in which students work in pairs to master academic skills or content. Peer tutoring can involve partners who are the same age or different ages (cross-age). Cross-age peer tutoring involves older students serving as tutors for younger, lower-functioning students. Cross-age tutoring occurs, for example, when students in a high school child development class spend regularly scheduled time each week reading with struggling students in a fourth grade class. In this instance, the tutors might be expected to gain less from the content being tutored but may be expected to gain more in social responsibility or understanding of learning as a process.

In same-age tutoring, in which students of the same age tutor each other, more skilled students may be paired with less skilled students. In this case, students with stronger skills may provide the first responses, providing a model for the less skilled partner. In other cases, the teacher may decide to pair students of similar ability and have them alternate tutoring roles, which is sometimes referred to as reciprocal peer tutoring. Class-wide Peer Tutoring (CWPT) occurs when the teacher creates highly structured tutoring materials for use during the tutoring session. Peer tutoring is differentiated from tutoring between adults, such as community volunteers, and students. It is also distinguished from cooperative learning, in which students work collaboratively in groups.

Clearly, peer tutoring is a general term that encompasses many tutoring models. All methods are designed to increase practice, responding, and feedback for students, and they often result in increased student motivation and achievement. These models differ, however, in how tutoring pairs are assigned, how tutoring content is developed, and how extensively the tutoring is employed. For example, in cross-age tutoring the expert tutor is typically the older student, while in reciprocal peer tutoring and CWPT the paired students are the same age and can take turns assuming the expert role. In cross-age and reciprocal tutoring, the student tutor is typically responsible for learning the content and then teaching the information to the tutee, while in CWPT the teacher is more responsible.

The instructional components of the peer tutoring model include: (a) explicit teaching of students in how to be tutoring experts, (b) purposeful partner assignment, (c) careful preparation of tutoring materials, (d) highly structured tutoring procedures that include specific feedback for tutors to provide tutees, (e) expert role reversal, and (f) active teacher monitoring. Also, some type of systematic performance is typically included. Explicit teaching of students in how to be tutoring experts can include modeling examples and non-examples of appropriate tutoring interactions, posting tutoring guidelines as reminders for students, giving feedback on how well students are meeting expectations for tutoring, and re-teaching procedures as necessary. Partner assignment can be based on student academic skills, tutoring activity content, and/or interpersonal relationships between students. Preparing tutoring materials carefully is necessary to ensure success in the tutoring experience and may include differentiation of materials. Materials typically include highly structured tutoring procedures that indicate how tutors can determine if a response is correct and how to respond to both correct and incorrect responses. Finally, teachers actively monitor peer tutoring and may give feedback to students both on content and procedures.

Peer Assisted Learning Strategies (PALS) is one peer tutoring activity that has been researched for grades kindergarten through 12. This tutoring program is designed to help students improve in reading and other academic skill areas. The steps to the program for reading are: (a) predicting, (b) partner reading, (c) retelling, and (d) summarizing. In this program, the stronger reader is the expert tutor. Students begin by making a prediction about the passage they are about to read. They then take turns reading the same passage with the stronger reader going first. Then the stronger reader prompts the weaker reader to retell the passage and then summarize the information with the following steps: (a) "Name the who or what the passage is about," (b) "Tell the most important thing about the who or what," and (c) "Say the main idea in 10 words or less." A modified version of this peer tutoring model has also been used in mathematics.

Another example is peer tutoring with differentiated instructional materials targeted toward classrooms with students of different learning needs. Differentiation of materials can include: (a) differential practice time, (b) embedded strategic information, and (c) increasing levels of difficulty. Differential practice time allows for students to have as much time needed to master a concept before proceeding to the next skill set. Embedded strategic information can include specific strategies for improving memory or comprehension of important concepts, such a mnemonic strategies or comprehension questioning. Increasing levels of difficulty might include varying levels of supports that can be provided to students on an as needed basis. For example, students can begin with identification formats (in which they are asked to identify the correct response from an array) and advance to production formats (in which they produce the correct response independently) or to answering tutor questions under prompted or non-prompted conditions.

Peer tutoring models were applied systematically as early as 1789, but they gained popularity in toward the end of the twentieth century, with accumulating research evidence in support of the practice. Learning gains commonly observed in peer tutoring programs are generally attributed to increased active academic engagement and opportunities to respond on the part of students, particularly in contrast to models in which all instruction is delivered by the teacher or by independent seat work. Peer tutoring has been studied in many academic areas, including science and social studies, in addition to skill areas such as reading and spelling. Peer tutoring has also been effectively implemented in classrooms that include students with diverse learning needs, such as students with disabilities and students for whom English is a second language.

Academic gains have been consistently observed in peer tutoring programs, with treatment effects in the medium to high range for both tutors and tutees. Effects have also been observed for students acting as tutors in the role of expert. Social benefits of peer tutoring, including improved self-esteem and self-efficacy, improved attitude toward school, and improved interpersonal functioning, are commonly reported anecdotally. Research support for these more general outcomes has been inconsistent, although students commonly improve in their attitude toward the content being tutored and in their attitude toward their tutoring partner. Teachers who have implemented peer tutoring typically respond favorably to the practice.

SEE ALSO *Communities of Learners.*

BIBLIOGRAPHY

Greenwood, C. R. (2002). Classwide peer tutoring programs. In M. R. Shinn, H. M. Walker, & G. Stoner (Eds.), *Interventions for academic and behavior problems: 2. Preventative and remedial programs* (pp. 611–649). Washington, DC: National Association of School Psychologists.

McMaster, K. L., Fuchs, D., & Fuchs, L. S. (2006). Research on peer-assisted learning strategies: The promise and limitations of peer-mediated instruction. *Reading and Writing Quarterly: Overcoming Learning Difficulties, 22,* 5–25.

Mastropieri, M. A., Scruggs, T. E., & Berkeley, S. L. (2007). Peers helping peers. *Educational Leadership, 64*(5), 54–58.

Topping, K. (2001). *Peer assisted learning.* Cambridge, MA: Brookline Books.

Topping, K., & Elhy, S. (Eds.). (1998). *Peer assisted learning.* Mahwah, NJ: Erlbaum.

Thomas E. Scruggs
Margo A. Mastropieri
Sheri Berkeley

PIAGET, JEAN
1896–1980

Jean Piaget was born in 1896 in Neuchâtel, Switzerland, and died in Geneva in 1980. He graduated from the University of Neuchâtel in 1918 as a Doctor of Natural Sciences with a dissertation on mollusks, but he had always been deeply interested in philosophy. Subsequently, he studied psychology, logic, and philosophy of sciences in Zurich and at the Sorbonne in Paris. He held various professorships in sociology, philosophy of sciences, history of scientific thought, experimental psychology, and developmental psychology at the Universities of Neuchâtel, Geneva, and Lausanne, and the Sorbonne, but his research interest starting in the 1920s was in epistemology. He is often viewed as a psychologist,

Jean Piaget ARCHIVES OF THE HISTORY OF AMERICAN PSYCHOLOGY. THE UNIVERSITY OF AKRON.

but child psychology for him was a means for answering epistemological questions such as: How do we know what we think we know, and how did humanity build knowledge since its prehistoric beginnings? As a scientist, he insisted that such questions had to be answered scientifically, but historical evidence was no longer available. He studied children's construction of knowledge because children furnished empirical data that seemed most relevant to humanity's construction of knowledge.

PIAGET'S CONTRIBUTION TO THE PSYCHOLOGY OF CLASSROOM LEARNING

Piaget made many contributions to the psychology of classroom learning. Two will be highlighted here. One is his constructivism, the theory that states that human beings acquire knowledge and moral values by constructing them from the inside in interaction with the environment, rather than by internalizing them directly from the environment. Young children's construction of language illustrates the constructive process. Because most American children learn English, and most French children learn French, it is easy to think that children learn language by internalization from their environment. When one looks more carefully,

however, one finds that babies begin by uttering one word such as "Ball!" and go on to say two words, such as "Ball gone." By the time they go to school, children utter sentences like "I thinked it in my head." These examples cannot be said to have been acquired by internalization because no one in the environment talks in these ways.

In the moral realm, too, most adults in the early 21st century believe that moral values and rules are acquired by direct internalization from the environment. However, Piaget showed that moral values, too, are constructed by each child from the inside in interaction with the environment. For example, he asked 6-to-14-year-olds why it was bad to tell lies. Young, heteronomous children replied, "Because you get punished when you lie." By contrast, older, more autonomous children tended to say that lies are bad even when one is not punished for them because lies destroy the bond of trust. The importance of mutual trust is an example of a moral value that has been constructed from the inside. For older, more autonomous children, lies are bad independently of reward and punishment.

Many psychologists think that Piaget's major contribution was the stages of development he found, but the stages are important only because they furnish the evidence that supports constructivism. Many bits of knowledge and morality can be learned by internalization, but this learning is often superficial and/or temporary.

An important part of Piaget's constructivism is his epistemological position against empiricism.

For centuries, philosophers had been arguing about the truth of two major epistemological traditions—empiricism and rationalism. Piaget's sympathy was with the rationalist side of the fence as can be seen in the conservation-of-number task. In this task, if the child uses one-to-one correspondence to put out as many chips as the interviewer has aligned, the interviewer says, "Watch what I am going to do," and moves the chips to make one of the rows look longer than the other. The crucial question then put to the child is: Are there as many chips in my row as in your row, or are there more in yours, or more in mine? Nonconservers usually say that the longer row has more because it looks like more. Nonconservers thus base their judgments on the empirical knowledge of what they can see. When their logico-mathematical knowledge later becomes stronger, they begin to deduce logically that the two rows have to have the same number.

Piaget's method of data collection must be noted here. At a time when only standardized questions were considered to be "objective" and "scientific," he invented the "clinical method," arguing that researchers must probe into each child's reasoning to get valid data. For example, if a child gave the correct answer in the conservation-of-number task,

Piaget believed that the interviewer should ask, "How do you know (that the two rows have the same number)?" If the child's response was "I just knew it," he further probed into the child's reasoning to ascertain the strength of his or her logic.

A second major contribution Piaget made to the psychology of classroom learning is his conceptualization of autonomy as the aim of education. In his theory, autonomy does not mean the right to make decisions. It means the ability to make decisions by taking relevant factors into account, independently of reward and punishment. These decisions are about right and wrong in the moral realm, and about truth and untruth in the intellectual realm. Autonomy is the opposite of heteronomy, which means being unable to make decisions for oneself and therefore being governed by others. For an autonomous person like Copernicus, the heliocentric theory had to be promulgated even though it was rejected by his fellow scientists.

Schools are now generally run with ready-made rules and curricula supported by reward and punishment, as if heteronomy (obedience) were the aim of education. Piaget's theory has changed some classroom practices in the early grades, but its influence is yet to take roots. When educators adopt moral and intellectual autonomy as the aim of education, schools will be run very differently and produce graduates with a strong sense of responsibility about themselves as well as the welfare of others. Schools will also endeavor to produce thinkers capable of creating new knowledge rather than merely repeating what others have said.

SEE ALSO *Cognitive Development: Piaget's Theory.*

BIBLIOGRAPHY

WORKS BY

Inhelder, B., & Piaget, J. (1958). *The growth of logical thinking from childhood to adolescence.* New York: Basic Books.

Inhelder, B., & Piaget, J. (1964). *The early growth of logic in the child.* New York: Harper & Row.

Piaget, J. (1954). *The construction of reality in the child.* New York: Basic Books.

Piaget, J. (1965). *The moral judgment of the child.* New York: Free Press.

Piaget, J., & Szeminska, A. (1965). *The child's conception of number.* New York: Norton.

WORKS ABOUT

Kohler, R. (2008). *Jean Piaget.* New York, NY: Continuum International.

Perret-Clermont, A.-N. & Barrelet, J. M. (Eds.). (2007). *Jean Piaget and Neuchâtel: the learner and the scholar.* New York: Psychology Press.

Constance Kamii

PINTRICH, PAUL ROBERT
1953–2003

Paul Pintrich was born on November 4, 1953. He died of a heart attack July 12, 2003, while riding with a group of bicyclists on the road back from Hell, Michigan.

Pintrich received a B.A. in psychology from Clark University in 1975 and a Ph.D. in education and psychology from the University of Michigan in 1982. He remained at Michigan until his death, rising through the ranks to become professor and chair of the Combined Program in Education and Psychology and associate dean for research in the School of Education.

Although Pintrich died before reaching the age of 50, he was unusually productive, publishing well over 100 articles and book chapters as well as coauthoring or co-editing nine books. He was an excellent mentor and colleague, publishing with many collaborators in the United States and abroad. He helped build bridges to psychology in Europe, participating in the European Association for Research in Learning and Instruction (EARLI) and serving as president of the Division of Learning, Instruction, and School Psychology of the International Association of Applied Psychology. His professional service also included the editorship of the *Educational Psychologist*, the presidency of APA Division 15 (Educational Psychology), and president of the AERA Special Interest Group on Motivation.

In the early 1980s Pintrich and Wilbert J. McKeachie developed one of the first courses in Learning to Learn. This course differed from traditional study skills courses in that students not only learned strategies for learning but also learned the cognitive and motivational theories that underlie student learning so that they could apply the theories in new learning situations (Pintrich, McKeachie, & Lin, 1985). Followup studies showed that the course improved learning in later courses (McKeachie, Pintrich, & Lin, 1985). An outgrowth of that work was the development of the Motivated Strategies for Learning Questionnaire (MSLQ), which was used all over the world (Pintrich, Smith, Garcia, & McKeachie, 1991).

Beginning with studies of student self-efficacy (Pintrich & Blumenfeld, 1985), Pintrich was soon writing about the dynamic interactions between cognition and motivation in learning (Pintrich, 1988, 1989, Marx, & Boyle, 1993). In their seminal research on self-directed learning, Pintrich and his wife, Elizabeth De Groot, integrated cognitive, motivational, and behavioral factors affecting learning (Pintrich & De Groot, 1990). Well before self-regulation became a major research area, Pintrich was publishing research and theory that formed a foundation for later work. He and his students expanded the original cognitive approach to self-regulation to include regulation of motivation and emotion as well (Garcia & Pintrich, 1994; VanderStoep, Pintrich, & Fagerlin, 1996).

Shortly thereafter Pintrich and his students became involved in research on goal theory. Their work was designed to answer questions such as the following: Are students primarily studying to get a good grade or is their primary goal to gain a good understanding of the subject? Are they more concerned with doing better than other students (performance motivation) than with mastering the subject (mastery motivation)? Although goals are usually thought of in positive terms, Pintrich and his collaborators also looked at avoidance goals (Zusho & Pintrich, 2000).

In later years Pintrich and Barbara Hofer (his student) began studying epistemological beliefs. Their paper "The development of epistemological beliefs: Beliefs about knowledge and knowing and their relation to learning" (Hofer & Pintrich, 2002) won the AERA award for best review article of the year.

Pintrich was a pioneer in developing an integrated theory of motivation and cognition and in showing how classrooms influence the development of student motivation for learning. He was one of the world's leading scholars in the area of student motivation, cognition, and self-regulation.

BIBLIOGRAPHY

WORKS BY

Boekaerts, M., Pintrich, P. R., & Ziegler, M. (Eds.). (2000). *Handbook of self-regulation.* San Diego, CA: Academic Press.

Hoefer, B. K., & Pintrich, P. R. (Eds.). (2002). *Personal epistemology: The psychology of beliefs about knowledge and knowing.* Mahwah, NJ: Erlbaum.

Pintrich, P. R., Brown, D. R., & Weinstein, C. E. (Eds.). (1994). *Student motivation, cognition, and learning: Essays in honor of Wilbert J. McKeachie.* Hillsdale, NJ: Erlbaum.

Pintrich, P. R., & Schunk, D. H. (1996). *Motivation in education: Theory, research, and applications.* Englewood Cliffs, NJ: Merrill.

Pintrich, P. R., & Schunk, D. H. (2002). *Motivation in education: Theory, research, and applications* (2nd ed.). Upper Saddle River, NJ: Merrill.

Schunk, D. H., Pintrich, P. R., & Meece, J. L. (2008). *Motivation in education: Theory, research, and applications* (3rd ed.). Upper Saddle River, NJ: Pearson/Merrill Prentice Hall.

Sinatra, G. M., & Pintrich, P. R. (2003). *Intentional conceptual change.* Mahwah, NJ: Erlbaum.

VanderStoep, S. W., & Pintrich, P. R. (2003, 2008). *Learning to learn: The skill and will of college success.* Upper Saddle River, NJ: Prentice Hall.

Wilbert J. McKeachie

PORTFOLIO ASSESSMENT

Portfolio assessment is an evaluation tool used to document student learning through a series of student-developed artifacts. Considered a form of authentic assessment, it offers an alternative or an addition to traditional methods of grading and high stakes exams. Portfolio assessment gives both teachers and students a controlled space to document, review, and analyze content leaning. In short, portfolios are a collection of student work that allows assessment by providing evidence of effort and accomplishments in relation to specific instructional goals (Jardine, 1996). At its best, portfolio assessment demands the following: clarity of goals, explicit criteria for evaluation, work samples tied to those goals, student participation in selection of entries, teacher and student involvement in the assessment process, and self-reflections that demonstrate students' metacognitive ability, that is, their understanding of what worked for them in the learning process, what did not, and why. These elements enhance the learning experience and the self-understanding of the student as learner.

ASSUMPTIONS AND PROCEDURES

Portfolio assessment is not defined by a single procedure, nor is there a single best way to use portfolios. However, the following components are generally assumed integral. The portfolio itself is a container of some sort, for example, a folder, crate, file, or virtual space for online portfolios. The selected contents should demonstrate student accomplishments over time. All selections and parts are authentic in that the included pieces provide evidence that the goals and objectives of the curriculum have been met, with added student reflections that review the process and /or products of learning. Participants in the portfolio assessment process (instructors, students and parents or administrators, if applicable), should be aware of assessment standards in advance. Depending on the type of portfolio, the contents may vary widely. Possible contents include writing samples that may vary in genre, content, and style, laboratory reports, journals, taped performances, recordings, art, research papers, projects, photos, interviews, conferences, tests, quizzes, observations, and reflections.

In some schools, material from a semester's or year's portfolio is digitalized and stored for future reference as a record of student accomplishments over a specified time. Colleges requiring licensure for a profession may require students to keep evidence of each standard met in an online or physical portfolio, ensuring ready access to reviewers or accrediting agencies that all work has been completed. Because a portfolio contains a variety of artifacts that provide evidence of work completed, it is particularly useful in these assessment circumstances.

KEY ELEMENTS FOR EFFECTIVE PORTFOLIO ASSESSMENT

Clear criteria for evaluation, including what must be included in the portfolio and rubrics for evaluation, are vital to successful portfolio assessment. When teachers develop unambiguous assessment criteria, they necessarily use a shared discourse, clarify beforehand any unfamiliar vocabulary (Rodgers, 2002), and assure that they and students have a mutual understanding regarding the theoretical foundations of the task before it takes place. Understanding these criteria can help reduce or eliminate criticism about subjectivity or unfairness of grading, a common criticism of those who prefer standardized assessments. The use of comprehensive rubrics that present structured information about organization, required components, length and content of entries and reflections, in addition to any specific assignment rubrics that clearly outline the goals, obligations, and constraints of particular entries, are valuable. The more precise and comprehensive the rubric, the more objective the assessment. Through explicit direction, instructors should make clear all guiding principles or policies for what may or may not be included in the portfolio.

Reflective pieces require students to articulate and review components of the portfolio and are a part of a comprehensive assessment. Reflections allow students the time and space to analyze their achievement in relation to class standards, evaluate their final products, and determine growth as well as needs (Fernsten & Fernsten 2005). The metacognitive exercise of figuring out how they know what they know about the learning that has taken place can be an invaluable learning tool and helps participants take responsibility for their own learning.

TYPES OF PORTFOLIOS

There are a variety of portfolio types, each designed to help assess either the process or the products of learning.

Showcase portfolios. Showcase portfolios highlight the best products over a particular time period or course. For example, a showcase portfolio in a composition class may include the best examples of different writing genres, such as an essay, a poem, a short story, a biographical piece, or a literary analysis. In a business class, the showcase portfolio may include a resume, sample business letters, a marketing project, and a collaborative assignment that demonstrates the individual's ability to work in a team. Students are often allowed to choose what they believe to be their best work, highlighting their achievements and skills. Showcase reflections typically focus on the strengths of selected pieces and discuss how each met or exceeded required standards.

Process portfolios. Process portfolios, by contrast, concentrate more on the journey of learning rather than the final destination or end products of the learning process. In the composition class, for example, different stages of the process—an outline, first draft, peer and teacher responses, early revisions, and a final edited draft—may be required. A process reflection may discuss why a particular strategy was used, what was useful or ineffective for the individual in the writing process, and how the student went about making progress in the face of difficulty in meeting requirements. A process reflection typically focuses on many aspects of the learning process, including the following: what approaches work best, which are ineffective, information about oneself as a learner, and strategies or approaches to remember in future assignments.

Evaluation portfolios. Evaluation portfolios may vary substantially in their content. Their basic purpose, however, remains to exhibit a series of evaluations over a course and the learning or accomplishments of the student in regard to previously determined criteria or goals. Essentially, this type of portfolio documents tests, observations, records, or other assessment artifacts required for successful completion of the course. A math evaluation portfolio may include tests, quizzes, and written explanations of how one went about solving a problem or determining which formula to use, whereas a science evaluation portfolio might also include laboratory experiments, science project outcomes with photos or other artifacts, and research reports, as well as tests and quizzes. Unlike the showcase portfolio, evaluation portfolios do not simply include the best work, but rather a selection of predetermined evaluations that may also demonstrate students' difficulties and unsuccessful struggles as well as their better work. Students who reflect on why some work was successful and other work was less so continue their learning as they develop their metacognitive skills.

Online or e-portfolios. Online or e-portfolios may be one of the above portfolio types or a combination of different types, a general requirement being that all information and artifacts are somehow accessible online. A number of colleges require students to maintain a virtual portfolio that may include digital, video, or Web-based products. The portfolio assessment process may be linked to a specific course or an entire program. As with all portfolios, students are able to visually track and show their accomplishments to a wide audience.

BENEFITS OF PORTFOLIO ASSESSMENT

Portfolio assessment research substantiates the idea that students greatly benefit from assessments that go beyond simple letter grades and involve participants in the evaluation process. By taking part in the development of their portfolios, analyzing the criteria for what constitutes good work, and learning to evaluate their own work through guided reflective practices, students grow and develop in their knowledge and understandings. Portfolio assessment is part of a substantial body of research documenting the student benefits that emerge from an awareness of the processes and strategies involved in learning. (Hamp-Lyons & Congdon, 2000; Martin-Kniep, Cunningham, Feige, 1998)

The benefits of portfolio assessment are numerous. To begin with, they are a more individualized way of assessing students and have the advantage of demonstrating a wide range of work. They may also be used in conjunction with other types of required assessments, such as standardized or norm referenced tests. Often, portfolio contents are selected collaboratively, allowing students an opportunity to make decisions about their work and encouraging them to set goals regarding what has been accomplished and what needs further work, an important skill that may serve them well in life endeavors.

Portfolio assessment can promote a dialog between teacher and students about the individualized nature of the work. Too often, students may have papers or projects returned with a number or letter grade only and fail to understand what might be necessary for improvement. Required reflections in conjunction with conferencing reduce the possibility that students will be unclear about the assessment or what must be done to make improvements. This one-to-one aspect is an additional bonus for those students who may be too shy to initiate conversations with instructors as well as for those who enjoy speaking about their work and may better understand what worked and what did not through a verbal exchange.

Most importantly, portfolio assessments provide an authentic way of demonstrating skills and accomplishments. They encourage a real world experience that demands organization, decision making, and metacognition. Used in a thoughtful, carefully planned way, portfolio assessment can foster a positive outlook on learning and achievement.

SEE ALSO *Classroom Assessment.*

BIBLIOGRAPHY

Fernsten, L., & Fernsten, J. (2005). Portfolio assessment and reflection: Enhancing learning through effective practice. *Reflective Practice 6*(2), 303–309.

Hamp-Lyons, L., & Condon, W. (2000). *Assessing the portfolio: Principles for practice, theory, and research.* Cresskill, NJ: Hampton Press.

Jardine, A. S. (1996). Key points of the authentic assessment portfolio. *Intervention in School and Clinic, 31*(4), 252–253.

Martin-Kniep, G.O., Cunningham, D. & Feige, D. M. (1998). *Why am I doing this?: Purposeful teaching through portfolio assessment.* Portsmouth, NH: Heinemann.

Rodgers, C. R. (2002). Voices inside schools, seeing student learning: Teacher change and the role of reflection. *Harvard Educational Review 72*(2), 230–253.

Linda A. Fernsten

POSSIBLE SELVES THEORY

Self-concept is one's theory about oneself, the person one was in the past, is now, and can become in the future, including social roles and group memberships. A well-functioning self-concept helps make sense of one's present, preserves positive self-feelings, makes predictions about the future, and guides motivation. The contents of the future-oriented component of self-concept have been termed *possible selves* (Markus & Nurius, 1986). Possible selves are the selves one believes one might become in the near and the more distal future and are therefore important in goal setting and motivation (for a review, see Oyserman & James, in press). Possible selves are valenced; that is, each individual has both positive images of the selves he or she desires and expects to become and negative images of the selves he or she wishes to avoid becoming.

While current self-concept focuses on who one is now, by focusing on the future, possible selves allow for self-improvement, malleability, and personal growth. They provide a chance to experiment with and try on various potential futures ("Maybe I'll be a teacher or maybe I'll be a nurse. What would it be like to become a teacher or a nurse? How would I get there? What are the stages and obstacles along the way?"). The future is the target of much of our efforts as individuals. Homework is done and broccoli is eaten all in pursuit of some future state. As noted by Oyserman & James (in press), doing or not doing homework one night really does not make that much difference, but if each night's homework is viewed in this way, homework will rarely get done— and that does matter. Whether one eats or does not eat the potato chips with lunch today does not make or break one's likelihood of being overweight, but, over time, each of these small choices adds up. In this sense, current actions are taken due to individuals' beliefs about their consequences in the future. Generally speaking, individuals are motivated to reduce the gap between their present and future positive possible selves while increasing the gap between their present and future negative possible selves.

Because possible selves provide both positive images of one's self attaining future goals and negative images of one's self failing to attain these goals (and of the feared selves one might become instead), possible selves are an integral part of a well-functioning self-concept. By focusing on the future, possible selves can improve well-being and optimism about the future. Things may not be going well now, but a possible self suggests the promise of change. Possible selves can improve one's ability to self-control and self-regulate because possible selves help one to focus on goals and lessen the influence of distractions in one's social world. Possible selves are most likely to improve self-regulatory ability when they are salient, linked with strategies, feel congruent with other aspects of self-concept, and when difficulty attaining them feels like proof one really cares rather than evidence for withdrawing effort (Oyserman & James, in press).

In terms of content, school-focused selves are common in childhood and adolescence regardless of socioeconomic status (for a review, see Oyserman & Fryberg, 2006). School-focused possible selves describe positive expectations regarding one's school success and academic attainment, including specific, immediate goals such as passing eighth grade or not failing the math test and more general long-term views such as being smart or getting a GED (Oyserman, Bybee, Terry, & Hart-Johnson, 2004). Youth are likely to have multiple, potentially competing possible selves, not all of which will influence behavior at any particular point in time (Oyserman & James, in press).

DEVELOPMENT OF POSSIBLE SELVES: INDIVIDUAL AND CONTEXTUAL FACTORS

Possible selves are influenced by both individual and contextual factors. Others can serve as role models and anti-models for both positive and negative possible selves. These others can be particular individuals with whom one has a relationship or simply a general sense of what others like oneself have been able to do.

Past Experiences. One's own past experiences of success or failure in a domain clearly influences one's beliefs about the relevance or attainability of possible selves in that domain as well as one's ability to articulate strategies to work on the possible self. Past failures may make it harder to articulate both what success would look like in a particular domain and which strategies are likely to be effective. Past successes may make it easier to articulate both what success would look like and which steps are needed to attain a desired possible self. For example, youth with a history of juvenile delinquency and school failure are less likely to articulate education and job focused possible

selves, students from low income families are less likely to generate multiple strategies for how to attain school-focused possible selves like doing well and getting good grades (Oyserman & Fryberg, 2006; Oyserman & James, in press; Oyserman & Markus, 1990).

Developmental Context. Content of possible selves reflects developmentally relevant self-tasks. During the school years, these tasks focus on being competent in school, being connected to others, and developing a sense of self. Not surprisingly, common possible selves are focused on school, relationships and avoiding becoming off-track such as using drugs or becoming pregnant (Oyserman & Fryberg, 2006). With development, the focus of these tasks evolves. College students and young adults are focused on occupational, educational, and interpersonal possible selves (such as getting married), whereas family and parenting possible selves become more important in young and middle adult years. As adults age, job-focused possible selves recede and physical health related possible selves become more prominent. However, some possible selves persist even when they are not easy to attain (for a review, see Oyserman & James, in press).

Social Context. Possible selves are also influenced by others' expectations and by historical and sociopolitical contexts. Some social contexts provide easy access to role models and reminders to focus on school while other contexts rarely provide these cues. Minority, low-income, and rural youth may be less able to imagine school-focused possible selves or to sustain these possible selves if their contexts include few models of overcoming barriers to success or are rife with stereotypes that are not congruent with school-focused possible selves. Research has shown that if going to college does not feel like an option as early as middle school, students withdraw academic effort (Oyserman & Fryberg, 2006; Oyserman, Gant, & Ager, 1995).

ASSESSING POSSIBLE SELVES

This section draws heavily from the review of measures and measurement strategies presented in Oyserman and Fryberg (2006). Oyserman and Fryberg (2006) provide specific references for both close- and open-ended measures used to assess possible selves and the interested reader is referred to their more detailed discussion.

Close-Ended Measures. Respondents are provided a list of possible selves and either asked to check off which possible selves are relevant or rate their likelihood of attaining each possible self or sort and rank the importance of these possible selves. Close-ended measures are easy to code but require preparation to be sure that the content is relevant to the sample of interest. Moreover, with close-ended measures, one can only learn how much respondents endorse the items provided, not what they would have said given free rein. Though past research results can form a basis, to make sure that content is relevant, pilot work is needed. Given the potential diversity of possible selves, a pre-set checklist may not accurately reflect content of possible selves.

Open-Ended Measures. Open-ended tools typically open with a brief statement of what possible selves are and ask respondents to generate their own possible selves and, where relevant, their strategies for attaining them. The strengths of an open-ended measure are that it allows participants to describe their possible selves without constraint and that the format is easily adapted to different groups and contexts. The limitations of this method are that it requires content-coding of responses and generating one's own responses (rather than simply endorsing a pre-set list as is done in the close-ended method) is likely to be more effortful.

MOTIVATIONAL CONSEQUENCES OF POSSIBLE SELVES ON CHOICE, PERSISTENCE, ACHIEVEMENT

The future is an important component of self-concept and doing well in school is a common element of youths' future possible selves (Oyserman & Fryberg, 2006). In their review, Oyserman and Fryberg report on studies linking possible selves with reduced risk of substance use and sexual activity. Thus, sixth through ninth graders with fewer positive possible selves were more likely to report cigarette smoking and alcohol consumption and eighth graders whose possible selves focused on being popular rather than academic success were more likely to report smoking and drinking alcohol in the ninth grade. Seventh grade African American boys reported less initiation of sexual activity after participating in an intervention to develop possible selves.

However, possible selves do not always sustain self-regulatory action. Youth do fail algebra and engage in risk-taking behavior. Possible selves succeed in focusing effort when they are linked to behavioral strategies, they feel congruent with important social identities, and they are balanced so that difficulty working on the possible self is not construed to mean that the possible self is unimportant (much as the 'no pain, no gain' metaphor in sports, see Oyserman, et al., 2006). Each of these issues is described below.

Strategies to Attain Possible Selves. Imagining what is possible for one's future can increase optimism, but articulating a possible self is not enough to produce sustained effort and behavior change. For that to occur, possible selves need to be linked with specific strategies (Oyserman et al., 2004). Strategies are concrete behaviors such as studying or setting an alarm clock. Strategies help one to focus on goals while anticipating and planning for setbacks by developing plans of action and fall back plans. In one study, by the end of the school year, students whose school-focused possible selves included detailed strategies reported feeling more efficacious; results were not limited to positive feelings, according to school records, students with strategies attained better grades than those without them (Oyserman et al., 2004). In another study, an intervention increased students' possible selves and strategies to attain them succeed in improving outcomes, including grades and in-class behaviors, even when other conditions suggested risk of school failure (Oyserman, Brickman, Rhodes, 2007).

Social Identity. One is more likely to engage in strategies to attain a possible self when the possible self and the strategies feel congruent with one's important social identities (e.g., racial-ethnic, gender, social class). Otherwise, the possible self itself or working on attaining the possible self will feel like it conflicts with the rest of who one is. For example, if boys believe that only girls raise their hands to participate or do their homework or stay after class for help, they are less likely to engage in these activities, even if they believe that these strategies would help them attain school-focused positive possible selves (for the general model, see Oyserman, et al., 2006).

The Carrot and the Stick: Balance in Possible Selves. It is tempting to focus only on the positive since thinking about how things can go wrong may feel discouraging. However, focusing on both positive and negative possible selves in the same domain improves focus and is associated with better outcomes. Balanced school-focused possible selves occur when one has both a positive possible self (e.g., going to college) and a feared or to-be-avoided possible self (e.g., being an unemployed drop-out) in the same domain (Oyserman, et al., 2006). Having both images serves as a carrot and a stick, simultaneously reminding the student of the goal (the carrot) and of where the student may end up if effort is not sustained (the stick). Students with school-focused balance in possible selves are less likely to be involved in delinquent activities (Oyserman & Markus, 1990) and are more likely to attain better grades (Oyserman et al., 2006), and the presence of balance in possible selves may be particularly important in social contexts in which one is likely to encounter obstacles to achieving one's goals.

IMPLICATIONS OF POSSIBLE SELF THEORY FOR TEACHERS

Teachers, parents, and students all have possible selves—images of how things might be in the near and more distal future. These images illustrate that change is possible. Possible selves can undergird self-improvement by showing a path toward the future and by highlighting where one might end up if effort is not maintained. Intervention to help teachers, parents, and students focus on what they want to become and avoid becoming, what they value, and how they expect to engage in becoming like their desired selves and avoiding becoming like their undesired selves can be highly effective. Indeed, the theory of possible selves has been used to understand progress and life transitions for both youth learners and adults in continuing education and other settings.

Perhaps the most important message that educators can take from the research on possible selves is that possible selves are malleable and can be influenced by intervention to enhance the content of possible selves. Changing possible selves through intervention can lead to positive changes in academic behavior, in better academic performance and lower risk of depression (Oyserman et al., 2002; 2006). Of particular note is the School-to-Jobs (STJ) intervention that focused explicitly on improving academic outcomes by changing possible selves. STJ was tested both as an after-school and an in-school intervention, running twice per week for six weeks so that it was completed by Thanksgiving break.

Each STJ session focused on developing an aspect of possible selves. Beginning sessions linked school-focused possible selves to important social identities (e.g., gender or racial-ethnic groups), linked proximal possible selves (e.g., graduating from eighth grade) to desired but distant adult possible selves (e.g., going to college, getting a good job), discussed how possible selves are influenced by role models, and linked present action to possible selves. Later sessions focused on identifying specific strategies to be enacted in the present that would help youth obtain their possible selves. Students' articulated how they would cope with difficulty that they might encounter in attaining their desired possible selves. Program activities involved individualized activities such as creating a timeline into one's future, active participation by students, and group exercises. Two final sessions involved parents, with the goal of providing youth and parents structured activities in which to talk about possible selves and strategies to attain them (see Oyserman et al., 2006). Evaluation indicated that STJ successfully improved time spent engaged in strategies (e.g., improved in-class behavior, time spent doing homework) and long-term academic attainment, as measured by standardized test scores and attendance (Oyserman et al., 2004; Oyserman et al.,

2002). Additionally, participation in STJ reduced participants' depressive symptoms (Oyserman et al., 2006) and buffered youth from the negative effects on grades and behavior of low parent involvement in school (Oyserman, et al, 2007). Effects were sustained through two years of follow-up assessment. In sum, possible selves are useful as descriptive and predictive tools and can be modified by in-school activities resulting in significant long-term benefits for children.

SEE ALSO *Relevance of Self-Evaluations to Classroom Learning.*

BIBLIOGRAPHY
Markus, H. R., & Nurius, P. (1986). Possible selves. *American Psychologist, 41,* 954–969.
Oyserman, D., Brickman, D., & Rhodes, M. (2007). School success, possible selves and parent school-involvement. *Family Relations, 56,* 479–489.
Oyserman, D., Bybee, D., & Terry, K. (2006). Possible selves and academic outcomes: How and when possible selves impel action. *Journal of Personality and Social Psychology, 91,* 188–204.
Oyserman, D., Bybee, D., Terry, K., & Hart-Johnson, T. (2004). Possible selves as roadmaps. *Journal of Research in Personality, 38,* 130–149.
Oyserman, D., & Fryberg, S. (2006). The possible selves of diverse adolescents: Content and function across gender, race and national origin. In C. Dunkel & J. Kerpelman (Eds.), *Possible selves: Theory, research, and application.* Huntington, NY: Nova.
Oyserman, D., Gant, L., & Ager, J. (1995). A socially contextualized model of African-American identity: Possible selves and school persistence. *Journal of Personality and Social Psychology, 69,* 1216–1232.
Oyserman, D., & James, L. (in press). Possible selves: From content to process. In: Markman, Klein, & Suhr (Eds.). *The Handbook of Imagination and Mental Stimulation.* Psychology Press.
Oyserman, D., & Markus, H. R. (1990). Possible selves and delinquency. *Journal of Personality and Social Psychology, 59,* 112–125.
Oyserman, D., & Saltz, E. (1993). Competence, delinquency, and attempts to attain possible selves. *Journal of Personality and Social Psychology, 65,* 360–374.
Oyserman, D., Terry, K., & Bybee, D. (2002). A possible selves intervention to enhance school involvement. *Journal of Adolescence, 25,* 313–326.

Shawna J. Lee
Daphna Oyserman

PRAISE

The word praise originates from the Latin verb *pretiare,* meaning to highly value. The seminal work on the use of praise within the classroom context was produced by J. Brophy who defined praise as "commending the worth of" or "to express approval or admiration" (1981, p.5). J. Thomas (1991) used the term "descriptive reinforcement" to describe praise. He outlined a three stage model for providing praise in the classroom as follows: (a) personalize the praise by using the student's name, (b) use one of 110 praise statements, and (c) outline what the student did to merit being praised. P. C. Burnett (2001) referred to Thomas's 110 statements as general praise noting examples such as "that's great," "well done," "terrific job," and "that's fantastic." In summary, teacher praise involves positive words, accompanied by positive affect, and as such is a targeted, affective response to students' behaviors or performance.

The term feedback is often used alongside praise but is quite different. Feedback is used to guide students in ways to improve their performance by providing information about their ability or inability to achieve success (Hattie, 1993). One type of feedback is attributional feedback. Teachers who note that students' success is attributed to their hard work are providing effort feedback (for example, "Tim, your great results reflect your hard work"), while teachers who ascribe success to ability (for example, "Great result, Rachel, you are clever at math") are providing ability feedback. Effort and ability feedback are referred to as attributional feedback because they attribute success and performance to either effort or ability.

EFFECTIVE AND INEFFECTIVE PRAISE

Brophy conducted a functional analysis of praise in the classroom and noted that teachers' verbal praise did not equate to positive reinforcement because praise was typically used infrequently, without reference to specific behaviors and often without credibility and sincerity. Brophy noted that classroom research suggested that only 6% of interactions involved praise, and he concluded that high rates of praise were not evident in classrooms. Brophy described 12 guidelines for both effective and ineffective praise.

The key ingredients for effective praise according to Brophy (1981) are:

Praise should be delivered in response to a specific behavior.

The behavior, deserving of praise, should described in specific terms.

Praise should be sincere, credible, and spontaneous.

Praise should reward the attainment of clearly defined and understood performance criteria.

Praise should provide information about the student's competencies.

Praise should be given in recognition of noteworthy effort or success at a difficult task for that particular student.

Praise should attribute success to effort and ability implying that similar success in the future.

Ineffective praise:

Is delivered randomly or unsystematically,

Is restricted to global positive reactions delivered in a bland fashion with minimal attention to the student or behavior,

Rewards participation unrelated to performance,

Compares the student's performance to other students,

Is given without regard to the effort needed to complete the task,

Attributes success to ability alone or to external factors such as luck or the ease of the task, and

Is given by the teacher who acts as a power figure and external authority in a manipulative manner.

Not all of the literature is supportive of the use of praise in the classroom even when used effectively. R. Hitz and A. Driscoll (1994) noted literature that suggested that praise led to low expectations of success, discouraged children from judging for themselves, created anxiety, invited dependency, evoked defensiveness, and was delivered in the context of a power relationship. The major concern expressed was that praise was intrusive and controlling. Hitz and Driscoll advocated giving encouragement not praise and hence the mantra, encourage don't praise, emerged and formed part of many teacher training programs.

There has also been some debate regarding the use of ability feedback by teachers following a student's success. Brophy's guidelines noted ability feedback in the effective list but also noted a limitation by including the use of ability feedback alone in the ineffective list. Those who advocate the use of ability feedback highlight the impact that it has on the formation and development of students' self-concept (Craven, Marsh, & Debus, 1991). In addition, D. H. Schunk (1983) and B. Weiner (1986) noted that ability feedback produced higher expectations for future performance, greater skill acquisition, higher self-concept, enhanced satisfaction with performance, and further striving for achievement. Opposing the use of ability feedback in the classroom was C. M. Mueller and C. S. Dweck (1998) who argued against its use when they found that students who faced failure after receiving ability feedback showed low effort, poor persistence at a task and high frustration due to attributing their poor performance to lack of ability. Of further interest is the fact that the use of effort feedback in the classroom has limitations. J. Henderlong and M. R. Lepper (2002) noted that the positive impact of effort feedback might be restricted if effort is overemphasised and the student perceives this as an indication that they lack ability and have to work hard to get anywhere. Furthermore, providing effort feedback may also be negative if hard work and effort result in failure.

DEVELOPMENTAL DIFFERENCES

Burnett (2001) investigated 747 elementary students' preferences for classroom praise. The students were in grades 3 to 7 and aged 8 to 12 years. Students reported that they wanted to be praised in classroom. Forty percent wanted to be praised often, 51% wanted to be praised sometimes, and only 9% never wanted to be praised. Interestingly, 84% wanted to be praised for trying hard and effort, while only 16% wanted to be praised for their ability and being smart. Most of students (52%) wanted to be praised quietly, while 31% wanted to be praised loudly in front of the class, leaving 17% who did not want to be praised publicly or quietly.

Developmental differences across the grades were noted. The need for praise increased from grade 3 to 5 and then declined over the next two grades levels. Students in grades 3 and 7 wanted to be praised at similar levels with the intermediate grades reporting that they wished to be praised more frequently. The students wanting the highest amount of praise were those in grades 4 to 6, suggesting that this is a developmental phase where students seek recognition and reassurance from their teachers. There were also developmental differences across the grades for effort and ability feedback. As students progressed through the grades they reported wanting more effort feedback and less ability feedback. Grade 3 students reported that they wanted about the same level of both effort and ability feedback, while grade 7 students reported wanting more effort feedback and less ability feedback. This suggests that younger students prefer to hear that they are smart and capable, but once this information is integrated into their self-concept they prefer to have their achievements attributed to their efforts.

Elwell and Tiberio (1994) investigated 620 high school students' preferences for the use of praise in their classrooms. Students in grades 9 and 10 wanted to be praised less frequently and less publicly than their younger and older counterparts in grades 7 and 8 and grades 11 and 12 respectively. The students in this study perceived the use of praise in the classroom as appropriate and expected to receive it for academic-related behaviors but not for socially appropriate behaviors. Nearly 60% of the students surveyed preferred quiet and private praise or no praise at all for academic success, while 41%

wanted to be praised loudly and publicly for their achievements. Elwell and Tiberio noted that students respond differently to praise, and teachers need to know about when, where, and under what circumstances praise should be delivered in the classroom.

USING PRAISE IN THE CLASSROOM

The research findings on the use of praise and feedback in the classroom have been integrated into guidelines for teachers. Burnett (2003) described a summary of what has been learned about praise and feedback in the classroom as a result of research.

Positive statements. Positive statements by teachers have a powerful impact and should be used in the classroom. Positive statements must be related to a behavior or performance. General praise that is not targeted or related to a specific behavior or performance has little impact on students and is not related to students' perceptions of the classroom environment or relationship with teacher. Thomas's 1991 descriptive reinforcement model (that is, name the student, use positive statements, describe the behavior) has merit.

Individual feedback. Praise and feedback should mostly be given individually. Only 31% of elementary students and 24% of high school students reported having a preference for public praise. Teachers should monitor a student's reaction to feedback as nearly one in five students reported not wanting to be praised at all, but this preference depends on circumstances and the student's grade level. Students should be praised for both effort and ability where warranted and appropriate for the grade level. Both types of feedback can be used despite having advantages and limitations.

Importance of grade level. The grade of the student is important. Students in grades 4 to 6 like to be praised more frequently and more publicly than students in grades 3 and 7, while students in grades 9 and 10 have a lower need for praise when compared with their older and younger high school peers. In the elementary school classroom students' preference for receiving effort feedback increases with grade, while preference for receiving ability feedback declines with grade.

SEE ALSO *Teacher Expectations.*

BIBLIOGRAPHY

Brophy, J. (1981). Teacher praise: A functional analysis. *Review of Educational Research, 51,* 5–32.

Burnett, P. C. (2001). Elementary students' preferences for teacher praise. *Journal of Classroom Interaction, 36(1),* 16–23.

Burnett, P. C. (2003). Positive statements, positive students, positive classrooms. *Australian Journal of Guidance and Counselling, 13,* 1–10.

Craven, R. G., Marsh, H.W., & Debus, R.L. (1991). Effects of internally focused feedback and attributional feedback on enhancement of academic self-concept. *Journal of Educational Psychology, 83,* 17–27.

Elwell, W. C., & Tiberio, J. (1994). Teacher praise. *Journal of Instructional Psychology, 21,* 322–328.

Hattie, J. (1993). *Measuring the effects of schooling.* SET: Research Information for Teachers, 2, 1–4.

Henderlong, J., & Lepper, M. R. (2002). The effects of praise on children's intrinsic motivation: A review and synthesis. *Psychological Bulletin, 128,* 774–795.

Hitz, R., & Driscoll, A. (1994). Give encouragement, not praise. *Texas Child Care, 21,* 3–11.

Mueller, C. M., & Dweck, C. S. (1998). Praise for intelligence can undermine children's motivation and performance. *Journal of Personality and Social Psychology, 75,* 33–52.

Schunk. D. H. (1983). Ability versus effort attributional feedback; Differential effects on self-efficacy and achievement. *Journal of Educational Psychology, 75,* 848–856.

Thomas, J. (1991). You're the greatest. *Principal, 71(1):* 32–33.

Weiner, B. (1986). *An Attributional Theory of Motivation and Emotion.* New York: Springer Verlag.

Paul Burnett

PRESSLEY, G. MICHAEL
1951–2006

On May 23, 2006, the academic community lost one of its most brilliant and influential scholars in the fields of psychology and education. Michael Pressley, esteemed researcher and academic, died from complications associated with his fourth battle with cancer.

During his career, Pressley published more than 350 articles and book chapters and edited more than 25 books on psychology, literacy, and education. He especially was recognized for his senior authorship of the McGraw-Hill/ SRA Open Course K-6 literacy program (also known as Open Court). He served as editor and board member for many prominent journals including *Journal of Educational Psychology* and the *Journal of Reading Behaviour.*

Pressley's dedication as a researcher was matched by his commitment to junior scholars. Pressley served as an advisor and mentor to dozens of doctoral and master's students throughout the United States and Canada, involving them extensively in his research and publication activities. Pressley also held great passion for K–12 schooling and involved himself in teacher preparation programs and the daily functions of elementary classrooms across America.

Pressley's schooling experiences, in part, shaped his interests in the psychology of learning. A student in the post-Sputnik era, Pressley participated in a science-enriched curriculum that concluded in his senior year with an 8-week research psychology summer session at Western Michigan University. This experience was profound in that it provided him with foundational insights about the enormous potential of research psychology to inform the field of education—insights that would subsequently be transformed into a professional passion.

Pressley completed his undergraduate studies at Northwestern University and earned a doctoral degree from the Institute of Child Development at Minnesota, specializing in cognitive development. Over the course of his career Pressley held positions at nine esteemed institutions including the University of Maryland-College Park, State University of New York, and Michigan State University.

A vigorous scholar, his research interests ranged from explorations in basic memory development to reading instruction. Pressley's initial explorations were largely quantitative and deepened understanding of effective learning strategies and study techniques, as well as factors that affected the learning process (good strategy user model). Adopting a variety of qualitative and mixed-methods methodologies, Pressley extended his research attentions to transforming educational practice and defining the essence of exemplary classroom instruction. His later interests focused in the area of reading comprehension and in monitoring and shaping teacher-student interactions as they negotiated meaning from text. Whether in the laboratory or in the classroom, students' positive learning experiences formed the foundation of Pressley's research and quickly earned him recognition as one of the nation's foremost educational researchers.

Pressley was the recipient of several prestigious career awards honoring his outstanding overall contributions to the fields of psychology and education, as well as his specific contributions in reading research and remedial reading diagnosis and programming for students at risk for reading and writing failure. These honors include induction into the Reading Hall of Fame, the Oscar Causey Award from the National Reading Conference, the Sylvia Scriber Award from the American Educational Research Association, and the Thorndike Award from the American Psychological Association. Pressley was honored with the University Distinguished Professor Award from Michigan State University and recognized as one of the top 100 University of Minnesota Distinguished Alumni from the College of Education and Human Development.

Pressley's contributions to the social science and education fields were unprecedented, as was his commitment to the universities, programs, and individuals he served. His intellect and leadership were matched by his compassion and unselfishness. Pressley was an individual who truly made a difference in the lives of his students and colleagues and his legacy remains with those who serve in America's classrooms.

BIBLIOGRAPHY

WORKS BY

Block, C., Gambrell, L. B., & Pressley, M. (Eds.). (2002). *Improving comprehension instruction: Rethinking research, theory, and classroom practice.* San Francisco: Jossey-Bass.

Pressley, M. (1998). *Reading instruction that works: the case for balanced teaching.* New York: Guilford.

Pressley, M. (2006). *Reading instruction that works: The case for balanced teaching* (3rd ed.). New York: Guilford.

Pressley, M., Ailington, R. L., Wharton-McDonald, R., Block, C. C., & Morrow, L. M. (2001). *Learning to read: Lessons from exemplary first-grade classrooms.* New York: Guilford.

Pressley, M., et al. (2003). *Motivating primary-grade students.* New York: Guilford.

Schneider, W., & Pressley, M. (1997) *Memory development between two and twenty* (2nd ed.). Mahwah, NJ: Erlbaum.

Vera Ella Woloshyn

PRIMARY LANGUAGE ACQUISITION

SEE *First (Primary) Language Acquisition.*

PROBLEM-BASED LEARNING

SEE *Constructivism: Problem-Based Learning.*

PROBLEM SOLVING

A major goal of education is to help students learn in ways that enable them to use what they have learned to solve problems in new situations. In short, problem solving is fundamental to education because educators are interested in improving students' ability to solve problems. This entry defines key terms, types of problems, and processes in problem solving and then examines theories of problem solving, ways of teaching for problem solving transfer, and ways of teaching of problem solving skill.

DEFINITIONS

What is a Problem? A problem exists when a problem solver has a goal but does not know how to accomplish it.

Specifically, a problem occurs when a situation is in a given state, a problem solver wants the situation to be in a goal state, and the problem solver is not aware of an obvious way to transform the situation from the given state to the goal state. In his classic monograph, *On Problem Solving,* the Gestalt psychologist Karl Duncker defined a problem as follows:

> A problem arises when a living creature has a goal but does not know how this goal is to be reached. Whenever one cannot go from the given situation to the desired situation simply by action, then there has to be recourse to thinking. Such thinking has the task of devising some action, which may mediate between the existing and desired situations. (1945, p. 1)

This definition includes high-level academic tasks for a typical middle school student such as writing a convincing essay, solving an unfamiliar algebra word problem, or figuring out how an electric motor works, but does not include low-level academic tasks such as pronouncing the sound of the printed word "cat," stating the answer to "2 + 2 =___," or changing a word from singular to plural form.

What is Problem Solving? According to Mayer and Wittrock, problem solving is "cognitive processing directed at achieving a goal when no solution method is obvious to the problem solver" (2006, p. 287). This definition consists of four parts: (1) problem solving is cognitive, that is, problem solving occurs within the problem solver's cognitive system and can only be inferred from the problem solver's behavior, (2) problem solving is a process, that is, problem solving involves applying cognitive processes to cognitive representations in the problem solver's cognitive system, (3) problem solving is directed, that is, problem solving is guided by the problem solver's goals, and (4) problem solving is personal, that is, problem solving depends on the knowledge and skill of the problem solver. In sum, problem solving is cognitive processing directed at transforming a problem from the given state to the goal state when the problem solver is not immediately aware of a solution method. For example, problem solving occurs when a high school student writes a convincing essay on the causes of the American Civil War, understands how the heart works from reading a biology textbook, or solves a complex arithmetic word problem.

PROBLEM SOLVING AS A KIND OF THINKING

Problem solving is related to other terms such as thinking, reasoning, decision making, critical thinking, and creative thinking. Thinking refers to a problem solver's cognitive processing, but it includes both directed thinking (which is problem solving) and undirected thinking (such as day-dreaming). Thus, thinking is a broader term that includes problem solving as a subset of thinking (i.e., a kind of thinking, i.e., directed thinking).

Reasoning, decision making, critical thinking, and creative thinking are subsets of problem solving, that is, kinds of problem solving. Reasoning refers to problem solving with a specific task in which the goal is to draw a conclusion from premises using logical rules based on deduction or induction. For example, if students know that all four-sided figures are quadrilaterals and that all squares have four sides, then by using deduction they can conclude that all squares are quadrilaterals. If they are given the sequence 2–4–6–8, then by induction they can conclude that the next number should be 10. Decision making refers to problem solving with a specific task in which the goal is to choose one of two or more alternatives based on some criteria. For example, a decision making task is to decide whether someone would rather have $100 for sure or a 1% chance of getting $100,000. Thus, both reasoning and decision-making are kinds of problem solving that are characterized by specific kinds of tasks.

Finally, creative thinking and critical thinking refer to specific aspects of problem solving, respectively. Creative thinking involves generating alternatives that meet some criteria, such as listing all the possible uses for a brick, whereas critical thinking involves evaluating how well various alternatives meet some criteria, such as determining which are the best answers for the brick problem. For example, in scientific problem solving situations, creative thinking is involved in generating hypotheses and critical thinking is involved in testing them. Creative thinking and critical thinking can be involved in reasoning and decision making.

TYPES OF PROBLEMS

Problems can be well-defined or ill-defined. A well-defined problem has a clearly specified given state, a clearly specified goal state, and a clearly specified set of allowable operations. For example, "Solve for x: $2x + 11 = 33$" is a well-defined problem because there is clear given state (i.e., $2x + 11 = 33$), a clear goal state (i.e., $x =$ ___) and a clear set of operations (i.e., the rules of algebra and arithmetic). An ill-defined problem lacks a clearly specified given state, goal state, and/or set of allowable operators. For example, "develop a research plan for a senior honors thesis" is an ill-defined problem for most students because the goal state is not clear (e.g., the requirements for the plan) and the allowable operators are not clear (e.g., the places where students may find information). What makes a problem well-defined or ill-defined depends on the characteristics of the problem. Although most important

and challenging problems in life are ill-defined, most problem solving in schools involves well-defined problems.

Moreover, it is also customary to distinguish between routine and non-routine problems. When a problem solver knows how to go about solving a problem, the problem is routine. For example, two-column multiplication problems, such as 25 x 12 = ___, are routine for most high school students because they know the procedure. When a problem solver does not initially know how to go about solving a problem, the problem is non-routine. For example, the following problem is non-routine for most high-school students: "If the area covered by water lilies in a lake doubles every 24 hours, and the entire lake is covered in 60 days, how long does it take to cover half the lake?" Robert Sternberg and Janet Davidson (1995) refer to this kind of problem as an *insight problem* because problem solvers need to invent a solution method (e.g., in this case the answer is 59 days). What makes problems either routine or non-routine depends on the knowledge of the problem solver because the same problem can be routine for one person and non-routine for another. Although the goal of education is to prepare students for solving non-routine problems, most of the problems that students are asked to solve in school are routine.

COGNITIVE PROCESSES IN PROBLEM SOLVING

Mayer and Wittrock (2006) distinguished among four major cognitive processes in problem solving: representing, in which the problem solver constructs a cognitive representation of the problem; planning, in which the problem solver devises a plan for solving the problem; executing, in which the problem solver carries out the plan; and self-regulating, in which the problem solver evaluates the effectiveness of cognitive processing during problem solving and adjusts accordingly. During representing, the problem solver seeks to understand the problem, including the given state, goal state, and allowable operators, and the problem solver may build a situation model—that is, a concrete representation of the situation being described in the problem. Although solution execution is often emphasized in mathematics textbooks and in mathematics classrooms, successful mathematical problem solving also depends on representing, planning, and self-regulating. In a 2001 review, Jeremy Kilpatrick, Jane Swafford, and Bradford Findell concluded that mathematical proficiency depends on intertwining of procedural fluency (for executing) with conceptual understanding (for representing), strategic competence (for planning), adaptive reasoning, and productive disposition (for self-regulating).

According to Mayer and Wittrock (2006), students need to have five kinds of knowledge in order to be successful problem solvers:

facts: knowledge about characteristics of elements or events, such as "there are 100 cents in a dollar";

concepts: knowledge of a categories, principles, or models, such as knowing what place value means in arithmetic or how hot air rises in science;

strategies: knowledge of general methods, such as how to break a problem into parts or how to find a related problem;

procedures: knowledge of specific procedures, such as how to carry out long division or how to change words from singular to plural form; and

beliefs: cognitions about one's problem-solving competence (such as "I am not good in math") or about the nature of problem solving (e.g., "If someone can't solve a problem right away, the person never will be able to solve it").

Facts and concepts are useful for representing a problem, strategies are needed for planning a solution, procedures are needed for carrying out the plan, and beliefs can influence the process of self-regulating.

THEORIES OF PROBLEM SOLVING

Many current views of problem solving, such as described in Keith Holyoak and Robert Morrison's *Cambridge Handbook of Thinking and Reasoning* (2005) or Marsha Lovett's 2002 review of research on problem solving, have their roots in Gestalt theory or information processing theory.

Gestalt Theory. The Gestalt theory of problem solving, described by Karl Duncker (1945) and Max Wertheimer (1959), holds that problem solving occurs with a flash of insight. Richard Mayer (1995) noted that insight occurs when a problem solver moves from a state of not knowing how to solve a problem to knowing how to solve a problem. During insight, problem solvers devise a way of representing the problem that enables solution. Gestalt psychologists offered several ways of conceptualizing what happens during insight: insight involves building a schema in which all the parts fit together, insight involves suddenly reorganizing the visual information so it fits together to solve the problem, insight involves restating a problem's givens or problem goal in a new way that makes the problem easier to solve, insight involves removing mental blocks, and insight involves finding a problem analog (i.e., a similar problem that the problem solver already knows how to solve). Gestalt theory

informs educational programs aimed at teaching students how to represent problems.

Information Processing Theory. The information processing theory of problem solving, as described by Allen Newell and Herbert Simon (1972), is based on a human-computer metaphor in which problem solving involves carrying out a series of mental computations on mental representations. The key components in the theory are as follows: the idea that a problem can be represented as a problem space—a representation of the initial state, goal state, and all possible intervening states—and search heuristics—a strategy for moving through the problem space from one state of the problem to the next. The problem begins in the given state, the problem solver applies an operator that generates a new state, and so on until the goal state is reached. For example, a common search heuristic is means-ends analysis, in which the problem solver seeks to apply an operator that will satisfy the problem-solver's current goal; if there is a constraint that blocks the application of the operator, then a goal is set to remove the constraint, and so on. Information processing theory informs educational programs aimed at teaching strategies for solving problems.

TEACHING FOR PROBLEM SOLVING

Max Wertheimer (1959) made the classic distinction between learning by rote and learning by understanding. For example, in teaching students how to compute the area of a parallelogram by a rote method, students are shown how to measure the height, how to measure the base, and how to multiply height times base using the formula, area = height x base. According to Wertheimer, this rote method of instruction leads to good performance on retention tests (i.e., solving similar problems) and poor performance on transfer tests (i.e., solving new problems). In contrast, learning by understanding involves helping students see that if they can cut off the triangle from one end of the parallelogram and place it on the other side to form a rectangle; then, they can put 1 x 1 squares over the surface of the rectangle to determine how many squares form the area. According to Wertheimer, this meaningful method of instruction leads to good retention and good transfer performance. Wertheimer claimed that rote instruction creates reproductive thinking—applying already learned procedures to a problem—whereas meaningful instruction leads to productive thinking—adapting what was learned to new kinds of problems.

Mayer and Wittrock (2006) identified instructional methods that are intended to promote meaningful learning, such as providing advance organizers that prime appropriate prior knowledge during learning, asking learners to explain aloud a text they are reading, presenting worked out examples along with commentary, or providing hints and guidance as students work on an example problem. A major goal of meaningful methods of instruction is to promote problem-solving transfer, that is, the ability to use what was learned in new situations. Wittrock (1974) referred to meaningful learning as a generative process because it requires active cognitive processing during learning.

TEACHING OF PROBLEM SOLVING

In the previous section, instructional methods were examined that are intended to promote problem-solving transfer. However, a more direct approach is to teach people the knowledge and skills they need to be better problem solvers. Mayer (2008) identified four issues that are involved in designing a problem-solving course.

What to Teach. Should problem-solving courses attempt to teach problem solving as a single, monolithic skill (e.g., a mental muscle that needs to be strengthened) or as a collection of smaller, component skills? Although conventional wisdom is that problem solving involves a single skill, research in cognitive science suggests that problem solving ability is a collection of small component skills.

How to Teach. Should problem-solving courses focus on the product of problem solving (i.e., getting the right answer) or the process of problem solving (i.e., figuring out how to solve the problem)? While it makes sense that students need practice in getting the right answer (i.e., the product of problem solving), research in cognitive science suggests that students benefit from training in describing and evaluating the methods used to solve problems (i.e., the process of problem solving). For example, one technique that emphasizes the process of problem solving is modeling, in which teachers and students demonstrate their problem-solving methods.

Where to Teach. Should problem solving be taught as a general, stand-alone course or within specific domains (such as problem solving in history, in science, in mathematics, ETC.)? Although conventional wisdom is that students should be taught general skills in stand-alone courses, there is sufficient cognitive science research to propose that it would be effective to teach problem solving within the context of specific subject domains.

When to Teach. Should problem solving be taught before or after students have mastered corresponding lower-levels? Although it seems to make sense that higher-order thinking skills should be taught only after lower-level skills have been mastered, there is sufficient

cognitive science research to propose that it would be effective to teach higher-order skills before lower-level skills are mastered.

In this section, three classic problem-solving courses are described that meet these four criteria and that have been subjected to rigorous research study: the Productive Thinking Program developed by Martin Covington, Richard Crutchfield, and Lillian Davies (1966), Instrumental Enrichment developed by Reuven Feuerstein (1980), and Odyssey described by Raymond Nickerson (1994). The Productive Thinking Program consisted of 15 cartoon-like booklets intended to teach thinking skills to elementary school children. Each booklet presented a detective-type story—such a story about a bank robbery—and students learned how to generate hypotheses—such as who might have done it—and evaluate hypotheses using information in the booklet. Child characters in the booklet modeled problem-solving methods, and adult characters offered commentary and hints. Overall, Richard Mansfield, Thomas Busse, and Ernest Krepelka (1978) reported that students who learned with the Productive Thinking Program showed greater improvements in their ability to solve similar detective-type problems as compared to students who had not received the training.

In Instrumental Enrichment, students who had been identified as mentally retarded based on a traditional intelligence test were given concentrated classroom instruction in how to solve traditional intelligence test items. In a typical lesson, the teacher introduces the class to an intelligence test item; then, the class breaks down into small groups to devise ways to solve the problem; next, each group reports on its solution method to the whole class; and finally, a teacher-led discussion ensues in which students focus on describing effective methods for solving the problem. Evaluation studies reported by Feuerstein (1980) show that students who received this training on a regular basis over several years showed greater gains in non-verbal intelligence than did non-trained students.

Finally, in Odyssey, middle-school students received training in how to solve intelligence test problems, using a procedure somewhat like Instrumental Enrichment, and with similar results. David Perkins and Tina Grotzer reported that the training "enhanced the magnitude of students' intelligent behavior [on] authentic tasks at least in the short term" (2000, p. 496). Overall, each of these courses met the criteria for what to teach (i.e., a collection of small component skills), how to teach (i.e., using modeling to focus on the process of problem solving), where to teach (i.e., teaching specific skills), and when to teach (i.e., teaching before all lower-level skills were mastered). Although none of these programs is currently popular, courses based on these four criteria are likely to be successful.

SEE ALSO *Creativity; Critical Thinking; Decision Making; Learning and Teaching Mathematics; Reasoning.*

BIBLIOGRAPHY

Covington, M. V., Crutchfield, R. S., & Davies, L. B. (1966). *The productive thinking program.* Columbus, OH: Merrill.

Duncker, K. (1945). On problem solving. *Psychological Monographs, 58*(5), Whole No. 270.

Feuerstein, R. (1980). *Instrumental enrichment.* Baltimore: University Park Press.

Holyoak, K. J., & Morrison, R. G. (Eds.). (2005). *The Cambridge handbook of thinking and reasoning.* New York: Cambridge University Press.

Kilpatrick, J., Swafford, J., & Findell, B. (2001). *Adding it up: Helping children learn mathematics.* Washington, DC: National Academy Press.

Lovett, M. C., (2002). Problem solving. In D. Medin (Ed.), *Stevens' handbook of experimental psychology:* Vol. 2, *Memory and cognitive processes* (3rd ed., pp. 317–362). New York: Wiley.

Mansfield, R. S., Busse, T. V., & Krepelka, E. J. (1978). The effectiveness of creativity training. *Review of Educational Research, 48,* 517–536.

Mayer, R. E. (1995). The search for insight: Grappling with Gestalt psychology's unanswered questions. In R. J. Sternberg & J. E. Davidson (Eds.), *The nature of insight* (pp. 3–32). Cambridge, MA: MIT Press.

Mayer, R. E. (2008*). Learning and instruction* (2nd ed.). Upper Saddle River, NJ: Pearson Merrill Prentice Hall.

Mayer, R. E., & Wittrock, R. C. (2006). Problem solving. In P. A. Alexander & P. H. Winne (Eds.), *Handbook of educational psychology* (2nd ed., pp. 287–304). Mahwah, NJ: Erlbaum.

Newell, A., & Simon, H. A. (1972). *Human problem solving.* Englewood Cliffs, NJ: Prentice Hall.

Nickerson, R. S. (1994). Project intelligence. In R. J. Sternberg (Ed.), *Encyclopedia of human intelligence* (pp. 392–430). New York: Cambridge University Press.

Perkins, D. N., & Grotzer, T. A. (1997). Teaching intelligence. *American Psychologist, 52,* 1125–1133.

Sternberg, R. J. & Davidson, J. E. (Eds.). (1995). *The nature of insight* (pp. 3–32). Cambridge, MA: MIT Press.

Wertheimer, M. (1959). *Productive thinking.* New York: Harper & Row.

Wittrock, M. C. (1974). Learning as a generative process. *Educational Psychologist, 11,* 87–95.

Richard E. Mayer
Merlin C. Wittrock

PROJECT-BASED LEARNING

SEE *Constructivism: Project-Based Learning.*

PROSOCIAL BEHAVIOR

Prosocial behaviors are voluntary behaviors made with the intention of benefiting others (Eisenberg & Fabes, 1998). This definition carefully circumvents the potential benefits to the person performing the prosocial behavior. Prosocial behavior is often accompanied with psychological and social rewards for its performer. In the long run, individuals can benefit from living in a society where prosociality is common (which, in evolutionary terms, increases reproductive potential). It has therefore been difficult for researchers to identify purely altruistic behaviors, benefiting only the recipient and not the performer. Nevertheless, behaviors benefiting others, but whose main goal is self-advantageous (e.g. cooperative behaviors intended to obtain a common resource), typically are not considered prosocial. Typical examples include: volunteering; sharing toys, treats, or food with friends; instrumental help (e.g., helping a peer with school assignments); costly help (e.g. risking one's own life to save others); and emotionally supporting others in distress (e.g., comforting a peer following a disappointing experience or caring for a person who is ill).

DEVELOPMENTAL CHANGES

Prosocial behavior has roots in human evolutionary history as de Waal's comparison with other species shows. Nevertheless, Fehr and Fischbacher note that humans are unique in their degree of prosociality. Hoffman's theory proposes that prosocial behavior becomes increasingly other-oriented as children mature. Infants feel self-distress in reaction to the distress of others because they are incapable of differentiating their own experiences from those of others. Gradually, self-distress is replaced by other-oriented concern, requiring some understanding of others' mental states (Hoffman, 2000). Zahn-Waxler, Robinson, and Emde show that by age 4, many children can react empathically to others, including offering help to those in distress.

The 1998 Eisenberg and Fabes meta-analysis found that prosocial behavior increases with age, although increases varied in size, depending on the methodological aspects of each study. In one study by Benenson, Pascoe, and Radmore, about 60 percent of 4-year old children donated at least one of 10 stickers they received to a peer, and about 85 percent did so at age 9. This increase was markedly elevated for higher-SES children compared to lower-SES children. From childhood to adolescence further increases are found in sharing, but not in helping or providing emotional support (Eisenberg & Fabes, 1998). The boost in prosocial behavior with age is attributed to developmental increases in cognitive abilities associated with detecting others' needs and determining ways to help, in empathy-related responding, and in the moral understanding of the importance of helping others (Eisenberg et al., 2006).

CONTEXTUAL AND INDIVIDUAL INFLUENCES

Many contextual factors are associated with prosocial behavior. For example, Cole and colleagues report short-term success for television programs designed to increase children's prosociality. Social psychological experiments consistently show that recognizing a situation as requiring assistance, involving personal responsibility, and enabling oneself to help, all increase helping behavior (Penner, Dovidio, Piliavin, & Schroeder, 2005). Individuals are more likely to provide support in situations that promote personal psychological and material rewards, or where the costs (e.g., guilt) associated with not helping are prominent. Finally, individuals are more likely to behave prosocially towards similar or likable others (Penner et al., 2005), and towards others considered to be close, especially kin (Graziano et al., 2007). This pattern may reflect an ultimate evolutionary goal of kin selection as described by Hamilton, although de Waal notes that helpers' psychological goals may be quite different. Genetic relatedness aside, prosocial behavior towards family members probably involves a sense of duty, reciprocity, and affective relationships.

Rushton describes moderate consistency in individuals' prosocial behavior across varying situations and contexts, demonstrating both stable individual differences in prosociality and the importance of contextual factors. Research following children from early childhood to adulthood supports the existence of the long-debated altruistic or prosocial personality (Eisenberg et al., 1999). Individual differences in prosociality are linked to sociability, low shyness, extroversion, and agreeableness, although specific prosocial behaviors may require a combination of additional traits, such as perceived self-efficacy in the case of helping (Penner et al., 2005). Researchers Bardi and Schwartz highlight the importance of individuals' specific prosocial values, including emphasizing the importance of the welfare of others, as an additional variable likely to influence prosocial behavior. Personality and contextual variables are likely to interact in determining prosocial behavior. For example, agreeable individuals were more likely to help an outgroup member than low-agreeableness individuals, but agreeableness was not associated with helping an ingroup member (Graziano et al., 2007).

Environmental factors linked to individual differences in children's prosociality include parental modeling of helping behavior and use of inductive discipline (e.g., explaining to children the consequences of their behavior) as opposed to power-assertive discipline (e.g., punishment) (Eisenberg & Fabes, 1998). Beyond parental influence, siblings, peers, and schools also may affect prosociality. For example, as Wentzel, McNamara, and Caldwell point out, children's prosociality may be influenced by close friends. Furthermore, the better the affective quality of the friendship, the more influential friends are to each other's prosociality.

Genetics also contribute to individual variation in prosociality. Research on adults finds that prosociality is substantially heritable. Research on young children shows lower heritability, demonstrated by one longitudinal twin study showing increases in the heritability of parent-rated prosociality, from 30 percent at age 2 to 60 percent at age 7 (Knafo & Plomin, 2006).

Genetic and environmental effects are often intertwined. For example, parental reasoning may be more effective with highly attentive children, while external rewards may work better for other children. These gene-environment interactions, in which children's genetically influenced tendencies interact with environmental influences in determining behavior, are highly likely. Further investigation is necessary of gene-environment interactions with regard to prosociality. Gene-environment correlations can also shape individual differences in prosociality. For example, children's low prosociality is related to parents' use of negative discipline and affection. This relationship can be traced back to children's genetic tendencies, implying that the genetically influenced low prosociality can initiate a negative reaction from parents (Knafo & Plomin, 2006).

Gender and culture are additional predictors of prosocial behavior. A meta-analysis found small differences favoring girls in prosocial behavior, smaller than expected based on gender stereotypes and lower for instrumental help than for other prosocial behaviors (Eisenberg & Fabes, 1998). Some evidence suggests that children in Western societies are less prosocial than children in other cultures, but some studies find no differences along these lines (see review by Eisenberg et al., 2006). A field study by Levine, Norenzayan, and Philbrick found large cultural differences in spontaneously helping strangers. For example, the proportion of individuals helping a stranger with a hurt leg pick up dropped magazines ranged from 22 percent to 95 percent across 23 cultures. Although national wealth was negatively associated with helping rates, the closely related cultural value of individualism-collectivism (individualism is on average higher in richer countries) was not related. A compelling cultural explanation for cross-national differences in prosocial behavior was still needed as of 2008. Perhaps, cultures differ substantially in what each promotes as prosocial behavior (Eisenberg et al., 2006).

RELATION TO OTHER ASPECTS OF SCHOOL FUNCTIONING

Clark and Ladd find that prosocial children are relatively well adjusted and have better peer relationships than less prosocial children. Highly prosocial children have more friends and report a better quality of friendship, relative to less prosocial children.

Caprara and colleagues find positive relationships between children's early prosocial behavior and later academic achievement, and positive peer relations (statistically controlling for earlier achievement). The exact nature of these relationships has yet to be determined. Possibly, prosocial children's superior social skills enable them to work better with peers and to get along better with teachers. Alternatively, earlier prosociality represents self-regulation abilities needed for later achievement. Similarly, a finding by Johnson and colleagues that volunteering adolescents have higher grade point averages and intrinsic motivation toward schoolwork may indicate that volunteering increases academic self-esteem. Furthermore, adolescents who volunteer may receive preferential treatment from teachers, increasing their achievement.

HOW TEACHERS AND SCHOOLS CAN PROMOTE PROSOCIAL BEHAVIOR

Although observational studies suggest that preschool teachers usually do little to encourage prosocial behavior, teachers' behavior and school policies can promote prosociality. Positive, warm, and secure teacher-student relationships are associated with children's prosociality (Eisenberg et al., 2006).

To overrule the possibility that highly adjusted children are both prosocial and elicit positive reactions from teachers, intervention studies are essential. A five-year longitudinal study by Solomon and colleagues finds that training teachers to promote children's prosociality and developmental discipline increases children's prosocial values and behaviors. The program provided children with an opportunity to work collaboratively in small groups and participate in activities designed to promote social understanding. It emphasized prosocial values through the use of relevant media and highlighting children's positive behaviors and provided opportunities for active helping such as a buddy program that assigned older children to help younger peers.

In another school intervention reported by Fraser and colleagues, children received training designed to teach social problem-solving skills and to reduce peer rejection. Simultaneously, parents participated in home lessons designed to improve parenting skills (e.g., child development, parent-child communication, problem-solving, and discipline). Intervention children increased in prosocial behavior in comparison to the control group. Another experimental school program reported by Flannery and colleagues shows longitudinal gains in children's prosocial behavior by altering school climate by teaching students and staff five simple rules and activities: (a) praise people, (b) avoid put-downs, (c) seek wise people as advisers and friends, (d) notice and correct hurts one causes, and (e) right wrongs.

McMahon and Washburn point out that effective interventions often work to address students' empathy and problem-solving skills and are often tailored to the cultural, developmental, and behavioral characteristics of students. Research by Kazdin, Bass, Siegel, and Thomas reveals the effectiveness of cognitive-behavioral therapy in increasing prosociality in children with severe antisocial behavior. Another violence prevention program reported by DeCarlo and Hockman improves male urban African American students' prosocial skills through analysis of relevant RAP music lyrics. Furthermore, Lakes and Hoyt show the effectiveness of tae-kwon-do training at primary school to improve self-regulation and prosocial behavior among boys and, to a lesser extent, girls. Attention/play interventions by school psychologists with highly aggressive boys (modeling, role-playing, coaching, feedback, and discussion of play strategies), by Dubow and colleagues longitudinally decrease aggression and increase prosocial behavior. These studies demonstrate the usefulness of non-preaching approaches to prosocial development.

SEE ALSO *Moral Development; Social Skills.*

BIBLIOGRAPHY

Bardi, A., & Schwartz, S.H. (2000). Values and behavior: Strength and structure of relations. *Personality and Social Psychology Bulletin,* 29(10),1207–1220.

Benenson, J. F., Pascoe, J., & Radmore, N. (2007). Children's altruistic behavior in the dictator game. *Evolution and Human Behavior, 28,* 168–175.

Caprara, G. V., Barbaranelli, C., Pastorelli, C., Bandura, A., & Zimbardo, P. G. (2000). Prosocial foundations of children's academic achievement. *Psychological Science, 11*(4), 302–306.

Clark, K. E., & Ladd, G. W. (2000). Connectedness and autonomy support in parent-child relationships: Links to children's socioemotional orientation and peer relationships. *Developmental Psychology, 36,* 485–498.

Cole, C. F., Arafat, C., Tidhar, C., Tafesh, W. Z., Fox, N. A., et al. (2003). The educational impact of Rechov Sumsum/ Shara'a Simsim: A Sesame Street television series to promote respect and understanding among children living in Israel, the

West Bank and Gaza. *International Journal of Behavioral Development, 27,* 409–422.

DeCarlo, A., & Hockman, E. (2003). RAP therapy: A group work intervention method for urban adolescents. *Social Work with Groups, 26*(3), 45–59.

De Waal, F. B. M. (2007). Putting the altruism back into altruism: The evolution of empathy. *Annual Review of Psychology, 59(4),* 4.1–4.22.

Dubow, E. F., Huesmann, L. R., & Eron, L. D. (1987). Mitigating aggression and promoting prosocial behavior in aggressive elementary schoolboys. *Behaviour Research and Therapy, 25*(6), 527–531.

Eisenberg, N., & Fabes, R. A. (1998). Prosocial Development. In W. Damon, (Ed.), *Handbook of child psychology: Social, emotional, and personality development* (Vol. 3, pp. 701–778). New York: Wiley.

Eisenberg, N., Fabes, R. A., & Spinrad, T. L. (2006). Prosocial development. In N. Eisenberg (Vol. Ed.), W. Damon & R. M. Lerner (Series Eds.), *Handbook of child psychology: Social, emotional, and personality development* (Vol. 3, pp. 646–718). New York: Wiley.

Eisenberg, N., Guthrie, B., Murphy, C., Shepard, S. A., Cumberland, A., & Carlo, G. (1999). Consistency and development of prosocial dispositions: A longitudinal study. *Child Development, 70*(6), 1360–1372.

Fehr, E., & Fischbacher, U. (2003). The nature of human altruism. *Nature, 425*(6960), 785–791.

Flannery, D. J., Liau, A. K., Powell, K. E., Vesterdal, W., Vazsonyi, A.T., Guo, S., et al. (2003). Initial behavior outcomes for the peacebuilders universal school-based violence prevention program. *Developmental Psychology, 39,* 292–308.

Fraser, M. W., Day, S. H., Galinsky, M. J., Hodges, V. G., & Smokowski, P. R. (2004). Conduct problems and peer rejection in childhood: A randomized trial of the making choices and strong families programs. *Research on Social Work Practice, 14,* 313–324.

Graziano, W. G., Habashi, M. M., Sheese, B. E., & Tobin, R. M. (2007). Agreeableness, empathy, and helping: A person X situation perspective. *Journal of Personality and Social Psychology, 93*(4), 583–59.

Hamilton, W. D. (1964). The genetical evolution of social behaviour I and II. *Journal of Theoretical Biology* 7, 1–52.

Hoffman, M. L. (2000). *Empathy and moral development: Implications for caring and justice.* New York: Cambridge University Press.

Johnson, M. K., Beebe, T., Mortimer, J. T., & Snyder, M. (1998). Volunteerism in adolescence: A process perspective. *Journal of Research on Adolescence, 8*(3), 309–332.

Kazdin, A. E., Bass, D., Siegel, T., & Thomas, C. (1989). Cognitive-behavioral therapy and relationship therapy in the treatment of children referred for antisocial behavior. *Journal of Consulting and Clinical Psychology, 57*(4), 522–535.

Knafo, A., & Plomin, R. (2006). Parental discipline and affection and children's prosocial behavior: Genetic and environmental links. *Journal of Personality and Social Psychology, 90,* 147–164.

Lakes, K. D., & Hoyt, W. T. (2004). Promoting self-regulation through school-based martial arts training. *Applied Developmental Psychology, 25,* 283–302.

Levine, R. V., Norenzayan, A., & Philbrick, K. (2001). Cross-cultural differences in helping strangers. *Journal of Cross-Cultural Psychology, 32,* 543–560.

McMahon, S. D., & Washburn, J. J. (2003). Violence prevention: An evaluation of program effects with urban African American students. *Journal of Primary Prevention, 24*(1), 43–62.

Penner, L. A., Dovidio, J. F., Piliavin, J. A., & Schroeder, D. A. (2005). Prosocial behavior: multilevel perspectives. *Annual Reviews of Psychology, 56,* 365–392.

Rushton, J. P. (1984). The altruistic personality: Evidence from laboratory, naturalistic, and self-report perspectives. In E. Staub, D. Bar-Tal, J. Karylowski, & J. Reykowski (Eds.), *The Development and Maintenance of Prosocial Behavior: International Perspectives on Positive Development* (pp. 271–290). New York: Plenum.

Solomon, D., Watson, M. S., Delucchi, K. L., Scraps, E., & Battistich, V. (1988). Enhancing children's prosocial behavior in the classroom. *American Educational Research Journal, 25,* 527–554.

Wentzel, K. R., McNamara, B. C., & Caldwell, K. A. (2004). Friendships in middle school: influences on motivation and school adjustment. *Journal of Education Psychology, 96*(2), 195–203.

Zahn-Waxler, C., Robinson, J. L., & Emde, R. N. (1992). The development of empathy in twins. *Developmental Psychology, 28*(6), 1038–1047.

Ariel Knafo
Michelle Weiner
Irit Dubrovsky

PROVIDING EXPLANATIONS

Written explanations in classrooms have the goal of teaching a new understanding to students. According to genre theory, writers build a set of characteristics into explanations that readers use to learn from their reading. Cognitive load theory and educational psychology specify how the set of characteristics in an explanation could be designed to teach new domain understandings to students who do not yet have expertise. A synthesis of these separate areas of scholarship suggests guidelines for providing explanations that effectively teach important content to particular students.

EXPLANATION AS A GENRE

Genre theory specifies the characteristics of different genres and proposes a mechanism for how genres have developed. According to the theory, the identifiable patterns of structure and content that characterize any genre result from the work of communities of people completing recurring tasks and fulfilling shared purposes. A writer with a particular purpose in mind composes a text with content, structure, and style characteristics that a prospective audience also knows and can use to fulfill a purpose, which may or may not match the goal intended by the author. The author who would write an explanation chooses characteristics with the purpose of communicating a new understanding to potential readers. Well-designed explanations present information, examples, analogies, diagrams, pictures, and models as subexplanations. These subexplanations follow a logical order to form a bridge between readers' current understandings and the new understanding. The goal for the reader is to construct a new understanding by attending to the subexplanations and following the text's logical order.

For example, the British physicist and astronomer, Sir James Jeans (1877–1946), wrote a short explanation titled "Why the Sky Is Blue" based on a series of radio talks for an audience with no formal knowledge of science. Jeans began by asking the reader to imagine standing on an ocean pier watching the waves roll in and strike the columns supporting the pier. This first subexplanation contrasted what happened to short and long ocean waves with the purpose of reminding the reader of an experience that the reader could readily imagine. The second subexplanation chronicled the movement of light waves through the atmosphere, a series of events that cannot be directly perceived. The third subexplanation mapped the model of water waves onto the model of light. The explanation ended with an explicit description of light waves moving through the atmosphere and ended with the two short sentences, "Consequently the blue waves of the sunlight enter our eyes from all directions. And that is why the sky looks blue." This explanation presents four subexplanations logically ordered to juxtapose a readily perceivable and imaginable phenomenon that readers may have actually seen with a scientific model to bridge the knowledge of a novice and the understanding of an expert.

Explanations with these features appear in science textbooks in the United States, in science and social studies textbooks internationally, in science and social studies trade books, and in magazine articles and books written for the general public. They also appear in composition books prepared to teach important genres to novice writers (e.g. the anthology that includes Jeans's explanation). The educational community seems to have developed this genre to help learners gain new understanding.

COGNITIVE LOAD THEORY

Whereas rhetoricians have proposed a theory to explain the characteristics and development of genres, Cognitive load theory, developed by cognitive psychologists, explains how learning occurs and suggests constraints on the design of successful explanations. According to

the theory, the mind is composed of a limited working memory through which information enters the mind and a limitless long-term memory, which stores information that has successfully been processed in working memory as organized schemas. The schemas are abstract structures that store large amounts of information. Working memory can hold only a small number of discrete "bits" of information, and thus can be something of a bottleneck. Learning cannot occur if incoming information overloads working memory capacity; if the cognitive load is too great. But a schema is processed as a single bit. Schemas effectively reduce cognitive load.

Cognitive load can be intrinsic, germane, or extraneous. Intrinsic cognitive load depends on the complexity of the information and whether the learner already has at least one relevant schema. If intrinsic load is not too great, the learner may have the capacity in working memory to engage in processes that are germane to learning, including constructing new schemas. Instruction is effective to the extent that it enhances germane cognitive load. In contrast, instruction may actually impede schema acquisition by enhancing extraneous cognitive load, such as requiring readers to search for or organize information within instructional materials rather than presenting information coherently.

Cognitive load theory provides a framework for understanding how well-designed explanations enhance learning. Psychologically, domain understandings, such as understandings about light developed by physicists, are stored in long-term memory as schemas. The purpose of classroom explanation is to reduce intrinsic and extrinsic cognitive load so that the reader has the working memory capacity to construct a new schema. The design of the subexplanations and how they are ordered must meet this goal in order for learning to occur.

REDUCING INTRINSIC COGNITIVE LOAD

Originally the theory specified that instruction could not modify intrinsic cognitive load. However, research by psychologists John Sweller and Richard Catrambone and others using explanations of chemistry models and written mathematics tasks suggests that presenting instruction as a series of simplified tasks can reduce intrinsic cognitive load. Young adolescent boys following instructions to build molecular models completed the tasks more quickly for 10 simple models with only two related elements each than for 2 complex models with several related elements. Other work using written mathematics tasks suggests that presenting instruction as a series of simplified versions of a complex task can reduce intrinsic cognitive load. Intrinsic cognitive load can be reduced by restricting the number of related elements that the learner must consider at a single point in time. Choosing incoming information that matches a known schema also reduces intrinsic cognitive load. The adolescentswere faster for the complex models if the instructions were diagrammatic rather than text, matching the structure of a common graphic organizer used in school. Apparently, they had a schema that they could use to reduce the intrinsic cognitive load for even complex models. "Why the Sky Is Blue" offers an example of this process. It presents a sequence of subexplanations, each of which has a smaller number of related elements than is true for the explanation as a whole. It also begins with the ocean wave example, for which readers may well have a schema. Both of these features could reduce intrinsic load and thereby allow readers to understand the subexplanations about light waves.

REDUCING EXTRANEOUS COGNITIVE LOAD

In an explanation, any example, diagram, information, analogy and so on that does not relate directly to the schema to be acquired would increase extraneous cognitive load. Eliminating unnecessary input would reduce cognitive load and facilitate comprehension. For example, research by psychologist Richard Mayer and others has shown that learners reading a text with only a qualitative description of a model of ocean waves learned more than learners reading a text with quantitative data interspersed within the qualitative description. In the "Why the Sky Is Blue" example, this criterion is met, as each subexplanation relates to the light wave schema.

Texts that require the reader to expend working memory resources figuring out how to process the input also increase extraneous cognitive load. Designing a text to minimize processing unrelated to schema acquisition reduces this load. Research has shown that learners reading a text with captions that point out the relevant features in a diagram or highlighting that signals important relations in a text learn more than learners reading texts without these features. Reducing extraneous cognitive load is particularly important if intrinsic cognitive load is high. Reading diagrams that depicted the relations among chemical elements facilitated how quickly adolescents constructed complex models over reading prose explanations. Prose explanations would not directly represent the relations among elements in the model and might well require learners to create in working memory their own images, adding to the overall cognitive load.

Local coherence also reduces extraneous cognitive load. Readers reading texts with clear pronoun referents, paragraphs organized around a single idea, and paragraph topic sentences learn more than readers reading texts without local coherence, who must dedicate working memory capacity to creating the local coherence themselves. Topic sentences from "Why the Sky Is Blue" such as, "We have been watching a sort of working model of the way in which sunlight struggles through the earth's atmosphere"; (p. 703) and "The waves of the sea represent the sunlight" (p. 704), draw the reader's attention to important relations in the text and also could help readers connect the subexplanations, therefore decreasing extraneous cognitive load.

Eliminating redundancy can decrease cognitive load as well. If an explanation only has content that relates to the expert schema, provides enough support so that the learner does not have to figure out how to process the input, and is coherent, adding additional explanatory support is redundant. Processing this redundancy increases extraneous cognitive load. Learners who read more concise explanations without additional, less central explanatory content learned more than learners who read elaborated versions with additional explanatory content. Redundancy only exists when an explanation has been designed well enough to lead to schema acquisition without the additional content. "Why the Sky Is Blue" is short, and it is likely that this explanation would have redundant content only for readers who already have the light wave schema.

ENHANCING GERMANE COGNITIVE LOAD

Germane cognitive load results from input that can stimulate the higher cognitive processes necessary for schema acquisition. The same features that decrease intrinsic and extrinsic cognitive load can also contribute to germane cognitive load if they enhance schema acquisition. For example, if all subexplanations are related to the schema, readers have the input to compare and contrast the subexplanations, abstract general similarities, and construct a schema that incorporates the separate subexplanations. If the explanation signals the similarities explicitly through captions on diagrams, explicitly noting the relationships between analogs, or worked out mathematical examples, readers' attention will be further directed away from extraneous content and toward the similarities.

Research has suggested that providing subexplanations with different surface features can encourage learners to abstract the general similarities and construct a schema. The subexplanations in "Why the Sky Is Blue" present an analogy, the light wave model, a mapping of the analogy onto the model, and the sequence that results in the perception of the color blue. These multiple subexplanations could be expected to enhance germane cognitive load and learning because they all exemplify the underlying relationships in the schema and are not so numerous as to become redundant. Learners would be thus more likely to focus cognitive effort on the relevant parts of the subexplanations.

The order in which an explanation presents subexplanations can also enhance germane cognitive load. Research on the development of expertise suggests that novices begin with simple schemas, and through practice, construct progressively more complex and useful schemas that ultimately are so well known that they are automatic and bypass working memory altogether. An explanation that begins with a simple, known schema followed by subexplanations that present progressively more complex schemas, could provide the input that a novice would be able to use to construct an expert schema. The subexplanations for "Why the Sky Is Blue" follow this simple to complex order.

EXPLANATIONS TO PROMOTE DOMAIN LEARNING

The challenge in providing explanations to promote domain learning is that typically students either lack obvious schemas upon which to construct new understanding or the schemas that they do have are misleading and interfere with domain learning. First, learners may lack schemas for letter-sound correspondences and grammatical patterns in English. Consequently, they may require so much working memory capacity to process the symbols on the page that no capacity is left for schema construction. Second, students may not have a schema for the generic characteristics of explanation and therefore be unable to take advantage of the subexplanations and logical order in the text. Rather than processing the text as a single unit in working memory, they may instead be overwhelmed by the individual pieces of information in the explanation. Third, students may either have no schemas for the content in the text, or the schemas that they do have may be based on everyday experiences that interfere with their construction of counterintuitive domain-based understandings. Naïve understandings most obviously interfere with new understandings in science, but they can also occur for formalistic vocabulary in mathematics and stereotypes in social studies and English.

LACKING DECODING SCHEMAS

Students who lack letter-sound and sentence grammar schemas struggle with almost all reading tasks. Because their struggles to decode and maintain fluency take up so much working memory capacity, it is of utmost importance that intrinsic load be minimal and other types of extrinsic load be eliminated. Intrinsic load can be minimized by providing explanations that rely heavily on pictures and familiar types of diagrams accompanied by a limited amount of text. Presenting the content in diagrams and pictures will eliminate the need for large

amounts of decoding; accompanying these features with a limited amount of text will give the readers practice in decoding successfully and thereby constructing the decoding schemas that they are lacking. "Why the Sky Is Blue" has no features that would support readers who lack decoding schemas. It was written for adults who presumably have these schemas.

Firmly established content schemas can also minimize intrinsic cognitive load. Students who struggle to decode otherwise can at times read content about which they have well-established schemas quite fluently. The problem, of course, is that the purpose of explanations is to lead to new understanding. The optimal balance between known and new for readers who struggle to decode is an important area for future research.

LACKING TEXT SCHEMAS

Explanations can be designed to build on text schemas that students typically have and compensate for text schemas that they lack. The most firmly established text schema for most students is narrative. Educational psychologists Linda Kucan and Isabel Beck, for example, have demonstrated that fourth graders seem to be able to follow the logic in narratives and fail to follow the logic in expositions. Asked to recall after reading, children up through fifth grade and beyond tend to recall the gist of stories and unconnected bits and pieces of expository texts—what educational psychologist Bonnie Meyer has called the default list. Overall, explanation is exposition. It is structured as a series of subexplanations, not as a plot with characters. It might be expected that many students would lack a schema for explanation. However, subexplanations within explanations can be narrative. "Why the Sky Is Blue" starts with a narrative-like example with the reader as the main character, the waves and the pier as the setting, and what happens to the waves as the plot. It is possible that readers could use a narrative schema to process the remaining subexplanations even though the explanation as a whole is exposition.

Readers lacking a text schema can begin to construct one through signaling. Across a number of studies, research has demonstrated that introductions that synopsize the text structure; paragraph topic sentences and words such as "first," "then," and "however" that signal the structure of the text; and conclusions that summarize direct a reader's attention to the generic patterns in a text. Explanations with these features would prompt readers to process an explanation within working memory as a single unit rather than a succession of unrelated bits of information. "Why the Sky Is Blue" has no signals that would help readers process it as an explanation.

HAVING WELL-ESTABLISHED NAÏVE UNDERSTANDINGS

A challenge in most scholarly domains is to help students use expert models to explain everyday experience. In economics, models of supply and demand can explain fluctuations in price. In history, models of limited resources can explain why one country would invade another. In science, scholars have proposed and demonstrated causal models that can be used to explain and predict a wide range of phenomena. These models reduce phenomena to a set of core theoretical ideas that are often very different from the realm of everyday knowing. Indeed, a challenge in all domains, but particularly science, is to help students use expert models to explain everyday phenomena. Unfortunately, the schemas that students have, rather than guiding their understanding, can actually interfere with their construction of a new schema. Often texts for use in classrooms begin with the target model to be taught and do not address students' naïve models, typically failing to prompt students to construct a new schema. "Why the Sky Is Blue" fits this pattern, in that it does not directly address students' prior ideas about light.

A type of explanation called *refutational text* has proven to be an effective way to help readers adopt scientific models that may even be at odds with their naïve experience-based schemas. Refutational texts begin with a subexplanation that presents the naïve model based on everyday experiences, and follow with subexplanations that are logically ordered to demonstrate the limitations of the naïve model, present the scientific model, and point out how it addresses the limitations. Students who demonstrated naïve understandings before reading were more likely to demonstrate expert understanding after reading refutational texts than other students who conducted experiments, discussed in small groups, or read typical textbook material that did not "refute" their naïve understandings.

IMPLICATIONS FOR TEACHERS

The most important implication for teachers is to choose and compose explanations carefully. The well-designed explanation begins with a schema that the teacher could expect students in the class to have. If the children's schema contrasts with the expert understanding, the explanation is designed as a refutational text. The effective explanation has no extraneous content and is locally coherent. Subexplanations are varied, including diagrams and pictures to highlight the relationships in the schema where appropriate, as well as narrative examples. The explanation is as explicit as possible, drawing connections among each successive subexplanation, highlighting important relationships and including informative dia-gram captions. Subexplanations follow a logical order, from part to whole, from simple to complex, from familiar to unfamiliar. Knowing the students well, the teacher chooses or develops an explanation with the optimal relationship between known and new to maximize germane cognitive load and student learning.

Most explanations will not match this set of characteristics perfectly. For example, "Why the Sky Is Blue" does not include diagrams and pictures, nor does it address possible naïve understandings. For less than perfect explanations, classroom instruction would need to provide what the explanation lacks. Students could draw missing diagrams or write captions for diagrams that are in the text, brainstorm before reading to access relevant schemas, and create graphic representations of the ideas in the explanation to highlight relevant content. Students could process more than one explanation, each of which could make up for lacks in the other. Even though research suggests that reading print may lead to learning more effectively than watching or listening to other types of media, students who lack decoding or relevant content schemas can learn better from a combination of print and other media than either by itself.

SEE ALSO *Cognitive Load Theory.*

BIBLIOGRAPHY

Carlson, R., Chandler, P., & Sweller, J. (2003). Learning and understanding science instructional material. *Journal of Educational Psychology, 95,* 629–640.

Chambliss, M. J., & Calfee, R. C. (1998). *Textbooks for learning.* Malden, MA: Blackwell.

Gerjets, P., Scheiter, K., & Catrambone, R. (2004). Designing instructional examples to reduce intrinsic cognitive load: Molar versus modular presentation of solution procedures. *Instructional Science, 32,* 33–58.

Graves, M. F., Prenn, M. C., Earle, J., Thompson, J., Johnson, V., & Slater, W. H. (1991). Commentary: Improving instructional text: Some lessons learned. *Reading Research Quarterly, 26,* 110–122.

Hynd, C. R., McWhorter, J. Y., Phares, V. L., & Suttles, C. W. (1994). The role of instructional variables in conceptual change in high school physics topics. *Journal of Research in Science Teaching, 31,* 933–946.

Jeans, J. (2007). Why the sky is blue. In N. R. Comley, D. Hamilton, C. H. Klaus, R. Scholes, & N. Sommers (Eds.), *Fields of reading: Motives for writing* (pp. 703–704), New York: Bedford/St. Martin's.

Kucan, L., & Beck, I. L. (1996). Four fourth graders thinking aloud: An investigation of genre effects. *Journal of Literacy Research, 28,* 259–287.

Mayer, R. E., & Jackson, J. (2005). The case for coherence in scientific explanations: Quantitative details can hurt qualitative understanding. *Journal of Experimental Psychology, 11,* 13–18.

Mayer, R. E., Steinhoff, K., Bower, G., Mars, R. (1995). A generative theory of textbook design: Using annotated illustrations to foster meaningful learning of science text. *Educational Technology Research and Development, 43,* 31–43.

Meyer, B. J. F. (1985). Prose analysis: Purposes, procedures, and problems: Parts 1 and 2. In B. K. Britton & J. Black (Eds.), *Understanding expository text* (pp. 11–64, 269–304). Hillsdale, NJ: Erlbaum.

Swales, J. M. (1990). *Genre analysis: English in academic and research settings.* Cambridge, England: Cambridge University Press.

Sweller, J., Van Merrienboer, J. J. G., & Paas, F. (1998). Cognitive architecture and instructional design. *Educational Psychology Review, 10,* 251–296.

Van Merrienboer, J. J. G., & Sweller, J. (2005). Cognitive load theory and complex learning: Recent developments and future directions. *Educational Psychology Review, 17,* 147–177.

Marilyn J. Chambliss

PUNISHMENT

SEE *Classroom Management: Punishment.*

Q

QUALITATIVE RESEARCH

A doctoral student collecting data for her dissertation visits a third grade classroom where two children labeled autistic are regular members. She goes there several days per week staying approximately four hours each time. She tries to remain as unobtrusive as possible observing the natural class environment and activities as they occur. When she leaves each day she goes to her home computer and writes detailed notes of everything she has seen and heard. In addition, she keeps a diary of her personal reactions and evolving thoughts. After she has been there six weeks, she begins conducting recorded interviews with the teacher and other school staff. She even interviews some of the parents of children in the classroom. Rather than using a questionnaire she asks general questions, leaving room for the respondents to raise issues and to freely express themselves. In conjunction with this interview information she gathers various official documents, student evaluations, and other information related to the class.

This researcher is interested in social relationships and learning in the room especially the experiences of the children labeled disabled. She wants to understand the classroom both from the teacher's point of view and that of other people involved. Although these are her general interests she did not state specific hypotheses or questions before she started. When she finishes the data collection she reads, rereads, and codes her descriptive data. She relies on one of the computer software programs available to help organize and analyze her qualitative date. Then she writes a dissertation about what she has learned.

DEFINITION OF QUALITATIVE RESEARCH

The researcher is engaging in qualitative research in the classroom. Her comprehensive data collection approach is not the only one qualitative researchers use to study classrooms. Some rely solely on in-depth interviews, others limit their data collection to intense observation, others on first person document analysis. Other techniques exist as well but what those who practice qualitative research in education have in common are the following:

1. Their data is descriptive (e.g. field notes, interview transcripts).

2. Their analysis is inductive (the questions and focus are not predetermined but evolve as the data are collected).

3. Their data are typically collected in natural settings, in classrooms, and in other places teachers and students spend their time. They try to conduct interviews on location and in a conversational style.

4. Their data are not reduced to numbers and they do not employ advanced statistical procedures. During data analysis some qualitative researchers use frequency counts and other simple quantitative procedures, but, for the most part, their reports are descriptive and conceptual.

5. Their goal is to understand basic social processes (e.g. how children play and learn in a group) and in developing insights in the form of sensitizing concepts. In addition they try to grasp the view of the world from the point of view of the participants (the

teachers, students and others related to the classroom). Their concern is not with prediction and the relationship between discrete variables.

IS IT A QUALITATIVE STUDY?

The example of the doctoral student collecting data for her dissertation is an exemplar of qualitative research of classroom learning. Her study contains all of the elements of this kind of research. Not all studies that people refer to as qualitative research incorporate all of these characteristics however. For example, some researchers might start with stated questions, others may emphasize interviews with teachers thereby straying from observations in the classroom. Whether a particular study is called qualitative is a judgment regarding the degree it contains the above elements rather than whether it meets all the criteria. As discussed below, researchers have different ideas about where to draw the line. Thus some researchers call what they do qualitative research, whereas others would not.

Terms previously used and currently associated with this form of research include: fieldwork, naturalistic, ethnographic, symbolic interaction, inner perspective, Chicago School, phenomenological, case study, interpretive, ethnomethodological, ecological and descriptive. These terms are not synonymous with qualitative research. Rather qualitative research is an umbrella for them all. The exact definition of each varies within particular research traditions and from user to user and from time to time. But each refers to approaches with many of the elements that are part of qualitative research as defined above.

EARLY HISTORY

Researchers employing the general approach described above have existed since the systematic inquiry began. Academic anthropologists and sociologists have used it since the late 1890s. Typically the former conducted studies in cultures other than their own, in so-called less developed or unindustrialized societies. Sociologists did similar work in Western countries. Although the approach was widely employed, the term *qualitative research* was not coined until the late 1960s. In 1967 scholars Barney Glaser and Anslem Strauss first used the phrase in the title of a book, *The Discovery of Grounded Theory: Strategies for Qualitative Research*. William Filstead followed in 1970 with his edited collection, *Qualitative Methodology*. In the late 1960s and early 70s some researchers, including those in education, began a dialogue about the approach outside the academic boundaries of anthropology and sociology.

HISTORY OF QUALITATIVE RESEARCH IN EDUCATION

Two of the earliest researchers to apply qualitative approaches to education in the United States were Margaret Mead and Willard Waller. In the 1940s Mead, an anthropologist, used her fieldwork in less technically developed societies to reflect on the rapidly changing education system in the United States. She examined how what she called little red schoolhouses, city schools, and academies required particular kinds of interaction between teacher and student. She advocated that teachers use first-hand observation to study changes in schools and pupils as a way for them to become better teachers.

When Willard Waller published his work in the 1930s sociology was dominated by quantitative approaches. His book *Sociology of Teaching* (1932) relied on various kinds of descriptive data to analyze the social world of teachers and their students. He saw schools as people tied together in a complex maze of social interconnections. His book was designed to help teachers develop insight into the social nature of school life as a way of facilitating learning in the classroom.

In 1951 Howard Becker, a sociologist who would become very influential in the development of qualitative approaches to research, wrote his dissertation on the careers of Chicago school teacher and social-class variation in teacher-pupil relations. He used qualitative interviews to collect his data. Becker went on to launch a series of qualitative research studies on various aspects of education and encouraged a number of graduate students to follow his lead.

COMING OF AGE

Few important qualitative studies in education appeared prior to the 1960s. Quantitative methods continued to dominate research about schools and classrooms. Change began in the sixties as qualitative research began finding a small but enthusiastic following. During this decade the nation began focusing on educational problems, especially de facto segregation and the underachievement of minority students in the classroom. Civil rights leaders and other concerned citizens demanded that people take into account what teaching and learning was actually like in the classroom. Popular journalistic accounts of school life and autobiographical writings by teachers which documented the lack of learning in ghetto schools grabbed the attention of the public. In 1968 Jonathan Kozol's *Death at an Early Age: The Destruction of the Hearts and Minds of Negro Children in the Boston Public Schools*, his poignant account of his first year of teaching in a ghetto school in Boston, won a National Book Award. People wanted to know more about what was actually going on in schools.

Educational researchers began practicing qualitative strategies themselves in the 1960s rather than depending upon sociologists and anthropologists. Federal agencies began to see the promise in this research approach and started to fund qualitative research. A number of these studies addressed inequality in schools. In 1963 Project True at Hunter College in New York City relied on interviews to examine the experiences of new teachers in urban schools and school integration (Eddy, 1967; Fuchs, 1969). Other researchers recognized that education had failed poor children and that this chronic problem needed to be studied in new ways. Eleanor Leacock focused her influential inquiry on the effect of school authorities on student behavior and learning. Jules Henry studied racism in elementary schools in St. Louis. It was through this project that Ray Rist, an important practitioner of qualitative research, started his career. His book, *Urban School: Factory for Failure,* a systematic observational study of learning in one classroom, was widely read by policymakers and researchers alike.

EMERGENCE OF THE FIELD OF QUALITATIVE RESEARCH

The 1960s were both the launching period of qualitative studies and the time that qualitative research emerged as a field. Prior to the 1960s courses in qualitative research were uncommon. Instruction in the method was mainly in anthropology and sociology through apprenticeships with professors engaged in research projects. A well-developed literature on the theories underlying the method and how to do it had not developed. In the late 1960s and early 1970s such a literature began to emerge and courses began to be offered. In 1966 Severyn Bruyn published *The Human Perspective in Sociology,* a comprehensive theoretical methodological treatise on the qualitative tradition. His book was followed by Glaser and Strauss's *Discovery of Grounded Theory: Strategies for Qualitative Research,* which for the first time presented the logic behind qualitative analysis. In 1971 Rosalie Wax published one of the first qualitative methods books, *Doing Fieldwork: Warning and Advice.* The literature grew. The early 1970s also saw courses in the approach being offered for the first time. Additionally, a literature began appearing in education and in other professional schools that addressed the research dilemmas inherent in classrooms and in other places where human service professionals practiced their trade.

The 1970s and 1980s saw qualitative research flower in education. Not only did well established educational research journals start regularly publishing articles that employed qualitative research, but also new journals favoring the approach first appeared. Book publishers welcomed titles on qualitative research and special sessions at meetings of professional educational researchers were devoted to the subject. Organizations emphasizing the qualitative approach arose and conferences devoted

to the approach became regular features of educational researchers' calendars.

CONFLICT AND DEBATE

Not all educational researchers embraced qualitative research during the 1970s and 1980s, however. Some professors and other researchers who were trained in quantitative approaches applied their method's criteria for good research to the encroaching approach and found it wanting. They resisted the movement, opposed its widespread use, and were skeptical about its contribution. The 1970s and 1980s became a time—at least at some universities and within some professional groups—of debate and conflict. Although a number of researchers trained in the quantitative tradition began integrating the qualitative approach into their work, others regarded the different methods as competing and in some universities became identified as being in one camp or another—qualitative verses quantitative. By the end of the 1980s, doctoral students trained with broader ideas about research began entering the field of educational research and staunch detractors of the qualitative approach began to mellow. By this time there was an armistice of sorts with some researchers preferring one approach over the other and others attempting to integrate the two. Still others switched back and forth, choosing to adjust their approaches to the problems at hand.

ADDITIONAL ISSUES AND DEBATES

Although by the late 1980s and early 1990s the qualitative/quantitative debate had subsided, the qualitative researcher faced other issues and changes that continued being reformulated each decade. Some researchers trained in quantitative approaches who became practitioners of qualitative research as well as qualitative researchers responding to critics who wanted more structure in their research developed more rigid research designs. Authors such as Miles and Huberman advocated formal data collection protocols and standardized data analysis procedures in their work. They championed the development and use of computer software programs to do more thorough and systematic data analysis. Not all qualitative researchers were comfortable with these efforts and charged that such formalization of the method robbed it of its strengths, the discovery of new ways of thinking.

While some qualitative researchers moved toward more structure and accountability another group of scholars went in the opposite direction. People traditionally associated with the humanities (i.e., historical, literary, and philosophical scholars) began to embrace the label of qualitative research. A number of influential books such as James Clifford and George Marcus's *Writing Culture: The Poetics and Politics of Ethnography* and

J. Van Maaen's *Tales of the Field: On Writing Ethnography*, discussed the interpretive nature of qualitative research and how its writing was a product of the author's predispositions and characteristics. Rather than trying to control the author's predilections, a new brand of scholars embraced their own point of view and abandoned the goal of objectivity. They tended to de-emphasize rigorous data collection and concerned themselves less with the empirical world than did more traditional qualitative researchers. In addition to welcoming the humanities into the realm of qualitative research, some qualitative researchers embraced feminist, post-structural, conflict, and critical theory for the underpinnings of their work. Some more traditional qualitative researchers joined their ranks. This group of researchers became much more theory driven than traditional qualitative researchers had been. They also became less data based.

Thus starting in the early 1990s and continuing into the 21st century, qualitative research was pulled in many directions, some of them antagonistic. These movements led some to question whether the term qualitative research had expanded so much that the phrase had lost its meaning. While some cheered the expansion of the field, others thought that qualitative research should return to the basics, to just the elements included in the definition provided above in this entry.

STRENGTHS AND WEAKNESSES

Although general acceptance of qualitative research as defined here exists, some in the field of education continued to express concerns about its use. Qualitative researchers and skeptics would agree that one drawback of the approach is the time it takes to do a good study. Qualitative research is labor intensive; it takes hundreds of hours in the field to collect the data, and data analysis is complex and vexing.

More serious concerns among critics involve the topics of researcher bias and the generalizability of qualitative findings. Qualitative researchers use less standardized instruments and codified procedures than do quantitative researchers. The former approach resembles a craft in which the outcomes are dependent on the skills of the researcher to establish rapport, collect, and then analyze descriptive data. Researchers vary considerably in their talent, interests, points of view, and political disposition. In addition, few external checks on the researcher's data collection and analysis procedures exist. The descriptive data do not readily lend themselves to outside review. Because the data are filtered through the human instrument critics argue that the approach is wrought with observer effect and so its integrity is undermined.

Since most qualitative research involves small samples or studies of one particular classroom or school, critics question whether what is found can be generalized. They point out, for example, that third grade classes vary so much from place to place and time to time, what is found in a case study of one class tells people little about other classrooms. They point to the danger of thinking that because a person knows one third grade well that person understands third grade classes in general.

Sufficient room is not present here to detail how advocates of qualitative research respond to questions of researcher bias and generalizability. Qualitative researchers acknowledge the unstructured nature of the inquiry and the influence the researcher might have on the outcome. In addressing bias, some point to the careful procedures they have built into the various stages of their research projects. As already indicated, some qualitative researchers, to the consternation of others, have attempted to become even more systematic and formal in their approach, thereby abandoning the evolving design that is characteristic of traditional qualitative studies. Others say the bias that critics are concerned with is overstated. After all, they say, just because other forms of research use instruments and more formal procedures does not mean that the researcher's point of view is not built into the researcher's studies. Further, they point out, in most qualitative studies the researcher carefully states his or her perspective and the concerns that drove the project, a practice that quantitative researchers do not follow.

How do qualitative researchers address the criticism that their findings are idiosyncratic and cannot be generalized? They take the position that critics do not understand the basic premise and logic of the approach. Rather than carrying out rigorous sampling, testing hypotheses, and coming up with a precise list of facts and findings that can be applied across settings and populations, qualitative researchers concern themselves with the dynamics of basic social processes and are interested in developing sensitizing concepts and grounded theory. They believe that behavior is not random and idiosyncratic. If they discover a process or develop a concept in one setting it has to exist in other places. They do not assume that it occurs in all places, for example, called third grade classrooms. Part of the analysis is speculating about other settings in which their findings might apply. Further, they say that if people are interested in generalizability as traditionally defined, it can be checked by additional studies.

Qualitative research comes in many forms and is widely practiced as a part of educational research. Once new and controversial, it has become a regular part of the curriculum for those studying for advanced degrees in education. While it will never replace quantitative approaches, it contributes a different kind of information and understanding to what researchers know about learning in the classroom.

SEE ALSO *Research Methods: An Overview.*

BIBLIOGRAPHY

Becker, H. S. (1952). Social-class variations in teacher-pupil relationships, *Journal of Educational Sociology, 25,* 251–265.

Bogdan, R. C., & Biklen, S. K. (2007). *Qualitative research for education: An introduction to theories and methods* (5th ed.). Boston: Allyn & Bacon.

Bruyn, S. (1966). *The human perspective in sociology.* Englewood Cliffs, NJ: Prentice-Hall.

Clifford, J., & Marcus, G.E. (Eds.). (1986). *Writing culture: The poetics and politics of ethnography.* Berkley: University of California Press.

Eddy, E. (1967). *Walk the white line.* Garden City, NY: Doubleday.

Filstead, W. (Ed.). (1970). *Qualitative methodology.* Chicago: Markham.

Fuchs, E. (1969). *Teachers talk.* Garden City, NY: Doubleday.

Glaser, B., & Strauss, A. (1967). *The discovery of grounded theory: strategies for qualitative research.* Chicago: Aldine.

Henry, J. (1963). *Culture against man.* New York: Random House.

Kozol, J. (1967). *Death at an early age: The destruction of the hearts and minds of Negro children in the Boston Public Schools.* New York: Bantam.

Leacock, E. (1969). *Teaching and learning in city schools.* New York: Basic Books.

Mead, M. (1942). An anthropologist looks at looks at the teacher's role. *Educational Method, 21,* 219–223.

Miles, M. B., & Huberman, A. M. (1994). *Qualitative data analysis: An expanded source book* (2nd ed.). Thousand Oaks, CA: Sage.

Rist, R. (1973). *Urban school: Factory for failure.* Cambridge, MA: MIT Press.

Van Maanen, J. (1988). *Tales of the field: On writing ethnography.* Chicago: University of Chicago Press.

Waller, W. (1932). *Sociology of teaching.* New York: Wiley.

Wax, R. (1971). *Doing fieldwork: Warning and advice.* Chicago: University of Chicago.

Robert Bogdan

QUASIEXPERIMENTAL RESEARCH

There are two general categories of experimental research—true experimental design and quasiexperimental design (Gribbons & Herman, 1997). The word "quasi" in Latin means *as if* or *almost.* Considering this, quasiexperimental research could be described as a best attempt at an experiment when it is impossible, or not reasonable, to meet all the criteria of a true experiment. This type of research is typically identified as being void of randomization of either subjects or treatment and/or the lack of comparison groups. Yet, there is still an attempt to isolate the treatment. As an overarching goal, the body of quasiexperimental research attempts to answer questions such as: "Does a treatment or intervention have an impact?" and "What is the relationship between program practices and outcomes?" (Dimsdale and Kutner, 2004).

True experiments are ideal when it comes to being able to isolate any type of statistical relationship, with the potential to infer causality. Even so, prior to designing an experiment, it is necessary to consider a few key elements. Can the individuals and/or other elements in your study be precisely classified? Can you select random individuals or other elements in your study? Is the process of randomization fair to all involved in the study? Should the answer be "no" to any of these questions, quasiexperimental designs then surface. Educational research, and the techniques or interventions that are introduced, seem relatively harmless to the general eye; thus, many researchers continue to emphasize true experiments (Kidder, 1981). It is never so simple; however, as effectiveness, efficiency, and feasibility also need to be considered. There are other ethical considerations as well. If there is any risk of harm from delivering or withholding services to someone in the sample, then an experimental design cannot be employed. For these reasons, in fields such as education, psychology, and criminal justice, quasiexperimental research is often utilized. As a whole, the research community tends to support the use of and recognize the utility of quasiexperimental research (Campbell & Stanley, 1963; Cook & Campbell, 1979).

A COMPARISON TO EXPERIMENTAL RESEARCH

Quasiexperimental research and experimental research both attempt to create a design scheme in which the concluded results can be thought of as the best, most logical solution to the question at hand. Quasiexperimental designs tend to do this through a comparison of existing groups. Experimental designs accomplish the same goal through random assignment of individuals to interventions or treatments (Michigan State University, College of Education, 2004).

Experiments, especially large-scale, are designed to control for the influences of extraneous variables. The goal is to allow for a maximum level of certainty regarding the impact of an intervention. Specifically, experimental designs must have random selection of subject, use of control groups, random assignments of individuals to the control and experimental groups, and random assignment of groups to the intervention (Henrichsen, Smith & Baker, 1997). The strongest comparisons are made through the ability to conduct a true experiment (Gribbons & Herman, 1997). To this extent, quasiexperimental designs attempt to rule out unrelated explanations so that the outcome can be attributed only to the experimental intervention. The task is not as straightforward, but through efforts such as matching subjects and statistical analysis, the true experiment is mimicked (Morgan, Gliner & Harmon, 2000; SERVE Center, 2007). Specifically, *trend* replaces the word *cause* in quasiexperimental research. The goal of quasiexperimental research is to discover the one trend that is a result of the treatment or intervention. Clearly, this is not a simple or direct task and error exists in that process.

The data collection and analyses are a point of overlap and a point of distinction between experimental and quasiexperimental research. While standardized assessments are utilized in both approaches, they are the singular mechanism to the experimental design. In contrast, quasiexperimental design also utilizes such means as surveys, interviews, and observations. The statistical techniques also have the same appearance, clean and simple. In contrast, quasiexperimental research uses an array of analysis techniques including the t-test, but also extending to correlation, regression, and factor analysis (Dimsdale & Kutner, 2004).

Quasiexperimental designs are typically employed if random assignment is not practical, or even impossible. Without randomization, typical issues surface. Even with a comparison group, the concern surfaces of how alike the groups are from the onset. Also, with the loss of control in quasiexperimental designs, it is of concern whether both groups are in some manner exposed to the intervention, intentionally or not. Nonetheless, the biggest weakness of quasiexperimental designs may also indicate the greatest strength—a broader scope of the research design. The controlled, randomized design of true experiments typically lends itself to a very limited, narrow view of the topic of interest (Gribbons & Herman, 1997). In all cases, when human subjects are involved, there is never a 100% guarantee that the results of an intervention can be completely attributed to the intervention itself, with no regard for the opinions and practice of the individuals involved. Simply stated, true experiments work well in laboratory settings. Quasiexperiments work well in natural settings (Schoenfeld, 2006).

EXAMPLES OF QUASIEXPERIMENTAL RESEARCH

Quasiexperimental research is designed with the intent to be as much like a true experiment as possible. The two traditional platforms are: (1) matching studies, in which participants are compared with individuals that are comparable on variables of interest that do not receive the intervention; and (2) interrupted time series, in which observations made prior to an intervention are compared

again and additional observations are made after the intervention has happened. These types of studies present themselves in various formats (Prater, 1983).

The general goal of quasiexperimental research is to investigate cause and effect relationships. This approach to research allows for greater understanding of program features and practices. Because there is a loss of control in the quasiexperimental design, it is necessary for the researcher to decide what and when to measure (Dawson, 1997). What follows is a sample outline of designs. An *X* represents the group being exposed to a treatment or intervention. An *O* represents an observation or measurement. Temporal order of events is designated from left to right. The dotted line in each design is an indication of the lack of random assignment of subjects to the groups (Prater, 1983).

One-group posttest design

$$X \qquad O$$

The One-Group Posttest Design is a one-shot case study. It simply has a treatment, *X*, and posttest, *O* with no control group. This design is best implemented as an evaluation model. It should be used only when there is no available comparison group or pretest data.

Static-group comparison design

$$X \qquad O$$
$$------$$
$$O$$

In the Static-Group Comparison Design, a pre-test, *X*, is given to only one group, while the post-test, *O*, is given to both the control and experimental group. This design is comparable to the One-Group Posttest Design, with the addition of a control group for comparison purposes. No randomization is present, instead two groups are arbitrarily selected, and one is labeled as experimental and the other control.

Nonequivalent control-group design

$$O_1 \qquad X \qquad O_2$$
$$------$$
$$O_2 \qquad \qquad O_2$$

The most common quasiexperimental design is the Nonequivalent Control-Group Design, illustrated above. The design includes at least an experimental and control group. It mirrors the Pretest-Posttest control group experimental design, but instead of randomization, naturally occurring comparison groups are selected to be as alike as possible (Gribbons & Herman, 1997).

Time series design

$$O_1 \quad O_2 \quad O_3 \quad X \quad O_4 \quad O_5 \quad O_6$$

Pre-test   Post-test

With a Time Series Design, observations are taken (in this case three) to establish a baseline; a treatment then occurs, *X*, followed by additional observations being made. From this, an estimate of the impact the treatment made is computed (Gribbons & Herman, 1997; Morgan, Gliner & Harmon, 2000). The design can be employed to establish a baseline measure, describe a change over time or to keep track of trends. Data are almost always presented in a graph.

Multiple time series design

$$O_1 \quad O_2 \quad O_3 \quad X \quad O_4 \quad O_5 \quad O_6$$
$$- - - - - - - - - - - - -$$
$$O_1 \quad O_2 \quad O_3 \quad \quad O_4 \quad O_5 \quad O_6$$

Pre-test   Post-test

The Multiple Time Series Design is simply an extension of the Time Series Design with the addition of a comparison group. It attempts to model what would have happened to the experimental group if the treatment or intervention had not taken place. The addition of the control adds credibility, even without randomization.

Equivalent materials design

$$M_a X_1 O \quad M_b X_0 O \quad M_c X_1 O \quad M_d X_0 O$$

In the Equivalent Materials Design, different, equivalent materials are represented throughout with $M_{a,b,c,d}$. The treatments and repeats of treatments, $X_{0,1}$, are applied and then observed. In addition to the aforementioned designs, there are elaborate extensions, such as the Latin-square Design (Fortune & Hutson, 1984).

ROLE OF QUASIEXPERIMENTAL RESEARCH IN EDUCATIONAL RESEARCH

It was not until the late 1900s that educational reform gave credence to research. Prior to that, untested interventions and innovations were commonplace. The U.S. government has come to demand a research base, as demonstrated by the Comprehensive School Reform Demonstration legislation of 1997 and the No Child Left Behind Act. In both cases, the emphasis is in the application of experimental or quasiexperimental research (Slavin, 2003).

Campbell and Stanley (1963) speak to traditional experimental and quasiexperimental methods. Cook and Campbell (1979) continued to explore these methods, building upon early investigations of validity. In 1993 Parker reviewed and synthesized both the works and further added to the mound of threats to validity. At the turn of the century, various authors were continuing to write about the issue of what constitutes an experimental design and the issues associated with a less than perfect experiment. The presence of true experimental designs in educational research has not been prevalent over time largely due to methodological constraints and on some accounts, more logistical issues like money and time. It is frequently not practical to randomly assign individuals to control and experimental groups, like in a clinical setting where groups are already intact (Dimsdale & Kutner, 2004; Heppner, Kivlighan & Wampold, 1992). Quasiexperimental designs offer a plausible solution to these dilemmas.

Other issues that typically surface in educational research include, but are not limited to, confounding and the assumption of independence. Independence states that the measure for an individual is independent of the measures of other individuals. Randomization of subjects is the only way to insure this. Confounding is another concern. When a variable in a research design is not controlled, but should be, it is identified as a confounding factor. Given that confounding cannot be dealt with in terms of statistical notions alone, quasiexperimental designs, and for the most part educational research as a whole, always have this as a limitation (Pearl, 2000).

If evidence-based school reform continues to be the golden standard, quasiexperimental research will play an instrumental role. Quasiexperimental research, and the scientifically based results that go along with it, can provide the educational community with a variety of models that have been shown to be effective. Reading First and other similar initiatives have created evidence-based reform that can be sustained. Because of this, it is plausible that the rigor associated with quasiexperimental designs will become commonplace (Slavin, 2003; U.S. Department of Education, 1998; U.S. Department of Education, 2002).

ANALYTIC APPLICATIONS APPLIED IN QUASIEXPERIMENTAL RESEARCH

Valentin (1997) made a claim that with an understanding of eight statistical procedures, it is reasonable to have an understanding of 90% of quantitative research. Experimental designs lend themselves to straightforward, often simpler, statistical analysis than quasiexperimenatal designs. Advanced statistical procedures are typically necessary in quasiexperimental research, largely due to the lack of randomization (Dimsdale & Kutner, 2004).

Two specific examples include multiple regression analysis and factor analysis. *Multiple regression analysis* is a statistical application that is utilized in studies in which impact is being measured. Using statistical methods, a control group is simulated, and multiple adjustments can be made for outside factors. Thus, the control that is in the design of an experiment is inserted through analytical techniques (SERVE Center, 2007). *Factor analysis* is a useful technique when a study has a large number of variables. This statistical application allows for a reduction in the number of variables while detecting possible relationships between those variables of interest (Dimsdale & Kutner, 2004). It is commonly applied when data is collected through a survey, especially when the survey contains a large number of items. *Analysis of covariance* (ANCOVA) is yet another analytical technique employed to increase the strength of the quasiexperimental design. By making compensating adjustments, ANCOVA reduces the effects of the initial differences between groups. This again is an attempt to respond to the lack of randomization.

STRENGTHS AND WEAKNESS OF QUASIEXPERIMENTAL RESEARCH

When considering what type of design to employ in a study, it is important to consider both validity and practicality. In general, quasiexperimental research is more feasible, given the typical time and logistical constraints. At the surface level, an easily identifiable weakness of employing quasiexperimental research, in contrast to a true experiment, is the lack of random assignment. Without random assignment, internal validity is reduced, and causal claims become quite difficult to make (Prater, 1983).

On the other side, quasiexperimental designs tend to present the situation under investigation in real-world conditions, increasing the external validity. Typically, quasiexperimental designs are pre-existing constructions. Because of this, fewer variables are able to be controlled; yet another factor limiting the ability to make causal claims (Henrichsen, Smith & Baker, 1997).

With the implementation of the No Child Left Behind statute, educational research put forth an agenda of scientifically based research. Shavelson and Towne (2002) outline criteria necessary for a scientific study, which include: direct, empirical investigation of an important question; consideration for the context in which the study took place; alignment with a conceptual framework; careful and thorough reasoning; and disclosure of results. Quasiexperimental research makes the

mark by meeting each criterion listed. While the controlled, experimental design is the ideal, at least statistically, when an experiment is not possible or practical, the best approach is to identify and eliminate threats to validity through the implementation of a quasiexperimental approach (Borg & Gall, 1989).

SEE ALSO *Research Methods: An Overview.*

BIBLIOGRAPHY

Borg, W. R., & Gall, M. D. (1989). *Educational research: An introduction.* New York: Longman.

Campbell, D., & J. Stanley. (1963). *Experimental and quasi-experimental Designs.* Chicago: Rand McNally.

Cook, T., & D. Campbell. (1979). *Quasi-experimental design.* Chicago: Rand McNally.

Dawson, T. E. (1997, January 23–25). *A primer on experimental and quasi-experimental design.* Paper presented at the Annual Meeting of the Southwest Educational Research Association, Austin, TX.

Dimsdale, T., & Kutner, M. (2004, December 9–11). *Becoming an educated consumer of research: A quick look at the basics of research methodologies and design.* Meeting of the Minds Practitioner-Researcher Symposium. American Institutes for Research, Sacramento, CA.

Fortune, J. C., & Hutson, B. A. (1984). Selecting models for measuring change when true experimental conditions do not exist. *Journal of Educational Research, 77*(4), 197–206.

Gribbons, B., & Herman, J. (1997) True and quasi-experimental designs. Washington, DC: ERIC Clearinghouse on Assessment and Evaluation.

Henrichsen, L., Smith, M. T. & Baker, D. S. (1997). Taming the Research Beast, Brigham Young University. Retrieved April 16, 2008, from http://linguistics.byu.edu/faculty/henrichsenl/researchmethods/RM_0_02.html.

Kidder, L. H. (1981). *Research methods in social relations.* Fort Worth, TX: Holt, Rinehart & Winston.

Morgan, G. A., Gliner, J. A., & Harmon, R. J. (2000). Quasi-experimental designs. *Journal of the American Academy of Child & Adolescent Psychiatry, 39*(6), 794–796.

Pearl, J. (2000). *Causality: Models, reasoning, and inference.* Cambridge, England: Cambridge University Press.

Prater, J. M. (1983). *An analysis of selected statistical techniques utilized in quasi-experimental designs.* Paper presented at the Annual Meeting of the Mid-South Educational Research Association, November 16–18, Nashville, TN.

Schoenfeld, A. H. (2006). Design Experiments. In Judith L. Green, Gregory Camilli, & Patricia B. Elmer (Eds.), *Handbook of complementary methods in educational research* (pp. 193–205). Mahwah, NJ: Erlbaum.

SERVE Center. (2007). Education Research: What is scientifically based research? University of North Carolina, Greensboro. Retrieved April 16, 2008, from http://www.serve.org/EdResearch/SBR/quasi.php.

Shavelson, R. J., & Towne, L. (2002). *Scientific research in education.* Washington, DC: National Academy Express.

Slavin, R. E. (February, 2003). A reader's guide to scientifically based research. *Educational Leadership*, 12–16.

U.S. Department of Education. (1998). *Guidance on the comprehensive school reform demonstration program.* Washington, DC: Author.

U.S. Department of Education. (2002, June 14). *Draft guidance on the comprehensive school reform program.* Washington, DC: Author.

Valentin, T. (1997). Understanding quantitative research about adult literacy. *Focus on basics, 1*(A), Cambridge, MA: National Center for the Study of Adult Literacy and Learning. Retrieved April 16, 2008, from http://www.ncsall.net/?id=470.

Kelly D. Bradley

QUESTIONING

Questioning consumes a considerable proportion of time in classrooms. It occurs most often within recitations, characterized by the initiate-respond-evaluate (IRE) pattern of discourse, as well as in more open-ended discussions. Interest in questioning as an instructional tool can be traced back to the fourth century BCE as evidenced in the Socratic dialogues recorded by Plato (424/423–348/347 BCE). In the 21st century, teachers use questions to manage student behavior and classroom activities, to promote students' inquiry and thinking, and to assess students' knowledge or understanding. The focus of this entry is predominantly on teachers and students' use of questions as a tool to promote inquiry, thinking, and ultimately learning.

RESEARCH STRANDS AND CURRENTS

The research on questioning is considerable both in volume and topics investigated. Research on questioning has investigated the incidence and types of questions teachers ask (e.g., Guszak, 1967); the sources of teacher questions (e.g., Shake & Allington, 1985); the effect of teacher questions as compared to other instructional methods (e.g., Gall, Ward, Berliner, Cahen, Winne, Elashoff, & Stanton, 1978); the effects of different types of questions (e.g., Wright & Nuthall, 1970); the effects of waiting for students to respond after asking questions (e.g., Rowe, 1986; see also Tobin, 1987); training teachers to use certain types of questions (e.g., Galassi, Gall, Dunnng, & Banks, 1974); teaching students how to answer questions (e.g., Raphael & Wonnacott; 1985); teaching students to generate their own questions (e.g., Commeyras & Sumner, 1998), and the psychology of question asking and answering (e.g., Graesser & Black, 1985). Table 1 lists the major reviews of this research.

Two trends are apparent in the research. One is movement from a focus on questions as isolated events to a focus on questions embedded within larger spatial and temporal contexts, including the contexts created by the ongoing classroom discourse. Up until the early 1980s, researchers classified and counted teacher questions and attempted to relate the frequencies of different types of questions to student achievement. Researchers employed correlational studies that capitalized on existing variation in teacher questioning behavior or experimental studies in which they manipulated teachers' use of questions (see Brophy & Good, 1986). In the late 1980s and 1990s, researchers examined questions as "sites of interaction" (Nystrand, 1997) and their relationship to student learning. These sites of interaction included the question asked, students' responses to the question, the teacher's valuation or follow-up to students' responses, and even the genre of the entire classroom discourse. Researchers also developed questioning routines to help students talk and think together in cooperative or collaborative learning environments. These routines included *Reciprocal Teaching* (Palincsar & Brown, 1984), *Questioning the Author* (Beck, McKeown, Hamilton, & Kucan, 1997), and various methods of structuring discourse to promote learning among peers (King, 1999).

This trend was motivated by research in sociolinguistics and language acquisition that highlighted the distinction between language form and communicative function, showing that the meaning of a question depended on its context of use. This context includes not only the situational context but also the contexts created by speakers in the give and take of discussion. From a sociolinguistic perspective, teacher questions are mutually constructed by teachers and students (Carlsen, 1991). Hence, the cognitive impact of questions depends on their placement within the larger discourse, the backgrounds of the students, relations among teachers and students, and other factors. (Cazden, 2001).

Another trend apparent in the research is movement from a focus on teacher-generated questions to a focus on student-generated questions. This trend is apparent in the research on questioning routines embedded in cooperative or collaborative learning environments mentioned earlier. It can also be seen in research on the K-W-L technique developed by Ogle (1986), a technique that requires students to ask themselves questions to promote comprehension of expository texts ("What do I *K*now about the text?" "What do I *W*ant to learn from the text?" "What did I *L*earn from the text?"). It is also evident in research by Commeyras (1995; Commeyras & Sumner, 1998) on the benefits of giving students responsibility for posing their own questions for discussion in response to literature. Wong (1985) reviewed 27 studies of student question generating and found positive

---

Chronological list of major reviews of questioning research

Year	Review
1970	Gall, M.D.(1970).The use of questions in teaching. *Review of Educational Research 40*, 707-721.
1971	Rosenshine, B. (1971). *Teaching behaviors and student achievement*. Windsor: NFER/Nelson.
1974	Dunkin, M. J., & Biddle, B. J. (1974). *The study of teaching*. NY: Holt, Rinehart and Winston.
1976	Rosenshine, B. (1976). Classroom instruction. In N. L. Gage (Ed.), *The psychology of teaching methods* (The Seventy-Fifth Year book of the National Society for the Study of Education, Part I, pp.335-371). Chicago: University of Chicago Press.
1979	Winne, P. H. (1979). Experiments relating teachers' use of higher cognitive questions to student achievement. *Review of Educational Research, 49*, 13-49.
1981	Redfield, D. L., & Rousseau, E. W. (1981). A meta-analysis of experimental research on teacher questioning behavior. *Review of Educational Research, 51*, 237-245.
1982	Dillon, J. T. (1982). The multi disciplinary study of questioning. *Journal of Educational Psychology 74*(2), 147-165.
1984	Dillon, J. T. (1984). Research on questioning and discussion. *Educational Leadership, 42*, 50-56.
1984	Gall, M. (1984). Synthesis of research on teachers' questioning. *Educational Leadership, 42*, 40-47
1985	Wong, B. Y. (1985). Self-questioning instructional research: A review. *Review of Educational Research, 55*, 227-268.
1986	Brophy, J., & Good, T. L. (1986). Teacher behavior and student achievement. In M. C. Wittrock (Ed.), *Handbook of Research on Teaching* (3rd ed., pp. 328-375). New York: Macmillan.
1986	Wilen, W. W. & Clegg, A. A. (1986). Effective questions and questioning: A research review. *Theory and Research in Social Education,14*, 153-161.
1987	Doenau, S. J. (1987). Soliciting. In M. J. Dunkin (Ed.), *The international encyclopedia of teaching and teacher education* (pp. 407-413). Oxford, England: Pergamon.
1987	Gall, M. D. & Rhody, T. (1987). Review of research on questioning techniques. In W. W. Wilen (Ed.), *Questions, questioning techniques, and effective teaching*. Washington, DC: National Education Association.
1987	Samson, G. E., Strykowski, B., Weinstein, T., & Walberg, H. J. (1987). The effects of teacher questioning levels on student achievement: A quantitative synthesis. *Journal of Educational Research, 80*, 290-295.
1988	Wong, B. (1988). Self-questioning strategy training: From theory to practice. *Australian Journal of Reading, 11,* 246-256.
1991	Carlsen, W. S. (1991). Questioning in classrooms: A sociolinguistic perspective. *Review of Educational Research, 61*, 157-178.
1991	Wilen,W. W.(1991).*Questioning skills for teachers: What research says to the teacher*. Washington, D. C., National Education Association.
1995	Gall, M. D., & Artero-Boname, M. (1995). Questioning. In L. W. Anderson (Ed.), *The international encyclopedia of teaching and teacher education* (pp. 242-248). Oxford, England: Pergamon.
1996	Rosenshine, B., Meister, C., & Chapman, S. (1996). Teaching students to generate questions: A review of the intervention studies. *Review of Educational Research, 66,* 181-221.
2006	Gayle, B. M., Preiss, R. W. , & Allen, M. (2006). How effective are teacher-initiated classroom questions in enhancing student learning? In B. M. Gayle, R. W. Preiss, N. Burrell & M. Allen (Eds.). *Classroom communication and instructional processes: Advances through meta-analysis* (pp. 279-293). Mahwah, NJ: Erlbaum.

Table 1 ILLUSTRATION BY GGS INFORMATION SERVICES. CENGAGE LEARNING, GALE.

---

effects on students' reading comprehension in the majority of studies. Rosenshine, Meister, and Chapman (1996) conducted a meta-analysis of 26 studies of student questioning and also found positive effects on students' comprehension.

QUESTIONS THAT VARY BY COGNITIVE DEMAND

Questions are typically classified by the nature of the cognitive demand they are presumed to make on students. Most classifications define cognitive demand in terms of Bloom's 1956 taxonomy of learning or some variant of it. Bloom defined learning in terms of six levels of increasingly complex requirements: knowledge, comprehension, application, analysis, synthesis, and evaluation. Lower-order questions are presumed to elicit a student's knowledge and comprehension of a topic or text; higher-order questions are presumed to elicit a student's application, analysis, synthesis, or evaluation of a topic or text.

A related framework often used in research in reading and the teaching of reading is Pearson and Johnson's 1978 taxonomy of questions or, more accurately, question-answer relations. This framework classifies questions according to source of information that must be used by the reader to generate a response: *textually explicit*, in which the information required for answering the question is stated explicitly in the text ("reading the lines"); *textually implicit*, in which the information required for answering the question is in the text but has to be inferred by integrating material from different parts of the text ("reading between the lines"); and *scriptally implicit*, in which the information required for answering the question involves the reader's store of prior knowledge ("reading beyond the lines").

Research in the United States as well as in other English-speaking countries has documented a higher incidence of lower-order than higher-order questions in classrooms for much of the 20th century. Stevens' 1912 study was possibly the first systematic study of teacher questioning in the United States. He observed teachers in 100 high-school classrooms in six subject areas and found that at least two-thirds of the questions teachers asked focused on recitation and memory of facts. Studies in the 1970s and 1980s (e.g., Sirotnik, 1983) showed little change in the preponderance of lower-order over higher-order questions (see Klinzing & Klinzing-Eurich, 1988). Data collected by Nystrand in 1997 also suggest little change. Nystrand observed the instructional practices in 58 eighth-grade and 54 ninth-grade language arts and English classes in eight Midwestern communities in the United States. He reported that 64% of questions in the eighth-grade classes involved recitation and reporting of facts whereas only 36% involved high-level thinking (analysis, generalization, speculation). Results in the ninth-grade classes revealed a somewhat different picture with 54% of questions involving recitation and reporting.

Similar trends are evident in observational studies of reading instruction in elementary grades. Guszak's 1967 study examined the kinds of questions 12 teachers asked in selected second-, fourth-, and sixth-grade classrooms in Texas during reading group lessons. He found that 70% of questions were recognition or recall questions that focused on literal comprehension. O'Flahavan, Hartman, and Pearson (1988) conducted a replication and extension of Guszak's study, videotaping teacher-led reading groups and story discussions conducted by 15 teachers in grades 2, 4, and 6 in four schools in Illinois. Results showed a lower incidence of recognition and recall questions (43%). Overall, relative to Guszak's findings, they noted a shift from literal questions to more inferential questions. However, other studies conducted at the time continued to report a preponderance of lower-level, text-based questions in reading lessons (Gambrell, 1983; Shake & Allington, 1985; Weber & Shake, 1988). Observational studies by Taylor and Pearson (Taylor, Pearson, Clark, & Walpole, 1999, 2000; Taylor, Peterson, Pearson, & Rodriguez, 2002; Taylor, Pearson, Peterson, & Rodriguez, 2003, 2005) of reading instruction in grades 1 to 5 in a number of high-poverty schools in the United States have shown similar results. Across all grades, they observed a relatively small amount of higher-level questioning (e.g., only 16% of the teachers in grades 1 to 3 were frequently observed asking higher-level questions).

It is presumed that asking more higher-order questions contributes to greater gains in students' high-level thinking, learning, and achievement. This presumption has received only weak support. Rosenshine (1971, 1976) and Dunkin and Biddle (1974) conducted reviews of studies relating teacher questioning to student learning, many of which were correlational studies, and found that results were inconsistent (in some studies, even lower-order questions were found to be more effective). Winne (1979) reviewed 18 experimental and quasi-experimental studies on levels of teacher questioning and concluded that "whether teachers use predominantly higher cognitive

questions or predominantly fact questions makes little difference in student achievement" (p. 43). Redfield and Rousseau (1981) conducted a meta-analysis of 14 experiments, 13 of which overlapped with those reviewed by Winne, and found that a predominant use of higher cognitive questions had an overall positive effect on student achievement (mean effect size = 0.73). Samson, Strykowski, Weinstein, and Walberg (1987) conducted another meta-analysis of 14 experiments, most of which overlapped with those of the previous reviews, and obtained results more in tune with the earlier findings by Winne and others. Samson and colleagues reported only a small positive effects of higher cognitive questions on student achievement (median effects size = 0.13). Gall and Artero-Boname (1995) attributed the inconsistency in results to a number of factors, not the least of which was that the individual studies failed to take account of the larger instructional context in which questions occurred.

Other studies have attempted to examine the role of questions within the larger instructional context but have still not shown consistent results. Nystrand's 1997 large-scale correlational study showed no relationship between the cognitive level of questions and students' performance. Taylor and Pearson's series of correlational studies of reading instruction in high-poverty schools (Taylor et al., 1999, 2000; Taylor et al., 2002; Taylor et al., 2003, 2005) have shown more consistent relationships between higher-level questioning and students' growth in reading and writing. However, even in these studies, there were inconsistencies. In their 2005 study, they found that high-level questioning made a modest contribution to growth in students' reading fluency but had no relationship to growth in their comprehension or writing.

QUESTIONS THAT VARY BY EPISTEMIC ROLE

Another way of classifying questions is in terms of the epistemic role they afford students. Authenticity and "uptake" are key features in giving students a role in orchestrating their own learning. Questions that give students considerable control over their learning are "authentic questions"—questions that the teacher is genuinely interested in exploring and that evoke a variety of responses from students (in other words, the answer is not prespecified). By contrast, questions that give students little to no control are known-answer questions (sometimes called "test questions") that allow only one possible right answer. Questions that incorporate responses from students, called uptake, offer another way of building on students' contributions and affording them a role in learning. This way of classifying questions is not independent of the level of cognitive demand described earlier. Authentic questions are more likely to elicit application, analysis, synthesis, or evaluations of information; whereas known-answer questions are more likely to elicit recall or literal understanding.

Nystrand (1997) and Applebee, Langer, Nystrand, & Gamoran (2003) documented the incidence of authentic questions and uptake in large numbers of language arts and English classes in middle and high schools in various states in the United States. Nystrand's data showed that, in the eighth-grade classes, only 10% of teacher questions were authentic and only 11% exhibited uptake. In the ninth-grade classes, 27% of teacher questions were authentic and 26% exhibited uptake (Nystrand noted that much of the increase in the incidence of authentic questions in the ninth grade was due to the use of authentic questions about nonacademic topics). Applebee and colleagues' data for grades 7, 8, 10, and 11 showed that 19% of teacher questions were authentic and 31% exhibited uptake.

Nystrand's 1997 correlational analyses showed that, in eighth-grade classes, authentic questions and those exhibiting uptake were significantly related to students' learning. However, in ninth-grade classes, results showed that authentic questions were not related or were even negatively related to learning. Questions exhibiting uptake still showed a significant and positive contribution. Further analyses showed that authentic questions had a positive relation in high-track classes but a negative relation in low-track classes. This was because most of the authentic questions in high-track classes pertained to literature, whereas most in low-track questions were about topics not related to literature. Nystrand concluded that authentic questions do not invariably produce learning but they at least signal to students "that *their* ideas ... are important and can provide opportunities for learning" (p. 90). The 2003 study by Applebee and colleagues largely confirmed the role of authentic questions and uptake, in combination with other discussion-based approaches to developing understanding, as contributors to student learning.

WHAT IS KNOWN AND NOT KNOWN ABOUT QUESTIONING

The considerable volume of research on questioning has shed light on a number of issues regarding questions as a tool for learning. It is known that the incidence of higher-order and authentic questions is low relative to lower-order and known-answer questions. It is known that waiting for students to respond to questions leads to enhanced quality of responses and improved student achievement. It is known that teachers can be taught to ask certain types of question, and that students can be taught how to answer questions based on the relationship to the text. It is also known that promoting student-generated questions has positive effects on learning.

However, there are several enduring issues about which research is unclear. It is not known whether teacher questioning as an instructional tool is any better than other instructional methods. Indeed, there is research and argument that a number of alternatives to questioning (e.g., declarative statements) are associated with longer and more complex responses from students (Dillon, 1985; 1991). It is not known, with any reasonable surety, that asking higher-level questions contributes cognitive benefits for students. Asking higher-level questions seems to have at least a small positive effect on learning but the inconsistency in results on this issue remains an enigma. Asking authentic questions and questions that involve uptake has more reliable associations with student achievement, but only to the extent that they assign meaningful epistemic roles to students—and little is known about the context and classroom culture that shape such conditions. These are questions about questions that are in need of exploring.

SEE ALSO *Bloom's Taxonomy; Discussion Methods.*

BIBLIOGRAPHY

Applebee, A., Langer, J., Nystrand, M., & Gamoran, A. (2003). Discussion-based approaches to developing understanding: Classroom instruction and student performance in middle and high school English. *American Educational Research Journal, 40,* 685–730.

Beck, I. L., McKeown, M. G., Hamilton, R. L., & Kucan, L. (1997). *Questioning the Author: An approach for enhancing student engagement with text.* Newark, NJ: International Reading Association.

Bloom, B. S. (1956). *Taxonomy of educational objectives, Handbook I: The cognitive domain.* NY: Guilford.

Brophy, J., & Good, T. L. (1986). Teacher behavior and student achievement. In M. C. Wittrock (Ed.), *Handbook of research on teaching* (3rd ed., pp. 328–375). New York: Macmillan.

Carlsen, W. S. (1991). Questioning in classrooms: A sociolinguistic perspective. *Review of Educational Research, 61,* 157–178.

Cazden, C. (2001). *Classroom discourse: The language of teaching and learning.* Portsmouth, NH: Heinemann.

Commeyras, M. (1995). What can we learn from students' questions. *Theory into Practice, 34,* 101–106.

Commeyras, M., & G. Sumner (1998). Literature questions children want to discuss: What teachers and students learned in a second-grade classroom. *The Elementary School Journal, 99,* 129–152.

Dillon, J. T. (1982). The multidisciplinary study of questioning. *Journal of Educational Psychology 74*(2), 147–165.

Dillon, J. T. (1984). Research on questioning and discussion. *Educational Leadership, 42,* 50–56.

Dillon, J. T. (1985). Using questions to foil discussion. *Teaching and Teacher Education, 1,* 109–121.

Dillon, J. T. (1991). Questioning the use of questions. *Journal of Educational Psychology, 83,* 163–164.

Doenau, S. J. (1987). Soliciting. In M. J. Dunkin (Ed.), *The international encyclopedia of teaching and teacher education* (pp. 407–413). Oxford, England: Pergamon.

Dunkin, M. J., & Biddle, B. J. (1974). *The study of teaching.* New York: Holt, Rinehart and Winston.

Galassi, J. P., Gall, M. D., Dunnng, B., & Banks, H. (1974). The use of written versus videotape instruction to train teachers in questioning skills. *Journal of Experimental Education, 43,* 16–23.

Gall, M. D. (1970). The use of questions in teaching. *Review of Educational Research 40,* 707–721.

Gall, M. D. (1984). Synthesis of research on teachers' questioning. *Educational Leadership, 42,* 40–47.

Gall, M. D., & Artero-Boname, M. (1995). Questioning. In L. W. Anderson (Ed.), *The international encyclopedia of teaching and teacher education* (pp. 242–248). Oxford, England: Pergamon.

Gall, M. D., & Rhody, T. (1987). Review of research on questioning techniques. In W. W. Wilen (Ed.), *Questions, questioning techniques, and effective teaching.* Washington, DC: National Education Association.

Gall, M. D., Ward, B. A., Berliner, D., Cahen, L. S., Winne, P. H., Elashoff, J. D., & Stanton, G. C. (1978). Effects of questioning techniques and recitation on student learning. *American Educational Research Journal, 15,* 175–199.

Gambrell, L. B. (1983). The occurrence of think-time during reading comprehension instruction. *Journal of Educational Research, 77,* 77–90.

Gayle, B. M., Preiss, R. W., & Allen, M. (2006). How effective are teacher-initiated classroom questions in enhancing student learning? In B. M. Gayle, R. W. Preiss, N. Burrell & M. Allen (Eds.), *Classroom communication and instructional processes: Advances through meta-analysis* (pp. 279–293). Mahwah, NJ: Erlbaum.

Graesser, A. C., & Black, J. B. (1985). *The psychology of questions.* Hillsdale, NJ: Erlbaum.

Graesser, A. C., McMahen, C. L., & Johnson, B. K. (1994). Question asking and answering. In M. A. Gernsbacher (Ed.), *Handbook of psycholinguistics* (pp. 517–538). San Diego, CA: Academic Press.

Guszak, F. J. (1967). Teacher questioning and reading. *The Reading Teacher, 21,* 227–234.

Hare, V. C., & Pulliam, C. P. (1980). Teacher questioning: verification and an extension. *Journal of Reading Behavior, 12,* 69–72.

King, A. (1999). Discourse patterns for mediating peer learning. In A. M. O'Donnell & A. King (Eds.), *Cognitive perspectives on peer learning* (pp. 87–116). Mahwah, NJ: Erlbaum.

Klinzing, H. G., & Klinzing-Eurich, G. (1988). Questions, responses, and reactions. In J. T. Dillon (Ed.), *Questioning and discussion* (pp. 212–239). Norwood, NJ: Ablex.

Nystrand, M. (1997). *Opening Dialogue: Understanding the dynamics of language and learning in the classroom.* New York: Teachers College Press.

O'Flahavan, J. F., Hartman, D. K., & Pearson, P. D. (1988). Teacher questioning and feedback practices: A twenty year retrospective. *National Reading Conference Yearbook, 37,* 183–208.

Ogle, D. (1986). K-W-L: A teaching model that develops active reading of expository text. *The Reading Teacher, 39,* 564–570.

Palincsar, A. S., & Brown, A. L. (1984). Reciprocal teaching of comprehension-fostering and comprehension-monitoring activities. *Cognition & Instruction, 1,* 117–175.

Pearson, P. D., & Johnson, D. D. (1978). *Teaching reading comprehension.* New York: Holt, Rinehart and Winston.

Raphael, T. E., & Au, K. H. (2005) QAR: Enhancing comprehension and test taking across grades and content areas. *The Reading Teacher, 59,* 206–221.

Raphael, T. E., & Wonnacott, C. A. (1985). Heightening fourth-grade students' sensitivity to sources of information for answering comprehension questions. *Reading Research Quarterly, 20,* 282–296.

Redfield, D. L., & E. W. Rousseau (1981). A meta-analysis of experimental research on teacher questioning behavior. *Review of Educational Research, 51,* 237–245.

Rosenshine, B. (1971). *Teaching behaviors and student achievement.* Windsor: NFER/Nelson.

Rosenshine, B. (1976). Classroom instruction. In N. L. Gage (Ed.), *The psychology of teaching methods* (The seventy-fifth yearbook of the National Society for the Study of Education, Part I, pp. 335–371). Chicago: University of Chicago Press.

Rosenshine, B., Meister, C., & Chapman, S. (1996). Teaching students to generate questions: A review of the intervention studies. *Review of Educational Research, 66,* 181–221.

Rowe, M. B. (1986). Wait time: Slowing down may be a way of speeding up. *Journal of Teacher Education, 37,* 43–50.

Samson, G. E., Strykowski, B., Weinstein, T., & Walberg, H. J. (1987). The effects of teacher questioning levels on student achievement: A quantitative synthesis. *Journal of Educational Research, 80,* 290–295.

Shake, M. C., & Allington, R. L. (1985). Where do teachers' questions come from? *The Reading Teacher, 38,* 432–438.

Sirotnik, K. A. (1983). What you see is what you get—consistency, persistency, and mediocrity in classrooms. *Harvard Educational Review, 53,* 16–31.

Slack, J. B. (1998). *Questioning strategies to improve student thinking and comprehension.* Austin, TX, Southwest Educational Development Laboratory.

Stevens, R. (1912). *The question as a measure of efficiency in instruction: A critical study of class-room practice.* New York: Teachers College Press.

Taylor, B. M., Pearson, P. D., Clark, K., & Walpole, S. (1999). Effective schools/accomplished teachers. *The Reading Teacher, 53,* 156–159.

Taylor, B. M., Pearson, P. D., Clark, K., & Walpole, S. (2000). Effective schools and accomplished teachers: Lessons about primary grade reading instruction in low-income schools. *Elementary School Journal, 101,* 121–166.

Taylor, B. M., Pearson, P. D., Peterson D. S., & Rodriguez, M. C. (2003). Reading growth in high-poverty classrooms: The influence of teacher practices that encourage cognitive engagement in literacy learning. *Elementary School Journal, 104,* 3–28.

Taylor, B. M., Pearson, P. D., Peterson D. S., & Rodriguez, M. C. (2005). The CIERA school change framework: An evidence-based approach to professional development and school reading improvement. *Reading Research Quarterly, 40,* 40–69.

Taylor, B. M., Peterson D. S., Pearson, P. D., & Rodriguez, M. C. (2002). Looking inside classrooms: Reflecting on the "how" as well as the "what" in effective reading instruction. *The Reading Teacher, 56,* 270–279.

Tobin, K. G. (1987). The role of wait time in higher cognitive level learning. *Review of Educational Research, 57,* 69–95.

Weber, R-M., & Shake, M. C. (1988). Teachers' rejoinders to students' responses in reading lessons. *Journal of Reading Behavior, 20,* 285–299.

Wilen, W. W. (1991). *Questioning skills for teachers: What research says to the teacher.* Washington, DC: National Education Association.

Wilen, W. W., & Clegg, A. A. (1986). Effective questions and questioning: A research review. *Theory and Research in Social Education, 14,* 153–161.

Winne, P. H. (1979). Experiments relating teachers' use of higher cognitive questions to student achievement. *Review of Educational Research, 49,* 13–49.

Wright, C. J., & Nuthall, G. (1970). Relationships between teacher behaviors and pupil achievement in three experimental elementary science lessons. *American Educational Research Journal, 7,* 477–491.

Wong, B. (1988). Self-questioning strategy training: From theory to practice. *Australian Journal of Reading, 11,* 246–256.

Wong, B. Y. (1985). Self-questioning instructional research: A review. *Review of Educational Research, 55,* 227–268.

Ian A. G. Wilkinson
Eun Hye Son

R

READING, LEARNING AND TEACHING

SEE *Learning and Teaching Reading.*

REASONING

Reasoning has long been a topic of study in logic and philosophy. Logical philosophical approaches are typically concerned with formal and epistemic aspects of reasoning: describing normative models of sound or valid reasoning. However, philosopher David Hume (1711–1776), who produced some of the most influential work on inductive reasoning, recognized the limitations of purely logical accounts of reasoning and noted that psychological processes were vital to a full account of reasoning. Formal or logical approaches to reasoning specify the syntactic form of valid inferences (i.e., those that do not lead to logical contradictions). In contrast, psychological approaches to reasoning explain cognitive performance or how people actually reason. Inferences that are syntactically valid from a logical perspective may be practically uninformative. For example, given the premises (a) Jane is taller than Mary, and (b) Mary is taller than Jill, it would be logically valid to deduce the following inference: Jane is taller than Mary, and Mary is taller than Jill, and Jane is taller than Mary and Jill. However, people are unlikely to make this particular inference from the premises (a) and (b) because it is not parsimonious. Instead, people are far more likely to draw the logically valid and parsimonious conclusion that Jane is taller than Jill.

People's knowledge of the world places pragmatic constraints on how they reason (Brewer & Samarapungavan, 1991; Giere, 1988; Johnson-Laird, 2006; Cheng, 1997). Classical models of reasoning based on logic or the laws of statistics and probability assume an ideal reasoner, unconstrained by cognitive resources. However, Gigerenzer & Goldstein (1996) argue that people display bounded rationality. Their reasoning is constrained by a number of factors such as the limited capacity of working memory and their cognitive goals (they often reason to find an acceptable solution, not necessarily the "best" solution).

DEFINITION OF REASONING

From a psychological perspective, reasoning may be defined as the set of mental processes used to derive inferences or conclusions from premises. Reasoning helps to generate new knowledge and to organize existing knowledge, rendering it more usable for future mental work. Reasoning is therefore central to many forms of thought such as scientific, critical, and creative thinking, argumentation, problem solving, and decision making. Each of these more complex forms of thought can employ inductive, deductive, and abductive reasoning which are described below.

Induction. *Inductive reasoning* is ampliative; it generates new knowledge. Inductive reasoning supports inferences but does not guarantee that the inferences are true. Vickers (2006) characterizes inductive reasoning as "contingent" (i.e., dependent on past experiences and observations). There are many forms of inductive reasoning such as *enumerative induction* and *analogical reasoning*. The best known form is enumerative induction in which the general properties of a class are inferred from a specific set of empirical observations. For example, upon observing that all the birds in the neighborhood have wings and fly, a person infers that all birds have wings and fly. Generalizations of this kind, though commonplace in human reasoning, are clearly fallible (ostriches and penguins are birds and have wings, but do not fly). The preceding example illustrates a general epistemic problem with inductive inferences, which philosophers refer to as the problem of underdetermination.

Analogical reasoning is another form of inductive reasoning that is important in generating new knowledge. Analogical reasoning involves the transfer of knowledge elements and relationships among knowledge elements (e.g., object properties and property relations such as correlated features) from a well-known domain, a "base," to an unknown or partially known domain, a "target" (see Gentner, Holyoak, & Koikinov, 2001). For example, the analogy of a biological cell as a factory allows people to transfer knowledge about how a factory works (it has parts that are specialized to perform certain tasks and that operate together to maintain the functioning of the whole) to understand how a cell works. Analogical reasoning is often employed in instruction to help student understand new concepts by analogical transfer from more familiar concepts (Clement, 1993; Baker & Lawson, 2001, Thagard, 2006). Inductive reasoning presumes principles of regularity or continuity in the world that allow the drawing of inferences about new instances from past experience. Induction plays a role in concept formation and concept learning in every domain of knowledge from natural language to science.

Deduction. Deduction refers to processes of inference which guarantee logically valid conclusions from a set of premises. In other words, assuming that the premises are correct, the conclusions deduced from these premises must also be correct. Transitive inferences of the kind described earlier (Jane is taller than Mary; Mary is taller than Jill; therefore Jane is taller than Jill) are one form of deductive inference. Deduction is a constituent of many varieties of cognitive performance such as text comprehension, scientific and mathematical reasoning, and argumentation. Deduction also plays an important role in categorical reasoning. If, for example, scientists were to discover the remains of a hitherto unknown animal in permafrost, conduct DNA analysis on the remains and conclude that the animal was a mammal. they could then deduce that this previously unknown species had defining mammalian characteristics (e.g., it gave birth to its young and had body hair). One of the main cognitive functions of deductive reasoning is to organize knowledge in ways that allow one to derive parsimonious conclusions from sets of premises.

Abduction. The term *abduction* was coined by Charles Peirce (1839–1914) to refer to a third mode of inference that was distinct from induction and deduction and played a crucial role in scientific reasoning and discovery. Adductive reasoning is a form of reasoning in which individuals start by attending to a particular phenomenon and try to construct a hypothesis that best explains their observation. The process is often called inference to the best explanation (Lipton, 1961; Thagard & Shelley, 1997). Many causal inferences are abductive in nature.

An example of abductive reasoning would be an inquiry into a car crash in which investigators try to reconstruct what happened from forensic evidence (e.g., patterns of damage to a car and its surroundings, data from physiological and toxicological exams conducted on the driver and passengers). From the forensic data, they reconstruct the most plausible or likely explanation for the crash.

SCIENTIFIC REASONING

A classic model of scientific reasoning in philosophy is the hypothetico-deductive model developed by Karl Popper (1902–1994) (1959, 1972). This model posits that hypotheses are deduced from theory and empirically verified by conducting tests that attempt to falsify them. Hypotheses that withstand repeated attempts at falsification may be regarded as better corroborated by the existing evidence than those that do not. However, according to Popper (following Hume), no matter how often a hypothesis is corroborated by empirical evidence, there can be no certainty that it is true.

Post-Popperian scholarship suggests that scientific reasoning is multi-faceted and includes inductive, deductive, and abductive reasoning (Giere, 1988). It is perhaps most useful to think of scientific reasoning as an umbrella term that encompasses all forms of inference that further the generation, evaluation, and revision of scientific knowledge. One important source of scholarship on scientific reasoning comes from the area of science studies. Much of this research draws upon the methods and data of historical research to understand how science is done (Conant, 1957; Giere, 1988; Kuhn, 1962; Thagard, 1990). Such studies analyze archival data, including the laboratory notebooks, correspondence, and the publications of scientists. Dunbar, Giere, Knorr-Cetina, and Sahdra and Thagard have undertaken cognitive analyses of the research practices of working scientists. Naturalistic research has highlighted the role of interpretation in scientific reasoning. Laudan (1990) suggests that scientific judgments are often based on pragmatic criteria such as the compatibility of new ideas with those that are considered to be "well founded."

VARIATIONS IN REASONING ACROSS DISCIPLINES

Naturalistic research suggests that reasoning within different disciplines and sub-disciplines is shaped by the specific conventions of disciplinary practice such as methodological conventions for collecting, analyzing, presenting, and evaluating data (Ericsson, Charness, Hoffman, & Feltovich, 2006; Giere, 1988; Thagard, 2003; Sahdra & Thagard, 2003). Deductive reasoning may play a greater role in disciplines or sub-disciplines with well-developed formal theories; for instance, certain areas of mathematics and physics. Inductive and abductive reasoning may play a greater role in contexts in which different causal patterns can result in similar outcomes (medical diagnosis) or where particular configurations of events are unique and unlikely to be repeated exactly (forensic science). For instance, Wineburg (1998, 1999) argues that history is a discipline with its own unique contextualized patterns of reasoning. It should be noted that most disciplines employ varied forms of reasoning. Although mathematics has historically been characterized as a deductive discipline (Kitcher, 1979; Netz, 2005; Russell, 1903), Kitcher (1985) and Lakatos (1976) suggest that inductive reasoning plays an important role in mathematical thinking.

DEVELOPMENT OF SCIENTIFIC REASONING

Research indicates that some aspects of reasoning develop early, even before the onset of formal schooling or instruction, and may be part of the basic cognitive machinery of humans. There is considerable evidence that people employ forms of inductive and abductive reasoning to construct concepts about the natural world spontaneously, even in the absence of formal instruction in science (Baillargeon, 2004; Carey, 1985; diSessa, 1993; Hatano & Inagaki, 2004; Vosniadou & Brewer, 1992). Young children can use prior knowledge of causal mechanisms to reason causally in new contexts and to make causal inferences. Brown's 1990 research shows that by the age of 3, children are able to use their causal knowledge about physical mechanisms to select tools of the right shape and material to help them retrieve a physical object. Given a set of tools of the same shape (rakes or hoes) but different materials, the children in Brown's experiments rejected non-rigid or "squishy" tools in favor of those that were made of rigid materials and would pick up the desired objects without bending or breaking.

Children can use category-based induction to infer new biological knowledge. Two-year-olds expect animals that belong to the same category or "kind" to have the same underlying properties (Gelman & Coley, 1991; Lawson & Kalish, 2006). Young children are also able

to use analogical reasoning to help them solve novel problems (Goswami, 1989; Holyoak, Junn, & Billman, 1984). Both adults and young children are able to induce causal structures from observed patterns of covariation in data (Cheng, 1997; Glymour, 2001; Sobel, Tennebaum, & Gopnik, 2004). Preshcoolers can use Bayesian knowledge about causal patterns to infer causal structure from data in some circumstances. In experiments, children observe patterns of data in which an outcome C varies as two putative causes A and B are presented either individually or together. For example, they might observe that A alone is followed by C, and A and B together are followed by C, but B alone is not followed by C. Children ages 3 and 4 are able to infer from such patterns that only A and not B causes C (Sobel, Tennebaum, & Gopnik, 2004; Schulz and Gopnik, 2004).

Certain aspects of reasoning develop late and may not be evident even in the thinking of college-educated adults in the absence of specific training. Research shows that complex forms of deductive reasoning such as syllogistic and conditional reasoning start to emerge in the late elementary school years and continue to develop through adolescence (Bara, Bucciarelli, & Johnson-Laird, 1995; Ward & Overton, 1990). One important psychological model of scientific reasoning is Klahr and Dunbar's model which characterizes scientific discovery as the search for hypotheses to account for patterns of relevant evidence. The model posits that during discovery, people simultaneously search in two related spaces, a "hypothesis space" and an "experiment space." When trying to account for patterns of data, people either invoke hypotheses from prior knowledge or induce them from the data. They then search for an experiment that can help them choose among rival hypotheses. The work of Klahr and his colleagues suggests that adolescents and adults have difficulty with the use of appropriate experimental design and evidence evaluation strategies. For instance, many people do not spontaneously employ a "control of variables" strategy in complex scientific discovery tasks where there are several potential causes that might influence an outcome (Chen & Klahr, 1999; Klahr, 2000).

On tasks that require the interpretation of covariation evidence (for instance, rates of illness among people who have eaten different combinations of foods) research shows that both children and adults often make unwarranted causal inferences from confounded experiments (Kuhn, 1989, 1991; Kuhn & Dean, 2004). Additionally, people reason differently about identical patterns of covariation evidence depending on whether the variables under consideration are believed to be causal or noncausal based on prior knowledge (Kuhn, 1991; Schauble, 1996). These findings parallel earlier work by Kahneman and Tversky (1979) on errors and biases in human reasoning which shows that given the same objective probability data, people's reasoning about probable gains differed from their reasoning about probable losses. Kuhn & Dean (2004, 2005) argue that part of learning to reason scientifically is the ability to generate genuine scientific questions (ones to which the answer is not known) that can be fruitfully addressed by empirical evidence. They point out that in richer and more realistic knowledge building and evaluation contexts, there is considerable variability in reasoning both across individuals (for example, by age and expertise) and within individuals (for instance, across domains and tasks). Thus, one aspect of developing reasoning competence is the range of contexts to which different forms of reasoning can be successfully applied.

THE ROLE OF CONCEPTUAL KNOWLEDGE

As noted earlier, one factor that influences how people reason is the nature of the conceptual base from which they reason. People reason with and about concepts, and one problem in evaluating reasoning is that different individuals may interpret the same situation differently and bring different assumptions to bear in reasoning. Prior knowledge and belief facilitate reasoning in some contexts. The work of Brown (1990) shows that prior knowledge facilitates causal reasoning even in young children. Pragmatic knowledge improves deductive reasoning on conditional reasoning tasks (e.g., tasks of the logical form: If P then Q for both children and adults (Cheng & Holyoak, 1985; Girotto, Light, & Colbourn, 1988). Samarapungavan (1992) has shown that elementary school children are able to reason scientifically in theory choice tasks if the competing theories are both plausible. For example, given two equally plausible theories, they prefer the theory that is consistent with the available empirical evidence. They also prefer theories that explain a wider range of data to narrower theories.

Prior knowledge and belief can also impede valid reasoning. For example, Kahneman and Tversky (1973) showed that people's predictions about the likelihood of future events were often based not on the actual (known) frequencies with which these events occurred in a target population (the "base rate") but on other heuristics such as how easily an example of the event came to mind (availability). In the context of scientific investigation tasks, differences in conceptual models lead people to adopt different strategies of investigation and evidence interpretation. When investigating electricity in a simulated microworld (a computer-based dynamic system that simulates how electricity works) called Votlaville, college students with more sophisticated initial causal models of electricity learned more than students with less sophisticated models because they used more fruitful investiga-

tive strategies and engaged in better reasoning (Schauble, Glaser, Raghavan, & Reiner, 1992).

SOCIOCULTURAL FACTORS IN REASONING

In contrast to traditional psychological approaches which focus on individual reasoning, sociocultural theories emphasize the socially shared or co-constructed aspects of reasoning (Boyd & Richerson, 2005; Bruner, 1966; Latour & Woolgar, 1986; Knorr-Cetina, 1999; Rogoff, 1990; Vygotsky, 1978). Jean Piaget (1896–1980) (1945) believed that encountering beliefs and opinions that countered one's own in the course of social interaction provided a powerful form of cognitive challenge which impelled a person to reason. The science studies research discussed above illustrates how sociocultural contexts and practices shape and support scientific reasoning in a variety of ways. Individuals learn prototypical forms or patterns of reasoning as they are acculturated into the practices of their discipline. For instance, social scientists become adept in the use of statistical models for reasoning about patterns of evidence. Giere (1988) and Knorr-Cetina (1989) have noted the role of peer discourse, both formal and informal (e.g., peer review, research group discussions), in shaping the reasoning and knowledge of scientists engaged in discovery. Expert reasoning is supported by cultural tools such as charts, laboratory notebooks, and computer programs for statistical analysis or data modeling (Latour, 1990). Such inscriptional tools allow users to externalize and share both the processes and products of reasoning and reduce cognitive load during complex tasks. For example, using computer programs such as SAS to perform multivariate regression reduces the computational burden of reasoning about covariation evidence with large data sets.

INSTRUCTIONAL STRATEGIES

Can good reasoning be developed through instruction? The research suggests that a variety of instructional approaches and strategies can support the development of reasoning in students. In some circumstances, explicit instruction and modeling can help students acquire patterns of reasoning that they are unfamiliar with (Nisbett, Fong, Lehman, & Cheng, 1987). Students who are explicitly taught to use a "control of variables" strategy on scientific reasoning and discovery tasks are more likely to transfer and use this strategy in novel reasoning contexts than students who receive no explicit instruction and are left to discover the strategy on their own (Klahr & Nigam, 2004).

Instructional scaffolding can be used to support and enhance students' reasoning. Adult support and guidance in the form of hints, questions, and prompts during classroom discourse can help students gain awareness and control over their reasoning (Hogan, Nastasi, & Pressley, 2000; Gleason & Schauble, 1999). Cultural tools (especially computer technology) can be used to enhance student thinking and reasoning in the classroom (Polman & Pea, 2001; Roschelle, Pea, Hoadley, & Gordin, 2000).

In addition to specific strategies to foster reasoning, many educators have discussed the general characteristics of learning environments that support habits of thought and reasoning. These include the use of knowledge-rich, challenging, and open-ended instructional tasks, such as those used in project-based, problem-based, and inquiry learning, that provide the students with affordances to reason (Barron, Schwartz, Vye, & Moore, 1998; Chinn & Malhotra, 2001; Duschl, 2000; Haskill, 2001, Hammer & Elby, 2002; Magnusson, & Palinscar, 1995; Penner, Lehrer, & Schauble, 1998). More generally, fostering a culture of communication in which children are encouraged to talk to one another, argue about ideas, explain concepts, and share their discoveries supports the development of reasoning (Bruner, 1996; Polman & Pea, 2001; Roth, 2005).

BIBLIOGRAPHY

Baker, W. P., & Lawson, A. E., (2001). Complex instructional analogies and theoretical concept acquisition in college genetics. *Science Education, 85*(6), 665–683.

Baillargeon, R. (2004). Infants' reasoning about hidden objects: evidence for event-general and event-specific expectations. *Developmental Science, 7*(4), 391–414.

Bara, G. B., Bucciarelli, M., & Johnson-Laird, P. N. (1995). Development of syllogistic reasoning. *American Journal of Psychology, 108*(2), 157–193.

Barron, B. J. S., Schwartz, D. L., Vye, N. J., & Moore, A. (1998). Doing with understanding: Lessons from research on problem-and project-based learning. *Journal of the Learning Sciences, 7*(3&4), 271–311.

Boyd, R., & Richerson, P. J. (2005). *The origin and evolution of cultures.* Oxford, England: Oxford University Press.

Brewer, W. F., & Samarapungavan, A. (1991). Children's theories versus scientific theories: Differences in reasoning or differences in knowledge? In R. R Hoffman & D. S. Palermo (Eds.), *Cognition and the symbolic processes: Vol. 3. Applied and ecological perspectives* (pp. 209–232). Hillsdale, NJ: Erlbaum.

Brown, A. L. (1990). Domain-specific principles affect learning and transfer in children. *Cognitive Science, 14*(1), 107–133.

Bruner, J. (1996). *The culture of education.* Cambridge, MA: Harvard University Press.

Carey, S. (1985). *Conceptual change in childhood.* Cambridge, MA: MIT Press.

Chen, Z., & Klahr, D. (1999). All other things being equal: the acquisition and transfer of the control of variables strategy. *Child Development, 70*(5), 1098–1120.

Cheng, P. W. (1997). From covariation to causation: A causal power theory. *Psychological Review, 104,* 367–405.

Cheng, P. W., & Holyoak, K. J. (1985). Pragmatic reasoning schemas. *Cognitive Psychology, 17,* 391–416.

Chinn, C. A., & Malhotra, B. A. (2001). Epistemologically authentic inquiry in schools: A theoretical framework for evaluating inquiry tasks. *Science Education, 86,* 175–218).

Clement, J. (1993). Using bridging analogies and anchoring intuitions to deal with students' misconceptions in physics. *Journal of Research in Science Teaching, 30*(10), 1241–1257.

Conant, J. B. (1957). The overthrow of the phlogiston theory. The chemical revolution of 1775–1789. In J. B. Conant & L. K. Nash (Eds.), *Harvard case histories in experimental science* (pp. 67–115). Cambridge, MA: Harvard University Press.

diSessa, A. (1993). Towards an epistemology of physics. *Cognition and instruction, 10,* 105–225.

Dunbar, K. (1995). How scientists really reason: Scientific reasoning in real-world laboratories. In R.J. Sternberg, & J. Davidson (Eds.), *Mechanisms of insight* (pp. 365–395). Cambridge MA: MIT Press.

Duschl, R. (2000). Making the nature of science explicit. In R. Millar, J. Osborne & J. Leach (Eds.), *Improving Science Education* (pp. 185–206). Philadelphia: Open University Press.

Ericsson, C. A., Charness, N., Hoffman, R. R., Feltovich, J. P. (Eds.) (2006). *The Cambridge handbook of expertise and expert performance.* Cambridge, England: Cambridge University Press.

Gelman, S. A., & Coley, J. D. (1991). The importance of knowing a dodo is a bird: Categories and inference in 2-year-old children. *Developmental Psychology, 26,* 796–804.

Gentner, D., Holyoak, K.J., & Koikinov, B. N. (Eds.) (2001). *The analogical mind.* Cambridge, MA: MIT Press.

Giere, R. (1988). *Explaining science: A cognitive approach.* Chicago: University of Chicago Press.

Gigerenzer, D., & Goldstein, D. (1996). Reasoning the fast and frugal way: Models of bounded rationality. *Psychological Review, 103*(4), 650–669.

Girotto, V., Light, P., & Colbourn, C. (1988). Pragmatic reasoning schemas and conditional reasoning in children. *Quarterly Journal of Experimental Psychology, 40A*(3), 469–482.

Gleason, M. E., & Schauble, L. (1999). Parents' assistance of their children's scientific reasoning. *Cognition & Instruction, 17*(4), 343–378.

Glymour, C. (2001). *The mind's arrows: Bayes nets and graphical causal models in psychology.* Cambridge, MA: MIT Press.

Goswami, U. (1989). Relational complexity and the development of analogical reasoning. *Cognitive Development, 4,* 251–268.

Hammer, D., & Elby, A. (2002). On the form of a personal epistemology. In B. K. Hofer & P. R. Pintrich, (Eds.), *Personal epistemology: The psychology of beliefs about knowledge and knowing* (pp 169–190). Mahwah, NJ: Erlbaum.

Haskill, R. E. (2001). *Transfer of learning. Cognition, instruction, & reasoning.* New York: Academic Press.

Hatano. G., & Inagaki, K. (1994). Young children's naïve theory of biology. *Cognition, 50,* 171–188.

Hogan, K., Nastasi, B. K., Pressley, M. (2000). Discourse patterns and collaborative scientific reasoning in peer and teacher-guided discussions. *Cognition & Instruction, 17*(4), 379–432.

Johnson-Laird, P. N. (2006). *How we reason.* Oxford, England: Oxford University Press.

Kahneman, D., & Tversky, A. (1973). On the psychology of prediction. *Psychological Review, 80,* 237–251.

Kahneman, D., & Tversky, A. (1979) Prospect Theory: An Analysis of Decision under Risk. *Econometrica, 47*(2), 263–292.

Kitcher, P. (1979). Frege's epistemology. *The Philosophical Review, 88*(2), 235–262.

Kitcher, P. (1985). *The nature of mathematical knowledge.* Oxford, England: Oxford University Press.

Klahr, D. (2000). *Exploring science: The cognition and development of discovery processes.* Cambridge, MA: MIT Press.

Klahr, D., & Dunbar, K. (1988). Dual space search during scientific reasoning. *Cognitive Science, 12*(1), 1–48.

Klahr, D., & Nigam, M. (2004). The equivalence of learning paths in early science instruction, *Psychological Science, 15*(10), 661–667.

Knorr-Cetina, K. K. (1999). *Epistemic cultures. How the sciences make knowledge.* Cambridge, MA: Harvard University Press.

Kuhn, D. (1989). Children and adults as intuitive scientists. *Psychological Review, 96,* 674–689.

Kuhn, D. (1991). *The skills of argument.* Cambridge, MA: MIT Press.

Kuhn, D., & Dean, D. (2004). Connecting scientific reasoning and causal inference. *Journal of Cognition and Development, 5*(2), 261–288.

Kuhn, D., & Dean, D. (2005). Is developing scientific thinking all about learning to control variables? *Psychological Science, 16*(11), 866–870.

Kuhn, T. (1962). *The structure of scientific revolutions.* Chicago: University of Chicago Press.

Lakatos, I. (1976). A renaissance of empiricism in recent philosophy of mathematics. *The British Journal for the Philosophy of Science, 27*(3), 201–223.

Latour, B. (1990). *Drawing things together. Representation in scientific practice.* Cambridge, MA: MIT Press.

Latour, B., & Woolgar, S. (1986). *Laboratory life: the construction of scientific facts.* Princeton, NJ: Princeton University Press.

Laudan, L. (1990). *Science and relativism: Some key controversies in the philosophy of science.* Chicago: Chicago University Press.

Lawson, C. A., & Kalish, C. W. (2006). Inductive inferences across time and identity: Are category members more like than single individuals? *Journal of Cognition and Development, 7(2),* 233–252.

Lipton. P. (1961). *Inference to the best explanation.* New York: Routledge.

Magnusson, S. J., & Palinscar, A. S. (1995). The learning environment as a site for science education reform. *Theory Into Practice, 34*(1), 43–59.

Netz, R. (2005). *The shaping of deduction in Greek mathematics. A study in cognitive history.* Cambridge, England: Cambridge University Press.

Nisbett, R. E., Fong, G. T., Lehman, D. R., & Cheng, P. W. (1987). Teaching reasoning. *Science, 238*(4827), 628–631.

Penner, D., Lehrer, R., & Schauble, L. (1998). From physical models to biomechanics: A design-based modeling approach. *Journal of the Learning Sciences, 7*(3–4), 429–449.

Piaget, J. (1945). *Sociological studies.* New York: Routledge.

Polman, J. L., & Pea, R. D. (2001). Transformative communication as a cultural tool for guiding inquiry science. *Science Education, 85*(3), 223–238.

Popper, K. (1959). *The logic of scientific discovery.* New York: Basic.

Popper, K. (1972). *Objective knowledge.* Oxford, England: Oxford University Press.

Rogoff, B. (1990). *Apprenticeship in thinking: Cognitive development in social context.* New York: Oxford University Press.

Roschelle, J. M., Pea, R., D., Hoadley, C. M., Gordin, D. N. (2000). Changing how and what children learn in school with computer-based technologies. *The Future of Children, 10*(2), 76–102.

Roth, W. M. (2005). *Talking science: Language and learning in science.* Lanham, MD: Rowman & Littlefield.

Russell, B. (1903). *The principles of mathematics.* London, England: Cambridge University Press.

Sahdra, B., & Thagard, P. (2003). Procedural knowledge in molecular biology. *Philosophical Psychology, 16,* 477–498.

Samarapungavan, A. (1992). Children's judgments in theory choice tasks: Scientific rationality in childhood. *Cognition, 45*(1), 1–32.

Schauble, L. (1996). The development of scientific reasoning in knowledge rich contexts. *Developmental Psychology, 32*(1), 102–119.

Schauble, L., Glaser, R., Ragahavan, K., & Reiner, M. (1992). The integration of knowledge and experimentation strategies in understanding a physical system. *Applied Cognitive Psychology, 6*(4), 321–343.

Schulz, L. E., & Gopnik. A. (2004). Causal learning across domains. *Developmental Psychology, 40*(2), 162–176.

Simon, H. A. (1997). *Models of bounded rationality.* Cambridge, MA: MIT Press.

Sobel, D., Tennebaum, J., B., & Gopnik, A. (2004). Children's causal inferences from indirect evidence: Backwards blocking and Bayesian reasoning in preschoolers. *Cognitive Science, 28*(3), 303–333.

Thagard, P. (1990). The conceptual structure of the chemical revolution. *Philosophy of Science, 57,* 183–209.

Thagard, P. (1993). *Explanatory coherence.* Cambridge, MA: MIT Press.

Thagard, P. (2003). Pathways to biomedical discovery. *Philosophy of Science, 70,* 235–254.

Thagard, P. (2006). Analogy, Explanation, & Education. *Journal of Research in Science Teaching, 29*(6), 537–544.

Thagard, P., & Shelley, C. P. (1997). Abductive reasoning: Logic, visual thinking, and coherence. In M.L. D. Chiara, K. Doets, D. Mundici, & J. van Benthem (Eds.), *Logic and scientific methods* (pp. 413–427). Dordrecht: Kluwer.

Vickers, J. (2006). The Problem of Induction. In E. N. Zalta (Ed.), *The Stanford Encyclopedia of Philosophy,* Retrieved April 16, 2008, from http://plato.stanford.edu/entries/induction-problem/.

Vosniadou, S., & Brewer, W. F. (1992). Mental models of the earth: A study of conceptual change in childhood. *Cognitive Psychology, 24*(4), 535–585.

Vygotsky, L. (1978). *Mind in society. The development of higher psychological processes* (M. Cole., V. John-Steiner, S. Scribner, & E. Souberman, Eds.). Cambridge, MA: Harvard University Press.

Ward, S. L., & Overton, W. F. (1990). Semantic familiarity, relevance, and the development of deductive reasoning. *Developmental Psychology, 26*(3), 488–493.

Wineburg, S. (1998). Historical Thinking and Other Unnatural Acts. *Phi Delta Kappan, 80*(7), 488–99.

Wineburg, S. (1999). Reading Abraham Lincoln: An expert/expert study in the interpretation of historical texts. *Cognitive Science, 22*(3), 319–346.

Ala Samarapungavan

RECIPROCAL TEACHING

Reciprocal teaching is one of the methods that are used to teach comprehension-fostering strategies to students. Reading scores have usually improved as a result of this instruction.

Until the 1980s, students were seldom provided with any help in reading comprehension. In a class study, Durkin (1979) observed 4,469 minutes of reading instruction in grade 4 and found that only 20 minutes of this time were spent in teaching students how to comprehend what they were reading. Durkin found that teachers spent almost all of the instructional time asking students questions, but they spent little time teaching students comprehension strategies they could use to answer the questions. Duffy, Lanier, and Roehler noted a similar lack of comprehension instruction in elementary classrooms: "There is little evidence of instruction of any kind ... Seldom does one observe teaching in which a teacher presents a skill, a strategy, or a process to pupils, shows them how to do it, provides assistance as they initiate attempts to perform the task and assures that they can be successful" (1980, p. 514). As a result of these astonishing findings, investigators developed and taught students to use specific cognitive strategies that were designed to help them perform higher-level operations in reading. Palincsar and Brown (1984) referred to these strategies as "comprehension-fostering" activities.

Teaching students to ask questions about the material they are reading is an example of a comprehension-fostering activity. Asking questions, by itself, does not directly lead in a step-by-step manner to comprehension. Rather, in the process of generating questions, students need to search the text and combine information, and these processes serve to help students comprehend what they read. A cognitive strategy, then, is a guide or a scaffold that serves to support the learners as they develop the internal procedures that enable them to perform the higher level operations.

TWO MAJOR COGNITIVE STRATEGIES

Two of the major and most researched cognitive strategies have been teaching students to ask questions about material they were reading and teaching students to summarize passages.

The cognitive strategy of asking questions was usually taught by providing students with a list of signal words—who, what, when, why, how—that students could use to form questions. The strategy of summarizing was frequently taught using a *legs and table* procedure in which students first list the major details (the legs) and then use the legs to compose a summary sentence (the table).

TEACHING COGNITIVE STRATEGIES

In many of these studies the cognitive strategies were taught directly by the teacher. The teacher first presented a list of signal words and then modeled the use of these words to ask questions about the material in a story or a passage. Then the teacher guided the students as they began to generate questions about the material, and, finally, the students asked questions independently, without much supervision.

Students were taught to use the legs and table strategy the same way. First, the teacher modeled how to select the main points (the legs) and then use these points to develop a summary (the table). Then the teacher supervised the students as they practiced identifying the legs and the table. The teacher would guide the students as they practiced by first summarizing a paragraph, then several paragraphs, then a passage, and then a larger unit. Finally, the students worked on their own, with minimal supervision from the teacher.

Reciprocal teaching, a term and practice developed by Palincsar and Brown (1984), is a variation on the traditional teaching method. In reciprocal teaching the focus is also upon teaching students specific comprehension-fostering strategies. Palincsar and Brown taught students four strategies: asking questions about the text, summarizing what was read, predicting what might happen next, and attempting to clarify words and phrases that were not understood. But in reciprocal teaching, the practice of applying these strategies takes place primarily in the context of a dialogue between the teacher and the students.

In reciprocal teaching, students read a passage of expository material paragraph by paragraph. During the early stages of the lesson, the teacher assumes the major responsibility for instruction by explicitly modeling the process of using these strategies on a selected text. The students then practice the strategies on the next section of text and the teacher supports each student's participation through specific feedback, additional modeling, coaching, hints, and explanations. The teacher adjusts the difficulty of the task according to the current level of the student. As Palincsar and Brown (1984) explained:

> The teacher models and explains, relinquishing part of the task to novices only at the level each one is capable of negotiating at any one time.

Increasingly, as the novice becomes more competent, the teacher increases her demands, requiring participation at a slightly more challenging level. (p. 13)

During this guided practice the teacher invites students to initiate discussion and to react to other students' statements. Student participation can include (a) elaborating or commenting on another student's summary, (b) suggesting other questions, (c) commenting on another's predictions, (d) requesting clarification of material not understood, and (e) helping to resolve misunderstandings.

The teacher supports the students by rephrasing or elaborating on their answers, comments, or questions, and by providing hints and instruction when needed. In the course of this guided practice, there is a gradual shift in responsibility from the teacher doing much of the work to the student taking over the major thinking while the teacher observes and helps only when needed.

At this point, the practice becomes a dialogue: one student asks questions, another answers, and a third comments on the answer; one student identifies a difficult word, and the other students help to infer the meaning and give reasons for the inferences they made. The emphasis throughout is on a cooperative effort by the teacher and students to bring meaning to the ideas in the text, rather than merely restating the words. In addition, during the dialogue, students are provided instruction in when, why, and where these activities should be applied to the text.

Reciprocal teaching, then, has two major features: instruction and practice of the four comprehension-fostering strategies and the use of the reciprocal teaching dialogue as a vehicle for learning and practicing these four strategies.

The process of gradual introduction of a skill by a teacher who provides assistance to students as they practice is similar to the guided practice described by Hunter (1982), Good and Grouws (1979), and Rosenshine and Stevens (1986). In reciprocal teaching, however, much greater emphasis is placed on encouraging students to provide instructional support for each other.

RESULTS

Two different types of tests were used to study the effect of using reciprocal teaching methods. Some investigators developed their own tests while other investigators used standardized tests in reading. Some investigators used both their own tests and standardized tests.

When experimenter-developed tests were used in the reciprocal teaching studies, the results were usually statistically significant and the average effect size was .88. An effect size of .88 means that students who scored at the 50th percentile in the experimental group would have scored at the 88th percentile if they had been in the control group (Rosenshine & Meister, 1994). When standardized tests were used the average effect size was .32. This result means that on the standardized tests, students who scored at the 50th percentile in the experimental group would have scored at the 63rd percentile if they had been in the control group. An effect size of .88 is considered to be very large.

As noted, asking questions has also been taught in traditional settings, without the reciprocal teaching addition. When experimenter-developed tests were used in these studies the results were also usually statistically significant and the average effect size was .89. When standardized tests were used the average effect size was .34 (Rosenshine, Meister and Chapman, 1996). This result means that the same statistically significant results were obtained for teacher-led instruction when only the question-asking strategy was taught as were obtained using the reciprocal teaching format when four cognitive strategies were taught. These results suggest that the teaching of cognitive strategies is a useful instructional procedure for raising student achievement, and these strategies can be successfully taught in both a traditional and a reciprocal teaching format.

Palincsar and Brown (1984) suggest that what the students learned was not simply how to ask questions and summarize. Rather, the new strategies enabled and required the students to perform deeper processing of what they read, to engage in making sense of what they read, to be aware of what they did not understand the material, and to engage in additional searching when they encountered comprehension difficulties, and it was the learning and practice of these processes that led to the improved comprehension.

SEE ALSO *Brown, Ann Leslie; Communities of Learners; Scaffolding; Tutoring.*

BIBLIOGRAPHY

Brown, A. L., & Palincsar, A. S. (1989). Guided, cooperative learning and individual knowledge acquisition. In L. B. Resnick (Ed.), *Knowing, learning, and instruction: Essays in honor of Robert Glaser* (pp. 393–451). Mahwah, NJ: Erlbaum.

Durkin, D. (1979). What classroom observations reveal about reading comprehension. *Reading Research Quarterly, 14,* 581–544.

Duffy, G., Lanier, J. E., & Roehler, L. R. (1980). On the need to consider instructional practice when looking for instructional implications. Paper presented at the Reading Expository Materials, University of Wisconsin–Madison.

Duffy, G., & Roehler, L. R. (1987). Improving reading instruction through the use of responsive elaboration. *The Reading Teacher, 40,* 514–521.

Hunter, M. (1982). *Mastery teaching.* El Segundo, CA: TIP.

Good, T. L., & Grouws, D. A. (1979). The Missouri mathematics effectiveness project. *Journal of Educational Psychology, 71,* 143–155.

Palinscar, A. S., & Brown, A. L. (1984). Reciprocal teaching of comprehension-fostering and comprehension-monitoring activities. *Cognition and Instruction, 2,* 117–175.

Rosenshine, B., & Meister, C. (1994). Reciprocal teaching: A review of the research. *Review of Educational Research, 64*(4), 479–530.

Rosenshine, B., Meister, C., & Chapman, S. (1996). Teaching students to generate questions: A review of the intervention studies. *Review of Educational Research, 66*(2), 181–221.

Rosenshine, B., & Stevens, R. (1986). Teaching functions. In M. C. Wittrock (Ed.), *Handbook of research on teaching* (3rd ed., pp. 376–391). New York: Macmillan.

Barak Rosenshine

REINFORCEMENT

Reinforcement is an event that increases behavior. In the classroom, reinforcement occurs as teachers manage the environmental events that follow students' desired ways of behaving so to increase the strength and future likelihood of that behavior.

Reinforcement comes in two types—positive and negative. Positive reinforcement occurs when desired behavior is strengthened by the presentation of a contingent stimulus. The attractive, behavior-increasing, contingent stimulus used during positive reinforcement is referred to as a positive reinforcer. A positive reinforcer is defined as any environmental event that, when given in response to the behavior, increases the strength and frequency of that behavior. Some commonly used positive reinforcers in the classroom are praise, attention, tokens, and stickers.

Negative reinforcement occurs when desired behavior is strengthened by the removal of a contingent stimulus. The aversive, behavior-increasing, contingent stimulus that is removed during negative reinforcement is referred to as a negative reinforcer. A negative reinforcer is defined as any environmental event that, when taken away in response to the behavior, increases the strength and frequency of that behavior. Some commonly used negative reinforcers in the classroom are taking away an aversive assignment (e.g., homework), withdrawing an intrusive stare, or canceling a chore.

Table 1 provides a sample of reinforcers commonly used in K-12 classrooms. The left side of the table lists a variety of positive reinforcers that teachers give to strengthen students' behavior, while the right side of the table lists a variety of negative reinforcers that teachers take away to strengthen students' behavior. What is common to all positive reinforcers in the list is the idea that after the student engages in a particular behavior, he or she receives an attractive consequence for doing so.

Examples of positive and negative reinforcers commonly-used in K–12 classrooms

Positive reinforcers	Negative reinforcers
Giving praise	Taking away a deadline
Giving stickers	Taking away surveillance
Giving privileges	Taking away an unattractive assignment
Giving tokens	Taking away a threat
Giving attention	Removing a negative evaluation
Giving good grades	Removing bad grades
Giving scholarships	Taking away criticism
Giving an honor	Stopping one's ridicule
Giving a trophy	Stopping one's teasing
Giving a prize	Stopping one's yelling or screaming
Giving an award	Stopping one's crying
Giving food	Stopping one's whining
Giving money	Stopping one's staring
Giving a smile	Stopping one's pleading or pouting
Giving positive feedback	Stopping laughing (at someone)

Table 1 ILLUSTRATION BY GGS INFORMATION SERVICES. CENGAGE LEARNING, GALE.

That is, when the student turns in her homework, the teacher then places a sticker on the paper. The sticker is given after the homework has been handed in and with the intention of strengthening the likelihood that future homework assignments will be forthcoming. What is common to all negative reinforcers in the list is the idea that when the student engages in a particular behavior, he or she gets a break from an unattractive or aversive consequence for doing so. That is, when the student turns in her homework, the teacher then exempts the student from an arduous assignment of long division problems. The arduous assignment is removed after the homework has been handed in and with the intention of strengthening the likelihood that future homework assignments will be forthcoming.

REINFORCERS AND REWARDS

Reinforcement is defined by its effect on behavior. Only environmental events that actually increase behavior are reinforcers. If an event such as a smile, candy bar, or break from chores does not increase the student's behavior, then the event is not actually a reinforcer. This qualification of which environmental events are reinforcers and which are not is an important point because teachers often implement consequences haphazardly (non-contingently) or inconsistently (Kauffman, 1996; Pullen, 2004). Praise represents a good example of commonly used attractive environmental event that is used for a dozen different reasons, only one of which is to reinforce (increase) students' behavior (Brophy, 1981). Further, teachers do not reinforce positive behavior as often as they could (Wehby, Symons, Canale, & Go, 1998). Instead of delivering contingent and strategic consequences for desired behavior (i.e., reinforcers), what teachers more typically offer to students are promises of reward.

A reward is the offering of an environmental event in exchange for the student's participation, service, or achievement (Craighead, Kazdin, & Mahoney, 1981). When a teacher promises an award if the student will complete an assignment or when a teacher promises a prize to acknowledge a successful performance, she introduces a reward into the learning environment. Adding a discussion of rewards to a discussion of reinforcement highlights the instructional practice of soliciting students' behavior or acknowledging their achievement, regardless of whether those rewards actually reinforce behavior. The discrepancy between reinforcers and rewards is that a reward functions as a reinforcer only when the student values it enough to affect a change in his or her behavior. Sometimes teachers use rewards that students do not value (e.g., public recognition), and unappealing rewards do not increase the frequency of the desired behavior. If the student is embarrassed, rather than gratified by, the public recognition then it will not reinforce (i.e., strengthen) the behavior, and it might even act as a punisher to some students. The important point is that teachers offer rewards in hopes of soliciting behavior, while they deliver contingent reinforcers to increase desired behavior which has already occurred.

ASSUMPTIONS THAT RELATE REINFORCEMENT TO LEARNING

Reinforcement is an educational concept rooted in behavioral learning theory (Baldwin & Baldwin, 1986). Behavioral learning theory does not focus on mental knowledge, such as learning information. Neither does it focus on cognitive and sociocultural concepts, such as creating meaning, understanding concepts, using memory, and the experience of conceptual change. Instead, behavioral learning theory focuses on behavior. Specifically, it focuses on voluntary, intentional, and situationally appropriate behavior. So, the learning highlighted by behavioral learning theory is learning how to adapt successfully to one's environment (e.g., raise one's hand before speaking, wait one's turn in the lunch line). Reinforcers play the important role they do in helping students learn how to adapt to the classroom (and school) environment by signaling which behaviors are desirable (those that are reinforced) and which are not (those that are not reinforced). Students learn which behaviors are desirable and adaptive by learning which behaviors are associated with reinforcers. The assumption that relates reinforcement to learning is that the presence of a rein-

forcer signals that a particular behavior is desirable, and this signaling process, therefore, helps students learn how to adapt more successfully to the classroom environment.

ASSUMPTIONS THAT RELATE REINFORCEMENT TO MOTIVATION

Reinforcing students' desirable behaviors with positive and negative contingencies is an extrinsic motivational strategy. Motivation researchers outside behavioral learning theory find that extrinsic rewards often undermine students' intrinsic motivation and capacity for autonomous self-regulation (Deci & Ryan, 1985; Deci, Koestner, & Ryan, 1999; Kohn, 1993). That is, reinforcers and rewards produce complicated, and often undesirable, motivational side-effects. The undermining effect that extrinsic rewards often have on intrinsic motivation and autonomous self-regulation is important for two reasons. First, many teachers incorrectly assume that adding extrinsic rewards on top of students' intrinsic motivation will create a supermotivation in which the two types of motivation (extrinsic and intrinsic) will combine and complement one another. Instead, extrinsic rewards typically interfere with and undermine intrinsic motivation and autonomous self-regulation. Second, teachers often offer students extrinsic rewards when introducing uninteresting activities in the hope that the reward will be able to generate the motivation to engage in the task that the task itself cannot generate (because it is uninteresting). From a motivational point of view, teachers therefore use positive reinforcers, negative reinforcers, and extrinsic rewards to bolster students' otherwise low motivation (Boggiano, Barrett, Weiher, McClelland, & Lusk, 1987). In doing so, teachers are essentially trying to set up (manage) conditions that make desired target behaviors, such as engaging in uninteresting (but educationally important) lessons, more likely.

CLASSROOM MANAGEMENT TO PROMOTE EDUCATIONAL OUTCOMES

Many positive educational outcomes can be framed in terms of desirable behavior. Teachers, administrators, and parents all consider behaviors such as attending school regularly and promptly, being actively engaged during classroom lessons, showing respect for others, making good grades, and graduating from school as desirable ways to behave. Because educators value these ways of behaving and because they would like to see students engage in these ways of behaving more frequently, they find merit in classroom management practices, the most popular and the most effective of which involves the strategic use of positive reinforcers, negative reinforcers, and extrinsic rewards (Landrum & Kauffman, 2006).

The fundamental task of classroom management is to create a caring, supportive, inclusive, and engaging community in which students frequently engage in desirable, constructive, and prosocial behavior (Weinstein, Curran, & Tomlinson-Clarke, 2003). When practiced effectively, classroom management is a proactive strategy that creates a classroom environment in which desirable behavior is expected, supported, and reinforced. From this point of view, reinforcement plays only one part in the teacher's larger effect to manage the classrooms. In addition to reinforcing desirable behavior after it occurs and in addition to offering extrinsic rewards to solicit students' desired behavior, teachers can further support students' desirable ways of behaving by adding additional classroom management strategies such as modeling and observational learning (Ozur & Bandura, 1990), scaffolding and tutoring (Chi, Siler, Jeong, Yamauchi, & Jausmann, 2001), behavioral supports (Casteel, Isom, & Jordan, 2000), and promoting students' effective self-management (Bohn, Roehrig, & Pressley, 2004).

SEE ALSO *Behaviorism; Rewards; Thorndike, E(dward) L(ee).*

BIBLIOGRAPHY

Baldwin, J. D., & Baldwin, J. I. (1986). *Behavior principles in everyday life* (2nd ed.). Englewood Cliffs, NJ: Prentice Hall.

Boggiano, A. K., Barrett, M., Weiher, A. W., McClelland, G. H., & Lusk, C. M. (1987). Use of the maximal-operant principle to motivate children's intrinsic interest. *Journal of Personality and Social Psychology, 53,* 866–879.

Bohn, C. M., Roehrig, A. D., & Pressley, M. (2004). The first day of school in the classroom of two more effective and four less effective primary grade teachers. *Elementary School Journal, 104,* 269–287.

Brophy, J. (1981). Teacher praise: A functional analysis. *Review of Educational Research, 51,* 5–32.

Casteel, C. P., Isom, B. A., & Jordan, K. F. (2000). Creating confident and competent readers: Transactional strategies instruction. *Intervention in School and Clinic, 36,* 67–77.

Chi, M. T. H., Siler, S. A., Jeong, H., Yamauchi, T., & Hausmann, R. G. (2001). Learning from human tutoring. *Cognitive Science, 25,* 71–533.

Craighead, W. E., Kazdin, A. E., & Mahoney, M. J. (1981). *Behavior modification: Principles, issues, and applications.* Boston: Houghton Mifflin.

Deci, E. L., Koestner, R., & Ryan, R. M. (1999). A meta-analytic review of experiments examining the effects of extrinsic rewards on intrinsic motivation. *Psychological Bulletin, 125,* 627–668.

Deci, E. L., & Ryan, R. M. (1985). *Intrinsic motivation and self-determination in human behavior.* New York: Plenum.

Kauffman, J. M. (1996). Research to practice issues. *Behavioral Disorders, 22,* 55–60.

Kohn, A. (1993). *Punished by rewards: The trouble with gold stars, incentive plans, A's, praise, and other bribes.* Boston: Houghton Mifflin.

Landrum, T. J., & Kauffman, J. M. (2006). Behavioral approaches to classroom management. In C. M. Evertson & C. S. Weinstein (Eds.), *Handbook of classroom management:* *Research, practice, and contemporary issues* (pp. 7–71). Mahwah, NJ: Lawrence Erlbaum.

Ozur, E. M., & Bandura, A. (1990). Mechanisms governing empowerment effects: A self-efficacy analysis. *Journal of Personality and Social psychology, 58,* 472–486.

Pullen, P. L. (2004). *Brighter beginnings for teachers.* Lanham, MD: Scarecrow Education.

Wehby, J. H., Symons, F. J., Canale, J. A., & Go, F. J. (1998). Teaching practices in classrooms for students with emotional and behavioral disorders: Discrepancies between recommendations and observations. *Behavioral Disorders, 24,* 51–56.

Weinstein, C., Curran, M. E., & Tomlinson-Clarke, S. (2003). Culturally responsive classroom management: Awareness into action. *Theory into Practice, 42, 269*–276.

Johnmarshall Reeve

RELEVANCE OF SELF-EVALUATIONS TO CLASSROOM LEARNING

There has been controversy in the psychological and educational literature about the role of self-concept and global self-esteem in the classroom. How are these constructs best defined, and distinguished from each other, as well as from self-efficacy? Is an understanding of students' perceptions of their scholastic ability related to their motivation to perform in the classroom room? How does the *accuracy* of students' perceptions of their academic performance impact their preference for intellectual challenge? What are the implications for educators, in terms of possible interventions in the classroom? Here there is also controversy. Should educators focus on the enhancement of scholastic skills themselves or should attention be directed toward impacting self-concept as the primary target? How is global self-esteem relevant to students in the classroom, as well as to interventions?

DEFINITIONAL ISSUES

Before addressing these substantive issues, it is important to untangle the often confusing terminology. For example, among the many terms are *self-concept, self-efficacy,* and *self-esteem,* to name three that are a source of confusion. The definitions offered here are those that appear to be the most useful, in terms of clarity. Self-concept refers to one's perceptions of competence or adequacy across specific domains, for example, scholastic competence, athletic competence, and social competence, as well as feelings of adequacy in such domains as perceptions of appearance and the evaluations of one's behavioral conduct or morality (see Harter, 1999). Thus, the concept of domain-specific self-concepts is particularly useful in discriminating differences between the various arenas in which one has self-perceptions of competence and/or adequacy.

This approach is particularly useful in identifying a profile of self-perceptions across the various domains that are included on any given instrument adopting this framework. That is, the vast majority of children and adolescents do not feel equally competent and/or adequate in every domain assessed. Their scores on domain-specific measures vary across domains, leading to different profiles for individuals. Summing or averaging such scores can mask the incredible differences that individuals report across domains. From an educator's perspective, perceptions of competence in the domain of scholastics may be particularly critical to discriminate from other domains, although the latter may also be of interest.

Another term that represents a source of confusion is self-efficacy, a construct identified by Bandura (1977). Self-efficacy refers to the belief that one can or will be efficacious in a particular arena. It has a futuristic connotation. For example, a student may feel that "when I am faced with new academic challenges, I will be successful." Domain-specific self-concept, in contrast, refers to self-evaluations in the present, for example, "I am very good at my schoolwork (right now)." While the two constructs, self-concept and self-efficacy, may be correlated with one another, they are not the same and therefore there can be discrepancies between the two. For example, students could feel competent in the present about their specific ability, if facing new challenges, associated with movement to a new grade, a new teacher, a new school, but not necessarily possess self-efficacy about their future ability to perform. Conversely, students may feel that they can be efficacious in the future, if a change favors their abilities, but may not experience domain-specific competence in their present educational environment. (In this entry, the focus will be on domain-specific competence, emphasizing the scholastic or academic domain, and will not address self-efficacy, although it is important to distinguish clearly between the two constructs.)

APPLICATIONS OF DOMAIN-SPECIFIC SCHOLASTIC COMPETENCE

Before addressing the third construct, self-esteem, which is not domain-specific but rather an overall evaluation of one's worth as a person, two classroom applications of domain-specific scholastic competence will be considered: (a) how perceptions of scholastic competence impact intrinsic versus extrinsic motivation in the classroom, and (b) whether the accuracy of perceptions of scholastic competence is predictive of preference for scholastic challenge, one motivational component.

An important motivational dimension critical to educators is whether children are *intrinsically* or *extrinsically* motivated in the classroom. Three dimension of motivation have been identified (Harter, 1981): First, are the students intrinsically motivated by curiosity and the love of learning or are they merely extrinsically motivated to do the schoolwork assigned? Second do the students prefer academic challenge or do they merely want easy work that they are sure they can accomplish? Third, do the students prefer to approach schoolwork independently or are they dependent on the teacher and need help and/or to be given the correct answer? These dimensions are highly correlated with one another and thus can be combined into a single score representing a student's average motivation along a dimension from intrinsic (highest score = 4) to extrinsic (lowest score = 1).

There is considerable variability in students' motivational level, across grade levels as well as within a given grade level. Developmentally, across grades 3 through 9, there is a systematic decline representing a gradual shift from intrinsic motivation in the third grade to extrinsic motivation during adolescence (Harter, 1981). Eccles, Midgley, and Adler (1984) have suggested that grade-related changes in educational practices are responsible. A focus on academic grades and test performance, including public posting of scores, social comparison, a shift from an emphasis on effort to ability, ability grouping, and a shift from an emphasis on the product of one's performance to the process of learning could all adaptively contribute to a decline in intrinsic motivation and an increase in extrinsic motivation.

Not all students show this unilateral shift. A longitudinal study by Riddle and Harter (reported in Harter, 1990) studied motivational patterns in children making the transition from a sixth grade elementary school to a middle school (seventh and eighth grades). Some showed the decline to extrinsic motivation over this transition, some reported no change, and yet a third group actually showed increases toward greater intrinsic motivation.

What might explain these three different patterns? The researchers found that the patterns were directly predicted by students' perceived scholastic competence. Students whose perceived scholastic competence increased across the transition from sixth to seventh grades, reported a shift toward greater intrinsic motivation, those reporting no changes in scholastic competence reported no changes in level of motivation, and those reporting a decrease in perceived scholastic competence reported a shift to more extrinsic motivation.

Why should children's perceived scholastic competence change as a function of the transition to a new school? In this study, students from three elementary feeder schools made the shift to one junior high school.

This means that two-thirds of the students were undoubtedly new to each individual. Social comparison processes would lead to the conclusion that the hierarchy of perceived competence would shift for many, leading to different perceptions of their perceived scholastic competence (see Harter, 1996). These, in turn, impacted the level of intrinsic vs. extrinsic motivation. Thus, the more students feel scholastically competent, the more they will be drawn to an intrinsic motivational orientation. Conversely, if students report a decline in scholastic competence, they will shift toward an extrinsic motivational style in which they may feel more assured of some success and less failure.

The second application of domain-specific competence concerns the accuracy of perceptions of scholastic competence and preference for challenge. Do the accuracy of self-perceptions have an impact? In one study of the component of preference for challenge, the researchers first established accuracy by comparing teachers' ratings of students' scholastic competence to the students' own perceptions of scholastic competence. Students were divided into "over-raters," those whose scores significantly exceeding the rating of the teacher, "under-raters," those whose scores were significantly lower than the teacher's ratings, and "accurate" raters, those whose scores were congruent with the teachers' (see Harter, 1999).

Next, students were brought into a university classroom in which research assistants acted as teachers. Students were given a booklet that contained anagrams of different levels of challenge, three-letter to seven-letter anagrams, to be unscrambled to make legitimate words. They were given a choice of which they wanted to attempt (see Harter, 1999, for details). Results revealed that the under-raters selected the easier anagrams, presumably because they did not feel scholastically competent. Surprisingly, perhaps, the over-raters who reported high perceived scholastic competence also selected the easiest anagrams. Accurate raters chose the most challenging anagrams.

Why should those reporting high levels of perceived competence select easier anagrams? it should be recalled that this group, the over-raters, were so designated because teachers were not in agreement with their perceptions, viewing them as less competent than the students themselves. The researchers interpreted these findings to reflect the fact that these over-raters, at some level, consciously or perhaps defensively, knew that they were not as competent as their ratings implied. Thus, rather than risk failure, they selected the easiest anagrams. This is an important finding because if over-raters select easier tasks in a simulated classroom, they are likely to select easier tasks in other arenas of their life. By avoiding challenges, they will limit their learning ability. Thus, it is not only the level of perceived scholastic competence that is relevant to the

prediction of certain forms of motivation but the accuracy of those judgments. The issue of why unrealistic evaluations can ultimately be psychologically debilitating will be further discussed below.

SELF-ESTEEM

Another term that is critical to define is self-esteem. Self-esteem, in this entry, refers to a *global* perception of one's overall worth as a person, such as "liking who one is as a person," "being satisfied, overall with who one is." (Negative content is also included.) It should be noted that in the framework of Harter (1999) and Rosenberg (1979) global self-esteem is *not* the sum or average of domain-specific scores. It is its own construct, assessed by its own set of items.

From a developmental perspective, the ability to construct a global view of one's esteem does not appear until about age 8. Younger children (ages 4 to 7) do not have the cognitive skills to integrate information about the self into an overall self-evaluation of their worth (see Harter, 1985, 1999). Rather, they can only make judgments about domain-specific self-concepts such as cognitive competence, social acceptance, and physical competence. This does not mean that young children do not have some sense of their overall worth. Rather, they do not have a verbalizable concept of their global self-esteem, as a cognitive construct that can be expressed through language. However, it has been demonstrated that young children exude or manifest a sense of self-esteem in their *behavior*.

An empirical effort to identify the relevant behaviors by Haltiwanger and Harter has been described in Harter (1985). The researchers first asked teachers to sort behavioral descriptors into groups, those describing high- and low-self-esteem children, ages 4 to 7. Those defining the high self-esteem child included curiosity, exploration, pride in their "work" (e.g., drawings), and confidence, to name the primary descriptors. Those identified with low self-esteem displayed the lack of these attributes. Agreement among teachers was extremely high. The researchers then cast these items in a behavioral rating scale such that teachers or relevant adults could evaluate children on a four-point scale in which they rated each item separately. These could then be averaged to arrive at a score that represented young children's behaviorally manifest self-esteem.

To return to older children and adolescents, separate self-report measures of both domain-specific self-concepts and global self-esteem are needed because global self-esteem is highly related to depression, which, in turn, is predictive of suicidal thinking and behavior (Harter, 1999). These are major mental health concerns, particularly in contemporary society. In fact, reports indicate that depression and suicide are on the rise among preadolescents, adolescents, and young adults. Thus, it is important to understand the causes of depression and suicide, namely lack of global self-esteem, as well as to understand the causes of different levels of global self-esteem. Often these factors are difficult for teachers to observe, and observing them is not the primary task of the educator. Thus, self-report measures that may be administered by school counselors, social workers, or mental health professionals, can aid in the identification of children at risk.

In understanding the causes of global self-esteem and the relevance of domain-specific self-concepts, it is critical to assess domain-specific self-concepts because they can contribute to global self-esteem, as was pointed out by an historical scholar of the self, William James (1842–1910) (1892). James argued that global self-esteem was the product of those domain-specific successes that individuals viewed as particularly important to their well-being (see Harter, 1985, 1999). For example, if scholastic competence is important to students and they are doing well academically, that may be one contributor to high global self-esteem. Conversely, if scholastic competence is important but the students are doing poorly at schoolwork, then they will experience low global self-esteem. The same logic applies to other domains. An example involves the domain of perceived physical attractiveness. In fact, this domain bears the highest correlation with global self-esteem (see Harter, 1985; 1999). The correlation between scholastic competence and self-esteem is the second highest correlation. Thus, to understand one's level of global self-esteem, it is critical to examine domain-specific self-concepts and the relationship they bear to how much one likes oneself as a person, overall.

Another influential theory of the causes of global self-esteem was put forth by Charles Horton Cooley (1864–1929) (1902), another historical scholar of the self. Unlike James, Cooley contended that the opinions of significant others were the key to understanding one's level of self-esteem. Cooley proposed the metaphor of the "looking glass self." Other people are social mirrors into which individuals psychologically gaze in order to divine how they are being perceived. If people feel that others hold them in esteem and approve of them as worthy individuals, then they will incorporate their view into their self-evaluation of their own overall self-esteem. Conversely, if they feel that significant others do not value them, they will report low self-esteem.

Harter (1985, 1999) consistently discovered that approval from classmates is the best predictor of global self-esteem. Classmates are the public significant others who can scrutinize the self and whose resulting opinions are critical to one's self-esteem. The opinions of classmates, expressed directly (e.g., through comments that may communicate negative evaluations of the self) or more indirectly (e.g., avoidance, conveying social rejection), are internalized in the form of low self-esteem. In contrast, the perceived positive acceptance by classmates will lead to positive acceptance of the self, in the form of high self-esteem. Thus, processes that occur within the classroom, namely, perceptions of domain-specific scholastic competence and perceptions of classmate approval are each critical to global self-esteem.

IMPLICATIONS FOR INTERVENTION

A comprehensive coverage of the implications for intervention can be found in Harter (1999). A few of these principles will be summarized here. One issue is whether the goal of interventions should be the enhancement of domain-specific self-evaluations, for example, scholastic competence, or efforts to promote the accuracy of self-evaluations. Some scholars advocate enhancement as the primary goal, such that students will feel good about themselves. However, others point to the dangers of promoting unrealistically high domain-specific evaluations and urge that interventions promote more realistic self-perceptions. The negative effects of over-rating one's scholastic competence were described above.

A similar controversy applies to the construct of global self-esteem. While "feel-good" approaches aimed at encouraging students to value themselves as individuals may give students a temporary psychological lift, in the long run they can have detrimental effects. Damon (1995) views such efforts as misguided, in that they lead to an inflated sense of self-esteem. He argues that they divert educators from teaching skills and deprive students the thrill of actual accomplishment. Damon contends that the importance of self-esteem as a commodity has been greatly exaggerated and that the effusive praise that parents or teachers heap on children to make them feel good is often met with suspicion by children. Moreover, it interferes with the goal of building specific skills in the service of genuine achievement.

Other strategies apply to interventions to influence social self-evaluations. For those reporting low social support from parents, one should determine whether they are withholding support because their children are not meeting parents' highly demanding and often unrealistic expectations. Encouraging parents to accept their children for who they are and for domains in which the child has talents is one goal. For example, parents of a child who has legitimate academic limitations (low intelligence, learning disabilities) but who is musically talented should reward musical accomplishments rather than critically hound the child for lack of academic success. If these strategies are unworkable, then providing some type of compensatory support, in the form of a special adult who can provide support, for example, an extended family member or those in programs like Big Sisters and Big Brothers.

Other students may lack peer support, contributing to low self-esteem. To the extent that they are realistic, attempts should focus on understanding the particular causes of their lack of acceptance. Do such children lack attributes that are valued by peers, for example, attractiveness, athletic ability, or interpersonal qualities that make them likable? Intervention efforts may be directed toward improving the child's skills in the relevant area(s), realizing that there will be natural limits on the extent to which the child may be able to improve. Another strategy may involve removing such children from an unsupportive peer-group situation and placing them with individuals who are likely to provide more support. Social skills programs may also be an option. Increasing social support from either parents or peers, in turn, enhance children's global self-esteem.

The present entry has focused on two critical constructs, students' domain-specific self-concepts and global self-esteem, and how they are relevant to the classroom. Research by Harter has revealed that students' motivation shifts from intrinsic to extrinsic motivation as a function of grade-level. Moreover, students' perceived scholastic competence is a powerful predictor of the level of intrinsic versus extrinsic motivation. In addition, Harter's research has demonstrated that those who over-rate and under-rate their scholastic competence are more likely to report low preference for challenge, which in turn can hamper efforts to approach challenging situations in the classroom as well as in other arenas of their life that can provide learning experiences.

SEE ALSO *Self-Esteem.*

BIBLIOGRAPHY
Bandura, A. (1977). Self-efficacy: Toward a unifying theory of behavioral change. *Psychological Review, 84,* 344–358.

Cooley, C. H. (1902). *Human Nature and the Social Order.* New York: Scribner's.

Eccles, J. S., Midgley, C., & Adler, T. (1984). Grade-related changes in the school environment: Effects on achievement motivation. In J. G. Nichols (Ed.), *The development of achievement motivation* (pp. 283–331). Greenwich, CT: JAI Press.

Harter, S. (1981). A new self-report scale of intrinsic versus extrinsic orientation in the classroom: Motivational and informational components. *Developmental Psychology, 17,* 300–312.

Harter, S. (1985). Competence as a dimension of self-evaluation: Toward a comprehensive model of self-esteem. In R. Leahy (Ed.). *The development of the self* (pp. 55–122). New York: Academic Press.

Harter, S. (1990). Causes, correlates, and the functional role of global self-esteem. In R. Stern & J. Kolligian, Jr. (Eds.),

Competence considered (pp. 67–68). New Haven, CT: Yale University Press.

Harter, S. (1996). Teacher and classmate influences on scholastic motivation, self-esteem, and choice. In K. Wentzel & J. Juvonen (Eds.), *Social motivation: Understanding children's school adjustment* (pp. 11–42). Cambridge, England: Cambridge University Press.

Harter, S. (1999). *The construction of the self.* New York: Guilford Press.

James, W. (1892). *Psychology: The briefer course.* New York: Henry Holt.

Rosenberg, M. (1979). *Conceiving the self.* New York: Basic.

Susan Harter

RELIABILITY

Reliability is the consistency of a measure. In educational testing, reliability refers to the confidence that the test score will be the same across repeated administrations of the test. There is a close relation between the construct of reliability and the construct of validity. Many sources discuss how a test can have reliability without validity and that a test cannot have validity without reliability. In the theoretical sense, these statements are true but not in any practical sense. A test is designed to be reliable and valid, consistent, and accurate. Practical conceptualizations of reliability cannot be discussed separately from examples with validity.

RELIABILITY AND VALIDITY

Reliability without validity would be similar to an archer consistently hitting the target in the same place but missing the bull's eye by a foot. The archer's aim is reliable because it is predictable but it is not accurate. The archer's aim never hits what it is expected to hit. In this analogy, validity without reliability would be the arrows hitting the target in a haphazard manner but close to the bull's eye and centering around the bull's eye. In this second example, it can be seen that the validity is evidence that the archer is aiming at the right place. However, it also demonstrates that, even though the reliability is low, there is still some degree of reliability. That is, at least the arrows are consistently hitting the target. In addition, if the arrows are centered around the bull's eye, the error of one aim leading too far to the right is balanced by another aim leading too far to the left. Looking at the unpainted backside of the target's canvas, someone would be able to identify where the bull's eye was by averaging the distance of all the shots from the bull's eye.

Reliability of a test is an important selling point for publishers of standardized test, especially in high-stakes testing. If an institute asserts that its instrument can identify children who qualify for a special education program, the users of that test would hope that it has a high reliability. Otherwise, some children requiring the special education may not be identified, whereas others who do not require the special education may be unnecessarily assigned to the special education program.

Even in situations perceived as low-stakes testing, such as classroom testing, reliability and validity are serious concerns. Classroom teachers are concerned that the tests they administer are truly reflective of their students' abilities. If a teacher administered a test that was reliable but not valid, it would not have much practical use. An example would be a teacher in a grade-school history class administering, as a midterm exam, a standardized test from a reputable publisher. If that exam was suggested by the test developer as the final exam, the results would most likely be reliable but not valid. The test results would be reliable because they would most likely reflect the students' rank order in class performance. However, the test would not be valid as most students would not be ready for half of the material being tested. If the grade-school history teacher administered as a midterm exam a standardized test recommended by the test developer as a midterm exam for the appropriate grade level, the test could be considered valid. However, if the students (for some strange reason) did not receive uniform instruction in grade-appropriate history, the test would most likely not be reliable.

From these examples, it is clear that it is easier to increase the validity of a reliable measure than to increase the reliability of an otherwise valid measure. The reliable archer could be trained, little by little, to move the aim in the direction of the bull's eye. However, the target could be moved over one foot, so that the bull's eye is at the spot on the target that the archer usually hits. The teacher could take the time necessary (half a school year) to teach the students what they need to know to pass the valid final exam. (This is similar to training the archer to shoot in the right direction.) Another solution for the classroom situation would be for the teacher to adapt the test items in the exam, so that it is more appropriate as a midterm exam, instead of as a final exam. (This is similar to moving the target so that the archer's aim hits the bull's eye.)

In the test publishing world, the reliability of a draft test instrument is often quickly established. However, after the test is used many times, its validity might be questioned. A test designed as a verbal reasoning test may rely heavily on the test-taker's knowledge of music, art, and history. Because the test is reliable, the publishers might redefine what construct it is measuring; in this case, it is a better measure of the students' knowledge of the humanities than of verbal reasoning. The publisher would recall all copies of the Verbal Reasoning test; then,

with little change to the test, the publisher could offer it again as the Humanities Achievement test.

Test reliability is explained through the true score theory and the theory of reliability. True score theory states that the observed score on a test is the result of a true score plus some error in measurement. The theory of reliability compares the reliability of a test of human characteristics with the reliability of measuring instruments in the physical sciences.

RELIABILITY IN TRUE SCORE THEORY

True score is the exact measure of the test taker's true ability in the area being tested. With a perfect test, the observed score would be equal to the true score. However, there is no perfect test. As one example of where the error may occur, the wording of test items may not be detailed enough for some test takers yet be too detailed for others. The examples of test errors are innumerable. According to true score theory, no one can know what the reliability of the test is unless one knows how much random error exists in the test. One cannot know how much error exists in the test unless one knows what the true score is. As a theoretical concept, the true score cannot be known. Therefore, what the reliability is can never be known with certainty. However, one can still estimate what the reliability is through repeated measures. As the error is assumed to be random, it should be balanced out over many administrations of the same test. If the test-taker's ability measured by the test is unchanging, when the error inflates the observed score one time it can be expected to deflate the observed score to the same degree at another time.

THE THEORY OF RELIABILITY

According to the theory of reliability, when a test is administered to a group of individuals, the observed variance in the distribution of scores should be due only to the true variance in the ability levels of the test takers. The degree that the two variances match is the reliability evaluation.

Another principle of the theory of reliability is that the reliability of a test is the ratio of the true score over the observed score. This relates to the true score theory because if the true score equals the observed score, then the error term must equal zero and the ratio of the true score to the observed score will be a perfect 1. Any deviation from this perfect ratio is caused by the strength of the error term (whether a positive or negative value). Therefore, expressing reliability as the ratio of the true score to observed score is in agreement with true score theory.

Reliability can also be expressed as the ratio of the variance of the true score to the variance of the observed score. Still, as noted above, one cannot know what the true score is, so one cannot know what the variance of the true score is. One way to estimate the variance of the true score is to calculate the covariance of two observed scores from the same test with the same test takers with unchanging ability.

The covariance of two measures is the variance that the two measures share. It is the numerator in the calculation of the correlation of the two measures. The denominator of the correlation is the standard deviation of one measure times the standard deviation of the second. Because the measures are assumed to be the same, their standard deviations should be the same. Therefore, the product of the two standard deviations should equal the square of the standard deviation of the one measure. Statistically, this is the same as the variance of the observed score. The conclusion is that the estimation of reliability is the same as the correlation of two distributions of matching scores from the same test.

In summary, according to reliability theory, reliability is equal to the ratio of the variance of the true score to the variance of the observed score. Calculating the ratio of the estimated variance of the true score to the variance of the observed score is the same as calculating the correlation between two observed scores. Therefore, the correlation of two repeated measures of the same test is accepted as an appropriate estimate of the reliability of the test.

TYPES OF RELIABILITY

Inter-rater (or inter-observer) reliability is an important consideration in the social sciences because there are many conditions for which the best means of measurement is the report of trained observers. Some classes such as gymnastics can only be assessed through the ratings of expert judges. As another example, external observers may be brought into a classroom to assess a student's inappropriate behavior. The observations of only one observer can be challenged from so many points of view. A lone observer may have some personal expectancies of what is supposed to occur. The lone observer may get tired and bored, so that earlier observations are more precise than later ones. It is less likely that the reports of two or more observers would be challenged. Particularly, the acceptability of the reports of two or more observers increases when their observations are similar. The measure of the similarities of the observations coming from two or more sources is the inter-rater reliability.

One method to establish inter-rater reliability is to calculate the proportion of agreement between or among the observers. This is appropriate if the ratings or observations are in mutually exclusive categories. The two observers recording the behavior of the student with the

inappropriate behavior would do well to have a common checklist of the likely behaviors. If they agree on the occurrence of 16 out of 20 behaviors, their inter-rater reliability would be 80 percent.

Another method is to calculate the correlation between the ratings of the two or more observers. This is possible if the ratings or observations are two or more sets of interval numbers. The gymnastic judges would have different ratings. Some may be consistently rating high while others consistently rating low. However, there should be some general agreement on the ranking of the different performers. The strength of this agreement would be reflected in the correlation of their ratings.

Inter-rater reliability is increased if the observers have appropriate training. The training should focus on what exactly is meant to be observed. The raters need to be given a clear description of the event to be observed. The classroom observers would need to know what is and is not appropriate behavior. The raters also need concrete examples of what constitutes an occurrence or what constitutes achievement at each criterion level. The gymnastic judges need to know the standards for each element of the gymnastic routine. Training is best when it includes much practice with feedback.

Test-retest reliability is appropriate for tests that measure a construct that is not likely to change. The construct that intelligence tests measure is not expected to change. Another well-known test with an expectedly unchanging construct is the Scholastic Aptitude Test (SAT). Although a test taker is allowed to take the SAT up to three times, the developers claim that the score on repeated administrations will not change. The construct that the SAT is measuring is the predicted adaptability to college. By the time students take the SAT, they are as prepared for college as they are going to be.

Test-retest reliability is described as the correlation between the distribution of scores on one administration and the distribution of scores on a subsequent administration. Test-retest reliability is also an important factor in some experimental designs in which the treatment group is administered a pretest and posttest with treatment in between and the control group only receives the pretest and the posttest. Any analysis of the difference noted in the results of the posttest (compared to the pretest) of the treatment group is confounded unless there is a strong reliability between the pretest and posttest of the control group.

Parallel-forms reliability evaluates the consistency of the results of two tests constructed in the same manner from the same content domain. For every item on the test, a similar item is developed with the same difficulty level. The items from each pair are then randomly assigned to one form of the test or the other. The resulting two tests are the same in content and difficulty but not expression. The reliability is described as the correlation of the two distributions of scores. This type of reliability is important in the development of standardized tests.

Split half reliability is similar to parallel forms except that the two forms are both incorporated into one test. After the test is administered, the scores are divided into the two forms and the correlation between the two distributions of scores is calculated. Like parallel forms it is important in the development of standardized tests. However, it could have classroom applications if the classroom teacher was willing to make the effort to develop a test with twice as many items as an ordinary test. In the classroom, split-half reliability could detect the effect of students' guessing on the test.

Inter-item reliability is another means of evaluating the reliability of one administration of one test. Most tests are made up of items that are related to one another because they are measuring similar concepts. Because the items are similar in design, there should be a measurable correlation between the items in any pair of items. The evaluation of inter-item reliability begins with predicting all correlations between all pairs of items. The inter-item reliability is expressed as the proportion of correct predictions. A classroom teacher might want to use inter-item reliability to identify the items that were not related to any other items or to identify the effects of students' guessing.

Cronbach's Alpha and the Kuder-Richardson methods are systems of reporting internal consistency of a test. The essential results of the internal consistency methods are comparable to the average of all correlations between all pairs of items. These methods can estimate reliability using the results of only one administration of the test. The main difference between the two approaches is how the items are scored. Cronbach's Alpha can be used on items with a range of responses such as a Likert scale. The Kuder-Richardson methods require that all items be scored dichotomously right or wrong (Borg and Gall, 1983).

PROCEDURES TO INCREASE RELIABILITY

The general goal to increase reliability of a measure is to increase the variance while reducing the variance error. Three recommended procedures to accomplish this are: 1) decrease the ambiguity of the test items; 2) increase the number of items per objective; and 3) provide clear test-taking instructions (Kerlinger, 1986).

If an item is ambiguous, it can be interpreted in more than one way. Two test takers of equal ability could conceivably interpret an ambiguous item two different ways, one getting it right and the other getting it wrong.

Their score would differ based on their interpretation of the item and not based on their differences in true ability.

Where there is error in a test item, it will have less effect if that item is one among many for the same objective than if that item is one among few. A test taker whose ability is mismeasured by a faulty item will need to balance the effect of that item with the effect of the items that are measuring more accurately.

Clear test-taking instructions help test takers to interpret the test items correctly and to indicate their chosen answers properly. Test instructions might remind the test takers of the types of items that require special attention. In addition, if there is a special procedure for answering such as using an answering sheet, test instructions can remind test takers how to respond correctly.

SEE ALSO *Standards for Educational and Psychological Testing; Validity.*

BIBLIOGRAPHY

Borg, W. R., Gall, M. D. (1983). *Educational research: An introduction* (4th ed.) White Plains, NY: Longman.

Kerlinger, F. N. (1986). *Foundations of behavioral research* (3rd ed.). Fort Worth, TX: Holt, Rinehart and Winston.

Shaughnessy, J. J., Zechmeister, E. B., & Zechmeister, J. S. (2006). *Research methods in psychology* (7th ed.). New York: McGraw-Hill.

Rudner, L. M., & Schafer, W. D. (2001). *Reliability: ERIC digest.* College Park MD: ERIC Clearinghouse on Assessment and Evaluation. ERIC Identifier: ED458213.

Ray Brogan

RESEARCH METHODS: AN OVERVIEW

There are many different methodologies that can be used to conduct educational research. The type of methodology selected by a researcher emanates directly from the research question that is being asked. In addition, some of the differing techniques for conducting educational research reflect different paradigms in scientific thought. In this entry, a review of the most commonly used methodologies is presented; in addition, the strengths and weaknesses of various methods are compared and contrasted.

OVERVIEW OF RESEARCH METHODS IN EDUCATION

Research methodologies can be classified in many different ways. For example, some researchers distinguish between quantitative and qualitative studies; others distinguish between experimental and non-experimental research; still others distinguish between research that is

Examples of strengths and weaknesses of various research methodologies

Methodology	Major strength	Major weakness
Correlational	Can be used to examine complex relations among many variables.	Can't draw conclusions about causality.
Experimental	Can draw conclusions about causality.	Often does not represent true learning environments in real classrooms.
Quasi-experimental	Can simulate an experiment in a true classroom setting.	More difficult to justify causal conclusions than in true experiments.
Qualitative	Can provide detailed, in-depth analyses of the contexts of learning environments.	Very time-consuming, both in terms of data collection and analysis.
Longitudinal	Can examine changes in variables over time.	Very costly, and subjects may drop out over the course of the study.
Cross-sectional	Efficient and rapid way to examine developmental differences.	Not nearly as accurate as longitudinal designs; cohorts may differ, and these differences may be mistaken for true developmental differences.
Design experiments	Occur in actual classrooms; experiments are constantly altered based on actual occurrences in the classrooms.	Very time-consuming; sometimes quite difficult to examine causality.
Microgenetic research	Allows for in-depth analyses of development in strategy usage over time.	Very time consuming; often uses very small samples.
Single-subjects	Provides detailed data about changes in a specific variable in one individual learner at a time; can be particularly useful in developing interventions for learners with special needs.	Difficult to generalize to larger populations.
Action research	Involves real classroom teachers investigating questions that are directly important to practicing educators.	Often does not meet the stringent criteria of other designs, and results may not be acceptable to the scientific community.

Table 1 ILLUSTRATION BY GGS INFORMATION SERVICES. CENGAGE LEARNING, GALE.

conducted in laboratories versus in the field (i.e., in classrooms). Obviously, there are many ways to categorize research methods. However, there also is much overlap in such categorizations. For example, a "non-experimental" study can be either quantitative or qualitative; an experimental study can include some qualitative components. This entry does not attempt to classify these methodologies; rather, the various methods are first briefly described and then compared and contrasted.

Correlational Research. *Correlational research* involves quantitatively studying the relations between and among variables. One of the hallmarks of correlational research is that cause and effect relations cannot be determined.

Researchers who engage in correlational research do not manipulate variables; rather, they collect data on existing variables and examine relations between those variables. A number of different statistical techniques can be used to analyze correlational data. An example of a correlational research would be an examination of the statistical relations between middle school students' standardized examination scores in mathematics, and the students' demographic characteristics (e.g., gender, ethnicity, socioeconomic status, etc.).

Experimental Research. In an experiment, participants are randomly assigned to one of several treatments. One

of the most basic experimental designs involves random assignment to either an experimental group (which receives some kind of treatment), or a control group (which does not receive the treatment). If the differences in treatment between the experimental and the control group are tightly controlled, and if subsequent to the experiment there are measurable differences between the two groups that were not present before the experiment, then researchers often conclude that the experimental manipulation "caused" the differences to occur.

Many researchers and government agencies consider true experiments to represent the gold standard in research; however, it is extraordinarily difficult to conduct true experiments in actual educational settings (i.e., schools). The primary reason for this difficulty is the fact that students can rarely be randomly assigned to conditions or classrooms in school settings. It is also important to distinguish between small-scale experiments and larger-scale clinical trials. Small-scale experiments can occur in settings such as laboratories or classrooms, whereas larger-scale clinical trials often occur across many classrooms or schools.

An example of an experiment would be a study examining the effects of a video presentation on learning multiplication skills. Students in a classroom where all students are learning about multiplication could be randomly assigned to either watch a video that demonstrates multiplication skills, or to watch another video (i.e., a video about how to make ice cream sundaes); the students would probably be asked to view the videos in a highly controlled environment, where the experimental and control conditions could be as similar as possible (except for the video presentation). If on a post-test the students who watched the multiplication video outperformed the other students, then a researcher could conclude that the video "caused" the improved performance.

Quasi-Experimental Research. In quasi-experimental studies, researchers do not randomly assign participants to groups (Cook & Campbell, 1979). Quasi-experimentation is used often in educational research, because it is often impossible and sometimes unethical to randomly assign students to settings.

In quasi-experimental studies, researchers attempt to control for differences between non-randomly assigned groups in a number of ways. Two of the most common methods include (a) matching, and (b) statistical control. The following example explains the concept. A researcher is interested in comparing the effects of a traditional third-grade reading curriculum with the effects of an enhanced version of the curriculum that includes extra homework assignments. If the two versions of the curricula are being administered in different classrooms, the researcher can try to "match" similar classrooms on certain variables. For example, the researcher might decide to match classrooms on years of experience of the teacher, wherein teachers with much experience (e.g., 20 or more years of teaching experience) might be paired, so that for each pair of highly experienced teachers, one is assigned to each condition.

In addition, the researcher can statistically control for variables that are related to the outcome. If the researcher knows that variables such as socioeconomic status and prior reading ability are related to reading achievement, then the researcher can statistically control for these variables, in order to better assess the unique effects of the new curriculum.

Qualitative Research. Qualitative research represents a broad framework for conducting educational studies. Whereas *quantitative* research focuses on measurable variations between and among variables, *qualitative* studies focus on holistic descriptions of learners and teachers in naturalistic settings.

Fraenkel and Wallen (1996) describe five general characteristics of qualitative research studies. These include:

1. Researchers collect their data in naturalistic settings (e.g., classrooms), by observing and participating in regular activities.

2. Data are collected via words or pictures (not via numerical or quantifiable indicators).

3. Processes (i.e., how individuals communicate with each other about a lesson) are as important as products (i.e., whether or not students obtain the correct answers to a problem).

4. Most qualitative researchers do not start out with specific hypotheses; rather, they use inductive methods to generate conclusions regarding their observations.

5. Qualitative researchers care about participants' perceptions; investigators are likely to question participants in depth about their beliefs, attitudes, and thought processes.

A variety of methods can be used to conduct qualitative studies. For example, qualitative researchers can collect their data from direct observations, from analyses of video or audio recordings, from interviews, or from long-term ethnographic studies.

There are a variety of different ways of analyzing qualitative data. Generally, researchers carefully examine their data and discover themes that emerge from the data. Sometimes several researchers will analyze the same sources of data and then compare their conclusions and examine the extent to which they agree or disagree (inter-rater reliability); in other studies, one researcher will conduct all of the analyses, and will also critically examine how his or her own biases may affect interpretations. Software packages have been developed to assist qualitative researchers with data analysis. Two of the most commonly used packages are Envivo and NUDIST.

Longitudinal and Cross-sectional Research. Many research studies in education focus on developmental issues (i.e., how individuals change over time). For example, it is known that the reading strategies that young children use are different from the reading strategies adopted by older children (Pressley & Harris, 2006). There are several different methods that can be used to examine such developmental phenomena.

In a *longitudinal* study, researchers collect data on the same individuals over a number of different time periods or "waves." Thus the same group of students might complete study assessments at the end of first grade, second grade, third grade, and fourth grade. Researchers can then examine changes in student data across those four years.

In a *cross-sectional* study, researchers collect data on individuals of differing ages or developmental levels, at the same time. Thus data are collected for many students, at one time interval only. For example, a researcher might give assessments to 200 first graders, 200 second graders,

748

200 third graders, and 200 fourth graders all at the same time. Then the researcher can compare the results of students in these four different grades and try to draw some conclusions about developmental differences.

Most researchers agree that when possible, longitudinal studies provide better developmental data than cross-sectional studies. The primary advantage of longitudinal studies is that the same individuals are assessed at different time points; therefore, it is easier to make inferences about true development over time, since the distinct data points represent the same individuals across different time periods. However, longitudinal research is often difficult to conduct, because it is very expensive, and it is often difficult to track individuals over time; many of the students who participate in the first wave of data collection may have moved or may not want to participate in later waves of the study.

Design Experiments. When researchers conduct design experiments, they examine the effects of educational interventions in actual classrooms while the interventions are being implemented. As results are obtained and analyzed, the intervention is changed and continuously re-evaluated (Brown, 1992).

Cobb, Confrey, diSessa, Lehrer, and Schauble (2003) identified five overarching features of design experiments:

1. The purpose of design experiments is to develop theories about learning (including how learning is supported).

2. Design experiments involve an intervention, or the introduction of a new instructional technique.

3. In design experiments, researchers attempt to develop new theoretical perspectives, but also must test and refine their theories along the way.

4. Design experiments have iterative designs; as theories change during the study, the design of the study must be revised and altered accordingly.

5. The theories that are developed in design experiments should affect future instruction.

An example of a design experiment might be a study of a new curriculum designed to teach adolescents about HIV and pregnancy prevention. The curriculum might be introduced into the classroom setting; then, after initial presentation of the first few units, the researchers might collect data and then make some alterations to the next units, based on those data. This process can continue until the curriculum is substantially improved.

It is important to note that in design experiments, the changes in instruction that occur across iterations are often confounded with greater teacher familiarity with the

approach as a whole. This can be problematic, because it hinders researchers' abilities to make causal inferences.

Microgenetic Research. In microgenetic research studies, the same individual is observed intensively over a long period of time; this could be for many weeks or even months. Data are collected in order to examine both large-scale and small-scale changes in learners' use of strategies over time (Kuhn, 1995). Data can be analyzed via either quantitative or qualitative methods, depending on the types of data that are collected.

As noted by Chinn (2006), most educational research using a microgenetic approach has examined learners' usage of cognitive strategies (e.g., problem solving). Microgenetic studies are time consuming and be expensive, but they also can provide researchers with rich and detailed information concerning cognitive processes in learners. An example of a microgenetic study would be an examination of a kindergartner's strategy usage in solving simple addition problems over a three-month period.

Single-Subject Research. In a single-subject study, there is only one participant. Researchers generally examine a variable at a baseline stage (prior to the start of an intervention), and then later examine how this variable changes at different time intervals, as an intervention is introduced. In single-subject research, control or comparison groups are not used. Researchers are particularly interested in whether or not patterns replicate over time within the same subject; in addition, researchers also examine whether or not similar patterns can be generated in new subjects.

Single-subject studies are particularly common in the special education literature, although this methodology can be used in other areas of educational research as well. An example of a single-subject study would be an examination of the effect of classical music on the ability of a learning-disabled child to solve single-digit addition problems. First, the child's baseline addition skills would be assessed; then, the student's skills in the presence of music would be measured. The music might then be alternately started and stopped several times, while the student's problem-solving skills are continuously assessed.

Action Research. Action research is research that is conducted by classroom teachers, examining their own practices. The goal of action research is to examine one's practices critically and then to make changes to those practices based on the results of the research. Action research can be conducted by a single teacher, or by a group of educators working together.

Ferrance (2000) summarizes five steps in action research. These include:

1. Identify the problem or question that is going to be investigated.

2. Gather data to help answer the driving question. Data can be collected in many forms (e.g., interviews with students, surveys, journals, video or audio tapes, samples of student work, etc.).

3. Interpret the data by critically examining all data sources, and identifying major themes.

4. Evaluate results; in particular, examine whether or not the research question has been answered.

5. Take next steps—develop additional research questions, or make changes to instructional methods.

Action research can improve instruction for students; in addition, it can empower teachers, since it is a tool that allows them to judge their own efforts and evaluate the outcomes of their practices.

STRENGTHS AND WEAKNESSES OF RESEARCH DESIGNS

Each of the aforementioned research designs has both strengths and weaknesses. Some of these differences are obvious but others are not. Table 1 presents some examples of the key strengths and weaknesses of the various research methodologies discussed in this entry. This is not an exhaustive list; rather, it is provided to demonstrate that each methodology is complex and has both pros and cons.

When researchers and consumers of research evaluate the strengths and weaknesses of various designs, there are many issues to consider. Specifically, there are several key questions that can serve as a framework for evaluating research designs. The main questions are discussed below.

The Research Question. The research question is by far the most important question to consider when selecting and evaluating a research design. In all educational studies, the major research question should be articulated before the methodology is selected; the appropriate methodology should then be chosen based on that question. Most social scientists agree that a preferred methodology should not be used as a framework to guide research.

For example, a large school district might want to know if high school students' foreign language pronunciation is better after two years of studying Spanish or two years of studying French. The research question might be: What is the relation between studying French versus studying Spanish, and foreign language pronunciation after two years of study?

The researcher then must decide which research design is the most appropriate to answer the specific research question. In this example, the researcher can easily eliminate several options. For example, an experiment would be

impossible, since students cannot be randomly assigned to Spanish or French classes. In addition, the researcher might decide that qualitative and microgenetic studies are inappropriate, since the researcher is not interested in the processes or developmental trends that occur over time. There are several other questions that the researcher must also address that will help to finalize the decision.

The Sample Being Studied. Researchers must consider the nature of their samples when selecting a methodology. This is an important question because some methodologies are challenging to implement with certain populations.

For example, most studies that use survey-based methodologies require the participants to be able to read the survey items. If the sample included young children, or individuals with impaired visual abilities, then this might preclude the use of a self-administered survey. In addition, if the researcher is studying a large sample, with more than 1000 participants, in many cases this would prohibit the investigator from implementing single-subject designs, since the sample is so large.

Resources Available to Do the Research. Many resources are needed to complete research studies. Novice researchers often do not realize the cost involved with educational studies. A college student doing a small study for a research methods course will certainly not have the same resources available as an experienced investigator with a multimillion dollar grant.

Resources involve more than money. Another important consideration is personnel. Some research methodologies require more personnel than others. For example, a microgenetic study might be carried out by one investigator who can focus on the progress of a few subjects. In contrast, a large experimental study that requires collection of large amounts of data from many participants will require many more personnel. Thus if fewer resources are available, a researcher might not be able to use the ideal methodology to conduct a study.

Time is another important resource that often affects the type of methodology that is chosen for a particular study. A design experiment that involves continuous evaluation of progress and setting of goals might be ideal if a researcher has enough time to devote to a long-term study. Some studies (e.g., longitudinal studies) take a long time to complete. Thus a researcher who is interested in examining developmental issues, but who does not have a lot of time and funding, might select a cross-sectional methodology instead.

The Intended Audience for the Research. Different audiences will benefit from different kinds of research studies. If the audience is practitioners, then action research might be highly appropriate. First, teachers can be directly involved in action research studies; second, other educators might be more willing to accept the results obtained from one of their peers via action research than from unknown researchers.

Certain funding agencies might be interested in only funding some types of studies. For example, there is much debate among educational researchers about the advantages and disadvantages of using experimental designs in educational research; whereas many funding agencies encourage experimental studies, many educational researchers argue that sometimes, true experiments are difficult to implement in actual classroom settings.

Using Mixed Methods. Many educational issues are multifaceted and complex; consequently, often one single methodology will not yield all of the essential information that researchers desire. Given the strengths and weaknesses of the various designs, and the many decisions that researchers must make before choosing a methodology, a number of scholars in recent years have begun to use mixed methods in educational research. When researcher use mixed methods, they use a variety of different methodologies within the same study.

A mixed methods study is usually challenging; the researchers must be able to utilize multiple designs appropriately. Some mixed methods studies involve two or more methodologies being carried out simultaneously, whereas others involve a succession of different studies, all designed to answer one general research question.

An example is a study conducted by Turner and her colleagues (Turner et al., 2002). In that study, the researchers were interested in examining the relations between early adolescents' perceptions of the classroom environment and the students' use of avoidance strategies (e.g., avoidance of asking for help from the teacher) in math classrooms. The researchers realized that the use of multiple methods would help them to best answer their research question. Therefore, they conducted a study in which longitudinal survey data were collected from a sample of more than 1,000 students. The researchers also randomly selected nine classrooms in which they conducted observations. The final analysis of data included quantitative results from the surveys as well as qualitative results from detailed discourse analyses from the classrooms. Each source of data provided different types of information, which allowed the researchers to examine a variety of indicators of the use of avoidance strategies by students. The quantitative survey data allowed the researchers to examine the relations of both student characteristics (e.g., gender) and students' perceptions of classroom environments to the use of avoidance strategies; the observational data allowed the researchers to

examine the discourse patterns in classrooms with different types of learning environments.

In summary, research methodology is a complex topic. This entry has described some of the most basic issues in the research enterprise, some of the methods that educational researchers use in their work, and some of the complexities involved in deciding upon an appropriate methodology. Ultimately, the methodology that is chosen will be determined by the specific research question and by the resources that are available.

Most research studies have limitations, which often are related to the design of the study. Research can always be improved, and it is important for scholars engaged in educational research critically to evaluate their designs and to acknowledge the limitations of their studies. As new researchers replicate previous studies, they often will attempt to eliminate the design problems encountered by previous researchers. This is one of the most important ways in which educational researchers can continue to improve and enhance knowledge about teaching and learning.

BIBLIOGRAPHY

Brown, A. L. (1992). Design experiments: Theoretical and methodological challenges in creating complex interventions. *Journal of the Learning Sciences, 2*, 141–178.

Chinn, C. (2006). The microgenetic method: Current work and extensions to classroom research. In J. L. Green, G. Cmailli, & P.B. Elmore (Eds.), *Handbook of complementary methods in education research* (pp. 439–456). Mahwah, NJ: Erlbaum.

Cobb, P., Confrey, J., diSessa, A., Lehrer, R., & Schauble, L. (2003). Design experiments in educational research. *Educational Researcher, 32*, 9–13.

Cook, T. D., & Campbell, D. T. (1979). *Quasi-experimentation: Design and analysis issues for field settings.* Boston: Houghton Mifflin.

Ferrance, E. (2000). *Action research.* Providence, RI: Northeast and Islands Regional Educational Laboratory at Brown University.

Fraenkel, J.R., & Wallen, N.E. (1996). *How to design and evaluate research in education* (3rd ed.). New York: McGraw-Hill.

Kuhn, D. (1995). Microgenetic study of change: What has it told us? *Psychological Science, 6*, 133–139.

Pressley, M., & Harris, J.R. (2006). Cognitive strategies instruction: From basic research to classroom instruction. In P. A. Alexander & P. H. Winne (Eds.), *Handbook of educational psychology* (2nd ed., pp. 265–286). Mahwah, NJ: Erlbaum.

Turner, J. C., Midgley, C., Meyer, D. K., Gheen, M., Anderman, E. M., Kang, Y., & Patrick, H. (2002). The classroom environment and students' reports of avoidance strategies in mathematics: A multimethod study. *Journal of Educational Psychology, 94*, 88–106.

Eric M. Anderman

RESISTANCE THEORY

School classrooms involve complex human and environmental interactions. The classroom-based cultural landscapes hold unique teacher-student and student-student interrelationships that can mirror socioeconomic experiences of the larger community. In all these relationships, human agency permeates teachers' and students' interactions. Students' interpretation of and their responses to classroom culture can have profound effects on their achievement. Belonging, cultural relatedness, and autonomy are some of many issues that play key roles in determining students' motivation to approach or resist participation in learning activities. Resistance theories, in particular, provide a unique description of the classroom culture by examining how students or teachers perceive and respond to cultural dominance. Generally, resistance involves actions that passively or actively oppose the dominant culture. These actions serve to preserve students' or teachers' (as the case may be) sense of autonomy and identity.

CULTURAL OPPOSITIONAL THEORY

John Ogbu and Signithia Fordham (Fordham, 1996; Fordham & Ogbu, 1986; Ogbu, 1991; Ogbu, 2003) propose a resistance theory that explores minority students' reactions to cultural dominance. Originating with John Ogbu, this theory explores how different ethnic groups respond to different cultural landscapes. Ogbu suggests that ethnic-minority groups in the United States fall into one of two categories: voluntary minorities or involuntary minorities. These categories matter in the interpretation of mainstream cultures. Voluntary minorities are those who came or whose ancestors came to the United States out of their own free will (e.g., Vietnamese, Irish). Involuntary minorities are those whose ancestors were brought to the United States by force (e.g., African Americans) or whose ancestors were forced into ethnic minority status by military force (e.g., Native Americans).

Ogbu posits that voluntary minorities hold positive beliefs about the dominant society and, as a result, are more likely to adopt the attitudes and practices of the dominant group. In contrast, involuntary minorities hold less positive beliefs about the dominant society. These groups, such as the African Americans and Native Americans, see the United States as taking away or compromising their civil liberties. Ogbu suggests that, for many involuntary minorities, adopting dominant attitudes or behaviors is perceived as supporting their oppression. These beliefs for involuntary minorities have been substantially investigated by Ogbu and Fordham (Fordham, 1996; Fordham & Ogbu, 1986; Ogbu, 1991; Ogbu, 2003). In school context, Ogbu's 1991 findings suggest that voluntary minorities have more positive attitudes toward schooling, teachers, and the curriculum. Whereas

Southeast Asian and Chinese students accepted greater responsibility for academic underachievement, involuntary minorities avoided responsibility and asserted blame on teachers and school administrators.

In addition to attitudes, Ogbu and Fordham argue that perspectives of involuntary minorities manifest themselves in "oppositional behavior." That is, involuntary minorities react according to their beliefs about the dominant culture by engaging in behaviors that is in opposition to it. To support this notion, Ogbu (2003) reports that, in school contexts, involuntary minorities are more likely to disengage in academic activities than voluntary minorities. Ogbu called such behavior the "norm of minimal effort." Ogbu also found that these behavioral norms to disengage from academic activities were reinforced by African Americans who label other African American students who pursue academic achievement as "acting white." Such labels reinforce the notion that participating in dominant institutions by involuntary minorities contributes to the power of the dominant culture. In other words, if one succumbs to participating in the institutions of the dominant culture, then one becomes a member of that culture.

Furthermore, it is common to hear the expression, "talking white," a similar label to "acting white," applied to African Americans who use standard English. Limiting standard English in school is an important oppositional behavior that resists the dominant school culture. Similarly, a study by Bryan Brown (2003) explored how minority students in a science class avoided using scientific terms during classroom discourse, thus continuing to oppose the standard curriculum and pedagogy. These oppositional behaviors can have significant negative results on students' achievement. Ogbu (2003) observed an interesting phenomenon among students who resisted succumbing to the dominant academic culture: These students, while believing that education can lead them to economic stability, also held beliefs that athletics and entertainment could also serve as pathways to similar, if not better economic outcome.

Finn (1999), while using Ogbu's notions to describe reasons for students' resistance, brings together research of other scholars to expand sociological reasons for students' resistance beyond resistance of involuntary minority communities. Finn synthesizes a body of research on resistance of students from working-class families (Anyon, 1981; Weis, 1990; Willis, 1977) to suggest that the mismatch between working-class students' goals and their teachers' goals creates a social environment that is reminiscent of the relationship between management and workers within a factory. Within such a relationship, the management's goals have to do with meeting production quotas whereas the workers' goals have to do with managing and lowering the amount of work that is required while maintaining salaries that can support their families. Finn reports that in such work environments, workers often develop systems that slow down the productivity. Likewise, Finn makes the connection to working-class students who challenge their teachers, sometimes subversively, by developing mechanisms to lower the amount of required work. An example of such a mechanism is students' asking a series of relevant and irrelevant questions to waste class time.

Finn, then, makes an explicit connection between Ogbu's work on resistance of involuntary minorities and that of scholars who describe resistance of working-class students by describing the relationship between unions and management. Union members who are seen as not cooperating with the union and collaborating with management are often harassed by other union members. For example, workers who beat their quota are often called derogatory names, reminiscent of the "acting white" term that is described by Ogbu. Likewise, working-class students who are seen to increase the amount of work in the classroom are also alienated by their classmates. Such oppositional social structures are natural spawning grounds for oppositional identities that enable resistance to school work.

CRITIQUE OF OPPOSITIONAL THEORY

While Ogbu's notions are well known in the education research community, his ideas are not without critics. The first set of criticism comes from Solorzano and Dolores Delgado-Bernal (2001), who challenge Ogbu's theory by suggesting that Ogbu focuses on "self-defeating" resistance. They, instead, posit that resistance can also have transformative effects. In their reconceptualization of Ogbu's work, they argue that there are four main types of students' resistance. The first type of resistance focuses on opposition with no orientation or awareness of social justice or the dominant culture. During such resistance, students exhibit poor classroom behavior for the sake of disrupting classroom instructional activities. Another type of resistance is self-defeating resistance. As a part of this type of resistance, students engage in oppositional behaviors with no real goal for bringing about social justice, although they may have some notion about societal inequities. This is most similar to Ogbu's notions of oppositional behavior. The third type of resistance is labeled as the conformist resistance. These students are very much aware of social injustice but do not respond to these beliefs by their actions. These students adopt dominant behaviors, in spite of their knowledge about society and school contexts. Finally, Solorzano and Delgado-Bernal describe the final type of resistance, transformative resistance. These students see the world as unjust and engage in oppositional behavior to bring out social

justice. These behaviors may include students' working harder to disprove negative expectations about their academic abilities or to challenge poor and racist classroom curricula or pedagogy.

Interestingly, in addition to describing development of oppositional identities of working-class students, Finn (1999) also identifies transformative people who have the power to create educational environments. While he describes resistance from the perspective of differentiated goals for education between students and teachers, he also describes societal leaders as having the option to be transformative. Finn does not believe that education in which students unconditionally do the work that teachers assign is "powerful." He believes that students must participate in their own education and that educators should establish educational environments in which students have access to empower themselves. To this end, Finn draws on the work of Aronowitz and Giroux (1993) to describe three types of educators: hegemonic, critical, and transformative. Hegemonic educators work to maintain the status quo by recreating an educational environment that, in its own right, recreates the social classes of students. In such classrooms, working-class students attempt to lower their workload while middle-class students do all their assigned work and learn how to glean information from textbooks. Critical educators believe themselves to be free of bias and think that they provide the same education to all students, regardless of students' backgrounds, including ethnicity and socio-economic class. Nonetheless, critical educators maintain the status quo by not actively challenging it by empowering students to take control of their education. Transformative educators help their students actively resist societal hegemony and take the power of education into their control. This, of course, fits directly into Solorzano and Delgado-Bernal's 2001 notion of transformative resistance.

Research on resilience highlights this notion of transformative resistance. Researchers such as Hassinger and Plourde (2005) suggest that students adopt adaptive behaviors to disprove prevailing expectations or stereotypes. Solorzano and Delgado-Bernal (2001) describe how students engaged in resistance behavior in order to announce their opposition to California state policy limiting bilingual education. Their resistance was aimed at promoting, in their mind, social justice.

The work of Horvat and Lewis (2003) counters Ogbu's notions about the significance of the "acting white" label by suggesting two counter examples. First, they review literature that suggests that the behaviors associated with negatively labeling students who participate in academic pursuits reflect students' in-group/outgroup school hierarchies that are typical of teen-agers, regardless of ethnicity, similar to the description above of working-class students resisting schoolwork. Second, Horvat and Lewis describe their own research in which they found that "acting white" was not a dominant force in African American female students' academic decisions. They report that African American females who participated in their research navigated among diverse set of African American peers from various socioeconomic strata of society. This challenge to Fordham and Ogbu's notions does not negate the phenomena of resistance, but it certainly complicates the occurrence of resistance among involuntary minorities.

IMPLICATIONS FOR CLASSROOMS AND TEACHERS

Research on resistance theory highlights the need for some students to actively engage in oppositional behaviors. This is a choice that they make and this choice may be based on awareness of the dominant culture and social injustice. The reasons for students' resistance may be difficult for teachers to assess. Oppositional behaviors may be the result of peer cultural norms (Horvat & Lewis, 2003), disparate goals of students and teachers (Finn, 1999), or awareness of social injustice (Solorzano & Delgado-Bernal, 2001). In light of the latter two reasons, the teacher needs to facilitate students' autonomy by allowing students to critique the curriculum and classroom pedagogy. Some researchers suggest that autonomy-supportive behaviors, such as permitting students' opportunities to voice opinions and oppositions to classroom activities, promote engagement in and positive attitudes about the classroom (Assor et al., 2002).

Students who engage in oppositional behavior as a result of cultural norms, however, require a different set of responses from teachers. One solution comes from Freire's 1993 notions regarding the pedagogy of the oppressed. While some students may resist standard curriculum as a tool designed to oppress them, teachers can use strategies that raise students' awareness about societal inequities and provide tools by which students may combat social injustice.

Another task for teachers is to carefully examine what activities, behaviors, and artifacts are valued by the class culture and school administration. Oakes and Lipton (2003) suggests that some schools and teachers show what is important in schools by way of rewarding key behaviors or attitudes. For example, schools show that they value high grades by posting names of students with excellent academic achievement. For many schools, these students may be racially identifiable. Other talents or abilities that reflect more student diversity may not be highly valued by a school. Teachers and school communities should take a critical examination of what gets praised and rewarded, determine whether these values

favor one ethnicity over another, and search for activities that value and convey social justice.

Finally, Gloria Ladson Billings (1997; 1998; 2000) and Geneava Gay (2002; 2004; 2005) write extensively about teachers' making their curriculum culturally relevant. They suggest that classrooms should be spaces in which students find a sense of belonging, in which students believe that their teachers understand them, and in which instructional activities reflect students' experiences by building on their prior knowledge. In these classrooms, students should work with and not in opposition to the teachers because their experiences are a part of the classroom culture; there is a symbiotic relationship that supports and promotes positive learning experiences for students as well as teachers.

BIBLIOGRAPHY

Anyon, J. (1980). Social class and the hidden curriculum of work. *Journal of Education, 162,* 67–92.

Anyon, J. (1981). Social class and school knowledge. *Curriculum Inquiry, 11,* 3–42.

Aronowitz, S., & Giroux, H. (1993). *Education still under siege.* Westport, CT: Bergin and Harvey.

Assor, A., Kaplan, H., & Roth, G. (2002). Choice is good, but relevance is excellent: Autonomy-enhancing and suppressing teacher behaviours predicting students' engagement in schoolwork. *British Journal of Educational Psychology, 72*(2), 261–278.

Brown, B. (2003). Discursive identity: Assimilation into the culture of science and its implications for minority students. *Journal of Research in Science Teaching, 41*(8), 810–834.

Finn, P. J. (1999). *Literacy with an attitude: Educating working-class children in their own self-interest.* Albany: State University of New York Press.

Fordham, S. (1996). *Blacked out: Dilemmas of race, identity, and success at capital high.* Chicago: University of Chicago Press.

Fordham, S., & Ogbu, J. U. (1986). Black students' school success: Coping with the burden of "acting white." *Urban Review, 18,* 176–206.

Freire, P. (1993). *Pedagogy of the oppressed* (Rev. ed.). New York: Continuum.

Gay, G. (2002). Preparing for culturally responsive teaching. *Journal of Teacher Education, 53*(2), 106–116.

Gay, G. (2004). The importance of multicultural education. *Educational Leadership, 61*(4), 30–35.

Gay, G. (2005). Politics of multicultural teacher education. *Journal of Teacher Education, 56*(3), 221–228.

Hassinger, M., & Plourde, L. A. (2005). "Beating the odds": How bi-lingual Hispanic youth work through adversity to become high achieving students. *Education, 126*(2), 316–327.

Horvat, E. M., & Lewis, K. S. (2003). Reassessing the "burden of 'acting white'": The importance of peer groups in managing academic success. *Sociology of Education, 76*(4), 265–280.

Ladson-Billings, G. (1997). It doesn't add up: African American students' mathematics achievement. *Journal for Research in Mathematics Education, 28,* 697–708.

Ladson-Billings, G. (1998). Teaching in dangerous times: Culturally relevant approaches to teacher assessment. *Journal of Negro Education, 67*(3), 255–267.

Ladson-Billings, G. (2000). Fighting for our lives: Preparing teachers to teach African American students. *Journal of Teacher Education, 51*(3), 206–214.

Oakes, J., & Lipton, M. (2003). *Teaching to change the world* (2nd ed.). New York: McGraw-Hill.

Ogbu, J. U. (1991). Cultural diversity and school experience. In C. E. Walsh (Ed.), *Literacy as praxis: Culture, language, and pedagogy* (pp. 25–50). Norwood, NJ: Ablex.

Ogbu, J. U. (2003). Black American students in an affluent suburb: A study of academic disengagement. Mahwah, NJ: Erlbaum.

Solorzano, D. G., & Delgado-Bernal, D. (2001). Examining transformational resistance through a critical race and LatCrit theory framework: Chicana and Chicano students in an urban context. *Urban Education, 36*(3), 308–342.

Weis, L. (1990). *Working class without work: High school students in a de-industrializing economy.* New York: Routledge.

Willis, P. E. (1977). *Learning to labor: How working class kids get working class jobs.* Westmead, UK: Saxon House.

Estella W. Chizhik
Alexander W. Chizhik

REWARDS

Every teacher in every classroom throughout the United States uses strategies to acknowledge and encourage appropriate social and academic behavior by their students. These strategies take many forms, some overt and dramatic (presentation of tokens or recognition at an assembly), others more subtle and embedded in natural activities (a smile, the organization of a successful academic effort). This process of encouraging appropriate behavior and how best to incorporate this process in education has been a major focus of both research and professional controversy. As a result, understanding the role and function of rewards is in the early 2000s a central concern for many educators.

Since 1898, when E. L. Thorndike (1874–1949) described the law of effect, educators and psychologists have noted that when a behavior is successful it is more likely to occur again in similar circumstances. The success of a behavior lies in the result, effect, or consequence that behavior has on the environment. The simple message is that the consequences of a behavior affect future performance of that behavior. If, following the contingent delivery of a consequence, a behavior becomes more likely in the future, then that consequence was reinforcing or rewarding. This basic idea has been among the most intensely studied and validated phenomena associated with human behavior. The use of rewards in education remains a controversy, not over the principles governing its function, but in part due to two issues: (a)

the precise definition of rewards, and (b) the perceived effect of rewards on intrinsic motivation.

DEFINING REWARDS

Rewards (or the more technical term, reinforcers) are defined as any contingently delivered consequence (e.g., event, activity, object) associated with an increase in the future likelihood of a behavior in similar situations. This definition presents many problems when used in natural contexts such as homes, schools, and communities. When applied in a rigorous and precise manner, the definition allows an object or event to be classified as a reward, or reinforcer, only after demonstration that (a) the object/event was delivered contingent upon the performance of a behavior, and (b) the behavior became more likely to occur under similar conditions in the future. In practice, teachers and parents seldom wait to see the effect of a consequence on future occurrences of the behavior. It is far more likely that a teacher will simply presume that she or he has provided rewards when praise is delivered following sharing or points are assigned for correct problem completion, or access to preferred toys follows work completion.

An important distinction here is that the technical definition of a reward (reinforcer) always adopts the perspective of the learner, not the intentions of the person delivering the reward. If the contingent delivery of a consequence resulted in increased likelihood of that behavior, then the consequence was a reward. If the consequence was a piece of preferred fruit, and the behavior increased, then the fruit was a reward; if the consequence was a sticker, and the behavior increased, then the sticker was a reward; if the consequence was a reprimand (which included adult attention), and the behavior increased, then the reprimand was a reward. It is the effect of the consequence on future behavior that determines if that consequence is a reward (reinforcer).

If a consequence does not lead to increased likelihood of the behavior, then it was not a reward, even if the person delivering the consequence had the best of intensions. If a teacher's praise for on-task working is followed by a reduction in level of being on-task, then the teacher's praise was not a functional reward (reinforcer). If the delivery of tokens for sharing on the playground does not lead to increased sharing, then the tokens were not a reward. From a technical perspective, rewards are defined by the effect they have on behavior, not on their intended desirability. In this way, an event, activity, or object can never be defined as a reward without connecting it to the behavior that was affected by contingent access to that event, activity, or object. Practically, teachers will deliver feedback and consequences that they presume are rewards. Those teachers with technical knowledge, however, will always check the effect of that presumed reward on student behavior.

Understanding rewards is of special importance because teachers not only want desirable behavior to be rewarded, but they also want to avoid rewarding undesirable behavior. A reprimand, for example, may not have been intended to be a reward, but may still function in that capacity. One of the more common findings in schools is that teachers inadvertently reward inappropriate child behavior by attending to talking out or disruptive acts. Similarly being sent to the office may be rewarding to some students if it involves escaping from aversive or difficult work. If a behavior is contingently followed by (a) obtaining a desirable event/activity/object or (b) avoiding an aversive event/activity/object, then the behavior will become more likely to occur in similar situations in the future. Said differently, the behavior has been rewarded.

Rewards are important for both encouraging appropriate behavior and preventing the encouragement of inappropriate behavior. What the science of human behavior teaches, is that teachers should adopt the perspective of the learner when they plan how to select and deliver rewards. The following are some basic guidelines:

Reward behavior not people. When rewards are provided be clear about the specific behavior that led to the reward.

Include the learner in identification of possible rewards. Use consequences that are likely to be rewarding to the students.

Use small rewards frequently, rather than large rewards infrequently.

Embed rewards in the activity/behavior that is to be encouraged.

Ensure that rewards closely follow the behavior that is to be encouraged.

Try to reward quickly because doing so tends to be more effective that delaying the reward.

Use rewards that are natural to the context, appropriate to the developmental age of the learner, and easy to administer.

Use many different kinds of rewards (objects, activities, privileges, attention, natural consequences) rather than relying on one strategy or pattern.

Use rewards more often than negative consequences. Students should experience at least five times the number of rewards as they do corrections or punishers.

Avoid delivering rewards (even inadvertently) for problem behaviors.

THE IMPACT OF REWARDS ON INTRINSIC MOTIVATION

Some people wonder if the formal use of rewards in schools may result in children failing to develop intrinsic, or self-managed, motivation. Reading should be a behavior that becomes more frequent because the content of what is read is rewarding, not because a token or play period will follow reading. Sharing on the playground should occur because a child experiences personal satisfaction from behaving well, not because the child receives candy if she shares. Similarly, some people wonder if a teacher provides a reward to Child A for excellent math work, it will be a negative, or punishing, experience for Child B who did not receive a reward, tried just as hard, but did not get as many problems correct. These concerns were substantiated in research conducted in the 1970s (Deci, 1971; 1975; Lepper, Greene & Nisbett, 1973) and have led to strong recommendations against the formal use of praise and extrinsic rewards (e.g., tokens, food, activities, privileges) in schools (Deci, Koestner, & Ryan, 2001; Kohn, 1993; 1996). There is evidence that rewards can be used poorly. The primary errors involve (a) providing rewards without being clear about the behavior being rewarded, (b) inadvertently providing rewards for problem behavior, (c) providing large rewards and then suddenly (rather than gradually) withdrawing the rewards, and (d) providing rewards so infrequently that a child never builds the skill fluency needed to attain the natural benefit of a skill (e.g., does not learn to read fast enough or well enough to enjoy reading). These errors are worth considering and avoiding.

The concern that rewards damage the intrinsic motivation of students is less well supported by research. Most educators will agree that academic and social skills learned in schools should be maintained by natural consequence, not artificial rewards. Reading, math and play skills should not end when a teacher is no longer present to offer verbal praise, toys, or stickers. The rewards provided for the behavior of one student should not function as a punisher for all others. There is less agreement (and much less evidence) that the use of rewards in schools leads to these ill effects.

To address these concerns several scholars examined the full body of research literature and concluded that have schools successfully employed the use of external rewards for decades (Slavin, 1997) and the use of rewards following appropriate behavior is directly related to both initial and durable academic and social success. Rewards are an effective, important, and functional part of any educational context and need not be detrimental to intrinsic motivation (Akin-Little, Eckert, Lovett, & Little, 2004; Cameron, Banko, & Pierce, 2001). Rewards are especially important for helping motivate a child to build early competence (fluency) with reading, math, or social skills. Encouragement, guidance, and reward of appropriate approximations of successful behavior are helpful for students in building the skills that can then be sustained by the natural consequences from reading well, joining games with peers, or playing a musical instrument. Rewards also are important for building a predictable, positive social culture in a school. Schools with clearly defined behavioral expectations and formal strategies for acknowledging (rewarding) appropriate behavior are perceived as safer, more effective learning environments. The delivery of rewards is one overt way in which children learn that adults are serious about the social and academic goals they are teaching.

Understanding and using rewards is an essential skill for any educator. Selecting the right type, level, and form of rewards to encourage student behavior is a competence developed over time and is a hallmark of effective teaching.

SEE ALSO *Feedback in Learning.*

BIBLIOGRAPHY

Akin-Little, K., Eckert, T., Lovett, B., & Little, S. (2004). Extrinsic reinforcement in the classroom: Bribery or best practice. *School Psychology Review, 33,* 344–362.

Cameron, J., Banko, K., & Pierce, W. (2001). Pervasive negative effects of rewards on intrinsic motivation: The myth continues. *Behavior Analyst, 24,* 1–44.

Deci, E. (1971). Effects of externally mediated rewards on intrinsic motivation. *Journal of Personality and Social Psychology, 18,* 105–115.

Deci, E., (1975). *Intrinsic Motivation.* New York: Plenum Press.

Deci, E., Koestner, R., & Ryan R. (2001). Extrinsic rewards and intrinsic motivation in education: Reconsidered once again. *Review of Educational Research, 71,* 1–27.

Kohn, A. (1993). *Punished by rewards: The trouble with gold stars, incentive plans, A's, praise and other bribes.* Boston: Houghton Mifflin.

Lepper, M., Greene, D., & Nisbett, R. (1973). Undermining children's intrinsic interest with extrinsic reward: A test of the "overjustification" hypothesis. *Journal of Personality and Social Psychology, 28,* 129–137.

Slavin, R. E. (1997). *Educational Psychology* (5th ed). Needham Heights. MA: Allyn & Bacon.

Robert H. Horner
Scott A. Spaulding

ROGOFF, BARBARA
1950–

Born in 1950, Barbara Rogoff received her B.A. in psychology with honors from Pomona College in 1971. From 1971 to 1972 she attended the École de Psychologie et Sciences de l'Education at the University of Geneva, where she studied with Barbel Inhelder. In 1977 Rogoff received her Ph.D. in developmental psychology from Harvard University, where she was mentored by Sheldon H. White, Jerome Kagan, and Beatrice Whiting. During her graduate training, she spent a year in Guatemala as a field psychologist at the Institute of Nutrition of Central America and Panama, which began a decades long involvement with the Tz'utujil Mayan community of San Pedro, Guatemala. There she collaborated with the anthropologists Benjamin and Lois Paul. From 1977 to 1992 she was a member of the Department of Psychology at the University of Utah. In 1992 she joined the faculty at the University of California at Santa Cruz, where as of 2008 she was the UCSC Foundation Professor of Psychology. She is a Fellow of the American Psychological Association, the American Psychological Society, and the California Academy of Science, as well as a member of the National Academy of Education. She has been a Fellow at the Center for Advanced Study in the Behavioral Sciences and a Kellogg Fellow.

Rogoff has advanced theory and research on the cultural and social bases of human development. In 1975 she collaborated in a landmark study that examined the ethnographies of 50 cultural communities and documented a shift between 5 and 7 years of age in children's roles and responsibilities across these settings. This research contains two themes that came to be central to Rogoff's research: the cultural variability of child development and the developmental processes in these culturally diverse paths. 1n 1981 Rogoff drew on a wide range of anthropological and psychological research to describe how the cultural institution of formal schooling relates to cognitive development. She concluded that contemporary understanding of cognitive development is deeply entwined with children's experiences with formal schooling and, thus, limited in its ability to account for the range of human intellectual development.

From the 1970s into the early 2000s, Rogoff pursued these ideas in empirical research on memory, problem solving, planning, communication, and attention. She examined cultural contributions to development as well as how cultural ways of thinking are fostered in children through social interaction. This research, coupled with her ethnographic work in Guatemala, led to the concept of guided participation, a concept that pointed out that children's learning is based on their own participation in cultural activities, at the same time that other people and the community also provide them with varying forms of guidance. In one form of guided participation, learning through intent community participation, Rogoff described learning as children participate in the range of everyday activities of their community, in the company of more experienced cultural members. Although these activities are sometimes instructional, they often occur in the midst of adult activities in which the primary purpose is not to instruct the child but to carry out the activity. An important component of her approach is the idea that children are participants in cultural activities from the outset of development, in one form or another. For Rogoff (2003), intent community participation, in which children seek opportunities to observed, initiate, and engage in the activities that are important in their community, is one of the most prevalent forms of children's learning.

Rogoff's approach redefines development in a fundamental way with her view that the proper level of developmental analysis is not the solitary child but rather the child's changing participation in socially and culturally organized activity. This approach, integrating the social and cognitive processes of human development is described in her 2003 book, *The Cultural Nature of Human Development*, which was awarded the APA William James Award for advancing the field of psychology.

SEE ALSO *Guided Participation.*

BIBLIOGRAPHY

WORKS BY

Rogoff, B., Sellers, M. J., Pirotta, S., Fox, N., & White, S. H. (1975). Age of assignment of roles and responsibilities to children: A cross-cultural survey. *Human Development, 18,* 353–369.

Rogoff, B. (1981). Schooling and the development of cognitive skills. In H.C. Triandis & A. Heron (Eds.), *Handbook of cross-cultural psychology* (Vol. 4, pp. 233–294). Rockleigh, NJ: Allyn & Bacon.

Rogoff, B. (1990). *Apprenticeship in thinking: Cognitive development in social context.* New York: Oxford University Press.

Rogoff, B., Goodman Turkanis, C., & Bartlett, L., (2001). *Learning together: Children and adults in a school community.* New York: Oxford University Press.

Rogoff, B. (2003). *The cultural nature of human development.* New York: Oxford University Press.

Mary Gauvain

RULES AND PROCEDURES

SEE *Classroom Management: Rules and Procedures.*

S

SCAFFOLDING

Scaffolding is an often-used construct to describe the ongoing support provided to a learner by an expert. In this entry, the original notion of scaffolding and its key tenets are discussed, followed by a description of the use of the construct in classrooms and in computer-based systems. The challenges of providing scaffolding to students in a classroom are also discussed.

Scaffolding has been defined by Wood, Bruner, and Ross (1976) as an "adult controlling those elements of the task that are essentially beyond the learner's capacity, thus permitting him to concentrate upon and complete only those elements that are within his range of competence." The notion of scaffolding has been linked to the work of Soviet psychologist Lev Vygotsky (1896–1934). However, Vygotsky never used the term *scaffolding* (Stone, 1998), but emphasized the role of social interaction as being crucial to cognitive development, so that learning first occurs at the social or interindividual level. Thus, when a child (or a novice) learns with an adult or a more capable peer, the learning occurs within the child's *zone of proximal development* (ZPD). ZPD is defined as the "distance between the child's actual developmental level as determined by independent problem solving and the higher level of potential development as determined through problem solving under adult guidance and in collaboration with more capable peers" (Vygotksy, 1978, p. 86). Enabling the learner to bridge this gap between the actual and the potential depends on the resources or the kind of support that is provided.

KEY FEATURES OF SCAFFOLDING

The original notion of scaffolding assumed that a single more knowledgeable person, such as a parent or a teacher, helps individual learners, providing them with exactly the support they need to move forward (e.g., Bruner, 1975; Wood et al., 1976). One of the most critical aspects of scaffolding is the role of the adult or the expert. The expert is knowledgeable about the content of instruction as well as a facilitator with the skills, strategies and processes required for teaching. The expert not only helps motivate learners by providing just enough support to enable them to accomplish the goal, but also provides support in the form of modeling, highlighting the critical features of the task, and providing hints and questions that might help learners to reflect (Wood et al., 1976). In this conception then, the adult's role has perceptual and cognitive as well as affective components (Stone, 1998).

Although the role of the adult is crucial, descriptions of the notion of scaffolding (Langer & Applebee, 1986; Palincsar, 1998; Reid, 1998; Stone, 1998) point to several other key elements of scaffolded instruction:

1. *Common goal.* Shared understanding, described as *intersubjectivity* (Rogoff, 1990), is of critical importance in scaffolded instruction. Intersubjectivity refers to the combined ownership of the task between the adult and the child, and setting a common goal.

2. *Ongoing diagnosis and adaptive support.* Perhaps the most important feature of scaffolding is the fact that the adult is constantly evaluating the child's progress and providing support that is appropriate for "*this*

tutee, in *this task* at *this* point in task mastering" (Wood et al., 1976, p. 97). This results in interactions that are different in "content and form from individual to individual" (Hogan & Tudge, 1999), and for the same individual at different times. As Wood and colleagues (1976) described, scaffolded interactions comprise of a theory of the task and a theory of the tutee. The adult needs to have a thorough knowledge of the task and its components, the subgoals that need to be accomplished, as well as knowledge of the child's capabilities as they change throughout the instruction.

3. *Dialogues and interactions.* A critical factor in the ongoing diagnosis and calibrated support is the dialogic nature of scaffolding interactions, so that the learner is an active participant and a partner in deciding the direction of the interaction, and not a passive recipient. The dialogic nature of scaffolding is best illustrated in the reciprocal teaching studies of reading (Brown & Palincsar, 1985; Palincsar & Brown, 1984), in which students took turns leading the group discussion, engaging in comprehension monitoring strategies.

4. *Fading and transfer of responsibility.* The final feature of scaffolding is reducing the support provided to learners so that they are in control and take responsibility for their learning. The best scaffolding will eventually lead learners to internalize the processes they are being helped to accomplish (Rogoff, 1990). In the original description by Wood and colleagues (1976), the important aspect of the transfer of responsibility is that the child has not only learned how to complete a specific task, but has also abstracted the process of completing the particular task.

EXAMPLES OF SCAFFOLDING

The early studies that described scaffolding, be they descriptions of parent-child interactions (Greenfield, 1999) or classroom interactions (Langer and Applebee, 1986), were observational rather than interventionist studies. One of the earliest accounts of an interventionist study of scaffolding is Wood, Bruner and Ross's 1976 study in which 3-, 4-, and 5-year-olds engaged in a task of building a pyramid from interlocking blocks, with guidance from a tutor. Each child was tutored individually and the tutor followed a set of guidelines for her tutoring. But the tutor did not always follow pre-set rules in her interactions; instead she provided just enough assistance to help the child move forward—assistance that was sensitive to, and adapted based on, the child's progress. Wood and colleagues documented six types of support that an adult can provide: recruiting the child's interest, reducing the degrees of freedom by simplifying the task, maintaining

direction, highlighting the critical task features, controlling frustration, and demonstrating ideal solution paths.

Perhaps the most well-known example of the notion of scaffolding in the classroom is the work on reciprocal teaching (Palinscar & Brown, 1984; Brown & Palinscar, 1985). In this study, groups of students were supported in the process of reading by strategies such as self-directed summarizing (review), questioning, clarifying, and predicting. A teacher or a more capable peer took the lead in modeling the strategies until students in the group could apply them on their own. The teacher or the peer modeled the strategies and used prompts and questions to enable students to apply the four strategies. As described by Palinscar and Brown (1984), the teacher used strategies such as prompting ("What question did you think a teacher might ask?"); instruction ("Remember, a summary is a shortened version, it doesn't include detail"); and modifying the activity ("If you're having a hard time thinking of a question, why don't you summarize first?") (Palinscar & Brown, 1984, p. 131). Both the Wood, Bruner, and Ross study and the reciprocal teaching studies highlight how the key features—intersubjectivity, ongoing diagnosis, tailored assistance, and fading—were attained in the dynamic, interactive environment. Whereas the study by Wood and colleagues illustrates the tutorial interventions in a one-on-one situation, the reciprocal teaching studies were conducted with small groups of learners. In addition, both the quality and the quantity of support were varied, based on the needs of a particular learner. As the learners attained competence, the scaffolding was faded, giving them more control.

SCAFFOLDING IN CLASSROOM SITUATIONS

The notion of scaffolding is increasingly being used to describe the support provided for students to learn successfully in classrooms, especially the use of project- or design-based activities to teach math and science (e.g., Kafai, 1994; Kolodner et al., 2003; Krajcik et al., 1998). Many of these approaches are based on a socioconstructivist model (Vygotsky, 1978; Wertsch, Mcnamee, McLare, & Budwig, 1980) emphasizing that learning occurs in a rich social context, marked by interaction, negotiation, articulation, and collaboration. The original notion of scaffolding, as used in the initial studies of parent-child interactions (Bruner, 1975) or in teacher-student interactions, focused on situations that allowed for one-on-one interactions between the adult or the expert and the learner. The one-on-one nature of the tutoring allowed the adult/teacher to provide "titrated support" (Stone, 1998) that changed based on the progress made by the learner. However, classroom situations involving many students do not allow for the fine-tuned, sensitive, personalized exchange that occurs in one-on-

one or small-group scaffolding (Rogoff, 1990). There-fore, instead of one teacher working with each student, support is provided in a paper or software tool that individuals interact with, or classroom activities are rede-fined so that peers can help each other (e.g., Bell & Davis, 2000; Jackson, Krajcik, & Soloway, 1998; Pun-tambekar & Kolodner, 2002; Reiser et al., 2001).

SOFTWARE TOOLS IN THE CLASSROOM

Software environments that provide support have been developed with the goal of supporting students in the processes that they might find difficult in a complex task when it is not possible for a teacher to attend to each student in a class. Several software tools have been devel-oped to prompt students to reflect, articulate, and com-plete the steps of a complex task. Examples of such software include ThinkerTools (White & Fredrickson, 1998), Knowledge Integration Environment or KIE (Bell & Davis, 2000), Progress Portfolio (Loh et al., 1998), BGuILE (Reiser et al., 2001) and Model-It (Jackson, Krajcik, & Soloway, 1998).

Quintana and colleagues (2004) have put forth a comprehensive scaffolding design framework for building software tools to help students learn from inquiry-based science activities. Their framework is based on the diffi-culties that students have during science inquiry and focuses on such aspects of the inquiry process as process management, i.e., the ability to engage in processes and activities required for inquiry; sense making, which they describe as difficulties that learners experience in making sense of their work and finding a direction; and data recording and analysis and articulation.

Reiser (2004) proposed two mechanisms as being essential to software tools that scaffold complex learning: structuring and problematizing. Structuring is believed to scaffold students by decomposing the task and guiding them through the steps of a complex task. Structuring can be provided by using prompts that help students with reflection and articulation, helping them move forward in a complex task. For example, in the software tool Explanation Constructor (Reiser et al., 2001) is an elec-tronic journal that helps students construct their science explanations. In this tool, structuring is provided for articulation and reflection by having students record their research questions, construct explanations, and articulate their findings. In other words, structuring breaks down a complex task into constituent steps to make it more manageable to students. Problematizing, as Reiser described it, "is the flip side of structuring" (p. 287). It involves having learners confront the complexity of the task by helping them focus on aspects of the task that need to be resolved. For example, having students analyze

their findings based on a theoretical framework forces students to think about the theoretical constructs that they should use in their explanations, supporting the notion of problematizing.

Software tools and frameworks are based on the difficulties that students have and help students with complex tasks and several strategies that they need. They provide an important first step in the design of scaffold-ing; however, if the tools do not fade the support, and do not vary the support for different users, they lack the most critical elements of scaffolding, that of ongoing diagnosis and calibrated support.

PEER INTERACTIONS

In addition to software tools, peer interactions have also been considered important for scaffolding in classrooms. In contrast to the adult being the expert in the traditional notion of scaffolding, in peer interactions students support one another through their interactions. Brown and col-leagues (1993) emphasized the multidimensional nature of the interactions in a classroom embodying the commu-nities of learners approach. In this environment, the researchers note:

> [learners] of all ages and levels of expertise and interests seed the environment with ideas and knowledge that are appropriated by different learners at different rates, according to their needs and to the current states of the zones of proximal development in which they are engaged.

For example, a modified version of the jigsaw method is used in this approach in which a research theme is divided into subtopics and students in each research group are assigned different topics. Thus every group has a member who is working on a subtopic and every member in a group works on a different subtopic. All the students work on their subtopic and then students come together in reciprocal teaching groups to put their information together and complete the jigsaw. Expertise is therefore distributed amongst all participants, who are engaged in supporting and critiquing one another, justifying views and opinions, and offering suggestions and explanations. The teacher's role changes from that of being a knowledge giver to a facilitator of a community in which students engage in reasoning and justification, eventually helping them to adopt these crucial skills.

DISTRIBUTED SCAFFOLDING

With software tools and peer interactions being used as a way to support learning in classrooms, researchers theo-rize about a *system* of scaffolding that can describe the complex nature of providing support to multiple students in a classroom. Puntambekar and Kolodner (2005) put forth the notion of *distributed scaffolding* to explain multiple forms of support in the complex environment of a classroom. In this context, support for the design process was provided through the design diaries; in addition, tools such as pin-up sessions and gallery walks were used to help students discuss their designs, providing opportunities for support from teachers and peers. Puntambekar and Kolodner (2005) found that multiple forms of support, distributed across available tools, activities, and agents in the classroom, and integrated in ways that admit redundancy, enhance the learning and performance of a wide variety of students in the classroom. In a complex classroom environment, it can be difficult to align all the affordances in such a way that every student can recognize and take advantage of all of them. When support is distributed, integrated, and multiple, there are more chances for students to notice and take advantages of the affordances of the environment and the activity.

Tabak (2004) presents the notion of *synergistic* scaffolds, as a form of distributed scaffolding. According to Tabak, synergy refers to a pattern of scaffolding in which different kinds of support, such as software and teacher coaching, address the learning need but in different ways. Tabak (2004), states that "synergistic scaffolds are different supports that augment each other; they interact and work in concert to guide a single performance of a task or goal" (p. 318). For example, the software could help students reflect while the teacher might model the necessary strategies, so that the software and teacher support together provides students with a complete set of supports to help them successfully complete the task.

With the development of software tools and classrooms interactions as forms of scaffolds, the notion of scaffolding has evolved since its original conception and has changed considerably from the 1990s into the early 21st century. While later approaches have helped researchers understand the kinds of support that are needed to help classroom communities learn successfully, there have also been some aspects of scaffolding that have been difficult to achieve because of the reality of scaffolding in a classroom. Thus, although the notion of scaffolding has evolved, and understanding of providing support in multiple formats has been enriched, it is necessary to think about the critical elements that are missing, such as the ongoing diagnosis of student learning, the careful calibration of support, and fading, the transfer of responsibility to the student.

Current instantiations of the scaffolding construct have addressed a key aspect of scaffolding, i.e., that scaffolding be based on knowledge of the task and the difficulties that students have. However, the tools are permanent and unchanging; they provide structure and consistency by highlighting the aspects of the tasks that students should focus on. While this is by no means

trivial, support becomes scaffolding only when it is adaptive, based on an ongoing diagnosis of student learning, and helps students to eventually internalize the knowledge and skills when the scaffolds are removed. More research is needed into how a system of scaffolding can be built, so that ongoing diagnosis and fading can be achieved in classroom situations.

SEE ALSO *Sociocultural Theory; Vygotsky, Lev Semenovich.*

BIBLIOGRAPHY

Bell, P., & Davis, E. A. (2000). Designing Mildred: Scaffolding students' reflection and argumentation using a cognitive software guide. In S. O'Connor-Divelbiss (Ed.), *Proceedings of the 4th International Conference of the Learning Sciences* (pp. 142–149). Mahwah, NJ: Erlbaum.

Brown, A. L., Ash, D., Rutherford, M., Nakaguwa, K., Gordon, A., & Campione, J. C. (1993). Distributed expertise in the classroom. In G. Saloman (Ed.), *Distributed cognition: Psychological and educational considerations* (pp. 188–228). Cambridge, England: Cambridge University Press.

Brown, A. L., & Palincsar, A. S. (1985). Reciprocal teaching of comprehension strategies: A natural history of one program for enhancing learning. In J. D. Day & J. G. Borkowski (Eds.), *Intelligence and exceptionality: New directions for theory, assessment, and instructional practice.* Norwood, NJ: Ablex.

Bruner, J. S. (1975). From communication to language: A psychological perspective. *Cognition, 3,* 255–287.

Hogan, D. M., & Tudge, J. (1999). Implications of Vygotsky's theory for peer learning. In A. M. O' Donnell & A. King (Eds.), *Cognitive perspectives on peer learning* (pp. 39–65). Mahwah: NJ.: Erlbaum.

Jackson, S., Krajcik, J., & Soloway, E. (1998). The design of guided learner-adaptable scaffolding in interactive learning environments. In *Proceedings of the conference on Human Factors in Computing Systems* (pp. 187–194). Los Angeles: ACM.

Kafai, Y. B. (1994). *Minds in play: Computer game design as a context for children's learning.* Hillsdale, NJ: Erlbaum.

Kolodner, J. L., Crismond, D., Fasse, B., Gray, J., Holbrook, J., & Puntambekar, S. (2003). Putting a student-centered learning by design curriculum into practice: Lessons learned. *Journal of the Learning Sciences, 12*(4), 485–547.

Krajcik, J. S., Blumenfeld, P. C., Marx, R. W., & Soloway, E. (1991). A collaborative model for helping middle grade science teachers learn project-based instruction. *The Elementary School Journal, 94*(5), 483–497.

Langer, J. A., & Applebee, A. N. (1986). Reading and writing instruction: Toward a theory of teaching and learning. In E. Z. Rothkopf (Ed.), *Review of Research in Education* (Vol. 13, pp. 171–194). Washington, DC: American Educational Research Association.

Loh, B., Radinsky, J., Russell, E., Gomez, L. M., Reiser, B. J., & Edelson, D. C. (1998). The Progress Portfolio: Designing reflective tools for a classroom context. In *Proceedings of the conference on Human Factors in Computing Systems* (pp. 627–634). Los Angeles: ACM.

Palincsar, A. S., & Brown, A. L. (1984). Reciprocal teaching of comprehension-fostering and comprehension-monitoring activities. *Cognition and Instruction, 1*(2), 117–175.

Puntambekar, S., & Kolodner, J. L. (2005). Distributed scaffolding: Helping students learn science by design. *Journal of Research in Science Teaching, 42*(2), 185–217.

Quintana, C., Reiser, B. J., Davis, E. A., Krajcik, J., Golan, R., Kyza, E. A., et al. (2004). Evolving a scaffolding design framework for designing educational software. *Journal of the Learning Sciences, 13*(3), 337–386.

Reid, D. K. (1998). Scaffolding: A broader view. *Journal of Learning Disabilities, 31*(4), 386–396.

Reiser, Brian J. (2004). Scaffolding complex learning: The mechanisms of structuring and problematizing student work. *Journal of the Learning Sciences, 13*(3), 273–304.

Reiser, B. J., Tabak, I., Sandoval, W. A., Smith, B., Steinmuller, F., & Leone, A. J. (2001). BGuILE: Strategic and conceptual scaffolds for scientific inquiry in biology classrooms. In S. M. Carver & D. Klahr (Eds.), *Cognition and instruction: Twenty-five years of progress.* Mahwah, NJ: Erlbaum.

Rogoff, B. (1990). Apprenticeship in thinking: Cognitive development in sociocultural activity. New York: Oxford University Press.

Stone, C. A. (1998). The metaphor of scaffolding: Its utility for the field of learning disabilities. *Journal of Learning Disabilities, 31*(4), 344–364.

Tabak, I. (2004). Synergy: A complement to emerging patterns of distributed scaffolding, *Journal of the Learning Sciences, 13*(3), 305–335.

Vygotsky, L. S. (1978). *Mind in society: The development of higher psychological processes.* Cambridge, MA: Harvard University Press.

Wertsch, J. V. (1985). *Vygotsky and the social formation of mind.* Cambridge, MA: Harvard University Press.

Wertsch, J., Mcnamee, G., McLare, J., & Budwig, N. (1980). The adult-child dyad as a problem solving system. *Child Development, 51*, 1215–1221.

White, B., & Frederiksen, J. (1998). Inquiry, modeling, and metacognition: Making science accessible to all students. *Cognition and Instruction, 16*(1), 3–118.

Wood, D., Bruner, J. S., & Ross, G. (1976). The role of tutoring in problem solving. *Journal of Child Psychology & Psychiatry & Allied Disciplines, 17*(2), 89–100.

Sadhana Puntambekar

SCHOOL BELONGING

The term *school belonging* refers to students' subjective perception of being accepted and respected in their particular school setting. Some researchers have also examined the parallel perception in relation to specific classes; typically using the term *class belonging*. Baumeister and Leary (1995) have proposed that all people have an innate need to belong to social groups and to form positive interpersonal relationships with others. Given the amount of time children and adolescents spend in educational settings and the societal importance attached to school-related activities, students' sense of belonging in those settings is particularly important for their healthy development.

Carol Goodenow (1993) defined students' sense of belonging as the sense of "psychological membership in the school or classroom, that is, the extent to which students feel personally accepted, respected, included, and supported by others in the school environment" (p. 80). Other researchers have studied similar perceptions using terms such as *school connectedness* or *bonding to school*; however, these terms are less common (see Anderman & Freeman, 2004, for a review).

The fact that different researchers have examined similar psychological constructs using different terms can make it difficult to synthesize the findings of studies related to students' sense of belonging. Furthermore, this difficulty extends beyond simply the terminology that is used to include differences in both the psychological theories or models that researchers use and the specific ways in which they measure individuals' perceptions of belonging. Because the sense of belonging or connectedness is a subjective perception, it is best measured using students' self-reports. This is done, most commonly, through the use of questionnaire measures, although interviews with students can also be used (e.g., Kester, 1994). Even within the use of questionnaire measures, however, considerable differences exist in the specific measures available. Perhaps the most widely known measure of school or classroom belonging is the Psychological Sense of School Membership Scale (PSSM; Goodenow & Grady, 1993). This measure includes 18 items and was originally developed for use with students in middle school, focusing on students' sense of being liked, included, and respected in their school. More recently, several researchers have adapted the PSSM to develop shorter versions and for use with college-age students. In contrast to the PSSM, other researchers have used measures that include somewhat broader constructs that include the sense of belonging in conjunction with other perceptions and attitudes (such as valuing academic activities or holding shared group norms). These differences contribute to the sometimes mixed findings from research, which are described in more detail below.

CONSEQUENCES OF FEELING A SENSE OF BELONGING

Researchers interested in students' sense of belonging have examined the perception of subjective membership and acceptance at both the classroom and more general school level, although the latter is more common. Regardless of this distinction, and across a range of grade levels, students' sense of belonging has been associated consistently with a variety of positive academic and affective variables. Furthermore, there is growing evidence that the positive consequences of feeling a sense of belonging transcend ethnic and cultural differences in students (e.g., Sanchez, Colon, & Esparza, 2005).

In terms of academic variables, one of the most common findings is that students' sense of school belonging is associated with a range of adaptive motivational beliefs. For example, students' sense of belonging in a particular class has been associated with higher expectancies for success in that class; higher perceptions of class tasks as being interesting, important and useful; and intrinsic and mastery goal orientations related to the class. Sense of belonging at the school level has also been associated with more general measures of school-related motivation, self-reported effort, and reduced absenteeism. In contrast to the research on students' academic motivation, the literature is much less clear with regard to associations between students' sense of belonging and their academic achievement. In this area, findings are very mixed. Furthermore, the design of many studies does not allow for clear statements of the direction of effects. That is, although some researchers have reported a positive association between sense of belonging and achievement, it may be that students with a stronger record of prior achievement are more likely to feel as though they are accepted and respected in school, compared to their lower-achieving peers. It is not clear whether promoting a sense of belonging can help a student to achieve at higher levels in the future. Nevertheless, many researchers believe that students' sense of belonging and academic achievement may be reciprocally related over time, with each positive outcome reinforcing the other. Of course, for some students, low levels of perceived belonging and poor academic performance may similarly reinforce one another.

Finn (1989) proposed an Identification-Participation model to describe the process by which some students become alienated from, and eventually drop out of, school. In this model, Finn suggests that a sense of belonging combined with valuing of school-relevant goals (called "identification with school") leads to an increase in the quality, as well as the quantity, of students' participation in school activities. Such increased participation, when met with quality instruction, then leads to successful performances and achievement which, in turn, contribute to a greater sense of identification. In other words, Finn proposes that academic achievement can be both a precursor to and an outcome of the sense of belonging. An important point of Finn's model, however, is recognizing that the sense of belonging is necessary but not sufficient for students' achievement. Simply feeling accepted and respected, without accompanying valuing of school-related goals and appropriate instruction, will not lead to successful performance on academic tasks.

In addition to academic outcomes, researchers also have investigated associations between students' sense of belonging and a range of affective and well-being related outcomes. One highly influential study published by Resnick and his colleagues (1997) reported that the sense of school connectedness (another term for school belonging) was associated with lower levels of emotional distress, lower suicidal ideation, lower levels of involvement in violence, and less frequent use of tobacco, alcohol, and marijuana in adolescents. Subsequently, other researchers have found perceived school belonging to be associated with lower levels of depression and general negative school-related affect, along with avoidance of behavioral problems in school. In addition, belonging is associated with increased positive school-related affect, empathy, self-esteem, and higher levels of general optimism (E. Anderman, 2002; L. Anderman, 1999; Battistich, Solomon, Kim, Watson, & Schaps, 1995).

FACTORS THAT CONTRIBUTE TO THE SENSE OF BELONGING

Given the range of positive academic and affective outcomes associated with students' sense of belonging, it is important to understand those factors that support this perception. Unfortunately, the research in this area is less extensive than that described in the previous section (see Anderman & Freeman, 2004, for a review of this research). Some researchers have reported differences in the sense of belonging in terms of characteristics of the students themselves. For example, there is some evidence that, among adolescents, girls tend to report higher levels of school belonging than do boys. Similarly, as noted earlier, adolescents with lower levels of academic achievement may be less likely to report a sense of belonging than their higher-achieving peers.

Some researchers have also reported differences in reported school belonging related to students' ethnicity; however, the findings in this regard are quite mixed. Although some data suggest that minority students feel less sense of belonging in their schools than do White students, it may be that students' representation within the school population is a critical factor. That is, when African American or Hispanic students make up the majority of a school's population, and particularly when the teaching faculty is ethnically mixed, those minority students have been found to report higher levels of belonging than their White classmates. In other words, minority status in relation to the population of the school, rather than in the more usual sense of the term, may be the more important determinant of students' sense of belonging. Finally, in terms of individual characteristics, students' beliefs about the academic work presented in their classes and their self-concepts also are related to their sense of belonging. A strong global self-concept and high perceived task values (that is, the perception that tasks are interesting, important, and useful;

see Eccles & Wigfield, 1995) are strongly associated with higher levels of belonging.

Beyond individual and group differences in students' sense of belonging, there also is evidence that several characteristics of schools and classrooms themselves can help to foster the sense of belonging for all students. There is clear evidence that average levels of students' sense of belonging vary significantly across schools and classrooms (see Anderman & Freeman, 2004, for a review). Interestingly, these differences do not appear to be systematically related to school or class size, or school type (e.g., public, private, or parochial). In contrast, there is some evidence that students may report higher levels of belonging in rural schools compared to urban schools, and in K-8 or K-12 structured schools compared to traditional middle and high school structures. Finally, average levels of school belonging in adolescents may tend to be higher in schools in which larger numbers of students participate in extra-curricular activities.

Beyond characteristics of the school in general, the instructional and interpersonal characteristics of specific classes also contribute to students' perceptions of belonging at both the class and general school level. In fact, these more proximal influences may be more important in shaping students' day-to-day experiences than are school-level factors. Furthermore, the variables that have been associated with higher levels of belonging are quite consistent across students of different ages, ranging from elementary school to undergraduate students in college.

Battistich, Solomon and their colleagues conducted a long-term intervention in elementary schools, known as the Child Development Project (CDP), aimed at creating a greater sense of community in students. In this work, a sense of community included students' sense of belonging, along with the development of shared values and having a role in decision-making. Schools in the CDP program adopted a range of policies and practices, including the use of cooperative learning activities, developmental discipline strategies, emphasizing interpersonal helping and prosocial behavior, and promoting non-exclusionary attitudes in their students. Direct observation of teachers' classroom behaviors demonstrated that warmth and supportiveness, emphasis on prosocial values, encouragement of cooperation, and elicitation of student thinking all were associated with an increased sense of community among students.

Research conducted in middle-school settings also supports the importance of a classroom social environment characterized by mutual interpersonal respect. L. Anderman (2003) examined change in middle school students' sense of belonging over time and found that, in spite of an overall decline in belonging between sixth and seventh grades, this decline was partially corrected when students

perceived their teachers as requiring students to treat one another respectfully. In addition, that study showed strong support for the importance of a classroom context that focused on individual mastery and learning as the purpose for academic tasks (that is, a mastery goal focus, Ames, 1992). Across the sixth and seventh grades, a perceived focus on meaning and understanding in academic tasks was the single strongest predictor of students' sense of belonging in school, even after other characteristics were taken into account. Finally, preliminary research conducted in college classrooms suggests that very similar characteristics may help promote a sense of class belonging for undergraduate students. Not only is a sense of belonging still important for students at the college level, but their sense of belonging is higher in classes where instructors encourage student participation, are perceived as warm, friendly, and helpful, and as being well organized and prepared for classes (Freeman, Anderman, & Jensen, 2007). Less research has been conducted on promoting a sense of belonging in high schools. This remains an important area to be developed.

IMPLICATIONS FOR TEACHERS

As described in the preceding section, empirical research has demonstrated the importance of a number of school- and classroom-level policies and practices for fostering and maintaining students' subjective sense of belonging. What is particularly notable about these findings is, first, the remarkable consistency in findings across widely varying age groups and, second, that many of the characteristics identified are able to be modified. In other words, students' sense of belonging seems to be shaped less by fixed and objective characteristics of their schooling (such as school size) and more by those attitudes and practices that are within educators' power to control.

Perhaps the first and most important implication of this body of research for teachers is that they need to recognize the value of students' sense of belonging, both in their classes and in the school as a whole. Being aware of students' subjective sense of acceptance, respect and inclusion, as distinct from their objective membership of the school community, may be an important first step in sustaining students' academic and affective development and well-being. Beyond this initial awareness, the research literature also points to a number of specific characteristics of classes that are likely to foster students' sense of belonging at all levels.

In terms of instructional practices and pedagogy, teachers who encourage high levels of student participation in activities, particularly those who ensure equal participation from all students, are likely to foster a sense of class belonging. Importantly, this benefit is most likely to occur when participation is designed as cooperative and focused on the individual pursuit of understanding and mastery, rather than as demonstrating one's knowledge before classmates or competing. Students' sense of belonging can also be fostered through participation in decision-making within class, such as helping to develop class rules for behavior, or having some limited choices in terms of academic tasks. Teachers who are perceived as committed to their students' learning, holding high expectations for student success and providing assistance when it is needed, also are likely to promote a sense of belonging. Beyond the strictly pedagogical aspects of classes, the interpersonal and affective tone of classes also will support students' sense of belonging. Teachers need to communicate their own warmth and availability to students but they also play a critical role in setting the climate for interactions among students in class. Teachers can communicate the importance of prosocial and cooperative attitudes, active participation and mutual respect among class participants. Taken together, this research suggests that teachers will be most likely to promote and maintain students' sense of belonging when they are able to balance a strong focus on students' learning and academic progress with a climate of warm and supportive interpersonal relationships in class.

SEE ALSO *Classroom Environment; School Climate.*

BIBLIOGRAPHY

Anderman, E. M. (2002). School effects on psychological outcomes during adolescence. *Journal of Educational Psychology, 94,* 795–809.

Anderman, L. H. (1999). Classroom goal orientation, school belonging and social goals as predictors of students' positive and negative affect following the transition to middle school. *Journal of Research and Development in Education, 32,* 89–103.

Anderman, L. H. (2003). Academic and social perceptions as predictors of change in middle school students' sense of school belonging. *Journal of Experimental Education, 72,* 5–22.

Anderman, L. H., & Freeman, T. M. (2004). Students' sense of belonging in school. In M. Maehr & P. Pintrich (Eds.), *Advances in motivation and achievement: Vol. 13. Motivating students, improving schools: The legacy of Carol Midgley* (pp. 27–63). Oxford: Elsevier, JAI.

Battistich, V., Solomon, D., Kim, D., Watson, M., & Schaps, E. (1995). Schools as communities, poverty levels of student populations, and students' attitudes, motives, and performance: A multilevel analysis. *American Educational Research Journal, 32,* 627–658.

Battistich, V., Solomon, D., Watson, M., & Schaps, E. (1997). Caring school communities. *Educational Psychologist, 32,* 137–151.

Baumeister, R. F. & Leary, M. R. (1995). The need to belong: desire for interpersonal attachments as a fundamental human motivation. *Psychological Bulletin, 117,* 497–529.

Eccles, J. S., & Wigfield, A. (1995). In the mind of the actor: The structure of adolescents' achievement task values and

expectancy-related beliefs. *Personality and Social Psychology Bulletin, 21,* 215–225.

Finn, J. D. (1989). Withdrawing from school. *Review of Educational Research 59,* 117–142.

Freeman, T. M., Anderman, L. H., & Jensen, J. M. (2007). Sense of belonging in college freshmen at the classroom and campus levels. *Journal of Experimental Education, 75,* 203–220.

Sanchez, B., Colon, Y., & Esparza, P. (2005). The role of sense of school belonging and gender in the academic achievement of Latino adolescents. *Journal of Youth and Adolescence, 34,* 619–628.

Lynley H. Anderman

SCHOOL CLIMATE

Definitions of school climate include a critical core set of common elements. The definition of school climate usually encompasses dimensions of the perceived social environment that: (a) have a contextual influence on the learning and development of students, (b) remain stable over time, and (c) can be meaningfully aggregated across raters. Definitions of climate characteristically focus on conditions as they are perceived by students, teachers, or other participants in a school setting, rather than on objective aspects of the setting. Illustratively, school climate may be reflected in the frequency with which teachers go out of their way to explain material to students, a behavior that can be observed by students. However, objective characteristics of the school, such as the percentage of teachers who are certified in the area that they teach, would not fall within the scope of climate assessment. School climate has been conceived as a set of conditions that influence student outcomes, in part by establishing norms and expectations for behavior. Climate dimensions mediate the effects of educational interventions on student outcomes, rather than being the final outcomes themselves. For example, the amount of emphasis that is placed on learning is a common focus of climate assessment, while students' grade point averages would be viewed as an outcome indicator.

Climate assessments are thought to have a contextual effect in the sense that school-level differences in climate dimensions are thought to be associated with differences between schools in student outcomes in ways that are not accounted for by individual differences in students' background characteristics and prior achievement. Climate dimensions are thought to be stable across time, absent any systematic effort to change them. For example, climate scores in middle schools remain stable over 2 years, even when the student membership of the building turns over (Brand, Felner, Shim, Seitsinger, & Dumas, 2003), suggesting that climate persists over time independent of the individuals who comprise the membership of a building. Finally, while students may offer diverse opinions about the climate of their school building, their ratings can be meaningfully and reliably aggregated to create school-level scores (Brand et al., 2008; Griffith, 2000).

Research on school climate has focused on the proximal conditions affecting students' learning, focusing on students' and teachers' experiences of the school as a learning environment. A related body of work on the organizational climate of the school also considers teachers' experiences of the school as a workplace (Halpin & Croft, 1963; Hoy & Tarter, 1997; Kelly et al., 1986; Rentoul & Fraser, 1983). Illustratively, the educational climate literature considers such dimensions as teacher support or achievement emphasis, while the organizational climate literature considers teachers' experiences of participation in decision-making at work. The present review focuses on the educational climate of the school, although the influence of organizational climate variables on students' learning and adjustment must also be acknowledged.

Implicitly, many educators and researchers think of school climate as being one-dimensional, in the sense that climate is generally positive or negative. Another form of one-dimensional thinking associates the entire domain of school climate with a specific dimension. In this vein, the domain of climate is equated with just teacher support, personalization, sense of community, relationships, achievement emphasis, or school safety. While each of these may be important aspects of school climate, no single dimension encompasses the entire domain of school climate. Rather, numerous studies suggest that a comprehensive assessment of school climate should encompass multiple dimensions.

An early, and very influential, conceptual framework was proposed by Trickett and Moos (1973), who suggested that classroom climate assessment should address three overarching conceptual dimensions: Relationships, Personal Growth or Goal Orientation, and System Maintenance and Change. This conception of climate dimensions has broadened the perspective of investigators on the multidimensional nature of climate, and has lead to efforts to empirically differentiate underlying dimensions of climate through factor analysis. Illustratively, Brand and his colleagues (2003) report that students' ratings of the ten ISC-S scales reflect the following higher-order dimensions: Developmental Sensitivity, Pro-social Emphasis, Contextual Negativity, and Safety Problems. Cumulatively, these perspectives suggest that efforts to improve school climate need to be cognizant of how school conditions vary on multiple dimensions.

ASSESSMENT OF CLASSROOM AND SCHOOL CLIMATE

School and classroom climate dimensions have been assessed through structured inventories that ask participants to indicate the extent to which they agree or disagree with specific statements about the social environment. Scale scores are computed by summing or averaging responses to the items that comprise a dimension. Pioneering work on the development of structured climate inventories was undertaken during the 1960s by Herbert Walberg and colleagues (Walberg & Anderson, 1968) and George Stern (1970). During the 1970s Walberg's work led to the development of the Learning Environment Inventory (LEI) (Fraser, Anderson, & Walberg, 1982) for secondary level classrooms, and the My Class Inventory (MCI) (Fraser et al., 1982), for elementary classrooms. During the same period, Edison Trickett and Rudy Moos published the Classroom Environment Scale (CES) (Trickett & Moos, 1973; Moos, 1979). Though the CES was initially developed for use in secondary level classrooms, this instrument was adapted to assess school-level climate in high schools (Felner, Aber, Cauce, & Primavera, 1985), and classroom climate in the early elementary grades (Toro et al., 1985). Research using the LEI and CES proved to be critical in establishing the importance of climate assessment for research and intervention.

Investigations of climate have often focused on the social climate of classrooms, even in secondary level schools where students occupy multiple classes throughout the school day. The classroom-level focus reflects the interest of investigators in changing instructional practices and conditions in particular subject-specific classrooms. Over the past two decades, increased attention has been given to the assessment of whole school climate, reflecting growing interest in implementing and evaluating the effects of comprehensive school reform models. The emphasis on school-level climate is reflected in the work of James Comer's School Development Program on the School Climate Scale (Haynes, Emmons, & Comer, 1993), as well as climate studies by Shaps (Battisch, Solomon, Kim, Watson, & Shaps, 1995) and Raudenbush (Raudenbush, Rowan, & Kang, 1991), and the Project on High Performance Learning Communities (HiPlaces) (Felner, Seitsinger, Brand, Burns, & Bolton, 2008) As part of the HiPlaces project the Inventory of School Climate (ISC) (Brand, Felner, Shim, Seitsinger, & Dumas, 2003) has been administered in more than 3,000 whole-school assessments in the past two decades. This instrument has also been widely adopted in other projects in the United States and internationally. The ISC assesses the perceived social environment of middle level and secondary schools, and is also available in a form that is appropriate for elementary school children.

In addition, the teacher version of the ISC has been found to predict students' climate ratings and outcomes (Brand, Felner, Seitsinger, Burns, & Bolton, 2008). Drawing upon the work of the authors cited above, and factor analytic research in large and diverse samples, the ISC assesses ten dimensions of school climate, including teacher support, consistency and clarity of rules and expectations, student commitment to achievement, negative peer interactions, positive peer interactions, disciplinary harshness, student input in decision-making, instructional innovation and relevance, support for cultural pluralism, and safety problems. Each of these dimensions of perceived school climate has been found to be associated with multiple indices of students' learning and adjustment, as is shown in the following section.

SIGNIFICANCE OF SCHOOL CLIMATE FOR STUDENTS' LEARNING AND DEVELOPMENT

School climate has been found to be associated with multiple areas of students' learning and development. A pervasive pattern of relationships has been found between climate dimensions and students' academic, behavioral, and socioemotional adjustment, even after partialling out the effects of poverty on student outcomes. The relationship of climate to each of these adjustment domains are considered in turn, focusing on findings from large-scale studies of young adolescents (Brand et al., 2003). The dimensions of school climate discussed below have also been found to be associated with student learning and adjustment in large scale samples of students at the elementary and high school levels (Brand, Felner, Seitsinger, & Hupkau, 2006).

To assess the impact of climate on students' learning, it is critically important to examine variation in students' academic motivation, as well as in their scores on standardized achievement tests. Academic motivation merits attention because students' aspirations, expectations, and sense of self-efficacy influence their long-term adaptation to school as well as decisions about the pursuit of advanced training and education. In schools with higher levels of student commitment to achievement, students attain higher scores on standardized tests of reading and math. In addition, multiple dimensions have been found to be associated with students' academic motivation. Higher teacher expectations, academic aspirations, and academic efficacy have been found in schools with higher school mean levels of teacher support, structure, positive peer interactions, and instructional innovation. In schools that students rated as having fewer safety problems, students reported higher self and teacher expectations, academic aspirations, and efficacy. Better grades and teacher expectations were associated with higher

mean levels of student participation in decision-making, and lower levels of disciplinary harshness and negative peer interactions, while higher student self-expectations and academic aspirations were related consistently with higher mean levels of support for cultural pluralism.

Turning to indicators of students' behavioral adjustment, higher levels of smoking, drinking and drug use, and more favorable attitudes toward these activities, were found in schools that students rated as lower in teacher support, student commitment to achievement, and instructional innovation, and higher in safety problems. Higher levels of delinquency and teacher-rated aggression were found in schools that students rated as having higher levels of negative peer interactions, disciplinary harshness, and safety problems. Higher levels of delinquency and classroom aggression were also found in schools that students rated as having lower levels of teacher support, student commitment to achievement, structure, and positive peer interactions. Turning to indices of socioemotional adjustment, higher levels of peer self-esteem, and lower levels of depression, have been found in schools in which students report higher levels of teacher support, structure, student commitment to achievement, positive peer interactions, and instructional innovation, as well as lower levels of safety problems. In addition to the climate dimensions noted above, support for cultural pluralism appears to be particularly important for academic performance, aspirations, and self-expectations among minority students (Brand, Felner, Seitsinger, Burns, & Jung, 2007). Support for pluralism also moderates the impact of poverty on students' academic performance and motivation. Gaps between students from low-income families and those from more affluent families are significantly smaller in schools that have higher levels of support for cultural pluralism.

While the majority of studies on school climate have been cross-sectional in nature, initial studies have examined the longitudinal impact of climate dimensions on trajectories of adjustment, particularly in early adolescence (e.g., Brand et al., 2007; Kuperminc, Leadbeater, & Blatt, 2001; Loukas & Murphy, 2007). Teacher expectations often decline during the middle school years. However, these declines were not evident in schools that were characterized by higher levels of structure, student commitment to achievement, positive peer interaction, and instructional innovation, as well as lower levels of disciplinary harshness. Gains over time in students' self-expectations and sense of efficacy were associated with higher levels of student commitment to achievement, positive peer interaction, and instructional innovation (Brand et al., 2007). School climate dimensions are associated with differential rates of onset for smoking, drinking, and drug use during early adolescence (Brand, Felner, Seitsinger, Shim, & Hupkau, 2005). Students who did not smoke, drink or use drugs in sixth grade were less likely to initiate these behaviors by eighth grade in schools that had higher levels of teacher support, student commitment to achievement, student involvement in decision-making, and instructional innovation and relevance, as well as lower levels of disciplinary harshness, negative peer interactions, and safety problems. Cumulatively, findings from the cross-sectional and longitudinal studies again emphasize the importance of a comprehensive, multi-dimensional perspective on school climate.

CURRENT ISSUES IN THE CONCEPTION AND MEASUREMENT OF SCHOOL CLIMATE

The metaphor of "climate" has often, unintentionally, suggested that the perceived social environment of the school is like the weather: critically important, but difficult to control. This view of school climate can, implicitly, lead to the assumption that climate is simply a given, or the product of complex forces that cannot be systematically and deliberately addressed by educators. However, the findings of numerous studies suggest that school climate can be enhanced by systematic changes in the social organization and instructional regularities of the school (e.g., Maehr & Midgley, 1996). Numerous dimensions of school climate are associated with differences in the size, structure, and activities of interdisciplinary teams in middle grade schools (Brand et al., 2007). Other factors affecting school climate include classroom instructional practices, teacher attitudes toward the implementation of research-based practices, teacher readiness and professional development, and teacher role strain and job satisfaction. Change in school climate can result from systematic changes in school organization, instruction, and other regularities of the school. Indeed, the effects of structural and organizational changes on students' learning may be mediated by dimensions of school climate.

STUDENT PERCEPTIONS OF SCHOOL CLIMATE

Initially, theories of social climate (e.g., Moos,1979) proposed that social climate reflected consensual perceptions of the social environment of the school that were shared by occupants of the classroom or school building. However, since the late 1990s, numerous studies have shown that ratings of social climate vary much more within school buildings than they do between school buildings. Illustratively, Griffith (2000) reports that only 3% to 6% of the variance in school climate ratings is accounted for by differences between school buildings. Such findings suggest that the average rating of climate in a school does not necessarily reflect the perceptions that are shared by all students. However, even though a

school-level mean score on a climate scale may not reflect a consensus of opinion among students about their building, variation in this score account for a substantial portion of the variance between buildings in indices of students' learning and adjustment (Brand et al., 2003). Further, school mean scores also tend to be highly correlated when they are drawn from randomly selected sub-samples of students from the same building (Brand et al., 2003; Griffith, 2000). Obtaining a consensus of opinion across students might not be a necessary condition for obtaining a reliable and predictive assessment of school climate dimension.

ANALYSIS OF MULTI-LEVEL DATA FROM STUDENTS, CLASSROOMS, AND SCHOOLS

Efforts to assess the school-level impact of climate dimensions have been greatly enhanced by advances in the field of Hierarchical Linear Modeling (HLM) (Raudenbush, Rowan, & Kang, 1991). HLM is a statistical technique that has been developed specifically for analysis of multi-level, hierarchical data. Initial efforts to relate climate with adjustment examined correlations at the level of the individual student (which looks at a conceptually quite different level of analysis), or else carried out correlational analyses of the relationship between school mean scores on climate and adjustment (which tends to over-estimate school-level effects). HLM has enabled investigators to make more accurate estimates of school-level effects of climate on students' developmental trajectories, and to better understand how school-level climate can moderate the effects of students' background characteristics on learning and school adaptation.

ALTERNATIVE METHODS OF ASSESSING CLIMATE

While standard methods for assessing school climate rely on the collection of data from students, circumstances can arise in which reliable survey data from a representative sample of students is not available. In such circumstances, investigators may need to rely on alternate sources of information to assess climate dimensions. Illustratively, Pianta and colleagues (Pianta et al., 2002) have developed an observational system to assess climate conditions, as well as instructional and organizational regularities, in kindergarten classrooms. This approach is particularly critical for the investigation of climate among children who are too young to complete climate inventories. In addition to using observational data, investigators may turn to teacher ratings to assess climate when representative and reliable student data are not available. However, caution should be exercised when using teacher ratings as a proxy for student ratings. It may be particularly important to choose a teacher instrument that has been validated for the purpose of predicting students' ratings and outcomes (Brand, et al., 2008).

SEE ALSO *Classroom Environment; School Belonging.*

BIBLIOGRAPHY

Battisch, V., Solomon, D., Kim, D., Watson, M. & Shaps, E. (1995). Schools as communities, poverty levels of student populations, and students' attitudes, motives, and performance: a multi-level analysis. *American Educational Research Journal, 32,* 627–658.

Brand, S., Felner, R., Seitsinger, A., Burns, A, & Bolton, A. (2008). Assessing the social environment of middle schools: The validity and utility of teachers' ratings of school climate, cultural pluralism, and safety problems for understanding and assessing the impact of school improvement. *Journal of School Psychology.*

Brand, S., Felner, R. D., Seitsinger, A, Burns, A. & Jung, E. (April, 2007). *The longitudinal influence of school climate on developmental trajectories during early adolescence.* Annual meeting of the American Educational Research Association, Chicago.

Brand, S., Felner, R. D, Seitsinger, A., Shim, M., & Hupkau, A. (2005, August). *Prevention of adolescent substance use: Protective factors at school.* Annual meeting of the American Psychological Association, Washington, DC.

Brand, S., Felner, R. D., Seitsinger, A., & Hupkau, A. (2006, April). *Learning support indicators: School climate.* Annual meeting of the American Educational Research Association, San Francisco.

Brand, S., Felner, R. D., Shim, M., Seitsinger, A., & Dumas, T. (2003). Middle school improvement and reform: Development and validation of a school-level assessment of climate, cultural pluralism and school safety. *Journal of Educational Psychology, 95,* 570–588.

Felner, R.D., Aber, M.S., Cauce, A. & Primavera, J. (1985). Adaptation and vulnerability in high-risk adolescents: An examination of environmental mediators. *American Journal of Community Psychology, 13,* 365–379.

Felner, R.D., Seitsinger, A., Brand, S., Burns, A., & Bolton. A. (2008). Whole school, ecological approaches to understanding and enhancing student motivation, expectations, and performance: Enhancing opportunities to learn through the Project on High Performance Learning Communities. *Educational Researcher.*

Fraser, B. J., Anderson, G. J., & Walberg, H. J. (1982). *Assessment of learning environments: Manual for Learning Environment Inventory (LEI) and My Class Inventory (MCI).* Perth: Western Australian Institute of Technology.

Griffith, J. (2000). School climate as group evaluation and group consensus: Student and parent perceptions of the elementary school environment. *Elementary School Journal, 101,* 35–61.

Halpin, A.W., & Croft, D.B. (1963). *The organizational climate of schools.* Chicago: University of Chicago Midwest Administration Center.

Haynes, N.M., Emmons, C.L., & Comer, J.P. (1993). *Elementary and middle school climate survey.* New Haven, CT: Yale University Child Study Center.

Hoy, W.K., & Tarter, C.J. (1997). *The road to open and healthy schools: A handbook for change* (Elementary ed.). Thousand Oaks, CA: Corwin Press.

Kelly, E. A., Glover, J. A., Keefe, J. W., Halderson, C., Sorenson, C., & Speth, C. (1986). *School climate scale* (Modified). Reston, VA: National Association of Secondary School Principals.

Kuperminc, G. P., Leadbeater, B. J., & Blatt, S. J. (2001). School social climate and individual differences in vulnerability to psychopathology among middle school students. *Journal of School Psychology, 39,* 141–159.

Loukas, A., & Murphy, J. L. (2007). Middle school student perceptions of school climate: Examining protective functions on subsequent adjustment problems. *Journal of School Psychology, 45,* 293–309.

Maehr, M. L., & Midgley, C. (1996). *Transforming school cultures.* Boulder, CO: Westview Press.

Moos, R. H. (1979). *Evaluating educational environments.* San Francisco: Jossey-Bass.

Pianta, R., La Pero, K. M., Payne, C., Cox, M. J., & Bradley, R. (2002). The relationship of kindergarten classroom environment to teacher, family, and school characteristics and child outcomes. *Elementary School Journal, 102,* 225–238.

Raudenbush, S. W., Rowan, B., & Kang, S. J. (1991). A multilevel, multivariate model for studying school climate with estimation via the EM algorithm and application to U.S. high school data. *Journal of Educational Statistics, 16,* 295–330.

Rentoul, A.J., & Fraser, B.J. (1983). Development of a school level environment questionnaire. *Journal of Educational Administration, 21,* 21–39.

Stern, G. G. (1970). *People in context: Measuring person-environment congruence in education and industry.* New York: Wiley.

Toro, P. A., Cowen, E. L., Gesten, E. L., Weissberg, R. P., Rapkin, B. D., & Davidson, E. (1985). Social environmental predictors of children's adjustment in elementary school classrooms. *American Journal of Community Psychology, 13,* 353–364.

Trickett, E., & Moos, R. H. (1973). The social environment of junior high and high school classrooms. *Journal of Educational Psychology, 65,* 93–102.

Walberg, H. J., & Anderson, H. J. (1968). Classroom climate and individual learning. *Journal of Educational Psychology, 59,* 414–419.

Stephen Brand

SCHOOL TRANSITIONS

This entry contains the following:

OVERVIEW

School transitions mark the time period when students move from one school environment into another. Transitions occur at a variety of ages and vary greatly across school districts. Students often experience problems adjusting to changes in educational environments; consequently, teachers need to receive professional development training to assist students in making successful school transitions.

MAJOR TRANSITIONS

Although transitions can occur at many different time periods, several periods are typical. The transition into kindergarten is the first major school transition; however, for some children, who already have attended childcare or preschool, the transition into kindergarten may be much easier than for other children, who have stayed at home until just prior to kindergarten. Data from the National Center for Education Statistics indicate that most children

Mortorboards against the sky signal school transitions. **CHRIS CHEADLE /ALL CANADA PHOTOS/GETTY IMAGES.**

do experience at least some care before kindergarten from non-parental caretakers; for example, in 2001, only 26.1% of preschool children were cared for solely by parents (U.S. Department of Education National Center for Education Statistics, 2006). Consequently, for most children, the transition into kindergarten is not the first time they have been out of the home.

The second major transition for most students is the transition from elementary school into middle or junior high school. Much research has been conducted examining the effects of this transition on a variety of outcomes. Research generally indicates that the transition into middle school often is problematic for early adolescents because the instructional practices of many middle schools do not meet the developmental needs of early adolescents (e.g., Anderman & Maehr, 1994; Eccles & Midgley, 1989; Simmons & Blyth, 1987). Many students become less motivated and begin to lose interest in school after this transition.

The third transition often is the transition from middle or junior high school into high school. There is less research on this transition than on some of the other school transitions. Nevertheless, a growing body of evidence suggests that this transition often is traumatic and problematic for some students (Eccles, 2008).

For some students, high school represents the final stage of formal education. However, for many students, the transition from high school into college represents another very important school transition. Some students attend two-year community colleges, whereas others attend four-year colleges or universities. The transition into college for many students represents the first time that the student attends school while simultaneously living away from home. Many students do not adapt well to college life and experience academic difficulties during their first year of school, which can eventually lead to dropping out (Tinto, 2006).

EFFECTS OF SCHOOL TRANSITIONS

Transitions are extremely important because they represent major shifts in the daily contexts in which children and adolescents interact. For some students, the transition is smooth and peaceful, whereas for others it is stressful.

School transitions are related to a variety of behavioral and psychological changes. Research indicates that across transitions, students often experience changes in relationships with peers, parents, and teachers. In addition, behavioral problems often become evident after a school transition, which is particularly true when students interact with new peer groups after the transition. Much research has examined changes in academic variables after transitions; many transitions are related to notable changes in students' motivation to learn, academic performance, and attitudes toward school.

IMPLICATIONS FOR EDUCATORS

It is very important for educators to be well prepared to assist students during transitional periods. Teachers cannot assume that students will naturally adjust to new learning environments with little difficulty. Educators must attend to the developmental needs of children and work collaboratively with parents, school counselors, and administrators to ease transitions for students of all ages. Programmatic efforts to facilitate such transitions are growing in number.

BIBLIOGRAPHY

Anderman, E. M., & Maehr, M. L. (1994). Motivation and schooling in the middle grades. *Review of Educational Research, 64,* 287–309.

Eccles, J. S. (2008). High school transitions. In J. Meece & J. S. Eccles (Eds.), *Schooling and development: Theory, methods, and applications.*

Eccles, J. S., & Midgley, C. (1989). Stage-environment fit: Developmentally appropriate classrooms for young adolescents. In C. Ames & R. Ames (Eds.), *Research on motivation in education: Goals and cognitions* (Vol. 3, pp. 139–186). New York: Academic Press.

Simmons, R. G., & Blyth, D. A. (1987). *Moving into adolescence: The impact of pubertal change and school context.* New York: Aldine de Gruyter.

United States Department of Education, National Center for Education Statistics. (2006). *Digest of education statistics* (NCES 2006–030).

Tinto, V. (2006). Research and practice of student retention: What next? *Journal of College Student Retention, Research, Theory, and Practice, 8,* 1–19.

Eric M. Anderman

ELEMENTARY SCHOOL

Kindergarten marks the entrance to formal schooling and is an important time of transition for children and families (Pianta, Rimm-Kaufman, & Cox, 1999). Children are changing developmentally in ways that potentially support adaptation to the expectations and demands of the kindergarten setting. Given the number of changes that characterize the transition period, identification of factors that support successful transition are critical. This entry describes the changes children experience as they transition to kindergarten and discusses factors related to successful adjustment to schooling.

TRANSITION TO KINDERGARTEN

Contextual changes from preschool to kindergarten coincide with developmental changes. As children physically mature, their experiences change, providing additional opportunities for skill development in a repeating and reciprocal cycle. Through the preschool years, basic skills increase rapidly. Greater motor coordination allows children to engage in more physical activity (e.g., running, climbing) essential for interactive play and group games that become more prominent in kindergarten. Changes in fine motor skills allow children to participate in academic tasks (e.g., writing, using scissors) and support adaptive skills (e.g., dressing, tying shoes) that promote independence. Language and communication skills become more sophisticated and refined, allowing greater expression and understanding of ideas, feelings, and knowledge. These basic developmental changes that are readily observed are accompanied by changes in cognition and psychosocial development that are explained by theoretical perspectives.

Jean Piaget (1896–1980) developed a theory of cognitive development that placed children of transition age near the end of the preoperational period, moving toward the concrete operational period. This movement is characterized by decreasing egocentrism and increasing flexibility in thinking, leading to increased perspective taking, understanding of functions and relations, cause and effect, and simultaneous consideration of features of objects (e.g., length and width). From an information-processing perspective, changes in cognition are accompanied by increases in learning and memory capacity that result in diversified strategies for learning (Miller, 2002). As cognitive capabilities change, children interact with and store knowledge in a way that increases capacity for learning and connecting new information to existing information. These cognitive advances contribute to effective problem-solving in an academic sense and in interpersonal interactions. Flexibility in thinking, greater memory capacity, and more effective problem-solving can support focused attention, task persistence, and increased motivation to learn. Increased perspective taking can facilitate social problem-solving, the development of empathy, self-regulation and self-control, necessary skills for school success.

Developmental changes are also reflected in theories of social development. According to the psychosocial perspective of Erik Erikson (1902–1994), as an individual develops, new skills create opportunities and demands. Physical and cognitive changes contribute to increasing autonomy and a developing sense of self through participation in new experiences. Adaptation to the opportunities and challenges in school is an important element of Erikson's theory of identity development, which places children of transition age in the stage of

Industry vs. Inferiority, characterized by the sentiment "I am what I learn." Further, emotional and moral development reflects a shift toward social comparisons and an internalized sense of standards, rules and values based on fairness and equality. Success in school, academically and interpersonally, provides children with a sense of mastery and competence that supports continued development.

Sociocultural theory provides a larger context in which to consider the cognitive and psychosocial changes that children experience during transition. Social interaction is critical to development, and the nature of interaction shifts to accommodate and challenge the growing child. As children mature, their participation in sociocultural activities and interactions with others changes, affording greater opportunities for development as evident in the different experiences from preschool to kindergarten. Key to this process is the notion of the zone of proximal development, developed by Lev Vygotsky (1896–1934), which can be defined as the difference between what a child can do independently and what the child can do with adult support. Successful learning within the zone in academic or social domains is characterized by shared goals, scaffolding, and social interactions between a child and a more competent individual. Thus, teachers, caregivers, and competent peers play a significant role in supporting adjustment to formal schooling.

In sum, developmental changes that characterize the age of transition to formal schooling prepare children to become more active learners and more social beings during a time of increased demands for social competence, both of a learning-related and peer-related nature. In kindergarten children enter a world of opportunities and challenges different from their preschool or home environments, and their experiences in that context set the stage for continued development.

CONTEXTUAL CHANGES IN TRANSITION TO KINDERGARTEN

Preschool and kindergarten settings vary a great deal in curricular content, structure, and focus. In general, preschool settings tend to be characterized by an approach to education that emphasizes child-directed learning through play, whereas kindergarten settings are more likely to emphasize the acquisition of skills and knowledge through direct instruction approaches and structured activities (Hemmeter, 2000). From a sociopolitical context several factors may contribute to observed differences in the two settings. Preschool programs have historically operated independently from the formal schooling system, and evaluation outcomes in preschool have been more likely to focus on health and safety than on early academic performance or development of social competence. Coupled with a significant emphasis on child-directed learning and play,

this has resulted in few formal instructional curricula for preschoolers. In contrast, physically located in schools and conceptually linked to formal schooling, kindergartens may experience accountability demands, attention to performance and standards, and emphasis on foundational academic skills. As such, formal curricula for kindergarten are widely available and used in schools with an eye toward academic outcomes (e.g., learning to read) that change the nature of children's experiences.

Changing experiences are accompanied by changing expectations related to learning and social interaction. As time on learning increases, classroom daily activities shift from more play-based in preschool to more structured and academically focused in kindergarten. Further, because more children are enrolled in kindergarten classrooms than in preschool classrooms, children may be interacting with a larger and more heterogeneous group of children in the context of higher child-teacher ratios. Learning-related social skills (McClelland & Morrison, 2003) that enable children to attend to instruction, follow directions, participate in group activities, organize materials, and persist in challenging tasks become more important. In addition, membership in group and individual relationships (Schwartz, Garfinkle, & Davis, 2000) becomes increasingly complex to negotiate and requires effective peer-related and adult-related social skills, such as initiating and maintaining positive interactions, sharing, turn-taking (McClelland & Morrison, 2003), effective social communication, and regulation of emotions (Izard, Trentacosta, King, & Mostow, 2004). Behaviors that may be tolerated in preschool settings and viewed as within the range of developmentally appropriate may be considered inappropriate and problematic in terms of school adjustment. For example, difficulty following directions, sharing, compliance, or lack of social interaction is likely to generate more concern in kindergarten settings. As such, it is important to understand expectations of kindergarten settings to facilitate transition.

FACTORS THAT CONTRIBUTE TO SUCCESSFUL TRANSITION

Research suggests that academic development at kindergarten entry has both direct and indirect effects on first grade schooling outcomes, and the link between early performance and later achievement has been demonstrated through grade 10 (Stevenson & Newman, 1986). Thus, upon entrance to kindergarten children need to have foundational skills to support continued development. Critical early literacy skills in language development, phonological awareness, letter-sound correspondence, concepts about print, and alphabetic principles need to be in place for a child to be prepared to read and write (Snow, Burns, & Griffin, 1998). Children's language structures and word knowledge continues to grow, facilitating development of more complex phonological neighborhoods that support early literacy skills such as rhyming (Snow et al., 1998). Similarly, children's early informal numerical understanding provides a structure for formal instruction in skills and concepts that expand their ability to use mathematics in abstract ways (Bowman, Donovan, & Burns, 2001). Facility with a mental number line constitutes an important conceptual framework for mathematical learning (Griffin & Case, 1997). Without foundational skills in key academic areas, the gap between children with skills and those without is likely to continue to grow throughout kindergarten and subsequent grades (Bowman et al., 2001).

Although necessary, early academic skills alone are not sufficient for successful transition to elementary. The degree to which children successfully navigate the kindergarten social environment in terms of classroom rules and expectations (learning-related social skills), peer relationships (peer-related social skills), and adult relationships (adult-related social skills), can dramatically affect short-term and long-term adjustment to kindergarten and to school in general.

Acquisition of *learning-related social skills* such as task completion, listening, following directions, active participation, attentiveness, compliance, self-regulation, and independence are necessary for kindergarten success as they facilitate the ability to attend to, participate in, and benefit from instruction (McClelland & Morrison, 2003). Kindergarten children rated by their teachers as having high levels of learning-related social skills have significantly less risk for being identified with behavior problems (Cooper & Farran, 1988). Kindergarten teachers have also specified that key behaviors such as listening to the teacher and complying with teacher directions are critical to successful adjustment to kindergarten (Pianta et al., 1999). Moreover, in a survey of 3,500 kindergarten teachers across the United States, 46% indicated their biggest concern was that entering children "had difficulty following directions" (Rimm-Kaufman, Pianta, & Cox, 2000). Studies have shown connections between learning-related skills at the beginning of kindergarten and later academic success, with learning-related skills accounting for unique variance in children's reading, mathematics, vocabulary, general information and alphabet skills in kindergarten and through the end of second grade (McClelland & Morrison, 2003).

Acquisition of *peer-related social skills* such as the ability to initiate and maintain interactions, share, cooperate, and demonstrate respect for other children (McClelland & Morrison, 2003) significantly affect a child's transition to school and subsequent adjustment (Ladd & Coleman, 1997), and is commonly reflected in the number of mutual friendships that children have, peer social

status, and general climate of peer interactions (Phillipsen, Deptula, & Cohen, 1999). Research suggests that children who engage in high rates of positive initiations toward peers receive high rates of positive initiations from peers (McConnell et al., 1984), and that children tend to maintain similar relationship patterns across kindergarten (Ladd & Coleman, 1997). Children who maintain friendships during the first two months of kindergarten are more likely to view school favorably (Ladd & Coleman, 1997) and children with high levels of prosocial skills tend to have more mutual friendships (Ladd, Birch, & Buhs, 1999). In addition, children who engage in positive peer interactions demonstrate more positive overall engagement in the classroom (Fantuzzo, Bulotsky-Shearer, Fusco, & McWayne, 2005), suggesting a relation between learning-related and peer-related social skills.

Adult-related social skills have an important role in the transition to elementary because children transitioning to kindergarten are still quite young, and have largely relied on adult modeling and nurturance from birth. Because parents and caregivers are the first socialization agents of young children, their influence has lasting effects on their child's social development. Children who report closeness with their parents tend to adjust best to school with more friends, fewer conflicts, and higher levels of peer acceptance, with teachers reporting frequent on-task behavior, following directions, and overall classroom competency (Clark & Ladd, 2000). This is important because children tend to develop relationships with teachers that mirror their relationships with parents, that is, if a child is clingy and needy or distant with a parent, they are likely to interact similarly with a teacher (Clark & Ladd, 2000). Children with appropriate teacher relationships are more likely to have important social skills, including self regulation and independent work habits (Pianta, Nimetz, & Bennett, 1997) as well as higher academic achievement, more mutual friends, and a higher level of peer acceptance (DeMulder, Denham, Schmidt, & Mitchell, 2000). Some research has suggested that parent involvement in school activities starting at kindergarten strongly impacts a child's adjustment to school, which can maintain through at least sixth grade (Pettit, Bates, & Dodge, 1997).

In conclusion, the transition to kindergarten is marked by important changes. Children are changing developmentally in ways that can support their adjustment and growth cognitively and socially when fostered in sensitive interactions with others. Further, the context of learning and social interaction changes as children move from preschool and home settings to formal school environments, resulting in new opportunities and challenges for skill development. With changes in context, typically there are changes in expectations for early academic performance and social behavior that require a solid foundation as well as continued development of skills and knowledge (Pianta et al., 1999). School success is largely determined by competence in the areas of academic skills and relationships with peers and adults. Key elements from these areas have collective and significant influence on a child's transition to elementary school and subsequent school adjustment (Pianta et al., 1999). Viewed together, a detailed picture emerges of the skills and experiences most likely to lead to successful transition to elementary, providing direction for early education and kindergarten settings in their efforts to support young children's development.

BIBLIOGRAPHY

Bowman, B. T., Donovan, S., & Burns, M. S. (Eds.) (2001). *Eager to learn: Educating our preschoolers.* Washington, DC: National Academy Press.

Clark, K. E., & Ladd, G. W. (2000). Connectedness and autonomy support in parent-child relationships: Links to children's socioemotional orientation and peer relationships. *Developmental Psychology, 36*(4), 485–498.

Cooper, D. H., & Farran, D. C. (1988). Behavioral risk factors in kindergarten. *Early Childhood Research Quarterly, 3,* 1–19.

DeMulder, E. K., Denham, S., Schmidt, M., & Mitchell, J. (2000). Q-Sort assessment of attachment security during the preschool years: Links for home to school. *Developmental Psychology, 36*(2), 274–282.

Fantuzzo, J.W., Bulotsky-Shearer, R., Fusco, R., & McWayne, C. (2005). An investigation of preschool classroom behavioral adjustment problems and social-emotional school readiness competencies. *Early Childhood Research Quarterly, 20,* 259–275.

Griffin, S., & Case, R. (1997). Re-thinking the primary school math curriculum: An approach based on cognitive science. *Issues in Education, 3*(1), 1–49.

Hemmeter, M. L. (2000). Classroom-based interventions: Evaluating the past and looking toward the future. *Topics in Early Childhood Special Education, 20*(1), 56–61.

Izard, C. E., Trentacosta, C. J., King, K. A., & Mostow, A.J. (2004). An emotion-based prevention program for Head Start children. *Early Education and Development, 15*(4), 407–422.

Ladd, G. W., Birch, S. H., & Buhs, E. (1999). Children's social and scholastic lives in kindergarten: Related spheres of influence? *Child Development, 70,* 1373–1400.

Ladd, G.W., & Coleman, C. C. (1997). Children's classroom peer relationships and early school attitudes: Concurrent and longitudinal associations. *Early Education and Development, 8*(1), 51–66.

McClelland, M. M., & Morrison, F., J. (2003). The emergence of learning-related social skills in preschool children. *Early Childhood Research Quarterly, 18,* 206–224.

McConnell, S. R., Strain, P. S., Kerr, M. M., Stagg, V., Lenkner, D. A., & Lambert, D. L. (1984). An empirical definition of elementary school adjustment: Selection of target behaviors for a comprehensive treatment program. *Behavior Modification, 8*(4), 451–473.

Pettit, G. S., Bates, J. E., & Dodge, K. A. (1997). Supportive parenting, ecological context, and children's adjustment: A seven-year longitudinal study. *Child Development, 68*(5), 908–923.

Phillipsen, L. C., Deptula, D. P., & Cohen, R. (1999). Relating characteristics of children and their friends to relational and overt aggression. *Child Study Journal, 29*(4), 269–289.

Pianta, R. C., Nimetz, S. L., & Bennett, E. (1997). Mother-child relationships, teacher-child relationships, and school outcomes in preschool and kindergarten. *Early Childhood Research Quarterly, 12,* 263–280.

Pianta, R. C., Rimm-Kaufman, S. E., & Cox, M. J. (1999). An ecological approach to kindergarten transition. In R. C. Pianta & M. J. Cox (Eds.), *The transition to kindergarten* (pp. 3–12). Baltimore: Brookes.

Rimm-Kaufman, S. E., Pianta, R. C., & Cox, M. J. (2000). Teachers' judgments of problems in the transition to kindergarten. *Early Childhood Research Quarterly, 15*(2), 147–166.

Schwartz, I. S., Garfinkle, A., N., & Davis, C. (2000). Arranging preschool environments to facilitate valued social and educational outcomes. In M. R. Shinn, H. M. Walker, & G. Stoner (Eds.), *Interventions for academic and behavior problems II: Preventive and remedial approaches* (pp. 455–468). Baltimore: National Association of School Psychologists.

Snow, C. E., Burns, M. S., & Griffin, P. (Eds.). (1998). *Preventing reading difficulties in young children.* Washington, DC: National Academy Press.

Stevenson, H. W., & Newman, R. S. (1986). Long-term prediction of achievement and attitudes in mathematics and reading. *Child Development, 57,* 646–659.

Kristen N. Missall
Robin L. Hojnoski

MIDDLE SCHOOL

Most educational systems in the United States involve students attending a middle school (traditionally called junior high school) for two to three years, sandwiched between the elementary and high school grades. There is considerable variability in the grades included in middle schools, although sixth through eighth are the most common. Grade configuration is influenced primarily by social, demographic, and space considerations within school districts. Middle schools span elementary schools' focus on providing all students with a breadth of educational experiences and developing core knowledge and skills, and high schools' educational specialization that prepares students for the workforce or post-secondary education. They typically offer new subjects that students can elect to study, different levels of a subject within the same grade, and teachers with subject-specific specialization for academic subjects (resulting in students being taught by multiple teachers).

The transition to middle school coincides with early adolescence—the developmental transition period between childhood and adulthood. Developmental changes associated with adolescence have bearing on all students' experiences.

DEVELOPMENTAL CHANGES COINCIDING WITH THE TRANSITION TO MIDDLE SCHOOL

The early adolescent period is a time of dramatic physical, cognitive, social, and psychological growth and development. Not only must adolescents adjust to their own changes, they must also adjust to others treating them differently because of that development.

Physical Development. The onset of puberty usually marks the beginning of adolescence. Females begin puberty approximately eighteen months earlier, on average, than males; however, timing varies widely. Adolescents experience a dramatic growth spurt, with significant gains in height and weight, development of secondary sexual characteristics, and changes in fat and muscle distribution. Sexual interest also develops. Adolescents often appear awkward with their bodies, because of their rapid and irregular growth. Pubertal timing, relative to peers, is related to adolescents' body image and satisfaction with their appearance; late-developing females and early-developing males hold the most positive perceptions.

Cognitive Development. Adolescence is characterized by steady improvement in a range of cognitive abilities, both because of biological maturing and experiences. Adolescents process information faster and more efficiently, and their memory is better than in childhood. They become more meta-cognitive, or able to think about their thoughts and actions. However, they also tend to overestimate their abilities and underestimate their vulnerabilities. Adolescents become increasingly able to engage in complex and abstract thinking, reasoning, decision making, and problem solving. With their improved cognitive abilities they appreciate others' perspectives better, reflect on themselves more, and become more self-aware. With these changes come greater self-consciousness and a tendency to believe that their experiences and feelings are unique to themselves. Finally, adolescents become better at regulating and coordinating their thinking, emotions, and behavior.

Social Relationships. Another dramatic change associated with adolescence is the increased importance of peer relationships. Young adolescents spend more time with peers, and friendships become more intense, close, and involve more self-disclosure. Distinct peer groups, with different characteristics, reputations, and status hierarchies, appear during early adolescence. With this emergence of cliques and crowds comes concern about social image. The desire to fit in and be like others is also strongest in early adolescence. This desire for acceptance is accompanied by greater use of strategies designed to project a particular image.

Psychological Development. With the development of adult-like characteristics comes a desire for greater independence and autonomy. Changes in young adolescents' physical characteristics, cognitive abilities, and social relationships influence their identity development—perceptions of who they are, what they are good or not good at, what they value or devalue, and what they aspire to or fear becoming. Establishing an identity involves the process of exploring and embarking on commitments (both emotionally, and with time and resources) to particular paths and outcomes. Although identity continues to develop through adulthood, it is especially important during adolescence; choices made at this time can have far-reaching consequences for education, employment, and relationships.

CHANGES WHEN STUDENTS MOVE TO MIDDLE SCHOOL

Middle schools typically afford experiences quite different from those students were accustomed to. The school buildings tend to be larger, serving students from multiple elementary schools, and employ subject-specific specialist teachers. Students also experience changes in what and how they are taught, how they are evaluated, their interactions with teachers and peers, and institutional norms and requirements. The nature of these changes has profound implications for young adolescents' academic and emotional thriving.

Middle Grade Schools (1980s). Research during the 1980s by Roberta Simmons and Dale Blyth showed that the transition to junior high school (as it was called then) was typically accompanied by worrying changes. Compared to students in K-8 schools, those in junior high had lower grades, lower self-esteem, and more negative attitudes about school. Other researchers (most notably Jacquelynne Eccles, Carol Midgley, and their colleagues) identified similar and additional negative outcomes, including lower achievement, perceived ability, and interest in school, less positive and personal student-teacher relationships, and more anxiety and absenteeism. Because the comparison was between students in the same grade, with only the schools' grade configuration differing, prevailing notions that hormones and puberty were responsible for students' difficulties in junior high were shown to be incorrect.

Eccles and Midgley argued that these changes were a result of a mismatch between the school environment and students' development, and they coined the term *stage-environment fit*. They noted that the nature of junior high schools was antithetical to the developmental needs of young adolescents. That is, at a time when social connections and interpersonal relationships become particularly important, students had less opportunity for personal connections because they moved from class to class, with different teachers and different classmates and experienced predominantly whole class instruction. At a time of dramatic and uneven cognitive development, homogenous classes were formed by ability grouping and students received different learning opportunities. It was then extremely difficult for students in lower tracks to learn material necessary for college entry, and this design worked against those with later, but normal, cognitive development. Worksheets and whole class instruction predominated, so students' lessons were less varied and individualized compared to elementary school. Also of concern, junior high school teachers were less confident about teaching their students than were elementary teachers in the same grades.

When students are particularly concerned about fitting in and are sensitive about how they are viewed by others, they experienced more public and socially comparative grading practices and recognition policies. Also, although students are able to view situations more complexly, understand more abstract and nuanced ideas, and are developing their reasoning and argumentation skills, their lessons were slotted rigidly into short periods. Thus, time constrained the type and complexity of activities they could engage in. When students desire more independence and responsibility, they had fewer choices and opportunities for input. Teachers trusted students less than did elementary teachers of the same grades, and their management and discipline practices were controlling and custodial rather than student-centered.

Middle School Reform (1990s). Concern that junior high schools were not meeting young adolescents' needs led to calls for reform, with the objective of creating middle-level educational environments that are congruent developmentally with their needs. *Turning Points*, the Carnegie Council on Adolescent Development's prominent and influential report, advocated widespread changes to all aspects of the middle grades experience. The National Middle School Association advocated similar changes. Their recommendations included: (1) creating smaller learning environments to promote positive teacher-student relationships and connectedness to school (e.g., interdisciplinary team teaching, advisory programs), (2) teaching more challenging and complex material (e.g., emphasizing critical thinking skills, interdisciplinary curricula, flexible or block scheduling), (3) ensuring all students have common core classes and can be successful (e.g., heterogeneous classes), and (4) preparing teachers for the middle grades (e.g., learning about ado-

lescent development, gaining certification with a middle grade specialty).

Middle Schools between the 1990s and Early 2000s. The middle school reform recommendations were adopted unevenly, according to reviews by the Carnegie Corporation and the RAND Corporation. Organizational changes were adopted more often than recommendations involving instruction. More than half the middle schools introduced home room classes and team teaching, however, often not as intended, thwarting objectives. For example, team teaching was premised on teachers having time together for shared planning and communicating about students, but teachers' planning times were often not coordinated. Flexible scheduling, which allows longer time periods for more complex activities, had been introduced infrequently. Integration across disciplines was difficult because teaching methods and beliefs vary for different subjects. Students continued to be placed in classes by ability groups in most schools. Although there were promising teaching reforms to increase students' conceptual understanding in mathematics and science (advocated by the National Council of Teachers of Mathematics and the National Research Council, respectively), in the early 2000s these efforts had been supplanted by consequences of high-stakes standardized testing, with its emphasis on knowledge that can be assessed quickly and easily.

Research in the 1990s and early 2000s showed that students' attitudes about school and feeling of connectedness no longer declined after the transition to middle school. Thus, the changes that targeted improving student-teacher relationships and creating a positive school climate had positive results for students. However, students did not fare better academically compared to pre-reform levels. Researchers expressed concern with the nature of instruction and the shortage of qualified teachers. Students viewed their classrooms as emphasizing learning and understanding to a lesser extent than their elementary school classrooms did.

FACTORS THAT PREDICT STUDENTS' TRANSITION EXPERIENCES

Students who are confident about themselves and their learning are most likely to experience the transition to middle school positively, whereas those who begin with academic difficulties are at risk for academic and behavioral problems. Participation in school-affiliated extracurricular activities strengthens school commitment and achievement, especially for low-achieving males. Early pubertal development is a risk factor, particularly for girls. They are more likely to experience low self-esteem, to have older friends, be sexually active, and drink alcohol; therefore, their social lives may generate tensions with academic demands before they have developed sound coping strategies.

Friends and peers reinforce each others' actions and, therefore, support and encourage positive or negative behaviors and attitudes, depending on peer group characteristics and the intensity of the relationship. Consequently, strong friendships with peers who value school and achievement are positive predictors of transition experiences, whereas socializing with peers whose norms are counter to those promoted by school predicts future academic and social difficulties.

Students are most likely to make a positive transition to middle school when their classroom and school environments promote both their learning and understanding and supportive interpersonal relationships. This transition outcome involves a classroom emphasis on learning and understanding, not just memorization of facts, where success is viewed as self-improvement or in criterion-referenced terms, students have some autonomy, teachers have high expectations for all students, and learning activities are challenging, valued, and relevant to students. Furthermore, positive outcomes are more likely when students believe their teachers are enthusiastic and committed to helping them learn and are able to do so, feel respected as learners and as people, and view their classmates as encouraging them academically and emotionally. In contrast, competitive learning environments in which students' progress is public and expressed relative to others, and teachers' practices are controlling, inconsistent, or inflexible are likely to elicit less positive transition outcomes.

Characteristics of schools and staff affect the nature of the middle school transition. Having student-teacher advisory teams and a consistent group of classmates ease the transition. Also, having teachers who are confident in teaching their students, knowledgeable about their subject-matter and how to teach it, understand and like young adolescents, have opportunities for their own professional decision making, and feel supported by their principal and school administrators, predict middle school students' achievement and socio-emotional well-being. Conversely, students are less likely to thrive when their teachers experience high teaching demands and stress, low autonomy, and feel pressed to cover content, rather than having flexibility to pace material in response to students' understanding.

POST-TRANSITION INDICTORS OF POTENTIAL DIFFICULTIES

Academic and social aspects of school are closely related; socio-emotional and behavioral difficulties lead easily to academic problems, however academic problems can pre-cipitate poor socio-emotional well-being. In general, "standing out and not fitting in are especially detrimental during the middle school years" (Juvonen et al., 2004, p. 48). Indicators of possible difficulties are increases in absenteeism, tardiness, missed homework assignments, and declining class preparedness, interest, participation in lessons, and grades. Also, repeating a middle grade is a strong predictor of dropping out of school. Depression, with its lethargy, decreased emotionality, and sleep disturbances can lead to academic problems. Displaying problem behaviors, such as aggressiveness, disruptiveness, or impulsivity are warning signs of difficulties, as is having relationships with deviant peers. Being socially isolated increases risk for depression, interpersonal difficulties (including bullying or being bullied), poor school performance, and dropping out of school. Finally, likelihood of difficulties at middle school increases with multiple stressors; these also include stressors outside school, such as illness, financial problems, or conflict within the family, divorce, and students' job commitments.

BIBLIOGRAPHY

Eccles, J. S., & Midgley, C. (1989). Stage-environment fit: Developmentally appropriate classrooms for early adolescents. In C. Ames & R. Ames (Eds.), *Research on motivation in education*: Volume 3. *Goals and cognitions* (pp. 139–186). New York: Academic Press.

Eccles, J. S., Midgley, C., Wigfield, A., Buchanan, C. M., Reuman, D. Flanagan, C., et al. (1993). Development during adolescence: The impact of stage-environment fit on young adolescents' experiences in schools and in families. *American Psychologist, 48,* 90–101.

Jackson, A. W., & Davis, G. A. (2000). *Turning points 2000: Educating adolescents in the 21st century.* New York: Teachers College Press.

Juvonen, J., Le, V-N, Kaganoff, T., Augustine, C., & Constant, L. (2004). *Focus on the wonder years: Challenges facing the American middle school.* Santa Monica, CA: RAND Corporation.

Midgley, C., & Edelin, K. C. (1998). Middle school reform and early adolescent well-being: The good news and the bad. *Educational Psychologist, 33,* 195–206.

Midgley, C., Middleton, M. J. Gheen, M. H., & Kumar, R. (2002). Stage-environment fit revisited: A goal theory approach to examining school transitions. In C. Midgley (Ed.), *Goals, goal structures, and patterns of adaptive learning* (pp. 109–142). Mahwah, NJ: Erlbaum.

National Middle School Association. (1995). *This we believe: Developmentally responsive middle level schools.* Columbus, OH: author.

Simmons, R. G., & Blyth, D. A. (1987). *Moving into adolescence: The impact of pubertal change and social context.* Hawthorne, NY: Aldine de Gruyter.

Helen Patrick
Brent M. Drake

HIGH SCHOOL

School transition research has included consideration of transitions from elementary to middle and from middle to high school as well as transitions across grades within schools and across schools in adolescence and has documented many problems for adolescents. Jacquelynne Eccles and her colleagues produced the seminal work in this area published in the *American Psychologist* (1993) as well as many other scholarly journals. She hypothesized that most middle and high schools in the United States do not meet the developmental needs of adolescents. She further argued that school transitions are largely discontinuous and disruptive for development. Much data support this hypothesis across diverse populations and strong longitudinal study designs that controlled for many confounding variables (e.g., Simmons, et al., 1987; Eccles, 2004; Isakson, & Jarvis, 1999; Gutman, & Midgley, 2000; Barber & Olsen, 2004).

Generally, students making the transition to high school experience a decrease in self-esteem, participate less in school and extracurricular activities, see a drop in grade point average, miss more school days, and suffer from anonymity. Additionally anxiety is high concerning school procedures and the presence of older peers. Yet characteristics of schools as well as differences between adolescents may influence such adjustment. According to Barber and Olsen, high school students have been assumed to have fewer problems than middle school students given that they have had experience with middle school transitions and are more mature than early adolescents, all of which makes them less vulnerable to peer influence. These authors and many others argue that these assumptions are incorrect, as high school students in middle adolescence also experience significant stressors as they strive to meet the challenges associated with school/grade transitions. The focus of this entry is on empirical findings from research on adolescent adjustment during the transition to high school.

MAJOR DEVELOPMENTAL CHALLENGES FOR ADOLESCENTS

Based on John Hill's 1983 theoretical framework for studying adolescents, biological, cognitive, and social changes are fundamental to the transition from childhood to adolescence. Such changes occur across developmental contexts, including family, peers, schools, work, and leisure. Psychosocial issues, including identity, intimacy, sexuality, autonomy, and achievement, are paramount for adolescent development as well as across the lifespan generally. Adolescents face challenges associated with these psychosocial issues as they move through adolescence and experience the fundamental biological, cognitive, and social changes across contexts that give the issues greater significance than in childhood. Specific developmental challenges following this theoretical framework for adolescents making the transition to high school include the increased importance of academic achievement (unfortunately largely focused on grade point average) for success after graduation, the increased social significance of peer associations, and high school environments that require more self-reliance in students than was required of them in middle school.

The increased emphasis on social interactions in high school creates an environment in which fitting in and belonging serves an added source of pressure while at the same time peers (and parents) provide support for adolescents during this transitional period. Teacher expectations and demands increase in high school and students experience a higher level of stress than they did in middle school. Stark and colleagues and Phelps and Jarvis found that high school students reported their main problems to be in the areas of school, parents, friends, and dating, which is consistent with the types of developmental adjustments adolescents typically encounter and the high school atmosphere itself. Males reported more school problems, whereas females reported more interpersonal problems in both studies. Thus, adaptive coping strategies are needed by adolescents to handle such challenges. Success or failure at developmental tasks in adolescence sets the pathway for adult adjustment.

MAJOR STRUCTURAL AND ACADEMIC CHANGES IN HIGH SCHOOL

Structural changes in peer groups and schools influence the student transitioning to high school. This transition engenders changes in peer contacts such that adolescents begin to come into contact with older peers who are perceived as having more antisocial values. As with literature on early maturing adolescents, students entering the high school environment may not be prepared to cope with the influences of older, more experienced peers.

In most high schools, the structure of classes is also potentially problematic for adolescents in that classes are even less decentralized than in middle school leaving students without clear connections to caring adults who know their academic and social strengths well. Brief contact with numerous teachers in a more anonymous and bureaucratic setting makes it difficult for adolescents to feel valued and special, especially in overcrowded, resource-impoverished schools. This lack of connections to adults who can listen to adolescents' concerns undermines healthy adjustment, as Barber and Olsen discussed and the Carnegie Council on Adolescent Development noted in their task force report on preparing adolescents for the 21st century. Barber and Olsen assessed transitions to middle and high school in the same students and found that, although in high school students reported fewer negative changes than they had two years earlier in middle school transition, the types of problems reported were consistent across both school transitions. Specifically, students perceived the school environment negatively (feeling less positive about school, feeling the need for more organization, and perceiving less support) and indicated decreased psychological adjustment (e.g., lower self-esteem, more depressive and anxiety symptoms).

Similarly, the research teams of both Simmons and Eccles noted academic changes such as stricter grading standards and structural changes common to high schools such as more impersonal environments and larger schools that increase anonymity of students. Goodenow found that students' feelings of belongingness in their school positively affected their motivation for school, effort, level of participation, and eventual achievement in school. Finally, Resnick and colleagues, reporting on the first wave of the Add Health data (a longitudinal study of adolescent health involving some 90,000 students in grades 7–12), found that both older and younger students who felt connected to their school reported less emotional distress and violent behavior. These researchers also found that a sense of connection to school protected youth from cigarette, alcohol, and marijuana use, and was associated with delay of first sexual intercourse. Both the structural and academic changes in high schools compared to middle schools alienate adolescents from school.

FACTORS PREDICTING SCHOOL TRANSITION ADJUSTMENT

Among the factors considered that predict school transition adjustment, the consensus is that a myriad of variables interact to explain variability (and resiliency) across populations of students. The main variables that have been found to predict adjustment are parent, peer, and teacher support, and development of effective coping strategies. Social class and ethnicity have also been variables identified as important mediators of adolescent adjustment. Each of these variables is considered below.

Gender differences in coping have been found that support consideration of the complexity of experience for particular adolescents. For example, Phelps and Jarvis found that females tended to use emotion-focused coping such as seeking social support; yet faced with a new, more impersonal high school environment, this coping style may not work if close friends are not present to support the adolescent in times of stress. Either new friends are needed or effective coping styles must be used. This view presumes adolescents do not make school transitions with their friends. In some instances (especially in private schools), such transitions are made from school to school as a group, and problems are less pronounced. Phelps and

Jarvis also found that adolescents identified humor and religion as possible coping strategies but did not indicate that they had used such strategies when faced with stressors; thus, one intervention option is to encourage and support the development and use of adaptive coping strategies (generally defined in the coping literature as active problem solving or seeking instrumental support more than emotional support with solvable problems) in these adolescents.

Furthermore, the role of peers is less clear if one considers the peer group's orientation toward school. Generally, peers provide support for adolescents as they face new challenges. Felner and colleagues found that the level of social support from peers and teachers was positively related to school adjustment after the transition to high school for students involved in a support project. Compared to students not involved in the project, the students in the project had higher GPAs, better attendance, more positive self-concepts, and viewed school more favorably.

Some schools have mentorship programs to help students adjust to high school transitions whereby senior students accepted into the program via an application process serve as mentors for entering freshmen (even meeting with new students before the first day of school to help them find their classes). The students then meet with their mentors (one mentor per three incoming students) weekly to acclimate to the new environment with an experienced partner. The overall effectiveness of such programs has not been adequately studied however.

Parents also play an important role in school adjustment for high school students. Fuligni and Eccles found that parents who treat their adolescents in a more adult-like fashion and grant more autonomy than in childhood ease the transition to high school more than parents who restrict opportunities for growth and development in this transitional stage. Steinberg and colleagues also noted that some parents may be experiencing midlife identity issues of their own and as a result restrict their adolescents' life choices such that their adolescents actually experience greater dependency rather than the more healthy process of becoming autonomous adults.

The role of social class must be considered as well as it is generally concluded in literature on schooling in the United States that the rich get richer and the poor stay the same or fall further behind. Similarly, in school transition literature regarding large urban schools that were resource poor, students showed increasing disengagement from school. Seidman and colleagues documented the same declines in school engagement and academics with more ethnically diverse students at such schools as had been documented previously with more middle class, less diverse, samples but also found an increase in daily hassles for poor adolescents in poor schools that turned such adolescents even more toward their peers and gravitated toward more antisocial values. It is fairly well documented that students of color are alienated and marginalized in schools in which they are the minority and/or where tracking places them in inferior classes. Taylor and colleagues and Midgley and her colleagues argue that high schools can and must do more to support rather than undermine school engagement and motivation in students, and doing so especially needed for students who are in a racial minority in their school and even more for those minority students who also experience impoverished living conditions. Overall, poor students in poor schools in poor communities suffer the most during times of stress such as a school or life transition and are the most at risk for developmental problems associated with such stressors.

PROBLEM BEHAVIORS AFTER HIGH SCHOOL TRANSITIONS

Academic problems are the most common difficulties students experience after school transitions followed by psychological and interpersonal adjustment difficulties. These findings have been replicated across many studies in the United States as well as in Australia (see the work of Cotterell with adolescents in Australia). Some students recover from transition losses as they develop positive coping skills and if they receive parental, peer, and teacher support while other students fall further behind over the high school years and may even drop out of school. It has been difficult to adequately study such students over time as students who fell too far behind dropped out and are thus not represented in such samples.

Identifying students experiencing school transition stressors early in the first year of high school may guide interventions to prevent greater problems later. For example, students who do not feel they are a part of their school (lower sense of school membership, according to Goodenow) evince misbehavior, decreased motivation, and academic problems during high school. Although a successful transition into high school implies forming social networks with one's peers and increased support from friends may improve feelings of belongingness in the school, such support may also lead to lower academic achievement if students are distracted from academic work by spending too much time with peers.

A compromise position is to set limits such that it is clearly defined which nights of the week an adolescent may spend time with friends and which nights must be devoted to school work (this would include limits on computer and cell phone usage). Both parents and teachers should foster ongoing communication with transitioning adolescents regarding school progress.

Finally, school administrators and teachers who reach out to students suffering from anonymity and provide "a school within a school," as termed by the Carnegie Council on Adolescent Development, such that these students form appropriate close relationships with at least one adult in the school may reverse negative trajectories for such students. It is considered fundamental for intellectual and personal growth that adolescents have stable, close, mutually respectful relationships with adults and peers. Such relationships can develop best if schools support them through this or similar types of school-within-a-school contexts.

BIBLIOGRAPHY
Barber, B. K., & Olsen, J. A. (2004). Assessing the transitions to middle and high school. *Journal of Adolescent Research, 19,* 3–30.
Carnegie Commission on Adolescent Development. (1989). *Turning Points: Preparing American youth for the 21st century: The report of the task force on the education of young adolescents.* Washington, DC: Carnegie Council on Adolescent Development.
Cotterell, J. L. (1992). The relation of attachments and supports to adolescent well-being and school adjustment. *Journal of Adolescent Research, 7,* 28–42.
Eccles, J. (2004). Schools, academic motivation, and stage-environment fit. In R. Lerner & L. Steinberg (Eds.), *Handbook of adolescent psychology.* New York: Wiley.
Eccles, J. S., Midgley, C., Wigfield, A., Buchanan, C. M., Reuman, D., Flanagan, C. et al. (1993). Development during adolescence: The impact of stage-environment fit on young adolescents' experiences in schools and families. *American Psychologist, 48,* 90–101.
Felner, R. D., Primavera, J., & Cauce, A. M. (1981). The impact of school transitions: A focus for preventive efforts. *American Journal of Community Psychology, 9,* 449–459.
Fuligni, A. J., & Eccles, J. S. (1993). Perceived parent-child relationships and early adolescents' orientation toward peers. *Developmental Psychology, 29,* 622–632.
Goodenow, C. (1993). The psychological sense of school membership among adolescents: Scale development and educational correlates. *Psychology in the Schools, 30,* 79–90.
Gutman, L. M., & Midgley, C. (2000). The role of protective factors in supporting the academic achievement of poor African American students during the middle school transition. *Journal of Youth and Adolescence, 29,* 223–248.
Harter, S., Whitesell, N. R., & Kowalski, P. (1992). Individual differences in the effects of educational transitions on young adolescent's perceptions of competence and motivational orientation. *American Educational Research Journal, 29,* 777–780.
Hill, J. (1983). Early adolescence: A framework. *Journal of early adolescence, 3,* 1–21.
Hirsch, B. J., & DuBois, D. L. (1992). The relation of peer social support and psychological symptomatology during the transition to junior high school: A two-year longitudinal analysis. *American Journal of Community Psychology, 20,* 333–347.

Isakson, K., & Jarvis, P. A. (1999). The adjustment of adolescents during the transition into high school: A short-term longitudinal study. *Journal of Youth and Adolescence, 28,* 1–26.

Phelps, S. B., & Jarvis, P. A. (1994). Coping in adolescence: Empirical evidence for a theoretically based approach to assessing coping. *Journal of Youth and Adolescence, 23,* 359–371.

Resnick, M., Bearman, P., Blum, R., Bauman, K., Harris, K., Jones, J., et al. (1997). Protecting adolescents from harm: Findings from the National Longitudinal Study on Adolescent Health. *Journal of the American Medical Association, 278,* 823–832.

Seidman, E, LaRue, A., Aber, J., Mitchell, C., & Feinman, J. (1994). The impact of school transitions in early adolescence on the self-system and perceived social context of poor urban youth. *Child Development, 65,* 507–522.

Simmons, R. G., Burgeson, R., Carlton-Ford, S., & Blyth, D. A. (1987). The impact of cumulative change in early adolescence. *Child Development, 58,* 1220–1234.

Stark, L. J., Spirito, A., Williams, C. A., & Guevremont, D. C. (1989). Common problems and coping strategies 1: Findings with normal adolescents. *Journal of Abnormal Child Psychology, 17,* 203–212.

Steinberg, L., & Steinberg, W. (1994). *Crossing paths: How your child's adolescence triggers your own crisis.* New York: Simon and Schuster.

Taylor, R. D., Casten, R., Flickinger, S., Roberts, D., & Fulmore, C. D. (1994). Explaining the school performance of African-American adolescents. *Journal of Research on Adolescence, 4,* 21–44.

Patricia Jarvis

SCT

SEE *Social Cognitive Theory.*

SECOND LANGUAGE ACQUISITION

Second language acquisition is learning of a nonnative language (i.e., second language) sometime after learning a native language (i.e., first language) has begun. A central characteristic defining second language acquisition is that it occurs in the context in which that language is spoken. For example, native Spanish speakers learning English in the United States or native German speakers learning Japanese in Japan are considered second language learners. However, learning a second language may or may not take place in the context of classroom instruction.

FIRST LANGUAGE VERSUS SECOND LANGUAGE

Second language acquisition is different from learning a foreign language. Second language acquisition of a nonnative language occurs in an environment in which the nonnative speaker has easy access to speakers of the language being learned. In contrast, foreign language learning refers to the learning of a nonnative language in the environment of one's native language. For example, a native English speaker learning French in the United States would be learning a foreign language (Gass & Selinker, 2001).

Understanding second language acquisition requires understanding the difference between learning a first language and a second language. First language develops without formal instruction by children being constantly exposed to language rich environments over the course of many years. The richness of the language environments in which children learn—the amount of language they are exposed to and type of language they are exposed to—influences how thoroughly children learn their native language. Also, as children learn their native language what they learn influences how well and how rapidly native language learning will occur (Hart & Risley, 1995). In contrast, learning a second language usually depends heavily on learning experiences in more constricted environments associated with the classroom or some other formal setting. In these settings, a major goal frequently is to formally teach children the elements of language that are learned much more informally in their native language. Consequently, assumptions regarding teaching and learning a second language are very different from assumptions about children learning their native language.

THE FIVE PRIMARY LINGUISTIC ELEMENTS.

Acquiring any language means learning five primary linguistic elements: phonology, syntax, morphology, semantics, and pragmatics. Phonology is the knowledge of the sound system in a language. It involves knowing what happens in words in fast speech as opposed to more carefully articulated speech. For example in the sentence: "I'm going to ride my bike", it is plausible that a second language learner would believe the correct pronunciation would be: "I'm goin to RIDEMYBIKE" (i.e., the learner does not articulate all of the phonemes in words and runs words together because she does not hear the words and sounds distinctly).

Phonology. Phonology includes knowing all of the sounds that are included in a language and knowing how the sounds are combined. For example, the English letter combinations *sc, sp,* and *st,* do not exist in Spanish at the beginning of words. Thus, to pronounce these letter combinations, native Spanish speakers learning English tend to add an /e/ sound to the beginning of these letter combinations (e.g. /esc/, /esp/, as in eschool, especial) because in Spanish words with *sc, sp,* and *st* combinations begin with an /e/ sound (e.g. "escuela", "especial").

Syntax. Syntax is grammar, the rules that govern word order in sentences. Knowing the grammatical rules allows the speaker to produce an infinite set of sentences that can be easily understood by any individual proficient in that language. For example, the sentence: "The green turtle ran across the street to look for her friend the duck," can be understood by proficient native English speakers even though it is unlikely that the individual has encountered this particular sentence before (Gass & Selinker, 2001).

Morphology. Morphology is the study of word formation. Morphemes represent the minimal unit of meaning in words. For example, the word *fitness* is made up of two morphemes: *fit* and *ness. Ness* is considered a *bound* morpheme because it can never be a word by itself, while *fit* is defined as a *free* morpheme because it is a word in and of itself like the words *man, woman,* and *moon.* Words can be created by adding morphemes, as in *entangle*: dis+entangle, dis+entangl+ing. The ways words are used in sentences also follow accepted patterns. For example, English speakers say, "Mt. Everest is a high mountain," but not "The Empire State Building is a high building." (They would say, "The Empire State Building is a tall building.") Sometimes the reason certain word combinations are appropriate is clear, while at other times the combination appears to be quite arbitrary (Gass & Selinker, 2001).

Semantics. Semantics is the study of meaning. Knowledge of the semantics of a language also includes knowledge of the reference of words, word combinations, and limitation of word meanings. For example, in English the word *bank* has multiple meanings. When a reader encounters the word *bank* in text such as "The children sat very close to the river bank admiring the elegant movements of the swans," he knows from the context that the word *bank* is being used to represent a margin. Knowing that words may have multiple meanings, and knowing those meanings, allows listeners and readers to interpret messages appropriately. Word combinations also affect the meaning of a sentence. For example, the meaning of the sentence: "The dog bit the man" is different from the meaning of "The man bit the dog" although both sentences include exactly the same words.

Pragmatics. Pragmatics refers to the way language is used in context. For example, when a teacher says: "Eyes on me," a direction is being given and the expectation is that students will look at the teacher. The teacher is not suggesting she has eyes on her body somewhere. Word order has also an effect on pragmatics. For example, when a child orders a chocolate and vanilla ice cream cone, the order of the flavors may be important to understand which flavor comes first and which comes second.

The level of importance of each of these elements varies at different points in the development of language proficiency. A mature speaker of a second language uses the language differently from a novice speaker, and the differences follow predictable stages of development. For example, reading development depends on knowing the sounds in words and being able to accurately read words contained in text. Similarly, understanding the pragmatics of a language requires that second language learners understand phonology, morphology, and semantics.

THREE MODELS FOR SECOND LANGUAGE ACQUISITION

Several linguistic models attempt to explain the development of second language acquisition. The three most common models are the Universal Grammar Model, the Competition Model, and the Monitor Model. The Universal Grammar Model refers to the system of principles, conditions, and rules that are properties or elements of all human languages. At the same time, each language has grammatical rules that vary from one language to another. Thus, different languages have a limited possibility of different grammatical structures (Chomsky, 1975). Therefore, second language learners base their second language acquisition on universal principles common to all languages, and on the constraints of the particular rules of each language. For example, adjectives in English usually precede nouns. By contrast, in Spanish adjectives follow nouns. Although adjectives in both languages have the same function, their position depends on the constraints of each of the languages.

The Competition Model is based in the assumption that forms of natural language are created to communicate. Thus, second language learners are faced with the conflict between native language and target language cues and cue strengths. Learners will first resort to their native language interpretation strategies, and when these do not match the target language, then they resort to a universal selection of meaning based on cues as opposed to syntax-based cues. Positive and negative evidence is necessary for learners to realize which cues are correct for the target language (Bates & MacWhinney, 1982).

The Monitor Model (Krashen, 1985) has been very influential in school settings. This model is based on five hypotheses: the Acquisition-Learning Hypothesis (acquisition occurs unconsciously, learning is conscious knowledge of the second language); the Natural Order Hypothesis (language rules are acquired in a predictable order); the Monitor Hypothesis (the learned system acts as a monitor of the acquired system), the Input Hypothesis; and the Affective Filter Hypothesis (motivation, attitude, self-confidence, and anxiety affect second language acquisition).

Krashen's 1985 Input Hypothesis, central to his theory of second language acquisition, suggests that language instruction just slightly above the student's current level of language proficiency (i.e., comprehensible input) is useful for second language acquisition. Generally, a silent period in the beginning of second language acquisition is natural and desirable until learners feel comfortable expressing themselves. Speaking cannot be taught directly; it is a result of internalizing comprehensible input.

Cummins (1979) hypothesized that second language acquisition includes the development of two proficiencies, conversational skills and academic language. Conversational skills (also called Basic Interpersonal Communication Skills, BICS) refer to the ability of children to use everyday language with adults and peers. The more formal academic language is the language of the classroom, as it is frequently characterized. Academic language enables students to understand and apply academic content in school. Conversational language is easier to learn and is learned more quickly than academic language.

VARIATIONS AND SUBGROUPS

Second language learners in the United States are typically referred as English language learners (ELLs). According to the National Research Council (1998), ELLs are "students who come from language backgrounds other than English and whose proficiency is not developed enough where they can profit fully from English-only instruction" (August & Hakuta, 1997, p. 15). The term Limited English Proficiency (LEP) is the formal term used by the federal government to describe and identify ELLs. The term ELLs is considered more descriptive and less pejorative than other terms (LaCelle-Peterson & Rivera, 1994; August & Shanahan, 2006). Approximately 67% of ELLs are in elementary school settings (Kindler, 2002). This statistic means that over 3 million ELLs attend elementary schools, representing more than 11.7% of the elementary school population. The vast majority of ELLs speak Spanish (79.2%) as their first language, but there are more than 460 native languages spoken by school-age students nationwide. The largest language groups after Spanish are Vietnamese

(2%), Hmong (1.6%), Cantonese (1%), and Korean (1%) (Kindler, 2002).

Approximately two out of every three ELLs reside in five states: California, Texas, New York, Florida, and Illinois. Despite this concentration of ELLs in specific states, virtually all states in the United States have seen dramatic increases in their ELL populations since 1990 when the wave of immigration to the United States rose substantially. Many of these states are experiencing the emergence of ELLs in significant numbers for the first time.

For a high percentage of ELLs, schools have difficulty providing the learning environments necessary for them to succeed academically and keep pace with their native English-speaking peers. A major challenge is teaching ELLs a second language (i.e., English) and academic content simultaneously. Since 1998 the federal government has tracked the progress of ELLs as a separate group on the National Assessment of Educational Progress. In important subjects such as reading and math, ELLs lag considerably behind other students. How to close this achievement gap concerns the research community and bilingual educators (August & Shanahan, 2006).

INTERVENTIONS AND INSTRUCTIONAL PROCEDURES TO ENHANCE EDUCATION OUTCOMES

A central question regarding ELLs acquiring English as a second language is whether it is better to teach them English language and academic content directly in English or to first make sure they have developed literacy skills in their first language. A number of research syntheses have been conducted to address this question. Francis, Lesaux, and August (2006) reviewed these syntheses and also conducted their own analysis. Although the quality of this research is not particularly strong, Francis, Lesaux, and August concluded there is a benefit to literacy development in English when ELLs are instructed in their native language (Francis et al., 2006). Overall, native language instruction resulted in a small positive impact on English reading development. They also noted the effect was strongest in those studies that paired native language instruction with English literacy instruction.

Regardless of the timing of English instruction in relation to primary language instruction, it is essential that English is taught with a strong focus placed on both learning the language and learning academic content in that language. In terms of academic content, much of the instructional approaches that are effective for native English-speaking students should also be effective for students learning English as a second language. For example, Shanahan and Beck (2006) concluded that in terms of English literacy development, the core instructional components that are effective with native English speakers, such as phonemic awareness, phonics, fluency, vocabulary, and comprehension, are effective with students learning English as a second language. Further, many of the same instructional approaches that are effective in delivering instruction with native English speakers, such as instruction that is systematic and explicit, will be effective with second language students.

In terms of acquiring English as a second language, approaches referred to generally as sheltered instruction, in which students learn English under conditions of high language support, are advocated. In sheltered instruction, the English demands are lower than they are for native English speakers, and the acquisition of English is promoted through instruction in the language and instruction in academic content simultaneously. Frequently, however, explicit instruction in English gets less emphasis and it is more a hope that "language develop occurs" (Gersten & Baker, 2000, p. 459) during content area lessons than a clear instructional objective. This circumstance can pose a particular problem when teachers are required to cover extensive content in science, social studies, and mathematics, and there is insufficient time for English language development, particularly formal academic English.

Although the research on specific instructional variables that affect second language learning is minimal, five variables have some empirical support as well as conceptual merit: (a) vocabulary as a major curricular objective, (b) using visuals to reinforce concepts and vocabulary, (c) implementing cooperative learning and peer- tutoring strategies, (d) using native language strategically, and (e) modulation of cognitive and language demands (Gersten & Baker, 2000). Vocabulary is a key instruction target in second language learning. Vocabulary instruction should include concentration on Tier 2 words, (i.e., words that are likely to appear in a wide variety of texts and in the written and oral language of mature users (Beck, 2002). However, second language learners in the initial stages of language acquisition also benefit from instruction in Tier 1 words (i.e., words that are common in everyday life) because they frequently are not familiar to second language learners.

Using visuals and prompts helps learners visualize the abstractions of language and provide second language learners with the opportunity to practice vocabulary in formats such as small group instruction. Instructional interactions with peers increases the likelihood that information will be retained. In modulating cognitive and language demands, skillful teachers increase second language demands when students are practicing familiar academic content and decrease language demands (e.g., the use of complete sentences) when instruction focuses on the learning of new content. Strategic use of the student's native primary language in learning new content can help second language learners attach new labels to concepts they know in their primary language. One problem in using the student's native language to explain concepts is that sometimes second language learners do not understand the concept in their primary language. As of the early 2000s, research in all of these areas is badly needed.

ISSUES RELATED TO ASSESSMENT AND INSTRUCTION

School-based assessments of students learning a second language are done for two broad purposes: to assess their English language proficiency and to assess their academic content knowledge. A number of problems are associated with both types of assessments, although they can provide information that is useful in school decision-making, such as identifying students for academic programs. For example, measures of English language proficiency do not predict very accurately performance on academic measures. Assessments of language proficiency also may underestimate how well students are prepared academically because performance of second language learners on academic assessments may be influenced by their knowledge of English.

Thus, low language proficiency may obscure what the learner really knows about the academic content being assessed. For example, in the early elementary grades, measures of language proficiency in English are sometimes used to delay literacy instruction until students have acquired the oral language skills considered necessary to learn academic content. A common assumption has been that teaching reading in English should occur after oral language proficiency is developed. Empirical evidence contradicts this position. Measures of oral English proficiency do not predict how well second language learners will learn English literacy skills. Even students whose oral English is very low can make significant progress learning foundations of reading in a second language such as phonemic awareness and understanding of the alphabetic principle (Chiappe, Siegel, & Wade-Woolley, 2002; Geva & Yaghoub Zadeh, 2006; Lesaux & Siegel, 2003).

In the United States, second language instruction has been heavily influenced by Krashen's 1985 input hypothesis. However, this hypothesis has been criticized for being vague in terms of instructional specificity and lacking empirical support. Many studies have shown that speaking helps comprehension and acquisition of a second language (Pica et al., 1987; Ellis et al., 1994; Gas & Varonis, 1994; Klingner & Vaughn, 1996; Mackey, 1999). Further, in school contexts, Klingner and Vaughn (1996) suggest that providing students plenty of opportunities to practice newly learned vocabulary words in complete sentences in different contexts throughout the school day, providing immediate feedback and frequent monitoring, helps children increase English language acquisition. In fact, several researchers have found that a major issue in instructional contexts is the lack of opportunities second language students have to use English in the classroom (Arreaga-Mayer & Perdomo-Rivera, 1996; Gersten & Baker, 2000; Ramírez, 1992). In other words, the lack of opportunities for students to engage in meaningful language use that is cognitively challenging may hinder second language acquisition.

Another issue extensively discussed has been whether there is a critical period in second language learning, generally considered to be around puberty, beyond which it is difficult or impossible to learn a second language to the same degree as a native speaker. This hypothesis suggests that young children are more likely to attain native-like proficiency in a second language than are adolescents or adults. Children appear to master the phonology of a language faster than adults, but adults appear to learn morphology and syntax faster.

However, the advantage children appear to have in attaining mastery of a second language (particularly phonology) is not uniformly apparent in all languages. Learning a second language is influenced by the alignment between the native language and the second language, and mastery of skills in the native language influences second language acquisition.

SEE ALSO *First (Primary) Language Acquisition.*

BIBLIOGRAPHY

Arreaga-Mayer, C., & Perdomo-Rivera, C. (1996). Ecobehavioral analysis of instruction for at-risk language-minority students. *Elementary School Journal, 96,* 245–258.

August, D., & Hakuta, K. (1997). *Improving schooling for language-minority children: A research agenda.* Washington, DC: National Academy Press.

August, D., & Shanahan, L. (2006). *Developing literacy in second-language learners: Report of the National Literacy Panel on Language Minority Children and Youth.* Washington, DC: National Literacy Panel on Language-Minority Children and Youth (U.S.).

Bates, E., & MacWhinney, B. (1982). Functionalist approaches to grammar. In E. Wanner & L. R. Gleitman (Eds.), *Language acquisition: The state of the art* (pp. 173–218). New York: Cambridge University Press.

Chiappe, P., Siegel, L., & Wade-Woolley, L. (2002). Linguistic diversity and the development of reading skills: A longitudinal study. *Scientific Studies of Reading, 6*(4), 369–400.

Chomsky, N. (1975). *Reflections on language* (1st ed.). New York: Pantheon Books.

Cummins, J. (1979). Linguistic interdependence and the educational development of bilingual children. *Review of Educational Research, 49*(2), 222–251.

Ellis, R., Tanaka, Y., & Yamazaki, A. (1994). Classroom interaction, comprehension, and the acquisition of L2 word meanings. *Language Learning, 44*(3), 449–491.

Francis, D., Lesaux, N. K., & August, D. (2006). Language of instruction. In D. L. August & T. Shanahan (Eds.), *Developing literacy in a second language: Report of the National Literacy Panel* (pp. 365–410). Mahwah, NJ: Erlbaum.

Gass, S. M., & Selinker, L. (2001). *Second language acquisition: An introductory course* (2nd ed.). Mahwah, NJ: Erlbaum.

Gass, S. M., & Varonis, E. M. (1994). Input, interaction, and second language production. *Studies in Second Language Acquisition, 16*(3), 283–302.

Gersten, R., & Baker, S. (2000). What we know about effective instructional practices for English-language learners. *Exceptional Children, 66*(4), 454–470.

Geva, E., & Yaghoub-Zadeh, Z. (2006). Reading efficiency in native English-speaking and English-as-a-second-language children: The role of oral proficiency and underlying cognitive-linguistic processes. *Scientific Studies of Reading, 10*(1), 31–57.

Hart, B., & Risley, T. R. (1995). Meaningful differences in the everyday experience of young American children. Towson, MD: Brookes.

Hedges, L. V. (1981). Distribution theory for Glass's estimator of effect size and related estimators. *Journal of Educational Statistics, 6*(2), 107–128.

Kindler, A. (2002). *Survey of the states' limited English proficient students and available educational programs and services 2000–2001* (Summary Report). Washington DC: National Clearinghouse for English Language Acquisition and Language Instruction Educational Programs.

Klingner, J. K., & Vaughn, S. (1996). Reciprocal teaching of reading comprehension strategies for students with learning disabilities who use English as a second language. *Elementary School Journal, 96*(3), 275–293.

Krashen, S. D. (1985). *The input hypothesis: Issues and implications.* White Plains, NY: Longman.

LaCelle-Peterson, M. W., & Rivera, C. (1994). Is it real for all kids? A framework for equitable assessment policies for English language learners. *Harvard Educational Review, 64*(1), 55–75.

Lesaux, N., & Siegel, L. (2003). The development of reading in children who speak English as a second language. *Developmental Psychology, 39*(6), 1005–1020.

National Research Council. (1998). *Preventing reading difficulties in young children.* Washington, DC: National Academy Press.

Pica, T., Young, R., & Doughty, C. (1987). The impact of interaction on comprehension. *TESOL Quarterly, 21*(4), 737–759.

Ramírez, J. D. (1992). Executive summary: Longitudinal study of structured English immersion strategy, early-exit and late-exit transitional bilingual education programs for language-minority children. *Bilingual Research Journal, 16*(1 & 2), 1–62.

Shanahan, T., & Beck, I. (2006). Effective literacy teaching for English-language learners. In D. L. August & T. Shanahan (Eds.), *Developing literacy in a second language: Report of the National Literacy Panel* (pp. 415–488). Mahwah, NJ: Erlbaum.

Doris Luft Baker
Scott K. Baker

SELF-CONCEPT

SEE *Relevance of Self-Evaluations to Classroom Learning.*

SELF-DETERMINATION THEORY OF MOTIVATION

Teachers and parents frequently find themselves frustrated with their students or children, wondering how to motivate them to try harder on their schoolwork. Self-determination theory (SDT) is a broad motivational theory that addresses that issue. The theory begins by distinguishing between two different types of motivation—namely, autonomous motivation and controlled motivation—and it then considers the different consequences of these two motivations as well as their different antecedents. SDT also looks at the concept of goals as well as motivations and considers them in a differentiated manner. This entry discusses each of these ideas in turn, beginning with an explanation of the types of motivation.

AUTONOMOUS AND CONTROLLED MOTIVATIONS

Autonomous motivation involves engaging in an activity with eagerness and volition, with a sense of choice and willingness. It is made up of two subtypes: (1) intrinsic motivation, which means doing a task because it is interesting and spontaneously satisfying; and (2) identified motivation, which is a well internalized form of extrinsic motivation and involves doing the task because it feels personally important. A girl is intrinsically motivated when she takes a music class just because it is fun and challenging; a boy's motivation is identified when he studies biology because he is deeply committed to becoming a doctor.

In contrast, controlled motivation involves doing a task with a sense of pressure, demand, or coercion. It comprises two subtypes of extrinsic motivation that have not been well internalized: (1) external motivation, which means doing the activity in order to receive a reward or avoid a punishment; and (2) introjected motivation, which results from partial internalization of the extrinsic contingencies and involves doing an activity because the person would feel approved of for doing it, or guilty and unworthy for not. A boy is externally motivated when he does his homework because his parents pay him for doing it; a girl's motivation is introjected when she takes calculus because she thinks she should and would be ashamed of herself if she did not.

Both autonomy and control are types of motivation; they move students to exert energy and perform tasks. These are clearly distinct from amotivation, which means

not to be motivated for a particular activity or in a particular setting. A student who is daydreaming or paying no attention to a history lesson would be amotivated for history, at least at that time.

When one thinks about the various students in a classroom it is likely that the range of motivations will be present, for example, with some students seeming relatively autonomous and others seeming relatively controlled in their motivations. Self-determination theory focuses both on the outcomes of being more autonomous versus more controlled in one's motivation for schoolwork and on the conditions in classrooms and homes that promote the different types of motivation. Why is it, for example, that some students tend to become more interested in and committed to their school subjects over the course of an academic year, whereas other students come to value school less and become less engaged with learning over the year?

AUTONOMY AND CONTROL: THEIR CONSEQUENCES

Both types of motivation can lead to learning, but the quality of that learning is very different for the two motivations. Wendy Grolnick and Richard Ryan found, for example, that when late-elementary students tended to be autonomous in their motivation because they found the learning material interesting or because they believed the learning was personally important, the students tended to learn the material more deeply—they learned concepts rather than just memorizing facts. But if the students were studying the material because they were told they would be tested on it, they did tend just to memorize facts and not to understand how these facts fit together thematically. In short, the quality of their learning was very different, with autonomy being associated with deeper and fuller learning and control being associated with more superficial learning.

Further, Ryan, along with Richard Koestner, Frank Bernieri, and Kathleen Holt examined school children's motivation for painting pictures and found that when their motivation was more autonomous the students produced paintings that were judged to be more creative than were the paintings produced by students who were more controlled.

Several studies have also linked autonomous motivation to students' adjustment and well-being in school. For example, Grolnick and Ryan found that teachers rated students who were autonomously motivated to be more competent and to have fewer adjustment problem than students who were controlled in their motivation.

In sum, when students are more autonomously motivated because they are interested in learning the material or believe it to be personally valuable, they learn better conceptually, tend to be more creative, and are better adjusted than when their motivation is controlled. As such, it seems very important to give careful consideration to the factors that tend to increase students' autonomous, relative to controlled, motivation.

THE ANTECEDENTS OF AUTONOMY AND CONTROL

An enormous amount of research has examined how specific events such as the offer of a reward, the provision of feedback, or the imposition of a deadline affect students' motivation. As well, many studies have explored how the general interpersonal climates in classrooms or homes influence students' motivation.

Experiments on Antecedents. Many studies have shown that giving students tangible rewards such as money, prizes, and awards for doing an activity tends to make the students more controlled rather than autonomous in their motivation for the activity. In other words, it tends to diminish their interest in the activity and also makes them dependent on the reward so they will be less likely to do the activity unless the rewards continue. In fact, Edward Deci, with Koestner and Ryan, reviewed more than one hundred experiments that examined the effects of rewards on autonomous motivation and found that overall the effects of tangible rewards were negative. Rewards can indeed prompt students to do well at school work that is routine and memory focused, but when it comes to more interesting and conceptual kinds of schoolwork, reward effects are more negative, diminishing autonomous motivation and performance. Some schools reward students with pizza parties for completing work or passing tests. Unfortunately, that is not likely to help them maintain motivation for such work. It is fine to have pizza parties, but motivationally, it is best not to make them contingent on certain behaviors or outcomes.

Other external motivators such as competition (i.e., telling students to try to beat their fellow students), evaluations (i.e., telling students that their performance will be evaluated), surveillance (i.e., watching closely at what the students are doing), and threats (i.e., telling students they will be punished if they do not do just what they are told to do) also tend to undermine the students autonomous motivation because, like rewards, they also tend to be controlling. In contrast, offering students choice about what activities to focus on and allowing them to regulate the time they devote to each was found in an experiment to increase their interest and autonomous motivation.

The thing that ties together these various results is that the typical external motivators such as rewards, deadlines, punishments, and evaluations tend to diminish people's sense of initiation, self-regulation, and volition, whereas offering them opportunities to make choices and guide their own activities tends to allow a greater sense of autonomy. It has become clear, from a huge amount of research, that people need to feel a sense of autonomy or self-determination in order to perform effectively and be well adjusted. In other words, based on many different studies, SDT maintains that autonomy is a basic psychological need—something that must be satisfied for people to be optimally motivated, function effectively, and be psychologically healthy. Factors that help students satisfy this need promote autonomous motivation and positive outcomes, whereas those that are likely to thwart satisfaction of this need diminish autonomous motivation and lead to poorer outcomes.

Other research related to autonomous and controlled motivations has highlighted two other basic psychological needs that are operative in people and affect their motivation. First, it seems that everyone needs to feel competent or effective in dealing with his or her environment. Accordingly, studies have shown that positive feedback enhances students' autonomous motivation because it signifies competence, whereas negative feedback decreases autonomous motivation and leaves students amotivated. Studies also show that satisfaction of the need for competence leads people to be healthier and more effective, but thwarting of this need leads to a sense of ill-being and poorer achievement. Thus, it is important to recognize that students who get continual negative feedback about their work may get into a spiral of feeling ineffective and amotivated, performing even worse and showing signs of poor adjustment, which leads to more of the same. Second, all people need to feel a sense of relatedness, a sense that there are other people who know and care about them. Students who feel a satisfying relationship with one or more teachers tend to do better in school than those who do not. In fact, studies have shown that feeling a sense of relatedness to important others supports the students' autonomous motivation, which in turn leads to better performance and adjustment.

Indeed, looking across a range of studies, it seems that external forces that promote satisfaction of all three needs—that is, the needs for autonomy, competence, and relatedness—lead to the most optimal school engagement and adjustment. Students who experience such need satisfaction feel a sense of vitality, interest, and flexibility; but those who do not are uninterested and disaffected, and they show signs of greater adjustment problems.

Classroom Studies. Research conducted in public schools has shown that the interpersonal climate or ambience of classrooms relates to the motivation and well-being of students in those classrooms. For example, Deci and

Ryan, with Allan Schwartz and Louise Sheinman, examined whether teachers in fourth through sixth grade classes were oriented toward controlling the students' behavior versus supporting the students' autonomy. When teachers are controlling, they make all the decisions, tell the students what they have to do, and use rewards and punishments to ensure that the students do what they—the teachers—demand. This is an extreme version of the traditional classroom that is sometimes called a teacher-centered classroom. Supporting students' autonomy, in contrast, means understanding and acknowledging the students' perspectives, encouraging them to take initiative and solve problems for themselves, allowing students to make choices when possible, and minimizing the use of rewards, punishments, and controlling language (e.g., "should" and "have to"). Such classrooms involve the teachers being supportive of the students' basic need satisfaction and are sometimes referred to as more student-centered classrooms.

At the beginning of a school year, Deci and colleagues did a study in which teachers completed a questionnaire from which the researchers were able to glean whether the teachers were more oriented toward controlling the students' behavior or supporting their autonomy. As well, students in those classrooms completed a set of questionnaires during the first week of school and then two months later. These questionnaires assessed the students' intrinsic motivation, feelings of competence at schoolwork, and general sense of self-worth. Results of the studies showed clear relationships between the teachers' orientations and the students' motivation, perceived competence, and self-worth. In classrooms where teachers were more oriented toward supporting the students' own motivation, the students became more intrinsically motivated and felt more competent and personally worthy, whereas in the classrooms where the teachers were more controlling the students tended to show decreases in intrinsic motivation, perceived competence, and self-worth.

Johnmarshall Reeve and Hyungshim Jang did a study in which they found that specific teacher autonomy-supportive behaviors such as being responsive to students' comments and questions, making time for students' independent work, acknowledging signs of improvement and mastery, offering progress-enabling hints when students seemed stuck, and acknowledging students' experiences and perspectives were linked positively to students' autonomous motivation.

Studies of Parents. Other studies have shown that parents' orientations toward controlling children versus supporting the children's autonomy also affected their children's autonomous motivation for schoolwork and classroom outcomes. For example, Grolnick and Ryan did in-home interviews with parents concerning how

they motivated their late-elementary-school children concerning homework and chores around the house. Mothers and fathers were interviewed separately and two interviewers rated each parent on the degree to which the responses represented autonomy support versus control. The researchers then assessed the children's autonomous motivation and perceived competence in their classrooms and gathered information from the teachers about each student's adjustment and academic competence. Results indicated that parents who were judged to be more autonomy supportive—who understood their children's feelings, while supporting and encouraging them—had children who reported more autonomous motivation and higher perceived competence than the children of parents judged to be more controlling. Further, the students who were rated by teachers as more academically competent and better adjusted were the ones who had more autonomy-supportive parents.

Some studies have examined students' perceptions of autonomy support from both teachers and parents and have found that each contributes predictability to students' motivation, performance, and adjustment. A study of Russian and American high school students, for example, showed that autonomy support from parents and teachers led students to be focused on learning instead of just on grades and to display greater well-being. A study of Canadians indicated that high school students' perceptions of their parents and teachers being high in autonomy support led the students to be less likely to have dropped out of school a year later.

To summarize, considerable research conducted in the psychology laboratory, in school classrooms, and in homes has indicated that external factors as well as interpersonal climates affect students' sense of volition and autonomy versus their sense of being pressure and control, as well as their school engagement, learning, performance, and psychological growth. Those teachers who are supportive of students' autonomy, competence, and relatedness enhance autonomous motivation, learning, and well-being, whereas those who thwart any of these basic needs tend to diminish the important developmental and educational outcomes.

GOALS AND STUDENT PERFORMANCE

As mentioned above, self-determination theory also studies the kinds of goals people use to guide their life pursuits. Some people, for example, place the strongest emphasis on accumulating wealth, whereas others place the strongest emphasis on having meaningful relationships. Research has shown that these types of goals can be categorized into two broad groups: extrinsic goals and intrinsic goals. For example, Tim Kasser and Ryan found that wealth, fame, and attractive image fell into the category labeled extrinsic goals because they are concerned with external indicators of worth and do not provide direct satisfaction of the basic psychological needs. In contrast, relationships, personal growth, health, and community involvement fell into the category labeled intrinsic goals because they are satisfying in their own right and lead more directly to basic need satisfaction.

Vansteenkiste and colleagues did research that applied these goal concepts to classrooms. They introduced classroom activities by telling students that learning the material would be useful in the future either for achieving one of the extrinsic goals (e.g., making money) or for attaining one of the intrinsic goals (e.g., contributing to the community). It turned out that when learning activities were framed in terms of the intrinsic goal of helping the community, students learned the material more fully, performed better when using it, and persisted longer in learning about the topic than when it was said to be useful for making money for themselves. Further, in the experiments, the goal framing was done in either an autonomy-supportive or a controlling manner, and results indicated that intrinsic goal framing and the autonomy-supportive style each contributed to better learning outcomes. In short, orienting students learning more toward intrinsic goals and communicating with them in a more responsive and supportive way facilitates autonomous motivation, deep learning, and effective performance.

INFLUENCES ON TEACHERS' AUTONOMY SUPPORT

The fact that teachers' orientations toward autonomy support versus control in their classroom behaviors has been found to have a significant impact on students' motivation, engagement, achievement, and well-being led researchers to consider what school conditions might affect the teachers' orientations with their students. Research by Deci, Ryan, and Koestner, with Nancy Spiegel and Manette Kauffman, hypothesized that when teachers are pressured for accountability, they will tend to become more controlling with their students. The researchers then did an experiment in which teachers were given the task of teaching students how to solve a particular set of problems. In one group, teachers were told it was their responsibility to ensure that their students performed up to high standards, whereas this accountability statement was not made to teachers in another group. Results indicated that those teachers who were reminded of accountability talked much more during the teaching session, made more commands, used language that contained more control words such as "should," and, remarkably, gave the students the answers rather than giving them hints and encouraging them to find the problem solutions themselves. In short, when teachers are pressured, they in turn pressure their students

and teach in ways that have been found to be detrimental to motivation, performance, and psychological adjustment. Facilitating optimal motivation in students is thus not just an issue for teachers, for it is influenced by the school, the district, and political forces acting upon them.

Substantial research has shown that autonomous motivation, in which students read, study, and discuss their work out of interest and the belief in its importance for themselves, is the optimal motivation for deep learning, creativity, and psychological health. It is also clear that this optimal motivation requires teachers and parents to provide supports that allow students to satisfy their basic needs for feeling competence, relatedness, and autonomy by encouraging the students' initiations, respecting them as individuals, listening to their perspectives, creating opportunities for choice and self-regulation, helping out when they run into barriers, and providing positive and constructive feedback. In these ways, teachers and parents will be supporting students' motivation, engagement, achievement, and psychological well-being. When schools, districts, and states create and reinforce conditions that allow teachers to satisfy their own needs for competence, relatedness, and autonomy on the job, schools will be characterized by more effective teaching and learning.

SEE ALSO *Autonomy Support; Interest; Intrinsic and Extrinsic Motivation.*

BIBLIOGRAPHY

Deci, E. L., Koestner, R., & Ryan, R. M. (1999). A meta-analytic review of experiments examining the effects of extrinsic rewards on intrinsic motivation. *Psychological Bulletin, 125,* 627–668.

Deci, E. L., Schwartz, A. J., Sheinman, L., & Ryan, R. M. (1981). An Instrument to assess adults' orientations toward control versus autonomy with children: Reflections on intrinsic motivation and perceived competence. *Journal of Educational Psychology, 73,* 642–650.

Deci, E. L., Spiegel, N. H., Ryan, R. M., Koestner, R., & Kauffman, M. (1982). Effects of performance standards on teaching styles: Behavior of controlling teachers. *Journal of Educational Psychology, 74,* 852–859.

Grolnick, W. S., & Ryan, R. M. (1987). Autonomy in children's learning: An experimental and individual difference investigation. *Journal of Personality and Social Psychology, 52,* 890–898.

Grolnick, W. S., & Ryan, R. M. (1989). Parent styles associated with children's self-regulation and competence in school. *Journal of Educational Psychology, 81,* 143–154.

Kasser, T., & Ryan, R. M. (1996). Further examining the American dream: Differential correlates of intrinsic and extrinsic goals. *Personality and Social Psychology Bulletin 22,* 80–87.

Koestner, R., Ryan, R. M., Bernieri, F., & Holt, K. (1984). Setting limits on children's behavior: The differential effects of controlling versus informational styles on intrinsic motivation and creativity. *Journal of Personality, 52,* 233–248.

Reeve, J., & Jang, H. (2006). What teachers say and do to support students' autonomy during a learning activity. *Journal of Educational Psychology, 98,* 209–218.

Vansteenkiste, M., Simons, J., Lens, W., Sheldon, K. M., & Deci, E. L. (2004). Motivating learning, performance, and persistence: The synergistic effects of intrinsic goal contents and autonomy-supportive contexts. *Journal of Personality and Social Psychology, 87,* 246–260.

Edward L. Deci
Richard M. Ryan

SELF-EFFICACY THEORY

In 1986, when he put forth a social cognitive theory of human functioning, *Social Foundations of Thought and Action: A Social Cognitive Theory,* psychologist Albert Bandura painted a portrait of human behavior and motivation in which individuals' self-beliefs are critical elements. His subsequent work, *Self-efficacy: The exercise of control* (1997), advanced the discussion. Of all the beliefs that people hold about themselves and that affect their day-to-day functioning, and standing at the core of social cognitive theory, are *self-efficacy beliefs,* which can be defined as the judgments that individuals hold about their capabilities to learn or to perform courses of action at designated levels. In essence, self-efficacy beliefs are the self-perceptions that individuals hold about their capabilities.

According to social cognitive theory, self-efficacy beliefs provide the foundation for human motivation, well-being, and personal accomplishment: Unless people believe that their actions can produce the outcomes they desire, they have little incentive to act or to persevere in the face of difficulties. These self-perceptions touch virtually every aspect of people's lives—whether they think productively, self-debilitatingly, pessimistically or optimistically; how well they motivate themselves and persevere in the face of adversities; their vulnerability to stress and depression; and the life choices they make. Self-efficacy is also a critical determinant of the self-regulatory practices in which individuals engage as they go about the important task of self-correcting their actions and cognitions.

Self-efficacy beliefs should not be confused with outcome expectations, which are people's judgments of the consequences that their behavior will produce. Typically, self-efficacy beliefs help foster the outcome one expects. Confident individuals anticipate successful outcomes. Students confident in their social skills anticipate successful social encounters. Those confident in their academic skills expect high marks on exams and expect the quality of their work to reap academic benefits. The opposite is true of those who lack confidence. People who doubt their social skills often envision rejection or ridicule even before they establish social contact. Students who lack confidence in their academic skills envision a low grade even before they begin an exam or enroll in a course. The expected results of these imagined performances will be differently envisioned: social success or greater career options for the former, social isolation or curtailed academic possibilities for the latter.

When self-efficacy belief and outcome expectation differ, the self-efficacy belief is more likely to determine the behavior. Students may well realize that strong academic skills are essential for obtaining a good SAT score and being admitted to the college of their choice, and this, in turn, may ensure a comfortable future lifestyle. But if students lack confidence in their academic capabilities, they may well shy away from challenging courses, will approach the SAT with apprehension and self-doubt, and may not even consider college attendance. In the social interaction, individuals may realize that pleasing manners and physical attractiveness are essential for attracting the attention of others, which is the first step toward building long-lasting relationships. If, however, they have low confidence in their social skills and doubt their physical attractiveness, they may hesitate to make contact and hence miss potentially promising opportunities.

Because individuals operate collectively as well as individually, self-efficacy is both a personal and a social construct. Collective systems develop a sense of collective efficacy—a group's shared belief in its capability to attain goals and accomplish desired tasks. For example, schools develop collective beliefs about the capability of their students to learn, of their teachers to teach and otherwise enhance the lives of their students, and of their administrators and policy makers to create environments conducive to these tasks. Organizations with a strong sense of collective efficacy exercise empowering and vitalizing influences on their constituents, and these effects are palpable and evident.

SOURCES OF SELF-EFFICACY BELIEFS

Individuals form their self-efficacy beliefs by interpreting information primarily from four sources: mastery experience, vicarious experience, social persuasions, and physiological reactions. For most people, the most influential source is the interpreted result of one's own performance, or mastery experience. Simply put, individuals gauge the effects of their actions, and their interpretations of these effects help create their efficacy beliefs. Success raises self-efficacy; failure lowers it. Students who perform well on mathematics tests and earn high grades in mathematics classes develop confidence in their mathematics capabilities. This sense of efficacy helps ensure that they will enroll in subsequent mathematics-related classes, approach mathematics tasks with serenity, and increase their efforts when a difficulty arises.

In addition to interpreting the results of their mastery experiences, young people form their efficacy beliefs through the vicarious experience of observing others perform tasks. Observing the successes and failures of peers perceived as similar in capability contributes to beliefs one's own capabilities (i.e., "If he can do it, so can I!"). Although this source of information is usually weaker than is mastery experience, when adolescents are uncertain about their own abilities or have limited previous experience, they become especially sensitive to it. If there is one finding that is incontrovertible in education and psychology, it is that young people learn from the actions of models, and so this is a prominent area of research in the study of self-efficacy. Vicarious experience also involves the social comparisons that individuals make with each other. These comparisons, along with peer modeling, can be powerful influences on self-efficacy beliefs. In situations in which young people have little experience with which to form a judgment of their competence in a particular area, peer models are especially useful.

Self-efficacy beliefs are also influenced by the verbal messages and social persuasions individuals receive from others, whether these are intentional or accidental. These messages can help one to exert the extra effort and persistence required to succeed, resulting in the continued development of skills and of personal efficacy. Or they can be powerfully disheartening. Persuaders play an important part in the development of an individual's self-efficacy beliefs. But social persuasions should not be confused with knee-jerk praise or empty inspirational homilies. Effective persuaders must cultivate people's beliefs in their capabilities while at the same time ensuring that the envisioned success is attainable. And, just as positive persuasions may work to encourage and empower, negative persuasions can work to defeat and weaken self-efficacy beliefs. In fact, it is usually easier to weaken self-efficacy beliefs through negative appraisals than to strengthen such beliefs through positive encouragement.

Physiological and emotional states such as anxiety and stress, along with one's mood, provide information about efficacy beliefs. Typically, optimism or a positive mood enhances self-efficacy, whereas depression, despair, or a sense of despondency diminishes it. As with the other sources, it is not the intensity of the physical indicator or mood state itself that is important, but the individual's interpretation of it. Adolescents with strong self-efficacy will view the emotional state as energizing, whereas those beset by self-doubt may regard it as debilitating.

MOTIVATIONAL CONSEQUENCES OF SELF-EFFICACY BELIEFS

Self-efficacy beliefs can enhance human accomplishment and well-being in countless ways. They influence the choices people make and the courses of action they pursue. Individuals tend to select tasks and activities in which they feel competent and confident and avoid those in which they do not. Unless people believe that their actions will have the desired consequences, they have little incentive to engage in those actions. How far will an interest in medicine take a student who feels hopeless while studying anatomy? Whatever factors operate to influence behavior, they are rooted in the core belief that one has the capability to accomplish that behavior.

Self-efficacy beliefs also help determine how much effort people will expend on an activity, how long they will persevere when confronting obstacles, and how resilient they will be in the face of adverse situations. People with a strong sense of personal competence approach difficult tasks as challenges to be mastered rather than as threats to be avoided. They have greater intrinsic interest and deep engrossment in activities, set themselves challenging goals and maintain strong commitment to them, and heighten and sustain their efforts in the face of failure. Moreover, they more quickly recover their sense of efficacy after failures or setbacks.

Self-efficacy beliefs also influence an individual's thought patterns and emotional reactions. High self-efficacy helps create feelings of serenity in approaching difficult tasks and activities. Conversely, people with low self-efficacy may believe that things are tougher than they really are, a belief that fosters anxiety, stress, depression, and a narrow vision of how best to solve a problem.

Human motivation, cognition, and behavior are influenced by many factors. The success or failure that people experience as they engage the myriad tasks that comprise their life naturally influence the many decisions they must make. Also, the knowledge and skills they possess will certainly play critical roles in what they choose to do and not do. But people must invariably interpret the results of their attainments, just as they must make judgments about the quality of the knowledge and skills they possess. Imagine, for example, two students who receive a B on an important mathematics exam. In and of itself, a B has no inherent meaning, and certainly no causal properties. How will receiving such a grade affect a particular student? A student accustomed to receiving A's in math class and who worked hard throughout the term and studied for the exam will view the B in ways quite dissimilar from those of a student accustomed to receiving C's and who worked equally hard. For the former, the B will be received with distress; for the latter, the B is likely to be received with elation. The student accustomed to receiving A's is likely to have bruised self-efficacy; the C-acquainted student is sure to have boosted self-efficacy.

SELF-EFFICACY BELIEFS AND ACADEMIC ATTAINMENTS

Self-efficacy has been the focus of research in areas as diverse as business, athletics, medicine and health, media studies, social and political change, moral development, psychiatry, psychopathology, and international affairs. In psychology, it has been the focus of studies on clinical problems such as phobias, depression, social skills, assertiveness, smoking behavior, and moral development. Self-efficacy has been especially prominent in educational research, where scholars have reported that, regardless of previous achievement or ability, self-efficacious students work harder, persist longer, persevere in the face of adversity, have greater optimism and lower anxiety, and achieve more. Students who believe they are capable of performing academic tasks also use more cognitive and metacognitive strategies than those who do not. Academic self-efficacy influences cognitive strategy use and self-regulation through the use of metacognitive strategies, and self-efficacy is associated with in-class seatwork and homework, exams and quizzes, and essays and reports.

In psychology, intelligence (in the form of IQ) has typically been acknowledged the most powerful cognitive predictor of achievement. But when researchers tested the joint contribution of self-efficacy and intelligence to the prediction of achievement, they found that students' self-efficacy beliefs made a powerful and independent contribution to the prediction of their academic performance. Self-efficacy is also a critical determinant of the life choices that students make and of the courses of action they pursue. Typically, they engage in activities in which they feel competent and avoid those in which they do not. Doing so is particularly critical at the high school and college levels, where young people progressively have more academic options.

Students with high self-efficacy engage in more effective self-regulatory strategies at differing levels of ability, and self-efficacy enhances students' memory performance by enhancing persistence. In studies of college students who pursue science and engineering courses, high self-efficacy has been demonstrated to influence the academic persistence necessary to maintain high academic achievement.

In general, researchers have established that self-efficacy beliefs and behavior changes and outcomes are highly correlated and that self-efficacy is an excellent predictor of behavior. The depth of this support prompted Graham and Weiner (1996) to conclude that, particularly in psychology and education, self-efficacy has proven to be a more consistent predictor of behavioral outcomes than have any other motivational constructs.

IMPLICATIONS FOR TEACHERS AND SCHOOLS

The first and major implication that arises from research findings on the role and function of self-efficacy beliefs in academic contexts is that teachers do well to take seriously their share of responsibility in nurturing the self-efficacy beliefs of their pupils, for it is clear that these beliefs can have beneficial or destructive influences. Bandura has argued that beliefs of personal competence constitute the key factor of human agency, the ability to act intentionally and exercise a measure of control over one's environment and social structures. As children strive to exercise control over their world, their first transactions are mediated by adults who can empower them with self-assurance or diminish their fledgling self-beliefs. Because young children are not proficient at making accurate self-appraisals, they naturally rely on the judgments of others to create their own judgments of their capabilities. Teachers who provide children with challenging tasks and meaningful activities that can be mastered, and who chaperone these efforts with support and encouragement, help ensure the development of a robust sense of efficacy. Effective teachers know their students' capabilities. They also know that trying very hard and continually failing can have a devastating effect on one's confidence. For this reason, they are careful to assign work that will indeed be challenging but that they are sure can be accomplished with proper effort.

An incontrovertible finding in educational research is that students learn from the actions of models. Different modeling practices in school can differently affect self-efficacy beliefs. For example, when models make errors, engage in coping behaviors in front of students, and verbalize emotive statements reflecting low confidence and achievement (such as "Gosh, I seem to be having some trouble with this, don't I?"), low-achieving students perceive the models as more similar to themselves and subsequently experience greater achievement and self-efficacy under their tutelage. Social cognitive theorists recommend that teachers engage in effective modeling practices and that they select peers for classroom models judiciously so as to ensure that students view themselves as comparable in learning ability to the models. Peer models should also share similar attributes to the students for whom they are serving as models.

Children inevitably compare themselves to other children, and these social comparisons are critical to the development of self-efficacy beliefs. Social-comparative school practices that emphasize standardized, normative assessments, involve ability grouping and lock-step instruction, use competitive grading practices, and encourage students to compare their achievement with that of their peers work to destroy the fragile self-beliefs of those who are less academically talented or prepared. As Bandura (1997) has noted, these are practices that can work to convert "instructional experiences into education in inefficacy" (p. 175).

When classroom structures are individualized and instruction is tailored to students' capabilities, social comparisons are minimized and students are more likely to gauge their academic progress according to their own standards rather than compare it to the progress of their classmates. In cooperative and individualized learning settings, students can more easily select the peers with whom to compare themselves. Individualized and cooperative structures that lower the competitive orientation of a classroom and school are more likely than traditional, competitive structures to increase self-efficacy. Similarly, classrooms that emphasize a mastery goal orientation, which is to say that they emphasize the view that learning is an enjoyable activity and should be undertaken for its own sake rather than for extrinsic or performance oriented reasons, also have beneficial effects on students' self-efficacy beliefs.

Some researchers have suggested that teachers should pay as much attention to students' perceptions of competence as to actual competence, for it is the perceptions that may more accurately influence students' motivation and future academic choices. Assessing students' self-efficacy beliefs can provide teachers with important insights about their pupils' academic motivation, behavior, and future choices. For example, unrealistically low self-efficacy, not lack of capability or skill, can be responsible for maladaptive academic behaviors, avoidance of courses and careers, and diminishing school interest and achievement. Students who lack confidence in skills they possess are less likely to engage in tasks in which those skills are required, and they will more quickly give up in the face of difficulty. In such cases, in addition to continued skill improvement, schools must work to identify their students' inaccurate judgments and design and implement interventions to challenge them. Researchers have identified various ways in which self-efficacy perceptions can be challenged. For example, teachers can set goals for students that are close at hand rather than goals that require a large investment in time. Teachers can also provide frequent and appropriate feedback as students are engaged in a task. Of course, it has been amply shown that effort-focused feedback (such as "Well done, you're working hard.") enhance students' self-efficacy and performance to a greater degree than does ability-focused feedback (such as "Well done, you're so smart.").

It seems clear that many of the difficulties that people experience throughout their lives are closely con-nected with the beliefs they hold about what they can and cannot do. Sound research evidence suggests that students' academic failures in basic subjects, as well as the misdirected motivation and lack of commitment often characteristic of the underachiever, the dropout, the student labeled at risk, and the socially disabled, are in good measure the consequence of, or certainly exacerbated by, the beliefs that students develop about their ability to exercise a measure of control over their environments.

Empirical findings have amply strengthen the claim of social cognitive theorists that self-efficacy beliefs play an influential role in human agency, and they support the contention of theorists and researchers that students' self-efficacy beliefs in academic areas powerfully influence their subsequent motivation and performance in these areas. Clearly, researchers and school practitioners should continue to look to students' beliefs about their academic capabilities as important predictors and determinants of academic achievement, for they are critical components of motivation and behavior.

SEE ALSO *Bandura, Albert; Social Comparisons; Volition.*

BIBLIOGRAPHY

Bandura, A. (1986). *Social foundations of thought and action: A social cognitive theory.* Englewood Cliffs, NJ: Prentice-Hall.

Bandura, A. (1997). *Self-efficacy: The exercise of control.* New York: W. H. Freeman.

Graham, S., & Weiner, B. (1996). Theories and principles of motivation. In D. C. Berliner & R. C. Calfee (Eds.), *Handbook of educational psychology* (Macmillan Research on Education Handbook Series) (pp. 63–84). New York: Macmillan.

Pajares, F. (1997). Current directions in self-efficacy research. In M. Maehr & P. R. Pintrich (Eds.), *Advances in motivation and achievement* (Vol. 10, pp. 1–49). Greenwich, CT: JAI Press.

Pajares, F., & Urdan, T. (Eds.). (2006). *Adolescence and education: Vol. 5. Self-efficacy beliefs of adolescents.* Greenwich, CT: Information Age Publishing.

Frank Pajares

SELF-ESTEEM

Self-esteem refers to an individual's or in some cases a group's evaluative judgment about himself, herself, or itself. The term and concept were relatively unnoticed prior to the 1960s, at which time various thinkers and researchers began to suspect that it could be an important factor in behavior. By the late 1970s self-esteem had become a major focus of a great deal of research, and people began to seek to raise self-esteem in connection with a broad assortment of interventions, including clinical practice and education.

During the 1980s self-esteem became a national buzz-word and was being studied and applied in a staggering variety of settings. Leading proponents such as Nathaniel Branden (1984) contended that deficient self-esteem was a causal factor behind nearly every sort of personal and social problem and pathology. A high point of sorts was reached late that decade, when the state of California established the California Task Force to Promote Self-esteem and Personal and Social Responsibility. Its manifesto (California Task Force, 1990) asserted that raising the self-esteem of California's citizens would help solve many of the state's problems, including violence, drug abuse, unwanted pregnancy, and school underachievement.

Criticism began to mount in the 1990s, and since the early 2000s the value of self-esteem has become the focus of serious debate. As of 2008 there are many programs for boosting self-esteem, especially among schools, and some groups whose livelihoods depend on administering these are fiercely resistant to criticism. On the other side, accumulated research findings have led many experts to question whether high self-esteem or boosting self-esteem has any practical value at all. Most likely an intermediate conclusion is correct.

In 1999 the American Psychological Society (subsequently renamed the Association for Psychological Science) commissioned a panel of experts to review the research findings and provide a summary evaluation of the benefits of high self-esteem. The governing board sought to compose the panel of persons with widely different initial views about self-esteem (i.e., both proponents and critics) and selected a leader (Baumeister) who had held different opinions at different times, reflecting a presumptive willingness to revise his opinions in light of new evidence. Its report filled an entire issue of the journal *Psychological Science in the Public Interest* (Baumeister, Campbell, Krueger, & Vohs, 2003). That report, and a condensed version for lay readers published by the same authors in *Scientific American* in January 2005, offers a relatively thorough overview for interested readers.

DEFINITION AND MEASUREMENT

Self-esteem literally means a person's valuing of himself or herself. It is thus the evaluative dimension of the self-concept. This may include both thoughts and feelings. Related terms include self-love, self-worth, self-respect, self-regard, and narcissism.

Self-esteem is typically measured with a questionnaire inviting respondents to rate how they think and feel about themselves. For better or worse, the brief scale developed by Rosenberg (1965) has become the standard way of measuring self-esteem. Items on self-esteem scales typically include assessment of liking for oneself overall, appraisal of one's confidence at being able to perform well at work and in school, and ability to get along with others and be liked. Moral self-appraisals are included in some scales.

Self-esteem is thus opinion, not objective appraisal. High self-esteem may refer to accurate, healthy appreciation of one's genuine capabilities and worth as a person, or it may refer to unrealistic, conceited overestimates of the self. Efforts to distinguish inflated egotism or narcissistic conceitedness from so-called true self-esteem have not had much success thus far. One general implication, therefore, is that several different kinds of people score high in self-esteem.

Nearly all research samples find that self-esteem, at least among modern Americans, is relatively high on average. That is, the distribution of scores runs from close to the maximum possible score on the scale down to a bit below the scale midpoint, with then relatively few scores in the bottom register. When researchers compare high and low scores on self-esteem, they divide the sample in its middle, but some critics have suggested that this in effect compares truly high self-esteem against medium self-esteem. Nonetheless, the distribution refutes widespread claims that the American population suffers from an epidemic of low self-esteem. In fact, American self-esteem scores have long been relatively high and have been increasing steadily in recent decades (Twenge & Campbell, 2001).

One important question is whether self-esteem should be measured as a general attitude toward the self overall or, instead, in specific domains. It seems eminently possible for a person to believe himself or herself to be good at math and poor at music; is there a core overall evaluation of self that coexists with these? Most research has focused on global self-esteem, but there are notable exceptions, particularly the work of Herbert Marsh (e.g., 2006), which focuses on academic self-esteem and indeed sometimes emphasizes self-esteem as separate for specific areas of study.

A persistent source of bias in the research literature stems from relying on self-reports. People score high in self-esteem by saying favorable things about themselves on a questionnaire, and so people who tend to flatter themselves on questionnaires end up classified as high in self-esteem. That may sound obvious, but many researchers then give people another questionnaire to ask about other sorts of behaviors and attributes, and when these same people say favorable things about themselves on those questionnaires, researchers sometimes mistakenly conclude that self-esteem contributes to positive outcomes. For example, when researchers ask people how intelligent or physically attractive they are, people with high self-esteem rate themselves higher than those with low self-esteem, which seemingly suggests that high self-esteem is linked to intelligence and good looks. But when researchers get objective data (e.g., giving an IQ test, or having judges rate how good-looking participants are), those differences disappear completely.

BENEFITS OF HIGH SELF-ESTEEM: SCHOOL PERFORMANCE

Much interest in self-esteem was stimulated by the claim that raising self-esteem could contribute to improving schoolwork. Although these hopes appear now to be false, they were plausible. In theory, high self-esteem might improve performance by increasing confidence, by making people willing to persist despite initial failure, by means of self-fulfilling prophecies, by eagerness to seek out challenges, and by other means. These hopes have been fueled by persistent findings that correlate self-esteem with grades in school and test performance, typically around .21 to .26, as noted already by Hansford and Hattie (1982), though the results varied widely from one study to another.

The fact that students with higher grades have higher self-esteem does not necessarily mean that bolstering self-esteem will cause other students to improve performance, however, for two reasons. The first reason is the familiar gap between correlation and causation. High self-esteem appears to be the result, not the cause, of doing well in school, as gradually emerged from painstaking longitudinal studies (e.g., Bachman & O'Malley, 1977). In other words, the good grades come first, and high self-esteem follows, so boosting self-esteem to improve grades may be backwards and hence futile.

Second, even if there were direct causal links between a stable trait of self-esteem and school performance, this does not guarantee that artificially boosting the trait or attitude will lead to improvements in performance. The many programs aimed at increasing self-esteem among students have generally failed to provide any evidence that they improve learning. An early review of such interventions and programs by Scheirer and Kraut (1979) concluded that such interventions were not effective. Subsequently, many professional programs advertised as bolstering self-esteem among students have added modules on study skills and socially desirable behavior, seemingly in tacit acknowledgement that self-esteem boosting alone does not work, but programs originating in the schools themselves may not uniformly recognize this need.

Almost no studies have employed experimental designs with proper controls to investigate the effects of boosting self-esteem. One exception was reported by Forsyth, Kerr, Burnette, and Baumeister (2007). College students with C, D, or F midterm grades were randomly assigned to receive weekly messages containing (1) review questions, (2) review questions plus self-esteem boosting, or (3) review questions plus reminders to take personal responsibility. Students whose self-esteem was boosted actually got significantly poorer grades on the final examination than on the midterm and poorer than students in the control condition. Thus, boosting self-esteem actually caused a significant decline in performance. The authors were surprised by this result and wished to conduct further studies, but obviously it would be unethical to conduct research that expects to cause students to get bad grades. Still, this result should give pause to anyone interested in improving school performance. Some have pointed out that the widespread embracing of self-esteem in school curriculums has coincided with a general decline in American student performance, though drawing firm causal conclusions from mass societal phenomena is generally unwarranted, especially in comparison with controlled experimentation.

Why might self-esteem cause school performance to get worse? Even proponents of self-esteem such as Nathaniel Branden have begun to suggest that self-esteem has most positive effects when it is earned via legitimate accomplishment. Hence simply telling people to think they are wonderful in the absence of such achievement may foster a sense of being too good to be willing to work hard or other sorts of entitlements. Overconfidence is also a possibility.

OTHER POTENTIAL BENEFITS OF HIGH SELF-ESTEEM

Self-esteem has been investigated for a variety of possible benefits beyond school performance. Given the limited space, this entry provides only a brief overview: For a more thorough review, see Baumeister and colleagues (2003).

Interpersonally, people with high self-esteem report and consider themselves to be charming and popular, with good relationship skills and many friends, but when they are rated by other people, most of these advantages disappear. In laboratory studies that assign people to interact with strangers and then report their impressions, high self-esteem persons generally think they have made better impressions than people with low self-esteem, but the actual impressions are no different or in some cases worse.

A longstanding view has surmised that violence and aggression stem from low self-esteem, but the actual evidence for this is extremely sparse and consists mainly of self-reports. Behavioral studies generally find self-esteem to make no difference and people high in narcissism, which can be regarded as one of the less appealing kinds of high self-esteem, are the most aggressive, especially when someone has criticized them. Thus, violence stems more from threatened egotism than from inadequate self-love (Baumeister, Smart, & Boden, 1996). There is some evidence of a correlation between some forms of delinquent, externalizing, antisocial behavior and low self-esteem, though it is not known which causes which.

The effects of self-esteem on work and task performance resemble those on school performance. Self-reports vary widely but generally point toward a mildly positive relationship, possibly because people with high self-esteem are prouder of their work than are people low in self-esteem. Objective data on task performance generally show little or no difference, with one important exception: High self-esteem leads to better persistence in the face of failure than low self-esteem, as shown in many studies.

Happiness is correlated with high self-esteem. Obviously these studies rely on self-reports of happiness (because no objective measures exist), but the pattern seems robust across many methods and samples, and experimental manipulations that raise or lower self-esteem produce corresponding emotional changes to support the conclusion. There is also a longstanding hypothesis that high self-esteem acts as a buffer to shield the person from the harmful effects of stress and trauma, and some rigorous studies have supported that conclusion. Although other studies have shown somewhat different patterns of results, none finds that low self-esteem leads to better coping or more happiness. Low self-esteem is persistently correlated with depression, though it is very difficult to say which causes the other.

The hope that high self-esteem would help young people resist smoking, drug abuse, early sexual behavior, and other unhealthy patterns has not generally been supported. If anything, more findings link high than low self-esteem to early experimentation with sex and drugs, possibly because popularity contributes to both high self-esteem and experimentation. Among all these domains surveyed by Baumeister and colleagues (2003), the best results were found with eating disorders. Low self-esteem appears to be a risk factor that significantly increases the risk that young women and possibly young men will develop eating disorders, though the effect of self-esteem is only in combination with other factors and possibly indirect.

Overall, two benefits of high self-esteem stood out. High self-esteem promotes initiative, presumably because confidence makes people more willing to take action and rely on their own judgment. This can produce negative effects, but initiative is mostly considered a good thing, and so this is one important benefit.

The other benefit is positive feelings and happiness. High self-esteem seems to be linked to a stock of pleasant, happy feelings that enable the person to enjoy life when it is good and/or avoid depression and misery when things are not going well.

Although these two established benefits of high self-esteem fall far short of what was once hoped, they are far

from trivial, and in combination they can contribute to making life good for people whose self-esteem is high. The question of how much effort and other resources should be devoted to boosting self-esteem in order to increase these two benefits is left to policymakers. It is however noteworthy that these benefits of high self-esteem accrue mainly to the individuals rather than to their relationship partners or to society as a whole. Some experts caution that simply flattering young people or otherwise seeking to boost their self-esteem directly will more likely contribute to increased narcissism and other less desirable forms of self-esteem, and the societal consequences of narcissism (which has been increasing throughout the U.S. population in the last decades of the 20th century; Twenge & Campbell, in press) are if anything negative.

UNDERSTANDING SELF-ESTEEM

The question of what are the benefits of high self-esteem is hardly the only important question about self-esteem. Considerable work has been invested in understanding how the behavioral, mental, and emotional reactions of people with high self-esteem differ from those with low or medium self-esteem. Presumably most educators and other leaders will have to deal with people having a variety of levels of self-esteem, and so understanding these differences may be useful for helping them deal effectively with each individual.

In general, low self-esteem is a greater puzzle than high self-esteem. Researchers have found it relatively easy to characterize people with high self-esteem, who like themselves and generally expect life to go well. Competing theories about low self-esteem have flourished, however.

Regarding emotional differences, high self-esteem is associated with generally higher levels of happiness and good feelings than low self-esteem (as noted above). Another difference is in emotional lability (Campbell, Chew, & Scratchley, 1991). People with low self-esteem have more frequent emotional ups and downs. This may indicate that people with low self-esteem lack the stabilizing influence that is associated with the emotional resources that go with high self-esteem.

Regarding cognition, people with low self-esteem experience more uncertainty and instability of self-knowledge (Campbell, 1990). Their self-concepts fluctuate more than those of people with high self-esteem. They are more likely to describe themselves in inconsistent and contradictory ways and to change how they rate themselves from one time to another. They are also more likely to respond "I don't know" to questions about themselves. This is an important clue to the nature of self-esteem. High self-esteem means having firm, clear ideas about who one is and what one wants. Low self-esteem does not apparently mean being convinced that one is a bad person. Instead, it is the absence of well-defined positive views of self rather than the presence of well-defined negative views.

People with high self-esteem engage in many self-flattering biases, such as assuming and in many cases overestimating how much that others will agree with their opinions and that their abilities are unique. They take credit for success and deny blame for failure. People with low self-esteem have fewer such biases. These mental tricks contribute to some of the biases noted earlier, such as that people with high self-esteem consider themselves smarter, more popular, and better-looking than other people, whereas objective evidence generally disconfirms these self-flattering views. Thus, an essential part of high self-esteem in many cases is convincing oneself that one is better than one really is.

Turning to motivation, what do people with low self-esteem want? Mostly they do not seek failure and rejection. Instead, they seem to want the same things that people high in self-esteem want (such as success and social approval), but they are less certain than others that they will achieve these goals (McFarlin & Blascovich, 1981).

The level of aspiration is different, and as a result, the overarching social motivations are different. People with high self-esteem want and expect to succeed, and so they are willing to take chances to stand out. They have a self-enhancing orientation, which means they look for ways to increase their stock of successes and to improve how others see them. In contrast, low self-esteem is associated with a prevention orientation: These people go through life seeking to remedy problems and avoid failures. They may focus on their weaknesses (whereas people with high self-esteem focus on their strengths) and avoid risky situations (for review, see Baumeister, Tice, & Hutton, 1989).

People with low self-esteem lack confidence in their own views and ideas, and so they are relatively willing to do what others tell them. Indeed, some of the earliest research on self-esteem emphasized that low self-esteem produces a relatively high susceptibility to persuasion and influence (Janis, 1954; for review, see Brockner, 1983). The behavior of these people varies across situations as they yield to current pressures. High self-esteem, in contrast, tends to promote acting on one's own and disregarding the influences and even the good advice of others.

Abundant research has shown that people desire high self-esteem: They strive to think well of themselves. Why is the concern with self-esteem seemingly so deeply rooted in the psyche? If high self-esteem conferred many positive benefits, the desire for it would be understandable, but given the relatively few advantages, it presents a puzzle. Noting that high self-esteem feels good provides a partial answer, but because emotions are presumably there to help people survive and prosper, the question again arises, why are emotions tied to self-esteem?

One answer offered by Mark Leary and his colleagues is that self-esteem is a kind of internal measure of something that is vitally important, namely one's prospects for social acceptance (Leary, Tambor, Terdal, & Downs, 1995). High self-esteem is typically based on thinking one has the traits that will bring acceptance: attractiveness, likeability, and competence. Low self-esteem in this view is essentially a belief that one does not have what it takes to attract and keep relationship partners and group memberships. Human survival has long depended on belonging to important groups, and so self-esteem may be one's internal measure of how likely that is.

SEE ALSO *Relevance of Self-Evaluations to Classroom Learning.*

BIBLIOGRAPHY
Bachman, J. G., & O'Malley, P. M. (1977). Self-esteem in young men: A longitudinal analysis of the impact of educational and occupational attainment. *Journal of Personality and Social Psychology, 35,* 365–380.
Baumeister, R. F., Campbell, J. D., Krueger, J. I., & Vohs, K. D. (2003). Does high self-esteem cause better performance interpersonal success, happiness, or healthier lifestyles? *Psychological Science in the Public Interest, 4,* 1–44.
Baumeister, R. F., Campbell, J. D., Krueger, J. I., & Vohs, K. D. (2005, January). Exploding the self-esteem myth. *Scientific American, 292*(1), 84–91.
Baumeister, R. F., Smart, L., & Boden, J. M. (1996). Relation of threatened egotism to violence and aggression: The dark side of high self-esteem. *Psychological Review, 103,* 5–33.
Baumeister, R. F., Tice, D. M., & Hutton, D. G. (1989). Self-presentational motivations and personality differences in self-esteem. *Journal of Personality, 57,* 547–579.
Branden, N. (1984). In defense of self. *Association for Humanistic Psychology,* (August–September), 12–13.
Brockner, J. (1983). Low self-esteem and behavioral plasticity: Some implications. In L. Wheeler & P. Shaver (Eds.), *Review of Personality and Social Psychology,* Vol. 4 (pp. 237–271). Beverly Hills, CA: Sage.
California Task Force to Promote Self-esteem and Personal and Social Responsibility (1990). Toward a state of self-esteem. Sacramento, CA: California State Department of Education.
Campbell, J. D. (1990). Self-esteem and clarity of the self-concept. *Journal of Personality and Social Psychology, 59,* 538–549.
Campbell, J. D., Chew, B., & Scratchley, L. S. (1991). Cognitive and emotional reactions to daily events: The effects of self-esteem and self-complexity. *Journal of Personality, 59,* 473–505.
Forsyth, D. R., Kerr, N. A., Burnette, J. L., & Baumeister, R. F. (2007). Attempting to improve the academic performance of struggling college students. *Journal of Social and Clinical Psychology, 26*(4), 447–459.
Hansford, B. C., & Hattie, J. A. (1982). The relationship between self and achievement/performance measures. *Review of Educational Research, 52,* 123–142.

Janis, I. L. (1954). Personality correlates of susceptibility to persuasion. *Journal of Personality, 22,* 504–518.

Leary, M. R., Tambor, E. S., Terdal, S. K., Downs, D. L. (1995). Self-esteem as an interpersonal monitor: The sociometer hypothesis. *Journal of Personality & Social Psychology, 68,* 518–530.

Marsh, H., & Craven, R. G. (2006). Reciprocal effects of self concept and performance from a multidimensional perspective: Beyond seductive pleasure and unidimensional perspectives. *Perspectives on Psychological Science, 1,* 133–163.

McFarlin, D. B., & Blascovich, J. (1981). Effects of self-esteem and performance feedback on future affective preferences and cognitive expectations. *Journal of Personality and Social Psychology, 40,* 521–531.

Rosenberg, M. (1965). *Society and the adolescent self-image.* Princeton, NJ: Princeton University Press.

Scheirer, M. A., & Kraut, R. E. (1979). Increased educational achievement via self-concept change. *Review of Educational Research, 49,* 131–150.

Twenge, J. M., & Campbell, W. K. (2001). Age and birth cohort differences in self-esteem: A cross-temporal meta-analysis. *Personality and Social Psychology Review, 5,* 321–344.

Roy F. Baumeister

SELF-EVALUATIONS

SEE *Relevance of Self-Evaluations to Classroom Learning.*

SELF-EXPLANATION

Simply defined, learning involves the use of existing knowledge to make meaning of new information (Driscoll, 2000). The process of explaining to-be-learned materials to oneself has been called *self-explanation* and is considered to be a constructive activity (e.g., Calin-Jageman & Ratner, 2005; Tajika, Nakatsu, Nozaki, Neumann, & Maruno, 2007). Self-explanation facilitates learning in one of two manners. The process prompts students to form inferences beyond the provided information, extending and supporting their knowledge revision (McNamara, 2004; Taboada & Guthrie, 2006). This form of self-explanation helps students compensate for text inadequacies, inconsistencies, and incompleteness. Self-explanation also encourages students to revise their current understandings of concepts by prompting them to compare their inaccurate and/or incomplete understandings with those presented in text. New learning unfolds as students attempt to reduce inconsistencies between their existing knowledge structures and new information (Ainsworth & Burcham, 2007).

EFFECTIVENESS OF SELF-EXPLANATIONS

In their seminal work, Chi and colleagues (Chi, Bassok, Lewis, Reimann, & Glaser, 1989; Chi & Bassok, 1989) instructed undergraduate students to provide self-explanations in response to worked examples. The researchers observed that undergraduates who demonstrated proficiency in problem solving (82% correct or higher) produced twice as many self-explanations, confirming earlier findings that providing justifications for solution steps while problem solving improves learning (e.g., Gagné & Smith, 1962). Moreover, Chi and colleagues observed that the nature of students' explanations differed qualitatively. Successful problem solvers provided self-explanations that refined, defined, and expanded action components of the examples, and used them as references to principles and concepts outlined in the text. These students' explanations indicated self-monitoring of new understandings and misunderstandings. Students who were less successful problem solvers generated insufficient and/or superficial explanations and did not monitor their learning with subsequent analyses confirming these distinctions (Chi & VanLehn, 1991; Renkel, 1997). Equally important, these studies revealed that, in the absence of specific instructions or supports, most students either do not generate self-explanations or generate superficial ones only (e.g., Atkinson, Renkl, & Merrill, 2003; Chi & Bassok, 1989; Chi, Leeuw, Chiu, & LaVancher, 1994; McNamara, O'Reilly, Best, & Ozuru, 2006; Schworm & Renkl, 2007).

Findings from earlier research documented that undergraduates who generated self-explanations demonstrated greater learning than students who did not produce self-explanations. However, they learned less overall than students who were provided with expert-generated explanations (Stein & Bransford, 1979). Closer analysis revealed that expert-generated effects were limited to instances in which students generated imprecise elaborations, corroborating that self-explanation effects are contingent on having students produce meaningful explanations that either establish connections between text ideas or integrate them with relevant prior knowledge (Chi, 2000; King & Rosenshine, 1993; McNamara & Kintsch, 1996; Rosenshine, Meister, & Chapman, 1996; Scardamalia & Bereiter, 1992).

The quality of instructor-generated explanations is also an important instructional factor. When experts or instructors verbalize "why-type" explanations, they encourage students to practice self-explanation. This is especially true when working with young students (Crowley & Siegler, 1999; Peters, Messer, Smith, & Davey, 1999; Pine & Messer, 2000; Siegler, 1995). When prompted to describe the instructor's problem-solving strategy, kindergarten students produced superior self-explanations and used this problem-solving strategy more frequently than did students who responded to their own thinking (Calin-Jageman & Ratner, 2005). Modeling provides students with the opportunity to reflect on instructors' rationales and reasoning, and provides them with opportunities to gain proficiency in the use of self-explanation.

There is substantial evidence that all students can be taught to produce self-explanations and that doing so produces subsequent learning gains relative to not doing so or being provided with generated explanations (post-secondary: Aleven & Koedinger, 2002; Bielaczyc, Pirolli & Brown, 1995; de Bruin, Rikers, & Schmidt, 2007; Reimann & Neubert, 2000; secondary: Chi et al., 1994; Siegler, 2002; Wong, Lawson & Keeves, 2002; elementary: Davis, 2003; Tajika & Nakatsu, 2005; Tajika, Nakatsu, & Nozaki, 2006). For example, Rittle-Johnson's 2006 study (2006) demonstrated that students in grades 3 to 5 were able to solve more mathematical equivalency problems following instructions to generate self-explanations than were students who were not provided with such instructions. Students' learning gains held across measures of immediate and delayed learning and were especially pronounced for measures of procedural learning and transfer.

ENHANCING QUALITY OF SELF-EXPLANATIONS

Providing students with instruction in the use of specific thinking prompts and learning strategies can enhance the quality of self-explanation. The use of thought-provoking question stems is one technique for assisting students to generate quality self-explanations when processing text independently, in pairs or in small groups (King, 1989; 1990; 1991; 1992; 1994). Question stems are based on higher-level thinking skills and are intended to encourage students to draw upon their existing knowledge to generate applications (e.g., "How would you use _____ to _____?"), explanations (e.g., "Explain why . . .") evaluations (e.g., "Which one is the best _____ and why?"), and other forms of higher-level thought (e.g., "What do you think would happen if . . .?"). Students who generate self-explanations that extend beyond the literal level of the text demonstrate enhanced retention and understanding (e.g., National Reading Panel, 2000; Taboada & Guthrie, 2006).

Students have also benefited from receiving instruction intended to promote the use of multiple strategies that promote self-explanation and metacognitive awareness (McNamara, 2004). McNamara found that undergraduates instructed to generate elaborations and predictions, use logic, make bridging inferences, and paraphrase and monitor comprehension, demonstrated superior learning for unfamiliar materials compared to their uninstructed peers. They titled their program the

Self-Explanation Reading Training (SERT). While students with high and low levels of prior knowledge benefited from instruction, gains were especially pronounced for participants with low prior knowledge when responding to text-based questions.

Self-explanation may benefit certain students more than others. Specifically, students who possess relatively low levels of prior knowledge demonstrate greater learning following self-explanation than those with higher levels of prior knowledge (Renkl, Stark, Gruber, & Mandl, 1998). The former group of students typically do not activate prior knowledge or engage in other elaborative processes during new learning experiences (McNamara, 2001; McNamara & Kintsch, 1996). Presumably, engaging in the process of self-explanation is more helpful for these students than their peers who possess higher levels of prior knowledge as it encourages them to adopt strategic processes while studying and allows them to maximize working memory capacity (Best, Rowe, Ozuru & McNamara, 2005). There is also evidence that the accuracy of the self-explanation does not dramatically affect students' learning gains. That is, the process of producing self-explanations, regardless of the accuracy of the explanations, seems sufficient to enhance the learning process. To this end, some researchers have argued that the process of generating self-explanations itself induces greater understanding of domain principles (Chi, 2000; Chi & VanLehn, 1991).

Having instructors or experts provide students with instructions to produce self-explanations is not always feasible. However, research supports the conclusion that paraprofessionals and tutors can also promote processing that involves self-explanation. Students working with tutors trained to prompt self-explanation demonstrated superior learning relative to those whose tutors engaged in the typical processes of initiating questions, providing constructive feedback and assessing comprehension. Presumably, scaffolding and prompting in this manner encourages students to control their own learning. Self-explanations in tutoring are especially conducive to addressing students' misconceptions (Anderson, Boyle & Reiser, 1985; Chi, 1996; Chi, Siler, Jeong, Yamauchi, & Hausmann, 2001).

Peers can also encourage each other to generate self-explanations (Chin & Brown, 2000; Minick, 1989). For instance, Webb and her colleagues (Webb, 1991; Webb & Palincsar, 1996) demonstrated that students can be trained to encourage explanations from each other (rather than provide responses) when working in cooperative learning groups. In these learning situations, how instructors interact with students as part of their large group instruction influences the nature of small group interactions (Webb, Nemer, & Ing, 2006). If students are encouraged to verbalize their thinking or ask "why-type" questions as part of teacher-led instruction, they are also likely to adopt these behaviors as part of small group interactions. In essence, students' small-group behaviors mirror instructors' discourse and expectations (Webb et al., 2006). Instructional environments that are entrenched in cultures of low-level questions and sparse explanations produce long-term learning effects that are difficult to overcome.

USING COMPUTER MODELS TO REPRODUCE SELF-EXPLANATION EFFECT

Computer-based learning environments also provide alternative instructional venues for the promotion of self-explanations. One of the earliest computer models devised to account for and reproduce the self-explanation effect through the use of analogies was Cascade (Van-Lehn, Jones, & Chi, 1992). More recent computer-based learning environments provide students with tutorial-like dialogues that analyze their explanations while problem solving, recognize omissions in their explanations, and provide appropriate feedback. For instance, students who explained their problem-solving steps using Cognitive Tutor demonstrated greater learning for target questions and transfer problems than students who did not use the program and were not required to explain their problem-solving steps (Anderson, Corbett, Koedinger, & Pelletier, 1995; Aleven & Koedinger, 2002; Aleven, Popescu & Koedinger, 2001a; 2001b).

Other computer-based learning environments promote self-explanation through the use of inquiry and metacognitive prompts (Graesser, McNamara, & Van-Lehn, 2005). In the computer-based program, Point & Query (Graesser, Langston, & Baggett, 1993) students are encouraged to ask questions and form deep causal questions. Students control the question-answering process through hypertext, hypermedia, and other learning environments. Similarly, the computer-based program, Autotutor (Graesser, Lu, Jackson, Mitchell, Ventura, Olney, & Louwerse, 2004; Graesser, Person, & Harter, 2001; Graesser, VanLehn, Rose, Jordan, & Harter, 2001), coaches students to produce explanations by responding to their questions in natural language.

One of the most recent computer-based learning environments to assist students' acquisition of metacognitive strategies and reading comprehension is iSTART. The iSTART program (Interactive Strategy Trainer for Active Reading and Thinking; McNamara, Levinstein, & Boonthum, 2004; McNamara et al., 2006) is a computer-based learning environment modeled after the face-to-face reading comprehension instructional program SERT. The program is designed to assess the quality of students' self-explanations, provide them with

elaborative feedback, and promote the use of active reading strategies.

As part of the iSTART program, students observe a simulated classroom, identifying the strategies that simulated learners use to explain the actions of the simulated instructor. They then produce self-explanations under the guidance of the simulated instructor (McNamara et al., 2004). Adolescents using iSTART demonstrated greater learning for science text than their peers who were provided with a demonstration on how to self-explain text (McNamara, et al., 2006). Applications of iSTART confirm that all students benefited from participating in this program, although learning gains vary as a function of students' prior knowledge. Those with low prior knowledge demonstrate substantial improvement when responding to text-based questions while students with high levels of prior knowledge demonstrate greatest growth when responding to inferential questions (McNamara et al., 2006).

In summary, self-explanation is a versatile, effective strategy that students can use independently or as part of group processing to enhance their learning across a variety of instructional tasks, including the processing of expository texts, mathematical problem solving, and the studying of worked examples. Students from kindergarten through postsecondary school have benefited from instruction in the generation of self-explanations, demonstrating enhanced learning and metacognitive awareness. Learning gains associated with self-explanation are especially powerful for students who possess relatively low levels of prior knowledge for target materials. Instructors, tutors, and peers can effectively encourage students to adopt self-explanation practices with minimal training. Alternatively, computer-based learning environments also hold great promise with respect to enhancing students' use of this effective learning strategy.

SEE ALSO *Cognitive Strategies.*

BIBLIOGRAPHY

Ainsworth, S., & Burcham, S. (2007). The impact of text coherence on learning by self-explanation. *Learning and Instruction, 17*, 286–303.

Aleven, V., & Koedinger, K. (2002). An effective metacognitive strategy: learning by doing and explaining with a computer-based cognitive tutor. *Cognitive Science, 26*, 147–179.

Aleven, V., Popescu, O., & Koedinger, K. R. (2001a). Towards tutorial dialog to support self-explanations: adding natural language understanding to a cognitive tutor. In J. D. Moore, C. L. Redfield, & W. L. Johnson (Eds.), *Artificial intelligence in education: AI-ED in the wired and wireless future* (pp. 246–255). Amsterdam: IOS Press.

Aleven V., Popescu, O. & Koedinger, K. R. (2001b). Pedagogical content knowledge in a tutorial dialogue system to support self-explanation. In *Papers of the AIED-2001 Workshop on Tutorial Dialogue Systems*, 59–70.

Anderson, J. R., Boyle, C. F., & Reiser, B. J. (1985). Intelligent tutoring systems. *Science, 228*, 456–468.

Anderson, J. R., Corbett, A. T., Koedinger, K. R., & Pelletier, R. (1995). Cognitive tutors: Lessons learned. *The Journal of the Learning Sciences, 4*, 167–207.

Atkinson, R. K., Renkl, A., & Merrill, M. M. (2003). Transitioning from studying examples to solving problems: Combining fading with prompting fosters learning. *Journal of Educational Psychology, 95*, 774–783.

Best, R.M., Rowe, M., Ozuru, Y., & McNamara, D. (2005). Deep-level comprehension of science texts. *Topics in Language Disorders, 25*(1), 65–83.

Bielaczyc, K., Pirolli, P., & Brown, A. (1995). Training in self-explanation and self-regulation strategies: Investigating the effects of knowledge acquisition activities on problem solving. *Cognition and Instruction, 13*(2), 221–252.

Calin-Jageman, R., & Ratner, H. (2005). The role of encoding in the self-explanation effect. *Cognition and Instruction, 23*(4), 523–543.

Chi, M. T. H. (1996). Constructing self-explanations and scaffolded explanations in tutoring. *Applied Cognitive Psychology, 10*, 33–49.

Chi, M. T. H. (2000). Self-explaining expository texts: The dual processes of generating inferences and repairing mental models. In R. Glaser (Ed.), *Advances in instructional psychology: Educational design and cognitive science* (Vol. 5, pp. 161–238). Mahwah, NJ: Erlbaum.

Chi, M. T. H., & Bassok, M. (1989). Learning from examples via self-explanations. In L. B. Resnick (Ed.), *Knowing, learning, and instruction: Essays in honor of Robert Glaser* (pp. 251–282). Hillsdale, NJ: Erlbaum.

Chi, M. T. H., Bassok, M., Lewis, M., Reimann, P., & Glasser, R. (1989). Self-explanations: How students study and use examples in learning to solve problems. *Cognitive Science, 13*, 145–182.

Chi, M. T. H., Leeuw, N., Chiu, M., & LaVancher, C. (1994). Eliciting self-explanations improves understanding. *Cognitive Science, 18*, 439–477.

Chi, M. T. H., Siler, S. A., Jeong, H., Yamauchi, T., & Hausmann, R. G. (2001). Learning from human tutoring. *Cognitive Science, 25*(4), 471–533.

Chi, M. T. H., & VanLehn, K. A. (1991). The content of physics self-explanations. *The Journal of the Learning Sciences, 1*(1), 69–105.

Chin, C., & Brown, D. (2000). Learning in science: A comparison of deep and surface approaches. *Journal of Research in Science Teaching, 37*(2), 109–138.

Crowley, K., & Siegler, R. (1999). Explanation and generalization in young children's strategy learning. *Child Development, 70*, 304–316.

Davis, E. (2003). Prompting middle school science students for productive reflection: generic and directed prompts. *The Journal of the Learning Sciences, 12*(1), 91–142.

de Bruin, A., Rikers, R., & Schmidt, H. (2007). The effect of self-explanation and prediction on the development of principled understanding of chess in novices. *Contemporary Educational Psychologist, 32*, 188–205.

Driscoll, M. (2000). *Psychology of learning for instruction.* (2nd ed.). Boston: Allyn & Bacon.

Gagné, R. M., & Smith, E. C. Jr. (1962). A study of the effects of verbalization on problem solving. *Journal of Experimental Psychology, 63*, 12–18.

Graesser, A. C., Langston, M. C., & Baggett, W. B. (1993). Exploring information about concepts by asking questions. In G. V. Nakamura, R. M. Taraban, & D. Medin (Eds.), *The psychology of learning and motivation: Vol. 29. Categorization by humans and machines* (pp.411–436). Orlando, FL: Academic Press.

Graesser, A. C., Lu, S., Jackson, G. T., Mitchell, H., Ventura, M., Olney, A., et al. (2004). AutoTutor: A tutor with dialogue in natural language. *Behavioral Research Methods, Instruments, and Computers, 36*, 180–192.

Graesser, A., McNamara, D., & VanLehn, K. (2005). Scaffolding deep comprehension strategies through Point&Query, AutoTutor, and iSTART. *Educational Psychologist, 40*(4), 225–234.

Graesser, A. C., Person, N. K., & Harter, D. (2001). Teaching tactics and dialogue in AutoTutor. *International Journal of Artificial Intelligence in Education, 12*, 257–279.

Graesser, A. C., VanLehn, K., Rose, C., Jordan, P., & Harter, D. (2001). Intelligent tutoring systems with conversational dialogue. *AI Magazine, 22*, 39–51.

King, A. (1989). Effects of self-questioning training on college students' comprehension of lectures. *Contemporary Educational Psychology, 14*(4), 1–16.

King, A. (1990). Enhancing peer interaction and learning in the classroom. *American Educational Research Journal, 27*, 664–687.

King, A. (1991). Improving lecture comprehension: Effects of a metacognitive strategy. *Applied Cognitive Psychology, 5*, 331–346.

King, A. (1992). Facilitating elaborative learning through guided student-generated questioning. *Educational Psychologist, 27*(1), 111–126.

King, A. (1994). Guiding knowledge construction in the classroom: Effects of teaching children how to question and how to explain. *American Educational Research Journal, 31*(2), 338–368.

King, A., & Rosenshine, B. (1993). Effects of guided cooperative questioning on children's knowledge construction. *Journal of Experimental Education, 61*, 127–148.

McNamara, D. S. (2001). Reading both high-coherence and low coherence texts: Effects of text sequence and prior knowledge. *Canadian Journal of Experimental Psychology, 55*, 51–62.

McNamara, D. S. (2004). SERT: Self-explanation reading training. *Discourse Processes, 38*(1), 1–30.

McNamara, D. S., & Kintsch, W (1996). Learning from text: Effects of prior knowledge and text coherence. *Discourse Processes, 22*, 247–287.

McNamara, D. S., Levinstein, I. B., & Boonthum, C. (2004). iSTART: Interactive strategy trainer for active reading and thinking. *Behavioral Research Methods, Instruments, and Computers, 36*, 222–233.

McNamara, D. S., O'Reilly, T. Best, R., & Ozuru, Y. (2006). Improving adolescent students' reading comprehensions with iSTART. *Journal of Educational Computing Research, 34*(2), 147–171.

Minick, N. (1989). Mind and activity in Vygotsky's work: an expanded frame of reference. *Cultural Dynamics, 2*, 162–187.

National Reading Panel. (2000). *Teaching children to read: An evidence-based assessment of the scientific research literature on reading and its implications for reading instruction.* Washington, DC: National Institute of Child Health and Human Development, and Department of Education.

Peters, L., Messer, D., Smith, P., & Davey, N. (1999). An investigation into Karmiloff-Smith's RR model: The effects of structure tuition. *British Journal of Developmental Psychology, 17,* 277–292.

Pine, K., & Messer, D. (2000). The effect of explaining another's actions on children's implicit theories of balance. *Cognition and Instruction, 18,* 35–51.

Reimann, P., & Neubert, C. (2000). The role of self-explanation in learning to use a spreadsheet through examples. *Journal of Computer Assisted Learning, 16,* 316–325.

Renkl, A. (1997). Learning from worked out examples: A study on individual differences. *Cognitive Science, 21*(1), 1–2.

Renkl, A., Stark, R., Gruber, H., & Mandl, H. (1998). Learning from worked-out examples: The effects of example variability and elicited self-explanations. *Contemporary Educational Psychology, 23,* 90–108.

Rittle-Johnson, B. (2006). Promoting transfer: Effects of self-explanation and direct instruction. *Child Development, 77*(1), 1–15.

Rosenshine, B., Meister, C., & Chapman, S. (1996). Teaching students to generate questions: A review of intervention studies. *Review of Educational Research, 66,* 181–221.

Scardamalia, M., & Bereiter, C. (1992). Text-based and knowledge-based questioning by children. *Cognition and Instruction, 9,* 177–199.

Schworn, S., & Renkl, A. (2007). Computer-supported example-based learning: When instructional explanations reduce self-explanations. *Computers and Education, 46,* 426–445.

Siegler, R. (1995). How does change occur: A microgenetic study of number conservation. *Cognitive Psychology, 28,* 225–273.

Siegler, R. (2002). Microgenetic studies of self-explanation. In N. Granott & J. Parziale (Eds.), *Microdevelopment: Transition processes in development and learning* (pp. 31–58). Cambridge, England: Cambridge University Press.

Stein, B. S., & Bransford, J. D. (1979). Constraints on effective elaboration: Effects of precision and subject generation. *Journal of Verbal Learning and Verbal Behavior, 18,* 769–777.

Taboada, A., & Guthrie, T. (2006). Contributions of student questioning and prior knowledge to construction of knowledge from reading information text. *Journal of Literacy Research, 38*(1), 1–35.

Tajika, H., & Nakatsu, N. (2005). Using a metacognitive strategy to solve mathematical problems. *Bulletin of the Aichi University of Education, 54,* 1–9.

Tajika, H., Nakatsu, N., & Nozaki, H. (2006). The effect of self-explanation on solving mathematical word problems. *Bulletin of Educational Research and Curriculum Development of the Aichi University of Education, 9,* 1–8.

Tajika, H., Nakatsu, N., Nozaki, H., Neumann, E., & Maruno, S. (2007). Effects of self-explanation as a metacognitive strategy for solving mathematical word problems. *Japanese Psychological Research, 49*(3), 222–233.

VanLehn, K., Jones, R., & Chi, M. T. H. (1992). A model of the self-explanation effect. *The Journal of the Learning Sciences, 2*(1), 1–59.

Webb, N. M. (1991). Task-related verbal interaction and mathematics learning in small groups. *Journal for Research in Mathematics Education, 22,* 366–389.

Webb, N. M., Nemer, K., & Ing, M. (2006). Small-group reflections: Parallels between teacher discourse and student behavior in peer-directed groups. *The Journal of the Learning Sciences, 15*(1), 63–119.

Webb, N. M., & Palincsar, A. S. (1996). Group processes in the classroom. In D. Berliner & R. Calfee (Eds.), *Handbook of educational psychology* (pp. 841–873). New York: Macmillan.

Wong, R., Lawson, M. J., & Keeves, J. P. (2002). The effects of self-explanation training on students' problem solving in high school mathematics. *Learning and Instruction, 12,* 233–262.

Vera E. Woloshyn
Tiffany L. Gallagher

SELF-HANDICAPPING

Self-handicapping refers to the undermining of one's own performance, usually for the sake of impression management (Kolditz & Arkin, 1982). When individuals fear or expect they may fail at tasks that are important to them, they often engage in practices that may actually increase the probability of failure (or at least lower achievement) so they have an excuse, other than lack of ability, for the failure. For example, individuals who value romantic relationships but doubt their ability to sustain one often engage in relationship-destructive behavior (e.g., infidelity, verbal abuse, neglect) so that, when the relationship inevitably fails, they can attribute the failure to their controllable behavior rather than some unchangeable characteristic of themselves. This "shooting-oneself-in-the-foot" can and does appear in any activity or domain, but academic self-handicapping has received a considerable amount of attention because academic achievement reflects on a valued characteristic (i.e., intelligence) and there are frequent opportunities for students to display their abilities, or lack thereof, in public ways. In other words, students often worry that they will appear unintelligent if they perform poorly on a test or assignment, so they sometimes engage in self-handicapping behavior that provides an excuse, other than lack of ability, for the poor performance.

Procrastinating, becoming overly busy with too many activities, placing oneself in a loud or noisy environment to study, getting drunk the night before an important exam, selecting tasks that are much to difficult for one's ability level, failing to study, and failing to get enough sleep are just a few of the many possible self-handicapping behaviors that individuals can engage in. Self-handicapping behavior can range from active (e.g., getting drunk before a test) to passive (failing to study), but they all have the same effect of potentially undermining performance.

To be considered self-handicapping, the behavior must include several features. First, it must occur before the activity that provides the opportunity for poor performance. Students who simply tell their friends they did not study for the exam after taking the exam are providing an excuse for their potentially low performance, but if they actually did study for the exam they did not self-handicap. Second, many agree that self-handicapping is intentional. Student who do not study because they forgot that there was an exam the next day are not self-handicapping. But purposefully failing to study so that one can have a ready excuse for low performance on the test is self-handicapping. Finally, self-handicapping is a behavior undertaken for the specific purpose of influencing the judgments, or attributions, of others, and possibly oneself. Student who procrastinate until 2:00 a.m. before starting to write their term paper may well perform badly on the paper and may reasonably attribute his or her poor performance to procrastination. But the procrastination behavior would only be considered self-handicapping if the purpose of the procrastination was to provide an excuse for the poor performance, should it occur. Self-handicapping, then, is the intentional, *a priori*, performance-undermining behavior that individuals engage in to create the impression that it is this behavior, and not a lack of ability, that causes the low performance (Berglas & Jones, 1978).

ANTECEDENTS OF SELF-HANDICAPPING

Self-handicapping has been conceptualized as a trait-like tendency (Jones & Rhodewalt, 1982) and as a situationally induced behavior (Tice, 1991). Those who have described it as a trait argue that some individuals are simply more inclined to self-handicap than others, and this inclination is present across situations. Sources for the development of such a trait may be biological (i.e., more anxious personality) or can arise from socialization experiences in childhood, such as a strong emphasis on the importance of appearing able. Self-handicapping is also associated with a variety of stable characteristics that may contribute to self-handicapping behavior such as low self-esteem, low perceptions of control, high self-consciousness, and a belief that intelligence is a fixed trait (Berglas, 1985; Rhodewalt, 1994; Knee & Zuckerman, 1998). Researchers who have conceptualized self-handicapping as a situation-specific behavior tend to focus on environmental factors as the sources for the self-handicapping behavior. For example, Midgley and Urdan have examined the association between an emphasis on performance goals in the classroom and self-handicapping behavior (Midgley & Urdan, 2001; Urdan,

Midgley & Anderman, 1998; Urdan, 2004). According to this research, students are more likely to self-handicap in classrooms where they perceive an emphasis on competition and trying to outperform classmates. Similarly, experimental research often creates situations in which participants are told that they will be given a difficult task and that performance on the task is indicative of ability (e.g., Tice, 1991). When individuals can be primed to fear that they may not succeed and that any lack of success may indicate a general lack of ability, self-handicapping is more likely to occur.

Perhaps the strongest experiential predictor of self-handicapping is a history of low achievement. Individuals who perform poorly can develop the expectation of low achievement on similar tasks in the future, especially if they believe the failure is caused by stable and uncontrollable causes, such as a lack of ability. Once individuals develop the belief that they may fail on an upcoming task, they become more likely to engage in self-handicapping behavior, which increases the probability that they will fail again. This cycle of failure→self-handicapping→failure can result in a gradual withdrawal of effort in school (or in any domain), leading to dropping out of the activity altogether (Urdan & Midgley, 2003; Zuckerman, Kieffer, & Knee, 1998).

A fair amount of research examining the association between motivation and self-handicapping has revealed that certain motivational characteristics of students and teacher instructional practices are associated with self-handicapping behavior. When students are concerned with not performing worse than other students, and with not appearing academically unable, they are more likely to self-handicap (Kaplan, Middleton, Urdan, & Midgley, 2002; Urdan, 2004). These concerns, known as *performance-avoidance goals*, can be influenced by teacher behaviors. Teachers who emphasize social comparison and competition in the classroom and publicly display reports of student achievement (e.g., test scores, grades) can promote the adoption of performance-avoidance goals in the classroom (L. Anderman & E. Anderman, 1999). In contrast, Turner and her colleagues found that in classrooms where teachers explicitly supported student autonomy and intrinsic motivation, performance-avoidance goals and self-handicapping were reduced (Turner, Meyer, Midgley, & Patrick, 2003).

CORRELATES AND CONSEQUENCES OF SELF-HANDICAPPING

Self-handicapping behavior is associated with lower achievement. Because self-handicapping behavior represents a reduction or withdrawal of effort toward a given task (e.g., not studying for a test), it is not surprising that self-handicapping is associated with lower performance on these tasks. But there may also be some benefits of self-handicapping. Some research indicates that self-handicappers do feel better about themselves after failure than do students who do not handicap (Drexler, Ahrens & Haaga, 1995; Feick & Rhodewalt, 1997). So there does appear to be some ego-protective function of self-handicapping in failure situations. In addition, there may be benefits for students who are able to succeed despite self-handicapping (Feick & Rhodewalt, 1997). Tice (1991) found that students with low self-esteem were more likely to self-handicap when they feared failing at a task, whereas students with high self-esteem were more likely to handicap when they believed they had a chance to stand out as exceptionally able by succeeding at a task. Some evidence suggests that students who succeed even after engaging in self-handicapping behavior do experience temporary increases in self-esteem. In addition, research indicates that self-handicapping is often successful at helping individuals divert the judgments of others away from low-ability attributions for failure.

Unfortunately, even though self-handicappers are often successful at their attempt to provide excuses other than low ability for their low achievement, they usually do not delude themselves. Self-handicappers describe themselves with words such as "lazy" and "shiftless" (Covington, 1992). Moreover, observers of self-handicappers developed negative attitudes about the personalities and work habits of self-handicappers (Rhodewalt et al., 1995; Smith & Strube, 1991).

PRACTICAL IMPLICATIONS

Because self-handicapping behavior undermines achievement and can lead to long-term withdrawal from achievement activities (such as school), it is important for parents and teachers to discourage self-handicapping and to avoid behaviors that might encourage it. Dweck (1999) and her colleagues have long argued that teachers and parents should promote a view of intelligence as a modifiable characteristic, something that can be improved through effort. They suggest that teachers and parents praise children for using the correct strategies rather than simply telling them how smart they are, as the latter may encourage them to think of ability as fixed, a view that contributes to self-handicapping. Midgley, Urdan, and their colleagues have suggested that teachers should emphasize individual growth, improvement, and understanding of the academic material rather than social comparison and competition, as the latter can make students concerned with appearing able or, more importantly, fearing they might appear stupid. Because it is this fear that leads students to engage in self-handicapping, efforts to reduce this fear will likely result in reduction in self-handicapping as well.

BIBLIOGRAPHY

Anderman, L. H., & Anderman, E. M. (1999). Social predictors of changes in students' achievement goal orientations. *Contemporary Educational Psychology, 25,* 21–37.

Berglas, S. (1985). Self-handicapping and self-handicappers: A cognitive/attributional model of interpersonal self-protective behavior. *Perspectives in Personality, 1,* 235–270.

Berglas, S., & Jones, E. E. (1978). Drug choice as a self-handicapping strategy in response to noncontingent success. *Journal of Personality and Social Psychology, 36,* 405–417.

Covington, M. V. (1992). *Making the grade: A self-worth perspective on motivation and school reform.* New York: Cambridge University Press.

Drexler, L. P., Ahrens, A., H., & Haaga, D. A. (1995). The affective consequences of self-handicapping. *Journal of Behavioral Personality, 10,* 861–870.

Dweck, C. S. (1999). Caution—praise can be dangerous. *American Educator 23(1),* 4–9.

Feick, D. L., & Rhodewalt, F. (1997). The double-edged sword of self-handicapping: Discounting, augmentation, and the protection and enhancement of self-esteem. *Motivation and Emotion 21,* 147–163.

Jones, E. E., & Rhodewalt, F. (1982). *The self-handicapping scale.* Princeton, NJ: Princeton University Press.

Kaplan, A., Middleton, M. J., Urdan, T., & Midgley, C. (2002). Achievement goals and goal structures. In C. Midgley (Ed.), *Understanding adolescent students' motivation: A longitudinal study* (pp. 21–54). Mahwah, NJ: Erlbaum.

Knee, C. R., & Zuckerman, M. (1998). A nondefensive personality: Autonomy control as moderators of defensive coping and self-handicapping. *Journal of Research in Personality, 32,* 115–130.

Kolditz, T. A., & Arkin, R. M. (1982). An impression management interpretation of self-handicapping strategy. *Journal of Personality and Social Psychology 43,* 492–502.

Midgley, C., & Urdan, T. (2001). Academic self-handicapping and performance goals: A further examination. *Contemporary Educational Psychology, 26,* 61–75.

Rhodewalt, F. (1994). Conceptions of ability, achievement goals, and individual differences in self-handicapping behavior: On the application of implicit theories. *Journal of Personality, 62,* 67–85.

Rhodewalt, F., Sanbonmatsu, D. M., Tschanz, B., Feick, D. L., & Waller, A. (1995). Self-handicapping and interpersonal trade-offs: The effects of claimed self-handicaps on observers' performance evaluations and feedback. *Personality and Social Psychology Bulletin, 21,* 1042–1050.

Smith, D. S., & Strube, M. J. (1991). Self-protective tendencies as moderators of self-handicapping impressions. *Basic and Applied Social Psychology, 12,* 63–80.

Tice, D. M. (1991). Esteem protection or enhancement? Self-handicapping motives and attributions differ by trait self-esteem. *Journal of Personality and Social Psychology, 60,* 711–725.

Turner, J. C., Meyer, D. K., Midgley, C., & Patrick, H. (2003). Teacher discourse and sixth graders' reported affect and achievement behaviors in two high-mastery/high-performance mathematics classrooms. *Elementary School Journal, 103,* 359–382.

Urdan, T. (2004). Predictors of academic self-handicapping and achievement: Examining achievement goals, classroom goal structures, and culture. *Journal of Educational Psychology, 96,* 251–264.

Urdan, T., & Midgley, C., (2003). Changes in the perceived classroom goal structure and patterns of adaptive learning during early adolescence. *Contemporary Educational Psychology, 28,* 524–551.

Urdan, T., Midgley, C., & Anderman, E. A. (1998). The role of classroom goal structure in students' use of self-handicapping. *American Educational Research Journal, 35,* 101–122.

Zuckerman, M., Kieffer, S. C., & Knee, C. R., (1998). Consequences of self-handicapping: Effects on coping, academic performance, and adjustment. *Journal of Personality and Social Psychology, 74,* 1619–1628.

Tim C. Urdan

SELF-REGULATED LEARNING

Educators increasingly are emphasizing self-regulated learning as a means of raising students' achievement outcomes. Self-regulated learning (or self-regulation) refers to learning that results from students' self-generated thoughts and behaviors that are oriented systematically toward the attainment of their goals (Zimmerman, 2001). Researchers have identified several self-regulatory processes that students instigate, modify, and sustain, such as attending to instruction, cognitively processing information, rehearsing and relating new learning to prior learning, believing that one is capable of learning, and establishing productive work and social environments. Research shows that increases in self-regulation result in higher student learning and achievement.

BACKGROUND OF SELF-REGULATED LEARNING

The emphasis on self-regulated learning in education began as an outgrowth of behaviorally oriented research on self-control in which individuals learned ways to reduce dysfunctional behaviors such as impulsive or disruptive actions. Behavioral researchers (e.g., Mace, Belfiore, & Hutchinson) stress self-regulating processes such as self-monitoring (self-observation and self-recording of one's own behaviors), self-instruction (rules or strategic steps that one applies and often verbalizes during a task), self-evaluation (comparing some aspects of one's behaviors with standards), self-correction (correcting one's behaviors to better match standards), and self-reinforcement (rewarding oneself with reinforcers such as points or free time when behaviors meet or exceed standards).

An issue with behavioral theories is that because they do not consider learners' internal states such as thoughts, beliefs, and emotions, they offer incomplete explanations

of learning. Against this backdrop cognitive theories of learning began their ascendance in the 1960s and soon became the dominant focus of human learning. But researchers often found that cognitive skills and abilities did not fully account for students' learning, which suggested that other factors such as motivation and self-regulation were important (Zimmerman, 2001). These findings led to the emergence of cognitive theories of self-regulated learning.

THEORIES OF SELF-REGULATED LEARNING

Cognitive theories of self-regulated learning differ in many ways but share some common features (Zimmerman, 2001). One common feature is an emphasis on learners being proactive and exerting control on their learning processes and environments. Self-regulated learners do not passively take in information but rather proactively develop their skills and strategies. Cognitive theories also assume that self-regulated learning is a cyclical process in which learners set goals, implement strategies, monitor their learning progress, and modify their strategies when they believe they are not effective. A third common feature is an emphasis on motivation. Self-regulated learning does not occur automatically; rather, students approach learning with goals and the extent to which they self-regulate depends on motivational factors such as their commitment to their goals, their beliefs about the likely outcomes of their actions, and their self-efficacy, or personal beliefs about their capabilities to learn or perform actions at designated levels.

Although there are various cognitive self-regulated learning theories, three that have been applied extensively to school learning are information processing, social constructivist, and social cognitive theories. Information processing theory stresses cognitive functions such as attending to, perceiving, storing, and transforming information. For example, Winne and Hadwin postulated that self-regulated learning comprises four phases: defining the task, setting goals and planning how to reach them, enacting tactics, and adapting metacognition. Initially learners process information about the conditions that characterize the task to clearly define it. Sources of information include task conditions (task information that learners interpret based on the environment such as a teacher's directions) and cognitive conditions that learners retrieve from long-term memory such as how they did on prior tasks and motivational information (e.g., perceived competence). In the second phase learners set a goal and a plan for attaining it to include the learning strategies they will use. During the third phase learners apply their strategies, and in the fourth phase they adapt their plans and strategies based on self-evaluations of their success (this phase is optional if no adaptation is needed).

Within each phase, cognitive information processing constructs new information or information products. Information processing works on existing information and includes processes characterized by the acronym SMART: searching, monitoring, assembling, rehearsing, and translating. While working on a task, students fill in slots in a script that includes conditions, operations, products, evaluations, and standards. Information processing outcomes are judged against standards and these evaluations (e.g., progress is on target or too low) are used to bring new conditions to bear on students' learning activities.

Vygotsky's theory of development provides a social constructivist account of self-regulation. Lev Vygotsky (1896–1934) believed that people and their cultural environments constitute an interacting social system. Through their communications and actions people in children's environments teach children tools (e.g., language, symbols) needed for developing competence. By using these tools within the social system, learners develop higher-level cognitive functions such as problem solving and self-regulation. Self-regulated learning includes the coordination of such mental processes as memory, planning, synthesis, and evaluation. These coordinated processes do not operate independently of the context in which they are formed. A student's self-regulated learning processes reflect those that are valued and taught in the culture of the student's home and school.

Vygotsky believed that people learn to self-regulate through control of their own actions. The primary mechanisms affecting self-regulation are language and the zone of proximal development (ZPD), or the amount of learning possible by a student given the proper instructional conditions. Initially children's actions are directed by the language (speech) of others but children gradually internalize this self-directing language and use it to self-regulate. Through interactions with adults in the ZPD children make the transition from behaviors regulated by others to behaviors regulated by themselves, or self-regulated learning.

Bandura's social cognitive theory posits that human functioning results from reciprocal interactions among personal factors (e.g., cognitions, emotions), behaviors, and environmental conditions. Self-regulated learning fits well with this idea of reciprocal interactions because personal factors, behaviors, and environmental conditions change during learning and must be monitored. Such self-monitoring can lead to additional changes in students' strategies, cognitions, affects, and behaviors.

This process is reflected in Zimmerman's 2000 three-phase self-regulated learning model comprising forethought, performance/volitional control, and self-reflection. The forethought phase precedes performance and refers to processes that set the stage for action. The performance/volitional control phase includes processes that occur during learning and that affect motivation and action. During the self-reflection phase, learners mentally review their performances and determine whether changes in behaviors or strategies are needed.

Various self-regulatory components come into play during the different phases. Two processes active throughout the model are goals and self-efficacy, In the forethought phase, learners set goals and hold a sense of self-efficacy for attaining them. During the performance phase they implement learning strategies and cognitively compare their performances with their goals to determine progress. Their self-efficacy is sustained when they believe that they are making goal progress. During self-reflection learners determine whether their present strategy is effective. If they feel self-efficacious for succeeding but believe that their present strategy is not working well enough, they may alter their strategy such as by working harder, persisting longer, deciding to use a different method, or seeking help from others. These self-regulatory processes promote learning, motivation, and self-efficacy.

DEVELOPMENT OF SELF-REGULATED LEARNING

The self-regulated learning processes discussed in the preceding section do not appear automatically in learners. Rather, students become more proficient self-regulators as a function of cognitive development and learning.

The development of self-regulation depends heavily on the use of self-regulatory or private speech (speech that is non-socially communicative). According to Kopp, increasing self-regulation involves a transition from responding to the commands of others to the use of speech and other cognitive tools to plan, monitor, and direct one's activities. Young children's actions are directed by adults. The meaning of actions depends on both the context and the tools (e.g., language, symbols) used to describe the actions. Through interactions with adults in the ZPD, children make the transition from behaviors regulated by others to behaviors regulated by themselves. This transition occurs as children develop the capability for using private speech to direct their actions. Such speech—which often may be talking aloud—eventually becomes internalized. The internalization of self-regulatory speech does not imply the absence of adult influence. Children's private speech may heavily reflect the directive speech of key adults (e.g., parents, teachers).

Research has identified other developmental changes. Zimmerman and Martinez-Pons found that between grades five and eight children increase their use of planning, sequencing, and goal-setting. Academic studying also undergoes changes. Meece noted that younger children equate studying with rereading material, whereas older students make greater use of note taking and underlining. Younger children also are less capable of monitoring their comprehension. Older children are better able to determine inconsistencies in text and when they find them they act to resolve them such as by rereading the passage to ensure that they read it accurately or by reading the broader passage to better determine the context.

Thus, improvements in self-regulated learning involve cognitive development and learning. As children become older they are better able to cognitively engage in such self-regulatory activities as planning, goal setting, monitoring comprehension, evaluating progress, and adjusting strategies as needed. But teaching also is important because students can learn to be better self-regulators, as discussed below.

RESEARCH ON IMPROVING SELF-REGULATION SKILLS

As discussed by Schunk and Ertmer, much educational research shows that children, adolescents, and adults can be taught self-regulated learning skills, that their use of these skills improves learning, and that skills can maintain themselves over time and generalize to new learning settings. For example, teaching students to use goal setting can improve their self-regulated learning. There are different distinctions among goals, but one is between a process goal (what skill or strategy students are attempting to learn) and an outcome goal (the intended performance). In algebra a student may be trying to learn how to use the binomial theorem (process goal) or trying to finish a problem set (outcome goal). Researchers have found that focusing students' attention on process goals—especially in the early stages of learning—improves self-regulated learning better than focusing on outcome goals. However, Zimmerman and Kitsantas found benefits from shifting from process to outcome goals. High school students were taught a writing revision strategy. Students received a process goal (following steps in the strategy), an outcome goal (number of words in sentences), or initially a process goal but then were advised to shift to an outcome goal. Learners who changed goals as their revision skills developed demonstrated higher self-efficacy and skill than students who pursued either the process or the outcome goal.

Self-monitoring and perceptions of progress are key self-regulated learning processes. Researchers have found that students can be taught self-monitoring skills and that giving them feedback on their learning progress improves their use of self-regulatory skills. Schunk and Swartz found that providing students with a process goal of learning to use a writing strategy and feedback that linked strategy use with improved writing performance led to the highest use of a writing strategy and that this strategy usage maintained itself over time and generalized to writing tasks on which students had received no instruction.

Self-evaluations of progress help students focus on self-regulation processes and can raise their motivation and self-efficacy for continuing to improve. Research shows that allowing students to periodically evaluate their learning capabilities raises their self-efficacy, motivation to self-regulate, and use of self-regulated learning strategies. A particularly effective approach is to give students a learning process goal (e.g., learn to use a strategy to solve problems) and allow them to self-evaluate their capabilities for using the strategy successfully.

There are formal programs designed to improve students' self-regulation skills. Weinstein, Husman, and Dierking described a university course in strategic learning that teaches students to use several steps in working on academic material: set a goal, reflect on the task and one's personal resources, develop a plan, select potential strategies, implement strategies, monitor and evaluate the strategies and one's progress, modify strategies as needed, and evaluate the outcomes to determine if this approach should continue to be used. Prior to the course students complete the Learning and Study Strategies Inventory, and instructors use this information to help students improve their skills, motivation, self-regulation, and academic environment.

EDUCATIONAL IMPLICATIONS

The preceding research makes clear the connection between effective self-regulation and gains in students' learning and achievement. Research findings also suggest ways to help students improve their self-regulated learning skills.

One suggestion is that, although students may discover effective self-regulated learning strategies on their own, they benefit from sound instruction and models that explain and demonstrate strategies. This does not imply that strategy instruction programs must be formally structured, but some guidance to students is important especially in the early stages of learning. As students become more proficient they are better able to construct effective strategies on their own and, as Zimmerman and Kitsantas found, pursue outcome rather than learning process goals.

A second point is that self-regulation should be taught in conjunction with an academic subject and not separately. Students benefit from seeing how they can use what they learn. Many self-regulation strategies are generic and can be applied to different content, but their implementation typically will vary depending on the content area. Thus, self-monitoring is a general strategy but what students self-monitor will vary depending whether they are reading passages in text, writing essays, or solving problems in geometry. When general strategies are taught it is important also to show students how the strategy can be adapted for use with other content.

Students should be taught how to evaluate their learning progress and given opportunities to do so. Typically in school students have their learning evaluated for them by teachers. But self-regulation is a cyclical process in which students self-regulate, check their progress, and adjust their approach as needed. Students need opportunities for self-evaluation because they may not do it automatically and it affects their motivation and self-regulated learning.

Developmental factors must be taken into account in teaching students to be better self-regulated learners. Self-monitoring is best kept simple for young children, such as by having them use a check list or count how many problems they have completed. With development, students can implement more elaborate self-regulation strategies; however, they are apt to benefit from instruction showing how to evaluate progress in areas where progress may be difficult to assess, such as writing improvement or reading comprehension.

Motivational variables also should be included in self-regulation programs. Developing effective self-regulation strategies takes time and effort, and students may not be motivated to self-regulate unless they see benefits compared with their usual approaches. They also may not feel self-efficacious about improving their self-regulation. Providing students with progress feedback linking strategy use with improved performance can raise their self-efficacy and motivation and enhance their self-evaluations of progress.

School learning typically is focused on academic content. Self-regulated learning skills do not develop automatically, but these skills will benefit students for life-long learning. Therefore, it behooves teachers and parents to help students develop their self-regulatory competencies and encourage them to practice using them in all facets of their lives.

SEE ALSO *Learning Styles; Self-Efficacy Theory.*

BIBLIOGRAPHY

Bandura, A. (1986). *Social foundations of thought and action: A social cognitive theory.* Englewood Cliffs, NJ: Prentice Hall.

Kopp, C. B. (1982). Antecedents of self-regulation: A developmental perspective. *Developmental Psychology, 18,* 199–214.

Mace, F. C., Belfiore, P. J., & Hutchinson, J. M. (2001). Operant theory and research on self-regulation. In B. J. Zimmerman & D. H. Schunk (Eds.), *Self-regulated learning and academic achievement: Theoretical perspectives* (2nd ed., pp. 39–65). Mahwah, NJ: Erlbaum.

Meece, J. L. (2002). *Child and adolescent development for educators* (2nd ed.). Boston: McGraw-Hill.

Schunk, D. H., & Ertmer, P. A. (2000). Self-regulation and academic learning: Self-efficacy enhancing interventions. In M. Boekaerts, P. R. Pintrich, & M. Zeidner (Eds.), *Handbook of self-regulation* (pp. 631–649). San Diego, CA: Academic Press.

Schunk, D. H., & Swartz, C. W. (1993). Goals and progress feedback: Effects on self-efficacy and writing achievement. *Contemporary Educational Psychology, 18,* 337–354.

Vygotsky, L. (1962). *Thought and language.* Cambridge, MA: MIT Press.

Weinstein, C. E., Husman, J., & Dierking, D. R. (2000). Self-regulation interventions with a focus on learning strategies. In M. Boekaerts, P. R. Pintrich, & M. Zeidner (Eds.), *Handbook of self-regulation* (pp. 727–747). San Diego, CA: Academic Press.

Winne, P. H., & Hadwin, A. F. (1998). Studying as self-regulated learning. In D. J. Hacker, J. Dunlosky, & A. C. Graesser (Eds.), *Metacognition in educational theory and practice* (pp. 277–304). Hillsdale, NJ: Erlbaum.

Zimmerman, B. J. (2000). Attaining self-regulation: A social cognitive perspective. In M. Boekaerts, P. R. Pintrich, & M. Zeidner (Eds.), *Handbook of self-regulation* (pp. 13–39). San Diego, CA: Academic Press.

Zimmerman, B. J. (2001). Theories of self-regulated learning and academic achievement: An overview and analysis. In B. J. Zimmerman & D. H. Schunk (Eds.), *Self-regulated learning and academic achievement: Theoretical perspectives* (2nd ed., pp. 1–37). Mahwah, NJ: Erlbaum.

Zimmerman, B. J., & Kitsantas, A. (1999). Acquiring writing revision skill: Shifting from process to outcome self-regulatory goals. *Journal of Educational Psychology, 91,* 241–250.

Zimmerman, B. J., & Martinez-Pons, M. (1990). Student differences in self-regulated learning: Relating grade, sex, and giftedness to self-efficacy and strategy use. *Journal of Educational Psychology, 82,* 51–59.

Dale Schunk

SENSATION-SEEKING

Sensation-seeking is characterized by researchers as a basic human need and as a component of human personality. The need for sensation runs along a continuum, wherein some individuals have a high need for sensation, whereas others have a low need for sensation. An individual who has a high need for sensation seeks sensation in the form of novelty, complexity, or physical stimulation from the environment (Zuckerman, 1979, 1988). Some researchers argue that sensation-seeking includes the willingness to actually take risks, whereas others argue that the willingness to take risks is a separate but related construct (e.g., Arnett, 1994).

The concept of sensation-seeking primarily has been studied in the domains of clinical psychology, personality psychology, health psychology, and communications. From an evolutionary perspective, attention to novel stimuli in the environment was necessary for human survival. Specifically, the detection of new stimuli alerted humans to potential dangers (Franklin, Donohew, Dhoundiyal, & Cook, 1988). For example, an awareness of new sounds in the environment could alert an individual to the approach of a potential predator. Most researchers in the early 2000s view sensation-seeking as an important personality trait of humans, albeit not one that is necessary for survival. The fact that sensation-seeking is viewed as a personality variable is important because personality variables are often not easily malleable; thus an individual who expresses a high need for sensation is unlikely to change much over time.

Research from the field of communications generally indicates that individuals with a high need for sensation are more likely to attune to and pay attention to messages (i.e., communications from teachers, messages from television commercials, etc.), when such messages or communications are presented in ways that catch and hold the attention of the individual.

THE IMPORTANCE OF SENSATION-SEEKING

Much of the research on sensation-seeking that is relevant to education and to educational psychology emanates from the field of health communications. In addition, much of this work has been applied research, often in school settings, and often with adolescent populations. Specifically, communication researchers have found that individuals pay attention to messages (e.g., media messages such as radio or television advertisements) based on (a) the individuals' need for sensation and (b) the level of sensation or stimulation that is provided by a given message. A media message that provides high levels of sensation is typically loud, colorful, and filled with motion and action. Intervention studies have found that when the sensation-value of a message is increased (i.e., it is made to be more stimulating by making it loud, including more colors and motion, etc.), the message is more attractive to individuals with a high need for sensation and thus has more effect on individuals' subsequent attitudes and behaviors (Donohew, Lorch, & Palmgreen, 1998).

Individuals who have high sensation needs typically engage in certain predictable behaviors. Most notably, the research indicates that individuals who exhibit a high need for sensation often are more likely to engage in risky or dangerous behaviors, such as abusing substances and having unprotected sexual intercourse (Baer, 2002; Donohew, Zimmerman, Novak, Feist-Price, & Cupp, 2000). However, research also indicates that high-sensation seekers exhibit other diverse characteristics. For example, one

study found that these individuals report greater use of the Internet than do individuals with lower reported levels of sensation-seeking (Lin & Tsai, 2002).

Research indicates that sensation-seeking rises markedly during early adolescence (Donohew et al., 1994). For many adolescents, this increase coincides with the transition from elementary school into middle school. Thus although students with high needs for sensation are present in elementary, middle, and high schools, these students may be particularly prevalent in middle school settings.

SENSATION-SEEKING IN THE CLASSROOM

Students with high need for sensation are likely to display certain predictable characteristics. First, these students may engage in risky activities in school, such as running in the hallway, jumping off desks, throwing food in the cafeteria, or more serious activities such as using illicit substances or getting into physical fights. Second, these students may be particularly attracted to stimulating experiences in school; such students may want to listen to loud music or to look at highly visually stimulating materials (e.g., colorful books with many bright pictures). Third, these students are likely to get bored easily; they may not fare well in classrooms in which they are required to sit for long periods of time and listen to lectures.

Nevertheless, these students still pay attention to tasks, activities, and media messages that are low in sensation-value, if the topic is particularly salient to them. For example, individuals may attend to a seemingly boring documentary on cancer research, if they have close relatives or friends who is suffering from the disease; they may attend to a lecture on the stock market if they have just received the gift of a larger sum of money.

SUGGESTIONS FOR EDUCATORS

Scholars who study sensation-seeking have examined in particular how media (e.g., television programs or commercials) and general communication in the classroom (e.g., the ways that teachers communicate information to students) affect learning. Students with a high sensation needs benefit from instructional practices that meet those needs. It certainly is not possible to meet the needs of these students at all times, but some lessons can be altered to better hold their attention. Clear suggestions for educators emerge from this literature.

First, these students are more academically engaged in classrooms in which novel, unpredictable activities occur. These students get bored easily in monotonous settings in which activities are repeated daily. Thus, these students benefit from changes in daily routines and the presentation of new instructional materials from time to time (e.g., the use of new texts, the introduction of novel activities, the use of videos and the Internet, holding class outside on a nice day).

Second, educators can adapt curricular materials and classroom activities to make them more appealing to students who have high sensation needs. Whereas these adaptations benefit the high sensation-seeking students, they also may be interesting and novel for students who do not have such high needs. Researchers have identified specific ways in which curricula can be adapted for students with high sensation needs. These adaptations include: (a) the use of dramatic role-playing activities (including the videotaping of such activities), (b) the incorporation of videos and music into traditional lessons, (c) the inclusion of outside speakers with real-world experiences, and (d) the opportunity for students to facilitate conversations and activities in the classrooms (Anderman, Noar, Zimmerman, & Donohew, 2004).

Donohew and his colleagues have identified the characteristics of academic tasks and media messages that are likely to be attractive to adolescents with a high sensation needs (Donohew et al., 1998). These include: (a) tasks that are novel or unusual, (b) tasks that are complex, (c) tasks that provide auditory and visual stimulation, (d) tasks that are unconventional, (e) tasks that are fast-paced, (f) tasks that are complex or ambiguous, and (g) tasks that are suspenseful.

Third, educators need to be aware that students with high sensation needs may also experience problems with behavior in the classroom. These students are more likely to get out of their seats, to talk to their neighbors, and to seek attention from the teacher. Thus targeting students with high needs for sensation early on and setting up classroom contexts to provide for these students' needs may alleviate some potential behavioral problems in the classroom.

Finally, although most of the research has focused on students who exhibit high needs for sensation, educators must be aware of students who have a low need for sensation as well. Although research suggests that tasks that are low in sensation value appeal to students with a low need for sensation (Zuckerman, 1988), it is incorrect to assume that all academic tasks or media messages that are low in sensation-value will always be attractive to these individuals. Donohew and others suggest that these messages may simply be boring and ineffective for all learners. However, educators also must be aware that students with low needs for sensation may find tasks that are high in sensation value particularly over-stimulating.

SEE ALSO *Impulsive Decision Making.*

BIBLIOGRAPHY

Anderman, E. M., Noar, S., Zimmerman, R. S., & Donohew, L. (2004). The need for sensation as a prerequisite for motivation to engage in academic tasks. In M. L. Maehr & P.

R. Pintrich (Eds.), *Advances in motivation and achievement: Motivating students, improving schools: The legacy of Carol Midgley* (Vol. 13). Greenwich: JAI Press.

Arnett, J. (1994). Sensation seeking: A new conceptualization and a new scale. *Personality and Individual Differences, 16,* 289–296.

Baer, J. S. (2002). Understanding individual variation in college drinking. *Journal of Studies on Alcohol, 14,* 40–53.

Donohew, L., Lorch, E. P., & Palmgreen, P. (1998). Applications of a theoretical model of information exposure to health interventions. *Human Communication Research, 24,* 454–468.

Donohew, L. D., Zimmerman, R. S., Novak, S. P., Feist-Price, S., & Cupp, P. (2000). Sensation-seeking, impulsive decision making, and risky sex: Implications of individual differences for risk-taking and design of interventions. *Journal of Personality and Individual Differences, 28,* 1079–1091.

Franklin, J., Donohew, L., Dhoundiyal, V., & Cook, P. L. (1988). Attention and our ancient past: The scaly thumb of the reptile. *American Behavioral Scientist, 31,* 312–326.

Zuckerman, M. (1979). *Sensation seeking: Beyond the optimal level of arousal.* Hillsdale: Erlbaum.

Zuckerman, M. (1988). Behavior and biology: Research on sensation-seeking and reactions to media. In L. Donohew, H. Spher, & T. Higgins (Eds.), *Communication, social cognition, and affect* (pp. 173–194). Hillsdale, NJ: Erlbaum.

Eric M. Anderman

SERVICE-LEARNING

Students and faculty are engaged in service-learning at every level of the educational ecology; state and international communities, K-12 schools, and colleges and universities in the United States and abroad. The National Center for Education Statistics (NCES) estimates that more than 13 million K-12 students participated in service and service-learning during the 2000–2001 academic year (Fiske, 2001). During the 2005–2006 academic year more than 6 million college and university students attending more than 1,000 institutions of higher education also were engaged in some type of service-learning (Campus Compact, 2007). These data suggest that service-learning is a comprehensive and innovative pedagogy in college, universities, and K-12 schools.

DEFINITION

In the early 2000s, service-learning projects continue to grow and evolve in schools and institutions of higher education in such a way that a common definition has not yet emerged; however, a number of accepted definitions for service-learning are used by researchers and practitioners. One definition proposed by Campus Compact (2001) focuses on service-learning as pedagogy: "service learning is an educational methodology which combines community service with academic learning objectives, preparation for community work and deliberate reflection" (p. v.). A second definition offered by Campus Compact states: "service-learning means a method under which students learn and develop through thoughtfully organized service that is conducted in and meets the needs of a community and is coordinated with an institution of higher education (or K-12 school), and with the community; helps foster civic responsibility; is integrated into and enhances the academic curriculum of the students enrolled; and include structured time for students to reflect on the service experience" (p. 15). Tom Ehrlich of the Carnegie Foundation for the Advancement of Teaching defines services learning as follows: "the various pedagogies that link community service and academic study so that each strengthens the other. The basic theory of service learning is Dewey's: the interaction of knowledge and skills with experience is key to learning" (1996). Researchers Robert Bringle and Julie Hatcher (1995) define service-learning as "a credit-bearing, educational experience in which students participate in an organized service activity that meets identified community needs and reflect on the service activity in such a way as to gain further understanding of course content, a broader appreciation of the discipline, and an enhanced sense of civic responsibility."

Staff at Learn and Serve America offer a core concept of service-learning, which holds wide agreement among both researchers and practitioners: "service learning combines service objectives with learning objectives with the intent that the activity change both the recipient and the provider of the service. This is accomplished by combining service tasks with structured opportunities that link the task to self-reflection, self-discovery, and the acquisition and comprehension of values, skills, and knowledge content" (retrieved from http://www.servicelearning.org. on April 15, 2008).

The National Commission on Service-Learning (Fiske, 2001) suggests that service-learning is a teaching and learning approach that integrates community service with academic study to enrich learning, teach civic responsibility, and strengthen communities. The intentional and planned link to the curriculum is the hallmark of service-learning. A second distinction is the reciprocal nature of the partnership between campus and community in the identification of the need and in the benefits resulting from the partnership. In other words, service-learning activities provide a mechanism for active learning and the construction of authentic learning experiences. It allows students to translate and reflect on their experience and to work in teams with other students and community members who may be different from themselves toward solving authentic problems in the community. Service-learning projects are group projects that prepare students for membership in teams in schools and

future professions. Finally, service-learning projects provide faculty with a strategy for moving away from the role of lecturer to the role of a facilitator and guide who facilitates the incorporation of new knowledge with old and the application of information to authentic, new, and varied contexts or persons.

One challenge in the implementation of service-learning activities is the misconception that these are equivalent to other community-based activities such as experiential education, volunteerism, internships, practica, and field experience. Furco (1996) provides a conceptual model for differentiating service-learning from other forms of experiential education that uses two factors: the intended beneficiary and the overall balance between service and learning as the discriminating variables. For example, volunteerism may be defined as an experience in which students provide a service and the intended beneficiary is the community partner. Community service is the engagement of students in activities with a primary focus on the service provided and the benefits accrued for the community partner. Students may acquire some benefit, but it is not necessarily tied to their discipline. At the other end of the continuum, internships engage students in service activities with the purpose of providing hands-on learning opportunities to enhance the learning and application of a set of skills or knowledge: The focus is the student.

Field experiences provide students with the opportunity to perform a service as part of a program designed primarily to enhance the understanding of a field of study: The emphasis is on the student's acquisition of skills within the field of study. Service-learning is distinguished from these other forms of experiential education by the intention to benefit the student and the community in a reciprocal and equal partnership. The focus is equally divided between the service provided and the learning that occurs. Weigert (1998) identifies six elements of service-learning that further differentiate it from other community-based outreach activities: (1) the service is meaningful to the community; (2) the service meets a need or goal; (3) the service is defined and identified by the community; (4) the service is embedded in course objectives; (5) assignments which require reflection are used to link service with objectives; and (6) the assignment has value and is assessed and evaluated.

THEORETICAL MODEL AND IMPLEMENTATION

The conceptual model that has guided service-learning was proposed by David Kolb (1984) and was built on the process of experiential inquiry proposed by John Dewey. The six step process of inquiry (encountering a problem; proposing a problem or question to be answered; gathering information to answer the question or solve the problem; making hypotheses; testing hypotheses; and making judgments or assertions) was used by Kolb to develop a learning cycle that included four phases: concrete experiences, reflective observations, abstract conceptualization (with faculty mentoring and guidance), and active experimentation. These phases are cyclical and generative.

Billig (2006) provides eight principles of effective practice in the development of service-learning activities within the curriculum: (1) service must be integrated in the curriculum; (2) diverse perspectives and experiences foster civic discourse and democratic values for all participants, both student and community partners; (3) the service is meaningful, requiring problem-solving and critical thinking; (4) reflection is used to encourage critical and creative thinking; (5) students contribute ideas in each phase of the experience; (6) the process is monitored by knowledgeable faculty and staff; (7) the experience is of sufficient intensity and duration; and (8) partnership is reciprocal and collaborative.

Faculty implementing service-learning generally move through four stages. First, community needs are identified and defined by community and campus partners, goals are then set for both learning and service. Faculty and community partners clearly delineate responsibilities and expectations and typically provide some type of orientation for students and staff if needed. The service experience constitutes the second phase and provides authentic and meaningful experience linked to the discipline and course objectives. Reflection is phase three and may occur in multiple ways: by analyzing concepts, evaluating experiences, positing questions, and reflecting on the problem/need and potential solutions. Evaluation and celebration is the final stage and recognizes the work of the student and community partner and provides a public mechanism to share the accomplishments of the students and community partners in meeting the need and/or solving the problem.

IMPACT

A number of large and small sample studies have demonstrated the positive impact of service-learning on personal outcomes, such as efficacy, identify, spiritual growth, and moral development (Astin & Sax, 1998; Eyler & Giles, 1999), the ability to work with others, leadership, and communication skills (Driscoll, Holland, Gelmon, & Kerrigan, 1996). Social outcomes such as the reduction of stereotypes, facilitation of cultural and racial understanding, sense of social responsibility, and citizenship skills (Eyler & Giles, 1999) have also been positively impacted (Bringle & Kremer, 1993). Participation in service-learning has also been documented to affect community involvement and volunteerism after graduation (Astin, Sax, & Avalos, 1999).

Faculty report that service-learning has a positive impact on academic learning and improves students' ability to apply what they have learned in the real world (Driscoll et al., 1996; Eyler & Giles, 1999). For example, a study of California high school students found that those students who participated in service-learning scored higher on all of the study's academic measures than those students enrolled in the comparison group who did not participate (Furco, 2002). These findings have been replicated in Philadelphia, Denver, and Hawaii (Billig, 2006). A study of fifth graders in Michigan also found that participation in service-learning activities was positively correlated with state test scores (Klute & Billig, 2002). Similar findings are reported for sixth grade students in Philadelphia (Billig, 2006). Participation in service-learning has been associated with higher attendance rates (Shumer, 1994) and decreased referral for disciplinary reasons (Follman, 1998). Service-learning also contributes to career development (Astin & Sax, 1998) and to students' greater sense of belonging and identification with their school (Eyler & Giles, 1999). Most importantly, students who are engaged in service-learning are more likely to graduate (Astin & Sax, 1998).

As of 2008, increased attention to service-learning was occurring concurrently with a focus on engaged teaching and learning. Researchers, scholars, and professional organizations have encouraged U.S. schools, colleges, and universities to focus on student learning and academic outcomes. Faculty state that their involvement in service-learning is motivated by one of three philosophical questions. First. is the value of service-learning for enhancing academic and interdisciplinary learning? If so, this philosophy would also support service-learning as a methodology that allows students to deepen their understanding of their discipline while developing strategies of inquiry appropriate across all disciplines and life experience. Second, is the use of service-learning for the acquisition of the skills and behaviors of leadership? Knowledge of and skills necessary for effective leadership are best experienced and gained firsthand in the real world. Third, is the service-learning conducive to civic engagement? This connection is frequently explored in published research.

In summary, service-learning has been demonstrated to benefit all members of the partnership: students, faculty, and community. Students have the opportunity to apply knowledge in meaningful ways, to work in interdisciplinary partnership with students from other disciplines and communities, and to acquire and/or change disposition and lifelong behaviors and attitudes. Community partners are able to meet an identified goal and establish positive relationships with students and the sponsoring institution. Faculty have the opportunity to support the expansion of student knowledge in application and applied settings; to demonstrate or model the application of discipline specific knowledge in applied settings; to establish partners in the application of research, and to respond to the needs identified by community partners for engaged research. Schools and other educational institutions are able to make connections to the community and form trusting and authentic partnerships with community members and organizations in engaged research and service.

RESOURCES

After the devastation of Katrina and other hurricanes in the Gulf Coast region of the United States, student organizations and faculties across the country responded through service-learning and other community outreach and engagement efforts. Student groups organized efforts to provide books, school supplies, clothing, and other necessities. Campuses offered displaced students and faculty places to live, tuition waivers, and opportunities to complete degrees that would have otherwise been abandoned. In 2005 the U. S. Housing and Urban Development and the Corporation for National and Community Service funded the Gulf Coast Universities Rebuilding America Partnership in response to the needs of communities affected by the hurricanes. This program provides an organized mechanism for supporting and engaging college and university students, faculty, and staff in helping rebuild the Gulf Coast region (for more information, see http://www.learnandserve.org/about/programs/index.asp).

Serve America (the predecessor of Learn and Serve America) was created in 1990 through funding by the National and Community Service Act (As amended through December 17, 1999, 170, P.L. 106–170) and the Domestic Volunteer Service Act (as amended by Public Law 106–170, approved December 17, 1999) to integrate community service with curricula through service-learning. In 1993 President Clinton signed legislation to create the Corporation for National and Community Service whose mission is to improve lives of Americans, strengthen communities, and foster civic engagement through service and volunteering. The corporation provides opportunities for more than two million Americans of all ages and backgrounds to serve their communities and country through Senior Corps, AmeriCorps, and Learn and Serve America, which provides support to K-12 schools, institutions of higher education, and community groups. The mission of Learn and Serve America is to facilitate service-learning projects by providing grant support for school-community partnerships, technical support and training, and the collection and dissemination of information about model programs, curricula, and research (for more information, see http://www.learnandserve.org).

Campus Compact, which is funded by a number of public and private sources (i.e., Corporation for National

and Community Service, Ford Foundation, Andrew Mellon Foundation, Pew Charitable Trusts, and the Carnegie Corporation of New York), began in 1985 as a collaboration of the presidents of Brown, Georgetown, and Stanford universities in cooperation with the Education Commission of the States. These university presidents believed that students on their campuses were socially and politically responsive to the needs of their communities and neighbors and were actively involved in community service. They sought a mechanism to document these efforts and to encourage supportive structures to increase the participation of other students. By 1991 the Compact had funded more than 120 grants and 130 service-learning workshops across the nation to faculty who linked community serve with the academic mission of higher education, and in 1999, a total of 51 college and university presidents crafted the Presidents' Declaration on the Civic Responsibility of Higher Education. By 2003, one-fourth of all higher education institutions in the United States were members of Campus Compact. These members promote civic engagement through shared knowledge and resources in the provision of service-learning efforts in the areas of literacy, health care, hunger, homelessness, the environment, and senior services. The Campus Compact mission is "to advance the public purposes of colleges and universities by deepening their ability to improve community life and to educate students for civic and social responsibility" (retrieved April 15, 2008, from www.compact.org).

Students at Campus Compact's more than 1,000 member colleges and universities contributed an estimated $7.1 billion in services to their communities during the 2005–2006 academic year. Nearly one-third of students participated in volunteer and service-learning work coordinated by campuses, performing an average of 5.6 hours of work each week, for a total of 377 million hours of service. It is important to note that these figures represent only work organized or supported by member colleges and universities; it does not capture other student volunteer work. The most common service programs on member campuses focused on tutoring and mentoring, a reflection of the high number of member institutions that have partnerships with local K-12 schools and other youth-serving organizations. Other commonly addressed issues included poverty, reading/writing, housing/homelessness, hunger, the environment, health care, multi-cultural issues, and services to seniors (Campus Compact, 2007).

BIBLIOGRAPHY

Astin, A. W., & Sax, L. J. (1998). How undergraduates are affected by service participation. *Journal of College Student Development, 39*(3), 251–263.

Astin, A. W., Sax, L. J., & Avalos, J. (1999). Long term effects of volunteerism during the undergraduate years. *Review of Higher Education, 22*(2), 187–202.

Billig, S. H. (2006). Empowering youth to change their world: Identifying key components of a community service program to promote positive development. *Journal of School Psychology, 44*(6), 513–531.

Billig, S. H., & Meyer, S. (2002). Evaluation of the Hawaiian Studies Program at Waianae High School for CREDE. Denver, CO: RMC Research.

Boyer, E. T. (1996). The scholarship of engagement. *Journal of Public Service and Outreach 1*(1) 9–20.

Bringle, R., & Hatcher, J. (1995). A service learning curriculum for faculty. *Michigan Journal of Community Service Learning, 2,* 112–122.

Bringle, R. G., & Kremer, J. F. (1993). Evaluation of an intergenerational service-learning project for undergraduates. *Educational Gerontology, 19*(5), 407–6.

Campus Compact. (2007). Campus Compact annual membership survey, 2006. Providence, RI: Author.

Driscoll, A., Holland, B., Gelmon, S., & Kerringa, S. (1996). An assessment model for service-learning: Comprehensive case studies of impact of faculty, students, community, and institutions. *Michigan Journal of Community Service Learning, 3,* 66–71.

Ehrlich, T. (1996). Foreward. In B. Jacoby & Associates (Eds.), *Service-Learning in Higher Education: Concepts and Practices.* San Francisco: Jossey-Bass.

Eyler, J. S., & Giles, D. E., Jr. (1999). *Where's the Learning in Service-Learning?* San Francisco: Jossey-Bass.

Eyler, J. S., Giles, D. E., Stenson, C. M., & Gray, C. J. (2001). At a glance: What we know about the effects of service-learning on college students, faculty, institutions, and communities, 1993–2000. In *Introduction to Service-Learning Toolkit* (3rd ed.). Providence, RI: Brown University and Campus Compact.

Fiske, E. B. (2001). *Learning in deed: The power of service-learning for American schools.* Battle Creek, MI: W. K. Kellogg Foundation.

Follman, J. (1998). *Florida learn and serve, 1996–1997: Outcomes and correlations with 1944–1995 and 1995–1996.* Tallahassee: Florida State University, Center for Civic Education and Service.

Furco, A. (1996). *Service-learning, a balanced approach to experiential education: Expanding boundaries, serving and learning.* Washington, DC Corporation for National Service, pp. 2–6.

Furco, A. (2002). Is service-learning really better than community service? A study of high school service. In A. Furco & S. H. Billig, (Eds.), *Advances in Service-Learning Research* (Vol. 1). Greenwich, CT: Information Age.

Klute, M. M., & Billig, S. H. (2002). *The impact of service-learning on MEAP: A large-scale study of Michigan learn and serve grantees.* Denver: RMC Research.

Kolb, D. A. (1984). *Experiential learning: Experience as a source of learning and development.* Inglewood, Cliffs, NJ: Prentice-Hall.

Shumer, R. (1994). Community-based learning: Humanizing education. *Journal of Adolescence, 17*(4), 357–367.

Weigert, K. M. (1998). Academic service learning: Its meaning and relevance. In R.A. Rhoads & J. P. J. Howard (Eds.), *Academic Service Learning: Pedagogy of Actions and Reflection* (pp. 3–10). San Francisco: Jossey-Bass.

Katherine M. McCormick

SEXUAL ORIENTATION

While commonly considered a way to divide the world into dichotomous and unambiguous categories of heterosexual/homosexual or gay/straight, sexual orientation is, in reality, a complex configuration of sexual attraction/desire, sexual behavior, and sexual identity. For many individuals, these three aspects of sexual orientation are neither neatly aligned nor stable across the lifespan. For example, a young adolescent female may only engage in sexual intercourse with her boyfriend, may experience sexual/romantic attractions to both males and females, live in a heterosexual marriage for a number of years during early adulthood, and claim a lesbian or bisexual identity in mid-adulthood. Likewise, a young male may be aware from an early age that his attraction is oriented to other males; he may engage in insertive-only sexual behaviors with other male sex partners, and he may claim a heterosexual identity throughout adulthood. Therefore, those who identify as gay, lesbian, or bisexual (GLB) or even heterosexual, do not form distinct, homogenous groups. Each of the three aspects of sexual orientation exist on a continuum, with fewer individuals endorsing exclusive attraction or behavior toward one sex, and with many other individuals endorsing some level of attraction to or behavior toward each sex.

Even this generally accepted tripartite conceptualization of sexual orientation vastly oversimplifies the human experience of sexuality. By focusing on the anatomy of the chosen sex partner(s) as the determining factor of sexual identity, the understanding of the complexities of sexuality and how it develops within the social context of family, peers, schools, and communities is truncated. Acknowledging this oversimplification of a complex phenomenon, the remainder of this article focuses on youth who are (or who are perceived to be) same-sex attracted.

Given this necessarily limited scope, readers are urged to consult other resources on transgender youth, another distinct and non-homogenous social identity. Transgender individuals represent the *T* in the common acronym GLBT (gay, lesbian, bisexual, transgender). However, transgender identities are constructed around the experience of the self as male or female rather than one's sexual orientation toward other persons perceived as male or female. That is, a trangender person may identify as either male or female (in contrast to the perceived and assigned sex) and then separately as heterosexual, homosexual, or bisexual depending on the perceived/assigned sex of those to whom the person is sexually attracted. Transgender youth share with GLB youth the experience of having to negotiate a stigmatized identity in often hostile or rejecting environments. However, their experiences and needs cannot be assumed to be the same. Further information and focused discussion of the important and unique needs of transgender youth in schools can be found in most of the resources suggested at the end of this entry.

As with other socially constructed categories (e.g. race, ethnicity, sex, age), sexual orientation categories reinforce power hierarchies within the culture. Heterosexual identities are privileged and non-heterosexual identities are invisible or even oppressed. For example, displays of heterosexuality in the form of social dating opportunities, proms, homecoming kings and queens, are "embellished, protected, and promoted" in schools (Leck, 2000, p. 344). In stark contrast, several states have passed legislation forbidding positive representations of homosexuality in schools (Kosciw & Diaz, 2006).

The realities of heterosexism and homophobia are the social context in which sexual minorities (the term commonly used to refer to all of those who are perceived to be or who claim to be non-heterosexual) develop their identities. In response to heterosexist and/or homophobic social contexts and social interactions, sexual minority adolescents and adults frequently conceal their same-sex sexuality (even on confidential research surveys), making it impossible to know with certainty the distribution of sexual minority identities in the general population. Additionally, for other individuals, the available categorical labels for those who experience same-sex attractions do not adequately describe their experience and thus they chose not to check a box on surveys or in their self-referent discourse (Diamond, 2005; 2006). With these caveats in mind, the best and most recent (as of 2007) population studies have determined that approximately 2 to 4 percent of the general population has a homosexual orientation (Laumann, Gagnon, Michael, & Michaels, 1994). In real numbers, this statistic implies that in a high school of 1,000 students, approximately 20 to 40 individuals will, by adulthood, identify as gay, lesbian, or bisexual. While a relatively small percentage of youth in any one school may identify as GLB, exponentially more heterosexually identified youth have at least one GLB parent, sibling, or other close family member.

School communities, thus, are filled with students, teachers, and staff who either are non-heterosexual themselves or have a close affiliation (friend or family member) to someone with a non-heterosexual identity. Public education that promotes democratic values and produces an informed citizenry that will positively contribute to a diverse, global society requires multicultural (rather than monocultural) competence that includes accurate information about and respectful interaction with sexual minorities. The respectful, professional, and inclusive treatment of sexual minority teachers, school personnel, and students provides a powerful opportunity for increasing multicultural competence among all. The absence of strong modeling of this kind of inclusivity perpetuates heterosexism and is detrimental to the goals of social justice and democracy. Having now emphasized that school communities include GLB teachers, GLB staff, GLB students, children of GLB parents, and family members of GLB individuals, the remainder of this article focuses on the needs of GLB youth in the school context.

NORMATIVE DEVELOPMENT OF SEXUAL MINORITY YOUTH

Like all adolescents, sexual minority youth face the developmental task of consolidating their identities within the context of their families, peers, and communities. That is, like heterosexual youth, sexual minority youth are trying to answer the question of who they are in relation to others and the world around them. To the extent that youths live in a social context that is characterized by homophobic attitudes and the heterosexist assumption that all so-called normal youth are heterosexual, sexual minority youths must weigh the risks of disclosing their sexual orientation. Conforming feminine or masculine appearance may make concealment a realistic option for some sexual minority youths. In any case, the on-going decisions to disclose or conceal one's identity from various people in the social network (e.g., family members, friends, teachers, and other adults) can be a significant source of chronic stress for some youths, particularly for those from racial/ethnic groups, religious groups, families, schools and/or communities that are intolerant of same-sex sexuality. Such adolescents may remain closeted rather than risk the loss of family and/or community support. In some cases, disclosure could result in the threat of violence and/or homelessness. Overall, however, same-sex attracted youths (particularly boys) are acknowledging same-sex attraction, questioning their sexual orientation and/or coming out at younger ages than in past generations (D'Augelli, 2005), perhaps due to increasing visibility of sexual minority individuals and families in the media and in many communities.

Regardless of the decision to disclose or conceal same-sex attraction, this milestone is considered the beginning of the coming out process for sexual minority youth. While identity models have portrayed a linear, lock-step process of gay and lesbian identity development that begins with acknowledgment and acceptance of one's same-sex sexuality and ends with claiming a stable identity and disclosing it to others, the actual experiences of this process have been demonstrated (most notably in young women) to be rarely this simple, tidy, and final (Diamond, 2005; 2006). Some youths altogether reject sexual identity labels and categories and others identify as *queer* rather than gay, lesbian, or bisexual as a way to reclaim or reframe a derogatory label as one of power and pride.

RISK AND PROTECTIVE FACTORS

As noted above, sexual minority youths face chronic stressors that are typically not a part of heterosexual youths' life experience. These chronic stressors, referred to collectively as "minority stress" (Meyer, 2003) include experiences of discrimination and prejudice, anticipation of rejection, internalized homophobia (i.e., negative attitudes and feelings incorporated into the self-image), and, as mentioned above, disclosing or concealing one's identity in various social contexts and relationships. Perhaps the most pervasive and destructive minority stressor frequently experienced by GLBT students in schools is peer harassment, bullying, and violence (Russell, Franz & Driscoll, 2001; Human Rights Watch, 2001; Udry & Chantala, 2002). A 2005 national survey of sexual minority youths' perceptions and experiences of their school climate found that two out of three students had been verbally harassed because of their perceived sexual orientation. Half of the participants had been verbally harassed because of the way they expressed their gender. A full three out of four participants felt unsafe at school because of treatment they received because of one personal characteristic, usually sexual orientation or gender expression (Kosciw & Diaz, 2006).

Harassment affects the educational outcomes of sexual minority youth. Large population-based studies have found that sexual minority youth are significantly more likely than their heterosexual peers to be threatened or harassed at school and to skip school because they feel unsafe (Goodenow, Szalacha, & Westheimer, 2006; Robin et al., 2002). Sexual minority youth also report lower levels of school belonging (Galliher, Rostosky, & Hughes, 2004; Rostosky, Owens, Zimmerman, & Riggle, 2003) and more negative attitudes about school and difficulties in school (Russell, Seif, & Truong, 2001). Sexual minority students are also less likely to perceive that there is an adult at school that is available to them for support (Goodenow, Szalacha, & Westheimer, 2006). The combined effect of a negative school environment and meager social support increases the risk for poor educational outcomes (Kosciw & Diaz, 2006; Murdock & Bolch, 2005).

Strong social support from family, from peers, or from other gay-affirmative adults (including teachers and other school personnel) may buffer at least some of the effects of minority stress on sexual minority youths. However, sexual minority youths who do not enjoy adequate social support or who have difficulty coping with the levels of minority stress in their lives may be at increased risk for poor psychosocial outcomes. While the majority of sexual minority youths develop coping strategies and coping resources that help to minimize the effects of minority stress, the overall higher rates of

psychological distress (Elze, 2002; Udry & Chantala, 2002) and substance abuse problems (Rostosky, Owens, & Zimmerman & Riggle, 2003; Russell, Driscoll, & Truong, 2002) among these youths are of serious concern. For example, research has established links between the school bullying and victimization experiences of sexual minority youth and their higher rates of suicidality and depressive symptoms (Bontempo & D'Augelli, 2002; Goodenow, Szalacha, & Westheimer, 2006).

CHARACTERISTICS OF SCHOOLS AND CLASSROOMS REGARDING RISK

Providing access to safe schools for all children and adolescents is a necessary requirement for positive educational outcomes. The increased risks of harassment and educational disruption and interruption for sexual minority youths must be addressed at multiple levels. First, state-wide legislation that comprehensively and specifically protects students of all socially disadvantaged groups must be enacted. The majority of GLB students in the United States are not protected, and research has demonstrated that blanket coverage through generic legislation that does not enumerate protected categories is no more effective in reducing harassment than no legislation at all (Kosciw & Diaz, 2006).

District-wide and school-level establishment and enforcement of strong anti-bullying policies that are comprehensive and inclusive of sexual orientation sends a strong message that all students will be protected from physical and psychological harm. Research findings indicate that GLB students in schools with comprehensive anti-bullying policies that include sexual orientation are more likely to report harassment, and teachers in such schools are more likely to intervene in such harassment than those GLB students and teachers in schools with generic anti-bullying policies (Kosciw & Diaz, 2006).

Safe schools create and adopt inclusive curricula that affirm the intrinsic worth of all individuals, including those who are sexual minorities. All students, including sexual minority students, have a right to a school environment that is safe and that facilitates rather than inhibits learning. Integrating sexual minority lives into classroom curricula models acceptance and appreciation of diversity. Resources on GLBT-related topics should be made available in the library and on the Internet. Students should be exposed to positive representations of GLBT issues, achievements and contributions, and current events.

At the classroom level, appropriate professional training on issues related to sexual minority youths and families should be provided since the majority of GLBT students indicate that they talked with a teacher at least once during the previous school year (Kosciw & Diaz,

2006). Unfortunately, many teachers and school staff lack even basic knowledge about sexual orientation and, therefore, are unprepared to provide information, protection, or support to their sexual minority students (Ryan & Rivers, 2003). Beyond providing support to these students, however, teachers and staff need to be trained in and encouraged to exercise skills in confronting the use of derogatory language and in effectively intervening in anti-gay bullying and harassment. Such training has been demonstrated to be significantly associated with an improved school climate (Szalacha, 2003).

School personnel should also be provided with resources (time, expertise, rewards) for grappling with their own assumptions about and biases toward others who are different from themselves. To provide effective multicultural education for students, school personnel must first have opportunities to address the ways they as individuals have personally benefited from and suffered from power hierarchies attached to social categories. This type of professional development requires a safe and trusting environment and investments of time, effort, and resources. However, the effect of this investment on school climate and educational outcomes can be significant.

At the student level, research has shown that sexual minority youths who perceive that their teachers are supportive of them and that their school environment is not rejecting of them report better school-related adjustment (Murdock & Bolch, 2005). Schools should be safe places for both GLBT students and teachers. In the 2005 school climate survey, over half of sexual minority students reported that they did not know an *out* teacher or school staff member (Kosciw & Diaz, 2006).

Finally, sexual minority youths in schools with gay/straight alliances (GSAs) or other types of groups aimed at providing support and ending discrimination and prejudice are less than half as likely as sexual minority students in other schools to report school victimization or to skip school due to fear of victimization (Goodenow, Szalacha, & Westheimer, 2006). Attending a school with a GSA (or similar support group) or perceiving that one has access to a school staff person to whom one could go for support is associated with lower rates of suicidality (Goodenow, Szalacha, & Westheimer, 2006). Principals and other school administrations need to visibly and vocally support of these groups.

SOME SUGGESTED RESOURCES FOR EDUCATORS

Safe Schools Coalition (http://www.safeschoolscoalition.org) has lesson plans and handouts for addressing issues of sexual diversity in age appropriate ways in the classroom. There are also many resources for sexual minority youths and their friends and allies, including greeting cards that can be downloaded.

The American Psychological Association's Healthy Lesbian, Gay, and Bisexual Students Project was founded "to strengthen the capacity of the nation's schools to prevent the behavioral health risks of lesbian, gay, and bisexual students through knowledge development, dissemination, and application, working with and through national organizations of school stakeholders." Their Web site (http://www.apa.org/ed/hlgbaboutus.html) provides links to national education organizations' policies and the latest research on sexual minority youths, including a link to *Just the Facts About Sexual Orientation & Youth: A Primer for Principals, Educators and School Personnel.*

The Gay, Lesbian, and Straight Education Network (http://www.glsen.org) "strives to assure that each member of every school community is valued and respected regardless of sexual orientation or gender identity/expression." More than 1,000 resources related to current events and issues, tools for ensuring safe schools, policies and legal issues, and lesson plans and curricula for the classroom are available from its Web site.

Advocates For Youth Gay, Lesbian, Bisexual, Transgender and Questioning (GLBT) Youth Initiative (http://www.advocatesforyouth.org/about/glbtq.htm) "works to address homophobia within communities, sensitize youth-serving professionals to the needs of GLBTQ youth and to encourage GLBTQ youth to become powerful advocates for themselves and other youth by sharing culturally relevant information and access to tailored services." Available at this Web site are tips for teachers and teens for dealing with harassment and for creating inclusive programs. Several fact sheets and tip sheets are available for transgender youth and for the adults in their lives.

Parents, Friends, and Families of Lesbians and Gays (http://www.pflag.org) offers support and information for families of LGBT people with more than 400 chapters nationwide. PFLAG offers Safe Schools Training for school personnel.

Children of Lesbian and Gays Everywhere (http://colage.org/) was formed "to engage, connect, and empower people to make the world a better place for children of lesbian, gay, bisexual, and/or transgender parents and families." The Web site offers a link to "Tips for making the classroom safe for children with LGBT parents," as well as lists of books and films.

SEE ALSO *Bullies and Victims; School Belonging; School Climate.*

BIBLIOGRAPHY

Bontempo, D. E. & D'Augelli, A. R. (2002). Effects of at-school victimization and sexual orientation on lesbian, gay, bisexual youths' health risk behavior. *Journal of Adolescent Health, 30,* 364–374.

D'Augelli, A. R. (2005). Developmental and contextual factors and mental health among lesbian, gay, and bisexual youths. In A. M. Omoto and H.S. Kurtzman (Eds.), *Sexual orientation and mental health: Examining identity and development in lesbian, gay, and bisexual people* (pp. 37–53). Washington, DC: American Psychological Association.

Diamond, L. M. (2005). A new view of lesbian subtypes, Stable vs. fluid identity trajectories over an 8-year period. *Psychology of Women Quarterly, 29,* 119–228.

Diamond, L. M. (2006). What we got wrong about sexual identity development: Unexpected findings from a longitudinal study of young women. In A. M. Omoto and H. S. Kurtzman (Eds), *Sexual orientation and mental health: Examining identity and development in lesbian, gay, and bisexual people* (pp. 73–94). Washington, DC: American Psychological Association.

Elze, D. E. (2002). Risk factors for internalizing and externalizing problems among gay, lesbian, and bisexual adolescents. *Social Work Research, 26,* 89–100.

Galliher, R. V., Rostosky, S. S., & Hughes, H. K. (2004). School belonging, self-esteem, and depressive symptoms in adolescents: An examination of sex, sexual attraction status, and urbanicity. *Journal of Youth and Adolescence, 33,* 235–245.

Goodenow, C., Szalacha, L., & Westheimer, K. (2006). School support groups, other school factors, and the safety of sexual minority adolescents. *Psychology in the Schools, 43,* 573–587.

Human Rights Watch. (2001). *Hatred in the hallways: Violence and discrimination against lesbian, gay, bisexual and transgender students in U.S. schools.* New York: Author.

Kosciw, J. G. & Diaz, E. M. (2006). *The 2005 National School Climate Survey: The experiences of lesbian, gay, bisexual and transgender youth in our nation's schools.* New York: GLSEN.

Laumann, E., Gagnon, J., Michael, R., & Michaels, S. (1994). *The social organization of sexuality: Sexual practices in the United States.* Chicago: University of Chicago Press.

Leck, G. M. (2000). Heterosexual or homosexual? Reconsidering binary narratives on sexual identities in urban schools. *Education and Urban Society, 32,* 324–348.

Meyer, I. H. (2003). Prejudice, social stress, and mental health in lesbian, gay, and bisexual populations: Conceptual issues and research evidence. *Psychological Bulletin, 129,* 674–697.

Murdock, T. B., & Bolch, M. B. (2005). Risk and protective factors for poor school adjustment in lesbian, gay, and bisexual (LGB) high school youth: Variable and person-centered analyses. *Psychology in the Schools, 42,* 159–117.

Robin, L., Brener, N., Emberley, N., Donahue, S., Hack, T., & Goodenow, C. (2002). Association between health-risk behaviors and gender of sexual partner in representative samples of Vermont and Massachusetts high school students. *Archives of Pediatric and Adolescent Medicine, 156,* 349–355.

Rostosky, S. S., Owens, G. P., Zimmerman, R. S., & Riggle, E. (2003). Associations among sexual attraction status, school belonging, and alcohol and marijuana use in rural high school students. *Journal of Adolescence, 26,* 741–751.

Russell, S. T., Driscoll, A. K., & Truong, N. (2002). Adolescent same-sex romantic attractions and relationships: Implications for substance use and abuse. *American Journal of Public Health, 92,* 198–202.

Russell, S. T., Franz, B.T., & Driscoll, A.K. (2001). Same-sex romantic attraction and experiences of violence in adolescence. *American Journal of Public Health, 91,* 903–906.

Russell, S. T., Seif, H., & Truong, B. L. (2001). School outcomes of sexual minority youth in the United States: Evidence from a national study. *Journal of Adolescence, 24,* 111–127.

Ryan, C., & Rivers, I. (2003). Lesbian, gay, bisexual and transgender youth: Victimization and its correlates in the USA and UK. *Culture, Health, & Sexuality, 5,* 103–119.

Szalacha, L. A. (2003). Safer sexual diversity climates: Lessons learned from an evaluation of Massachusetts Safe Schools Program for Gay and Lesbian Students. *American Journal of Education, 110,* 58–88.

Udry, J. R., & Chantala, K. (2002). Risk assessment of adolescents with same-sex relationships. *Journal of Adolescent Health, 31,* 84–92.

Sharon Scales Rostosky

SHARED COGNITION

Shared cognition occurs when two or more people intertwine their thinking processes, yielding feelings of "being on the same page" and often leading to intellectual accomplishments that "belong to us." In some settings, such as when a mother and child playfully plan a tea party, shared cognition may appear to occur naturally and effortlessly. Indeed, the basic mechanisms underlying shared cognition are readily available to school-age children and adults. Yet in many situations, shared cognition does not easily occur. Partners can bring very different life experiences, assumptions, and knowledge to their joint efforts, creating the need for strategies that can bridge their unique perspectives. Shared cognition, then, is an achievement realized in a designed environment through intentional and skillful interaction.

Both formal and informal learning settings can encourage the development of shared cognition, and doing so can have benefits both for individual learning and for students' future life opportunities. Research has shown that collaborative approaches to learning are beneficial for individual and collective knowledge growth, including the development of disciplinary practices. Studies also indicate that collaborative approaches can help students develop positive affective qualities, such as confidence and motivation. Teachers can support the expression and development of collaborative capacities through the careful design of activities, assessments, and methods for establishing and maintaining classroom norms that support productive joint work.

TRADITIONAL AND KNOWLEDGE WORK PERSPECTIVES

Traditional perspectives on learning view collaboration instrumentally. For example, a teacher may ask students to work together, but only count their individual test results toward their grade. Alternatively, a knowledge work perspective can lead to seeing collaborative learning as valuable in itself, because collaborative learning reproduces a desirable cultural practice of sharing cognition. For example, *Science for All Americans, Project 2061* (American Association for the Advancement of Science, 1989) argues:

> The collaborative nature of scientific and technological work should be strongly reinforced by frequent group activity in the classroom. Scientists and engineers work mostly in groups and less often as isolated investigators. Similarly, students should gain experiences sharing responsibility for learning with each other. In the process of coming to understandings, students in a group must frequently inform each other about procedures and meanings, argue over findings, and assess how the task is progressing. In the context of team responsibility, feedback and communication become more realistic and have a character very different from the usual individualistic textbook-homework-recitation approach. (p. 202)

THE SCOPE OF SHARED COGNITION

Shared cognition is one of several overlapping concepts: Intersubjectivity, social cognition, collective cognition, distributed cognition, group cognition, team cognition, collective consciousness, communities of practice, grounding processes in conversations, and transactive memory are all foci of research on how people learn together. To give a sense of the possible scope of shared cognition, we briefly review two concepts, intersubjectivity & joint problem solving, that are closely related to the notion of shared cognition, and the somewhat contrasting perspective of distributed cognition.

Intersubjectivity. Intersubjectivity refers to shared understanding of what has been happening and what is going to happen next. The concept of intersubjectivity has also been central in studies of infant-parent interaction. Some definitions of intersubjectivity build on a sharing metaphor, highlighting overlap and coming to consensus. Other definitions focus on the dynamics of mutual engagement and pay equal attention to disagreement, diversity of views, and conflict (Matusov, 1996). In this view coordination of perspectives is emphasized and intersubjectivity can be achieved without agreement or complete overlap of perspectives.

Joint Problem Solving. Problem solving emerged in cognitive psychology as the signature cognitive activity. When solving problems together, people often find the need to share goals, ideas, plans, explanations, justifications, judgments, and many other aspects of intellectual life. For example, students can develop shared understanding of an "if-then" problem-solving rule (e.g., if the slope is steeper, the rate is faster) by spreading the parts across utterances ("Look, it's steeper!" "So, we *know* it's going faster.") A distinction is made between cooperation or coordination, in which partners merely agree on breakdown of work, and true collaboration, in which partners help each other think the problem through (Teasley & Roschelle, 1993).

Distributed Cognition. Distributed cognition expands the unit of analyses beyond interacting partners to include the cognitive affordances of multiple partners, tools, and representations. A well-known example comes from Ed Hutchins (1995) who analyzed the navigation of a ship coming into harbor and showed that successful navigation of the ship was dependent on complex coordinations between the knowledge of team members, measurement tools, and representational systems. Based on this and other analyses he argued that human intelligent action is productively conceived as an accomplishment that arises from *properties of interactions* between people or between people and artifacts in the world.

BUILDING BLOCKS OF SHARED COGNITION

Close analyses of conversations have led to deeper understanding of building blocks that support the accomplishment of shared cognition. Four building blocks are discussed below.

Joint Attention. Joint attention is first observed between 9 and 15 months (Adamson & Bakeman, 1991). Studies of infant-mother interaction provide interesting insights about the subtle ways in which partners help regulate the attention of the other and highlight how both partners are active contributors to the process. Achieving joint attention during problem-solving situations depends on the mutual intent of group members to share a focus and come to a common understanding.

Making and Acknowledging Contributions. Participants build a sense of shared cognition through interactions that make and acknowledge contributions (Clark, 1996). Participants take knowledge to be shared only after a first participant's bid to introduce an idea is accepted by a second participant. This can occur in two short utterances or be the result of a lengthy deliberation.

Grounding. The everyday phrase "finding common ground" is a practical solution to a pervasive problem in sharing cognition: How can participants tell if an idea is mutually understood? A simple "uh, huh" provides weaker evidence than a more elaborate paraphrase that participants agree on. Common ground can also be found in action; smooth translation of ideas to satisfactory joint actions is good evidence the ideas were shared. Conversational analysis shows that people flexibly apply a variety of grounding strategies and criteria of mutuality depending on the purposes of communication and the channels of communication available (Clark & Brennan, 1991).

Repair. Of course, attempts to share cognition often go astray. Successful collaborators notice divergence and engage in repairs. For example, in baking a cake one might have the following exchange: "The recipe called for 1 teaspoon of baking soda." "No, baking *powder*." "OK, I'll put in 1 teaspoon of baking powder." In this set of three utterances, by saying no and emphasizing the word *powder* the second person repairs the misconception of the first and the two people achieve shared knowledge of the right ingredient.

Although these building blocks have been described in generic terms, one can imagine their application to classroom situations. In order to share cognition, teachers and students must also achieve joint focus of attention, make and acknowledge contributions, find common ground, and repair misunderstandings.

In one example, researchers observed students constructing a "joint problem space" (Roschelle, 1992; Teasley & Roschelle, 1993). A joint problem-solving space was defined as a shared conceptual structure developed in the course of collaborative work. In a study of two girls using a computer simulation designed to provide a dynamic view of velocity and acceleration, Roschelle (1992) argued that the creation of a joint problem-solving space was accomplished through repeated cycles of displaying, confirming, and repairing understandings. As the conversation progressed, the students expected increasingly explicit evidence that they understood one another.

HOW SHARED COGNITION CONTRIBUTES TO LEARNING

Theorists have given varied accounts of how shared cognition leads to learning. More recently, researchers have developed more specific accounts and analyses.

Conflict was central in the theory of Jean Piaget (1896–1980) about how social exchange can result in cognitive development (Piaget, 1932). Different perspectives on the same problem can lead to disagreements, decentering from one's own perspective, more advanced stages of cognitive development, and sometimes mutual understanding.

Interaction within a *zone of proximal development* was central to the theory of development put forward by Lev Vygotsky (1896–1954) (Vygotsky, 1978). This zone represents the level of challenge at which a learner cannot independently accomplish a task but can do so with the help of a more expert peer or teacher. *Internalization* occurs because the child is actively playing a role in the joint activity and the more expert partner is attending to when and where assistance is needed. The child comes to own not only skills but the cultural tools that have been developed over long periods of time, such as writing systems, maps, language, and numerical systems.

More recently, investigators have offered more detailed explanations of how group work can support individual learning. These include opportunities to share original insights (Bos, 1937), resolve differing perspectives through argument (Amigues, 1988; Phelps & Damon, 1989), explain one's thinking about a phenomenon (King, 1990; Webb, Troper, & Fall, 1995), provide critique (Bos, 1937), observe the strategies of others (Azmitia, 1988), listen to explanations (Coleman, 1988; Hatano & Iganaki, 1991), and generate new insights through shared abstract representations, such as diagrams (Jeong & Chi, 2007; Schwartz, 1995).

Increasingly it is recognized that asking learners to work in groups does not automatically lead to interactions that capitalize on the knowledge and skills of all group members. One of the most challenging aspects of group projects involves developing an understanding of what knowledge is shared and what knowledge members hold uniquely. The extent to which learners come to a common or shared understanding of their efforts can vary, depending on multiple factors including their prior experiences, their personal relationships, broader power structures in society, and the extent to which their goals for the task are aligned.

Research that attends explicitly to variability in group interaction has provided information about how relational challenges can interfere with the shared cognition, even when collaborators have similar levels of prior knowledge. Barron (2003) analyzed the interactions of 16 triads in order to understand the sources of variability in how well the students collaborated and how much individuals learned. She found less joint attention in groups in which partners were competing, and this translated into poorer performance even when correct solutions were voiced. If a collaboration is going well: (1) many students will be involved in the discussion as contributors and responders, (2) the contributions are coordinated rather than consisting of many independent, unrelated conversational turns; (3) students attend to one another and to their work in common as indicated by eye gaze and body position. These are good markers of *mutual engagement and joint attention,* important elements of collaborative work.

SCHOOLING PRACTICES

A great deal of work has been done to specify the kinds of tasks, accountability structures, and roles that help students collaborate well. It is generally agreed that tasks requiring interdependence of team members, accountability structures at the group and individual level, and opportunities to reflect on group progress and interaction are key element Two approaches, complex instruction and jigsaw, are described below.

Complex Instruction. Cohen and her colleagues developed *Complex Instruction,* one of the best-known and well-researched approaches. Complex Instruction uses carefully designed activities that require a diversity of talents and interdependence among group members. Teachers are encouraged to pay attention to unequal participation that often results from status differences among peers and are given strategies that will allow them to bolster the status of infrequent contributors (Cohen & Lotan, 1997). In addition, roles are assigned that support equal participation. The roles include a recorder, a reporter, a materials manager, a resource manager, a communication facilitator, and a harmonizer. A major aspect of the approach is the development of "group-worthy tasks" that are both sufficiently open-ended and multi-faceted in their cognitive demands to require and benefit from the participation of every member of the group.

Jigsaw Method. The jigsaw method divides topics among students so that each class member becomes an expert in a subtopic. Experts then teach their group members what they know so that the group benefits from the distributed work. For example, groups of four to five students might be asked to write proposals to study a specific animal species (Engle & Conant, 2002). The groups are then assigned an animal based on the quality of their group proposal. A final product of the group is required, such as a written report to which all members of the group contribute. Individual students become expert on a specific subtopic, such as reproduction strategies or defense mechanisms, and contribute chapters that focus on these subtopics. After they have shared this knowledge with their group, the entire group writes the introduction and conclusion.

IMPLICATIONS

Education traditionally downplays the importance of shared cognition in favor of sequestered test-taking skills. This bias appears shortsighted in an era driven by the intellectual accomplishments of teams. By understanding the building blocks of shared cognition, the ways in which shared cognition can enhance learning, and research-based school practices, educators can enable students to learn both subject matter content and how to succeed in realistic adult tasks.

BIBLIOGRAPHY

Adamson, L. B. & Bakeman, R. (1991). The development of shared attention during infancy. In Ross Vasta (Ed), *Annals of child development* (pp. 1–41). London: Jessica Kingsley.

American Association for the Advancement of Science. *Science for all Americans: Project 2061.* New York: Oxford University Press, 1989.

Amigues, R. (1988). Peer interaction in solving physics problems: Sociocognitive confrontation and metacognitive aspects. *Journal of Experimental Child Psychology, 45*(1), 141–158.

Azmitia, M. (1988). Peer interaction and problem solving: When are two heads better than one? *Child Development, 59*(1), 87–96.

Barron, B. (2003). When smart groups fail. *Journal of the Learning Sciences, 12*(3), 307–359.

Bos, M. C. (1937). Experimental study of productive collaboration. *Acta Psychologica, 3,* 315–426.

Clark, H. (1996). *Using language.* Cambridge, England: Cambridge University Press.

Clark, H. H., & Brennan, S. A. (1991). Grounding in communication. In L. B. Resnick, J. M. Levine, & S. D. Teasley (Eds.). *Perspectives on socially shared cognition* (pp. 127–149). Washington DC: American Psychological Association.

Cohen, E. (1994.) *Designing groupwork: Strategies for the heterogeneous classroom.* New York: Teachers College Press.

Cohen, E. G., & Lotan, R. A. (1995). Producing equal-status interaction in the heterogeneous classroom. *American Educational Research Journal, 32*(1), 99–120.

Coleman, E. (1998). Using explanatory knowledge during collaborative problem solving in science. *Journal of Learning Sciences, 7,* 387–427.

Engle, R. A., & Conant, F. R. (2002). Guiding principles for fostering productive disciplinary engagement: Explaining an emergent argument in a community of learners classroom. *Cognition and Instruction, 20*(4), 399–483.

Hatano, G., & Ignaki, K. (1991). Sharing cognition through collective comprehension activity. In L. B. Resnick, J. Levine, & S. Teasley (Eds.), *Perspectives on socially shared cognition* (pp. 331–348). Washington, DC: American Psychological Association.

Hutchins, E. (1995). *Cognition in the wild.* Cambridge, MA: MIT Press.

King, A. (1990). Facilitating elaborative learning in the classroom through reciprocal questioning. *American Educational Research Journal, 27,* 664–687.

Matusov, E. (1996). Intersubjectivity without agreement. *Mind, Culture, and Activity, 3*(1), 25–45.

Phelps, E., & Damon, W. (1989). Problem solving with equals: Peer collaboration as a context for learning mathematics and spatial concepts. *Journal of Educational Psychology, 81*(4), 639–646.

Piaget, J. (1932). *The moral judgement of the child.* New York: Harcourt Brace.

Roschelle, J. (1992). Learning by collaborating: Convergent conceptual change. *Journal of the Learning Sciences, 2*(3), 235–276.

Schwartz, D. L. (1995). The emergence of abstract representations in dyad problem solving. *Journal of the Learning Sciences, 4*(3), 321–354.

Teasley, S. D., & Roschelle, J. (1993). *Constructing a joint problem space: The computer as a tool for sharing knowledge.* Hillsdale, NJ: Erlbaum.

Vygotsky, L. (1978). *Mind in society. The development of higher psychological processes* (M. Cole., V. John-Steiner, S. Scribner, & E. Souberman (Eds.)). Cambridge, MA: Harvard University Press.

Webb, N. M., Troper, J. D., & Fall, R. (1995). Constructive activity and learning in collaborative small groups. *Journal of Educational Psychology, 87,* 406–423.

Brigid Barron
Jeremy Roschelle

SIMON, HERBERT (ALEXANDER)
1916–2001

To the outside world American psychologist and computer scientist Herbert Alexander Simon (1916–2001) appeared to be a Renaissance man. A political scientist who won a Nobel Prize in economics (1978) and the first National Medal of Science for behavioral sciences, Simon pioneered artificial intelligence and made significant contributions in diverse fields, including philosophy, physics, the history of science, business administration, and the psychology of learning. Yet Simon described himself as a monomaniac singularly focused on understanding the processes of human learning, problem solving, and decision making.

Born and raised in Milwaukee, Wisconsin, Simon became interested in decision-making processes as an undergraduate at the University of Chicago. There he conducted a study on the administration of the Milwaukee Recreation Department for Clarence Ridley's course on evaluating city government. After earning his BA in political science in 1936, Simon became Ridley's assistant at the International City Managers' Association in Chicago. In 1939 Simon moved to the University of California at Berkeley to head a three-year study on local government, while completing his doctorate from Chicago on decision-making in organizations.

In 1942 Simon joined the political science faculty at the Illinois Institute of Technology, becoming department chair in 1946. There he continued his collaborations at the University of Chicago and the Cowles Commission for Research in Economics. In 1949 Simon joined the new Graduate School of Industrial Administration at the Carnegie Institute of Technology (later Carnegie-Mellon University) in Pittsburgh, Pennsylvania. He remained there for the rest of his life, from 1965 on as the Richard King Mellon University Professor of computer science and psychology.

Simon challenged a basic tenet of classic economic theory when he argued that business decision-makers could not have enough information to maximize profits. He developed the theory of "satisficing" or "bounded rationality" to describe the balancing of factors for making satisfactory rather than optimal decisions. Later Simon applied his theory to the teaching of algebra.

In the 1950s Simon began using computers to study how humans think and learn, with a goal of improving teaching methods. In early experiments with Allen Newell and Clifford Shaw of the RAND Corporation, Simon had subjects verbalize their reasoning while working through problems in logic. These human problem-solving processes were then codified as computer programs. The Logic Theorist program and subsequent General Problem Solver were the first computer programs to simulate human reasoning and the forerunners of artificial intelligence. Simon and his colleagues subsequently developed computer programs as models of other human cognitive processes, including learning.

According to Simon, educational programs should first determine what students need to know and then design experiences that result in learning the desired skills and information. For example, geometry teachers should begin by determining what students need to know to solve problems and prove theorems and then design the appropriate learning experiences. Simon and his colleagues found that working through step-by-step examples of solutions to problems was a powerful learning method. As the students worked through the examples, they learned how to get from one step to the next. Subsequently Simon developed computer programs that learned new skills by examining worked-out solutions to problems. In other experiments Simon and K. Anders Ericsson demonstrated that the verbalizing of thought processes often improved student learning.

While developing computer programs for playing chess, Simon found that pattern recognition—rather than analysis—was a key to learning and developing expertise. He concluded that more emphasis should be placed on teaching pattern recognition. During the 1980s Simon also studied short-term memory with Chinese colleagues and used computers to simulate human memory processing and determine the limits of short-term memory. The researchers discovered that it takes eight seconds to learn a pattern for one day, but substantially longer to learn a pattern permanently.

Using computer programs as models Simon and colleagues at the Chinese Academy of Sciences designed a middle-school curriculum in algebra and geometry. Traditional algebra textbooks explained the rules for solving equations, but not how to decide which rule to use. In their experimental classrooms, large groups of students learned algebra by working through examples, while the teacher tutored individual students rather then lecturing. Simon found that the children learned algebra about 50% faster than with traditional methods. By 1998 the curriculum was being used in some 200 Chinese schools.

Simon and his colleagues at Carnegie-Mellon were pioneers in the use of computers in education. To design computer displays for teaching, Simon set out to determine what humans were capable of visualizing, how they visualized, and how students utilized visual material. For example he observed what students doodled as they tried to understand complex problems in math and physics. Simon died in Pittsburgh at the age of 84.

Ericsson and others subsequently extended Simon's findings on learning and the acquisition of expertise and applied it to K-12 education.

SEE ALSO *Decision Making.*

BIBLIOGRAPHY

WORKS BY

Simon, H. (1991). *Models of my life.* New York: Basic Books.

Simon, H. (1998). What we know about learning. *Journal of Engineering Education, 87,* 343–348.

Simon, H. (2001). Achieving excellence through education. In M. Ferrari (Ed.), *The pursuit of excellence through education* (pp. 181–194). Mahwah, NJ: Erlbaum.

Simon, H. (2001). Seek and ye shall find: How curiosity engenders discovery. In K. Crowley, C. D. Schunn, & T. Okada (Eds.), *Designing for science: Implications from everyday, classroom, and professional settings* (pp. 3–18). Mahwah, NJ: Erlbaum.

Simon, H. & Zhu, X. (1987). Learning mathematics from examples and by doing. *Cognition and Instruction, 4,* 137–166.

WORKS ABOUT

Augier, M. (2000). Models of Herbert A. Simon. *Perspectives on Science, 8,* 407–444.

Ross, P. E. (1998). Flash of genius as I see it. *Forbes, 162,* 98–100.

Simon, H. A. (2001). Psychology Research. Retrieved April 10, 2008, from http://www.psy.cmu.edu/psy/faculty/hsimon/hsimon.html.

Stewart D. (1994). Herbert A. Simon (artificial intelligence pioneer) (interview). *Omni, 16,* 70–77.

Margaret Alic

SINGLE-CASE DESIGNS

The term *single-case designs* refers to a family of research designs that are true experiments. They can be used to infer causal relationships between an intervention program (e.g., in education, therapy, rehabilitation) and change in client functioning and behavior. The unique feature of these designs is the capacity to conduct experimental investigations with the single case, that is, one subject or one group. However, the designs can evaluate the effects of interventions with multiple subjects and groups.

CHARACTERISTICS AND UNDERPINNINGS OF THE DESIGNS

There are key features of the designs that are pivotal for drawing causal inferences. As with designs in the quantitative-group tradition, control and comparison of conditions, prediction, and testing of predictions are all central. These are accomplished in novel ways in single-case designs.

Logic of the Designs. The designs draw causal inferences based on how the assessment information is used over the course of the design. Each design includes phases or periods of time (e.g., week, month) in which baseline (no intervention) or intervention are presented (e.g., to one or a few individuals or a group). The designs usually begin with a baseline phase, a period of observations before the intervention is implemented. The data in this phase have two purposes: to describe current performance and predict what performance is likely to be in the immediate future without an intervention. After the baseline pattern is clear, an intervention is implemented in a new phase, all the while data are being collected. Data in the intervention (and any subsequent phases) have three purposes: to describe as in baseline; to predict what performance would be likely if the intervention were to continue, and to test the prior prediction from baseline. Baseline is used to predict likely performance; if the intervention is having any effect in the next phase the data ought to depart from that projected level of performance.

Essentially, single-case designs are based on describing, predicting, and testing predictions. The logic of this is exactly like that of experiments in the quantitative-group tradition, in which describing performance without intervention and testing whether the intervention departs from that is achieved by a control group of subjects (e.g., no treatment, waiting list). In single-case and group research methods, the question is whether the intervention (variable, experimental manipulation) made a difference in a way that departs from the control phase or group, respectively.

Assessment Requirements. The most fundamental design requirement is repeated observations of performance over time. The performance of one or more clients is observed on several occasions, usually before the intervention is applied and continuously over the period while the intervention is in effect. Typically, observations are conducted on a daily basis or at least on multiple occasions each week to provide the information to describe, predict, and test predictions, as noted previously. Continuous assessment provides the observations that allow the comparisons of interest (e.g., intervention versus no intervention) within the individual subject.

Because baseline performance is used to predict how the client will behave in the future, it is important that the data are stable. Data stability refers to minimal fluctuation or variability in the subject's performance over time. Excessive variability in the data during baseline or other phases can interfere with drawing conclusions about treatment. Whether the variability is excessive and interferes with drawing conclusions about the intervention depends on many factors, such as the initial level of behavior during the baseline phase and the magnitude of behavior change when the intervention is implemented.

MAJOR EXPERIMENTAL DESIGN STRATEGIES

There are many single-case designs that vary in the way the intervention is presented and evaluated over time. Three designs are presented here to illustrate the methodology.

ABAB Design. As with all of the designs, continuous observations of performance are made over time for a given client (or group of clients). In ABAB design, typically two separate phases are alternated over time, including the baseline (A phase), when no intervention is in effect, and the intervention (B phase). The A and B phases are repeated again to complete the four phases. The effects of the intervention are clear if performance improves during the first intervention phase, reverts to or approaches original baseline levels of performance when the intervention is withdrawn, improves when the intervention is reinstated in the second intervention phase, and again changes in the final intervention phase.

The most commonly used version of the ABAB design has been discussed here as a four-phase design

that alternates a single intervention with baseline phases. However, designs are available that include more than one treatment and more than four phases or that end with a new phase in which procedures are included to maintain the gains. For example, suppose that the treatment (B1) does not change behavior after the baseline phase. The investigator would not continue the phase but would try another treatment (B2). This latter treatment would constitute a new phase and would probably be implemented later in the design. The design could be represented as an AB1 B2 AB2 design.

As a general rule, problems related to reversing behavior make the ABAB design and its variations undesirable in educational and other applied settings. If a reversal does occur, that may be problematic if the behavior is important for the clients or for those in contact with them. If a reversal does not occur, this raises obstacles in concluding that the intervention led to the change. Yet the power of the design in demonstrating control of an intervention over behavior is very compelling. If behavior can, in effect, be turned on and off as a function of the intervention, this is a potent demonstration of a causal relation. Other designs can also demonstrate a causal relation without using a reversal of conditions.

Multiple-Baseline Designs. These designs evaluate change across different baselines that refer to two or more: behaviors of a given individual, individuals, settings, or time periods. The intervention is introduced to the different baselines at different points in time, for example, in a staggered fashion. Ideally, change occurs when the intervention is introduced in sequence to each of the baselines. The different baselines might, for example, consist of three children in a classroom (or three entire classrooms). Each child's behavior is observed and graphed separately. After baseline observations, the intervention is introduced to one of the children. The other children continue to be observed and remain in a baseline phase. Later the intervention is introduced to the other children in a staggered fashion so that by the end each is receiving the intervention. The effect of the intervention is demonstrated by showing that the behavior of each child changed when and only when the intervention was introduced.

Multiple-baseline designs are user friendly in educational and clinical applications because the intervention is applied in a gradual or sequential fashion across different responses of the individual (or different individuals, or different situations). If the intervention is effective, then it can be extended to all of the other responses for which change is desired. As important, if the intervention is not effective or not effective enough to achieve important changes, it can be altered or improved before it is extended.

Changing-Criterion Design. This design demonstrates the effect of an intervention by showing that behavior changes in increments to match a performance criterion. The design begins with a baseline phase after which the intervention is introduced. When the intervention is introduced, a specific level of performance is chosen as a criterion for the client. The daily criterion may be used as a basis for providing response consequences or an incentive (e.g., token reinforcement). When the performance meets or surpasses the criterion level on a given day (e.g., certain number of cigarettes smoked, number of calories consumed), the response consequence (e.g., tokens) is provided.

A specific criterion usually is invoked continuously for at least a few days. When performance consistently meets the criterion, the criterion is made more stringent (e.g., fewer cigarettes or calories consumed daily). Consequences are provided only for meeting the new criterion on a given day, and the criterion again is changed if the performance meets the criterion consistently. The criterion is repeatedly changed throughout the intervention phase until the terminal goal of the program is achieved. A causal relation between an intervention and behavior is demonstrated if behavior matches a constantly changing criterion for performance over the course of treatment. By implementing a given criterion for at least a few days (or even longer), the behavior shows a step-like effect that is not likely to result from a general incremental change occurring as a function of extraneous events.

As with the multiple-baseline design, the changing-criterion design can be quite compatible with demands of the applied settings. Many therapeutic regimens focus on gradual development of behavior or skills (e.g., improving reading comprehension or participation of activities) or reduction of problematic function (e.g., overcoming anxiety). Shaping these behaviors or gradually exposing individuals to an anxiety-provoking situations may proceed in ways that can reflect increasing the performance criteria as changes are evident. Thus, progress can be monitored and evaluated in a changing-criterion design.

DATA EVALUATION

Data evaluation refers to the way the numbers are examined to infer whether there was a veridical intervention effect. Investigators working with single-case designs as a matter of choice often prefer nonstatistical evaluation of the data, a method referred to as visual inspection. Visual inspection depends primarily on examining four characteristics of the data across phases of the design:

Changes in means: Consistent changes in means (average) across phases;

Changes in level: A shift or discontinuity of the data point from the end of one phase to the beginning the next phase; an index of the immediacy of change;

Changes in slope or trend: Changes the direction (e.g., accelerating or decelerating slope) of behavior as the intervention is applied or withdrawn; and

Latency of the change: The more immediate the change after a phase is altered, the more likely the intervention can be inferred to be responsible for change.

Although visual inspection is the most frequently used method of data evaluation, statistical tests are available and often applied to the data. Statistical tests for single-case designs consist of methods (e.g., time-series analyses, randomization tests) not usually taught in social and biological sciences. Characteristics of single case data (autocorrelation) often preclude the straightforward application of more familiar statistical tests.

STRENGTHS AND LIMITATIONS

There are strengths of the designs. First, they are well suited to evaluating interventions in diverse settings. Most programs in schools, institutions, the home, and the community at large are not evaluated empirically and have no evidence in their behalf in part because randomized controlled trials are not feasible. Single-case designs permit careful and rigorous evaluation. Second, the designs allow for changes during a study, a feature that is well suited to applied settings. If the intervention is not working well or optimally, modifications can be made, and the design can continue to provide a rigorous evaluation. Third, the designs can address many questions of interest in intervention research beyond the effects of a particular intervention such as the components of the intervention that contribute to change and the relative effectiveness of two or more interventions.

There are limitations as well. First, when only one or a few subjects are used, there is difficulty in identifying characteristics (moderators) that might explain why some individuals respond better than others or do not respond. The sample is inherently too small to conduct post hoc analyses of characteristics (e.g., by age, sex, ethnicity) that might influence responsiveness to treatment.

Second, an oft-cited but probably misunderstood concern or limitation is the extent to which the results with one or a few subjects can generalize to others not included in the study. This concern has not proven to be an issue. Also, the concern reflects a misunderstanding of group research; when means are compared one has no idea within a study how many individuals responded. In addition, unless the group was randomly selected from a population, generalizing beyond the sample is a problem.

Tests of generality invariably require replication. The limitation of single-case designs is not generality of the effects but identifying the dimensions or categories which may influence the extent to which the intervention exerted impact.

Finally, the use of visual inspection can be a limitation of the designs. When the visual inspection criteria are not clearly met, agreement on interpretation of the data becomes less clear. Studies of how individuals invoke the criteria for visual inspection have shown that judges, even when experts in the field, often disagree about particular data patterns and whether the effects were reliable.

APPLICATIONS IN EDUCATIONAL SETTINGS

Single-case designs have been used extensively in educational settings, from preschool through college. There is a special role for these designs in schools because school is often a place in which diverse programs are implemented and at different levels (e.g., classroom, schools, districts, and states and provinces). Among the many examples are programs with an academic focus (e.g., reading comprehension), study habits (e.g., homework compliance and completion), classroom deportment (e.g., decreases in disruptive behavior), risky behaviors among adolescents (e.g., substance use, unprotected sex), skill acquisition (e.g., voice, musical instrument), and safety (e.g., driving). It is not feasible to even consider randomized trials to evaluate such programs. Single-case designs are quite useful for evaluation in general and in the many situations in which there is or cannot be a control group. Single-case designs and programs in educational (but other institutional settings) are a natural combination because one can develop the program by examining its impact on student functioning, can make changes during the evaluation to improve the program, and identify causal relation between interventions and outcomes without the constraints of large samples, random assignment, and control condition.

Single-case designs are rarely taught in graduate training in social and biological sciences. This is unfortunate because people in education, psychology, counseling, medicine, and other disciplines frequently are interested in evaluating interventions at the level of the individual, groups, and institutions. The designs can be used in applied settings and hence serve as a way to translate laboratory findings to real world settings as well as identifying promising interventions that might warrant further research in laboratory settings.

SEE ALSO *Applied Behavior Analysis; Research Methods: An Overview.*

BIBLIOGRAPHY

Cooper, J. O., Heron, T. E., & Heward, W. L. (2007). *Applied behavior analysis.* 2nd ed. Upper Saddle River, NJ: Pearson Prentice Hall.

Kazdin, A. E. (1982). *Single-case research designs: Methods for clinical and applied settings.* New York: Oxford University Press.

Kazdin, A. E. (2001). *Behavior modification in applied settings* (6th ed.). Belmont, CA: Wadsworth.

Kazdin, A. E. (2003). *Research design in clinical psychology* (4th ed.). Needham Heights, MA: Allyn & Bacon.

Kennedy, C. H. (2005). *Single-case designs for educational research.* Boston: Allyn & Bacon.

Kratochwill, T. R., & Levin, J. R. (Eds.). (1992). *Single-case research design and analysis.* Hillsdale, NJ: Erlbaum.

Alan E. Kazdin

SITUATED COGNITION

Many practices of conventional schooling consider knowledge and skill as discrete structures of cognition that can be adequately transferred from teachers to students in classrooms and studied in laboratories. Knowing and thinking, in this view, are assumed to go on in individual minds isolated from the complexity of the world outside, from which abstract knowledge can be successfully distilled. However, a growing body of research that considers cognition and learning in activities outside specialized learning environments is undermining the plausibility of these presuppositions (e.g., Brown, Collins & Duguid, 1989; Engeström, 2001; Greeno, Collins, & Resnick, 1996; Hutchins, 1995a; Lave & Wenger, 1991; Nersessian et al., 2003; Rogoff, 1990; Rogoff & Lave, 1984). This research supports the view that knowing and learning by individuals are inextricably situated in the physical and social contexts of their acquisition and use. It is a mistake to think that classrooms or laboratory experiments produce knowledge or follow principles of learning that are somehow context-free. Cognition and learning by individuals always occur in a context; the issue has to be what the context is, not whether there is one.

For most of time between 1950 and the early 2000s, active research programs have been studying structures and processes of social interaction, as well as cognitive processes of representing and transforming information. But these research programs have been largely separate from each other. Situative research and theorizing attempts to unify the two perspectives of individual cognitive theory and the analysis of interactional structures and processes. The primary level of a situative analysis is an activity system, in which one or more individuals participate along with material and informational resources in the environment. Cognitive processes are understood as aspects of the practices of a community or group. Studies include analyses of perceiving (Goodwin, 1996), remembering (Hutchins, 1995b), reasoning and understanding (Greeno & Van de Sande, 2007; Ochs, Gonzales, & Jacoby, 1996), and learning (Bowers, Cobb, & McClain, 1999; Engeström, 2001; Engle, 2006; Stenning et al., 2002). In these analyses, successful cognitive performances are considered as part of an interactive system, and analyses focus on how the multiple participants coordinate their contributions. Information structures, which the individual cognitive perspective attributes to individual minds, are attributed in the situative perspective to the interacting group as achievements of communication that enter the group's common ground (cf. Clark, 1996). Such analyses do not preclude also having analyses of the same events that focus on one or more individual participants, identifying their respective contributions to the interactions and explaining these in terms of their individual capabilities, and with other participants and systems considered as the context (cf. Bowers, Cobb & McClain, 1999; Hatano & Inagaki, 2003).

If knowing is understood as successful situated participation, then many conventional assumptions must be questioned. In particular, a situative theory of knowing challenges the widely held belief that abstraction of knowledge from situations is the key to transferability. An examination of the role of situations in structuring knowledge suggests that abstraction and explication provide an inherently impoverished and often misleading view of knowing. Knowing by an individual is fundamentally a capability of the person to interact in the world. In this view, hypotheses or assessments of an individual's or group's knowing are about their capabilities for interacting in situations. Hypotheses that represent knowledge only as abstract propositions do not capture the densely interwoven nature of knowing.

The situative perspective views knowing as distributed among people and their environments, including the objects, artifacts, tools, books, and the communities of which they are a part. Analyses of activity focus on processes of interaction of individuals with other people and with physical and technological systems. Several research traditions have contributed to the situative perspective. The best established of these is ethnography, including the study of cultural practices and patterns of social interactions, as well as discourse analysis and conversation analysis in activity theory, sociolinguistics, anthropology, and sociology. Another research tradition is ecological psychology, which studies behavior as physical interaction in which animals, including people, participate in physical and technological systems. A third research tradition is situation theory in logic and philosophy, which analyzes meaning and action as relational systems and is developing a reformulation of logic to support these relational analyses. Knowing in this per-

spective is both an attribute of groups that carry out cooperative activities and an attribute of individuals who participate in the groups. Learning by a group or individual involves becoming attuned to constraints and affordances of the material and social systems with which they interact. Discussions of motivation in this perspective often emphasize engagement of individuals with the functions and goals of the community, including interpersonal commitments and ways in which individuals' identities are enhanced or diminished by their participation.

APPRENTICESHIP AND IDENTITY

When knowing is viewed as practices of communities and of the abilities of individuals to participate in those practices, then learning is the strengthening of those practices and participatory abilities. Systems in which individuals learn to participate in social practices are very common and include apprenticeship and other forms of being initiated into the practices of a group. Lave and Wenger (1991) reviewed several studies of learning by newcomers to communities of practice and concluded that a crucial factor in the success of such a system is that learners must be afforded legitimate peripheral participation, which involves access to the practices that they are expected to learn and genuine participation in the activities and concerns of the group.

Lave and Wenger characterized learning of practices as processes of participation in which beginners are relatively peripheral in the activities of a community, and as they become more experienced and adept, they progress toward fuller participation. A crucial issue in the nature of learning is whether, and in what ways, the peripheral participation of beginners is legitimate. They described four cases of learning by newcomers and emphasized how learners' identities derive from being part of the community as they become more fully participating members in the community. They also noted that an apprenticeship relationship can be unproductive for learning, as in a case of meat cutters they cited, where the apprentices worked in a separate room and were isolated from the working community. For an environment of apprenticeship to be a productive environment of learning, learners need to have opportunities to observe and practice activities in order to progress toward more full participation.

The degree to which people participate fully and are respected by other members of a community determines their sense of identity (Lave & Wenger, 1991; Wenger, 1998). The fully participative roles are those that most directly contribute to the collective activities and knowledge of the community. The motivation to participate more fully in a community of practice can provide a powerful incentive for learning. Smith (1988) argued that children learn to read and write if the people they admire read and write. That is, they will want to join the "literacy club" and will work hard to become members. Learning to read is part of becoming the kind of person they want to become. Identity is central to deep learning.

An important aspect of learners' identities are the ways that they are positioned in the participant structures (Phillips, 1972) of learning activities. An important distinction by Pickering (1995) involves different kinds of agency, called conceptual and disciplinary. Students who are positioned with disciplinary agency only participate as receivers and reproducers of the established meanings and procedures of the discipline, and their learning is evaluated only by whether they can perform procedures and explanations correctly. Students who are positioned with conceptual agency are expected to question and adapt concepts and methods of the discipline. For example, they might construct understandings that utilize disciplinary concepts in novel ways or consider alternatives to standard definitions of concepts. As an example, research by Boaler (2002) compared learning of mathematics in two English secondary schools and found that students who learned primarily through investigations understood mathematics as a general resource for understanding and problem solving, whereas students whose learning was primarily mastery of set procedures understood mathematics as a set of rules to be followed.

Wenger (1998) argued that people participate in a variety of communities—at home, at work, at school, and in hobbies. In his view a community of practice is a group of people participating together to carry out different activities, such as garage bands, ham-radio operators, recovering alcoholics, and research scientists. Wenger stated: "For individuals, it means that learning is an issue of engaging in and contributing to the practices of their communities. For communities, it means that learning is an issue of refining their practice and ensuring new generations of members. For organizations, it means that learning is an issue of sustaining the interconnected communities of practice through which an organization knows what it knows and thus becomes effective and valuable as an organization." (pp. 7–8).

The view that learning occurs through participation is at the root of the practices of apprenticeship, where apprentices are guided and supervised by masters. In successful apprenticeship learning, masters teach by showing apprentices how to do a task (modeling), and then helping them as they try to do it on their own (coaching and fading). Lave and Wenger (1991) emphasized how an apprentice's identity derives from becoming part of the community of practitioners. The motive for becoming a more full participant in a community of practice can provide a powerful motivation for learning. Of course, what is learned in apprenticeship may not

generalize easily to other contexts. Collins, Brown, and Newman (1989) attempted to characterize how the modeling, coaching, and fading paradigm of apprenticeship might be applied to learning the cognitive subjects of school in an approach they called "cognitive apprenticeship."

EDUCATIONAL APPLICATIONS OF THE SITUATIVE VIEW

A major goal of educational reform is to have students participate more actively and legitimately in learning communities, including participation in formulating and evaluating questions and problems, and constructing and evaluating hypotheses, evidence, arguments, and conclusions (Brown & Campione, 1996). Abilities for participating in these activities have to be learned, and the research literature on that kind of learning is sparse. Several projects have been focused on creating classroom practices of discussion and inquiry, and the investigators in those projects have discussed some aspects of the process of establishing norms and expectations by the students that support productive collaborative learning (Cohen, 1986; Lampert, 1990; Slavin, 1983).

In the view of learning as coming to participate more fully in a community of practice, transfer is often thought to be a problematic issue (e.g., Anderson, Reder & Simon, 1996). Viewed in the situative perspective, transfer can occur when learning leads to better performance or learning of new practices within a community (e.g., for school communities this might mean working new problems or accomplishing new kinds of tasks) or outside the community (e.g., for school these might be work environments such as those studied by Beach, 1995, and Saxe, 1990). Many of the resources and supports that occur within a community of practice do not carry over to a different community, and so the problem of transfer becomes one of marshalling the resources needed to be successful in a new environment. Doing so requires sophisticated social and information-processing skills, which are the kinds of skills that businesses think they will need in the future.

In a view of transfer in the situative perspective proposed by Greeno, Smith, and Moore (1993), transfer depends on constraints and/or affordances that are invariant under the transformations that change the learning situation into the transfer situation. For transfer to occur, learners must become attuned to those invariants in their initial learning. One of the ways to be attuned is to have an abstract representation that can apply in the new situation, but this is only one possible way for attunement to occur and may not be the typical way for many learned activities to generalize (Greeno, 1997).

Although the situative view insists that all cognition and learning are situated, learning designers who take a situative perspective generally attend to the activity settings in which learning is to occur. For example, in goal-based scenarios (Schank et al., 1994; Nowakowski et al., 1994) learners are given real-world tasks and the scaffolding they need to carry out such tasks. They can be set either in computer-based environments or naturalistic environments. In one computerized goal-based scenario, learners are asked to advise married couples as to whether their children are likely to have sickle-cell anemia, a genetically linked disease. In order to advise the couples, learners must use the facilities in the system to find out how different genetic combinations lead to the disease and run tests to determine the parents' genetic makeup. There are scaffolds in the system to support the learners, such as various recorded experts who offer advice. Other goal-based scenarios support learners in a wide variety of challenging tasks, such as putting together a news broadcast, solving an environmental problem, or developing a computer-reservation system. Goal-based scenarios make it possible to embed cognitive skills and knowledge in the kinds of contexts where they are to be used. So people learn the basic competencies they will need and also when and how to apply these competencies.

Video and computer technology has enhanced the ability to create simulation environments in which students are learning skills in context. A novel use of video technology is the Jasper series developed by the Cognition and Technology Group (1997) at Vanderbilt University to teach middle-school mathematics. In a series of 15 to 20 minute videos students are put into various problem-solving contexts, for example, deciding on a business plan for a school fair or a rescue plan for a wounded eagle. The problems are quite difficult to solve and reflect the complex problem solving and planning that occurs in real life. Middle-school students work in groups for several days to solve each problem. Solving the problems develops a much richer understanding of the underlying mathematical concepts than the traditional school-mathematics problems.

Another novel use of technology is the curriculum developed by the Middle-school Mathematics through Applications Project (MMAP) at the Institute for Research on Learning (Goldman & Moschkovich, 1995; Greeno et al., 1999). The leading activities in the MMAP curriculum are design problems, supported by software that provide computer-aided design environments in which students design floor plans of buildings, models of population growth and decline, lexicographic codes, or geographical analyses of environmental quality. Mathematical reasoning and problem solving involving topics such as proportional reasoning, linear and exponential functions, and geometrical properties of geographical space are required for successful progress in the design activities. Printed curriculum materials are provided to support teachers in organizing activities for students to encounter, recognize, and learn important mathematical concepts and methods.

These kinds of learning tasks are different from most school tasks because the contexts of most school tasks lack characteristics of practices that occur outside of school. Traditionally, academic material has been taught abstractly without practical real-world context; the equivalent to which might be learning tennis by being told the rules and practicing the forehand, backhand, and serve without ever playing or seeing a tennis match. If tennis were taught that way, it would be hard to see the point of what the students were learning. Yet in school, students are taught algebra and the works of Shakespeare without being given any idea of how they might be useful in their lives. That is not how a coach would teach students to play tennis. A coach might first show them how to grip and swing the racket, but very soon they would be hitting the ball and playing games. A good coach would have the students go back and forth between playing games and working on particular skills—combining global learning with focused local knowledge. The essential idea in the situative view of cognition is to consider learning and cognition as participation in an activity system. This view supports designers' and educators' efforts to tightly couple a focus on accomplishing authentic tasks with a focus on the underlying competencies needed to carry out the tasks.

For centuries, the epistemology that has guided educational practice has concentrated on abstract representations of concepts, assuming that knowing abstract concepts is a condition for acting and perceiving effectively in a broad range of situations. A situative theory of cognition suggests that conceptualization is embedded in activity and perception and that more attention needs to be focused on them. Learning through legitimate peripheral participation, enables learners to acquire and develop tools and skills, including conceptualizations, through authentic work and membership in communities of practice. Through this process, novices enter the culture of practice. So the concept of learning through legitimate participation helps to emphasize the centrality of activity in learning and knowledge and highlights the inherently content-dependent and enculturating nature of learning.

BIBLIOGRAPHY

Anderson, J.R., Reder, L. M., & Simon, H. A. (1996). Situated learning and education. *Educational Researcher, 25*(4), 5–11.

Beach, K. (1995). Activity as a mediator of sociocultural change and individual development: The case of school-work transition in Nepal. *Mind, Culture, and Activity, 2*, 285–302.

Boaler, J. (2002). *Experiencing school mathematics: Traditional and reform approaches to teaching and their impact on student learning* (Rev. ed.). Mahwah, NJ: Erlbaum.

Bowers, J., Cobb, P., & McClain, K. (1999). The evolution of mathematical practices: A case study. *Cognition and Instruction, 17,* 25–64.

Brown, A., & Campione, J. (1996). Psychological theory and the design of innovative learning environments: On procedures, principles, and systems. In L. Schauble & R. Glaser (Eds.), *Innovations in learning: New environments for education* (pp. 289–325). Mahwah NJ: Erlbaum.

Brown, J. S., Collins, J., & Duguid, P. (1989) Situated cognition and the culture of learning. *Educational Researcher, 18*(1), 32–42.

Clark, H. H. (1996). *Using language.* Cambridge, U.K.: Cambridge University Press.

Cognition and Technology Group at Vanderbilt. (1997). *The Jasper Project: Lessons in curriculum, instruction, assessment, and professional development.* Mahwah NJ: Erlbaum.

Cohen, E. G. (1986). *Designing groupwork.* New York: Teachers College Press.

Collins, A., Brown, J. S., & Newman, S. E. (1989). Cognitive apprenticeship: Teaching the craft of reading, writing, and mathematics. In L. B. Resnick (Ed.), *Knowing, learning, and instruction: Essays in honor of Robert Glaser* (pp. 453–494). Hillsdale, NJ: Erlbaum.

Engeström, Y. (2001). Expansive learning at work: Toward an activity theoretical reconceptualization. *Journal of Education and Work, 14,* 133–156.

Engle, R. A. (2006). Framing interactions to foster generative learning: A situative explanation of transfer in a community of learners classroom. *Journal of the Learning Sciences, 15,* 451–498.

Goldman, S., & Moschkovich, J. (1995). Environments for collaborating mathematically: The Middle-school Mathematics through Applications Project. *CSCL '95 Proceedings.*

Goodwin, C. (1996). Transparent vision. In E. Ochs, E. A. Schegloff, & S. A. Thompson (Eds.), *Interaction and grammar* (pp. 370–404). Cambridge, U.K.: Cambridge University Press.

Greeno, J. G. (1997). On claims that answer the wrong questions. *Educational Researcher, 26*(1), 5–17.

Greeno, J. G., Collins, A., & Resnick, L. B. (1996). Cognition and learning (Ch. 2). In D. C. Berliner & R. C. Calfee (Eds.), *Handbook of Educational Psychology* (pp. 15–46). New York: Macmillan.

Greeno, J. G., McDermott, R., Cole, K., Engle, R. A., Goldman, S., Knudsen, J., et al. (1999). Research, reform, and aims in education: Modes of action in search of each other. In E. Lagemann & L. Shulman (Eds.), *Issues in education research: Problems and possibilities* (pp. 299–335). San Francisco: Jossey-Bass.

Greeno, J. G., Smith, D. R., & Moore, J. L. (1993). Transfer of situated learning. In D. K. Detterman & R. J. Sternberg (Eds.), *Transfer on trial: Intelligence, cognition, and instruction* (pp. 99–167). Norwood, NJ: Ablex.

Greeno, J. G., & Van de Sande, C. (2007). Perspectival understanding of conceptions and conceptual growth in interaction. *Educational Psychologist, 42,* 9–23.

Hatano, G., & Inagaki, K. (2003). When is conceptual change intentional? A cognitive-sociocultural view. In G. M. Sinatra & P. R. Pintrich (Eds.), *Intentional conceptual change.* Mahwah NJ: Erlbaum.

Hutchins, E. (1995a). *Cognition in the wild.* Cambridge, MA: MIT Press.

Hutchins, E. (1995b). How a cockpit remembers its speeds. *Cognitive Science, 19,* 265–288.

Lampert, M. (1990). When the problem is not the question and the solution is not the answer: Mathematical knowing and teaching. *American Educational Research Journal, 17,* 29–64.

Lave, J., & Wenger, E. (1991). *Situated Learning: Legitimate Peripheral Participation.* New York: Cambridge University Press.

Nersessian, N. J., Kurz-Milcke, E., Newstetter, W. C., & Davies, J. (2003). Research laboratories as evolving distributed cognitive systems. In R. Alterman & D. Kirsh (Eds.), *Proceedings of the Twenty-Fifth Annual Conference of the Cognitive Science Society.* Mahwah, NJ: Erlbaum.

Nowakowski, A., Campbell, R., Monson, D. Montgomery, J., Moffett, C., Acovelli, M., et al. (1994). Goal-based scenarios: A new approach to professional education. *Educational Technology, 34*(9), 3–32.

Ochs, E., Gonzales, P., & Jacoby, S. (1996). When I come down I'm in the domain state: Grammar and graphic representation in the interpretive activity of physicists. In E. Ochs, A. Schegloff, & S. A. Thompson (Eds.). *Interaction and grammar* (pp. 328–369). Cambridge, U.K.: Cambridge University Press.

Phillips, S. U. (1972). Participant structures and communicative competence: Warm Springs children in community and classroom. In C. B. Cazden, V. P. John, & D. Hymes (Eds.), *Functions of language in the classroom* (pp. 370–394). New York: Teachers College Press.

Pickering, A. (1995). *The mangle of practice.* Chicago: University of Chicago Press.

Rogoff, B. (1990). *Apprenticeship in thinking: Cognitive development in social context.* New York: Oxford University Press.

Rogoff, B., & Lave J. (1984). *Everyday cognition: Its development in social context.* Cambridge, MA: Harvard University Press.

Saxe, G. (1990). *Culture and cognitive development: Studies in mathematical understanding.* Hillsdale, NJ: Erlbaum.

Schank, R. C., Fano, A., Bell, B., & Jona, M. (1994). The design of goal-based scenarios. *Journal of the Learning Sciences, 3*(4), 305–346.

Slavin, R. E. (1983). *Cooperative learning.* New York: Longman.

Smith, F. (1988). *Joining the literacy club.* Portsmouth, NH: Heinemann.

Stenning, K., Greeno, J. G., Hall, R., Sommerfeld, M., & Wiebe, M. (2002). Coordinating mathematical with biological multiplication: Conceptual learning as the development of heterogeneous reasoning systems. In M. Baker, P. Brna, K. Stenning, & A. Tiberghien (Eds.), *The role of communication in learning to model* (pp. 3–48). Mahwah, NJ: Erlbaum.

Wenger, E. (1998). *Communities of practice: Learning, meaning, and identity.* New York: Cambridge University Press.

Allan Collins
James G. Greeno

SKINNER, B(URRHUS) F(REDERIC)
1904–1990

Burrhus Frederic Skinner (1904–1990) is considered by many to be the most influential psychologist of all time and by some to be one of the most influential people in history. A research scientist, author, and philosopher, his work has had a lasting impact on psychology, education, psychotherapy, psychopharmacology, philosophy, and even the business world.

Skinner was born March 20, 1904, in the small town of Susquehana, in Pennsylvania, the son of a lawyer father and a housewife mother. He earned his undergraduate degree at Hamilton College in New York, intending to become a professional writer. Soon discouraged, a book about behaviorism by psychologist John B. Watson inspired him to enter graduate school at Harvard University in 1928. There his extraordinary mechanical skills allowed him to invent a series of devices for studying rat behavior. Ultimately one of those devices, subsequently known as the Skinner Box, gave him unprecedented control over ongoing behavior, summar-

B. F. Skinner, April 1, 1987. **YVONNE HEMSEY/GETTY IMAGES.**

ized in his first book, *The Behavior of Organisms: An Experimental Analysis* (1938).

Behaviorists inspired by the work of Russian physiologist Ivan Pavlov (1849–1936) had focused on relatively simple stimulus-response reflexes, whereas Skinner was able to show a high degree of orderliness in more common, fluid, everyday behavior, which Skinner called *operant behavior*. Skinner showed that a great deal of behavior that appeared to be spontaneous and voluntary was the product of a "history of reinforcement," and he also showed how a *reinforcer* (a stimulus that strengthens the behavior it follows) could be delivered in optimal ways to alter future behavior. In a major breakthrough, Skinner showed that entirely new behaviors could quickly be taught simply by selectively reinforcing successive approximations to that behavior, a process he called *shaping*.

During the 1940s, 1950s, and 1960s, Skinner extended his laboratory discoveries to a number of practical human domains. During World War II he trained pigeons to guide missiles for the U.S. military (a project never fully implemented). In 1948 Skinner published a novel called *Walden Two*, in which he speculated about how a science of behavior might be used to create an ideal community. During the 1950s, in work with psychotic patients, he laid the foundations for modern *behavior therapy*, a term that was coined by his research team. He also invented sophisticated mechanical teaching machines and developed the first programmed textbook, advances which helped lead the way toward modern computer-aided instruction.

During the 1960s Skinner's students and adherents guided by his numerous essays on education (brought together in 1968 in his book, *The Technology of Teaching*) developed successful reinforcement-based classroom management techniques, which were subsequently widely used in countries around the world. His work also inspired business professionals to develop new management techniques and incentive systems, and professionals working with developmentally disabled individuals were inspired to develop powerful new training and treatment techniques, which later became standard in virtually all treatment facilities for such individuals.

In its impact on education, Skinner's work is similar to that of Edward L. Thorndike. In the late 1890s, while a graduate student at Harvard, Thorndike conducted animal experiments that convinced him of the enormous power of behavioral consequences, which led to Thorndike's formulation of the Law of Effect, which remains influential in education in the early 2000s. Thorndike's experiments had been relatively crude and were conducted in open chambers. Skinner eventually learned how to conduct such experiments in closed chambers, which eliminated distractions and the need for handling the animals, thus allowing

Skinner to determine much more precisely how behavior actually works. It was the precision in Skinner's research that helped lay the foundations for a true science of both animal and human behavior.

SEE ALSO *Operant Conditioning.*

BIBLIOGRAPHY

WORKS BY

Holland, J. G., & Skinner, B. F. (1961). *The analysis of behavior: A program for self-instruction.* New York: McGraw-Hill.

Skinner, B. F. (1938). *The behavior of organisms: An experimental analysis* (The Century Psychology Series). New York: Appleton-Century.

Skinner, B. F. (1948). *Walden two.* New York: Macmillan.

Skinner, B. F. (1953). *Science and human behavior.* New York: Free Press.

Skinner, B. F. (1968). *The technology of teaching.* New York: Appleton-Century-Crofts.

Skinner, B. F. (1971). *Beyond freedom and dignity.* New York: Alfred A. Knopf.

WORKS ABOUT

Demorest, A. (2005). *Psychology's grand theorists: how personal experiences shaped professional ideas.* Mahwah, NJ: Erlbaum.

Nye, R. D. (2000). *Three psychologies: perspectives from Freud, Skinner, and Rogers* (6th ed.). Pacific Grove, CA: Brooks/Cole.

O'Donohue, W. & Ferguson, K. E. (2001). *The psychology of B.F. Skinner.* Thousand Oaks, CA: Sage.

Robert Epstein

SOCIAL COGNITIVE THEORY

Social cognitive theory (SCT) refers to a psychological model of behavior that emerged primarily from the work of Albert Bandura (1977; 1986). Initially developed with an emphasis on the acquisition of social behaviors, SCT continues to emphasize that learning occurs in a social context and that much of what is learned is gained through observation. SCT has been applied broadly to such diverse areas of human functioning as career choice, organizational behavior, athletics, and mental and physical health. SCT also has been applied extensively by those interested in understanding classroom motivation, learning, and achievement (Pajares, 1996; Schunk & Zimmerman, 1994; 1998).

SCT rests on several basic assumptions about learning and behavior. One assumption concerns triadic reciprocality, or the view that personal, behavioral, and environmental factors influence one another in a bidirectional, reciprocal fashion. That is, a person's on-going functioning is a product of a continuous interaction between cognitive, behavioral, and contextual factors. For instance, classroom learning is shaped by factors within the academic environment, especially the reinforcements experienced by oneself and by others. At the same time, learning is affected by students' own thoughts and self-beliefs and their interpretation of the classroom context.

A closely related assumption within SCT is that people have an agency or ability to influence their own behavior and the environment in a purposeful, goal-directed fashion (Bandura, 2001). This belief conflicts with earlier forms of behaviorism that advocated a more rigorous form of environmental determinism. SCT does not deny the importance of the environment in determining behavior, but it does argue that people can also, through forethought, self-reflection, and self-regulatory processes, exert substantial influence over their own outcomes and the environment more broadly.

A third assumption within SCT is that learning can occur without an immediate change in behavior or more broadly that learning and the demonstration of what has been learned are distinct processes. One reason for this separation is that SCT also assumes that learning involves not just the acquisition of new behaviors, but also of knowledge, cognitive skills, concepts, abstract rules, values, and other cognitive constructs. This division of learning and behavior is a shift from the position advocated by behavioral theories that defined learning stridently as a change in the form or frequency of behavior. It also means that students can learn but not demonstrate that learning until motivated to do so.

HISTORICAL ORIGINS OF SCT

Born in 1925, Albert Bandura was trained and began his career in the mid-twentieth century when explanations of human functioning, including classroom learning, were dominated by behavioral models advocated by researchers such as B. F. Skinner, Clark Hull, Kenneth Spence, and Edward Tolman. In this context, Bandura, along with his students and colleagues, initiated a series of studies designed to examine social explanations for why and when children displayed aggressive behaviors. These studies demonstrated the value of modeling for acquiring novel behaviors and provided initial evidence for the separation of learning and performance. They also indicated the importance of the learner's perceptions of the environment generally, of the person modeling a behavior specifically, and of the learner's expectations regarding the consequences of behavior. In doing so, findings from this systematic research contradicted assumptions within behavioral models that learning was the result of trial and error learning or that changes in behavior were due primarily to the consequences of one's own actions.

Children learn by observing others. JENNY ACHESON/RISER/
GETTY IMAGES.

By the mid 1970s these studies helped form the foundation for what Bandura initially called observational learning theory and then later social learning theory (Bandura, 1977). This precursor to SCT established a viable model for understanding how people learned through observation of models. Additional work during this time expanded aspects of the theory dealing with abstract modeling, language, and conceptual learning. In the years that followed, SCT continued to evolve, spurred by the work of Bandura and his colleagues stressing the processes of goal setting, self-efficacy, and self-regulation. The evolution of SCT also drew ideas from information processing models of psychological functioning to describe the cognitive processes that mediate learning. Ultimately, Bandura noted in the preface to his 1986 treatise, *Social Foundations of Thought and Action: A Social-Cognitive Theory,* that, in an effort to be inclusive of these more motivational and cognitive processes, he was using the label "social cognitive theory" rather than social learning to describe his framework. Throughout this book, Ban-

dura describes the philosophical and conceptual foundation for SCT and reviews empirical evidence for its main components. Hence, it provides a concrete milestone for the birth of contemporary SCT. Since that time, SCT has continued to grow and expand especially with regard to the work on self-efficacy, self-regulation, and agency (Bandura, 1997; 2001; Zimmerman, 2000).

CORE CONCEPTS WITHIN SCT

SCT integrates a large number of discrete ideas, concepts, and sub-processes into an overall framework for understanding human functioning. Five of the central concepts are described below. For a more complete explanation of SCT, readers are directed to works by Bandura and to the relevant chapters within textbooks on learning.

Observational Learning/Modeling. From its inception one core premise within SCT has been that people learn through observation. This process is also described as vicarious learning or modeling because learning is a result of watching the behavior and consequences of models in the environment. Although observational learning is dependent upon the availability of models, who or what can serve this role is defined broadly. Live demonstrations of a behavior or skill by a teacher or classmate, of course, typify the notion of modeling. Verbal or written descriptions, video or audio recordings, and other less direct forms of performance are also considered forms of modeling. There also distinctions among different types of models. Mastery models are proficient when demonstrating a skills, whereas coping models struggle, make mistakes, and only eventually show proficiency. Abstract modeling occurs when the skill or knowledge being learned is conveyed only indirectly, and cognitive modeling occurs when a model verbalizes her thoughts while demonstrating a cognitive process or skill.

According to SCT, observational learning of novel behaviors or skills is dependent on four inter-related processes involving attention, retention, production, and motivation. Attentional processes are critical because students must attend to a model and the relevant aspects of behavior in order to learn. Retention refers to the processes necessary for reducing and transforming what is observed into a symbolic form that can be stored for later use. Production processes are necessary when students draw on their stored codes and make an effort to perform what they have observed. Finally, motivational processes are key for understanding why students engage in the prior subprocesses, including whether they ever attempt to use or recreate the new skills they have observed. Each of these processes, furthermore, are affected by factors such as the developmental level of the learner and characteristics of the model and modeled behavior.

Beyond new learning, modeling is also important for understanding when or why previously learned behaviors are exhibited. Students' may inhibit their engagement in a behavior if they observe a model suffer consequences they would prefer to avoid. For instance, if a teacher glares at one student who is talking out of turn, other students may suppress this behavior to avoid a similar reaction. In a related fashion, students may disinhibit or engage in a behavior they had initially suppressed when they fail to see any negative consequences accrue to a model. For example, students may refrain from shouting out answers unless they are called upon only until they see others do so without repercussions. Finally, through a process labeled response facilitation, models can simply prompt others to behave in known ways.

Outcome Expectations. Outcome expectations reflect individuals' beliefs about what consequences are most likely to ensue if particular behaviors are performed. For instance, children may believe that if they get a hit during a baseball game the crowd will cheer, they will feel good and will be admired by their teammates. These beliefs are formed enactively through students' own past experiences and vicariously through the observation of others. Outcome expectations are important in SCT because they shape the decisions people make about what actions to take and which behaviors to suppress. The frequency of a behavior should increase when the outcomes expected are valued, whereas behaviors associated with unfavorable or irrelevant outcomes will be avoided.

Perceived Self-efficacy. Self-efficacy also has emerged as a prominent and influential concept within SCT. Self-efficacy reflects individuals' beliefs about whether they can achieve a given level of successful at a particular task (Bandura, 1997). Students with greater self-efficacy are more confident in their abilities to be successful when compared to their peers with lower self-efficacy. Self-efficacy has proven useful for understanding students' motivation and achievement in academic contexts. Higher levels of perceived self-efficacy have been associated with greater choice, persistence, and with more effective strategy use (Pajares, 1996).

Consistent with the tenets of SCT, self-efficacy is viewed as a product of individuals' own past performances, the observation and verbal persuasion of others in the environment, and individuals' on-going physiological state (Bandura, 1997). Rather than directly affecting their self-efficacy, however, these sources of information are weighed and filtered through a process known as cognitive appraisal. For instance, a prior failure may not be detrimental to self-efficacy if students believe there was some no-longer relevant reason for the poor performance (e.g., prior sickness). Interventions based on SCT and designed to increase self-efficacy in school-aged children have proven effective (Pajares, 1996).

Goal Setting. Goal setting is another central process within SCT (Bandura, 1986; Schunk, 1990). Goals reflect cognitive representations of anticipated, desired, or preferred outcomes. Hence, goals exemplify the agency view within SCT that people not only learn, they use forethought to envision the future, identify desired outcomes, and generate plans of action. Goals are also closely related to other important processes within SCT. For instance, models can provide goals in the form of specific behavioral outcomes or more general standards for acceptable levels of performance. Goals also are intricately related to students' outcome expectations and their perceived self-efficacy. Goals are a function of the outcomes students expect from engaging in particular behaviors and the confidence they have for completing those behaviors successfully. Finally, goals are an important prerequisite for self-regulation because they provide objectives that students are trying to achieve and benchmarks against which to judge progress.

Self-regulation. Research on self-regulation or, when applied to academic contexts, self-regulated learning, blossomed in the 1980s and continued into the early 2000s to expand. Explanations for students' management or control of their own learning behaviors have arisen from within many distinct theoretical perspectives (Zimmerman & Schunk, 2001). Many of the most common models, however, have strong roots in SCT. SCT models of self-regulation assume that self-regulation is dependent on goal setting, in that students are thought to manage their thoughts and actions in order to reach particular outcomes (Schunk, 2001; Zimmerman, 2000). SCT views of self-regulation initially emphasized three sub-processes (Bandura, 1986; 1991). Self-observation reflects students' ability to monitor or keep track of their own behaviors and outcomes. Self-judgment is the process through which students' evaluate whether their actions are effective and allow them to make progress toward their goals. Finally, self-reaction occurs when students' respond to the evaluations they have made by modifying their behavior, rewarding it, or discontinuing it.

Self-regulation is a prominent and increasing aspect of SCT that exemplifies the underlying assumptions regarding agency and the influence of personal factors on behavior and the environment. As noted above, self-regulation is also dependent on other processes within SCT, including goal setting and self-efficacy. Unless students have goals and feel efficacious about reaching them, they may not activate the processes needed for self-regulation. Modeling can also affect students' self-regulated learning. The skills needed to manage one's behavior, as well the beliefs and attitudes that serve to motivate self-regulation, can be obtained through modeling.

TELEVISION: EDUCATOR'S FRIEND OR FOE?

From its inception, television has been considered a behavioral stimulus (Vos Post, 1995). Factors that impact research on the influence television has on behavior include socio-economic status and rural versus urban settings, as well as factors that are pertinent to the nature and culture of the local society. Is a "shoot 'em up" cops and robbers television programming any more violent than a news report of a suicide bomber in the Middle East? Should children be shielded from viewing either or both of those programs on television? The social cognitive theory of behavior learned through observation expounded by Bandura (2001) has been related to television as well as to the classroom and home environments. Young children are particularly unable to discriminate between the fiction of television and real life. Research shows that they are likely to apply the aggressive behaviors they have seen on television to the playground as early as nursery school age. According to Ortiz (2007), they internalize behaviors that they observe even though they have not experienced them directly.

In 1995 Aronson defined aggression as "behavior causing harm or pain." In that same year, Vos Post added that "we still have no widely-accepted, clear-cut, and scientific definition for either the aggressive acts on television or those purportedly caused by television by its audience." In the mid-1990s researchers counted an average of 18 acts of aggression per hour during the Saturday morning cartoons that continue in the 21st century to be popular with young children. George Gerbner has reported that violent acts take place five or six times per hour during prime time and Saturday morning television. In addition, eight of ten television programs include some sort of violence.

Vos Post (1995) stated that programming on U.S. television was no more aggressive than it had been historically. He went on to report that television programming in Japan had a much higher level of violence than television programming in the United States. However, there are considerably lower rates of aggression in Japan than in the United States, which contradicts the argument that aggressive behavior is learned or encouraged by viewing violence on television.

When Bandura's social cognitive theory, which suggests that children learn through observation, is extended to television viewing, it would seem to indicate that children would learn aggressive behavior through observation of violence on television. It also means that if children observe positive behaviors in television programming, they should emulate those behaviors as well. Bandura's theory states that when children see behavior modeled, they will accept it and use it when they deem it appropriate. It also explains the need for positive role models on television for children.

According to Bandura's social cognitive theory, when children see family members or friends working together on a television situation comedy to resolve a problem, it follows that they will try to resolve problems with their own family members or friends peacefully, by working together, instead of fighting with them. Research on the results of this type of modeled behavior is reported to be difficult, with inconclusive results.

According to Hoffner (1996), Bandura's theory of behaviors learned by observation means that young viewers have to identify with the characters to model either pro-social or violent behavior. In other words, if a child observes television characters that she or he perceives as being similar to herself or himself, that child will be more likely to behave in a manner similar to those characters.

Educational programming is based on Bandura's theory of modeled behavior. To be effective with pro-social behaviors, television programmers have to conduct extensive research and make sure characters and events portrayed in their shows have a relation to real-world situations. They also have to carefully create characters who are positive, with good results from their actions; negative, with undesirable results from their actions; and transitional, who start the show as negative characters but change because of decisions made and actions taken, so they become positive role models by the end of the show.

Violent acts in regular television programming have more of an effect on children's behavior than sports programming. The results of research on the effect that violence on television has on students generally are in agreement that children who observe violence in prime time television or on Saturday morning children's shows that do not include sports programming will behave aggressively whether or not they had were pre-disposed to behave aggressively.

A real concern with the effects of television violence and aggressive behavior learned by observation of incidents of violent programming is that this learning has been proven to continue through adolescence and into adulthood. Vos Post (1995) concluded: "Not only because television violence is a reality, and aggression is a fact of life, but because an effective social psychology understanding of the relationship between television and behavior may help to not only reduce socially unacceptable aggression, but may actually enable us to increase socially desirable effects."

BIBLIOGRAPHY

Ortiz, Michelle, and Jake Harwood (Dec. 2007). "A social cognitive theory approach to the effects of mediated intergroup contact on intergroup attitudes." Broadcast Education Association. Retrieved January 24, 2008, from www.entrepreneur.com/tradejournals/article/172978815.html.

Pajares, Frank (2002). *Overview of social cognitive theory and of self-efficacy.* Retrieved January 24, 2008, from http://www.emory.edu/EDUCATION/mfp/eff.html.

Smith, Deborah (October 2002). "The theory heard 'round the world." *Monitor on Psychology.* Retrieved January 24, 2008, from http://www.apa.org/monitor/oct02/theory.html.

Vos Post, Jonathan (1995). "Open Questions on the Correlation Between Television and Violence." Magic Dragon Multimedia. Retrieved January 24, 2008, from http://www.magicdragon.com/EmeraldCity/Nonfiction/socphil.html.

Heidi H. Denler

IMPLICATIONS FOR CLASSROOM INSTRUCTION

One strength of SCT is that it provides a clear foundation for classroom interventions designed to improve students' learning. In this section, several general implications for instruction derived from the key concepts described above are described. More complete treatments of the instructional implications of SCT readers are available elsewhere (e.g., Linares et al., 2005; Paris & Paris, 2001; Zimmerman, Bonner, & Kovach, 1996).

Observational Learning/Modeling. The most basic instructional implication of SCT is that students should be provided frequent access to models of the knowledge, skills, and behaviors they are expected to learn. For example, teachers should model the behaviors and cognitive processes they want students to learn. Effective instruction, moreover, should include multiple types of models (e.g., teacher, peers, parents) and various forms of modeling (e.g. cognitive, verbal, mastery, coping). The inhibitory and disinhibitory effects of modeling, further, necessitate that educators administer rewards and punishments in a careful and consistent manner.

More specifically, instruction based on SCT should support students' engagement in each of the four subprocesses of observational learning. Students' attention can be increased by using models that are viewed as competent, prestigious, and similar to themselves. Students also pay closer attention when the skill or material being demonstrated is considered more personally relevant or interesting. Instruction should support students' retention by facilitating the creation of verbal labels or images through the use of mnemonics, graphic organizers, or other similar learning strategies. Opportunities for rehearsal, both in the form of repeated exposure to models and in the form of time to reflect on the material or skills also assist retention. The effective use of models depends on providing students multiple opportunities to practice the behaviors or skills they have observed. This process will be improved if students are provided feedback about their efforts that is specific, more immediate, and insightful about what the learner is doing well and what needs improvement. Teachers should support the motivational aspects of observational learning through the purposeful use of rewards and punishments. These consequences, further, should shape students' behavior when they are provided either to the learner or to a model. To improve motivation, teachers should also model attitudes that they want students to adopt such as enthusiasm or interest in the material.

Outcome Expectations. Instruction should help students to see that classroom learning and the demonstration of that learning leads to personally valued or important outcomes. Students must believe that, if they complete learning tasks successfully, the outcomes they achieve are meaningful, useful, or worthy of the effort necessary to reach them. To encourage these beliefs, teachers should create lessons that emphasize real-world applications and the relevance of material to students' own lives. Decontextualized instructional practices that obfuscate the benefits of learning should be avoided.

Perceived Self-Efficacy. Students will be more active, effortful, and effective learners when they are confident in their ability to complete academic tasks successfully. Hence, instruction should be designed in a way that helps them to develop and sustain their self-efficacy for learning. Most simply, tasks should be moderately challenging so that students do well and make progress when providing reasonable effort. Teachers should ensure that students have the prerequisite knowledge and strategies needed to be successful at more complex and rigorous tasks. In this way, students will develop a pattern of success that fosters positive levels of self-efficacy. Self-efficacy can also be improved when students are exposed to peer models who initially struggle but who ultimately are able to complete tasks effectively (i.e., coping models). Finally, teachers can make direct statements to learners or models as a way to boost their confidence. Such statements, however, must be credible or they will be discounted or ignored by learners.

Goal Setting. Instruction should help students to set effective goals by addressing the properties found in the most effective goals (Schunk, 1990). Instructional practices should promote students' efforts to set attainable goals that are clear, specific, and moderately challenging. In order to show progress and to maintain self-efficacy, learning goals should be attainable with moderate levels of effort. These goals will also reduce disappointment and frustration that students might feel if they fail to reach their goals. Specific goals are more effective than general or vague goals in spurring students to action and in guiding their behavior. Students should have both distal and more short-term goals for their learning in school. However, proximal goals are more effective at guiding behavior because they allow for more immediate feedback about progress. Finally, goals that students set or endorse themselves have a bigger impact on their behavior than goals that are assigned. Hence, instruction should help students develop the ability and willingness to form their own academic goals.

Self-Regulation. According to SCT, all students should be supported in their efforts to be self-regulated learners. In addition to fostering self-efficacy and effective goal setting, teachers should help students become skilled at self-observation, self-judgment, and self-reaction (see Zimmerman et al., 1996). Teachers can promote self-observation by helping students learn how to monitor different aspects of their academic behavior. Practices such as journal writing, checklists, and time for self-reflection help students develop these skills. For self-judgment, students must learn how to evaluate their performance in light of the goals or standards they have set. Teachers can facilitate this process through modeling and by supporting students' own efforts to compare their performance to both absolute and normative standards. Teachers should also help students see the value and relevance of the standards in order to encourage their self-judgment. The self-reaction process depends on students' ability to respond adaptively both when they are making progress and when they are not. For the former,

instructional practices should assist students in learning how to self-administer reinforcements for their own efforts using both concrete and internal rewards. For the latter, instruction should support students in their efforts to evaluate and modify their learning strategies in order to improve progress. As with all skills, students can development these self-regulatory abilities vicariously and with guided opportunities to practice them firsthand.

SEE ALSO *Bandura, Albert.*

BIBLIOGRAPHY

Bandura, A. (1977). *Social learning theory.* Englewood Cliffs, NJ: Prentice Hall.

Bandura, A. (1986). *Social foundations of thought and action: A social-cognitive theory.* Englewood Cliffs, NJ: Prentice Hall.

Bandura, A. (1991). Social cognitive theory of self-regulation. *Organizational Behavior and Human Decision Processes, 50,* 248–287.

Bandura, A. (1997). *Self-efficacy: The exercise of control.* New York: W. H. Freeman.

Bandura, A. (2001). Social cognitive theory: An agentic perspective. *Annual Review of Psychology, 52,* 1–26.

Driscoll, M. (2005). *Psychology of learning for instruction* (3rd ed.). Boston: Allyn & Bacon.

Linares, L. O., Rosbruch, N., Stern, M. B., Edwards, M. E., Walker, G., Abikoff, H. B., et al. (2005). Developing cognitive-social-emotional competencies to enhance academic learning. *Psychology in the Schools, 42,* 405–417.

Ormrod, J. E. (2008). *Human learning* (5th ed.). Upper Saddle River, MJ: Pearson Education.

Pajares, F. (1996). Self–efficacy beliefs in academic settings. *Review of Educational Research, 66,* 543–578.

Paris, S. G., & Paris, A. H. (2001). Classroom applications of research on self-regulated learning. *Educational Psychologist, 36,* 89–101.

Schunk, D. (1990). Goal setting and self-efficacy during self-regulated learning. *Educational Psychologist, 25,* 71–86.

Schunk, D. (2001). Social–cognitive theory and self-regulated learning. In B. Zimmerman & D. Schunk (Eds.), *Self-regulated learning and academic achievement: Theoretical perspectives* (2nd ed., pp. 125–151). Mahwah, NJ: Erlbaum.

Schunk, D. (2008). *Learning theories: An educational perspective* (5th ed.). Upper Saddle River, NJ: Prentice Hall.

Schunk, D., & Zimmerman, B. (Eds.). (1994). *Self-regulation of learning and performance: Issues and educational applications.* Hillsdale, NJ: Erlbaum.

Schunk, D., & Zimmerman, B. (Eds.) (1998). *Self-regulated learning: From teaching to self–reflective practice.* New York: Guilford Press.

Zimmerman, B. (2000). Attaining self-regulation: A social cognitive perspective. In M. Boekaerts, P. R. Pintrich, & M. Zeidner (Eds.), *Handbook of self–regulation: Theory, research, and applications* (pp. 13–29). San Diego, CA: Academic Press.

Zimmerman, B. J., Bonner, S., & Kovach, R. (1996). *Developing self-regulated learners: Beyond achievement to self-efficacy.* Washington, DC: American Psychological Association.

Zimmerman, B., & Schunk, D. (Eds.). (2001). *Self-regulated learning and academic achievement: Theoretical perspectives* (2nd ed.). Mahwah, NJ: Erlbaum.

Zimmerman, B., & Schunk, D. (2003). Albert Bandura: The scholar and his contributions to educational psychology. In B. Zimmerman and D. Schunk (Eds.), *Educational psychology: A century to contributions* (pp. 431–457). Mahwah, NJ: Erlbaum.

Christopher A. Wolters
Maria B. Benzon

SOCIAL COMPARISONS

Social comparisons are carried out when a person relates abilities, opinions, or other characteristics of one person or group to abilities, opinions, or other characteristics of another person or group. In academic settings, social comparisons occur (intentionally or unintentionally), for example, when a student compares his own exam grade with the grade of a class mate or when a teacher thinks of the best or worst students in mathematics in his class. Referring to educational theory and research, social comparisons are important and valid predictors of students' self-evaluations and achievement behavior.

FESTINGER'S THEORY OF SOCIAL COMPARISON

The study of social comparison was initiated by the social psychologist Leon Festinger (1954). In his model, Festinger outlines the central processes underlying the formation of the beliefs about one's own abilities and opinions held by a person. Festinger hypothesizes that a motive for self-evaluation triggers social comparisons, in particular when objective means are not available. Following Festinger, people tend to use similar other persons as comparison targets to maximize the information resulting from comparisons. Goethals and Darley (1977) defined similarity in terms of related attributes. Therefore, comparisons are more useful when the comparison target shares relevant attributes (for example, gender or age) with the person carrying out the comparison. Comparing one's math performance with the math performance of a same age student is much more informative than comparing the math performance with a younger or older student.

UPWARD AND DOWNWARD COMPARISONS

Studies on spontaneous comparisons using diary methods revealed insight in the occurrence of social comparisons in daily life. According to Wheeler and Miyake (1992) situations such as school exams actually encourage social comparisons.

When students are free to choose a particular classmate as a comparison target, the majority prefers slightly higher achieving classmates. This finding corresponds to the "unidirectional drive upward" hypothesis. Such comparisons with slightly better classmates are called upward comparisons. They often seem to be caused by the aspiration to get hints from analyzing the work of better-off students. Therefore, a self-improvement motive may trigger upward comparisons.

If a student chooses to compare with a lower achieving classmate downward comparisons are carried out. Downward comparisons often seem to be caused by the motive to feel good or better; self-enhancement or self-protection motives may trigger downward comparisons.

The frequency of upward and downward comparisons is affected by performance level and pre-comparison affect. Good performance and positive mood predict downward social comparisons whereas poor performance and negative mood predict upward social comparisons (Blanton, Buunk, Gibbons, and Kuyper, 1999).

HOW SOCIAL COMPARISON INFLUENCES STUDENTS' SELF-BELIEFS

If a student gets better grades than others, and feels to be more competent in a particular subject in relation to other students, relatively positive self-evaluations may be the consequence. Thus, good grades and downward comparisons lead to a relatively high academic self-concept in that subject. If a student gets worse grades than others, and feels to be less competent in a particular subject in relation to other students, relatively negative self-evaluations may be the consequence. Therefore, bad grades and upward comparisons lead to a relatively low academic self-concept in that subject.

However, each comparison direction may reveal opposite consequences as well. On the one hand, upward comparisons may boost self-concepts when individuals believe that they can improve their own performance and become as good as the comparison target. On the other hand, downward comparisons may reduce self-concepts when people believe that they may become as worse as their comparison target.

Researchers have to distinguish social comparison effects on different kinds of self-beliefs. At first, social comparisons are relevant for the self-concept formation as described above. In addition, they are relevant for more affective evaluations such as self-esteem. For example, in the Wheeler and Miyake study, the direction of comparison had an impact on the affective reaction—upward social comparisons reduced, and downward social comparisons enhanced subjective well-being.

Social comparisons are less important for self-efficacy measures which include different questions concerning specific tasks ("How many of these particular tasks will you solve within 30 minutes?") Answering these questions does not necessarily require social comparison processes but prior experience with similar tasks.

HOW SOCIAL COMPARISON INFLUENCES STUDENTS PERFORMANCE

Social comparisons not only influence students' self-concepts but also improve their performance. Blanton et al. (1999) longitudinally investigated the effects of comparison processes on academic performance. They asked students to nominate a particular classmate with whom they typically compared their grades. One of the central results was that students, on average, preferred upward comparisons which improved their grades in longitudinal analyses controlling for prior grades.

BIG-FISH-IN-A-LITTLE-POND EFFECT

The big-fish-little-pond effect (BFLPE) is based on students' comparisons of their own ability or performance with the abilities of their classmates. This social comparison process leads to a lower self-concept when the class level is high and to a higher self-concept when the class level is low. Therefore, two students with equal performance in a domain may develop different self-concepts when they belong to different classes with different performance levels.

Whereas social comparison research usually analyses the consequences of comparisons with particular other persons, research on the BFLPE assumes that students compare their own ability with the class or school level. Marsh, Trautwein, Lüdtke, and Köller (2007) assume that such a generalized other serves as an (unintentionally chosen) comparison target leading to a self-concept decrease following upward comparisons (small fish in a big pond) or to a self-concept increase following downward comparisons (big fish in a little pond).

Moreover, Marsh et al. (2007) compared results based on comparisons with a generalized other (class-average achievement) and comparisons with a specific classmate. Both sources of social comparison information contributed negatively to self-beliefs with regard to math ability. Selecting higher achieving classmates as comparison targets as well as attending high performing classes reduced self-beliefs. Comparing downward with worse performing classmates as well as attending a low performing class increased self-beliefs.

OTHER TYPES OF COMPARISONS

Clearly, a lot more comparisons take place in schools; students (as well as teachers) can compare their performance, motivation, effort, and other characteristics to each standard they want. Following Skaalvik and Skaalvik

(2002), students use multiple external and internal frames of reference while making self-judgments. They may compare their achievement with goals and aspirations, with effort in those subjects, or with other external standards such as school grades and class rankings.

According to the Internal/External-Frame-of-Reference model (I/E model, Marsh, 1986), students compare their levels of academic ability using two different, but connected, frames of reference: internal (dimensional) and external (social) comparison processes. Within the external frame of reference, students conduct social comparisons: that is, they compare their accomplishments with those of their classmates. If their verbal achievement is higher than their classmates', their verbal self-concept will also be higher. Because achievements in school subjects typically are positively correlated, it would seem reasonable to assume that these social comparison processes will lead to domain-specific self-concepts that are also positively correlated.

Processes of internal or dimensional (Möller & Köller, 2001a) comparison have been drawn on to explain the domain-specificity of academic self-concepts and the often very low correlations observed between verbal and math self-concept. According to this internal frame of reference, students evaluate their achievements in any given subject in relation to their own achievements in other subjects. Therefore, talented students may develop an average self-concept in their worst subject, even though their performance in this subject is well above the average performance of their peers. Hence, social and dimensional comparisons affect the development of domain-specific self-concepts. Based on external comparisons with one's classmates' achievements in mathematics, low math ability tends to lead to low math self-concept. Based on internal comparisons between one's own achievement in mathematics and one's achievement in verbal domains, low math ability seems to lead to an increase in verbal self-concept (see the meta-analyses by Möller, Pohlmann, Köller & Marsh, 2007).

EDUCATIONAL IMPLICATIONS OF SOCIAL COMPARISON RESEARCH

Social comparisons matter in different ways. Teachers can affect the types of social comparisons carried out by themselves and their students. Teachers who overly compare the low performances of their poorer students to the performances of their better students may further reduce the poorer students' self-concepts and self-esteem. In particular, poorer students who did not expect to be able to improve their performance significantly may suffer in a highly competitive class. It may be more useful for teachers to compare students' performance intra-individually and over time. Such temporal comparisons should outline the progress even poorly performing students reveal. Teachers' encouraging comments particularly following academic failure may reduce the amount and importance of unfavorable social comparisons, which could protect poorly achieving students' self-beliefs and motivation to a certain degree.

Moreover, teachers may use the positive effects of upward comparisons with slightly better-off classmates. If a student is convinced that he is able to reach the comparison target's performance level, it is useful to analyze the better performance of a classmate in order to improve his own performance. In particular, within cooperative learning settings the positive effects of social learning may be fostered when students are taught to cooperate and not to compete.

SEE ALSO *Goal Orientation Theory; Relevance of Self-Evaluations to Classroom Learning; Self-Esteem.*

BIBLIOGRAPHY

Blanton, H., Buunk, B. P., Gibbons, F. X., & Kuyper, H. (1999). When better-than-others compare upward: Choice of comparison and comparative evaluation as independent predictors of academic performance. *Journal of Personality and Social Psychology, 76,* 420–430.

Festinger, L. (1954). A theory of social comparison processes. *Human Relations, 7,* 117–140.

Goethals, G. R. & Darley, J. (1977). Social comparison theory: An attributional approach. In J. Suls and R. L. Miller (Eds.*),* *Social comparison processes: Theoretical and empirical perspectives* (pp. 259–278). Washington, DC: Hemisphere Publishing.

Marsh, H. W. (1986). Verbal and math self-concepts: An internal/external frame of reference model. *American Educational Research Journal, 23,* 129–149.

Marsh, H. W., Trautwein, U., Lüdtke, O., & Köller, O. (2007). Social comparison and big-fish-little-pond effects on self-concept and other self-belief constructs: Role of generalized and specific others. Under review.

Möller, J., & Köller, O. (2001). Dimensional comparisons: An experimental approach to the internal/external frame of reference model. *Journal of Educational Psychology, 93,* 826–835.

Skaalvik, E. M., & Skaalvik, S. (2002). Internal and external frames of reference for academic self-concept. *Educational Psychologist, 37,* 233–244.

Wheeler, L., & Miyake, K. (1992). Social comparison in everyday life. *Journal of Personality and Social Psychology, 62,* 760–773.

Jens Möller

SOCIAL GOALS

Social goals are increasingly being appreciated as important to understanding engagement and achievement in school. In general, social goals refer to what students are focused on and trying to accomplish with their peers. Three main approaches have been used to investigate students' social goals in relation to academic adjustment: a content approach, an achievement goal approach, and a hybrid social-academic goal approach.

DIFFERENT CONCEPTUALIZATIONS OF SOCIAL GOALS

First, social goals have been conceptualized as how often students focus on or try to do various things with their peers (e.g., have fun, follow rules). This approach is often referred to as a goal content approach and assumes students strive for certain outcomes that direct their behavior (Anderman & Anderman, 1999; Ford, 1992; Jarvinan & Nicholls, 1996). Some of the main social goals that have been identified within this approach are: responsibility goals, prosocial and intimacy goals, popularity goals, and dominance goals. Responsibility goals refer to a focus on conforming to the social and moral rules, meeting obligations, and keeping commitments. Prosocial goals refer to forming friendships as well as helping, sharing, and cooperating with peers. Intimacy goals are similar to prosocial goals but focus more specifically on establishing intimate friendships characterized by mutual support and disclosure of thoughts and feelings. Popularity goals refer to a focus on establishing high social status characterized by visibility and prestige within the larger peer group at school. Dominance goals refer to a focus on having power over peers characterized by getting peers to comply with one's wishes and instilling fear in peers.

Second, social goals have been conceptualized as distinct orientations toward social competence and linked to adjustment in the classroom (an achievement goal approach, encompassing development and demonstration goals; Erdley, Cain, Loomis, Dumas-Hines & Dweck, 1997; Host, Finney, & Barron, 2007; Ryan & Shim, in press). A social development goal concerns a focus on developing social competence with peers. The focus is on learning new material and skills, growth, and improvement. Success would be judged by whether one is improving social skills, deepening the quality of relationships, or developing one's social life in general. A social demonstration-approach goal concerns a focus on demonstrating social competence and gaining from peers positive judgments that one is socially desirable. A social demonstration-avoid goal concerns a focus on demonstrating that one does not lack social competence. The focus is on avoiding doing something that would incur negative judgments from peers and indicate social undesirability. With both social demonstration goals, attention is focused on the appearance of the self, especially in relation to others. For a social demonstration-approach goal, success is garnering positive feedback from peers, social prestige, and having a good reputation compared to others (e.g., being popular or seen as important), and for a social demonstration-avoid goal, success is avoiding negative judgments from peers compared to others and lack of a reputation as socially awkward or ineffective (e.g., not being seen as a loser or *geek*). These social achievement goals are analogous to those identified in other domains, although described with different terms (e.g., *mastery* and *performance* in the academic domain).

Third, social goals have been conceptualized as the social reasons students have for the pursuit of academic achievement (a hybrid social-academic goal approach; Dowson & McInerney, 2001; Urdan & Maehr, 1995). Social goals identified in this approach are affiliation goals, approval goals, concern goals, and responsibility goals. A social affiliation goal is the desire to do well academically to enhance one's sense of belonging in the group. A social approval goal is the desire to do well academically to gain approval from others (parents, teachers, or peers). A social concern goal is the desire to do well academically so one can help or assist others in their personal or academic development. A social responsibility goal is the desire to do well academically to maintain an interpersonal commitment, fulfill one's obligation, or follow the social/moral rules.

SOCIAL GOALS AND ADJUSTMENT IN SCHOOL

Research on social goals has provided insight into students' academic adjustment in school. Social goals have implications for academic adjustment via the behaviors as well as the types of social relationships they promote (Wentzel, 2005). Responsibility and prosocial goals have been found to be positively related to academic engagement and achievement (e.g., Wentzel, 1996). Similarly, intimacy goals have been found to be positively associated with positive attitudes toward school (Anderman, 1999), engagement and achievement (Kiefer & Ryan, in press). Striving for responsibility, prosocial outcomes, and intimacy with peers are positive orientations towards social relations that also facilitate academic adjustment in the classroom. In contrast, popularity goals are less adaptive for students' academic adjustment. The pursuit of popularity goals has been found to be related to negative attitudes about school (Andermann, 1999) and disengagement in the form of help avoidance (Ryan, Hicks & Midgley, 1997). However, popularity goals are often found to be not related to engagement and achievement at school (Kiefer & Ryan, in press). Finally, social dominance goals seem the most detrimental for academic adjustment as they are negatively associated with effort, positively associated with disruptive behavior, and negatively associated with grades in school (Kiefer & Ryan, in press).

When students are focused on establishing power over their peers (making others do what they want and establishing their toughness) they are more likely to act in ways that disrupts the class and less likely to put effort into their schoolwork, and not surprisingly this undermines their achievement.

The social achievement goal approach to social goals has found that a social development goal is adaptive for classroom adjustment whereas social demonstration-approach and avoid goals are maladaptive, although for different reasons. A social development goal has been associated with prosocial behavior with peers in the classroom (e.g., cooperation and sharing). A social development goal has been negatively associated with disruptive and aggressive behavior (Ryan & Shim, in press).

A focus on developing social competence seems to be a positive orientation towards the social world that sets in motion adaptive beliefs and behaviors in the classroom. In contrast, a social demonstration-approach goal has been found to be positively associated with disruptive and aggressive behavior and negatively associated with prosocial behavior with peers in the classroom. A social demonstration-avoid goal has been found to be positively associated with anxious solitary behavior and worry (Ryan & Shim, in press). Thus, a focus on demonstrating social competence seems to lead to maladaptive behavior in the form of inappropriate actions that are active or external to the student. A social demonstration-avoid goal also has drawbacks but is manifested in actions that are more passive or internal to the student.

Some research suggests that it may be important to consider the fact that students may pursue multiple social achievement goals in the classroom. For example, a social development goal was found to ameliorate the positive relation between a social demonstration-approach goal and aggressive behavior (Ryan & Shim, in press). This suggests that an additional benefit of a social development goal is that it can minimize the aggressive behavior that is associated with a social demonstration-approach goal.

Concerning the social-academic hybrid approach to goals, qualitative research has found that these social goals (affiliative, approval, concern, and responsibility) are intertwined with students' comments about their affect, engagement, and achievement in school (Dowson & McInerney, 2001). A quantitative study found these social-academic goals to be distinct factors from their cognitive and metacognitive strategies for their work (Dowson & McInerney, 2004). An interesting area of future research will be further investigation of the relation of the relation of these social-academic goals to engagement and achievement.

IMPLICATIONS FOR TEACHERS

Teachers need to attend to students' social goals as research has found them to be important to engagement and achievement. When students are not successful in the classroom, part of the explanation may be related to their social goals. Teachers should encourage adaptive social goals (e.g. procosial and development goals), redirect maladaptive social goals into more appropriate ones (e.g., steer from dominance goals to leadership goals) and vary the opportunities and nature of academic tasks so that social goals do not compete with or undermine academic goals and behaviors (e.g., seating and grouping of students; opportunities to collaborate with peers).

In sum, there are three key perspectives on social goals: (a) a goal content approach, (b) an achievement goal approach, and (c) a hybrid social-academic goal approach. For theory and research related to the social goal content perspective, see Martin Ford (1992), Kathryn Wentzel (1996), and Lynley Anderman (1999). For theory and research related to the achievement goal approach, see Carol Dweck (e.g., Erdley et al., 1997), Allison Ryan (Ryan & Shim, in press), Jeanne Horst (Horst, Finney, & Barron, 2007), and Andrew Elliot (Elliot, Gable, & Mapes, 2006). For theory and research related to a hybrid social-academic goal approach, see Tim Urdan (Urdan & Maehr, 1995) and Martin Dowson and Dennis McInerney (2001; 2004).

SEE ALSO *Caring Teachers; Goal Orientation Theory; Impression Management; Prosocial Behavior.*

BIBLIOGRAPHY

Anderman, L. H. (1999). Classroom goal orientation, school belonging and social goals as predictors of students' positive and negative affect following the transition to middle school. *Journal of Research and Development in Education, 32,* 89–103.

Anderman, L. H. & Anderman, E. M. (1999). Social predictors of changes in students' achievement goal orientations. *Contemporary Educational Psychology, 24,* 21–37.

Dowson, M., & McInerney, D. M. (2001). Psychological parameters of students' social and work-avoidance goals: A qualitative investigation. *Journal of Educational Psychology, 93,* 35–42.

Dowson, M., & McInerney, D. M. (2004). The development and validation of the goal orientation and learning strategies survey (GOALS_A). *Educational and Psychological Measurement, 64,* 290–310.

Elliot, A. J., Gable, S. L., & Mapes, R. R. (2006). Approach and avoidance motivation in the social domain. *Personality and Social Psychology Bulletin, 32,* 378–391.

Erdley, C. A., Cain, K. M., Loomis, C. C., Dumas-Hines, F., & Dweck, C. (1997). Relations among children's social goals, implicit personality theories, and responses to social failure. *Developmental Psychology, 33,* 263–272.

Ford, M. E. (1992). *Motivating humans: Goals, emotions, and personal agency beliefs.* Newbury Park, CA: Sage.

Horst, S. J., Finney, S. J., & Barron, K. E. (2007). Moving beyond academic achievement measures: A study of social achievement goals. *Contemporary Educational Psychology, 32,* 667–698.

Jarvinen, D. W., & Nicholls, J. G. (1996). Adolescents' social goals, beliefs about the causes of social success, and satisfaction in peer relations. *Developmental Psychology 32,* 435–441.

Kiefer, S. M., & Ryan, A. M. (in press). Different implications of dominance, popularity and intimacy goals for academic adjustment during early adolescence.

Ryan, A. M., & Shim, S. O. (in press). An exploration of young adolescents' social achievement goals and social adjustment in middle school. *Journal of Educational Psychology.*

Ryan, A. M., Hicks, L., & Midgley, C. (1997). Social goals, academic goals, and avoidance of help seeking in the classroom. *Journal of Early Adolescence, 17,* 152–171.

Urdan, T., & Maehr, M. (1995). Beyond a two-goal theory of motivation: A case for social goals. *Review of Educational Research, 65,* 213–244.

Wentzel, K. R. (1996). Social and academic motivation in middle school: Concurrent and long-term relations to academic effort. *Journal of Early Adolescence, 16,* 390–406.

Wentzel, K. (2005). Peer relationships, motivation, and academic performance at school. In A. J. Elliot, & C. S. Dweck, (Eds.), *Handbook of competence and motivation* (pp. 279–296). New York: Guilford Publications.

Allison M. Ryan

SOCIAL SKILLS

Children's social skills are important for early school success and later adjustment. Research has documented that children without adequate social skills are at risk for difficulties including peer rejection, behavior problems, and poor academic achievement. Moreover, recent research shows disturbing rates of expulsion in preschool and kindergarten, which has fueled efforts to promote these skills (Gilliam & Shahar, 2006). Broadly speaking, social skills describe how children navigate social and learning contexts and can be conceptualized as including interpersonal skills and learning-related skills. *Interpersonal skills* refers to the ability to perform competently in social situations, including interacting positively with others, cooperating, sharing, and respecting peers. Research has found that interpersonal skills are important for peer acceptance and social adjustment throughout childhood and adolescence (Masten et al., 2005).

In contrast to interpersonal skills, *learning-related skills* are important for learning and achievement in childhood and adolescence. These skills include self-regulation and social competence (e.g., cooperation, independence, and responsibility) on classroom tasks and in learning situations. There is strong evidence that learning-related skills predict academic achievement in kindergarten and throughout elementary school (McClelland, Acock, & Morrison, 2006). Aspects of learning-related skills are also important for achievement in adolescence (Duckworth & Seligman, 2005).

Although interpersonal skills and learning-related skills fall under the broad social skills construct, they are separate but related constructs with differing relations to outcomes in childhood and adolescence. Whereas interpersonal skills have been mostly linked to children's social development, learning-related skills have been related to doing well in classroom settings and to academic success.

PROCESSES THAT SUPPORT DEVELOPMENT OF SOCIAL SKILLS

One of the most important influences in early childhood is neurological maturation in the areas of the brain that help children control, direct, and plan their actions. Evidence from brain research shows these skills are associated with particular patterns of frontal lobe activity, specifically in the prefrontal cortex (Blair, 2002). Rapid development in the prefrontal cortex between ages 3 to 6 means the preschool period is a crucial time for acquiring social skills (Shonkoff & Phillips, 2000). Children's social skills vary widely, however, which may be related to differences in prefrontal cortex development, as well as other individual and environmental factors throughout childhood and adolescence (Calkins, 2004). For example, recent research has suggested that growing up in poverty is related to increased stress levels for young children, which can alter brain development in ways that are linked to social skill and self-regulation difficulties (Dearing, Berry, & Zaslow, 2006; Gunnar, 2006).

Child temperament, including children's level of reactivity and regulation, also plays a significant role in the social development of children and adolescents. One aspect of temperament, effortful control, helps children regulate their emotions and behavior, and has emerged as being especially important for self-regulation and social competence (Rothbart & Rueda, 2005).

A large body of research has also examined the vital role that parents play in the development of their children (Collins, Maccoby, Steinberg, Hetherington, & Bornstein, 2000). Although many aspects of parenting are important for children's development, parental warmth and sensitivity have emerged as two of the most salient predictors of children's social development (NICHD Early Child Care Research Network, 2006).

The quality of the parent-child attachment relationship also predicts children's social skills. A number of studies have found that having a secure attachment with a parent allows children to express emotion effectively and develop strong self-regulatory skills. Moreover, studies of attachment highlight the importance of the child's behavior, including reactivity and responsiveness, in helping to shape the attachment relationship (Calkins, 2004).

NORMATIVE DEVELOPMENTAL CHANGES IN SOCIAL SKILLS

From early childhood through adolescence, social skill development occurs through a reciprocal and bidirectional relationship between a child's individual characteristics (e.g., temperament) and the environment (e.g., parent warmth and sensitivity, family factors, and peers). Children begin developing social skills within the context of the parent-child attachment relationship (Rubin, Bulkowski, & Parker, 2006). It is from this relationship that children learn to read emotional cues, regulate their own emotions and behavior, and incorporate the responses of their parents into their own experiences with people and situations; a process known as social referencing (Thompson & Lagattuta, 2006). From observing family members, children learn appropriate social rules and behaviors, which they apply to interactions outside of the family.

In early childhood, children have exposure to other children in childcare settings. As toddlers, children engage primarily in solitary play, but interactions with other children increase with age. Positive interactions with peers help children develop interpersonal skills, communication skills, emotional understanding/regulation, the ability to control aggressive behaviors, and early learning-related skills. A number of developmental changes occur in early childhood that also facilitate the development of social skills, including a significant increase in vocabulary (Thompson & Lagattuta, 2006) and brain maturation in the prefrontal cortex (Blair, 2002). These developmental changes lead to an improved ability to communicate and regulate feelings and behaviors. Children also begin to develop empathy and gain an understanding of the feelings, desires, and beliefs of their peers; skills which continue to impact social development throughout childhood and adolescence.

Friendships become increasingly important in middle childhood and adolescence, especially for the development of social skills. As children improve their ability to understand the emotions of others, they build increasingly mature friendships and strengthen their interpersonal and learning-related skills. Children and adolescents who have difficulty empathizing or self-regulating have few positive social interactions and are likely to be rejected or neglected by peers, which can significantly impact social well-being and academic outcomes (Rubin et al., 2006).

SOCIAL SKILLS DEVELOPMENT AND SCHOOL ADJUSTMENT

A large body of evidence supports the role that children's social skills (including interpersonal skills and learning-related skills) play in social and academic success. In general, children's interpersonal skills have been linked to social outcomes whereas learning-related skills have predicted academic success. Interpersonal skills are especially important for social adjustment in childhood and adolescence. For example, one study found that poor interpersonal skills (e.g., externalizing problems) in childhood, predicted academic problems in adolescence, which in turn led to internalizing problems in adulthood (Masten et al., 2005).

There is also strong evidence that learning-related skills predict early academic achievement (McClelland et al., 2006). For example, one study found that prekindergarteners who had difficulty using learning-related skills to complete goal-directed activities scored lower on a standardized cognitive achievement measure. These children also exhibited more risk factors, such as family problems, lower parental education, and behavioral or emotional problems (Bronson, Tivnan, & Seppanen, 1995). Another study found that the gains in learning-related skills, specifically self-regulation, predicted gains made in early literacy, vocabulary, and math skills over the prekindergarten year in a diverse sample of children across two sites in the United States (McClelland et al., 2007).

Other research in elementary school has demonstrated that kindergarten learning-related skills significantly predicted reading and math achievement between kindergarten and sixth grade, and growth in literacy and math from kindergarten to second grade (McClelland et al., 2006). Finally, in one recent study, aspects of learning-related skills, such as self-discipline, were stronger predictors of academic performance than intelligence test scores in adolescents (Duckworth & Seligman, 2005).

A number of studies also support relations between interpersonal skills and learning-related skills for children's school adjustment. For example, research has shown that children's self-regulation positively relates to social competence, and that strong self-regulation can buffer otherwise negative outcomes (Lengua, 2002). Taken together, research suggests that promoting interpersonal skills and learning-related skills in young children and adolescents is one way to ensure strong social and academic skills.

ASSESSING STUDENTS' SOCIAL SKILLS

A variety of methods are used to assess children's social skills. When determining a method of assessment, it is essential to select instruments that are reliable, valid, and feasible given cost and time limitations. It is also critical to choose measures that are appropriate for the age, developmental stage, and special needs of the target population (McClelland & Scalzo, 2006).

Naturalistic observations are one of the best methods for assessing interpersonal and learning-related skills. Typically, observations are conducted at school where there is ample opportunity to observe children interacting within social and learning environments. Observers should be objective and trained in how to code and record the frequency, duration, and interval of behaviors that are being assessed. Although observation provides a rich source of information, it is time-consuming and most useful for initial assessments rather than ongoing evaluation (McClelland & Scalzo, 2006).

Behavior rating scales also measure interpersonal and learning-related skills, but are less time-intensive and more cost effective than observations. They have high levels of reliability and validity and can be used to assess children who are too young to report their own behaviors. They do not, however, provide information about the antecedents and consequences of behavior.

Structured and unstructured interviews provide useful information regarding a child's social context, although they lack reliability and validity. Another limitation of interviews is that children often provide biased responses as they can be suggestible and influenced by social desirability.

Role-play, most commonly used by clinicians, allows direct observation of social skills when naturalistic observation is not possible. In role-play, children are asked to respond to a scenario or staged interaction. Although they can be used to elicit low-frequency behaviors that might not otherwise occur, role-play lacks generalizability because children may not respond to role-play as they would to real-world situations (Merrell, 2001).

Sociometric techniques assess peer relationships and interpersonal skills by asking children to rank classmates and identify peers they like/dislike and peers who exhibit specific behaviors, such as aggression. The reliability and validity of sociometric techniques are very strong, but there are many practical constraints. Sociometric techniques often require consent from all parents in a classroom, and parents are often reluctant to consent for fear that participation will reinforce social rejection (Merrell, 2001).

RISK AND PROTECTIVE FACTORS

Research documents that children who are disadvantaged or of minority status may be at risk for having difficulty socially and academically in early childhood. For example, studies have linked growing up in poverty to a number of risk factors, including poor achievement on cognitive and language outcomes, increased behavior problems (both externalizing and internalizing), increased stress levels, and difficulties with self-regulation and emotion regulation (Dearing et al., 2006). Children from disadvantaged backgrounds also have been found to exhibit poorer learning-related skills and do worse on academic indices throughout elementary school compared to their peers (McClelland et al., 2006). These results suggest that income level and minority status can be risk factors in the development of social skills for children and adolescents.

One protective factor of children's social skills development is parenting. Parents who are warm and sensitive and set appropriate limits for children are more likely to have children with strong interpersonal and learning-related skills. For example, research has found that children's stress levels can be buffered by sensitive parenting, which can enhance children's social and emotional development (Gunnar, 2006). Finally, children of chronically depressed parents are more likely to have lower social skills in early childhood (NICHD Early Child Care Research Network, 2003), making it especially important to work with parents to effectively promote children's social skill development.

A number of studies have found that social skills deficits have been more often documented in boys than girls. Compared with girls, boys are more likely to be suspended and expelled at every grade level, drop out of school, exhibit behavior problems, and have lower education levels (Gilliam & Shahar, 2006). Research also indicates that girls have stronger aspects of learning-related skills and more adaptive classroom behavior than boys. One recent study found that girls had significantly stronger levels of self-regulation in kindergarten than boys, and there were greater numbers of boys scoring at the lowest levels on self-regulation over the school year compared to girls (Matthews, Ponitz, & Morrison, 2007).

Taken together, it is clear that a number of factors contribute to children's positive social skill development. Effective strategies for strengthening social skills involve a multi-faceted approach to working with children and parents.

EFFECTIVE CLASSROOM STRATEGIES

The teacher-child relationship plays a significant role in facilitating social skill development. Numerous studies have found that warm teacher-child relationships are associated with high levels of cooperation, social competence, and learning-related skills in early childhood and elementary school. Teacher-reported negativity, however, has been associated with social difficulties in children. The ratio of teachers to children in the classroom also relates to children's social skills. A smaller teacher-child ratio allows opportunities for children to work with teachers in small groups or one-on-one, and organization of children into smaller groups has been found to pro-

mote positive interpersonal and learning-related skills (Rimm-Kaufman, La Paro, Downer, & Pianta, 2005).

In addition to teacher factors, the classroom environment can facilitate the development of social skills. Classrooms that best promote these skills are child-centered and provide a stimulating, organized environment with ample opportunity for interaction (Cameron, Connor, & Morrison, 2005). Children demonstrate higher interpersonal and learning-related skills in classrooms where teachers provide organization and guidance, such as modeling appropriate social behaviors and problem-solving skills. Teachers can facilitate social problem-solving by demonstrating how to talk through the steps of a problem and by creating opportunities for children to practice social skills.

Children with social skills deficits most often have difficulties with one or more of the following areas: cooperation, communication, emotional understanding and regulation, aggression, and problem-solving (Bierman & Erath, 2006). To effectively help children who have social skills deficits, teachers can provide instruction and modeling of appropriate behaviors and responses. In young children, teachers can also create opportunities for children to practice and generalize social skills through classroom interactions. As children practice social skills, teachers should provide positive feedback to promote appropriate behaviors and redirect inappropriate behaviors.

Social skills (interpersonal skills and learning-related skills) are important for academic success and social well-being from early childhood through adolescence. Children without adequate social skills are at risk of peer rejection, behavior problems, and poor academic achievement. A combination of child, parent, and environmental factors influence the development of social skills and it is therefore essential for teachers and researchers to consider a child's context and use multi-faceted strategies to effectively promote positive social skills development.

BIBLIOGRAPHY

Bierman, K. L., & Erath, S. A. (2006). Promoting social competence in early childhood: Classroom curricula and social skills coaching programs. In K. McCartney & D. Phillips (Eds.), *Blackwell handbook of early childhood development* (pp. 595–615). Malden, MA: Blackwell.

Blair, C. (2002). School readiness: Integrating cognition and emotion in a neurobiological conceptualization of children's functioning at school entry. *American Psychologist, 57,* 111–127.

Bronson, M. B., Tivnan, T., & Seppanen, P. S. (1995). Relations between teacher and classroom activity variables and the classroom behaviors of prekindergarten children in Chapter 1 funded programs. *Journal of Applied Developmental Psychology, 16,* 253–282.

Calkins, S. D. (2004). Early attachment processes and the development of emotional self-regulation. In R. F. Baumeister

& K. D. Vohs (Eds.), *Handbook of self-regulation: Research, theory, and applications* (pp. 324–339). New York: Guildford Press.

Cameron, C., Connor, C. M., & Morrison, F. J. (2005). Effects of variation in teacher organization on classroom functioning. *Journal of School Psychology, 43*, 61–85.

Collins, W., Maccoby, E. E., Steinberg, L., Hetherington, E., & Bornstein, M. H. (2000). Contemporary research on parenting: The case for nature and nurture. *American Psychologist, 55*(2), 218–232.

Dearing, E., Berry, D., & Zaslow, M. (2006). Poverty during early childhood. In K. McCartney & D. Phillips (Eds.), *Blackwell handbook of early childhood development* (pp. 399–423). Malden, MA: Blackwell.

Duckworth, A. L., & Seligman, M. E. P. (2005). Self-discipline outdoes IQ in predicting academic performance of adolescents. *Psychological Science, 16*(12), 939–944.

Gilliam, W. S., & Shahar, G. (2006). Preschool and child care expulsion and suspension: Rates and predictors in one state. *Infants and Young Children, 19*(3), 228–245.

Gunnar, M. R. (2006). Social regulation of stress in early child development. In K. McCartney & D. Phillips (Eds.), *Blackwell handbook of early childhood development* (pp. 106–125). Malden, MA: Blackwell.

Lengua, L. J. (2002). The contribution of emotionality and self-regulation to the understanding of children's response to multiple risk. *Child Development, 73*, 144–161.

Masten, A. S., Roisman, G. I., Long, J. D., Burt, K. B., Obradovic, J., Riley, J. R., et al. (2005). Developmental cascades: Linking academic achievement and externalizing and internalizing symptoms over 20 years. *Developmental Psychology, 41*(5), 733–746.

McClelland, M. M., Acock, A. C., & Morrison, F. J. (2006). The impact of kindergarten learning-related skills on academic trajectories at the end of elementary school. *Early Childhood Research Quarterly, 21*, 471–490.

McClelland, M. M., Cameron, C. E., Connor, C. M., Farris, C. L., Jewkes, A. M., & Morrison, F. J. (2007). Links between behavioral regulation and preschoolers' literacy, vocabulary and math skills. *Developmental Psychology, 43*(4), 947–959.

McClelland, M. M., & Scalzo, C. (2006). Social skills deficits. In M. Hersen (Ed.), *Clinician's handbook of child behavioral assessment* (pp. 313–335). San Diego, CA: Elsevier.

Merrell, K. W. (2001). Assessment of children's social skills: Recent developments, best practices, and new directions. *Exceptionality, 9*, 3–18.

NICHD Early Child Care Research Network. (2003). Social functioning in first grade: Associations with earlier home and child care predictors and with current classroom experiences. *Child Development, 74*, 1639–1662.

NICHD Early Child Care Research Network. (2006). Child-care effect sizes for the NICHD Study of Early Child Care and Youth Development. *American Psychologist, 61*(2), 99–116.

Rimm-Kaufman, S. E., La Paro, K. M., Downer, J. T., & Pianta, R. C. (2005). The contribution of classroom setting and quality of instruction to children's behavior in the kindergarten classroom. *Elementary School Journal, 105*(4), 377–394.

Rothbart, M. K., & Rueda, M. R. (2005). The development of effortful control. In U. Mayr, E. Awh, & S. Keele (Eds.), *Developing individuality in the human brain: A tribute to Michael I. Posner* (pp. 167–188). Washington, D.C.: American Psychological Association.

Rubin, K. H., Bulkowski, W. M., & Parker, J. G. (2006). Peer interactions, relationships, and groups. In N. Eisenberg (Ed.), *Handbook on child psychology, Vol. 3, Social, emotional, and personality development* (6th ed., pp. 619–700). New York: Wiley.

Shonkoff, J. P., & Phillips, D. A. (2000). *From neurons to neighborhoods: The science of early childhood development.* Washington, DC: National Academy Press.

Thompson, R. A., & Lagattuta, K. H. (2006). Feeling and understanding: Early emotional development. In K. McCartney & D. Phillips (Eds.), *Blackwell handbook of early childhood development* (pp. 317–337). Malden, MA: Blackwell.

Megan M. McClelland
Shauna Tominey

SOCIOCULTURAL THEORIES OF MOTIVATION

For most educators, motivation is central to understanding and improving their students' classroom learning. While there is disagreement over its exact nature, most theories describe motivation as an *individual* phenomenon. Study of motivation has increasingly concerned the contexts in which motivated activity occurs. Of particular concern are specific *social* aspects of contexts (e.g. peers and classmates) and broader *cultural* aspects (e.g., societal values, cultural norms). Motivation theories that focus strongly on context are often described as *sociocultural* theories of motivation. This entry considers socioculturally oriented theories of motivation and, more broadly, the role of context in motivation theories. It contrasts sociocultural theories with more conventional theories, considers the distinctions between different sociocultural theories of motivation, and considers the practical implications of such theories of motivating classroom learning.

PRIOR THEORIES OF MOTIVATION

Most of the well-known individually oriented theories of motivation focus on either the behavior or the cognition of individuals. Following from the ideas of the behaviorist B.F. Skinner (1904–1990), theories that focus on behavior generally do not recognize motivation as something different from learning. Behavioral theories generally describe both motivation and learning in terms of how behavior is or is not reinforced by the environment. Because of this, behavioral theories describe contexts in terms of the patterns and relationships in the environment. Behavioral motivation theories argue that teachers should structure classroom contexts so that learning can proceed in a very systematic fashion, and that students are appropriately rewarded for mastering very specific learning objectives.

The cognitive development theories of Jean Piaget (1896–1980) and the emergence of cognitive psychology in the 1970s led to very different theories of motivation. While still focusing on individuals, these theories made a clear distinction between learning and motivation. Well-known types of cognitive theories of motivation include social cognitive theories (e.g., *self-efficacy* and *self-regulation*) and intrinsic motivation theories (e.g., *self-determination, expectancy theory,* and *personal interest*). Historically, cognitive theories of motivation treated the sociocultural context as one of many factors that influence the motivation of individuals. Concern over the relevance of these theories by leading theorists such as Weiner (1990) led to increased concern with classroom and cultural contexts, particularly among motivation researchers who were concerned with education. This led to increased attention to the ways that classroom contexts, ethnicity, and culture influenced goals (e.g., Maehr & Pintrich, 1995), efficacy (Bandura, 2000), and interests (Hidi & Anderson, 1992). The implication of this trend for teachers was that their students' motivation was much more influenced by the classroom context and by the broader sociocultural context than had previously been assumed. In particular, this trend led away from explanations of motivation that focused on the individuals' genetic inheritance.

SOCIOCULTURAL THEORIES

Increased concern with sociocultural contexts in motivation and education more broadly reflects the influence of the Soviet theorist Lev Vygotsky (1896–1934). This influence began after Vygotsky's earlier works were translated into English (e.g., 1978). Vygotsky used the ideas of the philosopher Friedrich Engels (1820–1895) to understand how history and society impact the way that humans develop and learn. This led him to argue that knowledge originates in the social context. For some motivation theorists, Vygotsky's theories, when compared to theories that focused on individuals, provided a more useful explanation of the way that factors such as poverty and racism interfere with motivation for classroom learning. For example, Sivan (1986) proposed that the individual goals and values that motivate learning originate in the sociohistoric context, just as Vygotsky argued that language originated in the sociohistoric context. The practical implication of these theories is that explanations for differences in motivation should begin with the classroom, home, and sociocultural context, rather than the individual.

One well-known Vygotskian strand of motivational research involved studies of *adaptive learning* (e.g., McCaslin & Murdock, 1991) and *co-regulated learning* (McCaslin & Good, 1996). McCaslin and colleagues studied social and instructional environments found in the home and in the classroom. These studies provided detailed accounts of the way that students' regulation of their own thinking processes originated in the negotiation of goals and norms among students, teacher, and families. These studies were important because they identified the source of motivation as the relationships that students developed. This included relationships with school activities and relationships with the many other participants in school learning. Therefore, motivating classroom learners meant helping them coordinate the goals implied by a range of different relationships, and recognizing that some of the goals will conflict with other goals. This implies that before searching for strategies to motivate individual learners, teachers need to help students learn to negotiate worthwhile goals for themselves and their classmates. In doing so, teachers need to acknowledging the influence of other goals which might interfere with classroom learning, but which have real value for students.

McCaslin's studies helped pave the way for other studies that focused on the relationships that students had with other participants in the classroom and cultural contexts, including Järvelä and Salovaara (2004), Nolen (2007), Turner and Meyer (2000), and Yowell and Smylie (1999). By the start of the 21st century, "motivation in context" had emerged as an important theme among motivation researchers. This is particularly apparent in the treatment of motivation in educational psychology textbooks. While continuing to give ample treatment to motivational strategies that focus on individual learners, many also point out that teachers need to help the classroom community negotiate worthwhile goals, acknowledging that the students themselves help create and change these very goals.

SITUATIVE THEORIES

The most distinctively sociocultural theories of motivation are rooted in the "situative" theories of cognition that began taking shape in the 1990s. Like Vygotskian theories, situative theories assume that knowledge originates in social interaction and in cultural activity. However, situative theories assume that the knowledge primarily resides in these contexts as well. Situativity theorists argue that the abstract concepts that make up knowledge in cognitive theories and the specific associations that make up knowledge in the behavioral theories are "secondary" ways of describing knowledge. From this perspective, strictly behavioral or strictly cognitive explanations of individual activity reflect the beliefs of particular researchers and the methods they use (Greeno & the MMAP, 1998). Situativity theorists believe that knowledge is "distributed" across tools, technologies, and social rituals that human cultures construct to let them work together. This means that knowledge and meaning are primarily rooted in the actual collective experiences people have in the world. According to Gee (2004), the abstract generalizations that are taken for granted in modern cognitive perspectives come at the end of a long process of socially situated activity—if they come at all. Because of this, situative theorists believe that students' learning is strongly attached to their participation in the construction of situated knowledge in socially meaningful activity.

Situative considerations of motivation for classroom learning first ask whether a particular learning context affords collective engagement in situated learning. In other words, are students and teachers negotiating a shared understanding of the concepts, terms, and rituals of the domain? This leads to a very different approach to motivation than prior approaches that focused on the activity of individuals. In one initial consideration, Hickey (1997) examined the motivational implications of situative instructional approaches that achieved prominence in the 1990s. This included the *cognitive apprenticeship* model defined by Collins, Brown, and Newman (1989). That paper suggested that the negative motivational consequences of competition might be more the result of lack of opportunity to engage in meaningful shared activity, rather than any fundamental consequence of competition.

Likewise, Hickey explored Bereiter and Scardamalia's 1989 *intentional learning* perspective, which argued that learning environments first need to give students opportunities to participate in the construction of new knowledge in shared activity. They suggested that the widely held distinction between intrinsic and extrinsic motivation was too crude to be of much use in developing intentional learning environments. Both of these seminal considerations of situated learning suggested that the motivational strategies from earlier individually oriented theories of motivation might actually interfere with efforts to motivate engagement in situated learning. Given that situative theorists consider all learning to be socially situated, situative perspectives on learning seemed to have profound implications for motivating classroom learning.

One implication of this trend towards situated theories of motivation is that efforts to improve motivation for classroom learning should focus on *engagement*. This is because focusing on engagement requires being more specific about assumptions about learning. This issue was elaborated in Hickey and McCaslin (2001) who examined the implications of situative theories for motivating engage-

ment in learning. They argued that a situative focus on *learning to* participate in shared discourse (rather than *learning from* that participation) meant that teachers should focus their efforts at motivating that participation. Prior theories would focus on motivating students to encourage them to engage in discourse, and search for individual explanations when they failed to do so. Behaviorally oriented theorists would consider how the environment rewarded or punished individuals for participating in that activity. Cognitively oriented theorists would consider how the goals or values of the individuals affected the desirability of that activity.

In contrast, situative theories focus more directly on fostering worthwhile discourse among their students. This discourse occurs as students work together to make meaning of the terms, representations, and ideas that have already been negotiated by the community of experts in the particular academic domain. For example, the prevailing social norms in a math class should motivate students and teachers to encourage one another to use the mathematical term *vector* rather than the everyday term *point* during a lesson on geometry. Given the limits of human attention, this shift has major implications of teachers. This is because asking teachers to focus directly on such situated considerations of learning draws limited resources away from focusing on the behavior and/or cognition of each of their students.

Hickey and McCaslin (2001) also described the basic tension between earlier behavioral and cognitive views of motivation. As illustrated by the seemingly intractable debate over extrinsic incentives (e.g., prizes, competition, and grades), they argued that these tensions were a major obstacle to educational reform. Reflecting their very different views of learning, cognitive theorists have long argued that incentives interfere with natural learning processes, while behavioral theorists have long argued that incentive are useful for encouraging learning. Hickey and McCaslin argued that a relatively neutral situative view of motivation might offer a more useful lens for studying and comparing behavioral and cognitive strategies for motivating engagement. From a situative perspective, incentives and competition are not inherently good or bad. Rather, all motivational practices should first be analyzed in terms of their impact on students' success at negotiating meaningfulness of the language and concepts of the particular academic domain. Importantly, a situative theory of motivation assumes that the success of these negotiations is the primary source of individual motivation towards the domain. Therefore it is the collective success of these negotiations that predicts whether or not those individuals will be motivated to engage in the practices of the domain in the future.

The notion of *engaged participation*, which was introduced by Greeno and colleagues (1998) provides a particularly appealing theoretical basis for a situated theory of motivation. This theory focuses concern with motivation on participation in the rituals and practices of content domains that represent those domains in the activities of classrooms. This viewpoint argues that if the community of learners that makes up the classroom does not value participation in those rituals and practices, it is difficult for a particular individual to participate in them (Hickey, 2003). In contrast to sociocultural views that assume socially constructed goals and values are internalized by individuals, this viewpoint argues that goal and values remain alongside the knowledge practices in the sociocultural environment. While this distinction is philosophical rather than scientific, it has an important practical implication: as one's view of knowledge becomes more situated, the assumption that goals and values are internalized becomes less useful for motivating engagement (Hickey & Granade, 2005).

This raises fundamental questions about the scope of research that might inform teachers' efforts to motivate classroom learning. It argues that the wealth of existing sociocultural research on topics like identity (Holland, Lachicotte, Skinner, & Cain, 1998) and discourse (Gee & Green, 1998) are directly relevant for understanding motivated classroom learning. A particularly useful aspect of this research is that much of it concerns particular content areas, such as mathematics or science. When motivated classroom learning is viewed as engaged participation, this research becomes directly relevant for motivating that learning. Because this perspective assumes that specific motivational practices will have different consequences in different situations, teachers must be able to continually assess collective participation and adjust their practices accordingly. The current focus on individually oriented models of motivation in teacher education programs may be distracting from (or even undermining) the development of this ability.

One potential advantage of situative models of motivation is that they lend themselves well to the design-based research methods advanced by many situative educational theorists (e.g., Barab & Squire, 2004). These approaches build theory within efforts to reform educational practice. This is very different from the building of theory in highly controlled experiments or surveys (as in traditional studies of motivation) or naturalistic investigations of classroom or cultural activity (as in many of the recent study of motivation in context). Design-based methods are particularly relevant to educators because they highlight the value of theories that are developed in specific contexts for improving learning in those same contexts. Hickey and Schaffer (2006) proposed a model for improving classroom motivation over a series increasingly formal design-based studies. This first study would focus on highly situated analyses of motivation, using discourse analytic methods to increase collective partic-

ipation; this would be followed by more experimental studies of individual goals and values. A final cycle would use traditional program evaluation methods to look at the motivated behavior of all of the students. While elements of such an approach have been examined in initial studies (Hickey & Zuiker, 2005), the entire model has yet to be fully implemented or validated. The practical implications of such an approach is that if teachers focus their attention on directly enhancing their students' collective participation in domain-specific discourse, they will indirectly enhance the intrinsic motivation (e.g., goals and self-determination) of their individual students while improving the overall behavior (e.g., disciplinary actions and enrollments in advanced courses) over the student body.

BIBLIOGRAPHY

Bandura, A. (2000). Exercise of human agency through collective efficacy. *Current Directions in Psychological Science, 9,* 75–78.

Barab, S., & Squire, K. (2004). Design-based research: Putting a stake in the ground. *Journal of the Learning Sciences, 13,* 1–14.

Bereiter, C., & Scardamalia, S. (1989). Intentional learning as the goal of instruction. In L. B. Resnick (Ed.), *Knowing, learning, & instruction: Essays in honor of Robert Glaser* (pp. 361–385). Hillsdale, NJ: Erlbaum.

Collins, A., Brown, J. S., & Newman, S. E. (1989). Cognitive apprenticeship: Teaching the craft of reading, writing, & mathematics. In L. B. Resnick (Ed.), *Knowing, learning, & instruction: Essays in honor of Robert Glaser* (pp. 453–494). Hillsdale, NJ: Erlbaum.

Gee, J. P. (2004). *Situated learning and language: A critique of traditional schooling.* London: Routledge.

Gee, J. P., & Green, J. L. (1998). Discourse analysis, learning, and social practice: A methodological study. *Review of Research in Education, 22,* 119–165.

Greeno, J. G., & the Middle School Mathematics through Application Project. (1998). The situativity of knowing, learning, and research. *American Psychologist, 53,* 5–26.

Hickey, D. T. (1997). Motivation and contemporary socio-constructivist instructional perspectives. *Educational Psychologist, 32,* 175–193.

Hickey, D. T. (2003). Engaged participation vs. marginal non-participation: A stridently sociocultural model of achievement motivation. *Elementary School Journal, 103,* 401–429.

Hickey, D. T., & Granade, J. (2004). The influence of sociocultural theory on our theories of engagement and motivation. In D. M. McInerney & S. Van Etten (Eds.), *Big theories revisited: Research on sociocultural influences on motivation and learning* (Vol. 4, pp. 223–247). Greenwich, CO: Information Age.

Hickey, D. T., & McCaslin, M. (2001). Comparative and sociocultural analyses of context and motivation. In S. S. Volet & S. Järvelä (Eds.), *Motivation in learning contexts: Theoretical and methodological implications* (pp. 33–56). Amsterdam: Pergamon/Elsevier.

Hickey, D. T., & Schafer, N. J. (2006). Design-based, participation-centered approaches to classroom management. In C. Evertson & C. Weinstein (Eds.), *The Handbook of classroom management: Research, practice, & contemporary issues* (pp. 281–308). New York: Simon & Schuster Macmillan.

Hickey, D. T., & Zuiker, S. J. (2005). Engaged participation: A sociocultural model of motivation with implications for assessment. *Educational Assessment, 10,* 277–305.

Hidi, S., & Anderson, R. (1992). Situational interest and its impact on reading and expository writing. In K. A. Renninger, S. Hidi, & A. Krapp (Eds.), *The role of interest in learning and development* (pp. 215–238). Hillsdale, NJ: Erlbaum.

Holland, D., Lachicotte, D., Skinner, D., & Cain, C. (1998). *Agency and identity in cultural worlds.* Cambridge, MA: Harvard University Press.

Järvelä, S., & Salovaara, H. (2004). The interplay of motivational goals and cognitive strategies in a new pedagogical culture: A context-oriented and qualitative approach. *European Psychologist, 9,* 232–244.

Maehr, M. L., & Pintrich, P. R. (Eds.). (1995). *Advances in motivation and achievement: Culture, motivation, and achievement.* Greenwich, CT: JAI Press.

McCaslin, M., & Good, T. (1996). The informal curriculum. In D. Berliner & R. Calfee (Eds.), *The handbook of educational psychology* (pp. 622–673). New York: Macmillan.

McCaslin, M., & Murdock, T. B. (1991). The emergent interaction of home and school in the development of adaptive learning. In M. L. Maehr & P. Pintrich (Eds.), *Advances in Motivation and Achievement* (pp. 213–259). Greenwich, CT: JAI Press.

Nolen, S. B. (2007). Young children's motivation to read and write: Development in social contexts. *Cognition and Instruction, 25,* 219–270.

Sivan, E. (1986). Motivation in social constructivist theory. *Educational Psychologist, 21,* 209–233.

Turner, J. C., & Meyer, D. K. (2000). Studying and understanding the instructional contexts of classrooms: Using our past to forge our future. *Educational Psychologist, 90,* 730–745.

Vygotsky, L. S. (1978). *Mind in society: The development of higher psychological processes.* Cambridge MA: Harvard University Press.

Weiner, B. (1990). The history of motivation research in education. *Journal of Educational Psychology, 82,* 616–622.

Yowell, C M., & Smylie, M. (1999). Self regulation in democratic communities. *The Elementary School Journal* 99(5), 469–490.

Daniel Hickey

SOCIOCULTURAL THEORY

The work of *sociocultural theory* is to explain how individual mental functioning is related to cultural, institutional, and historical context; hence, the focus of the sociocultural perspective is on the roles that participation in social interactions and culturally organized activities play in influencing psychological development. While much of the framework for sociocultural theory was put forth by Lev Vygotsky (1931/1997), extensions, elabo-

rations, and refinements of sociocultural theory can be found in writings regarding *activity theory* (Chaiklin & Lave, 1993; Leontiev, 1981) and *cultural-historical activity theory* (Cole, 1996; Cole & Engestrom, 1994).

THE HISTORICAL ROOTS OF SOCIOCULTURAL THEORY

Lev S. Vygotksy, a psychologist in Russia who began his work following the Russian Revolution of 1917, is most closely identified with sociocultural theory. Vygotsky, argued: "The social dimension of consciousness is primary in time and in fact. The individual dimension of consciousness is derivative and secondary" (Vygotsky, 1979, p. 30, cited in Wertsch & Bivens, 1992). From this perspective, mental functioning of the individual is not simply derived from social interaction; rather, the specific structures and processes revealed by individuals can be traced to their interactions with others.

Wertsch (1991) proposed three major themes in Vygotsky's writings that elucidate the nature of this interdependence between individual and social processes in learning and development. The first is that individual development, including higher mental functioning, has its origins in social sources. This theme is best represented in Vygotsky's "genetic law of development": "Any function of the child's cultural development appears on the stage twice, or on two planes, first the social, then the psychological, first between people as an intermental category, then within the child as an intramental category" (Vygotsky, 1931/1997, pp. 105–106).

From this perspective, as learners participate in a broad range of joint activities and internalize the effects of working together, they acquire new strategies and knowledge of the world and culture. Typically this tenet has been illustrated by examining the interactions between individuals with disparate knowledge levels; for example, children and their caregivers, or experts and novices. However, as Tudge and Scrimsher (2003) note, Vygotsky was not only interested in what more knowledgeable others brought to the interaction, but also in what the child himself or herself brought to the interaction, as well as how the broader cultural and historical setting shaped the interaction.

The second Vygotskian theme that Wertsch (1991) has identified is that human action, on both the social and individual planes, is mediated by tools and signs— semiotics. These semiotic means include: "language; various systems of counting; mnemonic techniques; algebraic symbol systems; works of art; writing; schemes, diagrams, maps and mechanical drawings; all sorts of conventional signs and so on" (Vygotsky, 1981, p. 137). Additional semiotic means include: computers, calculators, paint brushes and the like, all of which are useful in representational activity. These semiotic means are both the tools that facilitate the co-construction of knowledge and the means that are internalized to aid future independent problem solving activity.

Leontiev (1981), a colleague of Vygotsky, used the term "appropriation" to characterize this process of internalization:

> [Children] cannot and need not reinvent artifacts that have taken millennia to evolve in order to appropriate such objects into their own system of activity. The child has only to come to an understanding that it is adequate for using the culturally elaborated object in the novel life circumstances he encounters. (Quoted in Newman, Griffin, & Cole, 1989, p. 63)

The third theme that Wertsch (1991) proposes from Vygotsky's writing is that the first two themes are best examined through genetic, or developmental, analysis:

> To study something historically means to study it in the process of change; that is the dialectical method's basic demand. To encompass in research the process of a given thing's development in all its phases and changes—from birth to death—fundamentally means to discover its nature, its essence, for it is only in movement that a body shows what it is. Thus the historical study of behavior is not an auxiliary aspect of theoretical study, but rather forms its very base. (Vygotsky, 1978, pp. 64–65)

In contrast to prevailing views of his time, in which learning was regarded as an external process and development an internal process, Vygotsky was concerned with the unity and interdependence of learning and development. For example, he was critical of Piaget's theory in which "maturation is viewed as a precondition of learning but never the result of it" (Vygotsky, 1978, p. 80). In contrast, Vygotsky proposed:

> Learning awakens a variety of internal developmental processes that are able to operate only when the child is interacting with people in his environment and with his peers. . . . learning is not development; however, properly organized learning results in mental development and sets in motion a variety of developmental processes that would be impossible apart from learning. Thus learning is a necessary and universal aspect of the process of developing culturally organized, specifically human, psychological functions. (p. 90)

In support of this perspective, Vygotsky (1978) introduced the construct of the *zone of proximal development* (ZPD) as a fundamentally new approach to the problem that learning should be matched in some man-

ner with the child's level of development. He argued that to understand the relationship between development and learning, two developmental levels must be distinguished: the actual and the potential levels of development. The actual refers to those accomplishments a child can demonstrate alone or perform independently; in contrast to potential levels of development as suggested by the ZPD—what children can do with assistance: "The distance between the actual developmental level as determined by independent problem solving and the level of potential development as determined through problem solving under adult guidance or in collaboration with more capable peers" (p. 85). The ZPD was regarded as a better, more dynamic and relative indicator of cognitive development than what children accomplished alone. In summary, productive interactions are those which orient instruction toward the ZPD; otherwise, instruction lags behind the development of the child. "The only good learning is that which is in advance of development." (Vygotsky, 1978, p. 89). Hence, from a Vygotskian perspective, cognitive development is studied by examining the processes that one participates in when engaged in shared endeavors and how this engagement influences engagement in other activities. Development occurs as children learn general concepts and principles that can be applied to new tasks and problems; whereas from a Piagetian perspective, learning is constrained by development.

Vygotksy was a prolific writer; he advanced a vast number of ideas in his brief life as a scholar (he died when he was but 37), some of which are appropriately characterized as underspecified and emergent. One of the most frequently criticized facets of Vygotksy's theory is its model of internalization. For example, Cobb and Yackel (1996) have argued that this aspect of Vygotskian theory constitutes a transmission model in which "students inherit the cultural meanings that constitute their intellectual bequest from prior generations" (p. 186). There is an alternative model, the *participation model of cultural development* (Lave and Wenger, 1991; Rogoff, 1990), which seems useful to overcoming dualisms, such as the society and the individual. The participation model represents development as the transformation of individual participation in sociocultural activity. Transformation (rather than internalization) occurs as participants in the activity assume increasing responsibility for the activity; in essence, redefining membership in a community of practice, and, in fact, changing the sociocultural practice itself. These ideas are elaborated on below.

THE CONCEPT OF GUIDED PARTICIPATION

The concept of guided participation highlights that cognitive development occurs in a social context while extending sociocultural theory beyond language-based dialogue. Importantly, guided participation builds on and extends Vygotsky's notion of ZPD. Rogoff (1990) writes, "Children's cognitive development is an apprenticeship—it occurs through guided participation in social activity with companions who support and stretch children's understanding of and skill in using the tools of the culture" (p. vii). While this sounds very similar to ZPD, Rogoff explicitly states that guided participation focuses more centrally on the interrelatedness of children and caregiver interactions and the fact that the "guided" does not necessarily mean face to face. For example, a student working on a research report in isolation is still "guided" by the teacher, librarians, classmates, the publishing industry, and parents who help shape the writing of the research report as a cultural activity. Emphasis on tacit, distal, and non-verbal forms of communication stands in contrast to Vygotsky's emphasis on didactic dialogue. This helps broaden the lens of sociocultural theory beyond language-based interactions as the primary source of learning culture. Finally, socioculturally oriented research, generally, and research on guided participation, specifically, have played important roles in bridging research on in-school and out-of-school learning.

HOW SOCIOCULTURAL THEORY DIFFERS FROM CONSTRUCTIVIST THEORY

Similar to sociocultural theory, constructivism emerged as a theory of knowledge in response to behaviorism. Immanuel Kant (1724–1804) and Jean Piaget (1896–1980) are two theorists whose thinking and research significantly shaped constructivist theory. Kant (1951) significantly influenced Piaget's thinking when he proposed that it is the mind that provides the categories of knowing, while experience yields the content. Piaget (1955) argued that it is through the child's experiences manipulating and changing the world that the child acquires knowledge about relations within and between people and objects.

Both constructivism and sociocultural theory, when applied to learning, are concerned with the activities that children engage in to learn. However, constructivist theory suggests one should attend to the learning and mental representations of the individual while sociocultural theory is more concerned with the ways in which learning is an act of enculturation. Many learning situations attempt to accommodate both, for example, the mathematics teach-

ing of Ball (1993). Cobb (1994), in looking at Ball's dilemma of attending to students' individual knowledge (math as an active construction) and the traditions that have grown out of centuries of mathematics as a discipline (math learning as enculturation), notes that the dual presence of both sociocultural and constructivist theory can act as competing aims for teachers.

The lens of sociocultural theory is considerably wide when compared to constructivist theory. A sociocultural theorist, when interpreting a learning situation, might attend to the broader social system in which the learning is happening and will draw interpretations about an individual's thinking and development based on his or her participation in culturally organized activities. An account of learning and development through the lens of constructivist theory, in contrast, is concerned with the individual—and the ways in which sense making happens through the individual's accommodation of experience (Cobb, 1994).

Giyoo Hatano was most skillful at bridging sociocultural perspectives on learning with constructivist theories of learning that resulted in a "mixed" theory of conceptual knowledge that successfully accommodated both perspectives (Cole & Miyake, 2006). In an attempt to understand whether cognitive development proceeded along a predetermined innate set of principles, Hatano and Inagaki (1994) explored the long-held theory, first put forth by Piaget (1929) that children come to develop theories of biology rather late in the course of development. Through experimental work with Japanese schoolchildren, they demonstrated that theories of cognitive development must also account for the role that experience plays in advancing development, thus accommodating Vygotskian ideas about the social nature of learning.

THE EDUCATIONAL IMPLICATIONS OF SOCIOCULTURAL THEORY

Given the comprehensive nature of sociocultural theory, its educational implications for assessment, curriculum, and instruction are broad-ranging, and only a glimpse of them can be provided in this entry. For example, sociocultural theory—in particular the notion of zones of proximal development—would suggest that the goals of educational assessment should be to: (a) identify abilities that are in the process of developing, and (b) attempt to predict what the learner will do independently in the future. A line of inquiry consistent with these assessment goals is *dynamic assessment*. Dynamic assessment is a term used to characterize a number of distinct approaches that feature guided learning for the purpose of determining a learner's potential for change. In contrast to traditional and static procedures that focus on the products of assessment, dynamic assessment is concerned with the different ways in which individuals who earned the same score achieved that score. Furthermore, while traditional measures reveal only those abilities that are completely developed, dynamic measures are concerned with how well a learner performs when provided assistance. Initial inquiry into the design and use of dynamic assessment used domain-general types of problem-solving tasks (e.g., Campione & Brown, 1984; Feuerstein, 1980). These studies suggested that dynamic assessment measures did indeed reveal a different picture of competence than do static measures, which typically underestimate children's ability to learn in a domain in which they initially performed poorly.

More recent research suggests that the principles of dynamic assessment can also be applied within academic contexts. For example, Magnusson, Templin, and Boyle (1997) conducted research on the use of dynamic assessment to determine students' conceptions regarding the flow of electricity. They devised a context in which students could test out their conceptions and revise their thinking based upon the outcomes of their investigations. In this context, the researchers determined that students were, indeed, able to understand more about electrical behavior than had been determined on static measures used in previous research.

Instructional Implications. Informed by a sociocultural perspective, learning is thought to occur through interaction, negotiation, and collaboration. While these features are characteristic of "cooperative learning," what sets instruction that is informed by sociocultural theory apart is that there is also attention to the discourse, norms, and practices associated with particular discourse and practice communities. The goal of instruction is to support students to engage in the activities, talk, and use of tools in a manner that is consistent with the practices of the community to which students are being introduced (e.g., scientists, mathematicians, historians).

These tenets are consistent with inquiry-based approaches, in which teachers and students are co-inquirers, but with teachers mediating among students' personal meanings, the meanings emerging from the collective thinking and talk of the students, and the culturally established (scientific, mathematical, historical, literary) meanings of the wider society. Examples of research of this kind can be found in mathematics (Ball, 1993; Cobb, Wood, & Yackel, 1993; science (Engle & Conant, 2002; Magnusson & Palincsar, 2005; Wells & Chang-Wells, 1992), history (Bain, 2006), and literary studies (Smagorinsky & O'Donnell-Allen, 2000; Lee, 2007).

Sociocultural theory has also been called upon to advance instructional practice that might redress disparities in the current educational system. Forty-two percent of school-aged children in the United States struggle to advance beyond basic levels of reading comprehension.

Minority students and children living in poverty disproportionately perform in the lowest quartile on standardized measures of reading ability (Perie, Grigg, & Donahue, 2005). Given these distressing statistics, the increasing diversity in U.S. classrooms, and the proliferation of literacy technologies (e.g, multimedia and information and communications technologies), teachers have been challenged to reconsider the canonical approach to literacy instruction (e.g., Lee, 2007). A view of literacy instruction through the lens of sociocultural theory helps educators understand the situational specificity of literacy practice. From this perspective, educators would consider literacy as a tool for use in specific contexts; thus, children would be taught how to negotiate multiple literacies for use in multiple contexts.

Some researchers (Bhaba, 1994; Gutiérrez, Baquedano-Lopez, & Tejeda, 1999; Moje et al., 2004; Soja, 1996) have advanced the idea that educators work to develop a *third space* in which students' primary discourses (those used in the home, community, and informal social interactions) and students' secondary discourses (those endorsed in school and other formal institutions) intersect to form this third space, where primary and secondary discourses are merged. Were educators to be more attentive to the creation of these third spaces in school, greater attention would be paid to incorporating students' prior knowledge and experience, as well as current literacy practices in the school curriculum. Research conducted by Varellas and Pappas (2006) illustrates the productive instructional use of discourse in third spaces to promote science learning. Working in primary-grade classrooms in an urban school, teachers encouraged their students to draw upon: (a) their own explorations of scientific phenomena (such as the water cycle) in classroom, home, and community settings; (b) prior conversations, and (c) other books read in and out of school in the course of read-aloud sessions. Varellas and Pappas documented numerous examples of young children bringing their own funds of knowledge to the classroom setting, but they also documented how the teachers made facile use of these funds and promoted the children's learning of scientific language and concepts.

Use of New Technologies. With the proliferation of information and communication technologies in educational and everyday settings, scholars, working from a sociocultural perspective, are working to expand concepts, such as distributed cognition, to include not only people and artifacts, but also digital technologies. For example, Shaffer and Clinton (2006) introduce a new category of tool, which they call, *toolforthoughts* and, in doing so, challenge the idea that humans occupy a privileged position in psychological analyses. They argue that media, such as video games, word processors, and analytical tools create new skills and habits of mind, in addition to shifting the focus from reading and writing the printed word to multimodal literacy.

Recently, sociocultural theory has been taken into consideration in the design of online distance education technologies. Research on the social context of learning has provided ample evidence that traditional teacher-centered approaches would be inappropriate in an online setting. It is less clear, however, how to design online learning environments in which students feel connected to peers and professors in a virtual classroom community. Community building in asynchronous learning networks poses a particular challenge from the perspective of sociocultural theory because students are often not together physically or even virtually. Brigham Young University (BYU), a large provider of accredited online distance education in the United States, has adopted a model of online distance learning that is designed with sociocultural theory in mind. ProfessorsPlus™ carefully integrates social interaction among participants, substantive and interactive assistance from the course facilitators, and dynamic course content that is responsive to student learning (Teemant, 2005).

Research Applied to Institutional Settings. Research conducted from a sociocultural perspective has focused traditionally on the interactions of individuals and groups of individuals. However, research has also applied this lens to much larger institutional settings. For example, Cobb and McClain (2006) illustrate how efforts toward a mathematics reform effort need to be analyzed at a teacher, classroom, school, district, and indeed state and federal policy levels, to provide a more complete accounting of the reform effort.

Broad-scale use of assessments represent another approach to educational reform, and similarly, must also attend to the larger institutional settings in which the assessment instrument is positioned. Moss and her colleagues (Moss, Girard, & Haniford, 2006), in their work on validity theory, describe educational measurement as a cultural tool situated within a larger institutional, social, and national context. Applying the lens of sociocultural theory, they urge that interpretations of student performance on these tests must be made with attention to the local context, the purposes for which the test was written, and the larger policy context in which the test is situated.

BIBLIOGRAPHY

Bain, R. B. (2006). Rounding Up Unusual Suspects: Facing the Authority Hidden in the History Classroom. *Teachers College Record, 108*(10), 2080–2114.

Ball, D. L. (1993). With an eye on the mathematical horizon: Dilemmas of teaching elementary school mathematics. *Elementary School Journal, 93*, 373–397.

Bhaba, H. K. (1994). *The location of culture.* New York: Routledge.

Campione, J. C., & Brown, A. L. (1984). Learning ability and transfer propensity as sources of individual differences in intelligence. In P.H. Brooks, R. Sperber, & C. McCauley (Eds.) *Learning and Cognition in the Mentally Retarded* (pp. 137–150). Baltimore: University Park Press.

Chaiklin, S., & Lave, J. (1993). *Understanding practice: Perspectives on activity and context.* Cambridge, England: Cambridge University Press.

Cobb, P. (1994). Where Is the Mind? Constructivist and Sociocultural Perspectives on Mathematical Development, *Educational Researcher, 23,* 13–20.

Cobb, P., & McClain, K. (2006). The collective mediation of a high-stakes accountability program: Communities and networks of practice. *Mind, Culture, and Activity, 13*(2), 80–100.

Cobb P., Wood T., & Yackel, E. (1993). Discourse, mathematical thinking, and classroom practice. In E. A. Forman, N. Minich, & C. A. Stone (Eds.), *Contexts for Learning* (pp. 91–119). New York: Oxford University Press.

Cobb, P., & Yackel, E. (1996). Constructivism, emergent, and sociocultural perspectives in the context of developmental research. *Educational Psychology, 31,* 175–190.

Cole, M. (1996). *Cultural Psychology.* Cambridge, MA: Harvard University Press.

Cole, M., & Engeström, Y. (1994). Introduction. Mind, culture and activity. *An International Journal, 1*(4), 201.

Cole, M., & Miyake, N. (2006). Remembering Giyoo Hatano. *Journal of the Learning Sciences, 13*(3), 429–430.

Engle, R.A., & Conant, F.R. (2002). Guiding Principles for Fostering Productive Disciplinary Engagement: Explaining an Emergent Argument in a Community of Learners Classroom. *Cognition and Instruction, 20,* 399–484.

Feuerstein, R. (1980). *Instrumental Enrichment: An Intervention Program for Cognitive Modifiability.* Baltimore: University Park Press.

Gutiérrez, K., Baquedano-Lopez, P., and Tejeda, C. (1999). Rethinking diversity: Hybridity and hybrid language practices in the third space. *Mind, Culture, & Activity, 6*(4), 286–303.

Hatano, G., & Inagaki, K. (1994). Young children's naive theory of biology. *Cognition, 50,* 171–188.

Kant, I. (1951). *Critique of judgment* (J. H. Bernard, Trans.). New York: Hafner. (Original work published 1790)

Lave, J., & Wenger, E. (1991). *Situated learning: Legitimate peripheral participation.* Cambridge, England: Cambridge University Press.

Lee, C. D. (2007). *Culture, literacy, and learning: Blooming in the midst of the whirlwind.* New York: Teachers College Press.

Leontiev, A.N. (1981). *Problems of the development of mind.* Moscow: Progress Press.

Magnusson, S. J., & Palincsar, A S. (2005). Teaching to promote the development of scientific knowledge and reasoning about light at the elementary school level. In J. Bransford and S. Donovan (Eds.), *How students learn: History, mathematics, and science in the classroom* (pp. 421–474). Washington, DC: National Academies Press.

Magnusson, S. J., Templin, M., and Boyle, R. (1997). Documenting and promoting conceptual change toward scientific knowledge: Children's emerging understandings of electricity. *Journal of Learning Sciences, 6,* 91–142.

Moje, E. B., McIntosh-Ciechanowski, K., Kramer, K., Ellis, L., Carrillo, R., & Collazo, T. (2004). Working toward third space in content area literacy: An examination of everyday funds of knowledge and discourse. *Reading Research Quarterly, 39*(1), 38–71.

Moss, P. A., Girard, B. J., and Haniford, L. C. (2006) Validity in Educational Assessment. *Review of Research in Education, 30,* 109–162.

Newman, D., Griffin P., and Cole, M. (1989). *The construction zone: Working for cognitive change in schools.* Cambridge, England: Cambridge University Press.

Piaget, J. (1929). *The child's conception of the world.* New York: Harcourt, Brace Jovanovich.

Piaget, J. (1955). *The Child's Construction of Reality.* London: Routledge and Kegan Paul.

Rogoff, B. (1990). *Apprenticeship in thinking: Cognitive development in social context.* New York: Oxford University Press.

Shaffer, D. W., & Clinton, K. A. (2006). Toolforthoughts: Reexamining thinking in the digital age. *Mind, Culture, and Activity, 13*(4), pp. 283–300.

Smagorinsky, P., & O'Donnell-Allen, C. (2000). Idiocultural diversity in small groups: The role of the relational framework in collaborative learning. In C.D. Lee & P. Smagorinsky (Eds.), *Vygotskian perspectives on literacy research: Constructing meaning through collaborative inquiry* (pp. 165–190). New York: Cambridge University Press.

Soja, E.W. (1996) *Thirdspace: Journeys to Los Angeles and other real-and-imagined places.* Oxford: Blackwell.

Teemant, A. (2005). Evaluating socio-cultural pedagogy in a distance teacher education program. *Teacher Education Quarterly, 32*(3) 49–62.

Tudge, J., & Scrimsher, S. (2003). Lev S. Vygotsky on education: A cultural-historical, interpersonal, and individual approach to development. In B. J. Zimmerman & D. H. Schunk (Eds.), *Educational psychology: A century of contributions* (pp. 207–228) Mahwah, NJ: Erlbaum.

Varellas, M., & Pappas, C. (2006). Intertextuality in read-alouds of integrated science-literacy units in urban primary classrooms: Opportunities for the development of thought and language. *Cognition and Instruction, 24* (2), 211–259.

Vygotsky, L. S. (1997). *The collected works of L. S. Vygotsky, Vol. 4: The history of the development of higher mental functions* (R. W. Rieber, Vol. Ed; M. J. Hall, Trans.). New York: Plenum Press. (Original work published 1941)

Vygotsky, L. S. (1978). *Mind in Society: The Development of Higher Psychological Processes.* M. Cole, V. John-Steiner, S. Scribner, & E. Souberman (Eds.). Cambridge, MA: Harvard University Press.

Vygotsky, L. S. (1979). Consciousness as a problem in the psychology of behaviour. *Soviet Psychology, 17*(4), 3–35.

Wells, G., & Chang-Wells, G. L. (1992). *Constructing knowledge together.* Portsmouth, NH: Heinemann.

Wertsch J. (1991). *Voices of the mind: A Sociocultural approach to mediated action.* Cambridge, MA: Harvard University Press.

Wertsch, J. V., & Bivens, J. A. (1992). The social origins of individual mental functioning: Alternatives and perspectives. *Quarterly Newsletter of the Laboratoryof Comparative Human Cognition, 14*(2), 35–44.

Sarah E. Scott
Annemarie Sullivan Palincsar

SOCIOECONOMIC STATUS

Socioeconomic status (SES) is the measure of the influence that the social environment has on individuals, families, communities, and schools. In many ways SES is related to the concept of social class. Both have financial stability as a foundation for classification. Both are important to a child's optimal development and an adult's satisfaction with life. However, the concept of social class is considered to be continuous throughout one's lifetime and from one generation to the next. The SES classifications are established in an effort to find the means of identifying and changing inequalities. In addition, social class has economic differences as a primary influence. The concept of SES considers other influences such as the chance for social or economic advancement, influence on policy, availability of resources, and prestige of the primary occupation.

DEFINITION

The definitions of SES emphasize that, as a construct, (1) it is conditional, (2) it is imposed on people, (3) it is used for comparisons, (4) it is based on economics, opportunity, and means of influence. Santrock (2004) defines it as "the grouping of people with similar occupational, educational, and economic characteristics" (p. 583). Woolfolk (2007) calls SES "the relative standing in society based on income, power, background and prestige" (p. 165). Santrock (2004) adds that an important qualification is "the ability to control resources and participate in society's rewards" (p. 583). Woolfolk (2007) also notes that every researcher will define it differently based on the nature of the study. In most discussions, there are three levels of SES: low, moderate, and high. Because most problems associated with low SES are related to poverty, sometimes poverty level is used as a similar concept to low SES. Race may also be considered a factor because Blacks and Latinos are disproportionately represented in the low SES.

MEASUREMENT OF SES AND VARIOUS COMPONENTS

The factors that are usually considered in establishing SES are income, occupation, education, neighborhood, and political power. For each of these five factors, the consideration of how fixed each one is also contributes to SES. For example, if a family is considered low income because one of the parents is in school to eventually get a better job, then the family is not really in the same SES as their neighbors who have little hope of a better job.

Individuals' SES is usually determined by the SES of their family. The SES of the family is calculated based on the measure of the five factors noted above. How well can the family members meet their financial responsibilities?

What prestige is associated with the occupation of the head of the household? What level of education have the parents achieved? What is the safety and upkeep of the neighborhood in which the family lives? What hope do the family members reasonably have to influence the government and community policies that affect their lives? A school's SES is determined by the neighborhood in which it is located and by the SES of the families whose children attend the school.

SCHOOL OUTCOMES
AND PERSONAL SES

The negative effects of low SES can interfere with a child's cognitive development. Among families of low SES, there are more occurrences of lead poisoning, fetal alcohol syndrome, and premature birth. Lead poisoning, caused by the child ingesting bits of the lead paint found in old buildings, produces neurological disorders. Children born to women who drink alcohol during pregnancy develop fetal alcohol syndrome, a condition that includes mental retardation. The child from a premature birth experiences a diminished brain development. All of these problems lead to language delays, attention problems, and learning disabilities.

Observed family differences based on SES include those constituting parenting styles. Comparing high SES parents to low SES parents, the high SES parents tend to be less directive and more conversational in their communication with their children. Low SES parents are more likely than the high SES parents to expect obedience without question from their children. Low SES parents encourage their children to conform to society's expectations, while the high SES parents encourage creativity and exploration. These differences foster self-confidence in the high SES students and an uncertainty about life in the low SES students.

Young people in the low SES neighborhood report as many pleasant experiences as the young people in high SES neighborhoods. However, children growing up in a low SES neighborhood are more likely to experience distressing events than their counterparts in the higher SES neighborhoods. These include physical punishment in the home, domestic violence in their home building, and serious crime in the neighborhood. Such demoralizing experiences lead to higher rates of depression, low self-esteem, and juvenile delinquency among children from the low SES neighborhoods.

Some children are resilient and able to develop normally under difficult conditions. However, for most children long-term problems are associated with the amount of time living in poverty.

RELATIONS BETWEEN SCHOOL
OUTCOMES AND SCHOOL SES

Schools in low SES neighborhoods tend to have fewer resources. Their students, beginning school with little preparation, require an educational system with a more skillful and focused approach. However, the teachers in the low SES schools are often less paid and less trained than the teachers in the higher SES schools. The results are low achievement rates for the students. Few high school students in the low SES schools plan to attend college; therefore, the graduation rate is low.

One of the big problems in school for children of low SES is the self-fulfilling prophecy of failure. If the children do not dress well or are too shy, the teacher may not feel they are very bright. The teacher will call on these students less often and not regularly engage them in class discussion. These students are then left feeling as if they do not belong in school and as if they do not have hope of doing well. If learned helplessness builds in the students' self-concept, they will look for experiences that confirm this self-concept. This process is especially strong if the students are from an ethnic minority and face discrimination.

In mixed SES schools, the practice of tracking can negatively affect the low SES student. Tracking involves assigning students to classes in one grade based on their achievement level in the previous year. There are different expectations for the hierarchy of tracks; the high tracks set higher academic priorities and offer more encouragement than the lower tracks. Tracking disproportionately assigns low-SES students to low-achieving classrooms. Thus, the students who need the most stimulation and motivation are given the least. The original disparity between the achievement levels of the high-track students and the low-track students widens as tracking continues.

The schools in low SES neighborhoods suffer from the lack of support from the students' homes. The home environment contributes substantially to the development of academic skills. Enriching experiences in the home can contribute up to one-half of the measured achievement in verbal skills, reading, and mathematics. Three main factors distinguish the home environment of the high SES student from that of the low SES student. The high SES student is likely to do more reading, more skill building, and less television watching in the home than the low SES student, even during summer vacation (Woolfolk, 2007).

These factors are most closely associated with the educational level of the mother. The mother in the high SES family can be expected to have graduated from college. The college-graduate mother recognizes the need for home enrichment; the low-education mother likely does not. However, these problems can be resolved if the low SES schools help the parents recognize ways to improve the home learning environment, such as turning off the television. As a passive activity, watching television discourages critical thinking. Parents have to recognize that television is an educational medium that does not always present accurate information.

There are examples of low-SES students keeping up with (or even surpassing) the higher SES students. There are two serious conditions that have to be considered regarding these cases. Often, the achievement is only seen during the school year. During the summer the low SES student is likely to fall behind. The other condition occurs when the achievement level is continuous. There is usually one or both parents making the necessary sacrifices to ensure that the home life provides enrichment for (and prevents interference with) the child's academic achievement.

The detrimental effects of low SES on early childhood can be ameliorated by quality preschool programs. One such program, Head Start, has existed since the 1960s. Its goal is to give children of low SES families a chance to be better prepared for school. Similar programs include the High/Scope Preschool in Michigan, Abecedarian Intervention program in North Carolina, and Child-Parent Center in Illinois. These programs have been shown to have longitudinal effects on the cognitive development of the children attending. The results are higher reading and math scores than other children of low SES families. Furthermore, the programs' attendees are more likely to finish high school and less likely to commit a crime than their peers.

SEE ALSO *At-risk Students.*

BIBLIOGRAPHY
Santrock J. W. (2004). *Child development* (10th ed.). New York: McGraw-Hill.
Woolfolk, A. (2007). *Educational psychology* (10th ed.). Boston: Allyn and Bacon.

Ray Brogan

SOCIOMETRIC ASSESSMENT

Sociometric assessment can be defined as the measurement of interpersonal relationships in a social group. Sociometric measurement or assessment methods provide information about an individual's social competence and standing within a peer group. School-based sociometric assessment often focuses on a child's relationships with regard to social popularity, peer acceptance, peer rejection, and reputation. Some sociometric assessment methods derive information on social relationships by assessing children's positive and negative social perceptions of one another, whereas other methods involve adult (teacher, parent) and self perceptions of children's social competencies or standing. Sociometric assessment methods were introduced in the 1930s and advanced in the journal Sociometry. In the 1950s, several books were published on the topic and sociometric measurements often were part of research and school-based assessments of social relationships. The use of classic sociometric procedures declined in the following decades, due to the advancement of social behavior rating scales and ethical concerns regarding the use of peer nomination methods with children.

SOCIOMETRIC ASSESSMENT METHODS

There are a variety of what can be referred to as classic sociometric assessment techniques derived from the work of the 1930s, including peer nomination, peer rankings, and sociometric rankings. In the peer nomination technique, children in a social group or school classroom anonymously identify social preferences for their classmates. For example, children may be asked to provide a list of the three classmates with whom they would most like to play and the three with whom they would least like to play. Another peer nomination technique (see Figure 1) is to provide a list of the names of the children in a classroom along with social acceptance items (e.g., "Who do you like to play with?" "Who is most likely to be alone during recess?" "Who gets into trouble the most?"). The children are asked to identify perhaps one to three classmates who they perceive best fit the item description.

An alternative peer nomination method for early readers is to use photographs with an adult reading the items aloud in either an individual or classroom setting while the children provide a nomination for a child, perhaps by assigning a smiling or frowning face to the photograph that applies. Another variation of the peer nomination method is the class play. In this procedure children cast their peers in positive and negative roles in an imaginary play. The class play has the potential advantage of being more acceptable in school settings because the positive and negative role assignments may be perceived as a more discreet method for identifying children's social standing. For each of the methods described, the nominations may be summed for each child and the results are used to identify those children who are perceived as most socially positive or negative by their peers.

Two other sociometric techniques can be described as peer ratings and sociometric rankings. Peer ratings are conducted by providing a list of children's names in the social group or classroom along with a rating for social acceptance items such as "The most fun to play with,"

Example of a peer nomination technique

Place an X under the name of one classmate in answer to each question below	Alma	Bart	Carl	Dave	Edna	Fayd	Gigi	Holz	Inez
Who would you most like to play with?		X							
Who would you least like to play with?							X		
Who gets into trouble the most?				X					
Who is most likely to be alone during recess?		X							
Who gets along best with others?	X								

Figure 1 ILLUSTRATION BY GGS INFORMATION SERVICES. CENGAGE LEARNING, GALE.

"The least fun to play with," and "Has the most friends." The rating methods that are used may vary, typically ranging from three- to five-point Likert-type responses (e.g., Agree, Neutral, Disagree). In contrast to peer nominations and ratings, sociometric rankings are completed by an adult, most often the classroom teacher who has had the opportunity to observe the children in multiple social settings such as the classroom, playground, and cafeteria. In this method, teachers rank the children on social dimensions similar to those provided by peers.

Each of these sociometric assessment methods has strengths and limitations. Researchers have found that each method appears to be valid for identifying children's social standing. Peer ratings and adult rankings appear to provide the most reliable or stable measurements and, as such, may be more useful than the peer nomination method. A major issue that arises with each of these methods is the concept of social validity, which refers to the acceptance, usefulness, and potential harm of an assessment procedure. The applications of sociometric assessment methods have resulted in controversy and ethical concerns regarding their use. These concerns center on the use of negative peer nominations and the possibility that children will compare responses which may result in negative social and emotional consequences for children who are not positively perceived by their peers. These concerns contributed to the decline in the acceptance and use of sociometric assessment methods, particularly in school settings. However, researchers have found no strong evidence that negative consequences occur for either the children who are rating or those being rated; therefore, sociometric assessment continues to be used as a research tool for understanding children's social relationships.

RELATED ASSESSMENT METHODS

Although the term sociometrics has been most often applied to the assessment methods described above, in a broader context the term can be applied to related assessment measures of social functioning. These methods tend to focus on children's social competencies and skills rather than measuring only social standing or peer acceptance. Because these methods are more often used in practical applications in school settings, they are briefly described here.

Social Behavior Rating Scales. Social behavior rating scales represent one of the most frequently used measures of social competence. These rating scales are designed for gathering data on the frequency of occurrence of specific skills or behaviors. Some rating scales focus on social problem behaviors and others are designed specifically to assess children's social skills. For example, a social skills rating scale may contain items such as "Appropriately invites friends to play" or "Controls temper in conflicts with adults" which are rated on a frequency scale (e.g., Never, Sometimes, Always). Depending on the measure, ratings can be gathered from parents or parent surrogates, teachers, and when appropriate from the children themselves. Rating scales in essence provide summary observations of a child's social behavior. Gathering data from these multiple sources can facilitate understanding different perspectives regarding a child's social skills in home and school settings. Well designed social skills rating scales have been found to be reliable and valid measures.

Observation Methods. Observation methods are used to gather information about a child's social skills in natural settings, such as in the classroom, in the cafeteria, and on the playground. Observation methods can be highly structured wherein defined behaviors are measured for frequency of occurrence or measured for occurrence during specified time periods or intervals. For example, a child's play behavior may be observed during recess by a school psychologist who records every 30 seconds whether the child was playing alone or with others. Other observation methods are less structured and rely on a narrative approach for describing a child's social interactions. Observation methods often include focus on the environmental variables that may increase or decrease a child's social skills, such as the reactions of peers and adults to a child's attempts at initiating conversation. Observations also can be conducted in what is known as analogue assessment, which involves having a child role-play social scenarios and observing the child's performance. Whereas rating scales provide summary measures that rely on some level of recall, observations have the advantage of directly sampling a child's behavior in actual social contexts or settings, thereby increasing the validity of the assessment. The limitations of observations are that multiple observers are required to ensure reliable assessment (interobserver agreement) and observations are more time intensive. Thus in applied settings they may provide limited information due to time constraints.

Interview Methods. Interview methods are used to gather information about a child's social skill strengths and weaknesses, and to aid in the identification of specific skill deficits for intervention. Interviews can be used separately with children, parents or parent surrogates, and teachers, or conjointly with multiple sources. Interviews can be structured, with a focus on the identification and treatment of specific social skills, or interviews can be less structured, with a greater focus on feelings and perceptions about a child's social skills. As with rating scales, interview data can be viewed as summary recall information which should be validated with direct observation.

The assessment methods described often are combined in a comprehensive social skills assessment that may include rating scales, observations, and interviews. Using multiple methods of assessment is considered best practice because the use of more than one assessment method increases the likelihood that the behaviors which are targeted for classification or intervention are valid, and that specific social skills strengths and deficits are clearly defined. It is also important to use multiple assessment methods to monitor a child's progress and to assess the effectiveness of an intervention.

IMPLICATIONS OF SOCIOMETRIC ASSESSMENT FOR EDUCATIONAL PRACTICE

In educational practice, sociometric assessment most often is used to determine eligibility for special education and for intervention for adaptive behaviors or socio-emotional problems. Children identified with special education needs, such as learning problems, mental retardation, attention deficit disorders, and autism spectrum disorders, including Asperger's syndrome, may benefit from assessment and intervention toward enhancing their social skills. In the general education population, children may benefit who are shy, rejected, or engage in bullying or aggressive

behaviors or who simply have limited social skills. Most of the classic sociometric assessment methods are not used in educational practice, partly due to issues with acceptability. Furthermore, although these methods have been found to be useful in research, they may not be viewed as being useful in school settings because they do not lead to specific classification for special education nor do they provide specific data that can directly assist in the intervention process. Related sociometric assessment measures such as rating scales often are used because these methods provide more specific information that can be linked to classification and intervention.

One classic sociometric assessment method that has been shown to be effective in educational practice is sociometric rankings. In this procedure teachers rank the children in their classroom who the teacher views as having social behavior problems, sometimes in relation to internalizing and externalizing problem behaviors. (Internalizing behaviors refer to problems such as depression, anxiety, and social withdrawal; externalizing behaviors refer to problems such as aggression, conduct problems, and hyperactivity.) The use of teacher rankings serves as an initial screening device for identifying children who may need additional assessment and intervention. Once identified, the children are screened further with a rating scale or related method to determine the extent of their social difficulties. Those children who are found to have problems are then referred for more assessment intended to specify their problems and provide an intervention, such as social skills training. Researchers have found this method of assessment, known as a multiple gating procedure, to be acceptable and effective in applied settings.

Assessing and understanding children's and adolescents' peer relations is important in educational settings for several reasons. From a developmental standpoint, it is important to understand how children develop social skills as they mature. Researchers have found that sociometric assessment can be useful in identifying children's social standing and predicting positive or negative social outcomes for children. The establishment of friendships and positive social interactions are important for children's social development and for interacting in the social world, including the school setting. Children with poor peer and adult relationships often experience negative social and emotional consequences that can continue throughout adulthood. These negative consequences can include lower academic achievement, higher rates of school dropout, depression, anxiety, low self-esteem, poor self-concept, social withdrawal, fewer positive employment opportunities, and anti-social behaviors such as aggression and criminality. Researchers have estimated that at least 10%, or one in ten children experience consistent negative peer relationships. Therefore, a large number of children with inadequate social relationships may be at-risk for developing behavioral and emotional difficulties. Children with poor or limited social skills also are at risk for becoming victims of bullying and other aggressive behaviors. Children with disabilities often have social skills deficits and negative peer perceptions that put them at heightened risk.

Given these potentially negative outcomes, social skills assessment is important in educational settings. In research, the identification of the development of social standing and social skills can facilitate understanding the behaviors of socially successful and unsuccessful children. In research settings, both classic sociometric assessment and social skills assessment methods are used to achieve better understanding of social types and behaviors. These behaviors can in turn be used to understand children's and adolescents' social skill deficits and can aid in the design and study of social skills assessments and interventions.

SEE ALSO *Classroom Assessment; Social Skills.*

BIBLIOGRAPHY

Elliott, S. N., & Busse, R. T. (1991). Social skills assessment and intervention with children and adolescents. *School Psychology International, 12,* 63–83.

Gresham, F. M. (2002). Best practices in social skills training. In A. Thomas & J. Grimes (Eds.), *Best practices in school psychology IV* (pp. 1029–1040). Bethesda, MD: National Association of School Psychologists.

McConnell, S. R., & Odom, S. L. (1986). Sociometrics: Peer-referenced measures and the assessment of social competence. In P. Strain, M. J. Guralnick, & H. M. Walker (Eds.), *Children's social behavior: Development, assessment, and modification* (pp. 215–284). New York: Academic Press.

Merrell, K. W. (1999). *Behavioral, social, and emotional assessment of children and adolescents.* Mahwah, NJ: Erlbaum.

Sheridan, S. M., & Walker, D. (1999). Social skills in context: Considerations for assessment, intervention, and generalization. In C. R. Reynolds & T. B. Gutkin (Eds.), *The handbook of school psychology* (3rd ed., pp. 686–708). New York: Wiley.

R. T. Busse

SOCIOMETRIC STATUS

SEE *Peer Relationships: Sociometric Status.*

SPEARMAN, CHARLES EDWARD
1863–1945

Charles Edward Spearman was born in London on September 10, 1863, into a respected family. As a student, he demonstrated a superb mastery of mathematics and

Charles Spearman ARCHIVES OF THE HISTORY OF AMERICAN PSYCHOLOGY. THE UNIVERSITY OF AKRON.

science but held a "secret devotion to philosophy" that would last his entire life (1930, p. 299). Following graduation from college, Spearman secured a commission as an officer in the Royal Engineers of the British Army. Spearman was assigned to a post in Burma, where he served honorably and rose to the rank of major. During this time, his continued interests in philosophy led to the belief that many of the debated issues of philosophy could be resolved successfully by applying the empiricism of psychology. So at the age of 34, Spearman abandoned a successful military career and began study in the Leipzig laboratory of Wilhelm Wundt. Despite his obvious military success, Spearman later portrayed his 14 years of service as "the greatest mistake of my life, [based on] the youthful delusion that life is long." (1930, p. 300).

Although Wundt is considered a founding father of psychology, Spearman's greatest influence came from Sir Frances Galton (1822–1911). After reading Galton's *Hereditary Genius* (1869) and *Inquiries into Human Faculty and Its Development* (1883), Spearman seized on two principles that guided the remainder of his life's work. First, individual differences in sensory, motor, and cognitive abilities may be measured precisely using standardized techniques. Second, there exists a biologically based general mental ability that enters into every kind of mental activity.

At his own personal expense and without the support of Wundt, Spearman conducted a study to test the Galtonian notion that individual differences in sensory discrimination and modality were positively correlated with varied measures of cognitive ability. As the logic goes, positive correlations among the variables would demonstrate the existence of a common source of variation (i.e., the presence of a general ability). To accomplish his aim, Spearman invented the statistical technique of factor analysis to analyze the matrix of correlations among variables. Spearman published this study as a 1904 article titled "'General Intelligence', Objectively Determined and Measured." The article garnered considerable scientific interest, both for its surprising support of Galton's theory of general ability, as well as its innovative statistical methodology. Following further military service in the Boer War, Spearman finally completed his doctoral study in experimental psychology in 1906. By that time he was 42 years of age but with "more distinguished scientific accomplishments to his credit than probably any other new Ph.D. in the history of psychology" (Jensen, 2000, p. 4).

Spearman joined the Department of Experimental Psychology at University College, London, where he was promoted to full professor in 1911. He continued his research into general ability and expanded investigations to include group differences, psychometrics, eugenics, and learning. Spearman retired in 1931, but continued to play an active role in field of educational psychology. After retirement, Spearman taught in North America at Columbia University, where his students included David Wechsler and Raymond B. Cattell.

During his esteemed career, Spearman received numerous honors, including Fellow of the Royal Society and membership in the United States National Academy of Science. In 1945, with failing health at age 82, Spearman reportedly committed suicide by jumping from a window of the London University Hospital, where he was a patient.

Spearman is credited with offering the first truly tenable psychometric definition of intelligence and is, therefore, considered to be the founding father of classical test theory. This approach, which considers an individual's observed score as consisting of a *true score* plus *error score* has been particularly influential in test development and conceptions of reliability. Spearman's best known contribution to statistics is the rank-order correlation coefficient, a nonparametric index of association between two ordinal variables. Additionally, Spearman's development of factor analysis is the first direct application of latent trait theory, which advances that individual differences in observed test scores serve as reflections of some smaller number of hypothetical, or latent, variables. This technique is routinely used to determine the construct validity of tests. Undoubtedly, Spearman's most important discovery was the identification of a general factor of mental ability (i.e., Spearman's *g* or *g factor*). A century of research finds that Spearman's *g* is the largest singular source of individual differences in mental ability and learning, regularly accounting for approximately half of the variance in test scores (Jensen, 1998).

Since its explication in Spearman's seminal 1904 article, the *g factor* has garnered considerable support and controversy. The continued interest and influence of Spearman's research can be traced to a number of developments, including the spread of universal public education, an increased range in the intelligence and scholastic achievement of the school population, and the rising cognitive demands of a complex modern society and workplace. In the early 2000s, one of the liveliest and most productive lines of research in cognitive neuroscience and biogenetics is the search for the physiological/genetic provenance of Spearman's *g* (Brand, 1996; Meisenberg, 2005). As testimony to his originality and continued influence, Spearman is one of the few psychologists showing an increasing rate of citations since his death.

SEE ALSO *Intelligence: An Overview.*

BIBLIOGRAPHY

WORKS BY

Spearman, C. (1904). 'General intelligence', objectively determined and measured. *American Journal of Psychology, 15,* 201–293.

Spearman, C. (1923). *The nature of intelligence and the principles of cognition.* London: Macmillan.

Spearman, C. (1927). *The abilities of man: Their nature and measurement.* London: Macmillan.

Spearman, C. (1930). Autobiography. In C. Murchison (Ed.), *A history of psychology in autobiography* (Vol. 1, pp. 199–333). Worcester, MA: Clark University Press.

Spearman, C., & Jones, L. W. (1950). *Human ability.* London: Macmillan.

WORKS ABOUT

Brand, C, R, (1996). *The g factor: General intelligence and its implications.* New York: Wiley & Sons.

Jensen, A. R. (1998). *The g factor: The science of mental ability.* Westport, CT: Praeger.

Jensen, A. R. (2000, March). *Portraits of the pioneers: Charles Spearman. Newsletter of the Galton Institute, 36,* 3–7.

Meisenberg, G. (2005). Genes for intelligence. A review of recent progress. *Mankind Quarterly, 36,* 139–164.

Harrison Kane
Ayesha Khurshid

SPECIAL EDUCATION

As defined by U. S. law, special education is: "specially designed instruction, at no cost to parents, to meet the unique needs of a child with a disability, including instruction conducted in the classroom, in the home, in hospitals and institutions, and other settings; and instruction in physical education" (Individuals with Disabilities Education Improvement Act, 2004) 20 U.S.C. § 1401 (29). The law also stipulates that students with disabilities are entitled to related services, as needed. Related services include such services as transportation, occupational and physical therapy, and psychological, counseling, speech/language pathology, audiology, and interpreting services.

SPECIALLY DESIGNED INSTRUCTION

For most students with disabilities, "specially designed instruction" is defined as involving intensive, relentless, structured, appropriately paced instruction, in small groups in which each student's progress is monitored frequently (Kauffman & Hallahan, 2005). According to Kauffman and Hallahan, all of these characteristics should usually be more evident in special education than is typically the case in general education. Intensive instruction translates into more teacher instructional time and more opportunities for students to respond to the instruction and more time to practice and review what they have learned. Relentless instruction involves repeating this sequence or parts of this sequence more often than is typically done with non-disabled students. Structured instruction refers to teachers being more directive, instituting more explicit rules, and providing more frequent consequences for appropriate or inappropriate behavior. The pace of the instruction in special education is tailored more to the needs of the student and is often slower, with teachers waiting for a longer period of time for a response after querying the student. Instruction in small groups facilitates the intensity, relentlessness, structured nature, and the individualized pace of instruction. Moreover, specially designed instruction means that a student's progress in learning is monitored frequently, often several times per week.

In addition to these general principles of instruction that apply to most students with disabilities, there are some that apply to specific categories of special education students. For example, for students with blindness or low vision, the "specialized designed instruction" may take the form of reading materials in Braille, large print, or audio recordings, and instruction in the use of a cane for mobility. For students who are deaf or hard of hearing, the instruction may involve sign language or hearing aids. Additionally, for students with emotional or behavioral disorders, instruction may require highly structured classrooms and teaching routines and use of functional behav-

ioral assessment (FBA) and positive behavioral intervention and support (PBIS). FBA involves determining what factors help to set off and maintain inappropriate behaviors. And PBIS emphasizes "rewarding positive behavior, to make problem behavior less effective, efficient, and relevant and to make desired behavior more functional" (Hallahan, Kauffman, & Pullen, 2009, pp. 163–164).

SPECIAL EDUCATION CATEGORIES

Students served by special education fall into 13 disability categories. In order of prevalence they are learning disabilities, speech or language impairments, mental retardation, emotional disturbance, other health impairments (including attention deficit hyperactivity disorder), multiple disabilities, autism, orthopedic impairments, hearing impairments, developmental delay, visual impairments, traumatic brain injury, deaf-blindness. The federal government has provided definitions for each of these categories in order to give guidance to schools in finding students eligible for special education services.

Learning Disabilities. Students with learning disabilities are by far the largest category of special education, comprising between 5 and 6 percent of the school-age population and nearly half of all students identified for special education services. Although its historical roots can be traced back to work done in the 1800s in Europe (Hallahan & Mercer, 2002), learning disabilities as a condition and as a discipline was not formally recognized until the 1960s and 1970s. A major reason for the eventual recognition of learning disabilities as a condition warranting special education services came from parents and professionals who pointed out that there were many students who, although not scoring low enough on intelligence tests to qualify as mentally retarded, were nevertheless still displaying learning problems, especially in reading.

The federal definition of learning disabilities is as follows:

General—The term "specific learning disability" means a disorder in one or more of the basic psychological processes involved in understanding or in using language, spoken or written, which disorder may manifest itself in an imperfect ability to listen, think, speak, read, write, spell, or do mathematical calculations.).

Disorders Included—Such term includes such conditions as perceptual disabilities, brain injury, minimal brain dysfunction, dyslexia, and developmental aphasia.).

Disorders Not Included—Such term does not include a learning problem that is primarily the result of visual, hearing, or motor disabilities, of mental retardation, of emotional disturbance, or of environmental, cultural, or economic disadvantage (Individuals with Disabilities Education Act Amendments of 1997, Sec. 602(26), p. 13.).

Speech or Language Impairments. Speech impairments include disorders of articulation, fluency, and/or voice (American Speech-Language-Hearing Association, 1993). Articulation disorders often result from neuromuscular abnormalities resulting in omission, substitution, or distortion of speech sounds. Fluency refers to being able to produce smooth speech flow. Disorders of voice include such characteristics as abnormal pitch, loudness, or resonance.

Language impairments can include problems in production and/or comprehension that violate the rules of language pertaining to phonology, morphology, syntax, semantics, or pragmatics. Phonology rules govern how speech sounds are sequenced. Morphology refers to parts of words that indicate such factors as verb tense and plurals. Syntax involves word order that reflects proper grammar. Semantics refers to the meanings of words and sentences, and pragmatics involves using language for social purposes.

Mental Retardation. Most professionals use the definition of mental retardation provided by the American Association on Intellectual and Developmental Disabilities (AAIDD): "Mental retardation is a disability characterized by significant limitations both in intellectual functioning and in adaptive behavior as expressed in conceptual, social, and practical adaptive skills. This disability originates before age 18" (AAMR Ad Hoc Committee on Terminology and Classification, 2002, p. 1). The AAIDD considers the following five points as crucial to understanding the context of the definition:

1. Limitations in present functioning must be considered within the context of community environments typical of the individual's age peers and culture.

2. Valid assessment considers cultural and linguistic diversity as well as differences in communication, sensory, motor, and behavioral factors.

3. Within an individual, limitations often coexist with strengths.

4. An important purpose of describing limitations is to develop a profile of needed supports.

5. With appropriate personalized supports over a sustained period, the life functioning of the person with mental retardation (intellectual disability) generally will improve. (AAMR Ad Hoc Committee on Terminology and Classification, 2002, p. 1).

Emotional Disturbance. There is considerable controversy concerning the definition of emotional disturbance, which stems from the relatively subjective nature of the condition. In fact, even though the federal government uses the term emotionally disturbed, there are many professionals who prefer the term *emotional or behavioral disorders* because it more accurately conveys the socialization problems these students exhibit.

With respect to definition, many authorities agree on the following three features of emotional or behavioral disorders:

Behavior that goes to an extreme—that is not just slightly different from the usual;

A problem that is chronic—one that does not quickly disappear; and

Behavior that is unacceptable because of social or cultural expectations (Hallahan et al., 2009).

Other Health Impairments. According to the federal definition, other health impairments (OHIs) are medical conditions, such as asthma, diabetes, epilepsy, sickle cell anemia, which impair to such a degree that they adversely affect a student's educational performance. The key to the definition is that the condition must interfere with the student's educational performance. For example, not all students who have asthma have it to such a degree that it affects their ability to function in school.

Students with attention deficit hyperactivity disorder (ADHD) are also included in the federal government's category of OHI. The American Psychiatric Association (2000) recognizes three types of ADHD: (1) ADHD, predominantly inattentive type; (2) ADHD, predominantly hyperactive-impulsive type; (3) ADHD, combined type.

The reason behind the decision to place ADHD in the OHI category is an interesting lesson in disability advocacy and politics (Hallahan et al., 2009). In the late 1980s and early 1990s, parents of affected children lobbied intensely for ADHD as a new category of special education. Many surmise that the U. S. Department of Education was worried about creating yet another category, especially one that could potentially attract large numbers of students. Therefore, in 1991, they came up with the compromise of stating that students with ADHD could receive special education services if they were identified as having OHI, i.e., had a condition that interfered with their educational performance, thus leaving open the possibility that some students with ADHD would not meet the criteria of OHI because their educational performance was not adversely affected.

Multiple Disabilities. The multiple disabilities category consists of students who have two or more disabilities, "the combination of which causes such severe educational problems that they cannot be accommodated in special education programs solely for one of the impairments" (34 CFR, Sec. 300 [b][6]).

Autism. Many authorities in the early 2000s consider autism to be one of several similar conditions that fall on a spectrum, hence the term *autism spectrum disorders*. The conditions on the spectrum share impairments in three areas: (1) communication skills, (2) social interactions, and (3) repetitive and stereotyped patterns of behavior (Strock, 2004). Classic autism and Asperger syndrome are the most common conditions. Whereas students with autism have relatively severe deficits in all three areas plus severe cognitive deficits, those with Asperger syndrome generally have less severe deficits in all three areas, with their major problem lying in the area of social interactions and some having very high intelligence.

Orthopedic Impairments. Orthopedic impairments include physical disabilities of the muscles and/or bones that negatively affect school learning. Two examples are muscular dystrophy (a hereditary condition resulting in muscle fiber degeneration) and juvenile rheumatoid arthritis.

Hearing Impairments. Students with hearing impairments fall into two categories: those who are deaf and those who are hard of hearing. How one differentiates between the two depends on whether one adopts a physiological or an educational orientation. A physiologically based definition relies on the measurable degree of hearing loss, with those having an impairment of 90 decibels or greater being deaf (0 dB is the level at which the average person can hear the faintest sound). An educationally based definition focuses on the ability to process linguistic information, with deafness indicating that the person cannot process linguistic information through audition even with a hearing aid (Brill, MacNeil, & Newman, 1986).

Developmental Delay. For many infants and preschoolers, it is often difficult to determine whether they have a true disability or have a temporary delay in maturation. In addition, it is sometimes difficult to determine the exact nature of very young children's disability. For these reasons, professionals are often reluctant to make a clinical diagnosis and, instead, refer to them as having a developmental delay.

Visual Impairments. Like hearing impairments, visual impairments are divided into two groups based on severity: blindness and low vision. Additionally, like hear-

ing impairments, these two groups are defined differently according to whether one uses a physiological versus an educational approach. A physiological orientation (also referred to as the legal definition because it is used to determine certain government benefits) relies on measurement of visual acuity and field of vision. Visual acuity of 20/200 (normal acuity is 20/20, being able to see at 20 feet what a person with normal vision sees at 20 feet) or less in the better eye, even with correction (e.g., eyeglasses), or visual field of less than 20 degrees qualifies an individual as legally blind. Those having visual acuity between 20/70 and 20/200 are referred to as having low vision or being partially sighted. The educational definition focuses on mode of reading, with those needing to use Braille being considered blind, and those who can read print, even with magnifying devices or large-print books, being considered as having low vision or being partially sighted.

Traumatic Brain Injury. In 1990, the federal government added students with traumatic brain injury (TBI) to the list of those eligible for special education services. This decision was in recognition of the fact that TBI occurs much more frequently than was previously thought. For example, estimates are that about one million children and adolescents receive head injuries each year, with 15,000 to 20,000 incurring lasting effects (Council for Exceptional Children, 2001). TBI refers to trauma to the brain caused by an external force that results in behavioral dysfunction. Such injuries can be open head injuries (i.e., penetrating head wounds) or closed head injuries (i.e., damage caused by internal compression or shearing motion inside the head) (Adelson & Kochanek, 1998).

Deaf-Blindness. Basically, students with deaf-blindness meet the educational definitions of both deafness and blindness. The vast majority of students with deaf-blindness also have one or more other disabilities, such as mental retardation. Deaf-blindness can result from (a) prenatal causes, such as rubella, (b) postnatal causes, such as meningitis, or (c) genetic/chromosomal syndromes (Hallahan et al., 2009).

HISTORY OF SPECIAL EDUCATION

The history of special education reveals a pattern characterized by alternating periods of progress and optimism and regress and pessimism. In spite of these fluctuations, overall special education has progressed from a relatively primitive state to its present-day robust status as a viable service option in public schools and as a field of scientific inquiry. Special education history is presented below in four time periods, starting with its birth in the late eighteenth and early nineteenth centuries.

LATE EIGHTEENTH AND EARLY NINETEENTH CENTURIES.

Historians of special education usually trace its roots back to the end of the eighteenth century and beginning of the nineteenth century (Hallahan et al., 2009; Kauffman, 1981). Prior to the French and American Revolutions, care for people with disabilities came largely in the form of asylums, created almost as much to protect the larger society from those considered *idiotic* or *insane* as to protect those housed within the institutions. With the revolutions, however, came principles of democracy and egalitarianism. Fueled by this idealism, many European and American physicians, clergymen, and other reformers tackled the issue of rehabilitating and educating children with a variety of disabilities.

Jean-Marc-Gaspard Itard (1775–1838) is generally credited as being the creator of many of the basic instructional principles upon which special education is built. A French physician, Itard was a specialist in deafness. In fact, it was his specialization in deafness that serendipitously led to his groundbreaking work with Victor, the "wild boy of Aveyron" (Lane, 1984). Found wandering in the forest in 1801, Victor was brought to the National Institution for the Deaf because he was thought to be deaf. Itard, who worked at a nearby hospital was called to the Institute to attend to a resident who had broken his leg on the very day that Victor arrived. Itard saw in Victor the opportunity to demonstrate that intensive instruction could ameliorate even the most intractable learning difficulties. Although Itard was not able to cure Victor and, in fact, considered his efforts largely a failure, others after him considered Victor's progress to be quite remarkable.

Eduoard Seguin (1812–1880), along with other students of Itard, carried forward many ideas that served as the foundation of special education: individualized instruction, careful sequencing of instruction, stimulation of the senses, careful structuring of the educational environment, immediate reward for correct performance, instruction in functional skills for independence, and an assumption that all children can make some progress (Hallahan et al., 2009). Seguin established the first known school to serve mentally retarded children in France in 1839 before immigrating to the United States. In 1866, he published *Idiocy* and its treatment by the physiological method, which is often cited as the first textbook on instruction for persons with mental retardation.

In addition to Seguin, several other reformers were influential in establishing educational programming for students with disabilities in the United States. The physician Samuel Gridley Howe (1801–1876), who had been the one inviting Seguin to the United States, helped establish the first school for the blind in 1832 in Watertown, Massachusetts, the Perkins School for the Blind.

The minister Thomas Hopkins Gallaudet (1787–1851), after visiting European educators of the deaf, founded the first residential school for the deaf in the United States in 1817 in Harford, Connecticut. In 1841 the social crusader Dorthea Dix (1802–1887) lobbied state and federal legislatures to provide funding for asylums for the insane.

LATE NINETEENTH CENTURY

Much of the optimism and interest in quality care that characterized the early part of the century began to wane in the late nineteenth century (Kauffman, 1981). Depressing economic conditions in the aftermath of the American Civil War (1860–1865), combined with an influx of immigrants and rapid industrialization and urbanization, led to a decrease in interest in educating and rehabilitating those with disabilities.

But even in the face of dwindling interest and resources, several positive developments occurred, including Congress establishing a U. S. Department of Education, special classes and day schools for children who were deaf, the addition of a Department of Special Education in the National Education Association, and special education teacher training programs usually housed in institutions for those with disabilities. It was during this time, too, that numerous professional organizations sprung up for those working with students with disabilities.

But counteracting these positive developments, the close of the nineteenth century witnessed a growing pessimism about what could be done for students with disabilities, especially those who were mentally retarded. The prevailing professional opinion was that mental retardation was incurable and that the most that could be done was to provide protection from and for retarded individuals by housing them in large institutions.

EARLY TWENTIETH CENTURY

The early twentieth century brought mostly positive developments for students with disabilities, with a smattering of negativism, especially toward those with mental retardation. During this time, the eugenics movement gained influence. Henry H. Goddard's *The Kallikak Family: A Study pf The Heredity of Feeblemindedness* in 1912, purportedly showing the hereditary spread of mental retardation, fueled the passage of legislation in several states to sterilize residents in institutions of mental retardation. Interestingly, later examination revealed strong evidence that he fabricated or altered much of his so-called data (Smith, 1985).

During this time, some of the more progressive public schools began to offer special education classes and resource rooms for students with various disabilities. Elizabeth Farrell (1870–1932), a New York City special education teacher, advocated for the establishment of classes for students with disabilities. In 1922 she helped found the Council for Exceptional Children, which remained into the early 2000s as the major professional organization for educators of students with disabilities. With the spread of these programs, special education began to be recognized as part of the curricular offerings in school systems.

This period also saw the emergence of many issues concerning education of students with disabilities that persist into the 21st century. For example, there were vigorous debates in the professional literature about segregation versus mainstreaming of students with disabilities, early identification and prevention of disabilities, more federal aid for special education services. In short, the stage was being set for special education to become a discipline of study.

LATE TWENTIETH CENTURY

One of the most, if not the most important development of the late 1900s was the emergence of parent groups and organizations. For example, the National Association for Retarded Children (subsequently called The Arc) was founded in 1950 and the Association for Children with Learning Disabilities (later called the Learning Disabilities Association of America) was founded in 1963. Such organizations were instrumental, along with professional organizations, in lobbying for legislation and services for students with disabilities.

The end of the 20th century was a time of increased expansion of special education research and services. In the research domain, the federal government funded research that generated an expanding body of literature on best practices in identification and intervention for students with disabilities. These competitive research grant programs focused on individual researchers or small teams of researchers as well as large, interdisciplinary research centers. Additionally, personnel preparation grants helped fill the growing need for pre-service and in-service special education teachers, as well as university-level teacher educators.

During this time, too, several pieces of landmark legislation were passed that mandated special education as a civil right for children with disabilities and their families. This legislation, discussed in the following section, established special education as a major piece of the educational landscape in U.S. K-12 schools and universities.

RELEVANT LEGISLATION

Beginning in 1975 and continuing into the 21st century, federal legislation has worked to define the needs of special students and through laws to design ways of serving this population.

Public Law 94-142. The 1975 Education for All Handicapped Children Act (PL 94–142) was a groundbreaking law that established the fundamental parameters of how special education services are defined and implemented in the United States. Key provisions such as a free appropriate public education (FAPE), individualized education programs (IEP), least restrictive environment (LRE), and procedural safeguards (such as due process procedures) defined in the original statute remained primary to the law in subsequent reauthorizations.

Prior to the passage of PL 94–142, many children and youth with disabilities were excluded from public schooling. For the majority of those students, that meant lack of access to appropriate assessment, education, rehabilitative services, and community support. Other federal legislation laid the groundwork for PL 94–142, but these statues did not wield the same power in terms of firmly establishing the rights of individuals with disabilities access to public education. Notable legislation includes the Training of Professional Personnel Act of 1959 (teacher training for working with individuals with mental retardation), Teachers of the Deaf Act of 1961 (teacher training for working with individuals who are deaf or hard of hearing), the Elementary and Secondary Education Act of 1965 (funding for the education of children with disabilities), and the Handicapped Children's Early Education Assistance Act of 1968 and the Economic Opportunities Amendments of 1972 (establishment of early childhood programs for children with disabilities). These laws helped to articulate instructional practices specific to the needs of students with disabilities and establish models for teacher training that would be included in PL 94–142.

Since 1975 several substantive changes have been made to the law through the reauthorization process. The 1986 reauthorization extended FAPE to include children ages 3 to 5 and established Early Intervention Programs (EIP) and the Individualized Family Service Plan (IFSP) for children ages from birth to 3 years.

More significant changes occurred in the 1990 reauthorization. First, the law was renamed the Individuals with Disabilities Education Act (IDEA). The title change reflected three important points. First, the reach of the law expanded (birth to age 21) with the term "individuals" replacing "children." Second, people-first language "individuals with disabilities" replaced "handicapped children" to emphasize the individual nature of disability—people with disabilities should not be defined by their disability and individuals with the same disability will demonstrate great diversity. Third, the term "disability" replaced "handicapped" to more accurately define the population served. The 1990 reauthorization also included the provision of transition services for students, created new categories of autism and traumatic brain injury, and re-crafted the language of LRE to place greater emphasis on the need for students with disabilities to receive education with their non-disabled peers.

The 1997 reauthorization extended this LRE position by including specific language that students with disabilities should have "access to the general education curriculum" (PL 105–17). The 1997 reauthorization also included more explicit guidelines regarding disciplinary procedures for students with disabilities. Specifically, the law recommended the use of FBA, discussed earlier, in order to provide preventative instruction or conditions to promote pro-social or desired behaviors. Taken together the reauthorizations of IDEA that occurred between 1986 and 1997 served to strengthen the core mission of the law and provide increased clarity on who is served under the law and what practices should surround the development of special education.

The Role of the Federal Government in Education. To understand how IDEA and other federal statutes affect local educational decision-making, it is important to examine the relationship between the federal government and the fifty states. The U.S. Constitution does not allocate specific power to the federal government in terms of education. As a result, states determine the policies, procedures, and requirements school districts must follow. The federal government does not possess the power to establish a national curriculum or set national standards for performance. From time to time, however, the federal government passes legislation that allows for the provision of funds to states for the purpose of improving education. Examples include grants to build infrastructure (e.g., land grants) or grants to improve educational outcomes for children in poverty (e.g., Head Start). When states accept these funds, they must also uphold the specific requirements associated with that funding stream. Even though the funding provided by the federal government has historically not exceeded 10% of a state's education budget, states do rely on these funds (Yell & Drasgow, 2005). This relationship supplies the power to the federal government to shape and influence education.

Standards and Special Education. In 1983, under the leadership of the Secretary of Education, the Commission on Excellence in Education issued the *Nation at Risk* report. Many viewed the report as a wake-up call to the mediocre levels of student achievement in the country. One recommendation contained in the report urged the development of challenging, measurable academic standards. The push for standards came again in 1989 when President George H. W. Bush convened the fifty governors at the first National Education Summit. Many of the goals and priorities established as a result of the

summit became a part of the educational plans of President Bush and then of President Clinton.

In 1994 President Clinton reauthorized the Elementary and Secondary Education Act of 1965 (ESEA). The reauthorized act, renamed Improving America's Schools Act, reflected the standards framework recommended by the *Nation at Risk* report and articulated in President Bush's America 2000 and President Clinton's Goals 2000: Educate America Act. This reauthorization established a precedent for an expanded role of government in education and lay the groundwork for the next reauthorization, which would prove to be both controversial and far-reaching.

No Child Left Behind Act. The 2001 reauthorization of ESEA brought yet another title change for the law. The No Child Left Behind Act of 2001 (NCLB), under President George W. Bush, adopted many of the principal features (e.g., academic standards, accountability, and adequate yearly progress) included in the 1994 reauthorization of ESEA (Yell & Glasgow, 2005). The departure from prior educational legislation came in the form of demands—to bring all students up to standards within a certain time frame and the establishment of sanctions for schools that did not perform. In essence, NCLB was the first instance of federal educational legislation that had the power to enforce itself. NCLB passed by an overwhelming bipartisan majority in both the House and Senate, yet shortly after its passage political schisms in regard to implementation of the law occurred.

The confluence of standards/accountability represented in NCLB and the increasing emphasis on access to the general education curriculum in IDEA resulted in a federal position on the education of students with disabilities that looked more similar to general education policies than ever before in the history of special education. Several provisions in NCLB had direct influence on the reauthorization of IDEA in 2004 and on the ensuing instructional practices for students with disabilities. Specifically, NCLB required (a) accountability for results, including the results of students from identified subgroups (i.e., students with disabilities, ethnic and racial minorities, students who are economically disadvantaged, and students who are limited English proficient); (b) the use of instructional practices based upon scientifically based research; and (c) that necessity that all students be taught by a teacher who meets the federal definition of "highly qualified." The 2004 reauthorization of IDEA included NCLB's definition of highly qualified special education teacher and a similar requirement for the use of materials and practices based upon scientifically based research.

Under NCLB, states were required to report disaggregated data on the various sub-groups, including students with disabilities. Although these data led to greater transparency in regard to the educational outcomes of students with disabilities and greater accountability for demonstrating educational progress, the fact that at least 95% of students with disabilities were required to participate in the state-wide assessments caused concern for some. In addition, only 2% of students with disabilities could participate in modified achievement standards or alternate tests. Questions related to which assessments (grade-level or ability-level), accommodations or supports, and populations of students under IDEA should be selected challenged states' initial implementation of the law. NCLB's highly qualified teacher requirement also proved challenging in its implementation.

In addition to incorporating the language and fundamental principles of NCLB, IDEA 2004 included several other important provisions that would have direct influence on the identification of and instructional practices for students with disabilities. For example, the concept "universal design" was used throughout the amendments to underscore the importance of selecting materials, methods, and assessment techniques and technologies that allow for access by a wide-range of students. For teachers, universal design means selecting instructional strategies that provide benefit to a range of learners—from students with disabilities to high-achieving students—or creating assessments that allow a range of students to demonstrate knowledge of high academic standards.

Two other changes to IDEA 2004 reflected the trend towards unifying general education and special education practices. These changes included providing more flexibility to schools in terms of the discipline of students with disabilities and the removal of short-term objectives on the IEP for the majority of students with disabilities. In terms of discipline, the law shifted the burden of proof in manifestation determination reviews to the parents and made it easier for schools to remove children for disciplinary infractions other than weapons, drugs, or dangerous behavior. The removal of short-term objectives for all students, except those who participate in alternate assessments and follow alternate standards (less than 1% of students with disabilities), reflected the increasing emphasis on participation in general education standards and accountability.

Perhaps the most significant addition to IDEA 2004, though, was the inclusion of additional procedures for the identification of students with specific learning disabilities. States were no longer required to use a "severe discrepancy" between achievement and intellectual ability as an identifying factor. In addition, states could now allow processes that measured a "child's response to

scientific, research-based interventions" as a gauge for identification. Commonly referred to as *response to instruction* or RTI, this provision dramatically changed the language (and some would argue, practice) of special education. Special educators would differentiate between "core instruction," the instruction received by the majority of students in general education, and "levels of intervention," the qualitatively different instruction that was delivered to students not making progress in the core program. These levels of intervention were not necessarily delivered in settings outside the general education classroom but could be.

Other Influential Laws. Two other laws directly influence the education of students with disabilities: Section 504 of the Rehabilitation Act of 1973 (Section 504) and the Americans with Disabilities Act (ADA) of 1990. Both Section 504 and ADA are civil rights acts that protect qualified individuals with disabilities from discrimination of benefits or services on the basis of disability. These nondiscrimination laws apply to any organization receiving federal financial assistance, which would include public schools. Although 504 and ADA have much in common with IDEA, the fundamental purposes of these laws differs from the charge of IDEA.

The purpose of Section 504 is to create equal opportunity for students with disabilities through the elimination of barriers or the provision of accommodations for equal access. In other words, for students who can be successful the general education classroom with the provision of minor instructional accommodations or structural changes, Section 504 may be the only law these students need. In contrast, the intent of IDEA is to provide specialized services and supports that differ in some way from the education received by students without disabilities. Students with disabilities who require more intensive instructional modifications or supports (regardless of placement—in the general education setting or in a more restrictive setting) would benefit from the protections and services provided under IDEA.

To qualify under Section 504, students must (a) have a physical or mental impairment that substantially limits a major life activity (e.g., learning, walking, seeing, hearing), (b) have a record of an impairment, or (c) be regarded as having an impairment. Some students with disabilities who would not qualify under one of IDEA's 13 disability categories may qualify under Section 504's broad definition of disability. Section 504 protections can be important for students with communicable diseases, chronic health conditions, and students with ADHD who would not or choose not to qualify under IDEA but are in need of instructional supports. Unlike IDEA, schools do not receive funding for Section 504 services, but schools are under the same federal obligation to comply with the law. As such, some schools are hesitant about offering such services or making Section 504 information widely available to parents. Yet, Section 504 protections must be in place and available for interested parents, teachers, and student advocates.

The Americans with Disabilities Act reflects similar language (e.g., definition of disability) and objectives as Section 504 but applies to a broader spectrum of organizations—public transportation, employment, and state and local government. Basic provisions under ADA require organizations to provide "reasonable accommodations," physical access (e.g., ramps for individuals who use wheelchairs), and freedom from discrimination based upon disability status. Both ADA and Section 504 are administer by the Office of Civil Rights and are considered identical for the purposes of compliance monitoring.

RESPONSE TO INTERVENTION IN SPECIAL EDUCATION

In the context of increased accountability, greater emphasis on the use of scientifically based practices, and a focus on high standards for students with disabilities, the landscape of special education has become simultaneously more uncertain and more articulated. One example of this contradictory position occurred in the introduction of the concept of responsiveness to intervention (RTI). With the passage of the 2004 amendments to IDEA, RTI was established as an alternative to the use of ability-achievement discrepancy as a means for identifying learning disabilities. The law also positioned RTI practices as a tool for ensuring the systematic delivery of research-based interventions to all students not making appropriate gains in the general curriculum. Many heralded the inclusion of RTI in the 2004 statute, yet questions remained regarding issues of implementation and scale (Hallahan & Cohen, in press; Fletcher, Lyon, Fuchs, & Barnes, 2007). Specifically, some in special education have questioned whether the distinction between specialized services and general education practices would be blurred and result in less intensive supports for students with disabilities, while others felt that the move would result in even clearer articulation of levels of instruction and the identification of specific interventions for students with disabilities.

In 2005 the National Joint Committee on Learning Disabilities (NJCLD), consisting of representation from the major professional organizations devoted to learning disabilities, issued a report on RTI in which it identified potential strengths and highlighted areas of future research. In underscoring the potential of RTI methodologies, the NJCLD noted the promise of early and/or preventative remediation, the application of high-quality interventions, and the ability to yield a "true population" of students with learning disabilities. The underlying assumption of RTI is that the application of effective instructional methodologies will result in the majority of students making satisfactory gains while other students will fail to respond to the instruction. These students who continue to struggle while receiving high-quality instruction are students with learning disabilities. Therefore, these students require the more intensive, specialized instruction provided under IDEA.

One example of an RTI model is as follows:

Implementation of Tier 1 (high-quality general education instruction) with universal screening to identify at-risk students and the use of regular progress monitoring.

The provision of Tier 2 interventions (typically 8–12 weeks in duration) provided within the general education classroom for the identified at-risk students.

Continual progress monitoring is provided in order to determine responsiveness to the intervention.

Finally, students failing to respond to Tier 2 are referred for eligibility for special education in Tier 3, which consists of more individualized, intensive tertiary interventions, thus defining Tier 3 interventions as special education.

RESPONSE TO INSTRUCTION IN SPECIAL EDUCATION

Instructional practices for students with disabilities take into consideration (a) the unique characteristics of the learner, (b) the nature of the content or skill to be taught, and (c) the intersection of those characteristics and content. Given the fundamental role both learner and content play in the development of special education practices, special educators need to be well-versed in both the characteristics of the students they serve and the nature of the content to be taught. Some characteristics may be unique to a category of disability identified under IDEA, such as social impairments associated with autism, or the characteristics may cut across a range of categories, such as difficulty with memory and information processing associated with students with learning disabilities and students with mental retardation.

Fundamental to the practice of designing specialized instruction is task-analysis—breaking down the content of instruction to all the requisite skills and constructs. Identification of requisite skills and constructs allows teachers to select appropriate strategies, scaffolds/supports, and accommodations or modifications to meet the unique needs of the individual student. Three common elements to the implementation of effective special education instruction are: (a) explicit, systematic instruction, (b) continual progress monitoring, and (c) behavioral analysis and supports.

As stated previously, the hallmark of special education instruction is the delivery of intensive, relentless instruction with frequent opportunities for student response. Research on effective practices in special education has demonstrated the power of explicit instructional practices such as direct instruction—fast-paced, well-sequence, highly focused instruction with high student responses rates—and strategy instruction that focus on organization, elaboration, or generative thinking for students with disabilities (Gersten, Schiller, & Vaughn, 2000). Key features of explicit instruction include careful sequencing and organization, enhancing student motivation through early and frequent success, and scaffolding (decreasing levels of support to foster mastery). Specific instructional strategies that reflect these principles and have been demonstrated as effective for students with disabilities include: structured peer-tutoring (Fuchs, & Fuchs, 1998), direct instruction (Adams & Engleman, 1996), mnemonic instruction (Mastropieri, Sweda, & Scruggs, 2000), and learning strategies (NICHY, 1997).

Progress monitoring was first introduced in the field of special education in the 1970s as data-based program monitoring and later as curriculum-based measurement (Deno, 2003). The underlying concept was that teachers would use repeated measures of student performance in order to determine the effectiveness of instruction and then make needed changes to their teaching if students were not responding. Incarnations of curriculum-based measurement/progress monitoring as of 2008 involve tracking student performance over time and instructional decision-making using predetermined targets or benchmarks. Decades after its inception the fundamental constructs of progress monitoring and instructional decision-making based upon data have become paramount in the field of special education. Further, what began as a special education practice came in time to influence the conceptualization of effective instruction for all students.

Another component of effective special education is the application of behavioral analysis for the purpose of determining appropriate supports, frequently referred to in special education as *positive behavioral supports*. Meta-analyses, statistical procedures that measure the overall efficacy of a strategy or approach, have demonstrated the power of positive behavioral supports to reduce undesirable behaviors and increase pro-social or desired behaviors (Gersten, Schiller, & Vaughn, 2000). The development of positive behavioral supports begins with an analysis of environment and student behavior. The environment includes all elements associated with the delivery of instruction (e.g., instructional methods or strategies used, materials selected, physical design), and student behavior includes communication, social interactions, and maladaptive responses. Special educators or IEP teams collect data on the behavior(s) of concern in an attempt to determine the function or purpose of the behavior. Analysis of the data leads to the development of a hypothesis of the function of the behavior. The educator or team then identifies teaching procedures intended to (a) reduce the undesirable behavior and (b) teach a more acceptable or adaptive behavior. Data continue to be collected in order to determine the efficacy of the supports and instruction selected.

In summary, the basic principles that served as the foundation of special education remain a vibrant part of the instruction of students with disabilities today. Research in the field of special education has served to refine and improve specific practices such as progress monitoring, the delivery of instruction, cognitive strategy instruction, functional behavioral analysis and positive behavioral supports, and the identification of a range of disabilities. Legislation in the early 2000s and to come will continue to influence and shape the context of the education of students with disabilities, but fundamental principles of individualization, remediation, and measured-growth will remain an essential part of what special educators do.

SEE ALSO *Attention Deficit Hyperactivity Disorder (ADHD); Deaf and Hard of Hearing; Gifted Education; Individualized Education Program (IEP); Learning Disabilities; Mental Retardation; Speech and Language Impairments; Visual Impairments.*

BIBLIOGRAPHY

AAMR Ad Hoc Committee on Terminology and Classification. (2002). *Mental retardation: Definition, classification, and systems of supports* (10th ed.). Washington, DC: American Association on Mental Retardation.

Adams, G., & Engleman S. (1996). *Research on direct instruction: 25 years beyond Distar.* Seattle, WA: Educational Achievement Systems.

Adelson, P. D., & Kochanek, P. M. (1998). Head injury in children. *Journal of Child Neurology, 13,* 2–15.

American Speech-Language-Hearing Association. (1993). Definitions of communication disorders and variations. *ASHA, 35*(Suppl. 10), 40–41.

Council for Exceptional Children. (2001). Traumatic brain injury: The silent epidemic. *CEC Today, 7*(7), 1, 5, 15.

Deno, S. L. (2003). Developments in curriculum-based measurement. *Journal of Special Education, 37*(3), 184–192.

Fletcher, J. M., Lyon, G. R., Fuchs, L. S., & Barnes, M. A. (2007). *Learning disabilities: From identification to intervention.* New York: Guilford.

Fuchs, D., & Fuchs, L. S. (1998). Researchers and teachers working closely together to adapt instruction for diverse learners. *Learning Disability Research and Practice, 13,* 126–137.

Gersten, R., Schiller, E. P., & Vaughn, S. R. (2000). *Contemporary special education research: Synthesis of the knowledge base on critical instructional issues.* Mahwah, NJ: Erlbaum.

Goddard, H. H. (1912). *The Kallikak family: A study in the heredity of feeble-mindedness.* New York: Macmillan.

Hallahan, D. P., & Cohen, S. B. (in press). Many students with learning disabilities are not receiving special education. *Learning Disabilities: A Multidisciplinary Journal.*

Hallahan, D. P., Kauffman, J. M., & Pullen, P. C. (2009). *Exceptional learners: Introduction to special education* (11th ed.). Boston: Allyn & Bacon.

Hallahan, D. P., & Mercer, C. D. (2002). Learning disabilities: Historical perspectives. In R. Bradley, L. Danielson, & D. P. Hallahan (Eds.), *Identification in learning disabilities: Research to practice* (pp. 1–67). Mahwah, NJ: Erlbaum.

Individuals with Disabilities Education Act Amendments of 1997, P.L. 95–17, 20 U.S.C. Section 1400 et. seq.

Individuals with Disabilities Education Improvement Act, 20 U.S.C. § 600 et seq. (2004).

Kauffman, J. M. (1981). Introduction: Historical trends and contemporary issues in special education in the United States. In J. M. Kauffman & D. P. Hallahan (Eds.). *Handbook of special education* (pp. 3–23). Englewood Cliffs, NJ: Prentice-Hall.

Kauffman, J. M., & Hallahan, D. P. (2005). *Special education: What it is and why we need it.* Boston: Allyn & Bacon.

Lane, H. (1984). *When the mind hears: A history of the deaf.* New York: Random House.

Mastropieri, M. A., Sweda, J., & Scruggs, T. E. (2000). Teacher use of mnemonic strategy instruction. *Learning Disabilities Research and Practice, 15,* 69–74.

National Joint Committee on Learning Disabilities (2005). Responsiveness to intervention and learning disabilities. *Learning Disability Quarterly, 28,* 249–260.

NICHCY. (1997). *Interventions for students with learning disabilities (News Digest 25).* Washington, DC: National Dissemination Center for Children with Disabilities.

Office of Special Education Programs. (2005). *History: 25 years of progress in educating children with disabilities through IDEA.* Washington, DC: Author.

Smith, J. D. (1985). *Minds made feeble: The myth and legacy of the Kallikaks.* Rockville, MD: Aspen Systems.

Strock, M. (2004). *Autism spectrum disorders (pervasive developmental disorders).* Bethesda, MD: U.S. Department of Health and Human Services, National Institutes of Health, National Institute of Mental Health. Retrieved April 2, 2008, from http://www.nimh.nih.gov/health/publications/autism/complete-publications.html.

Yell, M. L., & Drasgow, E. (2005). *No child left behind: A guide for professionals.* Upper Saddle River, NJ: Pearson.

Daniel P. Hallahan
Kristin L. Sayeski

SPEECH AND LANGUAGE IMPAIRMENTS

According to the U.S. Department of Education, in 2006 there were 1,486,960 children with diagnoses of speech and language impairments in U.S. public schools. Even greater numbers of children had speech and language

impairments associated with other diagnoses such as learning disabilities, autism spectrum disorders, or hearing impairment. The school-based speech and language pathologist (SLP) works to promote the functional skills of children affected by speech and language impairments and "to provide support in the general educational environment for students with communication handicaps to facilitate their successful participation, socialization, and learning" (American Speech-Language-Hearing Association, ASHA, 2000, p. 11). The impact of the impairment on the child's educational functioning is the paramount consideration.

DEFINITIONS

Speech and language impairments may be classified by *symptomology*, the particular aspects of speech or language that are affected; *specificity*, whether or not the impairment is part of a broader deficit; and *etiology*, whether the impairment is developmental or acquired. In the following sections, these classifications are defined.

Speech. Children affected by speech impairment most often have deficits in producing the sounds of the language as compared to their same-age peers. They may leave out sounds (e.g., tar for star) or substitute one sound for another (e.g., cawot for carrot). In some cases the child does not understand the rules that govern the production and combination of speech sounds, which is commonly referred to as phonological impairment. In other cases, the root of the problem is motoric, which is commonly referred to as articulation impairment. Often, because the roots are not completely understood, the terms are used interchangeably. Articulation/phonological impairment is the single most frequent diagnostic category represented on the caseload of the school SLP (ASHA, 2006).

Speech impairments broadly defined also include abnormal voice, nasal resonance, and fluency (ASHA, 1993). Children with voice problems present with deviations in pitch, quality, or loudness of their speech as compared to other children of their same sex and age. Nasal resonance problems involve either hypo- or hypernasality. The former results when a blockage (e.g., swollen adenoids) prevents air from resonating within the nasal cavity during speech. The latter results when the soft palate does not make adequate closure with the pharyngeal wall during production of the oral sounds of the language. The speech of children who stutter is characterized by disruptions in rate and rhythm as well as repetitions of sounds, syllables, words or phrases. Affected children may struggle or tense when they stutter.

Language. Children affected by language impairments have deficits in understanding or expressing words, sentences, or extended discourse in either spoken or written modalities. This deficit may involve problems with semantics, the meaning of language (e.g., understanding the meaningful relationship between the words *animal, cat,* and *Tabby*); morphology and syntax, the grammar of language (e.g., inflecting verbs with *–ed* to indicate past tense); or pragmatics, the social use of language (e.g., judging the right amount of information to convey to a listener). Childhood language impairments may be referred to as language delays or language disorders. The term *delay* implies slow but typical development whereas *disorder* implies atypical development.

Primary or Secondary Impairment. Developmental speech and language impairments may be primary or secondary diagnoses. Children with primary impairments are otherwise normally developing. The cause of the impairment is usually unknown though central nervous dysfunction is presumed (ASHA, 1997) and, according to Bruce Tomblin and colleagues (1997), such impairments run in families. Children with primary language impairments affecting the oral modality are often said to have specific language impairment; those with primary impairments affecting the written modality are often said to have language learning disabilities, but either diagnostic category can encompass impairments in both modalities. Other children have speech and language impairments that are secondary to another deficit. For example, children with attention deficit hyperactivity disorder may have difficulty planning and organizing discourse as well as problems using language in a pragmatically appropriate manner, whereas children with cerebral palsy may have difficulty pronouncing speech sounds.

Developmental or Acquired Impairment. Most speech and language impairments exhibited by school children are developmental, that is, roots of the problem exist from birth and manifestations of the problem emerge as the child develops and it becomes obvious that the child is slower or atypical compared to peers. In a minority of cases, speech and language impairments are acquired when a child suffers an illness or accident that affects brain function. In these cases, the impairment may be referred to as aphasia. Rhea Paul (2001) summarizes these aphasias as follows. In cases of stroke and traumatic brain injury, children tend to be initially mute but have generally good recovery over time. A stroke, especially one that results in focal damage to the left hemisphere, typically results in long-term but subtle deficits in verbal memory, grammatical complexity, word finding, and reading. Traumatic brain injuries, such as those sustained from falls or car accidents, may result in long-term problems with word

finding, discourse, and pragmatics. Speech motor control may also be compromised. A seizure disorder known as Landau-Kleffner syndrome has its onset in childhood and usually results in permanent impairments in the comprehension and expression of language.

DIAGNOSIS AND ASSESSMENT OF SPEECH AND LANGUAGE IMPAIRMENTS

In school settings, diagnosis and assessment are typically accomplished by teams of professionals who collaborate to make decisions regarding a given child's strengths and weaknesses. When speech and language development is a potential area of weakness, the SLP will be part of that team. The diagnosis of speech and language impairments is, in general, a two-pronged process. First, the child is referred for diagnostic testing, usually because a family member or teacher is concerned about his or her ability to function successfully in situations that demand verbal performance. Such situations include expressing basic needs, making friends, communicating in the classroom, taking tests, and learning to read and write. The SLP explores these concerns as well as the child's developmental and educational history via parent and teacher interviews.

Second, via standardized norm-referenced testing, observations in natural settings, and descriptive criterion-referenced assessments (e.g., review of classroom work portfolios, probes of response to intervention) the SLP determines whether the child is functioning more poorly than peers of the same chronological age in one or more domains (e.g., speech, semantics, morpho-syntax, pragmatics) and whether the child is apt to improve functioning in response to various supports. There is no universally agreed upon cut-off score on standardized tests for identifying speech and language impairments. Instead, the decision varies with the extent of the real-life impact, the number of domains affected, and the resources available for intervening on the child's behalf. State codes may establish eligibility criteria as well as recommended amounts of service and service delivery options in school settings (ASHA, 2000).

In cases of secondary impairments, speech and language problems may be one symptom leading to the diagnosis of the primary impairment. For example, late talking may be the first sign that a child is affected by a hearing impairment. In other cases, the primary impairment is diagnosed first and speech and language is monitored because the child is known to be at risk. This situation is illustrated in Down syndrome, an impairment typically diagnosed *in utero*. Children with Down syndrome are known to have particular difficulties with speech-motor control and expressive language development; therefore, they are frequently placed in speech and language intervention programs as babies. In cases in which speech and language problems are secondary to a deficit that involves mental retardation, the extent of the speech and language problem may be determined relative to mental-age peers (i.e., younger normally developing children) rather than chronological-age peers. In cases of acquired language impairments, the child may also be compared to his or her own previous level of functioning, if that is known.

CHARACTERISTICS OF SPEECH AND LANGUAGE IMPAIRMENTS BY DIAGNOSTIC CATEGORY

Implicit in the above definitions is the enormous variability between children with speech and language impairments. One child may have a very mild deficit affecting only a few speech sounds whereas another may have a very severe deficit that prevents oral language altogether. In between are numerous other profiles, some of which are predictable if the roots of the impairment are known. For example, Laurence Leonard (1998) notes that children with specific language impairment are typically late to acquire first words. Their acquisition of grammar lags even further behind (in English this is often manifested as omission of inflections on verbs across an extended developmental period). Abbeduto and Hagerman (1997) note that children with fragile X syndrome, especially boys, often present with variability in rate of speech, delays in the development of words and word inflections, and perseverations of words during discourse. Finally, Krista Wilkinson (1998) notes that children with autism spectrum disorders have difficulty establishing and maintaining joint attention with communicative partners. Their speech may sound monotonous and the information that they convey via speech may strike the listener as odd or tangential. Although researchers can make generalizations like these for almost any diagnostic category, the value of the exercise is questionable. Two children who share a diagnosis may be less similar than two children with different diagnoses. Moreover, knowing the child's diagnostic category is of limited help in designing an intervention. Instead, the SLP typically meets with more success by selecting goals and strategies based on what is known about the child rather than the diagnosis.

CURRENT INTERVENTIONS AND INSTRUCTIONAL PROCEDURES

In school settings, interventions for children with speech and language impairments are specified by an Individual Family Service Plan (IFSP) for children younger than three or an Individual Educational Program (IEP) for children who are three or more years of age. These plans are mandated by the Individuals with Disabilities Educa-

tion Act of 1997 (IDEA). In the case of a child with or at risk for speech and language impairments, either plan will specify goals for speech and language development and the services and program accommodations necessary to reach those goals. Typically the SLP will set both long-term and short-term goals. If, for example, a long-term goal for the child is to master new grammatical forms, a more intermediate goal might be to learn to use helping verbs and the short-term targets of focus might be *will, can,* and *does.*

According to Rebecca McCauley and Marc Fey (2006), to approach these goals, the SLP must determine the context for the intervention (e.g., classroom-based, pull-out group, pull-out individual, self-contained classroom), the intervention agent (e.g., SLP, teacher, peer, parent), and the dosage (e.g., minutes per week). These decisions are made with consideration of the needs of the child, the wishes of the parents, and state codes. The SLP then determines the activities and strategies that will work best for a given child. Activities may include picture naming drills, joint book reading, dramatic play, computerized language comprehension exercises, and writing assignments, to name a few. During those activities, the SLP employs strategies that may include asking the child to listen to or imitate models of correct target productions, to correct mistakes when given feedback, or to respond when given scaffolds such as cues and simplifications of the task. The SLP chooses materials that will provide focused stimulation, that is, those which will allow many opportunities for the child to experience and to practice the target. The SLP may recast, revise, or expand the child's spontaneous utterances as a way to further model targets. When the SLP is not the primary agent of intervention, she serves as a collaborative consultant to teachers, parents, or peers by explaining the goals, activities, and strategies to be used with the child. An additional important component of intervention is on-going reassessment to ensure that the child is making progress; if not, program modification is necessary.

Best practice requires that decisions made about the intervention program are guided by the expertise of the SLP in light of the needs and values of the child and family and the research evidence that demonstrates the utility of various program options. Learning about the child and family is an on-going process that begins with the case-history interviews and observations, continues during the IFSP or IEP process, and grows as the SLP manages the child's intervention. SLPs who adhere to evidence-based practice seek independent confirmation and converging evidence for clinical decisions from the research literature. They evaluate research evidence to ensure that it is characterized by adequate experimental control and that it is free from bias. They determine whether the effects of any reported clinical procedure are sizeable, relevant to the child in question, and feasible in the school setting (ASHA, 2004).

ISSUES RELATED TO ASSESSMENT AND INTERVENTION

As in any profession, the state-of-the-art in speech and language pathology is dynamic. A number of issues have prompted important changes in service delivery to children with speech and language impairments. Three issues are highlighted below.

Inclusion. The IDEA amendments of 1997 encouraged the participation of children with special needs in the general education curriculum. As a result, children with speech and language impairments are now often assessed and treated, at least in part, within the regular classroom. According to Rhea Paul (2001) and Carol Westby (2006), during curriculum-based assessment, the SLP analyzes the spoken or written features of the student's school work (homework, tests, projects), observes the child's successes and failures during school activities, and tests the utility of various scaffolds for the child's verbal performance during such activities. Curriculum-based intervention requires the SLP to move away from contrived exercises outside the classroom and towards consultant or collaborative roles within the classroom. As consultants to classroom teachers, SLPs suggest modified verbal instructions that enhance comprehension and verbal responding in the moment as well as strategies, materials, and activities that promote improvements in speech and language development over time. As collaborators, SLPs plan and implement lessons along with teachers. In either role, the SLP is concerned with supporting the child's communication in the classroom as well as his or her performance on language-related academic tasks whether they are taking a spelling test or comprehending a social studies text. Curriculum-based practice in schools is highly compatible with a broader emphasis in the field of speech pathology on intervening via purposeful and functional activities in naturalistic settings.

Diversity. According to a 1994 report from the U.S. General Accounting Office, bilingual students learning English as a second language were common in nearly every state. SLPs recognize that differences between communities in dialect or language are to be cherished, not pathologized or stigmatized (ASHA, 1983). Therefore, one of the key roles played by the SLP in increasingly diverse school settings is to help assessment teams distinguish speech and language patterns that reflect the learning of English as a second language from those indicative of true impairments. To make this distinction effectively, IDEA mandates that the child's native language development be assessed. Such assessment is complicated by a lack of professionals who are familiar with more than a mere handful of the 311 languages reported by the National Virtual Translation Center to be spoken in the United States as well as a lack of standardized tests that are normed for students who are bilingual. The limited availability of appropriate standardized tests represents yet another impetus in the movement towards curriculum-based assessments in naturalistic classroom settings. In cases in which true impairments have been discerned in the bilingual child, intervention is also complicated. For example, as noted by Celeste Roseberry-McKibben (2007), cultural and linguistic differences between the parents and the SLP may impede effective involvement of the family in the intervention. Such challenges may increase as the diversity of the U.S. population continues to grow; however, that growth will surely motivate useful changes in the design of tests and the education of SLPs and other professionals.

Evidence-based Practice. SLPs have long been aware that collecting data from individual children is important for planning interventions and monitoring their success. They have known that keeping current with research in the field is important. What changed with the advent of the evidence-based practice movement in the early 2000s was the emphasis on finding high levels of evidence, evaluating the quality of that evidence, and applying that evidence in decision making for individual children. Various guidelines exist for determining levels of evidence and evaluating quality (ASHA 2004). The SLP can also make use of published systematic reviews and meta-analyses and searchable online databases that summarize findings over multiple studies and include quality appraisals for each. Evidence-based practice is the joint responsibility of clinicians and scientists. As school-based SLPs retool to master evidence-based decision making; scientists must continue to fill gaps in the quantity and quality of available evidence. These joint efforts stand to further enhance the assessment and intervention services provided to school children with speech and language impairments.

SEE ALSO *First (Primary) Language Acquisition; Second Language Acquisition; Special Education.*

BIBLIOGRAPHY

Abbeduto, L., & Hagerman, R. J. (1997). Language and communication in fragile x syndrome. *Mental Retardation and Developmental Disabilities Research Reviews, 3,* 313–322.

American Speech-Language-Hearing Association. (1983). Social dialects [Position Statement]. Retrieved April 15, 2008, from http://www.asha.org/docs/html/PS1983-00115.html.

American Speech-Language-Hearing Association. (1993). Definitions of communication disorders and variations [Relevant Paper]. Retrieved April 15, 2008, from http://www.asha.org/docs/html/RP1993-00208.html.

American Speech-Language-Hearing Association. (1997). Operationalizing the NJCLD definition of learning disabilities for ongoing assessment in schools [Relevant Paper]. Retrieved April 15, 2008, from http://www.asha.org/docs/html/RP1998-00130.html.

American Speech-Language-Hearing Association. (2000). Guidelines for the roles and responsibilities of the school-based speech-language pathologist [Guidelines]. Retrieved April 15, 2008, from http://www.asha.org/docs/html/GL2000-00053.html.

American Speech-Language-Hearing Association. (2004). Evidence-based practice in communication disorders: An introduction [Technical Report]. Retrieved April 15, 2008, from http://www.asha.org/docs/html/TR2004-00001.html.

American Speech-Language-Hearing Association. (2006). ASHA 2006 schools survey-caseload characteristics report. Retrieved April 15, 2008, from http://www.asha.org/NR/rdonlyres/22D66325-4CE6-460D-8D61-9E0388219EC3/0/SchoolsSurveyCaseloads.pdf.

105th Congress of the United States. (1997). Individuals with Disabilities Education Act of 1997. Retrieved April 15, 2008, from http://frwebgate.access.gpo.gov/cgi-bin/getdoc.cgi?dbname=105_cong_public_laws&docid=f:publ17.105.

Johnston, J. (2006). *Thinking about child language: Research to practice.* Eau Claire, WI: Thinking Publications.

Leonard, L. B. (1998). *Children with specific language impairment.* Cambridge: MIT Press.

McCauley, R. J., & Fey, M. E. (2006). *Treatment of language disorders in children.* Baltimore: Paul H. Brookes.

National Virtual Translations Center, Languages of the World (2007). *Languages spoken in the U.S.* Retrieved April 15, 2008, from http://www.nvtc.gov/lotw/months/november/USlanguages.html.

Paul, R. (2001). *Language disorders from infancy through adolescence: Assessment & intervention* (2nd ed.). St. Louis, MO: Mosby.

Roseberry-McKibbin, C. (2007). *Language disorders in children: A multicultural and case perspective.* Boston: Pearson Education.

Tomblin, J. B., Smith, E., & Zhang, X. (1997). Epidemiology of specific language impairment: Prenatal and perinatal risk factors. *Journal of Communication Disorders, 30,* 325–344.

U.S. Department of Education, Office of Special Education Programs, Data Analysis System, OMB#1820-0043: *Children with disabilities receiving special education under Part B of IDEA-2005 (2006).* Retrieved April 15, 2008, from https://www.ideadata.org/tables29th/ar_1-7.xls.

U.S. General Accounting Office. (1994). *Limited English proficiency: A growing and costly educational challenge facing many school districts (GAO/HEHS-94-38).* Washington, DC: U.S. General Accounting Office. Retrieved April 15, 2008, from http://161.203.16.4/t2pbat4/150611.pdf.

Ukrainetz, T. A. (2006). *Contextualized language intervention: Scaffolding PreK-12 literacy achievement.* Eau Claire, WI: Thinking Publications.

Westby, C. (2006). There's more to passing than knowing the answers: Learning to do school. In T. A. Ukrainetz (Ed.), *Contextualized language intervention: Scaffolding PreK-12 literacy achievement* (pp. 319–387). Eau Claire, WI: Thinking Publications.

Wilkinson, K. M. (1998). Profiles of language and communication skills in autism. *Mental Retardation and Developmental Disabilities Research Reviews, 4,* 73–79.

Karla K. McGregor

STANDARDIZED TESTING

Standardized testing involves using testing instruments that are administered and scored in a pre-established standard or consistent manner. There are two types of standardized testing instruments: *norm-referenced tests* and *criterion-referenced tests* (IRA/NCTE Joint Task Force on Assessment, 1994). The former testing instruments yield scores that compare the examinee's scores to that of a representative sample (the normative group) of same-age or grade peers. The latter type of testing instrument involves comparing an examinee's score to a pre-determined criterion (such as a school curriculum).

Norm-referenced Tests. Academic achievement tests and cognitive tests, commonly referred to as IQ tests, are well known examples of norm-referenced, standardized tests given to individuals. Most norm-referenced test batteries include a manual and/or computerized scoring program that (1) provides information regarding the normative, or standardization, sample; (2) provides information on reliability and validity, (3) provides language and presentation of items administration and scoring information, and (4) provides guidelines for the interpretation of the test results. Norm-referenced test performance is generally summarized as one or more types of scores such as age-equivalent, grade-equivalent, percentile rankings, stanine, scaled scores, indexes, clusters, or quotients (Mercer, 1997). Newer editions of test instruments follow an item-response-theory procedure in their development which can allow for a new type of scores. These scores (called W-, Growth, Change-Sensitive, Growth-Score-Value) allow an examinee's performance to be measured against themselves by establishing the difficulty level of the items.

Criterion-referenced Tests. Criterion-referenced tests are similar to norm-referenced tests in terms of administration, scoring, and format; however, they differ in terms of interpretation. Criterion-referenced test interpretation involves evaluating an examinee's performance in relation to a specific criterion. For instance, if a criterion were "the ability to subtract single digit numbers," the interpretation would involve indicating simply whether or not the student answered the administered subtraction problem items correctly. A norm-referenced test interpretation, however, would involve whether this student correctly answered more questions compared to others in the normative group. Generally, criterion-referenced performance is summarized as percentage correct or represented as a grade-equivalent score (Weaver, 1990; Witt, Elliot, Daly, Gresham, & Kramer, 1998).

Criterion-referenced tests are sometimes misunderstood. Although these types of test can involve the use of a cutoff score (e.g., the point at which the examinee passes if the score exceeds this number), the cutoff score is not the criterion. Rather, the criterion refers to the content area domain that the test is intended to assess (Witt et al., 1998).

QUALITY OF STANDARDIZED TESTING INSTRUMENTS

The quality, or adequacy, of any standardized testing instrument, whether norm-referenced or criterion-referenced, is directly empirically supported by both reliability and validity studies. Professional testing associations or organizations often publish standards that practitioners can refer to when evaluating the quality of a testing instrument. For instance, in the field of psychometrics, there is a set of standards titled, "Standards for Educational and Psychological Testing" which psychologists and other related practitioners can refer to when interested in the standards of test development or construction, fairness in testing, and testing applications. Additionally, practitioners can learn about the psychometric properties (e.g., reliability, validity) of tests by consulting sources such as *Mental Measurements Yearbooks* and *Tests in Print*, both available from the Buros Institute of Mental Measurements and housed within most major libraries (Mercer, 1997) or *Test Critiques*, available from Pro-Ed Publishers.

ADVANTAGES OF STANDARDIZED TESTING

Using standardized tests to conduct assessments is advantageous for several reasons. First, because standardized tests yield quantifiable information (scores, proficiency levels, and so forth), results can be used in screening programs (e.g., identifying those students in need of further assessment). Second, standardized test results provide information regarding an examinee's areas of strength and weakness. Third, standardized test results allow a student to be compared to age- or grade-peers. Finally, standardized tests can be used to assess students' progress over time (e.g., readministering tests after the application of an intervention or following the institution of a remedial program) (IRA/NCTE Joint Task Force on Assessment, 1997; Witt et al., 1998). The most important advantage of results from a test administered in a standardized fashion is that the results can be documented and empirically veri-

fied. This then allows for the results to be interpreted and ideas about an individual's skills generalized.

DISADVANTAGES OF STANDARDIZED TESTING

Although standardized testing is beneficial in some situations, its use has been criticized, specifically because such measures fail to inform instruction adequately. Standardized administrations may not be possible for some students with disabilities. Some disabled students can take some test in the established standardized way with some accommodations. Some accommodations, however, can become modifications to the trait or concept attempting to be measured. Some other common criticisms or disadvantages of standardized tests are as follows: (1) standardized test items frequently are unrelated to those tasks and behaviors required in the classroom setting, (2) standardized test results reflect behavior or ability that has been measured during a single point in time and, as such, are greatly influenced by noncognitive factors (e.g., fatigue, attention, and so forth); (3) standardized test results do not provide the type of information required for making curricular modifications or instructional change, and (4) standardized administration procedures often prevent the examiner from obtaining useful information regarding the conditions under which the examinee may be able to improve performance (e.g., could a student with a language deficit benefit from clarification of test directions?) (Fuchs & Fuchs, 1986; Haywood & Tzuriel, 1992; Quinto & McKenna, 1977; Tzuriel, 2001; Tzuriel & Samuels, 2000).

ALTERNATIVES TO STANDARDIZED TESTING

Partly due to the criticisms of standardized testing and the need to generate information that can more directly guide instruction, alternatives to standardized testing have arisen. While there are various alternatives, three of the most commonly used alternatives are curriculum-based assessment, dynamic assessment, and alternative, or portfolio-based, assessment approaches.

Curriculum-Based Assessment. Although *curriculum-based assessment* (CBA) falls under the umbrella of criterion-referenced testing, it is thought of as an alternative to traditional, standardized norm-referenced academic testing. Curriculum-based assessment refers to a measurement method that relies on "direct observation and recording of a student's performance in the local curriculum as a basis for gathering information to make instructional decisions" (Deno, 1987, p. 41). CBA has also been referred to as *direct assessment* of the mastery of academic skills, and although models of CBA may differ, all share the common foundational assumption that one should assess what is taught, or more simply, "test what one teaches." Typically, CBA approaches involve repeated assessment of specific academic skills (Lentz, 1988). In each academic area, *probes* are developed (e.g., short reading passages, samples of math computation items, and brief spelling word lists, and so forth) and used to collect student performance data. The curricular materials from the examinee's immediate learning environment are used to develop CBA probes. Given this, CBA provides a structured method for evaluating students' performances on curricular assignments used in their actual academic setting.

Generally, a student's responses are evaluated in terms of speed or proficiency, as well as for accuracy. Performance criteria are then developed to determine acceptable levels of student performance or mastery (Witt et al., 1998). Normative sampling is one procedure employed for establishing mastery criteria (Idol, 1993). This procedure involves collecting samples of average or acceptable student performance in the general education setting and using such samples to decide what the absolute mastery criteria should be. In some cases, a referred student may be so far below the levels of acceptable performance that a type of changing criterion design might have to be implemented. This type of design, which would allow the mastery criteria to reflect the classroom average, would permit a lowering of the criteria for subsequent instruction, and then allow the criteria to be made more stringent until the student reached the changed classroom average.

Overall, the basic assumption of a CBA approach is that in evaluating students' progress in reading and writing, researchers should observe them reading and writing in their academic environment, and should collect such data often so that they can efficiently ascertain whether a student is progressing adequately or falling behind. The ability to generalize from the results of CBA tests is limited.

Dynamic Assessment. *Dynamic assessment* refers to a particular type of learning assessment that involves the use of an active teaching process (Lidz, 1987). The goal of this teaching process is to "modify" an individual's cognitive functioning and to observe subsequent changes in the examinee's learning and use of problem-solving strategies. The primary goals of dynamic assessment are to (1) assess a student's ability to understand principles underlying a problem and to use that understanding to generate a solution, (2) assess the type and amount of teaching necessary to teach a student a specific rule or principle, and (3) identify any cognitive deficits and noncognitive factors that assist in explaining performance failures and to determine whether such factors can be modified by teaching alone (Lidz, 1987).

Dynamic assessment directly contrasts with static assessment procedures (i.e., standardized assessment), which involve examiners presenting items to examinees without any guidance, assistance, or any other intervention designed to change or improve the examinee's performance. A static test is usually based on a "question, record, and score" format wherein the examiner presents the question, records the examinee's response, and awards a prescribed number of points, based on the examinee's given response.

The difference between static and dynamic assessment approaches stems from the paradigms from which they emerged. Static assessment generally involves "passive acceptance," wherein a child's deficits or disabilities are accepted and the environment is modified to help the child work within any identified limitations (Haywood, 1997). In contrast, dynamic assessment is based on "active modification," wherein a concentrated effort is made to remediate any identified deficit or at least provide the child with compensatory strategies to circumvent the impact of any identified weakness (Haywood & Tzuriel, 1992).

The inherent limitations or inadequacy of standardized tests has motivated, in part, the development of dynamic assessment approaches. Static assessments have been criticized widely. Major criticisms involve the fact that (1) static tests do not provide important information about a child's learning processes or mediational strategies that can facilitate learning, (2) they do not result in clear recommendations for prescriptive teaching or remedial activities, and (3) they do not focus on noncognitive factors that influence an examinee's performance on standardized, cognitive assessments. Compared to static assessment, dynamic assessment is intended to provide information about (1) examinees' overall learning ability and information regarding how they learn, (2) specific cognitive factors that can assist in problem solving and can help the examiner understand potential factors related to academic successes and failures, (3) teaching strategies that seem to work for a given examinee, and (4) noncognitive factors that exert beneficial or negative influences on cognitive performance (e.g., heightened anxiety can impact performance on tests of perceptual speed).

The zone of proximal development (ZPD) developed by Lev Vygotsky (1896–1934) and Reuben Feuerstein's theory of mediated learning experience (MLE) served as the primary foundations for most of the dynamic assessment approaches (Feuerstein, Rand, & Hoffman, 1979; Tzuriel, 1999). It is important to note that dynamic assessment is intended to supplement, not replace, standardized testing. It is a broad assessment approach, rather than a particular test. Some standardized test batteries have features of dynamic assessment (e.g., KABC-II contains teaching items that can be used with examinees before the administration of sample items).

Disadvantages of dynamic assessment include: (1) the time and skill required to implement a dynamic assessment approach, (2) the extent to which cognitive modifiability can occur across all cognitive domains is largely unknown, and (3) the validation of DA is far more complex than validating static assessment approaches because dynamic assessment has broad goals (e.g., assess initial performance, assess cognitive functions, identify any deficit functions, determine the nature and amount of remediation needed to address the deficit, identify noncognitive factors and the role they play in cognitive performance, and identify the parameters or goals for future change). By allowing the examiner to administer a test instrument in a non-standardized way, the ability to replicate the test results is more limited due to the potentially inconsistent nature of test administration. Overall, to validate dynamic assessment approaches, one needs to develop criteria variables that measure changes that are directly relatable to any applied cognitive intervention.

Alternative, or Portfolio-Based Assessment. Another type of assessment is *alternative assessment,* or *portfolio-based assessment.* This type of assessment is often longitudinal and very idiosyncratic in nature, as teachers, students, and even parents at times, select pieces from a student's work over several years (four years, on average) to demonstrate what learning progress has occurred over the years. Alternative assessments encourage all relevant individuals (teachers, students, parents) to become active participants in the documentation of the learning process (Quinto & McKenna, 1977). Although the terms portfolio-assessment and performance assessment sound similar, the latter involves looking at actual student work produced over time and the processes by which the students produced such work, be it individually or collaboratively. In contrast, the former involves focusing on the products and processes of learning as well as other factors, such as the students' interest in learning, their concept of themselves as readers and/or writers, and their ability to evaluate their own work and set learning goals for themselves. Examples of portfolio- or performance-based assessment include such things as tape-recorded samples of students' oral reading, results of reading interviews focused on identifying students' understanding of the reading process (e.g., strategies they used to decode problem words or comprehend text), records of students' reading lists to gain information regarding reading interests, and so forth.

Overall, alternative assessment is derived from student's daily classroom work. Minimally, it involves collecting student work samples, recording observations of learning processes, and student and/or teacher evaluation of students' processes and products. While such information can be summarized quantitatively for grading purposes, the primary goal of such assessment is to improve both teaching methods and students' learning.

Other Forms of Assessment and Testing. While static assessment approaches such as norm-referenced testing and criterion-referenced testing, curriculum-based assessment, and dynamic assessment approaches are used to varying extents in academic settings, other assessment techniques are also used, including interviews, anecdotal records, rating scales, classroom quizzes and tests, observation, and self-report techniques (Mercer, 1997; National Commission on Testing and Public Policy, 1990).

Each form of testing gathers information regarding a student or group of students and allows for a different type of interpretation and usage of data applied. Like the sides of a cut diamond, each shines in areas in which it is strong but is only a limited facet of the whole.

SEE ALSO *Norm-Referenced Testing.*

BIBLIOGRAPHY

American Psychological Association, National Council on Measurement in Education, & American Educational Research Association. (1999). *Standards for educational and psychological testing.* Washington, DC: American Psychological Association.

Deno, S. L. (1987). Curriculum-based measurement. *Teaching Exceptional Children (20),* 41.

Feuerstein, R., Rand, Y., & Hoffman, M. B. (1979). *The dynamic assessment of retarded performers: The learning potential assessment device: Theory, instruments, and techniques.* Baltimore, MD: University Park Press.

Fuchs, L. S., & Fuchs, D. (1986). Linking assessment to instructional intervention: An overview. *School Psychology Review (15),* 319–322.

Haywood, H. C. (1997). Interactive assessment. In R. L. Taylor (Ed.), *Assessment of individuals with mental retardation* (pp. 108–129). San Diego, CA: Singular.

Haywood, H. C., & Tzuriel, D. (1992). *Interactive assessment.* Berlin: Springer.

Idol, L. (1993). *Special educator's consultation handbook.* Austin, TX: Pro-Ed.

IRA/NCTE Joint Task Force on Assessment (1994). *Standards for the assessment of reading and writing.* Newark, DE: International Reading Association, and Urbana, IL: National Council of Teachers of English.

Lentz, F. E. (1988). Direct observation and measurement of academic skills: A conceptual review. In E. S. Shapiro & T. R. Kratochwill (Eds.). *Behavioral assessment in schools* (pp. 76–120). New York: Guilford.

Lidz, C. S. (1987). *Dynamic assessment.* New York: Guilford.

Mercer, C. D. (1997). *Students with learning disabilities* (5th ed.). Upper Saddle River, NJ: Prentice-Hall.

National Commission on Testing and Public Policy (1990). *From gatekeeper to gateway: Transforming testing in America.* Chestnut Hill, MA: Boston College.

Quinto, F., & McKenna, B. (1977). *Alternatives to standardized testing.* Washington, DC: National Education Association, Division of Instruction and Professional Development.

Tzuriel, D. (1999). Parent-child mediated learning transactions as determinants of cognitive modifiability: Recent research and future directions. *Genetic, Social, and General Psychology Monographs, 125,* 109–156.

Tzuriel, D. (2001). *Dynamic assessment of young children.* New York: Kluwer Academic/Plenum.

Tzuriel, D., & Samuels, M. T. (2000). Dynamic assessment of learning potential: Inter-rater reliability of deficient cognitive functions, type of mediation, and non-intellective factors. *Journal of Cognitive Education and Psychology, (1),* 41–64.

Weaver, C. (1990). *Understanding whole language: From principles to practice.* Portsmouth, NH: Heinemann.

Witt, J. C., Elliot, S. N., Daly III, E. J., Gresham, F. M., & Kramer, J. J. (1998). *Assessment of at-risk and special needs children* (2nd ed.). Boston: McGraw-Hill.

Dawn P. Flanagan
Jennifer T. Mascolo
Steven Hardy-Braz

STANDARDS FOR EDUCATIONAL AND PSYCHOLOGICAL TESTING

The appropriate development and use of assessments are essential requirements for responsible professional practice in educational testing and measurement. The American Educational Research Association (AERA), the American Psychological Association (APA), and the National Council on Measurement in Education (NCME) have collaborated on the development of Standards for Educational and Psychological Testing (hereafter referred to as the Standards) since 1966. There have been four revisions to these joint standards since they were first issued as separate technical recommendations for achievement tests and psychological tests by AERA and NCME in 1955, and APA in 1954. A subsequent edition of the Standards was published in 1999, and another revision was scheduled to begin in 2008.

When the Standards were developed the test user was assumed to be a trained professional who generally had some graduate training and supervised experience in assessment. These *primary test users* would include test developers, testing contractors, state and district assessment directors, and school counselors who develop or use tests for decision making purposes (Camara, 1997).

In the early 2000s, the term *test user* encompasses a much broader group of *secondary test users*, including individuals with little or no training in measurement and assessment such as teachers, parents, policymakers, and the media (Camara, 1997). Policymakers and educational administrators may have great influence over the use of assessment results and may misuse assessments in the 21st-century accountability environment (Berliner & Biddle, 1995). The further the test users are from the assessment, the less familiar they may be with the intended use of the assessment, evidence supporting the validity of inferences concerning the use of assessment results, and test content and characteristics of the test-taking population, which increases the likelihood of test misuse (Camara and Lane, 2006).

PURPOSE AND USE OF THE STANDARDS

The Standards have continued to emphasize that their primary purpose is to provide criteria for evaluating tests and testing practices and to encourage test developers, sponsors, publishers, and users to adopt the Standards, but there is no requirement on members of the professional associations or testing organizations and users to do so. They also note that the Standards do not attempt to provide psychometric answers to policy or legal questions. In 1999 the Standards abandoned the former designations of each standard as primary (required for all tests before operational use), secondary (desirable, but not required), or conditional (applicable in some instances and settings) (AERA et al., 1999). This change met with some criticism and controversy because it appeared to remove any absolute criteria or requirements for testing and test use and relied more on professional judgment in adherence to each standard.

The Standards also apply broadly to a wide range of standardized instruments and procedures which sample an individual's behavior that can include tests, assessments, inventories, and scales, for example. The main exceptions in applying the Standards are for unstandardized questionnaires (e.g., unstructured behavioral checklists or observational forms), teacher-made tests, and subjective decision processes (e.g., teacher evaluating classroom participation over the semester). The Standards apply equally to standardized multiple-choice tests as they do to performance assessments (including tests comprised only of open-ended essays) and hands-on assessments or simulations.

There is no mechanism to enforce compliance to the Standards on the part of the test developer or test user. As of 2008, many tests are sold and marketed that do not provide documentation required concerning their appropriate use, validation evidence to support such uses, and basic technical documentation such as the reliability of the score scale or a description of the normative or standard setting samples used for score reporting. Some publishers have ignored requests for technical manuals or validation studies, citing the proprietary nature of their clients, while some test users have used tests for unintended and multiple purposes with no concern for collecting additional evidence to support such uses. Requests for proposals from states and local educational departments nearly always refer to the Standards and frequently include a broad statement to the effect that vendors responding to the RFP must comply with the Standards; yet few states have conducted detailed audits of their assessment programs in direct reference to all the applicable standards.

Wise (2006) describes how technical advisory committees (TACs) and the peer review process used by the U.S. Department of Education for assessment systems under No Child Left Behind (NCLB) are efforts to improve the quality of testing but do not base reviews on all relevant components of the Standards. Madaus, Lynch, and Lynch (2001) and Kortz (2006) have described the need for some independent mechanisms to interpret, encourage compliance with, or even enforce the Standards. However, the Standards have been referred to in law and cited in Supreme Court and other judicial decisions, lending additional authority to the document. For example, they have been cited in Goals 2000: Educate America Act[1] and Title I (Elementary and Secondary Education Act)[2]. They were also cited in several major court decisions involving employment testing, including a Supreme Court case in 1988[3].

ADDITIONAL STANDARDS AND GUIDELINES IN TESTING

The APA adopted the first formal ethics code for any profession using assessments in 1952. Eighteen of approximately 100 principles in that Code (APA, 1953) addressed issues such as qualifications of test users, security of testing materials, documentation required in test manuals, and responsibilities of test publishers and test users. Ethical standards for assessment are one of nine areas addressed by the current code (APA, 2002). Many other professional associations with members involved in assessment similarly adopted ethical standards and professional codes between the mid-1980s and 2005. Increased public awareness of ethical issues, the variety of proposed and actual use of assessments, and the increased visibility and importance placed on assessments for accountability have resulted in greater attention to ethical and professional responsibilities by many professional associations (Eyde & Quaintance, 1988; Schmeiser, 1992).

In the early 1990s the American Counseling Association (ACA) and AERA each approved ethical standards that cover a broad range of standards for behavior in counseling and educational research but make only passing reference to assessment. Ethical standards of ACA (1998), APA, and the National Association of School Psychologists (NASP, 1997; 2000) are unique in that these associations support formal enforcement mechanisms that can result in suspension and expulsion of members, respectively (Camara, 1997)[4]. Ethical standards were first adopted by AERA in 1992 and revised twice thereafter. The standards as of 2008 (AERA, 1999) are designed to guide the work of educational researchers but are not enforceable.

In contrast to laws and regulations that are designed to protect the public from specific abuses, ethical standards and codes attempt to establish a higher normative standard for a broad range of professional activities and behaviors. For example, APA's Ethics Principles state: "if this Ethics Code establishes a higher standard of conduct than is required by law, psychologists must meet the higher ethical standards" (2002, p. 1062). ACA, AERA, APA and the Society for Industrial and Organizational Psychology (SIOP) have followed up the development of ethics codes with casebooks that attempt to guide users in interpreting and applying their standards.

The increased use of tests for accountability has also increased the urgency of informing and educating secondary users of their responsibilities in the appropriate and ethical use of tests and test data. In 2000 the U.S. Department of Education's Office of Civil Rights drafted a resource *Guide on High Stakes Testing* for educators and policy makers (2000) that attempted to interpret the technical and professional testing standards and legal principles and apply them to high stakes uses in schools, but as of 2008 the guide had not been disseminated following a change of administrations. Standards for Educational Accountability Systems (CRESST, 2002), which attempt to apply professional standards to accountability systems for a broad group of educators, were developed after passage of educational reform law.

The Code of Fair Testing Practices in Education (Joint Committee on Testing Practices, 2004) attempts to condense the most salient statements concerning the responsibilities of test users and test developers from existing codes and standards in four areas: (a) development and selection of tests; (b) administration and scoring of tests: (c) reporting and interpretation of test results; and (d) informing test takers. The Code has been endorsed by most of the major test publishers and is frequently reproduced on Web pages and publications in an attempt to guide educational professionals in appropriate practice and use of assessments. Most other technical and professional standards have a much more limited distribution, primarily to members, while the Code encourages reproduction and dissemination. A similar document, *Responsibilities of Users of Standardized Tests* (Association for Assessment in Counseling, 2003), was developed to enhance ethical standards and assist counselors in the ethical practice of testing.

TEST DEVELOPMENT

Ethical and professional issues relating to the development of assessments is a broad area that includes test construction (the technical qualities of assessments, evidence supporting the validity of inferences made from test results, and norms and scales) as well as modifications to the test, technical documentation, statements and claims made about assessments, and appropriate use of copyright materials. Technical competence in the development and selection of assessments is an ethical issue. APA's Ethics Code states that persons who develop tests "use appropriate psychometric procedures and current scientific or professional knowledge for test design, standardization, validation, reduction or elimination of bias and recommendations for use" (2002, p. 1072). Test developers are responsible for ensuring that assessment products and services meet applicable professional and technical standards and should be familiar with the Standards and other applicable requirements. They also have a responsibility for providing technical documentation on their tests, including evidence of reliability and validity that supports inferences that will be made from test scores. Technical qualities for many educational tests also include construct representation and curriculum relevance (Messick, 1989). Educators who select among *off-the-shelf* tests should ensure that the content specifications of the tests align with the curriculum and that assessment formats are relevant. The Standards reiterate the importance of construct relevance as a central requirement in the validation argument (AERA et al., 1999).

Test developers need to employ appropriate processes for item development, review, and test assembly to ensure potentially offensive (or biased) content or language is avoided and test content is relevant for the intended use. Evidence that differences in performance across major subgroups are related to the construct being measured and not due to construct irrelevant variance is also a professional responsibility of developers (Joint Committee on Testing Practices, 2004). Test development also includes obtaining appropriate permissions when copyrighted texts or art work are used for an assessment. The Standards reiterate that tests should be developed on a sound scientific basis (AERA et al., 1999).

A number of potential dilemmas may arise for test developers who produce off-the-shelf, as well as those who purchase these tests. For example, a test contract may require a developer to produce many more items in a short period of time than the organization is capable of developing while meeting acceptable quality standards. The increased assessment demands from local, state, and federal arenas may require test developers to take actions to meet scheduling and economic constraints that can threaten the technical quality of an assessment program. Sometimes the demand of test production may outstrip the resources of a test publisher and result in errors that may have been prevented with a more reasonable schedule (Phillips and Camara, 2006).

Test users who attempt to use a test for multiple purposes must provide evidence to support the use of the test for each proposed purpose unless existing evidence has been provided by the publisher or other sources. Educators often propose using the same test for both formative and summative purposes or to provide student, teacher, and school accountability functions as well as instructional, diagnostic, and placement purposes for the student. Evidence to support each specific use should be provided according to the Standards.

Rhoades and Madaus (2003) report on several instances in which insufficient piloting and pretesting led to spurious results, and time schedules for accountability tests did not allow for all the quality control procedures needed to detect and correct errors prior to test administration. In some situations, the desire to have tests drive the curriculum may conflict with any accountability uses for test results. For example, math teachers recruited to determine test specifications for a state accountability test may insist that a new eighth grade assessment require the use of graphing calculators to send a signal to students and all teachers about the need to introduce students to this technology and to compel the state to support the purchase of graphing calculators and appropriate professional development. However, if students are required to take the test before they are proficient in the use of graphing calculators, then the assessment is measuring construct irrelevant variance. Opportunity to learn is an important component of tests designed to measure achievement. In each of these instances, the technical quality of the assessment raises professional and even ethical issues that are more serious when the stakes associated with the testing program are higher.

The development of standardized administrative procedures and appropriately modified forms of tests and administrative procedures is also a responsibility of test developers (AERA et al., 1999; Joint Committee on Testing Practices, 2004; NCME, 1995). Modifications in test forms, response format, and test setting or content for students with disabling conditions or diverse linguistic backgrounds should be clearly described so that test users can reduce potential misuse of assessments.

Finally, technical documentation is a major requirement of any testing program. The first technical recommendations and standards produced by a professional association (APA, 1954) were largely developed to address the concern that tests were often released without adequate supporting documentation and research (Novick, 1981). NCME's Code (1995) notes that current technical information to support the reliability, validity, scoring and reporting processes, and other relevant characteristics of the assessment should be made available to the appropriate persons. The *Code of Fair Testing Practices in Education* (2004) and Standards (AERA et al., 1999) add that technical information provided to users should also include the level of precision of test scores, descriptions of test content and skills assessed, and representative samples of test items, directions, answer sheets, and score reports.

The increased importance placed on the use and results of high stakes assessments has not only placed enormous pressure on students, teachers, principles, school boards, and other parties inside the educational system; it has created additional professional and ethnical demands on measurement and testing professionals. The increased stakes associated with educational testing has led to a variety of unintended consequences that impact curriculum, teacher training, and professionalism in areas not directly tied to assessment as well as errors in the testing process itself (Cizek, 2001; Phillips and Camara, 2006). The Standards (AERA et al., 1999) and other professional, technical, and ethical guidelines that address assessment professionals provide guidance on many of the issues measurement professionals have long encountered in test development, test use, and test reporting.

NOTES

1. PL 103-227–Goals 2000: Educate America Act–Sec. 211 Purpose States "the National Education Standards and Improvement Council shall. (5) certify State assessments submitted by States or groups of States on a voluntary basis, if such assessments–(A) are aligned with and support State content standards certified by such Council; and (B) are valid, reliable, and consistent with relevant, nationally recognized, professional and technical standards for assessment when used for their intended purposes." The Federal Register, 43, pp. 38290-38315.) defines assessment under Goals 2000 act as, "ASSESSMENT–Any method used to measure characteristics of people, programs, or objects. (American Educational Research Association, American Psychological Association, & National Council on Measurement in Education. [1985]. Standards for educational and psychological testing. Washington, DC: American Psychological Association.)"

2. Title I–ESEA (Guidance on Standards, Assessments, and Accountability) "Title I requires that the assessment system be used for purposes that are valid and

reliable and that it meet nationally recognized professional and technical standards...The primary reference for technical quality of educational assessments is *Standards for Educational and Psychological Testing* (1985), developed by the American Educational Research Association, the American Psychological Association, and the National Council on Measurement in Education." (see http://www.ed.gov/policy/elsec/guid/standardsassessment/guidance_pg4.html).

3. *WATSON v. FORT WORTH BANK & TRUST*, 487 U.S. 977 (1988) 487 U.S. 977

4. The National Association for College Admission Counseling (NACAC) has developed standards of practice and other policy guidelines that are enforceable to its institutional members.

SEE ALSO *Reliability; Validity.*

BIBLIOGRAPHY

American Educational Research Association. (2000). *Ethical standards of AERA.* Washington, DC: Author.

American Educational Research Association, American Psychological Association, & National Council of Measurement in Education. (1999). *Standards for educational and psychological testing.* Washington, DC: AERA.

American Psychological Association. (2002). Ethical principles of psychologists and code of conduct. *American Psychologist, 57*(12), 1060–1073.

American Psychological Association. (1953). *Ethical standards for psychologists.* Washington, DC: Author.

American Psychological Association. (1954). *Technical recommendations for psychological test and diagnostic techniques.* Washington, DC: Author.

Association for Assessment in Counseling. (2003). *Responsibilities of Users of Standard Tests (RUST).* Alexandria, VA: Author.

Berliner, D. C., & Biddle, B. J. (1995). *The manufactured crisis: Myths, fraud, and the attack on America's public schools.* Reading, MA: Addison-Wesley.

Camara, W. J. (1997). Use and consequences of assessments in the USA: Professional, educational, and legal issues. *European Journal of Psychological Assessment, 13*(2), 140–152.

Camara, W. J., & Lane S. (2006). A historical perspective and current views on the Standards for Educational and Psychological Testing. *Educational Measurement: Issues and Practice, 25*(3), 35–45.

Cizek, G. J. (2001). More unintended consequences of high-stakes testing. *Educational Measurement: Issues and Practices, 20*(4), 19–27.

CRESST. (2002, Winter). *Standards for educational accountability systems.* Policy Brief 5. Los Angeles, CA: Author.

Joint Committee on Testing Practices. (2004). *Code of Fair Testing Practices in Education.* Retrieved November 1, 2007, from http://www.apa.org/science/FinalCode.pdf.

Kortz, D. (2006). Steps toward more effective implementation of the Standards for Educational and Psychological Testing. *Educational Measurement: Issues and Practice, 25*(3), 46–50.

Madaus, G. F., Lynch, C. A., & Lynch, P. S. (2001). A brief history of attempts to monitor testing. *National Board of Educational Testing and Public Policy Statements, 2*(2). Boston, MA: NBETPP.

Messick, S. (1989). Validity. In R. L. Linn (Ed.), *Educational measurement* (3rd ed., pp. 13–103). Washington, DC: American Council on Education-Macmillan.

National Association of Collegiate Admissions Counseling. (2001). *Statement of Principles of Good Practice.* Alexandria, VA: Author.

National Association of School Psychologists. (1997). *Procedural guidelines for the adjudications of ethical complaints.* Bethesda, MD: Author.

National Association of School Psychologists. (2000). *Professional Conduct Manual* (4th ed.). Bethesda, MD: Author.

National Council of Measurement in Education. (1995). *Code of professional responsibilities in education.* Washington, DC: Author.

Novick, M. R. (1981). Federal guidelines and professional standards. *American Psychologist, 36,* 1035–1046.

Phillips, S. E., & Camara, W. J. (2006). Legal and ethical issues. In Brennan, R. (Ed.), *Educational measurement* (ACE/Praeger Series on Higher Education) (4th ed., pp. 734–755). Westport, CT: Praeger.

Rhoades, K., & Madaus, G. (2003, May). *Errors in standardized testing: A systematic problem.* Retrieved November 1, 2007, from http://www.bc.edu/research/nbetpp/statements/M1N4.pdf.

Schmeiser, C. B. (1992). Ethical codes in the professions. *Educational Measurement: Issues and Practice, 11*(3), 5–11.

Wise, L. (2006). Encouraging and supporting compliance with standards for educational testing. *Educational Measurement: Issues and Practice, 25*(3), 51–56.

Wayne J. Camara

STANFORD-BINET INTELLIGENCE SCALES

The Stanford-Binet Intelligence Scales: Fifth Edition (SB-5; Roid, 2003a) is a test of intelligence/cognitive abilities for individuals 2 to over 85 years of age (child, adolescent, and adult). It is a major revision of the Stanford-Binet Intelligence Scales: Fourth Edition (SB-4; Thorndike, Hagen, & Sattler, 1986) and took seven years to complete. The complete SB-5 takes between 45 and 75 minutes to administer while the Abbreviated Battery takes between 15 and 20 minutes to complete. The Abbreviated Battery was included to allow for quick estimation of general intellectual abilities for screening purposes and includes the Nonverbal Fluid Reasoning and Verbal Knowledge subtests. These subtests are also used as routing subtests to provide estimates of intellectual functioning for placement into the appropriate level of test items better matching the individual's abilities. Use of the SB-5 may be for assessing mental retardation,

learning disabilities, developmental disabilities, and intellectual giftedness, although diagnosis of mental retardation also requires assessment of and significant deficits in adaptive behaviors. The SB-5 examiner's manual articulates test user qualifications, including college and/or graduate training in statistics and measurement for understanding test scores; thorough understanding of standardized administration, scoring, and calculation of standardized scores; and supervised training in administration via training workshops and/or graduate school testing courses.

HISTORICAL BACKGROUND AND DEVELOPMENT

The SB-5 evolved out of the original pioneering work of Alfred Binet (1857–1911), Victor Henri, and Théodore Simon in France during the late 1800s and early 1900s. Binet and Henri (1895) defined intelligence in terms of complex mental abilities (i.e., memory, abstraction, judgment, and reasoning) whereas Sir Francis Galton (1822–1911) had previously relied primarily on measuring physical and sensory abilities in assessing individual differences. Binet and Henri also developed tasks to measure these complex mental abilities. In 1904 the Minister of Public Instruction in Paris established a committee charged with finding a means to differentiate mentally retarded from normal children, and Binet was appointed to this committee. Earlier work by Binet and Henri and collaboration with Simon evolved into the first practical test of intellectual abilities for the diagnosis of mental retardation: the Binet-Simon Scale of Intelligence (Binet & Simon, 1905). Revisions and improvements of the Binet-Simon Scale of Intelligence were published in 1908 and 1911. Due to the success of the Binet-Simon Scale in France; Henry H. Goddard, Frederick Kuhlmann, J. E. Wallace Wallin, and Robert M. Yerkes each created translations of the Binet-Simon Scale of Intelligence for their use in the United States (Kaufman, 1990), but these different translations were not comparable and proved problematic. It was Lewis M. Termin who provided the most comprehensive translation and adaptation of the Binet-Simon Scale of Intelligence and provided better standardization. Termin's measure has survived to the present day through numerous revisions.

STANFORD-BINET INTELLIGENCE SCALES-FIFTH EDITION (SB-5)

The Stanford-Binet Intelligence Scales: Fifth Edition, (SB-5; Roid, 2003a), is a major revision and restructuring based on the hierarchical model of intelligence measurement illustrated by John B. Carroll (1993) and previous work by Raymond B. Cattell (1943, 1963) and John L. Horn (Cattell & Horn, 1978). The Cattell-Horn-Carroll

<table>
<tr><td colspan="3">**Stanford-Binet Intelligence Scales: Fifth Edition subtests and activities in relation to verbal and nonverbal domains and CHC Stratum II Factors**</td></tr>
<tr><td></td><td colspan="2">**Domains**</td></tr>
<tr><td>**Factors**</td><td>**Nonverbal**</td><td>**Verbal**</td></tr>
<tr><td>Fluid reasoning</td><td>**Nonverbal fluid reasoning**
*Object series/matrices**</td><td>**Verbal fluid reasoning**
Early reasoning (Levels 2–3)
Verbal absurdities (Level 4)
Verbal analogies (Levels 5–6)</td></tr>
<tr><td>Knowledge</td><td>**Nonverbal knowledge**
Procedural knowledge (Levels 2–3)
Picture absurdities (Levels 4–6)</td><td>**Verbal knowledge**
*Vocabulary**</td></tr>
<tr><td>Quantitative reasoning</td><td>**Nonverbal quantitative reasoning**
Quantitative reasoning (Levels 2–6)</td><td>**Verbal quantitative reasoning**
Quantitative reasoning (Levels 2–6)</td></tr>
<tr><td>Visual-spatial processing</td><td>**Nonverbal visual-spatial processing**
Form board (Levels 1–2)
Form patterns (Levels 3–6)</td><td>**Verbal visual-spatial processing**
Position and direction (Levels 2–6)</td></tr>
<tr><td>Working memory</td><td>**Nonverbal working memory**
Delayed response (Level 1)
Block span (Levels 2–6)</td><td>**Verbal working memory**
Memory for sentences (Levels 2–3)
Last word (Levels 4–6)</td></tr>
<tr><td colspan="3">Note: *Routing subtests. Subtests presented in bold. Table adapted from Roid (2003b) Figure 2.1.</td></tr>
</table>

Table 1 ILLUSTRATION BY GGS INFORMATION SERVICES. CENGAGE LEARNING, GALE.

(CHC) model of the structure of intellectual abilities is hierarchical with 50 to 60 narrow abilities at the bottom (Stratum I), 8 to 10 broad ability factors in the middle (Stratum II), and the general (*g*) ability factor at the top (Stratum III). The SB-5 activities and subtests measure a number of Stratum I dimensions, SB-5 Factors measure five Stratum II dimensions, and the Full Scale IQ measures Stratum III (*g* [general intelligence]). A number of subtests from the SB-4 were eliminated while new subtests were created and included in the SB-5.

The SB-5 (Roid, 2003a) includes ten subtests selected and designed to measure five CHC factors (fluid reasoning, knowledge, quantitative reasoning, visual-spatial processing, and working memory) within verbal and nonverbal domains. A global, Full Scale IQ score is provided in addition to Verbal IQ, Nonverbal IQ, and five composite factor scores. All scores are based on a mean of 100 and standard deviation of 15. Table 1 presents the SB-5 subtests (in bold) and the activities within subtests (in italics) used to measure the subtests specific to the different levels. Performance on the two routing subtests (nonverbal fluid reasoning and verbal knowledge) place individuals into the level appropriate for assessment. Recommendations for interpretation of SB-5 scores include the Full Scale IQ, comparisons of the Verbal and Nonverbal IQs, and the five factor scores (Roid, 2003b, 2003c).

Full Scale IQ scores range from 40 to 190, covering a wide range of intellectual abilities (±4 *SD*s). This allows for assessment to the lower levels of moderate mental retardation to the higher levels of intellectual giftedness. Verbal IQs range from 43 to 156 and Nonverbal IQs range from 42 to 158, providing a wide range. Factor scores also have wide ranges of possible scores (fluid reasoning: 47–153, knowledge: 49–151, quantitative reasoning: 50–149, visual–spatial processing: 48–152, working memory: 48–152).

The standardization sample of the SB-5 was stratified to closely match the 1998 United States Census data on key demographic variables of geographic region, race/ethnicity, age, and socioeconomic level for generalizing performance to the population. Socioeconomic level was estimated by the number of years of education completed or in the case of children, their parent's education level. Other technical characteristics, such as reliability (internal consistency, stability, and interrater agreement) and validity of SB-5 scores were generally considered positive in two independent reviews (Johnson & D'Amato, 2005; Kush, 2005). Both reviews noted improvements over the SB-4 but both also noted some problems.

INDEPENDENT RESEARCH WITH STANFORD-BINET INTELLIGENCE SCALES-FIFTH EDITION

Gale H. Roid (2003a, 2003b, 2003c) claimed the Stanford-Binet Intelligence Scales-Fifth Edition (SB-5) measured five CHC intelligence factors within verbal and nonverbal domains based on the test design and on use of confirmatory factor analysis (CFA) procedures. Factor analysis includes several approaches to investigate how a variety of measures relate and thus, how they define underlying dimensions. Generally, CFA procedures examine competing structural models to see which fits the data best while exploratory factor analysis (EFA) examines a correlation matrix to determine how many factors or dimensions should be extracted and retained to reflect the underlying structure.

Independent studies have seriously challenged the claim that the SB-5 measures five-factors using SB-5 standardization data. Christine DiStefano and Stefan C. Dombrowski (2006) recognized the problem of not using, or reporting, EFA and set to rectify this in their study of the SB-5 standardization data. They used both EFA and CFA procedures to determine the underlying structure of the SB-5. None of the analyses (EFA or CFA) performed by DiStefano and Dombrowski on the SB-5 standardization sample data found evidence for a five-factor model and only modest support was found for two-factors (verbal and nonverbal) and only with the two youngest age groups. The verbal and nonverbal dimensions were so moderately (EFA) to highly (CFA) correlated, DiStefano and Dombrowski concluded that the SB-5 was probably best explained as a unidimensional test of intelligence.

Gary L. Canivez (2007a, 2007b), like DiStefano and Dombrowski (2006), also failed to find empirical evidence for a five-factor model and further investigated the viability of the two-factor (verbal & nonverbal) SB-5 model for the child and adolescent subsamples from the SB-5 standardization sample. Using a hierarchical exploratory factor analysis method (Schmid & Leiman, 1957), which is a recommended procedure to understand how variance is apportioned at different interpretive levels (Carroll, 1993; Carretta & Ree, 2001), Canivez (2007a, 2007b) found that the overwhelming majority of variance measured by the SB-5 was at the general intelligence factor level (Carroll's Stratum III) and little variance seems to be measured at the lower level (verbal and nonverbal, Carroll's Stratum II). Failure to find support for Roid's (2003c) five factors and limited support for even two factors (Canivez, 2007a, 2007b; DiStefano & Dombrowski, 2006) may be the result of Roid extracting too many factors due to not considering exploratory factor analyses and multiple factor extraction criteria (Frazier & Youngstrom, 2007). As a result, clinical interpretation of the SB-5 should primarily reside at the global, general intelligence level until research adequately supports interpretation of lower-order (Stratum II) dimensions.

In summary, the SB-5 appears to be a very good measure of general intelligence across a wide age range, and the standardization sample appears to be a close match to the population on key demographic variables.

IQ scores also cover a wide range of ability from the lower levels of moderate mental retardation to the higher levels of intellectual giftedness. As such, they will be helpful in assessing students with mental retardation, learning disabilities, and intellectual giftedness, and interpretation of the global Full Scale IQ appears to have strong empirical support. However, as of 2007 much more research is required before interpretation of two- or five-factor models can be supported or recommended.

SEE ALSO *Intelligence Testing.*

BIBLIOGRAPHY

Binet, A. (1911). Nouvelle recherches sur la mesure du niveau intellectuel chez les enfants d'école. *L'Année Psychologique, 17,* 145–210.

Binet, A., & Henri, V. (1895). La psychologie individuelle. *L'Année Psychologique, 2,* 411–465.

Binet, A., & Simon, T. (1905). Methodes nouvelles pour le diagnostic du niveau intellectual des anormaux. *L'Année Psychologique, 11,* 191–244.

Binet, A., & Simon, T. (1908). Le developpement de l'intelligence chez les enfants. *L'Année Psychologique, 14,* 1–94.

Canivez, G. L. (2007a). Orthogonal higher-order factor structure of the Stanford-Binet Intelligence Scales for children and adolescents. Manuscript submitted for publication.

Canivez, G. L. (2007b, August). Hierarchical Factor Structure of the Stanford-Binet Intelligence Scales-Fifth Edition. Paper presented at the 2007 Annual Convention of the American Psychological Association, San Francisco, CA.

Carretta, T. R., & Ree, J. J. (2001). Pitfalls of ability research. *International Journal of Selection and Assessment, 9,* 325–335.

Carroll, J. B. (1993). *Human cognitive abilities: A survey of factor analytic studies.* New York: Cambridge University Press.

Cattell, R. B. (1943). The measurement of adult intelligence. *Psychological Bulletin, 40,* 153–193.

Cattell, R. B. (1963). Theory of fluid and crystallized intelligence: A critical experiment. *Journal of Educational Psychology, 54,* 1–22.

Cattell, R. B., & Horn, J. L. (1978). A check on the theory of fluid and crystallized intelligence with description of new subtest designs. *Journal of Educational Measurement, 15,* 139–164.

DiStefano, C., & Dombrowski, S. C. (2006). Investigating the theoretical structure of the Stanford-Binet-Fifth Edition. *Journal of Psychoeducational Assessment, 24,* 123–136.

Frazier, T. W., & Youngstrom, E. A. (2007). Historical increase in the number of factors measured by commercial tests of cognitive ability: Are we overfactoring? *Intelligence, 35,* 169–182.

Johnson, J. A., & D'Amato, R. C. (2005). Review of the Stanford-Binet Intelligence Scales: Fifth Edition. In R. S. Spies & B. S. Plake (Eds.), *The sixteenth mental measurements yearbook* (pp. 976–979). Lincoln, NE: Buros Institute of Mental Measurements.

Kaufman, A. (1990). *Assessing adolescent and adult intelligence.* Boston: Allyn & Bacon.

Kush, J. C. (2005). Review of the *Stanford-Binet Intelligence Scales: Fifth Edition.* In R. S. Spies & B. S. Plake (Eds.), *The sixteenth mental measurements yearbook* (pp. 979–984). Lincoln, NE: Buros Institute of Mental Measurements.

Roid, G. H. (2003a). *Stanford-Binet Intelligence Scales: Fifth Edition.* Itasca, IL: Riverside.

Roid, G. H. (2003b). *Stanford-Binet Intelligence Scales: Fifth Edition, Examiner's Manual.* Itasca, IL: Riverside.

Roid, G. H. (2003c). *Stanford-Binet Intelligence Scales: Fifth Edition, Technical Manual.* Itasca, IL: Riverside.

Schmid, J., & Leiman, J. M. (1957). The development of hierarchical factor solutions. *Psychometrika, 22,* 53–61.

Terman, L. M. (1916). The measurement of intelligence. Boston: Houghton Mifflin.

Terman, L. M., & Merrill, M. A. (1937). *Measuring intelligence.* Boston: Houghton Mifflin.

Terman, L. M., & Merrill, M. A. (1960). *Stanford-Binet Intelligence Scale.* Boston: Houghton Mifflin.

Terman, L. M., & Merrill, M. A. (1973). *Stanford-Binet Intelligence Scale: 1972 Norms Editions.* Boston: Houghton Mifflin.

Thorndike, R. L., Hagen, E. P., & Sattler, J. M. (1986). *Stanford-Binet Intelligence Scale: Fourth Edition.* Chicago: Riverside.

Gary L. Canivez

STEREOTYPE THREAT

According to Steele and Aronson (1995), stereotype threat is defined as a "socially premised psychological threat that arises when one is in a situation or doing something for which a negative stereotype about one's group applies" (Steele, 1997, p. 614). Another description of stereotype threat suggests that individuals are at risk of confirming a negative stereotype about their group. Here, individuals who experience stereotype threat are 1) acknowledging that a negative stereotype exists (i.e., salient in a given context or is explicitly stated) about the capabilities of their social group (i.e., race/ethnicity, gender, age, socioeconomic status) and 2) demonstrating apprehension about confirming the negative stereotype by engaging in particular activities.

An example of stereotype threat is a member of a stigmatized group (i.e., African American students, women) feeling apprehension about performing on an academic task because the individual is afraid that a possible poor performance may confirm a pre-existing negative stereotype about the individual's group (i.e., intellectual capabilities of African Americans or perceived underperformance of women in science and mathematics). For Steele, it is unnecessary for the group member to believe the stereotype to be true for stereotype threat to produce negative psychological consequences for the individual. That is, the psychological reactions to stereotype threat—exposure to contexts in which negative stereotypes about the capabilities and behaviors of a given group are or have been salient—are enough to alter the attitudes and behaviors of individual group members and produce maladaptive psychological functioning.

TASK PERFORMANCE SUBVERSION

Much of the research on stereotype threat has shown that the task performance of otherwise capable individuals is hindered when such a social-psychological threat is presented at the time of the performance (Aronson et al., 1999; Steele & Aronson, 1995; Steele, 1997). Steele (1997) and Aronson (2002) write that, for many stigmatized groups—namely women and ethnic minority populations—stereotype threat is a common reality. In particular, low-income African American and Latino students are often exposed to academic contexts in which, historically, negative beliefs regarding their perceived intelligence have been held. The awareness and salience of the belief regarding their intelligence can disrupt academic performance for these students.

The consequences of stereotype threat have been noted. For example, in a review, Aronson (2002) notes that perceptions of negative stereotypes lead many individuals to engage in activities such as self-handicapping (Smith, 2004), challenge avoidance (Good, Aronson, & Inzlicht, 2003), self-suppression (Steele, 1997; Pronin, Steele, & Ross, 2002), and disidentification or disengagement with the task or the context in which the task is to be performed (Steele, 1997; Aronson, 2002; Major et al., 1998). In addition to these poor academic performance correlates, stereotype threat has also been linked to high blood pressure among African Americans (Blascovich et al., 2001), altered career and/or professional aspirations and belonging (Steele, James, & Barnett, 2002), and social distancing, particularly from the stigmatized social group of which the participants are members (Pronin, Steele, & Ross, 2002).

These psychological and behavioral outcomes found among low-income African American and Latino and women students are not typically the result of negative stereotypes being communicated directly to them from others within the given social context. Rather, these behaviors typically result from exposure to a context in which historically 1) the performance of a given group is evaluated and compared with that of others, 2) such performance has been valued by the group and the larger society, and 3) the performance of one's group has been consistently negatively evaluated and thus stereotyped more than other groups.

MAJOR FINDINGS ON STEREOTYPE THREAT IN ACADEMIC DOMAINS

Much of the support for the presence and effects of stereotype threat has been garnered through experimentally designed studies that have been based on the research of Claude Steele and Joshua Aronson (Steele & Aronson, 1995; Steele, 1997). In each study, participants were primed toward greater awareness of a negative stereotype either about their group or a group believed to be superior to their group. The psychological effects of this priming were the major dependent variables of interest across their works.

For example, Steele and Aronson (1995) first tested the effects and corollaries of stereotype threat with African American college students. In the first of four experimentally designed studies, Steele and Aronson (1995) gave a 30-minute GRE verbal exam to 114 undergraduates. Using a 2 (race) x 3 (threat condition) factorial design, Steele and Aronson (1995) created and analyzed the effects of race (African American and White) and testing condition on students' performance on the graduate records exam (GRE). Similar to the research on stereotype threat and women's math performance, Steele and Aronson (1995) noted that African American and White students were matched on verbal ability prior to being recruited for participation in the study.

In the first testing condition, African American and White students were exposed to the stereotype threat condition in which the GRE exam was described by the researchers as a test to determine diagnostic ability on verbal competence. The second condition, non-stereotype threat, consisted of communication by the researchers that the students' test taking and performance were not diagnostic of ability and was only considered to be a routine laboratory task. Finally, the third condition consisted of communication by researchers indicating that the non-diagnostic task should be considered a challenge, but not indicative of their fixed intelligence. Results from the first study indicated that, after controlling for differences in SAT scores, African American students in the diagnostic (stereotype threat) condition fared worse on the GRE verbal examination than their White counterparts in the same condition and also African American students in the non-diagnostic and challenge conditions.

In study two, 40 undergraduates were recruited to participate in the study in which the same experimental conditions and procedures were employed. Here, a significant interaction emerged, with African American students in the diagnostic (stereotype threat) condition performing significantly worse than all other students in the remaining experimental conditions. Also noted were the findings that African American students in the stereotype threat condition yielded lower response accuracy and had more incomplete responses than their African American counterparts in the non-diagnostic condition. White students in both conditions also had higher response accuracy than African American students in the diagnostic, stereotype threat condition.

In addition to research with African American students, Steele and colleagues also carried out research on stereotype threat with another stigmatized group: women. Throughout these studies, stereotype threat was operationalized by stating a phrase that would evoke knowledge of and reactions to negative stereotypical beliefs about a particular group's ability on an academically premised experimental task. For example, Spencer, Steele, and Quinn (1999) tested the belief that women generally perform less well on standardized mathematics examinations as a result of stereotype threat. The study sample included undergraduate males and females deemed equally competent in mathematics performance. The criteria for such included completion of one semester in calculus with a grade of B and a score above the 85th percentile on the math subsection of the Scholastic Aptitude Test or American College Test (Steele, 1997).

To operationalize stereotype threat for the participants, students were told that the test had shown gender performance differences in the past. This would "explicitly evoke the stereotype about women's math ability" (p.11). In the other condition, students were told that the math examination did not yield gender performance differences. In this study, women in the stereotype threat condition were outperformed by men in the same condition, even though students from both gender groups had equitable ability and exposure to mathematics. In the non-stereotype condition, women performed equally to the men. A significant interaction between gender and test condition (gender difference/stereotype threat and no gender difference/non-stereotype threat) found that women in the stereotype threat condition scored the lowest on the math exam whereas no other significant differences among the four conditions emerged.

While much research on stereotype threat has shown that many persons from low-income and ethnic minority and gender minority statuses can experience the psychological threat of negative stereotypes, research has also shown that virtually any member of any group can experience stereotype threat (Aronson, 2002; Smith, 2004; Steele, 1997). For example, some research has shown negative or maladaptive effects of stereotype threat on a variety of groups, including the elderly (Levy, 1996), White males (Aronson et al., 1999), elementary and middle grade school students (Ambady et al., 2001), and low-income French and American students (Croizet & Claire, 1998; Spencer & Castano, 2007). In one study, elderly participants performed significantly worse on a short-term memory task when they were exposed to negative stereotypes regarding societal perceptions of old age and senility than their counterparts who did not receive such messages (Levy, 1996). Another study showed that White male mathematics majors could fall victim to stereotype threat, even though this population is typically not viewed as being stigmatized or marginalized.

In particular, Aronson and colleagues (1999) had White male undergraduate mathematics majors complete math tasks in one of two conditions: a stereotype threat condition and a non-stereotype threat condition. The stereotype threat prompt that they read suggested that they were participating in a study designed to determine why Asians seem to perform better on math examinations. Findings from this study showed that White male math majors in the stereotype threat condition performed significantly less well than their counterparts in the non-stereotype threat condition.

WAYS TEACHERS CAN STRUCTURE CLASSROOMS TO REDUCE STEREOTYPE THREAT

These studies and others by Steele and his colleagues have affirmed the idea that many students, but particularly low-income African American and female students, face added stressors in testing situations. These psychological stressors have little to do with students' sense of competence regarding intellectual tasks, but rather they stem from the societal-premised, negative stereotypes associated with African Americans' performance in testing situations. Given these findings, Steele (1997) and Aronson (2002) have noted that the challenge for minimizing the effects of stereotype threat often relies in the ability of educators to successfully counter societal-premised group stereotypes.

One solution, proposed formally by Steele, is the creation of "wise schooling." Through wise schooling, Steele and others have sought to replace the intangible, yet omnipresent stereotype of academic difficulty and cognitive and intellectual inferiority with instructor-based behaviors and activities that express the idea that such stigmatized students can and are fully expected to fare well in general and successfully meet the high academic standard found in and across various academic domains and settings (Cohen, Steele, & Ross, 1999). In addition, wise schooling for Steele and colleagues duly includes communicating to and believing that the stigmatized students are capable of achieving high standards and expectations.

Some research has empirically supported the use of wise schooling to reduce the effects of stereotype threat. Using experimental methods, Cohen, Steele, and Ross (1999) studied White and African American college students, all of whom were matched on language arts/writing ability. These individuals were given an essay assignment to complete under one of three feedback conditions, each of which was characterized by written feedback to the students' essays to indicate condition. The first condition, unbuffered criticism, was believed to be typical of the

college performance evaluation experience. Here, feedback was largely directive and provided in a neutral, disaffected voice/manner that did not consider the emotional impact such an evaluation may have on students. A sample statement from the unbuffered criticism letter to students in this condition is as follows: "Your letter needs work in several areas before it can be considered for publication" (1999, p. 1306).

Another condition was the wise criticism condition, which included language that communicated high and tangible achievement standards. The first line of the wise criticism letter to students in this condition stated: "It's obvious to me that you've taken your task seriously and I'm going to do likewise by giving you some straight forward, honest feedback." Additional wording in the feedback letter stated: "I wouldn't go to the trouble of giving you this feedback if I didn't think, based on what I've read in your letter/essay, that you are capable of meeting the higher standard" (p. 1307). Finally, in the positive buffer condition, the same feedback was present as that in the wise criticism condition. However, the feedback was preceded by a paragraph that offered the student some praise for the work, prior to the revisions it needed. A sample sentence there was: "Overall, nice job" (p. 1307).

The independent variables in the study were student race and criticism condition whereas the dependent variables included task motivation and perception of teacher/instructor bias. The authors found that African American students in the unbuffered criticism condition were significantly lower in their task motivation and significantly higher in their reports of perceived instructor bias than White students in the same condition. The researchers state that the difference in task motivation and bias perception between White and African American students was virtually removed in the wise criticism and positive buffer conditions.

In addition to wise schooling techniques to reduce stereotype threat effects, Aronson (2002) identified several ways in which teachers can work to minimize stereotype threat in the elementary and secondary classrooms. Teachers should reframe how standardized tests, evaluations, and even grades are presented to students. This can be done by shifting the emphasis of assessment from a measure of ability to what Aronson refers to as a non-evaluative task. For example, a teacher can suggest to students that a test is actually examining how well the teacher has instructed the students rather than how well the students have learned and retained the material. Teachers can reduce stereotype threat by dispelling the idea that ability, skill, and intelligence are static characteristics. For Aronson, communicating to students that their skills and intelligence can be further developed and are, therefore, malleable rather than unalterable or fixed can minimize the threat of stereotypes. Additional research has shown that teachers can deemphasize stereotype threat by emphasizing self-affirmation among the students and providing same-sex, same-gender role models to students in the classroom prior to their participation on an academic task (Cohen et al. 2006; McIntyre, Paulson, & Lord, 2003).

SEE ALSO *Cultural Bias in Teaching; Gender Bias in Teaching.*

BIBLIOGRAPHY

Ambady, N., Shih, M., Kim, A., & Pittinsky, T. L. (2001). Stereotype susceptibility in children: Effects of identity activation on quantitative performance. *Psychological Science, 12,* 385–390.

Aronson, J. (2002). Stereotype threat: Contending and coping with unnerving expectation. In J. Aronson (Ed.), *Improving academic achievement: Impact of psychological factors on education* (pp. 279–301). New York: Academic Press.

Aronson, J., Lustina, M. J., Good, C., Keough, K., Steele, C. M., & Brown, J. (1999). When White men can't do math: Necessary and sufficient factors in stereotype threat. *Journal of Experimental Social Psychology, 35,* 29–46.

Blascovich, J., Spencer, S. J., Quinn, D., & Steele, C.M. (2001). African American and high blood pressure: The role of stereotype threat. *Psychological Science, 12,* 225–229.

Cohen, G. L., Garcia, J., Apfel, N., & Master, A. (2006). Reducing the racial achievement gap: A social-psychological intervention. *Science, 313,* 1307–1310.

Cohen, G. L., Steele, C. M., & Ross, L. D. (1999). The mentor's dilemma: Providing critical feedback across the racial divide. *Personality and Social Psychology Bulletin, 25,* 1302–1318.

Croizet, J. C., & Claire, T. (1998). Extending the concept of stereotype threat to social class: The intellectual underperformance of students low socioeconomic backgrounds. *Personality and Social Psychology Bulletin, 24,* 588–594.

Good, C., Aronson, J., & Inzlicht, M. (2003). Improving adolescents' standardized test performance: An intervention to reduce the effects of stereotype threat. *Journal of Applied Developmental Psychology, 24,* 645–662.

Levy, B. (1996). Improving memory in old age through implicit self-stereotyping. *Journal of Personality and Social Psychology, 71,* 1092–1107.

Major, B., Spencer, S., Schmader, T., Wolfe, C., & Crocker, J. (1998). Coping with negative stereotypes about intellectual performance. The role of psychological disengagement. *Personality and Social Psychology Bulletin, 24,* 34–50.

McIntyre, R. B., Paulson, R., & Lord, C. (2003). Alleviating women's mathematics stereotype threat through salience of group achievements. *Journal of Experimental Social Psychology, 39,* 83–90.

Pronin, E., Steele, C. M., & Ross, L. (2004). Identity bifurcation in response to stereotype threat: Women and mathematics. *Journal of Experimental Social Psychology, 40,* 152–168.

Smith, J. L. (2004). Understanding the process of stereotype threat: A review of mediational variables and new performance goal directions. *Educational Psychology Review, 16*(3), 177–206.

Spencer, B., & Castano, E. (2007). Social class is dead. Long live social class! Stereotype threat among low socioeconomic status individuals. *Social Justice Research, 20,* 418–432.

Spencer, S. J., Steele, C. M., & Quinn, D. M. (1999). Stereotype threat and women's math performance. *Journal of Experimental Social Psychology, 35,* 4–28.

Steele, C. M. (1997). A threat in the air: How stereotypes shape intellectual identity and performance. *American Psychologist, 52,* 613–629.

Steele, C. M. & Aronson, J. (1995). Stereotype threat and the intellectual test performance of African Americans. *Journal of Personality and Social Psychology, 69,* 797–811.

Steele, J., James, J. B., & Barnett, R. (2002). Learning in a man's world: Examining the perceptions of undergraduate women in male-dominated academic areas. *Psychology of Women Quarterly, 26,* 46–50.

Kenneth M. Tyler
Christina Tyler

STERNBERG, ROBERT J(EFFREY)
1949–

Robert Jeffrey Sternberg was born on December 8, 1949, in Newark, New Jersey. He received his B.A. in psychology from Yale University in 1972, under the mentorship of Endel Tulving; and his Ph.D. in psychology from Stanford University in 1975, where he worked with Gordon Bower. After completion of his dissertation, Sternberg began his professional career at Yale University, where he remained for 30 years. Sternberg's career at Yale was extremely productive and resulted in the publication of more than 1,200 scientific and popular works and the establishment of the Center for the Psychology of Abilities, Competencies, and Expertise (PACE Center) in

Robert J. Sternberg, March 1, 2005. AP IMAGES.

2000. In 2005 Sternberg and the PACE Center relocated to Tufts University, where Sternberg accepted the positions of dean of the School of Arts and Sciences and professor of psychology.

Sternberg held many elected offices in professional organizations, including president of the American Psychological Association. He led as editor two major professional journals of the American Psychological Association, and served as associate editor, consulting editor, or member of the editorial board of more than 30 other psychological and educational journals. Sternberg's work has been recognized by honorary doctoral degrees from eight universities throughout the world and by 25 scholarly prizes and awards.

Sternberg has collaborated and published with a number of distinguished scientists, both senior (Endel Tulving and Gordon Bower) and peer (e.g., Douglas Detterman, Paul Ackerman and Howard Gardner). He also has a remarkable track record of publishing with his numerous current and former students, enhancing, stimulating, and promoting their careers.

The research of Robert Sternberg is extremely diverse, spanning the fields of cognitive, educational, personality, abnormal, and organizational psychology. In educational psychology, the main focus of his research has been the implications for teachers and students of individual differences in cognition and learning. For educators, the two most important theories are the theory of successful intelligence (also known as the triarchic theory of intelligence) and the theory of mental self government (also known as the theory of thinking styles).

The theory of successful intelligence defines intelligence as the ability of individuals to succeed in life by capitalizing on their strengths and compensating for their weaknesses.

According to Sternberg, abilities cannot be reduced to a single general measure of intelligence but should be developed and assessed in a multi-faceted manner. He defines three fundamental cognitive abilities; hence the original name triarchic theory of intelligence. Analytical abilities are needed for analyzing, evaluating, judging, comparing, and contrasting. Creative abilities are called for when there is a need to generate new knowledge. Practical abilities are required for the application and use of knowledge. The psychological building blocks of these abilities are the same, but individuals may demonstrate both integrated and uneven profiles across these dimensions. The theory of successful intelligence has been the subject of a wide range of studies. These range from the development and validation of the theory (see, for example, Sternberg, 1980) to application of the theory to college admission policies (e.g., Sternberg et al., 2006).

The theory of mental self-government postulates the presence of styles of thinking (or mental government) that form psychological bridges between individuals' intelligence and personalities. Sternberg differentiates 13 different styles of thinking. The primary types of styles are legislative, judicial, and executive, matching the three major functions of government. There are also four forms of styles (anarchic, oligarchic, monarchic, and hierarchic); two levels (liberal and conservative); two focuses (extra- and intro) and two dimensions (local and global). His empirical work validates the importance of recognizing the existence of different styles of thinking among both teachers and students to maximize the effectiveness of teaching and learning.

At the later stages of his career, Sternberg became interested in wisdom and developed an all-encompassing framework that embraces various components of his work; this framework is referred to as Wisdom, Intelligence, and Creativity Synthesized (WISC).

Sternberg's work has penetrated and influenced the field of education at all levels—research, practice and policy. His prolific writing has generated widespread attention and all contemporary textbooks in psychology and education mention his theoretical and empirical research.

SEE ALSO *Intelligence: An Overview; Triarchic Theory of Intelligence.*

BIBLIOGRAPHY
Sternberg, R. J. (1980). Sketch of a componential subtheory of human intelligence. *Behavioral and Brain Sciences, 3,* 573–584.
Sternberg, R. J. (1996). *Successful intelligence.* New York: Simon & Schuster.
Sternberg, R. J. (1997). *Thinking styles.* New York: Cambridge University Press.
Sternberg, R. J. (2003). *Wisdom, intelligence, and creativity synthesized.* New York: Cambridge University Press.
Sternberg, R. J., & Rainbow Project Collaborators (2006). The Rainbow Project: Enhancing the SAT through assessments of analytical, practical and creative skills. *Intelligence, 34,* 321–350.

Elena L. Grigorenko

STRATEGIES INSTRUCTION

A strategy is a plan of action for achieving a purpose (Harvey & Goudvis, 2007). With respect to classroom learning, purposes for employing strategies include the need to comprehend, compose, problem solve, remember, reason, evaluate, and decode. Students who have been taught strategies for accomplishing these purposes have a distinct advantage over the uninstructed (Pressley, Graham, & Harris, 2006; Torgesen, 2004). Yet, researchers have found that most teachers do not teach the strategies students need to comprehend and learn (Durkin, 1978–1979; Pressley, Wharton-McDonald, Mistretta, & Echevarria, 1998). Neglecting to teach strategies for accomplishing classroom tasks is a serious oversight, especially when people realize that the learners who are most successful are also the ones who are able to, and do, employ many strategies (Bransford, Brown, & Cocking, 2000; Trabasso & Bouchard, 2002). Strategies put students in control of their mental processes (Duffy, 2002); thus, it would be in students' best interest if teachers in all areas of the curriculum taught strategies.

Appropriate strategies for accomplishing learning tasks vary depending on the desired outcomes and structure of the domain. In the domains of history, mathematics, and science, Donovan and Bransford (2005) note that students benefit from strategies which enable them to access and evaluate their preconceptions, develop a deep foundation of factual knowledge, understand facts and ideas in the context of a conceptual framework, and organize knowledge in ways that facilitate retrieval and application. In conducting science investigations, strategies include generating a research question, designing a study, and explaining the results. In literature, strategies for detecting theme, analyzing character traits, and recognizing different genres are important (Gaskins, 2005; Harmon, Martinez, & Deckard, 2004). Common to the domains of history, mathematics, science, and literature are the basic skills of reading and writing. In these two areas researchers suggest that students be taught strategies for decoding and encoding words, as well as for comprehending and composing. Research-based comprehension strategies include accessing background knowledge, predicting, self-questioning, constructing mental images, and summarizing (Pressley, 2006). In writing, a meta-analysis suggests that students need to learn strategies for planning, drafting, reflecting, and revising (Graham, 2006). In all areas of the curriculum, researchers recommend that students be taught strategies for taking control of their thinking (Donovan & Bransford, 2005; Schunk & Zimmerman, 1997).

This entry on strategy instruction is divided into three sections: (1) major approaches to strategies instruction, (2) characteristics of explicit, teacher-led strategies instruction, and (3) effective instructional supports for strategies instruction.

MAJOR APPROACHES TO STRATEGIES INSTRUCTION

There is little debate in the 21st century about the benefits to be gained from teaching students strategies that will allow them to read, write, and learn independently (Deshler, Palincsar, Biancarosa, & Nair, 2007). The debate, with respect to strategies instruction, centers on which instructional approaches and contexts work best for which students and whose responsibility it is to teach strategies. This question is particularly relevant for students in grades 4 through 12, when the density of texts and concepts dramatically increase, and for students in all grades who have learning and reading difficulties (Alexander & Winne, 2006). There are at least three broad categories into which approaches to strategies instruction can be divided: (1) stand alone, in which strategies, heuristics, and/or study skills are taught as a separate course, usually with texts that are not part of the mainstream curriculum; (2) teachable moment, in which strategies are taught as students demonstrate a need for them; and (3) explicit, teacher-led instruction, in which teachers explain, model, scaffold, and guide practice regarding strategies that will be of immediate use in the completion of specific learning tasks that are part of the mainstream curriculum.

Different approaches may be beneficial for different people, depending on their backgrounds of knowledge in a domain, their learning strengths and challenges, and the context for learning. For students who read and write at levels significantly below their grade-level placement, particularly students who lack basic decoding and encoding strategies, stand-alone courses are sometimes needed as a supplement to the mainstream curriculum. For students with strong backgrounds in a domain, teachable-moment approaches may better meet their needs. Explicit, teacher-led instruction is the approach documented to be successful with students who demonstrate learning problems (Deshler, et al., 2007; Pressley & Harris, 2006; Swanson, 1999). There are also possible combinations and variations of the three main approaches described below.

Stand-alone Approach. In stand-alone approaches, strategies are taught outside the authentic situation in which they are expected to be applied. For example, students participating in a study skills course may be explicitly taught strategies for identifying main ideas, taking notes, and studying for tests, followed by teacher-directed, scaffolded practice in content-area materials. Often, however, the practice materials are not the same as those the students use in their content-area classes. For students who are motivated to learn these strategies and who also are aware of the appropriate occasions to apply them, a stand-alone course can be beneficial. The chances for application are increased if the students' regular classroom teachers are aware of the strategies that have been taught in the study skills course and can cue students when it is appropriate to use those strategies. The likelihood of transfer to authentic classroom situations is less likely, unfortunately, for struggling students who most need to apply these strategies (Pressley & Harris, 2006).

Teachable-moment Approach. Those who favor the teachable-moment approach assert that teachers should wait until a student encounters a problem in completing a task or asks for clarification, and then coach the student in his or her application of appropriate strategies. A classic debate regarding teachable-moment interventions has for decades surrounded the teaching of strategies for decoding. There are those who believe that decoding strategies should not be explicitly taught, but rather students should be taught to problem solve when they encounter an unknown word. For example, when a student encounters the unknown word "turtle," the teacher might ask: "What would make sense in the sentence and begins with *t-*?" If this clue is not helpful, the teacher might continue, "Do the pictures give you any clues that you could combine with the sense of the sentence and the sound for the first letter?" The goal of the teacher's questioning is to model questions students might ask themselves when they encounter an unknown word.

Similarly, when students are stuck solving a math problem or understanding a science experiment, the teacher might mediate the application of the needed strategy by asking questions the students could ask themselves on another occasion when they are perplexed. Two possible concerns about using this approach are that it relies on teachers being skillful in asking mediating questions (rather than telling too much) and on teachers having a deep understanding of the developmental sequence of strategies that would be beneficial for students to employ in completing classroom learning tasks. Another consideration is that the teachable-moment approach can be labor intensive; thus it may work best in small classes and one-on-one tutoring.

Explicit Teacher-led Approach. The approach to strategies instruction most frequently supported by research, especially for children with learning problems, is the approach that features explicit teacher explanations of the what, why, when, and how of using strategies, accompanied by teacher modeling, scaffolding, and guided practice (Lipson, 2007; Gaskins, 2005). As noted earlier, explicit explanation of strategies is not practiced in most classrooms; however, two such programs that have received empirical support are Project CRISS (Santa, Havens, & Valdes, 2005) and Transactional Strategies Instruction (Pressley, El-Dinary, Gaskins, Schuder, Bergman, et al., 1992). These are examples of programs in which direct and explicit instruction in the reading, writing, and thinking strategies needed for success in content-area courses are taught as essential parts of the courses. Both programs emphasize professional develop-

ment. In part, explicit teacher-led approaches are not commonplace in classrooms because they are dependent on excellent pre-service and in-service professional development. The explicit approach has also been found to be difficult for teachers to put into practice (Hilden & Pressley, 2007). Explicit teacher-led instruction is discussed in greater detail in the next section.

CHARACTERISTICS OF EXPLICIT, TEACHER-LED STRATEGIES INSTRUCTION

Research regarding reading comprehension in all areas of the curriculum strongly suggests that effective strategies instruction includes explicit explanations, modeling, scaffolding, and practice (Duffy, 2002; Pressley, 2006). Teachers of effective strategies instruction explicitly explain to students (1) what the strategy is that can be used to accomplish a specific task, (2) why and how the strategy facilitates learning, and (3) how and when to use the strategy (Gaskins, 2005). In addition, as recommended by Dimino (2007) and others, teachers use think-alouds (Meichenbaum & Biemiller, 1998) or mental modeling (Duffy, Roehler, & Herrmann, 1988) to share their thinking as they demonstrate using the strategy in authentic situations.

Thinking aloud, as described by Meichenbaum and Biemiller (1998), is verbally guiding oneself while carrying out a task. Teachers' think-alouds may be in the form of self-questioning or directive self-instructional statements sharing with students what they think before, during, and after completing a task. In contrast, the goal of mental modeling, as discussed by Duffy, Roehler, and Herrmann (1988), is to make reasoning visible. Mental modeling is differentiated from the "modeling of procedures which consist of telling students directions or steps to follow in completing a specific task" (Duffy, et al., p. 765). Instead, in mental modeling, the focus is on the thinking one does to complete the steps, not on the steps themselves. The intent is to convey the flexibility associated with reasoning as opposed to rigid following of steps. Mental modeling is implemented "in tandem with fluid teacher-student dialogues to ensure that students do not misinterpret the modeling and end up with misconceptions" (p. 766).

As part of explicit strategies instruction, teachers also guide, support, and cue students as they gradually release responsibility to students for putting a strategy, or a bundle of strategies, to work. The teacher scaffolds (supports) students in the application of strategies during guided practice, turning as much responsibility over to each student as that student can successfully handle, with the goal being that each student achieves independence in strategy use at his or her own pace.

EFFECTIVE INSTRUCTIONAL SUPPORTS FOR STRATEGIES INSTRUCTION

The success of strategies instruction depends on more than explicit explanations, modeling, scaffolding, and gradual release of responsibility. Other instructional supports need to be incorporated into strategies instruction, if the use of strategies is to become habitual for students. These supports include: emphasizing metacognition; making strategies use meaningful by sharing learning principles and brain-related rationale; teaching strategies school-wide and across the curriculum; and providing opportunities for professional development. Each of these instructional supports is discussed below.

Emphasizing Metacognition. Dimino (2007) postulates that one essential component of an instructional design for effective and explicit instruction of strategies is metacognition, a concept introduced in the 1970s but as of the early 2000s still not commonly discussed in classrooms. Metacognition is composed of two parts: (1) knowledge about thinking and (2) self-regulation of thinking. Knowledge of thinking includes knowledge of high-utility strategies that enhance thinking, as well as how and when to employ them. It is also the knowledge gained from self-evaluation regarding which strategies are personally effective and work well in which situations. As part of developing student awareness, teachers encourage students to share strategies that have led to successful learning and problem solving, and they praise students for their effort in applying appropriate strategies. They also engage students in self-assessing their work and in attributing satisfactory attainment of academic goals to strategy use. The second aspect of metacognition is executive function or volition, taking control of thinking by self-monitoring and putting into action a plan to successfully meet a goal. Awareness alone does not produce success.

As strategies are practiced, teachers gradually transfer control of implementing the strategies to students. Students assume responsibility for knowing where and when to use the strategies and for independently using them. Thus, they become self-regulated (Schunk & Zimmerman, 1997). This ownership is possible because students have gained awareness and control of their thinking. Students who have been engaged in a systematic strategies program have been taught how to monitor progress toward a goal (e.g., solving a math problem, composing a science report, decoding a word, or understanding a text) (Gaskins, 2005). They know how to manage accomplishing their goals by such tactics as adapting strategies to their purposes, engaging in an inner conversation so they can catch themselves when they need to mend understanding, and matching the appropriate strategy to the situation so they can make renewed progress toward their goals.

Making Strategies Use Meaningful. Explicitly teaching strategies and adding all the components outlined above may still not be enough to develop self-regulated students who independently employ strategies. Instructional experts and researchers recommend including a motivational component to strategies instruction that focuses on meaningfulness, including interest and value (Alexander, 2006; Anderman & Wolters, 2006; Gaskins, 2008). Because learning and applying strategies initially takes quite a lot of effort, students want to see some value in putting forth the extra work. They often need to be convinced of how what they are asked to do will benefit them. This calls for personal or situational interest.

Students are more likely to be interested in and take strategies instruction seriously if teachers provide a convincing rationale for each strategy they teach (Paris, Lipson, & Wixson, 1983). For example, teaching students how strategies help the brain work more effectively has proved a convincing rationale (Gaskins, 1991, 2005, 2008). Perhaps this is the case because students enjoy hearing interesting stories and sophisticated information about learning theory and knowledge about how the brain functions that is usually reserved for college courses. Teachers share both why they are teaching a particular strategy and how the strategy helps the brain work more effectively.

For example, in teaching students to survey, the teacher's explanation of why might sound something like this: "We survey to hook our interest and to get a sense of what the text is about. In addition, the information you gain while surveying provides an outline that you can fill in with new information as you read" (Gaskins, 2005, p. 197). The teacher's explanation of how surveying helps the brain might sound like this: "Surveying helps your brain by telling it what background knowledge to get ready to assist you in understanding the new information" (p. 197). Similarly, in teaching students to access background knowledge, the teacher might say: "We access background knowledge to help us become actively involved by relating what we are reading to what we know" (p. 197). An explanation of how might include that accessing background knowledge helps the brain make sense of and remember what is read "because our brains don't remember things that don't make sense. We also want to hook new information to what we already know, because it is easier to get information back out of our brain if it is hooked to what we already know" (p. 197).

In the same vein, teachers explain how learning works by sharing principles of learning with students (Gaskins, 2008). Examples of principles that might be shared with students include: organized knowledge is easier to recall than random information; information that is thoughtfully and deeply processed is likely to be understood and used; and concepts and strategies that are repeatedly practiced and applied are not easily forgotten

(Gaskins, 2008). To make these principles even more convincing, teachers can conduct mini-experiments with students to illustrate the principles (Gaskins, 1991).

Teaching Strategies School-wide and Across the Curriculum. Strategies instruction and application must take place in authentic settings across the entire school (Allington, 2006). Effective teachers make strategies instruction an integral part of all classroom instruction all year long in all areas of the curriculum. Each year they teach a small repertoire of strategies, bundling a newly taught strategy with those that have been previously learned. For example, a teacher might initially teach beginning readers to survey a pre-primer story. After students have practiced surveying until they are comfortable with the strategy, the teacher then bundles surveying with accessing background knowledge by explicitly explaining and modeling how to access background knowledge related to the information gained from surveying. This lesson is ideally followed by teaching students to make predictions based on information gained from surveying and accessing background knowledge. For each strategy taught and bundled with other strategies, teachers explicitly explain, model, scaffold, and guide practice, and they guide students to apply or adapt strategies to all areas of the curriculum.

The goal of strategies instruction is that the application of strategies to comprehend, compose, problem solve, remember, reason, evaluate, and decode is self-regulated by students. This occurs when students receive explicit strategies instruction as described above throughout at least their elementary and middle school years, and they are guided in their application of high-utility strategies to authentic situations until strategies use is each student's chosen way of addressing learning, thinking, and problem-solving tasks in all areas of the curriculum..

Ideally, there is a school-wide or district-wide plan for strategies instruction in order to provide continuity and consistency of strategy instruction across the curriculum and across grades. With such a plan, each teacher knows what his or her responsibility is for introducing and reinforcing specific strategies, and students are much more likely to be strategic in their learning, thinking, and problem solving because strategies introduced during one school year are reinforced, expanded, and bundled with other strategies in each consecutive year of schooling (Pressley, 2006).

Providing Opportunities for Professional Development. Given that what is known about strategies teaching is underused in the late 2000s, it is imperative that there be ongoing professional development so that students have the benefit of instruction from teachers who know what works and how to implement instruction based on evidence from scientific investigations (Pressley, Graham, & Harris,

2006). In addition, because experience and research have indicated that teaching strategies has initially proved difficult for teachers to implement (Hilden & Pressley, 2006), there must be frequent professional-development support, especially for teachers new to strategies instruction. Ideally, this support would include both workshops and in-class coaching by supervisors, principals, or instructional coaches, who support staff in employing approaches for teaching and reinforcing strategies with their students.

IMPLICATIONS FOR EDUCATORS

Despite ample research evidence upon which to base decisions about strategies instruction and despite the many college textbooks published since 1995 that introduce pre-service teachers to strategies instruction, strategies instruction is not commonplace in K-12 classrooms in the United States.. It is particularly absent in content-area classes such as mathematics, social studies, and science. That the need for strategies instruction is being recognized is evidenced by the burgeoning number of commercial programs to teach general and specific strategies. The drawback to these commercial programs is that, although many attempt to address strategies instruction, they do so outside the context of the core curriculum where these strategies need to be applied. For example, only 12 of the 48 programs reviewed by Deshler and colleagues (2007) were identified as core curricula, whereas 36 were designated supplemental or remedial intervention programs. An alternative to these commercial programs is for teachers to provide strategy instruction as an integrated part of all mainstream language arts and content-area instruction with the goal of enabling all levels of learners to participate in courses with more challenging content.

In order for the United States to produce young people who are well prepared to succeed in whatever they undertake, every teacher at every grade level in every domain must become a strategies teacher. Strategies instruction needs to be adopted across the curriculum and throughout schools and school districts. It needs to begin when children enter school and continue through 12th grade. Because the need for strategies is often specific to each discipline and transfer between disciplines is not automatic, students should receive instruction in strategies for reading, writing, and learning that is differentiated for each content area (Deshler, et al., 2007). Ongoing professional development and support for strategies teachers are keys to the success of a school-wide effort to make every teacher a strategies teacher and every student a self-regulated strategy user.

SEE ALSO *Cognitive Strategies; Metacognition; Problem Solving; Reasoning; Self-Regulated Learning; Strategy Development.*

BIBLIOGRAPHY

Alexander, P. A. (2006). *Psychology in learning and instruction.* Upper Saddle River, NJ: Pearson Education.

Alexander, P. A., & Winne, P. H. (Eds.). (2006). *Handbook of educational psychology* (2nd ed.). Mahwah, NJ: Erlbaum.

Allington, R. L. (2006). *What really matters for struggling readers: Designing research-based programs.* Boston: Pearson.

Anderman, E. M., & Wolters, C. A. (2006). Goals, values, and affect: Influences on student motivation. In P. A. Alexander & P. H. Winne (Eds.), *Handbook of educational psychology* (2nd ed., pp. 369–389). Mahwah, NJ: Erlbaum.

Bransford, J., Brown, A., & Cocking, R. (Eds.). (2000). *How people learn: Brain, mind, experience, and school* (Exp. ed.). Washington, DC: National Academy Press.

Deshler, D. D., Palincsar, A. S., Biancarosa, G., & Nair, M. (2007). *Informed choices for struggling adolescent readers: A research-based guide to instructional programs and practices.* Newark, DE: International Reading Association.

Dimino, J. A. (2007). Bridging the gap between research and practice. *Journal of Learning Disabilities, 40,* 183–189.

Donovan, M. S., & Bransford, J. D. (Eds.). (2005). *How students learn: History, mathematics, and Science in the classroom.* Washington, DC: National Academies Press.

Duffy, G. G. (2002). The case for direct explanation of strategies. In C. Block & M. Pressley (Eds.), *Comprehension instruction: Research-based best practices* (pp. 28–11). New York: Guilford Press.

Duffy, G. G., Roehler, L,. & Herrmann, B. A. (1988). Modeling mental processes helps poor readers become strategic readers. *Reading Teacher, 41,* 762–767.

Durkin, D. (1978–1979). What classroom observations reveal about reading comprehension instruction. *Reading Research Quarterly, 14,* 202–224.

Gaskins, I. W. (2005). *Success with struggling readers: The Benchmark School approach.* New York: Guilford Press.

Gaskins, I. W. (2008). Ten tenets of motivation for teaching struggling readers—And the rest of the class. In R. Fink & S. J. Samuels (Eds.), *Inspiring reading success: Interest and motivation in an age of high-stakes testing.* Newark, DE: International Reading Association.

Gaskins, I. W., & Elliot, T. T. (1991). *Implementing cognitive strategy instruction across the school: The Benchmark manual for teachers.* Cambridge, MA: Brookline Books.

Graham, S. (2006). Strategy instruction and the teaching of writing: A meta-analysis. In C. MacArthur, S. Graham, & J. Fitzgerald (Eds.), *Handbook of writing research.* New York: Guilford Press.

Graham, S., & Harris, K.R. (2005). *Writing better: Effective strategies for teaching students with learning difficulties.* Baltimore: Paul H. Brookes.

Harmon, J. M., Martinez, M. G., & Deckard, A. (2004). Children's strategic awareness for reading different genres and text types. In J. Worthy, B. Maloch, J. Hoffman, D. Schallert, & C. Fairbanks (Eds.), *53rd Yearbook of the National Reading Conference* (pp. 218–232). Oak Creek, WI: National Reading Conference.

Harvey, S., & Goudvis, A. (2007). *Strategies that work: Teaching comprehension for understanding and engagement* (2nd ed.). Portland, ME: Stenhouse Publishers.

Hilden, K. R., & Pressley, M. (2007). Self-regulation through transactional strategies instruction. *Reading and Writing Quarterly, 23,* 51–75.

Lipson, M. Y. (2007). *Teaching reading beyond the primary grades.* New York: Scholastic.

Meichenbaum, D., & Biemiller, A. (1998). *Nurturing independent learners: Helping students take charge of their learning.* Cambridge, MA: Brookline Books.

Paris, S. D., Lipson, M. Y., & Wixson, K. K. (1983). Becoming a strategic reader. *Contemporary educational Psychology, 8,* 293–316.

Pressley, M. (2006). *Reading instruction that works: The case for balanced teaching* (3rd ed.). New York: Guilford Press.

Pressley, M., El-Dinary, P. M., Gaskins, I. W., Schuder, T., Bergman, J. L., Almasi, J., et al. (1992). Beyond direct explanation: Transactional instruction of reading comprehension strategies. *Elementary School Journal, 92,* 511–554.

Pressley, M., Graham, S., & Harris, K. (2006). The state of educational intervention research as viewed through the lens of literacy intervention. *British Journal of Educational Psychology, 76,* 1–19.

Pressley, M., & Harris, K. (2006). Cognitive strategies instruction: From basic research to classroom instruction. In P. Alexander & P. Winne (Eds.), *Handbook of educational psychology* (2nd Ed., pp. 265–286). Mahwah, NJ: Erlbaum.

Pressley, M., Wharton-McDonald, R., Mistretta, J., & Echevarria, M. (1998). The nature of literacy instruction in ten grade-4/5 classrooms in upstate New York. *Scientific Studies of Reading, 2,* 159–191.

Santa, C. M., Havens, L., & Valdes, B. (2005). *Project CRISS: Helping teachers teach and learners learn.* Kalispell, MT: Project CRISS.

Schunk, D. H., & Zimmerman, B. J. (1997). Social origins of self-regulatory competence. *Educational Psychologist, 32,* 195–208.

Swanson, H. L., with Hoskyn, M., & Lee, C. (1999). *Interventions for students with learning disabilities: A meta-analysis of treatment outcomes.* New York: Guilford Press.

Torgesen, J. K. (2004). Lessons learned from research on interventions for students who have difficulty learning to read. In P. McCardle & V Chhabra (Eds.), *The voice of evidence in reading research* (pp. 355–382). Baltimore, MD: Paul H. Brookes.

Trabasso, T., & Bouchard, E. (2002). Teaching readers how to comprehend text strategically. In C. Block & M. Pressley, *Comprehension instruction: Research-based best practices* (pp. 176–200). New York: Guilford Press.

Irene W. Gaskins

STRATEGY DEVELOPMENT

A strategy is a purposeful action, or sequence of actions, executed in the interest of achieving a goal. The mistaken idea that children do not exhibit strategies prior to school age arose from studies asking preschool and older children to remember a set of items (for review, see Pressley & Hilden, 2006). Preschoolers did no better in remembering the items than they did when merely asked to look at them. Older children asked to remember the items, in contrast, were likely to employ strategies, such as organization or rehearsal. But this finding did not mean that children do not use strategies until they are 7 or 8 years old. An infant who uses a stick to bring a toy within reach is employing a strategy to reach a goal. The important questions are what strategies is a child able to employ, what is the degree of conscious control under which strategies operate, does the child know to apply the strategy or can the child be taught when and how to do so, and can strategies be employed more effectively to aid performance.

Strategies are not autonomous, multi-purpose tools stored away in a toolkit and brought out and applied when needed. Most often, people are unable to say definitively that a child either has or lacks possession of a particular strategy. Instead, strategies are linked to the contexts in which they are employed and the goals they serve. A child may exhibit a strategy in one context and not in another seemingly equivalent one.

Children's memory may differ, for example, when asked to retrieve a list of items from a mock grocery store and when asked to memorize a list of words. Multiple factors, however, are likely to contribute to such differences (Weissberg & Paris, 1986). The use of deliberate strategies, such as rehearsal, is one factor, but additional possibilities need to be weighed. These include the differing goal (and hence motivational) structures linked to the tasks and the differing familiarity of the task materials and the task activity itself. Moreover, these different contributors themselves interact with one another. A powerful memory strategy, for example, is elaboration, in which an association is formed between separate entities by identifying a theme that links them (e.g., the digit sequence 312 is remembered as a telephone area code or a batting average). In order to make use of this strategy, however, the learner needs to be familiar with such content domains.

In classroom settings, teachers need to be sensitive to these contexts of strategy use. A strategy may appear in one context but not another. A child faced with multiplying three times five, for example, may use a successive-addition strategy of laying out three groups of five objects and adding them. When the child later encounters the problem five times three, however, the child may be unable to apply the same strategy. The most common challenge teachers encounter is that students fail to apply a strategy that has been taught explicitly in one context when they later encounter problems for which it is appropriate. Simply learning how to execute the strategy is not enough.

ASSESSING STRATEGIES IN SITUATED CONTEXTS

Identifying what strategies a student is using can be difficult. Mental strategies most often are not detectable from overt performance. Asking people how they performed a task or solved a problem is one way of gaining information about strategy use, but not always a reliable one. How someone reports having solved a problem may not be identical or even similar to the mental operations that were actually performed to reach a solution. Asking the person to think aloud while engaged in the task is a better method, but it too can be misleading, because the think-aloud talk can disrupt or otherwise alter performance.

Mostly, cognitive psychologists must employ indirect methods in making inferences about strategy use, for example, by examining performance over different kinds of problems and observing response times or patterns of correctness as a way of testing hypotheses about the strategies the performer used. Nonverbal behavior (such as visual fixation patterns and gesture) may also be informative.

Teachers are in effect researchers-in-practice in the classroom, as they seek to diagnose the strategies that individual students apply to their work. They do best to treat their interpretations as hypotheses and then seek multiple kinds of evidence—by talking to the child about what he is doing as well as observing his work on different kinds of problems—that will either support or disconfirm such hypotheses. Teachers also need to be sensitive to two kinds of variation. One is the wide individual variation across children in how they approach a problem. Children of similar age and ability within a single classroom are likely to exhibit quite different strategies for the same task, including some that even the teacher may not have previously considered. The other kind of variation, discussed below, is variation in strategy usage within a single child.

STRATEGIC DEVELOPMENT

Adding to the assessment challenge, strategies must always be considered in relation to a task, a goal, and a situation. Still another challenge comes from the need to consider any strategy in a context of its alternatives. One of the major discoveries psychologists have made about strategies is that multiple alternative strategies applicable to a task typically exist in a learner's repertory. These strategies are of differing degrees of correctness or effectiveness. They also have different probabilities of application (see Figure 1). The instructional goal, then, is to reduce the strength, that is, probability of occurrence, of less effective strategies and increase the strength of more effective ones. New strategies do, of course, appear, but first emergence rarely indicates the beginning of consistent usage. The majority of change is thus of this

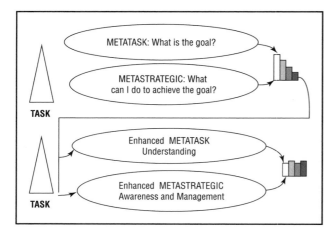

Figure 1 ILLUSTRATION BY GGS INFORMATION SERVICES. CENGAGE LEARNING, GALE.

shifting-frequency variety. Siegler (2000) proposes an "overlapping waves" model to portray this process. A particular less-than-ideal strategy initially appears infrequently, begins to increase in frequency, enjoys a period of ascendance, and then diminishes in frequency, while another strategy follows this same course but at a later, although overlapping, time. Siegler and his colleagues tracked the course of various strategies children use in performing simple single-digit addition and subtraction problems. When faced with adding nine plus three, a first-grade child may first count one subset, then the other, and then the entire set, to produce the answer, twelve—an unnecessarily burdensome and inefficient strategy. Asked to carry out a series of such calculations, the child may after a time discover a more efficient strategy—which Siegler calls the Min strategy—which involves simply counting up from the first addend, i.e., "ten, eleven, twelve," and requires enumerating only the second subset. Students may use these two (and several other) strategies as they tackle a set of problems. Over time, however, use of the less efficient strategy diminishes in frequency and use of the more efficient strategy increases.

What is entailed in this change process? Microgenetic studies (Kuhn, 1995; Siegler, 2006), in which an individual is observed engaged in the same or a similar set of problems over an extended period of weeks or months, show that the exercise afforded by this rich problem environment is sufficient to induce strategy change in a majority of cases, enabling researchers to examine its characteristics. One point that has become clear is that two distinct components are involved. The more familiar is the desired increasing strength of the more advanced strategy or strategies. But equally important is inhibition of less advanced strategies. In postulating mechanisms,

Siegler (2000, 2006; Siegler & Jenkins, 1989) emphasized the need for associations with the more frequent, less effective strategies to be weakened, as well as associations with more effective strategies strengthened.

Consistent with such a model is the finding that strategies when they first appear may not be used effectively enough to enhance performance. Researchers studying the development of memory strategies have in fact found this to be the case, giving rise to what has been called a *utilization deficiency*. A strategy such as categorization (of the to-be-remembered items), for example, even (or especially) if it has been explicitly taught, may not be used when a child later is free to approach a memory task as the child chooses, or, if it is used, may fail to improve or even diminish performance. The educational implication is that new strategies must be included in the repertory with sufficient frequency so as to allow them to be practiced, consolidated, and perfected until the user is able to experience their utility.

METASTRATEGIC DEVELOPMENT

While similarly emphasizing the relinquishment of less effective strategies as a more formidable obstacle than strengthening new ones, Kuhn and colleagues (Kuhn, 2001; Kuhn & Dean, 2004) proposed that knowledge at a meta-level is as important as that at the performance level and plays a major role in what happens there. The meta-level entails understanding of strategies—recognizing what they do or do not buy one—in relation to task goals. Portrayed in the right side of Figure 1 (Kuhn, 2001) are the strategies that co-exist and are available for use (analogous to Siegler's "overlapping waves" model). In the progress depicted from the upper to the lower half of the diagram in Figure 1, the less effective strategies to the left become less frequent and the more effective strategies to the right more frequent (in this case, yielding a temporary, transitional result of all strategies of roughly equal strategy). Implicated in this change are the meta-level operators that appear in the center of the diagram, representing the individual's understanding of the task goal, understanding of the strategies the individual has available to apply, and awareness of the need to coordinate the two in selecting a strategy. Feedback from the performance level should enhance meta-level understanding, further enhancing performance, in a continuous process.

Kuhn and colleagues have made use of this model in research on the scientific thinking of children and adults, in particular how they coordinate their own preexisting beliefs with new evidence and draw conclusions about the causal roles of various factors in producing an outcome. Even many adults have difficulty *bracketing*, that is, holding in suspension, their own beliefs in interpreting new evidence. Community college students, for example, were presented data regarding an experiment conducted by a school district on ways to improve reading instruction (Kuhn, Katz, & Dean, 2004). Three factors were investigated: a new reading curriculum, teacher aides, and reduced class size. Among six outcomes students were asked to examine were these two:

> Classrooms with the new reading curriculum and teacher aides reported an outcome of greatly improved.

> Classrooms with the new reading curriculum, teacher aides, and reduced class size reported an outcome of greatly improved.

Application of a control of variables strategy (in which all variables but the one being investigated are held constant) would dictate the conclusion that reduced class size played no role in the outcome.

Although some students did apply this strategy and come to the appropriate conclusion, a good number did not. One common response reflected the inference strategy that anything present in the context played a role in the outcome. For example, in one student's words: "Yes (class size makes a difference) because this class had it and they improved."

Other students, despite explicit instructions to interpret the presented data, ignored it and relied on their own preexisting knowledge, leading them to offer responses like this one: "Yes (class size makes a difference) because the numbers of children are small so they can learn faster and better."

To apply the more advanced, scientifically correct strategy individuals need to have good metastrategic control over their own thinking. In a problem like this one, this control makes it possible to monitor and manage the dual representations of the evidence and one's own knowledge state, as well as the cognitive strategies that are involved in coordinating them.

MANAGING ONE'S OWN LEARNING

How can teachers promote strategy development? The evidence suggests that a rich problem environment, in which students are given frequent and dense opportunities to engage problems requiring more advanced strategies will in a majority of cases lead to improvement in strategy use (Kuhn et al., 1995; Dean & Kuhn, 2007). Teachers can assist by supporting students' inclinations to take charge of their own learning. This points leads back to the contextual message with which this discussion began. If students develop their own firm understandings of what they are undertaking to learn in a particular situation and why, they are more likely to take charge of finding the most effective ways to enable them to

accomplish the job (Kuhn, 2005). This meta-level awareness and management in turn enhances the likelihood of transfer of strategies to new contexts.

The directions in which individual development progresses are consistent with the growing metastrategic capabilities that older children begin to display (Kuhn & Franklin, 2006). Older children and adolescents are less pliable than young children. They are more likely to question, and they want to try things their way. Expressed differently, they want to assume control of what they do. Growing cognitive and social skills make them more able to do so, and the indications are that in academic settings teachers should give them the space to try their own approaches to problems, to collaborate with others and to revise their strategies as warranted, and to gain from the experience that doing so affords.

SEE ALSO *Microgenetic Research; Strategies Instruction.*

BIBLIOGRAPHY

Dean, D., & Kuhn, D. (2007). Direct instruction vs. discovery: The long view. *Science Education, 91,* 384–397.

Kuhn, D. (2001). Why development does (and doesn't) occur: Evidence from the domain of inductive reasoning. In R. Siegler & J. McClelland (Eds.), *Mechanisms of cognitive development: Neural and behavioral perspectives.* Mahwah, NJ: Erlbaum.

Kuhn, D. (2005). *Education for thinking.* Cambridge, MA: Harvard University Press.

Kuhn, D., & Dean, D. (2004). Metacognition as a conceptual bridge between cognitive psychology and educational practice. *Theory into Practice, 43,* 268–273.

Kuhn, D., & Franklin, S. (2006). The second decade: What develops (and how)? In W. Damon & R. Lerner (Series Eds.) & D. Kuhn & R. Siegler (Eds.), *Handbook of Child Psychology: Vol. 2. Cognition, Perception, and Language* (6th ed.). Hoboken, NJ: Wiley.

Kuhn, D., Katz, J., & Dean, D. (2004). Developing reason. *Thinking and Reasoning, 10.* 197–219.

Siegler, R. S. (2000). The rebirth of children's learning. *Child Development, 71,* 26–35.

Siegler, R. S. (2006). Microgenetic studies of learning. In W. Damon & R. Lerner (Series Eds.) & D. Kuhn & R. Siegler (Eds.), *Handbook of Child Psychology: Vol. 2. Cognition, Perception, and Language* (6th ed.). Hoboken, NJ: Wiley.

Siegler, R. S., & Jenkins, E. A. (1989). *How children discover new strategies.* Hillsdale, NJ: Erlbaum.

Weissberg, J., & Paris, S. (1986). Young children's remembering in different contexts. *Child Development, 57,* 1123–1129.

Deanna Kuhn

STUDENT EMOTIONS

The classroom is an emotional place. The fact that learning and achievement are critical for students' educational careers implies that academic activities and attainments often arouse intense emotions. Relevant achievement emotions include positive emotions such as enjoyment of learning, hope, and pride, as well as negative emotions such as anger, anxiety, shame, or boredom in class. Due to the interactive nature of classroom settings, social emotions such as admiration, contempt, or envy can also play a major role in these settings. Furthermore, emotions are functionally important by influencing students' academic motivation, behavior, performance, health, and personality development. Nevertheless, as of 2008, there still was a lack of empirical research on student emotions. Research has thoroughly examined students' test anxiety since the 1950s (Zeidner, 1998, 2007) and has produced cumulative knowledge that can inform educational practice. There is little research on student emotions other than anxiety, however, implying that it is difficult to draw firm conclusions for most emotions experienced by students (Schutz & Pekrun, 2007).

DEFINITION AND ASSESSMENT OF EMOTION

Emotions are reactions to significant events and objects. Serving the preparation and adaptive organization of subsequent perception, cognition, and action, emotions are defined as involving multiple coordinated processes (Lewis & Haviland-Jones, 2000). Important components include the following. (1) Affective components comprise emotional feelings that are physiologically bound to the activation of subcortical systems such as the amygdala (e.g., uneasy, nervous feelings in anxiety experienced before an exam). (2) Cognitive components involve emotion-specific thoughts (such as worries about the threat of failing an exam). (3) Physiological components serve the preparation of action (e.g., peripheral physiological activation in anxiety, as indicated by symptoms such as increased heart rate, respiration rate, and sweating). (4) Motivational components comprise behavioral impulses and wishes (e.g., avoidance motivation in anxiety). (5) Expressive components include facial, postural, and vocal expression of emotion.

Due to the multi-component nature of emotion, there are various ways to assess student emotions. Self-report instruments assess self-perceptions of emotion. In test anxiety research, questionnaires such as the Test Anxiety Inventory (TAI; Spielberger, 1980) play an important role. An instrument measuring various achievement emotions experienced by students is the Achievement Emotions Questionnaire (AEQ; Pekrun, Goetz, Titz, & Perry, 2002). Recordings of physiological processes such as heart rate, respiration rate, or changes of skin conductance are used to infer emotions from their peripheral physiological components. Brain imaging techniques such as EEG and fMRI serve to identify central physiological processes underlying emotions. Finally, emotions can be assessed by observation of facial and postural expression. However, emotion observation is not an easy task with students beyond the early elementary years who control emotion expression by adhering to socially defined display rules.

CATEGORIES AND DIMENSIONS OF STUDENT EMOTIONS

Two distinct ways of describing emotions are provided by categorical and dimensional approaches. In categorical approaches, qualitatively different types of discrete emotions are differentiated, such as enjoyment, anger, anxiety, or boredom. This approach allows taking into account the unique patterns of components and functions that are typical for different emotions. Within the dimensional approach, a small number of dimensions are held to be sufficient to describe human emotion. Two important dimensions are valence (positive versus negative, or pleasant versus unpleasant) and activation (activating versus deactivating). Categorical and dimensional approaches can be integrated in hierarchical models that regard discrete emotions as lower-level factors, and affective dimensions as higher-order factors describing common properties of discrete emotions (Feldman, Barrett, & Russell, 1998).

The two dimensions valence and activation can also be used to classify students' achievement emotions (Pekrun, 2006; see Table 1). Achievement emotions are defined as emotions that relate to achievement activities (such as academic learning) and their outcomes (such as academic success and failure). The two dimensions render four broad categories of achievement emotions: (1) activating positive emotions (e.g., joy, hope, pride); (2) deactivating positive emotions (e.g., relief, relaxation); (3) activating negative emotions (e.g., anger, anxiety, shame); and (4) deactivating negative emotions (e.g., hopelessness, boredom).

In addition, achievement emotions differ according to their object focus, relating either to achievement activities such as learning, or to the success and failure outcomes of these activities. Furthermore, some achievement emotions render an affective self-evaluation by linking positively versus negatively valenced activities and outcomes to the self (e.g., pride after success and shame after failure). Self-evaluative emotions are critical for students' development of self-worth (Covington & Berry, 1976).

Taxonomy of achievement emotions

Object focus	Positive		Negative	
	Activating	Deactivating	Activating	Deactivating
Activity (Learning)	Enjoyment	Relaxation	Anger	Boredom Frustration
Outcome (Success/Failure)	Joy Hope Pride Gratitude	Contentment Relief	Anxiety Shame Anger	Sadness Disappointment Hopelessness

Table 1 ILLUSTRATION BY GGS INFORMATION SERVICES. CENGAGE LEARNING, GALE.

IMPORTANCE OF STUDENT EMOTIONS FOR ACADEMIC LEARNING AND PERFORMANCE

Two lines of evidence suggest that students' emotions profoundly affect their learning and performance. The first line of evidence originates in experimental mood research, the second in situated field studies directly analyzing students' emotions. Experimental mood research has shown that mood and emotions facilitate mood-congruent memory processes, such that positive self-related information is more easily stored and retrieved when in a positive mood and negative information when in a negative mood (e.g., Olafson & Ferraro, 2001). By implication, a positive mood can enhance students' motivation to approach learning tasks, whereas a negative mood can trigger mood-congruent avoidance motivation. Furthermore, the findings indicate that positive versus negative mood can promote different styles of information processing. Whereas creative, flexible, and holistic ways of thinking are facilitated by a positive mood, more analytical, rigid, and detailed ways of processing of information can be enhanced by a negative mood (Lewis & Haviland-Jones, 2000).

The ecological validity of these experimental findings, however, may be limited due to differences between the laboratory and real-life classroom situations, including ethical constraints preventing an induction of more intense emotions in the laboratory. Therefore, field studies have directly addressed the effects of students' emotions as experienced in classroom situations. Most of these studies focused on students' test anxiety (summaries in Zeidner, 1998, 2007). Research on test anxiety has shown that anxiety impairs performance on complex or difficult tasks that demand cognitive resources (e.g., difficult mathematical tasks). Performance on easy and less complex tasks is not impaired or enhanced. Interference and attentional deficit models have been proposed to explain negative performance effects of anxiety. These models assume that anxiety involves task-irrelevant thinking which reduces task-related attention thus interfers with performance on tasks requiring attentional resources: Students who worry about possible failure cannot focus their attention on learning.

In line with findings on task-related effects, test anxiety correlates negatively with students' academic achievement, typically explaining about 10% of the variance in achievement scores (Hembree, 1988). However, these correlations should be interpreted cautiously. First, they may be due to effects of failure on the development of students' anxiety, rather than effects of anxiety on achievement. Second, correlations were not uniformly negative across studies and individuals. Zero and positive relationships were found as well. One reason may be the ambiguous motivational effects which anxiety can exert: Anxiety reduces students' interest and intrinsic motivation, but it can also motivate students to invest extra effort to avoid failure. In individual cases, these motivating effects can be so strong that negative effects on attention and intrinsic motivation are compensated. From an educator's perspective, however, any positive effect of anxiety in an individual student is certainly outweighed by the negative effect on subject-matter interest and academic performance in the majority of students.

The available evidence for effects of student emotions other than anxiety is limited. For positive emotions such as enjoyment of learning, positive correlations with academic achievement have been reported (Pekrun et al., 2002). For anger and shame, findings suggest that overall relationships with students' achievement are negative. As with anxiety, however, the effects need not uniformly be negative. For example, in students who believe in their capabilities, shame about failure on an exam can fuel motivation to invest more effort in the future (Turner & Schallert, 2001). In contrast, findings on boredom and hopelessness suggest that these two emotions are just detrimental by exerting negative effects on cognitive resources, motivation, information processing, and any kind of academic performance (Pekrun et al., 2002).

In sum, the available evidence implies that it would be inappropriate to assume that positive emotions always exert positive effects and negative emotions always negative effects. Rather, the effects depend on the mediating processes and specific task demands under consideration. More specifically, positive activating emotions such as enjoyment of learning likely are beneficial for students' learning and performance under most task conditions. Conversely, negative deactivating emotions such as hopelessness and boredom can be assumed to be devastative to any kind of academic performance. The effects of positive deactivating emotions such as relief and relaxation, however, probably are more ambiguous. Similarly, negative activating emotions such as anxiety, shame, and anger can exert ambiguous effects by reducing attention and interest, but also by being able to strengthen extrinsic motivation as well as more rigid modes of information processing such as simple rehearsal of learning material. Therefore, negative activating emotions can enhance performance in specific cases, although their average affects across students are negative.

INDIVIDUAL ANTECEDENTS AND DEVELOPMENT OF STUDENT EMOTIONS

Students' achievement-related appraisals are important proximal determinants of their emotions. The impact of factors such as achievement goals and gender likely is mediated by students' appraisals. Also, the development of students' emotions largely depends on the development of their achievement-related thinking.

The impact of appraisals on anticipatory anxiety has been addressed by R. S. Lazarus's transactional stress model, and their impact on emotions following success and failure by B. Weiner's atttributional theory. The transactional stress model (Lazarus & Folkman, 1984) assumes that individuals first evaluate the threat implied by a stressful situation such as an exam ("primary appraisal") and then judge the possibilities of coping with the situation ("secondary appraisal"). In case of threat and insufficient perceived control over the situation, anxiety is assumed to be instigated. Weiner's 1985 attributional theory proposes that achievement outcomes immediately produce "attribution-independent" emotions such as happiness after success and frustration after failure. These emotions do not need any more cognitive elaboration. In contrast, attribution-dependent emotions are shaped by the causal attribution of the outcome. Pride is assumed to depend on an attribution of success to internal factors (such as ability). Shame and guilt are induced by failure that is attributed to internal factors that are subjectively controllable (such as lack of effort). Gratitude is expected to be aroused by an attribution of

success to external factors that are under control by others (e.g., help), and anger by attributions of failure to such factors. In line with Lazarus's and Weiner's theories, empirical research has corroborated that indicators of subjective lack of controllability, such as low self-concepts of ability and failure expectancies, are related to students' anxiety and their attributions of success and failure to emotions such as pride, shame, guilt, and anger (Heckhausen, 1991; Zeidner, 1998, 2007).

Different appraisal theories of achievement emotions, such as Lazarus's and Weiner's theories, are complementary rather than mutually exclusive. The control-value theory of achievement emotions (Pekrun, 2006) aims at integrating the assumptions of different theories. In addition, whereas previous theories have focused on outcome-related emotions such as anxiety, pride, and shame, the control-value theory also addresses activity-related emotions such as enjoyment and boredom experienced during learning. The theory assumes that students experience emotions when they feel in control of, or out of control of, activities and outcomes that are subjectively important to them, which suggests that control appraisals and value appraisals are the proximal determinants of their emotions. Occurrence and intensity of achievement emotions are seen as a joint product of these two kinds of appraisals. For example, anxiety is seen to be induced when the outcome of an exam is perceived as not being sufficiently controllable, but subjectively important. Conversely, if a student feels in control and does not expect failure or does not care about the exam, there is no need to be anxious. Similarly, enjoyment of learning is seen to be instigated if a student feels competent to master the material and values the material. If the student feels incompetent or is disinterested, negative activity emotions such as boredom are induced rather than enjoyment.

Achievement goals likely influence students' emotions by shaping emotion-inducing appraisals. Mastery goals can focus attention on the controllability and positive value of achievement activities. Performance-approach goals can facilitate positive appraisals of success, while performance-avoidance goals can sustain appraisals of the uncontrollability and negative value of failure. In line with these assumptions, empirical evidence shows that students' mastery goals relate positively to their enjoyment of learning and performance-avoidance goals to their anxiety (Linnenbrink & Pintrich, 2002; Pekrun, Elliot, & Maier, 2006).

Similarly, the impact of factors such as gender, race, and culture is likely mediated by their influence on students' appraisals of achievement. Specifically, while there is too little research on the impact on race and culture to draw firm conclusions, there is consistent evidence showing gender differences in achievement emotions. Anxiety research has shown that mean scores for achievement-related anxiety are higher for female than for male students. This is especially true for students' anxiety in mathematics. Gender differences in mathematics anxiety, however, are at least partially due to lower self-concepts of ability for female students in this domain (Frenzel, Pekrun, & Goetz, in press), suggesting that these gender differences are mediated by students' appraisals.

Finally, congruency between appraisals and emotions has also been found for the development of achievement emotions across students' educational career. Developmental research has shown that the occurrence of cognitively mediated emotions (such as pride and shame) in the preschool years is linked to the level of cognitive development (Heckhausen, 1991). Beyond the preschool years, all major achievement emotions are experienced by students. Subsequent development over the school years likely depends on the development of individual appraisals of capabilities and the subjective value of academic achievement. For test anxiety, research has shown that average levels of anxiety are low at the beginning of elementary school, increase substantially over the elementary school years, and remain at high levels throughout the middle school, high school, and university years (Hembree, 1988). This finding is congruent to the high levels of students' self-concepts of ability that are prevalent at the beginning of schooling and are adjusted downward during elementary school.

REGULATION AND THERAPY OF EMOTIONS

Emotion regulation involves up-regulating adaptive emotions such as enjoyment of learning and down-regulating maladaptive emotions such as anxiety. Cognitive competencies for doing so have been labeled emotional intelligence (Matthews, Zeidner, & Roberts, 2002). Concerning student emotions, research has focused on students' regulation of test anxiety (i.e., coping). Three broad categories of coping strategies have been identified (Zeidner, 1998, 2007). Emotion-oriented coping aims to reduce anxiety without changing the situation (e.g., by using relaxation techniques, taking drugs, or changing appraisals). Problem-oriented coping reduces anxiety by attempting to solve the problem (e.g., by investing effort in preparing an exam). Avoidance-oriented coping implies escaping the situation behaviorally or mentally (as implied by procrastination, absenteeism, and dropping out of school). In an academic achievement context, problem-oriented coping often is most adaptive. However, emotion-oriented coping can be adaptive as well (e.g., in situations providing no opportunities for successfully solving the problem).

Similarly, therapy of maladaptive student emotions can aim at directly changing the emotion or at changing underlying causal factors. Therapy of test anxiety has been researched most often and is among the most successful kinds of psychotherapy as of the late 1990s (Zeidner, 1998). Emotion-oriented treatment includes anxiety induction (e.g., flooding), biofeedback procedures, relaxation techniques, and systematic desensibilization. Cognitive therapies modify anxiety-inducing control appraisals, value beliefs, and styles of self-related thinking. Examples are cognitive-attentional training and cognitive restructuring therapy. Study-skills training teaches students to use task-oriented strategies of learning enabling them to be academically successful, thus alleviating their anxiety. Finally, multimodal therapies integrate several of these procedures.

Cognitive and multimodal therapy proved to be especially effective, both for reducing test anxiety and for improving academic performance. For students with deficits of learning strategies, study-skills training also turned out to be successful. Therapy focusing exclusively on emotion-oriented procedures is successful in terms of reducing anxiety but less effective as to students' academic improvement (Zeidner, 1998).

THE ROLE OF THE CLASSROOM CONTEXT AND IMPLICATIONS FOR EDUCATORS

Research in the late 1990s and early 2000s has focused on individual functions, antecedents, and therapy of student emotions. The role of classroom instruction remains largely unexplored. Again, research on test anxiety is an exception. Judging from test anxiety studies (Zeidner, 1998, 2007) and assumptions of appraisal theories (Pekrun, 2006), the following factors that are under the control of educators likely are important for the development of students' emotions.

1. Cognitive quality of instruction. Factors reducing students' perceived control, such as lack of structure, lack of clarity, and excessive task demands, are known to enhance students' test anxiety. With exams as well, lack of structure and transparency has been shown to contribute to students' anxiety (e.g., lack of information on demands, materials, and grading practices; Zeidner, 1998). Conversely, well-structured instruction and clear explanations likely contribute to adaptive student emotions by raising students' competencies and feelings of control. By implication, adaptive student emotions likely can be fostered, and maladaptive emotions reduced, by raising the cognitive quality of instruction.

2. Motivational quality of instruction. Teachers deliver direct messages conveying academic values, as well as more indirect messages implied by their behavior. Two ways of inducing values and related emotions may be most important. First, if learning environments meet the needs of students, positive activity-related emotions likely are fostered. For example, learning environments that support cooperative learning should help students to fulfill needs for social relatedness, thus making learning enjoyable. Second, teachers' own enthusiasm can facilitate students' adoption of positive emotions by way of observational learning and emotional contagion (Hatfield, Cacioppo, & Rapson, 1994).

3. Support of autonomy and self-regulated learning. Learning environments supporting students' self-regulated learning can be assumed to increase their sense of control and related positive emotions. In addition, such environments can foster positive emotions by meeting students' need for autonomy. However, these beneficial effects probably depend on the match between students' competence and individual need for academic autonomy, on the one hand, and the affordances of these environments, on the other. In case of a mismatch, loss of control and negative emotions can result. By implication, teachers should attend to matching demands for autonomy to students' competencies and needs.

4. Goal structures and achievement expectations. Academic achievement can be defined by standards of individual mastery, by normative standards based on competitive social comparison, or by standards pertaining to cooperative group performance instead of individual performance. These different standards imply individualistic (mastery), competitive (normative performance), and cooperative goal structures in the classroom (Johnson & Johnson, 1974). Goal structures and grading practices determine students' opportunities for experiencing success and perceiving control, thus influencing their emotions. Specifically, competitive goal structures imply, by definition, that some students experience success, whereas others have to experience failure, thus increasing levels of anxiety and hopelessness. Similarly, the demands implied by excessively high achievement expectancies of teachers and parents can lead to lowered control perceptions and related negative emotions. The available evidence corroborates that competitive classroom climates and excessive achievement expectancies correlate positively with students' test anxiety. Accordingly, as seen from an emotion perspective, educators should adapt expectancies to students' competencies and should refrain from using goal structures which induce individual competition between students.

5. Feedback and consequences of achievement. Research suggests that cumulative failure feedback is a major factor underlying students' test anxiety (Zeidner, 1998). Success experiences likely strengthen perceived control and related positive emotions, whereas repeated failure can undermine subjective control and, therefore, instigate negative emotions. In addition, the perceived consequences of success and failure are important. Positive future-related student emotions can be increased if academic success is seen to produce beneficial long-term outcomes (such as future occupational chances). Negative outcomes of academic failure, by contrast, can increase students' achievement-related anxiety and hopelessness. By implication, providing success experiences, defining mistakes as opportunities for learning rather than as personal failure, and linking attainment to beneficial outcomes also is important for helping students to develop adaptive emotions.

SEE ALSO *Anxiety; Evaluation (Test) Anxiety.*

BIBLIOGRAPHY
Covington, M. V., & Beery, R. G. (1976). *Self-worth and school learning.* Oxford, England: Holt, Rinehart, & Winston.
Feldman Barrett, L., & Russell, J. A. (1998). Independence and bipolarity in the structure of current affect. *Journal of Personality and Social Psychology, 74,* 967–984.
Frenzel, A. C., Pekrun, R., & Goetz, T. (in press). Girls and mathematics—a "hopeless" issue? A control-value approach to gender differences in emotions towards mathematics. *European Journal of Psychology of Education.*
Hatfield, E., Cacioppo, J. T., & Rapson, R. L. (1994). *Emotional contagion.* New York: Cambridge University Press.
Heckhausen, H. (1991). *Motivation and action.* New York: Springer.
Hembree, R. (1988). Correlates, causes, effects, and treatment of test anxiety. *Review of Educational Research, 58,* 47–77.
Johnson, D. W., & Johnson, R. T. (1974). Instructional goal structure: Cooperative, competitive or individualistic. *Review of Educational Research, 4,* 213–240.
Lazarus, R. S., & Folkman, S. (1984). *Stress, appraisal, and coping.* New York: Springer.
Lewis, M., & Haviland-Jones, J. M. (Eds.). (2000). *Handbook of emotions.* New York: Guilford Press.
Linnenbrink, E. A., & Pintrich, P. R. (2002). Achievement goal theory and affect: An asymmetrical bidirectional model. *Educational Psychologist, 37,* 69–78.
Matthews, G., Zeidner, M., and Roberts, R. D. (2002). *Emotional intelligence: Science and myth.* Cambridge, MA: MIT Press.
Olafson, K. M., & Ferraro, F. R. (2001). Effects of emotional state on lexical decision performance. *Brain and Cognition, 45,* 15–20.
Pekrun, R. (2006). The control-value theory of achievement emotions: Assumptions, corollaries, and implications for

educational research and practice. *Educational Psychology Review, 18,* 315–341.

Pekrun, R., Elliot, A. J., & Maier, M. A. (2006). Achievement goals and discrete achievement emotions: A theoretical model and prospective test. *Journal of Educational Psychology, 98,* 583–597.

Pekrun, R., Goetz, T., Titz, W., & Perry, R. P. (2002). Academic emotions in students' self-regulated learning and achievement: A program of quantitative and qualitative research. *Educational Psychologist, 37,* 91–106.

Schutz, P. A., & Pekrun, R. (Eds.). (2007). *Emotion in education.* San Diego, CA: Academic Press.

Spielberger, C. D. (1980). *Test Anxiety Inventory: Preliminary Professional Manual.* Palo Alto, CA: Consulting Psychologist Press.

Turner, J. E., & Schallert, D. L. (2001). Expectancy-value relationships of shame reactions and shame resiliency. *Journal of Educational Psychology, 93,* 320–329.

Weiner, B. (1985). An attributional theory of achievement motivation and emotion. *Psychological Review, 92,* 548–573.

Zeidner, M. (1998). *Test anxiety: The state of the art.* New York: Plenum.

Zeidner, M. (2007). Test anxiety in educational contexts: What I have learned so far. In P. A. Schutz & R. Pekrun (Eds.), *Emotion in education* (pp. 165–184). San Diego, CA: Academic Press.

Reinhard Pekrun

SUBJECTIVE TEST ITEMS

Subjective test items are more commonly called constructed response (CR) items. They require examinees to create their own responses, rather than selecting a response from a list of options (American Educational Research Association, American Psychological Association, and National Council on Measurement in Education, 1999). No single wording (or set of actions) can be regarded as the only correct response, and a response may earn full or partial credit. Responses must be scored subjectively by content experts. The term *constructed response item* may refer to an essay item or performance assessment. Measurement experts traditionally distinguish between two variations of these subjective item types: the restricted response item and the extended response item.

Restricted response items. On restricted response items examinees provide brief answers, usually no more than a few words or sentences, to fairly structured questions. An example in seventh grade science could be: Why are day lengths shorter in December than in July in the northern hemisphere?

Extended response items. Extended response items require lengthy responses that count heavily in scoring.

Ideally these items focus on major concepts of the content unit and demand higher level thinking. Typically examinees must organize multiple ideas and provide supporting information for major points in crafting responses. An example of such an item from 12th grade literature might be: The title of Steinbeck's novel, *The Winter of Our Discontent*, is found the opening line of the Shakespeare's play, *Richard III*. Having read both works, explain why you do, or do not, think this title is appropriate. Support your reasoning by comparing main characters, plots, and use of symbolism in these two works.

Performance assessment, as conceived in personnel psychology, requires the examinee to create a product or deliver a performance in a real world situation or simulation that could be evaluated using specified criteria. Raters typically score the performance using checklists or rating scales (Fitzpatrick & Morrison, 1971). When educators transported this procedure to classroom settings, their early performance exercises reflected this definition as shown in the following examples: determine the cost of carpeting a classroom, given a tape measure and carpet cost per square foot; determine the chemical composition of an unknown powdered compound.

Gradually, educators' views of performance assessment evolved to include pencil and paper items couched in real-world contexts. Coffman (1971) successfully argued that an essay item could be a performance assessment in some content areas. In performance assessments in the early 2000s, examinees may respond to questions containing diagrams, data tables, written scenarios, or text passages, but quite often their responses are written essays. In modern usage, the defining characteristic of a performance assessment is that it requires behaviors that are meaningful end-products of instruction derived from content standards (Lane & Stone, 2006). Performance assessments may also include portfolios or assigned out-of-class projects, but the principles for construction and scoring are the same as for essay items.

CONSTRUCTING THE ITEM

Content standards and test specifications operationally define the domain of subject matter knowledge and levels of cognitive complexity that are sampled by the achievement test items. Within these parameters, the test developer must develop the questions (or prompts), create scoring rubrics (or keys), and plan the scoring process. Welch (2006) provides a comprehensive summary of this process.

Developing the prompt. The prompt for a subjective item poses a question, presents a problem, or prescribes a task. It sets forth a scenario or set of circumstances to provide a common context for framing responses. Action verbs direct the examinee to focus on the desired behavior (e.g., solve, interpret, compare, contrast, discuss, or explain). Appropriate directions indicate expected length and format of the response, allowable resources or equipment, time limits, and features of the response that count in scoring (e.g., originality, organization, grammar, labeling diagrams, or numeric precision; see Gronlund & Linn, 1995).

Creating the scoring rubric. Scoring rubrics are usually analytic or holistic in nature. For an analytic rubric the item writer lists desired features of the response with a number of points awarded for each specific feature. A holistic rubric provides a scale for assigning points to the response based on overall impression. A range of possible points is specified (e.g. 0–8 or 0–3), and verbal descriptors are developed to characterize a response located at each possible point on the scale. Illustrative responses that correspond to each scale point are often developed or selected from actual examinee responses. These exemplars are called anchor papers because the scorer uses them as benchmarks for comparison when deciding where an examinee's response falls on the score scale.

Scoring responses. During subjective scoring at least four types of rater errors may occur as the rater (a) becomes more lenient or severe over time or scores erratically due to fatigue or distractions; (b) has knowledge or belief about an examinee that influences perception of the response; (c) is influenced by the examinee's good or poor performance on items previously scored; or (d) is influenced by the strength or weakness of a preceding examinee's response. To reduce these effects, a scoring process recommended for classroom teachers includes the following:

1. Mask student names to facilitate "blind" scoring;

2. Use the key on a trial basis for a small sample of papers and revise as necessary;

3. Grade all responses to a single item at one sitting if possible;

4. Shuffle papers between scoring different items so that examinees' responses are scored in varying order;

5. Mask the scores after initial scoring and rescore at least a sample of responses.

In large-scale testing programs, many raters participate in the scoring process. Prior to scoring, raters are trained to use common standards in extensive practice sessions using previously scored anchor papers. During scoring, each response is typically scored by at least two raters. Rater performance is monitored throughout the scoring process (Lane & Stone, 2006).

PERSISTENT ISSUES IN CONSTRUCTED RESPONSE TESTING

Using constructed response items presents issues that do not arise with objective item formats. Lane and Stone (2006) identify and discuss a number of these, but a few selected examples are as follows: Should the assessment present a few important tasks that demand complex, lengthy responses or more items, requiring briefer responses that provide broader sampling of the content and more reliable scores? Should examinees have a choice of prompts or should all respond to the same prompts? Does handwriting quality affect scores? Should examinees have a choice between handwriting or composing their responses at a computer keyboard? Do electronic scoring programs yield comparable results to those of human raters?

Such questions spark continuing debate for two reasons. First, research results from published studies on the issue may be conflicting or may not apply to other testing situations or populations. Second, these issues involve often value judgments rooted in differing educational philosophies. The final decision on such issues in a specific situation should rest on a rationale that weighs available research evidence, viewpoints of stakeholders, and possible consequences.

EVALUATING THE ITEMS

Despite the item writer's best efforts, subjective item prompts and rubrics will contain flaws. The most serious flaws are: mismatch to the content standards; ambiguity of wording; incorrect information in rubrics; inappropriate level of difficulty; content or wording that is offensive to some examinees, and potential for creating gender or ethnic bias due to the problem context or particular wording. Classroom teachers may ask colleagues to review a draft of items and critique them for such flaws. In large scale testing programs such reviews are conducted by multiple independent panels of experts (Welch, 2006).

After item administration, the examinees' numeric scores on each item provide a data set that can be analyzed to determine if the item functioned properly. This analysis typically includes computations of (a) mean item score and distribution statistics; (b) rater consistency indices (i.e., percentage of examinees receiving identical and contiguous scores from multiple raters or the correlations between the raters' scores); (c) consistency of examinee performance across different subjective items; and (d) relationship between item score and score on an objective section of the test (Schmeiser & Welch, 2006). In large scale assessments, these analyses are conducted after the items are field tested prior to live use. Flawed items can be revised or eliminated. At the classroom level, when the item analysis reveals a problem, adjustments to the scoring rubric can be made and responses can be rescored before examinees' scores are reported.

SEE ALSO *Classroom Assessment.*

BIBLIOGRAPHY

American Educational Research Association, American Psychological Association, and National Council on Measurement in Education (1999). *Standards for educational and psychological tests.* Washington DC: author.

Coffman, W. E. (1971). Essay examination. In R. L. Thorndike (Ed.), *Educational measurement* (2nd ed., pp. 271–302). Washington DC: American Council on Education.

Fitzpatrick, R., & Morrison, E. J. (1971). Performance and product evaluation. In R. L. Thorndike (Ed.), *Educational measurement* (2nd ed., pp. 237–270). Washington DC: American Council on Education.

Gronlund, N. E., & Linn, R. L. (1995). *Measurement and evaluation in teaching.* Englewood Cliffs, NJ: Merrill.

Lane, S., & Stone, C. (2006). Performance assessment. In R. L. Brennan (Ed.), *Educational measurement* (4th ed., pp. 387–431). Washington DC: American Council on Education.

Schmeiser, C. B., & Welch, C. J. (2006). Test development. In R. L. Brennan (Ed.), *Educational measurement* (4th ed., pp. 307–353). Washington DC: American Council on Education.

Welch C. J. (2006). Item and prompt development in performance testing. In S. M. Downing & T. M. Haladyna (Eds.). *Handbook of test development* (pp. 303–327). Mahwah, NJ: Erlbaum.

Linda Crocker

T

TA (TEST ANXIETY)

SEE *Evaluation (Test) Anxiety.*

TEACHER BELIEFS

In 1975 Dan Lortie coined the term *apprenticeship of observation* to describe the phenomenon that the majority of teachers teach very similarly to their own teachers:

> Teaching is unusual in that those who decide to enter it have had exceptional opportunity to observe members of the occupation at work; unlike most occupations today, the activities of teachers are not shielded from youngsters. Teachers-to-be underestimate the difficulties involved, but this supports the contention that those planning to teach form definite ideas about the nature of the role (p. 65).

Lortie contends many beliefs teachers hold about teaching originate from personal experiences as students. Some beliefs may derive from other personal experiences such as family traditions and values, social encounters, community participation, popular culture, teacher preparation, observing teachers, professional development, and scholarly literature.

Inasmuch as they originate from personal experience, beliefs are similar to attitudes and knowledge. Much scholarly debate attempts to determine just how beliefs, attitudes, and knowledge differ. In a 1992 article, M. Frank Pajares echoed Lortie's findings and described the difficulty in distinguishing attitudes from beliefs in the ways researchers have defined and studied them. Likewise, Patricia Alexander has described the challenges in deciphering what knowledge and beliefs have in common and how they are distinct. What is undisputed is beliefs have a motivational component and play a role in driving behavior.

Teachers' beliefs exist on many levels from global to personal and serve as overarching frameworks for understanding and engaging with the world. They can be thought of as guiding principles teachers' hold to be true that serve as lenses through which new experiences can be understood. Teachers' beliefs may be formed without evidence and sometimes in the face of contradictory evidence. They are a part of teachers' identities. Beliefs, and their influence, tend to be unexamined by teachers because many are implicit, unarticulated, or unconscious. The literature suggests failing to examine beliefs can have negative consequences as they guide practice and priorities, determined what is ignored, influence decision making, and shape what types of interactions are valued.

KINDS OF BELIEFS TEACHERS HOLD

Fundamentally, teachers' beliefs shape their professional practice. However, the study of teachers' beliefs has been tricky because of the multi-dimensionality of beliefs and the traditional boundaries drawn in educational psychology and teacher education about which beliefs constitute a relevant subset. For example, though teachers' beliefs as parents or as members of a religious group matter, much of the literature has focused on the beliefs most directly related to classroom practice. These beliefs can be

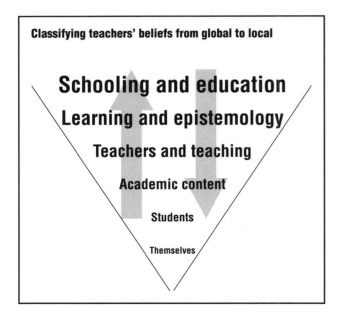

Figure 1 ILLUSTRATION BY GGS INFORMATION SERVICES. CENGAGE LEARNING, GALE.

organized into categories, each of which operates on a different level ranging from societal to personal. Figure 1 presents these categories as an inverted pyramid with the most global beliefs located at the top and filtering down toward to the most local beliefs teachers have about who they are. Placing teachers' beliefs about themselves as the most local should not, however, suggest they are of lesser importance or that they do not impact other beliefs. In fact, change in teachers' beliefs, at any level, can create a ripple effect throughout the teachers' entire system of beliefs.

Table 1 describes each category of belief along with a working definition synthesizing the related literature and a list of scholars whose work is directly related to that category. The categories are: schooling and education, epistemology, learning, teaching and teachers, academic content, students, and themselves.

BELIEFS ABOUT SCHOOLING, EPISTEMOLOGY, LEARNING, AND TEACHING

At the most global level, teachers hold beliefs about the purpose of schooling. For some teachers, these beliefs are rooted in a holistic perspective wherein the purpose of education is to help all children reach their full potential in every facet of their lives. Other teachers' beliefs, however, are rooted in more essentialist models that position schools as places in which students acquire knowledge critical to becoming productive members of society. Still others believe schooling should envision a new society,

help students become lifelong learners, or enhance the students' individuality.

Beliefs about the role of education can filter down and impact teachers' epistemological beliefs. These include "beliefs about the nature of knowledge and the processes of knowing" (Hofer & Pintrich, 1997, p. 117). They include beliefs about what criteria should be used to determine the validity and value of different types of knowledge. When identifying their epistemological orientation, teachers must ask themselves: Is knowledge singular or multiple? Must all knowledge be consistent or is there room for contradiction? And, who can be the source of knowledge: the teacher, society as a collective, or some singular, external authority?

Just as these epistemological beliefs are shaped by beliefs about the role of schooling, teachers' beliefs about learning are influenced by their epistemological beliefs. Beliefs about learning include those related to how people learn and what it means to have learned (Hofer & Pintrich, 1997). For example, teachers who have essentialist views of education are likely to believe that only certain kinds of knowledge are valid. They, therefore, are likely to focus their efforts on having students learn those kinds knowledge. Similarly, epistemological beliefs impact teachers' understandings of what it means to teach and how teaching is best accomplished. For example, teachers who believe authority figures (e.g., teachers, doctors, scientists) are the only real sources of knowledge may adopt a more behaviorist perspective about learning. They are also likely to enact transmissionist instructional techniques, such as direct instruction, founded on the notions that teachers know and students learn when teachers give them knowledge.

Alternatively, teachers who believe the self can be a valid source of knowing are likely to structure their classrooms in ways that emphasize students' contribution to the learning process. Furthermore, these teachers tend to believe that teachers and students know and learn together and that learning happens best through dialogue and shared interaction. Discussion and discovery learning pedagogies were founded in the belief that individuals and groups can create meaningful understandings.

TEACHERS' BELIEFS ABOUT ACADEMIC CONTENT, STUDENT POPULATIONS, AND THEMSELVES

Global beliefs have local impact on teachers' beliefs about the content they teach, their students, and themselves as teachers. Susan Stodolsky and colleagues argue teachers' beliefs about academic content, particularly with regard to status, stability, sequence, and scope, shape their practice. These beliefs inform the concepts teachers emphasize, the way they order and organize material, the student understandings and misunderstandings they anticipate, and their instructional and assessment decisions.

910

Teacher beliefs and prominent programs of research

Type of belief	Working definition	Eminent scholars
Schooling and education	Teachers hold beliefs about the nature and purpose of schooling including the reasons why we send children to school; what it means to educate; and what should be the ultimate goals of an (public or privately funded) education system.	Mortimer Adler, George Counts, John Dewey, Paulo Freire, Barbara Finkelstein, Maxine Greene, Eric Donald Hirsch, Jr., Bell Hooks, Nel Noddings
Epistemology	Teachers hold beliefs about the nature of knowing and knowledge including what types of knowledge are valued and what are the trusted sources of knowledge.	Patricia Alexander, Barbara Hofer, Paul Pintrich, Gregory Schraw, Gale Sinatra
Learning	Teachers hold beliefs about how people learn and the 'best' ways to support conceptual change.	Hilda Borko, James Greeno, Hugh Munby, Tom Russell
Behaviorist	Teachers who endorse behaviorist views of learning believe in the power of external forces, like rewards and consequences, to shape new learning.	Clark Hull, Ivan Pavlov, B. F. Skinner, Edward Tolman, Edward Thorndike, John Watson
Social cognitivist	Teachers who endorse social-cognitive views of learning emphasize the ways in which environmental factors work in combination with students' prior knowledge and their personal motives to create opportunities for performing different behaviors and intellectual tasks.	Albert Bandura, Dan C. Lortie, M. Frank Pajares, Barry Zimmerman
Social constructivist	Teachers who endorse social-constructivist views of learning believe in the power of culture, be it family culture, classroom culture or school culture. They view their role in the classroom as that of a gatekeeper—providing students with intellectual tools that can help them to increase their participation in the school and larger community.	Barbara Rogoff, Lev Vygotsky, Reggio Emelia Approach
Cognitivist	Teachers who endorse a cognitive view of learning emphasize the potentials and limits of students' understanding based on their prior knowledge, their memory capacity, their mental strategies, and their abilities to connect new understandings to what they already know.	Noam Chomsky, Jerome Bruner, Richard Mayer
Constructivist	Teachers who endorse a constructivist view of learning emphasize the individual nature of knowledge construction and emphasize the importance of students' experiential learning.	Paul Cobb, Maria Montesorri, Jean Piaget, Virginia Richardson
Teaching and teachers	Teachers hold beliefs about what it means to be a teacher including what roles and responsibilities teachers bear, what it means to serve students, what norms and mores are appropriate for classrooms, and what instruction "should" look like.	Douwe Beijaard, Marilyn Cochran Smith, Linda Darling-Hammond, Lisa Delpit, Fred Korthagen, Lee Shulman, Nancy Zimpher
Classroom management	Embedded in teachers' beliefs about instruction are their understandings of how to best manage a classroom to promote learning. These are, in part, a reflection of their beliefs about the nature and value of student-teacher and peer interactions.	Edmund Emmer, Carolyn Evertson, Nancy K. Martin, H. Richard Milner, Leslie Soodak, Carol Weinstein, Charles H. Wolfgang
Culturally relevant pedagogy	Embedded in teachers' beliefs about instruction are their beliefs about culture in general and classroom culture specifically. These beliefs include beliefs about the role students' home culture should play in the classroom. They focus teachers' efforts on either helping students to assimilate to a predetermined culture or on facilitating students' contributions to a negotiated culture.	David Brown, Geneva Gay, Jacqueline Irvine, Gloria Ladson-Billings
Subject matter/ academic content	Teachers hold beliefs about the nature and structure of the subject matter being taught. These beliefs guide them when planning what the important ideas are in their field, how to sequence their instruction, and what standards should be used in judging student mastery.	Pam Grossman, John Guthrie, Deborah Stipek, Susan Stodolsky
Students	Teaches hold beliefs about the nature of being a student including what it means to be a good student, how students should behave, how students can best spend their time, and the nature of ideal teacher-student relationships.	Jere E. Brophy, Mary McCaslin, Robert Rosenthall, Richard E. Snow, Thomas L. Good
Individual differences in learning	Teachers' beliefs about the impact of learner differences on classroom practice are closely tied with beliefs about the nature of intelligence. They shape teachers' conceptions about the amount of their time and energy different students will require to be successful.	Scott Danforth, Carol Dweck, Howard Gardner, Leslie Soodak, Robert J. Sternberg
Individual differences in interactions	Teachers' beliefs about the nature of students' stable identity characteristics such as their gender, race, religion, or sexual orientation. These beliefs shape can their instruction and interactions with students, privileging some and marginalizing others.	Molly Blackburn, Beverly Cross, Geneva Gay, Etta Hollins, Robert Pianta, Susan Talburt
Themselves	Teachers hold beliefs about themselves in the role of teacher. These include beliefs about their identity, knowledge, capabilities, values, desires, and needs.	Robert Bullough, Jane Danielewicz, Adrienne Dixson, Gail McCutchen, Beverly Tatum, Bruce Toroff
Self-efficacy	Teachers hold beliefs about their own abilities including the extent to which they believe they can be successful in all of their teaching tasks.	Patricia Ashton, Anita Woolfolk Hoy, M. Frank Pajares
Sense of responsibility	Teachers hold beliefs about outcomes they are, and are not, responsible for in their classroom, in their school, with their students.	Thomas Gusky, Julian Rotter

Table 1 ILLUSTRATION BY GGS INFORMATION SERVICES. CENGAGE LEARNING, GALE.

Even more local than beliefs about content are teachers' beliefs about their students. These beliefs include what it means to be a student, how students should relate to teachers, and the impact of student differences on classroom practice and culture. Scholars such as Richard Ryan, Edward Deci, and Johnmarshall Reeve assert that in order for students to assume responsibility for their own learning they must feel autonomous, competent, and connected to their classmates and teachers. Underlying their theories is the assumption that in order to be self-determined, students must to have these fundamental needs met. However, their research suggests teachers' beliefs about their own need to be in control may be in conflict with students' needs.

Likewise, teachers' beliefs about whether their students need relationships with them may be in conflict with what the literature says students actually need. Robert Pianta argues that all students need to experience close relationships with their teachers. However, the literature (see Davis, 2003) suggests that teachers may regard this need as varying with students' development or social group. Similarly, the work of Jere Brophy and Mary McCaslin (McCaslin has also published under the name Mary Rohrkemper) investigates teachers' definitions of and interactions with problem students. When teachers believe the source of behavior problems is a lack of competence as opposed to an attempt to usurp control in the class, they tend to respond with more caring and are more likely to help those students achieve competence. Other researchers have explored the causes of behavior understood by teachers to be disruptive. For example, Molly Blackburn writes about the experience of lesbian, gay, and bisexual students who are perceived as disruptive but who in actuality may be expressing malcontent with an irrelevant curriculum. More generally, Jacqueline Irvine's work highlights that teachers' beliefs about the way students should behave at school may prevent them from recognizing and appropriately responding to student behavior that critiques marginalizing curriculum. Irvine introduced the concept of *cultural synchronization* to describe how teachers' beliefs about certain student groups may be in conflict with the actual motives, values, and needs of those students. Clashes between teachers' and students' beliefs may have negative instructional and interpersonal consequences.

At the most local level, teachers hold beliefs about themselves—who they are in relation to curriculum, colleagues, and students; perceived strengths and weaknesses; values; self-efficacy; and matters about which they feel responsible. These beliefs may be domain specific; teachers may hold beliefs about who they are as instructors that are different from their beliefs about themselves as classroom managers or content experts. These beliefs may be hierarchically organized such that a teacher may believe they are experts in their fields, they are strong instructors, but they struggle with classroom management. Because teachers may weigh these domains differently (i.e., placing the most value on being a strong instructor), when asked if they are good teachers, they may respond based on a global perception that they are. Finally, beliefs may not necessarily be calibrated with actual behaviors. In her study of pre-service teachers, Carol Weinstein documented how novice teachers are likely to be unrealistically optimistic regarding their ability to manage classroom tasks.

Finally, it is important to note the majority of the literature on teachers' beliefs has been based predominantly on studies of white, middle class, female teachers (Woolfolk Hoy, Davis, & Pape, 2006). In "The Silenced Dialogue," Lisa Delpit reinforces the notion that teachers from underrepresented or marginalized populations may hold different beliefs about teaching minority students and, therefore, view themselves and their tasks very differently. One African American principal in Delpit's study expressed her experience of being ill-represented in the literature and of her majority colleagues using this literature to ignore her perspective. The principal was quoted as saying: "If you try to suggest that's not quite the way it is, they get defensive, then you get defensive, then they'll start reciting research. I try to give them my experiences, to explain ... they don't really hear me" (Delpit, 1995, p. 22). Delpit argues alternative, and perhaps transformative, perspectives of minority teachers are not represented in the research base and deserve to be voiced.

THE IMPORTANCE OF TEACHERS' BELIEFS

In the 1960s, Robert Rosenthal (b. 1933) began examining expectancy beliefs and self-fulfilling prophecies—research that has remained robust into the early 2000s. When teachers expect students to perform (i.e., high or low), they behave in differential ways that bring about the expected performance. In *Pygmalion in the Classroom: Teacher Expectations and Pupil's Intellectual Development* (1968), Rosenthal and Jacobsen documented how teachers' beliefs about student ability can be subtly manipulated such that teachers believe some students to be more able than their peers and how their beliefs about student ability affect students' actual achievement. Rosenthal's research was extended to understand systemic differences in the way teachers approach students from lower economic standing (Alvidrez & Weinstein, 1999), students in urban settings (Causey, Thomas, & Armento, 2000), and special education students (Soodak, Podell, & Lehman, 1998).

Measuring the power of teachers' beliefs about student intelligence became important. In 1973 W. Burleigh Seaver conducted a naturalistic experiment to examine the effects of teachers' expectations of students' performance given the performance of a high or low achieving sibling in their class in a previous year. Underlying this study was the assumption that teachers expect siblings to perform similarly given their shared family context and/or genetic makeup. Using school records, and controlling for the younger siblings' actual intelligence, older siblings were classified as either high or low performers and younger siblings' performances when they had the same or different teacher were examined. "When the older sibling had performed at a high level, the expectancy group [i.e., having the same teacher] scored better than the control; when the older sibling had performed poorly, the expectancy group scored lower than the control group" (p. 337). The average size of the effects was .30 on a grade equivalency score, approximately the achievement that happens across one-third of an academic year.

Self-fulfilling prophecies, such as those about student ability, operate through two forms of messages teachers send to students: the explicit (i.e., what is consciously said) and implicit (i.e., what is unconsciously said). In 1973 Rosenthal "derived four major types of teacher behaviors that appear to be associated with [teacher] expectancy effects. These are (1) climate—is the teacher warm and encouraging to the pupil? (2) feedback—does the teacher offer evaluative comments on the pupil's ongoing performance? (3) input—how much does the teacher try to teach the child? (4) output—how many opportunities does the teacher give the child to respond?" (Hall et al., 2001, p. 163).

Teachers' beliefs are a form of subjective reality: What they believe is real and true. Their beliefs guide their decision-making, behavior, and interactions with students and, in turn, create an objective reality in the classroom, what students experience as real and true. Teachers' beliefs shape their planning and curricular decisions, in effect determining what should be taught and what path instruction should follow. Moreover, their beliefs are not always a reflection of accepted notions in the field. In a 1998 study of teachers' and students' understandings of knowledge (from prior experience and formal instruction in school) and beliefs, Patricia Alexander and colleagues found teachers and students recognize beliefs and knowledge may not overlap:

> Our students and teachers in both Singapore and the United States suggest that there are those objective dimensions of one's understanding (i.e., knowledge) that are factual in nature and learned in school but of limited importance or value. In contrast, there are those personal tenets (i.e., beliefs) that may be unproven or even questioned in schools and society, but which are nonetheless true and which serve as the guiding forces in one's life. (p. 114)

These findings suggest teachers may hold beliefs that are in conflict with their physical and social realities; but that, nonetheless, inform their practice. Moreover, these findings suggest that teachers cannot assume an understanding of another person's (i.e. another teacher or their students) decision-making even when they share a knowledge base. Teachers need to dig deeper to try to uncover the beliefs, the personal tenets that drive their own, their colleagues', and their students' behavior.

HOW TEACHERS' BELIEFS OPERATE

Essentially beliefs function in a way similar to a lens on a magnifying glass. They clarify and guide interpretation of what may be ambiguous or unfocused. Generally, teachers interpret ambiguous situations in ways that are consistent with their beliefs. Beliefs also serve as a foundation for setting goals and standards by framing what is viewed in detail and focusing teachers' attention and energy. Similarly, they delimit what is peripheral, determining what teachers do not see, emphasize, or examine. Because beliefs help teachers to make sense of what they experience in the classroom, they create meaning for teachers. Moreover, they prepare teachers to experience certain emotions by mapping pleasant feelings onto some experiences (i.e., success or failure) and unpleasant feelings onto others.

Debate continues about the extent to which teachers' beliefs and their identity as teachers are the same. The literature on teachers' beliefs suggests teachers may simultaneously hold beliefs that are inconsistent, in conflict, and even contradictory and still see themselves as a teacher. Fred Korthagen posits teachers are likely to be the most effective when their beliefs are aligned with each other and with the field.

That beliefs are intimately tied with teachers' sense of self (be it their personal identities or their teaching identities) is consistent across the literature, and, for this reason, beliefs tend to be resistant to change. In the face of information that challenges their beliefs, such as policy inducement to reform, to modify/include new populations of students, or to innovate with new technologies, teachers tend to feel threatened (Fecho, 2001; Gregoire, 2003). This reaction constitutes a fundamental challenge and, at times the paradox, of practicing and pre-service teacher education. The problem is to figure out how can teachers be encouraged to approach research in education, professional development, and policy reform with open minds.

HOW TEACHERS' BELIEFS CHANGE

There is an inherent tension in the field of teacher beliefs between the call for teachers to habitually confront and revise their beliefs and the need for teachers to identify and preserve beliefs that serve them well. On one hand, at some point teachers inevitably have some maladaptive beliefs because the nature of childhood, the demands of society, and the curriculum change. On the other hand, there is an assumption in the literature, particularly with regard to beliefs about diverse students and best practice, that teachers' beliefs are bad and need to be changed. The danger of this thinking is that in order to protect their sense of self as good persons and as effective and altruistic teachers, teachers may defensively hold on to beliefs that do not serve their students. What appears to be a dichotomy here need not be. What teachers need to be encouraged to do is honestly face their beliefs in their entirety, evaluating which beliefs serve them, their content, and their students and which do not.

The question is what teachers should do when they confront beliefs that do not work anymore. The malleability, or persistence, of beliefs and ways to bring about belief change are highly debated issues. In general, the more beliefs are tied to a teacher's sense of self, the more they will resist change. Literature in the field of teacher education often suggests that the ideal conditions for belief change include: 1) bringing pre-existing beliefs to consciousness, 2) creating conditions in which pre-existing beliefs break down, 3) helping teachers to judge the conflict as challenging rather than threatening (Gregoire, 2003), and 4) providing teachers with the necessary time to reflect on their beliefs and reconcile them with the field and their current teaching context (Davis, 2006).

Mere awareness of beliefs may not be motivating enough to create change. Nearly all theories of conceptual change would argue that there needs to be some cognitive dissonance by which teachers see their beliefs do not work given serving a specific student population, teaching a specific concept, or enacting desired outcomes. Dissonance challenges teachers by forcing them to face failures, however small. When studying adaptive teaching Lyn Corno and colleagues (Corno & Snow, 1985; Rohrkemper & Corno, 1988) describe how adaptive teachers face dissonance and learn from it. Corno contends adaptive teaching involves monitoring which students are struggling and identifying the sources of the struggle. She argues that failures can have meaning and can transform teaching. In some cases, student failure can point to beliefs teachers have that are holding students back. Can teachers reframe failure to help themselves grow professionally? By thinking of students' struggles as "functional failures" (Rohrkemper & Corno, 1988; p. 303) teachers can modify what they are doing to help their students learn and, in doing so, help themselves to work more effectively with all students and their subject matter. What makes this so hard, according to Michelle Gregoire Gill, is helping teachers learn to interpret failure (or educational reform) as a challenge and an opportunity for growth rather than as a threat.

Perhaps the most challenging parts for administrators and teacher educators are building in the time and

providing teachers with the tools necessary to engage in productive reflection (Davis, 2006). Elizabeth Davis describes the ways reflection on beliefs can go awry and makes three recommendations. First, teachers should be encouraged to move beyond describing what they see and experience and to analyzing what is happening in their classrooms. Second, teachers should be encouraged to think about problems from an alternate perspective, particularly their students'. Third, to put an end to dichotomous thinking, teachers should be encouraged to integrate what may feel like competing tensions and create space for new solutions. Fundamentally, doing so entails a shift from either-or to both-and thinking. In other words, instead of teachers feeling like they have to choose between following their beliefs or participating in reform, when reform is important, teachers should seek ways to align their beliefs with the reform.

IMPLICATIONS FOR CLASSROOM TEACHERS

If there are three clear messages throughout the literature on teachers' beliefs, they are, first and foremost, that teachers' beliefs have profound impact on classroom life; that the beliefs that impact students are layered, multi-dimensional, sometimes implicit, and difficult to change; and that teachers who fail to examine their beliefs may bring about unanticipated consequences in the classroom. Without intending to, teachers may set aside valuable curriculum, overlook or marginalize students who need them, misinterpret students' motives or behavior, and limit their potential as professionals. Conversely, teachers who are willing to explore their beliefs, and how their beliefs relate to practice and the professional knowledge base, can capitalize on the beliefs they hold to promote students' intellectual growth, autonomy and reciprocity, and equity in their classrooms. Moreover, they create spaces for their own growth as they identify and revise beliefs that do not serve them, their students, or their schools.

SEE ALSO *Conceptual Change; Epistemological Beliefs; Identity Development; Knowledge; Metacognition; Teacher Efficacy; Theories of Learning.*

BIBLIOGRAPHY

Alexander, P. A., Murphy, P. K., Guan, J., & Murphy, P. A. (1998). How students and teachers in Singapore and the United States conceptualize knowledge and beliefs: Positioning learning within epistemological frameworks. *Learning and Instruction, 8,* 97–116.

Alvidrez, J., & Weinstein, R. S. (1999). Early teacher perceptions and later student achievement. *Journal of Educational Psychology, 91,* 31–39.

Blackburn, M. (2004). Understanding agency beyond school sanctioned activities. *Theory into Practice, 43,* 102–110.

Brophy, J. E., & Good, T. L. (1970). Teachers' communication of differential expectations for children's classroom performance: Some behavioral data. *Journal of Educational Psychology, 61,* 365–374.

Calderhead, J. (1996). Teachers: Beliefs and knowledge. In D. Berliner & R. Calfee (Eds.), *Handbook of educational psychology* (pp. 709–725). New York: Macmillan.

Causey, V. E., Thomas, C. D., & Armento, B. J. (2000). Cultural diversity is basically a foreign term to me: The challenges of diversity for pre-service teacher education. *Teaching and Teacher Education, 16,* 33–45.

Corno, L., & Snow, R. (1985). Adapting teaching to individual differences among learners. In M. C. Wittrock (Ed.), *Handbook of research on teaching* (3rd ed., pp. 605–629). New York: Macmillan.

Davis, E. A. (2006). Characterizing productive reflection among pre-service elementary teachers: Seeing what matters. *Teaching and Teacher Education, 22,* 281–301.

Davis, H. A. (2003). Conceptualizing the role and influence of student-teacher relationships on children's social and cognitive development. *Educational Psychologist, 38*(4), 207–234.

Davis, H. A. (2006). Exploring the contexts of relationship quality between middle school students and teachers. *Elementary School Journal, 106,* 193–223.

Delpit, L. (1995). The silenced dialogue: Power and pedagogy in educating other people's children. In *Other people's children: Cultural conflict in the classroom* (pp. 21–47). New York: New Press.

Fecho, B. (2001). "Why are you doing this?": Acknowledging and transcending threat in a critical inquiry classroom. *Research in the Teaching of English, 36,* 9–37.

Gregoire, M. (2003). Is it a challenge or a threat? A dual process model of teacher's cognition and appraisal processes during conceptual change. *Educational Psychology Review, 15,* 147–179.

Hall, J. A., Rosenthal, R., Archer, D., DiMatteo, M. R., & Rogers, P. L. (2001). Nonverbal skills in the classroom. *Theory into Practice, 16,* 162–166.

Hofer, B. K., & Pintrich, P. R. (1997). The development of epistemological theories: Beliefs about knowledge and knowing and their relation to learning. *Review of Educational Research, 67,* 88–140.

Kagan, D. M. (1992). Implications of research on teacher beliefs. *Educational Psychologist, 27,* 65–90.

Korthagen, F. A. J. (2004). In search of the essence of a good teacher: Towards a more holistic approach in teacher education. *Teaching and Teacher Education, 20,* 77–97.

Lortie, D. C. (1975). *Schoolteacher: A sociological study.* Chicago: University of Chicago Press.

Munby, H., Russell, T., & Martin, A. K. (2001). Teachers' knowledge and how it develops. In V. Richardson (Ed.), *Handbook of research on teaching* (4th ed., pp. 877–904). Washington, DC: American Educational Researcher.

Pajares, F. (1992). Teachers' beliefs and educational research: Cleaning up a messy construct. *Review of Educational Research, 62,* 307–332.

Patrick, H., & Pintrich, P. R. (2001). Conceptual change in teachers' intuitive conceptions of learning, motivation, and instruction: The role of motivational and epistemological beliefs. In B. Torff & R. J. Sternberg (Eds.), *Understanding and teaching the intuitive mind: Student and teacher learning* (pp. 117–143). Mahwah, NJ: Erlbaum.

Pianta, R. C. (1999). *Enhancing relationships between children and teachers.* Washington, DC: American Psychological Association.

Reeve, J. (2006). Teachers as facilitators: What autonomy-supportive teachers do and why their students benefit. *Elementary School Journal, 106,* 225–236.

Rohrkemper, M., & Corno, L. (1988). Success and failure on classroom tasks: Adaptive learning and classroom teaching. *Elementary School Journal, 88,* 296–312.

Rosenthal, R., & Jacobson, L. (1968). *Pygmalion in the classroom: Teacher expectations and pupils' intellectual development.* New York: Holt, Rinehart, & Winston.

Ryan, R. M., & Deci, E. L. (2000). Intrinsic and extrinsic motivation: Classic definitions and new directions. *Contemporary Educational Psychology, 25,* 54–67.

Seaver, W. B. (1973). Effects of naturally induced teacher expectancies. *Journal of Personality, 28,* 33–342.

Sookak, L. C., Podell, D., & Lehman, L. R. (1998). Teacher and student and school attributes as predictors of teachers' responses to inclusion. *Journal of Special Education, 31,* 480–497.

Stodolsky, S. S., & Grossman, P. L. (1995). The impact of subject matter on curricular activity: An analysis of five academic subject areas. *American Educational Research Journal, 32,* 227–249.

Weinstein, C. (1988). Pre-service teachers' expectations about the first year of teaching. *Teaching and Teacher Education, 4,* 31–41.

Woolfolk Hoy, A., Hoy, W. K., & Davis, H. (in press). Teachers' self-efficacy beliefs. In K. Wentzel & A. Wigfield (Eds.), *Handbook of motivation in school.* Mahwah, NJ: Erlbaum.

Woolfolk Hoy, A., Davis, H., & Pape, S. (2006). Teachers' knowledge, beliefs, and thinking. In P. A. Alexander & P. H, Winne (Eds.), *Handbook of educational psychology* (2nd ed., pp. 715–737.). Mahwah, NJ: Erlbaum.

Woolfolk Hoy, A., & Weinstein, C. S. (2006). Students' and teachers' perspectives on classroom management. In C. Evertson & C. S. Weinstein (Eds.), *Handbook for classroom management: Research, practice, and contemporary issue* (pp. 181–220). Mahwah, NJ: Erlbaum.

Heather A. Davis
Carey E. Andrzejewski

TEACHER EFFICACY

The concept of self-efficacy was pioneered by Albert Bandura (1925–) who characterized self-efficacy as the extent to which individuals believe they can organize and execute actions necessary to bring about a desired outcome. Self-efficacy is fundamentally concerned with the execution of control rather than the outcome action produces.

In 1984, Patricia Ashton (1946–) published a groundbreaking study that fundamentally expanded the concept of efficacy to include the extent to which teachers feel confident they are capable of bringing about learning outcomes. Ashton identified two dimensions of teaching efficacy: general, the extent to which a teacher believes her students can learn material; and personal, the extent to which a teacher believes her students can learn under her instruction. Ashton argued that teachers' beliefs

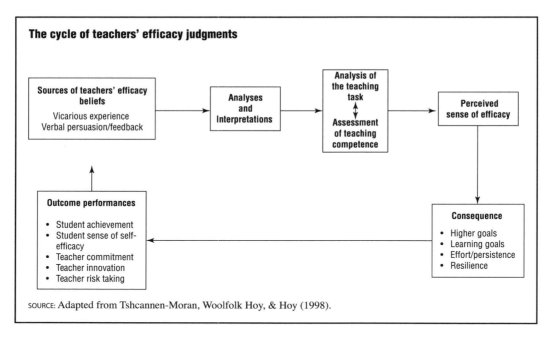

The cycle of teachers' efficacy judgments

SOURCE: Adapted from Tshcannen-Moran, Woolfolk Hoy, & Hoy (1998).

Figure 1 ILLUSTRATION BY GGS INFORMATION SERVICES. CENGAGE LEARNING, GALE.

about their ability to bring about outcomes in their classrooms, and their confidence in teaching in general, play a central role in their abilities to effectively serve their students. Since then, studies of teaching efficacy and its inclusion in studies of teacher effectiveness have grown exponentially.

Subsequent understandings of teaching efficacy have refined Ashton's understanding of personal efficacy. In a seminal review of teacher efficacy, Megan Tschannen-Moran (1956–) and Anita Woolfolk Hoy (1947–) operationalized teachers' sense of control over student outcomes in the Teachers' Sense of Efficacy Scale (TSES) (Tshannen-Moran & Woolfolk Hoy 2001). Rather than thinking about efficacy as a proxy for a global sense of confidence, they defined teacher efficacy as teachers' perceptions of their resources and strategies for bringing about student behavioral and instructional outcomes. Rather than ask, "How much can you help your students think critically?" the TSES asks, "How much can you do to help your students think critically?" This minor change in wording illustrates a critical issue in teacher efficacy research: that teachers' sense of efficacy reflects the judgments they make about their capabilities given the emotional and instrumental resources they can gather in a specific context. Because teachers' judgments of their resources and strategies may vary across teaching contexts, Woolfolk Hoy argues that teachers' efficacy beliefs may not be uniform across all disciplines or even across all student populations. It is therefore important to account for context and discipline in order to accurately assess teacher efficacy.

HOW TEACHERS DEVELOP SELF-EFFICACY BELIEFS

Tshcannen-Moran and colleagues (1998) developed a model of teacher efficacy identifying the ways in which efficacy judgments result as a function of the interaction between teachers' analysis of teaching task in context and their teachers' assessment of their personal teaching capabilities as they relate to the task (see Figure 1). In addition, Bandura also identified four specific sources of efficacy beliefs: mastery experiences, vicarious experiences, verbal persuasion, and arousal. Mastery experiences are direct encounters with success through engagement in a behavior that brings about a desired outcome. For example, student-teachers who facilitate laboratory experiments in which students demonstrate conceptual understanding may believe their actions led to student learning. These judgments are likely to increase their efficacy for conducting lab experiments in the future. This may be why some studies have found a connection between teacher education coursework and pre-service teacher efficacy. If student-teachers watch experienced teachers successfully facilitate laboratory experiments, they might also develop a sense of efficacy because they saw how to implement the actions necessary to bring about students' success. This would be an example of a vicarious, or observed experience leading to higher efficacy.

When student-teachers do not have opportunities to observe, their mentor teachers might remind them of the teaching skills they have developed and provide them with specific suggestions. This would be an example of verbal persuasion, which appeals to the teacher's ability to bring about success. Finally, arousal is a physiological state involving the release of hormones that signal an individual to prepare for action. Arousal can be interpreted as both pleasant and unpleasant. On the one hand, the body's natural release of hormones while teaching can help teachers feel alert or excited to take on the challenges of the lesson. On the other hand, heavy release of hormones (as in the case of extreme nervousness) can be paralyzing rather than helpful.

Calibrating and Re-Calibrating Teacher Efficacy. There is little consistency across the literature regarding the stability of teacher efficacy over time; some studies indicate efficacy may increase over time and others suggest it may decline. What is clear is that teachers' efficacy judgments tend to calibrate when they move into new contexts. For example, Woolfolk Hoy and Burke-Spero (2005) found teacher efficacy declined as they entered the field. One explanation for possible initial declines in efficacy may be that when new teachers enter the teaching force, they encounter a "reality shock" as they confront the complexity of the teaching task. Carol Weinstein (1988) suggests this may indicate a tempering, or calibration of overly optimistic efficacy beliefs, or what she termed "unrealistic optimism." Those who continue to feel incompetent are likely to leave the field, while teachers who remain in the field appear to experience a rebound in their efficacy judgments.

THE CONTEXT AND MEASUREMENT OF TEACHER EFFICACY

Teacher efficacy beliefs are one type of belief within a system of interrelated self-beliefs. Moreover, teacher efficacy beliefs emerge, in part, as a function of teachers' global and specific judgments about themselves within the context of their classroom. In the field of teacher beliefs, there has been a lot of debate about how best to study the relationship between teachers' beliefs about themselves and the impact of these beliefs on classroom learning. In part, this is because scholars from across a variety of research traditions developed frameworks for understanding self-beliefs, with each framework critiquing the level at which we should evaluate teachers' beliefs, the domains that matter, and which judgments inevitably lead to action. In an effort to delineate what teacher efficacy is and how it should be measured Table 1 outlines conceptual distinctions among the prominent programs of research on teachers' other self-beliefs.

Although teacher efficacy is related to self-concept, self-esteem, locus of control, and sense of responsibility, it is theoretically and empirically distinct from these constructs. On a global level, teachers hold beliefs about who

they are in their classroom, their teaching self-concept, and how they feel about themselves in their classrooms, their teaching self-esteem. Teachers' self-concepts and self-esteem are considered global because they are broad, descriptive mental representations teachers hold about the work they do in their classrooms. In contrast, scholars studying teacher efficacy attempt to identify specific, task-related judgments teachers make about their ability to bring about task-specific outcomes.

Carl Rogers (1902–1987) defined self-concept as a personal understanding of the self relative to other people and environments but unaffected by tasks or contexts. Teacher self-concept goes beyond merely identifying characteristics, "I am a teacher," to classifying those characteristics, "I am a good teacher." Whereas self-concept is based upon comparative judgments, self-esteem is based upon affective judgments. Teacher self-esteem may be defined as the evaluation of each characteristic contained in teachers' self-concepts. For example, "I am good at motivating students" may be evaluated in terms of satisfaction, or the extent to which being a good teacher is desirable. Although self-esteem may change over time, it is not variable across tasks or contexts.

Scholars studying teachers' locus of control and their sense of responsibility are primarily focused on teachers' perceptions of their roles in student achievement. Role attributes are beliefs about the part a teacher can play in bringing about outcomes. Thomas Guskey (1950–) characterizes teachers' perceptions of control as based primarily in the teacher (internal) or other factors (external) and variable across situations. If control over an outcome is attributed internally, individuals are more likely to engage in a behavior. The critical distinction between locus of control and self-efficacy is the emphasis on product rather than process; locus of control asserts that individuals are motivated to act based upon perception of control over the outcome. If teachers believe control lies within the student (e.g., smart/dull) or other external factors (e.g. family/community), they may be less likely to engage in actions that bring about desired outcomes even if they feel they can successfully execute those actions.

Responsibility models address teachers' underlying beliefs about who should bring about outcomes. Teachers' sense of responsibility is both an internal and external orientation deriving from perceptions of professional/ethical and personal/moral obligation. Perceptions of control and responsibility can impact teachers' efficacy judgments. In an environment where schools are becoming increasingly culturally diverse and where teachers are held strictly accountable for their students' success on standardized tests, teachers' ability to serve minority students and address politically sensitive issues is limited. Yet, many teachers are motivated to serve students who

Differentiating between teachers' sense of efficacy and their self-concept, self-esteem and self-worth

Construct	Definition	Characteristics	Sample items	Related articles
Teachers' sense of efficacy	Teachers' perceptions of their ability to accomplish specific tasks in a given context.	Task and context specific; Future-oriented; Not based on comparisons with other people or with other aspects of the self—rather question is "Can I do it?" Judgment of capability.	"How much can you do to help your students think critically?" (Instructional) "How much can you do to control disruptive behavior in the classroom?" (Classroom Management) "How much can you do to motivate students who show low interest in school work?" (Motivation) "Students would come to me when they have problems in their daily life because they know I can help." (Relationships)	Tschannen-Moran, Woolfolk Hoy, & Hoy (1998) TSES: Tschannen-Moran & Woolfolk Hoy (2001) Ho & Hau, 2004
Teacher self-concept	Global perceptions of my competence as a teacher.	Global; present orientation; includes self-efficacy and other self-judgments; based on comparisons with others (e.g., "I work with parents better than most teachers") or with self ("I'm better at lecturing than guiding group work").	"I am a good teacher." "My students learn many important things from me."	Friedman & Farber (1992) Brown (2004)
Teacher self-esteem	Global affective statements reflecting teachers' self-evaluations of their accomplishments.	Judgment of self-worth; not necessarily related to self-efficacy—can have low efficacy for a task, but not value the task, so self-esteem is unaffected.	"On the whole, I am satisfied with myself." "I wish I could have more respect for myself."	Singh (1984) Juhasz (1990) Christou, Phillipou, & Menon (2001)
Locus of control and teachers' sense of responsibility	Teachers' beliefs about their responsibility for student outcomes.	Teachers' attributions for student outcomes (Guskey). Teachers' acceptance or rejection of responsibility for implementing culturally relevant pedagogy (Kozel).	"If a student does well in your class, would it probably be: a. because that student had the natural ability to do well, or b. because of the encouragement you offered?" "It is my responsibility to ensure that all students are able to participate in every lesson." (Global beliefs about inclusion) "It is my responsibility to provide accurate information about sexual orientations." (Specific beliefs about racial, religious, and social minorities)	Guskey (1988) Kozel (2007)

Table 1 ILLUSTRATION BY GGS INFORMATION SERVICES. CENGAGE LEARNING, GALE.

need the most help (Winfield, 1986). Teachers may engage in activities designed to serve such students even when they do not feel efficacious or believe the outcome is outside of their control.

HOW TEACHER EFFICACY AFFECTS CLASSROOM LEARNING

In light of so many different ways of defining teachers' beliefs about themselves, why is teacher efficacy such an important construct? Simply put, empirical studies have recognized teacher efficacy as a major predictor of teachers' competence and commitment to teaching—more powerful than self-concept, self-esteem, and perceived control. Four seminal reviews of the impact of teacher efficacy by Ross (1998), Goddard et al. (2000), Labone (2004), and Wheatley (2005) reveal consistent findings: teachers who report a higher sense of efficacy, both individually and as a school collective, tend to be more likely to enter the field, report higher overall satisfaction with their jobs, display greater effort and motivation, take on extra roles in their schools, and are more resilient across the span of their career. Moreover, the extent to which shifts in teacher efficacy take place as teachers transition into new contexts appears to depend upon the level of support in the context; greater support from administrators and colleagues buffers against declines.

Individual Teacher Efficacy. Teachers with higher levels of efficacy are more likely to learn and use innovative strategies for teaching, implement management techniques that provide for student autonomy, set attainable goals, persist in the face of student failure, willingly offer special assistance to low achieving students, and design instruction that develops students' self-perceptions of their academic skills. Moreover, Woolfolk Hoy and Davis (2005) argue that teachers who feel efficacious about their instruction, management, and relationships with students may have more cognitive and emotional resources available to press students towards completing more complex tasks and developing deeper understandings. This is because teachers with a high sense of efficacy may be less afraid of student conflict and more likely to take greater intellectual and interpersonal risks in the classroom.

Teachers' Collective Sense of Efficacy. Collective teacher efficacy is "the perception of teachers in a school that the efforts of the faculty as a whole will have a positive effect on students" (Woolfolk Hoy, et al., in press). Hoy and Miskel (2008) argue that a school's system of shared beliefs binds the teachers together and gives the school a distinctive identity. Like self-efficacy, collective efficacy is associated with the tasks, level of effort, persistence, shared thoughts, stress levels, and achievement of groups. Studies have demonstrated that higher aggregate teacher and collective efficacy is associated with increased rates of parental involvement, increased school orderliness, teacher innovation, teacher familiarity with colleague's courses, reduced suspensions and dropout rates, and higher achievement across elementary and secondary schools. In a series of studies Roger Goddard (1966–) and colleagues found the collective efficacy of a school had a greater positive impact on student achievement than the locale of the school (i.e. urban, suburban, rural) and individual student demographic variables (e.g. race, gender, socio-economic status).

IMPLICATIONS FOR TEACHERS

The literature on teacher efficacy has important implications for the induction of new teachers and the professional development of practicing teachers. Broadly, research on teacher efficacy can help teachers think about the ways in which they approach tasks in their classrooms including how accurate they are in identifying the challenge level of tasks and the extent to which they try to break down complex, challenging tasks into something more manageable. Teachers can think about the ways in which they attempt to structure their teaching tasks (e.g. selecting activities, employing new strategies/methods) in such a way that allows them to both grow professionally and feel competent. Moreover, teachers need to be reflective about the areas where they feel most and least competent. How do discrete experiences of success and failure shape their beliefs about their ability to carry out similar behaviors in the future? Teachers need to be aware that feeling incompetent may lead them to avoid important classroom tasks. Over time, teachers may purposely make decisions to avoid certain schools and students or even avoid examining data as a way to protect their sense of self. When faced with feelings of failure, teachers need to engage in active help seeking aimed at building their efficacy through mastery experiences or observing colleagues.

Preservice and Early Career. The task of teacher education is, fundamentally, to develop competent and confident teachers. Preservice teachers with little or no teaching experience may lack a sense of efficacy, and program developers need to think carefully about how to structure entry into the field in a way that promotes mastery. On the other hand, if all of their early experiences lead to success, preservice teachers may enter the field with a false, or uncalibrated, sense of efficacy because it was developed without the demands of running one's own classroom, dealing with parents and teachers or managing student problems. In a seminal paper by Rohrkemper and Corno (1985), teachers were cautioned not to ignore the value of "functional failure." They encouraged teachers to create context in which students can learn from mistakes and learn to persist even when unsuccessful. Their work also has important implications for teacher educators, encouraging programs to rank task difficulty, complexity and frustration of field placements for student-teachers.

Experienced and Veteran Teachers. Throughout their careers, practicing teachers must strive to maintain a "competent teacher" identity while continuing to serve their students. This can be challenging particularly in light of the increasing complexity of the teaching task (Woolfolk Hoy, Davis, & Pape, 2005). Some scholars argue that teachers with higher sense of efficacy may be more prone to experience burnout because they tend to set higher standards and expectations (Fives et al., 2007). Faced with rapid changes in student populations and reform movements, practicing teachers may feel threatened and, in lieu of seeking professional development to build mastery, may engage in behaviors designed to preserve their sense of self. While it may preserve sense of self, resistance to change may come at the cost of serving important populations of students. For this reason, it is important for administrators to consult teachers prior to and during reform movements to identify the types of professional development experiences necessary for building mastery, carefully monitoring and adjusting the level of arousal, and providing the feedback that persuades teachers they can be successful (Gregoire, 2003). Several studies suggest practicing teachers' efficacy can be enhanced through participation in action research (Henson, 2001), reviewing lessons with colleagues (Puchner & Taylor, 2006), regular feedback on their goal pursuit (Labone, 2004), and self-reflection that helps identify and interpret mastery experiences while developing self-regulatory skills.

SEE ALSO *Attribution Theory; Caring Teachers; Relevance of Self-Evaluations to Classroom Learning; Self-Efficacy Theory; Social Cognitive Theory; Teacher Beliefs; Weiner, Bernard.*

BIBLIOGRAPHY

Ashton, P. (1984). Teacher efficacy: A motivational paradigm for effective teacher education. *Journal of Teacher Education, 35*, 287–232.

Bandura, A. (1997). *Self-efficacy: The exercise of control.* New York: W. H. Freeman.

Brown, E. L. (2004). The relationship of self-concepts to changes in cultural diversity awareness: Implications for urban teacher educators. *Urban Review, 36*, 119–145.

Christou, C., Phillipou, G., & Menon, M. E. (2001). Preservice teachers' self-esteem and mathematics achievement. *Contemporary Educational Psychology, 26*, 44–60.

Friedman, I. A., & Farber, B. A. (1992). Professional self-concept as a predictor of teacher burnout. *Journal of Educational Research, 86*, 28–36.

Goddard, R. G., Hoy, W. K., & Woolfolk Hoy, A. (2000). Collective teacher efficacy: Its meaning, measure, and impact on student achievement. *American Educational Research Journal, 37*, 479–508.

Guskey, T. R. (1988). Teacher efficacy, self-concept, and attitudes toward the implementation of instructional innovation. *Teaching and Teacher Education, 4*(1), 63–69.

Henson, R. K. (2001). Effect of participation in teacher research on teacher efficacy. *Teaching and Teacher Education, 17*, 819–836.

Ho, I. T., & Hau, K. T. (2004). Australian and Chinese teachers' efficacy: Similarities and differences in personal instruction, discipline, guidance efficacy and beliefs in external determinants. *Teaching and Teacher Education, 20*, 313–323.

Hoy, W. K., & Miskel, C. G. (2008). *Educational administration: Theory, research, and practice* (8th ed.). New York: McGraw-Hill.

Juhasz, A. M. (1990). Teacher self-esteem: A triple-role approach to this forgotten dimension. *Education 111*, 234–241.

Kozel, S. (2007). *Exploring preservice teachers' sense of responsibility for multiculturalism and diversity: Scale construction and construct validation.* Unpublished master's thesis, Ohio State University, Columbus.

Labone, E. (2004). Teacher efficacy: Maturing the construct through research in alternative paradigms. *Teaching and Teacher Education, 20*, 341–359.

Puchner, L. D., & Taylor, A. R. (2006). Lesson study, collaboration and teacher efficacy: Stories from two school-based math lesson study groups. *Teaching and Teacher Education, 22*, 922–934.

Ross, J. A. (1998). The antecedents and consequences of teacher efficacy. In J. Brophy (Ed.), *Advances in research on teaching* (Vol. 7, pp. 49–73). Greenwich, CT: JAI Press.

Singh, R. (1984). Peer-evaluation: A process that could enhance the self-esteem and professional growth of teachers. *Education, 105*, 73–75.

Tschannen-Moran, M., & Woolfolk Hoy, A. (2001). Teacher efficacy: Capturing and elusive construct. *Teaching and Teacher Education, 17*, 783–805.

Tschannen-Moran, M., Woolfolk Hoy, A., & Hoy, W. K. (1998). Teacher efficacy: Its meaning and measure. *Review of Educational Research, 68*, 202–248.

Weinstein, C. (1988). Preservice teachers' expectations about the first year of teaching. *Teaching and Teacher Education, 4*, 31–41.

Wheatley, K. F. (2005). The case for reconceptualizing teacher efficacy research. *Teaching and Teacher Education, 21*, 747–766.

Winfield, L. F. (1986). Teacher beliefs toward academically at risk students in inner urban schools. *Urban Review, 18*, 253–268.

Woolfolk Hoy, A., & Davis, H. (2005). Teachers' sense of efficacy and adolescent achievement. In T. Urdan & F. Pajares (Eds.), *Adolescence and education: Vol. 5: Self-efficacy beliefs during adolescence* (pp. 117–137). Greenwich, CT: Information Age.

Sarah Kozel Silverman
Heather A. Davis

TEACHER EXPECTATIONS

How are teacher expectations related to student achievement? For much of the last part of the 20th century social psychologists emphasized the power of expectations to create and distort social reality through self-fulfilling prophecies and expectancy-confirming biases, whereas educational psychologists typically emphasized the accuracy of teacher expectations. This entry conveys why 40 years of research on teacher expectations shows that teacher expectations are indeed mostly accurate and that they lead to typically small but occasionally large self-fulfilling prophecies.

TEACHER EXPECTATIONS AND RELATED CONSTRUCTS DEFINED

In studies on *teacher expectations*, the term has referred to everything from predictions to beliefs about current levels of ability and performance, to beliefs about students' *normative* behavior (essentially, cooperativeness, rule-following, etc.). This application of the term has been justified because such perceptions and beliefs are often the foundations for predictions, and, to the extent that they are inaccurate, may also produce *expectancy effects*, a term that refers to either of two related yet very different phenomena.

Two Types of Expectation Effects. First, erroneous expectations may bias or distort the expectancy-holder's judgments, a phenomenon sometimes referred to as *expectancy-confirming bias*, *perceptual bias*, or *confirmatory bias*. Sometimes perceivers' (including teachers') erroneous expectations lead them to judge, evaluate, interpret, or explain targets' (including students') behavior in ways consistent with those expectations. For example, if a teacher overestimates a student's academic competence, that teacher may evaluate the student's performance (on tests, homework, etc.) more positively than the same teacher evaluates identical work produced by a student whose academic competence the teacher underestimates. These types of expectancy biases influence the teacher's judgments about students' learning or achievement, but they do not necessarily influence students' actual learning or achievement.

The second type of expectancy effect is a self-fulfilling prophecy, which occurs when a perceiver's originally false expectation leads to its own actual (not merely perceived) confirmation. A teacher's erroneous expectation leads to its own fulfillment when it leads the teacher to behave differently towards high and low expectancy students, and when those students' achievement changes to confirm the teacher's (originally false, but now true) expectation. Thus, the high expectancy student achieves at higher levels, and the low expectancy student achieves at lower levels than they otherwise would have had the teacher's expectation been accurate.

Expectancy-confirming biases and self-fulfilling prophecies are similar because both involve expectations causing their own confirmation in some sense (which is why both are termed expectancy effects). They differ, however, in that expectancy-confirming biases occur entirely in the mind of the perceiver (or teacher), whereas the confirmation in self-fulfilling prophecy occurs as a result of an actual change in the behavior (or achievement) of the target (or student).

Accuracy. Teacher accuracy refers to correspondence between teachers' beliefs (expectations, perceptions, judgments, etc.) about one or more students and those students' characteristics or accomplishments, if the teachers' beliefs have not caused those characteristics or accomplishments. Accuracy is important for two reasons. First, accuracy constitutes a very different explanation (than bias or self-fulfilling prophecy) for why students may sometimes confirm teachers' expectations. When *expectancy confirmation* results from accuracy, it reflects teachers' expertise and competence, rather than their flaws and weaknesses. Second, accuracy represents a plausible alternative explanation (to self-fulfilling prophecy or bias) for evidence that students confirm teachers' expectations.

THE PYGMALION STUDY

The scientific study of teacher expectations was launched by the classic and controversial Pygmalion study (Rosenthal & Jacobson, 1968). Rosenthal and Jacobson led teachers to believe that some students in their classes were "late bloomers"—destined to show dramatic increases in IQ over the school year. In fact, these students had been selected at random. Results showed that, especially in the earlier grade levels, the "late bloomers" gained more in IQ than other students. Teacher expectations created a self-fulfilling prophecy.

Rosenthal and Jacobson's study (1968) received considerable attention in the social sciences and the popular press because it seemed to provide a powerful explanation for the low achievement of so-called disadvantaged students. However, it was also criticized by educational psychologists on conceptual, methodological, and statistical grounds. A controversy over the existence of the phenomenon continued through the 1970s, which included numerous attempts to replicate it in classrooms and other contexts (work settings, job training programs, laboratories, etc.). Consistently, only about one-third of the studies attempting to demonstrate a self-fulfilling prophecy succeeded (Rosenthal & Rubin, 1978). This pattern was often interpreted by critics as demonstrating that the phenomenon did not exist because support was unreliable. It was interpreted by proponents as demonstrating the existence of self-fulfilling prophecies because, if only chance differences were occurring, replications would only succeed about 5% of the time.

This controversy was resolved in 1978 by Rosenthal and Rubin's meta-analysis of the first 345 studies of interpersonal expectancy effects, which conclusively demonstrated the existence of self-fulfilling prophecies. The overall expectancy effect size was equal to a correlation of about .30 between teacher expectations and student achievement, and the probability of finding the observed expectancy effects, if the phenomenon did not exist, was essentially zero.

REMAINING CONTROVERSY ON TEACHER EXPECTATIONS AND STUDENT INTELLIGENCE

The most stunning claim that emerged from Rosenthal and Jacobson's 1968 study was that teacher expectations have self-fulfilling effects on intelligence. Although IQ test scores often are the best predictors of many important life outcomes, they are also notoriously resistant to change in response to social interventions designed to increase them. In this context, the claim that teacher expectations influence IQ was extremely important, controversial, and difficult (for some) to believe.

Unfortunately, the original Pygmalion study included some results that some researchers found difficult to believe. Although the methodological and statistical issues were numerous, one particular finding was especially problematic. There were five "bloomers" with wild IQ score gains: 17–110, 18–122, 133–202, 111–208, and 113–211. If one simply excluded these five bizarre gains, the difference between the bloomers and the controls evaporated.

Thus, the claim that the Pygmalion study showed that teacher expectations can have self-fulfilling effects on student intelligence was not universally accepted. Unfortunately, the subsequent evidence was also unclear on this issue, with some reviews concluding that the effect of teacher expectations on student intelligence averages near zero, and others concluding that such effects are small, but above zero. The fairest conclusion that can be reached as of 2008, therefore, may be that, if teacher expectations do have an effect on student intelligence, it is typically quite small.

NATURALLY OCCURRING VERSUS EXPERIMENTALLY INDUCED TEACHER EXPECTATIONS

A limitation of the original Pygmalion study and many follow up experiments was that researchers intentionally misled teachers into believing that some students were likely to show dramatic achievement gains. In general, however, teachers do not develop expectations based on falsified information. Thus, some researchers examined whether self-fulfilling prophecies also occurred when teachers developed their expectations naturally, without intervention by experimenters.

Identifying causal effects of teacher expectations is much more difficult in nonexperimental research than in experimental research. In nonexperimental research any particular correlation between teacher expectations and student achievement might occur because teacher expectations caused student achievement (self-fulfilling prophecy), student achievement caused teacher expectations, or some other variable or variables caused them both.

To address this issue, most naturalistic studies took two precautions. First, they used a longitudinal (over time) design, which takes advantage of the fact that the future cannot possibly cause the past. This rules out one possible causal direction. If teacher expectations are measured early in the year, and student achievement late in the year, that student achievement cannot have caused those teacher expectations. Second, naturalistic studies also typically statistically controlled for many of the most plausible predictors of teacher expectations and student future achievement, including student past achievement and demographics, and, sometimes, student self-concept and motivation. If teacher expectations early in the year predict student achievement late in the year, after controlling for all these variables, many third-variable explanations can be eliminated.

The naturalistic research found consistent evidence of self-fulfilling prophecy. In most studies, teacher expectations early in the year predicted student achievement late in the year, even after controlling for student prior achievement, demographics, motivation, and self-concept. The self-fulfilling prophecy effect sizes in such studies was typically about .1 to .2 (in terms of standardized regression coefficients relating teacher expectations to student achievement). Although statistically significant, these effects were consistently lower than found in Rosenthal and Rubin's 1978 meta-analysis of the experiments. Why might this be?

The most likely explanation was that under naturally occurring conditions, teachers' expectations may often be accurate. Indeed, nearly all naturalistic studies of teacher expectations find: 1) student past achievement has large effects on teachers' expectations; and 2) teacher expectations predict (correlate with) student future achievement much more highly than they cause student achievement. These findings are extremely important because they reflect two types of accuracy. The first shows that teacher impression accuracy is high (*impression accuracy* is the extent to which teachers' expectations correspond with students' current characteristics or achievement). The second shows that teacher predictive accuracy is high (*predictive accuracy* is the extent to which teacher expectations predict but do not cause student achievement). Overall, the naturalistic research has shown that about two-thirds to three-fourths of the reason teacher expectations predict student achievement is that those expectations are accurate, and that one-fourth to one-third of the reason they predict student achievement is that they create self-fulfilling prophecies.

The naturalistic research has also consistently found that teacher expectations predict student grades more strongly than they predict standardized test scores (even after controlling for prior grades, achievement, and demographics). Because teachers assign grades but not standardized test scores, this result most likely reflects expectancy-confirmation bias—teacher expectations biasing their evaluations of students, rather than influencing students' objective achievement. Both bias and self-fulfilling prophecy can and often do occur for grades, so that their effects are cumulative. Thus, expectancy effects (both bias and self-fulfilling prophecy) for grades often account for about half of the reason teacher expectations early in the year predict student grades (the remaining half being accuracy).

BASES OF TEACHER EXPECTATIONS

Teacher expectations are primarily based on student prior achievement and grades, which helps account for their relatively high levels of predictive accuracy. Because of the obvious social implications, both experimental and nonexperimental research has been concerned with whether teacher expectations are also based on social stereotypes. Again, the results partially diverge. In experimental studies, the most common methodology has been to provide teachers with little or ambiguous information about students from different groups (e.g., boys/girls, African Americans/Whites, etc.), and to assess whether teachers hold higher expectations for students from one group. They often do.

Because in real life, however, groups often do differ in average levels of achievement, such results do not necessarily show that stereotypes cause inaccuracy in teacher expectations. This issue, however, has also been addressed in naturalistic research, which has examined the extent to which student demographics predict teacher expectations, even after controlling for students' actual differences in achievement. Such research most often finds little or no effect of student demographic characteristics, meaning that, when teachers do perceive demographic differences there usually are corresponding bona fide demographic differences. The most notable exception seems to involve student gender and teacher perceptions of effort. Teachers routinely assume that girls try harder at school than do boys, even though there is little evidence that they actually do. Because there is good evidence that, in general, girls are more cooperative and obedient than boys, it seems likely that this reflects a halo effect (the presence of one positive trait in a target leads the perceiver to infer other positive attributes).

In contrast to stereotypes, diagnostic labels (ADHD, learning disabled, neurologically impaired, etc.), presumably because they come with greater scientific credibility, are often powerful sources of teacher expectations. Unfortunately, however, large minorities of students are often mislabeled, and, even when students are appropriately diagnosed, many teachers lack the training to understand how best to maximize such students' learning and achievement. Thus, diagnostic labels are often a culprit in negative self-fulfilling prophecies.

INTERPERSONAL PROCESSES

Much research has addressed how teachers act on their expectations in such a manner as to produce a self-fulfilling prophecy. This research has shown that teachers hold high expectancy students to higher standards of performance and, at the same time, provide a warmer and more supportive environment to them. Differential treatment can lead to self-fulfilling prophecies through either or both of two general routes. High standards means providing high expectancy students with more opportunities to master difficult material. When coupled with the support for doing so, highs may simply learn more material more quickly. In addition, however, differential treatment also may indirectly affect achievement, by enhancing or undermining student motivation. High standards and emotional support are likely to increase students' psychological investment in school, intrinsic motivation, and self-expectations, all of which have well-established beneficial effects on achievement (and, of course, low standards and a cold emotional environment are likely to be demotivating).

MODERATING CONDITIONS

Research has also examined moderators of self-fulfilling prophecies—the conditions under which self-fulfilling prophecies are stronger or weaker. This research has shown that self-fulfilling prophecies are stronger under the following conditions:

When experimental studies manipulate teachers' expectations early rather than late in the year. It is much harder to mislead teachers later in the year, after they have gotten to know their students.

In first, second, and seventh grades, a result that suggests that it is not younger children per se who are more vulnerable, but children who enter new and unfamiliar situations (seventh grade was the first grade of junior high school in many of the studies).

Among teachers high in dogmatism or cognitive rigidity. Even inaccurate expectations will not lead to self-fulfilling prophecies if teachers readily correct their expectations with new information. Teachers high in dogmatism or cognitive rigidity are unlikely to do so.

Among students with some sort of perceived difference from the majority. Some of the largest self-fulfilling prophecy effects ever obtained have been found to occur among some minority students, those from lower social class backgrounds, and those with histories of low achievement.

Many early researchers speculated that negative expectancy effects (those that undermine student achievement) were also more powerful than positive ones (those that enhance student achievement). The evidence regarding this issue, however, is quite mixed, with some studies showing that positive teacher expectations have more powerful self-fulfilling effects, and others showing that negative teacher expectations have more powerful self-fulfilling effects.

IMPLICATIONS FOR TEACHERS

First, teachers should take considerable comfort from the empirical evidence which, in contrast to some of the more extreme claims, shows that, in general, expectancy effects are small, fragile, and fleeting, rather than large, pervasive, and enduring. Second, any recommendation suggesting that teachers should simply adopt high expectations for all students would be oversimplified, unworkable, and probably dysfunctional. High expectations can work at raising student achievement, but only if they are backed up with the resources and institutional supports to do so.

The most constructive lessons to be learned for teachers from the research are the following:

Teachers should hold expectations flexibly. They might be wrong. The student's label might be wrong. Also, students change.

Teachers should remember that holding high standards without providing a warm environment is merely harsh. A warm environment without high standards is simply feel-good mush. But if teachers can create a combination of high standards with a warm and supportive environment, doing so will benefit all students, not just the high achievers.

High expectations will mean different things for different students. Attaining average performance might be high for one student and low for another. If teachers wants to purposely harness self-fulfilling prophecy processes to maximize student achievement, they need to integrate accuracy (a clear sense of students' current levels of skill and learning abilities and styles), with warmth and high standards for future performance in order to develop a clear plan for how those students will maximize their learning and achievement.

SEE ALSO *Caring Teachers.*

BIBLIOGRAPHY

Brophy, J. (1983). Research on the self-fulfilling prophecy and teacher expectations. *Journal of Educational Psychology, 75,* 631–661.

Brophy, J., & Good, T. (1974). *Teacher-student relationships: Causes and consequences.* New York: Holt, Rinehart, and Winston.

Harris, M. J., & Rosenthal, R. (1985). Mediation of interpersonal expectancy effects: 31 meta-analyses. *Psychological Bulletin, 97,* 363–386.

Jussim, L. (1986). Self-fulfilling prophecies: A theoretical and integrative review. *Psychological Review, 93,* 429–445.

Jussim, L., & Harber, K. (2005). Teacher expectations and self-fulfilling prophecies: Knowns and unknowns; resolved and unresolved controversies. *Personality and Social Psychology Review, 9*(2), 131–155.

Rosenthal, R., & Jacobson, L. (1968). *Pygmalion in the classroom: Teacher expectations and student intellectual development.* New York: Holt, Rinehart, and Winston.

Rosenthal R., & Rubin, D. B. (1978). Interpersonal expectancy effects: The first 345 studies. *Behavioral and Brain Sciences, 3,* 377–386.

Lee Jussim

TEMPERAMENT

Temperament is a general term referring to individual differences in behavior tendencies that are biologically based, present early in life, and relatively stable across situations and time (Bates & Wachs, 1994; Goldsmith et al., 1987). Individual differences in temperament are evidenced in the unique predispositions students bring to the school setting in terms of activity level, attention span, mood, approach to new experiences, and so on. Many have posited that individual differences in temperament during the early years constitute nascent personality (Caspi, 1998).

Evidence supports both genetic and environmental influences on temperament. Behavior-genetic research studies comparing correlations of temperament characteristics between monozygotic and dizygotic twins indicate significant genetic influences on some temperament characteristics from early childhood through adolescence. Monozygotic twins are much more temperamentally similar to each other than dizygotic twins (Caspi, 1998). Given the evidence supporting the role of genetic factors in temperament, researchers look to physiological, neurological, biochemical, and hormonal variables as the biological mechanisms by which temperament is transmitted across generations (Bates & Wachs, 1994). For example, Werner and colleagues (2007) reported that fetal heart rate activity predicted infant temperament assessed via parental report and behavioral observations at 4 months. With respect to environmental factors, children with difficult temperament are at increased risk of subsequent externalizing behavior problems when family conflict is present (Guerin et al., 2003).

CONCEPTUALIZATION AND MEASUREMENT OF TEMPERAMENT

Although temperament is an ancient concept (Kagan & Snidman, 2004), a large body of empirical research on temperament in children followed the dissemination of the theoretical perspective developed by Alexander Thomas, Stella Chess, and Herbert Birch (1968). They defined temperament as follows:

> Temperament may best be viewed as a general term referring to the *how* of behavior. It differs from ability, which is concerned with the *what* and how well of behaving, and from motivation, which seeks to account for *why* a person does what he is doing. When we refer to temperament, we are concerned with the way in which an individual behaves. (p. 4)

Thomas and colleagues identified nine dimensions of temperament, and these are listed in Table 1. Additionally, they observed three constellations or patterns characterizing young children's temperament. They labeled the largest temperament pattern, comprising about 40% of their sam-

ple, as "Easy" temperament: regular biological functioning, positive approach to new stimuli, quick adaptation to change, positive mood, and mild/moderate intensity in expression. About 10% exhibited the opposite pattern, labeled "Difficult" temperament. Thomas and Chess labeled the third pattern, seen in about 15% of their sample, as "Slow to Warm Up" temperament. These children's reactions to new stimuli were more often negative than those of children with "Easy" temperament, but they expressed themselves more mildly than children with "Difficult" temperament. Not all children fit into one of the three categories, however, and most research is based on one or more specific dimensions of temperament displayed in Table 1 rather than the constellations.

Subsequent to the Thomas and Chess model of temperament, other approaches to children's temperamental emerged. Arnold Buss and Robert Plomin viewed temperament as early-appearing inherited personality traits and focused on three temperaments: emotionality, activity, and sociability. Hill Goldsmith and Joseph Campos developed a conceptualization of temperament centering on infant primary emotions, such as fear, anger, sadness, pleasure, and interest, for example. Mary Rothbart and Douglas Derryberry proposed a developmental model defining temperament as constitutional differences in reactivity and self-regulation (Goldsmith et al., 1987). Jerome Kagan and colleagues (Kagan & Snidman, 2004) focused on a single temperament characteristic, children's initial reaction to unfamiliar events. At the extremes of this continuum are children who respond to unfamiliar stimuli with shyness and restraint (inhibited) and those who are sociable, talkative, and minimally fearful (uninhibited).

The most widely used method to measure temperament in infancy and early childhood is through caretaker (usually maternal) reports on standardized temperament inventories; child, youth, and adult self-report inventories are also available. Inventories for teachers to describe their students' temperament have also been developed (Keogh, 2003). Inventories offer the advantages of efficiency in assessing a range of temperament characteristics and established reliability and validity, with ratings based on individuals who are well-acquainted with the child over a range of situations and across time. In addition to inventories, a variety of behavioral assessment procedures are available (Goldsmith & Rothbart, 1991). Mechanical (e.g., actometers) and behavioral measures of activity have been employed.

Temperament dimensions identified by Thomas, Chess, et al.

Dimension	Description
Activity level	Level, tempo, and frequency of motor behavior
Biological rhythmicity	Regularity of biological functions, such as sleeping, feeding, elimination
Approach/withdrawal	Nature of initial response to new stimuli, such as people, food, toys
Adaptability	Ease with which child responds to new stimuli or changes in situation
Intensity of reaction	Energy level of response, ranging from mild to strong, regardless of whether reaction is positive or negative
Quality of mood	Balance of pleasant, joyful, friendly behavior compared to unpleasant, crying, unfriendly behavior
Persistence/attention span	Continuation of an activity in spite of obstacles and length of time a particular activity is pursued
Distractibility	Effectiveness of external stimuli in altering the direction of ongoing behavior
Threshold of responsiveness	Intensity level of stimulation necessary to evoke a response

SOURCE: Based on Thomas, Chess, and Birch (1968)

Table 1 ILLUSTRATION BY GGS INFORMATION SERVICES. CENGAGE LEARNING, GALE.

CONSISTENCY OF TEMPERAMENT ACROSS TIME

A growing literature documents the stability of children's temperament. In the United States, the Fullerton Longitudinal Study in California reported stability on eight of the nine

Thomas and Chess temperament dimensions from ages 2 through 12 years. Additionally, six of the nine dimensions were assessed at ages 14 and 16 years, and they also showed stability from middle childhood (Guerin et al., 2003). Mathiesen and Tambs (1999) reported strong stability of the Buss and Plomin temperament traits in a Norwegian sample followed from 18 through 50 months. Komsi and colleagues (2006) observed significant consistency across infancy and middle childhood in a sample of Finnish children for several temperament dimensions based on the Rothbart framework. In the early 2000s, evidence of stability in inhibited/uninhibited temperament was accumulating (Kagan & Snidman, 2004).

RESEARCH FINDINGS ON TEMPERAMENT AND SCHOOL FUNCTIONING

One question to consider is how these stable, individual differences relate to children's functioning in school. The tasks of school demand not only intellectual ability, but also characteristics such as flexibility and sustained effort (Keogh, 2003). Across the entire span of schooling, temperament characteristics relate to children's ability to successfully negotiate the multiple demands of school, whether in terms of academic achievement, socially appropriate behavior, or relationships.

In elementary school, three primary temperament characteristics relating to accomplishment are activity, distractibility, and persistence (Keogh, 2003). Either high or extremely low levels of activity, high levels of distractibility, and low levels of persistence relate to low levels of academic achievement. Similarly in early adolescence, persistence and distractibility relate to school success (Guerin et al., 2003). Children who can focus on their work and sustain an effort in spite of obstacles and length of time to completion achieve more in the academic realm.

During adolescence and early adulthood the characteristic of persistence, identified as task orientation, again stands out as important in terms of academic success. In the Fullerton Longitudinal Study, task orientation related positively to academic achievement as measured by standardized tests, parent reports, and self-reports. Task orientation related positively to high school GPA and college GPA, over and above socioeconomic status and IQ (Oliver, Guerin, & Gottfried, 2007).

In addition to the intellectual domain, children's temperament relates to classroom behavior as assessed by teachers. Guerin and colleagues found that high levels of persistence and adaptability as well as low levels of activity and distractibility were related to behaving appropriately, learning, and being happy in class (Guerin et al., 2003). Characteristics associated with the "Difficult" temperament constellation relate to children acting out in school, but there are also internalizing behavior problems related to temperament. Extremely inhibited children lack social competence and have high levels of social anxiety (Martin & Fox, 2006).

The quality of the student-teacher relationship has implications for children's competency and achievement in school. Teachers value certain characteristics such as adaptability, persistence, approach, and positive mood (Keogh, 2003). Thus, the behavior of some students with high activity levels, high distractibility, and low levels of persistence, can be misattributed by teachers as non-compliance and problem behavior. As evidence of the way in which temperament characteristics relate to child-teacher relationships, Guerin and colleagues found that children who are high in activity, low in adaptability, high in intensity, negative in mood, less persistent, and more distractible have greater levels of negative interaction and conflict with their teachers.

APPLYING TEMPERAMENT CONCEPTS IN SCHOOL

Given accumulating evidence that temperament characteristics show long-term stability and that individual differences in temperament relate to children's educational outcomes, numerous temperament researchers and clinicians have provided specific recommendations on using temperament research and theory in the classroom. Indeed, Rothbart and Jones (1998) advocate that college and university teacher-training programs include preparation on both children's temperament characteristics as well as their cognitive-processing capacities. A central tenet of the Thomas and Chess conceptualization of temperament is that development will be optimized when the environment and expectations experienced by children are consonant with their capacities and style of behaving ("goodness of fit"). Because individual children experience the same environment in unique ways, information on children's temperamental patterns could be used to modify classroom management techniques to be more in line with the children's style of behavior and reactivity (Rothbart & Jones, 1998). In addition, recognizing individual differences in temperament helps teachers to anticipate times or situations in which problems are most likely to occur (e.g., in transition periods) with the aim of planning techniques to alleviate or manage the stress of these times (Keogh, 2003). Sources providing specific suggestions to improve the goodness of fit between children's temperament and their classroom experience include Keogh (2003), Kristal (2005), and Rothbart and Jones (1998).

SEE ALSO *Caring Teachers.*

BIBLIOGRAPHY

Bates, J. E., & Wachs, T. D. (1994). *Temperament: Individual differences at the interface of biology and behavior.* Washington, D.C.: American Psychological Association.

Caspi, A. (1998). Personality development across the life course. In W. Damon & N. Eisenberg (Eds.), *Handbook of child psychology: Vol. 3. Social, emotional, and personality development* (5th ed., pp. 311–388). New York: Wiley.

Goldsmith, H. H., Buss, A. H., Plomin, R., Rothbart, M. K., Thomas, A., Chess, S., et al. (1987). Roundtable: What is temperament? Four approaches. *Child Development, 58,* 505–529.

Goldsmith, H. H., & Rothbart, M. K. (1991). Contemporary instruments for assessing early temperament by questionnaire and in the laboratory. In J. Strelau & A. Angleitner (Eds.), *Explorations in temperament: International perspectives on theory and measurement* (pp. 249–272). New York: Plenum.

Guerin, D. W., Gottfried, A. W., Oliver, P. H., & Thomas, C. W. (2003). *Temperament: Infancy through adolescence.* New York: Kluwer Academic/Plenum.

Kagan, J., & Snidman, N. (2004). *The long shadow of temperament.* Cambridge, MA: Harvard University Press.

Keogh, B. K. (2003). *Temperament in the classroom.* Baltimore, MD: Paul H. Brookes.

Komsi, N., Räikkönen, K., Pesonen, A., Heinonen, K., Keskivaara, P., Järvenpää, A., et al. (2006). Continuity of temperament from infancy to middle childhood. *Infant Behavior and Development, 29,* 494–508.

Kristal, J. (2005). *The temperament perspective: Working with children's behavioral styles.* New York: Paul H. Brookes.

Martin, J. N., & Fox, N. A. (2006). Temperament. In K. McCartney & D. Phillips (Eds.), *Blackwell handbook of early childhood development* (pp. 126–146). Malden, MA: Blackwell.

Mathiesen, K. S., & Tambs, K. (1999). The EAS temperament questionnaire: Factor structure, age trends, reliability, and stability in a Norwegian sample. *Journal of Child Psychology and Psychiatry, 40,* 431–439.

Oliver, P. H., Guerin, D. W., & Gottfried, A. W. (2007). Temperamental task orientation: Relation to high school and college educational achievements. *Learning and Individual Differences, 17,* 220–230.

Rothbart, M. K., & Jones, L. B. (1998). Temperament, self-regulation, and education. *School Psychology Review, 27,* 479–491.

Thomas, A., Chess, S., & Birch, H. G. (1968). *Temperament and behavior disorders in children.* New York: New York University Press.

Werner, E. A., Myers, M. M., Fifer, W. P., Cheng, B., Fang, Y., Allen, R., et al. (2007). Prenatal predictors of infant temperament. *Developmental Psychobiology, 49,* 474–484.

Diana Wright Guerin
Pamella H. Oliver
Allen W. Gottfried

TEST ANXIETY

SEE *Evaluation (Test) Anxiety.*

TEST TAKING SKILLS

In a seminal article, Millman, Bishop, and Ebel (1965) defined test wiseness as "a subject's capacity to utilize the characteristics and formats of the test and/or the test taking situation to receive a high score" (p. 707). The construct was first described in 1951 by Robert Thorndike, who considered its effect on test reliability. Test wiseness is generally thought to include an awareness of the process of test taking and knowledge of a number of individual test-taking skills that can be applied to a number of different testing formats to maximize test scores. Specific test-taking skills include using time wisely, answering all items, using effective guessing strategies, eliminating choices known to be incorrect, and making use of specific cues imbedded within individual test items. It has been suggested that there is individual variability in test wiseness, in that test-wise individuals have an advantage over individuals similar in knowledge or ability but lacking in test wiseness.

EFFECTIVE SKILLS

Effective test-takers possess a number of skills that go beyond the simple and direct knowledge of the content being tested. These skills include a complete understanding of the purpose(s) of the test, the specific requirements of the test, and any specific constraints placed upon performance, for example, time limits. Test wise test-takers use this awareness in order to employ strategies designed to meet these purposes, requirements, and constraints.

There has been some debate concerning whether test wiseness is a separate and distinct construct. However, specific tests of test-taking skills have been developed, suggesting that such skills do exist and can be described. Test wiseness tests may include items that are answerable only through the use of a test-taking strategy, imbedded within "real" test items. Following is an example of a test-taking skills item:

The Matharah tree is found most often in the following:

    a. arid areas;

    b. dry regions;

    c. rainy climates;

    d. barren locations.

Because the Matharah tree does not exist, test-taking skills must be employed to answer the question. In this case, items *a, b,* and *d,* all provide very similar information, and because they cannot all be chosen, the only logical choice is *c.* This strategy is referred to as *similar options.* It has been found that older test takers score higher than younger test takers on tests such as this. Other measures of test wiseness include passage independence tests (where test takers are asked to answer questions about a reading passage without having read the relevant passage), direct interviews (where test takers are asked to describe their thinking process as they answer test questions), and tests of the test taker's ability to use different test formats (such as separate answer sheets).

Finally, relative deficits in test-taking skills can be inferred by directly training participants in presumed areas of deficit and evaluating whether training results in increased test performance over participants who have not received such training. If this training includes skills only, and not the information being tested, any difference between the two groups can be considered deficits in test-taking skills. Overall, test-taking skills training has realized tangible, but modest effects. However, effects have been more pronounced for older (e.g., upper elementary) students and longer training periods; and for students with mild disabilities (e.g., learning disabilities) and those from lower socio-economic backgrounds. For some groups of test takers, test-taking skills training can make a significant difference in test scores.

TEACHING TEST WISENESS

A variety of procedures are employed to teach test wiseness. Without doubt, the most important strategy for improving test performance is academic preparation, particularly with respect to the specific purpose and anticipated requirements and format of the upcoming test. For example, a multiple choice test format may require broad, general, and shallower knowledge, while an essay format may require more focused, detailed, and elaborated knowledge. Another general strategy is physical preparation, which includes getting sufficient rest and nourishment prior to taking the test. Positive attitudes toward the test are also important and can be improved by setting realistic goals, taking practice tests, understanding the purpose of the particular test, rewarding effort, and understanding of specific test-taking skills.

While taking tests, people should use their time wisely. It is important to use time efficiently on familiar or easier items, and not to waste time on very difficult items unlikely to be answered correctly. Test-wise individuals monitor their time frequently and pace themselves as they take the test. That is, when the testing period is half over, test-takers generally should have completed about half the test. If the test is completed early, the additional time can be spent returning to the more difficult items. Efficient test-takers recognize that, when guessing is not directly penalized, it is important to answer every question.

In any test-taking situation, it is important for test takers to maximize the knowledge they have, even when it is not complete. Many standardized tests as well as classroom tests employ some type of identification format, such as multiple choice, in which test-takers identify a correct response from an array of choices. In these cases, efficient test-takers are careful to think first of a correct response, then consider all choices before answering. Test-wise individuals are aware that they may not only select the option most likely to be correct, they may also discard items unlikely to be correct, by using elimination strategies. In addition to the similar options strategy discussed previously, test-takers can also, based upon their prior or partial, eliminate responses known not to be correct. For example, even when the answer is not known, if an efficient test-taker can eliminate two of four possible answer choices, the probability of making a correct choice is increased to 50 percent from 25 percent. Over the course of a number of test items, this difference can increase a test score significantly. In other cases, particularly in the case of teacher-made tests, the syntactic or semantic content of the item stem (the "question") may provide a cue to the correct answer choice. This strategy can be enhanced if the test-taker has some partial knowledge of the item content. Test-wise individuals consider carefully choices that use absolutes such as *always* or *never*—because few statements allow for no exceptions—when choosing their answers.

DIFFERING TEST FORMATS

Some tests include specific formats unique to that particular test. For example, a multiple choice phonics test may require test takers to match sounds in different printed words, or a math test may require test takers to identify which missing information is required to solve a particular problem. Test-takers should practice applications of their knowledge in a variety of different contexts in order to be able to address such formats.

Test formats that require test takers to produce, rather than identify, correct responses also lend themselves to specific test-taking strategies. For example, for short answer or sentence completion items, it is important for test takers to guess if unsure, use partial knowledge when necessary, look for cues in the test item, and make the completed sentence appear logical and consistent. For essay tests, it is generally important to study the question and consider command words (e.g., *discuss, compare, justify*), note important points, organize thoughts, and write directly to the purpose of the question.

It has been argued that test-taking skills training should be discouraged because it encourages test-takers to outsmart the test, rather than by correctly applying content knowledge. Certainly, some strategies (e.g., the longest or most qualified answer choice will be correct) lend themselves to this criticism. However, in most cases, test-wise individuals employ appropriate strategies in conjunction with their content knowledge to maximize the impact of their knowledge on their test score. To the extent that a test-taker's score should reflect the test taker's level of content knowledge, and not be limited by relative awareness of test format requirements, test-taking skills training is an important overall component of educational measurement.

SEE ALSO *Classroom Assessment.*

BIBLIOGRAPHY

Mastropieri, M. A., & Scruggs, T. E. (2007). *The inclusive classroom.* Upper Saddle River, NJ: Prentice Hall.

Millman, J., Bishop, C. H., & Ebel, R. (1965). Analysis of test wiseness in the cognitive domain. *Educational and Psychological Measurement, 18,* 787–790.

Sarnacki, R. E. (1979). An examination of test-wiseness in the cognitive test domain. *Review of Educational Research, 49,* 252–279.

Scruggs, T. E., & Mastropieri, M. A. (1992). *Teaching test-taking skills: Helping students show what they know.* Cambridge, MA: Brookline Books.

Thorndike, E. L. (1951). Reliability. In E. F. Lindquist (Ed.), *Educational measurement* (pp. 560–620). Washington, DC: American Council on Education.

Thomas E. Scruggs
Margo A. Mastropieri

THEORIES (AS A FORM OF KNOWLEDGE)

The term *theory* has been historically used to describe forms of disciplinary knowledge. For example, one may speak of Einstein's theory of general relativity or Keynesian economic theory. However, despite or perhaps because of its common usage both in everyday and professional discourse, there is little agreement on just what a theory is. To illustrate, one traditional approach to describing formal disciplinary theories (such as scientific theories) is to think of them as axiomatic systems comprising of natural laws that correspond to empirical regularities in the world (Hempel & Oppenheim, 1948). Within the tradition of scholarship that construes laws as central to theory, there is disagreement about the nature of laws. Some scholars argue that true laws of nature are universal (Armstrong, 1983) while others argue that scientific laws such as Newton's laws are not universal generalizations and should be viewed as causal powers (Cartwright, 1983). More recently, scholars such as Giere have argued that laws serve no useful purpose in the context of scientific theory. Giere (2004) proposes that scientific knowledge is composed of families of models that selectively represent theoretically important features and relationships of things in the world.

THEORIES AS MENTAL REPRESENTATIONS

In the 1980s psychologists and educators who were interested in the nature of mental representation began to draw attention to theory-like properties of mental representations. Although the specific forms of mental representation proposed such as schemas (Rumelhart, 1980) mental models (Gentner & Stevens, 1983; Johnson-Laird, 1983) naïve theories (Carey & Spelke, 1994; Gopnik & Wellman, 1994), and explanatory frameworks (Samarapungavan & Wiers, 1997) vary greatly, they share certain features. These mental representations are molar or larger in scale and scope, and form structures that coordinate a variety of conceptual elements in complex and multi-faceted relationships. Such representations serve important explanatory functions, allowing people to organize, predict, and control their experiences of the world. For example, Rumelhart (1980, p. 37) says of schemas, "it is useful to think of a schema as a kind of informal, private, unarticulated theory about the nature of events."

The most explicit analogy between everyday mental representations and theories is drawn in the research on "naïve theories" (Gopnik & Wellman, 1994). "Novice-as-theorist" accounts assume that people are theory generators. Carey and Spelke (1994) have suggested that some conceptual frameworks, such as a naïve physics of object identity and motion, appear in early infancy and may be innate. A key issue for naïve-theoretic accounts of knowledge acquisition has to do with general structural and qualitative properties of naïve belief systems or their degree of "theoreticity." Three important aspects of theories are:

1. *Structure and content:* Theories comprise of a core of interrelated conceptual elements which constitute the explanatory principles for a target domain. The core explanatory principles are not mere empirical generalizations from experience but rather are abstract interpretations of experience. This is reflected in the fact that competing theoretical principles can provide different interpretations for the same body of experiential data. Theories form conceptual topographies. For example, in addition to domain-specific explanatory principles (e.g., natural selection in Darwinian theory), they contain ontological principles (Chi, Slotta, & de Leeuw, 1994) and epistemological principles or beliefs about what the central problems of the domain are, what sorts of data or evidence can be brought to bear in solving these problems, and how the explanatory fit of concepts can be evaluated (Samarapungavan & Wiers, 1997).

2. *Function:* Theories are explanatory devices. The core beliefs of a theory provide causal explanations for the

phenomena it circumscribes. Frameworks also allow for generative predictions;

3. *Corrigibility through epistemic processes:* Theories can be revised as a result of various epistemic processes of knowledge evaluation (Laudan et al., 1986).

The naïve theory approach has borrowed heavily from the work of historian and philosopher of science Thomas Kuhn (1962). Kuhn claimed that major historical changes in scientific theories are accompanied by changes in the explanatory core and boundaries of a discipline, whereby notions of what counts as data and which problems a theory should address change as well. Using similar ideas to explain why students have particular difficulty with the scientific concept of heat, Wiser (1988) suggests that novices have intensive rather than extensive concepts of heat that resemble a historical precursor of the current scientific theory, one in which heat and temperature were not differentiated. Thus, while students correctly predict that on identical burners, a big vessel of water must take longer to boil than a small one, they also make the "wrong" prediction that it would not take more heat to boil water in the big vessel because their concept of heat is intensional. In other words, in the latter situation the students are using the term "heat" in the sense of "temperature" and their predictions are correct with regard to temperature. Wiser concludes that like their historical counterparts, students' theories of heat are both different from and incommensurate with the expert theory.

Chi and her associates (Chi, Slotta, & de Leeuw, 1994) have proposed an interesting version of the incommensurability argument. They suggest that novices have ontological theories or beliefs about what "kinds" of things exist and what sorts of ontological properties each class or subclass in an ontological hierarchy of "kinds" can possess. Specifically, they propose that peoples' ontological knowledge is organized into at least three "trees" or taxonomies—matter, processes, and mental states. The three trees are defined by mutually exclusive ontological attributes. For example, objects in the category of matter (e.g., water, cars, and dogs) have ontological attributes such as having volume and mass. Similarly, processes have ontological attributes such as "occurring over time." Chi and colleagues argue that novices have difficulty with the acquisition of scientific concepts because these concepts require a restructuring of their ontologies. For example, while novices typically classify heat as a substance belonging to the ontological tree of matter, scientists see heat as a constraint-based interaction belonging to the ontological tree of processes.

THE DEBATE OVER NOVICE KNOWLEDGE

There is a vast body of research that shows that novice ideas about the natural world differ in conceptual content from those of scientists (Vosniadou & Brewer, 1992, 1994; Wiser, 1988). However, researchers disagree profoundly about the qualitative nature of such lay concepts. For example, based on research about naïve concepts in the domain of motion and force, diSessa and his colleagues (diSessa, 1993; diSessa, Gillespie, & Esterly, 2004) describe novice knowledge as a weakly organized system of beliefs that lacks internal coherence, is unstable over time and problem context, and malleable in the face of anomalous evidence. In a reinterpretation of the work in intuitive physics, diSessa and associates suggest that novices do not have anything like a naive "theory" of motion or force. According to diSessa (1993), what novices have is a fragmented, unstable, and malleable collection of beliefs which are low-level abstractions of everyday experience. diSessa refers to such beliefs as p-prims, short for *phenomenological primitives*. He argues that novice beliefs are unlike scientific theories because they are not constrained by epistemic requirements of coherence or "systematicity."

Research in several domains suggests that people's belief systems about some aspects of the natural world are theory-like, at least in some important respects. For example, children and lay adults appear to construct coherent and robust biological constructs based on principles of biological essentialism across a variety of cultures and task contexts (Ahn et al., 2001). Samarapungavan & Wiers, (1997) describe novice beliefs about species and speciation in terms of explanatory frameworks which they describe as a small set of explanatory principles that constrain but do not fully pre-specify the mental models that children construct when presented with novel biological problems about the nature of species and speciation. Part of the evidence for theoreticity comes from the observation that at least some of the core beliefs of novice biological frameworks cannot be induced directly from experience. For example, it is hard to conceive of any direct phenomenal experience that would lead elementary school children to a belief in the spontaneous generation of complex species (Samarapungavan & Wiers, 1997).

Vosniadou and Brewer and colleagues have conducted research on children's conceptual development in the domain observational astronomy. Their research shows that across a variety of cultures many elementary school children construct scientifically inaccurate but coherent and explanatory mental models of the earth's shape and the day-night cycle (Samarapungavan, Vosniadou & Brewer, 1996; Vosniadou & Brewer, 1992, Vosniadou,

Skopeliti, & Ikospentaki, 2004). These representations allow people to generate explanations for phenomena such as the seasons, eclipses, and the day/night cycle and to make and evaluate predictions about what will happen in novel scenarios. Additionally, their research shows that initial theory-like representations are corrigible because children revise their mental models over time to integrate new information presented in formal schooling.

Some researchers claim to have obtained empirical results that contradict Vosniadou and Brewer's findings in the domain of astronomy (Nobes et al., 2003). However, Brewer and Vosniadou and colleagues (Brewer, 2008; Vosniadou, Skopeliti, & Ikospentaki, 2004) point out serious methodological flaws in these studies.

THEORIES AS FORMS OF KNOWLEDGE: OPEN QUESTIONS

The debates about the utility of viewing knowledge as being organized in theory-like structures are hard to resolve definitively because of the great variability in the empirical studies on both sides of the issue. For one thing, findings about the degree of coherence and explanatory power in novice knowledge vary by domain. For example, Nakhleh and Samarapungavan (1999) found that elementary school children's ideas about the nature of matter cohered loosely at an ontological level but were not sufficiently coherent in terms of the specific explanations generated for phenomena such as phase transitions to be called explanatory frameworks. It may be that it is easier for people to form coherent knowledge structures in some domains than in others.

A second difficulty in resolving the debates about novice knowledge is the methodological variation in the studies. The studies draw from different populations; vary dramatically in sample size, in the nature and variety of tasks used to elicit data, and the methods for analyzing and aggregating data. One sub-domain in which two studies employed fairly similar methodologies but resulted in radically different conclusions about novice knowledge is that of force and motion. Ioannides and Vosniadou (2002) conducted a cross-sectional study with 105 Greek children (preschoolers through ninth graders) to investigate the development of concepts of force and motion and concluded that children used a small set of coherent constructs to explain phenomena in this domain. diSessa, Gillespie, and Esterly (2004) conducted a quasi-replication of the Ioannides and Vosniadou study with 30 American children across a similar age range. diSessa and colleagues found that the American children invoked a greater number of constructs to explain the phenomena of force and motion, and their use of these constructs varied contextually, showing a lack of coherence.

Although the two studies were relatively similar in the methods used to elicit data, there were nonetheless important differences. One difference was linguistic; the Greek children were tested in the Greek language while the American children were tested in English. Therefore, it is possible that at least some of the questions were not equivalent in translation between the two studies. A second, more important difference was that the American sample was much smaller, less than a quarter of the size of the Greek sample. Given the wide range of ages involved, the sub-samples at each age point may have been too small to be truly representative of the population at large. Thirdly and most importantly, although the procedures for data collection were similar in the two studies, the procedures for data analysis were not. Ioannides and Vosniadou (2002) scored children's explanations of their initial answers to each question while diSessa, Gillespie, and Esterly (2004) noted that they were unable to score children's explanations. Thus, despite the similarities in data collection procedures, the actual data set that was analyzed across the two studies was likely to be quite different.

Differences of the kind described above make it hard to render definitive judgments about the utility of regarding lay or everyday representations of the world as theory-like. In general, even if people represent some aspects of the natural world in theory-like ways, it would be implausible to suggest that all knowledge is organized in theories. Even highly regarded scientists such as Charles Darwin, Albert Einstein, or Michael Faraday, probably did not have good theories for every realm of experience. The extent to which knowledge representations are theory-like probably depends on a number of factors including the nature of domain phenomena, the individual's sustained interest and curiosity in the domain, as well as educational and cultural factors. For example, for American children, the dominant cultural model for observational astronomy corresponds to the scientific model. In other domains such as biology, there are often salient competing cultural models to the scientific theory of evolution for important phenomena such as speciation. The availability and salience of such competing cultural models, and the epistemic authority that students accord to various sources of information, are likely to affect both the content and the quality of students' representations.

Given the diversity of theoretical perspectives and empirical findings described above, it appears that while both children and adults may spontaneously construct theory-like representations of the world in some domains of knowledge, they are unlikely to do so uniformly across domains. Additionally, scientific theories are the products of the public institutions of science and their coherence stems in part from their development and modification under processes of rigorous evaluation and critique by the community of scientific practice. In contrast, individual knowledge representations used in everyday life are rarely subjected to such scrutiny and evaluation. Consequently, when compared with their scientific counterparts, naïve theories are invariably likely to be far less cohesive and consistent.

SEE ALSO *Concept Development; Knowledge Representation; Theory of Mind.*

BIBLIOGRAPHY

Ahn, W., Kalish, C., Gelman, S. A., Medin, D. L., Luhmann, C., Attran, S., et al. (2001). Why essences are essential in the psychology of concepts. *Cognition, 82,* 59–69.

Armstrong, D. (1983). *What is a law of nature?* Cambridge, England: Cambridge University Press.

Brewer, W. F. (2008). Naïve theories of observational astronomy: Review, analysis, and theoretical implications. In S. Vosniadou (Ed.), *International Handbook of Research on Conceptual Change.* London: Routledge.

Carey, S., & Spelke, E., (1994). Domain-specific knowledge and conceptual change. In L. A. Hirschfeld, & S. A. Gelman (Eds.), *Mapping the mind* (pp. 169–200). New York: Cambridge University Press.

Cartwright, N. (1983). *How the laws of physics lie.* Oxford, England: Oxford University Press.

Chi, M. T. H., Slotta, J. D., & deLeeuw, N. (1994). From things to processes: A theory of conceptual change for science learning. *Learning and Instruction, 4,* 27–43.

diSessa, A. (1993). Toward an epistemology of physics. *Cognition and Instruction, 10,* 105–225.

diSessa, A. A., Gillespie, N. M., & Esterly, J. B. (2004). Coherence versus fragmentation in the development of the concept of force. *Cognitive Science, 28,* 843–900.

Gentner, D., & Stevens, A. L. (1983). *Mental models.* Hillsdale, NJ: Erlbaum.

Giere, R. N. (2004). How models are used to represent reality. *Philosophy of Science, 71*(5), 742–752.

Gopnik, A., & Wellman, H. M. (1994). The theory theory. In L. A. Hirschfeld, & S. A. Gelman (Eds.), *Mapping the mind* (pp. 257–293). New York: Cambridge University Press.

Hempel, C., & Oppenheim, P. (1948). Studies in the Logic of Explanation. *Philosophy of Science, 15,* 135–175.

Ioannides, C., & Vosniadou, C. (2002). The changing meanings of force. *Cognitive Science Quarterly, 2,* 5–61.

Johnson-Laird, P. N. (1983). *Mental models.* Cambridge, MA: Harvard University Press.

Kuhn, T. S. (1962). *The structure of scientific revolutions.* Chicago: University of Chicago Press.

Laudan. L., Donovan, A., Laudan, R., Barker, P., Brown, H., Leplin, J., et al. (1986). Scientific change: Philosophical models and historical research. *Synthese, 69,* 141–223.

Nakhleh, M. B., & Samarapungavan, A. (1999). Elementary school children's theories of matter. *Journal of Research in Science Teaching, 36*(7), 777–805.

Nobes, G., Moore, D., Martin, A., Clifford, B., Butterworth, G., Panayiotaki, G., et al. (2003). Children's understanding of the earth in a multicultural community: Mental models or fragments of knowledge? *Developmental Science, 6*(1), 72–85.

Rumelhart, D. (1980). Schemata: the building blocks of cognition. In R. J. Spiro, B. Bruce, & W. F. Brewer (Eds.), *Theoretical issues in reading comprehension* (pp. 35–58). Hillsdale, NJ: Erlbaum.

Samarapungavan, A., & Wiers, R. (1997). Children's thoughts on the origin of species: A study of explanatory coherence. *Cognitive Science, 21*(2), 147–177.

Samarapungavan, A., Vosniadou, S., & Brewer, W. F. (1996). Thinking about the earth, sun, and moon: Indian children's cosmologies. *Cognitive Development, 11,* 491–521.

Vosniadou, S., & Brewer, W. F. (1992). Mental Models of the earth: A study of conceptual change in childhood. *Cognitive Psychology, 24,* 535–585.

Vosniadou, S., Skopeliti. I., & Ikospentaki, K. (2004). Modes of knowing and ways of reasoning in elementary astronomy. *Cognitive Development, 19*(2), 203–22.

Wiser, M. (1988). The differentiation of heat and temperature: History of science and novice expert shift. In S. Strauss (Ed.), *Ontogeny, phylogeny and historical development* (pp. 28–48). Norwood, NJ: Ablex.

Ala Samarapungavan

THEORIES OF INTELLIGENCE

Students' theories of intelligence are their beliefs about the nature and workings of their intellect. Some students believe that their intelligence is a fixed trait—that they have been given a certain amount of intelligence and that is that. This is called an *entity* theory of intelligence, and students with this view become very concerned with how much intelligence they have. Other students believe that their intelligence is a quality they can develop through their effort and education. This is called an *incremental* theory of intelligence, and students with this view are more focused on learning and becoming smarter. Each theory affects not only students' motivation to learn but also their success in learning and their achievement in school.

HISTORY OF THE CONCEPT

Research on theories of intelligence grew out of the study of students' achievement goals (Dweck, 2000). Research had found that some students were strongly oriented toward validating their ability (they pursued *performance goals*), whereas other students were oriented toward learning in the same situation (they pursued *learning* or *mastery* goals). This raised the question: What determined which goals students would favor? Research by Carol Dweck with Mary Bandura and later with Ellen Leggett, Ying-Yi Hong, and C.Y. Chiu (see Dweck, 2006) showed that students' theories of intelligence predicted which goals they would tend to pursue. Students who held a fixed (entity) view of intelligence tended to pursue performance goals in an attempt to document their ability (or in an attempt to avoid a negative judgment of their ability), whereas students who held a malleable (or incremental) view of their intelligence tended to pursue learning goals in an attempt to develop their ability (e.g., Dweck & Leggett, 1988).

As this work developed, it was shown that this concept applies to a wide range of abilities, including athletic ability and social skills. Individuals can have theories about the fixedness or malleability of many different abilities, and their theories will predict their goals and motivation in these different domains.

More and more research from cognitive psychology and neuroscience is supporting the idea that important parts of intelligence can be developed through educational programs and that the brain has far more plasticity throughout life than was previously believed. It is interesting to note that Alfred Binet (1857–1911), the inventor of the IQ test, had a very strong incremental theory. He developed the IQ test, not to measure fixed intelligence but to identify students who were not on course in the public schools in the hopes of developing better curricula for them.

PREVALENCE, STABILITY, GROUP DIFFERENCES, AND DEVELOPMENTAL CHANGES

It is found that about 40% of students endorse an entity theory, about 40% endorse an incremental theory, and about 20% do not indicate a preference for either theory. Students' theories tend to be relatively stable over time (Robins & Pals, 2002), but they can be changed by a workshop or an intervention. It is not consistently found that the endorsement of a particular theory of intelligence differs by a student's past achievement level, gender, race, or ethnicity. However, it is increasingly found that the theories of intelligence may matter more for females or for students in ethnic or racial groups that are subject to negative stereotypes about ability. In these cases, it is found that holding an entity theory makes students more susceptible to the harmful effects of these stereotypes, whereas holding an incremental theory makes students less vulnerable to them (e.g., Good, Aronson, & Inzlicht, 2003). Overall, it is found that holding an incremental theory of intelligence favors the growth of ability over time (see, e.g., Blackwell, Trzesniewski, & Dweck, 2007).

Researchers have detected the impact of children's theories in children as young as 5 years of age (Heyman, Dweck, & Cain, 1992). However, these are not theories of *intelligence* but rather theories about goodness and badness, which are the issues that young children are dealing with. Vulnerable young children tend to believe they are bad when they fail or are criticized, and they believe that badness is a stable trait. In contrast, resilient young children tend to believe they are still good children when they fail or are criticized, and that badness can be changed.

METHODS AND ASSESSMENT TOOLS

Students' theories of intelligence are studied in several ways. First, their theories of intelligence can be measured. This is typically done by asking them to disagree or agree (on a six-point scale) with statements such as "You have a certain amount of intelligence, and you really can't do much to change it" (entity theory) or "No matter who you are, you can change your intelligence a lot" (incremental theory) (see Dweck, 2000 for measures). Students' theories of intelligence are then used to predict their motivation or achievement. Measuring students' theories of intelligence works best with children 10 years of age and older.

Students' theories of intelligence can also be induced (temporarily) by exposing them to stories or articles that espouse an entity or incremental theory of intelligence or by telling them that a task measured a fixed ability or an ability that can be developed. It is then found that these induced theories will predict students' motivation and performance.

Finally, students' theories of intelligence can be changed through workshops or interventions. In these cases, students are taught an incremental theory by means of lessons that convey that the brain is like a muscle that gets stronger with use and that every time students work hard and learn new things, the neurons in their brains form new connections. Researchers then follow the students and look for changes in motivation and achievement.

MAJOR FINDINGS

The research shows that each theory of intelligence creates an entire psychological and motivational framework that has widespread effects (Blackwell et al., 2007). First, the theories, as noted earlier, affect students' goals, orienting them toward documenting their intelligence or toward learning. It has been shown that students with an entity theory will pass up important opportunities to learn if there is a danger that they will do poorly or expose a deficiency (e.g., Hong, Chiu, Dweck, Lin, & Wan, 1999). This is true even if it means that they are putting future achievement in jeopardy by passing up such opportunities. Students with an entity theory may also act defensively and conceal or lie about their deficiencies rather than confront and rectify them. For example, they are more likely to engage in self-handicapping (Rhodewalt, 1994). These are strategies that put students' performance at risk (e.g., watching television instead of studying the night before a test), but allow them to preserve their sense of their ability if they fail.

Next, students' theories of intelligence create different attitudes toward effort. Those with an entity theory believe that effort is a sign of low intelligence (Blackwell et al., 2007). They believe that if you have ability you would not need effort. In contrast, students with an incremental theory believe that effort is a good thing, something that helps build abilities. These different beliefs play an important role in dampening the achievement of entity students and enhancing the achievement of incremental students.

The theories of intelligence also influence students' reactions to setbacks. Students with an entity theory believe that failures, even at the beginning of a new course, signify a lack of ability (Blackwell et al., 2007). In line with this, they display a lack of persistence. For example, compared to students with an incremental theory, they report that they would study less after a poor grade in a new subject, that they would try never to take a course in that subject again, and that they would seriously consider cheating on the next test. Thus, when students believe they lack a fixed ability, they do not see good options for bringing about success in the future. Students with an incremental theory believe that school failures reflect more readily on their effort and their study or learning strategies. As a result, they react to challenges and setbacks with persistence. They step up their effort and they seek new learning and strategies.

When students have been tracked over challenging school transitions, researchers have found that those with the incremental theory out-achieve those with the entity theory (Blackwell et al., 2007). Those with an incremental theory also show increasing self-esteem over challenging times, in comparison to those with an entity theory, who show eroding self-esteem (Robins & Pals, 2002).

Finally, as noted above, several studies have sought to change students' theories of intelligence by creating workshops that teach students an incremental theory. After these workshops, students have shown significant increases in their motivation to learn, their grades, and their achievement test scores (Aronson, Fried, & Good, 2002; Blackwell et al., 2007; Good, Aronson, & Inzlicht, 2003).

TEACHERS' THEORIES OF INTELLIGENCE

There is less research available on teachers' theories of intelligence and how they affect students' achievement. However, work by Falko Rheinberg in Germany has shown that when teachers believe they have an impact on their students' intelligence, many students who were previously low achievers blossom in their classes. However, when teachers believe they have no impact on their students' intelligence, students who entered their classes as low achievers tend to remain low achievers.

It is interesting to note that in the famous Rosenthal and Jacobson research on the teacher expectancy effect, teachers were in a sense given an incremental theory of intelligence. They were told that certain students in their class would blossom intellectually that year (not, as commonly believed, that certain students were simply smart). Their results speak to the efficacy of teachers' holding an incremental theory of a student's ability.

Butler (2000) has examined the impact of teachers' theories of intelligence on their judgments of students' intelligence. She gave teachers information about two students, one whose performance increased over 10 tests and one whose performance decreased over 10 tests. Teachers with an incremental theory judged the student with the increasing performance to have higher ability than the one with decreasing performance, but teachers with an entity theory believed the opposite. Incremental teachers were focusing on progress over time as an index of ability, whereas entity teachers judged students by initial performance even if that performance was not maintained over time.

There has also been research on practices that foster an entity and incremental theory of intelligence in children (e.g., Mueller & Dweck, 1998). In experimental studies it has been shown that when adults praise children for their intelligence (*person praise*), as opposed to their effort (*process praise*), it fosters an entity theory of intelligence. Praising children for their intelligence also led them to care more about looking smart than about learning, made them lose confidence in their abilities when a task became difficult, led them to show impaired motivation and performance after difficulty, and led them to lie about their performance afterward. In contrast, praising children for their effort led them to embrace challenges, maintain confidence in the face of difficulty, maintain their motivation, and show enhanced performance after difficulty. Interestingly, the self-esteem movement has advocated praising children's intelligence and talents as a way to build their confidence and motivation. However, this research shows that, instead, praise for intelligence backfires by fostering an entity theory of intelligence with all of its vulnerabilities.

IMPLICATIONS FOR TEACHERS

The research reviewed shows that an incremental theory of intelligence promotes in students a greater desire to learn and enhanced resilience in the face of difficulty. It also predicts better performance on difficult tasks and across challenging school transitions, and it appears to be particularly important for the achievement of students who labor under negative stereotypes. It has been shown that an incremental theory of intelligence can be directly taught to students by teaching about the brain, for example, by telling them that the brain is a muscle that gets stronger with effort and learning and that every time they apply themselves and learn new things, their brain forms new connections. As discussed above, an incremental theory can also be encouraged by process praise. This would include praising children's effort, challenge-seeking, strategies, or improvement rather than their product, outcome, or ability. These are messages that can be readily incorporated into everyday classroom practices without altering the curriculum and without a great deal of additional time and effort on the part of teachers.

SEE ALSO *Goal Orientation Theory; Relevance of Self-Evaluations to Classroom Learning; Social Comparisons.*

BIBLIOGRAPHY

Aronson, J., Fried, C. B., & Good, C. (2002). Reducing the effects of stereotype threat on African American college students by shaping mindsets of intelligence. *Journal of Experimental Social Psychology, 38,* 113–125.

Blackwell, L. S., Trzesniewski, K. H., & Dweck, C. S. (2007). Implicit theories of intelligence predict achievement across an adolescent tradition: A longitudinal study and an intervention. *Child Development, 78,* 246–263.

Butler, R. (2000). Making judgments about ability: The role of implicit theories of ability in moderating inferences from temporal and social comparison information. *Journal of Personality and Social Psychology, 78,* 965–978.

Dweck, C. S. (2000). *Self-Theories: Their role in motivation, personality, and development.* Philadelphia: Psychology Press.

Dweck, C. S. (2006). *Mindset.* New York: Random House.

Dweck, C. S., & Leggett, E. L. (1988). A social-cognitive approach to motivation and personality, *Psychological Review, 95,* 256–273.

Good, C., Aronson, J., & Inzlicht, M. (2003). Improving adolescents' standardized test performance: An intervention to reduce the effects of stereotype threat. *Applied Developmental Psychology, 24,* 645–662.

Heyman, G. D., Dweck, C. S., & Cain, K. (1992) Young children's vulnerability to self-blame and helplessness. *Child Development, 63,* 401–415.

Hong, Y. Y., Chiu, C., Dweck, C. S., Lin, D., & Wan, W. (1999). Implicit theories, attributions, and coping: A meaning system approach. *Journal of Personality and Social Psychology, 77,* 588–599.

Mueller, C. M., & Dweck, C. S. (1998). Intelligence praise can undermine motivation and performance. *Journal of Personality and Social Psychology, 75,* 33–52.

Rhodewalt, F. (1994). Conceptions of ability, achievement goals, and individual differences in self-handicapping behavior: On the application of implicit theories. *Journal of Personality, 62,* 67–85.

Robins, R. W., & Pals, J. L. (2002). Implicit self-theories in the academic domain: Implications for goal orientation, attributions, affect, and self-esteem change. *Self and Identity, 1,* 313–336.

Rosenthal, R., & Jacobson, L. (1968). *Pygmalion in the classroom; teacher expectation and pupils' intellectual development.* New York: Holt, Rinehart & Winston.

Carol S. Dweck

THEORIES OF LEARNING

Learning is one of the most important activities in which humans engage. It is at the very core of the educational process, although most of what people learn occurs outside of school. For thousands of years, philosophers and psychologists have sought to understand the nature of learning, how it occurs, and how one person can influence the learning of another person through teaching and similar endeavors. Various theories of learning have been suggested, and these theories differ for a variety of reasons. A theory, most simply, is a combination of different factors or variables woven together in an effort to explain whatever the theory is about. In general, theories based on scientific evidence are considered more valid than theories based on opinion or personal experience. In any case, it is wise to be cautious when comparing the appropriateness of different theories.

In addition to formal theories, people hold personal theories, including theories of learning and teaching. Some typical questions such theories might involve are: How does one determine if learning has occurred? What factors determine whether or not learning occurs? Are these factors located in the environment or within the individual?

This entry focuses first on different conceptions and definitions of learning. Next, the evolution of theories and conceptions of learning over the past 100 years is discussed, highlighting some of the advantages and limitations of different theoretical perspectives. Following a discussion of the relationship between theory and practice, examples of different types of learning are presented, and the appropriateness of different theories for different learning situations is pointed out.

CONCEPTIONS OF "LEARNING"

Understanding any theory requires a clear idea of what the theory is trying to explain. When a particular word is used, people usually assume everyone has a common understanding of what the word means. Unfortunately, such is not always the case. In trying to understand the various theories of learning and their implications for education, it is helpful to realize that the term "learning" means different things to different people and is used somewhat differently in different theories. As theories of learning evolved over the past half-century, definitions of learning shifted from changes that occur in the mind or behavior of an individual to changes in participation in ongoing activities with other individuals to changes in a person's identity within a group (e.g., a change from being a follower to being a leader). Although, most definitions of learning involve a *change* in an individual's knowledge, ability to perform a skill, or participate in an activity with other individuals, there is considerable variation among the theories about the nature of this change.

Further difficulty in understanding similarities and differences among various theories results from the frequently overlooked fact that there are different types of learning. In many cases, the various theories are relevant to different types of learning and are not necessarily incompatible with one another. Rather, they provide different perspectives on the complex phenomena of learning and complement one another in their ability to explain different types of learning situations. Thus, radically different theories are relevant to the classroom by addressing different aspects of classroom learning, and it is wise to avoid comparing apples with oranges. Examples of different types of learning are presented later in this entry.

EVOLVING THEORIES OF LEARNING

The modern psychological study of learning can be dated from the work of Hermann Ebbinghaus (1850–1909), whose well-known study of memory was published in 1885. Other early studies of learning were by Edward L. Thorndike (1874–1949), whose dissertation on problem solving was published in 1898, and Ivan Pavlov (1849–1936), whose research on classical conditioning was begun in 1899 but first published in English in 1927. These theories focused on explaining the behavior of individuals and became known as behavioral theories. These theories use a stimulus-response framework to explain learning and dominated psychology and education for over half a century. Because behavioral theories focus on environmental factors such as reinforcement, feedback, and practice, they conceptualize learning as something that occurs from the outside in.

Behavioral theories provide very good explanations for certain kinds of learning but poor explanations for other types of learning. Operant conditioning, for example, is better than other theories at explaining the rote acquisition of information, the learning of physical and mental skills, and the development of behaviors conducive to a productive classroom (i.e., classroom management). In these situations, the focus is on performing behavioral tasks rather than developing a learner's cognitive structure or understanding. Although classical conditioning frequently is dismissed as irrelevant to human learning (Pavlov's initial research paradigm involved dogs salivating), this type of learning provides by far the best explanation of how and why people, including students, respond emotionally to a wide variety of stimuli and situations. The many types of emotional reactions acquired through classical conditioning include: anger toward or hatred for a particular person or group, phobias to a particular subject area or to school itself, and infatuation with another person. However, they are very poor at explaining how individuals come to understand complex ideas and phenomena.

But environmental factors are not the only ones that influence learning. Serious consideration of other perspectives began to enter mainstream psychological thinking about learning during the 1960s. For example, people clearly learn by observing others, and a learner's belief about his or her ability to perform a task (i.e., self-efficacy) plays an important role in their learning. In 1963 Albert Bandura and R. H. Walters published the first formal statement of social-learning theory in their book, *Social Learning and Personality Development.* Social-learning theory has clear roots in behavioral theory but differs from these theories in significant ways. During the 1980s the theory became known as social-cognitive theory. Although essentially the same theory, the new name more accurately reflects the cognitive features of the theory and aids in differentiating it from behavioral theories of learning.

During the 1970s and 1980s conceptions and definitions of learning began to change dramatically. Behavioral theories gave way to cognitive theories that focused on mental activities and the understanding of complex material. An information-processing metaphor replaced the stimulus-response framework of behavioral theories. These theories emphasized that learning occurred from the inside out rather than from the outside in. During the late 1970s John Flavell and Ann Brown each began to study metacognition—the learners' awareness of their own learning, an ability to reflect on their own thinking, and the capacity to monitor and manage their learning. During the mid 1980s the study of self-regulated learning began to emerge (see Zimmerman & Schunk, 2001).

Then, especially during the later 1980s and the 1990s, these cognitive theories were challenged by theories that emphasized the importance of social interactions and the sociocultural context of learning. The work of the Russian psychologist Lev Vygotsky (1896–1934) first became available in North America and along with the work of anthropologists such as Jean Lave began to have a major influence on theories of learning. Individuals were seen as initially participating in peripheral activities of a group (known as legitimate peripheral participation) before becoming fully integrated into group activities. Apprenticeship became a metaphor for the way people learn in natural settings. The notion that people learn by observing others, first articulated in social-cognitive theory, was expanded in a new context.

Traditionally, learning has been viewed as something that occurs within an individual. Individuals may participate and learn in groups, but it is the individual person that learns. With few exceptions, the educational systems in Europe and North America have adopted this perspective, if not entirely with regard to instructional practices, certainly in the evaluation of student performance and the assignment of grades. Many psychologists and educators currently consider learning to be a phenomenon that is distributed among several individuals and/or environmental affordances (such as calculators, computers, and textbooks) or situated (existing or occurring) within a "community of practice" (or community of learners). Both a social and a material dimension are involved in this distribution (Pea, 1993). For example, a student may use a calculator to help learn how to solve a three-digit multiplication problem (the material dimension) and/or work with another student to understand the proper procedures to follow (the social dimension). In either case, the student is not learning totally on his or her own but is taking advantages of resources (affordances) available in the environment. If the student is not able to solve a subsequent problem without the aid of the calculator or another student, then it is possible to see the distributed nature of learning. In such situations, participation or activity rather than acquisition becomes the defining metaphor (Greeno, 2006).

The evolution from behavioral to social to distributed to situated theories of learning was accompanied by new conceptions of knowledge (for a good discussion of these changes, see Schraw, 2006). Traditional theories conceive of knowledge as a commodity capable of being transmitted, more or less intact, from one individual to another. According to these theories, knowledge is something an individual acquires; when a student successfully learns it, he or she can reproduce the knowledge in its original form. In contrast, more recent theories conceive of knowledge as something each learner constructs or creates afresh rather than something that is assimilated in its preexisting form. According to current theories, truly "objective" knowledge does not exist, although something similar exists in the form of collective knowledge within a particular culture or discipline. Knowledge resides in the community of learners (individuals) that creates it and is distributed among members of the community and the various environmental affordances available to the group. Because each person constructs his or her own understandings, the knowledge they acquire is unique. Communities and cultures are composed of individuals with common understandings, and these groups provide opportunities for new members (e.g., children) to construct similar knowledge of the world through schools and/or a variety of informal activities.

The 1990s were dubbed "The Decade of the Brain," and huge advances were made in neuroscience and how the brain relates to human behavior and learning. The study of how the brain relates to learning is in its infancy (for an introduction to some of the issue, see Bransford et al., 2006). An understanding of how the neurophysiology of the brain affects learning and cognition will add greatly to our understanding of human learning and have a large influence on future theories of learning. Nevertheless, a psychological component to these theories will remain critical for learning in educational settings. Education as it is presently understood is based on psychological processes and interactions capable of being influenced by instruction, and it seems likely that psychological interventions will continue to be important for the foreseeable future.

THE RELATIONSHIP BETWEEN THEORY AND PRACTICE

The relationship between theories of learning and educational practices is complicated by several factors. One would think that instructional practices should be based on the best theories of learning available, but this relationship is not as straightforward as one might think. Schools and educational practices are far more likely to be based on philosophical beliefs than on empirical studies and theoretical understanding of learning. Schools are established according to different community and cultural beliefs about the world, the nature of humankind and children, locus of authority, and what should be learned. Schools also differ in their beliefs about teaching and learning, but the philosophical beliefs often come first. Every educational system and instructional program contains a theory of learning, although frequently this theory is implicit and goes unrecognized.

These philosophical and theoretical differences are formidable. Many have endured for centuries, and the debate is unlikely to end anytime soon. For example, the "factory model" of schooling dominated education in the United States for many years. This model is based on production and management procedures successful during the industrial revolution. It stands in sharp contrast to the voices of Henry David Thoreau (1817–1862), John Dewey (1859–1952), and others who advocated discovery, social reform, and freedom as the appropriate means of education. Both perspectives are clearly evident in modern-day discussions of education and instructional practices.

The correspondence between these philosophical perspectives and the various theories of learning is quite apparent. Classroom activities in a traditional classroom, for example, revolve around and are controlled by the teacher, who presents the to-be-learned material and dictates the type of learning activities in which students engage. Students are expected to study the information (via classroom activities and homework) until it is mastered. The knowledge being learned is seen as a commodity being passed from one individual (the teacher) to another (the student).

Very different classrooms emerge from different philosophical perspectives. If one believes, for example, that knowledge is something created afresh by each student, that learning occurs from working on authentic tasks in a social environment, and that the mental activities of the student determines what he or she learns, then the resulting classroom is likely to be one in which students work in groups and/or on projects, discussing how best to solve a problem, or negotiating the meaning of a concept. Once again consistency exists between theoretical beliefs and classroom practices. However, it is not always clear which comes first, for there is evidence that individuals seek out and accept information that confirms their existing beliefs while tending to reject information that would disconfirm those beliefs.

This reality leads to another realization regarding the relationship between theory and practice, namely that the relationship is two-way. A common belief is that knowledge flows from scientific theories to the development of effective practices, that sound theories of learning dictate effective educational practices. Science, however, does not always operate in such a linear fashion. In both the physical and social sciences, ideas often come from observing and questioning things that occur in the real world: "Why did that apple fall from the tree?" (a question asked by Isaac Newton [1643–1727] that led to his discovery of the three laws of motion). Scientific breakthroughs also come from trying to solve a practical problem (Stokes, 1997), such as "what is the best way to teach the concept of photosynthesis?" Established educational practices that teachers have found effective can and should be a source of ideas in developing a viable theory of learning.

A third caveat in understanding the relationship between theory and practice is realizing that the student is more important than the teacher in determining what is learned. This does not mean the teacher is not important; only that it is the students' perceptions, prior knowledge, and beliefs that determine what and if they learn something approximating the instructional goals of the teacher. The bottom line in the teaching-learning process is the learning activities in which the students engage, not the instructional activities in which the teacher engages.

Modern-day conceptions of learning and teaching recognize that students are active, often proactive, participants in the learning process, even if they appear otherwise. This dynamic nature of the learning process is one reason why instructional interventions that appear the same to the teacher can result in very different student outcomes and why rather different instructional methods can result in very similar outcomes (e.g., Nuthall & Alton-Lee, 1990; Olson, 2004).

DIFFERENT TYPES OF LEARNING

The relationship between theories of learning and educational practices is complicated by the reality that there is more than one type of learning. None of the present theories is capable of explaining learning in all situations, and scholars working within a particular theoretical perspective often ignore or deny the importance of other types of learning and the relevance of other theories for different situations. Nearly every educational setting involves several types of learning, each with its unique importance to the functioning of the classroom.

There is little agreement on how many types of learning actually exist. Nevertheless, it should not be too difficult to identify different types of learning in the following examples: (a) learning to tie a shoelace or necktie, (b) being afraid (fearful in a literal sense) to work in a math class after a lengthy public ridicule by a teacher two years earlier for being unable to explain a problem to the class, (c) understanding and explaining causes of the French and American revolutions, (d) learning to cook by watching one's father or mother, and (e) negotiating an understanding of "learning" with a person holding a different theoretical perspective. Different theories are good for explaining one example but poor for explaining other examples.

When evaluating the validity or usefulness of different theories, especially from the perspective of the student doing the learning, it is helpful to consider what the person is learning and what is taken as evidence that learning has occurred. Students do not always engage in the type of learning sought by the teacher. For example, a teacher conducts a lesson on the Civil War that includes authentic activities, having students question one another about the war, and finally giving the students a quiz. It would not be at all uncommon for the teacher to conclude that a particular student *understood* what happened at Gettysburg when in reality he or she only *memorized certain facts.*

Theories of learning are efforts to explain how people learn. Different theories are based on different assumptions and are appropriate for explaining some learning situations but not others. Theories of learning can inform teaching and the use of different instructional resources including technology, but ultimately the learning activities in which the student actually engages (mental, physical, and social) determine what a student learns in the classroom. Classroom learning involves social, emotional, and participatory factors in addition to cognitive ones, and theories of learning need to take these factors into account. Most current theories of learning presuppose that the goal of education is to develop the ability of students to understand the content and to think for themselves, presumptions that are consistent with the majority of modern-day schools.

SEE ALSO *Cognitive Load Theory; Constructivism; Distributed Cognition; Dual Coding Theory; Information Processing Theory; Self-Efficacy Theory; Self-Regulated Learning; Situated Cognition; Social Cognitive Theory; Sociocultural Theory.*

BIBLIOGRAPHY

Alexander, P. A., & Winne, P. H. (Eds.). (2006). *Handbook of educational psychology* (2nd ed.). Mahwah, NJ: Erlbaum.

Bransford, J., Stevens, R., Schwartz, D., Meltzoff, A., Pea, R., Roschelle, J., et al. (2006). Learning theories and education: Toward a decade of synergy. In P. A. Alexander & P. H. Winne (Eds.), *Handbook of educational psychology* (2nd ed., pp. 209–244). Mahwah, NJ: Erlbaum.

Greeno, J. G. (2006). Learning in activity. In R. K. Sawyer (Ed.), *The Cambridge handbook of the learning sciences* (pp. 79–96). New York: Cambridge University Press.

Nuthall, G., & Alton-Lee, A. (1990). Research on teaching and learning: Thirty years of change. *Elementary School Journal, 90,* 547–570.

Olson, D. R. (2004). The triumph of hope over experience in the search for "What Works": A response to Slavin. *Educational Researcher, 33*(1), 24–26.

Pea, R. D. (1993). Practices of distributed intelligence and designs for education. In G. Salomon (Ed.), *Distributed cognitions: psychological and educational considerations* (pp. 47–87). New York: Cambridge University Press.

Salomon, G. (Ed.). (1993). *Distributed cognitions: psychological and educational considerations.* New York: Cambridge University Press.

Sawyer, R. K. (Ed.). (2006). *The Cambridge handbook of the learning sciences.* New York: Cambridge University Press.

Schraw, G. (2006). Knowledge: Structures and processes. In P. A. Alexander & P. H. Winne (Eds.), *Handbook of educational psychology* (2nd ed., pp. 245–263). Mahwah, NJ: Erlbaum.

Stokes, D. E. (1997). *Pasteur's quadrant: Basic science and technological innovation.* Washington, DC: Brookings Institution Press.

Zimmerman, B. J., & Schunk, D. H. (Eds.). (2001). *Self-regulated learning and academic achievement: Theoretical perspectives* (2nd ed.). Mahwah, NJ: Erlbaum.

Thomas J. Shuell

THEORY OF MIND

Theory of mind (ToM) is the intuitive understanding of one's own and other people's minds or mental states—including thoughts, beliefs, perceptions, knowledge, intentions, desires, and emotions—and of how those mental states influence behavior. Sometimes called intuitive psychology, folk psychology, or even mind-reading, ToM is an innate human ability. The understanding that others have mental states different from one's own makes it possible to infer what others are thinking and to predict their behavior. This ability to recognize one's own state of mind and those of others is central to human consciousness. The study of ToM and identification of the skills comprising ToM is a rapidly changing field of developmental psychology.

THE THEORY OF TOM

The word *theory* in ToM refers to a person's tacit belief rather than to *theory* in the scientific sense. However, ToM is similar to a scientific theory in that it enables one to interpret and predict another's actions by evaluating their thoughts, beliefs, desires, or emotions. ToM also qualifies as a theory in the sense that the representations of reality generated by ToM are not directly observable.

The ability to develop a ToM is a cognitive ability that develops by degrees from infancy through childhood and adolescence on into adulthood. It forms a basis for a child's acquisition of language and the development of appropriate social behavior and skills. ToM includes the ability to understand that the representations generated in one's mind do not necessarily reflect the real world and that other people may hold different representations. Empathy—the ability to understand another person's perceptions on a deep level without reference to one's own perceptions—may be a culminating feature of ToM development.

ToM is involved in all aspects of daily living and social interactions. It underlies learning and teaching and the ability to follow directions and understand socially based information. ToM skills are essential for working cooperatively. They also underlie the ability to manipulate and deceive others. A lack of ToM skills is considered by many to be a core deficit in autism. and studies of autism have promoted research on the development and complex functioning of ToM.

As a basic component of human consciousness ToM has roots in philosophy, particularly in the groundwork for a science of the mind laid down by René Descartes (1596–1650). The Swiss psychologist Jean Piaget (1896–1980) suggested that before the age of 3 or 4 egocentrism prevents children from understanding that other people's thoughts and viewpoints may differ from their own. In 1978 Nicholas Humphrey proposed that introspective consciousness has a specific function; it enables social animals to predict each other's behavior. Being aware of the effects of emotions on one's own behavior enables humans to predict the reactions of others to those same emotions.

FALSE BELIEF

In 1978 David Premack and Guy Woodruff coined the term *theory of mind* as it is now used in developmental psychology. They argued that chimpanzees and perhaps other nonhuman primates could understand the intentions of others and therefore possessed ToM. Although that issue remains controversial, Premack and Woodruff's work was an inspiration for psychologists studying normal and abnormal child development.

In 1983 Josef Perner and Heinz Wimmer applied Premack and Woodruff's false-belief test to children using an "unexpected location" task. In one version of this test a puppet named Maxi puts a chocolate in the cupboard and leaves the scene. The experimenter moves the chocolate to a new location and asks the child where Maxi will look for it. In another version called the "Sally-Anne" task, Sally and Anne put a marble in a box. Sally leaves and Anne takes the marble out and puts it in a different box. Up until about the age of 4 most children ascribe their own beliefs to Maxi and Sally and tell the experimenter that Maxi or Sally will look for the chocolate or marble in its new location. However, older children understand that Maxi will look for the chocolate where he last saw it in the cupboard, and Sally will look in the first box. The task requires that children understand that other people's beliefs may differ from their own and then predict how those people will react based on their differing beliefs.

Over the years many permutations of the false-belief test have been developed to ensure that it does not require advanced language skills. In the "unexpected contents" or "Smarties" task a child opens a candy box expecting to find a candy called Smarties and finds pencils instead. Until the age of 3 or 4 children assume that someone else will expect to find pencils in the candy box. Furthermore, children claim that they expected to find pencils when they first opened the box, a phenomenon called hindsight bias. The ability to pass the false-belief test is seen as a major milestone in the development of ToM in young children.

TOM IN INFANTS AND TODDLERS

Although children clearly begin to develop ToM at an earlier age than Piaget thought, researchers disagree as to which behaviors indicate a developing ToM in children younger than 3, and it has been very difficult to assess ToM in preverbal children. Some researchers argue that mimicking by infants is indicative of a developing ToM.

Infants under 1 year expect hands and objects to move in ways that are goal-oriented. Between 6 and 12 months infants develop "joint attention"—looking in the direction of someone else's gaze. Between 12 and 18 months babies will look in the direction that someone is pointing, rather than at the person's finger, and will themselves point to draw someone's attention to something. In 2000 Charman and colleagues found that children who showed the highest rates of joint attention at 20 months scored the highest on ToM tests at 44 months.

Some researchers argue that as early as 14 months babies can understand intentional behavior and therefore understand that other people are intentional and mental beings. An 18-month-old who watches an adult try unsuccessfully to hang a loop on a hook will imitate the intended rather than the failed action, even though the baby has only seen the failed action. Toddlers begin to recognize that other people have desires and likes and dislikes that are different from their own. For example, a child can predict that another child who wants a cookie will go to the cookie jar. Two-year-olds understand and use words for their senses and their wants. They engage in pretend play and learn to distinguish between physical and mental events such as a real versus an imaginary playmate.

Three-year-olds begin to understand that other people's minds are distinct from their own but cannot yet clearly distinguish between what they know and what others know. Nevertheless, 3-year-olds have a fairly well-developed ToM. Most 3-year-olds can talk about mental states using words such as *think, know,* and *remember.* They can distinguish mental states such as dreams. They also understand that perception can lead to knowledge: Someone who looks inside a box will know what is in it, but someone who cannot see inside the box will not know.

TOM IN PRESCHOOLERS

At about age 4 children recognize that other people have minds and that their minds may hold different information. They also recognize that appearances may be deceptive and can mislead. The appearance-reality (A-R) task is used to assess a child's ability to distinguish between reality and representation. A child is given a sponge that is painted to look like a rock. When asked what the object looks like and what it is really, a 3-year-old will give the same answer to both questions—either a rock or a sponge. In contrast, a 4-year-old will correctly answer that it looks like a rock but is really a sponge. By the age of 5 children can understand that someone who appears happy may actually be sad. However, since the ability to recognize that others may have mistaken beliefs is central to ToM, the false-belief test remains the basic criterion for assessing ToM.

Although it is clear that the abilities to pass false-belief and A-R tasks at about age 4 represent important milestones in ToM development, the nature of these cognitive shifts is unclear. Simulation theory argues that children learn to understand other's beliefs through imagination—by imagining themselves in another person's situation. Other scientists believe that this milestone occurs through a process of conceptual change or through the maturing of structures in the brain that facilitate reasoning about the minds of others. Many psychologists believe that failure on false-belief and other ToM tasks is due to children's immature executive functioning.

Although understanding false belief is universal in normal children over the age of 5, a number of factors appear to affect the exact age at which the skill is acquired. Success on false-belief tests correlates with short-term memory ability. Children with larger vocabularies and those from larger families pass false-belief tests at earlier ages. However, attempts to teach younger children about false-belief have been unsuccessful; the children may show improvement on the specific task that is taught, but not on other false-belief tasks.

ToM development in young children is strongly correlated with language ability. Bilingual preschoolers have increased understanding of both mental and non-mental representations. The acquisition of ToM is delayed in children with some specific language impairments. Both language and ToM skills predict later metamemory—knowledge and beliefs about one's own memory—and metacognition—knowledge and beliefs about one's own cognitive processes.

ToM development appears to be advanced in children with older siblings, in children who participate in early pretend play, and in children whose families talk about mental states. Activities that seem to promote the development of ToM skills include:

• Pretend play and role playing

• Talking about past events

• Reading stories

• Discussing situations such as misunderstandings, teasing, and forgetfulness

• Imagining

• Discussing opinions and perspectives

Deaf children of deaf parents who are exposed to American Sign Language from birth perform similarly to hearing children on ToM tests. However, deaf children with hearing parents are significantly delayed in ToM development. A 2002 study by Schick and colleagues found that certain language skills of deaf children correlated with their ToM skills. For example, a deaf child who could understand the sentence "He thought his cake was in the cupboard" was more likely to pass ToM tests.

It has been suggested that deaf children undergo normal ToM development but lack the language necessary to understand the stories that are generally used in ToM tests.

TOM IN SCHOOL-AGE CHILDREN

By age 6 children can pass second-order false-belief tests. In contrast to first-order belief tests (Sally believes the marble is in the first box when it is really in the second), second-order tests require a child to understand that Sally thinks Mary thinks the marble is in the first box, but both Sally and Mary are wrong. By the age of 6 children have acquired another ToM skill—the ability to deceive others. In a 2007 study Talwar and colleagues found that among elementary-school children the ability to maintain consistency between an initial lie and subsequent statements increases with age and correlates with the children's scores on second-order false-belief tests.

ToM skills and knowledge about mental states and attitudes increase dramatically throughout childhood. Compared with younger children, 8-year-olds show more skill in first- and second-order false-belief tests involving physical facts and positive and negative emotions and have a much easier time explaining their responses. However, there are far fewer tests for evaluating ToM in children older than 6 and few ToM studies have focused on children older than about 7.

By elementary school children have gone from a state of self-recognition to a state of self-consciousness. At about age 7 they realize that thinking is an ongoing process or stream-of-consciousness, with each thought triggering a new thought. In contrast, preschoolers believe that mental activity starts and stops with each thought. Whereas very young children are unclear about what it means to know something and how they know it, and older preschoolers often insist that they have always known something that they learned just a few minutes ago, with middle childhood comes the realization that knowledge requires adequate information. Furthermore these children are starting to understand that interpretations of knowledge and situations can be influenced by expectations or biases. They are increasingly able to consider other people's points of view. ToM studies have shown that at about age 7 children come to understand that a person's facial expressions and thoughts do not necessarily coincide and they are increasingly able to link physical symptoms with anxiety. Researchers have found that sarcasm, irony, and bluffing are not well understood until about age 8.

Between the third and fifth grades children's understanding of the role of memory develops significantly. Although it has been both assumed and suggested by research that ToM is closely related to episodic memory—the ability to re-experience past events—recent research has suggested that ToM may function independently of episodic memory. Perner and colleagues reported in 2007 that episodic memory emerges later than false-belief skills, together with the ability to use imagery to solve visual rotation tasks.

A 1999 study by Simon Baron-Cohen and colleagues examined the ability of 7- to 11-year-olds to recognize a faux pas—saying something that is inappropriate or could be misconstrued—such as mistaking a boy for a girl or a customer in a restaurant for a waiter. The researchers found that the ability to recognize a faux pas developed by age 9 and that girls were better at it than boys.

TOM IN THE CLASSROOM

It is likely that ToM skills underlie a child's ability to understand and make up stories and therefore are important for developing reading skills. Astington and Pelletier (1996) have argued that there is a relationship between the degree of ToM development and the ability to learn by instruction and collaboration, and that ToM skills are linked to the development of scientific and critical thinking.

In a 1998 study Perry Klein found that students' skills in predicting or explaining a doll or cartoon character's behavior correlated with their abilities to plan controlled experiments and explain the causes of events. He suggested that first through fifth graders use science strategies that are dependent on their ToM development. Most 6-year-olds understand the concept of evidence, and 8-year-olds can distinguish between ambiguous and unambiguous evidence. Younger children often hold on to prior beliefs despite evidence to the contrary, whereas older children can revise their beliefs. Likewise, younger children manipulate multiple variables when planning science experiments, failing to hold any factor constant, whereas older children and adults understand the concept of testing only one variable at a time and holding the other factors constant.

In school children need to be able to discuss mutual understandings and misunderstandings and their own beliefs and those of others and to make conceptual changes. These activities all require ToM skills. Helping students to reflect on and talk about their thinking may help improve ToM abilities. Teachers report that children with more advanced ToM skills have better social skills. However, advanced ToM skills can also be utilized for antisocial purposes such as bullying.

The development of ToM may be particularly relevant to classroom learning during middle childhood and adolescence. Although all normal children develop ToM skills in basically the same sequence, the pace of ToM development may be different in different cultures, par-

ticularly among older children. This may be a function of the vocabularies about mental states in different languages or cultural differences in amount of thinking and talking about mental states. There also appear to be gender differences in the development of at least some aspects of ToM. In a 2000 study Bosacki found that 11-year-old girls scored higher than boys on tests of self-understanding and social understanding.

ToM development continues throughout adolescence and into adulthood. However most research with adolescents has focused on metacognition rather than on ToM. Adolescents are well known for a particular type of ToM error—believing that those around them, especially peers, are thinking about them and judging them when there is no evidence that this is the case.

THE NEUROSCIENCE OF TOM

Brain imaging while performing ToM tasks has suggested the involvement of a patch of neurons above the eyes called the anterior paracingulate cortex. Some researchers believe that this region is responsible for the central ToM task of distinguishing between one's own mind and that of another person. The frontal cortex is known to be important for both ToM and cognitive abilities and this region continues to develop during adolescence. Moriguchi and colleagues (2007) studied 9- to 16-year-olds and found that, as in adults, activation of the medial prefrontal cortex, the bilateral superior temporal sulcus (STS), and the temporal pole adjacent to the amygdala were associated with ToM, and that during late childhood and adolescence ToM activation of the medial prefrontal cortex switched from the ventral side to the dorsal. Researchers have found that the left medial prefrontal cortex is strongly activated when normal subjects read a story that requires understanding the mental states of characters, whereas this region is not activated when autistic subjects read the same story. The STS senses biological motion. It is activated by a moving hand but not a moving car and is particularly sensitive to eye and lip movements. The temporal pole is crucial for recalling memories. The amygdala, which is important for emotion, may also be involved in ToM.

Autism researchers have focused on the hypothesis that autistic children do not undergo normal ToM development. Autistic children who do manage to pass ToM tests usually have far more verbal knowledge than other 3- to 5-year-olds. They also laboriously explain their reasoning, whereas normal young children cannot explain their reasoning, suggesting that the autistic children use a different method to succeed on the test. In Baron-Cohen's 1999 study children with Asperger syndrome or high-functioning autism who passed false-belief tests were nonetheless unable to recognize faux pas or recognized them but continued to make them. Autistic children also have difficulty understanding and carrying out deception. Studies on autistic individuals have helped distinguish between ToM and cognition since autistics can have exceptional cognitive abilities while lacking ToM skills.

SEE ALSO *Cognitive Strategies; Metacognition.*

BIBLIOGRAPHY

Astington, J., & Pelletier, J. (1996). The language of the mind: Its role in teaching and learning. In D. R. Olson & N. Torrance (Eds.), *The handbook of education and human development: New models of learning, teaching, and schooling* (pp. 593–619). Cambridge, MA: Blackwell.

Baron-Cohen, S. (1995). *Mindblindness: An essay on autism and theory of mind.* Cambridge, MA: MIT Press.

Baron-Cohen, S., O'Riordan, M., Stone, V., Jones, R., & Plaisted, K. (1999). Recognition of faux pas by normally developing children and children with Asperger syndrome or high-functioning autism. *Journal of Autism and Developmental Disorders, 29,* 407–418.

Blacher, J., & Howell, E. (2007). Unlocking the mystery of social deficits in autism: theory of mind as key. *The Exceptional Parent, 37,* 96–97.

Bloom, P. (2004). *Descartes' baby: How the science of child development explains what makes us human.* New York: Basic Books.

Bosacki, S. L. (2000). Theory of mind and self-concept in preadolescents: links with gender and language. *Journal of Educational Psychology, 92,* 709–717.

Bower, B. (1993). A child's theory of mind: Mental life may change radically around age 4. *Science News, 144,* 40–42.

Carruthers, P., & Smith, P. K. (1996). *Theories of theories of mind.* New York: Cambridge University Press.

Charman, T., Baron-Cohen, S., Swettenham, J., Baird, G., Cox, A., & Drew, A. (2000). Testing joint attention, imitation, and play as infancy precursors to language and theory of mind. *Cognitive Development, 15,* 481–498.

Firth, C., & Firth, U. (1999). Interacting minds—a biological basis. *Science, 286,* 1692–1695.

Flavell, J. H. (2004). Theory-of-mind development: Retrospect and prospect. *Merrill-Palmer Quarterly, 50,* 274–290.

Humphrey, N. (1978, June 29). Nature's psychologists. *New Scientist, 78,* 900–903.

Klein, P. D. (1998). The role of children's theory of mind in science experimentation. *The Journal of Experimental Education, 66,* 101–124.

Miller, C. A. (2006). Developmental relationships between language and theory of mind. *American Journal of Speech-Language Pathology, 15,* 142–154.

Moriguchi, Y., Ohnishi, T., Mori, T., Matsuda, H., & Komaki, G. (2007). Changes of brain activity in the neural substrates for theory of mind during childhood and adolescence. *Psychiatry and Clinical Neurosciences, 61,* 355–363.

Perner, J., Kloo, D., & Stottinger. E. (2007). Introspection & remembering. *Synthese: An International Journal for Epistemology, Methodology and Philosophy of Science, 159,* 253–270.

Premack, D., & Woodruff, G. (1978). Does the chimpanzee have a theory of mind? *Behavioral and Brain Sciences, 4,* 515–526.

Saxe, R., & Baron-Cohen, S. (Eds.) (2006). *Theory of mind: A special issue of* Social Neuroscience. London: Psychology Press.

Schick, B., de Villiers, J., de Villiers, P., & Hoffmeister, B. (2002). Theory of mind: language and cognition in deaf children. *ASHA Leader, 7,* 6–8.

Schneider, W., Schumann-Hengsteler, R., & Sodian, B. (Eds.) (2005). *Young children's cognitive development: Interrelationships among executive functioning, working memory, verbal ability, and theory of mind.* Mahwah, NJ: Erlbaum.

Talwar, V., Gordon, H. M., & Lee, K. (2007). Lying in the elementary school years: Verbal deception and its relation to second-order belief understanding. *Developmental Psychology, 43,* 804–810.

Wimmer, H., & Perner, J. (1983). Beliefs about beliefs: Representation and constraining function of wrong beliefs in young children's understanding of deception. *Cognition, 13,* 103–128.

Zimmer, C. (2003). How the mind reads other minds: Understanding what others are thinking is a human exclusive. Now researchers are tracking how the brain performs this feat and speculating about how it evolved. *Science, 300,* 1079–1081.

Margaret Alic

THORNDIKE, E(DWARD) L(EE)
1874–1949

"Whatever exists at all exists in some amount. To know it thoroughly involves knowing its quantity as well as its quality" (Thorndike, 1918, p. 16). This quotation captures the attitude that E. L. Thorndike brought to the study of education. The hallmark of his work was his abiding faith in the quantifiability of all aspects of human experience.

LIFE EVENTS

Edward Lee Thorndike was born in Williamsburg, Massachusetts, on August 31, 1874, to Edward Roberts and Abbie (Ladd) Thorndike. E. R. Thorndike was a Methodist minister who served churches in Maine and Massachusetts. Perhaps in reaction to a strict religious upbringing, throughout his life, E. L. Thorndike favored science over religion.

Upon graduation from Wesleyan University in 1895, Thorndike went to Harvard University to study with William James and begin his psychological studies of learning. He soon moved from Harvard to James McKeen Cattell's lab at Columbia University where he undertook his famous puzzle box studies with cats. After earning his doctorate Thorndike spent a year at Western Reserve University before becoming a member of the founding faculty at Teachers College (TC), Columbia University, in the fall of 1899. He remained at TC until his retirement in 1940, publishing approximately 500

E. L. Thorndike THE LIBRARY OF CONGRESS.

books, monographs and papers. (For a list of publications, see Gates, 1949.)

Thorndike married Elizabeth Moulton on August 29, 1900. They had four children, all of whom earned PhDs. The second son, Robert L., followed in his father's footsteps at Teachers College.

E. L. Thorndike's work was widely recognized within his own lifetime. He was elected president of the American Psychological Association (1912), the American Association for the Advancement of Science (1933), and the Psychometric Society (1936). Cattell ranked him first among American psychologists in a 1921 poll for *American Men of Science.* Thorndike died of a massive cerebral hemorrhage on August 9, 1949.

THORNDIKE'S RESEARCH AND THEORY

E. L. Thorndike formulated a theory of mental associations called connectionism. He believed that the central nervous system was the basis of all behavior. Learning took place when connections were formed between neurons. The purpose of education was to facilitate the formation of desirable connections.

Thorndike was fascinated with individual differences, trying to measure them, explain them, and use them for prediction. He believed that science could solve human problems, and he applied scientific method to problems of education. Much of his career was spent trying to develop methods to measure individual differences and to use these measurements to make education more efficient and successful.

Thorndike set out to place education on a sound scientific footing. The prevalent educational practice in 1900 was the doctrine of mental discipline. Curriculum was founded on opinion, not evidence. Based on his studies he concluded that education must be conducted in the subject to be learned and tailored to the ability levels of the students. He continued his pursuit of quantification and scientific method in education in one of the first books on psychological and educational measurement (Thorndike, 1904).

In addition to his efforts to make education more efficient and scientifically sound, Thorndike expended considerable effort from 1900 to 1925 in developing measures of intellect. Beginning in 1903, he and his students developed a wide variety of measures of human abilities, culminating in the CAVD, a "test constructed (in 1922–1925) as a sample of what a measuring instrument for a mental ability should be" (Thorndike, 1949, p. v.). The acronym stood for Comprehension, Arithmetic, Vocabulary and Direction following, four of the more important dimensions of intellect in Thorndike's view.

In the 1930s, Thorndike turned his attention to problems of lexicography, and in this work, he revolutionized the way dictionaries were produced. For years he had been keeping records of the frequency of word usage in the English language. He used these counts to determine which words to include in his dictionaries and what the order of definitions should be. He also required that each word be defined only using words that were more frequently used than the word being defined. All modern dictionaries now apply these principles.

E. L. Thorndike's influence on education and psychology is so pervasive that it is hard to detect. He pioneered the scientific study of education and made major contributions to the measurement of human abilities, comparative psychology, and social psychology. The hundreds of students he taught have spread his ideas throughout American education and psychology. Most 21st-century education faculty can trace their intellectual ancestry to him through their mentors. A full biography of E. L. Thorndike is available in Joncich (1968).

SEE ALSO *Rewards.*

BIBLIOGRAPHY

WORKS BY

Thorndike, E. L. (1903). *Educational Psychology*. New York: Lemcke & Buechner.

Thorndike, E. L. (1904). *An introduction to the theory of mental and social measurements.* New York: Science Press.

Thorndike, E. L. (1913). *An introduction to the theory of mental and social measurements.* New York: Teachers College, Columbia University Press.

Thorndike, E. L. (1918). The nature, purposes, and general methods of measurement of educational products. In S. A. Courtis (Ed.), *The Measurement of Educational Products* (17th Yearbook of the National Society for the Study of Education, Pt. 2. pp. 16–24). Bloomington, IL: Public School.

Thorndike, E. L. (1949). *Selected Writings from a Connectionist's Psychology.* New York: Appleton-Century-Crofts.

WORKS ABOUT

Gates, A. I. (1949). The writings of Edward L. Thorndike. *Teachers College Record, 51,* 28–31.

Joncich, G. (1968). *The sane positivist: A biography of Edward Lee Thorndike.* Middletown, CT: Wesleyan University Press.

Robert Thorndike

TIME ON-TASK

Arguably, the primary goal of schooling is to provide students with a safe and engaging environment and ample opportunities to learn. A large portion of a student's typical school day is allocated towards providing these opportunities. However, once lunch, recess, and passing periods are accounted for, the amount of time teachers allocate for learning is far more than the amount of time students are actually engaged in learning. Martella, Nelson, and Marchand-Martella (2003) report that students only spend about 42% of their school day engaged in learning. Time on-task, also known as engaged time, is the amount of time actually spent learning (Slavin, 2003). It is important to acknowledge that engaged time is more than a behavioral concept; it also encompasses the emotional commitment to academics (VanDeWeghe, 2006). For example, students should demonstrate behaviors such as writing, participating in tasks, reading aloud, reading silently, and asking questions; they should also be attentive, interested, and invested in their learning (Greenwood, Horton, & Utley, 2002; Marks, 2000).

Some research concludes that engaged time is the most important influence on academic achievement (Greenwood et al., 2002; Marks, 2000; Slavin, 2003). According to Greenwood and colleagues (2002) academic engaged time increases through second grade and levels off through fifth grade. Conversely, off-task behavior is stable through second grade, increases momentarily through fourth grade, and then declines through fifth grade. Examples of off-task

behavior include talking out of turn, walking around the class, disturbing peers, and daydreaming. Students who engage to a high degree in off-task behavior "will be unable to respond to academic opportunities or manage subject matter tasks rapidly and accurately" (Greenwood et al., 2002, p. 328). This pattern "can lead to dysfunctional school behavior [which can] ultimately culminate in some students leaving school entirely" (Marks, 2000, p. 155).

Children from specific populations seem to experience lower levels of on-task behavior than others, particularly those with attention-deficit/hyperactivity disorder (ADHD; Brock, 2005). A literature review by Junod, DuPaul, Jitendra, Volpe, and Cleary (2006) reported that children with ADHD typically struggle academically because of their lower rates of academic engagement. More specifically, they reported that these individuals experience higher rates of retention and lower grade point averages, college enrolment, and socioeconomic status. Children with ADHD are typically 2.5 times more likely to engage in off-task behavior, which was suggested by Junod and colleagues to be the most influential variable associated with academic difficulties.

It is important to acknowledge that too much emphasis on academic engagement can have adverse outcomes on learning. An overemphasis on engagement as a teaching strategy can create an environment of mock participation, within which students pretend to be on-task but are not engaged in learning. While mock participation may achieve one's desire for students to stay on task behaviorally, it can negatively impact academic achievement as it lowers students' rate of emotional engagement (Slavin, 2003).

MEASURING ON-TASK BEHAVIOR

Direct observation can be used to assess levels of on- and off-task behavior. The observation might be conducted by a teacher, teacher's aid, behavior specialist, or school psychologist. Two considerations essential to obtaining accurate data are that (a) the observation be discrete and conducted in a way that does not alter the natural environment and (b) the behavior being observed must be concrete and measurable (O'Neil et al., 1997).

Two observation techniques often used to assess engaged time are frequency (the number of times a behavior occurs) and duration (the length of time that the behavior is expressed from beginning to end) strategies. For low frequency academic engagement behaviors event or frequency data is the easiest to collect and can be done as instruction occurs. For example, a teacher can tally the number of occurrences of a behavior throughout any given week, day, hour, or minute, and a behavioral rate calculated by dividing the number of occurrences by the duration of the observation. Examples of off-task behaviors often assessed via frequency data are calling out during instruction, number of worksheets completed, and getting out of one's seat. Duration recordings measure the length of time a behavior occurs. This type of recording is best for behaviors that occur over a period of time and have a clear beginning and ending. It requires the observer to attend to the behavior throughout its duration, typically with a stop watch. Examples of off-task behaviors often assessed via duration data are moderate temper tantrums and aggressive outbursts (Browning-Wright & Gurman, 2001).

Another common strategy for measuring on-task behaviors that occur relatively frequently is momentary interval time sampling. This technique entails dividing the observational period (usually 20 minutes) into equal time intervals (e.g., one minute intervals) and recording what the student is doing at each time interval. When measuring engaged time behaviors are typically coded using one of the following four categories: on-task (O), passively off-task (P), verbally off-task (V), or actively off-task (A). Once the observation is complete, the examined behavior is divided by the number of observation periods to obtain an estimate of on- and off-task behavior. Examples of off-task behaviors often assessed via momentary interval time sampling include talking to peers, walking around the classroom, or tapping a pencil.

BETWEEN AND WITHIN TASK TRANSITIONS

Transitioning from one activity to the next, although essential and inevitable, can negatively impact a student's engagement in academics (Martella et al., 2003). Effective transitions, either between-tasks or within-tasks, can have a positive effect on engaged learning as they increase allocated time and decrease the opportunity for disruptive behavior (Lee, 2006). Between-task transitions are tasks that include moving from one subject to another (e.g., math to reading, lunch to reading, or music to science; Martella et al., 2003). According to Slavin (2003) maintaining smoothness is important in decreasing the amount of time spent between tasks. Poor smoothness between tasks can cause abrupt breaks, possibly increasing disruptive behavior; instruction should be as seamless and sequential as possible. Within-tasks transitions are discrete activities that happen within a given task (e.g., passing out math worksheets during a math lesson or passing back graded papers during silent reading; Martella et al., 2003). Teachers can keep students on-task during within-task transitions by maintaining the momentum during the task. Momentum "refers to the avoidance of interruptions or slowdowns" once an activity has started (Slavin, 2003, p. 372).

In a literature review by Lee (2006), behavior momentum was examined in relation to facilitating between and within task transitions. It was found that when students are presented with several high-probability requests (i.e., those that evoke a high probability of compliance) prior to a low-probability request (i.e., those that evoke a low probability of compliance), task initiation increased and became more efficient. For example, when transitioning from silent reading to writing, a teacher could ask the students to take out a piece of paper, take out a pencil, and write their name on the paper immediately before asking the students to write about what they read; the momentum generated by positive responses to the high-probability request carried over to the low-probability request. The same idea can be used to facilitate within-task transitions in that several high-probability requests can be woven within low-probability requests to establish and maintain behavior momentum.

To alleviate the negative effects of transitions, teachers should be knowledgeable of strategies to maintain on-task behavior. Examples of such include the following:

Establish a consistent routine and illustrate such via a visual daily schedule (Brock, 2005).

Make lessons engaging and use materials that are interesting and motivating (Brock, 2005).

Reinforce on-task behavior and work completion (Brock, 2005).

Ensure that challenging lessons include relatively easy tasks (Lee, 2006).

Provide students with reminders as transitions approach; reminders can become more frequent as the transition approaches.

To maintain momentum and smoothness, avoid stopping instruction for longer than a minute to deal with missing papers, pencils, or other mild off-task behaviors (Slavin, 2003).

To decrease the amount of total class time spent transitioning, ask students to make transitions as a group and not individually (Slavin, 2003).

SEE ALSO *Behavioral Objectives; Feedback in Learning.*

BIBLIOGRAPHY

Brock, S. E. (2005). Time on-task. In S. W. Lee (Ed.), *Encyclopedia of school psychology* (pp. 567–568). Thousand Oaks, CA: Sage.

Browning-Wright, D., & Gurman, H. (2001). *Positive intervention for serious behavior problems: Best practices in implementing the positive behavioral intervention regulations.* Sacramento: California Department of Education.

Greenwood, C., Horton, B., & Utley, C. (2002). Academic engagement: Current perspectives on research and practice. *School Psychology Review, 31,* 328–349.

Junod, R., DuPaul, G., Jitendra, A., Volpe, R., Cleary, K. (2006). Classroom observations of students with and without

ADHD: Differences across types of engagement. *Journal of School Psychology, 44,* 87–104.

Lee, D. (2006). Facilitating transitions between and within academic tasks: An application of behavioral momentum. *Remedial and Special Education, 27,* 312–317.

Marks, H. (2000). Student engagement in instructional activity: Patterns in elementary, middle and high school years. *American Educational Research Journal, 37,* 153–184.

Martella, R., Nelson, J., & Marchand-Martella, N. (2003). *Managing disruptive behaviors in the schools.* Boston: Pearson Education.

O'Neill, R. E., Horner, R. H., Albin, R. W., Sprague, J. R., Storey, K., & Newton, J. S. (1997) *Functional assessment and program development for problem behavior: A practical guide.* (2nd ed.). Pacific Grove, CA: Brooks/Cole.

Slavin, R. (2003). *Educational psychology: Theory and practice.* Boston: Pearson Education.

VanDeWeghe, R. (2006). Research matters: What is engaged learning? *English Journal, 95*(3), 88–91.

Ellie Martinez
Stephen E. Brock

TOKEN ECONOMIES

SEE *Classroom Management: Token Economies.*

TOM

SEE *Theory of Mind.*

TRANSFER

Can humans benefit from their prior experience when attempting to solve novel problems? Transfer research suggests the complexity within this question. This entry describes the various complexities in studying transfer. First competing definitions of transfer are described, and then the discussion turns to the dimensions along which transfer may occur and the types of evidence that different researchers argue is needed to demonstrate the existence of transfer. Obstacles that prevent some from transferring their experience to new situations are described next, and the interventions that have been undertaken to surmount them. Finally, dominant approaches to studying and conceptualizing transfer are discussed, such as the preparation-for-future-learning view, information processing, and situated cognition approaches.

DEFINING TRANSFER

One definition of transfer is: "the carrying over of an act or way of acting from one performance to another" (Wood-

worth & Schlosberg, 1954, p. 734). Another definition is: "the ability to extend what has been learned in one context to new contexts" (Bransford, Brown, & Cocking, 1999, p. 39). A third definition is: "a situation where information learned at one point in time influences performance on information encountered at a later point in time" (Royer, Mestre, and Dufresne, 2005). The broadest of these conceptions suggests that transfer should be a widespread phenomenon: past learning must affect future performance frequently, and, indeed, formal schooling is predicated on this assumption. However, others disagree. Detterman points out: "Transfer has been one of the most actively studied phenomena in psychology ... Reviewers are in almost total agreement that little transfer occurs" (1993, p. 8). Detterman goes on to suggest, therefore, that the educational implications of the assumption of transfer are misplaced: "Cognitive psychologists, and other people who should know better, continue to advocate a philosophy of education that is totally lacking in empirical support" (1993, p. 16). One wonders who is correct.

The disparity lies, in part, in what qualifies as successful transfer, both in terms of the extent and nature of the initial learning experience and in terms of the novelty and difficulty of the transfer test. The history of this debate goes back over a century to the debate between two famous early psychologists, Edward L. Thorndike (1874–1949) and Charles Judd (1873–1946), about the implications of their findings. Beginning around 1900, Thorndike and his colleagues reported a series of experiments finding poor or uneven transfer across tasks, despite dependence upon similar operations. For example, after training subjects to estimate the area of certain geometric shapes (e.g., 100 sq. cm rectangles), they did not transfer their learning to solve other problems concerning estimating geometric area, such as estimating the area of other rectangles and triangles (see Thorndike & Woodworth, 1901). By contrast, in Judd's 1908 experiment, boys throwing darts at a submerged target, adapted better to a change in target depth if they were given an explanation of the principle of optical refraction that made the underwater target appear to be at a different depth.

This disparity in experimental evidence regarding transfer success has continued into the 2000s. For example, Gick and Holyoak (1980) employed an analogical transfer experiment using the classic Dunker tumor radiation problem (how to destroy cancer cells within the body without damaging surrounding flesh by converging on the diseased cells from many directions so as to spread out and dilute the potentially damaging effects of the rays) and an analogous military situation (troops spread over many roads to avoid detonating weight-sensitive mines). They found that if subjects were told to think about the training problem, when tackling the transfer test, transfer was superior. By contrast, Reed, Ernst, and

Banerji (1974) failed to demonstrate transfer on most performance measures, using the missionary-cannibal problem (how to get safely across a river in a limited-capacity boat without having the cannibals in the group ever outnumber the missionaries) and an analogous problem substituting wives and jealous husbands. Judd's underwater target findings suggest that a theoretical understanding of principles may be important for successful transfer, a claim supported by Brown's extensive body of work on transfer which also points to the need to foster theoretical understanding, though not necessarily by explicit instruction (e.g., Brown & Kane, 1988; Brown, 1989). (The above study by Gick and Holyoak also points to the need to foster a connection between the training and transfer materials.)

Given that the world outside of psychology experiments does not generally tell problem solvers which aspects of their experience are likely to be most relevant to current problem-solving situations, it could be argued that spontaneity is a requirement for true transfer and, therefore, that this work shows that such transfer is difficult to obtain. Further, much of the evidence for transfer described above is dismissed by some (e.g., Detterman, 1993) as demonstrating only near transfer, in which the transfer test is so close in some way to the training situation as to be trivial. This viewpoint argues that such near transfer does not count as true transfer because the situations in which society values transfer, such as from school learning to work performance, require far transfer, which is rarely obtained. However, others dispute this gloomy conclusion, claiming that training can enhance general thinking skills, which would constitute far transfer of learning (see, e.g., Perkins & Grotzer, 1997; Halpern, 1998). In sum, as of 2008, "There is little agreement in the scholarly community about the nature of transfer, the extent to which it occurs, and the nature of its underlying mechanisms" (Barnett & Ceci, 2002, p. 612).

DIFFERENT DIMENSIONS ALONG WHICH TRANSFER CAN OCCUR

The conflicting evidence concerning whether transfer occurs can be better understood if the disputed claims are dissected and the findings categorized according to the contextual and content dimensions along which transfer of learning has been assessed. Barnett and Ceci (2002) detailed a taxonomy of 6 context and 3 content dimensions along which transfer might be assessed and along which studies have suggested transfer success may differ, with near transfer (transfer to more similar contexts) generally resulting in easier transfer than far transfer (to more dissimilar contexts). The contextual dimensions include knowledge domain (e.g., physics vs. math), physical context (e.g., school vs. home), temporal context (e.g., in 5 minutes vs.

in a month), functional context (e.g., as an academic exercise vs. a task for earning money), social context (e.g., individual vs. group) and modality (e.g., written vs. verbal).

The content dimensions along which transfer success may vary involve the nature of the skill to be transferred (e.g., rote procedure vs. abstract principle), the performance change measured for this skill (e.g., percentage of correct answers vs. speed of response), and the memory demands of the transfer task used to measure it (e.g., spontaneous recall vs. prompted recognition). For example, as suggested by Gick and Holyoak's 1980 work, discussed earlier, transfer assessed after prompting may be easier to achieve than transfer assessed by spontaneous recall. Transfer may also be more likely when "learning contexts are framed as part of a larger ongoing intellectual conversation in which students are actively involved" (Engle, 2006, p. 451). Engle conducted a detailed case study of fifth graders in a Community of Learners classroom and suggested that future research should take into account not just the content to be transferred but also the framing of the wider learning context. The use of the terms *successful transfer* and *far transfer* without specifying and discriminating between these various dimensions has been the source of much confusion.

OBSTACLES TO SUCCESSFUL TRANSFER

Successful transfer requires encoding and subsequently identifying and retrieving relevant knowledge, followed by application of the knowledge to the transfer problem. Problems can occur at any or all of these stages. For example, knowledge may be adequately encoded but a student may fail to recognize its relevance. Successful near transfer combined with unsuccessful far transfer could be due to either a failure to recognize the relevance of the information, a failure to adapt the knowledge to the new situation, or encoding of such a specific interpretation of the initial learning situation that it is not applicable to the new situation. For example, Schliemann and Nunes (1990) found that school math class learning did not transfer to a fishing problem to which the same mathematical concepts could be applied (e.g., calculating proportions). This failure could be because the math class taught the material in a superficial manner, which did not lead to an understanding of the principles underlying the mathematical routines involved but merely showed the students how to mechanistically reproduce a very specific arithmetic procedure. Alternatively, it could be that the relevant knowledge was encoded, but the subjects failed to recognize the relevance of that knowledge to the fishing questions, perhaps because that knowledge was, for them, embedded in their knowledge of the school situation. This kind of situation-specificity was explored by Lave (1988) in her classic work with supermarket shoppers, which found a lack of evidence for

PERSPECTIVES ON TRANSFER

The process of prior knowledge influencing the way students solve a present task is known as *transfer*. The traditional view of transfer is known as *direct application*, where old knowledge is automatically applied to new tasks. So if a student is given the "know-how" to perform a mathematical procedure in an algebra class, such skills should transfer to chemistry class if needed. However, transfer fails to happen as often as we expect. Direct application theorists have viewed transfer as a relatively rare phenomenon but believe that transfer is more likely to happen when the new task resembles the original one.

Those who favor *high-road transfer* take a different perspective. From this view, transfer occurs when students are made aware that new knowledge or skills are in their "mental toolbox." In the algebra example, students learning a mathematical procedure might be told by their teacher, "Please keep in mind that this mathematical procedure will be used in your science class today." Later that day when students are solving a chemistry problem which calls for this procedure, the science teacher might remind them to "think about the skill you learned in math class today." Proponents of the high-road transfer perspective believe that a student's awareness of how his or her skills can be applied in other situations makes all the difference in whether or not transfer occurs.

These different perspectives have led to different methods for testing the occurrence of transfer, and

subsequently, different conditions under which transfer occurs. Those endorsing high-road transfer would say that students must correct their misconceptions through inquiry and discussion with their teacher; giving students a take-home message to be generally applied in other domains. Advocates of direct application transfer believe students must practice a skill over and over in similar scenarios, until the behavior becomes second nature. This way, there is little need for deliberation when confronted with a new, yet similar task.

The *situated cognition* offers a both an explanation and a potential solution for past difficulties in demonstrating and explaining transfer. Whereas repetition often may be initially helpful in mastering a given skill, students often maintain a narrow perception concerning when and where the skill should be employed. In other words, a strategy that has worked to solve a problem may only seem applicable in the context in which the student originally learned the strategy. For instance, students in a math class might see a particular algebraic formal as being used only for mathematics, because they never had the opportunity to use it in another context (e.g. science). From a situated cognition perspective, this problem can be aided by advising teachers to present information in various contexts and to switch the activities so that students will grasp the skill while thinking critically, and retaining basic strategies and themes.

DeLeon L. Gray

transfer from school math to shopping; despite knowing how to carry out elementary arithmetical operations on a math test, the same procedures were not used to determine unit prices at the market.

Some efforts to resolve these issues have focused on hypothesizing about the precise components of knowledge encoded in the initial training and mapping them onto the components of the transfer problem. Singley and Anderson's 1989 production rule approach to modeling computer programming learning is of this type. However, applying such approaches to modeling complex and less well structured learning situations, or those

in which similarities are abstract and less apparent, may be difficult.

Transfer processes may also be affected by motivation, which could influence initial learning, initiation of transfer attempts, spontaneity, and persistence in transfer tasks. Studies have shown that having mastery goals consistently predicts cognitive engagement and, in particular, results in activities such as deep processing and metacognitive strategies or insights into the workings of one's own cognitive systems (Pugh & Bergin, 2006). However, engagement does not always predict achievement, though this may be because of the kinds of achievement measures used, which may not reflect the deep processing associated with transfer

(Pugh & Bergin, 2006). Performance goals may have damaging effects on engagement and transfer because a focus on avoiding a display of incompetence hampers deep processing and a focus on trying to do well shows mixed results. For example, a study by Bereby-Meyer and Kaplan (2005) found that, for a group of grade-school children, the performance-approach goal condition did not differ from the control condition when the goal was induced before encoding and performed worse than the control when the goal was induced after encoding but prior to the transfer test.

INSTRUCTIONAL INTERVENTIONS THAT PROMOTE TRANSFER

Experimental studies have generally found that learning experiences that promote deep, theoretical understanding are most conducive to transfer to different domains (see Barnett & Ceci, 2002, for a review). Deep understanding can be facilitated by encouraging learners to compare and contrast a variety of examples and by requiring them to explain and justify their decisions. A number of researchers have reached similar conclusions and have investigated ways in which training can promote such understanding. Generally, these approaches focus on getting the learners to engage with the training materials at a deep, structural level. Catrambone and Holyoak (1989) used comparison questions with multiple examples, which improved transfer, for example. Similarly, Cummins (1992) found that inter-problem processing (focus on comparison questions) promoted more transfer than intra-problem processing (focus on specific wording or details). Needham and Begg (1991) encouraged their subjects to fruitfully engage with learning materials by using problem-oriented training (e.g., trying to explain) in contrast to memory-oriented training. However, it is not obvious what deep theoretical understanding really means. Wagner (2006) has suggested that it may not necessarily be more abstract but instead may be "increasingly complex sensitivity to the contextual differences ... encountered" (p. 4).

Halpern, Hansen, and Riefer (1990) suggested that hard work pays off in their study that enhanced subjects' ability to draw inferences from a studied passage by including far analogies in their training materials, presumably encouraging a focus on deep, structural processing. Their subjects did not derive the same benefit from a near analogy, which the authors suggest may be because they did not have to work as hard to make sense of it. Similarly, Reed and Saavedra (1986) showed that a task involving more concrete and effortful processing, termed the *discovery method* (running a computer simulation with feedback), improved performance more than a passive task (observing a computer-generated graph).

The merits of the discovery method of learning have been the subject of much debate. Chen and Klahr (1999) studied children's learning of the scientific method, specifically the "control of variables strategy" (the idea that one can figure out whether something is causal by changing it while holding all else the same). They compared training using probing questions with or without direct instruction and found that direct instruction was necessary for learning and transfer. Later, Klahr and Nigam (2004) compared the effectiveness of direct instruction and discovery learning on learning and transfer. They concluded that more children learned from direct instruction, challenging the "widely accepted claim in the science- and mathematics-education community ... that discovery learning, as opposed to direct instruction, is the best way to get deep and lasting understanding" (p. 661). However, Kuhn (2005, 2006) disputes this conclusion, suggesting that "direct instruction appears to be neither a necessary nor sufficient condition for robust acquisition or for maintenance over time" (2006, p. 384) based on her research. Klahr (2005) disagrees with her interpretation of her findings, instead stating that "they show how difficult it is to achieve long-term transfer with anything less than extremely detailed and direct instruction" (p. 871). Further research is needed to resolve this debate.

PREPARATION FOR FUTURE LEARNING

The constructivist view of learning argues that the challenge is for learners to construct new knowledge for themselves and that one factor which determines their ability to do so is their level of prior knowledge (Bransford et al., 2000). For example, Schwartz and Bransford (1998) demonstrated that preparatory work, such as generating distinctions between contrasting cases in psychological experiments, enhanced future learning from a lecture, as measured by transfer one week later. They proposed a distinction between this preparation-for-future-learning view and a sequestered approach which does not provide access to outside sources of information, suggesting that much classical transfer research is from the latter paradigm and advocating for the former. Sequestered problem solving is inadequate as an assessment of learning because it artificially restricts the problem solver's access to other sources of information which are an integral part of problem solving. Their preparation-for-future-learning view advocates exploration of how past learning prepares the learner for future learning in contrast to the sequestered problem-solving approach. However, learning and transfer could theoretically be assessed in an information-poor or an information-rich environment (sequestered or not), independent of the transfer measure used (problem-solving performance or enhanced future learning).

The broader concept of transfer suggested by the preparation-for-future-learning view fits within the tradition of studying more generalized outcomes such as the development of practical intelligence (see Sternberg & Kalmar, 1998) and metacognitive and critical thinking skills. As stated by the renowned transfer researcher, the late Ann Brown, "Effective learners operate best when they have insight into their own strengths and weaknesses and access to their own repertoires of strategies for learning. For the past 20 years or so, this type of knowledge and control over thinking has been termed *metacognition*" (Brown, 1997, p. 411). Halpern's 1998 critical thinking program is an attempt to boost such general reasoning skills: "to promote the learning of transcontextual thinking skills and the awareness of and the ability to direct one's own thinking and learning" (p. 451). Halpern's program of instruction builds skills such as verbal reasoning, argument analysis, hypothesis testing, probability, and decision-making. Training also aims to promote transfer by focusing on awareness of which skills to use and providing practice with a broad range of examples, supported by feedback and probing questions. One of the goals is to develop the rich, interconnected knowledge structures—the deep understanding that Brown (1989) suggested is important for transfer. In line with this view, the National Research Council's Committee on the Development of the Science of Learning (Bransford, Brown, & Cocking, 1999) concluded that transfer can be facilitated by training students in metacognitive awareness through activities that encourage introspective awareness and self-monitoring.

DIFFERENT THEORETICAL PERSPECTIVES TREATMENT OF TRANSFER

Some cognitive scientists have studied much more tightly specified learning and transfer processes. Holland and colleagues (1986) described the mechanism of analogical transfer, in terms of four steps: "encoding of the target, selection of a source analog, mapping of the source and target, and transfer of knowledge to the target by generation of new rules" (p. 307). Each step can then be broken down further, for example, encoding involves representing the problem in terms of the initial state, goal state, relevant operators, and path constraints. Singley and Anderson (1989; Anderson 1993) took this information processing approach further and proposed that cognitive skills can be understood in terms of production rules which represent knowledge, which can then be instantiated in, for example, computerized tutors for teaching programming skills.

Such decontextualised approaches have been criticized (see, e.g., Lave, 1988) for neglecting the embeddedness of learning and knowledge in context. Lave has advocated a strong view of this "situated cognition" hypothesis and suggests that learning is inextricably entwined with the context in which it was acquired: "Cognition . . . is distributed—

. . . not divided among—mind, body, activity and culturally organized settings (which include other actors)" (p. 1). More nuanced interpretations suggest that aspects of context may moderate transferability (Barnett & Ceci, 2002).

Lobato (2003) distinguished between what she called the classical transfer approach and actor-oriented transfer and suggested that the apparent failure to transfer in many traditional experiments was, in fact, a failure on the part of the experimenters to adopt the perspective of the learner. On this view, success or failure on the particular outcome measures the researcher had in mind is immaterial; what matters is how the learners make connections between the new and old situations. This approach often uses case studies as an investigative method, either alone (see, e.g., Lobato & Siebert, 2002) or in conjunction with group data (see, e.g., Dufresne et al., 2005). Lobato (2006) contrasts the classical transfer approach, of using highly controlled experiments and statistical analysis to assess whether particular learning opportunities result in predetermined differences on carefully designed transfer assessments, with her actor-oriented approach, using ethnographic methods to search for effects of prior learning on novel situations. This method increases the likelihood of capturing subtle effects on future performance that may not have been the intended lesson to be learned, but that may nevertheless provide insight into the mechanisms underlying the transfer process and generate hypotheses for further investigations. She emphasizes that generalization involves the construction of relationships rather than simply the reproduction of existing relations.

However, the implication that traditional transfer researchers have ignored the wider effects of prior learning and focused exclusively on a narrow, experimenter-imposed measure of transfer is somewhat misleading. Traditional researchers have often devised multiple assessments of learning outcomes and explored the consequences of many experimental manipulations to capture the richness of the learning and transfer processes, as well as used microgenetic methods to understand the step-by-step processes of learning (see, e.g., Brown & Kane, 1988; Chen & Klahr, 1999).

BIBLIOGRAPHY

Barnett, S. M., & Ceci, S. J. (2002). When and where do we apply what we learn? A taxonomy for far transfer. *Psychological Bulletin, 128*(4), 612–637.

Bereby-Meyer, Y., & Kaplan, A. (2005). Motivational influences on transfer of problem-solving strategies. *Contemporary Educational Psychology, 30,* 1–22.

Bransford, J. D., Brown, A. L,. Cocking, R. R. (eds). (2000*). How people learn: Brain, mind, experience, and school.* (Expanded ed.). Washington, D.C., National Academy Press.

Brown, A. L. (1989). Analogical learning and transfer: What develops? In S. Vosniadou & A. Ortony (Eds.), *Similarity and analogical reasoning.* New York: Cambridge University Press.

Brown, A. L. (1997). Transforming schools into communities of thinking and learning about serious matters. *American Psychologist, 52*(4), 399–413.

Brown, A. L., & Kane, M. J. (1988). Preschool children can learn to transfer: Learning to learn and learning from example. *Cognitive Psychology, 20*(4), 493–523.

Catrambone, R., & Holyoak, K. J. (1989). Overcoming contextual limitations on problem-solving transfer. *Journal of Experimental Psychology: Learning, Memory, and Cognition, 15*(6), 1147–1156.

Chen, Z., & Klahr, D. (1999). All other things being equal: Acquisition and transfer of the Control of Variables Strategy. *Child Development, 70*(5), 1098–1120.

Cummins, D. D. (1992). Role of analogical reasoning in the induction of problem categories. *Journal of Experimental Psychology: Learning, Memory, and Cognition, 18*(5), 1103–1124.

Dean, D., & Kuhn, D. (2007). Direct instruction vs. discovery: The long view. *Science Education, 91*(3), 384–397.

Detterman, D. K. (1993). The case for the prosecution: Transfer as an epiphenomenon. In D. K. Detterman & R. J. Sternberg (Eds.), *Transfer on trial: Intelligence, cognition, and instruction* (pp. 1–24). Norwood, NJ: Ablex.

Dufresne, R., et al. (2005). Knowledge representation and coordination in the transfer process. In J. P. Mestre (Ed.), *Transfer of learning from a modern multidisciplinary perspective.* Greenwich, CT: Information Age.

Engle, R.-A. (2006). Framing Interactions to Foster Generative Learning: A Situative Explanation of Transfer in a Community of Learners Classroom. *Journal of the Learning Sciences, 15*(4), 451–498.

Gick, M. L., & Holyoak. K. J. (1980). Analogical problem solving. *Cognitive Psychology, 12*(3), 306–355.

Halpern, D. F. (1998). Teaching critical thinking for transfer across domains. *American Psychologist, 53*(4), 449–455.

Halpern, D. F., Hansen, C. & Riefer, D. (1990). Analogies as an aid to understanding and memory. *Journal of Educational Psychology 82*(2), 298–305.

Holland, J. H., et al. (1986). *Induction: Processes of inference, learning, and discovery.* Cambridge, MA: MIT Press.

Judd, C. H. (1908). The relation of special training to general intelligence. *Educational Review, 36*, 28–42.

Klahr, D. (2005). Early science instruction: Addressing fundamental issues. *Psychological Science, 16*(11), 871–872.

Klahr, D., & Nigam, M. (2004). The equivalence of learning paths in early science instruction: Effects of direct instruction and discovery learning. *Psychological Science, 15*(10), 661–667.

Kuhn, D. (2005). What needs to be mastered in mastery of scientific method? *Psychological Science, 16*(11), 873–874.

Lave, J. (Ed.). (1988). *Cognition in practice: Mind, mathematics and culture in everyday life.* Cambridge, UK: Cambridge University Press.

Lobato, J. (2003). How design experiments can inform a rethinking of transfer and vice versa. *Educational Researcher, 32*(1), 17–20.

Lobato, J. (2006). Alternative perspectives on the transfer of learning: History, issues, and challenges for future research. *Journal of the Learning Sciences, 15*(4), 431–449.

Lobato, J., & Siebert, D. (2002). Quantitative reasoning in a reconceived view of transfer. *Journal of Mathematical Behavior, 21*(1), 87–116.

Mestre, J. P. (Ed.). (2005). *Transfer of learning from a modern multidisciplinary perspective: Current Perspectives on cognition, learning, and instruction.* Greenwich, CT: Information Age.

Needham, D. R., & Begg, I. M. (1991). Problem-oriented training promotes spontaneous analogical transfer: Memory-oriented training promotes memory for training. *Memory and Cognition, 19*(6), 543–557.

Perkins, D. N., & Grotzer, T. A. (1997). Teaching intelligence. *American Psychologist, 52*(10), 1125–1133.

Pugh, K. J., & Bergin, D. A. (2006). Motivational influences on transfer. *Educational Psychologist, 41*(3), 147–160.

Reed, S. K., Ernst, G. W., & Banerji, R. (1974). The role of analogy in transfer between similar problem states. *Cognitive Psychology, 6*(3), 436–450.

Reed, S. K., & Saavedra, N. C. (1986). A comparison of computation, discovery, and graph procedures for improving students' conception of average speed. *Cognition and Instruction, 3*(1), 31–62.

Royer, J. M., Mestre, J. P., & Dufresne, R. J. (2005). Introduction: Framing the transfer problem. In J. P. Mestre (Ed.), *Transfer of learning from a modern multidisciplinary perspective.* Greenwich, CT: Information Age.

Schliemann, A. D., & Nunes, T. (1990). A situated schema of proportionality. *British Journal of Developmental Psychology, 8*(3), 259–268.

Schwartz, D. L., & Bransford, J. D. (1998). A time for telling. *Cognition and Instruction, 16*(4), 475–522.

Singley, M. K., & Anderson, J. R. (1989). *The transfer of cognitive skill.* Cambridge, MA: Harvard University Press.

Thorndike, E. L., & Woodworth, R. S. (1901). The influence of improvement in one mental function upon the efficiency of other functions. (I). *Psychological Review, 8*(3), 247–261.

Wagner, J. F. (2006). Transfer in pieces. *Cognition and Instruction, 24*(1), 1–71.

Williams, W. M., Blythe, T., White, N., Li, J., Sternberg, R. J., & Gardner, H. (1996). *Practical intelligence for school.* New York: Harper Collins.

Susan M. Barnett
Stephen J. Ceci

TRIARCHIC THEORY OF INTELLIGENCE

Webster (1996) defines intelligence as the "capacity for learning, reasoning, understanding, and similar forms of mental activity" (p. 990). This definition implies that intelligence is both multifaceted (i.e., captures many aspects of mental ability) and reflective of differences in capacity, ability, and aptitude among individuals. Yet this definition is not necessarily embraced by all scientists. In fact, there is no consensus on the definition of intelligence among professionals who study it (e.g., psychologists, educators, and computer scientists), and many attempts have been made to define and generate supporting theories about exactly what constitutes intelligence. Among the many theories of intelligence are those that define intelligence as a cognitive "system." The overarching assumption of these systemic theories is that intelligence is not a single entity but a multifaceted structure and that traditional definitions of intelligence have been excessively narrow. The quest for theories that reflect the variety of ways in which humans think, learn, and adapt to their environment was initiated in the early 1980s in the United States. Most notable among systemic theories of intelligence is Robert Sternberg's *Triarchic Theory of Intelligence* (Sternberg, 1996). Other examples are Howard Gardner's *Theory of Multiple Intelligences* (Gardner, 1993) and the theory of *Emotional Intelligence*, initially presented in the scientific literature by Peter Salovey and Jack Mayer (Salovey & Mayer, 1990) and popularized by Daniel Goleman (Goleman, 1995).

Sternberg's Triarchic Theory of Intelligence was developed about the same time as Gardner's Theory of Multiple Intelligences. Rejecting traditionally narrow definitions of intelligence, Sternberg defined intelligence as mental activity central to one's life in real-world environments; individuals "succeed" in life when they use mental skills to adapt to, select, and shape external environments. Correspondingly, in the late 1990s, Sternberg changed the name of the theory to the *Theory of Successful Intelligence*. As per its original name, the theory comprises three types of intelligence: *analytical* (also referred to as componential); *practical* (also referred to as contextual) and *creative* (also referred to as experiential). *Analytical intelligence* is evoked while analyzing, evaluating, criticizing, reasoning, and judging. *Practical intelligence* is used while implying, implementing, and using. *Creative intelligence* is manifested while discovering, inventing, dealing with novelty, and creating. The theory predicts that "intelligent" people will identify their strengths and weaknesses, make the most of their strengths and compensate for their weaknesses. Individuals are not limited to strength in only one of the three areas; both integrated and uneven profiles of intelligence are possible.

Sternberg's work on the Theory of Successful Intelligence unfolded in three phases. The first phase was the validation of the fundamental importance of different abilities and the collection of supporting evidence from different cultures and societies. This work took place in a number of countries (e.g., China, India, Jamaica, Kenya, Russia, Taiwan, Tanzania, the United States, and Zambia) and in a variety of settings, both educational and occupational. These studies provided compelling evidence that the focus on traditionally-defined cognitive abilities (i.e., interpreting intelligence through the so-called *general factor* of intelligence, or *g*, as something common to all tests of intelligence) underestimates the importance of practical and creative abilities in human cultures. In one study, for example, Sternberg and his colleagues found that knowledge of herbal medicine among rural Kenyan children was perceived by adults in their communities as equal to or

more indicative of cognitive competence and, thus, as valuable or more highly valued, given the ecological conditions of a relatively isolated African village, than the children's performance on conventional tests of *g* (such as the Raven Matrices) or their achievement at school. A set of studies has been conducted to investigate implicit theories of intelligence in laypeople around the world. People from different cultures were found to differ widely in their emphasis of what they view as intelligence behavior. For example, even in the United States, people in some cultures, such as Latinos, value and emphasize social functioning facets of intelligence more than other cultures, such as Anglos. Around the globe, people also differ in their taste for when and how intelligence behaviors should be manifested. For example, Taiwanese Chinese appear to value a sensitivity to when one's intelligence should be shown off and when it should be concealed.

The second phase included studies designed to develop valid and reliable methods to assess analytical, practical, and creative abilities. This domain of research combined multiple efforts to design different instruments that can capture these abilities in both educational and employment settings. As an illustration, Sternberg and his colleagues worked with the U.S. Army to quantify the practical abilities of U.S. officers by capturing, describing. and measuring their "tacit" knowledge of military leadership so that this knowledge could be integrated into the training of military cadets preparing for future leadership roles. Similarly, the theory has been realized in the creation of different assessment instruments. An early version of such an instrument was referred to as The Sternberg Triarchic Abilities Test, or the STAT. The STAT had three subtests, analytical, practical, and creative, and contained items in two formats, multiple choice and essays. The latest generation of this instrument is referred to as the Aurora Battery.

The battery is designed for children in elementary and middle schools and captures their analytical, practical, and creative abilities in the domains of dealing with and manipulating words, numbers, and images (i.e., tapping into verbal, mathematical, and spatial representations). The Aurora Battery contains four components, engaging multiple methods and multiple informants. Specifically, it includes (a) group-administered assessment of abilities, which are captured by multiple-choice, right/wrong responses, and open-ended items; (b) a teacher rating scale; (c) a parent interview; and (d) a portfolio-based observation schedule (i.e., a collection of one-on-one assessments in which children are given a chance to generate specific products in situations modeling real life).

The third phase was designed to apply the Theory of Successful Intelligence to the educational environment. Sternberg and his colleagues completed multiple studies in U.S. schools in a variety of subject matters across

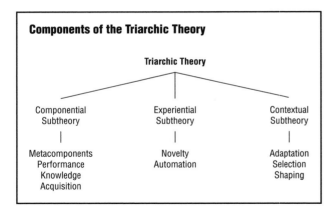

Components of the Triarchic Theory

Triarchic Theory

Componential
Subtheory

Experiential
Subtheory

Contextual
Subtheory

Metacomponents
Performance
Knowledge
Acquisition

Novelty
Automation

Adaptation
Selection
Shaping

ILLUSTRATION BY GGS INFORMATION SERVICES. CENGAGE LEARNING, GALE.

multiple grade levels. The main thrust of this research was to demonstrate the value of multiple pedagological approaches that ensure that children are taught in ways that challenge and develop their analytical, practical, and creative abilities. Pedagogical intervention studies based on the theory were carried out across different levels of schooling (elementary, middle, and high) and across a number of academic subjects (e.g., mathematics, science, language arts, social studies). In one of the largest studies, a triarchic theory-based curriculum was administered to a few thousand children enrolled in fourth grade in various locations in the United States. The curriculum was developed for language arts, mathematics, and sciences; it was based on the national standards and, prior to implementation, was adapted to specifics of requirements of the various states and districts where it was delivered. The study included three other comparison groups, all with a large number of children: (a) a group of children to whom a traditional (i.e., "treatment-as-usual") curriculum was delivered; (b) a group of children to whom a curriculum based on modern theories of memory was administered; and (c) a group of children who were taught with a curriculum based on theories of critical thinking. In each case, the study group was followed for approximately six months.

Although the profile of results is complex and variable for each domain of studies, there is a strong indication of an overall advantage of triarchic-based teaching. In general, this and similar studies have demonstrated the benefit of this approach: students not only developed competencies in thinking analytically, creatively, and practically, but also improved their performance on standardized tests. Capitalizing on empirical evidence obtained in his research studies, Sternberg has brought his work on the Theory of Successful Intelligence to a policy level. As the Director of the PACE (Psychology of Abilities, Competencies, and Expertise) Center at Yale Uni-

versity, Sternberg worked with the College Board on developing a triarchic assessment, referred to as the Rainbow Assessment, augmenting the SAT. As Dean of Arts and Sciences at Tufts University, within the framework of the Kaleidoscope Project, he ensured that, in addition to scores on standardized tests, assessments of creative and practical abilities are considered in student admission decisions.

Sternberg's theories have two main complements in the literature. The first is Howard Gardner's Theory of Multiple Intelligences. This theory (also referred to as the *MI* theory) was developed at roughly the same time as Sternberg's theory and also assumes the presence of a number of distinct forms of intelligence. Individuals possess these types of intelligence in varying degrees, which establishes their unique cognitive profiles. Like Sternberg's, Gardner's theory is based on the argument that traditional definitions of intelligence do not capture the wide variety of abilities humans display. To support his argument, Gardner analyzed case studies of individuals with unusual talents, such as child prodigies in music or mathematics; reviewed neuropsychological evidence on specialized areas of the brain that process particular types of information; and integrated evolutionary theory and results of psychometric tests.

According to Gardner, there are eight primary forms of intelligence: *linguistic* (manifested in dealing with spoken or written words); *musical* (demonstrated in dealing with rhythm, music and hearing); *logical-mathematical* (invoked while reasoning inductively or deductively and dealing with abstractions and numbers); *spatial* (engaged in vision and spatial judgment); *bodily-kinesthetic* (required for movement and doing); *interpersonal* (needed for interactions with others); *intrapersonal* (manifested in dealing with self) and *naturalistic* (demonstrated in dealing with nature, nurturing, and classification). The addition of a ninth form of intelligence, *existential* (descriptive of the capacity to raise and consider abstract philosophical questions), is still being considered.

Because of its humanistic approach to acknowledging and promoting the value and contributions of each individual student, the theory has been embraced and supported by the educational community around the world. A number of schools and many teachers claim to use this theory as the fundamental framework for their pedagogy. Yet the theory has been widely criticized as well; it has been argued that the theory is based primarily on Gardner's intuition and observations rather than evidence, that there are limited empirical data to support the evidence, that the separation between the constructs of multiple intelligences and personality types is blurry, that the assumption that all students are gifted in something might lead to intellectual relativism, and that there has been no systematic evaluation of the value of the theory in the classroom.

The second complementary stream of research, focused on the construct often called emotional intelligence, is associated with both Sternberg's theories (through his concept of practical intelligence) and Gardner's theories (through his concept of intrapersonal and interpersonal intelligences). Emotional intelligence is typically referred to as the ability, capacity, or skill to perceive and register, judge and assess, and manage and act on the emotions of self and others; yet there is currently no consensus definition for this term. The roots of the theory are in the use of the term *social intelligence* by American psychologist Edward Thorndike (Thorndike, 1920), who used this term to refer to the skill of getting along with other people. The term *emotional intelligence* is associated with the doctoral work of Wayne Payne (Payne, 1985); the systematic research on the construct definition and measurement is linked to Peter Salovey and Jack Mayer (Salovey & Mayer, 1990), and the popularization of the concept is associated with Daniel Goleman (Goleman, 1995). The field of emotional intelligence is relatively new, and a number of psychologists and educators are now working on the definition, assessment, and predictive power of this concept.

These three theories, although differing in detail, are aimed at diversifying the views and values of different abilities and competencies as they are exhibited by members of today's complex societies. All three theories stress the importance of expanding teaching approaches so that they encompass and target abilities and competencies that are distinct from those that only memorize and accumulate new knowledge. Although all three theories have been applied in the field of education, the Theory of Successful Intelligence appears to have accumulated the largest body of empirical evidence in its support.

Sternberg's theory has three major implications for educational psychology. First, teaching for all types of intelligence is important because students need to capitalize on their strongest abilities at the same time they work to develop the abilities in which they demonstrate weaknesses. Second, students' strongest abilities are directly connected to their most amenable learning styles. Teachers should know the learning preferences of their students and, when possible, capitalize on them. Third, because these variable abilities exist there should be many diverse assessments of school achievement, not only those that focus on traditional analytical abilities.

Sternberg's theory is widely referenced in the psychological and education literature and can be found in virtually any psychology or education textbook. Yet in the realm of practical applications, the theory has been regarded critically. The major points of criticism focus on the difficulties of reliably measuring "unconventional" (e.g., creative and practical) abilities and differentiating them psychometrically from abilities measured by more conventional tests of intelligence and achievement. These criticisms, however, are not specific to Sternberg's work and are often extended to the work on MI theory and the theory of Emotional Intelligence. Thus, study in the field continues with the goal of developing psychometrically sound assessment instruments suitable for quantifying these abilities, tracking them developmentally, and demonstrating their importance in educational and occupational contexts.

SEE ALSO *Intelligence: An Overview; Multiple Intelligences.*

BIBLIOGRAPHY

Gardner, H. (1993). *Multiple intelligences: The theory in practice.* New York: Basic Books.

Goleman, D. (1995). *Emotional intelligence.* New York: Bantam.

Payne, W. L. (1985). A study of emotion: Developing emotional intelligence; self integration; relating to fear, pain and desire. *Dissertation Abstracts International, 47,* 203A. (University Microfilms No. AAC 8605928).

Salovey, P., & Mayer, J. D. (1990). Emotional intelligence. *Imagination, Cognition, and Personality, 9,* 185–211.

Sternberg, R. J. (1996). *Successful intelligence.* New York: Simon & Schuster.

Thorndike, E. L. (1920). Intelligence and its uses. *Harper's Monthly Magazine, 140,* 227–235.

Webster's New Universal Dictionaries. (1996). *Webster's new universal unabridged dictionary of the English language, fully revised and updated.* New York: Barnes & Noble Books.

Elena L. Grigorenko

TUTORING

Tutoring refers to an instructional method in which a tutor teaches or guides a tutee about a specific subject matter or for a particular purpose by providing explanations, modeling targeted behaviors, and/or providing prompts and feedback to students' performance. Although one tutor can teach two or three tutees simultaneously, most tutoring involves one tutor teaching one student (thus the term "one-to-one" tutoring). Everyday tutors are often peers and other paraprofessionals with little experience in teaching, although they are knowledgeable about the content domains they teach (Bloom, 1984; Cohen, Kulik & Kulik, 1982). Terms such as *expert* and *novice* tutors are used to differentiate tutors with and without pedagogical expertise. The development of artificial intelligence and information technology has also made it possible for computers to serve as tutors.

EFFECTIVENESS OF TUTORING

One-to-one human tutoring has been shown to be a very effective form of instruction. The average tutored students achieved performance gains about two standard deviations (thus usually referred to as the *2 sigma effect*) above the average students in conventional classrooms with a class size of 30 students (Bloom, 1984). A meta-analysis of school tutoring programs reported superior academic performance of tutored students in 45 of the 52 studies. The average effect size was modest (.4), but it varied from study to study with the largest effect size reaching 2.3 (Cohen et al., 1982).

Tutoring effectiveness varied depending on a number of features of the tutoring program. The effect was larger when mathematics was taught as compared to reading and also when lower level skills were assessed. The effect was also larger in structured tutoring programs and also in programs of shorter durations. However, age difference between the tutor and the tutee did not seem to matter. Providing tutors with pre-training did not increase the effect sizes either (Cohen et al., 1982).

Tutoring produces effects not only on the cognitive level, but also on the affective level. In addition to higher achievement scores, tutored students developed positive attitudes toward the subject matter covered in the instruction. Tutoring also benefits both tutors and tutees. Although the amount of improvement was smaller than that of the tutee's learning, tutors' achievement test scores also improved in 33 out of the 38 studies (Cohen et al., 1982). This effect is often called *learning by teaching* (Bargh & Schul, 1980) or the *tutor learning effect* (Roscoe & Chi, 2007).

WHAT TUTORS DO

The tutoring session is predominantly controlled by tutors. Tutors, not the students, are the ones who set the agenda, introduced the subtopic, and/or proposed problems to solve. Tutors also speak first, take more turns, and make more statements than tutees (Chi, Siler, Jeong, Yamauch, & Hausmann, 2001; Graesser, Person, & Magliano, 1995; McArthur, Stasz, & Zmuidzinas, 1990). Given their dominance of the tutoring session, it is only natural to assume that tutoring is effective because of what tutors do. This leads to the conjecture that tutors would undertake an array of sophisticated pedagogical moves during tutoring. Research on tutoring, however, shows that although certain moves are frequently undertaken by tutors, they rarely undertake other, often more sophisticated pedagogical moves in spite of the conjectures and expectations that they would do so.

Feedback and Explanation. Earlier research on human and computer tutors highlighted the role of tutorial feedback (Anderson, Boyle, & Reiser, 1985; Anderson, Conrad, & Corbett, 1989; McArthur et al., 1990; Merrill, Reiser, Merrill, Landes, 1995; Merrill, Reiser, Ranney, & Trafton, 1992). For example, Merrill and colleagues (1995) studied natural human tutoring in computer programming and found that tutors kept the students' problem solving on track by providing ongoing confirmatory feedback and setting new goals. When errors were made, tutors immediately drew students' attention to them if students did not notice their errors first. Later studies of tutoring, however, reported that tutorial feedback was not only infrequent but also unimportant to student learning (Graesser et al., 1995; Chi et al., 2001). Because the majority of the studies emphasizing the role of tutorial feedback came from studies of tutoring procedural skills (e.g., programming language, algebra, and geometry), it is likely that the value of immediate feedback on errors might be most useful in the procedural domain where following the right problem solving steps is important. However, there is considerable variability in how tutors handle errors even in the procedural domain. Some tutors provide explicit feedback, sometimes even telling students how to solve a problem (McArthur et al., 1990), whereas other tutors give very subtle and indirect responses to student errors (Fox, 1990; Lepper, Woolverton, Mumme, & Gurtner, 1993).

Another frequent tutor move during tutoring is giving explanations. Graesser et al. (1995) examined the tutoring of algebra and research methods and reported that one of the noticeable tutor behaviors was providing explanations along with specific examples that connected student understanding to concrete real-world examples. Chi and colleagues (2001) analyzed various tutor statements made by novice biology tutors in a naturalistic tutoring session, such as: (a) giving explanations, (b) giving feedback followed by short corrective explanations when the feedback was negative, (c) reading text sentences aloud, (d) making self-monitoring comments (e.g., "I don't know whether this will help you"), (e) answering questions that students asked, (f) asking content questions, (g) scaffolding with generic and content prompts, and (h) asking comprehension gauging questions (e.g., "is this starting to stick?"). Of the eight types of tutor statements they coded, the most prevalent tutor statement was explanations. Giving explanations is also frequent in the procedural domain (Anderson et al., 1989; McKendree, 1990), but the prevalence of explanation might vary depending on the nature of the content domain. Conceptual domains such as biology are more conducive to tutor explanations than procedural domains such as algebra. In addition, the role of tutorial explanations seems to be limited as they only correlated with shallow measures of students' learning (Chi et al., 2001) or not at all (VanLehn, Siler, Murray, Yamauchi, & Baggett, 2003).

Socratic Technique and Error Diagnosis Rare. Although tutors dominate the tutoring dialogue, this does not necessarily mean that they employ sophisticated tutoring techniques. One such technique that is absent in typical tutoring is Socratic technique. Socratic technique refers to a tutoring method in which the tutors lead students to discover their own misconceptions and construct understanding through a line of questioning instead of giving out information to students directly (Collins & Stevens, 1982). Socratic tutoring appears to produce superior learning outcomes compared with didactic tutoring (Rosé, Moore, VanLehn, & Allbritton, 2001), but it is rare not only in typical tutoring session involving novice tutors (Graesser et al., 1995) but also when tutors have years of experience (VanLehn et al., 2003).

Another tutoring technique that has often been attributed to tutors is the ability to perform a detailed and accurate diagnosis of student understanding especially with respect to errors and misconceptions. An accurate diagnosis and monitoring of students' misunderstanding is essential for tutors to be able to decide how and when to deliver the feedback and explanations and also to tailor their moves to the needs of individual students. Chi, Siler, and Jeong (2004) analyzed how accurately novice biology tutors diagnose and monitor the status of students' misunderstandings. The results indicated that tutors could assess only what students did not know against the normative understanding that the tutors were teaching and were dismal at diagnosing the students' alternative understanding or misconception. Additional evidence indicated that even experienced tutors did not engage in detailed error diagnosis and monitoring (McArthur et al., 1990; Putnam, 1987). It seems that tutors have some sense of what students understand and are aware of the general level of their competence, but are insensitive to the specific errors or misconceptions students have.

REASONS FOR TUTORING EFFECTIVENESS

In spite of the initial belief that tutors would play a critical role in tutoring, a closer examination of tutor behaviors revealed that their contribution is rather limited. This led to a realization that tutoring effectiveness needs to be examined from a broader perspective that considers not only what tutors do but also what students do in the context of interactive tutorial dialogue.

Tutorial Dialogue. To examine the potential mechanisms responsible for the tutoring effect, Graesser et al. (1995) studied the tutoring dialogues of unskilled tutors as they tutored algebra and research methods in psychology and examined the extent to which tutoring dialogues manifest components that have been emphasized in contemporary pedagogical theories and intelligent tutoring systems. These components were: (a) active student learning, (b) sophisticated pedagogical strategies, (c) anchored learning in specific examples and cases, (d) collaborative problem solving and question answering, (e) deep explanatory reasoning, (f) convergence toward shared meanings, (g) feedback, error diagnosis and remediation, and (h) affect and motivation. Of these, only three components were prominent in a typical tutoring session: collaborative problem solving and question answering, explanatory reasoning, and anchoring in the context of specific examples.

Because most of the sophisticated techniques were underdeveloped or virtually non-existent in typical tutoring, Graesser and colleagues (1995) postulated that the tutoring effect would come from the use of localized strategies embedded within tutorial dialogues. They identified frequent dialogue patterns between tutors and tutees in the following five broad steps (p. 504):

1. Tutor asks a question.

2. Student answers question.

3. Tutor gives short feedback on the quality of the answer.

4. Tutor and student collaboratively improve the quality of the answer.

5. Tutor assesses student's understanding of the answer.

The first three steps of tutoring dialogue roughly correspond to the initiate, response, and evaluation cycle of the classroom dialogue in which the teacher initiates the dialogue typically by asking questions, the students respond, and then the teacher evaluates the responses. There are two extra steps in tutoring dialogue, however. Graesser and colleagues (1995) postulated that these extra steps of tutoring dialogue provided the advantage of tutoring over classroom instruction as tutors and tutees collaboratively construct knowledge during these steps.

Tutor-centered, Student-centered, and Interactive Hypothesis. Chi and colleagues (2001) conceptualized that tutoring effectiveness can be attributed to either what tutors do, what students do, or what tutors and tutees do together, and formulated three corresponding hypotheses: a tutor-centered, student-centered, and interactive hypothesis. The tutor-centered hypothesis states that tutors' pedagogical tactics are responsible for the effectiveness of tutoring and predicts that tutors not only employ sophisticated pedagogical moves during tutoring but also that their moves would make a significant contribution to students' learning. The student-centered hypothesis, derived from the findings that students' generative and constructive activities such as self-explanations aid learning (e.g., Chi, de Leeuw, Chiu, & Lavancher,

1994), states that tutoring is effective because it provides more opportunities for students to be generative and constructive. It predicts that students would be active during tutoring and that their active construction (e.g., question asking, self-explanations) would correlate with their learning outcomes. Lastly, the interactive hypothesis states that the key to tutoring effectiveness is not what the tutors or the students do alone, but the interaction between them. Tutorial interaction is critical because it elicits constructive responses from students. The hypothesis predicts that tutor and student would be interactive and that students' constructive and interactive responses (e.g., responding to tutor questions and scaffolding prompts) would foster learning more so than constructive but non-interactive responses (e.g., self-explanations) or interactive but non-constructive responses (e.g., acknowledgements).

In their analysis of naturalistic tutoring by novice biology tutors, Chi and colleagues (2001) found evidence for all three hypotheses. As for the tutor-centered hypothesis, tutors provided extensive amount of explanations, which was significantly correlated with student learning outcome. However, explanation was the only tutor move significantly correlated with student learning and did so only with shallow measures of learning. As for the student-centered hypothesis, they found that although tutors dominated the tutoring session, students were still more active during tutoring than in the classroom. Students asked far more questions during the tutoring sessions (e.g., about eight questions per hour) than in the classrooms (e.g.., less than one question per hour according to Graesser et al., 1995). They also found that some of the students' constructive moves were correlated with learning outcomes, but they were all interactive moves (i.e., responses to scaffolding prompts and comprehension gauging questions), lending support to the interactive hypothesis as well. As for the interactive hypothesis, although tutors were not very interactive (after all, they dominated the tutoring session), students were. They never ignored tutors and always responded to prompts and questions from tutors. Tutorial interaction was also essential to student learning in that interactive construction was correlated with learning outcomes, whereas non-interactive construction was not.

Tutoring is a complex process. On the surface, it appears that tutors play a critical role in making it so effective. However, tutors in general do not use sophisticated tutoring strategies such as the Socratic technique or error diagnosis. In addition, even the tutorial moves frequently used by tutors such as explanations only made a limited contribution to students' learning. A deeper look at the tutoring session suggests that what students do in response to tutorial interaction also plays an important role. Being in a one-to-one situation with a tutor gives students more chances to engage in active learning and to be constructive, but it is not merely students' construction that mattered. Student constructive responses elicited by tutor moves played a more important role in their learning than self-initiated constructive responses.

MAKING TUTORING MORE EFFECTIVE

Although tutoring is already a quite effective form of instruction, there is still room for further improvement. As Graesser and colleagues (1995) noted, many of the components that have been emphasized in contemporary pedagogical theories are either poorly executed or rare in typical tutoring situations. Thus, one obvious way to improve the effectiveness of tutoring is by training tutors in these missing pedagogical components. Although efforts to teach tutors to use specific strategies can be challenging, it seems that some of the strategies such as scaffolding seem to be relatively easy to implement (Chi et al., 2001).

Alternatively, tutoring can be made more effective by making tutors do less instead of trying to make them do more. Chi and colleagues (2001) also manipulated the kind of tutoring strategies tutors were permitted to use. In order to make tutoring less didactic and promote a more interactive style of dialogue, tutors were asked to refrain from giving explanations and feedback. They were encouraged to prompt the students instead. The results showed that students were just as effective at learning the materials even when tutors were suppressed from giving explanations and feedback. Even in the absence of tutor explanations and feedback, students were able to learn from a greater amount of scaffolding episodes as well as by taking greater control of their own learning by reading more.

COMPUTER-BASED INTELLIGENT TUTORS

Computer-based intelligent tutors began to appear in the mid 1980s. These Intelligent Tutoring Systems (ITSs) heavily relied on the cognitive model of competence about how students learn and solve problems (e.g., Anderson et al., 1985; Anderson, Corbett, Koedinger, & Pelletier, 1995). A detailed cognitive model of students allowed computer tutors to trace students' problem-solving behaviors closely and provide directive step-by-step feedback to ensure that students stayed on the right paths. There are now well-tested tutors of algebra, geometry, computer languages, physics, and electronics (e.g., Koedinger, Anderson, Hadley, & Mark, 1997; Lesgold, Lajoie, Bunzo, & Eggan, 1988; VanLehn et al., 2005). According to one estimate, they produce learning gains of approximately 1.0 standard deviation units compared with students learning the same content in a classroom (Corbett, Anderson,

Graesser, Koedinger, & VanLehn, 1999) and are actively implemented and used in schools in the United States (Aleven & Koedinger, 2002; Koedinger et al., 1997).

In spite of their success, existing ITSs are often too rigid, allowing only one strategy for problem solving and providing perhaps too much scaffolding in the form of error correction. They are also limited in promoting deep learning, failing to help students to articulate reasons behind the problem-solving procedures and to apply what they learn to more qualitative problems (Aleven & Koedinger, 2002; Graesser, VanLehn, Rosé, Jordan, & Harter, 2001; Ohlsson, 1986; VanLehn et al., 2000). Several attempts have been made to remedy these shortcomings and make computer tutors as competent as expert human tutors. One approach, based on the research showing the importance of students' own construction activities, is to provide more opportunities for students to self-construct their understanding (Aleven & Koedinger, 2002). Another approach is to endow ITSs with natural language capability so that computers could engage in tutorial dialogue with students using natural language, thereby eliciting collaborative knowledge construction more actively (Graesser et al., 2001; Person, Graesser, Kreuz, & Pomeroy, 2001; VanLehn et al., 2000). The preliminary results from these attempts look promising. Students who explained their steps during problem-solving practice with a computer tutor learned with greater understanding compared to students who did not explain steps (Aleven & Koedinger, 2002). Students tutored by an ITS with natural language enhancement also outperformed students tutored with an earlier version of ITS without the enhancement (Graesser et al., 2001).

INSIGHTS INTO IMPROVING CLASSROOM INSTRUCTION

The tutoring effect demonstrates that most of the students have a potential to reach a high level of learning. In spite of its effectiveness, tutoring has not been used as actively and widely as it should be. The main reason has been the cost. There are ways, however, to circumvent this limitation and introduce the benefits of one-to-one tutoring into classroom instruction. One traditional solution is to use peer tutors. Because the majority of tutors are novices and yet produce significant effects, pairing students with other students of either same-age or cross-age across grades can be an effective alternative to using professional tutors. Peer tutoring can also help those students who serve as tutors since tutors themselves engage in active knowledge construction processes as they tutor (Roscoe & Chi, 2007). Peer-tutoring also brings other benefits such as community building and integra-

tion of students with diverse cultural and linguistic backgrounds (O'Donnell, 2006; Webb & Palincsar, 1996).

Benefits of tutoring can also be obtained by combining collaborative learning with tutoring. For example, Chi, Roy, and Hausmann (in press) examined the effectiveness of collaborative observation of tutoring against several other instructional conditions such as one-on-one tutoring and collaboration without observation. The results showed that students learned to solve physics problems just as effectively from observing tutoring collaboratively as the students who were being tutored individually. It seems that learning conditions such as collaborative observation of tutoring can serve as a promising alternative to one-to-one tutoring while providing all the same benefits.

Research on tutoring has demonstrated and reinforced the idea that students learn best if they construct knowledge for themselves rather than being told the knowledge. Tutoring seems to be a particularly effective form of instruction because it facilitates active knowledge construction within the interactive context of tutorial dialogues. Regardless of whether teachers implement tutoring into the classroom, classroom instruction can benefit greatly by finding ways to elicit more active construction from students in interactive contexts.

SEE ALSO *Reciprocal Teaching.*

BIBLIOGRAPHY

Aleven, V. A. W. M. M., & Koedinger, K. R. (2002). An effective metacognitive strategy: learning by doing and explaining with a computer-based cognitive tutor. *Cognitive Science 26*, 147–179.

Anderson, J. R., Boyle, F. B., & Reiser, R. J. (1985). Intelligent tutoring system. *Science, 228,* 456–467.

Anderson, J. R., Conrad, F. G., & Corbett, A. T. (1989). Skill acquisition and the LISP tutor. *Cognitive Science, 13,* 467–505.

Anderson, J. R., Corbett, A. T., Koedinger, K. R., & Pelletier, R. (1995). Cognitive tutors: lessons learned. *Journal of the Learning Sciences, 4,* 167–207.

Bargh, J. A., & Schul, Y. (1980). On the cognitive benefits of teaching. *Journal of Educational Psychology, 72*(5), 593–604.

Bloom, B. S. (1984). The search for methods of group instruction as effective as one-to-one tutoring. *Educational Leadership, 41* (8), 4–17.

Chi, M. T. H., de Leeuw, N., Chiu, M., & LaVancher, C. (1994). Eliciting self-explanations improves understanding. *Cognitive Science, 18,* 439–477.

Chi, M. T. H., Roy, M., & Hausmann, R. G. (in press). Observing tutorial dialogues collaboratively. *Cognitive Science.*

Chi, M. T. H., Siler, S. A., Jeong, H., Yamauchi, T., & Hausmann, R. G. (2001). Learning from human tutoring. *Cognitive Science, 25,* 471–533.

Chi, M. T. H., Siler, S. A., & Jeong, H. (2004). Can tutors monitor students' understanding accurately? *Cognition and Instruction, 22*(3), 363–387.

Cohen, P., Kulik, J., & Kulik, C. (1982). Educational outcomes of tutoring: A meta-analysis of findings. *American Educational Research Journal, 19,* 237–248.

Collins, A., & Stevens, A. (1982). Goals and methods for inquiry teachers. In R. Glaser, (Ed.), *Advances in Instructional Psychology* (Vol. 2). Hillsdale, NJ: Erlbaum.

Corbett, A. T., Anderson, J. R., Graesser, A. Koedinger, K., & VanLehn, K. (1999). Third generation computer tutors: Learn from or ignore human tutors? *Proceedings of the 1999 Conference of Computer-Human Interaction* (pp. 85–86). New York: Association of Computing Machinery.

Fox, B. A. (1990). Cognitive and interactional aspects of correction in tutoring. In P. Goodyear (Ed.), *Teaching knowledge and intelligent tutoring.* Norwood, NJ: Ablex.

Graesser, A. C., Person, N. K., & Magliano, J. P. (1995). Collaborative dialogue patterns in naturalistic one-to-one tutoring. *Applied Cognitive Psychology, 9,* 495–522.

Graesser, A. C., VanLehn, K., Rosé, C. P., Jordan, P. W., & Harter, D. (2001). Intelligent tutoring systems with conversational dialogue. *AI Magazine, 22*(4), 39–51.

Koedinger, K. Anderson, J. R., Hadley, W. H., & Mark, M. A. (1997). Intelligent tutoring goes to school in the big city. *International Journal of Artificial Intelligence in Education 8,* 30–43.

Lepper, M. R. Woolverton, M. Mumme, D. L., & Gurtner, J. L. (1993). Motivational techniques of human expert tutors: lessons for the design of computer-based tutors. In S. P. Lajoie & S. J. Derry (Eds.), *Computers as cognitive tools* (pp. 75–105). Hillsdale, NJ: Lawrence Erlbaum.

Lesgold, A. Lajoie, S., Bunzo, M., & Eggan, G. (1988). SHERLOCK: A coached practice environment for an electronics trouble shooting job. In J. H. Larkin & R. W. Chabay (Eds.), *Computer-assisted instruction and intelligent tutoring systems.* Hillsdale, NJ: Erlbaum.

McArthur, D., Stasz, C., & Zmuidzinas, M. (1990). Tutoring techniques in Algebra. *Cognition and Instruction, 7*(3), 197–244.

McKendree, J. (1990). Effective feedback content for tutoring complex skills. *Human-Computer Interaction, 5,* 381–413.

Merrill, D. C., Reiser, B. J., Ranney, M., & Trafton, J. G. (1992). Effective tutoring techniques: A comparison of human tutors and intelligent tutoring system. *Journal of the Learning Sciences, 2*(3), 277–305.

Merrill, D. C. Reiser, B. J., Merrill, S. K., & Landes, S. (1995). Tutoring: Guided learning by doing. *Cognition and Instruction 13*(3), 315–372.

O'Donnell, A. M. (2006). The role of peers and group learning. In P. A. Alexander & P. H. Winne (Eds.), *Handbook of educational psychology* (2nd ed.). Hillsdale, NJ: Erlbaum.

Ohlsson, S. (1986). Some principles of intelligent tutoring. *Instructional Science, 14,* 293–326.

Person, N. K., Graesser, A. C., Kreuz, R. J., & Pomeroy, V. (2001). Simulating human dialogue moves in AUTOTUTOR. *International Journal of Artificial Intelligence in Education, 12,* 23–39.

Putnam, R. T. (1987). Structuring and adjusting content for students: A study of live and simulated tutoring of addition. *American Educational Research Journal, 24,* 13–48.

Roscoe, R. D., & Chi, M. T. H. (2007). Understanding tutor learning: Knowledge-building and knowledge-telling in peer tutors' explanation and questions. *Review of Educational Research, 77*(4), 534–574.

Rosé, C. P., Moore, J. D., VanLehn, K., & Allbritton, D. (2001). A comparative evaluation of Socratic versus didactic tutoring. *Proceedings of 23rd Annual Conference of the Cognitive Sciences Society.* Hillsdale, NJ: Erlbaum.

VanLehn, K., Freedman, R., Jordan, P., Murray, C., Rosé, C. P., Schulze, K., et al. (2000). Fading and deepening: The next steps for Andes and other model-tracing tutors. In G. Gauthier, C. Frasson, & K. VanLehn (Eds.), *Intelligent tutoring systems: 5th international conference: Vol. 1839. Lecture Notes in Computer Science* (pp. 474–483). Berlin: Springer-Verlag Berlin & Heidelberg GmbH.

VanLehn, K., Lynch, C., Schulze, K., Sapiro, J. A., R., S., Taylor, L., Treacy, D., et al. (2005). The Andes physics tutoring system: Five years of evaluation. In G. McCalla, C. K. Looi, B. Bredeweg, & J. Breuker (Eds.), *Artificial intelligence in education* (pp. 678–685). Amsterdam: IOS Press.

VanLehn, K., Siler, S. A., Murray, C., Yamauchi, T., & Baggett, W. B. (2003). Why do only some events cause learning during human tutoring? *Cognition and Instruction, 21*(3), 209–249.

Webb, N. M., & Palincsar, A. S. (1996). Group processes in the classroom. In D. C. Berliner & R. C. Calfee (Eds.), *Handbook of educational psychology* (pp. 841–873). New York: Simon & Schuster.

Heisawn Jeong

V

VALIDITY

Validity denotes the meaning of a test score or assessment result. Although historical notions of validity have suggested there are multiple forms of validity, contemporary views of validity consider it to be a unitary construct supported by distinct forms of evidence. Contrary to popular belief, validity is neither obvious nor intuitive. Therefore, the validity of any test or assessment, from teacher-made quizzes, tests, and assignments to published tests and procedures, should be established by collecting relevant forms of evidence so that educators can draw appropriate interpretations of assessment results.

HISTORICAL VERSUS CONTEMPORARY DEFINITIONS OF VALIDITY

Until the twentieth century, the validity of a test or assessment was determined primarily by the content of the assessment process. That is, a test was deemed to reflect mathematical skills if the questions on the test were primarily mathematical in nature; likewise, a test composed of questions about Elizabethan England was viewed as revealing a student's knowledge of history. However, advances in testing and assessment during the early twentieth century challenged these assumptions, in large part because the inferences about what tests were intended to measure changed from direct inferences (e.g., the student knows or does not know trigonometry) to less direct inferences (e.g., the student has strong or weak aptitude for quantitative reasoning). Therefore, the meaning of tests and assessments could not be directly inferred from test content. For example, the answer to the question "Who wrote Romeo and Juliet?" could reflect a student's understanding of a unit on British literature, or it could be a reflection of a student's ability to acquire knowledge incidentally from the environment (especially if the student had not yet had a course in British literature). Content analysis alone is insufficient to determine whether the question was a measure of literary knowledge or student ability.

By the 1980s, assessment experts generally agreed that there were three types of validity: content, construct, and criterion (AERA, APA, NCME, 1985). The meaning of a test result was determined in part by the test's content, but also by evidence that the test result behaved in ways consistent with its theoretical construct (e.g., raw scores on a test of intelligence should increase with age up to the mid- to late teens), and should predict socially valued criteria (e.g., a mechanical aptitude test should predict grades in an industrial arts class). Test users could expect to have all three forms of evidence (content, construct, and criterion) available for published tests, while also recognizing some forms of evidence were more important for some test uses than others.

However, by the end of the twentieth century, professional standards redefined validity so that there was only one "type" of validity—i.e., the meaning of a test score or assessment result (AERA, APA, NCME, 1999). However, standards outlined five forms of evidence needed to determine test score meaning: (1) content, (2) response processes, (3) internal structure, (4) relationships to other variables, and (5) test consequences. Test developers (and users) are expected to consider the forms of evidence most relevant to determining the meaning of a test result, and collect and provide relevant evidence to define the meaning of the test score or assessment result. Each of these forms of evidence is described to help those who use assessment results (e.g., teachers, psychologists, administrators) to understand, demand, and collect such evidence.

Content. Primary evidence in this domain includes the specification of the intended content and expert judgment of test items regarding adherence to those specifications. For example, tests of state standards (required by the No Child Left Behind Act of 2002) are validated in part by specifying what students are supposed to know and do in a given domain, the degree to which these skills should be represented in a given test, and the cognitive complexity and type of item to be used to assess the skill. A reading test at third grade might therefore have more items devoted to phonological skills (e.g., grapheme/phoneme correspondence), word attack, and vocabulary than an eighth-grade test of reading, which might have fewer items for phonological and word attack skills, but more items reflecting inferential comprehension. For domains with less clearly specified content (e.g., intelligence), judgments regarding content are more dependent on theory than on exact specification of intended domains. In all cases, judges evaluate the test content against the intended interpretation of the test to evaluate the degree to which the test content represents the intended meaning of the test. Additionally, panels of judges with expertise in diversity (e.g., linguistic, ethnic, gender, religious) may also evaluate the content to identify any content that may be problematic for diverse groups.

Response Processes. The psychological processes test takers use when responding to an assessment are known as *response processes*. Evidence that a test elicits the processes it intends to measure, and only those processes, is useful for establishing the meaning of the test score. One cannot assume that a test item will elicit the intended process; for example, the item "Use a barometer to calculate the height of a tall apartment building" could elicit use of air pressure to estimate altitude, but it might elicit social knowledge (e.g., "Offer to give the barometer to the building superintendent in return for telling you the height of the building"). Test takers may get an item right (or wrong) without ever using the process intended to be elicited by the item. Forms of evidence supporting response processes are direct (e.g., ask test-takers how they solved items), and indirect (e.g., analysis of eye gaze, brain activity, or error patterns).

Internal Structure. Simply put, tests should behave the way the developers expect them to behave—meaning items purporting to measure the same thing should be more related to each other than items purporting to measure something different. For example, a mathematics test might intend to measure probability and geometry; if so, the items and subscales measuring probability ought to be more related to each other than items and subscales measuring geometry. The primary forms of evidence, then, are internal consistency (items that measure the same thing should correlate with each other), and factor analysis (items should aggregate into common scales, and scales into expected patterns).

Relationships to other Variables. Assessment results ought to relate to measures outside of the assessment in ways that are consistent with the intended meaning. Evidence is often framed as *convergent* (i.e., the assessment should relate to things expected to be related), and *divergent* (i.e., the assessment should not relate to things that are expected to be unrelated). Forms of convergent evidence include grades given by teachers or scores on tests of similar constructs; forms of divergent evidence include a proposed independence between creativity and general intelligence (which rarely occurs, calling into question whether creativity is really different from general intelligence).

Test Consequences. Assessments are intended to benefit the test-giver and the test-taker. Therefore, test developers (and users) should collect and provide evidence that tests achieve their intended benefits, and avoid unintended consequences. For example, some argue testing mandates in No Child Left Behind benefit students by holding schools accountable for student achievement; critics argue that tests demoralize students and educators. The evidence needed to determine whether benefits are realized, or whether unintended consequences outweigh benefits, is often lacking from tests in educational settings. For example, in their 2005 study Braden and Niebling note that many popular cognitive ability tests claim to help educators match programs and instruction to student needs, but those promoting the tests do not actually provide supporting evidence.

A fundamental assumption is that no one form of evidence is sufficient to establish validity; rather, multiple forms of evidence must be presented and evaluated to support (or reject) an interpretation of a test score. Therefore, test users should obtain and weigh multiple forms of evidence to determine the validity of a test score or assessment result.

CRITICAL ISSUES IN ASSESSMENT VALIDITY

There are a number of issues that are particularly relevant to educators and educational settings. The following is a brief selection of critical issues.

Distinguishing Validity from Reliability. Validity refers to the meaning of a test score or assessment result, whereas reliability is the consistency of a score or result. Consistency of assessment results is established over time (i.e., test-retest reliability or "stability"), agreement among test items (internal consistency), and agreement between raters (i.e., inter-rater reliability). A test that is not reliable cannot be valid; therefore, educators should evaluate reliability evidence before they even consider validity evidence. Reliability is most often expressed as a number, which is somewhat analogous to a percentage; reliability indexes of .80 (i.e., 80%) or higher are generally considered to be adequate for use in making educational decisions.

Causes of Test Score Invalidity. In addition to poor reliability, Messick's 1995 study identified two causes of invalidity: *construct under-representation* and *construct-irrelevant variance*. Construct under-representation means the test inadequately taps what it intends to measure. For example, many multiple choice tests intend to measure skills ranging from lower order (e.g., recognition, recall) and higher order (e.g., analysis, synthesis, application, evaluation) skills. However, it takes time, energy, and expertise to create multiple choice items that tap higher order thinking skills, and so many multiple choice tests over-represent lower-order skills and under-represent higher-order skills. If the test purports to measure a broad range of cognitive skills, but has few items tapping evaluation and application, its scores will be invalid because they under-represent higher-order thinking in the domain.

Construct-irrelevant variance occurs when an assessment demands skills it does not intend to measure. For example, most reading comprehension tests intend to measure the test-taker's ability to decode and comprehend written text. However, tests demand that the test taker has the visual acuity to discriminate the letters and words in the text. If the test-taker does not have that ability (e.g., the test-taker has an uncorrected visual impairment), then the test score will not reflect reading comprehension; instead, it will reflect the test taker's skill in an unintended domain (i.e., visual acuity). In cases in which construct-irrelevant variance is high (e.g., limited visual acuity), the test-taker's score will be invalid if the test taker lacks the construct-irrelevant skill.

Test Accommodations. The principles of construct underrepresentation and construct-irrelevant variance can help identify ways in which tests can (and cannot) be changed to accommodate test takers. Essentially, changes that reduce construct-irrelevant variance without creating construct under-representation are valid accommodations; those that either fail to reduce construct-irrelevant variance, or that reduce construct representation, are invalid accommodations. Returning to the example of a reading comprehension test, enlarging the text print, or allowing the use of eye-glasses, reduces construct-irrelevant variance while maintaining construct representation, and is therefore a valid accommodation. However, reading the text to a person with a visual impairment is invalid, because it reduces construct representation (i.e., it under-represents decoding of text). It is important to note that test standards place the burden of proof for accommodation validity on the party recommending the change; the default assumption is that, in the absence of additional evidence, any changes to standardized assessment procedures and materials reduce the validity of the assessment result.

Assessment Bias. Assuming tests are equally reliable across groups (which is typically true), bias occurs when the meaning of the test score is different for one group relative to another (i.e., the validity is not consistent across groups). To determine if an assessment is biased, multiple forms of evidence must be presented showing different meanings for different groups. Simply looking at test content (e.g., claiming that a test is biased because it presumes cultural knowledge more prevalent in one group than in another) is insufficient to demonstrate bias. Most published assessments used in educational settings are not biased for groups whose native language is English; that is, the test scores represent the same thing for all groups of test-takers across ethnic, gender, and socioeconomic groups. Or to put it another way, tests generally reveal, rather than create, differences between groups. However, the validity evidence for test takers whose native language is not English is often limited, and less consistent, leaving open the possibility that assessment results have different meanings for native English versus non-English speakers. Simply noting that one group has lower scores than another is not in itself evidence of bias (i.e., groups can, and often do, differ).

Constructed versus Selected Response Assessments. Many educators and advocacy groups (e.g., Fairtest) are critical of selected-response or multiple choice tests. Critics contend that multiple choice tests emphasize low-level cognitive skills. Advocates of selected-response tests argue such claims are not supported by validity evidence, and they argue selected-response tests are reliable and cost effective. The bulk of evidence across the five validity domains suggests carefully developed assessments can overcome most limitations associated with item formats. For example, development of rubrics and rater training can produce adequate reliability in constructed-response assessments (e.g., performances, portfolios), and carefully constructed selected-response tests elicit higher-order cognitive processes. However, the greater costs in terms of time, scoring, and storing constructed-response assessments are not offset by better validity evidence, so most educational assessment programs primarily use selected-response assessments.

Teacher-developed Assessments. Most teachers have limited assessment training and even less time to develop and evaluate their own tests. Yet teachers routinely develop, administer, and score tests without considering validity issues. Some practical steps teachers can take to ensure student test scores reflect intended meanings include the following:

1. Develop student assessments before developing instructional units. By deciding in advance what students should know and do, teachers ensure content validity (e.g., breadth and depth of coverage), and can also align their instruction to ensure students learn the intended materials.

2. Specify assessment content and format with an item specification table. For example, a reading test might target 10% phonemic awareness, 20% alphabetic principle/phonics, 30% fluency, 15% vocabulary, and 25% comprehension distributed so that 50% of items are selected-response, 30% are fill-in-the-blank, and 20% are short answer. The resulting two-dimensional table helps teachers ensure content coverage is distributed as they intended, and also helps ensure that methods of assessment are distributed across content domains.

3. Provide multiple opportunities for students to demonstrate knowledge. Large-scale projects or final exams with a single score are less likely to be reliable, and therefore less likely to be valid, than a series of smaller, more frequent assessments.

4. Look for evidence that test scores might not convey intended meanings. Even tests developed by experts have unexpected problems; teacher-made tests are no exception. Teachers should look for evidence of unexpected outcomes (e.g., students who do well on quizzes do poorly on the unit test; items that nobody passes; evidence that groups differ in unusual ways on particular tests or items), and adjust tests if they conclude that the test did not accurately reflect its intended meaning.

Weighing the Evidence. Test makers and users want as much evidence as possible to understand what test scores mean. However, collecting and reporting evidence costs time and money, and so evidence is often incomplete. Test users must therefore weigh evidence to evaluate the degree to which it supports the validity, or intended meanings, of the test. Test users should invoke a four-step process to weigh evidence:

1. Identify the stated claims or purposes of the test.

2. Determine whether test scores have adequate reliability or consistency.

3. Decide which forms of evidence are most important.

4. Evaluate the degree to which the evidence supports intended meanings.

For example, suppose a test purports to measure mathematical knowledge and skills (step 1). Test users should decide what forms of consistency are most important (e.g., inter-rater agreement, stability), and then determine whether the test scores have reliability values greater than or equal to 0.80 (step 2). If the test has reasonable evidence of reliability, users should decide which forms of evidence are most salient. Achievement tests should have substantial evidence of test content (e.g., items should represent domains identified by the National Council of Teachers of Mathematics), internal structure (e.g., items purporting to measure common subdomains actually relate to each other), and relationships to other variables (e.g., the test correlates with other math tests). If the test also claims intended consequences (e.g., it will help plan educational interventions), then evidence showing how test scores enhance intervention selection, implementation, or outcomes should be provided. It should be noted that some domains (e.g., content) are more important than other domains (e.g., response processes). Finally, users should assess the evidence provided to judge the degree to which evidence supports the claims. Test reviews can be helpful, but test standards mandate that test users are personally responsible for ensuring that the tests they use have appropriate supporting evidence.

SEE ALSO *Normal Distribution; Reliability.*

BIBLIOGRAPHY

American Educational Research Association, American Psychological Association, & National Council on Measurement in Education (1985). *Standards for educational and psychological testing* (2nd ed.). Washington, DC: American Psychological Association.

American Educational Research Association, American Psychological Association, & National Council on Measurement in Education (1999). *Standards for educational and psychological testing* (3rd ed.). Washington, DC: American Educational Research Association.

Borsboom, D., Mellenbergh, G., & van Heerden, J. (2004). The concept of validity. *Psychological Review, 111*(4), 1061–1071.

Braden, J. P., & Joyce, L. B. (2008). Best practices in making assessment accommodations. In A. Thomas & J. Grimes. (Eds.), *Best practices in school psychology* (5th ed.). Silver Spring, MD: National Association of School Psychologists.

Braden, J. P., & Niebling, B. C. (2005). Using the joint test standards to evaluate the validity evidence for intelligence tests. In D. P. Flanagan & P. L. Harrison (Eds.), *Contemporary intellectual assessment: Theories, tests and issues* (2nd ed., pp. 615–630). New York: Guilford.

Kane, M. (2001). Current concerns in validity theory. *Journal of Educational Measurement, 38*(4), 319–342. (ERIC Document Reproduction Service No. EJ646472)

Messick, S. (1995). Validity of psychological assessment: Validation of inferences from persons' responses and performances as scientific inquiry into score meaning. *American Psychologist,* *50*(9), 741–749.

Sireci, S., & Parker, P. (2006). Validity on trial: Psychometric and legal conceptualizations of validity. *Educational Measurement: Issues and Practice, 25*(3), 27–34.

Jeffery P. Braden

VISUAL IMPAIRMENTS

Vision is an integral part to standardized learning. Students who lack visual abilities often feel lost in a confusing educational maze. Although the U.S. Department of Education reported that less than 1% of U.S. students had visual impairments in 2004, the actual number of children with visual impairments is higher. The consequences of visual impairment can range from missed opportunities in learning to obstacles to gaining independence.

At one point the term *visual impairment* referred to an eye disorder at the tissue level, but subsequently, visual impairments took on a broader meaning to include the consequence of a functional loss of vision caused by a number of eye disorders.

VISUAL IMPAIRMENT DEFINITION

The definition of visual impairment includes a range of vision loss, including low vision. Specifically, it is defined as "an impairment in vision that, even with correction, adversely affects a child's educational performance. The term includes both partial sight and blindness" (Pierangelo, 2007, p. 331). In the educational context, three terms describe levels of visual impairment.

The fist level, partially sighted, refers to a visual problem that has resulted in the need for special education.

Low vision is used generally to refer to a severe visual impairment. The impairment is not necessarily limited to distance vision, but includes students with sight who are unable to read a newspaper at normal viewing distance, even with the aid of contacts, eyeglasses, or electronic devices. Students with low vision use a combination of vision and other senses to learn; they may require adaptations to lighting, print size, or provision of written materials in Braille.

Legal blindness is defined by vision of 20/200 or less in the better eye after correction, or limited field of vision (measuring 20 degrees at its widest point). Limited field of vision results in some confusion for students. Legal blindness also includes total blindness, or a person with "no vision or only light perception." These are students who must receive instruction via aural methods, Braille, or other nonvisual media.

Visual impairments are caused by a number of eye disorders, including albinism, cataracts, retinal degeneration, diabetic retinopathy, glaucoma, corneal disorders, congenital disorders, and infection. Although the Department of Education listed fewer than 26,000 students age 6 to 21 as receiving special education services under the visual impairment category in 2004, the actual number is likely higher. Many students with visual impairments have other disabilities as well and are listed in those categories. Visual impairments actually occur at a rate of 12.2 per 1,000 people under age 18. Legal blindness occurs at a rate of .06 per 1,000 people under age 18.

ASSESSING VISUAL IMPAIRMENTS

Early assessment is key to helping a student benefit from appropriate intervention programs. Severe visual impairments are more easily identified in schools than milder vision losses. However, there are warning signs of visual impairment, such as lack of coordination in the eyes or excessive eye movement and blinking. Children who rub their eyes or who have frequent watering and signs of eye infections may need assessment for visual impairment. If children confuse colors, complain of headaches, or have poor posture when reading or writing, they may have vision impairment. More obvious signs include squinting, sitting very close to the chalkboard or screens, messy work, or complaining of difficulty seeing things clearly.

Among the goals set forth in the National Agenda for the Education of Children and Youths with Visual Impairments, Including Those with Multiple Disabilities, is Goal 6. It reads: "Assessment of students will be conducted, in collaboration with parents, by personnel having expertise in the education of students with visual impairments" (American Foundation for the Blind, 2005, p.1). Because the National Agenda emphasizes providing timely, quality educational services for children with visual impairments, initial and ongoing assessments are critical.

Students are assessed by a certified teacher of students with visual impairments (TVI). A functional visual assessment helps to determine how the children currently use any partial or low vision and what visual skills need further development or assistance. The TVI observes each child performing routine tasks and speaks with parents, teachers, and others involved in the child's care about how the child uses vision. The child's eye doctor also provides important clinical information on visual acuity, visual field, and diagnosis. A child with visual impairments may be examined by an ophthalmologist, who specializes in diagnosis and treatment of medical and surgical problems of the eye; an optometrist, who specializes in vision problems and treating vision conditions; and other providers such as an optician, who dispenses eyeglasses and other optical aids, or a low vision specialist.

The TVI will review the eye doctor's findings of visual acuity and summarize them on the report. The teacher also includes notes from observers and observes the child's visual skills from near and far distances. The teacher also observes how well the child sees objects that are to the sides, above or below the eye level to assess visual field, and notes other visual functions such as ability to localize, fixate, scan, track, and shift gaze. Eye preference and eye-hand coordination, as well as color vision, are additional concerns. The TVI observes the child in different settings and assesses visual abilities in relation to environmental considerations such as lighting, object size, and additional time to complete tasks. A team that consists of the TVI, parent or guardian, a general classroom teacher for the child, and other education professionals such as a school counselor or school psychologist, generally meet to make final recommendations and discuss the child's potential placement. The evaluation should include recommendations for services, adaptations, and instructional skills that will help the student learn.

Alternative media and tools such as books in Braille can aid the visually impaired student. WILL & DENI MCINTYRE/PHOTO RESEARCHERS, INC.

If a child has no vision, he or she still needs a functional visual assessment to confirm medical information and blindness, as well as noting recommendations for instruction modification.

CHARACTERISTICS OF CHILDREN WITH VISUAL IMPAIRMENTS

Many factors determine how visual impairments affect a child's learning experience. Age of onset and severity of vision loss, as well as presence of multiple disabilities, are some of the factors that make each child's situation unique. The U.S. Department of Education reported in 2004 that more boys than girls had visual impairment. As more and more infants are born prematurely, the incidence of visual impairments is expected to rise.

The cause of visual impairment and overall functioning level of a child also determine how the visual impairment affects a child's development. In general, visual impairments have cognitive, academic, social and emotional, and behavioral effects.

Restricted movement within the environment, particularly for children with congenital visual impairment, can affect a child's development. Children with visual impairments often have limited interactions with their environments, less reason to explore interesting objects, and as a result missed opportunities to learn. This lack of exploration may continue until some sort of intervention begins to motivate learning.

Academic performance may suffer for children with visual impairments, particularly in reading and writing. Alternative media and tools may help, such as Braille or an alternative form of print.

Children learn much about social behavior by observing others, so those with visual impairment may not understand nonverbal cues and other nuances of social behavior normally learned through imitation. The functional limitations caused by visual impairments may create obstacles to a child's independence as he or she ages. Studies have shown that some children with visual impairments can display social immaturity, more isolation, and less assertiveness than their peers.

Many myths surround children with low vision. In addition to later discovery of their visual impairment in some cases, those with low vision may not receive the adaptations and services they need as compared with their peers who are declared legally blind. Yet students who have low vision have unique social and emotional needs, such as identity issues, and they may need help with developing communication and self-advocacy skills.

Overall, children with visual impairments require assistance with technology, special print, auditory, or Braille materials. Other specialized needs depend on the functional visual assessment and ongoing assessments concerning the child's development.

EXAMPLES OF EYE DISORDERS

More than 30 specific diseases and conditions are associated with visual impairments. An ophthalmologist can make the definitive diagnosis as to the cause of the visual impairment based on a physical examination and associated tests. According to a report from the U.S. Preventive Services Task Force, the most common causes of visual impairment in children under age 5 years are amblyopia and its risk factors and refractive error not associated with amblyopia. The common name for amblyopia is lazy eye. It develops in early childhood and involves one eye not working well with the brain, resulting in reduced vision in the affected eye. Amblyopia affects about two to three out of every 100 children.

Amblyopia may be due to effects of other conditions that interfere with normal binocular vision, such as strabismus (ocular misalignment), anisometropia (a large difference in refractive power between the eyes), cataract (lens opacity), and ptosis (eyelid drooping). In anisometropic amblyopia, the two eyes have different refractive powers; one can be nearsighted, while the other is farsighted. The misalignment of the eyes in strabismic amblyopia causes one eye to be used less than the other. The nonpreferred eye does not receive adequate simulation, and the visual brain cells do not develop normally.

Refractive error not associated with amblyopia primarily includes myopia (nearsightedness) and hyperopia (farsightedness). These problems are correctable regardless of the child's age at detection.

Retinopathy of prematurity can blind a child. It generally develops in premature infants with low birth weights or less than 31 weeks of gestation. It is classified in five stages, from mild to severe. Diabetic retinopathy is a complication of diabetes, brought about by damage to tiny blood vessels in the retina. It is the leading cause of blindness in the United States. Retinoblastoma is a malignant tumor of the eye. Although it can occur at any age, it most often occurs in children younger than age five. The tumors may be present in one or both eyes.

Nystagmus is an involuntary movement of the eye that reduces vision. Typically, the movement is from side to side, but it can be up and down or circular. There are several forms of nystagmus. The condition may be hereditary and can result in severe reduction in vision. Students may need extra time for reading to scan text.

Strabismus is the misalignment of one eye and comes in several forms, such as esotropia, the inward turning of the eye, and exotropia, or outward deviation of the eye. Hypertropia refers to vertical deviation of the eye. Strabismus also can occur intermittently. The cause of strabismus generally is unknown. Other disorders often are associated with strabismus, including retinopathy of prematurity, retinoblastoma, traumatic brain injury, hemangioma near the eye, Apert syndrome, Noonan syndrome, Prader-Willi syndrome, and others.

EDUCATIONAL PRACTICES

At one time, students with visual impairments were taught only in residential schools for blind children. Early in the 20th century, local school districts began educating students with visual impairments, but primarily in special classrooms. In the early 2000s, itinerant teachers, resource rooms, general education classes, and special schools all may be used in the education of students with visual impairments. By 2004 the U.S. Department of Education reported that about 90 percent of children with visual impairments spent at least some time in regular classrooms with peers.

The Individuals with Disabilities Education Improvement Act (IDEA) was introduced in 1975 and passed in 1990. It was reauthorized in 1997 and 2004 and includes provisions for children with visual impairments as defined above. Students with visual impairments also may be eligible for accommodations for general classroom inclusion under Section 504 of the Vocational Rehabilitation Act, passed in 1973.

The National Agenda for the Education of Children and Youths with Visual Impairments, Including Those with Multiple Disabilities is a grassroots effort that has helped improve education for children with low vision and blindness. In 2003 the National Agenda was updated to include 10 goals. The goals range from ensuring referral to an appropriate education program within 30 days of identification of suspected visual impairment to recommending ongoing professional development for those providing services to students with visual impairments. The National Agenda also encourages implementation of policies that involve parents as equal partners in the education process, that local education programs ensure access to a full array of services, and that access to educational and developmental services include assurance that materials are available to students in the appropriate media and at the same time as their sighted peers. Educational goals should be based on the assessed need of students with visual impairments and goals and strategies should be set throughout the student's life continuum.

The TVI works with local and national professionals as needed to provide access to educational materials for students with visual impairments. Students who are blind may use raised maps and charts and other materials to facilitate tactile learning. Many rely on auditory information from books on tape or CD-ROMs, spoken output from a computer, or tape computers, in addition to large print or Braille materials. Each state has specific policies and practices for broad programming of curriculum. The National Agenda has an expanded core curriculum that describes the skill areas needed for students with visual impairments to prepare for a successful adult life. This curriculum goes beyond academic skills to include other considerations for the individualized education plan (IEP) team. Examples of expanded core curriculum areas are orientation and mobility, social interaction skills, career education, technology, independent living skills, and visual efficiency skills.

ASSESSMENT AND INSTRUCTIONAL ISSUES

Students with visual impairment should be included in general education when possible through careful assessment, strategies, and use of assistive equipment and materials. A TVI coordinates the instructional program. As children get older, it often is advisable to introduce them to adults with visual impairments so that they can experience normal work situations.

As stated previously, children with visual impairments may have difficulty with reading and writing and some low vision problems simply require more time for students. These issues can be particularly trying during standard testing at schools. The No Child Left Behind (NCLB) Act was signed into law in 2002 by President George W. Bush. The act revised the Elementary and Secondary Education Act, which is the primary federal law in precollegiate education. NCLB requires annual testing of all students in reading and math proficiency.

A student's functional visual assessment may need to include adaptation of achievement and other standardized tests such as those administered to satisfy school and state requirements under NCLB. The test may be conducted in Braille, on a computer, with magnification, or in a number of other ways, depending on the child's visual impairment. Responses may be given orally or through word processors or Braille writers. Scheduling accommodations such as extended time also may be made for students with visual impairments who need them.

There are challenges particular to educating students with visual impairments. Teachers who specialize in educating students with blindness and low vision often are isolated from their colleagues in the field because they may be the only TVI in the school district. They should remain connected with the larger community of professionals serving students with visual impairments. Some of the assistive devices for students can be difficult to find or expensive, so careful assessment, proof of need, and at times assistance from specialized resources may be required. Educators and parents of students with visual impairments should try to provide assistance to students

only when needed, within the guidelines of the assessment plan and IEP, and help students develop a sense of initiative and independence.

SEE ALSO *Individualized Education Program (IEP); Special Education.*

BIBLIOGRAPHY

American Foundation for the Blind. (2005). A teacher perspective. *National Agenda on the Education of Children and Youths with Visual Impairments, Including those with Multiple Disabilities.* Retrieved April 11, 2008, from http://www.afb.org/Section.asp?DocumentID=2669&SectionID=56.

Baumberger, J. P., & Harper R. E. (2007). *Assisting students with disabilities: A handbook for school counselors* (2nd ed.). Thousand Oaks, CA: Corwin Press.

Educating the child with a disability or other special needs. (2007). *The Exceptional Parent, 37,* 104–108.

Hannell, G. (2006) *Identifying children with special needs: Checklists and action plans for teachers.* Thousand Oaks, CA: Corwin Press.

Huebner, K. M. (2006). The expanded core curriculum: Finding the time. Retrieved April 11, 2008, from http://www.tsbvi.edu/agenda/core-ppt.htm.

National Dissemination Center for Children with Disabilities. (2004). Disability fact sheet no. 13: Visual Impairments. Retrieved April 11, 2008, from http://www.nichcy.org/pubs/factshe/fs13.pdf.

Olmstead, J.E. (n.d.) Itinerant teachers. Retrieved April 11, 2008, from http://www.afb.org/Section.asp?SectionID=44&TopicID=256.

Pierangelo, R., & Giuliani, G. (2007). *The educator's manual of disabilities and disorders.* San Francisco: John Wiley & Sons.

Riordan-Eva, P., & Whitcher, J. P. (2004). *Vaughan and Asbury's general ophthalmology* (16th ed.). New York: McGraw-Hill.

Topor, I. L. (n.d.) Fact sheet: Functional Vision Assessment. Retrieved April 11, 2008, from http://www.cde.state.co.us/cdesped/download/pdf/dbFuncVisionAssmt.pdf.

U.S. Preventive Services Task Force. (2005). Screening for visual impairment in children younger than five years: Recommendation statement. *American Family Physician, 71,* 333–336.

Teresa Odle

VOLITION

From the late 1980s to the late 2000s, psychologists analyzed personal qualities other than intelligence that predict accomplishments such as success in school. Qualities such as dependability and conscientiousness, which lead to high levels of competence, were recast in information processing terms. What underlies conscientiousness, for example, are wishes and desires that become goals and intentions, which must be implemented and protected from competing goals and other distractions (Kuhl, 1984). Duckworth and colleagues (2007) refer colloquially to a quality they call "grit," which they define as "perseverance and passion for long-term goals." Their "Grit Scale" reliably distinguishes students who attest to finishing tasks, persisting under difficulty, and overcoming obstacles from those students who say they tend to vacillate or are easily distracted on tasks. These authors find that "grit" plays a key role in leadership and other long-term achievements.

Cognitive-motivation researchers and positive psychologists alike recognized that there is something in the notion of purposive striving that cannot be captured within the concept of motivation, so they put a new interpretation on the old idea of willpower by returning to serious study of the psychological concept of volition. Volition is that quality of the will that takes a student from implementation to follow-through, reflecting an ability to persist in the face of difficulty. Whereas motivation denotes a process of goal setting leading to commitment, volition denotes a process of implementation leading to goal accomplishment. To the extent that volition helps a student to protect established goals and follow-through on tasks, it is highly important for success in academic settings such as classroom learning.

PROCESSES THAT CONTRIBUTE TO VOLITIONAL CONTROL

The key processes that define volition are the management, protection, and maintenance of attention, motivation, and emotion in tasks: Breaking a task into smaller pieces; beginning without procrastinating; resolving to avoid distraction and concentrate; thinking of the satisfaction completion will bring. Evidence of the ability for selective control of attention and emotion even in very young children has been shown to predict school performance later on (Shoda, Mischel, & Peake, 1990).

Psychologists offer a wide array of models that describe volitional processes. Some of the most cited are models of action control (Kuhl, 1984), effortful control, impulse control, emotion control, learned industriousness (Eisenberger, 1992), implementation intentions (Gollwitzer, 1999), and self-regulated learning or SRL (Corno, 2007). According to Boekaerts and Corno (2005), who reviewed research on self-regulation in education, there are several self-regulation processes that reflect volitional control; these include managing learning tasks, coping with distractions, focusing attention, and productively channeling emotions. In addition to these aspects of volition, SRL models highlight the role of motives and goals in strategy use and academic achievement (Zimmerman & Schunk, 2007).

Although volition theorists emphasize the conscious effort that a student makes to better manage learning, some go on to develop the idea that volitional processes can become automatized with repeated use and associated conditional feedback. Automization frees up mental resources for tasks over time, suggesting that volitional processes can

be transferred to new situations. Transfer across situations, as when there is evidence of automatically applied control on novel tasks, can lead students toward a volitional style of learning (a work style or work ethic) that again is suggestive of traits such as dependability.

STRATEGIES FOR MAINTAINING VOLITIONAL CONTROL

To better understand how volition develops, scholars identified the variety of explicit strategies used by students to manage, protect, and maintain their work efforts. For example, Corno and Kanfer (1993) adapted a list generated by Kuhl (1984) into two categories of covert and overt strategies used by students in educational settings. Both covert and overt (easily observable) strategies are aimed at protecting targeted goals from competing goals or other distractions, and managing negative affect.

The covert strategies studied by these authors included (a) metacognitive controls such as planning and self-monitoring; (b) motivation controls such as self-reinforcement, self-instructing, adapting tasks to make them more meaningful, and prioritizing target goals; and (c) emotion controls such as working out a timeline, controlled breathing in the face of difficulty, imagining rewards and satisfactions, and using available resources for conditional feedback. The overt strategies studied by these authors included controlling the task situation and others in the task setting. To control the task setting, students can create manageable sub-tasks, gather information and materials in advance, and avoid distractions. To control others in the task setting, students can take actions such as seeking assistance from teachers and supportive peers and asking bothersome peers to remove themselves. All of these strategies, whether overt or covert, are proactive, again aimed at managing, protecting, and maintaining focus on tasks.

To exemplify, imagine students who have decided to buckle down, pay attention, and do their schoolwork. Their challenge then is to avoid the idea of doing something else instead (e.g., to spend time with friends), however tempting and potentially more satisfying that alternative act might be. By prioritizing goals to get their work done over and above their competing social goals, and by regulating their emotional reactions to tasks (keeping negative affect at bay), students are using volitional control to manage an inner conflict. They are protecting their targeted goals and maintaining their efforts to achieve those goals. Imagine further that this scenario becomes automatic for more students in more academic task situations, so that the script for "concentrate—got to" gets used adaptively by students whenever it is needed. That is the goal for educators who seek to help students move toward better volitional control.

PERSON AND ENVIRONMENTAL FACTORS THAT INFLUENCE VOLITIONAL CONTROL

Researchers have also studied the individual and contextual factors that support or impede students' abilities to exercise volitional control adaptively. They find that some students are predisposed, by orientation or developmental experience, to be more or less conscientious in their academic endeavors. For example, Snow and Lohman (1984) related volitional strategy use to cognitive ability; using a variety of indicators, they found that college students who score highly on standardized tests of cognitive ability consistently use effective organization and control strategies that maintain concentration while they complete the items. Kuhl (1984) found that a self-reported orientation to take action rather than procrastinate when confronted with decision-making tasks was also predictive of volitional strategy use and task completion in adults. In a different vein, research by Dweck (see Dweck & Master, 2007) linked children's early understandings of the relationship between ability and effort to expressed beliefs about their own capabilities (their "self-theories"); Dweck found that even intellectually able students may have underdeveloped volition if they doubt their own capabilities.

In regards to aspects of the learning context that support and promote self-regulation in students, researchers highlight the importance of teacher modeling (many different explained examples) of self-regulation processes and strategies, with reinforced use in appropriate class assignments. The earlier and more frequent such explanation, the better; like metacognition, volitional control develops experientially (Corno, 2000). This means that parents, too, can serve as role models, particularly in the early grades and when working with children on homework (Xu & Corno, 1994). In general, the evidence supports the idea that acquiring higher-order skills such as self-regulation demands a co-constructive or social learning process that includes evaluative feedback.

In the early 2000s teachers commonly use various forms of collaborative learning activities to create cohesion in the classroom community. Cooperative work and projects are situations in which students with good work habits can model and encourage their peers. These same settings can disadvantage students, however, if poor work habits are being modeled instead, or if there is no conditional feedback. When tasks are carefully structured to maximize opportunities for learning about, carrying out, and receiving reinforcement for self-regulation and co-regulation (as when pairs of students work together in cooperative tasks), there is a positive influence on volitional control. Classrooms in which students share in planning decisions about what material will be covered, when, and in what

venues will also support volitional control because this creates an "implementation intention" (Gollwitzer, 1999).

EDUCATIONAL OUTCOMES RELATED TO VOLITIONAL CONTROL

Volition influences continued motivation and affect as well as learning and long-term performance. There are potential downsides as well as upsides to volitional control. Gollwitzer's 1999 research on intention suggests, paradoxically, that people tend not to look back once they have firmly established goals that they value. Although this is good for keeping students on task, it also implies that letting go of goals that are impossible to accomplish will be difficult. The person so focused uses volition as a form of denial. Another potential downside of particularly strong volition is the development of an over-controlling or compulsive learning style that can induce a stress response to schoolwork. Stress of course can also trigger related negative affect. Finally, particularly strong volition can mask a sense of inadequacy, just as an easy sense of agency can fuel movement toward goals. There are advantages if students can learn to self-regulate in natural, almost playful, ways, using volitional control automatically under many tasks and circumstances.

The strong upside of adaptive use of volitional control is that it tends to result in the display of good academic work habits. These are the strategies and tactics for effective completion of academic tasks that are honed through experience (Corno, 2007). Work habits studied by psychologists include class participation, using feedback and other available resources, managing a workload, planning, and studying (i.e., habitual use of volitional control strategies). Students with good work habits tend to perform well in school, in part because they are putting in the dedicated learning time. But they also excel because they are recognized and given status as full participants in their academic communities; this recognition fosters a sense of efficacy for academic work that then has its own momentum (Zimmerman & Schunk, 2007). When students are viewed by teachers and parents as responsible and diligent workers, they are likely, ultimately, to benefit in other ways as well. Appreciation and rewards for hard work are given all along the age range (e.g., teacher recommendations, academic awards, nominations for leadership positions). Such acknowledgements are influential in decisions about college admissions and employment because they are predictive of success in these settings (see Willingham, 1985).

DEVELOPING VOLITIONAL CONTROL IN STUDENTS

With respect to the combinations of instructional events that can promote development of volitional control in students, techniques range from simple manipulations to school-wide programs. An example of the former is illustrated by Oettingen, Honig, and Gollwitzer (2000) who taught students an algorithm for making an action plan: determine when, where, and first steps for doing homework. Results showed significantly more of these students actually completed homework relative to comparable peers in a control group. As already stated, individual teachers can use a variety of techniques for teaching students about self-regulated learning. Perry (1998) provides examples of strategies for teaching young children; Randi and Corno (2000) offer a secondary-level curriculum based on a quest theme in which literary characters are shown to embody self-regulation. Counseling psychologists and special educators have refined cognitive-behavior modification procedures such as self-monitoring to make them useful with children who have impulsivity and behavioral control issues or learning disabilities (Butler & Cartier, 2004). Programs for time management have been adapted from the workplace (Corno & Kanfer, 1994). Even students who are temperamentally or stylistically less self-regulating can learn to use the management aspects and many other strategies of volitional control, particularly if they are motivated by feedback and incentives (Zimmerman & Schunk, 2007).

A more ambitious effort is evident in an after-school program designed to support the self-regulation and academic performance of middle school students (Oyserman, Terry, & Bybee, 2002). In this program, adults helped students plan for their futures and construct paths for achieving their goals; they thought about obstacles and how to work past them and had students learn from interviews with others who followed a similar path. The authors' evaluation of this program with inner city students found increased emotional engagement with school and better attendance and behavior as a result of the experience, particularly among troubled boys. Boekaerts and Minnaert (2003) report on a similarly comprehensive program aimed at vocational secondary schools in the Netherlands. In all of these education efforts, it remains important for teachers to encourage students and provide opportunities for them to practice volitional control in regular class work as well, that is, to afford and reward rather than constrain volitional control.

Educational researchers define volition as a quality of human functioning that takes a student from commitment to follow-through in academic tasks. Volition reflects an ability to avoid procrastination and to persist in the face of difficulty. To the extent that volition helps a student to accomplish school tasks, it is important for success in academic learning and performance.

The key processes that underlie volition are the management, protection, and maintenance of attention, moti-

vation, and emotion, aspects of self-regulation that tend to mark the efforts of exceptional students. Volitional control is evidenced in strategic task management, coping with obstacles and distractions, efforts to focus attention, and productive channeling of emotions. In addition to conscious regulation of thinking as they work, students often have implicit, habitual or automatized processes in place to maintain their effort. Volitional control has been measured reliably in children and adults by observation, interview, and self-report, and the research confirms that it can be manipulated experimentally.

When students use volitional control to manage conflicting goals, they work strategically to protect targeted goals and maintain efforts to achieve those goals. Adaptive use of volitional strategies as needed comes easier for some students than for others. Predisposing orientations that have been identified include high cognitive ability, an action orientation, "grit," and what Dweck (Dweck & Master, 2007) calls an "incremental theory of intelligence" (an understanding that personal efforts will aid improvement after failure). Students with these and similar characteristics or experiences are also likely to develop good academic work habits from the exercise of volition.

Volition affects continued motivation and affects as well as school learning. A moderate level of volitional control used flexibly appears to be the best target for educators, because then students are viewed by teachers and parents as responsible and diligent workers who can benefit emotionally as well. Other motivation processes, such as expectations of success, a goal to get the most from the material, even a hope to earn a better grade, can benefit from protecting goals and follow-through. These motivators, in turn, help to reinforce volition.

To promote the development of volition directly, teachers can encourage students and provide opportunities for them to practice volitional control in regular classroom tasks where they can receive pointed and constructive feedback. Practitioners can enlist competent peers to model self-regulated learning and use collaborative activities that allow students to feel they are active participants in the learning process. Just as in many other endeavors, to reach high levels of competence learners need an understanding of the concept and guided practice using volitional strategies over extended periods of time.

SEE ALSO *Self-Regulated Learning.*

BIBLIOGRAPHY
Boekaerts, M., & Corno, L. (2005). Self-regulation in the classroom: A perspective on assessment and intervention. *Applied Psychology: An International Review, 54,* 99–232.
Boekaerts, M., & Minnaert, A. (2003). Measuring behavioral change processes during an ongoing innovation program: Scope and limits. In E. DeCorte (Ed.), *Powerful Learning*

Environments: Unraveling Basic Components and Dimensions (pp. 71–87). Amsterdam: Pergamon.

Butler, D., & Cartier, S. (2004). Promoting effective task interpretation as an important work habit: A key to successful teaching and learning. *Teachers College Record, 106,* 1729–1758.

Corno, L. (1994). Student volition and education: Outcomes, influences, and practices. In B. Zimmerman & D. Schunk (Eds.), *Self-regulated learning and academic achievement: Educational applications* (pp. 229-254). New York: Springer Verlag.

Corno, L. (Ed.). (2000). Conceptions of volition: Investigating theoretical questions; Studies of practice [Special double issue]. *International Journal of Educational Research, 33*(7, 8).

Corno, L. (2007). Work habits and self-regulated learning: Helping students to find a "will" from a "way." In B. Zimmerman & D. Schunk (Eds.), *Motivation and Self-Regulated Learning: Theory, Research, and Applications* (pp. 197–222). New York: Erlbaum/Taylor & Francis.

Corno, L., & Kanfer, R. (1993). The role of volition in learning and performance. In L. Darling-Hammond (Ed.), *Review of Research in Education* (Vol. 19, pp. 301–341). Washington, DC: American Educational Research Association.

Duckworth, A. L., Peterson, C., Matthews, M. D., & Kelly, D. R. (2007). Grit: Perseverance and passion for long-term goals. *Journal of Personality and Social Psychology, 92*(6), 1087–1101.

Dweck, C., & Master, A. (2007). Self-theories motivate self-regulated learning. In D. H. Schunk & B. J. Zimmerman (Eds.), *Motivation and self-regulated learning: Theory, research, and applications* (pp. 31–52). New York: Erlbaum/Taylor & Francis.

Eisenberger, R. (1992). Learned industriousness. *Psychological Review, 99,* 248–267.

Gollwitzer, P. M. (1999). Implementation intentions: Strong effects of simple plans. *American Psychologist, 54,* 493–503.

Kuhl, J. (1984). Volitional aspects of achievement motivation and learned helplessness: Toward a comprehensive theory of action control. In B. A. Maher (Ed.), *Progress in experimental personality research* (Vol. 13, pp. 99–171). New York: Academic Press.

Oettingen, G., Honig, G., & Gollwitzer, P. M. (2000). Effective self-regulation of goal attainment. *International Journal of Educational Research, 33,* 705–732.

Oyserman, D., Terry, K., & Bybee, D. (2002). A possible selves intervention to enhance school involvement. *Journal of Adolescence, 25*(3), 313–326.

Perry, N. (1998). Young children's self-regulated learning and contexts that support it. *Journal of Educational Psychology, 90,* 715–729.

Randi, J., & Corno, L. (2000). Teacher innovations in self-regulated learning. In P. Pintrich, M. Boekaerts, & M. Zeidner (Eds.), *Handbook of self-regulation* (pp. 651–685). San Diego, CA: Academic Press.

Shoda, Y., Mischel, W., & Peake, P. (1990). Predicting adolescent cognitive and self-regulatory competencies from preschool delay of gratification: Identifying diagnostic conditions. *Developmental Psychology, 26,* 978–986.

Snow, R. E., & Lohman, D. F. (1984). Toward a theory of cognitive aptitude for learning from instruction. *Journal of Educational Psychology, 76,* 347–376.

Willingham, W. (1985). *Success in college.* New York: College Board.

Xu, J. & Corno, L. (1994). Case studies of families doing third grade homework. *Teachers College Record, 100,* 402–436.

Zimmerman, B. & Schunk, D. (2007). *Motivation and Self-Regulated Learning: Theory, Research, and Applications.* Boca Raton, FL: Taylor & Francis.

CHILDREN'S LITERATURE

Bennett, W. (Ed.). (1995). *The children's book of virtues.* New York: Simon & Schuster. [Illustrated anthology of traditional stories and poems that teach the importance of qualities such as perseverance, responsibility, self-discipline, good work habits, and emotion control.]

Cecil, N. L., & Roberts, P. (1992). *Developing resiliency through children's literature: A guide for teachers and librarians, K-8.* Jefferson, NC: McFarland. [Annotated bibliography of children's books that can be used to teach resiliency, including such strategies as problem-solving, persistence, overcoming fears and obstacles, and positive thinking; contains numerous examples of classroom activities; valuable out-of-print resource worth seeking in libraries and used book outlets.]

Paulsen, G. (1986). *Hatchet.* New York: Macmillan. [Survival story in which a boy learns to survive in the wilderness after an airplane crash; offers a model for teaching resourcefulness.]

Piper, W. (2005). *The little engine that could.* New York: Philomel. [Classic tale retold by Watty Piper and illustrated by Loren Long; contains suggestions for reading the book to young children, including using the well-known refrain "I think I can" to reinforce the importance of effort.]

Polacco, P. (1998). *Thank you, Mr. Falker.* New York: Philomel. [Provides a model of how school children can overcome reading difficulties with persistence and a sense of self-efficacy.]

RESOURCES FOR CLASSROOM TEACHERS

Corno, L., & Randi, J. (1997). Motivation, volition, and collaborative innovation in classroom literacy. In J. T. Guthrie & A. Wigfield (Eds.), *Reading engagement: Motivating readers through integrated instruction* (pp. 51–67). Newark, DE: International Reading Association. [Includes "A Reference Guide for Addressing Motivational and Volitional Goals in Educational Settings," a brief synopsis teachers can keep on their desks (pp. 59–61).]

Israel, S. E. (2007). *Using metacognitive assessments to create individualized reading instruction.* Newark, DE: International Reading Association. [Includes a variety of reproducible student handouts and inventories for assessing students' metacognitive strategies.]

Johnson, E. (2004). *The hero in me: Reinforcing self-regulated learning as we connect to literary heroes.* Yale-New Haven Teachers Institute. Retrieved April 11, 2008, from http://www.yale.edu/ynhti/curriculum/units/2004/2/04.02.03.x.html. [Curriculum unit written developed by a teacher for use in upper elementary and middle school classes.]

Manning, B. H., & Payne, B. D. (1996). Self-talk for teachers and students: Metacognitive strategies for personal and classroom use. Boston: Allyn & Bacon. [Provides a teacher-friendly overview of self-regulation; includes examples and resources for applying metacognitive strategies for both students' and teachers' learning.]

Sternberg, R. E., & Grigorenko, E. (2000). *Teaching for successful intelligence.* Arlington Heights, IL: Skylight. [Provides classroom examples for implementing Sternberg's forms of "successful intelligence," one of which (practical intelligence) focuses on the development of personal traits that promote volition, including perseverance, impulse control, and commitment.]

RESOURCES FOR TEACHER EDUCATION

Snowman, J., & Biehler, R. (2006). *Psychology applied to teaching* (11th ed.). Boston: Houghton Mifflin. [Educational psychology textbook with an extensive treatment of self-regulated learning, including several models for promoting self-regulation among learners (see Chapter 9, "Social Cognitive Theory," pp. 276–308).]

Woolfolk, A. (2007). *Educational psychology* (10th ed.). Boston: Allyn & Bacon. (Library Course Reserve). [Widely adopted educational psychology textbook; summarizes the research on self-regulated learning and volition, provides guidelines for supporting self-regulated learning in the classroom, and suggests several Web sites that can serve as resources for parents and teachers interested in helping students develop volitional strategies.]

Lyn Corno
Judi Randi

VYGOTSKY, LEV SEMENOVICH
1896–1934

Lev Semenovich Vygotsky ARCHIVES OF THE HISTORY OF AMERICAN PSYCHOLOGY. THE UNIVERSITY OF AKRON.

Lev Semenovich Vygotsky (1896–1934) is best known for his theories of cognitive development in which he explored the importance of culture, language development, and the use of cognitive apprenticeships in the classroom. Although he was a prominent researcher in the Soviet Union during the cultural revolution, his writings were officially banned when Joseph Stalin (1879–1953) came to power and were overtaken in prominence by the growing influence of Jean Piaget (1896–1980). It was not until his works were translated from the original Russian several decades after his death that many European and American psychologists took note of Vygotsky's writings and began to incorporate his theories into their research and teaching practices.

Vygotsky graduated from Moscow University in 1917 with a degree in law and a specialization in literature. While attending Moscow University, Vygotsky concurrently attended an unofficial, anti-czarist institution known as Shinyavskii University where he studied a number of disciplines including history, philosophy, and psychology. These experiences led him to return to his hometown of Gomel, Byelorussia, to teach at a local teachers' training college, where he also established his first psychology laboratory to study handicapped and mentally retarded children. In 1924 Vygotsky accepted

an invitation to join the Institute of Psychology at Moscow State University (formerly Moscow University) where he completed his dissertation in 1925. He then founded the Experimental-Defectological Institute at Moscow State University II, where he advanced the field of special education by incorporating Marxist and other psychological influences into his research. At the end of Vygotsky's career, political and cultural changes in the Soviet Union caused him to lose the directorship of the Institute, though he continued to remain on its faculty until his premature death in 1934 at the age of 37. Vygotsky was associated with a number of prominent Russian and Soviet researchers and theorists during his career, including his friend and colleague Alexander Romanovich Luria, and A. N. Leontiev. He was a contemporary of many notable psychologists, including Jean Piaget.

Though Vygotsky was not well known in Western Europe or North America until the late 1950s, his work in special education and cognitive development has led to important developments in classroom learning. For example, Vygotsky was a firm advocate for integrated classrooms in which disabled students are educated alongside their peers, and he is known as one of the founders of special education. In addition, his theories on thought and language development are among the most well known of his contributions.

Vygotsky believed that "the most significant moment in the course of intellectual development, which gives birth to the purely human forms of practical and abstract intelligence, occurs when speech and practical activity, two previously completely independent lines of development, converge" (Vygotsky, L. S., 1978, p. 24). That is, when thought and language become one, the individual is able to analyze the world in more complex ways, to parse words and use them to form new meanings, and to organize thoughts. Vygotsky stressed that it is through the tools provided by language that meaning is assigned to what the child perceives, an act that is infused with cultural relevance. The words people use and the ways in which they use them convey certain elements of culture that are passed from one person to the next.

Through his theories of cognitive development, Vygotsky (1978) proposed that children develop most effectively and efficiently when they are engaged in tasks that are within their *zone of proximal development* which he defined as "the distance between the actual developmental level as determined by independent problem solving and the level of potential development as determined through problem solving under adult guidance or in collaboration with more capable peers" (p. 86). In other words, children often learn best when they are given tasks that are slightly beyond their ability to perform alone, but can perform when aided by someone who is more cognitively advanced.

A discussion of Vygotsky's work is not complete without reference to his proposition that development is situated within a culturally specific social-historical context. Vygotsky believed that development stems from relationships and social activities, whereby culture is imparted to the learner through both organized and unorganized activity. As Vygotsky sought to research various aspects of development, one of his primary concerns was to use appropriate methodologies. He believed that laboratory experiments, for example, were not appli-

cable to the real-world experiences of the participants. Instead, Vygotsky believed that it was important to study development within natural contexts. He also believed that the researcher should determine the most appropriate unit of analysis. In Vygotsky's research, for example, he often broadened his unit of analysis beyond the individual to include ecological factors.

As a result of Vygotsky's work, there have been a number of theoretical, methodological, and practical advances in psychology, education, and a wide variety of other disciplines. Barbara Rogoff's influential concept of guided participation is a contemporary idea inspired by Vygotsky's work. Also, many researchers have developed ecologically valid research methods. Developmental theorists have expanded Vygotsky's work to discuss the ways in which culture, history, and context play important roles in human development. Lastly, many pedagogical techniques used worldwide stem from Vygotsky's advocacy for the education of disabled students along with his theories of thought and language development and the zone of proximal development.

SEE ALSO *Cognitive Development: Vygotsky's Theory.*

BIBLIOGRAPHY

WORKS BY

Vygotsky, L. S. (1962). *Thought and language.* Cambridge, MA: MIT Press and Wiley.

Vygotsky, L. S. (1978). *Mind in society: The development of higher psychological processes.* Cambridge, MA: Harvard University Press.

Vygotsky, L. S. (1988–1999). *The collected works of L. S. Vygotsky* (Vols. 1–6). New York: Springer.

WORKS ABOUT

Moll, L. C. (Ed.). (1990). *Vygotsky and education: Instructional implications and applications of sociohistorical psychology.* New York: Cambridge University Press.

Newman, F., & Holman, L. (1993). *Lev Vygotsky: Revolutionary scientist.* New York: Routledge.

R. Trent Haines

WEINER, BERNARD
1935–

Bernard Weiner was born in 1935 in Chicago, Illinois, the youngest of three sons of Russian immigrants. A product of Chicago's public schools, he received his undergraduate degree in Liberal Arts from the University of Chicago in 1955 and an MBA, majoring in Industrial Relations, from the same university in 1957. Following two years of service in the U.S. Army, Weiner enrolled in a PhD program in personality at the University of Michigan, where he was mentored by John Atkinson, one of the leading personality and motivational psychologists of that era. Weiner completed his PhD from Michigan in 1963, spent two years as an assistant professor at the University of Minnesota before joining the psychology faculty at the University of California at Los Angeles (UCLA) in 1965, where he remained active into the early 2000s.

Drawing on his intellectual roots in the field of motivation, Weiner was a leader in the study of attribution theory, one of the major theories of motivation in contemporary psychology. Attribution theory is concerned with the perceived causes of success and failure—for example, did a student fail an important test because of low aptitude or lack of effort—and the motivational consequences of particular attributions. Fundamental to attribution theory are the properties of causes (including their locus in the person or the world, perceived stability, and controllability), causal linkages to emotions and expectancy of success, and achievement performance.

For example, lack of aptitude is perceived to be an internal, stable, and uncontrollable cause of failure. Being internal to the person, this attribution for failure reduces self-esteem; since it is stable, expectancy of future success is low; and because it is uncontrollable, feelings of shame are evoked. Low esteem, low expectancy, and shame give rise to poor performance. The factor of aptitude contrasts with lack of effort as the perceived cause of failure, which is unstable (thereby leading to high expectancy) and controllable (evoking guilt, a motivator of achievement rather than shame, an inhibitor). Attributional analyses help explain how individuals interpret their own achievement outcomes, but also the reactions of others. For example, teachers are likely to evaluate the failing student differently if his or her failure is perceived to be caused by low ability versus lack of effort. Thus attribution theory is both an intrapersonal theory of motivation (how one thinks about oneself) and an interpersonal theory of motivation (how others think about one).

Attribution theory provided educational psychology with the theoretical foundation for attribution retraining programs. Such programs are designed to improve motivation and achievement by changing maladaptive attributions for failure. For example, many attribution retraining studies with participants from elementary school through college have documented that students who are taught to attribute their failure to low effort rather than low aptitude are more likely to be optimistic about the future and to persist longer when they encounter academic challenges.

Weiner enjoyed an illustrious career as an attribution theorist. While he is best known to educational psychologists for his attribution research in the achievement domain, he also incorporated other social phenomena such as reactions to the stigmatized, help giving, aggression, excuse giving, punishment, and moral emotions. These phenomena are as

Bernard Weiner **PHOTO COURTESY OF BERNARD WEINER.**

relevant to educational psychology and classroom learning as the earlier attribution research on achievement strivings. Few other theories of motivation are amenable to such breadth of application.

As of 2008, Weiner had authored 13 books and published more than 200 articles in peer-reviewed journals. He was the recipient of numerous awards, including the Donald Campbell Research Award in Social Psychology from the American Psychological Association and the Palmer O. Johnson Publication Award from the American Educational Research Association. He holds honorary degrees from the Bielefeld University in Germany and Turku University in Finland.

Weiner is a recipient of a Distinguished Teaching Award from UCLA, a testament to his extraordinary ability to mentor students. Among his best known students who have had a significant impact in the field of education psychology are Jacqueline Eccles and Diane Ruble. His most frequent collaborator is a former student, Sandra Graham, also a colleague at UCLA.

SEE ALSO *Attribution Theory.*

BIBLIOGRAPHY

WORKS BY

Weiner, B. (1980). *Human motivation.* New York: Holt-Rinehart, & Winston. (Reprinted by Springer-Verlag, 1985; Erlbaum, 1989.)

Weiner, B. (1986). *An attributional theory of motivation and emotion.* New York: Springer-Verlag.

Weiner, B. (1992). *Human motivation: Metaphors, theories and research.* Newbury Park, CA: Sage.

Weiner, B. (1995). *Judgments of responsibility: A foundation for a theory of social conduct.* New York: Guilford.

Weiner, B. (2006). *Social motivation, justice, and the moral emotions.* Mahwah, NJ: Erlbaum.

Sandra Graham

WESCHLER INTELLIGENCE TEST

The Wechsler Intelligence Tests include three individually administered intelligence tests, appropriate for preschoolers through adulthood. The Wechsler Preschool and Primary Scale of Intelligence (3rd ed.) (WPPSI-III) is appropriate for children ages 2 years 6 months to 7 years, 3 months (Wechsler, 2002); the Wechsler Intelligence Scale for Children (4th ed.) (WISC-IV) is used for children and adolescents ages 6 through 16 (Wechsler, 2003); and the Wechsler Adult Intelligence Scale (3rd ed.) is used for assessment of those ages 16 and older (Wechsler, 1997). All scales are derived, directly or indirectly, from the Wechsler-Bellevue Intelligence Scale (Wechsler, 1939), and adult intelligence test developed by David Wechsler at Bellevue Hospital. The original WISC was a downward extension of the adult scale, and the WPPSI was a downward extension of the WISC. The three tests thus share a common heritage, structure, and interpretation. Although David Wechsler died in 1982, he continued into the early 2000s to be listed as the author of the Wechsler tests. This entry concentrates primarily on the WISC-IV, the measure most commonly used with school-age children, but many of the comments apply to the other Wechsler scales, as well.

In school settings, the WISC-IV is administered by school psychologists to children referred for a variety of academic and behavioral concerns. The test, administered as part of a battery of intellectual, academic, behavioral, and social-emotional measures, can be useful in differential diagnosis (e.g., mild mental retardation versus low average functioning) and in understanding a child's academic weaknesses (e.g., a problem in reading comprehension may be, in part, the result of low verbal reasoning skills).

Wechsler tests have traditionally included multiple subtests with both verbal and nonverbal content. Brief descriptions of the 15 WISC-IV subtests are shown in Table 1. Ten of the subtests are standard, or core subtests, and are given to all children. Five of the tests are supplemental, meaning that they are not generally used in the calculation of composite scores or IQs; they may

Scales and subtests of the Wechsler Intelligence Scale for Children—Fourth Edition

Scale	Subtest	Description
Verbal	Similarities	Explain what two words or concepts have in common
	Vocabulary	Defining words
	Comprehension	Answering practical problem-related questions (e.g., why do we put stamps on letters?)
	(Information)	Answering general information questions
	(Word reasoning)	Identifying the common concepts from verbal clues
Perceptual reasoning	Block design	Arranging red and white two-colored blocks to match a pattern
	Picture concepts	Picking pictures that share a common characteristic
	Matrix reasoning	Completing an unfinished matrix of symbols
	(Picture completion)	Identifying missing parts in drawn pictures
Working memory	Digit span	Repeating digits in forward and reversed order
	Letter-number sequencing	Series of letters & numbers are presented orally. Examinee recalls numbers in order first, then letters
	(Arithmetic)	Answering oral arithmetic word problems
Processing speed	Coding	Quickly writing symbols associated with numbers or shapes (younger children)
	Symbol search	Marking the re-occurrence of abstract symbols
	(Cancellation)	Speeded selection of a category (e.g., animals) of pictures

Note: Supplemental subtests are enclosed in parentheses.

Table 1 ILLUSTRATION BY GGS INFORMATION SERVICES. CENGAGE LEARNING, GALE.

be substituted for standard tests, however, if subtests are spoiled or are not given.

For previous versions of the WISC and the other Wechsler Scales, the subtests have traditionally been summed to create verbal and nonverbal (performance) IQs, as well as a full scale IQ designed to estimate general, overall, intelligence. Despite this traditional scoring, factor analyses have long suggested that the various Wechsler Scales were measuring more than just verbal, nonverbal, and general intelligence. The WISC-IV represents a major departure from this tradition; as shown in the Table, the WISC-IV subtests are combined to create verbal, perceptual reasoning, memory, and processing speed indexes (a full scale IQ, representing a composite of all 10 standard subtests, is still calculated). The structure for the WISC-IV was changed in order to make the instrument more consistent with research and with contemporary theory concerning the structure and nature of intelligence (Zhu & Weiss, 2005); presumably the subsequent revisions of the WAIS and WPPSI will also show considerable change.

Research (Keith, Fine, Reynolds, Taub, & Kranzler, 2006) suggests that the verbal scale of the WISC-IV indeed measures verbal reasoning skills, or crystallized intelligence from a three-stratum (Carroll, 1993) or Cattell-Horn-Carroll (CHC) (McGrew, 2005) theoretical orientation. Likewise, it appears that the processing speed index of the WISC-IV provides a measure of processing speed, and the full scale IQ is a valid measure of general

intelligence, or g. The perceptual reasoning tests of the WISC-IV, in contrast, appear to measure a mixture of visual spatial abilities and fluid intelligence (also know as novel reasoning). The working memory index of the WISC-IV, excluding the arithmetic subtest, appears to assess working and short-term memory skills. Arithmetic, however, may measure a mixture of intellectual abilities, chief among them quantitative knowledge or quantitative reasoning, a narrow ability subsumed under the broad ability of fluid intelligence. Interestingly, the arithmetic subtest is among the best single measures of general intelligence on the WISC-IV (Keith, Fine, Reynolds, Taub, & Kranzler, 2006).

The full scale IQ and the four index scores have a national mean of 100 and a standard deviation of 15 for each age level. Thus, because the scores conform to a normal curve, approximately 68% of children and adolescents will have scores between 85 and 115. The subtests use a different standard score metric: they have a mean of 10 and a SD of 3. A report of assessment results using the WISC-IV will generally include a listing of the full scale and index scores, including percentile ranks for those scores and confidence intervals around the scores. Such scores will often be interpreted with statements such as "Johnny's IQ score was higher than 34% of children his age, and there is a 90% chance that his true FSIQ is within the range of 90–98."

One perceived historic advantage of the Wechsler scales over the Stanford Binet, the most common individual intelligence test prior to the advent of the Wechsler scales, was that the multiple IQ (now index) scores and subtest scores allowed the analysis of a profile of scores for an individual. There is often considerable variability in children's performance on the various tasks, and many psychologists believe that a child's pattern of strengths and weaknesses is useful in understanding that child's cognitive functioning and in remediating academic weaknesses.

There is considerable debate about the efficacy of profile analysis, however, with critics contending that profiles rarely produce reliable information and that the most general score (the full scale IQ) is generally the only one that should be interpreted (Watkins, Glutting, & Youngstrom, 2005). It is certainly the case that profile analysis can be overdone, but its cautious use often is helpful in understanding the strengths and weaknesses of children referred for academic and behavioral concerns. Such an approach generally focuses on a top-down approach in which the most general score is interpreted and more specific scores are only interpreted when there is unusual variation in scores. This *intelligent testing* also proceeds in steps from interpretation of the IQ, to the indexes, to combinations of subtests that theory and research suggest measure common psychological constructs. Examiners look to other test results and background and interview information to support or reject hypotheses generated. Such an approach to interpretation of the WISC-IV is explained in Flanagan and Kaufman (2004). To use this approach validly, one obviously needs a strong understanding of the constructs measured by the test being interpreted.

The WISC-IV is well standardized and has a long clinical and research history. The test likely provides reliable and valid estimates of general intelligence and several important broad cognitive abilities. There are also inconsistencies in the scoring structure of the WISC-IV and what the test likely measures, which make interpretation of some of the scores produced difficult. Although more consistent with intelligence theory and research than previous versions of the WISC, the test still has room for improvement.

At one time the Wechsler Scales were among the few choices available for individual intellectual assessment. As of 2008 there are numerous other possibilities. Other possible measures include the Differential Abilities Scales, Second Edition (ages 2 years 6 months through 17) (Elliott, 2007), the Kaufman Assessment Battery for Children, Second Edition (age 3 to 18) (Kaufman & Kaufman, 2004), the Stanford Binet Intelligence Scales, Fifth Edition (ages 2 and older) (Roid, 2003), and the Woodcock Johnson III Tests of Cognitive Ability (ages 2 and older) (Woodcock, McGrew, & Mather, 2001, 2007).

SEE ALSO *Intelligence Testing.*

BIBLIOGRAPHY

Carroll, J. B. (1993). *Human cognitive abilities: A survey of factor-analytic studies.* New York: Cambridge University Press.

Elliott, C. D. (2007). *Differential ability scales* (2nd ed.). San Antonio, TX: Psychological Corporation.

Flanagan, D. P., & Kaufman, A. S. (2004). *Essentials of WISC-IV assessment.* New York: Wiley.

Kaufman, A. S., & Kaufman, N. L. (2004). *Kaufman assessment battery for children* (2nd ed.). Circle Pines, MN: American Guidance Service.

Keith, T. Z., Fine, J. G., Reynolds, M. R., Taub, G. E., & Kranzler, J. H. (2006). Higher-order, multi-sample, confirmatory factor analysis of the Wechsler Intelligence Scale for Children (4th ed.): What does it measure? *School Psychology Review, 35,* 108–127.

McGrew, K. S. (2005). The Cattell-Horn-Carroll theory of cogntive abilities: Past, present, and future. In D. P. Flanagan & P. L. Harrison (Eds.), *Contemporary intellectual assessment: Theories, tests, and issues* (2nd ed., pp. 136–181). New York: Guilford.

Roid, G. H. (2003). *Stanford Binet intelligence scales* (5th ed.). Itasca, IL: Riverside.

Watkins, M. W., Glutting, J. J., & Youngstrom, E. A. (2005). Issues in subtest profile analysis. In D. P. Flanagan & P. L. Harrison (Eds.), *Contemporary intellectual assessment: Theories, tests, and issues* (2nd ed., pp. 251–268). New York: Guilford.

Wechsler, D. (1939). *The measurement of adult intelligence.* Baltimore, MD: Williams & Wilkins.

Wechsler, D. (1997). *Wechsler adult intelligence scale* (3rd ed.). San Antonio, TX: Psychological Corporation.

Wechsler, D. (2002). *Wechsler preschool and primary scale of intelligence* (3rd ed.). San Antonio, TX: Psychological Corporation.

Wechsler, D. (2003). *Wechsler intelligence scale for children* (4th ed.). San Antonio, TX: Psychological Corporation.

Woodcock, R. W., McGrew, K. S., & Mather, N. (2001, 2007). *Woodcock-Johnson III tests of cognitive abilities.* Itasca, IL: Riverside.

Zhu, J., & Weiss, L. (2005). The Wechsler scales. In D. P. Flanagan & P. L. Harrison (Eds.), *Contemporary intellectual assessment: Theories, tests, and issues* (2nd ed., pp. 297–324). New York: Guilford.

Timothy Z. Keith

WITHITNESS

SEE *Classroom Management: Withitness.*

WRITING, LEARNING AND TEACHING

SEE *Learning and Teaching Writing.*

Index

This index is sorted word-by-word. Bold page numbers indicate main entries. Italic page numbers indicate photographs, tables, or figures.

A

5-E model, 561

AAMR (American Association on Mental Retardation), 597, 598–599

ABA (applied behavior analysis), **43–47**, 87, 98–99, 328, 450

Abductive reasoning, 730

Abecedarian Project, 60, 858

Ability grouping, **1–4**
    classroom environment and, 159
    giftedness and, 3, 434
    goal orientation theory on, 441
    mathematics instruction and, 2, 549–550
    school transitions and, 777
    tracking, 2–4, 777, 857

Absenteeism, 6–7, 817

Abuse, **4–8**, *5*

AC (America's Choice), 238

ACA (American Counseling Association), 881

Academic interventions. *See* Instructional methods

Academic press, **8–10**

Accelerated Schools, 238

Accommodation, 196

Accountability, **10–13**, 77, 868–869
    See also High stakes testing

Accountable talk discussion method, 332

Achenbach Child Behavior Checklist, 25

Achievement emotions. *See* Emotions

Achievement Emotions Questionnaire (AEQ), 900

Achievement expectations. *See* Instructional objectives

Achievement for Latinos for Academic Success program, 60

Achievement gap. *See* Opportunity/achievement gap

Achievement goal theory. *See* Goal orientation theory

Achievement motivation, **13–17**
    See also Goal orientation theory; Motivation

ACT (Adaptive Character of Thought) theory, 37, 530–531

Action research, **17–19**, 749–750

Activity theory, 564–565, 851
    See also Sociocultural theory

AD (Asperger disorder), 84, 85

ADA (Americans with Disabilities Act), 667, 869, 870

Adaptation, 195

Adaptive behavior, 597–598

Adaptive Behavior Assessment System, 598

Adaptive Character of Thought (ACT) theory, 37, 530–531

Adaptive learning, 848

Additive bilingualism, 106–107

ADHD (Attention Deficit Hyperactivity Disorder), 57, 64, **65–70**, 486, 864, 945

ADHD Rating Scale-IV, 67

ADI-R (Autism Diagnostic Interview), 86

Adolescence, **19–24**
    argumentation, 53
    attachment, 64
    cognitive development, 21, 776
    decision making, 315–316
    egocentrism, 356
    emotional development, 21–22, 366
    ethnic identity, 382, 383
    gender identity, 428
    home-school dissonance and, 464
    identity development, 21–22, 381–382, 479, 682
    motivation, 392
    and observational research methods, 26
    parent-child relationships and, 22, 366, 780
    peer relationships, 22–23, 676, 682–683, 776
    physical development, 20–21, 776
    Piagetian theory on, 21, 199
    school transitions and, 775–776, 779
    sensation-seeking, 810

ADOS-G (Autism Diagnostic Observation Schedule), 86

The Adventures of Jasper Woodbury, 34–35, 81, 124, 179, 550, 830

Advocacy, 139

Advocates For Gay Youth
    Lesbian, Bisexual, Transgender and Questioning (GLBT) Youth Initiative, 818

AEQ (Achievement Emotions Questionnaire), 900

AERA (American Educational Research Association), 880, 881

Brain, *continued*
  memory and, 111–112, 114–115, 117, 596
  micro- vs. macro-level structure, 113
  reading instruction and, 114, 115–117, *115*
  social skills and, 844
  theories of intelligence and, 933, 934–935
  theories of learning and, 937
  theory of mind and, 942
  writing instruction and, 114, *116*, 117–119
BrainPower Program, 27
Bransford, John D., 81, **123–124**
Bronfenbrenner, Urie, 59, *124*, **124–125**, 159
  See also Ecological model
Brophy, Jere Edward, **125–127**, 698–699
Brown, Ann Leslie, **127–128**, 195, 227, 316
Brown v. Board of Education, 147
BRT (Business Roundtable), 461
Bruner, Jerome Seymour, **128–130**, *129*, 227, 245–246, 268, 326
BTES (Beginning Teacher Evaluation Study), 102
Bull session discussion method, 332
Bully Busters, 134
Bullying, **130–136**
  academic press and, 9
  adolescence and, 23
  aggression and, 27, 130
  anxiety and, 41
  gender and, 23, 131
  peer relationships and, 132, 678
  prosocial behavior and, 23, 131
  school-wide policies and, 132, 134, 817
  self-esteem and, 23, 134
  sexual minority youth and, 817, 818
Business Roundtable (BRT), 461

C

CABAS (Comprehensive Application of Behavior Analysis to Schooling), 99
CAI (computer-assisted instruction), 68, 74, 179, 180–181, 550
Calfee, Robert C., **137–138**
Campione, Joe, 127, 227
Campus Compact, 814
Canonical correlation analysis, 276
Canter, Lee, 166
Canter, Marlene, 166
Carey, Susan, 251

Caring teachers, **138–141**, *139*, 295
Carnegie Council on Adolescent Development, 777
Carr, Edward, 46
Cartesian worldview, 18
CAS (Cognitive Abilities System), 501
Cascade, 801
Case, Robbie, 640–643
Case-based learning, 265, **267–268**
CASEL (Collaborative for Academic, Social, and Emotional Learning), 628
CAT (Consensual Assessment Technique), 280
Cattell-Horn-Carroll (CHC) theory of cognitive abilities, 49–50
Causal structure, 241–242
CBM (curriculum-based measurement), 417, 871, 877–878
CBT (cognitive-behavioral therapy), 27, 42
CDP (Child Development Project), 627, 765
Center for Learning Technologies in Urban Schools (LeTUS), 563
Centers, 556
Central conceptual structure theory, 640–643, *640, 641*
Cerebral palsy (CP), 666
CGI (Cognitively Guided Instruction), 552
Chaining, 656
CHC (Cattell-Horn-Carroll) theory of cognitive abilities, 49–50
Cheating, **141–146**, 462, 486
Checklists, 12, 25
Chicago Child-Parent Center program, 60
Child Behavior Checklist, 67
Child Behavior Questionnaire, 358
Child-centered (learner-centered) approach, 325, 351, 450, 846
Child Development Project (CDP), 627, 765
Child maltreatment, *See,* Abuse and neglect
Child-Parent Center, 858
Child-rearing practices. *See* Parenting styles
Childhood. *See* Early childhood development
Children of Lesbian and Gays Everywhere, 818
Children's Creative Response to Conflict, 257
Choice, 351, 393, 441, 512
Claim, in argumentation, 52

Clark, Kenneth Bancroft, *146*, **146–147**
Class belonging. *See* School belonging
Class meetings, 134
Class Play, 26
Class size, **147–150**, 159
Class-wide Peer Tutoring (CWPT), 689
Class-wide positive behavior support (CWPBS), 170–173, *171*
Classic analogy, 30
Classical conditioning, **150–152**, 936
Classical measurement theory (CMT), 517
Classical test theory (CTT), **152–155**, 517, 520–521, 862
Classical theory of concept learning, 243–244
Classism. *See* Socioeconomic status
Classroom assessment, **155–158**
Classroom environment, **158–162**
  class size and, 159
  classroom management and, 159–160, 164–165, 166
  early childhood development and, 351
  Eccles' contributions, 354
  help-seeking and, 459
  measurement strategies, 161–162, 351
  motivation and, 160–161, 344, 788–789
  peer relationships and, 679–680
  social skills and, 846
  stereotype threat and, 889–890
  teacher beliefs and, 910
  teacher efficacy and, 919
  See also Classroom management; School climate; Teacher roles
Classroom Environment Scale, 161
Classroom goal structures
  cheating and, 144
  classroom environment and, 161
  competition and, 231
  emotions and, 904
  goal orientation theory and, 437–438
  help-seeking and, 459
Classroom management
  aggression and, 27
  assertive discipline, **166–168**
  autism spectrum disorders and, 87
  behaviorism on, 97–98
  caring teachers and, 140
  class size and, 148–149
  classroom environment and, 159–160, 164–165, 166
  competition and, 233
  conflict resolution, 256–260

culturally relevant pedagogy and, 305–306

data collection/analysis, 163, *163, 164,* 165–166, *165*

emotion regulation and, 359–360

emotional development and, 367–368

gender bias and, 426–427

overview, **162–166**

positive behavior support, 170–173, *171*

punishment, 97, 164, **168–170,** 171, 655–656

reinforcement and, 164, 165, 738–739

rewards, 215–216, 359–360, 516, 737–738, 755–757, 788, 849

rules, **170–173,** *171*

school transitions and, 777

token economies, 68, **173–176,** 359–360

tracking and, 3

withitness, **176–177**

Classroom practice. *See* Classroom management; Instructional methods

Clonidine, 68

CLT (cognitive load theory), **205–209,** *206,* 249, 495, 710–712

CMP (Connected Mathematics Project), 551, 552

CMT (classical measurement theory), 517

Co-regulated learning, 848

Coaching, 178, 452, 529

Coca Cola Valued Youth Program, 60

Cochlear implants, 312

Code of Fair Testing Practices in Education, 881, 883

CogAT (Cognitive Abilities Test), 499, 500

Cognition

ACT theory, 37, 530–531

aggression and, 25, 27

analogical reasoning, 30–34

Bloom's taxonomy and, 108

Bransford's contributions, 123–124

Bruner's contributions, 129

cognitive load theory, 205–209, 249, 495, 710–712

cognitive strategies, 209–214, 215, 578

concept learning, 243–246

creativity and, 279–280

critical thinking, 195, 245, 284–287, 703

decision making, 313–316, 485–488

distributed, 336–339, 529, 820, 937

dual coding theory, 341–343, 531–532, 595

emotions and, 903

expertise and, 102

feedback and, 408

higher-order thinking skills, 8, 58, 77, 78, 725

mathematics instruction and, 546

modeling and, 618

motivation and, 14, 15–16

questioning and, 724–725

reasoning, 729–735

self-explanation, 799–803

shared, 819–823

situated, 81, 827–831, 848–850, 897, 949

theories, 929–932

theory of mind, 194, 939–943

transfer and, 951

volition and, 970

writing instruction and, 564, 566

See also Cognitive development; Information processing theory; Knowledge; Metacognition; Problem solving; Self-regulation

Cognitive Abilities System (CAS), 501

Cognitive Abilities Test (CogAT), 499, 500

Cognitive apprenticeship, **177–181,** 619–620, 849

Cognitive artifacts, 336–337

Cognitive-behavioral therapy (CBT), 27, 42

Cognitive conflict, 263

Cognitive development

adolescence, 21, 776

analogical reasoning, 32

aptitude testing and, 49

attribution theory and, 72

biological theories, 183–184, **187–191**

concept development, 240–243

constructivism and, 184–185

critical thinking and, 285–286

decision making, 315

ethnic identity and, 383

evolutionary theory and, 183, 187–191

guided participation and, 449–450

identity development and, 480–481

information processing theory and, 182–183, **191–195**

metacognition and, 605–606

modeling and, 618–620

overview, **182–187**

peer relationships and, 679

Piagetian theory, 184–185, **195–200,** 197–198, 355, 356, 480

school transitions and, 772, 776

self-regulation, 807–808

sociocultural theory on, 185–186, **200–205**

sociogenetic psychology on, 185–186

strategy development, 896–899

theory of mind, 940–942

Vygotsky's theory of, **200–205**

See also Cognition; Piagetian theory

Cognitive engagement, 80–81, 82

Cognitive learning theory, 247

Cognitive load theory (CLT), **205–209,** *206,* 249, 495, 710–712

Cognitive prompts, 217

Cognitive science approach to mathematics instruction, 546

Cognitive shortcuts, 314

Cognitive strategies, **209–214,** 215, 578

Cognitive task analysis (CTA), 405

Cognitive Tutor, 37, 801

Cognitively Guided Instruction (CGI), 552

Cohort gain model of accountability, 12–13

Coleman, James, 659–660

Collaborative for Academic, Social, and Emotional Learning (CASEL), 628

Collaborative learning, **214–219**

classroom environment and, 159

cognitive apprenticeship and, 179

communities of learners and, 228

competition and, 231

culturally relevant pedagogy and, 305

early childhood development and, 351

gender bias and, 426

jigsaw method, 180, 228, 229, 761, 822

mental retardation and, 599

motivation and, 392

peer tutoring, 68, 599, 689–690, 959

questioning and, 723

scaffolding and, 217, 761

science instruction, 561, 820

self-explanation and, 800–801

shared cognition, 819–823

social comparison and, 215, 841

socioeconomic status and, 58

teacher roles, 218, 761

tutoring and, 959

volition and, 970

See also Peer tutoring

Collaborative Reasoning, 38, 332

Collectivism, 458

College Board, 3

Colorblind ideology, 383, 385